Understanding Physics

JEE Main & Advanced

Mechanics

Volume 1

DC Pandey
[B.Tech, M.Tech, Pantnagar, ID 15722]

ARIHANT PRAKASHAN (Series), MEERUT

arihant

Arihant Prakashan (Series), Meerut

卐 **Administrative & Production Offices**

Regd. Office

'Ramchhaya' 4577/15, Agarwal Road, Darya Ganj, New Delhi -110002
Tele: 011- 47630600, 43518550

卐 **Head Office**

Kalindi, TP Nagar, Meerut (UP) - 250002
Tel: 0121-7156203, 7156204

卐 **Sales & Support Offices**

Agra, Ahmedabad, Bengaluru, Bareilly, Chennai, Delhi, Guwahati, Hyderabad, Jaipur, Jhansi, Kolkata, Lucknow, Nagpur & Pune.

卐 **ISBN** 978-93-26191-55-5

卐 **PRICE** ₹ 490.00

PO No. : TXT-59-T045940-3-22

Published by Arihant Publications (India) Ltd.

For further information about the books published by Arihant, log on to www.arihantbooks.com or e-mail at info@arihantbooks.com

Follow us on   

PREFACE

The overwhelming response to the previous editions of this book gives me an immense feeling of satisfaction and I take this an opportunity to thank all the teachers and the whole student community who have found this book really beneficial.

In the present scenario of ever-changing syllabus and the test pattern of JEE Main & Advanced, the NEW EDITION of this book is an effort to cater all the difficulties being faced by the students during their preparation of JEE Main & Advanced. Almost all types and levels of questions are included in this book. My aim is to present the students a fully comprehensive textbook which will help and guide them for all types of examinations. An attempt has been made to remove all the printing errors that had crept in the previous editions.

I am very thankful to (Dr.) Mrs. Sarita Pandey and Mr. Anoop Dhyani for completing this book.

Comments and criticism from readers will be highly appreciated and incorporated in the subsequent editions.

I also request the readers to drop me a mail if you find any corrections in the book at mail id arihantcorrections@gmail.com

---

DC Pandey

CONTENTS

SYLLABUS

JEE Main

Physics and Measurement

Physics, Technology and Society, SI units, Fundamental and derived units, Least count, Accuracy and Precision of measuring instruments, Errors in measurement, Dimensions of physical quantities, Dimensional analysis and its applications.

Kinematics

Frame of reference, Motion in a straight line, Position-time graph, Speed and velocity, Uniform and non-uniform motion, Average speed and instantaneous velocity, Uniformly accelerated motion, Velocity-time and position-time graphs, Relations for uniformly accelerated motion, Scalars and Vectors, vectors addition and subtraction, Zero vector, scalar and vector products, Unit vector, resolution of a vector, Relative velocity, motion in plane, Projectile motion, Uniform circular motion.

Laws of Motion

Force and inertia, Newton's first law of motion, Momentum, Newton's second law of motion, impulse, Newton's third Law of motion, law of conservation of linear momentum and its applications, Equilibrium of concurrent forces. Static and kinetic friction, Laws of friction, rolling friction. Dynamics of uniform circular motion, centripetal force and its applications.

Work, Energy and Power

Work done by a constant force and a variable force, Kinetic and potential energies, Work energy theorem, power. Potential energy of a spring, Conservation of mechanical energy, Conservative and non-conservative forces, Elastic and inelastic collisions in one and two dimensions.

Centre of Mass

Centre of mass of a two particle system, Centre of mass of a rigid body.

Experimental Skills

Vernier Callipers and its use to measure internal and external diameter and depth of a vessel. Screw gauge its use to determine thickness/diameter of thin sheet/wire.

JEE Advanced

General Physics

Units and dimensions, Dimensional analysis, Least count, Significant figures, Methods of measurement and error analysis for physical quantities pertaining to the following experiments, Experiments based on vernier callipers and screw gauge (micrometer).
Determination of *g* using simple pendulum, Young's modulus - elasticity of the material Surface tension of water by capillary rise and effect of detergents. Specific heat of a liquid using calorimeter, focal length of a concave mirror and a convex lens using u-v method, Speed of sound using resonance column, Verification of Ohm's law using voltmeter and ammeter, and specific resistance of the material of
a wire using meter bridge and post office box.

Kinematics

Kinematics in one and two dimensions (Cartesian coordinates only), Projectiles, Uniform circular motion, Relative velocity.

Laws of Motion

Newton's laws of motion, Inertial and uniformly accelerated frames of reference, Static and dynamic friction.

Work, Energy and Power

Kinetic and potential energy, Work and power, Conservation of linear momentum and mechanical energy.

Centre of Mass and Collision

System of particles, Centre of mass and its motion, Impulse, Elastic and inelastic collisions.

This book is dedicated to my honourable grandfather

(Late) Sh. Pitamber Pandey

a Kumaoni poet and a resident of Village
Dhaura (Almora), Uttarakhand

DEAR STUDENTS...

Many a times I have seen that students have a phobia of Physics. Based on my experience in the field of teaching and writing for about more than 25 years, I am suggesting some of the strategies which can make your Physics subject very strong.

1. Physics is a subject of concepts. So, don't chase after too many problems. Make your concepts very strong. Each and every concept should be lucid clear. Let us take a small example of normal reaction, so what are the important points in it? Perpendicular to the surface; towards the surface, equal and opposite acting on two different bodies, just like pressure (or pressure force PA) between two bodies in contact; minimum value is zero where two bodies leave contact with each other, there is some maximum limit also where the weaker body breaks, electromagnetic and component of net contact force in normal direction; work done by normal reaction is not always zero etc.
2. Don't miss a single class wherever you are studying.
3. Your concentration level in class should be 100%.
4. Keep only one standard book with you. There are many drawbacks when you keep so many books in front of you. A lot of concepts and problems are usually repeated in different books. So basically you are just wasting your valuable time on similar types of concepts/problems if you are solving different books. You have to cover all chapters in all the subjects. If you have too many books then what generally would happen is; you complete a chapter from one book and then repeat the same chapter from the other book. By doing so your course lags and when your exams are near, you are disturbed because of incompletion of many chapters.
5. In this one book theory, selection of that book is very important. Number of problems in the book should neither be too less nor too much. If the level of IIT-JEE is x, then the problems should start from zero level and reach up to $1.25x$. There is no need of touching $1.5x$ level. In complete theory, examples and exercises almost all concepts and types of problems, which are normally asked in the examinations, should be covered. Level of examples and questions should increase very gradually.
6. I have tried my level best to incorporate all the measures mentioned above in point number 5 in my books.

7. There are total 1364 solved examples and 5169 problems in all my five text book. The total of these two is 6533.

8. If you start preparing for IIT-JEE from class 11th in the month of April then try to complete all five text books till the August next year. So you have total 480 days. Per day target of problems is 13.61 or 14.

9. After finishing one chapter in your classes, read each and every word of above mentioned books and complete your daily target of examples/problems by all means. Some problems/examples will be very simple, increasing your coverage that particular day and that saved time can be utilized in tough problems. If you are unable to solve a particular problem, just mark it and in your free time think over it like a philosopher. After two or three attempts if you are further unable to solve then, just see the solution of it which is given at the end of books. If you attend all classes, read complete theory, see all examples and solve all problems, then I am sure by the August month (next year) you will feel very comfortable in Physics. You can't do too many problems. So if you follow the above strategy then don't try any other book/material. Problems in the above mentioned books are given in a systematic increasing order of difficulty level. So if you move step by step then you will not feel any difficulty, I assure you that.

   Note : *If you feel that theory of particular topic is very clear in your classes then you can skip theory of above books to save time and directly switch over to solved examples and exercises.*

10. From September to first Main Exam of January month, keep two more books in front of you. "New Pattern" written by myself and "IIT-JEE previous years' papers". Try to complete each and every problem of these two books. You can leave the subjective problems of IIT-JEE previous years' papers at this stage. If you qualify this stage then in the remaining months complete subjective problems of IIT-JEE previous years' papers, one another book written by me five hundred selected problems of Physics and all logical problems of Irodov. If you don't qualify JEE Main exam of January month then repeat those books once again (New Pattern and IIT-JEE previous years' papers, excluding its subjective problems) and just after the April Main exam, complete subjective problems of IIT-JEE previous years' papers, five hundred selected problems of Physics. That's it.

11. If you follow each and every word of above strategy, then I am sure you will give your best in the exams. And this is very important because due to wrong strategy and doing the things in mismanaged manner most of us are unable to deliver our best performance. Your personal talent in Physics subject and luck factor at the last moment also matters. That is beyond our control and I can't speak about it. Your school studies are also not covered in this message.

Good Luck Students

DC Pandey

1

Basic Mathematics

1.1 Logarithms

(i) $e \approx 2.7183$

(ii) If $e^x = y$, then $x = \log_e y = \ln y$

(iii) If $10^x = y$, then $x = \log_{10} y$

(iv) $\log_{10} y = 0.4343 \log_e y = 0.4343 \ln y$

(v) $\log (ab) = \log a + \log b$

(vi) $\log \left(\frac{a}{b}\right) = \log a - \log b$

(vii) $\log a^n = n \log a$

(viii) $\log_{10} 2 = 0.3010$

(ix) $\log_{10} 3 = 0.4771$

(x) $\log_e 2 = 0.6931$

(xi) $\log_e 3 = 1.0986$

(xii) $\log_{10} 10 = 1$

(xiii) $\log_e e = 1$

Example 1.1 *Find the values of*

(a) $\log_{10} 6$

(b) $\log_{10} 300$

(c) $\log_{10} 10^{-5}$

(d) $\log_{10}(4 \times 10^6)$

Solution (a) $\log_{10} 6 = \log_{10}(3 \times 2) = \log_{10} 3 + \log_{10} 2$

$$= (0.4771) + (0.3010)$$

$$= 0.7781$$ **Ans.**

(b) $\log_{10} 300 = \log_{10}(3 \times 10^2) = \log_{10} 3 + \log_{10} 10^2$

$$= \log_{10} 3 + 2\log_{10} 10$$

$$= (0.4771) + (2)(1)$$

$$= 2.4771$$ **Ans.**

(c) $\log_{10} 10^{-5} = -5\log_{10} 10 = -5(1) = -5$ **Ans.**

(d) $\log_{10}(4 \times 10^6) = \log_{10} 4 + \log_{10} 10^6$

$$= \log_{10}(2)^2 + 6\log_{10} 10$$

$$= 2\log_{10} 2 + 6\log_{10} 10$$

$$= (2)(0.3010) + (6)(1)$$

$$= 6.602$$ **Ans.**

1.2 Trigonometry

(i) **Angle**

$$1^\circ = 60' \text{ (minute)}$$

$$1' = 60'' \text{ (second)}$$

$$1 \text{ right angle} = 90^\circ \text{ (degrees)}$$

$$\text{also } 1 \text{ right angle} = \frac{\pi}{2} \text{ rad (radian)}$$

1 radian is the angle subtended at the centre of a circle by an arc of the circle, whose length is equal to the radius of the circle.

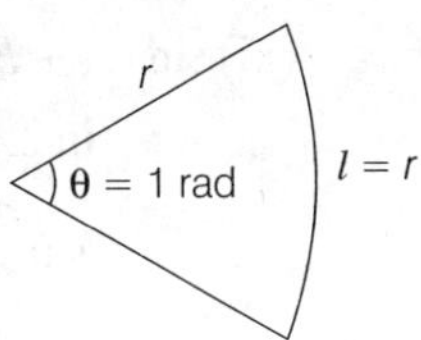

Fig. 1.1

$$1 \text{ rad} = \frac{180°}{\pi} \approx 57.3°$$

To convert an angle from degree to radian multiply it by $\frac{\pi}{180°}$.

To convert an angle from radian to degree multiply it by $\frac{180°}{\pi}$.

Note 1. *Angle (in radian)* $= \frac{\text{Arc}}{\text{Radius}}$

2. $180° = (\pi)$ *radian*

$$\frac{\pi}{2} = 90°, \frac{\pi}{4} = 45°, \frac{\pi}{6} = 30°, 2\pi = 360°$$

$$1 \text{ radian} = \left(\frac{180}{\pi}\right)^{\circ}, 1° = \left(\frac{\pi}{180}\right) \text{radian}$$

(ii)

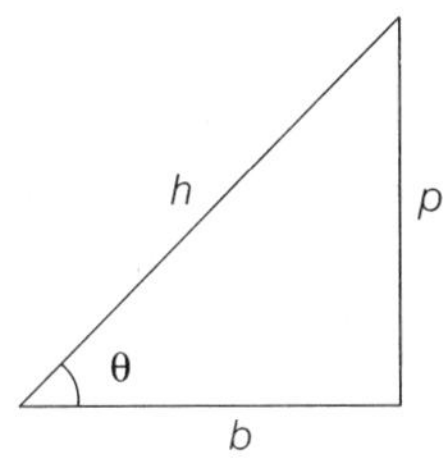

Fig. 1.2

$$h^2 = b^2 + p^2 \rightarrow \text{Pythagoras theorem}$$

(iii) $\sin\theta = \frac{p}{h}, \cos\theta = \frac{b}{h}, \tan\theta = \frac{p}{b}$

(iv) $\tan\theta = \frac{\sin\theta}{\cos\theta} = \frac{1}{\cot\theta}$

(v) $\cot\theta = \frac{\cos\theta}{\sin\theta} = \frac{1}{\tan\theta}$

(vi) $\sec\theta = \frac{1}{\cos\theta} = \frac{h}{b}$

(vii) $\operatorname{cosec}\theta = \frac{1}{\sin\theta} = \frac{h}{p}$

(viii) $\sin^2\theta + \cos^2\theta = 1 \Rightarrow \sin^2\theta = 1 - \cos^2\theta \Rightarrow \cos^2\theta = 1 - \sin^2\theta$

(ix) $\sec^2\theta = \tan^2\theta + 1 \Rightarrow \tan^2\theta = \sec^2\theta - 1$

(x) $\operatorname{cosec}^2\theta = 1 + \cot^2\theta$

(xi) $\sin(A+B) = \sin A \cos B + \cos A \sin B$

$\sin 2A = 2\sin A \cos A$ [put $B = A$]

$\sin A = 2\sin\frac{A}{2}\cos\frac{A}{2}$

(xii) $\sin(A-B) = \sin A \cos B - \cos A \sin B$

$\sin 0° = 0$ [put $B = A$]

(xiii) $\cos(A+B) = \cos A \cos B - \sin A \sin B$

$\cos 2A = \cos^2 A - \sin^2 A$ [put $B = A$]

$= 2\cos^2 A - 1$ [$\sin^2 A = 1 - \cos^2 A$]

$= 1 - 2\sin^2 A$

(xiv) $\cos A = \cos^2\frac{A}{2} - \sin^2\frac{A}{2} = 2\cos^2\frac{A}{2} - 1 = 1 - 2\sin^2\frac{A}{2}$

(xv) $\cos(A-B) = \cos A \cos B + \sin A \sin B$

$\cos 0° = \cos^2 A + \sin^2 A = 1$ [put $B = A$]

(xvi) $\tan(A+B) = \dfrac{\tan A + \tan B}{1 - \tan A \tan B}$

$\tan 2A = \dfrac{2\tan A}{1 - \tan^2 A}$ [put $B = A$]

$\tan A = \dfrac{2\tan\frac{A}{2}}{1 - \tan^2\frac{A}{2}}$

(xvii) $\tan(A-B) = \dfrac{\tan A - \tan B}{1 + \tan A \tan B}$

$\tan 0° = 0$ [put $B = A$]

(xviii) $\sin C + \sin D = 2\sin\dfrac{C+D}{2}\cos\dfrac{C-D}{2}$

$\sin C - \sin D = 2\sin\dfrac{C-D}{2}\cos\dfrac{C+D}{2}$

$\cos C + \cos D = 2\cos\dfrac{C+D}{2}\cos\dfrac{C-D}{2}$

$\cos C - \cos D = 2\sin\dfrac{C+D}{2}\sin\dfrac{D-C}{2}$

(xix) $(\cos\theta)(\cos\theta) = \cos^2\theta \neq \cos\theta^2 = (\cos\theta)^2$; $\cos\theta + \cos\theta = 2\cos\theta$

(xx) $\sin\theta \times \sin\theta = \sin^2\theta = (\sin\theta)^2 \neq \sin(\theta)^2$

(xxi)

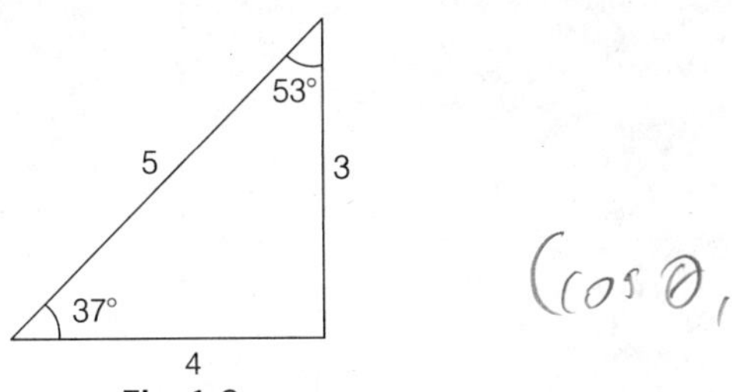

Fig. 1.3

Table 1.1

Angle	$\sin\theta$	$\cos\theta$	$\tan\theta = \dfrac{\sin\theta}{\cos\theta}$
0°	0	1	0
30°	1/2	$\sqrt{3}/2$	$1/\sqrt{3}$
37°	3/5	4/5	3/4
45°	$1/\sqrt{2}$	$1/\sqrt{2}$	1
53°	4/5	3/5	4/3
60°	$\sqrt{3}/2$	1/2	$\sqrt{3}$
90°	1	0	∞
180°	0	–1	0

(xxii) $\sin 20° = \cos 70°$, $\sin 10° = \cos 80°$,
$\sin 25° = \cos 65°$ etc.

(xxiii) Four quadrants and ASTC rule

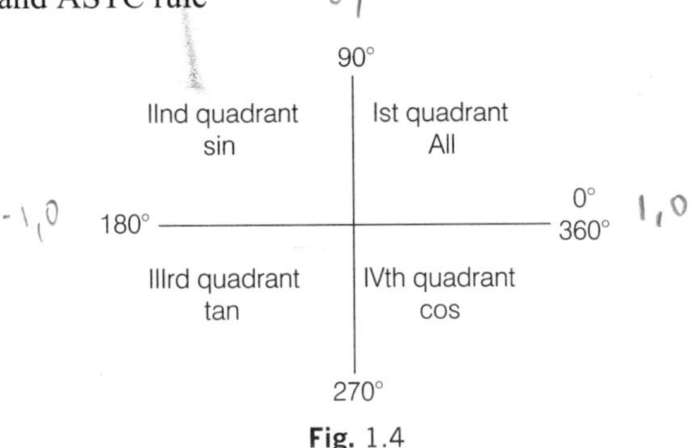

Fig. 1.4

0, -1

In first quadrant, all trigonometric ratios are positive.
In second quadrant, only $\sin\theta$ and $\text{cosec}\,\theta$ are positive.
In third quadrant, only $\tan\theta$ and $\cot\theta$ are positive.
In fourth quadrant, only $\cos\theta$ and $\sec\theta$ are positive.
Remember as **All Silver Tea Cups**.

(xxiv)

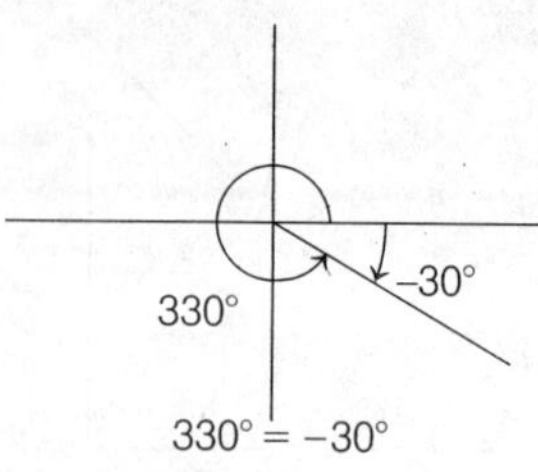

Fig. 1.5

(xxv)

$\sin(90° + \theta) = \cos\theta$ $\cos(90° + \theta) = -\sin\theta$ $\tan(90° + \theta) = -\cot\theta$	$\sin(180° - \theta) = \sin\theta$ $\cos(180° - \theta) = -\cos\theta$ $\tan(180° - \theta) = -\tan\theta$	$\sin(-\theta) = -\sin\theta$ $\cos(-\theta) = \cos\theta$ $\tan(-\theta) = -\tan\theta$
$\sin(90° - \theta) = \cos\theta$ $\cos(90° - \theta) = \sin\theta$ $\tan(90° - \theta) = \cot\theta$	$\sin(180° + \theta) = -\sin\theta$ $\cos(180° + \theta) = -\cos\theta$ $\tan(180° + \theta) = \tan\theta$	

(xxvi)

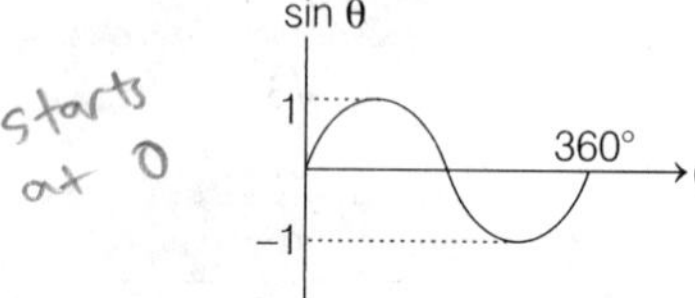

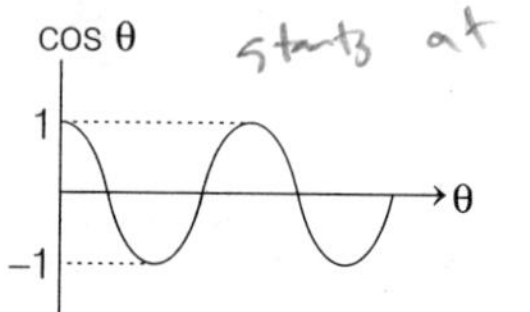

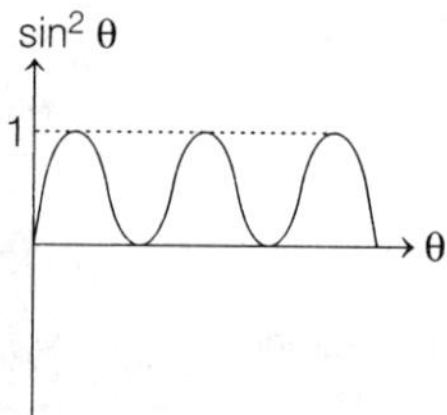

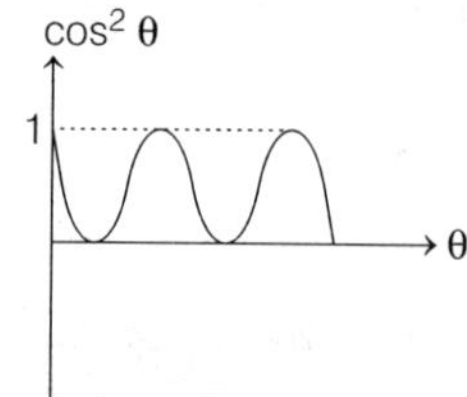

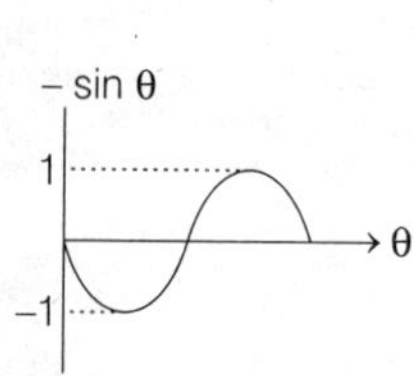

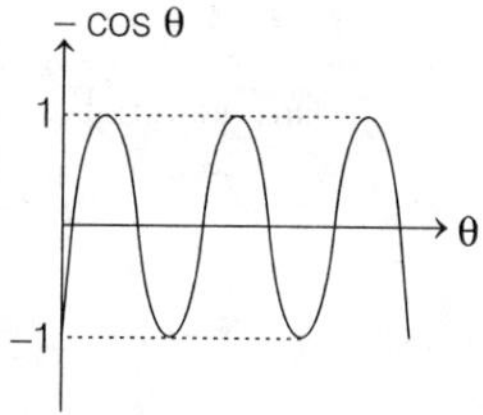

Fig. 1.6

(xxvii) $(\sin\theta)_{max} = (\cos\theta)_{max} = 1$

(xxviii) $(\sin\theta)_{min} = (\cos\theta)_{min} = -1$

(xxix) As θ increases from $0°$ to $90°$, $\sin\theta$ and $\tan\theta$ increases, but $\cos\theta$ decreases.

(xxx) For small values of θ

$$\sin\theta \approx \theta,\ \tan\theta \approx \theta \text{ and } \cos\theta \approx 1$$

Example 1.2 *A circular arc is of length π cm. Find angle subtended by it at the centre in radian and degree.*

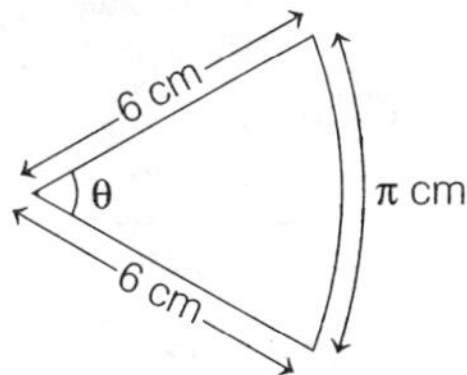

Solution $\theta = \frac{s}{r} = \frac{\pi \text{ cm}}{6 \text{ cm}} = \frac{\pi}{6} \text{ rad} = 30°$

$$\text{As } 1 \text{ rad} = \frac{180°}{\pi},$$

$$\text{So,} \quad \theta = \frac{\pi}{6} \times \frac{180°}{\pi} = 30°$$ **Ans.**

Example 1.3 *The moon's distance from the earth is 360000 km and its diameter subtends an angle of 42′ at the eye of the observer. Find the diameter of the moon.*

Solution Here, angle is very small so diameter ≈ arc

$$\text{Here } \theta = 42' = \left(42 \times \frac{1}{60}\right)^{o} = 42 \times \frac{1}{60} \times \frac{\pi}{180} = \frac{7\pi}{1800} \text{ rad}$$

$$\text{So, diameter} = R\theta = 360000 \times \frac{7}{1800} \times \frac{22}{7} = 4400 \text{ km}$$ **Ans.**

Example 1.4 *When a clock shows 4 o'clock, how much angle do its minute and hour needles make?*

(a) 120° *(b)* $\frac{\pi}{3}$ *rad*

(c) $\frac{2\pi}{3}$ *rad* *(d)* 160°

Solution

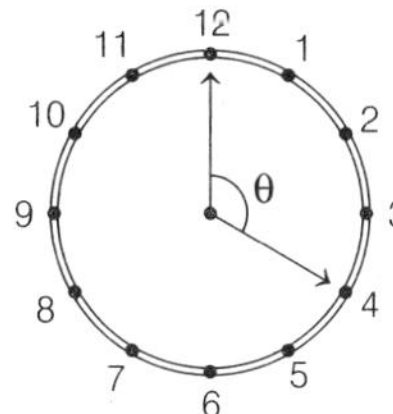

From the above diagram angle

$$\theta = 4 \times 30° = 120° = \frac{2\pi}{3} \text{ rad}$$ **Ans.**

The correct options are (a) and (c).

Example 1.5 *Given that* $\sin\theta = \frac{1}{4}$. *Find the values of* $\cos\theta$ *and* $\tan\theta$.

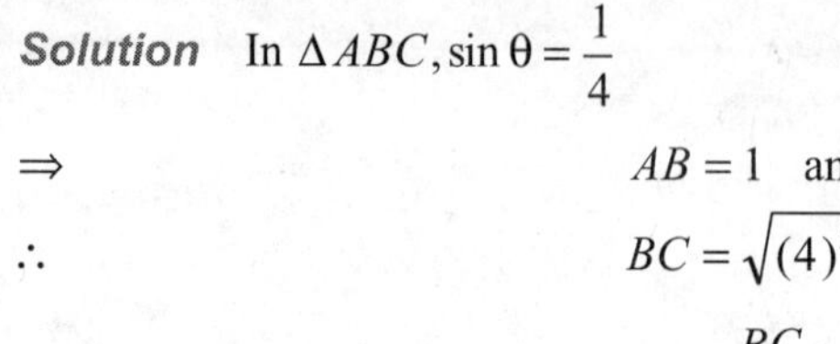

Solution In $\Delta ABC, \sin\theta = \frac{1}{4}$

$\Rightarrow$ $$AB = 1 \quad \text{and} \quad AC = 4$$

$\therefore$ $$BC = \sqrt{(4)^2 - (1)^2} = \sqrt{15}$$

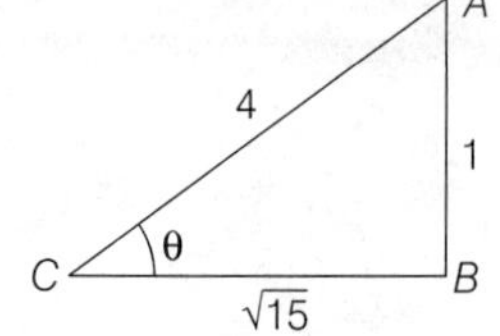

Now, $$\cos\theta = \frac{BC}{AC} = \frac{\sqrt{15}}{4}$$ **Ans.**

and $$\tan\theta = \frac{AB}{BC} = \frac{1}{\sqrt{15}}$$ **Ans.**

Example 1.6 *Find the values of*

(a) $\cos(-60°)$ *(b)* $\tan 210°$

(c) $\sin 300°$ *(d)* $\cos 120°$

Solution (a) $\cos(-60°) = \cos 60° = \frac{1}{2}$

(b) $\tan 210° = \tan(180° + 30°) = \tan 30° = \frac{1}{\sqrt{3}}$

(c) $\sin 300° = \sin(270° + 30°) = -\cos 30° = -\frac{\sqrt{3}}{2}$

(d) $\cos 120° = \cos(180° - 60°) = -\cos 60° = -\frac{1}{2}$ **Ans.**

1.3 Differentiation

(i) $\frac{d}{dx}(\text{constant}) = 0$

(ii) $\frac{d}{dx}(x^n) = nx^{n-1}$

(iii) $\frac{d}{dx}(\log_e x)$ or $\frac{d}{dx}(\ln x) = \frac{1}{x}$

(iv) $\frac{d}{dx}(\sin x) = \cos x$

(v) $\frac{d}{dx}(\cos x) = -\sin x$

(vi) $\frac{d}{dx}(\tan x) = \sec^2 x$

(vii) $\frac{d}{dx}(\cot x) = -\text{cosec}^2 x$

(viii) $\frac{d}{dx}(\sec x) = \sec x \tan x$

(ix) $\frac{d}{dx}(\text{cosec}\, x) = -\text{cosec}\, x \cot x$

(x) $\frac{d}{dx}(e^x) = e^x$

(xi) $\frac{d}{dx}\{f_1(x) . f_2(x)\} = f_1(x)\frac{d}{dx}f_2(x) + f_2(x)\frac{d}{dx}f_1(x)$

(xii) $$\frac{d}{dx}\frac{f_1(x)}{f_2(x)} = \frac{f_2(x)\frac{d}{dx}f_1(x) - f_1(x)\frac{d}{dx}f_2(x)}{\{f_2(x)\}^2}$$

(xiii) $\frac{d}{dx} f\,(ax+b) = a\frac{d}{dx} f(X)$, where $X = ax + b$

Note $\left\{ y = x^4, \frac{dy}{dx} = 4x^3, \frac{d^2y}{dx^2} = \frac{d}{dx}\left(\frac{dy}{dx}\right) = \frac{d}{dx}(4x^3) = 12x^2 \right\}$

(xiv) **Chain rule** Keep on differentiating and multiply the result.

For example :

$$\frac{d}{dx}(\sin e^{x^2}) = [\cos e^{x^2}][e^{x^2}][2x]$$

$$= 2xe^{x^2} \cos e^{x^2}$$

(xv) If $y = f(x)$ and we wish to find $\frac{dy}{dt}$, then

$$\frac{dy}{dt} = \left(\frac{dy}{dx}\right)\left(\frac{dx}{dt}\right) = \left[\frac{d}{dx} f(x)\right]\left(\frac{dx}{dt}\right)$$

(xvi) **Slope of a graph at some point**

(a) The slope of a line is the tangent of the angle made by the line with positive x-axis in the anti-clockwise direction.

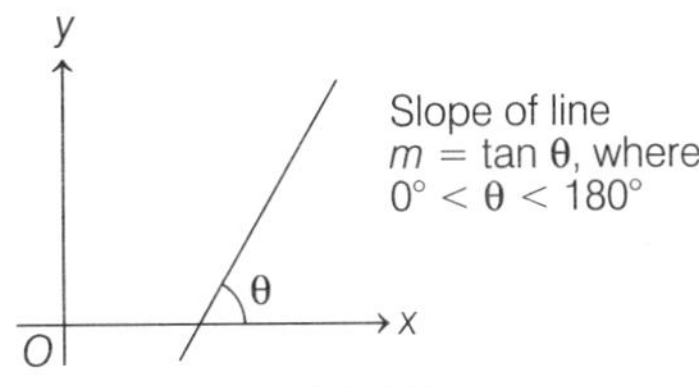

Fig. 1.7

If $0° < \theta < 90°$, θ lies between 0 to 90°, the slope is positive.

If $90° < \theta < 180°$, θ lies between 90° to 180°, the slope is negative.

If $\theta = 0°$ or 180°, the slope is zero ($m = 0$).

If $\theta = 90°$, the slope is not defined ($m = \infty$).

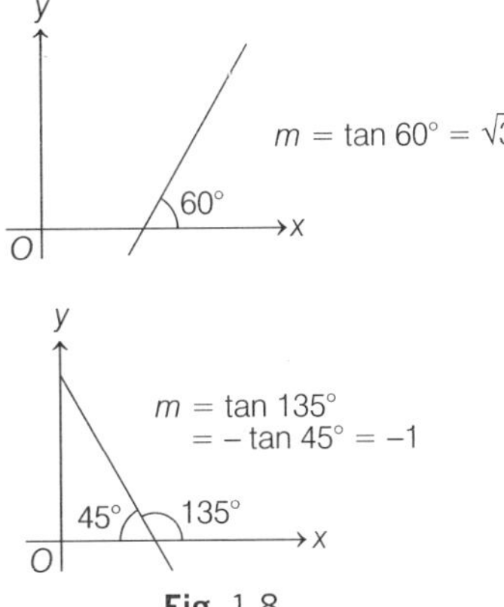

Fig. 1.8

(b) Slope can be calculated by rise over run

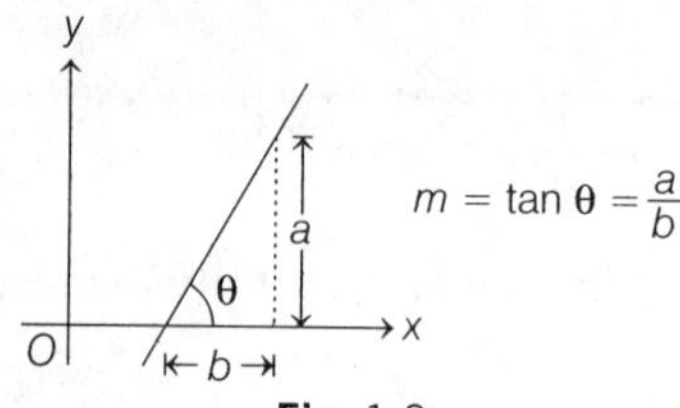

Fig. 1.9

(c) $\frac{dy}{dx}$: Differential coefficient of y w.r.t. x gives the slope of a line or a curve.

(i) $y = 4x + 7$

$\frac{dy}{dx} = 4$, slope is constant

(ii) $y = 2x^2$

$\frac{dy}{dx} = 4x$, slope is variable

At $x = 1, \frac{dy}{dx} = 4$

At $x = 2, \frac{dy}{dx} = 8$

(d) The slope of a curve at a point is the slope of the tangent line at that point.

(e) Slope of straight line curve ($= m$) is constant at all points. Slope of any other curve is different at different points.

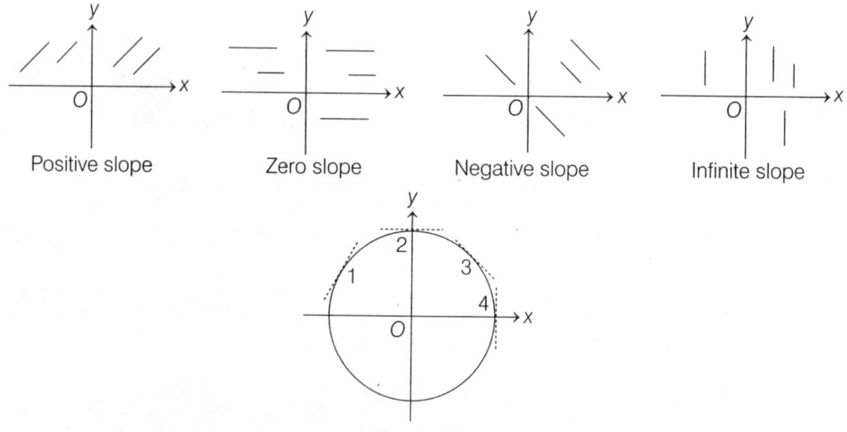

Fig. 1.10

$\text{Slope}_1 = \text{positive}$
$\text{Slope}_2 = \text{zero}$
$\text{Slope}_3 = \text{negative}$
$\text{Slope}_4 = \text{infinite}$

Maxima and Minima

Suppose y is a function of x. Or $y = f(x)$.

Then we can draw a graph between x and y. Let the graph is as shown in figure 1.11.

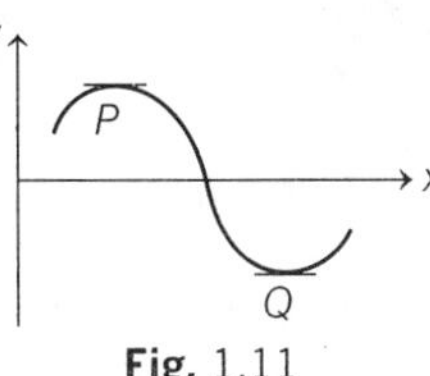

Fig. 1.11

Then from the graph we can see that at maximum or minimum value of y slope $\left(\text{or } \frac{dy}{dx}\right)$ to the graph is zero.

Thus, $\frac{dy}{dx} = 0$ at maximum or minimum value of y.

By putting $\frac{dy}{dx} = 0$, we will get different values of x. At these values of x, value of y is maximum if $\frac{d^2y}{dx^2}$ (double differentiation of y with respect to x) is negative at this value of x. Similarly, y is minimum if $\frac{d^2y}{dx^2}$ is positive.

Thus, $\frac{d^2y}{dx^2} = -\text{ve}$ for maximum value of y

and $\frac{d^2y}{dx^2} = +\text{ve}$ for minimum value of y

Note *That at constant value of y also* $\frac{dy}{dx} = 0$ *but in this case* $\frac{d^2y}{dx^2}$ *is zero.*

Example 1.7 *Differentiate the following functions with respect to x*

(a) $x^3 + 5x^2 - 2$ (b) $x \sin x$ (c) $(2x+3)^6$ (d) $\frac{x}{\sin x}$

(e) $e^{(5x+2)}$

Solution (a) $\frac{d}{dx}(x^3 + 5x^2 - 2) = \frac{d}{dx}(x^3) + 5\frac{d}{dx}(x^2) - \frac{d}{dx}(2)$

$$= 3x^2 + 5(2x) - 0$$

$$= 3x^2 + 10x$$

(b) $\frac{d}{dx}(x \sin x) = x\frac{d}{dx}(\sin x) + \sin x \cdot \frac{d}{dx}(x)$

$$= x \cos x + \sin x\,(1)$$

$$= x \cos x + \sin x$$

(c) $\frac{d}{dx}(2x+3)^6 = 2\frac{d}{dX}(X)^6$, where $X = 2x + 3$

$$= 2\{6X^5\} = 12X^5$$

$$= 12(2x+3)^5$$

(d) $$\frac{d}{dx}\left(\frac{x}{\sin x}\right) = \frac{\sin x \dfrac{d}{dx}(x) - x\dfrac{d}{dx}(\sin x)}{(\sin x)^2}$$

$$= \frac{(\sin x)(1) - x(\cos x)}{\sin^2 x} = \frac{\sin x - x\cos x}{\sin^2 x}$$

(e) $\frac{d}{dx} e^{(5x+2)} = 5\frac{d}{dX} e^X$, where $X = 5x + 2 = 5e^X = 5e^{5x+2}$

Example 1.8 *Find* $\frac{dy}{dx}$, *when*

(a) $y = \sqrt{x}$ *(b)* $y = x^5 + x^4 + 7$ *(c)* $y = x^2 + 4x^{-1/2} - 3x^{-2}$

Solution (a) $y = \sqrt{x}$

$$\frac{dy}{dx} = \frac{d}{dx}(\sqrt{x}) = \frac{d}{dx}(x^{1/2})$$

$$= \frac{1}{2}x^{1/2-1} = \frac{1}{2}x^{-1/2} = \frac{1}{2\sqrt{x}}$$ **Ans.**

(b) $y = x^5 + x^4 + 7$

$$\frac{dy}{dx} = \frac{d}{dx}(x^5 + x^4 + 7)$$

$$= \frac{d}{dx}(x^5) + \frac{d}{dx}(x^4) + \frac{d}{dx}(7)$$

$$= 5x^4 + 4x^3 + 0 = 5x^4 + 4x^3$$ **Ans.**

(c) $y = x^2 + 4x^{-1/2} - 3x^{-2}$

$$\frac{dy}{dx} = \frac{d}{dx}(x^2 + 4x^{-1/2} - 3x^{-2})$$

$$= \frac{d}{dx}(x^2) + \frac{d}{dx}(4x^{-1/2}) - \frac{d}{dx}(3x^{-2})$$

$$= \frac{d}{dx}(x^2) + 4\frac{d}{dx}(x^{-1/2}) - 3\frac{d}{dx}(x^{-2})$$

$$= 2x - \frac{1}{2}(4)x^{-3/2} - 3(-2)x^{-3}$$

$$= 2x - 2x^{-3/2} + 6x^{-3}$$ **Ans.**

Example 1.9 *Given,* $y = 3x^3$. *Find the value of* $\frac{dy}{dt}$.

Solution
$$\frac{dy}{dt} = \left(\frac{dy}{dx}\right)\left(\frac{dx}{dt}\right)$$

$$= \left[\frac{d}{dx}(3x^3)\right]\frac{dx}{dt} = 9x^2\left(\frac{dx}{dt}\right)$$ **Ans.**

Example 1.10 *If* $y = [x^2 + 3x + 2]^3 + [\log_e x^2]$. *Then, find* $\dfrac{dy}{dx}$.

Solution Using the chain rule, we have

$$\frac{dy}{dx} = 3(x^2 + 3x + 2)^{3-1} \cdot (2x + 3) + \frac{1}{x^2} \cdot 2x$$

$$= 3(2x + 3)(x^2 + 3x + 2)^2 + \frac{2}{x} \qquad \textbf{Ans.}$$

Example 1.11 *If* $y = \{(x^2 + 2x)^{1/2}\}$, *then find* $\dfrac{dy}{dx}$.

Solution Using the chain rule, we have

$$\frac{dy}{dx} = \frac{1}{2}(x^2 + 2x)^{\frac{1}{2}-1}(2x + 2)$$

$$= (x + 1)(x^2 + 2x)^{-1/2} \qquad \textbf{Ans.}$$

Example 1.12 *If* $y = \tan x$, *then using the chain rule find* $\dfrac{dy}{dx}$.

Solution

$$y = \tan x = \frac{\sin x}{\cos x}$$

$$\frac{dy}{dx} = \frac{\cos x \dfrac{d}{dx}(\sin x) - \sin x \dfrac{d}{dx}(\cos x)}{(\cos x)^2}$$

$$= \frac{\cos x \cdot \cos x - \sin x(-\sin x)}{\cos^2 x}$$

$$= \frac{\cos^2 x + \sin^2 x}{\cos^2 x} = \frac{1}{\cos^2 x} = \sec^2 x \qquad \textbf{Ans.}$$

Example 1.13 *Find maximum or minimum values of the functions*

(a) $y = 25x^2 + 5 - 10x$ *(b)* $y = 9 - (x - 3)^2$

Solution (a) For maximum and minimum value, we can put $\dfrac{dy}{dx} = 0$.

or
$$\frac{dy}{dx} = 50x - 10 = 0$$

∴
$$x = \frac{1}{5}$$

Further,
$$\frac{d^2y}{dx^2} = 50$$

or $\dfrac{d^2y}{dx^2}$ has positive value at $x = \dfrac{1}{5}$. Therefore, y has minimum value at $x = \dfrac{1}{5}$. **Ans.**

Substituting $x = \frac{1}{5}$ in given equation, we get

$$y_{min} = 25\left(\frac{1}{5}\right)^2 + 5 - 10\left(\frac{1}{5}\right) = 4$$ **Ans.**

(b) $y = 9 - (x-3)^2 = 9 - x^2 - 9 + 6x$

or $$y = 6x - x^2$$

$\therefore$ $$\frac{dy}{dx} = 6 - 2x$$

For minimum or maximum value of y, we will substitute $\frac{dy}{dx} = 0$

or $$6 - 2x = 0 \quad \text{or} \quad x = 3$$

To check whether value of y is maximum or minimum at $x = 3$, we will have to check whether $\frac{d^2y}{dx^2}$ is positive or negative.

$$\frac{d^2y}{dx^2} = -2$$

or $\frac{d^2y}{dx^2}$ is negative at $x = 3$. Hence, value of y is maximum. This maximum value of y is,

$$y_{max} = 9 - (3-3)^2 = 9$$ **Ans.**

Example 1.14 *Find the minimum value of* $y = 5x^2 - 2x + 1$.

Solution For maximum or minimum value, $\frac{dy}{dx} = 0$

$\Rightarrow$ $$5(2x) - 2(1) + 0 = 0$$

$\Rightarrow$ $$x = \frac{1}{5}$$

Now at $x = \frac{1}{5}$, $\frac{d^2y}{dx^2} = 10$ which is positive so minima at $x = \frac{1}{5}$.

Therefore, $y_{min} = 5\left(\frac{1}{5}\right)^2 - 2\left(\frac{1}{5}\right) + 1 = \frac{4}{5}$ **Ans.**

Example 1.15 *Divide a number* 100 *into two parts such that their product is maximum.*

Solution Let the two parts be x and $(100 - x)$

Product, $$P = x(100 - x) = 100x - x^2$$

For P to be maximum or minimum,

$$\frac{dP}{dx} = 100 - 2x = 0$$

$$\Rightarrow \qquad x = 50$$

$$\frac{d^2P}{dx^2} = -2,$$

i.e. P is maximum at $x = 50$

Dividing equally the two parts are (50, 50) **Ans.**

1.4 Integration

(i) $\int x^n \, dx = \frac{x^{n+1}}{n+1} + c \quad (n \neq -1)$

(ii) $\int \frac{dx}{x} = \log_e x + c$

or $\ln x + c$

(iii) $\int \sin x \, dx = -\cos x + c$

(iv) $\int \cos x \, dx = \sin x + c$

(v) $\int e^x dx = e^x + c$

(vi) $\int \sec^2 x \, dx = \tan x + c$

(vii) $\int \operatorname{cosec}^2 x \, dx = -\cot x + c$

(viii) $\int \sec x \tan x \, dx = \sec x + c$

(ix) $\int \operatorname{cosec} x \cot x \, dx = -\operatorname{cosec} x + c$

(x) $\int f(ax+b) \, dx = \frac{1}{a} \int f(X) \, dX,$

where $X = ax + b$

Here, c is constant of integration.

Definite integrals

When a function is integrated between a lower limit and an upper limit, it is called a definite integral.

If $\frac{d}{dx} f(x) = f'(x)$, then $\int f'(x)dx$ is called indefinite integral and $\int_a^b f'(x)dx$ is called definite integral.

Here, a and b are called lower and upper limits of the variable x.

After carrying out integration, the result is evaluated between upper and lower limits as explained below :

$$\int_a^b f'(x)dx = |f(x)|_a^b = f(b) - f(a)$$

Area under a curve and definite integration

Area of small shown element = $ydx = f(x)dx$

If we sum up all areas between $x = a$ and $x = b$, then $\int_a^b f(x)dx$ = shaded area between curve and x-axis.

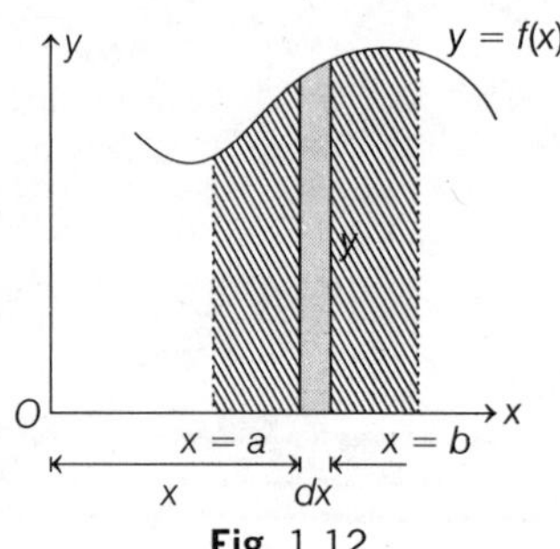

Fig. 1.12

Example 1.16 *Integrate the following functions with respect to x*

(a) $\int (5x^2 + 3x - 2)\, dx$ (b) $\int \left(4 \sin x - \dfrac{2}{x}\right) dx$

(c) $\int \dfrac{dx}{4x + 5}$ (d) $\int (6x + 2)^3\, dx$

Solution (a) $\int (5x^2 + 3x - 2)\, dx = 5\int x^2\, dx + 3\int x\, dx - 2\int dx = \dfrac{5x^3}{3} + \dfrac{3x^2}{2} - 2x + c$

(b) $\int \left(4 \sin x - \dfrac{2}{x}\right) dx = 4\int \sin x\, dx - 2\int \dfrac{dx}{x} = -4\cos x - 2\ln x + c$

(c) $\int \dfrac{dx}{4x + 5} = \dfrac{1}{4}\int \dfrac{dX}{X}$, where $X = 4x + 5 = \dfrac{1}{4}\ln X + c_1 = \dfrac{1}{4}\ln(4x + 5) + c_2$

(d) $\int (6x + 2)^3\, dx = \dfrac{1}{6}\int X^3\, dX$,

where $X = 6x + 2$

$$= \frac{1}{6}\left(\frac{X^4}{4}\right) + c_1 = \frac{(6x + 2)^4}{24} + c_2$$ **Ans.**

Example 1.17 *Find* $I = \int_0^{\pi/4} (\sin x + \cos x)dx.$

Solution $I = \int_0^{\pi/4} (\sin x + \cos x)dx = |-\cos x + \sin x|_0^{\pi/4}$

$$= \left\{-\cos\left(\frac{\pi}{4}\right) + \sin\left(\frac{\pi}{4}\right)\right\} - \{-\cos(0) + \sin(0)\}$$

$$= \left\{-\frac{1}{\sqrt{2}} + \frac{1}{\sqrt{2}}\right\} - \{-1 + 0\} = 1$$ **Ans.**

Example 1.18 *The integral* $\int_1^5 x^2\,dx$ *is equal to*

(a) $\frac{125}{3}$ (b) $\frac{124}{3}$ (c) $\frac{1}{3}$ (d) 45

Solution $\int_1^5 x^2\,dx = \left[\frac{x^3}{3}\right]_1^5 = \left[\frac{5^3}{3} - \frac{1^3}{3}\right] = \frac{125}{3} - \frac{1}{3} = \frac{124}{3}$ **Ans.**

∴ The correct option is (b).

1.5 Graphs

Following graphs and their corresponding equations are frequently used in Physics.

(i) $y = mx$, represents a straight line passing through origin. Here, $m = \tan\theta$ is also called the slope of line, where θ is the angle which the line makes with positive x-axis, when drawn in anti-clockwise direction from the positive x-axis towards the line.

The two possible cases are shown in Fig. 1.13. In Fig. 1.13 (i), $\theta < 90°$. Therefore, $\tan\theta$ or slope of line is positive. In Fig. 1.13 (ii), $90° < \theta < 180°$. Therefore, $\tan\theta$ or slope of line is negative.

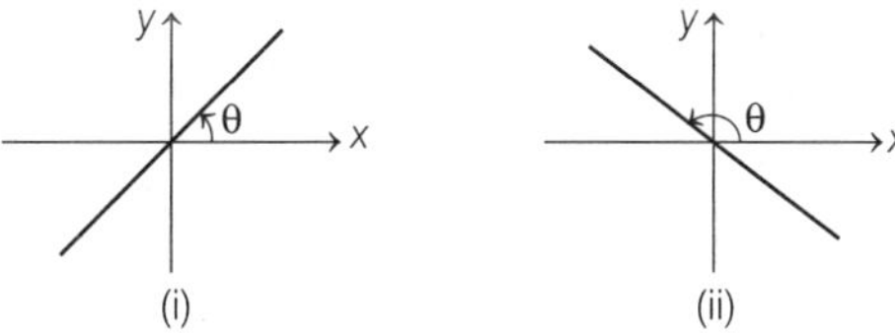

Fig. 1.13

Note *That $y = mx$ or $y \propto x$ also means that value of y becomes 2 times, if x is doubled. Or it will remain $\frac{1}{4}$th if x becomes $\frac{1}{4}$ times.*

(ii) $y = mx + c$, represents a straight line not passing through origin. Here, m is the slope of line as discussed above and c the intercept on y-axis.

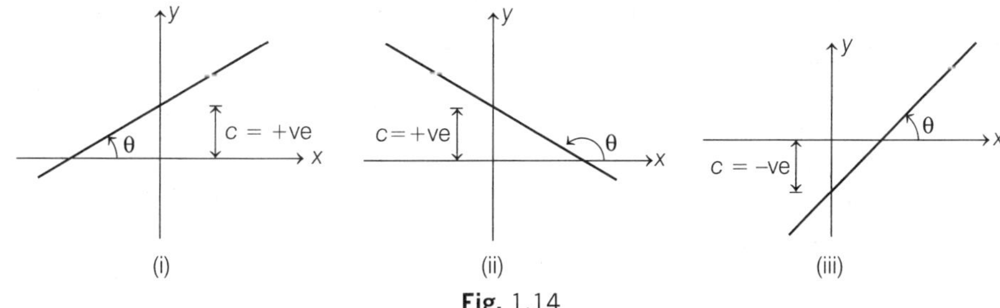

Fig. 1.14

In figure (i) : slope and intercept both are positive.

In figure (ii) : slope is negative but intercept is positive and

In figure (iii) : slope is positive but intercept is negative.

Note *That in $y = mx + c$, y does not become two times, if x is doubled.*

(iii) $y \propto \frac{1}{x}$ or $y=\frac{2}{x}$, etc., represents a rectangular hyperbola in first and third quadrants. The shape of rectangular hyperbola is shown in figure (i).

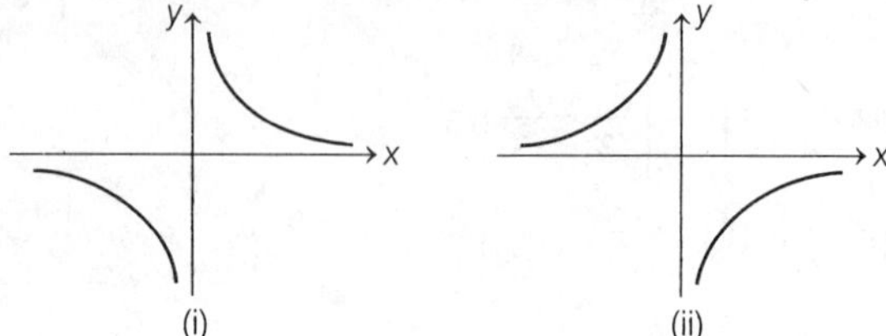

Fig. 1.15

From the graph we can see that $y \to 0$ as $x \to \infty$ or $x \to 0$ as $y \to \infty$.

Similarly, $y=-\frac{4}{x}$ represents a rectangular hyperbola in second and fourth quadrants as shown in figure (ii).

Note *That in case of rectangular hyperbola if x is doubled y will become half.*

(iv) $y \propto x^2$ or $y=2x^2$, etc., represents a parabola passing through origin as shown in Fig. 1.16 (i).

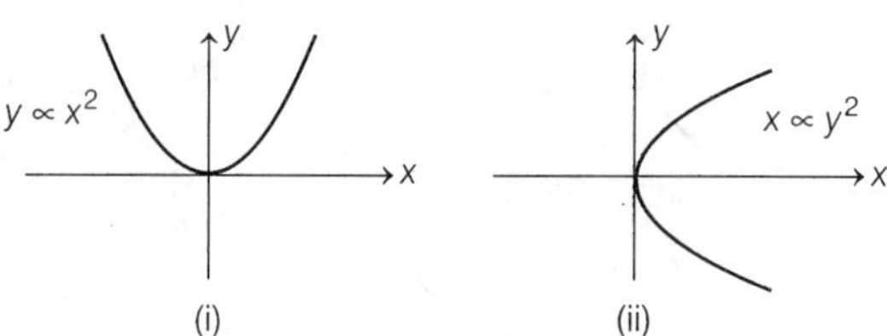

Fig. 1.16

Note *That in the parabola $y=2x^2$ or $y \propto x^2$, if x is doubled, y will become four times.*

Graph $x \propto y^2$ or $x=4y^2$ is again a parabola passing through origin as shown in Fig 1.16(ii). In this case if y is doubled, x will become four times.

(v) $y=x^2+4$ or $x=y^2-6$ will represent a parabola but not passing through origin. In the first equation ($y=x^2+4$), if x is doubled, y will not become four times.

(vi) $y=Ae^{-Kx}$; represents exponentially decreasing graph. The value of y decreases exponentially from A to 0. The graph is shown in Fig. 1.17.

From the graph and the equation, we can see that $y=A$ at $x=0$ and $y \to 0$ as $x \to \infty$.

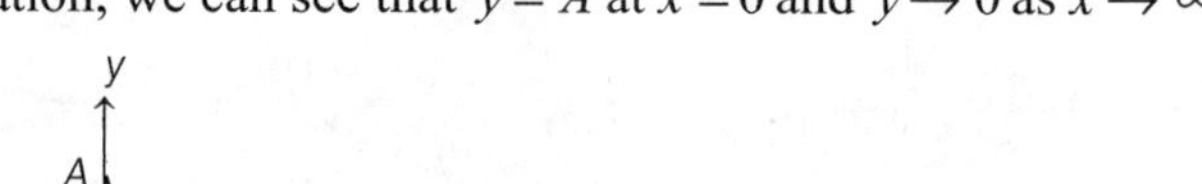

Fig. 1.17

(vii) $y = A(1 - e^{-Kx})$, represents an exponentially increasing graph. Value of y increases exponentially from 0 to A. The graph is shown in Fig. 1.18.

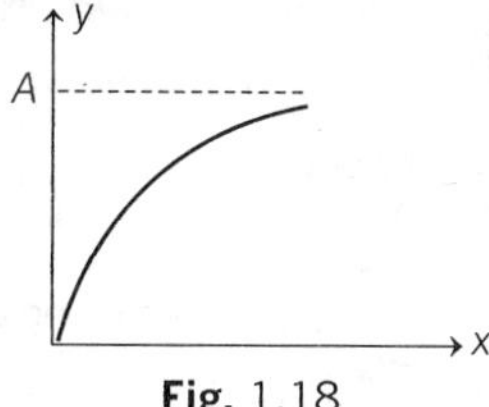

Fig. 1.18

From the graph and the equation, we can see that $y = 0$ at $x = 0$ and $y \to A$ as $x \to \infty$.

(viii) **Some standard graphs and their equations**

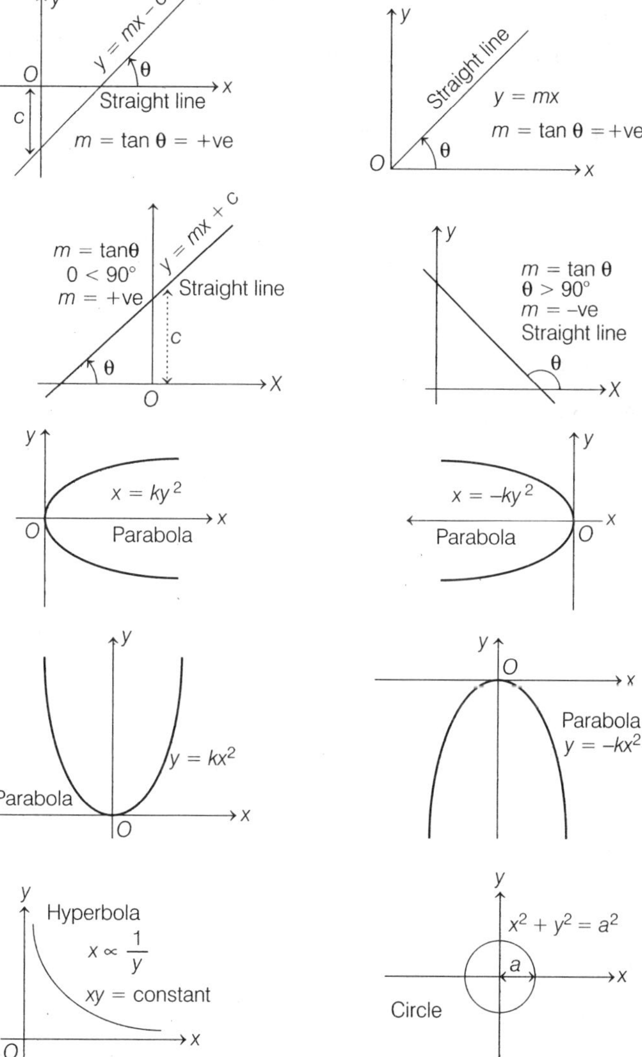

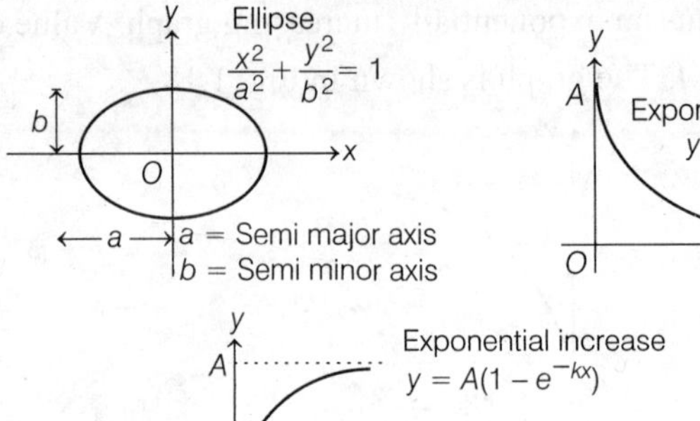

Fig. 1.19

Example 1.19 *Draw straight lines corresponding to following equations.*

(a) $y = 2x$ (b) $y = -6x$ (c) $y = 4x + 2$ (d) $y = 6x - 4$

Solution (a) In $y = 2x$, slope is 2 and intercept is zero. Hence, the graph is as shown below.

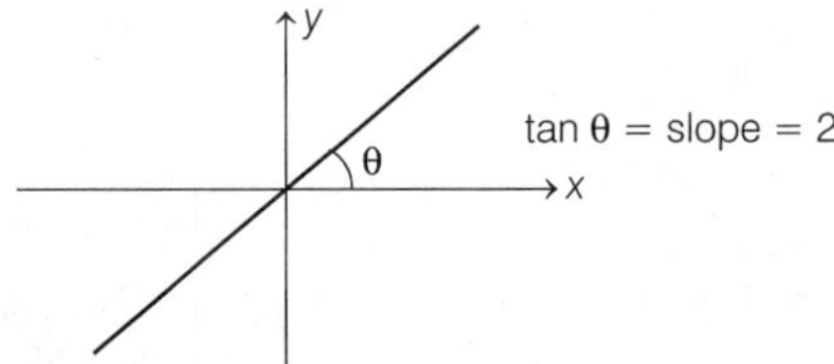

(b) In $y = -6x$, slope is -6 and intercept is zero. Hence, the graph is as shown below.

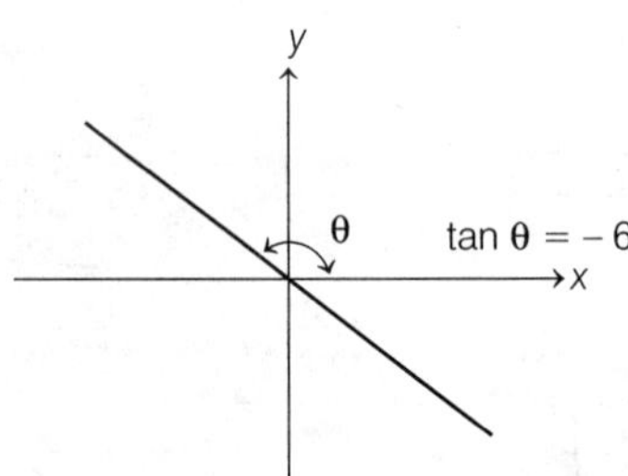

(c) In $y = 4x + 2$, slope is $+4$ and intercept is 2. The graph is as shown below.

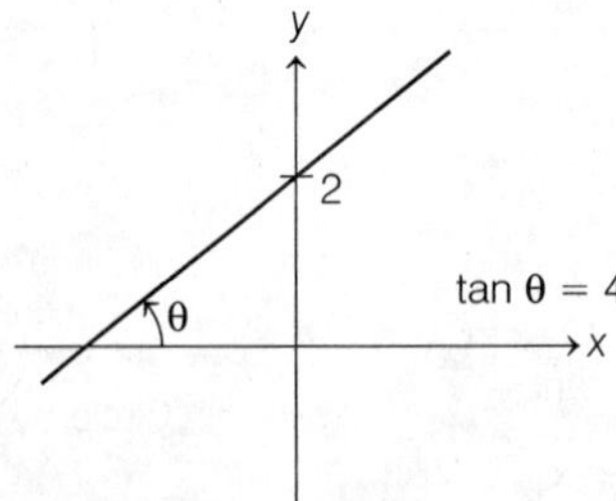

(d) In $y = 6x - 4$, slope is $+6$ and intercept is -4. Hence, the graph is as shown below.

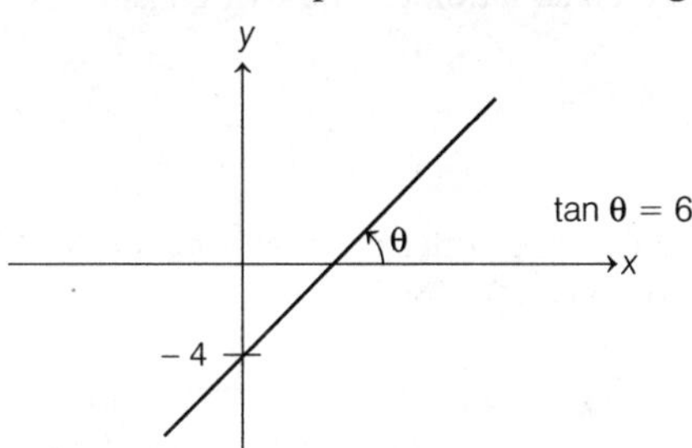

Example 1.20 *Plot the graphs corresponding to the following equations.*

(a) $y = 4x^2$ (b) $x = 4y^2$ (c) $y = \dfrac{4}{x}$ (d) $x^2 + y^2 = 16$

(e) $\dfrac{x^2}{16} + \dfrac{y^2}{9} = 1$

Solution (a) $\boldsymbol{y = 4x^2}$ Graph is a parabola.

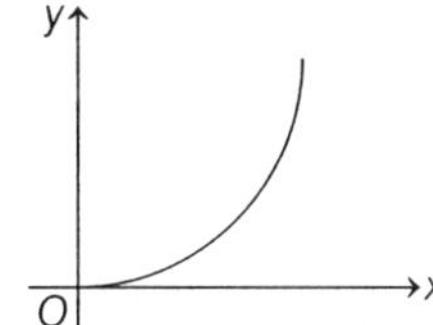

(b) $\boldsymbol{x = 4y^2}$ Graph is again a parabola.

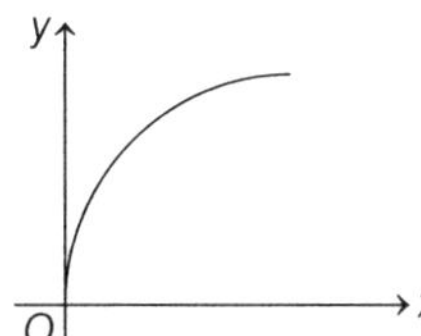

(c) $\boldsymbol{y = \dfrac{4}{x}}$ Graph is rectangular hyperbola.

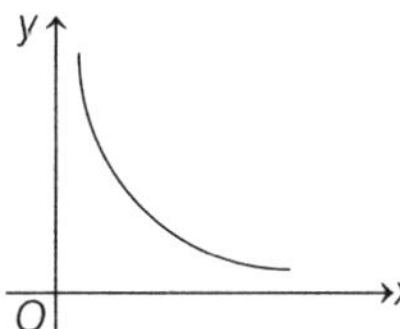

(d) $\boldsymbol{x^2 + y^2 = 16}$ The equation can be written as

$$x^2 + y^2 = (4)^2$$

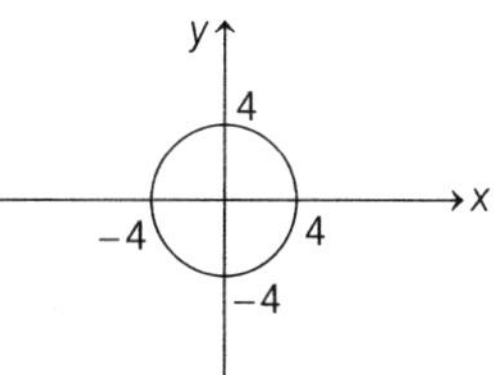

Hence, the graph is a circle with centre at origin and radius equal to 4.

(e) $\dfrac{x^2}{16}+\dfrac{y^2}{9}=1$ The given equation can be written as

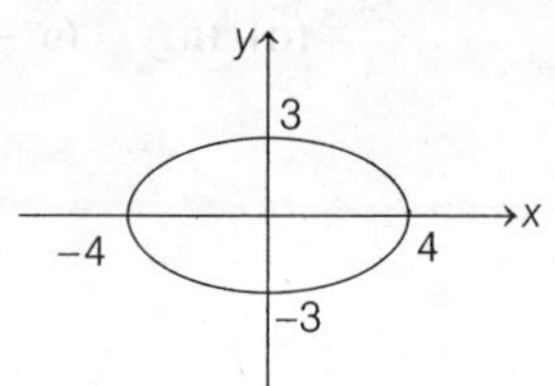

$$\frac{x^2}{(4)^2}+\frac{y^2}{(3)^2}=1$$

Hence, the graph is an ellipse with semi-major axis = 4, along x-axis and semi-minor axis = 3, along y-axis.

Example 1.21 *Velocity of a particle increases exponentially with time from 2 m/s to 6 m/s. Plot v-t graph and write v-t equation corresponding to it. Check the equation with graph at $t = 0$ and $t = \infty$.*

Solution v-t graph is as shown in figure,

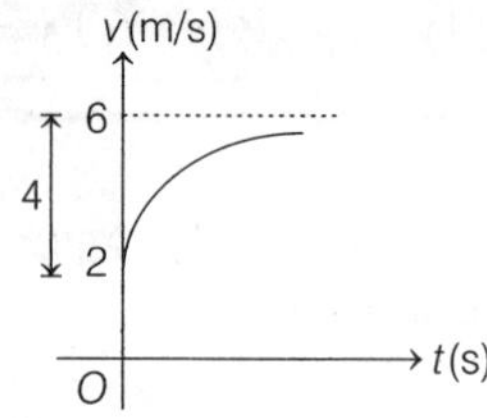

Above 2 m/s, the value 4 m/s increases exponentially. Hence, v-t equation is

$$v = 2 + 4\,(1 - e^{-kt})$$

Here k is a positive constant, which will depend on factors which are not given in the question.

At $t = 0$, $\quad v = 2 + 4\,(1 - e^{0})$

$= 2$ m/s $\quad$ as $e^0 = 1$

At $t = \infty$, $\quad v = 2 + 4\,(1 - e^{-\infty})$

$= 6$ m/s $\quad$ as $e^{-\infty} = 0$

Example 1.22 *Acceleration of a particle decreases exponentially from 10 m/s^2 to 6 m/s^2. Plot a-t graph. Write a-t equation and check the equation with graph at $t = 0$ and $t = \infty$.*

Solution a-t graph is as shown in figure.

Above 6 m/s^2 the value 4 m/s^2 decreases exponentially. Hence, a-t equation is

$$a = 6 + 4e^{-kt}$$

Here, k is a positive constant.

At $t = 0$, $\quad a = 6 + 4e^0 = 10$ m/s^2 as $e^0 = 1$

At $t = \infty$, $\quad a = 6 + 4e^{-\infty}$

$= 6$ m/s^2 as $e^{-\infty} = 0$

1.6 Algebra

(i) **Common formulae**

(a) $(a+b)^2 = a^2 + b^2 + 2ab$

(b) $(a-b)^2 = a^2 + b^2 - 2ab$

(c) $(a+b)^2 = (a-b)^2 + 4ab$

(d) $(a-b)^2 = (a+b)^2 - 4ab$

(e) $(a^2 - b^2) = (a+b)(a-b)$

(f) $(a+b)^3 = a^3 + b^3 + 3ab(a+b)$

(g) $(a-b)^3 = a^3 - b^3 - 3ab(a-b)$

(h) $a^3 + b^3 = (a+b)(a^2 - ab + b^2)$

(i) $a^3 - b^3 = (a-b)(a^2 + ab + b^2)$

(ii) **Quadratic equation and its solution**

An algebraic equation of second order (highest power of the variable is equal to 2) is called a quadratic equation. Equation $ax^2 + bx + c = 0$ is the general quadratic equation.

The general solution of the above quadratic equation or value of variable x is

$$x = \frac{-b \pm \sqrt{b^2 - 4ac}}{2a}$$

$$\Rightarrow \qquad x_1 = \frac{-b + \sqrt{b^2 - 4ac}}{2a}$$

$$\text{and} \qquad x_2 = \frac{-b - \sqrt{b^2 - 4ac}}{2a}$$

Sum of roots $= x_1 + x_2 = -\frac{b}{a}$ and product of roots $= x_1 x_2 = \frac{c}{a}$

For real roots $b^2 - 4ac \geq 0$ and for imaginary roots $b^2 - 4ac < 0$.

(iii) **Binomial approximation**

If x is very small, then $(1+x)^n \approx 1 + nx$

(iv) **Componendo and dividendo rule**

$$\text{If } \frac{p}{q} = \frac{a}{b}, \text{ then } \frac{p+q}{p-q} = \frac{a+b}{a-b}$$

(v) **Arithmetic progression (AP)**

General form : $a, a+d, a+2d, \ldots, a+(n-1)d$

Here, a = first term, d = common difference

Sum of n terms $S_n = \frac{n}{2}[a + a + (n-1)d] = \frac{n}{2}$ [Ist term + nth term]

(vi) **Geometric progression (GP)**

General form : $a, ar, ar^2, \ldots, ar^{n-1}$

Sum of n terms $S_n = \dfrac{a(1-r^n)}{1-r}$

Here, a = first term, r = common ratio

Sum of ∞ terms $S_\infty = \dfrac{a}{1-r}$ $(\because r<1 \therefore r^\infty \to 0)$

(vii) Sum of first n natural numbers

$$S_n = 1+2+,\ldots,+n = \frac{n}{2}[1+n] = \left[\frac{n(n+1)}{2}\right]$$

(viii) Sum of first n squared natural numbers

$$S_{n^2} = 1^2+2^2+3^2+,\ldots,+n^2 = \left[\frac{n(n+1)(2n+1)}{6}\right]$$

Example 1.23 *Solve the equation* $2x^2+5x-12=0$

Solution By comparison with the standard quadratic equation

$$a = 2, b = 5$$

and $$c = -12$$

$$x = \frac{-5 \pm \sqrt{(5)^2 - 4\times 2\times(-12)}}{2\times 2}$$

$$= \frac{-5\pm\sqrt{121}}{4} = \frac{-5\pm 11}{4}$$

$$= \frac{+6}{4}, \frac{-16}{4}$$

or $$x = \frac{3}{2}, -4$$

Example 1.24 *Calculate* $\sqrt{0.99}$.

Solution $\sqrt{0.99} = (1-0.01)^{1/2} = 1 - \frac{1}{2}(0.01) \approx 1 - 0.005 \approx 0.995$

Example 1.25 *Find the sum of given arithmetic progression*

$$4 + 8 + 12 + \ldots\ldots + 64$$

Solution Here, $a = 4, d = 4, n = 16$

So, $$\text{sum} = \frac{n}{2}[\text{first term} + \text{last term}]$$

$$= \frac{16}{2}[4+64] = 8(68) = 544$$

Example 1.26 *Find the sum of given geometric series* $1+2+4+8+,\dots\dots+256$

Solution Here, $a=1, r=2, n=9$ $[\because 256=2^8]$

So, $$S_9=\frac{(1)(1-2^9)}{(1-2)}$$

$$=2^9-1=512-1=511$$

Example 1.27 *Find* $1+\frac{1}{2}+\frac{1}{4}+\frac{1}{8}+\dots$ *upto* ∞.

Solution $a=1, r=\frac{1}{2}$

So, $$S_\infty=\frac{a}{1-r}=\frac{1}{1-\frac{1}{2}}=2$$

1.7 Geometry

(i) **Formulae for determination of area**

(a) Area of a square = $(\text{side})^2$

(b) Area of rectangle = length × breadth

(c) Area of a triangle = $\frac{1}{2}$(base × height)

(d) Area of trapezoid = $\frac{1}{2}$(distance between parallel side) × (sum of parallel side)

(e) Area enclosed by a circle = πr^2 (r = radius)

(f) Surface area of a sphere = $4\pi r^2$ (r = radius)

(g) Area of parallelogram = base × height

(h) Area of curved surface of cylinder = $2\pi rh$ (where, r = radius and h = length)

(i) Area of ellipse = πab

(a and b are semi major and semi minor axes respectively)

(j) Surface area of cube − 6 $(\text{side})^2$

(k) Total surface area of cone = $\pi r^2+\pi rl$

where, $\pi rl=\pi r\sqrt{r^2+h^2}$ = lateral area

(ii) **Formulae for determination of volume**

(a) Volume of rectangular slab = length × breadth × height = abt

(b) Volume of a cube = $(\text{side})^3$

(c) Volume of a sphere = $\frac{4}{3}\pi r^3$ (r = radius)

(d) Volume of a cylinder = $\pi r^2 h$ (r = radius and h is length)

(e) Volume of a cone $= \frac{1}{3}\pi r^2 h$

(r = radius and h is length)

Note $\pi = \frac{22}{7} = 3.14$, $\pi^2 = 9.8776 \approx 10$ *and* $\frac{1}{\pi} = 0.3182 \approx 0.3$

(iii) **Percentage change**

$$\text{Percentage change} = \left(\frac{\text{Final value}}{\text{Initial value}} - 1\right) \times 100$$

Note *If we have a formula* $y^m = 4x^n$ *or* $y^m \propto x^n$

Percentage change in x is small and percentage change in y is asked then we can use the approximate result,

$$m\,(\%\text{ change in } y) = n\,(\%\text{ change in } x)$$

Example 1.28 *Relation between kinetic energy K and momentum p of a particle is*

$$p = \sqrt{2Km}$$

Find percentage change in p, if

(a) K is increased by 1 % *(b) K is decreased by 36 %*

Solution (a) $p \propto \sqrt{K}$ [m = constant] or $p \propto K^{\frac{1}{2}}$

As % change is small. Hence,

$$(\%\text{ change in } p) = \frac{1}{2}(\%\text{ change in } K)$$
$$= \frac{1}{2}(+1\%) = +0.5\%$$

Therefore, momentum will increase by 0.5%.

(b) K is decreased by 36%. Therefore, new value of K is 64% of its original value or

$$K' = 0.64\,K$$

$$\therefore \quad p' = \sqrt{2K'm}$$
$$= \sqrt{2(0.64\,K)m}$$
$$= 0.8\sqrt{2Km}$$

Now, percentage change in momentum

$$= \left(\frac{\text{Final value}}{\text{Initial value}} - 1\right) \times 100$$
$$= \left(\frac{0.8\sqrt{2Km}}{\sqrt{2Km}} - 1\right) \times 100$$
$$= -20\%$$

Therefore, momentum will decrease by 20%.

1.8 Coordinate Geometry

(i) **Distance formula** The distance between two points (x_1, y_1) and (x_2, y_2) is given by

$$d = \sqrt{(x_2 - x_1)^2 + (y_2 - y_1)^2}$$

Note *In space* $d = \sqrt{(x_2 - x_1)^2 + (y_2 - y_1)^2 + (z_2 - z_1)^2}$

(ii) **Slope of a line** The slope of a line joining two points $A(x_1, y_1)$ and $B(x_2, y_2)$ is denoted by m and is given by

$$m = \frac{\Delta y}{\Delta x} = \frac{y_2 - y_1}{x_2 - x_1} = \tan\theta \qquad \text{[If both axes have identical scales]}$$

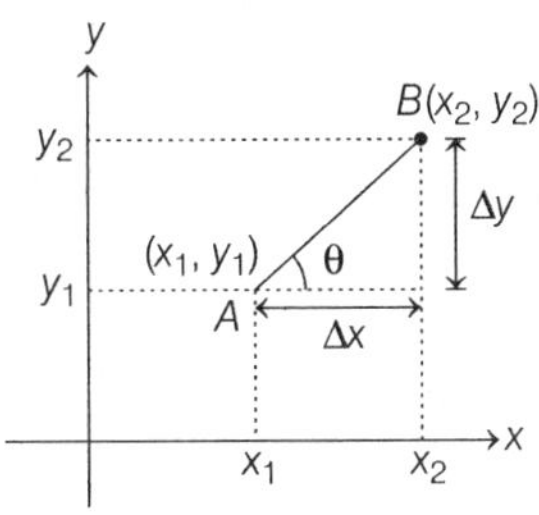

Fig. 1.20

Here, θ is the angle made by line with positive x-axis.

Example 1.29 *Find value of a if distance between the points (–9 cm, a cm) and (3 cm, 3 cm) is 13 cm.*

Solution By using distance formula,

$$d = \sqrt{(x_2 - x_1)^2 + (y_2 - y_1)^2}$$

$$\Rightarrow \quad 13^2 = 12^2 + (3 - a)^2$$

$$13^2 - 12^2 = (3 - a)^2 = 5^2$$

$$\Rightarrow \quad (3 - a) = \pm 5$$

$$\Rightarrow \quad a = -2 \text{ cm or } 8 \text{ cm}$$

Exercises

Subjective Questions

Trigonometry

1. In a circle of radius 4 m, find the angle of an arc of length 1 m subtended at centre.
2. If $\sin\theta = \frac{2}{5}$, then find the values of $\cos\theta$ and $\tan\theta$.
3. Find approximate value of $\tan 3°$.
4. Which of the following values are positive?
   (a) $\cos 120°$ (b) $\sin 210°$ (c) $\tan 240°$ (d) $\cos 315°$
5. Find the value of
   (a) $\cos 120°$ (b) $\sin 240°$ (c) $\tan(-60°)$ (d) $\cot 300°$
   (e) $\tan 330°$ (f) $\cos(-60°)$ (g) $\sin(-150°)$ (h) $\cos(-120°)$
6. Find the value of $\tan 105°$.
7. Find the value of $\cos 67°$.
8. Find the value of $\cos 105° + \cos 75°$.
9. Find the value of
   (a) $\sec^2\theta - \tan^2\theta$ (b) $\text{cosec}^2\theta - \cot^2\theta - 1$ (c) $2\sin 45° \cos 15°$ (d) $2\sin 15° \cos 45°$
10. Draw the following sinusoidal graphs
    (a) $y = 2 - 3\cos\theta$ (b) $y = -3 + 4\sin\theta$

Graphs

11. For the equations given below, tell the nature of graphs.
    (a) $y = 2x^2$ (b) $y = -4x^2 + 6$ (c) $y = 6e^{-4x}$ (d) $y = 4(1 - e^{-2x})$
    (e) $y = \frac{4}{x}$ (f) $y = -\frac{2}{x}$
12. Which of the following graphs do not pass through origin?
    (a) $y = 2x + 6$ (b) $y^2 - 2x = 0$ (c) $y^2 + 3x^2 + 5 = 0$ (d) $y + 6x = 0$
13. Check the quadrants for each part from where the following graphs will pass.
    (a) $y = -4x^2$ (b) $y = \frac{6}{x}$
14. After finding x-intercept C_x and y-intercept C_y, plot the straight line corresponding to the x-y equation given below.

$$6x - 2y + 5 = 0$$

15. Draw the graphs corresponding to the equations
    (a) $y = 4x$ (b) $y = -6x$ (c) $y = x + 4$ (d) $y = -2x + 4$
    (e) $y = 2x - 4$ (f) $y = -4x - 6$

16. For the graphs given below, write down their x-y equations

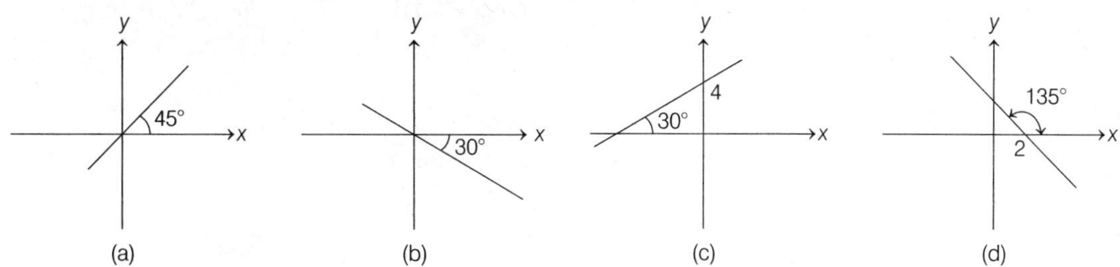

17. Value of y decreases exponentially from $y = 10$ to $y = 6$. Plot a x-y graph.

18. Value of y increases exponentially from $y = -4$ to $y = +4$. Plot a x-y graph.

19. The graph shown in figure is exponential. Write down the equation corresponding to the graph.

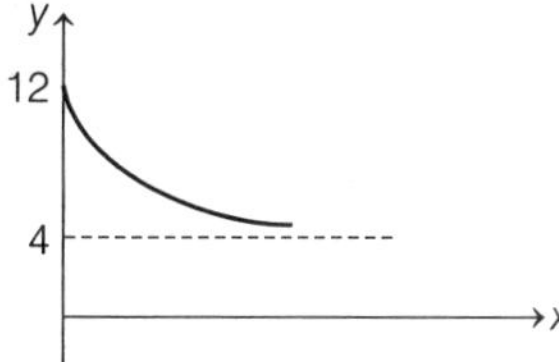

20. The graph shown in figure is exponential. Write down the equation corresponding to the graph.

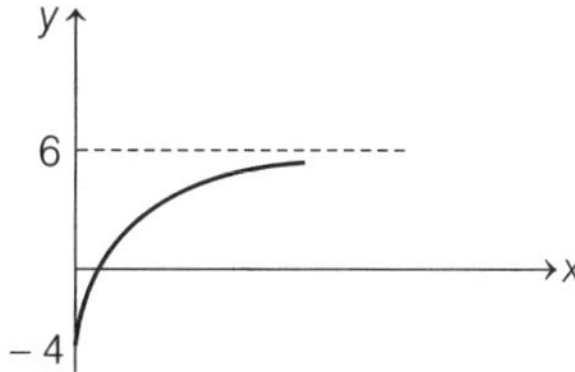

21. In the equation $y = 6 + 4(1 - e^{-kt})$, what is the maximum value of y?

22. In the equation $y = -4 - 6e^{-kt}$, what is the minimum value of y?

Differentiation

23. Differentiate the following with respect to x.

$$\sqrt{x} - \frac{1}{\sqrt{x}}$$

24. Differentiate the following with respect to x.

$$(5x^2 + 6)(2x^2 + 4)$$

25. Differentiate the following with respect to x.

$$\sqrt{x}\,(x^2 + 7)$$

26. Differentiate the following with respect to θ.

$$\frac{\cos\theta}{(1 - \sin\theta)}$$

27. Differentiate the following functions with respect to x.

(a) $x^4 + 3x^2 - 2x$ (b) $x^2 \cos x$ (c) $(6x + 7)^4$ (d) $e^x x^5$

(e) $\dfrac{(1 + x)}{e^x}$

28. Find the maximum/minimum value of y in the functions given below.

(a) $y = 5 - (x - 1)^2$ (b) $y = (\sin 2x - x)$, where $-\dfrac{\pi}{2} \le x \le \dfrac{\pi}{2}$

Integration

29. Integrate the following functions with respect to t

(a) $\int (3t^2 - 2t)\, dt$ (b) $\int (4 \cos t + t^2)\, dt$ (c) $\int (2t - 4)^{-4}\, dt$ (d) $\int \dfrac{dt}{(6t - 1)}$

30. Integrate the following functions

(a) $\int_0^2 2t\, dt$ (b) $\int_{\pi/6}^{\pi/3} \sin x\, dx$ (c) $\int_4^{10} \dfrac{dx}{x}$ (d) $\int_0^{\pi} \cos x\, dx$

(e) $\int_1^2 (2t - 4)\, dt$

Percentage Change

31. Momentum of a particle is increased by 2% without change in its mass. Find the percentage change in its kinetic energy.

32. Momentum of a particle is decreased by 20% without change in its mass. Find the percentage change in its kinetic energy.

33. Kinetic energy of a particle is decreased by 3% without change in its mass. Find the percentage change in its momentum.

34. Kinetic energy of a particle is increased by 50% without change in its mass. Find the percentage change in its momentum.

Ratio Division

35. Height of Kartik is 5ft and of Atharva 4ft. Divide ₹1000/- in inverse ratio of square of their heights.

Answers

Subjective Questions

1. (0.25) radian 2. $\cos\theta = \frac{\sqrt{21}}{5}, \tan\theta = \frac{2}{\sqrt{21}}$ 3. 0.052

4. (c) and (d) 5. (a) $-\frac{1}{2}$ (b) $-\frac{\sqrt{3}}{2}$ (c) $-\sqrt{3}$ (d) $-\frac{1}{\sqrt{3}}$ (e) $-\frac{1}{\sqrt{3}}$ (f) $\frac{1}{2}$ (g) $-\frac{1}{2}$ (h) $-\frac{1}{2}$

6. $\left(\frac{\sqrt{3}+1}{1-\sqrt{3}}\right)$ 7. $\left(\frac{4\sqrt{3}-3}{10}\right)$ 8. Zero

9. (a) 1 (b) 0 (c) $\left(\frac{\sqrt{3}+1}{2}\right)$ (d) $\left(\frac{\sqrt{3}-1}{2}\right)$

10.

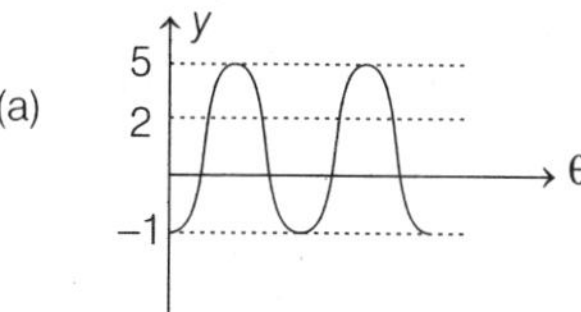

(a)

(b)

11. (a) Parabola passing through origin (b) Parabola not passing through origin
 (c) Exponentially decreasing graph (d) Exponentially increasing graph
 (e) Rectangular hyperbola in first and third quadrant
 (f) Rectangular hyperbola in second and fourth quadrant

12. (a) and (c) 13. (a) III and IV (b) III and I

14.

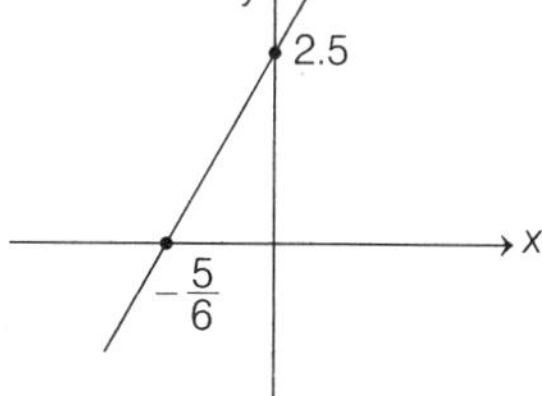

15.

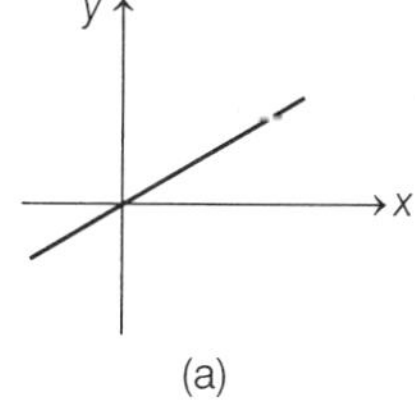

(a)

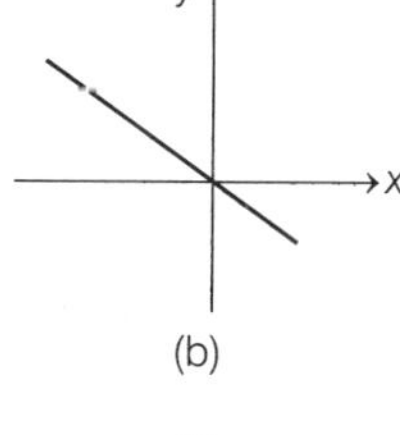

(b)

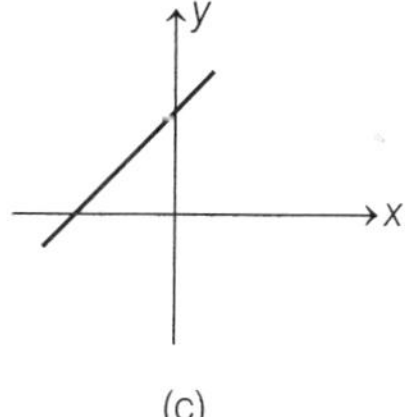

(c)

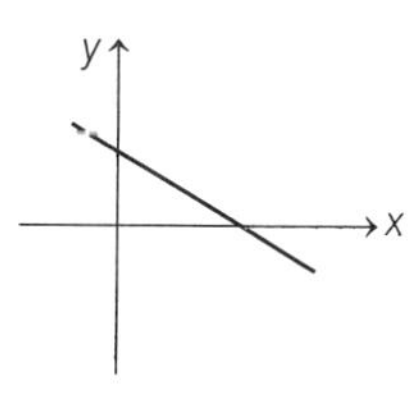

(d)

(e)

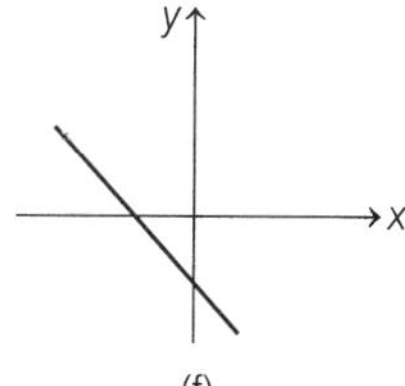

(f)

16. (a) $y = x$ (b) $y = -\frac{x}{\sqrt{3}}$ (c) $y = \frac{x}{\sqrt{3}} + 4$ (d) $y = -x + 2$

17. 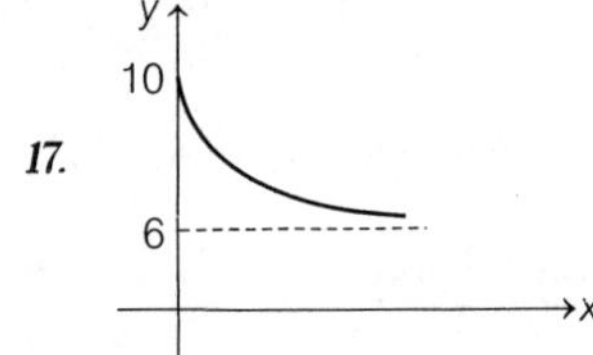

18. 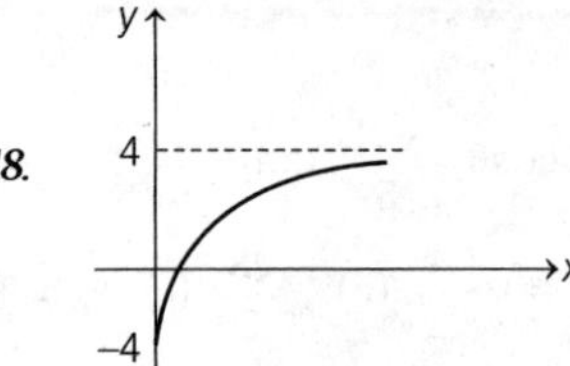

19. $y = 4 + 8e^{-Kx}$. Here, K is a positive constant

20. $y = -4 + 10(1 - e^{-Kx})$. Here, K is positive constant 21. 10

22. –10

23. $\frac{1}{2\sqrt{x}} + \frac{1}{2x^{\frac{3}{2}}} = \frac{1}{2\sqrt{x}}\left(1 + \frac{1}{x}\right)$

24. $40x^3 + 64x = 8x(5x^2 + 8)$

25. $\frac{5}{2}x^{\frac{3}{2}} + \frac{7}{2\sqrt{x}} = \frac{1}{2\sqrt{x}}(7 + 5x^2)$

26. $\frac{1}{1 - \sin\theta}$

27. (a) $4x^3 + 6x - 2$ (b) $2x\cos x - x^2\sin x$ (c) $24(6x + 7)^3$ (d) $5e^x x^4 + e^x x^5$ (e) $-xe^{-x}$

28. (a) $y_{max} = 5$ at $x = 1$ (b) $y_{min} = -\left(\frac{\sqrt{3}}{2} - \frac{\pi}{6}\right)$ at $x = -\pi/6$ and $y_{max} = \left(\frac{\sqrt{3}}{2} - \frac{\pi}{6}\right)$ at $x = \pi/6$

29. (a) $t^3 - t^2 + C$ (b) $4\sin t + \frac{t^3}{3} + C$ (c) $-\frac{1}{6(2t - 4)^3} + C$ (d) $\frac{1}{6}\ln(6t - 1) + C$

30. (a) 4 (b) $\frac{(\sqrt{3} - 1)}{2}$ (c) $\ln(5/2)$ (d) Zero (e) –1

31. 4% 32. –36% 33. –1.5% 34. Approximately 22%

35. ₹ $\frac{16000}{41}$, ₹ $\frac{25000}{41}$

2

Measurement and Errors

1.1 Errors in Measurement and Least Count

1.2 Significant Figures

1.3 Rounding Off a Digit

1.4 Algebraic Operations with Significant Figures

1.5 Error Analysis

2.1 Errors in Measurement and Least Count

To get some overview of error, least count and significant figures, let us have some examples.

Example 2.1 *Let us use a centimeter scale (on which only centimeter scales are there) to measure a length AB.*

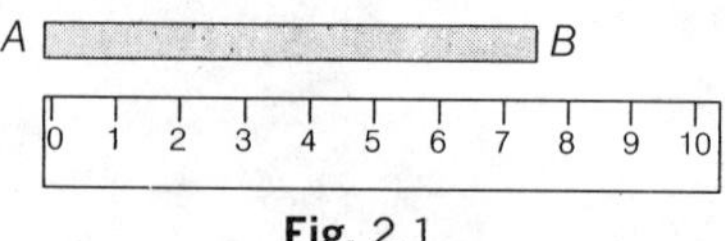

Fig. 2.1

From the figure, we can see that length AB is more than 7 cm and less than 8 cm. In this case, **Least Count (LC)** *of this centimeter scale is 1 cm, as it can measure accurately upto centimeters only. If we note down the length (l) of line AB as $l = 7$ cm then maximum uncertainty or maximum possible error in l can be 1 cm (= LC), because this scale can measure accurately only upto 1 cm.*

Example 2.2 *Let us now use a millimeter scale (on which millimeter marks are there). This is also our normal meter scale which we use in our routine life. From the figure, we can see that length AB is more than 3.3 cm and less than 3.4 cm. If we note down the length,*

$$l = AB = 3.4 \text{ cm}$$

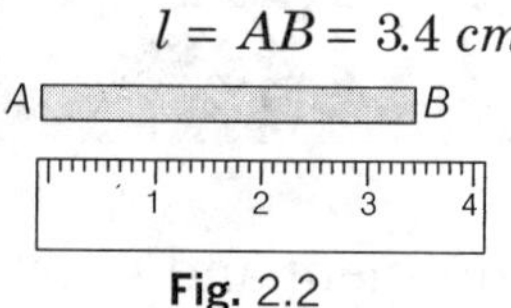

Fig. 2.2

Then, this measurement has two significant figures 3 and 4 in which 3 is absolutely correct and 4 is reasonably correct (doubtful). Least count of this scale is 0.1 cm because this scale can measure accurately only upto 0.1 cm. Further, maximum uncertainty or maximum possible error in l can also be 0.1 cm.

INTRODUCTORY EXERCISE 2.1

1. If we measure a length $l = 6.24$ cm with the help of a vernier callipers, then
   (a) what is least count of vernier callipers ?
   (b) how many significant figures are there in the measured length ?
   (c) which digits are absolutely correct and which is/are doubtful ?
2. If we measure a length $l = 3.267$ cm with the help of a screw gauge, then
   (a) what is maximum uncertainty or maximum possible error in l ?
   (b) how many significant figures are there in the measured length ?
   (c) which digits are absolutely correct and which is/are doubtful ?

2.2 Significant Figures

From example 2.2, we can conclude that:

"*In a measured quantity, significant figures are the digits which are absolutely correct plus the first uncertain digit*".

Rules for Counting Significant Figures

Rule 1 All non-zero digits are significant. For example, 126.28 has five significant figures.

Rule 2 The zeros appearing between two non-zero digits are significant. For example, 6.025 has four significant figures.

Rule 3 Trailing zeros after decimal places are significant. Measurement $l = 6.400$ cm has four significant figures. Let us take an example in its support.

Table 2.1

Measurement	Accuracy	l lies between (in cm)	Significant figures	Remarks
l = 6.4 cm	0.1 cm	6.3 – 6.5	Two	
l = 6.40 cm	0.01 cm	6.39 – 6.41	Three	closer
l = 6.400 cm	0.001 cm	6.399 – 6.401	Four	more closer

Thus, the significant figures depend on the accuracy of measurement. More the number of significant figures, more accurate is the measurement.

Rule 4 The powers of ten are not counted as significant figures. For example, 1.4×10^{-7} has only two significant figures 1 and 4.

Rule 5 If a measurement is less than one, then all zeros occurring to the left of last non-zero digit are not significant. For example, 0.0042 has two significant figures 4 and 2.

Rule 6 Change in units of measurement of a quantity does not change the number of significant figures. Suppose a measurement was done using mm scale and we get $l = 72$ mm (two significant figures).

We can write this measurement in other units also (without changing the number of significant figures) :

7.2 cm → Two significant figures.
0.072 m → Two significant figures.
0.000072 km → Two significant figures.
7.2×10^{7} nm → Two significant figures

Rule 7 The terminal or trailing zeros in a number without a decimal point are not significant. This also sometimes arises due to change of unit.

For example, 264 m = 26400 cm = 264000 mm

All have only three significant figures 2, 6 and 4. All trailing zeros are not significant.

Zeroes at the end of a number are significant only if they are behind a decimal point as in Rule-3. Otherwise, it is impossible to tell if they are significant. For example, in the number 8200, it is not clear if the zeros are significant or not. The number of significant digits in 8200 is at least two, but could be three or four. To avoid uncertainty, use scientific notation to place significant zeros behind a decimal point

8.200×10^{3} has four significant digits.

8.20×10^3 has three significant digits.

8.2×10^3 has two significant digits.

Therefore, if it is not expressed in scientific notations, then write least number of significant digits. Hence, in the number 8200, take significant digits as two.

Rule 8 Exact measurements have infinite number of significant figures. For example,

10 bananas in a basket

46 students in a class

speed of light in vacuum $= 299{,}792{,}458$ m/s (exact)

$\pi = \frac{22}{7}$ (exact)

All these measurements have infinite number of significant figures.

Example 2.3

Table 2.2

Measured value	Number of significant figures	Rule number
12376 cm	5	1
6024.7 cm	5	2
0.071 cm	2	5
4100 cm	2	7
2.40 cm	3	3
1.60×10^{14} km	3	4

INTRODUCTORY EXERCISE 2.2

1. Count total number of significant figures in the following measurements:
   (a) 4.080 cm (b) 0.079 m (c) 950
   (d) 10.00 cm (e) 4.07080 (f) 7.090×10^5

2.3 Rounding Off a Digit

Following are the rules for rounding off a measurement :

Rule 1 If the number lying to the right of cut off digit is less than 5, then the cut off digit is retained as such. However, if it is more than 5, then the cut off digit is increased by 1.

For example, $x = 6.24$ is rounded off to 6.2 to two significant digits and $x = 5.328$ is rounded off to 5.33 to three significant digits.

Rule 2 If the digit to be dropped is 5 followed by digits other than zero, then the preceding digit is increased by 1.

For example, $x = 14.252$ is rounded off to $x = 14.3$ to three significant digits.

Rule 3 If the digit to be dropped is simply 5 or 5 followed by zeros, then the preceding digit is left unchanged if it is even.

For example, $x = 6.250$ or $x = 6.25$ becomes $x = 6.2$ after rounding off to two significant digits.

Rule 4 If the digit to be dropped is 5 or 5 followed by zeros, then the preceding digit is raised by one if it is odd.

For example, $x = 6.350$ or $x = 6.35$ becomes $x = 6.4$ after rounding off to two significant digits.

Example 2.4

Table 2.3

Measured value	After rounding off to three significant digits	Rule
7.364	7.36	1
7.367	7.37	1
8.3251	8.33	2
9.445	9.44	3
9.4450	9.44	3
15.75	15.8	4
15.7500	15.8	4

INTRODUCTORY EXERCISE 2.3

1. Round off the following numbers to three significant figures :
   (a) 24572 (b) 24.937 (c) 36.350 (d) 42.450×10^9
2. Round 742396 to four, three and two significant digits.

2.4 Algebraic Operations with Significant Figures

The final result shall have significant figures corresponding to their number in the least accurate variable involved. To understand this, let us consider a chain of which all links are strong except the one. The chain will obviously break at the weakest link. Thus, the strength of the chain cannot be more than the strength of the weakest link in the chain.

Addition and Subtraction

Suppose, in the measured values to be added or subtracted the least number of digits after the decimal is n. Then, in the sum or difference also, the number of digits after the decimal should be n.

Example 2.5 $1.2 + 3.45 + 6.789 = 11.439 \approx 11.4$

Here, the least number of significant digits after the decimal is one. Hence, the result will be 11.4 (when rounded off to smallest number of decimal places).

Example 2.6 $12.63 - 10.2 = 2.43 \approx 2.4$

Multiplication or Division

Suppose in the measured values to be multiplied or divided the least number of significant digits be n. Then in the product or quotient, the number of significant digits should also be n.

Example 2.7 $1.2 \times 36.72 = 44.064 \approx 44$

The least number of significant digits in the measured values are two. Hence, the result when rounded off to two significant digits become 44. Therefore, the answer is 44.

Example 2.8 $\dfrac{1101\ \text{ms}^{-1}}{10.2\ \text{ms}^{-1}} = 107.94117647 \approx 108$

Example 2.9 *Find, volume of a cube of side $a = 1.4 \times 10^{-2}$ m.*

Solution Volume $V = a^3$

$$= (1.4 \times 10^{-2}) \times (1.4 \times 10^{-2}) \times (1.4 \times 10^{-2}) = 2.744 \times 10^{-6}\ \text{m}^3$$

Since, each value of a has two significant figures. Hence, we will round off the result to two significant figures.

$\therefore$ $$V = 2.7 \times 10^{-6}\ \text{m}^3$$ **Ans.**

Example 2.10 *Radius of a wire is 2.50 mm. The length of the wire is 50.0 cm. If mass of wire was measured as 25 g, then find the density of wire in correct significant figures.*
[Given, $\pi = 3.14$, exact]

Solution Given,

$r = 2.50$ mm (three significant figures)
$= 0.250$ cm (three significant figures)

Note *Change in the units of measurement of a quantity does not change the number of significant figures.*

Further given that,

$l = 50.0$ cm (three significant figures)
$m = 25$ g (two significant figures)
$\pi = 3.14$ exact (infinite significant figures)

$$\rho = \frac{m}{V} = \frac{m}{\pi r^2 l}$$

$$= \frac{25}{(3.14)(0.250)(0.250)(50.0)}$$

$$= 2.5477\ \text{g/cm}^3$$

But in the measured values, least number of significant figures are two. Hence, we will round off the result to two significant figures.

$\therefore$ $$\rho = 2.5\ \text{g/cm}^3$$ **Ans.**

INTRODUCTORY EXERCISE 2.4

1. Round to the appropriate number of significant digits
   (a) 13.214 + 234.6 + 7.0350 + 6.38
   (b) 1247 + 134.5 + 450 + 78
2. Simplify and round to the appropriate number of significant digits
   (a) $16.235 \times 0.217 \times 5$
   (b) 0.00435×4.6

2.5 Error Analysis

We have studied in the above articles that no measurement is perfect. Every instrument can measure upto a certain accuracy called **Least Count (LC)**.

Least Count

The smallest measurement that can be measured accurately by an instrument is called its least count.

Instrument	Its least count
mm scale	1 mm
Vernier callipers	0.1 mm
Screw gauge	0.01 mm
Stop watch	0.1 sec
Temperature thermometer	1°C

Permissible Error due to Least Count

Error in measurement due to the limitation (or least count) of the instrument is called permissible error. Least count of a millimeter scale is 1 mm. Therefore, maximum permissible error in the measurement of a length by a millimeter scale may be 1 mm.

If we measure a length $l = 26$ mm. Then, maximum value of true value may be $(26+1)$ mm $= 27$ mm and minimum value of true value may be $(26-1)$ mm $= 25$ mm.

Thus, we can write it like,

$$l = (26 \pm 1) \text{ mm}$$

If from any other instrument we measure a length $= 24.6$ mm, then the maximum permissible error (or least count) from this instrument is 0.1 mm. So, we can write the measurement like,

$$l = (24.6 \pm 0.1) \text{ mm}$$

Classification of Errors

Errors can be classified in two ways. First classification is based on the cause of error. Systematic error and random errors fall in this group. Second classification is based on the magnitude of errors. Absolute error, mean absolute error and relative (or fractional) error lie on this group. Now, let us discuss them separately.

Systematic Error

Systematic errors are the errors whose causes are known to us. Such errors can therefore be minimised. Following are few causes of these errors :

(a) Instrumental errors may be due to erroneous instruments. These errors can be reduced by using more accurate instruments and applying zero correction, when required.

(b) Sometimes errors arise on account of ignoring certain facts. For example in measuring time period of simple pendulum error may creep because no consideration is taken of air resistance. These errors can be reduced by applying proper corrections to the formula used.

(c) Change in temperature, pressure, humidity, etc., may also sometimes cause errors in the result. Relevant corrections can be made to minimise their effects.

Random Error

The causes of random errors are not known. Hence, it is not possible to remove them completely. These errors may arise due to a variety of reasons. For example the reading of a sensitive beam balance may change by the vibrations caused in the building due to persons moving in the laboratory or vehicles running nearby. The random errors can be minimized by repeating the observation a large number of times and taking the arithmetic mean of all the observations. The mean value would be very close to the most accurate reading. Thus,

$$a_{\text{mean}} = \frac{a_1 + a_2 + \ldots + a_n}{n}$$

Absolute Error

The difference between the true value and the measured value of a quantity is called an absolute error. Usually the mean value a_m is taken as the true value. So, if

$$a_m = \frac{a_1 + a_2 + \ldots + a_n}{n}$$

Now let us find the difference of a_m with measured values. Thus,

$$\Delta a_1 = a_m - a_1$$
$$\Delta a_2 = a_m - a_2$$
$$\ldots \quad \ldots \quad \ldots$$
$$\Delta a_n = a_m - a_n$$

Here, $\Delta a_1, \Delta a_2 \ldots \Delta a_n$ may be positive or negative but their magnitude $|\Delta a|$ which is always positive is called the absolute error.

Mean Absolute Error

Arithmetic mean of the magnitudes of absolute errors in all the measurements is called the mean absolute error. Thus,

$$\Delta a_{\text{mean}} = \frac{|\Delta a_1| + |\Delta a_2| + \ldots + |\Delta a_n|}{n}$$

The final result of measurement can be written as, $a = a_m \pm \Delta a_{mean}$
This implies that value of a is likely to lie between $a_m + \Delta a_{mean}$ and $a_m - \Delta a_{mean}$.

Relative or Fractional Error

The ratio of mean absolute error to the mean value of the quantity measured is called relative or fractional error. Thus,

$$\text{Relative error} = \frac{\Delta a_{\text{mean}}}{a_m}$$

Relative error expressed in percentage is called as the percentage error, i.e.

$$\text{Percentage error} = \frac{\Delta a_{\text{mean}}}{a_m} \times 100$$

Example 2.11 *The diameter of a wire as measured by screw gauge was found to be 2.620, 2.625, 2.630, 2.628 and 2.626 cm. Calculate*

(a) mean value of diameter
(b) absolute error in each measurement
(c) mean absolute error
(d) fractional error
(e) percentage error
(f) Express the result in terms of percentage error

Solution (a) Mean value of diameter

$$a_m = \frac{2.620 + 2.625 + 2.630 + 2.628 + 2.626}{5}$$

$$= 2.6258 \text{ cm}$$

$$= 2.626 \text{ cm} \quad \text{(rounding off to three decimal places)}$$

(b) Taking a_m as the true value, the absolute errors in different observations are,

$$\Delta a_1 = 2.626 - 2.620 = +0.006 \text{ cm}$$
$$\Delta a_2 = 2.626 - 2.625 = +0.001 \text{ cm}$$
$$\Delta a_3 = 2.626 - 2.630 = -0.004 \text{ cm}$$
$$\Delta a_4 = 2.626 - 2.628 = -0.002 \text{ cm}$$
$$\Delta a_5 = 2.626 - 2.626 = 0.000 \text{ cm}$$

(c) Mean absolute error,

$$\Delta a_{\text{mean}} = \frac{|\Delta a_1| + |\Delta a_2| + |\Delta a_3| + |\Delta a_4| + |\Delta a_5|}{5}$$

$$= \frac{0.006 + 0.001 + 0.004 + 0.002 + 0.000}{5}$$

$$= 0.0026 = 0.003 \quad \text{(rounding off to three decimal places)}$$

(d) Fractional error $= \pm \dfrac{\Delta a_{\text{mean}}}{a_m} = \dfrac{\pm 0.003}{2.626} = \pm 0.001$

(e) Percentage error $= \pm 0.001 \times 100 = \pm 0.1\%$

(f) Diameter of wire can be written as,

$$d = 2.626 \pm 0.1\%$$

Ans.

Combination of Errors

Errors in Sum or Difference

Let $x = a \pm b$

Further, let Δa is the absolute error in the measurement of a, Δb the absolute error in the measurement of b and Δx is the absolute error in the measurement of x.

Then,
$$x + \Delta x = (a \pm \Delta a) \pm (b \pm \Delta b)$$
$$= (a \pm b) \pm (\pm \Delta a \pm \Delta b)$$
$$= x \pm (\pm \Delta a \pm \Delta b)$$

or
$$\Delta x = \pm \Delta a \pm \Delta b$$

The four possible values of Δx are $(\Delta a - \Delta b)$, $(\Delta a + \Delta b)$, $(-\Delta a - \Delta b)$ and $(-\Delta a + \Delta b)$.

Therefore, the maximum absolute error in x is,

$$\Delta x = \pm (\Delta a + \Delta b)$$

i.e. the maximum absolute error in sum and difference of two quantities is equal to sum of the absolute errors in the individual quantities.

Example 2.12 *The volumes of two bodies are measured to be $V_1 = (10.2 \pm 0.02)\, cm^3$ and $V_2 = (6.4 \pm 0.01)\, cm^3$. Calculate sum and difference in volumes with error limits.*

Solution
$$V_1 = (10.2 \pm 0.02)\,\text{cm}^3$$

and
$$V_2 = (6.4 \pm 0.01)\,\text{cm}^3$$

$$\Delta V = \pm (\Delta V_1 + \Delta V_2)$$

$$= \pm (0.02 + 0.01)\,\text{cm}^3 = \pm 0.03\,\text{cm}^3$$

$$V_1 + V_2 = (10.2 + 6.4)\,\text{cm}^3 = 16.6\,\text{cm}^3$$

and
$$V_1 - V_2 = (10.2 - 6.4)\,\text{cm}^3 = 3.8\,\text{cm}^3$$

Hence, sum of volumes $= (16.6 \pm 0.03)\,\text{cm}^3$

and difference of volumes $= (3.8 \pm 0.03)\,\text{cm}^3$ **Ans.**

Errors in a Product

Let $x = ab$

Then,
$$(x \pm \Delta x) = (a \pm \Delta a)(b \pm \Delta b)$$

or
$$x\left(1 \pm \frac{\Delta x}{x}\right) = ab\left(1 \pm \frac{\Delta a}{a}\right)\left(1 \pm \frac{\Delta b}{b}\right)$$

or
$$1 \pm \frac{\Delta x}{x} = 1 \pm \frac{\Delta b}{b} \pm \frac{\Delta a}{a} \pm \frac{\Delta a}{a} \cdot \frac{\Delta b}{b} \qquad (\text{as } x = ab)$$

or
$$\pm \frac{\Delta x}{x} = \pm \frac{\Delta a}{a} \pm \frac{\Delta b}{b} \pm \frac{\Delta a}{a} \cdot \frac{\Delta b}{b}$$

Here, $\frac{\Delta a}{a} \cdot \frac{\Delta b}{b}$ is a small quantity, so can be neglected.

Hence,
$$\pm \frac{\Delta x}{x} = \pm \frac{\Delta a}{a} \pm \frac{\Delta b}{b}$$

Possible values of $\frac{\Delta x}{x}$ are $\left(\frac{\Delta a}{a} + \frac{\Delta b}{b}\right)$, $\left(\frac{\Delta a}{a} - \frac{\Delta b}{b}\right)$, $\left(-\frac{\Delta a}{a} + \frac{\Delta b}{b}\right)$ and $\left(-\frac{\Delta a}{a} - \frac{\Delta b}{b}\right)$.

Hence, maximum possible value of

$$\frac{\Delta x}{x} = \pm \left(\frac{\Delta a}{a} + \frac{\Delta b}{b}\right)$$

Therefore, maximum fractional error in product of two (or more) quantities is equal to sum of fractional errors in the individual quantities.

Errors in Division

Let $$x = \frac{a}{b}$$

Then, $$x \pm \Delta x = \frac{a \pm \Delta a}{b \pm \Delta b}$$

or $$x\left(1 \pm \frac{\Delta x}{x}\right) = \frac{a\left(1 \pm \frac{\Delta a}{a}\right)}{b\left(1 \pm \frac{\Delta b}{b}\right)}$$

or $$\left(1 \pm \frac{\Delta x}{x}\right) = \left(1 \pm \frac{\Delta a}{a}\right)\left(1 \pm \frac{\Delta b}{b}\right)^{-1} \qquad \left(\text{as } x = \frac{a}{b}\right)$$

As $\frac{\Delta b}{b} << 1$, so expanding binomially, we get

$$\left(1 \pm \frac{\Delta x}{x}\right) = \left(1 \pm \frac{\Delta a}{a}\right)\left(1 \mp \frac{\Delta b}{b}\right)$$

or $$1 \pm \frac{\Delta x}{x} = 1 \pm \frac{\Delta a}{a} \mp \frac{\Delta b}{b} \pm \frac{\Delta a}{a} \cdot \frac{\Delta b}{b}$$

Here, $\frac{\Delta a}{a} \cdot \frac{\Delta b}{b}$ is small quantity, so can be neglected. Therefore,

$$\pm \frac{\Delta x}{x} = \pm \frac{\Delta a}{a} \mp \frac{\Delta b}{b}$$

Possible values of $\frac{\Delta x}{x}$ are $\left(\frac{\Delta a}{a} - \frac{\Delta b}{b}\right)$, $\left(\frac{\Delta a}{a} + \frac{\Delta b}{b}\right)$, $\left(-\frac{\Delta a}{a} - \frac{\Delta b}{b}\right)$ and $\left(-\frac{\Delta a}{a} + \frac{\Delta b}{b}\right)$. Therefore, the maximum value of

$$\boxed{\frac{\Delta x}{x} = \pm\left(\frac{\Delta a}{a} + \frac{\Delta b}{b}\right)}$$

or the maximum value of fractional error in division of two quantities is equal to the sum of fractional errors in the individual quantities.

Error in Quantity Raised to Some Power

Let, $x = \frac{a^n}{b^m}$. Then, $\ln(x) = n\ln(a) - m\ln(b)$

Differentiating both sides, we get

$$\frac{dx}{x} = n \cdot \frac{da}{a} - m\frac{db}{b}$$

In terms of fractional error we may write,

$$\pm \frac{\Delta x}{x} = \pm n\frac{\Delta a}{a} \mp m\frac{\Delta b}{b}$$

Therefore, maximum value of

$$\boxed{\frac{\Delta x}{x} = \pm\left(n\frac{\Delta a}{a} + m\frac{\Delta b}{b}\right)}$$

Note *Errors in product and division can also be obtained by taking logarithm on both sides* $\left(\text{in } x = ab \text{ or } x = \frac{a}{b}\right)$ *and then differentiating.*

Example 2.13 *The mass and density of a solid sphere are measured to be* (12.4 ± 0.1) *kg and* (4.6 ± 0.2) *kg/m*^{3}*. Calculate the volume of the sphere with error limits.*

Solution Here, $m \pm \Delta m = (12.4 \pm 0.1)$ kg

and $\rho \pm \Delta\rho = (4.6 \pm 0.2)\ \text{kg/m}^3$

Volume $V = \frac{m}{\rho} = \frac{12.4}{4.6}$

$= 2.69\ \text{m}^3 = 2.7\ \text{m}^3$ (rounding off to one decimal place)

Now, $\frac{\Delta V}{V} = \pm\left(\frac{\Delta m}{m} + \frac{\Delta\rho}{\rho}\right)$

or $\Delta V = \pm\left(\frac{\Delta m}{m} + \frac{\Delta\rho}{\rho}\right) \times V$

$= \pm\left(\frac{0.1}{12.4} + \frac{0.2}{4.6}\right) \times 2.7$

$= \pm 0.14$

$\therefore$ $V \pm \Delta V = (2.7 \pm 0.14)\ \text{m}^3$ **Ans.**

Example 2.14 *Calculate percentage error in determination of time period of a pendulum*

$$T = 2\pi\sqrt{\frac{l}{g}}$$

where, l and g are measured with $\pm 1\%$ *and* $\pm 2\%$.

Solution $T = 2\pi\sqrt{\frac{l}{g}}$

or $T = (2\pi)(l)^{+1/2}(g)^{-1/2}$

Taking logarithm of both sides, we have

$$\ln(T) = \ln(2\pi) + \frac{1}{2}(\ln l) - \left(\frac{1}{2}\right)\ln(g) \quad \text{...(i)}$$

Here, 2π is a constant, therefore $\ln(2\pi)$ is also a constant.

Differentiating Eq. (i), we have

$$\frac{1}{T}dT = 0 + \frac{1}{2}\left(\frac{1}{l}\right)(dl) - \frac{1}{2}\left(\frac{1}{g}\right)(dg)$$

or $$\left(\frac{dT}{T}\right)_{max} = \text{maximum value of}\left(\pm\frac{1}{2}\frac{dl}{l} \mp \frac{1}{2}\frac{dg}{g}\right)$$

$$= \frac{1}{2}\left(\frac{dl}{l}\right) + \frac{1}{2}\left(\frac{dg}{g}\right)$$

This can also be written as

$$\left(\frac{\Delta T}{T} \times 100\right)_{max} = \frac{1}{2}\left[\frac{\Delta l}{l} \times 100\right] + \frac{1}{2}\left[\frac{\Delta g}{g} \times 100\right]$$

or percentage error in time period

$$= \pm\left[\frac{1}{2}(\text{percentage error in } l) + \frac{1}{2}(\text{percentage error in } g)\right]$$

$$= \pm\left[\frac{1}{2} \times 1 + \frac{1}{2} \times 2\right] = \pm 1.5\%$$ **Ans.**

Core Concepts

Order of Magnitude In physics, a number of times we come across quantities which vary over a wide range. For example, size of universe, mass of sun, radius of a nucleus etc. In this case, we use the powers of ten method. In this method, each number is expressed as $n \times 10^m$, where $1 \le n \le 10$ and m is a positive or negative integer. If n is less than or equal to 5, then order of number is 10^m and if n is greater than 5 then order of number is 10^{m+1}.

For example, diameter of the sun is 1.39×10^9 m. Therefore, the diameter of the sun is of the order of 10^9 m as n or $1.39 \le 5$.

Solved Examples

Example 1 *Round off 0.07284 to four, three and two significant digits.*

Solution

0.07284 (four significant digits)

0.0728 (three significant digits)

0.073 (two significant digits)

Example 2 *Round off 231.45 to four, three and two significant digits.*

Solution

231.5 (four significant digits)

231 (three significant digits)

230 (two significant digits)

Example 3 *Three measurements are $a = 483$, $b = 73.67$ and $c = 15.67$. Find the value $\frac{ab}{c}$ to correct significant figures.*

Solution

$$\frac{ab}{c} = \frac{483 \times 73.67}{15.67}$$

$$= 2270.7472$$

$$= 2.27 \times 10^3$$ **Ans.**

Note *The result is rounded off to least number of significant figures in the given measurement i.e. 3 (in 483).*

Example 4 *Three measurements are, $a = 25.6$, $b = 21.1$ and $c = 2.43$. Find the value $a - b - c$ to correct significant figures.*

Solution

$$a - b - c = 25.6 - 21.1 - 2.43$$

$$= 2.07 = 2.1$$ **Ans.**

Note *In the measurements, least number of significant digits after the decimal is one (in 25.6 and 21.1). Hence, the result will also be rounded off to one decimal place.*

Example 5 *A thin wire has a length of 21.7 cm and radius 0.46 mm. Calculate the volume of the wire to correct significant figures.*

Solution Given, $l = 21.7$ cm, $r = 0.46$ mm $= 0.046$ cm

$$\text{Volume of wire } V = \pi r^2 l$$

$$= \frac{22}{7}(0.046)^2(21.7)$$

$$= 0.1443 \text{ cm}^3$$

$$= 0.14 \text{ cm}^3$$ **Ans.**

Note *The result is rounded off to least number of significant figures in the given measurements i.e. 2 (in 0.46 mm).*

Example 6 *The radius of a sphere is measured to be* (1.2 ± 0.2) *cm. Calculate its volume with error limits.*

Solution Volume, $V = \frac{4}{3}\pi r^3 = \frac{4}{3}\left(\frac{22}{7}\right)(1.2)^3$

$$= 7.24 \text{ cm}^3 = 7.2 \text{ cm}^3$$

Further, $\frac{\Delta V}{V} = 3\left(\frac{\Delta r}{r}\right)$

$$\therefore \quad \Delta V = 3\left(\frac{\Delta r}{r}\right)V = \frac{3 \times 0.2 \times 7.2}{1.2}$$

$$= 3.6 \text{ cm}^3$$

$$\therefore \quad V = (7.2 \pm 3.6) \text{ cm}^3$$

Ans.

Example 7 *Calculate equivalent resistance of two resistors* R_1 *and* R_2 *in parallel where,* $R_1 = (6 \pm 0.2)$ *ohm and* $R_2 = (3 \pm 0.1)$ *ohm.*

Solution In parallel,

$$\frac{1}{R} = \frac{1}{R_1} + \frac{1}{R_2} \quad \text{...(i)}$$

or

$$R = \frac{R_1 R_2}{R_1 + R_2} = \frac{(6)(3)}{6+3} = 2 \text{ ohm}$$

Differentiating Eq. (i), we have

$$-\frac{dR}{R^2} = -\frac{dR_1}{R_1^2} - \frac{dR_2}{R_2^2}$$

Therefore, maximum permissible error in equivalent resistance may be

$$\Delta R = \left(\frac{\Delta R_1}{R_1^2} + \frac{\Delta R_2}{R_2^2}\right)(R^2)$$

Substituting the values we get,

$$\Delta R = \left[\frac{0.2}{(6)^2} + \frac{0.1}{(3)^2}\right](2)^2$$

$$= 0.07 \text{ ohm}$$

$$\therefore \quad R = (2 \pm 0.07) \text{ ohm}$$

Ans.

Exercises

Assertion and Reason

Directions : *Choose the correct option.*

(a) *If both* **Assertion** *and* **Reason** *are true and the* **Reason** *is the correct explanation of the* **Assertion.**

(b) *If both* **Assertion** *and* **Reason** *are true but* **Reason** *is not the correct explanation of* **Assertion.**

(c) *If* **Assertion** *is true, but the* **Reason** *is false.*

(d) *If* **Assertion** *is false but the* **Reason** *is true.*

(e) *If both* **Assertion** *and* **Reason** *are false.*

1. Assertion : Out of two measurements $l = 0.7$ m and $l = 0.70$ m, the second one is more accurate.

Reason : In every measurement, mostly the last digit is not accurately known.

2. Assertion : The watches having hour hand, minute hand and seconds hand have least count as 1 s.

Reason : Least count is the maximum measurement that can be measured accurately by an instrument.

Objective Questions

Single Correct Option

1. The number of significant figures in 3400 is

(a) 3 (b) 1
(c) 4 (d) 2

2. The significant figures in the number 6.0023 are

(a) 2 (b) 5
(c) 4 (d) 3

3. The respective number of significant figures for the numbers 23.023, 0.0003 and 2.1×10^{-3} are

(a) 5, 1, 2 (b) 5, 1, 5
(c) 5, 5, 2 (d) 4, 4, 2

4. Which of the following measurement is most accurate?

(a) 40 m (b) 0.04 m
(c) 4.00×10^{-4} m (d) 4×10^{2} m

5. Find the value of $525.5 + 10.81 - 53.15$.

(a) 483.16 (b) 483
(c) 483.2 (d) 483.1

6. Find the value of $\dfrac{3.008 \times 38.8}{2.8768}$

(a) 40.5695 (b) 40.5
(c) 40.57 (d) 40.6

7. The length and breadth of a metal sheet are 3.124 m and 3.002 m, respectively. The area of this sheet upto correct significant figure is
(a) 9.378 m^2
(b) 9.37 m^2
(c) 9.4 m^2
(d) None of these

8. The length, breadth and thickness of a block are given by $l = 12$ cm, $b = 6$ cm and $t = 2.45$ cm. The volume of the block according to the idea of significant figures should be
(a) 1×10^2 cm^3
(b) 2×10^2 cm^3
(c) 1.763×10^2 cm^3
(d) None of these

9. The mass of a ball is 1.76 kg. The mass of 25 such balls is
(a) 0.44×10^3 kg
(b) 44.0 kg
(c) 44 kg
(d) 44.00 kg

10. A body of mass $m = 3.513$ kg is moving along the X-axis with a speed of 5.00 ms^{-1}. The magnitude of its momentum is recorded as
(a) 17.6 kg-ms^{-1}
(b) 17.565 kg-ms^{-1}
(c) 17.56 kg-ms^{-1}
(d) 17.57 kg-ms^{-1}

11. In Ohm's law experiment, the reading of voltmeter across the resistor is 12.8 V and current through resistor is 0.30 A. Find the resistance of resistor.
(a) 42.67 Ω
(b) 42.667 Ω
(c) 42.3 Ω
(d) 43 Ω

12. In previous problem, find the maximum percentage error in measurement of resistance.
(a) 4.1%
(b) 4.2%
(c) 5%
(d) 10%

13. A student measures the thickness of a human hair by looking at it through a microscope of magnification 100. He makes 20 observations and finds that the average width of the hair is 3.5 mm. What is thickness of the hair?
(a) 0.0035 mm
(b) 0.035 mm
(c) 0.01 m
(d) 0.7 mm

14. If the random error in the arithmetic mean of 50 observations is α, then the random error in the arithmetic mean of 150 observations would be
(a) α
(b) 3α
(c) $\frac{\alpha}{3}$
(d) 2α

15. If error in measurement of radius of a sphere is 1%, what will be the error in measurement of volume?
(a) 1%
(b) $\frac{1}{3}$%
(c) 3%
(d) None of these

16. The density of a cube is measured by measuring its mass and length of its sides. If the maximum error in the measurement of mass and length are 4% and 3% respectively, the maximum error in the measurement of density will be
(a) 7%
(b) 9%
(c) 12%
(d) 13%

17. Percentage error in the measurement of mass and speed are 2% and 3%, respectively. The error in the measurement of kinetic energy obtained by measuring mass and speed will be
(a) 12%
(b) 10%
(c) 8%
(d) 5%

18. Let g be the acceleration due to gravity at the earth's surface and K be the rotational kinetic energy of the earth. Suppose the earth's radius decreases by 2%. Keeping all other quantities constant, then
(a) g increases by 2% and K increases by 2%
(b) g increases by 4% and K increases by 4%
(c) g decreases by 4% and K decreases by 2%
(d) g decreases by 2% and K decreases by 4%

19. If error in measuring diameter of a circle is 4%, the error in measuring radius of the circle would be
(a) 2% (b) 8%
(c) 4% (d) 1%

20. The length of a rod is (11.05 ± 0.2) cm. What is the length of the two rods?
(a) (22.1 ± 0.05) cm (b) (22.1 ± 0.1) cm
(c) (22.10 ± 0.05) cm (d) (22.10 ± 0.4) cm

21. The radius of a ball is (5.2 ± 0.2) cm. The percentage error in the volume of the ball is approximately
(a) 11% (b) 4%
(c) 7% (d) 9%

22. A body travels uniformly a distance of (13.8 ± 0.2) m in a time (4.0 ± 0.3) s. The velocity of the body within error limit is
(a) $(3.45 \pm 0.2)\ ms^{-1}$ (b) $(3.45 \pm 0.3)\ ms^{-1}$
(c) $(3.45 \pm 0.4)\ ms^{-1}$ (d) $(3.45 \pm 0.5)\ ms^{-1}$

23. If the error in the measurement of momentum of a particle is (+ 100%), then the error in the measurement of kinetic energy is
(a) 100% (b) 200%
(c) 300% (d) 400%

24. If $x = 10.0 \pm 0.1$ and $y = 10.0 \pm 0.1$, then $2x - 2y$ is equal to
(a) (0.1 ± 0.1) (b) zero
(c) (0.0 ± 0.4) (d) (20 ± 0.2)

25. The radius of a cylindrical wire is measured by screw gauge is 1.25 mm. The length of wire is 25.0 cm and the mass of wire is 12 g. The density of wire is
(a) $(9.8 \pm 1.0)\ gcm^{-3}$ (b) $(9.8 \pm 1.01267)\ gcm^{-3}$
(c) $(9.8 \pm 0.1)\ gcm^{-3}$ (d) $(9.80 \pm 0.01)\ gcm^{-3}$

26. The length of a simple pendulum is about 100 cm known to have an accuracy of 1 mm. Its period of oscillation is 2 s determined by measuring the time for 100 oscillations using a clock of 0.1 s resolution. What is the accuracy in the determined value of g?
(a) 0.2% (b) 0.5%
(c) 0.1% (d) 2%

27. The least count of a stop watch is 0.2 s. The time of 20 oscillations of a pendulum is measured to be 25 s. The percentage error in the time period is
(a) 1.2 % (b) 0.8 %
(c) 1.8 % (d) None of these

Subjective Questions

1. The mass of a box measured by a grocer's balance is 2.3 kg. Two gold pieces of masses 20.15 g and 20.17 g are added to the box. What is (a) the total mass of the box, (b) the difference in the masses of the pieces to correct significant figures ?
2. A thin wire has length of 21.7 cm and radius 0.46 mm. Calculate the volume of the wire to correct significant figures.
3. A cube has a side of length 2.342 m. Find the volume and surface area in correct significant figures.
4. Find density when a mass of 9.23 kg occupies a volume of 1.1 m^3. Take care of significant figures.
5. The radius of a sphere is measured to be (2.1 ± 0.5) cm. Calculate its surface area with error limits.
6. The temperature of two bodies measured by a thermometer are $(20 \pm 0.5)°$ C and $(50 \pm 0.5)°$ C. Calculate the temperature difference with error limits.
7. The resistance $R = \frac{V}{I}$, where $V = (100 \pm 5.0)$ V and $I = (10 \pm 0.2)$ A. Find the percentage error in R.
8. Find the percentage error in specific resistance given by $\rho = \frac{\pi r^2 R}{l}$, where r is the radius having value (0.2 ± 0.02) cm, R is the resistance of (60 ± 2) ohm and l is the length of (150 ± 0.1) cm.
9. A physical quantity ρ is related to four variables α, β, γ and η as
$$\rho = \frac{\alpha^3 \beta^2}{\eta \sqrt{\gamma}}$$
The percentage errors of measurements in α, β, γ and η are 1%, 3%, 4% and 2%, respectively. Find the percentage error in ρ.
10. The period of oscillation of a simple pendulum is $T = 2\pi\sqrt{L/g}$. Measured value of L is 20.0 cm known to 1 mm accuracy and time for 100 oscillations of the pendulum is found to be 90 s using a wrist watch of 1s resolution. What is the accuracy in the determination of g ?

Answers

Introductory Exercise 2.1

1. (a) 0.01 cm (b) 3
   (c) 6 and 2 are absolutely correct and 4 is doubtful.
2. (a) 0.001 cm (b) 4
   (c) 3, 2 and 6 are absolutely correct and 7 is doubtful.

Introductory Exercise 2.2

1. (a) 4 (b) 2 (c) 2 (d) 4
   (e) 6 (f) 4

Introductory Exercise 2.3

1. (a) 24600 (b) 24.9 (c) 36.4 (d) 42.4×10^9
2. 742400, 742000, 740000

Introductory Exercise 2.4

1. (a) 261.2 (b) 1910
2. (a) 20 (b) 0.020

Exercises

Assertion and Reason

1. (b) 2. (d)

Objective Questions

1. (d)	2. (b)	3. (a)	4. (c)	5. (c)	6. (d)	7. (a)	8. (b)	9. (d)	10. (a)
11. (d)	12. (a)	13. (b)	14. (c)	15. (c)	16. (d).	17. (c)	18. (b)	19. (c)	20. (d)
21. (a)	22. (b)	23. (c)	24. (c)	25. (a)	26. (a)	27. (b)			

Subjective Questions

1. (a) 2.3 kg (b) 0.02 g
2. 0.14 cm^3
3. Area = 5.485 m^2, Volume = 12.85 m^3
4. Density = 8.4 kg/m^3
5. $(55.4 \pm 26.4)\,cm^2$
6. $(30 \pm 1)°C$
7. 7%
8. 23.4 %
9. 13%
10. 2.7 %

3

Experiments

3.1 Vernier Callipers

Length is an elementary physical quantity. The device generally used in everyday life for measurement of length is a meter scale (we can also call it mm scale). It can be used for measurement of length with an accuracy of 1 mm. So, the least count of a meter scale is 1 mm. To measure length accurately upto 0.1 mm or 0.01 mm vernier callipers and screw gauge are used.

Vernier callipers has following three parts :

(i) Main scale It consists of a steel metallic strip *M*, graduated in cm and mm at one edge. It carries two fixed jaws *A* and *C* as shown in figure.

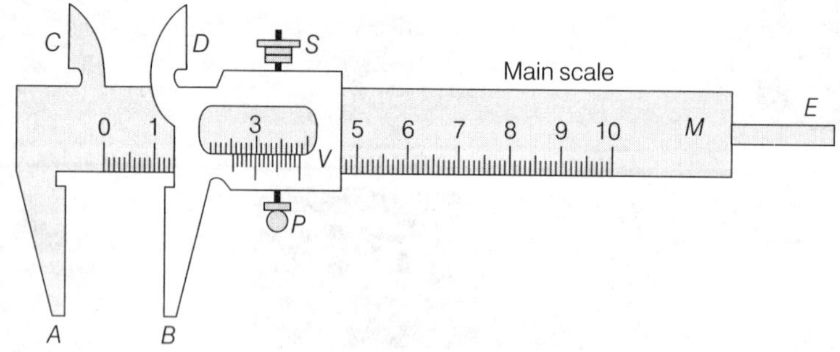

Fig. 3.1

(ii) Vernier scale Vernier scale *V* slides on metallic strip *M*. It can be fixed in any position by screw *S*. The side of the vernier scale which slide over the mm sides has ten divisions over a length of 9 mm. *B* and *D* two movable jaws are fixed with it. When vernier scale is pushed towards *A* and *C*, then *B* touches *A* and straight side of *C* will touch straight side of *D*. In this position, if the instrument is free from error, zeros of vernier scale will coincide with zeros of main scales. To measure the external diameter of an object it is held between the jaws *A* and *B*, while the straight edges of *C* and *D* are used for measuring the internal diameter of a hollow object.

(iii) Metallic strip There is a thin metallic strip *E* attached to the back side of *M* and connected with vernier scale. When jaws *A* and *B* touch each other, the edge of *E* touches the edge of *M*. When the jaws *A* and *B* are separated *E* moves outwards. This strip *E* is used for measuring the depth of a vessel.

Principle (Theory)

In the common form, the divisions on the vernier scale *V* are smaller in size than the smallest division on the main scale *M*, but in some special cases the size of the vernier division may be larger than the main scale division. Let n vernier scale divisions (VSD) coincide with $(n-1)$ main scale divisions (MSD). Then,

$$n \text{ VSD} = (n-1) \text{ MSD}$$

or

$$1 \text{ VSD} = \left(\frac{n-1}{n}\right) \text{MSD}$$

$$1 \text{ MSD} - 1 \text{ VSD} = 1 \text{ MSD} - \left(\frac{n-1}{n}\right) \text{MSD} = \frac{1}{n} \text{ MSD}$$

The difference between the values of one main scale division and one vernier scale division is known as **Vernier Constant (VC)** or the **Least Count (LC).** This is the smallest distance that can be accurately measured with the vernier scale. Thus,

$$\text{VC} = \text{LC} = 1\,\text{MSD} - 1\,\text{VSD} = \left(\frac{1}{n}\right)\text{MSD} = \frac{\text{Smallest division on main scale}}{\text{Number of divisions on vernier scale}}$$

In the ordinary vernier callipers one main scale division be 1 mm and 10 vernier scale divisions coincide with 9 main scale divisions.

$$1\text{ VSD} = \frac{9}{10}\text{ MSD} = 0.9\text{ mm}$$

$$\text{VC} = 1\text{ MSD} - 1\text{ VSD} = 1\text{ mm} - 0.9\text{ mm}$$

$$= 0.1\text{ mm} = 0.01\text{ cm}$$

Reading a Vernier Callipers

If we have to measure a length AB, the end A is coincided with the zero of main scale, suppose the end B lies between 1.0 cm and 1.1 cm on the main scale. Then,

$$1.0\text{ cm} < AB < 1.1\text{ cm}$$

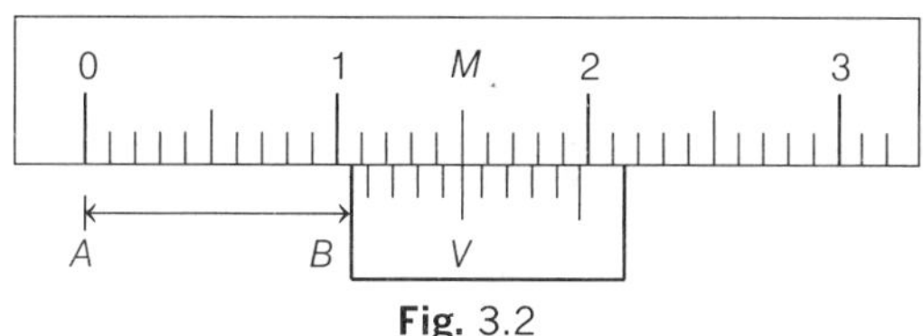

Fig. 3.2

Let 5th division of vernier scale coincides with 1.5 cm of main scale.

Then, $AB = 1.0 + 5 \times \text{VC} = (1.0 + 5 \times 0.01)\text{ cm} = 1.05\text{ cm}$

Thus, we can make the following formula,

$$\text{Total reading} = N + n \times \text{VC}$$

Here, N = main scale reading before on the left of the zero of the vernier scale.

n = number of vernier division which just coincides with any of the main scale division.

Note *That the main scale reading with which the vernier scale division coincides has no connection with reading.*

Zero Error and Zero Correction

If the zero of the vernier scale does not coincide with the zero of main scale when jaw B touches A and the straight edge of D touches the straight edge of C, then the instrument has an error called **zero error.** Zero error is always algebraically subtracted from measured length.

Zero correction has a magnitude equal to zero error but its sign is opposite to that of the zero error. Zero correction is always algebraically added to measured length.

$$\text{Zero error} \longrightarrow \text{algebraically subtracted}$$

$$\text{Zero correction} \longrightarrow \text{algebraically added}$$

Positive and Negative Zero Errors

If zero of vernier scale lies to the right of the main scale the zero error is positive and if it lies to the left of the main scale the zero error is negative (when jaws A and B are in contact).

$$\text{Positive zero error} = (N + x \times \text{VC})$$

Here, N = main scale reading on the left of zero of vernier scale.

x = vernier scale division which coincides with any main scale division.

When the vernier zero lies before the main scale zero the error is said to be negative zero error. If 3rd vernier scale division coincides with the main scale division, then

$$\begin{aligned}\text{Negative zero error} &= -[0.00 \text{ cm} + 3 \times \text{VC}]\\ &= -[0.00 \text{ cm} + 3 \times 0.01 \text{ cm}]\\ &= -0.03 \text{ cm}\end{aligned}$$

No Zero Error

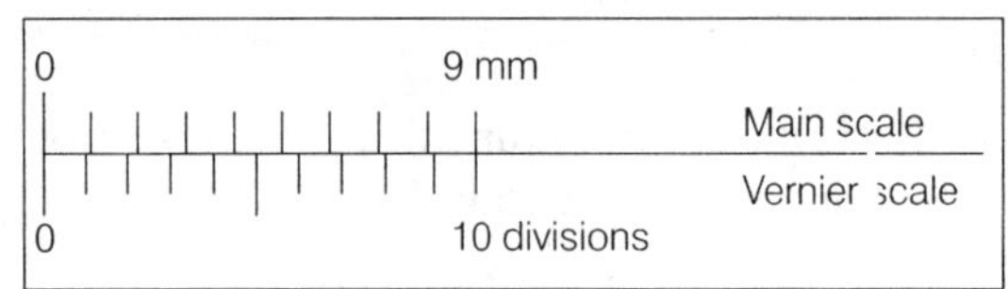

Negative Error

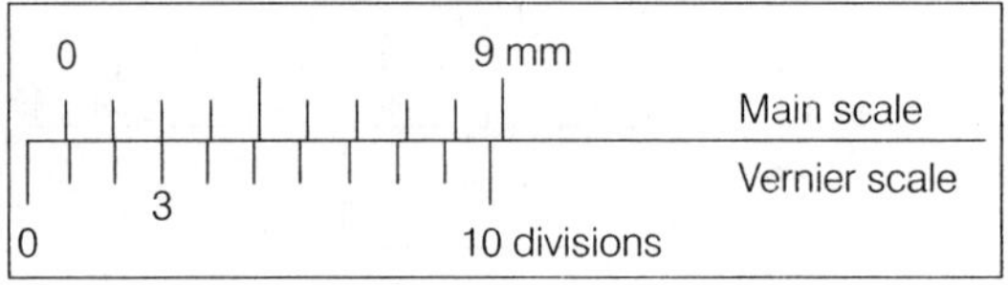

Positive Error

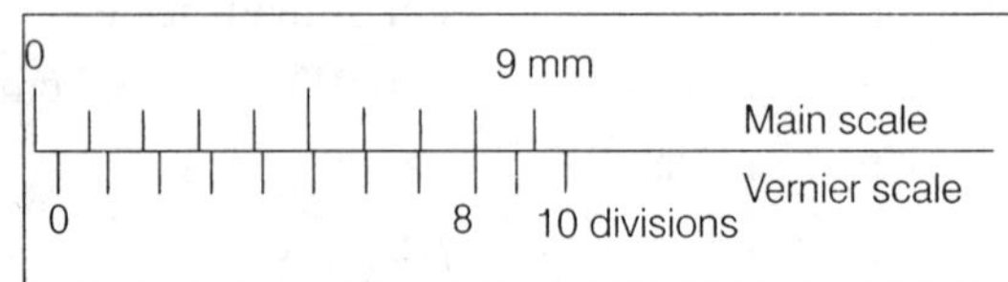

Fig. 3.3 Positive and negative zero error

Summary

1. $\text{VC} = \text{LC} = \dfrac{1 \text{ MSD}}{n} = \dfrac{\text{Smallest division on main scale}}{\text{Number of divisions on vernier scale}} = 1 \text{ MSD} - 1 \text{ VSD}$
2. In ordinary vernier callipers, 1 MSD = 1 mm and $n = 10$

   $\therefore \quad \text{VC} \text{ or } \text{LC} = \dfrac{1}{10} \text{ mm} = 0.01 \text{ cm}$
3. Total reading $= (N + n \times \text{VC})$
4. Zero correction = – zero error
5. Zero error is algebraically subtracted while the zero correction is algebraically added.

6. If zero of vernier scale lies to the right of zero of main scale the error is positive. The actual length in this case is less than observed length.
7. If zero of vernier scale lies to the left of zero of main scale the error is negative and the actual length is more than the observed length.
8. Positive zero error = $(N + x \times \text{VC})$

Example 3.1 *N divisions on the main scale of a vernier callipers coincide with N + 1 divisions on the vernier scale. If each division on the main scale is of a units, determine the least count of the instrument.* **(JEE 2003)**

Solution $(N+1)$ divisions on the vernier scale = N divisions on main scale

$\therefore$ 1 division on vernier scale $= \frac{N}{N+1}$ divisions on main scale

Each division on the main scale is of a units.

$\therefore$ 1 division on vernier scale $= \left(\frac{N}{N+1}\right) a$ units $= a'$ (say)

Least count = 1 main scale division – 1 vernier scale division

$$= a - a' = a - \left(\frac{N}{N+1}\right) a = \frac{a}{N+1}$$

Example 3.2 *In the diagram shown in figure, find the magnitude and nature of zero error.*

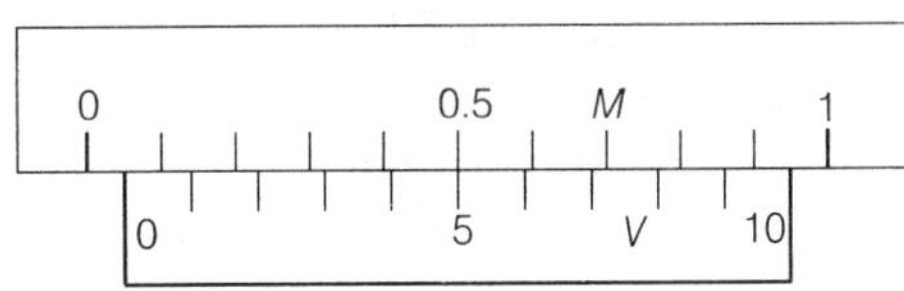

Fig. 3.4

Solution Here, zero of vernier scale lies to the right of zero of main scale, hence. it has positive zero error.

Further, $N = 0, \; x = 5$, LC or VC = 0.01 cm

Hence, Zero error $= N + x \times \text{VC}$

$= 0 + 5 \times 0.01 = 0.05$ cm

Zero correction = – 0.05 cm

$\therefore$ Actual length will be 0.05 cm less than the measured length.

Example 3.3 *The smallest division on main scale of a vernier callipers is 1 mm and 10 vernier divisions coincide with 9 main scale divisions. While measuring the length of a line, the zero mark of the vernier scale lies between 10.2 cm and 10.3 cm and the third division of vernier scale coincides with a main scale division.*

(a) Determine the least count of the callipers.

(b) Find the length of the line.

Solution (a) $\text{Least Count (LC)} = \dfrac{\text{Smallest division on main scale}}{\text{Number of divisions on vernier scale}}$

$$= \frac{1}{10}\ \text{mm} = 0.1\ \text{mm} = 0.01\ \text{cm}$$

(b) $L = N + n\,(\text{LC}) = (10.2 + 3 \times 0.01)\ \text{cm}$

$$= 10.23\ \text{cm}$$

INTRODUCTORY EXERCISE 3.1

1. The main scale of a vernier callipers reads 10 mm in 10 divisions. Ten divisions of vernier scale coincide with nine divisions of the main scale. When the two jaws of the callipers touch each other, the fifth division of the vernier coincides with 9 main scale divisions and the zero of the vernier is to the right of zero of main scale, when a cylinder is tightly placed between the two jaws, the zero of the vernier scale lies slightly to the right of 3.2 cm and the fourth vernier division coincides with a main scale division. Find diameter of the cylinder.
2. In a vernier callipers, N divisions of the main scale coincide with $N + m$ divisions of the vernier scale. What is the value of m for which the instrument has minimum least count?

3.2 Screw Gauge

Principle of a Micrometer Screw

The least count of vernier callipers ordinarily available in the laboratory is 0.01 cm. When lengths are to be measured with greater accuracy, say upto 0.001 cm, screw gauge and spherometer are used which are based on the principle of **micrometer screw** discussed below.

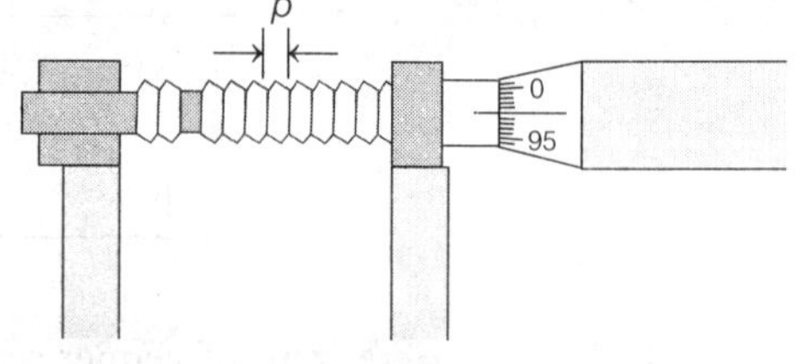

Fig. 3.5

If an accurately cut single threaded screw is rotated in a closely fitted nut, then in addition to the circular motion of the screw there is a linear motion of the screw head in the forward or backward direction, along the axis of the screw. The linear distance moved by the screw, when it is given one complete rotation is called the **pitch** (p) of the screw. This is equal to the distance between two consecutive threads as measured along the axis of the screw. In most of the cases, it is either 1 mm or 0.5 mm. A circular cap is fixed on one end of the screw and the circumference of the cap is normally divided into 100 or 50 equal parts. If it is divided into 100 equal parts, then the screw moves forward or backward by $\dfrac{1}{100}\left(\text{or } \dfrac{1}{50}\right)$ of the pitch, if the circular scale (we will discuss later about circular scale) is rotated through one circular scale division. It is the minimum distance which can be accurately measured and so called the **Least Count (LC)** of the screw.

Thus,
$$\text{Least count} = \frac{\text{Pitch}}{\text{Number of divisions on circular scale}}$$

If pitch is 1 mm and there are 100 divisions on circular scale then,

$$\text{LC} = \frac{1\text{ mm}}{100} = 0.01\text{ mm}$$

$$= 0.001\text{ cm} = 10\,\mu\text{m}$$

Since, LC is of the order of 10 μm, the screw is called micrometer screw.

Screw Gauge

Screw gauge works on the principle of micrometer screw. It consists of a U-shaped metal frame M. At one end of it is fixed a small metal piece A. It is called stud and it has a plane face. The other end N of M carries a cylindrical hub H. It is graduated in millimeter and half millimeter depending upon the pitch of the screw. This scale is called **linear scale** or **pitch scale.**

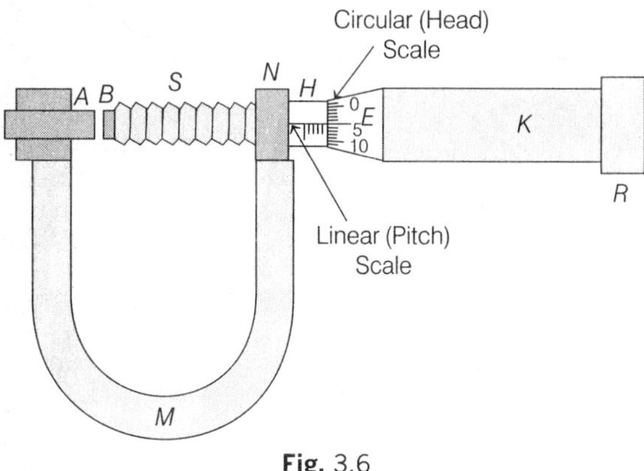

Fig. 3.6

A nut is threaded through the hub and the frame N. Through the nut moves a screw S. The front face B of the screw, facing the plane face A is also plane. A hollow cylindrical cap K is capable of rotating over the hub when screw is rotated. As the cap is rotated the screw either moves in or out. The surface E of the cap K is divided into 50 or 100 equal parts. It is called the **circular scale** or **head scale.** In an accurately adjusted instrument when the faces A and B are just touching each other. Zero of circular scale should coincide with zero of linear scale.

To Measure Diameter of a Given Wire Using a Screw Gauge

If with the wire between plane faces A and B, the edge of the cap lies ahead of Nth division of linear scale, and nth division of circular scale lies over reference line.

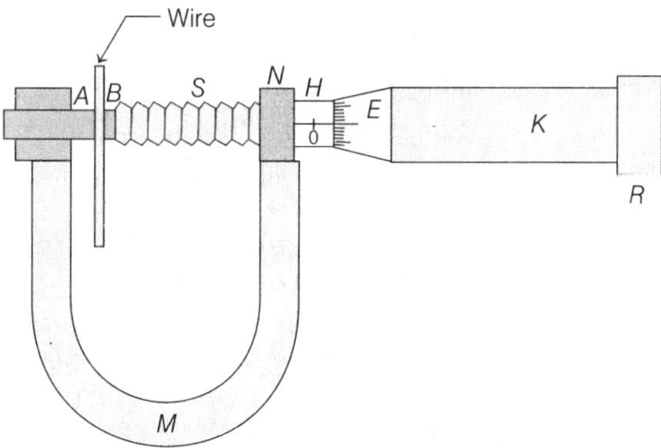

Fig. 3.7

Then, $$\boxed{\text{Total reading} = N + n \times \text{LC}}$$

Zero Error and Zero Correction

If zero mark of circular scale does not coincide with the zero of the pitch scale when the faces A and B are just touching each other, the instrument is said to possess zero error. If the zero of the circular scale advances beyond the reference line the zero error is **negative** and zero correction is **positive.** If it is left behind the reference line the zero is **positive** and zero correction is **negative.** For example, if zero of circular scale advances beyond the reference line by 5 divisions, zero correction $= +5 \times (\text{LC})$ and if the zero of circular scale is left behind the reference line by 5 divisions, zero correction $= -5 \times (\text{LC})$.

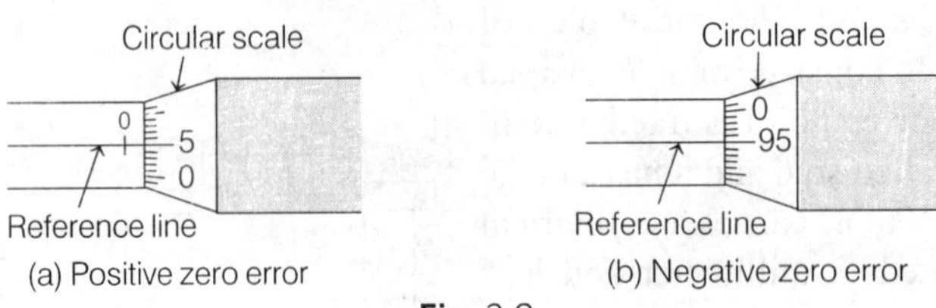

(a) Positive zero error (b) Negative zero error

Fig. 3.8

Note *In negative zero error 95th division of the circular scale is coinciding with the reference line. Hence there are 5 divisions between zero mark on the circular scale and the reference line.*

Back Lash Error

When the sense of rotation of the screw is suddenly changed, the screw head may rotate, but the screw itself may not move forward or backwards. Thus, the scale reading may change even by the actual movement of the screw. This is known as back lash error. This error is due to loose fitting of the screw. This arises due to wear and tear of the threading due to prolonged use of the screw. To reduce this error the screw must always be rotated in the same direction for a particular set of observations.

Example 3.4 *The pitch of a screw gauge is 1 mm and there are 100 divisions on the circular scale. In measuring the diameter of a sphere there are six divisions on the linear scale and forty divisions on circular scale coincide with the reference line. Find the diameter of the sphere.*

Solution

$$\text{LC} = \frac{1}{100} = 0.01 \text{ mm}$$

$$\text{Linear scale reading} = 6\,(\text{pitch}) = 6 \text{ mm}$$

$$\text{Circular scale reading} = n\,(\text{LC}) = 40 \times 0.01 = 0.4 \text{ mm}$$

$$\therefore \quad \text{Total reading} = (6 + 0.4) = 6.4 \text{ mm}$$

Example 3.5 *The pitch of a screw gauge is 1 mm and there are 100 divisions on circular scale. When faces A and B are just touching each without putting anything between the studs 32nd division of the circular scale coincides with the reference line. When a glass plate is placed between the studs, the linear scale reads 4 divisions and the circular scale reads 16 divisions. Find the thickness of the glass plate. Zero of linear scale is not hidden from circular scale when A and B touches each other.*

Solution

$$\text{Least count (LC)} = \frac{\text{Pitch}}{\text{Number of divisions on circular scale}} = \frac{1}{100} \text{ mm}$$

$$= 0.01 \text{ mm}$$

As zero is not hidden from circular scale when A and B touches each other. Hence, the screw gauge has positive error.

$$e = +n\,(\text{LC}) = 32 \times 0.01 = 0.32 \text{ mm}$$

$$\text{Linear scale reading} = 4 \times (1 \text{ mm}) = 4 \text{ mm}$$

$$\text{Circular scale reading} = 16 \times (0.01 \text{ mm}) = 0.16 \text{ mm}$$

$$\therefore \quad \text{Measured reading} = (4 + 0.16) \text{ mm} = 4.16 \text{ mm}$$

$$\therefore \quad \text{Absolute reading} = \text{Measured reading} - e$$

$$= (4.16 - 0.32) \text{ mm} = 3.84 \text{ mm}$$

Therefore, thickness of the glass plate is 3.84 mm.

INTRODUCTORY EXERCISE 3.2

1. Read the screw gauge shown below in the figure.
   Given that circular scale has 100 divisions and in one complete rotation the screw advances by 1mm.

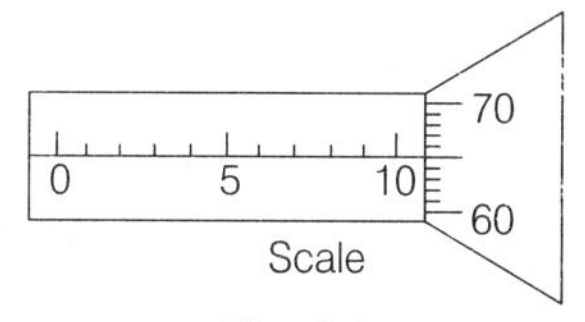

Fig. 3.9

2. The pitch of a screw gauge having 50 divisions on its circular scale is 1 mm. When the two jaws of the screw gauge are in contact with each other, the zero of the circular scale lies 6 divisions below the line of graduation. When a wire is placed between the jaws, 3 linear scale divisions are clearly visible while 31st division on the circular scale coincides with the reference line. Find diameter of the wire.

3.3 Determination of '*g*' using a Simple Pendulum

In this experiment, a small spherical bob is hanged with a cotton thread. This arrangement is called simple pendulum. The bob is displaced slightly and allowed to oscillate.

The period of small oscillations is given by

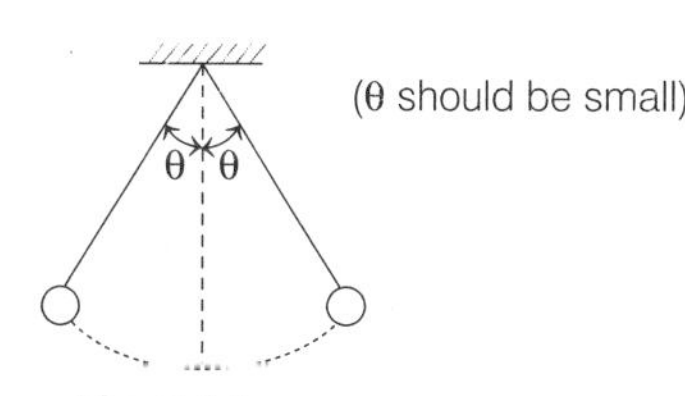

Fig. 3.10

$$T = 2\pi \sqrt{\frac{L}{g}}$$

where, $\quad L = l + r \quad$ (as shown in figure)

$$= \text{equivalent length of pendulum}$$

$$\therefore \quad \boxed{g = \frac{4\pi^2 L}{T^2}} \qquad \text{...(i)}$$

To find time period, time taken for 50 oscillations is noted using a stop watch.

$$\therefore \quad T = \frac{\text{Time taken for 50 oscillations}}{50}$$

Now, substituting the values of T and L in Eq. (i), we can easily find the value of 'g'.

Graphical Method of Finding Value of *g*

Eq. (i) can also be written as

$$T^2 = \left(\frac{4\pi^2}{g}\right) L \qquad \text{...(ii)}$$

$$\Rightarrow \qquad T^2 \propto L$$

Therefore, T^2 *versus* L graph is a straight line passing through origin with slope $= \left(\frac{4\pi^2}{g}\right)$

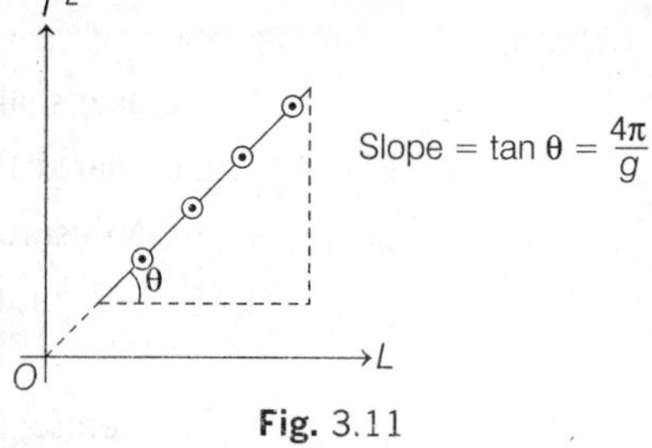

Fig. 3.11

Therefore, from the slope of this graph ($= 4\pi^2/g$) we can determine the value of g.

Example 3.6 *In a certain observation we get $l = 23.2$ cm, $r = 1.32$ cm and time taken for 20 oscillations was 20.0 sec. Taking $\pi^2 = 10$, find the value of g in proper significant figures.*

Solution Equivalent length of pendulum,

$$L = 23.2 \text{ cm} + 1.32 \text{ cm} = 24.52 \text{ cm}$$

$$= 24.5 \text{ cm} \qquad \text{(according to addition rule of significant figures)}$$

Time period, $T = \frac{20.0}{20} = 1.00$ s. Time period has 3 significant figures

Now, $$g = (4\pi^2)\frac{l}{T^2} = \frac{4 \times 10 \times 24.5 \times 10^{-2}}{(1.00)^2} = 9.80 \text{ m/s}^2$$ **Ans.**

Example 3.7 *For different values of L, we get different values of T^2. The graph between L versus T^2 is as shown in figure. Find the value of 'g' from the given graph. (Take $\pi^2 = 10$).*

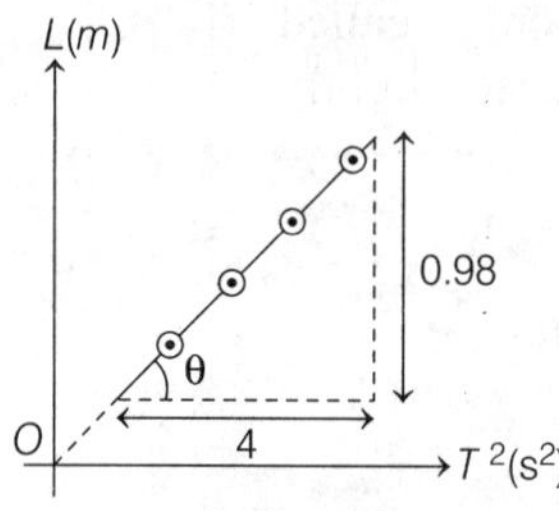

Fig. 3.12

Solution From the equation, $$T = 2\pi\sqrt{\frac{L}{g}}$$

we get, $$L = \left(\frac{g}{4\pi^2}\right) T^2 \quad \Rightarrow \quad L \propto T^2$$

i.e. L *versus* T^2 graph is a straight line passing through origin with slope $= \frac{g}{4\pi^2}$

$$\therefore \qquad \text{Slope} = \tan\theta = \frac{g}{4\pi^2} \quad \text{or} \quad g = (4\pi^2)\tan\theta$$

$$= \frac{4\times 10\times 0.98}{4} = 9.8 \text{ m/s}^2$$ **Ans.**

Example 3.8 *In a certain observation we got,* $l = 23.2$ *cm,* $r = 1.32$ *cm and time taken for* 10 *oscillations was* 10.0 s. *Find, maximum percentage error in determination of 'g'.*

Solution

$$l = 23.2 \text{ cm} \Rightarrow \Delta l = 0.1 \text{ cm}$$

$$r = 1.32 \text{ cm} \Rightarrow \Delta r = 0.01 \text{ cm}$$

$$t = 10.0 \text{ s} \Rightarrow \Delta t = 0.1 \text{ s}$$

Now,

$$g = 4\pi^2\left(\frac{L}{T^2}\right) = 4\pi^2\left[\frac{l+r}{(t/n)^2}\right]$$

$$g = 4\pi^2 n^2\left(\frac{l+r}{t^2}\right)$$

$\therefore$ Maximum percentage error in g will be

$$\left(\frac{\Delta g}{g}\right)\times 100 = \left[\frac{\Delta l + \Delta r}{l+r} + 2\left(\frac{\Delta t}{t}\right)\right]\times 100$$

$$= \left[\frac{0.1+0.01}{23.2+1.32} + 2\times\frac{0.1}{10.0}\right]\times 100$$

$$= 2.4\ \%$$ **Ans.**

INTRODUCTORY EXERCISE 3.3

1. What is a second's pendulum ?
2. Why should the amplitude be small for a simple pendulum experiment ?
3. Does the time period depend upon the mass and the material of the bob ?
4. What type of graph do you expect between (a) L and T and (b) L and T^2 ?
5. Why do the pendulum clocks go slow in summer and fast in winter ?
6. Why do we use Invar material for the pendulum of good clocks ?
7. A simple pendulum has a bob which is a hollow sphere full of sand and oscillates with certain period. If all that sand is drained out through a hole at its bottom, then its period
   (a) increases
   (b) decreases
   (c) remains same
   (d) is zero
8. The second's pendulum is taken from earth to moon, to keep the time period constant
   (a) the length of the second's pendulum should be decreased
   (b) the length of the second's pendulum should be increased
   (c) the amplitude should increase
   (d) the amplitude should decrease

3.4 Young's Modulus by Searle's Method

Young's modulus of a wire can be determined by an ordinary experiment as discussed below.

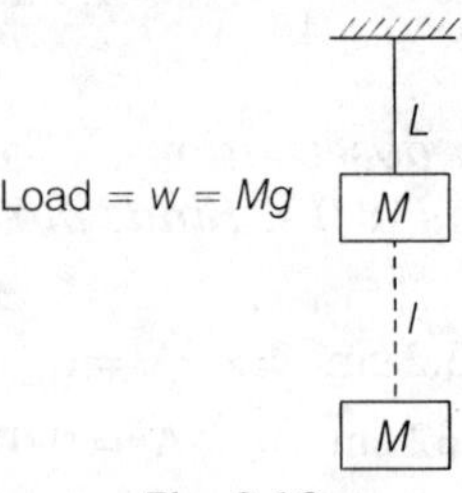

Fig. 3.13

A mass M is hanged from a wire of length L, cross sectional radius r and Young's modulus Y. Let change in length in wire is l. Then,

$$\text{Stress} = \frac{F}{A} = \frac{Mg}{\pi r^2}$$

$$\text{Strain} = \frac{l}{L}$$

and Young's modulus $Y = \dfrac{\text{Stress}}{\text{Strain}}$ or $Y = \dfrac{Mg/\pi r^2}{l/L}$

$\Rightarrow$ $$l = \left(\frac{L}{\pi r^2 Y}\right) Mg$$

or $$l = \left(\frac{L}{\pi r^2 Y}\right) w$$

$\Rightarrow$ $$l \propto w$$

Therefore, l *versus* w graph is a straight line passing through origin with

$$\text{Slope} = \frac{L}{\pi r^2 Y} = \tan\theta$$

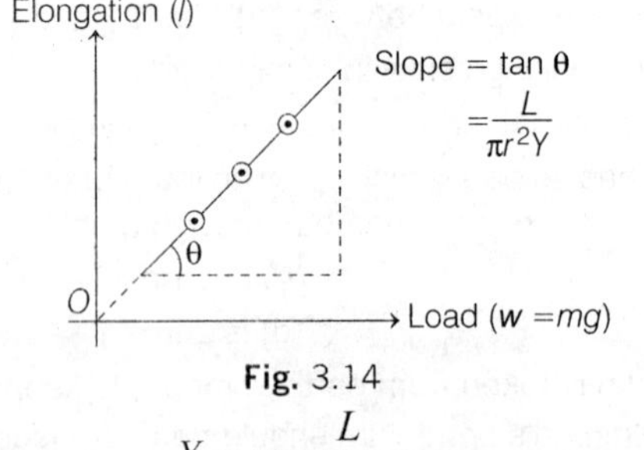

Fig. 3.14

$\therefore$ $$Y = \frac{L}{\pi r^2 (\tan\theta)} \quad \text{...(i)}$$

Thus, by measuring the slope (or tan θ) we can find Young's modulus Y from Eq. (i).

Note *We can also take load along y-axis and elongation along x-axis. In that case, slope* $= \dfrac{\pi r^2 Y}{L}$

Limitations of this Method

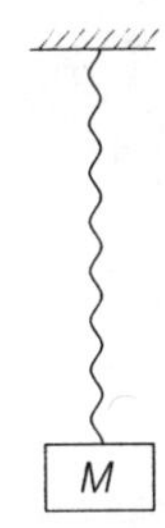

Fig. 3.15

1. For small loads, there may be some bends or kinks in the wire. So, it is better to start with some initial weight, so that wire becomes straight.
2. There is slight difference in behaviour of wire under loading and unloading load.

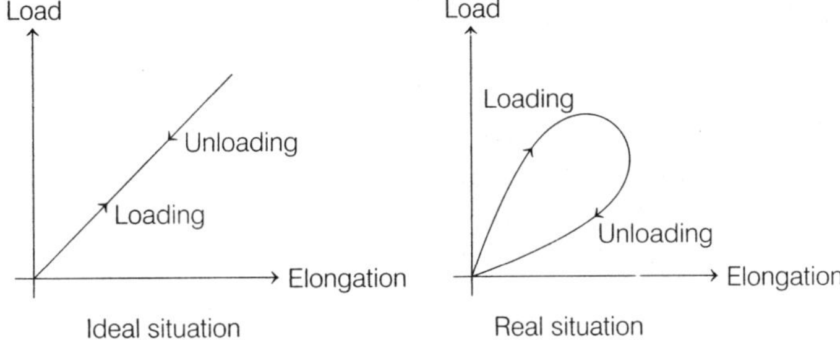

Fig. 3.16

Modification in Searle's Method

To keep the experimental wire straight and kink free we start with some dead load (say 2 kg). Now, we gradually increase the load and measure the extra elongation.

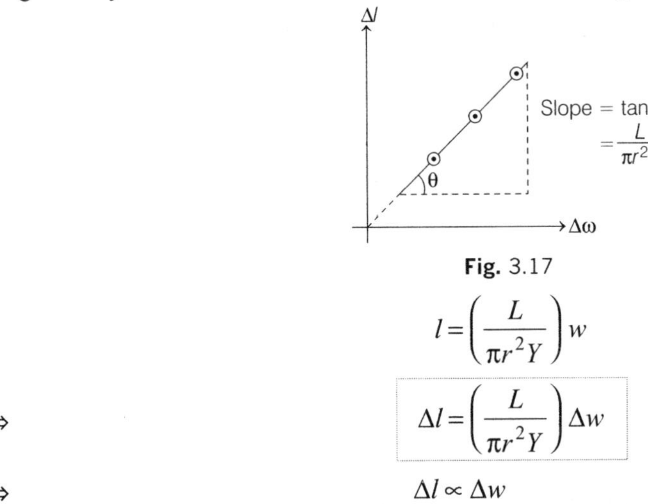

Fig. 3.17

$$l = \left(\frac{L}{\pi r^2 Y}\right) w$$

$$\Rightarrow \quad \boxed{\Delta l = \left(\frac{L}{\pi r^2 Y}\right) \Delta w}$$

$$\Rightarrow \quad \Delta l \propto \Delta w$$

or Δl *versus* Δw graph is again a straight line passing through origin with same slope, $\frac{L}{\pi r^2 Y}$

To measure extra elongation, compared to initial loaded position, we use a reference wire also carrying 2 kg.

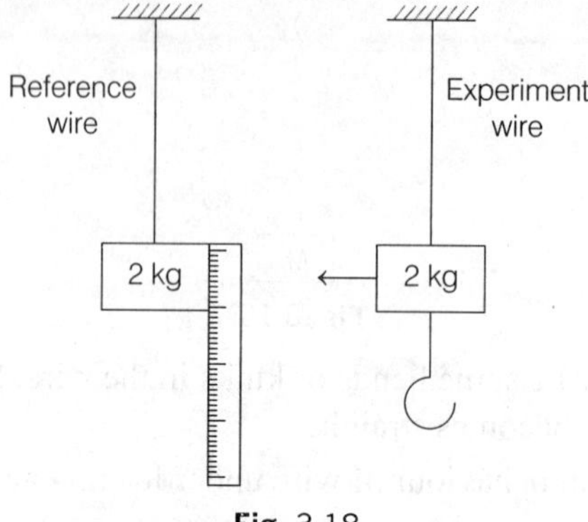

Fig. 3.18

Searle's Apparatus

It consists of two metal frames P and Q hinged together, such that they can have only vertical relative motion. A spirit level (S.L.) is supported at one end on a rigid cross bar frame whose other end rests on the tip of a micrometer screw C. If there is any relative motion between the two frames, the spirit level no longer remains horizontal and the bubble is displaced in the spirit level.

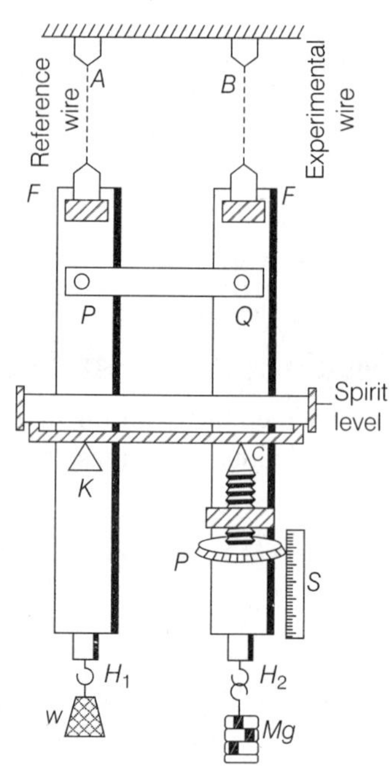

Fig. 3.19

To bring the bubble back to its original position, the screw has to be moved up or down. The distance through which the screw has to be moved gives the relative motion between the two frames.

The frames are suspended by two identical long wires of the same material, from the same rigid horizontal support. Wire B is the experimental wire and the wire A acts simply as a reference wire. The frames are provided with hooks H_1 and H_2 at their ends from which weights are suspended. The hook H_1 attached to the frame of the reference wire carries a constant weight W to keep the wire taut. To the hook H_2 of the experimental wire (i.e. wire B), is attached a hanger over which slotted weights can be placed to apply the stretching force, Mg.

Method

Step 1 Measure the length of the experimental wire.

Step 2 Measure the diameter of the experimental wire with the help of a screw gauge at about five different places.

Step 3 Find pitch and least count of the micrometer and adjust it such that the bubble in spirit level is exactly at the centre. Also note down the initial reading of micrometer.

Step 4 Gradually increase the load on the hanger H_2 in steps of 0.5 kg. Observe the reading on the micrometer at each step after levelling the instrument with the help of spirit level. To avoid the backlash error, all the final adjustments should be made by moving the screw in the upward direction only.

Step 5 Unload the wire by removing the weights in the same order and take the reading on the micrometer screw each time. The readings during loading and unloading should agree closely.

Step 6 Plot Δl *versus* Δw graph and from its slope determine the value of Y. We have seen above that,

$$\text{Slope} = \tan\theta = \frac{L}{\pi r^2 Y} \qquad \therefore \qquad Y = \frac{L}{(\pi r^2)\tan\theta}$$

Observation

Initial reading $l = 0.540$ mm , Radius of the wire $= 0.200$ mm

S.No.	Extra load on hanger Δm (kg)	Extra load Δw(N)	Micrometer reading		Mean reading $(p+q)/2$ (mm)	Extra elongation (mm)
			During loading (p) (mm)	During unloading (q) (mm)		
1	0.5	5	0.555	0.561	0.558	0.018
2	1.0	10	0.565	0.571	0.568	0.028
3	1.5	15	0.576	0.580	0.578	0.038
4	2.0	20	0.587	0.593	0.590	0.050
5	2.5	25	0.597	0.603	0.600	0.060
6	3.0	30	0.608	0.612	0.610	0.070
7	3.5	35	0.620	0.622	0.621	0.081
8	4.0	40	0.630	0.632	0.631	0.091
9	4.5	45	0.641	0.643	0.642	0.102
10	5.0	50	0.652	0.652	0.652	0.112

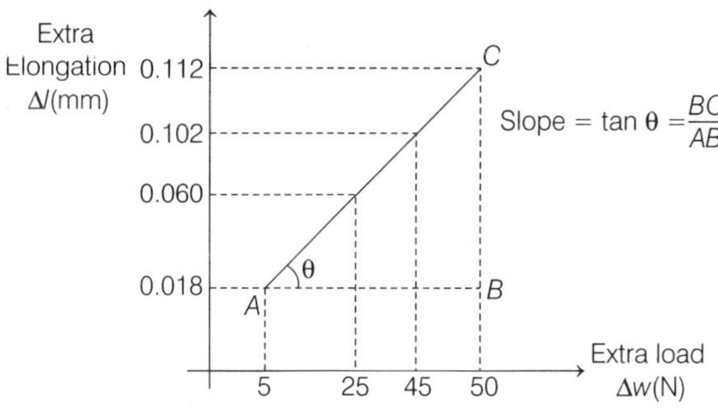

Fig. 3.20

$$\text{Slope} = \frac{BC}{AB}$$

Example 3.9 *The adjacent graph shows the extension (Δl) of a wire of length 1 m suspended from the top of a roof at one end and with a load w connected to the other end. If the cross-sectional area of the wire is 10^{-6} m^2, calculate from the graph the Young's modulus of the material of the wire.* **(JEE 2003)**

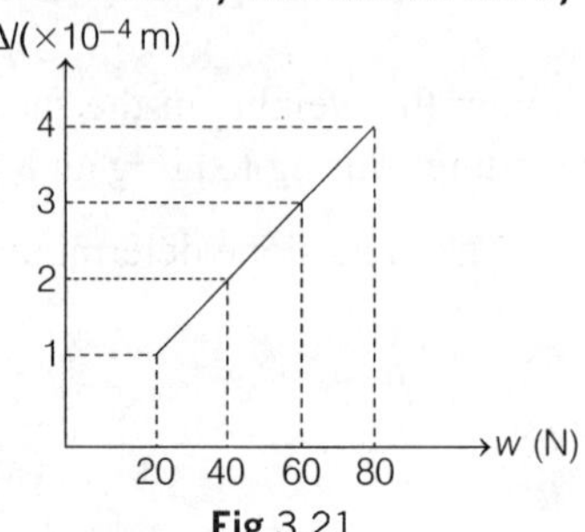

Fig 3.21

Solution $\Delta l = \left(\frac{l}{YA}\right) \cdot w \quad \Rightarrow \quad \Delta l \propto w$

i.e. Δl *versus* w graph is a straight line passing through origin (as shown in question also), the slope of which is $\frac{l}{YA}$.

$$\therefore \qquad \text{Slope} = \left(\frac{l}{YA}\right)$$

$$\therefore \qquad Y = \left(\frac{l}{A}\right)\left(\frac{1}{\text{slope}}\right)$$

$$= \left(\frac{1.0}{10^{-6}}\right)\frac{(80-20)}{(4-1)\times 10^{-4}}$$

$$= 2.0 \times 10^{11} \text{ N/m}^2$$ **Ans.**

Example 3.10 *In Searle's experiment, which is used to find Young's modulus of elasticity, the diameter of experimental wire is $D = 0.05$ cm (measured by a scale of least count 0.001 cm) and length is $L = 110$ cm (measured by a scale of least count 0.1 cm). A weight of 50 N causes an extension of $l = 0.125$ cm (measured by a micrometer of least count 0.001 cm). Find maximum possible error in the values of Young's modulus. Screw gauge and meter scale are free from error.* **(JEE 2004)**

Solution Young's modulus of elasticity is given by

$$Y = \frac{\text{stress}}{\text{strain}}$$

$$= \frac{F/A}{l/L} = \frac{FL}{lA} = \frac{FL}{l\left(\frac{\pi d^2}{4}\right)}$$

Substituting the values, we get

$$Y = \frac{50 \times 1.1 \times 4}{(1.25 \times 10^{-3}) \times \pi \times (5.0 \times 10^{-4})^2}$$

$$= 2.24 \times 10^{11} \text{ N/m}^2$$

Now,

$$\frac{\Delta Y}{Y} = \frac{\Delta L}{L} + \frac{\Delta l}{l} + 2\frac{\Delta d}{d}$$

$$= \left(\frac{0.1}{110}\right) + \left(\frac{0.001}{0.125}\right) + 2\left(\frac{0.001}{0.05}\right)$$

$$= 0.0489$$

$$\Delta Y = (0.0489) Y$$

$$= (0.0489) \times (2.24 \times 10^{11}) \text{ N/m}^2$$

$$= 1.09 \times 10^{10} \text{ N/m}^2$$

Ans.

INTRODUCTORY EXERCISE 3.4

1. A student performs an experiment to determine Young's modulus of a wire, exactly 2 m long by Searle's method. In a particular reading, the student measures the extension in the length of the wire to be 0.8 mm with an uncertainty of $\pm$ 0.05 mm at a load of 1.0 kg (exact). The student also measures the diameter of the wire to be 0.4 mm with an uncertainty of $\pm$ 0.01 mm. Take $g = 9.8 \text{ m/s}^2$ (exact). Find Young's modulus of elasticity with limits of error.
2. Which of the following is wrong regarding Searle's apparatus method in finding Young's modulus of a given wire ?
   (a) Average elongation of wire will be determined with a particular load while increasing the load and decreasing the load.
   (b) Reference wire will be just taut and experimental wire w ll undergo for elongation.
   (c) Air bubble in the spirit level will be disturbed from the central position due to relative displacement between the wires due to elongation.
   (d) Average elongation of the wires is to be determined by increasing the load attached to both the wires.

3.5 Determination of Specific Heat

Determination of Specific Heat Capacity of a given Solid

Specific heat of a solid can be determined by the **"Method of Mixture"** using the concept of the **"Law of Heat Exchange"** i.e.

Heat lost by hot body = Heat gained by cold body

The method of mixture is based on the fact that when a hot solid body is mixed with a cold body, the hot body loses heat and the cold body absorbs heat until thermal equilibrium is attained. At equilibrium, final temperature of mixture is measured. The specific heat of the solid is calculated with the help of the law of heat exchange.

Let

Mass of solid $= m_s$ kg
Mass of liquid $= m_l$ kg
Mass of calorimeter $= m_c$ kg
Initial temperature of solid $= T_s$K
Initial temperature of liquid $= T_l$K
Initial temperature of the calorimeter $= T_c$K
Specific heat of solid $= c_s$
Specific heat of liquid $= c_l$
Specific heat of the material of the calorimeter $= c_c$
Final temperature of the mixture $= T$ K

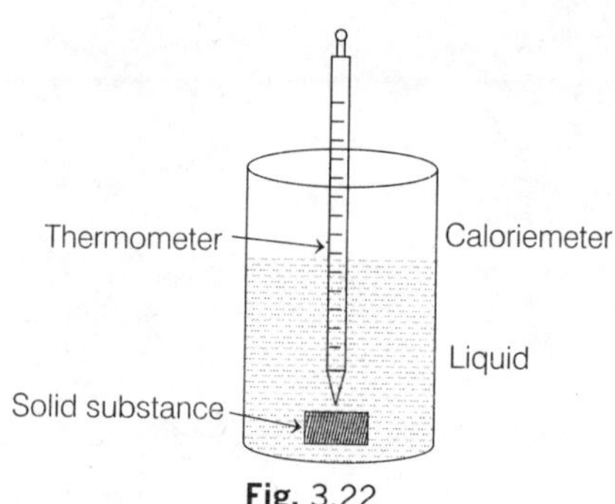

Fig. 3.22

According to the law of heat exchange

$$Q_{\text{Lost by solid}} = Q_{\text{Gained by liquid}} + Q_{\text{Gained by calorimeter}}$$

$$m_s c_s (T_s - T) = m_l c_l (T - T_l) + m_c c_c (T - T_c)$$

$$c_s = \frac{m_l c_l (T - T_1) + m_c c_c (T - T_c)}{m_s (T_s - T)}$$

Which is the required value of specific heat of solid in J/kg-K.

Determination of Specific Heat Capacity of the given Liquid by the Method of Mixtures

To determine the specific heat capacity of a liquid by the method of mixtures a solid of known specific heat capacity is taken and the given liquid is taken in the calorimeter in place of water. Suppose a solid of mass m_s and specific heat capacity c_s is heated to T_2°C and then mixed with m_1 mass of liquid of specific heat capacity c_1 at temperature T_1. The temperature of the mixture is T. Then,

Heat lost by the solid $= m_s c_s (T_2 - T)$

Heat gained by the liquid plus calorimeter $= (m_1 c_1 + m_c c_c)(T - T_1)$

By law of heat exchange,

$$\text{Heat lost} = \text{Heat gained}$$

$$\therefore \quad \boxed{m_s c_s (T_2 - T) = (m_1 c_1 + m_c c_c)(T - T_1)}$$

From this equation, we calculate the value of c_1. However, the procedure remains exactly the same as done previously.

Note *Specific heat is also called specific heat capacity and may be denoted by S, similarly temperature by θ.*

Example 3.11 *The mass, specific heat capacity and the temperature of a solid are* 1000 g, $\frac{1}{2}$ *cal/g-°C and* 80° C *respectively. The mass of the liquid and the calorimeter are* 900 g *and* 200 g. *Initially, both are at room temperature* 20° C. *Both calorimeter and the solid are made of same material. In the steady state, temperature of mixture is* 40° C, *then find the specific heat capacity of the unknown liquid.*

Solution m_1 = mass of solid = 1000 g,

S_1 = specific heat of solid = $\frac{1}{2}$ cal/g -° C

= S_2 or specific heat of calorimeter

m_2 = mass of calorimeter = 200 g

m_3 = mass of unknown liquid = 900 g

S_3 = specific heat of unknown liquid

From law of heat exchange,

Heat given by solid = Heat taken by calorimeter + Heat taken by unknown liquid

$$\therefore \quad m_1 S_1 |\Delta\theta_1| = m_2 S_2 |\Delta\theta_2| + m_3 S_3 |\Delta\theta_3|$$

$$\therefore \quad 1000 \times \frac{1}{2} \times (80 - 40) = 200 \times \frac{1}{2} (40 - 20) + 900 \times S_3 (40 - 20)$$

Solving this equation we get, $S_3 = 1$ cal/g-°C **Ans.**

Electrical Calorimeter

Figure shows an electrical calorimeter to determine specific heat capacity of an unknown liquid. We take a known quantity of liquid in an insulated calorimeter and heat it by passing a known current (i) through a heating coil immersed within the liquid. First of all, mass of empty calorimeter is measured and suppose it is m_1. Then, the unknown liquid is poured in it. Now, the combined mass (of calorimeter and liquid) is measured and let it be m_2. So, the mass of unknown liquid is $(m_2 - m_1)$. Initially, both are at room temperature (θ_0).

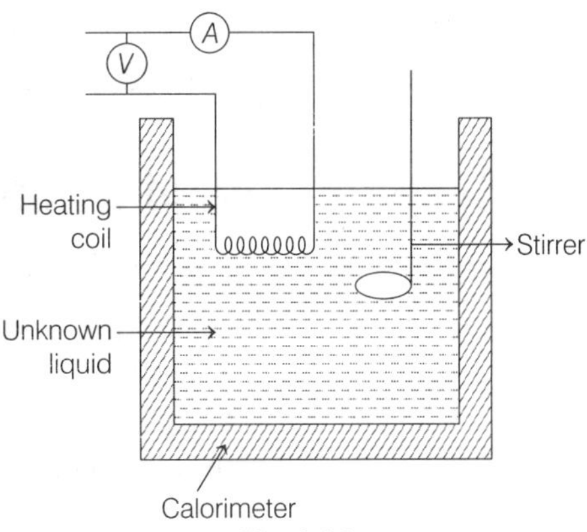

Fig. 3.23

Now, current i is passed through the heating coil at a potential difference V for time t. Due to this heat, the temperature of calorimeter and unknown liquid increase simultaneously. Suppose the final temperature is θ_f. If there is no heat loss to the surroundings, then

Heat supplied by the heating coil = heat absorbed by the liquid + heat absorbed by the calorimeter.

$$\therefore \quad Vit = (m_2 - m_1) S_l (\theta_f - \theta_0) + m_1 S_c (\theta_f - \theta_0)$$

Here S_l = Specific heat of unknown liquid and

S_c = Specific heat of calorimeter

Solving this equation we get,

$$S_l = \left(\frac{1}{m_2 - m_1}\right)\left[\frac{Vit}{\theta_f - \theta_0} - m_1 S_c\right]$$

Note *The sources of error in this experiment are errors due to improper connection of the heating coil and the radiation losses.*

Example 3.12 *In electrical calorimeter experiment, voltage across the heater is 100.0 V and current is 10.0 A. Heater is switched on for $t = 700.0$ s. Room temperature is $\theta_0 = 10.0°C$ and final temperature of calorimeter and unknown liquid is $\theta_f = 73.0°C$. Mass of empty calorimeter is $m_1 = 1.0$ kg and combined mass of calorimeter and unknown liquid is $m_2 = 3.0$ kg. Find the specific heat capacity of the unknown liquid in proper significant figures. Specific heat of calorimeter $= 3.0 \times 10^3$ J/kg°C*

Solution Given , $V = 100.0$ V, $i = 10.0$ A, $t = 700.0$ s, $\theta_0 = 10.0°C$, $\theta_f = 73.0°C$,

$m_1 = 1.0$ kg and $m_2 = 3.0$ kg

Substituting the values in the expression,

$$S_l = \left(\frac{1}{m_2 - m_1}\right)\left[\frac{Vit}{\theta_f - \theta_0} - m_1 S_c\right]$$

we have,

$$S_l = \frac{1}{3.0 - 1.0}\left[\frac{(100.0)(10.0)(700.0)}{73.0 - 10.0} - (1.0)(3.0 \times 10^3)\right]$$

$$= 4.1 \times 10^3 \text{ J/kg°C}$$ **Ans.**

(According to the rules of significant figures)

3.6 Speed of Sound using Resonance Tube

Apparatus

Figure shows a resonance tube. It consists of a long vertical glass tube T. A metre scale S (graduated in mm) is fixed adjacent to this tube. The zero of the scale coincides with the upper end of the tube. The lower end of the tube T is connected to a reservoir R of water tube through a pipe P. The water level in the tube can be adjusted by the adjustable screws attached with the reservoir. The vertical adjustment of the tube can be made with the help of levelling screws. For fine adjustments of the water level in the tube, the pinchcock is used.

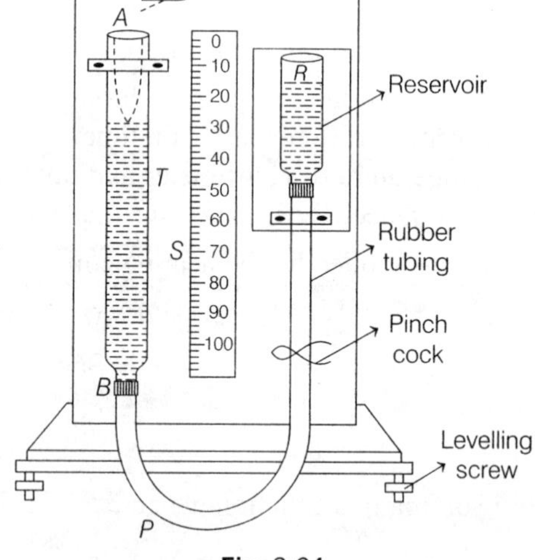

Fig. 3.24

Principle

If a vibrating tuning fork (of known frequency) is held over the open end of the resonance tube T, then resonance is obtained at some position as the level of water is lowered. If e is the end correction of the tube and l_1 is the length from the water level to the top of the tube, then

$$l_1 + e = \frac{\lambda}{4} = \frac{1}{4}\left(\frac{v}{f}\right) \quad \text{...(i)}$$

Here, v is the speed of sound in air and f is the frequency of tuning fork (or air column). Now, the water level is further lowered until a resonance is again obtained. If l_2 is the new length of air column, Then,

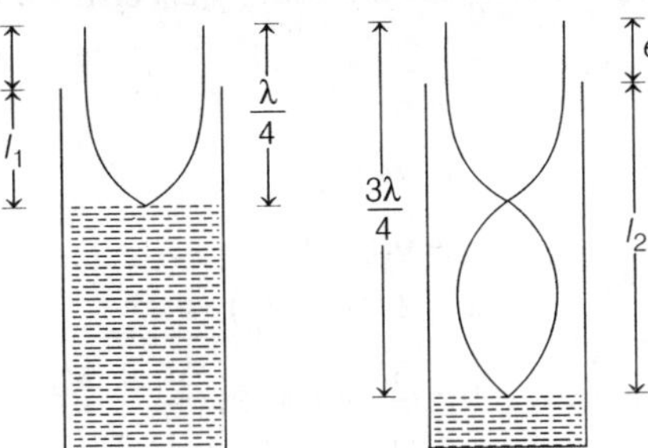

Fig. 3.25

$$l_2 + e = \frac{3\lambda}{4} = \frac{3}{4}\left(\frac{v}{f}\right) \qquad \text{...(ii)}$$

Subtracting Eq. (i) from Eq. (ii), we get

$$l_2 - l_1 = \frac{1}{2}\left(\frac{v}{f}\right) \quad \text{or} \quad \boxed{v = 2f\,(l_2 - l_1)} \qquad \text{...(iii)}$$

So, from Eq. (iii) we can find speed of sound v.

Note *We have nothing to do with the end correction e, as far as v is concerned.*

Example 3.13 *Corresponding to given observation calculate speed of sound. Frequency of tuning fork = 340 Hz*

Resonance	Length from the water level (in cm)	
	During falling	During rising
First	23.9	24.1
Second	73.9	74.1

Solution Mean length from the water level in first resonance is

$$l_1 = \frac{23.9 + 24.1}{2}$$
$$= 24.0 \text{ cm}$$

Similarly, mean length from the water level in second resonance is

$$l_2 = \frac{73.9 + 74.1}{2}$$
$$= 74.0 \text{ cm}$$

∴ Speed of sound,

$$v = 2f\,(l_2 - l_1)$$
$$= 2 \times 340\,(0.740 - 0.240)$$
$$= 340 \text{ m/s}$$

Ans.

Example 3.14 *If a tuning fork of frequency* (340 ± 1%) *is used in the resonance tube method and the first and second resonance lengths are* 20.0 cm *and* 74.0 cm *respectively. Find the maximum possible percentage error in speed of sound.*

Solution $l_1 = 20.0$ cm

$\Rightarrow$ $$\Delta l_1 = 0.1 \text{ cm}$$

$\Rightarrow$ $$l_2 = 74.0 \text{ cm}$$

$\Rightarrow$ $$\Delta l_2 = 0.1 \text{ cm}$$

$$v = 2f(l_2 - l_1)$$

$\therefore$ $$\frac{\Delta v}{v} \times 100 = \frac{\Delta f}{f} \times 100 + \left(\frac{\Delta l_1 + \Delta l_2}{l_2 - l_1}\right) \times 100$$

$$= 1\% + \left(\frac{0.1 + 0.1}{74.0 - 20.0}\right) \times 100$$

$$= 1\% + 0.37\% = 1.37\ \%$$ **Ans.**

INTRODUCTORY EXERCISE 3.5

1. In the experiment for the determination of the speed of sound in air using the resonance column method, the length of the air column that resonates in the fundamental mode, with a tuning fork is 0.1 m. When this length is changed to 0.35 m, the same tuning fork resonates with the first overtone. Calculate the end correction. **(JEE 2003)**
   (a) 0.012 m
   (b) 0.025 m
   (c) 0.05 m
   (d) 0.024 m

2. A student is performing the experiment of resonance column. The diameter of the column tube is 4 cm. The frequency of the tuning fork is 512 Hz. The air temperature is 38° C in which the speed of sound is 336 m/s. The zero of the meter scale coincides with the top end of the resonance column tube. When the first resonance occurs, the reading of the water level in the column is **(JEE 2012)**
   (a) 14.0 cm
   (b) 15.2 cm
   (c) 6.4 cm
   (d) 17.6 cm

3.7 Verification of Ohm's Law using Voltmeter and Ammeter

Ohm's law states that the electric current I flowing through a conductor is directly proportional to the potential difference (V) across its ends provided that the physical conditions of the conductor (such as temperature, dimensions, etc.) are kept constant. Mathematically,

$$V \propto I$$

or $$V = IR$$

Here, R is a constant known as resistance of the conductor and depends on the nature and dimensions of the conductor.

Circuit Diagram The circuit diagram is as shown below.

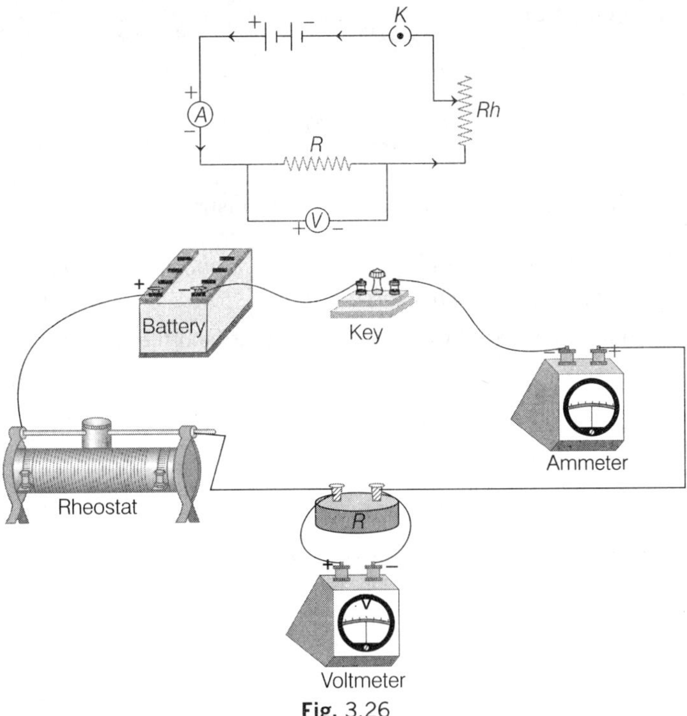

Fig. 3.26

Procedure

By shifting the rheostat contact, readings of ammeter and voltmeter are noted down. At least six set of observations are taken. Then, a graph is plotted between potential difference V and current I. The graph comes to be a straight line as shown in figure.

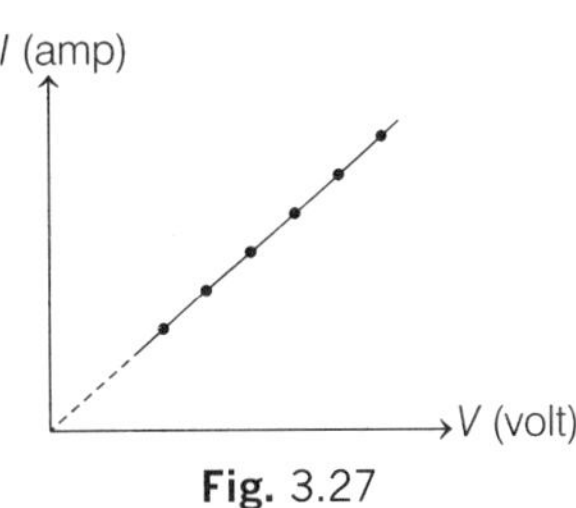

Fig. 3.27

Result

It is found from the graph that the ratio $\frac{V}{I}$ is constant. Hence, current voltage relationship is established, i.e. $V \propto I$. It means Ohm's law is established.

Precautions

1. The connections should be clean and tight.
2. Rheostat should be of low resistance.
3. Thick copper wire should be used for connections.
4. The key should be inserted only while taking observations to avoid heating of resistance.
5. The effect of finite resistance of the voltmeter can be over come by using a high resistance instrument or a potentiometer.
6. The lengths of connecting wires should be minimised as much as possible.

Error Analysis

The error in computing the ratio

$$R = \frac{V}{I} \text{ is given by}$$

$$\boxed{\frac{\Delta R}{R} = \frac{\Delta V}{V} + \frac{\Delta I}{I}}$$

where, ΔV and ΔI are the order of the least counts of the instruments used.

Example 3.15 *What result do you expect in above experiment, if by mistake, voltmeter is connected in series with the resistance.*

Solution Due to high resistance of voltmeter, current (and therefore reading of ammeter) in the circuit will be very low.

Example 3.16 *What result do you expect in above experiment if by mistake, ammeter is connected in parallel with voltmeter and resistance as shown in figure?*

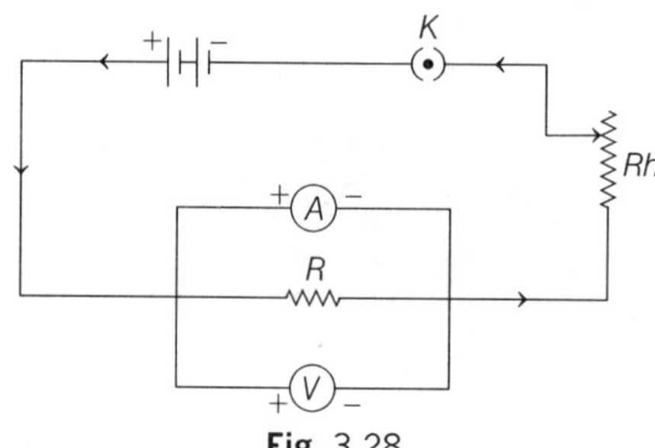

Fig. 3.28

Solution As ammeter has very low resistance, therefore most of the current will pass through the ammeter so reading of ammeter will be very large.

Example 3.17 *In the experiment of Ohm's law, when potential difference of* 10.0 V *is applied, current measured is* 1.00 A*. If length of wire is found to be* 10.0 cm *and diameter of wire* 2.50 mm*, then find maximum permissible percentage error in resistivity.*

Solution

$$R = \frac{\rho l}{A} = \frac{V}{I} \quad \text{...(i)}$$

where, ρ = resistivity

and A = cross sectional area

Therefore, from Eq. (i)

$$\rho = \frac{AV}{lI} = \frac{\pi d^2 V}{4lI} \quad \text{...(ii)}$$

where, $A = \frac{\pi d^2}{4}$ (d = diameter)

From Eq. (ii), we can see that maximum permissible percentage error in ρ will be

$$\frac{\Delta\rho}{\rho}\times 100=\left[2\left(\frac{\Delta d}{d}\right)+\left(\frac{\Delta V}{V}\right)+\left(\frac{\Delta l}{l}\right)+\left(\frac{\Delta I}{I}\right)\right]\times 100$$

$$=\left[2\times\frac{0.01}{2.50}+\frac{0.1}{10.0}+\frac{0.1}{10.0}+\frac{0.01}{1.00}\right]\times 100$$

$$=3.8\,\%$$

Ans.

Example 3.18 *Draw the circuit for experimental verification of Ohm's law using a source of variable DC voltage, a main resistance of 100 Ω, two galvanometers and two resistances of values 10^6 Ω and 10^{-3} Ω respectively. Clearly show the positions of the voltmeter and the ammeter.* **(JEE 2004)**

Solution

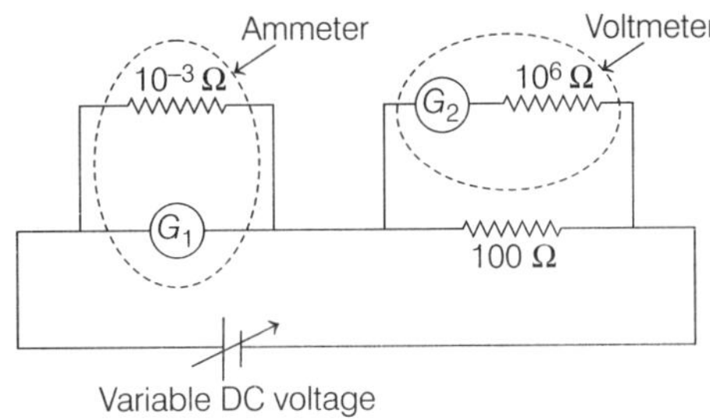

Fig. 3.29

INTRODUCTORY EXERCISE 3.6

1. In an experiment, current measured is $I = 10.0$ A, potential difference measured is $V = 100.0$ V, length of the wire is 31.4 cm and the diameter of the wire is 2.00 mm (all in correct significant figures). Find resistivity of the wire in correct significant figures. [Take, π = 3.14, (exact)]
2. In the previous question, find the maximum permissible percentage error in resistivity and resistance.
3. To verify Ohm's law, a student is provided with a test resistor R_T, a high resistance R_1, a small resistance R_2, two identical galvanometers G_1 and G_2, and a variable voltage source V. The correct circuit to carry out the experiment is

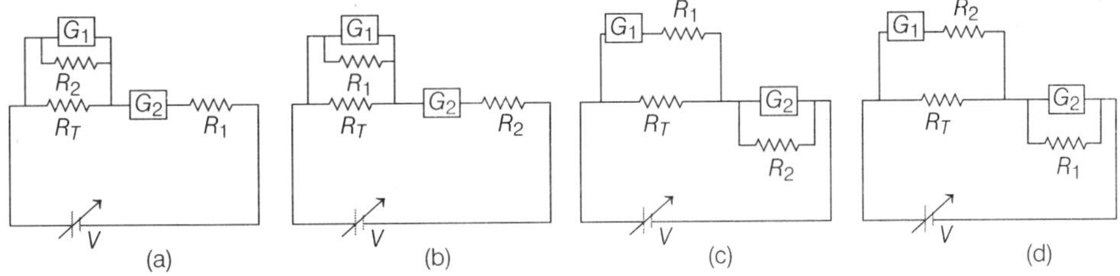

Fig. 3.30

3.8 Meter Bridge Experiment

Meter bridge works on Wheat stone's bridge principle and is used to find the unknown resistance (X) and its specific resistance (or resistivity).

Theory

As the metre bridge wire AC has uniform material density and area of cross-section, its resistance is proportional to its length. Hence, AB and BC are the ratio arms and their resistances correspond to P and Q respectively.

Thus,
$$\frac{\text{Resistance of } AB}{\text{Resistance of } BC} = \frac{P}{Q} = \frac{\lambda l}{\lambda (100 - l)} = \frac{l}{100 - l}$$

Here, λ is the resistance per unit length of the bridge wire.

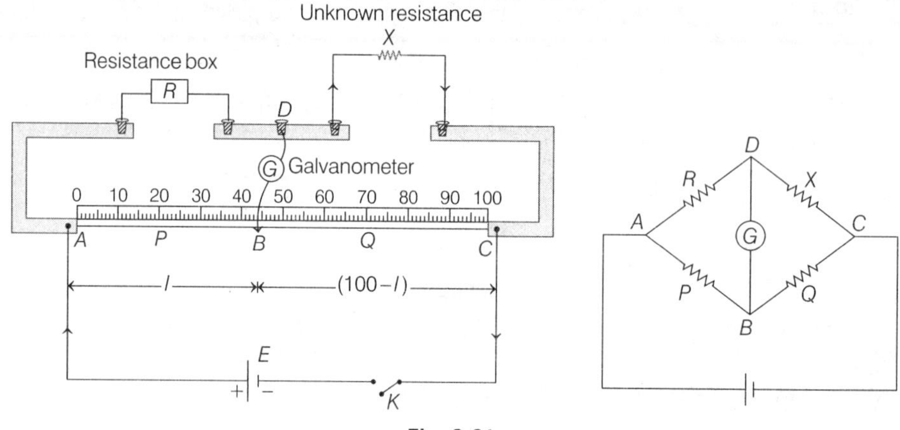

Fig. 3.31

Hence, according to Wheatstone's bridge principle,

When current through galvanometer is zero or bridge is balanced, then

$$\frac{P}{Q} = \frac{R}{X}$$

or
$$X = \frac{Q}{P} R$$

$\therefore$
$$\boxed{X = \left(\frac{100 - l}{l}\right) R} \qquad \text{...(i)}$$

So, by knowing R and l unknown resistance X can be determined.

Specific Resistance From resistance formula,

$$X = \rho \frac{L}{A}$$

or
$$\rho = \frac{XA}{L}$$

For a wire of radius r or diameter $D = 2r$,

$$A = \pi r^2 = \frac{\pi D^2}{4}$$

or
$$\rho = \frac{X\pi D^2}{4L} \qquad \text{...(ii)}$$

By knowing X, D and L we can find specific resistance of the given wire by Eq. (ii).

Precautions

1. The connections should be clean and tight.
2. Null point should be brought between 40 cm and 60 cm.
3. At one place, diameter of wire (D) should be measured in two mutually perpendicular directions.
4. The jockey should be moved gently over the bridge wire so that it does not rub the wire.

End Corrections

In meter bridge, some extra length (under the metallic strips) comes at points A and C. Therefore, some additional length (α and β) should be included at the ends. Here, α and β are called the end corrections. Hence in place of l we use $l + \alpha$ and in place of $100 - l$ we use $100 - l + \beta$.

To find α and β, use known resistors R_1 and R_2 in place of R and X and suppose we get null point length equal to l_1. Then,

$$\frac{R_1}{R_2} = \frac{l_1 + \alpha}{100 - l_1 + \beta} \qquad \text{...(i)}$$

Now, we interchange the positions of R_1 and R_2 and suppose the new null point length is l_2. Then,

$$\frac{R_2}{R_1} = \frac{l_2 + \alpha}{100 - l_2 + \beta} \qquad \text{...(ii)}$$

Solving Eqs. (i) and (ii), we can find α and β

$$\alpha = \frac{R_2 l_1 - R_1 l_2}{R_1 - R_2}$$

and
$$\beta = \frac{R_1 l_1 - R_2 l_2}{R_1 - R_2} - 100$$

Example 3.19 *If resistance R_1 in resistance box is 300 Ω, then the balanced length is found to be 75.0 cm from end A. The diameter of unknown wire is 1 mm and length of the unknown wire is 31.4 cm. Find the specific resistance of the unknown wire.*

Solution $\frac{R}{X} = \frac{l}{100 - l}$

$$\Rightarrow \qquad X = \left(\frac{100 - l}{l}\right) R = \left(\frac{100 - 75}{75}\right)(300) = 100\,\Omega$$

Now,
$$X = \frac{\rho l}{A} = \frac{\rho l}{(\pi d^2/4)}$$

$$\therefore \qquad \rho = \frac{\pi d^2 X}{4l}$$

$$= \frac{(22/7)(10^{-3})^2(100)}{(4)(0.314)}$$

$$= 2.5 \times 10^{-4}\ \Omega\text{-m}$$ **Ans.**

Example 3.20 *In a meter bridge, null point is 20 cm, when the known resistance R is shunted by 10 Ω resistance, null point is found to be shifted by 10 cm. Find the unknown resistance X.*

Solution $\frac{R}{X} = \frac{l}{100 - l}$

$$\therefore \qquad X = \left(\frac{100 - l}{l}\right) R$$

or $$X = \left(\frac{100 - 20}{20}\right) R = 4R \qquad \text{...(i)}$$

When known resistance R is shunted, its net resistance will decrease. Therefore, resistance parallel to this (i.e. P) should also decrease or its new null point length should also decrease.

$$\therefore \qquad \frac{R'}{X} = \frac{l'}{100 - l'}$$

$$= \frac{20 - 10}{100 - (20 - 10)} = \frac{1}{9}$$

or $$X = 9R' \qquad \text{...(ii)}$$

From Eqs. (i) and (ii), we have

$$4R = 9R' = 9\left[\frac{10R}{10 + R}\right]$$

Solving this equation, we get

$$R = \frac{50}{4}\ \Omega$$

Now, from Eq. (i), the unknown resistance

$$X = 4R = 4\left(\frac{50}{4}\right)$$

or $$X = 50\ \Omega$$ **Ans.**

Note *R′ is resultant of R and 10 Ω in parallel.*

$$\therefore \qquad \frac{1}{R'} = \frac{1}{10} + \frac{1}{R}$$

or $$R' = \frac{10R}{10 + R}$$

Example 3.21 *If we use 100 Ω and 200 Ω in place of R and X we get null point deflection, $l = 33$ cm. If we interchange the resistors, the null point length is found to be 67 cm. Find end corrections α and β.*

Solution

$$\alpha = \frac{R_2 l_1 - R_1 l_2}{R_1 - R_2} = \frac{(200)(33) - (100)(67)}{100 - 200} = 1\,\text{cm}$$ **Ans.**

$$\beta = \frac{R_1 l_1 - R_2 l_2}{R_1 - R_2} - 100$$

$$= \frac{(100)(33) - (200)(67)}{100 - 200} - 100$$

$$= 1\,\text{cm}$$ **Ans.**

INTRODUCTORY EXERCISE 3.7

1. A resistance of 2 Ω is connected across one gap of a meter bridge (the length of the wire is 100 cm) and an unknown resistance, greater than 2 Ω, is connected across the other gap. When these resistances are interchanged, the balance point shifts by 20 cm. Neglecting any corrections, the unknown resistance is **(JEE 2007)**
   (a) 3 Ω (b) 4 Ω (c) 5 Ω (d) 6 Ω
2. A meter bridge is set-up as shown in figure, to determine an unknown resistance X using a standard 10 Ω resistor. The galvanometer shows null point when tapping-key is at 52 cm mark. The end-corrections are 1 cm and 2 cm respectively for the ends A and B. The determined value of X is **(JEE 2011)**

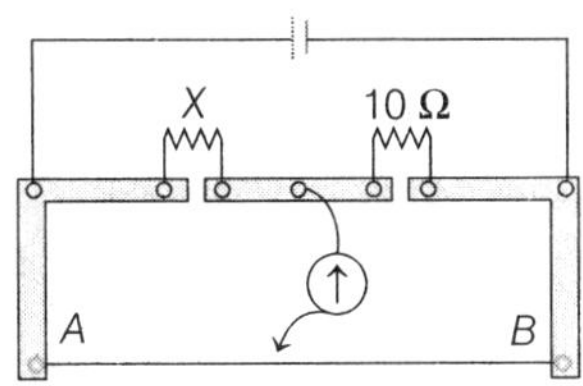

Fig. 3.32

   (a) 10.2 Ω (b) 10.6 Ω (c) 10.8 Ω (d) 11.1 Ω
3. R_1, R_2, R_3 are different values of R. A, B and C are the null points obtained corresponding to R_1, R_2 and R_3, respectively. For which resistor, the value of X will be the most accurate and why? **(JEE 2005)**

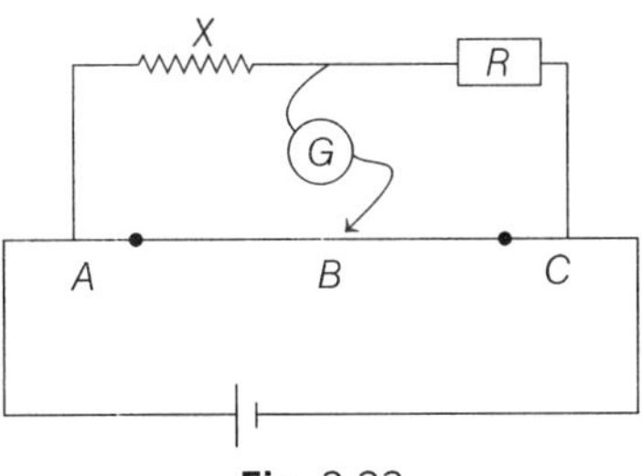

Fig. 3.33

3.9 Post Office Box

Post office box also works on the principle of Wheatstone's bridge.

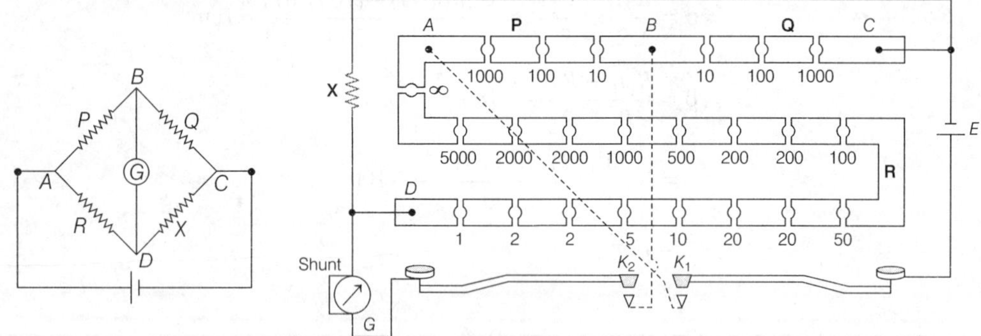

Fig. 3.34

In a Wheatstone's bridge circuit, if $\frac{P}{Q}=\frac{R}{X}$ then the bridge is balanced. So, unknown resistance $X=\frac{Q}{P}R$.

P and Q are set in arms AB and BC where we can have, $10\,\Omega, 100\,\Omega$ or $1000\,\Omega$ resistances to set any ratio $\frac{Q}{P}$.

These arms are called ratio arm, initially we take $Q=10\,\Omega$ and $P=10\,\Omega$ to set $\frac{Q}{P}=1$. The unknown resistance (X) is connected between C and D and battery is connected across A and C.

Now, put resistance in part A to D such that the bridge gets balanced. For this keep on increasing the resistance with $1\,\Omega$ interval, check the deflection in galvanometer by first pressing key K_1 then galvanometer key K_2.

Suppose at $R=4\,\Omega$, we get deflection towards left and at $R=5\,\Omega$, we get deflection towards right. Then, we can say that for balanced condition R should lie between $4\,\Omega$ to $5\,\Omega$.

Now, $X=\frac{Q}{P}R=\frac{10}{10}R=R=4\,\Omega$ to $5\,\Omega$

To get closer value of X, in the second observation, let us choose $\frac{Q}{P}=\frac{1}{10}$ i.e. $\left(\frac{P=100}{Q=10}\right)$

Suppose, now at $R=42$. We get deflection towards left and at $R=43$ deflection is towards right. So $R\in(42, 43)$.

Now, $X=\frac{Q}{P}R=\frac{10}{100}R=\frac{1}{10}R$, where $R\in(42, 43\,\Omega)$. Now, to get further closer value take $\frac{Q}{P}=\frac{1}{100}$ and so on.

The observation table is shown below.

S.No.	Resistance in the Ratio arm		Resistance in arm AD (R) (ohm)	Direction of deflection	Unknown resistance $X = \frac{Q}{P} \times R$ (ohm)
	AB (P) (ohm)	BC (Q) (ohm)			
1	10	10	4	Left	4 to 5
			5	Right	
2	100	10	40	Left (large)	(4.2 to 4.3)
			50	Right (large)	
			42	Left	
			43	Right	
3	1000	10	420	Left	4.25
			424	Left	
			425	No deflection	
			426	Right	

So, the correct value of X is 4.25 Ω.

Example 3.22 *To locate null point, deflection battery key (K_1) is pressed before the galvanometer key (K_2). Explain why?*

Solution If galvanometer key K_2 is pressed first then just after closing the battery key K_1 current suddenly increases.

So, due to self induction, a large back emf is generated in the galvanometer, which may damage the galvanometer.

Example 3.23 *What are the maximum and minimum values of unknown resistance X, which can be determined using the post office box shown in the Fig. 3.34 ?*

Solution

$$X = \frac{QR}{P}$$

$$\therefore \quad X_{max} = \frac{Q_{max}\, R_{max}}{P_{min}}$$

$$= \frac{1000}{10}(11110)$$

$$= 1111\,\text{k}\Omega \qquad \textbf{Ans.}$$

$$X_{min} = \frac{Q_{min}\, R_{min}}{P_{max}}$$

$$= \frac{(10)(1)}{1000}$$

$$= 0.01\,\Omega \qquad \textbf{Ans.}$$

INTRODUCTORY EXERCISE 3.8

1. In post office box experiment, if $\frac{Q}{P} = \frac{1}{10}$. In R, if 142 Ω is used, then we get deflection towards right and if $R = 143\ \Omega$, then deflection is towards left. What is the range of unknown resistance?
2. What is the change in experiment, if battery is connected between B and C and galvanometer is connected across A and C ?
3. For the post office box arrangement to determine the value of unknown resistance, the unknown resistance should be connected between **(JEE 2004)**

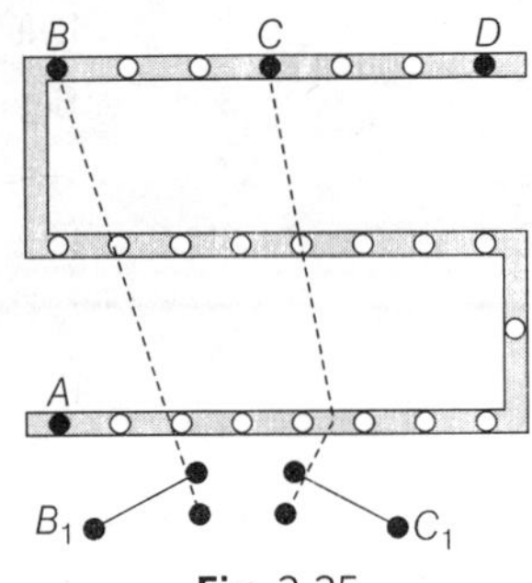

Fig. 3.35

(a) B and C (b) C and D (c) A and D (d) B_1 and C_1

3.10 Focal Length of a Concave Mirror using *u-v* Method

In this experiment, a knitting needle is used as an object O mounted in front of the concave mirror.

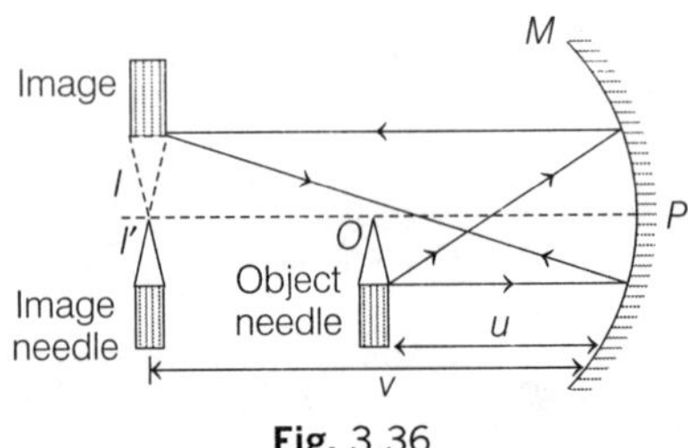

Fig. 3.36

First of all, we make a rough estimation of f. For this, make a sharp image of a far away object (like sun) on a filter paper. The image distance of the far object will be an approximate estimation of focal length f.

Now, the object needle is kept beyond F, so that its real and inverted image I can be formed. You can see this inverted image in the mirror by closing your one eye and keeping the other eye along the pole of the mirror.

To locate the position of the image use a second needle and shift this needle such that its peak coincide with the image. The second needle gives the distance of image v. This image is called image needle I. Note the object distance u and image distance v from the mm scale on optical bench.

Take some more observations in similar manner.

Determining f from u-v Observation

Method 1

Use mirror formula $\frac{1}{f} = \frac{1}{v} + \frac{1}{u}$ to find focal length from each u-v observation. Finally taking average of all we can find the focal length.

Method 2

The relation between object distance u and the image v from the pole of the mirror is given by

$$\frac{1}{v} + \frac{1}{u} = \frac{1}{f}.$$

where, f is the focal length of the mirror. The focal length of the concave mirror can be obtained from $\frac{1}{v}$ *versus* $\frac{1}{u}$ graph.

When the image is real (of course only upon then it can be obtained on screen), the object lies between focus (F) and infinity. In such a situation, u, v and f all are negative. Hence, the mirror formula,

$$\frac{1}{v} + \frac{1}{u} = \frac{1}{f}$$

becomes,

$$-\frac{1}{v} - \frac{1}{u} = -\frac{1}{f}$$

or again,

$$\frac{1}{v} + \frac{1}{u} = \frac{1}{f}$$

or

$$\frac{1}{v} = -\frac{1}{u} + \frac{1}{f}$$

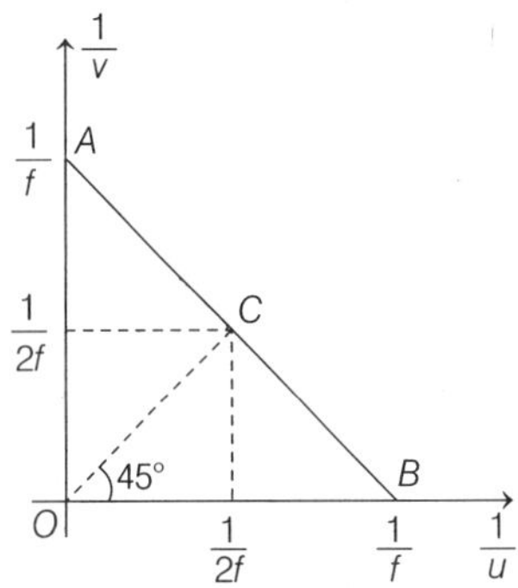

Fig. 3.37

Comparing with $y = mx + c$, the desired graph will be a straight line with slope -1 and intercept equal to $\frac{1}{f}$.

The corresponding $\frac{1}{v}$ *versus* $\frac{1}{u}$ graph is as shown in Fig. 3.37. The intercepts on the horizontal and vertical axes are equal. It is equal to $\frac{1}{f}$. A straight line OC at an angle 45° with the horizontal axis intersects line AB at C. The coordinates of point C are $\left(\frac{1}{2f}, \frac{1}{2f}\right)$. The focal length of the mirror can be calculated by measuring the coordinates of either of the points A, B or C.

Method 3

From u-v curve

Relation between u and v is

$$\frac{1}{v} + \frac{1}{u} = \frac{1}{f} \quad \text{...(i)}$$

After substituting u, v and f with sign (all negative) we get the same result.

For an object kept beyond F, u-v graph is as shown in figure. If we draw a line

$$u = v \qquad ...(ii)$$

then, it intersects the graph at point $P\ (2f, 2f)$.

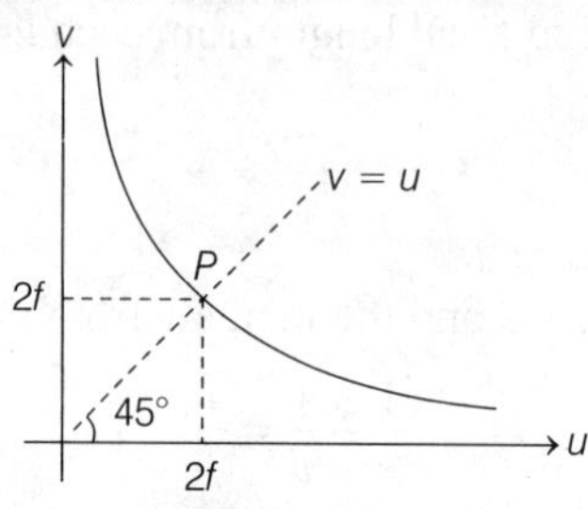

Fig. 3.38

From u-v data plot v *versus* u curve and draw a line at 45° as shown in figure. Find the intersection point and equate them to $(2f, 2f)$

By joining u_n and v_n : Mark $u_1, u_2, u_3 \ldots\ldots u_n$ along x-axis and $v_1, v_2, v_3 \ldots\ldots v_n$ along y-axis. If we join u_1 with v_1, u_2 with v_2, u_3 with v_3 and so on then all lines intersects at a common point (f, f).

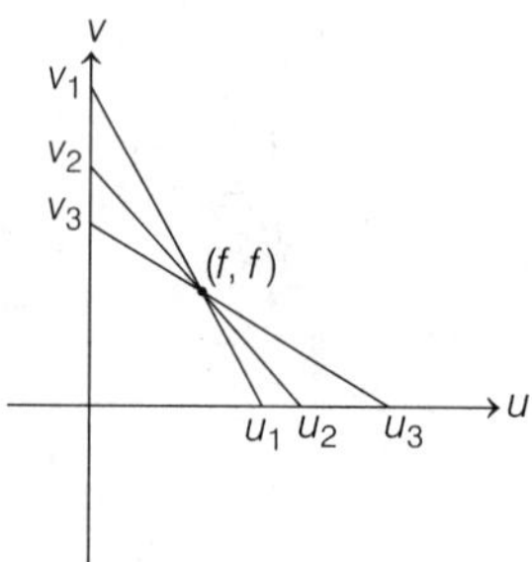

Fig. 3.39

Explanation

General equation of a line joining two points $P\ (a, 0)$ and $Q\ (0, b)$ is

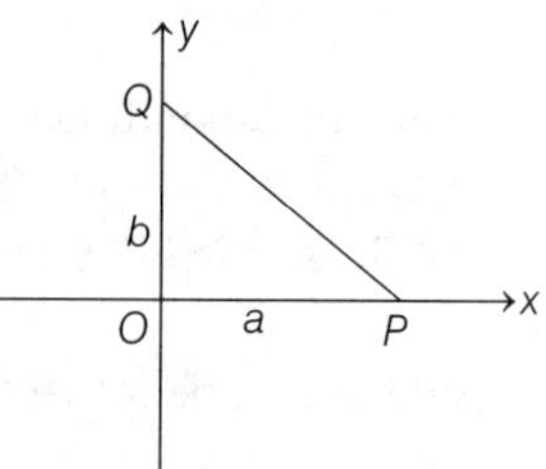

Fig. 3.40

$$y = mx + c$$

$$\Rightarrow \quad y = \frac{-b}{a}x + b$$

$$\Rightarrow \quad \frac{x}{a} + \frac{y}{b} = 1$$

Now, line joining u_1 and v_1 will be

$$\frac{x}{u_1} + \frac{y}{v_1} = 1 \qquad ...(iii)$$

where, $$\frac{1}{u_1} + \frac{1}{v_1} = \frac{1}{f}$$

or $$\frac{f}{u_1} + \frac{f}{v_1} = 1 \qquad ...(iv)$$

Similarly, line joining u_2 and v_2 is

$$\frac{x}{u_2}+\frac{y}{v_2}=1 \qquad ...(v)$$

where,

$$\frac{f}{u_2}+\frac{f}{v_2}=1 \qquad ...(vi)$$

and line joining u_n and v_n is

$$\frac{x}{v_n}+\frac{y}{u_n}=1 \qquad ...(vii)$$

where,

$$\frac{f}{u_n}+\frac{f}{v_n}=1 \qquad ...(viii)$$

From Eq. (iv), (vi), (viii), we can say that $x=f$ and $y=f$ will satisfy all Eq. (iii), (v), (vii). So, point (f, f) will be the common intersection point of all the lines.

From u-v data, draw $u_1, u_2 \ldots\ldots u_n$ along x-axis and $v_1, v_2, \ldots\ldots v_n$ along y-axis. Join u_1 with v_1, u_2 with v_2, ... u_n with v_n. Find common intersection point and equate it to (f, f).

Index Error

In u - v method, we require the distance between object or image from the pole P of the mirror. This is called actual distance. But practically, we measure the distance between the indices A and B. This is called the observed distance. The difference between two is called the index error (e). This is constant for every observation.

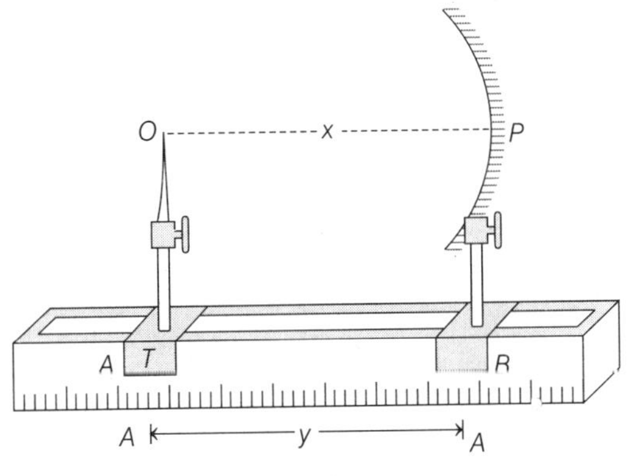

Fig. 3.41

$$\text{Index error} = \text{Observed distance} - \text{Actual distance}$$

To determine index error, mirror and object needle are placed at arbitery position. Measure the distances x and y as shown in figure.

So, index error is e = observed distance – Actual distance = $y-x$

once we get e, in every observation, we get

Actual distance = Observed distance (separation between the indices) – excess reading (e)

Example 3.24 *To find index error (e) distance between object needle and pole of the concave mirror is 20 cm. The separation between the indices of object needle and mirror was observed to be 20.2 cm. In some observation, the observed image distance is 20.2 cm and the object distance is 30.2 cm. Find*

(a) the index error e. *(b) focal length of the mirror f.*

Solution (a) Index error e = observed distance – actual distance

= separation between indices – distance between object needle and pole of the mirror

$= 20.2 - 20.0 = 0.2$ cm **Ans.**

(b) $|u| = 30.2 - 0.2 = 30\,\text{cm}$

$$\therefore \qquad u = -30\,\text{cm}$$

$$|v| = 20.2 - 0.2 = 20\,\text{cm}$$

$$\therefore \qquad v = -20\,\text{cm}$$

Using the mirror formula,

$$\frac{1}{f} = \frac{1}{v} + \frac{1}{u} = \frac{1}{-20} + \frac{1}{-30}$$

or $$f = -12\,\text{cm}$$ **Ans.**

Note *Since, it is a concave mirror, therefore focal length is negative.*

Example 3.25 *In u-v method to find focal length of a concave mirror, if object distance is found to be 10.0 cm and image distance was also found to be 10.0 cm, then find maximum permissible error in f.*

Solution Using the mirror formula,

$$\frac{1}{v} + \frac{1}{u} = \frac{1}{f} \qquad \text{...(i)}$$

we have, $$\frac{1}{-10} + \frac{1}{-10} = \frac{1}{f}$$

$$\Rightarrow \qquad f = -5\,\text{cm} \quad \text{or} \quad |f| = 5\,\text{cm}$$

Now, differentiating Eq. (i),

we have, $$\frac{-df}{f^2} = -\frac{du}{u^2} - \frac{dv}{v^2}$$

This equation can be written as

$$|\Delta f|_{\max} = \left[\frac{|\Delta u|}{u^2} + \frac{|\Delta v|}{v^2}\right](f^2)$$

Substituting the values we get,

$$|\Delta f|_{\max} = \left[\frac{0.1}{(10)^2} + \frac{0.1}{(10)^2}\right](5)^2 = 0.05\ \text{cm}$$

$$\therefore \qquad |f| = (5 \pm 0.05)\,\text{cm}$$ **Ans.**

Example 3.26 *A student performed the experiment of determination of focal length of a concave mirror by u-v method using an optical bench of length 1.5 m. The focal length of the mirror used is 24 cm. The maximum error in the location of the image can be 0.2 cm. The 5 sets of (u, v) values recorded by the student (in cm) are (42, 56), (48, 48), (60, 40), (66, 33), (78, 39). The data set(s) that cannot come from experiment and is (are) incorrectly recorded, is (are)* **(JEE 2009)**

(a) (42, 56) (b) (48, 48) (c) (66, 33) (d) (78, 39)

Solution Values of options (c) and (d) do not match with the mirror formula,

$$\frac{1}{v}+\frac{1}{u}=\frac{1}{f}$$

3.11 Focal Length of a Convex Lens using *u-v* Method

In this experiment, a convex lens is fixed in position L and a needle is used as an object mounted in front of the convex lens.

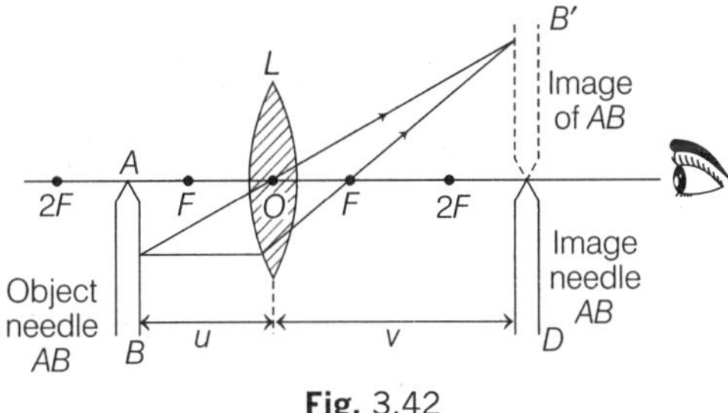

Fig. 3.42

First of all, we make a rough estimation of f. For estimating f roughly make a sharp image of a far away object (like sun) on a filter paper. The image distance of the far object will be an approximate estimation of focal length.

Now, the object needle is kept beyond F, so that its real and inverted image can be formed. To locate the position of the image, use a second needle and shift this needle such that its peak coincide with the image. The second needle gives the distance of image (v). Note the object distance u and image distance v from the mm scale on optical bench.

Take 4 to 5 more observations in similar manner.

Determining *f* from *u-v* Observations

Method 1

Use lens formula $\frac{1}{f}=\frac{1}{v}-\frac{1}{u}$ to find focal length corresponding to each u-v observation. Finally, take average of all.

Method 2

The relation between u, v and f for a convex lens is,

$$\frac{1}{v}-\frac{1}{u}=\frac{1}{f}$$

Using the proper sign convention, u is negative, v and f are positive. So, we have,

$$\frac{1}{v}-\frac{1}{-u}=\frac{1}{f}$$

or

$$\frac{1}{v}=-\frac{1}{u}+\frac{1}{f}$$

Comparing with $y=mx+c$, $\frac{1}{v}$ *versus* $\frac{1}{u}$ graph is a straight line with slope -1 and intercept $\frac{1}{f}$. The corresponding graph is as shown in Fig. 3.43. Proceeding in the similar manner as discussed in case of a concave mirror the focal length of the lens can be calculated by measuring the coordinates of either of the points A, B and C.

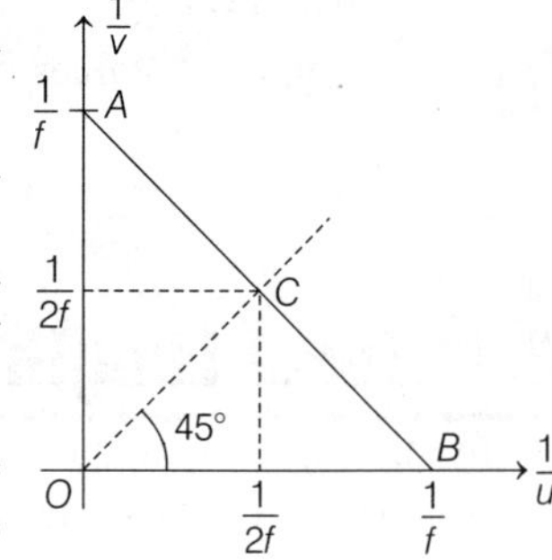

Fig. 3.43

The v *versus* u graph is as shown in the Fig. 3.44. By measuring the coordinates of point C whose coordinates are $(2f, 2f)$ we can calculate the focal length of the lens.

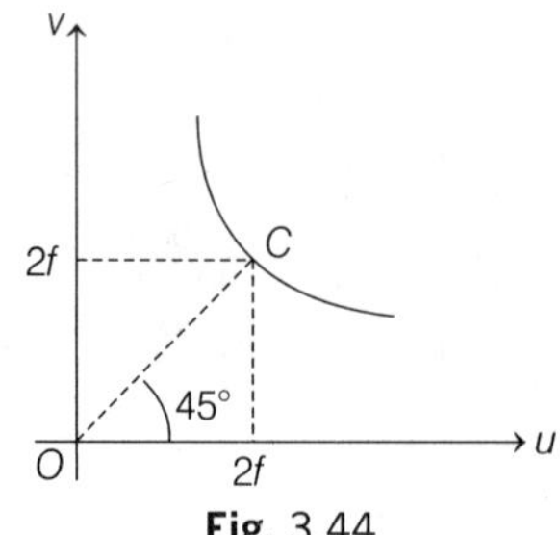

Fig. 3.44

Method 3

By joining u_n and v_n

Locate $u_1, u_2, u_3 \ldots\ldots u_n$ along x-axis and $v_1, v_2, v_3 \ldots\ldots v_n$ y-axis. If we join u_1 with v_1, u_2 with v_2, u_3 with v_3 and ………… so on. All lines intersect at a common point $(-f, f)$.

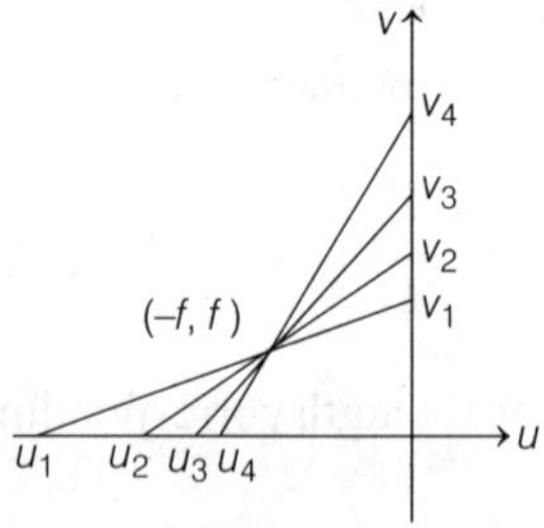

Fig. 3.45

From u-v data draw $u_1, u_2 \ldots\ldots u_n$ along x-axis and $v_1, v_2, \ldots\ldots v_n$ data on y-axis. Join u_1 and v_1, u_2 with v_2 …… u_n and v_n. Find common intersection point and equate it to $(-f, f)$.

Note *Index error is similar to the concave mirror.*

Example 3.27 *The graph between object distance u and image distance v for a lens is given below. The focal length of the lens is* **(JEE 2006)**

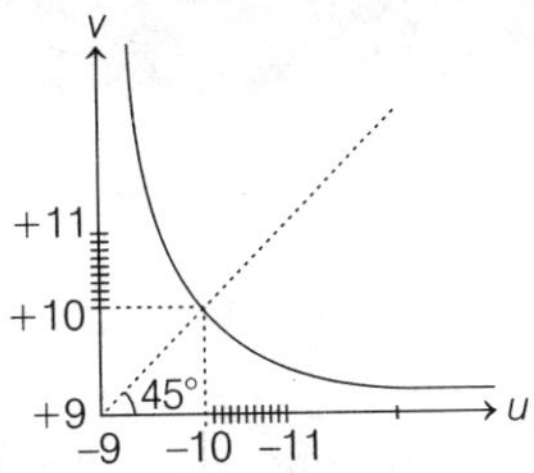

Fig. 3.46

(a) 5 ± 0.1 *(b)* 5 ± 0.05 *(c)* 0.5 ± 0.1 *(d)* 0.5 ± 0.05

Solution From the lens formula,

$$\frac{1}{f}=\frac{1}{v}-\frac{1}{u} \text{ we have,}$$

$$\frac{1}{f}=\frac{1}{10}-\frac{1}{-10} \text{ or } f=+5$$

Further, $$\Delta u = 0.1$$

and $$\Delta v = 0.1 \quad \text{(from the graph)}$$

Now, differentiating the lens formula, we have

$$\frac{\Delta f}{f^2}=\frac{\Delta v}{v^2}+\frac{\Delta u}{u^2}$$

or $$\Delta f=\left(\frac{\Delta v}{v^2}+\frac{\Delta u}{u^2}\right)f^2$$

Substituting the values, we have

$$\Delta f=\left(\frac{0.1}{10^2}+\frac{0.1}{10^2}\right)(5)^2=0.05$$

∴ $$f \pm \Delta f = 5 \pm 0.05$$

∴ The correct option is (b).

Exercises

Assertion and Reason

Directions : *Choose the correct option.*

(a) *If both* ***Assertion*** *and* ***Reason*** *are true and the* ***Reason*** *is correct explanation of the* ***Assertion.***

(b) *If both* ***Assertion*** *and* ***Reason*** *are true but* ***Reason*** *is not the correct explanation of* ***Assertion.***

(c) *If* ***Assertion*** *is true, but the* ***Reason*** *is false.*

(d) *If* ***Assertion*** *is false but the* ***Reason*** *is true.*

(e) *If both* ***Assertion*** *and* ***Reason*** *are false.*

1. Assertion : A screw gauge having a smaller value of pitch has greater accuracy.
Reason : The least count of screw gauge is directly proportional to the number of divisions on circular scale.

Objective Questions

Vernier Callipers

1. For positive error, the correction is
(a) positive (b) negative
(c) nill (d) may be positive or negative

2. The least count of a meter scale is 1 mm. Which of following lengths is/are measured by the meter scale? **(More than one correct options)**
(a) 2.8 cm (b) 2.80 cm (c) 2.834 cm (d) 2 mm

3. The least count of a wrist watch graduated at every second is **(More than one correct options)**
(a) one second, if it has hour hand, minute hand and second hand
(b) one minute, if it has only hour hand and minute hand
(c) one second in any case
(d) one minute in any case

4. Vernier constant is the
(a) value of one MSD divided by total number of divisions on the main scale
(b) value of one VSD divided by total number of divisions on the vernier scale
(c) total number of divisions on the main scale divided by total number of divisions on the vernier scale
(d) difference between the value of one main scale division and one vernier scale division

5. Select the **incorrect** statement.
(a) If the zero of vernier scale does not coincide with the zero of the main scale, then the vernier callipers is said to be having zero error
(b) Zero correction has a magnitude equal to zero error but sign is opposite to that of zero error
(c) Zero error is positive when the zero of vernier scale lies to the left of the zero of the main scale
(d) Zero error is negative when the zero of vernier scale lies to the left of the zero of the main scale

6. 1 cm on the main scale of a vernier callipers is divided into 10 equal parts. If 10 divisions of vernier coincide with 8 small divisions of main scale, then the least count of the calliper is

(a) 0.01 cm (b) 0.02 cm
(c) 0.05 cm (d) 0.005 cm

7. The vernier constant of a vernier callipers is 0.001 cm. If 49 main scale divisions coincide with 50 vernier scale divisions, then the value of 1 main scale division is

(a) 0.1 mm (b) 0.5 mm
(c) 0.4 mm (d) 1 mm

8. 1 cm of main scale of a vernier callipers is divided into 10 divisions. The least count of the callipers is 0.005 cm, then the vernier scale must have

(a) 10 divisions (b) 20 divisions
(c) 25 divisions (d) 50 divisions

9. Each division on the main scale is 1 mm. Which of the following vernier scales give vernier constant equal to 0.01 mm?

(a) 9 mm divided into 10 divisions (b) 90 mm divided into 100 divisions
(c) 99 mm divided into 100 divisions (d) 9 mm divided into 100 divisions

10. A vernier callipers having 1 main scale division = 0.1 cm is designed to have a least count of 0.02 cm. If n be the number of divisions on vernier scale and m be the length of vernier scale, then

(a) $n = 10, m = 0.5$ cm (b) $n = 9, m = 0.4$ cm
(c) $n = 10, m = 0.8$ cm (d) $n = 10, m = 0.2$ cm

11. The length of a rectangular plate is measured by a meter scale and is found to be 10.0 cm. Its width is measured by vernier callipers as 1.00 cm. The least count of the meter scale and vernier callipers are 0.1 cm and 0.01 cm, respectively. Maximum permissible error in area measurement is

(a) $\pm$ 0.2 cm^2 (b) $\pm$ 0.1 cm^2
(c) $\pm$ 0.3 cm^2 (d) zero

12. In the previous question, minimum possible error in area measurement can be

(a) $\pm$ 0.02 cm^2 (b) $\pm$ 0.01 cm^2
(c) $\pm$ 0.03 cm^2 (d) zero

13. The length of a strip measured with a metre rod is 10.0 cm. Its width measured with a vernier calipers is 1.00 cm. The least count of the metre rod is 0.1 cm and that of vernier calipers 0.01 cm. What will be error in its area?

(a) $\pm$ 13% (b) $\pm$ 7%
(c) $\pm$ 4% (d) $\pm$ 2%

14. The length of cylinder is measured with a metre rod having least count 0.1 cm. Its diameter is measured with vernier callipers having least count 0.01 cm. Given that length is 5.0 cm and radius is 2.0 cm. The percentage error in the calculated value of the volume will be

(a) 1.5% (b) 2.5%
(c) 3.5% (d) 4%

15. The diameter of a cylinder is measured using a vernier callipers with no zero error. It is found that the zero of the vernier scale lies between 5.10 cm and 5.15 cm of the main scale. The vernier scale has 50 division equivalent to 2.45 cm. The 24th division of the vernier scale exactly coincides with one of the main scale divisions. The diameter of the cylinder is

(a) 5.112 cm (b) 5.124 cm (c) 5.136 cm (d) 5.148 cm

16. A vernier callipers having main scale of 10 cm containing 100 divisions. If n be number of divisions on vernier scale of length l. Vernier calliper is designed to have a least count of 0.02 cm, then

(a) $l = 0.8$ cm, $n = 10$
(b) $l = 0.5$ cm, $n = 10$
(c) $l = 0.2$ cm, $n = 10$
(d) $l = 0.4$ cm, $n = 9$

17. A vernier calliper is having 1 main scale division = 1 mm. Ten divisions of vernier scale coincide with nine divisions of main scale. If two jaws of instrument touch each other, the 8th division of vernier scale coincide with a mark of main scale and the zero of the vernier scale lies to the right of the zero of main scale. While measuring the length of cylinder, the zero of the vernier scale lies slightly to the left of 3.2 cm and the fourth vernier division coincides with a mark of the length cylinder is

(a) 3.06 cm
(b) 3.15 cm
(c) 3.16 cm
(d) 3.22 cm

Screw Gauge

18. Screw gauge is said to have a negative error

(a) when circular scale zero coincides with base line of main scale
(b) when circular scale zero is above the base line of main scale
(c) when circular scale zero is below the base line of main scale
(d) None of the above

19. Least count of screw gauge is defined as

(a) $\dfrac{\text{distance moved by thimble on main scale}}{\text{number of rotation of thimble}}$

(b) $\dfrac{\text{pitch of the screw}}{\text{number of divisions on circular scale}}$

(c) $\dfrac{\text{number of rotation of thimble}}{\text{number of circular scale divisions}}$

(d) None of the above

20. Which of the following is the most precise device for measuring length?

(a) A vernier callipers with 20 divisions on the sliding scale
(b) An optical instrument that can measure length to within a wavelength of light
(c) A screw gauge of pitch 1 mm and 100 divisions on the circular scale
(d) All the above are equally precise

21. In four complete rotations, the distance moved by the screw on the linear scale is 2 mm. Its circular scale contains 50 divisions. Find the least count of the screw gauge.

(a) 0.05 mm
(b) 0.01 mm
(c) 0.1 mm
(d) 0.02 mm

22. The distance moved by the screw of a screw gauge is 2 mm in four rotations and there are 50 divisions on its cap. When nothing is put between its jaws, 20th division of circular scale coincides with reference line and zero of linear scale is hidden from circular scale when two jaws touch each other or zero of circular scale is lying above the reference line. When plate is placed between the jaws, main scale reads 2 divisions and circular scale reads 20 divisions. Thickness of plate is

(a) 1.1 mm
(b) 1.2 mm
(c) 1.4 mm
(d) 1.5 mm

23. The density of a solid ball is to be determined in an experiment. The diameter of the ball is measured with a screw gauge, whose pitch is 0.5 mm and there are 50 divisions on the circular scale. The reading on the main scale is 2.5 mm and that on the circular scale is 20 divisions. If the measured mass of the ball has a relative percentage error of 2%, the relative percentage error in the density is

(a) 0.9% (b) 2.4% (c) 3.1% (d) 4.2%

24. The pitch of screw gauge is 1 mm and there are 100 divisions on circular scale. Screw gauge is zero error free. While measuring diameter of a wire, the main scale reads 1 mm and 48th division on circular scale coincides with the reference line. The length of wire is 5.0 cm. Find the volume of the wire.

(a) 2.6 cm^3 (b) 0.086 cm^3
(c) 0.026 cm^3 (d) 0.036 cm^3

25. The pitch of the screw gauge is 1 mm. There are 100 divisions on the circular scale when the gap *AB* is just closed, 8th division of the circular scale coincides with reference line. While measuring the diameter of a wire, the linear scale reads 1 mm and 50th division on the circular scale coincides with the reference line. The length of the wire is 8.6 cm. Find the curved surface area of the cylinder.

(a) 3.8 cm^2 (b) 3.834 cm^2
(c) 2.6 cm^2 (d) 2.68 cm^2

26. In 10 complete rotations, the distance moved on the linear scale is 1 cm. There are 100 divisions on circular scale. When the gap *AB* is just closed, the 95th division of circular scale coincides with the reference line. While measuring the diameter of a wire, the linear scale reads 2 mm and 45th division on the circular scale coincides with the reference line. Find cross-sectional area of the wire.

(a) 3.8 cm^2 (b) 0.049 cm^2 (c) 0.098 cm^2 (d) 0.45 cm^2

27. In five complete rotations, the distance moved by screw on a linear scale is 0.5 cm. There are 100 divisions on circular scale. While measuring the thickness of a metal plate by the screw gauge, there are five divisions on the main scale and 35 divisions coincide with the reference line. Calculate the thickness of metal plate.

(a) 5.35 cm (b) 0.535 cm (c) 0.6 cm (d) 0.7 cm

Meter Bridge and Post Office Box

28. In a meter bridge set up, which of the following should be the properties of the one meter long wire?

(a) High resistivity and low temperature coefficient
(b) Low resistivity and low temperature coefficient
(c) Low resistivity and high temperature coefficient
(d) High resistivity and high temperature coefficient

29. *AB* is a wire of uniform resistance. The galvanometer *G* shows no deflection when the length $AC = 20$ cm and $CB = 80$ cm. The resistance *R* is equal to

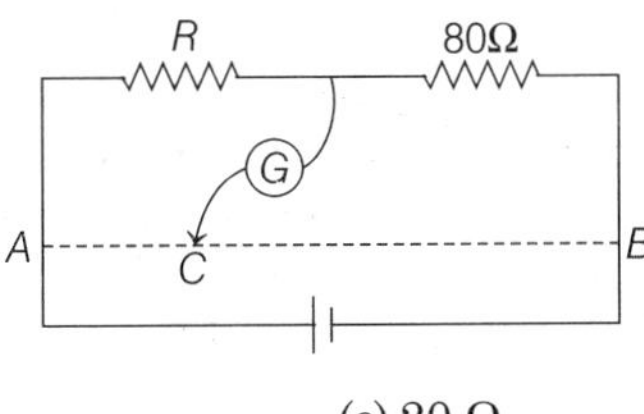

(a) 80 Ω (b) 10 Ω (c) 20 Ω (d) 40 Ω

30. For a post office box, the graph of galvanometer deflection *versus* R (resistance pulled out of resistance box) for the ratio 100 : 1 is given as shown. Find the value of unknown resistance.

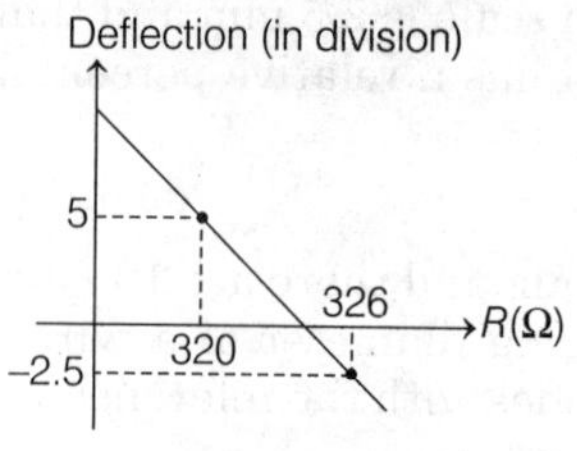

(a) 324 Ω
(b) 3.24 Ω
(c) 32.4 Ω
(d) None of these

31. The resistance in the left and right gaps of a balanced meter bridge are R_1 and R_2. The balanced point is 50 cm. If a resistance of 24 Ω is connected in parallel to R_2, the balance point is 70 cm. The value of R_1 or R_2 is
(a) 12 Ω
(b) 8 Ω
(c) 16 Ω
(d) 32 Ω

32. An unknown resistance R_1 is connected in series with a resistance of 10 Ω. This combination is connected to one gap of a meter bridge, while other gap is connected to another resistance R_2. The balance point is at 50 cm. Now, when the 10 Ω resistance is removed, the balance point shifts to 40 cm. Then, the value of R_1 is
(a) 60 Ω
(b) 40 Ω
(c) 20 Ω
(d) 10 Ω

33. In the post office box, if the connection of galvanometer and battery interchange, then
(a) we cannot get balanced condition
(b) experiment is less accurate
(c) experiment can be done in similar manner but battery is switched ON first, then galvanometer is switched ON
(d) experiment can be done in similar manner but galvanometer is switched ON first, then battery is switched ON

34. In the arrangement of meter bridge experiment, balancing length is x. What would be the value of balancing length, if length of wire AC is 2 m?

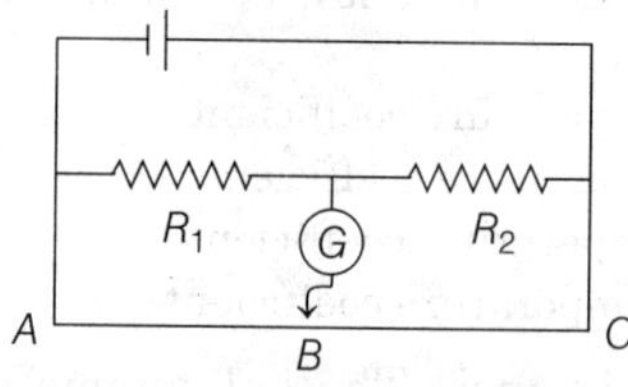

(a) x
(b) $2x$
(c) $\frac{2}{2-x}$
(d) $\frac{2-x}{2}$

35. Two resistances are connected in the two gaps of a meter bridge. The balance point is 20 cm from the zero end. When a resistance 15 Ω is connected in series with the smaller of two resistance, the null point shifts to 40 cm. The smaller of the two resistance has the value
(a) 8 Ω
(b) 9 Ω
(c) 10 Ω
(d) 12 Ω

36. In a meter bridge experiment, null point is obtained at 20 cm from one end of the wire when resistance X is balanced against another resistance Y. If $X < Y$, then the new position of the null point from the same end, if one decides to balance a resistance of $4X$ against Y will be at

(a) 50 cm
(b) 80 cm
(c) 40 cm
(d) 70 cm

37. In a meter bridge, the gaps are closed by two resistances P and Q and the balance point is obtained at 40 cm. When Q is shunted by a resistance of 10 Ω, the balance point shifts to 50 cm. The values of P and Q are

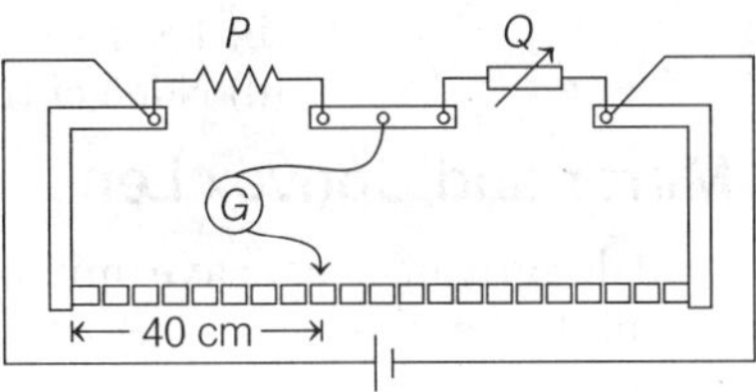

(a) $\frac{10}{3}$ Ω, 5 Ω
(b) 20 Ω, 30 Ω
(c) 10 Ω, 15 Ω
(d) 5 Ω, $\frac{15}{2}$ Ω

Resonance Column Experiment

38. The end correction (e) is (l_1 = length of air column at first resonance and l_2 is length of air column at second resonance)

(a) $e = \frac{l_2 - 3l_1}{2}$
(b) $e = \frac{l_1 - 3l_2}{2}$
(c) $e = \frac{l_2 - 2l_1}{2}$
(d) $e = \frac{l_1 - 2l_2}{2}$

39. The end correction of a resonance tube is 1 cm. If shortest resonating length is 15 cm, the next resonating length will be

(a) 47 cm
(b) 45 cm
(c) 50 cm
(d) 33 cm

40. A tuning fork of frequency 340 Hz is excited and held above a cylindrical tube of length 120 cm. It is slowly filled with water. The minimum height of water column required for resonance to be first heard (Velocity of sound = 340 ms^{-1}) is

(a) 25 cm
(b) 75 cm
(c) 45 cm
(d) 105 cm

41. Two unknown frequency tuning forks are used in resonance column apparatus. When only first tuning fork is excited the 1st and 2nd resonating lengths noted are 10 cm and 30 cm, respectively. When only second tuning fork is excited the 1st and 2nd resonating lengths noted are 30 cm and 90 cm respectively. The ratio of the frequency of the 1st to 2nd tuning fork is

(a) 1 : 3
(b) 1 : 2
(c) 3 : 1
(d) 2 : 1

42. In resonance column method to determine speed of sound in air, the first and second resonance lengths of air column are 25.0 cm and 75.0 cm, respectively. The frequency of tuning fork is exactly measured and is equal to 300 Hz. The speed of sound in air is

(a) (300 ± 1.2) ms^{-1}
(b) (330 ± 1.2) ms^{-1}
(c) $(300 - 1.2)$ ms^{-1}
(d) $(300 + 1.2)$ ms^{-1}

43. Resonance column method is applicable for finding speed of sound in air. The formula used for speed of sound in air is $v = 2(l_2 - l_1)f$.

Here, f = frequency of tuning fork, v = velocity of sound in air, l_1 = first resonance length of air column in the resonance tube, l_2 = second resonance length of air column in the resonance tube.

In resonance tube experiment, we find $l_1 = 20$ cm and $l_2 = 60$ cm and frequency of tuning fork is 400 Hz. The least count of the scale used to measure l_1 and l_2 is 0.1 cm and least count of the instrument measured the frequency of 0.5 Hz.

Find percentage error in measurement of speed of sound in air.

(a) 1.7%
(b) 1.8%
(c) 1.2%
(d) None of these

Focal Length of Concave Mirror and Convex Lens

44. In an experiment to find focal length of a concave mirror, a graph is drawn between the magnitudes of u and v. The graph looks like

(a)
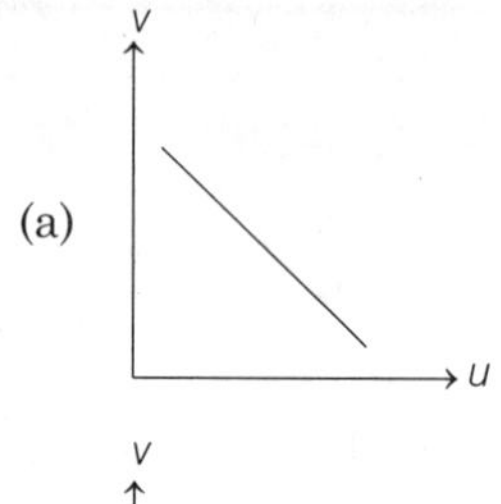

(b)
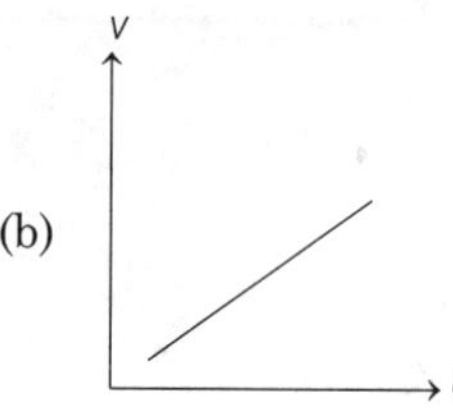

(c)
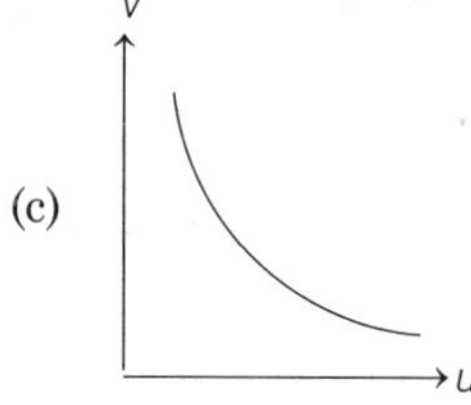

(d)
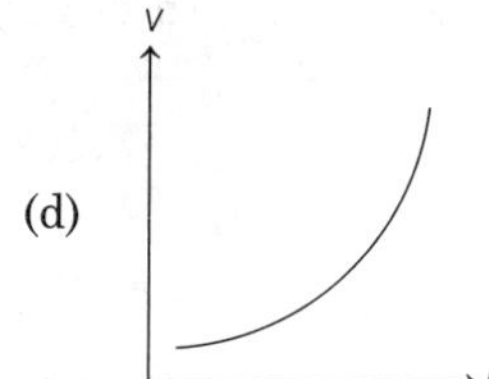

45. The graph between $\frac{1}{v}$ and $\frac{1}{u}$ for a concave mirror looks like

(a)
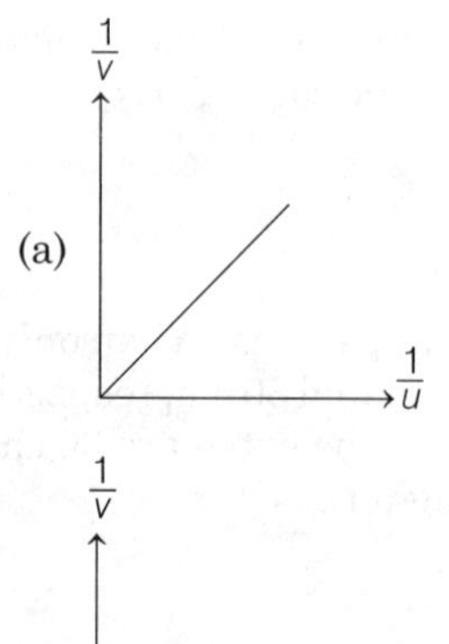

(b)
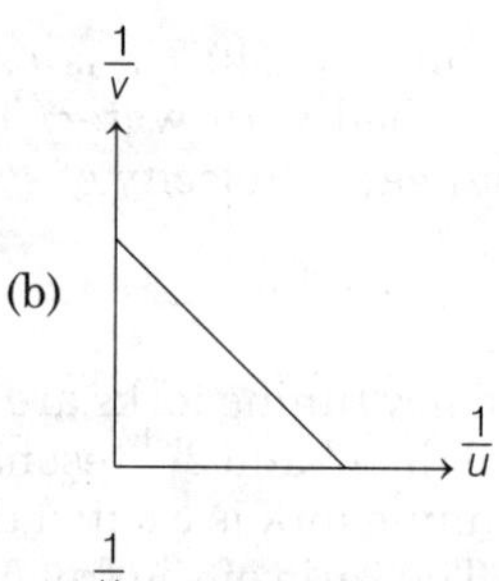

(c)
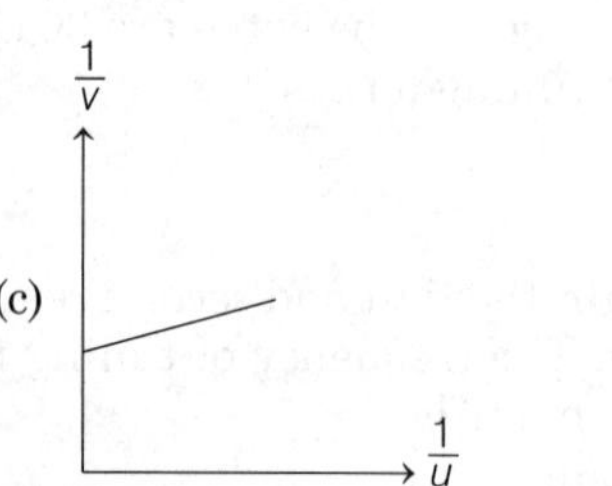

(d)
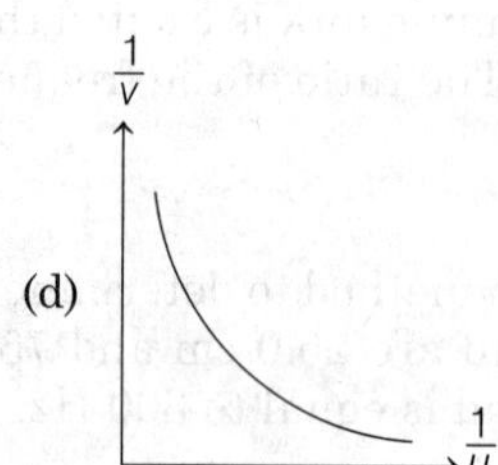

46. A graph is drawn with $\frac{1}{u}$ along x-axis and $\frac{1}{v}$ along the y-axis. If the intercept on the x-axis is $0.5\ m^{-1}$, the focal length of the lens is (in metre)

(a) 2.00
(b) 0.50
(c) 0.20
(d) 1.00

47. In the case of convex lens, if object distance is 30.0 cm and image distance is 60.0 cm. Find the focal length of lens.

(a) (20 ± 0.06) cm
(b) (20 ± 0.05) cm
(c) (10 ± 0.06) cm
(d) (40 ± 0.05) cm

Specific Heat

48. The mass of a copper calorimeter is 40 g and its specific heat in SI units is $4.2 \times 10^2\ J\ kg^{-1}\ ^\circ C^{-1}$. The thermal capacity is

(a) $4\ J\ ^\circ C^{-1}$
(b) 18.6 J
(c) 16.8 J /kg
(d) $16.8\ J\ ^\circ C^{-1}$

49. When 0.2 kg of brass at 100°C is dropped into 0.5 kg of water at 20 °C, the resulting temperature is 23°C. The specific heat of brass is

(a) $0.41 \times 10^3\ Jkg^{-1}\ ^\circ C^{-1}$
(b) $0.41 \times 10^2 Jkg^{-1}\ ^\circ C^{-1}$
(c) $0.41 \times 10^4 Jkg^{-1}\ ^\circ C^{-1}$
(d) $0.41\ Jkg^{-1}\ ^\circ C^{-1}$

50. In an experiment to determine the specific heat of a metal, a 0.20 kg block of the metal at 150°C is dropped in a copper calorimeter (of water equivalent 0.025 kg) containing 150 cm^3 of water at 27°C. The final temperature is 40°C. The specific heat of the metal is

(a) $0.1\ Jg^{-1}\ ^\circ C^{-1}$
(b) $0.2\ Jg^{-1}\ ^\circ C^{-1}$
(c) $0.3\ cal\ g^{-1}\ ^\circ C^{-1}$
(d) $0.1\ cal\ g^{-1}\ ^\circ C^{-1}$

51. In an experiment to determine the specific heat of aluminium, piece of aluminium weighing 500 g is heated to 100°C. It is then quickly transferred into a copper calorimeter of mass 500 g containing 300 g of water at 30°C. The final temperature of the mixture is found to be 46.8°C. If specific heat of copper is $0.093\ cal\ g^{-1}\ ^\circ C^{-1}$, then the specific heat of aluminium is

(a) $0.11\ cal\ g^{-1}\ ^\circ C^{-1}$
(b) $0.22\ cal\ g^{-1}\ ^\circ C^{-1}$
(c) $0.33\ cal\ g^{-1}\ ^\circ C^{-1}$
(d) $0.44\ cal\ g^{-1}\ ^\circ C^{-1}$

Miscellaneous Problems

52. In the Searle's experiment, after every step of loading, why should we wait for two minutes before taking the reading? **(More than one correct options)**

(a) So that the wire can have its desired change in length
(b) So that the wire can attain room temperature
(c) So that vertical oscillations can get subsided
(d) So that the wire has no change in its radius

53. To find the value of g using simple pendulum, $T = 2.0$ s, $l = 1.0$ m. The value of g is (Take, $\pi^2 = 10$)

(a) $(10 \pm 2\%)\ ms^{-2}$
(b) $(10 \pm 0.2\%)\ ms^{-2}$
(c) $(9.8 \pm 2\%)\ ms^{-2}$
(d) $(9.8 \pm 0.2\%)\ ms^{-2}$

Comprehension Based Questions

Passage 1 (Q.Nos. 1 to 2)

Verification of Ohm's law using voltmeter and ammeter :
According to Ohm's law,

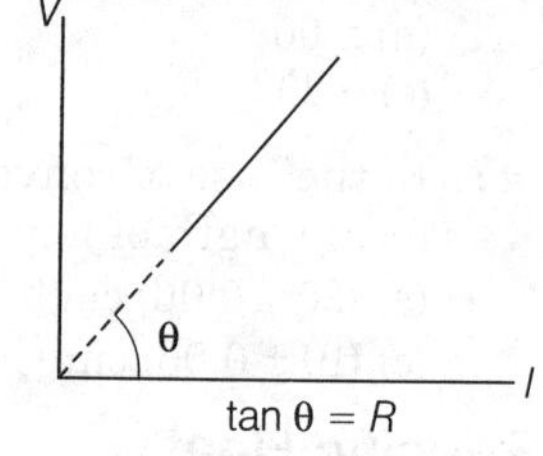

$$V \propto I, \quad \therefore \quad V = RI,$$

Here, V = *potential difference across wire,* I = *electric current,*
R = *electric resistance of the wire* $= \rho \dfrac{l}{A}$

ρ = *resistivity of material of wire,* l = *length of wire*

A = *cross-sectional area of the wire. For verification of Ohm's law, circuit used is shown in the figure.*

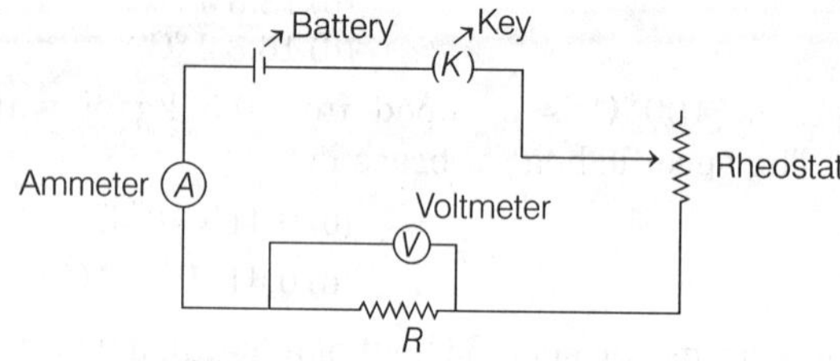

1. In the Ohm's experiment, 100.0 V is applied across a cylindrical wire of length 100.0 cm and diameter 5.000 mm, the current through wire is 1.00 A. The maximum percentage error in measurement of resistivity of the wire is approximately

(a) 2% (b) 3.8% (c) 1.2% (d) 1.8%

2. In previous problem, the resistance of wire is

(a) $(1.00 \times 10^2 \pm 1.1)\ \Omega$ (b) $(10.00 \times 10^2 \pm 1.1)\ \Omega$
(c) $(1.00 \times 10^2 \pm 0.11)\ \Omega$ (d) $(1.00 \times 10^2 \pm 2.2)\ \Omega$

Passage 2 (Q.Nos. 3 to 4)

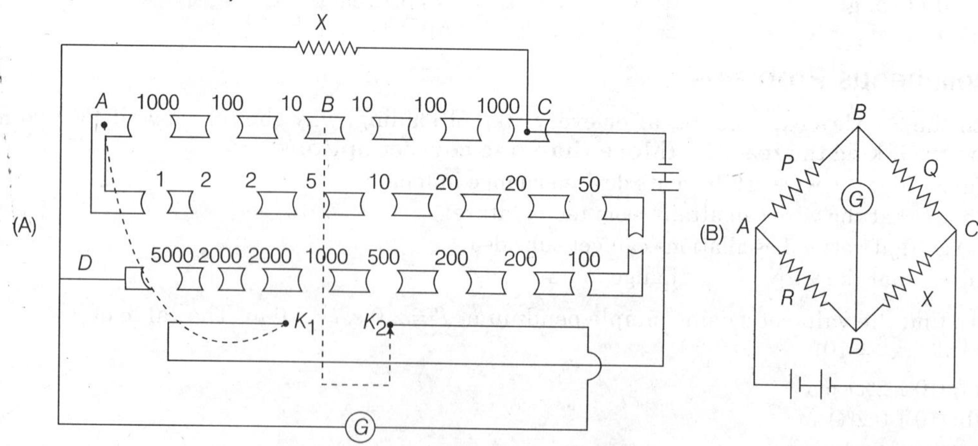

Post office box is useful to measure the value of unknown resistance correctly upto 2nd decimal place. It is based on Wheatstone bridge.

Systematic diagrams of post office box are shown in the given figures. Each of the arms AB and BC contains three resistances of 10 Ω, 100 Ω and 1000 Ω. These arms are generally known as ratio arms. With the help of these resistances, we can introduce resistance P in arm AB and resistance Q in arm BC. The resistance arm AD is a complete re~istance box containing resistances from 1 Ω to 5000 Ω. In this arm, we can introduce resistance R by taking out plugs of suitable values. The unknown resistance X is connected in fourth arm CD. These four arms actually form Wheatstone bridge shown in Fig (B). For balanced conditions, no deflection is formed in galvanometer.

At balanced condition, $PX = QR, \quad X = \frac{QR}{P}$.

3. What is the minimum and maximum possible resistance, which can be determined by using post office box?

(a) $0.01\,\Omega, 1111 \times 10^3\,\Omega$ (b) $0.1\,\Omega, 5000 \times 10^3\,\Omega$
(c) $0.01\,\Omega, 500 \times 10^3\,\Omega$ (d) $0.01\,\Omega, 1111\,\Omega$

4. In an experiment with a post office box, the ratio arms are 1000 : 10. The value of third resistance is 999 Ω, find the value of unknown resistance.

(a) 99.9 Ω (b) 999 Ω (c) 9.99 Ω (d) 1000 Ω

Subjective Questions

1. For determination of resistance of a coil, which of two methods is better Ohm's law method or meter bridge method ?

2. Which method is more accurate in the determination of f for a concave mirror

(i) u *versus* v or (ii) $\frac{1}{u}$ *versus* $\frac{1}{v}$ graphs ?

3. Why is the second resonance found feebler than the first ?

4. Why is the meter bridge suitable for resistance of moderate values only ?

5. Can we measure a resistance of the order of 0.160 Ω using a Wheatstone's bridge ? Support your answer with reasoning.

6. The edge of a cube is measured using a vernier callipers. [9 divisions of the main scale is equal to 10 divisions of vernier scale and 1 main scale division is 1 mm]. The main scale division reading is 10 and 1st division of vernier scale was found to be coinciding with the main scale. The mass of the cube is 2.736 g. Calculate the density (in g/ cm^3) upto correct significant figures.

Answers

Introductory Exercise 3.1

1. 3.19 cm 2. 1

Introductory Exercise 3.2

1. 10.65 mm 2. 3.50 mm

Introductory Exercise 3.3

3. No, No 4. (a) Parabolic (b) Straight line 7. (c) 8. (a)

Introductory Exercise 3.4

1. $(1.94 \pm 0.22) \times 10^{11}\ \text{N/m}^2$ 2. (d)

Introductory Exercise 3.5

1. (b) 2. (b)

Introductory Exercise 3.6

1. $1.00 \times 10^{-4}\ \Omega\cdot\text{m}$ 2. 2.41 %, 1.1 % 3. (c)

Introductory Exercise 3.7

1. (a) 2. (b) 3. *B* is most accurate

Introductory Exercise 3.8

1. $14.2\ \Omega$ to $14.3\ \Omega$ 3. (c)

Exercises

Assertion and Reason

1. (e)

Objective Questions

1. (b)	2. (a,d)	3. (a,b)	4. (d)	5. (c)	6. (b)	7. (b)	8. (b)	9. (c)	10. (c)
11. (a)	12. (d)	13. (d)	14. (b)	15. (b)	16. (a)	17. (a)	18. (b)	19. (b)	20. (b)
21. (b)	22. (d)	23. (c)	24. (b)	25. (a)	26. (b)	27. (b)	28. (a)	29. (c)	30. (b)
31. (d)	32. (c)	33. (c)	34. (b)	35. (b)	36. (a)	37. (a)	38. (a)	39. (a)	40. (c)
41. (c)	42. (a)	43. (d)	44. (c)	45. (b)	46. (a)	47. (a)	48. (d)	49. (a)	50. (d)
51. (b)	52. (a,b,c)	53. (a)							

Comprehension Based Questions

1. (c) 2. (a) 3. (a) 4. (c)

Subjective Questions

1. Meter bridge method 2. $\frac{1}{v}$ *versus* $\frac{1}{u}$ 3. See the hints

4. See the hints 5. No 6. $2.66\ \text{g/cm}^3$

4

Units and Dimensions

4.1 Units

To measure a physical quantity we need some standard unit of that quantity. The measurement of the quantity is specified in two parts, the first part gives how many times of the standard unit and the second part gives the name of the unit. Thus, suppose I say that length of this wire is 5 metre. The numeric part 5 says that it is 5 times of the unit of length and the second part metre says that unit chosen here is metre.

4.2 Fundamental and Derived Units

There are a large number of physical quantities and every quantity needs a unit.
However, not all the quantities are independent. For example, if a unit of length is defined, a unit of volume is automatically obtained. Thus, we can define a set of fundamental quantities and all other quantities may be expressed in terms of the fundamental quantities. Fundamental quantities are only seven in number. Units of all other quantities can be expressed in terms of the units of these seven quantities by multiplication or division.

Many different choices can be made about the fundamental quantities. For example, if we take length and time as the fundamental quantities then speed is a derived quantity and if we take speed and time as fundamental quantities then length is a derived quantity.

Several system of units are in use over the world. The units defined for the fundamental quantities are called fundamental units and those obtained for derived quantities are called the derived units.

SI Units

In 1971, General Conference on Weights and Measures held its meeting and decided a system of units which is known as the International System of Units. It is abbreviated as SI from the French name Le System International *d'* Unites. This system is widely used throughout the world. Table below gives the seven fundamental quantities and their SI units.

Table 4.1 Fundamental quantities and their SI units

S.No.	Quantity	SI Unit	Symbol
1.	Length	metre	m
2.	Mass	kilogram	kg
3.	Time	second	s
4.	Electric current	ampere	A
5.	Thermodynamic temperature	kelvin	K
6.	Amount of substance	mole	mol
7.	Luminous intensity	candela	cd

Two **supplementary** units, namely that of plane angle and solid angle are also defined. Their units are radian (rad) and steradian (st) respectively.

(i) **CGS System :** In this system, the units of length, mass and time are centimetre (cm), gram (g) and second (s) respectively. The unit of force is dyne and that of work or energy is erg.

(ii) **FPS System :** In this system, the units of length, mass and time are foot, pound and second. The unit of force in this system is poundal.

Definitions of Some Important SI Units

(i) **Metre** : $1\text{ m} = 1{,}650{,}763.73$ wavelengths in vacuum, of radiation corresponding to orange-red light of krypton-86.

(ii) **Second** : $1\text{ s} = 9{,}192{,}631{,}770$ time periods of a particular radiation from Cesium-133 atom.

(iii) **Kilogram** : 1 kg = mass of 1 litre of water at 4°C.

(iv) **Ampere** : It is the current which when flows through two infinitely long straight conductors of negligible cross-section placed at a distance of one metre in vacuum produces a force of 2×10^{-7} N/m between them.

(v) **Kelvin** : $1\text{ K} = 1/273.16$ part of the thermodynamic temperature of triple point of water.

(vi) **Mole** : It is the amount of substance of a system which contains as many elementary particles (atoms, molecules, ions etc.) as there are atoms in 12 g of carbon-12.

(vii) **Candela** : It is luminous intensity in a perpendicular direction of a surface of $\left(\frac{1}{600000}\right)\text{m}^2$ of a black body at the temperature of freezing platinum under a pressure of $1.013 \times 10^5\ \text{N/m}^2$.

(viii) **Radian** : It is the plane angle between two radii of a circle which cut-off on the circumference, an arc equal in length to the radius.

(ix) **Steradian** : The steradian is the solid angle having its vertex at the centre of the sphere, cut-off an area of the surface of sphere equal to that of a square with sides of length equal to the radius of the sphere.

SI Prefixes

The most commonly used prefixes are given below in tabular form.

Power of 10	Prefix	Symbol
6	mega	M
3	kilo	k
– 2	centi	c
– 3	milli	m
– 6	micro	μ
– 9	nano	n
– 12	pico	p

4.3 Dimensions

Dimensions of a physical quantity are the powers to which the fundamental quantities must be raised to represent the given physical quantity.

For example, density $= \frac{\text{mass}}{\text{volume}} = \frac{\text{mass}}{(\text{length})^3}$ or density = (mass) $(\text{length})^{-3}$ ...(i)

Thus, the dimensions of density are 1 in mass and -3 in length. The dimensions of all other fundamental quantities are zero.For convenience, the fundamental quantities are represented by one letter symbols. Generally mass is denoted by M, length by L, time by T and electric current by A.

The thermodynamic temperature, the amount of substance and the luminous intensity are denoted by the symbols of their units K, mol and cd respectively. The physical quantity that is expressed in terms of the base quantities is enclosed in square brackets.

Thus, Eq. (i) can be written as

$$[\text{density}] = [\text{ML}^{-3}]$$

Such an expression for a physical quantity in terms of the fundamental quantities is called the dimensional formula. Here, it is worthnoting that constants such as 5, π or trigonometrical functions such as $\sin\theta$, $\cos\theta$, etc., have no units and dimensions.

$$[\sin\theta]=[\cos\theta]=[\tan\theta]=[\log x]=[e^x]=[M^0L^0T^0]$$

Table 4.2 Dimensional formulae and SI units of some physical quantities frequently used in physics

S.No.	Physical Quantity	SI Units	Dimensional Formula
1.	Velocity = displacement/time	m/s	$[M^0LT^{-1}]$
2.	Acceleration = velocity/time	m/s^2	$[M^0LT^{-2}]$
3.	Force = mass × acceleration	kg-m/s^2 = newton or N	$[MLT^{-2}]$
4.	Work = force × displacement	kg-m^2/s^2 = N-m = joule or J	$[ML^2T^{-2}]$
5.	Energy	J	$[ML^2T^{-2}]$
6.	Torque = force × perpendicular distance	N-m	$[ML^2T^{-2}]$
7.	Power = work/time	J/s or watt	$[ML^2T^{-3}]$
8.	Momentum = mass × velocity	kg-m/s	$[MLT^{-1}]$
9.	Impulse = force × time	N-s	$[MLT^{-1}]$
10.	Angle = arc/radius	radian or rad	$[M^0L^0T^0]$
11.	Strain = $\frac{\Delta L}{L}$ or $\frac{\Delta V}{V}$	no units	$[M^0L^0T^0]$
12.	Stress = force/area	N/m^2	$[ML^{-1}T^{-2}]$
13.	Pressure = force/area	N/m^2	$[ML^{-1}T^{-2}]$
14.	Modulus of elasticity = stress/strain	N/m^2	$[ML^{-1}T^{-2}]$
15.	Frequency = 1/time period	per sec or hertz (Hz)	$[M^0L^0T^{-1}]$
16.	Angular velocity = angle/time	rad/s	$[M^0L^0T^{-1}]$
17.	Moment of inertia = (mass) × $(\text{distance})^2$	kg-m^2	$[ML^2T^0]$
18.	Surface tension = force/length	N/m	$[ML^0T^{-2}]$
19.	Gravitational constant $= \frac{\text{force} \times (\text{distance})^2}{(\text{mass})^2}$	N-m^2/kg^2	$[M^{-1}L^3T^{-2}]$
20.	Angular momentum	kg-m^2/s	$[ML^2T^{-1}]$
21.	Coefficient of viscosity	N-s/m^2	$[ML^{-1}T^{-1}]$
22.	Planck's constant	J-s	$[ML^2T^{-1}]$
23.	Specific heat (s)	J/kg-K	$[L^2T^{-2}K^{-1}]$
24.	Coefficient of thermal conductivity (K)	watt/m-K	$[MLT^{-3}K^{-1}]$
25.	Gas constant (R)	J/mol-K	$[ML^2T^{-2}K^{-1}\text{mol}^{-1}]$
26.	Boltzmann constant (k)	J/K	$[ML^2T^{-2}K^{-1}]$

S.No.	Physical Quantity	SI Units	Dimensional Formula
27.	Wien's constant (*b*)	m-K	[LK]
28.	Stefan's constant (σ)	watt/m^2-K^4	$[MT^{-3}K^{-4}]$
29.	Electric charge	C	[AT]
30.	Electric intensity	N/C	$[MLT^{-3}A^{-1}]$
31.	Electric potential	volt	$[ML^2T^{-3}A^{-1}]$
32.	Capacitance	farad	$[M^{-1}L^{-2}T^4A^2]$
33.	Permittivity of free space	$C^2N^{-1}m^{-2}$	$[M^{-1}L^{-3}T^4A^2]$
34.	Electric dipole moment	C-m	[LTA]
35.	Resistance	ohm	$[ML^2T^{-3}A^{-2}]$
36.	Magnetic field	tesla (T) or weber/m^2 (Wb/m^2)	$[MT^{-2}A^{-1}]$
37.	Coefficient of self induction	henry	$[ML^2T^{-2}A^{-2}]$

Example 4.1 *Find the dimensional formula of the following quantities :*

(a) Density *(b) Velocity* *(c) Acceleration*
(d) Momentum *(e) Force* *(f) Work or energy*
(g) Power *(h) Pressure*

Solution (a) Density $= \dfrac{\text{mass}}{\text{volume}}$

$$[\text{Density}] = \frac{[\text{mass}]}{[\text{volume}]} = \frac{[M]}{[L^{-3}]} = [ML^{-3}]$$

(b) Velocity $[v] = \dfrac{\text{displacement}}{\text{time}}$

$$[v] = \frac{[\text{displacement}]}{[\text{time}]} = \frac{[L]}{[T]} = [M^0LT^{-1}]$$

(c) Acceleration $[a] = \left[\dfrac{dv}{dt}\right]$

$$[a] = \frac{dv \rightarrow \text{kind of velocity}}{dt \rightarrow \text{kind of time}} = \frac{[LT^{-1}]}{[T]} = [LT^{-2}]$$

(d) Momentum $[P] = [mv]$

$$[P] = [M][v] = [M][LT^{-1}] = [MLT^{-1}]$$

(e) Force $[F] = [ma]$

$$[F] = [m][a] = [M][LT^{-2}] = [MLT^{-2}]$$

(f) Work or Energy = force × displacement

$$[\text{Work}] = [\text{force}][\text{displacement}]$$
$$= [MLT^{-2}][L] = [ML^2T^{-2}]$$

(g) Power = $\frac{\text{Work}}{\text{Time}}$

$$[\text{Power}] = \frac{[\text{Work}]}{[\text{Time}]} = \frac{[\text{M}\,\text{L}^2\text{T}^{-2}]}{[\text{T}]} = [\text{M}\,\text{L}^2\text{T}^{-3}]$$

(h) Pressure = $\frac{\text{Force}}{\text{Area}}$

$$[\text{Pressure}] = \frac{[\text{Force}]}{[\text{Area}]} = \frac{[\text{M}\,\text{L}\,\text{T}^{-2}]}{\text{L}^2}$$

$$= [\text{M}\,\text{L}^{-1}\text{T}^{-2}]$$

Example 4.2 *Find the dimensional formula of the following quantities :*

(a) Surface tension, T

(b) Universal constant of gravitation, G

(c) Impulse, J

(d) Torque, τ

The equations involving these equations are :

$T = F/l$, $F = \frac{Gm_1 m_2}{r^2}$, $J = F \times t$ *and* $\tau = F \times l$

Solution (a) $T = \frac{F}{l}$

$$\Rightarrow \qquad [\text{T}] = \frac{[\text{F}]}{[\text{l}]} = \frac{[\text{MLT}^{-2}]}{[\text{L}]}$$

$$= [\text{MT}^{-2}]$$ **Ans.**

(b) $F = \frac{Gm_1 m_2}{r^2} \quad \Rightarrow \quad G = \frac{Fr^2}{m_1 m_2}$

or

$$[G] = \frac{[\text{F}][\text{r}]^2}{[\text{m}]^2} = \frac{[\text{MLT}^{-2}][\text{L}^2]}{[\text{M}^2]}$$

$$= [\text{M}^{-1}\text{L}^3\text{T}^{-2}]$$ **Ans.**

(c) $J = F \times t$

∴

$$[\text{J}] = [\text{F}][\text{t}]$$

$$= [\text{MLT}^{-2}][\text{T}]$$

$$= [\text{MLT}^{-1}]$$ **Ans.**

(d) $\tau = F \times l$

∴

$$[\tau] = [\text{F}][\text{l}]$$

$$= [\text{MLT}^{-2}][\text{L}]$$

$$= [\text{ML}^2\text{T}^{-2}]$$ **Ans.**

4.4 Uses of Dimensions

Theory of dimensions have following main uses:

1. **Conversion of units** This is based on the fact that the product of the numerical value (n) and its corresponding unit (u) is a constant, i.e.

$$n[u] = \text{constant}$$

or

$$n_1[u_1] = n_2[u_2]$$

Suppose the dimensions of a physical quantity are a in mass, b in length and c in time. If the fundamental units in one system are M_1, L_1 and T_1 and in the other system are M_2, L_2 and T_2 respectively. Then, we can write

$$n_1[M_1^a L_1^b T_1^c] = n_2[M_2^a L_2^b T_2^c] \quad \ldots\text{(i)}$$

Here, n_1 and n_2 are the numerical values in two systems of units respectively. Using Eq. (i), we can convert the numerical value of a physical quantity from one system of units into the other system.

Example 4.3 *The value of gravitation constant is $G = 6.67 \times 10^{-11}$ N-m^2/kg^2 in SI units. Convert it into CGS system of units.*

Solution The dimensional formula of G is $[M^{-1} L^3 T^{-2}]$.

Using Eq. (i), i.e.

$$n_1[M_1^{-1} L_1^3 T_1^{-2}] = n_2[M_2^{-1} L_2^3 T_2^{-2}]$$

$$n_2 = n_1 \left[\frac{M_1}{M_2}\right]^{-1} \left[\frac{L_1}{L_2}\right]^{3} \left[\frac{T_1}{T_2}\right]^{-2}$$

Here, $$n_1 = 6.67 \times 10^{-11}$$

$$M_1 = 1\,\text{kg}, M_2 = 1\,\text{g} = 10^{-3}\,\text{kg}, L_1 = 1\,\text{m}, L_2 = 1\,\text{cm} = 10^{-2}\,\text{m}, T_1 = T_2 = 1\,\text{s}$$

Substituting in the above equation, we get

$$n_2 = 6.67 \times 10^{-11} \left[\frac{1\,\text{kg}}{10^{-3}\,\text{kg}}\right]^{-1} \left[\frac{1\,\text{m}}{10^{-2}\,\text{m}}\right]^{3} \left[\frac{1\,\text{s}}{1\,\text{s}}\right]^{-2}$$

or $$n_2 = 6.67 \times 10^{-8}$$

Thus, value of G in CGS system of units is 6.67×10^{-8} dyne cm^2/g^2.

2. **To check the dimensional correctness of a given physical equation** Every physical equation should be dimensionally balanced. This is called the 'Principle of Homogeneity'. The dimensions of each term on both sides of an equation must be the same. On this basis, we can judge whether a given equation is correct or not. But a dimensionally correct equation may or may not be physically correct.

Example 4.4 *Show that the expression of the time period T of a simple pendulum of length l given by $T = 2\pi\sqrt{\frac{l}{g}}$ is dimensionally correct.*

Solution $T = 2\pi\sqrt{\frac{l}{g}}$

Dimensionally $[T] = \sqrt{\frac{[L]}{[LT^{-2}]}} = [T]$

As in the above equation, the dimensions of both sides are same. The given formula is dimensionally correct.

Principle of Homogeneity of Dimensions

This principle states that the dimensions of all the terms in a physical expression should be same. For example, in the physical expression $s = ut + \frac{1}{2}at^2$, the dimensions of s, ut and $\frac{1}{2}at^2$ all are same.

Note *The physical quantities separated by the symbols +, –, =, >, < etc., have the same dimensions.*

Example 4.5 *The velocity v of a particle depends upon the time t according to the equation* $v = a + bt + \frac{c}{d+t}$. *Write the dimensions of a, b, c and d.*

Solution From principle of homogeneity,

$$[a] = [v] \quad \text{or} \quad [a] = [LT^{-1}]$$

$$[bt] = [v] \quad \text{or} \quad [b] = \frac{[v]}{[t]} = \frac{[LT^{-1}]}{[T]}$$

or $$[b] = [LT^{-2}]$$

Similarly, $$[d] = [t] = [T]$$

Further, $$\frac{[c]}{[d+t]} = [v] \quad \text{or} \quad [c] = [v][d+t]$$

or $$[c] = [LT^{-1}][T] \quad \text{or} \quad [c] = [L]$$

3. **To establish the relation among various physical quantities** If we know the factors on which a given physical quantity may depend, we can find a formula relating the quantity with those factors. Let us take an example.

Example 4.6 *The frequency (f) of a stretched string depends upon the tension F (dimensions of force), length l of the string and the mass per unit length μ of string. Derive the formula for frequency.*

Solution Suppose, that the frequency f depends on the tension raised to the power a, length raised to the power b and mass per unit length raised to the power c. Then,

$$f \propto F^a l^b \mu^c$$

or $$f = kF^a l^b \mu^c \qquad \text{...(i)}$$

Here, k is a dimensionless constant. Thus,

$$[f] = [F]^a\,[l]^b\,[\mu]^c$$

or $$[M^0L^0T^{-1}] = [MLT^{-2}]^a \, [L]^b \, [ML^{-1}]^c$$

or $$[M^0L^0T^{-1}] = [M^{a+c}L^{a+b-c}T^{-2a}]$$

For dimensional balance, the dimensions on both sides should be same.

Thus, $$a + c = 0 \qquad \text{...(ii)}$$

$$a + b - c = 0 \qquad \text{...(iii)}$$

and $$-2a = -1 \qquad \text{...(iv)}$$

Solving these three equations, we get

$$a = \frac{1}{2}, \quad c = -\frac{1}{2} \quad \text{and} \quad b = -1$$

Substituting these values in Eq. (i), we get

$$f = k(F)^{1/2}(l)^{-1}(\mu)^{-1/2}$$

or $$f = \frac{k}{l}\sqrt{\frac{F}{\mu}}$$

Experimentally, the value of k is found to be $\frac{1}{2}$.

Hence,

$$f = \frac{1}{2l}\sqrt{\frac{F}{\mu}}$$

Limitations of Dimensional Analysis

The method of dimensions has the following limitations :

(i) By this method, the value of dimensionless constant cannot be calculated.

(ii) By this method, the equation containing trigonometrical, exponential and logarithmic terms cannot be analysed.

(iii) This method is useful when a physical quantity depends on other quantities which are multiplied, divided or raised to some powers. It cannot be used if a physical quantity depends on sum or difference of two quantities. For example, we cannot get the relation, $s = ut + \frac{1}{2}at^2$ from dimensional analysis.

Core Concepts

1. There are some physical quantities which have the same dimensions. They are given in tabular form as below :

S.No.	Physical quantities or combination of physical quantities	Dimensions
1.	Angle, strain, $\sin\theta$, π, e^x	$[M^0 L^0 T^0]$
2.	Work, Energy, Torque, Rhc	$[ML^2 T^{-2}]$
3.	Time, $\frac{L}{R}$, CR, $\sqrt{LC}$	$[M^0 L^0 T]$
4.	Frequency, $\dot{\omega}$, $\frac{R}{L}$, $\frac{1}{CR}$, $\frac{1}{\sqrt{LC}}$, velocity gradient, Decay constant. Activity of a radioactive substance	$[M^0 L^0 T^{-1}]$
5.	Pressure, stress, modulus of elasticity, energy density (energy per unit volume), $\varepsilon_0 E^2$, $\frac{B^2}{\mu_0}$	$[ML^{-1}T^{-2}]$
6.	Angular impulse, angular momentum, Planck's constant	$[ML^2T^{-1}]$
7.	Linear momentum, linear impulse	$[MLT^{-1}]$
8.	Wavelength, radius of gyration, Light year	$[M^0 LT^0]$
9.	Velocity, $\frac{1}{\sqrt{\varepsilon_0\mu_0}}$, $\sqrt{\frac{GM}{R}}$, $\frac{E}{B}$	$[M^0 LT^{-1}]$

2. Astronomical unit : 1 AU = mean distance of earth from sun $\approx 1.5 \times 10^{11}$ m

Light year : 1 ly = distance travelled by light in vacuum in 1 year

$= 9.46 \times 10^{15}$ m

Parsec : 1 Parsec $= 3.07 \times 10^{16}$ m $= 3.26$ light year

X-ray unit : $1\text{U} = 10^{-3}$ m

1 shake $= 10^{-8}$ s

1 Bar $= 10^5$ N/m^2 $= 10^5$ Pa

1 torr = 1 mm of Hg = 133.3 Pa

1 barn $= 10^{-28}$ m^2

1 horse power = 746 W

1 pound = 453.6 g = 0.4536 kg

Solved Examples

Example 1 *Find the dimensional formulae of*

(a) coefficient of viscosity η *(b) charge q*

(c) potential V *(d) capacitance C and*

(e) resistance R

Some of the equations containing these quantities are

$$F = -\eta A\left(\frac{\Delta v}{\Delta l}\right),\ q = It,\ U = VIt,\ q = CV \text{ and } V = IR$$

where, A denotes the area, v the velocity, l is the length, I the electric current, t the time and U the energy.

Solution (a) $\eta = -\frac{F}{A}\frac{\Delta l}{\Delta v} \quad \Rightarrow \quad \therefore\ [\eta] = \frac{[F][l]}{[A][v]} = \frac{[\text{MLT}^{-2}][\text{L}]}{[\text{L}^2][\text{LT}^{-1}]} = [\text{ML}^{-1}\text{T}^{-1}]$

(b) $q = It \ \Rightarrow\ \therefore\ [q] = [I]\,[t] = [\text{AT}]$

(c) $U = VIt$

$$\therefore \qquad V = \frac{U}{It} \quad \text{or} \quad [V] = \frac{[U]}{[I]\,[t]} = \frac{[\text{ML}^2\text{T}^{-2}]}{[\text{A}][\text{T}]} = [\text{ML}^2\text{T}^{-3}\text{A}^{-1}]$$

(d) $q = CV$

$$\therefore \qquad C = \frac{q}{V} \quad \text{or} \quad [C] = \frac{[q]}{[V]} = \frac{[\text{AT}]}{[\text{ML}^2\text{T}^{-3}\text{A}^{-1}]} = [\text{M}^{-1}\text{L}^{-2}\text{T}^4\text{A}^2]$$

(e) $V = IR$

$$\therefore \qquad R = \frac{V}{I} \quad \text{or} \quad [R] = \frac{[V]}{[I]} = \frac{[\text{ML}^2\text{T}^{-3}\text{A}^{-1}]}{[\text{A}]} = [\text{ML}^2\text{T}^{-3}\text{A}^{-2}]$$

Example 2 *Write the dimensions of a and b in the relation, $P = \frac{b - x^2}{at}$, where P is power, x is distance and t is time.*

Solution The given equation can be written as, $Pat = b - x^2$

Now, $$[Pat] = [b] = [x^2] \quad \text{or} \quad [b] = [x^2] = [\text{M}^0\text{L}^2\text{T}^0]$$

and $$[a] = \frac{[x^2]}{[Pt]} = \frac{[\text{L}^2]}{[\text{ML}^2\text{T}^{-3}]\,[\text{T}]} = [\text{M}^{-1}\text{L}^0\text{T}^2]$$

Example 3 *The centripetal force F acting on a particle moving uniformly in a circle may depend upon mass (m), velocity (v) and radius (r) of the circle. Derive the formula for F using the method of dimensions.*

Solution Let $$F = k\,(m)^x\,(v)^y\,(r)^z \qquad \text{...(i)}$$

Here, k is a dimensionless constant of proportionality. Writing the dimensions of RHS and LHS in Eq. (i), we have

$$[\text{MLT}^{-2}] = [\text{M}]^x\,[\text{LT}^{-1}]^y\,[\text{L}]^z = [\text{M}^x\text{L}^{y+z}\text{T}^{-y}]$$

Equating the powers of M, L and T of both sides, we have,

$$x = 1, \quad y = 2 \quad \text{and} \quad y + z = 1 \quad \text{or} \quad z = 1 - y = -1$$

Putting the values in Eq. (i), we get

$$F = kmv^2r^{-1} = k\frac{mv^2}{r}$$

or $$F = \frac{mv^2}{r} \qquad \text{(where, } k = 1\text{)}$$

Example 4 *If velocity, time and force were chosen as basic quantities, find the dimensions of mass and energy.*

Solution (i) We know that,

$$\text{Force} = \text{mass} \times \text{acceleration}$$

$$= \text{mass} \times \frac{\text{velocity}}{\text{time}}$$

$$\Rightarrow \qquad \text{mass} = \frac{\text{force} \times \text{time}}{\text{velocity}}$$

or $$[\text{mass}] = \frac{[\text{force}] \times [\text{time}]}{[\text{velocity}]}$$

$$= \frac{[\text{F}]\,[\text{T}]}{[\text{v}]}$$

$$\therefore \qquad [\text{mass}] = [\text{F}\,\text{T}\,\text{v}^{-1}]$$ **Ans.**

(ii) Dimensions of energy are same as the dimensions of kinetic energy

$$\therefore \qquad [\text{Energy}] = \left[\frac{1}{2}\,\text{mv}^2\right] = [\text{m}]\,[\text{v}]^2$$

$$= [\text{FTv}^{-1}]\,[\text{v}]^2$$

$$= [\text{FTv}]$$ **Ans.**

Example 5 *Force acting on a particle is 5 N. If units of length and time are doubled and unit of mass is halved then find the numerical value of force in the new system of units.*

Solution Force $= 5\ \text{N} = \dfrac{5\ \text{kg-m}}{\text{s}^2}$

If unit of length and time are doubled and the unit of mass is halved.

Then unit of force will be $\left[\dfrac{\frac{1}{2} \times 2}{(2)^2}\right] = \dfrac{1}{4}$ times.

Hence the numberical value of force will be 4-times or answer is 20. **Ans.**

Example 6 *Can pressure (p), density (ρ) and velocity (v) be taken as fundamental quantities?*

Solution No, they cannot be taken as fundamental quantities, as they are related to each other by the relation,

$$p = \rho v^2$$

Exercises

Assertion and Reason

Directions : *Choose the correct option.*

(a) *If both* ***Assertion*** *and* ***Reason*** *are true and the* ***Reason*** *is correct explanation of the* ***Assertion.***

(b) *If both* ***Assertion*** *and* ***Reason*** *are true but* ***Reason*** *is not the correct explanation of* ***Assertion.***

(c) *If* ***Assertion*** *is true, but the* ***Reason*** *is false.*

(d) *If* ***Assertion*** *is false but the* ***Reason*** *is true.*

(e) *If both* ***Assertion*** *and* ***Reason*** *are false.*

1. **Assertion :** Velocity, volume and acceleration can be taken as fundamental quantities.

   Reason : All the three are independent from each other.

2. **Assertion :** If two physical quantities have same dimensions, then they can be certainly added or subtracted.

   Reason : If the dimensions of both the quantities are same, then both the physical quantities should be similar.

3. **Assertion :** Method of dimension cannot be used for deriving formulae containing trigonometrical ratios.

   Reason : This is because trigonometrical ratios have no dimensions.

4. **Assertion :** When we change the unit of measurement of a quantity, its numerical value changes.

   Reason : Smaller the unit of measurement smaller is its numerical value.

Objective Questions

Single Correct Option

1. The dimensional formula for Planck's constant and angular momentum are
   (a) $[ML^2T^{-2}]$ and $[MLT^{-1}]$
   (b) $[ML^2T^{-1}]$ and $[ML^2T^{-1}]$
   (c) $[ML^3T]$ and $[ML^2T^{-2}]$
   (d) $[MLT^{-1}]$ and $[MLT^{-2}]$

2. Dimension of velocity gradient is
   (a) $[M^0L^0T^{-1}]$
   (b) $[ML^{-1}T^{-1}]$
   (c) $[M^0LT^{-1}]$
   (d) $[ML^0T^{-1}]$

3. Which of the following is the dimension of the coefficient of friction?
   (a) $[M^2L^2T]$
   (b) $[M^0L^0T^0]$
   (c) $[ML^2T^{-2}]$
   (d) $[M^2L^2T^{-2}]$

4. Which of the following sets have different dimensions?
   (a) Pressure, Young's modulus, Stress
   (b) Emf, Potential difference, Electric potential
   (c) Heat, Work done, Energy
   (d) Dipole moment, Electric flux, Electric field

5. The viscous force F on a sphere of radius a moving in a medium with velocity v is given by $F = 6\pi\,\eta a v$. The dimensions of η are

(a) $[ML^{-3}]$ (b) $[MLT^{-2}]$
(c) $[MT^{-1}]$ (d) $[ML^{-1}T^{-1}]$

6. A force is given by $F = at + bt^2$, where t is the time. The dimensions of a and b are

(a) $[MLT^{-4}]$ and $[MLT]$ (b) $[MLT^{-1}]$ and $[MLT^0]$
(c) $[MLT^{-3}]$ and $[MLT^{-4}]$ (d) $[MLT^{-3}]$ and $[MLT^0]$

7. The physical quantity having the dimensions $[M^{-1}L^{-3}T^3A^2]$ is

(a) resistance (b) resistivity
(c) electrical conductivity (d) electromotive force

8. The dimensional formula for magnetic flux is

(a) $[ML^2T^{-2}A^{-1}]$ (b) $[ML^3T^{-2}A^{-2}]$
(c) $[M^0L^{-2}T^{-2}A^{-2}]$ (d) $[ML^2T^{-1}A^2]$

9. Choose the **wrong** statement.

(a) All quantities may be represented dimensionally in terms of the base quantities
(b) A base quantity cannot be represented dimensionally in terms of the rest of the base quantities
(c) The dimension of a base quantity in other base quantities is always zero
(d) The dimension of a derived quantity is never zero in any base quantity

10. Using mass (M), length (L), time (T) and current (A) as fundamental quantities, the dimension of permeability is

(a) $[M^{-1}LT^{-2}A]$ (b) $[ML^{-2}T^{-2}A^{-1}]$
(c) $[MLT^{-2}A^{-2}]$ (d) $[MLT^{-1}A^{-1}]$

11. If the energy (E), velocity (v) and force (F) be taken as fundamental quantities, then the dimensions of mass will be

(a) $[Fv^{-2}]$ (b) $[Fv^{-1}]$
(c) $[Ev^{-2}]$ (d) $[Ev^2]$

12. The ratio of the dimensions of Planck's constant and that of the moment of inertia is the dimension of

(a) frequency (b) velocity (c) angular momentum (d) time

13. Given that $y = A \sin\left[\left(\frac{2\pi}{\lambda}(ct - x)\right)\right]$, where y and x are measured in metres. Which of the following statements is true ?

(a) The unit of λ is same as that of x and A (b) The unit of λ is same as that of x but not of A
(c) The unit of c is same as that of $\frac{2\pi}{\lambda}$ (d) The unit of $(ct - x)$ is same as that of $\frac{2\pi}{\lambda}$

14. Which of the following sets cannot enter into the list of fundamental quantities in any system of units?

(a) Length, mass and acceleration (b) Length, time and velocity
(c) Mass, time and velocity (d) Length, time and density

15. In the formula $X = 3Y Z^2$, X and Z have dimensions of capacitance and magnetic induction respectively. What are the dimensions of Y in MKSQ system?

(a) $[M^{-3}L^{-1}T^3Q^4]$ (b) $[M^{-3}L^{-2}T^4Q^4]$
(c) $[M^{-2}L^{-2}T^4Q^4]$ (d) $[M^{-3}L^{-2}T^4Q]$

16. A quantity X is given by $\varepsilon_0 L \frac{\Delta V}{\Delta t}$, where ε_0 is the permittivity of free space, L is a length, ΔV is a potential difference and Δt is a time interval. The dimensional formula for X is the same as that of

(a) resistance (b) charge
(c) voltage (d) current

17. In the relation $p = \frac{\alpha}{\beta} e^{-\frac{\alpha Z}{k\theta}}$, p is pressure, Z is distance, k is Boltzmann constant and θ is the temperature. The dimensional formula of β will be

(a) $[M^0L^2T^0]$ (b) $[ML^2T]$
(c) $[ML^0T^{-1}]$ (d) $[M^0L^2T^{-1}]$

18. Joule × second is the unit of

(a) energy (b) momentum
(c) angular momentum (d) power

19. Which of the following is not equal to watt?

(a) Joule/second (b) Ampere × volt
(c) $(\text{Ampere})^2$ × ohm (d) Ampere/volt

20. Which of the following is not the units of surface tension?

(a) N/m (b) J/m^2
(c) kg/s^2 (d) None of these

21. A new unit of length is chosen such that the speed of light in vacuum is unity. What is the distance between the sun and the earth in terms of the new unit, if light takes 8 min and 20 s to cover this distance?

(a) 300 (b) 400
(c) 500 (d) 600

22. The dimensional formula for thermal resistance is

(a) $[ML^2T^{-3}K^{-1}]$ (b) $[ML^2T^{-2}K^{-1}]$
(c) $[ML^2T^{-3}K^{-2}]$ (d) $[M^{-1}L^{-2}T^3K]$

23. $[ML^2T^{-3}A^{-1}]$ is the dimensional formula for

(a) capacitance (b) resistance
(c) resistivity (d) potential difference

24. If p represents radiation pressure, c represent speed of light and Q represents radiation energy striking a unit area per second, then non-zero integers x, y and z such that $p^xQ^yc^z$ is dimensionless are

(a) $x = 1, y = 1, z = -1$ (b) $x = 1, y = -1, z = 1$
(c) $x = -1, y = 1, z = 1$ (d) $x = 1, y = 1, z = 1$

25. The units of length, velocity and force are doubled. Which of the following is the correct change in the other units?

(a) Unit of time is doubled (b) Unit of mass is doubled
(c) Unit of momentum is doubled (d) Unit of energy is doubled

26. The dimensional representation of specific resistance in terms of charge Q is

(a) $[ML^3T^{-1}Q^{-2}]$ (b) $[ML^2T^{-2}Q^2]$
(c) $[MLT^{-2}Q^{-1}]$ (d) $[ML^2T^{-2}Q^{-1}]$

27. Dimensions of 'ohm' are same as

(a) $\frac{h}{e}$ (b) $\frac{h^2}{e}$

(c) $\frac{h}{e^2}$ (d) $\frac{h^2}{e^2}$

(where, h is Planck's constant and e is charge)

28. If E = energy, G = gravitational constant, I = impulse and M = mass, then dimensions of $\frac{GIM^2}{E^2}$ are same as that of

(a) time (b) mass

(c) length (d) force

29. If y represents pressure and x represents velocity gradient, then the dimensions of $\frac{d^2y}{dx^2}$ are

(a) $[ML^{-1}T^{-2}]$ (b) $[M^2L^{-2}T^{-2}]$

(c) $[ML^{-1}T^0]$ (d) $[M^2L^{-2}T^{-4}]$

30. The density of a material in CGS system of units is 4 g/cm^3. In a system of units in which unit of length is 10 cm and unit of mass is 100 g, the value of density of material will be

(a) 0.04 (b) 0.4

(c) 40 (d) 400

31. If m, e, ε_0, h and c denote mass of electron, charge of electron, Planck's constant and speed of light, respectively. The dimensions of $\frac{me^4}{\varepsilon_0^2 h^3 c}$ are

(a) $[M^0L^0T^{-1}]$ (b) $[M^0L^{-1}T^{-1}]$

(c) $[M^2LT^{-3}]$ (d) $[M^0L^{-1}T^0]$

32. If m, e, ε_0 and h denote mass of electron, charge of electron, electric permittivity and Planck's constant, respectively. The unit of $\frac{me^4}{\varepsilon_0^2 h^2}$ is same as

(a) energy (b) power

(c) force (d) pressure

More than One Correct Options

1. The dimensions of the quantities in one (or more) of the following pairs are the same. Identify the pair (s).

(a) Torque and work

(b) Angular momentum and work

(c) Energy and Young's modulus

(d) Light year and wavelength

2. The pairs of physical quantities that have the same dimensions is (are)

(a) Reynold's number and coefficient of friction

(b) Curie and frequency of a light wave

(c) Latent heat and gravitational potential

(d) Planck's constant and torque

3. The SI unit of the inductance, the henry can by written as
(a) weber/ampere
(b) volt-second/ampere
(c) joule/(ampere)^2
(d) ohm-second

4. Let $[\varepsilon_0]$ denote the dimensional formula of the permittivity of the vacuum and $[\mu_0]$ that of the permeability of the vacuum. If M = mass, L = length, T = time and I = electric current, then
(a) $[\varepsilon_0] = [M^{-1}L^{-3}T^2 I]$
(b) $[\varepsilon_0] = [M^{-1}L^{-3}T^4 I^2]$
(c) $[\mu_0] = [MLT^{-2}I^{-2}]$
(d) $[\mu_0] = [ML^2T^{-1}I]$

5. L, C and R represent the physical quantities inductance, capacitance and resistance respectively. The combinations which have the dimensions of frequency are
(a) $\frac{1}{RC}$
(b) $\frac{R}{L}$
(c) $\frac{1}{\sqrt{LC}}$
(d) $\frac{C}{L}$

Match the Columns

1. Match the two columns.

Column I	Column II
(a) Boltzmann constant	(p) $[ML^2T^{-1}]$
(b) Coefficient of viscosity	(q) $[ML^{-1}T^{-1}]$
(c) Planck constant	(r) $[MLT^{-3}K^{-1}]$
(d) Thermal conductivity	(s) $[ML^2T^{-2}K^{-1}]$

2. Match the physical quantities given in Column I with dimensions expressed in terms of mass (M), length (L), time (T) and charge (Q) given in Column II.

Column I	Column II
(a) Angular momentum	(p) $[ML^2T^{-2}]$
(b) Latent heat	(q) $[ML^2Q^{-2}]$
(c) Torque	(r) $[ML^2T^{-1}]$
(d) Capacitance	(s) $[ML^3T^{-1}Q^{-2}]$
(e) Inductance	(t) $[M^{-1}L^{-2}T^2Q^2]$
(f) Resistivity	(u) $[L^2T^{-2}]$

3. Column I gives three physical quantities. Select the appropriate units for the choices given in Column II. Some of the physical quantities may have more than one choice.

Column I	Column II
(a) Capacitance	(p) ohm-second
(b) Inductance	(q) (coulomb)^2-joule^{-1}
(c) Magnetic induction	(r) coulomb (volt)$^{-1}$,
	(s) newton (ampere-metre)$^{-1}$,
	(t) volt-second (ampere)$^{-1}$

4. Some physical quantities are given in Column I and some possible SI units in which these quantities may be expressed are given in Column II. Match the physical quantities in Column I with the units in Column II.

Column I	Column II
(a) GM_eM_s G — universal gravitational constant, M_e — mass of the earth, M_s — mass of the sun.	(p) (volt) (coulomb) (metre)
(b) $\frac{3RT}{M}$ R — universal gas constant, T — absolute temperature, M — molar mass.	(q) (kilogram) $(\text{metre})^3$ $(\text{second})^{-2}$
(c) $\frac{F^2}{q^2B^2}$ F — force, q — charge, B — magnetic field.	(r) $(\text{metre})^2$ $(\text{second})^{-2}$
(d) $\frac{GM_e}{R_e}$ G — universal gravitational constant, M_e — mass of the earth, R_e — radius of the earth.	(s) (farad) $(\text{volt})^2$ $(\text{kg})^{-1}$

5. Match the two columns.

Column I	Column II
(a) $\frac{\text{Magnitude of electric dipole moment}}{\text{Magnitude of magnetic dipole moment}}$	(p) $[\text{KM}^{-1}\text{L}^{-3}\text{T}^4]$
(b) (Electric flux) × (Magnetic flux)	(q) $[\text{K mol M}^{-2}\text{L}]$
(c) $\frac{\text{Gravitational constant}}{\text{Universal gas constant}}$	(r) $[\text{A}^{-2}\text{M}^2\text{L}^5\text{T}^{-5}]$
(d) $\frac{\text{Inductance} \times \text{Electric permittivity}}{\text{Heat capacity}}$	(s) $[\text{L}^{-1}\text{T}]$

6. If G = gravitational constant, M = mass, R = radius, v = speed, λ = linear mass density, μ_0 = magnetic permeability, J = current density, q = charge, B = magnetic field. Match the two columns.

Column I	Column II
(a) $\sqrt{\frac{GM}{R}}$	(p) $[\text{M}^0\text{L}^0\text{T}]$
(b) λv^2	(q) $[\text{A}^{-1}\text{MT}^{-2}]$
(c) $\mu_0 Jr$	(r) $[\text{MLT}^{-2}]$
(d) $\frac{m}{qB}$	(s) $[\text{LT}^{-1}]$

Subjective Questions

1. Young's modulus of steel is $2.0 \times 10^{11}\ \text{N/m}^2$. Express it in dyne/cm^2.

2. Surface tension of water in the CGS system is 72 dyne/cm. What is its value in SI units?

3. A gas bubble, from an explosion under water, oscillates with a period T proportional to $p^a\ d^b\ E^c$, where p is the static pressure, d is the density of water and E is the total energy of the explosion. Find the values of a, b and c.

4. Show dimensionally that an expression, $Y = \dfrac{MgL}{\pi r^2 l}$ is dimensionally correct, where Y is Young's modulus of the material of wire, L is length of wire, Mg is the weight applied on the wire and l is the increase in the length of the wire.

5. The energy E of an oscillating body in simple harmonic motion depends on its mass m, frequency n and amplitude a. Using the method of dimensional analysis, find the relation between E, m, n and a.

6. $\dfrac{\alpha}{t^2} = Fv + \dfrac{\beta}{x^2}$. Find the dimension formula for $[\alpha]$ and $[\beta]$ (here t = time, F = force, v = velocity, x = distance)

7. For n moles of gas, van der Waals' equation is $\left(p + \dfrac{a}{V^2}\right)(V - b) = nRT$.

Find the dimensions of a and b, where p = pressure of gas, V = volume of gas and T = temperature of gas.

8. In the formula, $p = \dfrac{nRT}{V - b}\, e^{\frac{a}{RTV}}$, find the dimensions of a and b, where p = pressure, n = number of moles, T = temperature, V = volume and R = universal gas constant.

9. Let x and a stand for distance. Is $\int \dfrac{dx}{\sqrt{a^2 - x^2}} = \dfrac{1}{a} \sin^{-1} \dfrac{a}{x}$ dimensionally correct?

10. In the equation $\int \dfrac{dx}{\sqrt{2ax - x^2}} = a^n \sin^{-1}\left(\dfrac{x}{a} - 1\right)$. Find the value of n.

11. Taking force F, length L and time T to be the fundamental quantities, find the dimensions of

(a) density
(b) pressure
(c) momentum and
(d) energy

Answers

Assertion and Reason

1. (e) 2. (e) 3. (a) 4. (c)

Single Correct Option

1. (b) 2. (a) 3. (b) 4. (d) 5. (d) 6. (c) 7. (c) 8. (a) 9. (d) 10. (c)
11. (c) 12. (a) 13. (a) 14. (b) 15. (b) 16. (d) 17. (a) 18. (c) 19. (d) 20. (d)
21. (c) 22. (d) 23. (d) 24. (b) 25. (c) 26. (a) 27. (c) 28. (a) 29. (c) 30. (c)
31. (d) 32. (a)

More than One Correct Options

1. (a,d) 2. (a,b,c) 3. (all) 4. (b,c) 5. (a,b, c)

Match the Columns

1. (a) $\rightarrow$ s, (b) $\rightarrow$ q, (c) $\rightarrow$ p, (d) $\rightarrow$ r
2. (a) $\rightarrow$ r, (b) $\rightarrow$ u, (c) $\rightarrow$ p, (d) $\rightarrow$ t, (e) $\rightarrow$ q, (f) $\rightarrow$ s
3. (a) $\rightarrow$ q,r, (b) $\rightarrow$ p,t, (c) $\rightarrow$ s
4. (a) $\rightarrow$ p, q, (b) $\rightarrow$ r, s, (c) $\rightarrow$ r, s, (d) $\rightarrow$ r, s
5. (a) $\rightarrow$ s, (b) $\rightarrow$ r, (c) $\rightarrow$ q, (d) $\rightarrow$ p
6. (a) $\rightarrow$ s, (b) $\rightarrow$ r, (c) $\rightarrow$ q, (d) $\rightarrow$ p

Subjective Questions

1. $2.0 \times 10^{12}\ \text{dyne/cm}^2$
2. $0.072\ \text{N/m}$
3. $a = \dfrac{-5}{6}, b = \dfrac{1}{2}, c = \dfrac{1}{3}$
5. $E = kmn^2a^2$ (k = a dimensionless constant)
6. $[\beta] = [\text{ML}^4\text{T}^{-3}]$, $[\alpha] = [\text{ML}^2\ \text{T}^{-1}]$
7. $[a] = [\text{ML}^5\ \text{T}^{-2}]$, $[b] = [\text{L}^3]$
8. $[a] = [\text{ML}^5\ \text{T}^{-2}\ \text{mol}^{-1}], [b] = [\text{L}^3]$
9. No
10. zero
11. (a) $[\text{FL}^{-4}\ \text{T}^2]$ (b) $[\text{FL}^{-2}]$ (c) $[\text{FT}]$ (d) $[\text{FL}]$

5

Vectors

5.1 Vector and Scalar Quantities

Any physical quantity is either a scalar or a vector. A scalar quantity can be described completely by its magnitude only. Addition, subtraction, division or multiplication of scalar quantities can be done according to the ordinary rules of algebra. Mass, volume, density, etc., are few examples of scalar quantities. If a physical quantity in addition to magnitude has a specified direction as well as obeys the law of parallelogram of addition, then and then only it is said to be a vector quantity. Displacement, velocity, acceleration, etc., are few examples of vectors.

Any vector quantity should have a specified direction but it is not a sufficient condition for a quantity to be a vector. For example, current flowing in a wire is shown by a direction but it is not a vector because it does not obey the law of parallelogram of vector addition. According to the figure,

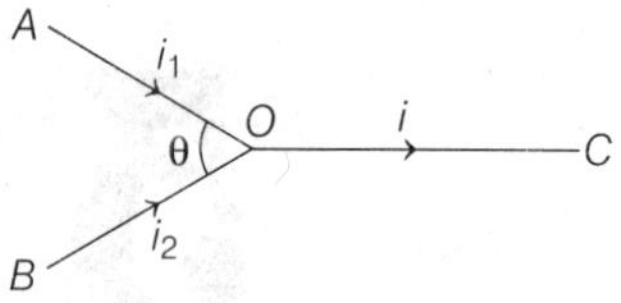

Fig. 5.1

Current flowing in wire OC = current in wire AO + current in wire BO

or $i = i_1 + i_2$ was the current a vector quantity, $i \neq i_1 + i_2$

It also depends on angle θ, the angle between i_1 and i_2.

1. **Scalar quantities** Mass, volume, distance, speed, density, work, power, energy, length, gravitation constant (G), specific heat, specific gravity, charge, current, potential, time, electric or magnetic flux, pressure, surface tension, temperature.
2. **Vector quantities** Displacement, velocity, acceleration, force, weight, acceleration due to gravity (g), gravitational field strength, electric field, magnetic field, dipole moment, torque, linear momentum, angular momentum.

5.2 General Points Regarding Vectors

Vector Notation

Usually a vector is represented by a bold capital letter with an arrow over it, as **A, B, C**, etc.

The magnitude of a vector **A** is represented by A or $|\mathbf{A}|$ and is always positive.

Graphical Representation of a Vector

Graphically a vector is represented by an arrow drawn to a chosen scale, parallel to the direction of the vector. The length and the direction of the arrow thus represent the magnitude and the direction of the vector respectively.

Thus, the arrow in Fig. 5.2 represents a vector **A** in xy-plane making an angle θ with x-axis.

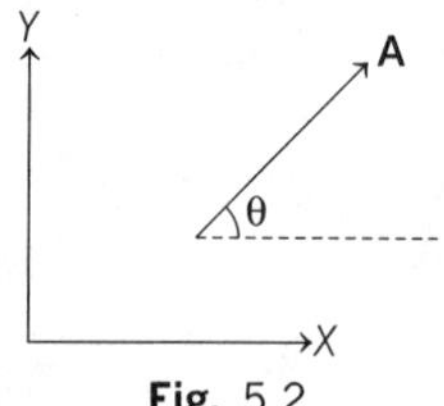

Fig. 5.2

Steps Involved in Representing a Vector

(i) By choosing a proper scale, draw a line whose length is proportional to the magnitude of the vector.

(ii) By following the standard convention to show direction, indicate the direction of the vector by marking an arrow head at one end of the line.

Example To represent the displacement of a body along x-axis.

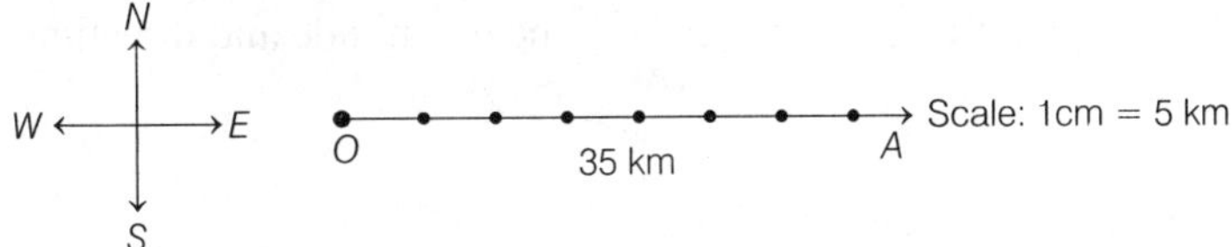

Fig. 5.3 Graphical representation of a vector

The vector represented by the directed line segment OA in Fig. 5.3 is denoted by **OA** (to be read as vector **OA**) or a simple notation as **A** (to be read as vector **A**). For vector **OA**, O is the initial point and A is the terminal point. In the figure shown, **OA** or **A** is a displacement vector of magnitude 35 km towards east.

Note *A vector can be displaced from one position to another. During the displacement if we do not change direction and magnitude then the vector remains unchanged.*

Angle between Two Vectors (θ)

To find angle between two vectors both the vectors are drawn from one point in such a manner that arrows of both the vectors are outwards from that point. Now, the smaller angle is called the angle between two vectors.

For example in Fig. 5.4, angle between **A** and **B** is 60° not 120°.Because in Fig.(a), they are wrongly drawn while in Fig. (b) they are drawn as we desire.

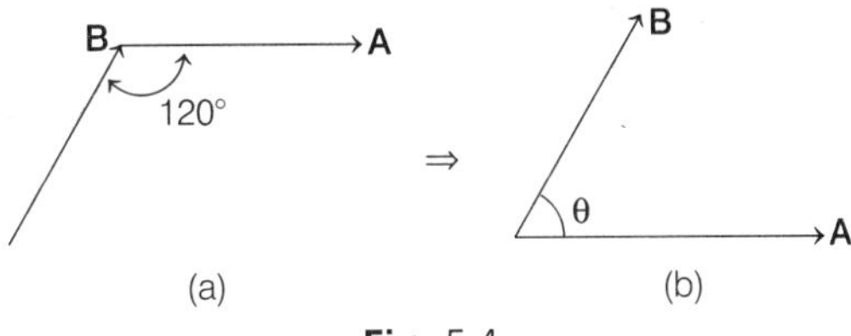

Fig. 5.4

Note $0° \leq \theta \leq 180°$

Kinds of Vectors

Unit Vector

A vector of unit magnitude is called a unit vector and the notation for it in the direction of **A** is $\hat{\mathbf{A}}$ read as 'A cap or A caret'.

Thus,
$$\mathbf{A} = A\hat{\mathbf{A}} \text{ or } \hat{\mathbf{A}} = \frac{\mathbf{A}}{|\mathbf{A}|} = \frac{\mathbf{A}}{A}$$

A unit vector merely indicates a direction. Unit vector along x, y and z-directions are $\hat{\mathbf{i}}$, $\hat{\mathbf{j}}$ and $\hat{\mathbf{k}}$.

Zero Vector or Null Vector

A vector having zero magnitude is called a null vector or zero vector.

Note *(i) Zero vector has no specific direction.*
(ii) The position vector of origin is a zero vector.
(iii) Zero vectors are only of mathematical importance.

Equal Vectors

Vectors are said to be equal if both vectors have same magnitude and direction.

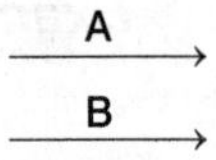

A

B

A = B

Fig. 5.5

Parallel Vectors

Vectors are said to be parallel if they have the same directions.

The vectors **A** and **B** shown in Fig. 5.6 represent parallel vectors.

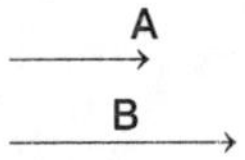

A

B

Fig. 5.6

Note *Two equal vectors are always parallel but, two parallel vectors may not be equal vectors.*

Anti-parallel Vectors (Unlike Vectors)

Vectors are said to be anti-parallel if they act in opposite direction.

The vectors **A** and **B** shown in Fig. 5.7 are anti-parallel vectors.

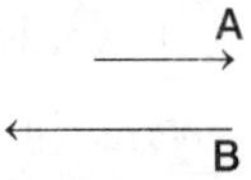

A

B

Fig. 5.7

Negative Vector

The negative vector of any vector is a vector having equal magnitude but acts in opposite direction.

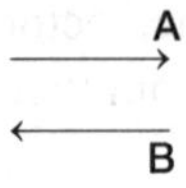

A

B

A = –B

or B = –A

Fig. 5.8

Concurrent Vectors (Co-initial Vectors)

Vectors having the same initial points are called concurrent vectors or co-initial vectors.

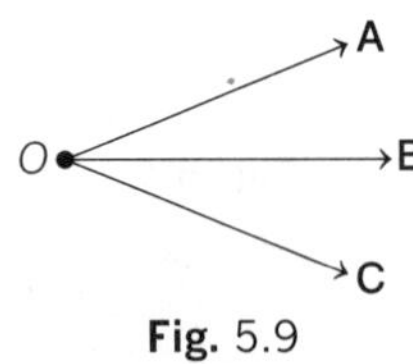

Fig. 5.9

A, B and **C** are concurrent at point *O*.

Coplanar Vectors

The vectors lying in the same plane are called coplanar vectors.

Fig. 5.10

The vector **A** and **B** are coplanar vectors. The vectors **A** and **B** shown in Fig. 5.10 (b) are concurrent coplanar vectors.

Orthogonal Vectors

Two vectors are said to be orthogonal if the angle between them is 90°.

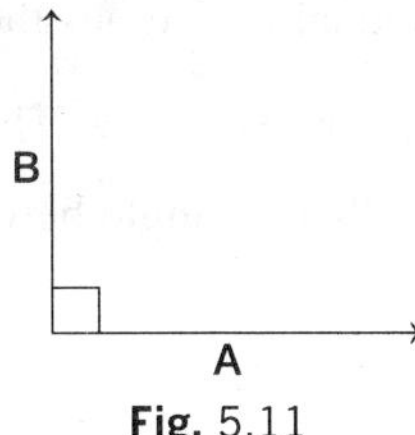

Fig. 5.11

The vector shown in Fig. 5.11, **A** and **B** are orthogonal to one another.

Multiplication and Division of Vectors by Scalars

The product of a vector **A** and a scalar m is a vector $m\mathbf{A}$ whose magnitude is m times the magnitude of **A** and which is in the direction or opposite to **A** according as the scalar m is positive or negative. Thus,

$$|m\mathbf{A}| = mA$$

Further, if m and n are two scalars, then

$$(m+n)\mathbf{A} = m\mathbf{A} + n\mathbf{A}$$

and

$$m(n\mathbf{A}) = n(m\mathbf{A}) = (mn)\mathbf{A}$$

The division of vector **A** by a non-zero scalar m is defined as the multiplication of **A** by $\frac{1}{m}$.

Example 5.1

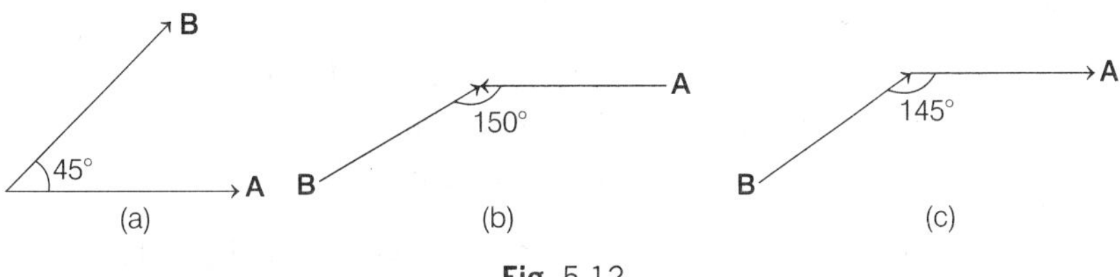

Fig. 5.12

In the shown Fig. 5.12 *(a), (b) and (c), find the angle between* **A** *and* **B**.

Solution If we draw both the vectors from one point with their arrows outwards, then they can be shown as below

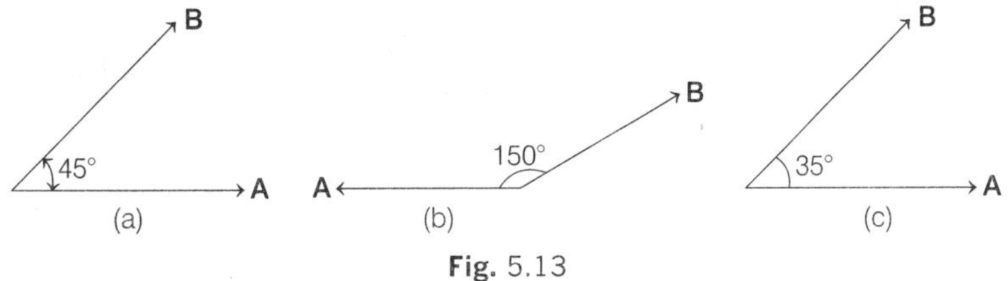

Fig. 5.13

In Fig. (a), $\theta = 45°$
In Fig. (b), $\theta = 150°$ and
In Fig. (c), $\theta = 35°$

Example 5.2 *What is the angle between* **a** *and* $-\frac{3}{2}$**a**.

Solution $-\frac{3}{2}$**a** has a magnitude equal to $\frac{3}{2}$ times the magnitude of **a** and its direction is opposite to **a**. Therefore, **a** and $-\frac{3}{2}$**a** are antiparallel to each other or angle between them is 180°.

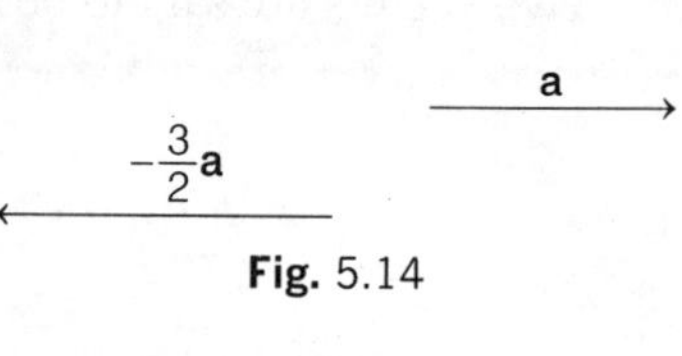

Fig. 5.14

5.3 Addition and Subtraction of Two Vectors

Addition

(i) **The parallelogram law** Let **R** be the resultant of two vectors **A** and **B**. According to parallelogram law of vector addition, the resultant **R** is the diagonal of the parallelogram of which **A** and **B** are the adjacent sides as shown in figure. Magnitude of **R** is given by

$$R = \sqrt{A^2 + B^2 + 2AB\cos\theta} \quad \text{...(i)}$$

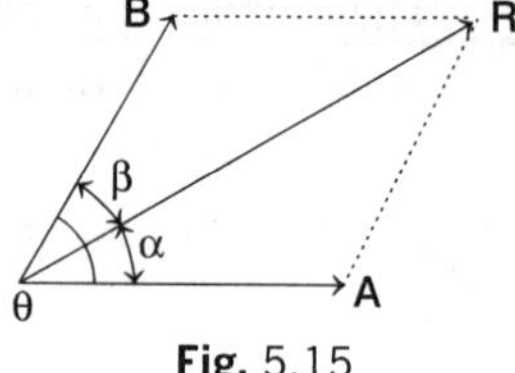

Fig. 5.15

Here, θ = angle between **A** and **B**. The direction of **R** can be found by angle α or β of **R** with **A** or **B**.

Here,
$$\tan\alpha = \frac{B\sin\theta}{A + B\cos\theta} \quad \text{and} \quad \tan\beta = \frac{A\sin\theta}{B + A\cos\theta} \quad \text{...(ii)}$$

Special cases

If $\theta = 0°$, $R = \text{maximum} = A + B$

$\theta = 180°$, $R = \text{minimum} = A \sim B$

and if $\theta = 90°$, $R = \sqrt{A^2 + B^2}$

In all other cases magnitude and direction of **R** can be calculated by using Eqs. (i) and (ii).

(ii) **The triangle law** According to this law, if the tail of one vector be placed at the head of the other, their sum or resultant **R** is drawn from the tail end of the first to the head end of the other. As is evident from the figure that the resultant **R** is the same irrespective of the order in which the vectors **A** and **B** are taken, Thus,
R = **A** + **B** = **B** + **A**

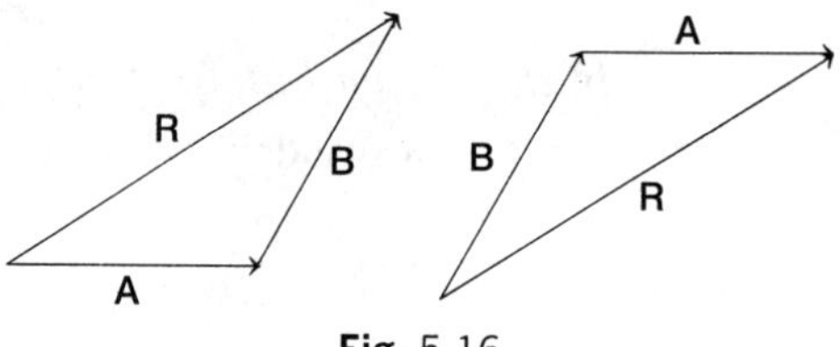

Fig. 5.16

Subtraction

Negative of a vector say −**A** is a vector of the same magnitude as vector **A** but pointing in a direction opposite to that of **A**.

Fig. 5.17

Thus, **A** – **B** can be written as **A** + (–**B**) or **A** – **B** is really the vector addition of **A** and –**B**. Suppose angle between two vectors **A** and **B** is θ. Then, angle between **A** and –**B** will be 180 – θ as shown in Fig. 5.18 (b).

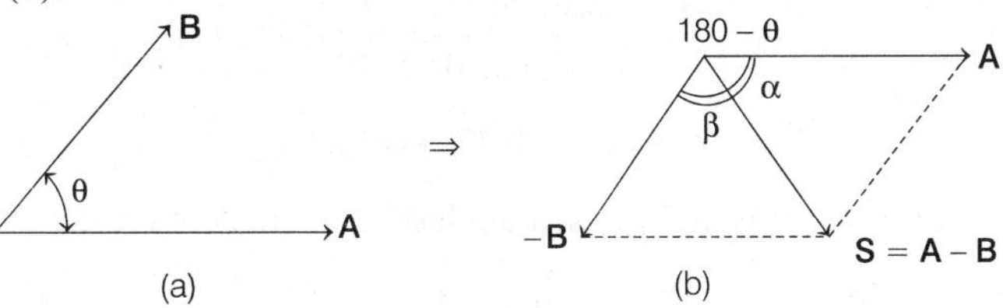

Fig. 5.18

Magnitude of **S** = **A** – **B** will be thus given by

$$S = |\mathbf{A} - \mathbf{B}| = |\mathbf{A} + (-\mathbf{B})|$$

$$= \sqrt{A^2 + B^2 + 2AB\cos(180 - \theta)}$$

or
$$S = \sqrt{A^2 + B^2 - 2AB\cos\theta} \quad \text{...(i)}$$

For direction of **S** we will either find angle α or β, where,

$$\tan\alpha = \frac{B\sin(180-\theta)}{A + B\cos(180-\theta)} = \frac{B\sin\theta}{A - B\cos\theta} \quad \text{...(ii)}$$

or
$$\tan\beta = \frac{A\sin(180-\theta)}{B + A\cos(180-\theta)} = \frac{A\sin\theta}{B - A\cos\theta} \quad \text{...(iii)}$$

Note **A** – **B** *or* **B** – **A** *can also be found by making triangles as shown in Fig. 5.19 (a) and (b).*

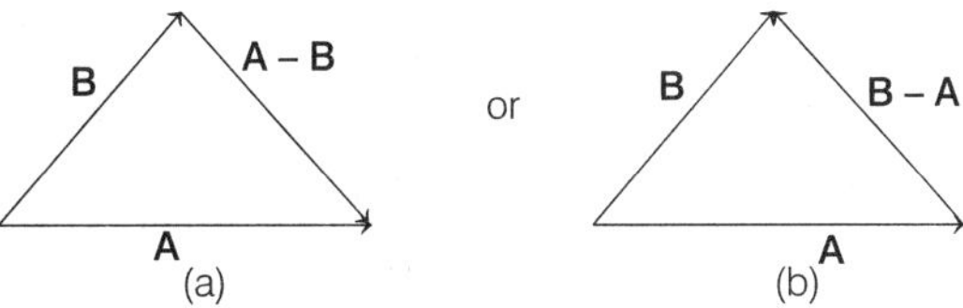

Fig. 5.19

● ***Example 5.3*** *Find* **A** + **B** *and* **A** – **B** *in the diagram shown in figure. Given* $A = 4$ *units and* $B = 3$ *units.*

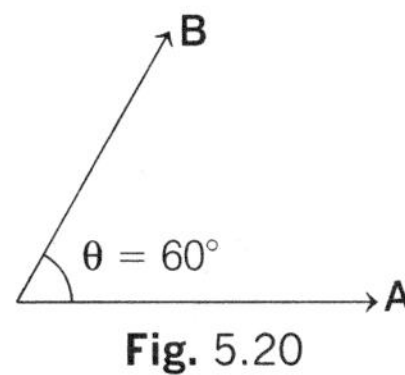

Fig. 5.20

Solution **Addition** $R = \sqrt{A^2 + B^2 + 2AB\cos\theta}$

$$= \sqrt{16 + 9 + 2 \times 4 \times 3\cos 60^\circ}$$

$$= \sqrt{37} \text{ units}$$

$$\tan\alpha = \frac{B\sin\theta}{A + B\cos\theta}$$

$$= \frac{3\sin 60°}{4 + 3\cos 60°} = 0.472$$

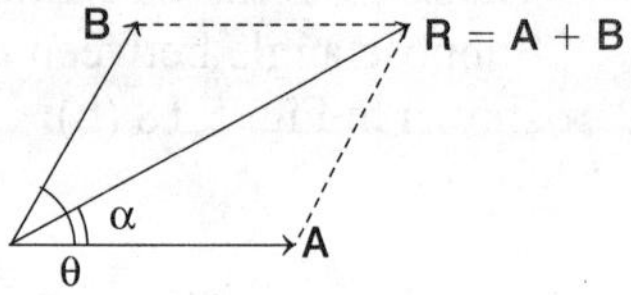

$\therefore \quad \alpha = \tan^{-1}(0.472) = 25.3°$

B R = A + B α θ A

Fig. 5.21

Thus, resultant of **A** and **B** is $\sqrt{37}$ units at angle 25.3° from **A** in the direction shown in figure.

Subtraction $\quad S = \sqrt{A^2 + B^2 - 2AB\cos\theta}$

$$= \sqrt{16 + 9 - 2\times 4\times 3\cos 60°} = \sqrt{13} \text{ units}$$

and $\quad \tan\alpha = \dfrac{B\sin\theta}{A - B\cos\theta}$

$$= \frac{3\sin 60°}{4 - 3\cos 60°} = 1.04$$

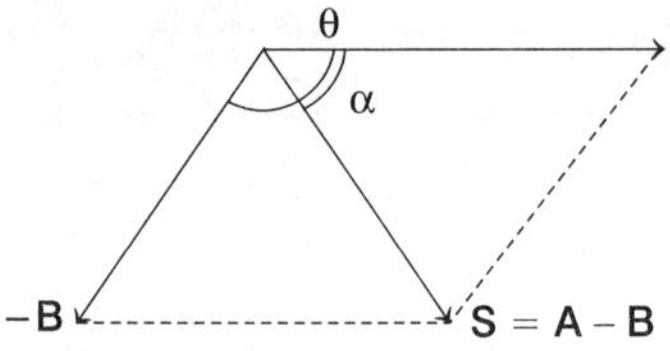

$\therefore \quad \alpha = \tan^{-1}(1.04) = 46.1°$

θ A α −B S = A − B

Fig. 5.22

Thus, **A** − **B** is $\sqrt{13}$ units at 46.1° from **A** in the direction shown in figure.

Polygon Law of Vector Addition for More than Two Vectors

This law states that if a vector polygon be drawn, placing the tail end of each succeeding vector at the head or the arrow end of the preceding one then their resultant **R** is drawn from the tail end of the first to the head or the arrow end of the last.

Thus, in the figure **R** = **A** + **B** + **C**

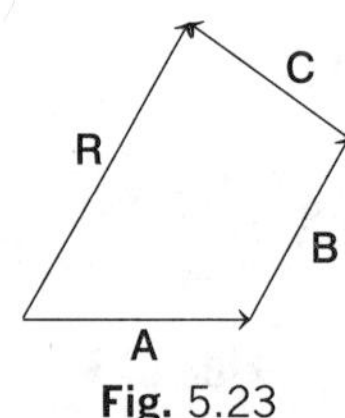

Fig. 5.23

INTRODUCTORY EXERCISE 5.1

1. What is the angle between 2**a** and 4**a**?
2. What is the angle between 3**a** and −5**a**? What is the ratio of magnitude of two vectors?
3. Two vectors have magnitudes 6 units and 8 units, respectively. Find magnitude of resultant of two vectors if angle between two vectors is
   (a) 0° (b) 180° (c) 60° (d) 120° (e) 90°
4. Two vectors **A** and **B** have magnitudes 6 units and 8 units, respectively. Find |**A** − **B**|, if the angle between two vectors is
   (a) 0° (b) 180° (c) 60° (d) 120° (e) 90°
5. For what angle between **A** and **B**, |**A** + **B**| = |**A** − **B**|?

5.4 Components of a Vector

Two or more vectors which, when compounded in accordance with the parallelogram law of vector **R** are said to be components of vector **R**. The most important components with which we are concerned are mutually perpendicular or rectangular ones along the three co-ordinate axes *ox, oy* and *oz* respectively. Thus, a vector **R** can be written as $\mathbf{R} = R_x\,\hat{\mathbf{i}} + R_y\hat{\mathbf{j}} + R_z\hat{\mathbf{k}}$.

Here, R_x, R_y and R_z are the components of **R** in *x, y* and *z*-axes respectively and $\hat{\mathbf{i}}$, $\hat{\mathbf{j}}$ and $\hat{\mathbf{k}}$ are unit vectors along these directions. The magnitude of **R** is given by

$$R = \sqrt{R_x^2 + R_y^2 + R_z^2}$$

This vector **R** makes an angle of $\alpha = \cos^{-1}\left(\frac{R_x}{R}\right)$ with *x*-axis or $\cos\alpha = \frac{R_x}{R}$

$$\beta = \cos^{-1}\left(\frac{R_y}{R}\right) \text{ with } y\text{-axis or } \cos\beta = \frac{R_y}{R}$$

and $$\gamma = \cos^{-1}\left(\frac{R_z}{R}\right) \text{ with } z\text{-axis or } \cos\gamma = \frac{R_z}{R}$$

Note *Here* $\cos\alpha$, $\cos\beta$ *and* $\cos\gamma$ *are called direction cosines of* **R** *with x, y and z-axes.*

Refer Fig. (a)

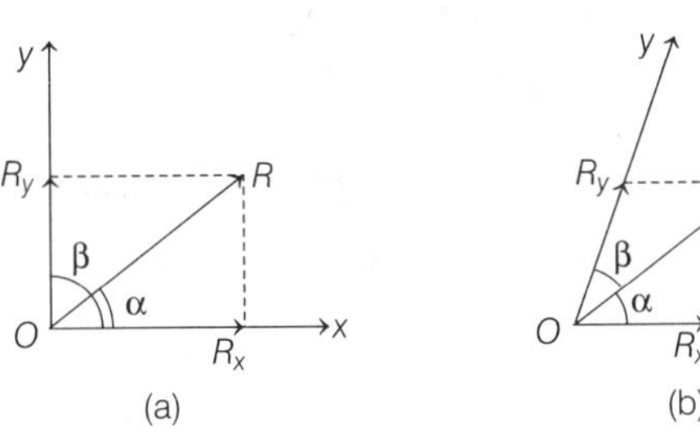

Fig. 5.24

We have resolved a two dimensional vector **R** (in *xy* plane) in mutually perpendicular directions *x* and *y*.

Component along *x*-axis $= R_x = R\cos\alpha$ or $R\sin\beta$ and component along *y*-axis $= R_y = R\cos\beta$ or $R\sin\alpha$.

If $\hat{\mathbf{i}}$ and $\hat{\mathbf{j}}$ be the unit vectors along *x* and *y*-axes respectively, we can write

$$\mathbf{R} = R_x\hat{\mathbf{i}} + R_y\hat{\mathbf{j}}$$

Refer Fig. (b)

Vector **R** has been resolved in two axes *x* and *y* not perpendicular to each other. Applying sine law in the triangle shown , we have

$$\frac{R}{\sin[180 - (\alpha+\beta)]} = \frac{R_x}{\sin\beta} = \frac{R_y}{\sin\alpha}$$

or $$R_x = \frac{R\sin\beta}{\sin(\alpha+\beta)} \quad \text{and} \quad R_y = \frac{R\sin\alpha}{\sin(\alpha+\beta)}$$

If $\alpha + \beta = 90°$, $R_x = R\sin\beta$ and $R_y = R\sin\alpha$

Position Vector

To locate the position of any point P in a plane or space, generally a fixed point of reference called the origin O is taken. The vector **OP** is called the position vector of P with respect to O as shown in figure. If coordinates of point P are (x, y) then position vector of point P with respect to point O is

$$\mathbf{OP} = \mathbf{r} = x\hat{\mathbf{i}} + y\hat{\mathbf{j}}$$

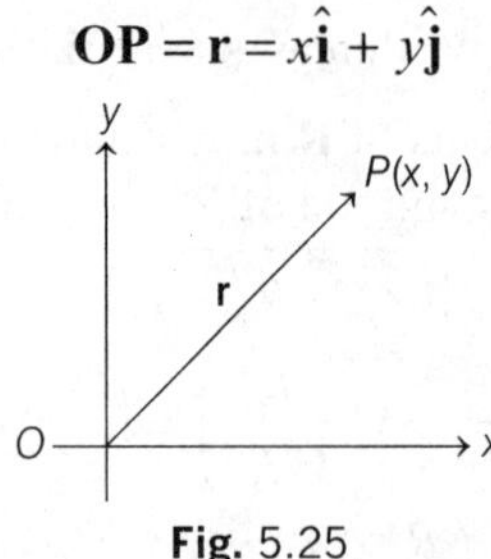

Fig. 5.25

Note *(i) For a point P, there is one and only one position vector with respect to the origin O.*
(ii) Position vector of a point P changes if the position of the origin O is changed.

Displacement Vector

If coordinates of point A are (x_1, y_1, z_1) and B are (x_2, y_2, z_2).

Then, position vector of $A = \mathbf{r}_A = \mathbf{OA} = x_1\hat{\mathbf{i}} + y_1\hat{\mathbf{j}} + z_1\hat{\mathbf{k}}$

Position vector of $B = \mathbf{r}_B = \mathbf{OB} = x_2\hat{\mathbf{i}} + y_2\hat{\mathbf{j}} + z_2\hat{\mathbf{k}}$

and $\mathbf{AB} = \mathbf{OB} - \mathbf{OA} = \mathbf{r}_B - \mathbf{r}_A$ = displacement vector (**s**)

$$= (x_2 - x_1)\hat{\mathbf{i}} + (y_2 - y_1)\hat{\mathbf{j}} + (z_2 - z_1)\hat{\mathbf{k}}$$

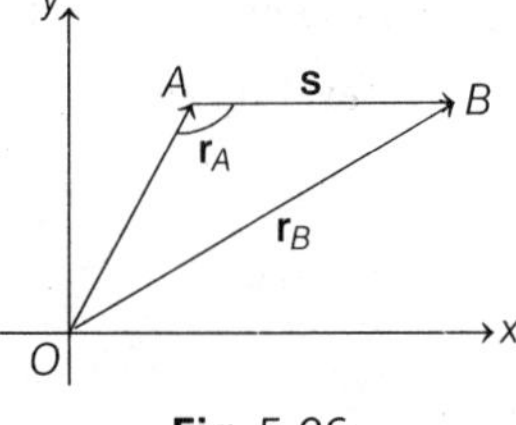

Fig. 5.26

Example 5.4 *A force* **F** *has magnitude of* 15 N. *Direction of* **F** *is at* 37° *from negative x-axis towards positive y-axis. Represent* **F** *in terms of* $\hat{\mathbf{i}}$ *and* $\hat{\mathbf{j}}$.

Solution The given force is as shown in figure. Let us find its x and y components.

$$F_x = F\cos 37°$$
$$= 15 \times \frac{4}{5}$$
$$= 12\,\text{N} \quad \text{(along negative } x\text{-axis)}$$
$$F_y = F\sin 37°$$
$$= 15 \times \frac{3}{5}$$
$$= 9\,\text{N} \quad \text{(along positive } y\text{-axis)}$$

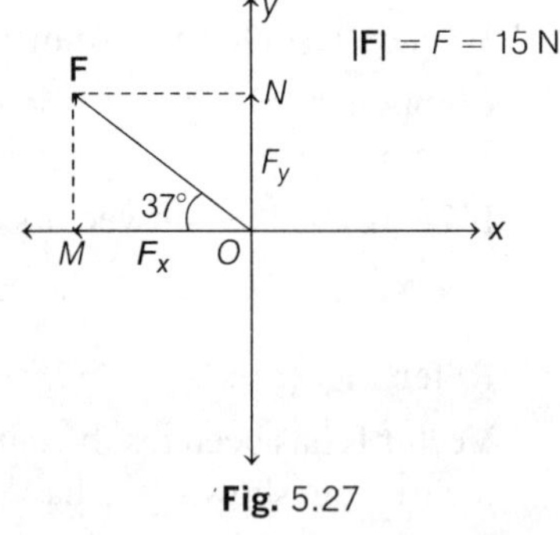

Fig. 5.27

From parallelogram law of vector addition, we can see that

$$\mathbf{F} = \mathbf{OM} + \mathbf{ON}$$
$$= F_x(-\hat{\mathbf{i}}) + F_y(\hat{\mathbf{j}})$$
$$= (-12\hat{\mathbf{i}} + 9\hat{\mathbf{j}})\,\text{N}$$ **Ans.**

Example 5.5 *Find magnitude and direction of a vector,* $\mathbf{A} = (6\hat{\mathbf{i}} - 8\hat{\mathbf{j}})$.

Solution **Magnitude of A**

$$|\mathbf{A}| \text{ or } A = \sqrt{(6)^2 + (-8)^2}$$

$$= 10 \text{ units} \qquad \textbf{Ans.}$$

Direction of A Vector **A** can be shown as

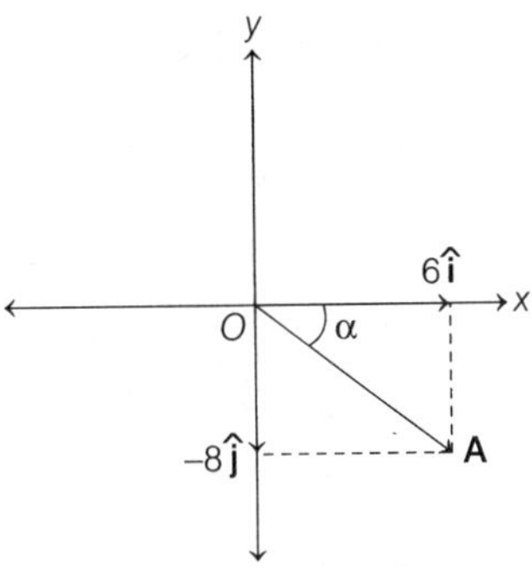

Fig. 5.28

$$\tan\alpha = \frac{8}{6} = \frac{4}{3}$$

$$\therefore \qquad \alpha = \tan^{-1}\left(\frac{4}{3}\right) = 53°$$

Therefore, **A** is making an angle of 53° from positive x-axis towards negative y-axis.

Example 5.6 *Resolve a weight of* 10 *N in two directions which are parallel and perpendicular to a slope inclined at* 30° *to the horizontal.*

Solution Component perpendicular to the plane

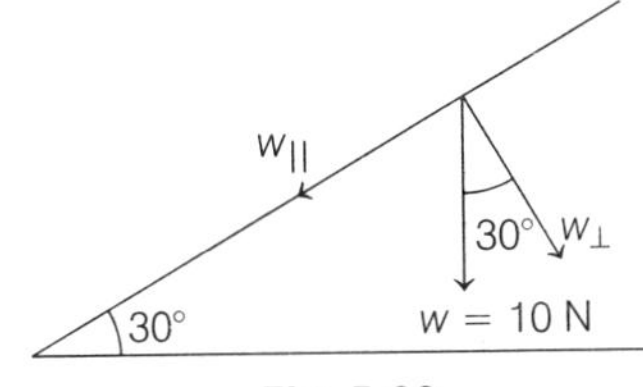

Fig. 5.29

$$w_{\perp} = w\cos 30°$$

$$= (10)\frac{\sqrt{3}}{2} = 5\sqrt{3} \text{ N}$$

and component parallel to the plane

$$w_{||} = w\sin 30° = (10)\left(\frac{1}{2}\right)$$

$$= 5 \text{ N}$$

Example 5.7 *Resolve horizontally and vertically a force $F = 8$ N which makes an angle of 45° with the horizontal.*

Solution Horizontal component of **F** is

$$F_H = F \cos 45° = (8)\left(\frac{1}{\sqrt{2}}\right) = 4\sqrt{2} \text{ N}$$

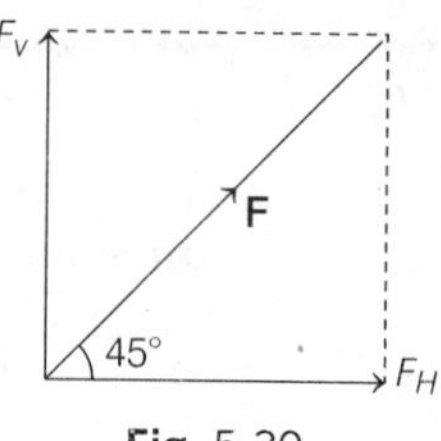

Fig. 5.30

and vertical component of **F** is

$$F_V = F \sin 45° = (8)\left(\frac{1}{\sqrt{2}}\right) = 4\sqrt{2} \text{ N}$$

Note *Two vectors given in the form of $\hat{\mathbf{i}}$, $\hat{\mathbf{j}}$ and $\hat{\mathbf{k}}$ can be added, subtracted or multiplied (by a scalar) directly as is done in the example 5.8.*

Example 5.8 *Obtain the magnitude of* $2\mathbf{A} - 3\mathbf{B}$ *if*

$$\mathbf{A} = \hat{\mathbf{i}} + \hat{\mathbf{j}} - 2\hat{\mathbf{k}} \quad and \quad \mathbf{B} = 2\hat{\mathbf{i}} - \hat{\mathbf{j}} + \hat{\mathbf{k}}$$

Solution $2\mathbf{A} - 3\mathbf{B} = 2(\hat{\mathbf{i}} + \hat{\mathbf{j}} - 2\hat{\mathbf{k}}) - 3(2\hat{\mathbf{i}} - \hat{\mathbf{j}} + \hat{\mathbf{k}}) = -4\hat{\mathbf{i}} + 5\hat{\mathbf{j}} - 7\hat{\mathbf{k}}$

$\therefore$ Magnitude of $2\mathbf{A} - 3\mathbf{B} = \sqrt{(-4)^2 + (5)^2 + (-7)^2} = \sqrt{16 + 25 + 49} = \sqrt{90}$

INTRODUCTORY EXERCISE 5.2

1. Find magnitude and direction cosines of the vector, $\mathbf{A} = (3\hat{\mathbf{i}} - 4\hat{\mathbf{j}} + 5\hat{\mathbf{k}})$.
2. Resolve a force $F = 10$ N along x and y-axes. Where this force vector is making an angle of 60° from negative x-axis towards negative y-axis?
3. Find magnitude of $\mathbf{A} - 2\mathbf{B} + 3\mathbf{C}$, where $\mathbf{A} = 2\hat{\mathbf{i}} + 3\hat{\mathbf{j}}$, $\mathbf{B} = \hat{\mathbf{i}} + \hat{\mathbf{j}}$ and $\mathbf{C} = \hat{\mathbf{k}}$.
4. Find angle between **A** and **B**, where
   (a) $\mathbf{A} = 2\hat{\mathbf{i}}$ and $\mathbf{B} = -6\hat{\mathbf{i}}$ (b) $\mathbf{A} = 6\hat{\mathbf{j}}$ and $\mathbf{B} = -2\hat{\mathbf{k}}$
   (c) $\mathbf{A} = (2\hat{\mathbf{i}} - 3\hat{\mathbf{j}})$ and $\mathbf{B} = 4\hat{\mathbf{k}}$ (d) $\mathbf{A} = 4\hat{\mathbf{i}}$ and $\mathbf{B} = (-3\hat{\mathbf{i}} + 3\hat{\mathbf{j}})$

5.5 Product of Two Vectors

The product of two vectors is of two kinds

(i) scalar or dot product.

(ii) a vector or a cross product.

Scalar or Dot Product

The scalar or dot product of two vectors **A** and **B** is denoted by $\mathbf{A} \cdot \mathbf{B}$ and is read as **A** dot **B**.

It is defined as the product of the magnitudes of the two vectors **A** and **B** and the cosine of their included angle θ.

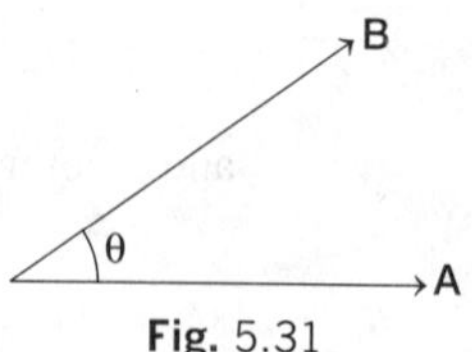

Fig. 5.31

Thus, $$\mathbf{A} \cdot \mathbf{B} = AB \cos \theta$$ (a scalar quantity)

Important Points Regarding Dot Product

The following points should be remembered regarding the dot product.

(i) $\mathbf{A}\cdot\mathbf{B}=\mathbf{B}\cdot\mathbf{A}$

(ii) $\mathbf{A}\cdot(\mathbf{B}+\mathbf{C})=\mathbf{A}\cdot\mathbf{B}+\mathbf{A}\cdot\mathbf{C}$

(iii) $\mathbf{A}\cdot\mathbf{A}=A^2$

(iv) $\mathbf{A}\cdot\mathbf{B}=A(B\cos\theta)=A$ (Component of **B** along **A**)
or $\mathbf{A}\cdot\mathbf{B}=B(A\cos\theta)=B$ (Component of **A** along **B**)

(v) $\hat{\mathbf{i}}\cdot\hat{\mathbf{i}}=\hat{\mathbf{j}}\cdot\hat{\mathbf{j}}=\hat{\mathbf{k}}\cdot\hat{\mathbf{k}}=(1)(1)\cos 0°=1$

(vi) $\hat{\mathbf{i}}\cdot\hat{\mathbf{j}}=\hat{\mathbf{j}}\cdot\hat{\mathbf{k}}=\hat{\mathbf{i}}\cdot\hat{\mathbf{k}}=(1)(1)\cos 90°=0$

(vii) $(a_1\hat{\mathbf{i}}+b_1\hat{\mathbf{j}}+c_1\hat{\mathbf{k}})\cdot(a_2\hat{\mathbf{i}}+b_2\hat{\mathbf{j}}+c_2\hat{\mathbf{k}})=a_1a_2+b_1b_2+c_1c_2$

(viii) $\cos\theta=\dfrac{\mathbf{A}\cdot\mathbf{B}}{AB}=$ (cosine of angle between **A** and **B**)

(ix) Two vectors are perpendicular if their dot product is zero. $(\theta=90°)$

Example 5.9 *Work done by a force* **F** *on a body is* $W=\mathbf{F}\bullet\mathbf{s}$, *where* **s** *is the displacement of body. Given that under a force* $\mathbf{F}=(2\hat{\mathbf{i}}+3\hat{\mathbf{j}}+4\hat{\mathbf{k}})$ *N a body is displaced from position vector* $\mathbf{r}_1=(2\hat{\mathbf{i}}+3\hat{\mathbf{j}}+\hat{\mathbf{k}})$ *m to the position vector* $\mathbf{r}_2=(\hat{\mathbf{i}}+\hat{\mathbf{j}}+\hat{\mathbf{k}})$ *m. Find the work done by this force.*

Solution The body is displaced from $\mathbf{r}_1$ to $\mathbf{r}_2$. Therefore, displacement of the body is

$$\begin{aligned}\mathbf{s}&=\mathbf{r}_2-\mathbf{r}_1\\&=(\hat{\mathbf{i}}+\hat{\mathbf{j}}+\hat{\mathbf{k}})-(2\hat{\mathbf{i}}+3\hat{\mathbf{j}}+\hat{\mathbf{k}})\\&=(-\hat{\mathbf{i}}-2\hat{\mathbf{j}})\text{ m}\end{aligned}$$

Now, work done by the force is

$$\begin{aligned}W&=\mathbf{F}\cdot\mathbf{s}\\&=(2\hat{\mathbf{i}}+3\hat{\mathbf{j}}+4\hat{\mathbf{k}})\cdot(-\hat{\mathbf{i}}-2\hat{\mathbf{j}})\\&=(2)(-1)+(3)(-2)+(4)(0)=-8\text{ J}\end{aligned}$$

Example 5.10 *Find the angle between two vectors* $\mathbf{A}=2\hat{\mathbf{i}}+\hat{\mathbf{j}}-\hat{\mathbf{k}}$ *and* $\mathbf{B}=\hat{\mathbf{i}}-\hat{\mathbf{k}}$.

Solution

$$A=|\mathbf{A}|=\sqrt{(2)^2+(1)^2\ (-1)^2}=\sqrt{6}$$

$$B=|\mathbf{B}|=\sqrt{(1)^2+(-1)^2}=\sqrt{2}$$

$$\begin{aligned}\mathbf{A}\cdot\mathbf{B}&=(2\hat{\mathbf{i}}+\hat{\mathbf{j}}-\hat{\mathbf{k}})\cdot(\hat{\mathbf{i}}-\hat{\mathbf{k}})\\&=(2)(1)+(1)(0)+(-1)(-1)=3\end{aligned}$$

Now,

$$\cos\theta=\frac{\mathbf{A}\cdot\mathbf{B}}{AB}=\frac{3}{\sqrt{6}\cdot\sqrt{2}}$$

$$=\frac{3}{\sqrt{12}}=\frac{\sqrt{3}}{2}$$

$\therefore$

$$\theta=30°$$

Example 5.11 *Prove that the vectors* $\mathbf{A} = 2\hat{\mathbf{i}} - 3\hat{\mathbf{j}} + \hat{\mathbf{k}}$ *and* $\mathbf{B} = \hat{\mathbf{i}} + \hat{\mathbf{j}} + \hat{\mathbf{k}}$ *are mutually perpendicular.*

Solution

$$\mathbf{A} \cdot \mathbf{B} = (2\hat{\mathbf{i}} - 3\hat{\mathbf{j}} + \hat{\mathbf{k}}) \cdot (\hat{\mathbf{i}} + \hat{\mathbf{j}} + \hat{\mathbf{k}})$$

$$= (2)(1) + (-3)(1) + (1)(1) = 0 = AB \cos \theta$$

$\therefore$ $\qquad \cos \theta = 0 \qquad$ (as $A \neq 0, B \neq 0$)

or $\qquad \theta = 90°$

or $\quad$ the vectors **A** and **B** are mutually perpendicular.

Vector or Cross Product

The cross product of two vectors **A** and **B** is denoted by $\mathbf{A} \times \mathbf{B}$ and read as **A** cross **B**. It is defined as a third vector **C** whose magnitude is equal to the product of the magnitudes of the two vectors **A** and **B** and the sine of their included angle θ.

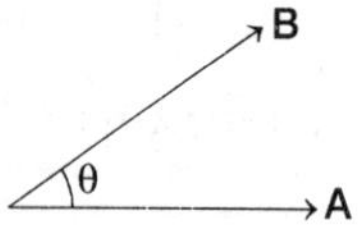

Thus, if $\boxed{\mathbf{C} = \mathbf{A} \times \mathbf{B}, \quad \text{then} \quad C = AB \sin \theta.}$

Fig. 5.32

The vector **C** is normal to the plane of **A** and **B** and points in the direction in which a right handed screw would advance when rotated about an axis perpendicular to the plane of the two vectors in the direction from **A** to **B** through the smaller angle θ between them or alternatively, we might state the rule as below

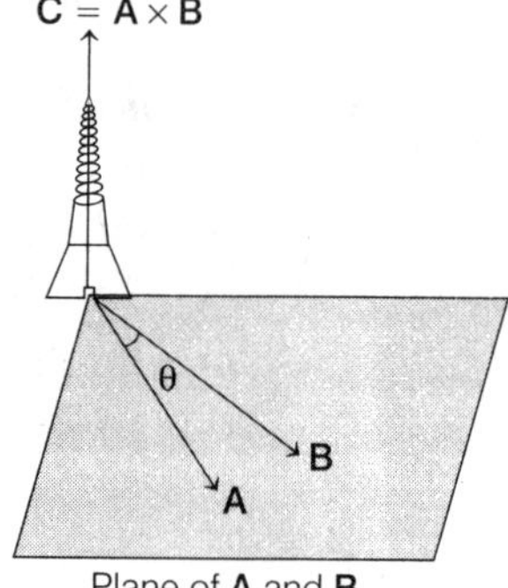

Plane of **A** and **B**

Fig. 5.33

If the fingers of the right hand be curled in the direction in which vector **A** must be turned through the smaller included angle θ to coincide with the direction of vector **B**, the thumb points in the direction of **C** as shown in Fig. 5.33.

Either of these rules is referred to as the right handed screw rule. Thus, if $\hat{\mathbf{n}}$ be the unit vector in the direction of **C**, we have

$$\mathbf{C} = \mathbf{A} \times \mathbf{B} = AB \sin \theta \, \hat{\mathbf{n}}$$

where, $\qquad 0 \leq \theta \leq \pi$

Important Points About Vector Product

(i) $\mathbf{A} \times \mathbf{B} = -\mathbf{B} \times \mathbf{A}$

(ii) The cross product of two parallel (or antiparallel) vectors is zero, as $|\mathbf{A} \times \mathbf{B}| = AB \sin \theta$ and $\theta = 0°$ or $\sin \theta = 0$ for two parallel vectors. Thus, $\hat{\mathbf{i}} \times \hat{\mathbf{i}} = \hat{\mathbf{j}} \times \hat{\mathbf{j}} = \hat{\mathbf{k}} \times \hat{\mathbf{k}} =$ a null vector.

(iii) If two vectors are perpendicular to each other, we have $\theta = 90°$ and therefore, $\sin \theta = 1$. So that $\mathbf{A} \times \mathbf{B} = AB \, \hat{\mathbf{n}}$. The vectors **A**, **B** and $\mathbf{A} \times \mathbf{B}$ thus form a right handed system of mutually perpendicular vectors. It follows at once from the above that in case of the orthogonal triad of unit vectors $\hat{\mathbf{i}}$, $\hat{\mathbf{j}}$ and $\hat{\mathbf{k}}$ (each perpendicular to each other)

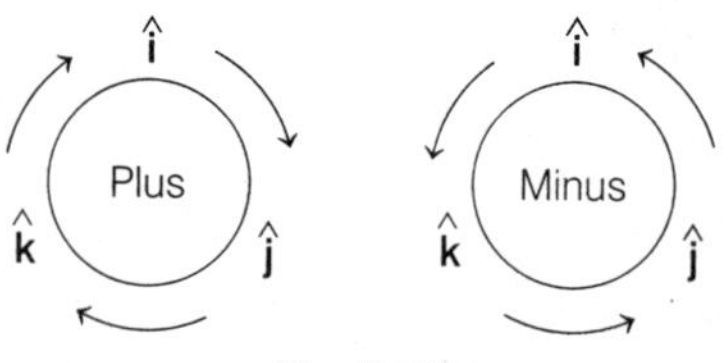

Fig. 5.34

$$\hat{\mathbf{i}} \times \hat{\mathbf{j}} = -\hat{\mathbf{j}} \times \hat{\mathbf{i}} = \hat{\mathbf{k}}$$

$$\hat{\mathbf{j}} \times \hat{\mathbf{k}} = -\hat{\mathbf{k}} \times \hat{\mathbf{j}} = \hat{\mathbf{i}} \quad \text{and} \quad \hat{\mathbf{k}} \times \hat{\mathbf{i}} = -\hat{\mathbf{i}} \times \hat{\mathbf{k}} = \hat{\mathbf{j}}$$

(iv) $\mathbf{A} \times (\mathbf{B} + \mathbf{C}) = \mathbf{A} \times \mathbf{B} + \mathbf{A} \times \mathbf{C}$

(v) A vector product can be expressed in terms of rectangular components of the two vectors and put in the determinant form as may be seen from the following:

Let $\mathbf{A} = a_1\hat{\mathbf{i}} + b_1\hat{\mathbf{j}} + c_1\hat{\mathbf{k}}$

and $\mathbf{B} = a_2\hat{\mathbf{i}} + b_2\hat{\mathbf{j}} + c_2\hat{\mathbf{k}}$

Then,

$$\mathbf{A}\times\mathbf{B} = (a_1\hat{\mathbf{i}} + b_1\hat{\mathbf{j}} + c_1\hat{\mathbf{k}})\times(a_2\hat{\mathbf{i}} + b_2\hat{\mathbf{j}} + c_2\hat{\mathbf{k}})$$

$$= a_1a_2(\hat{\mathbf{i}}\times\hat{\mathbf{i}}) + a_1b_2(\hat{\mathbf{i}}\times\hat{\mathbf{j}}) + a_1c_2\,(\hat{\mathbf{i}}\times\hat{\mathbf{k}}) + b_1a_2(\hat{\mathbf{j}}\times\hat{\mathbf{i}}) + b_1b_2\,(\hat{\mathbf{j}}\times\hat{\mathbf{j}})$$
$$+ b_1c_2(\hat{\mathbf{j}}\times\hat{\mathbf{k}}) + c_1a_2(\hat{\mathbf{k}}\times\hat{\mathbf{i}}) + c_1b_2(\hat{\mathbf{k}}\times\hat{\mathbf{j}}) + c_1c_2\,(\hat{\mathbf{k}}\times\hat{\mathbf{k}})$$

Since, $\hat{\mathbf{i}}\times\hat{\mathbf{i}} = \hat{\mathbf{j}}\times\hat{\mathbf{j}} = \hat{\mathbf{k}}\times\hat{\mathbf{k}}$ = a null vector and $\hat{\mathbf{i}}\times\hat{\mathbf{j}} = \hat{\mathbf{k}}$, etc., we have

$$\mathbf{A}\times\mathbf{B} = (b_1c_2 - c_1b_2)\,\hat{\mathbf{i}} + (c_1a_2 - a_1c_2)\,\hat{\mathbf{j}} + (a_1b_2 - b_1a_2)\,\hat{\mathbf{k}}$$

or putting it in determinant form, we have

$$\mathbf{A}\times\mathbf{B} = \begin{vmatrix} \hat{\mathbf{i}} & \hat{\mathbf{j}} & \hat{\mathbf{k}} \\ a_1 & b_1 & c_1 \\ a_2 & b_2 & c_2 \end{vmatrix}$$

It may be noted that the scalar components of the first vector **A** occupy the middle row of the determinant.

Example 5.12 *Find a unit vector perpendicular to* $\mathbf{A} = 2\hat{\mathbf{i}} + 3\hat{\mathbf{j}} + \hat{\mathbf{k}}$ *and* $\mathbf{B} = \hat{\mathbf{i}} - \hat{\mathbf{j}} + \hat{\mathbf{k}}$ *both.*

Solution As we have read, $\mathbf{C} = \mathbf{A}\times\mathbf{B}$ is a vector perpendicular to both **A** and **B**. Hence, a unit vector $\hat{\mathbf{n}}$ perpendicular to **A** and **B** can be written as

$$\hat{\mathbf{n}} = \frac{\mathbf{C}}{C} = \frac{\mathbf{A}\times\mathbf{B}}{|\mathbf{A}\times\mathbf{B}|}$$

Here,

$$\mathbf{A}\times\mathbf{B} = \begin{vmatrix} \hat{\mathbf{i}} & \hat{\mathbf{j}} & \hat{\mathbf{k}} \\ 2 & 3 & 1 \\ 1 & -1 & 1 \end{vmatrix}$$

$$= \hat{\mathbf{i}}(3+1) + \hat{\mathbf{j}}(1-2) + \hat{\mathbf{k}}(-2-3) = 4\hat{\mathbf{i}} - \hat{\mathbf{j}} - 5\hat{\mathbf{k}}$$

Further,

$$|\mathbf{A}\times\mathbf{B}| = \sqrt{(4)^2 + (-1)^2 + (-5)^2} = \sqrt{42}$$

∴ The desired unit vector is

$$\hat{\mathbf{n}} = \frac{\mathbf{A}\times\mathbf{B}}{|\mathbf{A}\times\mathbf{B}|} \quad \text{or} \quad \hat{\mathbf{n}} = \frac{1}{\sqrt{42}}(4\hat{\mathbf{i}} - \hat{\mathbf{j}} - 5\hat{\mathbf{k}})$$

Example 5.13 *Show that the vector* $\mathbf{A} = \hat{\mathbf{i}} - \hat{\mathbf{j}} + 2\hat{\mathbf{k}}$ *is parallel to a vector* $\mathbf{B} = 3\hat{\mathbf{i}} - 3\hat{\mathbf{j}} + 6\hat{\mathbf{k}}$.

Solution A vector **A** is parallel to an another vector **B** if it can be written as

$$\mathbf{A} = m\mathbf{B}$$

Here,

$$\mathbf{A} = (\hat{\mathbf{i}} - \hat{\mathbf{j}} + 2\hat{\mathbf{k}}) = \frac{1}{3}(3\hat{\mathbf{i}} - 3\hat{\mathbf{j}} + 6\hat{\mathbf{k}}) \quad \text{or} \quad \mathbf{A} = \frac{1}{3}\mathbf{B}$$

This implies that **A** is parallel to **B** and magnitude of **A** is $\frac{1}{3}$ times the magnitude of **B**.

Note *Two vectors can be shown parallel (or antiparallel) to one another if :*

(i) *The coefficients of* $\hat{\mathbf{i}}$, $\hat{\mathbf{j}}$ *and* $\hat{\mathbf{k}}$ *of both the vectors bear a constant ratio. For example, a vector* $\mathbf{A} = a_1\hat{\mathbf{i}} + b_1\hat{\mathbf{j}} + c_1\hat{\mathbf{k}}$ *is parallel to an another vector* $\mathbf{B} = a_2\hat{\mathbf{i}} + b_2\hat{\mathbf{j}} + c_2\hat{\mathbf{k}}$ *if :* $\frac{a_1}{a_2} = \frac{b_1}{b_2} = \frac{c_1}{c_2}$ = *constant. If this constant has positive value, then the vectors are parallel and if the constant has negative value then the vectors are antiparallel.*

(ii) *The cross product of both the vectors is a null vector. For instance,* **A** *and* **B** *are parallel (or antiparallel) to each other if* $\mathbf{A} \times \mathbf{B} = \begin{vmatrix} \hat{\mathbf{i}} & \hat{\mathbf{j}} & \hat{\mathbf{k}} \\ a_1 & b_1 & c_1 \\ a_2 & b_2 & c_2 \end{vmatrix}$ = *a null vector*

Example 5.14 *Let a force* **F** *be acting on a body free to rotate about a point O and let* **r** *the position vector of any point P on the line of action of the force. Then torque (τ) of this force about point O is defined as*

$$\tau = \mathbf{r} \times \mathbf{F}$$

Given, $\mathbf{F} = (2\hat{\mathbf{i}} + 3\hat{\mathbf{j}} - \hat{\mathbf{k}})\,N$ *and* $\mathbf{r} = (\hat{\mathbf{i}} - \hat{\mathbf{j}} + 6\hat{\mathbf{k}})\,m$

Find the torque of this force.

Solution

$$\tau = \mathbf{r} \times \mathbf{F} = \begin{vmatrix} \hat{\mathbf{i}} & \hat{\mathbf{j}} & \hat{\mathbf{k}} \\ 1 & -1 & 6 \\ 2 & 3 & -1 \end{vmatrix}$$

$$= \hat{\mathbf{i}}\,(1 - 18) + \hat{\mathbf{j}}(12 + 1) + \hat{\mathbf{k}}(3 + 2)$$

or $$\tau = (-17\hat{\mathbf{i}} + 13\hat{\mathbf{j}} + 5\hat{\mathbf{k}})\,\text{N-m}$$

INTRODUCTORY EXERCISE 5.3

1. Cross product of two parallel or antiparallel vectors is a null vector. Is this statement true or false?
2. Find the values of
   (a) $(4\hat{\mathbf{i}}) \times (-6\hat{\mathbf{k}})$
   (b) $(3\hat{\mathbf{j}}) \cdot (-4\hat{\mathbf{j}})$
   (c) $(2\hat{\mathbf{i}}) \cdot (-4\hat{\mathbf{k}})$
3. Two vectors **A** and **B** have magnitudes 2 units and 4 units, respectively. Find **A** · **B**, if angle between these two vectors is
   (a) 0° (b) 60°
   (c) 90° (d) 120°
   (e) 180°
4. Find $(2\mathbf{A}) \times (-3\mathbf{B})$, if $\mathbf{A} = 2\hat{\mathbf{i}} - \hat{\mathbf{j}}$ and $\mathbf{B} = (\hat{\mathbf{j}} + \hat{\mathbf{k}})$

Core Concepts

1. The moment of inertia has two forms, a scalar form I (used when the axis of rotation is known) and a more general tensor form that does not require knowing the axis of rotation. Although tensor is a generalized term which is characterized by its rank. For example, scalars are tensors of rank zero. Vectors are tensors of rank two.
2. Pressure is a scalar quantity, not a vector quantity. It has magnitude but no direction sense associated with it. Pressure acts in all directions at a point inside a fluid.
3. Surface tension is scalar because it has no specific direction.
4. Stress is neither a scalar nor a vector quantity, it is a tensor.
5. To qualify as a vector, a physical quantity must not only possess magnitude and direction but must also satisfy the parallelogram law of vector addition. For instance, the finite rotation of a rigid body about a given axis has magnitude (the angle of rotation) and also direction (the direction of the axis) but it is not a vector quantity. This is so for the simple reason that the two finite rotations of the body do not add up in accordance with the law of vector addition. However if the rotation be small or infinitesimal, it may be regarded as a vector quantity.
6. Area can behave either as a scalar or a vector and how it behaves depends on circumstances.
7. Area (vector), dipole moment and current density are defined as vectors with specific direction.
8. Vectors associated with a linear or directional effect are called polar vectors or simply as vectors and those associated with rotation about an axis are referred to as axial vectors. Thus, force, linear velocity and linear acceleration are polar vectors and angular velocity, angular acceleration are axial vectors.
9. Examples of dot-product and cross-product

Examples of Dot-product	Examples of Cross-product
$W = \mathbf{F} \cdot \mathbf{s}$	$\tau = \mathbf{r} \times \mathbf{F}$
$P = \mathbf{F} \cdot \mathbf{v}$	$\mathbf{L} = \mathbf{r} \times \mathbf{P}$
$d\phi_e = \mathbf{E} \cdot \mathbf{ds}$	$\mathbf{v} = \omega \times \mathbf{r}$
$d\phi_B = \mathbf{B} \cdot \mathbf{ds}$	$\tau_e = \mathbf{P} \times \mathbf{E}$
$U_e = \mathbf{P} \cdot \mathbf{E}$	$\tau_B = \mathbf{M} \times \mathbf{B}$
$U_B = \mathbf{M} \cdot \mathbf{B}$	$\mathbf{F}_B = q\ (\mathbf{v} \times \mathbf{B})$
	$\mathbf{dB} = \frac{\mu_0}{4\pi} \frac{i\ (\mathbf{dl} \times \mathbf{r})}{r^3}$

10. Students are often confused over the direction of cross product. Let us discuss a simple method. To find direction of $\mathbf{A} \times \mathbf{B}$ curl your fingers from **A** to **B** through smaller angle. If it is clockwise then $\mathbf{A} \times \mathbf{B}$ is perpendicular to the plane of **A** and **B** and away from you and if it is anti-clockwise then $\mathbf{A} \times \mathbf{B}$ is towards you perpendicular to the plane of **A** and **B**.
11. The area of triangle bounded by vectors **A** and **B** is $\frac{1}{2} |\mathbf{A} \times \mathbf{B}|$.

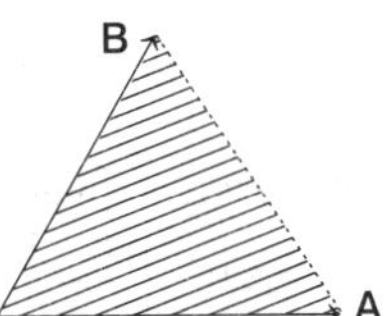

Exercise : Prove the above result.

12. Area of a parallelogram shown in figure is, Area = $|\mathbf{A} \times \mathbf{B}|$

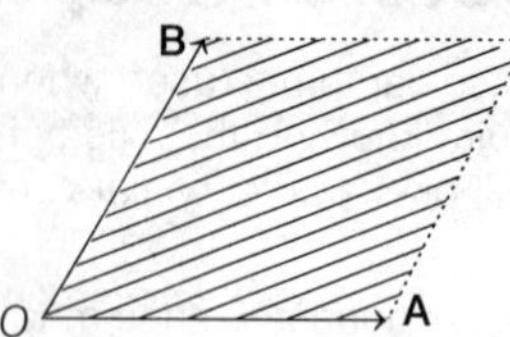

Exercise : Prove the above relation.

13. **Scalar triple product** : $\mathbf{A} \cdot (\mathbf{B} \times \mathbf{C})$ is called scalar triple product. It is a scalar quantity. We can show that $\mathbf{A} \cdot (\mathbf{B} \times \mathbf{C}) = (\mathbf{A} \times \mathbf{B}) \cdot \mathbf{C} = \mathbf{B} \cdot (\mathbf{C} \times \mathbf{A})$.
14. The volume of a parallelopiped bounded by vectors **A**,**B** and **C** can be obtained by $(\mathbf{A} \times \mathbf{B}) \cdot \mathbf{C}$.
15. If three vectors are coplanar then the volume of the parallelopiped bounded by these three vectors should be zero or we can say that their scalar triple product should be zero.
16. If $\mathbf{A} = a_1\hat{\mathbf{i}} + a_2\hat{\mathbf{j}} + a_3\hat{\mathbf{k}}$, $\mathbf{B} = b_1\hat{\mathbf{i}} + b_2\hat{\mathbf{j}} + b_3\hat{\mathbf{k}}$ and $\mathbf{C} = c_1\hat{\mathbf{i}} + c_2\hat{\mathbf{j}} + c_3\hat{\mathbf{k}}$ then $\mathbf{A} \cdot (\mathbf{B} \times \mathbf{C})$ is also written as [**ABC**] and it has the following value :

$$[\mathbf{ABC}] = \begin{vmatrix} a_1 & a_2 & a_3 \\ b_1 & b_2 & b_3 \\ c_1 & c_2 & c_3 \end{vmatrix}$$

= Volume of parallelopiped whose adjacent sides are along **A**, **B** and **C**.

17. If $|\mathbf{A}| = |\mathbf{B}| = A$ (say) then,

$$|\mathbf{R}| = |\mathbf{A} + \mathbf{B}| = 2A\cos\frac{\theta}{2}$$

Exercise : Prove the above result.

For $\theta = 0°$, $|\mathbf{R}| = 2A$
$\theta = 60°$, $|\mathbf{R}| = \sqrt{3}\,A$
$\theta = 90°$, $|\mathbf{R}| = \sqrt{2}\,A$
$\theta = 120°$, $|\mathbf{R}| = A$
and $\theta = 180°$, $|\mathbf{R}| = O$

In this case, resultant of **A** and **B** always passes through the bisector line of **A** and **B**.

18. If $|\mathbf{A}| = |\mathbf{B}| = A$ (say) then,

$$|\mathbf{S}| = |\mathbf{A} - \mathbf{B}| = 2A\sin\frac{\theta}{2}$$

Exercise : Prove the above result.

19. Angle between two vectors is obtained by their dot product (not from cross product) i.e.

$$\theta = \cos^{-1}\left(\frac{\mathbf{A} \cdot \mathbf{B}}{AB}\right)$$

It is not always, $\sin^{-1}\left\{\frac{|\mathbf{A} \times \mathbf{B}|}{AB}\right\}$

Exercise : Explain the reason why θ is not always given by the following relation?

$$\theta = \sin^{-1}\left\{\frac{|\mathbf{A} \times \mathbf{B}|}{AB}\right\}$$

20. A unit vector perpendicular to both **A** and **B**

$$\hat{\mathbf{C}} = \pm \frac{\mathbf{A} \times \mathbf{B}}{|\mathbf{A} \times \mathbf{B}|}$$

21. Component of **A** along **B** $= A \cos\theta = \dfrac{\mathbf{A} \cdot \mathbf{B}}{B}$

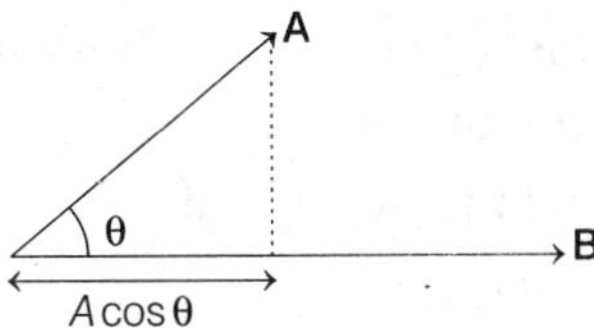

Similarly, component of **B** along **A**

$$= B \cos\theta = \frac{\mathbf{A} \cdot \mathbf{B}}{A}$$

Component of **A** along **B** = component of **B** along **A**

If $|\mathbf{A}| = |\mathbf{B}|$ or $A = B$. Otherwise they are not equal.

22. In the figure shown,

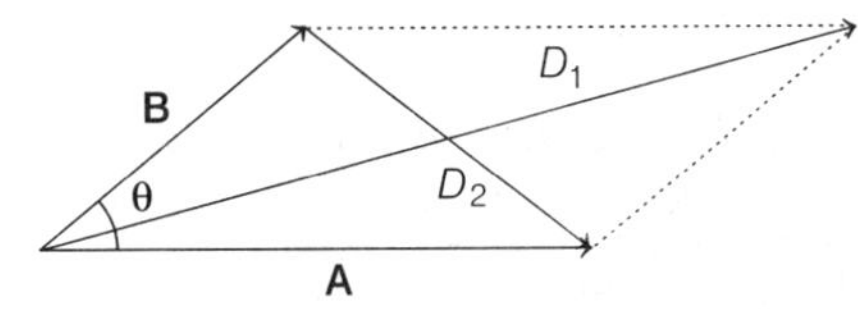

$$\text{diagonal } D_1 = |\mathbf{A} + \mathbf{B} \text{ or } \mathbf{R}| = \sqrt{A^2 + B^2 + 2AB\cos\theta}$$

$$\text{diagonal } D_2 = |\mathbf{A} - \mathbf{B} \text{ or } \mathbf{S}| = \sqrt{A^2 + B^2 - 2AB\cos\theta}$$

$$D_1 = D_2 = \sqrt{A^2 + B^2} \text{ if } \theta = 90^\circ$$

Solved Examples

Example 1 *Find component of vector* $\mathbf{A}+\mathbf{B}$ *along (i) x-axis, (ii)* $\mathbf{C}$.

Given $\mathbf{A}=\hat{\mathbf{i}}-2\hat{\mathbf{j}}$, $\mathbf{B}=2\hat{\mathbf{i}}+3\hat{\mathbf{k}}$ *and* $\mathbf{C}=\hat{\mathbf{i}}+\hat{\mathbf{j}}$.

Solution $\mathbf{A}+\mathbf{B}=(\hat{\mathbf{i}}-2\hat{\mathbf{j}})+(2\hat{\mathbf{i}}+3\hat{\mathbf{k}})=3\hat{\mathbf{i}}-2\hat{\mathbf{j}}+3\hat{\mathbf{k}}$

(i) Component of $\mathbf{A}+\mathbf{B}$ along x-axis is 3.

(ii) Component of $\mathbf{A}+\mathbf{B}=\mathbf{R}$ (say) along $\mathbf{C}$ is

$$R\cos\theta=\frac{\mathbf{R}\cdot\mathbf{C}}{C}$$

$$=\frac{(3\hat{\mathbf{i}}-2\hat{\mathbf{j}}+3\hat{\mathbf{k}})\cdot(\hat{\mathbf{i}}+\hat{\mathbf{j}})}{\sqrt{(1)^2+(1)^2}}$$

$$=\frac{3-2}{\sqrt{2}}=\frac{1}{\sqrt{2}}$$

Example 2 *Find the angle that the vector* $\mathbf{A}=2\hat{\mathbf{i}}+3\hat{\mathbf{j}}-\hat{\mathbf{k}}$ *makes with y-axis.*

Solution $\cos\theta=\dfrac{A_y}{A}=\dfrac{3}{\sqrt{(2)^2+(3)^2+(-1)^2}}=\dfrac{3}{\sqrt{14}}$

$\therefore$ $$\theta=\cos^{-1}\left(\frac{3}{\sqrt{14}}\right)$$

Example 3 *If* $\mathbf{a}$ *and* $\mathbf{b}$ *are the vectors* $\mathbf{AB}$ *and* $\mathbf{BC}$ *determined by the adjacent sides of a regular hexagon. What are the vectors determined by the other sides taken in order?*

Solution Given $\mathbf{AB}=\mathbf{a}$ and $\mathbf{BC}=\mathbf{b}$

From the method of vector addition (or subtraction) we can show that,

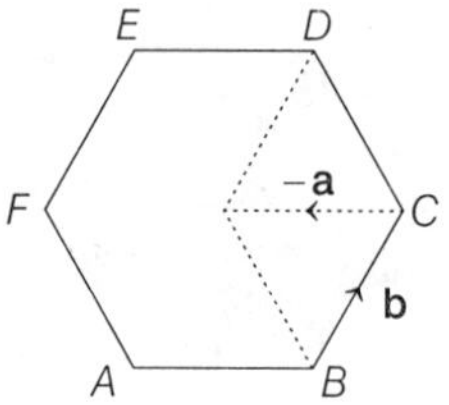

$$\mathbf{CD}=\mathbf{b}-\mathbf{a}$$

Then $$\mathbf{DE}=-\mathbf{AB}=-\mathbf{a}$$

$$\mathbf{EF}=-\mathbf{BC}=-\mathbf{b}$$

and $$\mathbf{FA}=-\mathbf{CD}=\mathbf{a}-\mathbf{b}$$

E D F −a C b A B

Example 4 *If* $\mathbf{a}\times\mathbf{b}=\mathbf{b}\times\mathbf{c}\neq\mathbf{0}$ *with* $\mathbf{a}\neq-\mathbf{c}$ *then show that* $\mathbf{a}+\mathbf{c}=k\mathbf{b}$, *where k is scalar.*

Solution $\mathbf{a}\times\mathbf{b}=\mathbf{b}\times\mathbf{c}$

$$\mathbf{a}\times\mathbf{b}=-\mathbf{c}\times\mathbf{b}$$

$\therefore$ $$\mathbf{a}\times\mathbf{b}+\mathbf{c}\times\mathbf{b}=0$$

$$(\mathbf{a}+\mathbf{c})\times\mathbf{b}=0$$

$\therefore$ $\mathbf{a}\times\mathbf{b}\neq 0$, $\mathbf{b}\times\mathbf{c}\neq 0$, $\mathbf{a},\mathbf{b},\mathbf{c}$ are non-zero vectors. $(\mathbf{a}+\mathbf{c})\neq\mathbf{0}$

Hence, $\mathbf{a}+\mathbf{c}$ is parallel to $\mathbf{b}$.

$\therefore$ $$\mathbf{a}+\mathbf{c}=k\mathbf{b}$$

Example 5 *If* $\mathbf{A} = 2\hat{\mathbf{i}} - 3\hat{\mathbf{j}} + 7\hat{\mathbf{k}}$, $\mathbf{B} = \hat{\mathbf{i}} + 2\hat{\mathbf{j}}$ *and* $\mathbf{C} = \hat{\mathbf{j}} - \hat{\mathbf{k}}$. *Find* $\mathbf{A} \cdot (\mathbf{B} \times \mathbf{C})$.

Solution $\mathbf{A} \cdot (\mathbf{B} \times \mathbf{C}) = [\mathbf{ABC}]$, volume of parallelopiped

$$= \begin{vmatrix} 2 & -3 & 7 \\ 1 & 2 & 0 \\ 0 & 1 & -1 \end{vmatrix} = 2(-2-0) + 3(-1-0) + 7(1-0) = -4 - 3 + 7 = 0$$

Therefore **A**, **B** and **C** are coplanar vectors.

Example 6 *Find the resultant of three vectors* **OA**, **OB** *and* **OC** *shown in figure. Radius of circle is 'R'.*

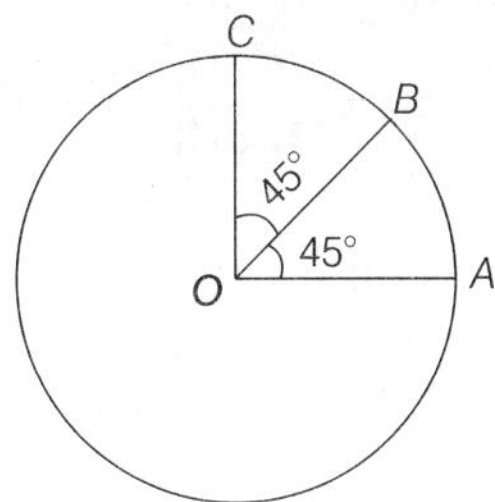

Solution $OA = OC$

$\mathbf{OA} + \mathbf{OC}$ is along **OB**, (bisector) and its magnitude is $2R \cos 45° = R\sqrt{2}$

$(\mathbf{OA} + \mathbf{OC}) + \mathbf{OB}$ is along **OB** and its magnitude is $R\sqrt{2} + R = R(1 + \sqrt{2})$

Example 7 *Prove that* $|\mathbf{a} \times \mathbf{b}|^2 = a^2 b^2 - (\mathbf{a} \cdot \mathbf{b})^2$

Solution Let $|\mathbf{a}| = a$, $|\mathbf{b}| = b$ and θ be the angle between them.

$$|\mathbf{a} \times \mathbf{b}|^2 = (ab \sin\theta)^2 = a^2 b^2 \sin^2\theta$$
$$= a^2 b^2 (1 - \cos^2\theta) = a^2 b^2 - (a \cdot b \cos\theta)^2$$
$$= a^2 b^2 - (\mathbf{a} \cdot \mathbf{b})^2$$

Hence Proved.

Example 8 *Show that the vectors* $\mathbf{a} = 3\hat{\mathbf{i}} - 2\hat{\mathbf{j}} + \hat{\mathbf{k}}$, $\mathbf{b} = \hat{\mathbf{i}} - 3\hat{\mathbf{j}} + 5\hat{\mathbf{k}}$ *and* $\mathbf{c} = 2\hat{\mathbf{i}} + \hat{\mathbf{j}} - 4\hat{\mathbf{k}}$ *form a right angled triangle.*

Solution We have $\mathbf{b} + \mathbf{c} = (\hat{\mathbf{i}} - 3\hat{\mathbf{j}} + 5\hat{\mathbf{k}}) + (2\hat{\mathbf{i}} + \hat{\mathbf{j}} - 4\hat{\mathbf{k}}) = 3\hat{\mathbf{i}} - 2\hat{\mathbf{j}} + \hat{\mathbf{k}} = \mathbf{a}$

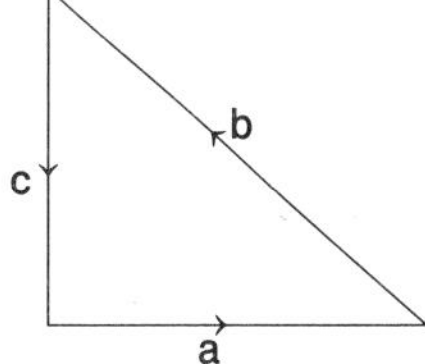

Hence, **a**, **b**, **c** are coplanar.

Also, we observe that no two of these vectors are parallel.

Further, $\mathbf{a} \cdot \mathbf{c} = (3\hat{\mathbf{i}} - 2\hat{\mathbf{j}} + \hat{\mathbf{k}}) \cdot (2\hat{\mathbf{i}} + \hat{\mathbf{j}} - 4\hat{\mathbf{k}}) = 0$

Dot product of two non-zero vectors is zero. Hence, they are perpendicular so they form a right angled triangle.

$$|\mathbf{a}| = \sqrt{9 + 4 + 1} = \sqrt{14},$$
$$|\mathbf{b}| = \sqrt{1 + 9 + 25} = \sqrt{35}$$

and $$|\mathbf{c}| = \sqrt{4 + 1 + 16} = \sqrt{21}$$

$\Rightarrow$ $$\sqrt{a^2 + c^2} = \sqrt{b^2}$$

Hence Proved.

Example 9 *Let* $\mathbf{A}, \mathbf{B}$ *and* $\mathbf{C}$ *be the unit vectors. Suppose that* $\mathbf{A} \cdot \mathbf{B} = \mathbf{A} \cdot \mathbf{C} = 0$ *and the angle between* $\mathbf{B}$ *and* $\mathbf{C}$ *is* $\frac{\pi}{6}$ *then prove that* $\mathbf{A} = \pm 2(\mathbf{B} \times \mathbf{C})$.

Solution Since, $\mathbf{A} \cdot \mathbf{B} = 0, \quad \mathbf{A} \cdot \mathbf{C} = 0$

Hence, $$(\mathbf{B} + \mathbf{C}) \cdot \mathbf{A} = 0$$

So, $\mathbf{A}$ is perpendicular to $(\mathbf{B} + \mathbf{C})$. Further, $\mathbf{A}$ is a unit vector perpendicular to the plane of vectors $\mathbf{B}$ and $\mathbf{C}$.

$$\mathbf{A} = \pm \frac{\mathbf{B} \times \mathbf{C}}{|\mathbf{B} \times \mathbf{C}|}$$

$$|\mathbf{B} \times \mathbf{C}| = |\mathbf{B}||\mathbf{C}| \sin \frac{\pi}{6} = 1 \times 1 \times \frac{1}{2} = \frac{1}{2}$$

$\therefore$ $$\mathbf{A} = \pm \frac{\mathbf{B} \times \mathbf{C}}{|\mathbf{B} \times \mathbf{C}|} = \pm 2(\mathbf{B} \times \mathbf{C})$$

Example 10 *A particle moves on a given line with a constant speed v. At a certain time, it is at a point P on its straight line path. O is a fixed point. Show that* $(\mathbf{OP} \times \mathbf{v})$ *is independent of the position P.*

Solution Let $\mathbf{v} = v\hat{\mathbf{i}}$

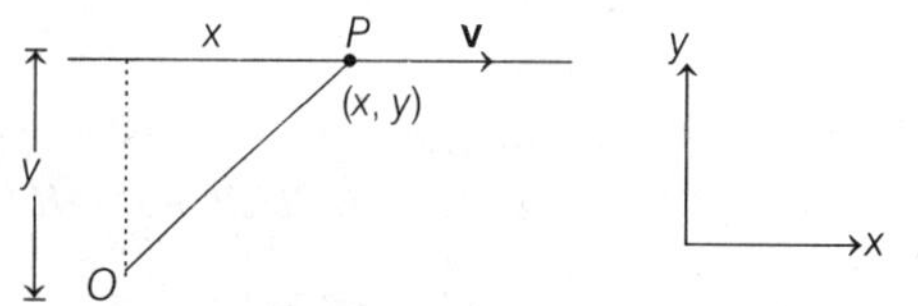

$$\mathbf{OP} = x\hat{\mathbf{i}} + y\hat{\mathbf{j}}$$

Take $$\mathbf{OP} \times \mathbf{v} = (x\hat{\mathbf{i}} + y\hat{\mathbf{j}}) \times v\hat{\mathbf{i}}$$

$$= -yv\hat{\mathbf{k}}$$

$$= \text{constant}$$ (because y is constant)

Hence, $\mathbf{OP} \times \mathbf{v}$, which is independent of position of P.

Example 11 *Prove that the mid-point of the hypotenuse of right angled triangle is equidistant from its vertices.*

Solution Here, $\angle CAB = 90°$, let D be the mid-point of hypotenuse, we have

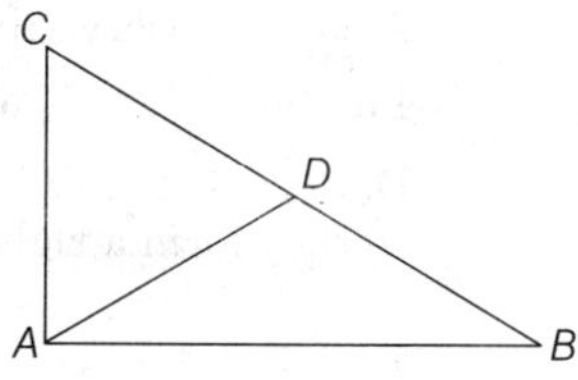

$$\mathbf{BD} = \mathbf{DC}$$

$$\mathbf{AB} = \mathbf{AD} + \mathbf{DB}$$

$$\mathbf{AC} = \mathbf{AD} + \mathbf{DC} = \mathbf{AD} + \mathbf{BD}$$

Since, $\angle BAC = 90°$ $\mathbf{AB} \perp \mathbf{AC}$

$$(\mathbf{AD} + \mathbf{DB}) \cdot (\mathbf{AD} + \mathbf{BD}) = 0$$

$$(\mathbf{AD} - \mathbf{BD}) \cdot (\mathbf{AD} + \mathbf{BD}) = 0$$

$$AD^2 - BD^2 = 0$$

$\therefore$ $$AD = BD \quad \text{also} \quad BD = DC$$

$\because$ D is mid-point of BC.

Thus, $|AD| = |BD| = |DC|$. Hence Proved.

Exercises

Objective Questions

Single Correct Option

1. Which one of the following is a scalar quantity?
(a) Dipole moment (b) Electric field (c) Acceleration (d) Work

2. Which one of the following is not a vector quantity?
(a) Torque (b) Displacement (c) Velocity (d) Speed

3. Which one is a vector quantity?
(a) Time (b) Temperature
(c) Magnetic flux (d) Magnetic field intensity

4. Minimum number of vectors of unequal magnitudes which can give zero resultant are
(a) two (b) three
(c) four (d) more than four

5. Which one of the following statement is **false**?
(a) A vector cannot be displaced from one point to another point
(b) Distance is a scalar quantity but displacement is a vector quantity
(c) Momentum, force and torque are vector quantities
(d) Mass, speed and energy are scalar quantities

6. A vector is not changed, if
(a) it is rotated through an arbitrary angle
(b) it is multiplied by an arbitrary scalar
(c) it is cross multiplied by a unit vector
(d) it is displaced parallel to itself

7. In a clockwise system,
(a) $\hat{\mathbf{j}} \times \hat{\mathbf{k}} = \hat{\mathbf{i}}$ (b) $\hat{\mathbf{k}} \cdot \hat{\mathbf{i}} = 1$ (c) $\hat{\mathbf{i}} \cdot \hat{\mathbf{i}} = 0$ (d) $\hat{\mathbf{j}} \times \hat{\mathbf{j}} = 1$

8. What is the dot product of two vectors of magnitudes 3 and 5, if angle between them is 60°?
(a) 5.2 (b) 7.5 (c) 8.4 (d) 8.6

9. The forces, which meet at one point but their lines of action do not lie in one plane, are called
(a) non-coplanar non-concurrent forces (b) non-coplanar concurrent forces
(c) coplanar concurrent forces (d) coplanar non-concurrent forces

10. A vector $\mathbf{A}$ points vertically upward and $\mathbf{B}$ points towards north. The vector product $\mathbf{A} \times \mathbf{B}$ is
(a) along west (b) along east
(c) zero (d) vertically downward

11. The magnitude of the vector product of two vectors $|\mathbf{A}|$ and $|\mathbf{B}|$ may be
(More than one correct options)
(a) greater than AB (b) equal to AB
(c) less than AB (d) equal to zero

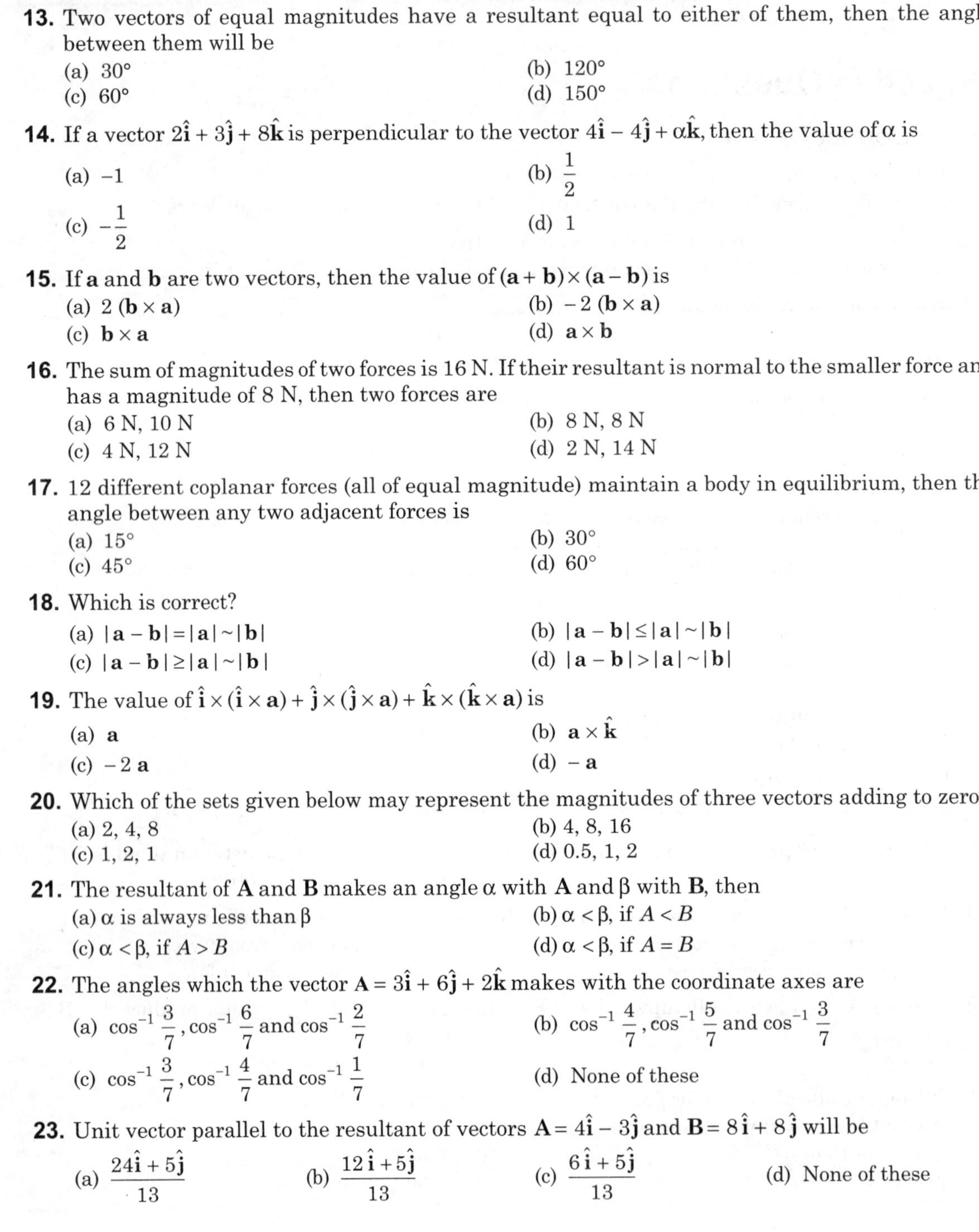

12. If a unit vector is represented by $0.5\,\hat{\mathbf{i}} + 0.8\,\hat{\mathbf{j}} + c\hat{\mathbf{k}}$, the value of c is

(a) 1 (b) $\sqrt{0.11}$
(c) $\sqrt{0.01}$ (d) 0.39

13. Two vectors of equal magnitudes have a resultant equal to either of them, then the angle between them will be

(a) 30° (b) 120°
(c) 60° (d) 150°

14. If a vector $2\hat{\mathbf{i}} + 3\hat{\mathbf{j}} + 8\hat{\mathbf{k}}$ is perpendicular to the vector $4\hat{\mathbf{i}} - 4\hat{\mathbf{j}} + \alpha\hat{\mathbf{k}}$, then the value of α is

(a) -1 (b) $\frac{1}{2}$
(c) $-\frac{1}{2}$ (d) 1

15. If $\mathbf{a}$ and $\mathbf{b}$ are two vectors, then the value of $(\mathbf{a} + \mathbf{b}) \times (\mathbf{a} - \mathbf{b})$ is

(a) $2\,(\mathbf{b} \times \mathbf{a})$ (b) $-2\,(\mathbf{b} \times \mathbf{a})$
(c) $\mathbf{b} \times \mathbf{a}$ (d) $\mathbf{a} \times \mathbf{b}$

16. The sum of magnitudes of two forces is 16 N. If their resultant is normal to the smaller force and has a magnitude of 8 N, then two forces are

(a) 6 N, 10 N (b) 8 N, 8 N
(c) 4 N, 12 N (d) 2 N, 14 N

17. 12 different coplanar forces (all of equal magnitude) maintain a body in equilibrium, then the angle between any two adjacent forces is

(a) 15° (b) 30°
(c) 45° (d) 60°

18. Which is correct?

(a) $|\mathbf{a} - \mathbf{b}| = |\mathbf{a}| \sim |\mathbf{b}|$ (b) $|\mathbf{a} - \mathbf{b}| \le |\mathbf{a}| \sim |\mathbf{b}|$
(c) $|\mathbf{a} - \mathbf{b}| \ge |\mathbf{a}| \sim |\mathbf{b}|$ (d) $|\mathbf{a} - \mathbf{b}| > |\mathbf{a}| \sim |\mathbf{b}|$

19. The value of $\hat{\mathbf{i}} \times (\hat{\mathbf{i}} \times \mathbf{a}) + \hat{\mathbf{j}} \times (\hat{\mathbf{j}} \times \mathbf{a}) + \hat{\mathbf{k}} \times (\hat{\mathbf{k}} \times \mathbf{a})$ is

(a) $\mathbf{a}$ (b) $\mathbf{a} \times \hat{\mathbf{k}}$
(c) $-2\,\mathbf{a}$ (d) $-\,\mathbf{a}$

20. Which of the sets given below may represent the magnitudes of three vectors adding to zero?

(a) 2, 4, 8 (b) 4, 8, 16
(c) 1, 2, 1 (d) 0.5, 1, 2

21. The resultant of $\mathbf{A}$ and $\mathbf{B}$ makes an angle α with $\mathbf{A}$ and β with $\mathbf{B}$, then

(a) α is always less than β (b) $\alpha < \beta$, if $A < B$
(c) $\alpha < \beta$, if $A > B$ (d) $\alpha < \beta$, if $A = B$

22. The angles which the vector $\mathbf{A} = 3\hat{\mathbf{i}} + 6\hat{\mathbf{j}} + 2\hat{\mathbf{k}}$ makes with the coordinate axes are

(a) $\cos^{-1}\frac{3}{7}, \cos^{-1}\frac{6}{7}$ and $\cos^{-1}\frac{2}{7}$ (b) $\cos^{-1}\frac{4}{7}, \cos^{-1}\frac{5}{7}$ and $\cos^{-1}\frac{3}{7}$
(c) $\cos^{-1}\frac{3}{7}, \cos^{-1}\frac{4}{7}$ and $\cos^{-1}\frac{1}{7}$ (d) None of these

23. Unit vector parallel to the resultant of vectors $\mathbf{A} = 4\hat{\mathbf{i}} - 3\hat{\mathbf{j}}$ and $\mathbf{B} = 8\hat{\mathbf{i}} + 8\hat{\mathbf{j}}$ will be

(a) $\frac{24\hat{\mathbf{i}} + 5\hat{\mathbf{j}}}{13}$ (b) $\frac{12\hat{\mathbf{i}} + 5\hat{\mathbf{j}}}{13}$ (c) $\frac{6\hat{\mathbf{i}} + 5\hat{\mathbf{j}}}{13}$ (d) None of these

24. If a vector **p** is making angles α, β and γ respectively with the X, Y and Z-axes, then $\sin^2\alpha + \sin^2\beta + \sin^2\gamma$ is equal to

(a) 0 (b) 1
(c) 2 (d) 3

25. Two vectors **A** and **B** are such that $\mathbf{A} + \mathbf{B} = \mathbf{C}$ and $A^2 + B^2 = C^2$. If θ is the angle between positive direction of **A** and **B**, then the correct statement is

(a) $\theta = \pi$ (b) $\theta = \frac{2\pi}{3}$
(c) $\theta = 0$ (d) $\theta = \frac{\pi}{2}$

26. If $|\mathbf{A} \times \mathbf{B}| = \sqrt{3}\mathbf{A} \cdot \mathbf{B}$, then the value of $|\mathbf{A} + \mathbf{B}|$ is

(a) $(A^2 + B^2 + AB)^{1/2}$ (b) $\left(A^2 + B^2 + \frac{AB}{\sqrt{3}}\right)^{1/2}$
(c) $(A + B)$ (d) $(A^2 + B^2 + \sqrt{3}AB)^{1/2}$

27. If the angle between the vectors **A** and **B** is θ, the value of the product $(\mathbf{B} \times \mathbf{A}) \cdot \mathbf{A}$ is equal to

(a) $BA^2 \cos\theta$ (b) $BA^2 \sin\theta$
(c) $BA^2 \sin\theta \cos\theta$ (d) zero

28. Given that $P = 12$, $Q = 5$ and $R = 13$ also $\mathbf{P} + \mathbf{Q} = \mathbf{R}$, then the angle between **P** and **Q** will be

(a) π (b) $\frac{\pi}{2}$
(c) zero (d) $\frac{\pi}{4}$

29. Given that $\mathbf{P} + \mathbf{Q} + \mathbf{R} = 0$. Two out of the three vectors are equal in magnitude. The magnitude of the third vector is $\sqrt{2}$ times that of the other two. Which of the following can be the angles between these vectors?

(a) 90°, 135°, 135° (b) 45°, 45°, 90°
(c) 30°, 60°, 90° (d) 45°, 90°, 135°

30. The angle between $\mathbf{P} + \mathbf{Q}$ and $\mathbf{P} - \mathbf{Q}$ will be

(a) 90° (b) between 0° and 180°
(c) 180° only (d) None of these

31. The resultant of two forces $3P$ and $2P$ is R. If the first force is doubled, then the resultant is also doubled. The angle between the two forces is

(a) 60° (b) 120°
(c) 30° (d) 135°

32. The resultant of two forces, one double the other in magnitude, is perpendicular to the smaller of the two forces. The angle between the two forces is

(a) 120° (b) 60°
(c) 90° (d) 150°

33. Three vectors satisfy the relation $\mathbf{A} \cdot \mathbf{B} = 0$ and $\mathbf{A} \cdot \mathbf{C} = 0$, then **A** is parallel or antiparallel to

(a) **C** (b) **B**
(c) $\mathbf{B} \times \mathbf{C}$ (d) $\mathbf{B} \cdot \mathbf{C}$

34. The sum of two vectors **A** and **B** is at right angles to their difference. Then,

(a) $A = B$ (b) $A = 2B$
(c) $B = 2A$ (d) **A** and **B** have the same direction

35. Let $\mathbf{C} = \mathbf{A} + \mathbf{B}$

(a) $|\mathbf{C}|$ is always greater than $|\mathbf{A}|$
(b) It is possible to have $|\mathbf{C}| < |\mathbf{A}|$ and $|\mathbf{C}| < |\mathbf{B}|$
(c) C is always equal to $A + B$
(d) C is never equal to $A + B$

36. Let the angle between two non-zero vectors **A** and **B** be 120° and its resultant be **C**.

(a) C must be equal to $|A - B|$
(b) C must be less than $|A - B|$
(c) C must be greater than $|A - B|$
(d) C may be equal to $|A - B|$

37. If the vectors $(\hat{\mathbf{i}} + \hat{\mathbf{j}} + \hat{\mathbf{k}})$ and $3\hat{\mathbf{i}}$ form two sides of a triangle, the area of the triangle is

(a) $\sqrt{3}$ unit
(b) $2\sqrt{3}$ unit
(c) $\frac{3}{\sqrt{2}}$ unit
(d) $3\sqrt{2}$ unit

38. A vector of length l is turned through an angle θ about its tail at origin. What is the change in the position vector of its head?

(a) $l \cos\theta/2$
(b) $2l \sin\theta/2$
(c) $2l \cos\theta/2$
(d) $l \sin\theta/2$

39. A cyclist is moving on a circular path with constant speed v. What is the change in its velocity after it has described an angle of 30°?

(a) $v\sqrt{2}$
(b) $\frac{v}{2}$
(c) $v\sqrt{3}$
(d) None of these

40. If $\mathbf{P} + \mathbf{Q} = \mathbf{R}$ and $|\mathbf{P}| = |\mathbf{Q}| = \sqrt{3}$ and $|\mathbf{R}| = 3$, then the angle between **P** and **Q** is

(a) $\pi/4$
(b) $\pi/6$
(c) $\pi/3$
(d) $\pi/2$

41. Given $\mathbf{A} = 3\hat{\mathbf{i}} + 4\hat{\mathbf{j}}$ and $\mathbf{B} = 6\hat{\mathbf{i}} + 8\hat{\mathbf{j}}$, which of the following statement is correct?

(a) $\mathbf{A} \times \mathbf{B} = 0$
(b) $\frac{|\mathbf{A}|}{|\mathbf{B}|} = \frac{1}{3}$
(c) $|\mathbf{A}| = 15$
(d) $\mathbf{A} \cdot \mathbf{B} = 48$

42. If three vectors along coordinate axis represent the adjacent sides of a cube of length b, then the unit vector along its diagonal passing through the origin will be

(a) $\frac{\hat{\mathbf{i}} + \hat{\mathbf{j}} + \hat{\mathbf{k}}}{\sqrt{2}}$
(b) $\frac{\hat{\mathbf{i}} + \hat{\mathbf{j}} + \hat{\mathbf{k}}}{\sqrt{36}}$
(c) $\hat{\mathbf{i}} + \hat{\mathbf{j}} + \hat{\mathbf{k}}$
(d) $\frac{\hat{\mathbf{i}} + \hat{\mathbf{j}} + \hat{\mathbf{k}}}{\sqrt{3}}$

43. If $\mathbf{A} = 3\hat{\mathbf{i}} + 4\hat{\mathbf{j}}$ and $\mathbf{B} = 7\hat{\mathbf{i}} + 24\hat{\mathbf{j}}$, the vector having the same magnitude as **B** and parallel to **A** is

(a) $5\hat{\mathbf{i}} + 20\hat{\mathbf{j}}$
(b) $15\hat{\mathbf{i}} + 10\hat{\mathbf{j}}$
(c) $20\hat{\mathbf{i}} + 15\hat{\mathbf{j}}$
(d) $15\hat{\mathbf{i}} + 20\hat{\mathbf{j}}$

44. If $\frac{|\mathbf{a} + \mathbf{b}|}{|\mathbf{a} - \mathbf{b}|} = 1$, then angle between **a** and **b** is

(a) 0°
(b) 45°
(c) 90°
(d) 60°

45. What is the value of $(\mathbf{A} + \mathbf{B}) \cdot (\mathbf{A} \times \mathbf{B})$?

(a) 0
(b) $A^2 - B^2$
(c) $A^2 + B^2 + 2AB$
(d) None of these

46. For the figure,

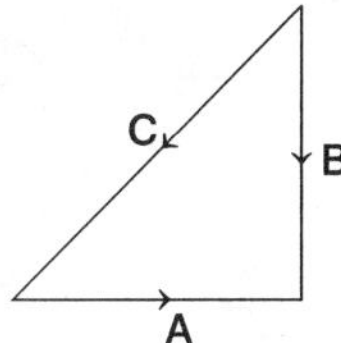

(a) $\mathbf{A}+\mathbf{B}=\mathbf{C}$ (b) $\mathbf{B}+\mathbf{C}=\mathbf{A}$
(c) $\mathbf{C}+\mathbf{A}=\mathbf{B}$ (d) $\mathbf{C}+\mathbf{A}+\mathbf{B}=0$

47. If **a** and **b** are two units vectors inclined at an angle of 60° to each other, then
(a) $|\mathbf{a}+\mathbf{b}|>1$ (b) $|\mathbf{a}+\mathbf{b}|<1$
(c) $|\mathbf{a}-\mathbf{b}|>1$ (d) $|\mathbf{a}-\mathbf{b}|<1$

48. If **A** and **B** are two vectors such that $|\mathbf{A}+\mathbf{B}| = 2|\mathbf{A}-\mathbf{B}|$, the angle between vectors **A** and **B** is
(a) 45° (b) 60°
(c) 30° (d) data insufficient

49. Given that $P = Q = R$. If $\mathbf{P}+\mathbf{Q}=\mathbf{R}$, then the angle between **P** and **R** is θ_1. If $\mathbf{P}+\mathbf{Q}+\mathbf{R}=0$, then the angle between **P** and **R** is θ_2. What is the relation between θ_1 and θ_2?
(a) $\theta_1=\theta_2$ (b) $\theta_1=\dfrac{\theta_2}{2}$
(c) $\theta_1=2\theta_2$ (d) None of these

50. Two vectors **A** and **B** have equal magnitudes. If magnitude of $\mathbf{A}+\mathbf{B}$ is equal to n times the magnitude of $\mathbf{A}-\mathbf{B}$, then the angle between **A** and **B** is
(a) $\cos^{-1}\left(\dfrac{n-1}{n+1}\right)$ (b) $\cos^{-1}\left(\dfrac{n^2-1}{n^2+1}\right)$
(c) $\sin^{-1}\left(\dfrac{n-1}{n+1}\right)$ (d) $\sin^{-1}\left(\dfrac{n^2-1}{n^2+1}\right)$

51. The resultant of **A** and **B** is $\mathbf{R}_1$. On reversing the vector **B**, the resultant becomes $\mathbf{R}_2$. What is the value of $R_1^2+R_2^2$?
(a) A^2+B^2 (b) A^2-B^2 (c) $2(A^2+B^2)$ (d) $2(A^2-B^2)$

52. Figure shown *ABCDEF* as a regular hexagon. What is the value of
AB + **AC** + **AD** + **AE** + **AF** ?

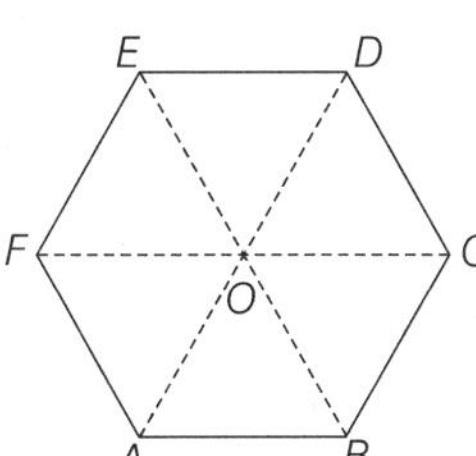

(a) **AO** (b) 2**AO** (c) 4**AO** (d) 6**AO**

53. If **A** is a unit vector in a given direction, then the value of $\hat{\mathbf{A}}\cdot\dfrac{d\hat{\mathbf{A}}}{dt}$ is
(a) 0 (b) 1 (c) $\dfrac{1}{2}$ (d) 2

54. Figure shows three vectors **p**, **q** and **r**, where C is the mid-point of AB. Then, which of the following relation is correct?

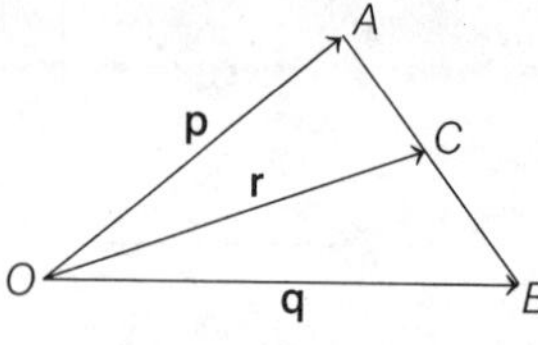

(a) $\mathbf{p}+\mathbf{q}=2\mathbf{r}$ (b) $\mathbf{p}+\mathbf{q}=\mathbf{r}$ (c) $\mathbf{p}-\mathbf{q}=2\mathbf{r}$ (d) $\mathbf{p}-\mathbf{q}=\mathbf{r}$

55. A vector **a** is turned without a change in its length through a small angle $\Delta\theta$. The value of $|\Delta\mathbf{a}|$ and Δa are respectively.

(a) $0, a\Delta\theta$ (b) $a\Delta\theta, 0$ (c) $0, 0$ (d) $a\Delta\theta, a\Delta\theta$

56. In the diagram shown in figure,

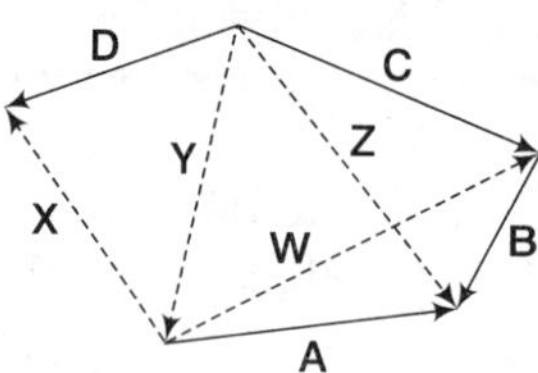

(a) $\mathbf{X}=\mathbf{A}+\mathbf{B}-\mathbf{C}+\mathbf{D}$ (b) $\mathbf{Y}=\mathbf{B}+\mathbf{C}+\mathbf{A}$
(c) $\mathbf{Z}=\mathbf{B}+\mathbf{C}$ (d) $\mathbf{W}=\mathbf{A}+\mathbf{B}$

57. Given that $\mathbf{A}+\mathbf{B}=\mathbf{C}$ and that **C** is perpendicular to **A** further if $|\mathbf{A}|=|\mathbf{C}|$, then what is the angle between **A** and **B**?

(a) $\frac{2\pi}{5}$ (b) $\frac{5\pi}{6}$ (c) $\frac{3\pi}{4}$ (d) $\frac{2\pi}{3}$

58. If $\mathbf{a}_1$ and $\mathbf{a}_2$ are two non-collinear unit vectors and if $|\mathbf{a}_1+\mathbf{a}_2|=\sqrt{3}$, then the value of $(\mathbf{a}_1-\mathbf{a}_2)\cdot(2\mathbf{a}_1+\mathbf{a}_2)$ is

(a) 2 (b) $\frac{3}{2}$ (c) $\frac{1}{2}$ (d) 1

59. If $\mathbf{a}+\mathbf{b}+\mathbf{c}=0$. The angle between **a** and **b**; and **b** and **c** are 150° and 120°, respectively. Then, the magnitude of vectors **a**, **b** and **c** are in ratio of

(a) 1 : 2 : 3 (b) $1:2:\sqrt{3}$ (c) $\sqrt{3}:2:1$ (d) $2:\sqrt{3}:1$

Match the Columns

1. Column I shows some vector equations. Match Column I with the value of angle between **A** and **B** given in Column II.

Column I	Column II
(a) $\lvert\mathbf{A}\times\mathbf{B}\rvert=\lvert\mathbf{A}\cdot\mathbf{B}\rvert$	(p) zero
(b) $\mathbf{A}\times\mathbf{B}=\mathbf{B}\times\mathbf{A}$	(q) $\frac{\pi}{2}$
(c) $\lvert\mathbf{A}+\mathbf{B}\rvert=\lvert\mathbf{A}-\mathbf{B}\rvert$	(r) $\frac{\pi}{4}$
(d) $\mathbf{A}+\mathbf{B}=\mathbf{C}$ and $A+B=C$	(s) $\frac{3\pi}{4}$

Subjective Questions

1. Two vectors have magnitudes 3 unit and 4 unit respectively. What should be the angle between them if the magnitude of the resultant is (a) 1 unit, (b) 5 unit and (c) 7 unit.

2. The work done by a force **F** during a displacement **r** is given by $\mathbf{F} \cdot \mathbf{r}$. Suppose a force of 12 N acts on a particle in vertically upward direction and the particle is displaced through 2.0 m in vertically downward direction. Find the work done by the force during this displacement.

3. If **A**, **B**, **C** are mutually perpendicular, then show that $\mathbf{C} \times (\mathbf{A} \times \mathbf{B}) = 0$.

4. Prove that $\mathbf{A} \cdot (\mathbf{A} \times \mathbf{B}) = 0$.

5. Find the resultant of the three vectors shown in figure.

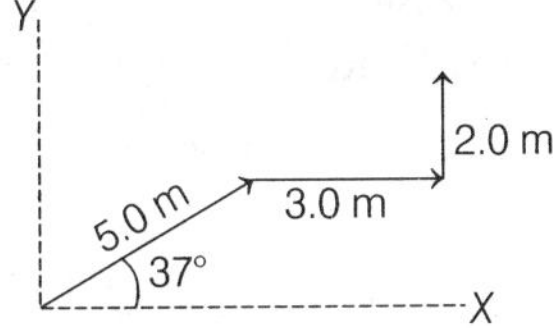

6. Give an example for which $\mathbf{A} \cdot \mathbf{B} = \mathbf{C} \cdot \mathbf{B}$ but $\mathbf{A} \neq \mathbf{C}$.

7. Obtain the angle between $\mathbf{A} + \mathbf{B}$ and $\mathbf{A} - \mathbf{B}$, if $\mathbf{A} = 2\hat{\mathbf{i}} + 3\hat{\mathbf{j}}$ and $\mathbf{B} = \hat{\mathbf{i}} - 2\hat{\mathbf{j}}$.

8. Deduce the condition for the vectors $2\hat{\mathbf{i}} + 3\hat{\mathbf{j}} - 4\hat{\mathbf{k}}$ and $3\hat{\mathbf{i}} - a\hat{\mathbf{j}} + b\hat{\mathbf{k}}$ to be parallel.

9. Find the area of the parallelogram whose sides are represented by $2\hat{\mathbf{i}} + 4\hat{\mathbf{j}} - 6\hat{\mathbf{k}}$ and $\hat{\mathbf{i}} + 2\hat{\mathbf{k}}$.

10. If $\mathbf{A} = 2\hat{\mathbf{i}} - 3\hat{\mathbf{j}} + 7\hat{\mathbf{k}}$, $\mathbf{B} = \hat{\mathbf{i}} + 2\hat{\mathbf{k}}$ and $\mathbf{C} = \hat{\mathbf{j}} - \hat{\mathbf{k}}$, then find $\mathbf{A} \cdot (\mathbf{B} \times \mathbf{C})$.

11. The x and y-components of vector **A** are 4 m and 6 m, respectively. The x and y-components of vector $\mathbf{A} + \mathbf{B}$ are 10 m and 9 m, respectively. Calculate for the vector **B** the following :

(a) its x and y-components

(b) its length

(c) the angle it makes with x-axis

12. Three vectors which are coplanar with respect to a certain rectangular coordinate system are given by $\mathbf{a} = 4\hat{\mathbf{i}} - \hat{\mathbf{j}}$, $\mathbf{b} = -3\hat{\mathbf{i}} + 2\hat{\mathbf{j}}$ and $\mathbf{c} = -3\hat{\mathbf{j}}$

Find

(a) $\mathbf{a} + \mathbf{b} + \mathbf{c}$ (b) $\mathbf{a} + \mathbf{b} - \mathbf{c}$ (c) the angle between $\mathbf{a} + \mathbf{b} + \mathbf{c}$ and $\mathbf{a} + \mathbf{b} - \mathbf{c}$.

13. Let **A** and **B** be the two vectors of magnitude 10 unit each. If they are inclined to the x-axis at angles 30° and 60° respectively, find the resultant.

14. The resultant of vectors **OA** and **OB** is perpendicular to **OA** as shown in figure. Find the angle AOB.

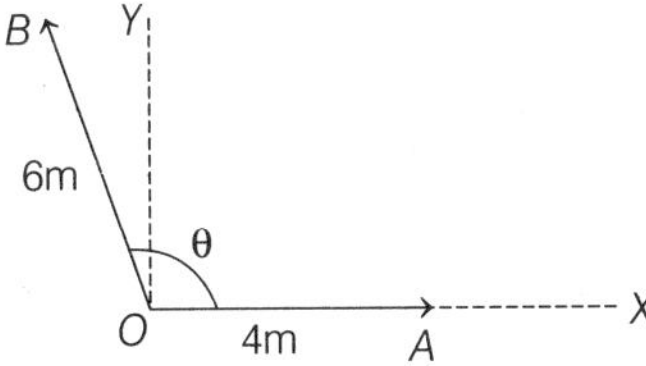

15. If two vectors are $\mathbf{A} = 2\hat{\mathbf{i}} + \hat{\mathbf{j}} - \hat{\mathbf{k}}$ and $\mathbf{B} = \hat{\mathbf{j}} - 4\hat{\mathbf{k}}$. By calculation, prove that $\mathbf{A} \times \mathbf{B}$ is perpendicular to both **A** and **B**.

16. Four forces of magnitude P, $2P$, $3P$ and $4P$ act along the four sides of a square $ABCD$ in cyclic order. Use the vector method to find the magnitude of resultant force.

17. Prove by the method of vectors that in a triangle $\frac{a}{\sin A} = \frac{b}{\sin B} = \frac{c}{\sin C}$

18. When two non-zero vectors **a** and **b** are perpendicular to each other, their magnitude of resultant is R. When they are opposite to each other, their resultant is of magnitude $\frac{R}{\sqrt{2}}$. Find the value of $\left(\frac{a}{b} + \frac{b}{a}\right)$.

19. The resultant of two vectors **a** and **b** has magnitude 2 N. The magnitude of **a** is $2\sqrt{3}$ N and makes an angle of 30° with the resultant. Find the magnitude of **b** (in newton).

20. Five vectors have equal magnitudes of 4 unit each angle between two sucessive vectors is 72°.
(a) Find resultant of these 5 vectors.
(b) If one vector is removed, then find resultant of remaining four vectors.

21. Resultant of two vectors of 5 units and 8 units is making an angle of 53° from first vector.
(a) Find angle between two vectors.
(b) Find magnitude of their resultant.

22. **A** and **B** have magnitudes 4 units and 5 units. Find magnitude and direction of **A** – **B**. If angle between two vectors is
(a) 0°
(b) 180°
(c) 150°

Answers

Introductory Exercise 5.1

1. $0°$ 2. $180°, 0.6$
3. (a) 14 units (b) 2 units (c) $2\sqrt{37}$ units (d) $2\sqrt{13}$ units (e) 10 units
4. (a) 2 units (b) 14 units (c) $2\sqrt{13}$ units (d) $2\sqrt{37}$ units (e) 10 units
5. $90°$

Introductory Exercise 5.2

1. $A = 5\sqrt{2}$ units, $\cos\alpha = \frac{3}{5\sqrt{2}}, \cos\beta = \frac{-4}{5\sqrt{2}}$ and $\cos\gamma = \frac{1}{\sqrt{2}}$
2. $F_x = -5$ N, $F_y = -5\sqrt{3}$ N
3. $\sqrt{10}$ units
4. (a) $180°$ (b) $90°$ (c) $90°$ (d) $135°$

Introductory Exercise 5.3

1. True
2. (a) $24\,\hat{\mathbf{j}}$ (b) -12 (c) zero
3. (a) 8 units (b) 4 units (c) zero (d) -4 units (e) -8 units
4. $(6\hat{\mathbf{i}} + 12\hat{\mathbf{j}} - 12\hat{\mathbf{k}})$

Exercises

Single Correct Option

1. (d)	2. (d)	3. (d)	4. (b)	5. (a)	6. (d)	7. (a)	8. (b)	9. (b)	10. (a)
11. (b,c,d)	12. (b)	13. (b)	14. (b)	15. (a)	16. (a)	17. (b)	18. (c)	19. (c)	20. (c)
21. (c)	22. (a)	23. (b)	24. (c)	25. (d)	26. (a)	27. (d)	28. (b)	29. (a)	30. (b)
31. (b)	32. (a)	33. (c)	34. (a)	35. (b)	36. (c)	37. (c)	38. (b)	39. (d)	40. (c)
41. (a)	42. (d)	43. (d)	44. (c)	45. (a)	46. (c)	47. (a)	48. (d)	49. (b)	50. (b)
51. (c)	52. (d)	53. (a)	54. (a)	55. (b)	56. (c)	57. (c)	58. (c)	59. (c)	

Match the Columns

1. (a) $\rightarrow$ r,s (b) $\rightarrow$ p (c) $\rightarrow$ q (d) $\rightarrow$ p

Subjective Questions

1. (a) $180°$ (b) $90°$ (c) $0°$
2. -24 J
5. $\sqrt{74}$ m at angle $\tan^{-1}\left(\frac{5}{7}\right)$ from x-axis towards y-axis
6. See the hints
7. $\cos^{-1}\left(\frac{4}{\sqrt{65}}\right)$
8. $a = -4.5, b = -6$
9. Area = 13.4 units
10. zero
11. (a) 6m, 3m (b) $3\sqrt{5}$ m (c) $\theta = \tan^{-1}\left(\frac{1}{2}\right)$
12. (a) $\hat{\mathbf{i}} - 2\hat{\mathbf{j}}$ (b) $\hat{\mathbf{i}} + 4\hat{\mathbf{j}}$ (c) $\cos^{-1}\left(\frac{-7}{\sqrt{85}}\right)$
13. $20\cos 15°$ unit at $45°$ with x-axis.
14. $\cos^{-1}\left(\frac{-2}{3}\right)$
16. $2\sqrt{2}\,P$
18. 4
19. 2
20. (a) 0 (b) 4 units
21. (a) $83°$ (b) $(3 + 4\sqrt{3})$ units
22. (a) 1 unit towards $-\mathbf{B}$. (b) 9 units towards $\mathbf{A}$ or $-\mathbf{B}$
    (c) $\sqrt{41 + 20\sqrt{3}}$ at an angle of $\alpha = \tan^{-1}\left[\frac{2.5}{4 + 2.5\sqrt{3}}\right]$ from $\mathbf{A}$ towards $-\mathbf{B}$.

6

Kinematics

6.1 Introduction to Mechanics and Kinematics

Mechanics is the branch of physics which deals with the motion of particles or bodies in space and time. Position and motion of a body can be determined only with respect to other bodies. Motion of the body involves position and time. For practical purposes a coordinate system, e.g. the cartesian system is fixed to the reference body and position of the body is determined with respect to this reference body. For calculation of time generally clock is used.

Kinematics is the branch of mechanics which deals with the motion regardless of the causes producing it. The study of causes of motion is called **dynamics.**

6.2 Few General Points of Motion

Kinematics is the branch of mechanics which deals with the motion regardless of the causes producing it.

1. Direction of velocity is in the direction of motion. But direction of acceleration is not necessarily in the direction of motion. Direction of acceleration is in the direction of net force acting on the body. For example, if we say that a body is moving due east, it means velocity of the body is towards east. From the above statement, we cannot find the direction of acceleration.
2. Motion in a straight line is called a one-dimensional motion.
3. Motion which is not one dimensional is called a curvilinear motion. Circular motion and projectile motion are the examples of curvilinear motion.

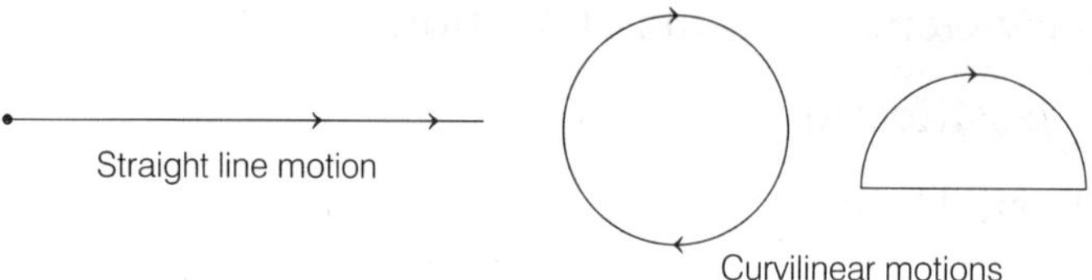

Fig. 6.1

4. Direction of velocity at any point on a curvilinear path is tangential to the path. But with direction of acceleration there is no such condition. As we have stated earlier also, it is in the direction of net force. For example, in the figure shown below a particle is moving on a curvilinear path.

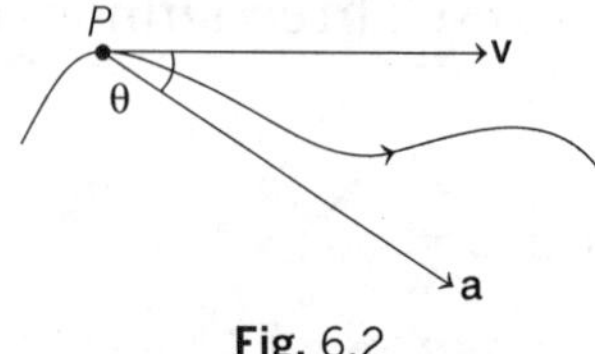

Fig. 6.2

At point P, velocity of the particle is tangential to the path but acceleration is making an angle θ with velocity. If θ is acute ($0° \le \theta < 90°$), then speed (which is also magnitude of velocity vector) of the particle increases. If θ is obtuse ($90° < \theta \le 180°$), then speed of the particle decreases.

Note $\theta = 90°$ *is a special case when speed remains constant. This point we shall discuss in our later discussions.*

Example 6.1 *Velocity of a particle at some instant is* $\mathbf{v} = (3\hat{\mathbf{i}} + 4\hat{\mathbf{j}} + 5\hat{\mathbf{k}})$ m/s. *Find speed of the particle at this instant.*

Solution Magnitude of velocity vector at any instant of time is the speed of particle. Hence,

$$\text{Speed} = v \text{ or } |\mathbf{v}| = \sqrt{(3)^2 + (4)^2 + (5)^2} = 5\sqrt{2} \text{ m/s}$$ **Ans.**

Example 6.2 *"A lift is ascending with decreasing speed". What are the directions of velocity and acceleration of the lift at the given instant.*

Solution (i) Direction of motion is the direction of velocity. Lift is ascending (means it is moving upwards). So, direction of velocity is upwards.

(ii) Speed of lift is decreasing. So, direction of acceleration should be in opposite direction or it should be downwards.

INTRODUCTORY EXERCISE 6.1

1. "A lift is descending with increasing speed". What are the directions of velocity and acceleration in the given statement?
2. Velocity and acceleration of a particle at some instant are

$$\mathbf{v} = (3\hat{\mathbf{i}} - 4\hat{\mathbf{j}} + 2\hat{\mathbf{k}}) \text{ m/s} \quad \text{and} \quad \mathbf{a} = (2\hat{\mathbf{i}} + \hat{\mathbf{j}} - 2\hat{\mathbf{k}}) \text{ m/s}^2$$

(a) What is the value of dot product of **v** and **a** at the given instant?
(b) What is the angle between **v** and **a**, acute, obtuse or 90°?
(c) At the given instant, whether speed of the particle is increasing, decreasing or constant?

6.3 Classification of Motion

A motion can be classified in following two ways :

First According to this way, a motion can be either

(i) One dimensional (1-D)
(ii) Two dimensional (2-D)
(iii) Three dimensional (3-D)

In one dimensional motion, particle (or a body) moves in a straight line, in two dimensional motion, it moves in a plane and in three dimensional motion body moves in space.

Second According to this way, a motion can be either

(i) Uniform motion
(ii) Uniformly accelerated
(iii) Non-uniformly accelerated.

In uniform motion, velocity of the particle is constant and in non-uniformly accelerated motion acceleration of the particle is not constant.

Equations, $\mathbf{v} = \mathbf{u} + \mathbf{a}t$ etc. can be applied directly, only for uniformly accelerated motion. If the motion is one dimensional then these equations can be written as, $v = u + at$ etc. For solving a problem of non-uniform acceleration, either integration or differentiation is required.

Extra Points to Remember

In uniform motion, velocity of particle is constant, therefore acceleration is zero. Velocity is constant, means its magnitude (or speed) is constant and direction of velocity is fixed. So, the particle moves in a straight line. Hence, it is always one dimensional motion.

Example 6.3 *Give two examples of two dimensional motion.*

Solution Two dimensional motion takes place in a plane. Its two examples are circular motion and projectile motion.

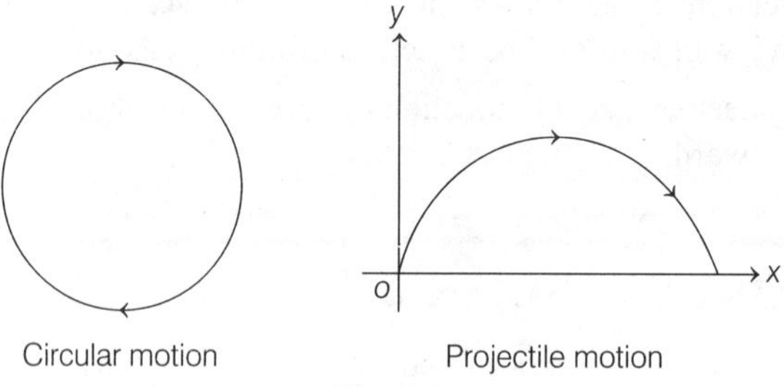

Fig. 6.3

Normally, the plane of circular motion is either horizontal or vertical and plane of projectile motion is vertical.

Example 6.4 *Velocity of a particle is* $\mathbf{v} = (2\hat{\mathbf{i}} + 3\hat{\mathbf{j}} - 4\hat{\mathbf{k}})$ *m/s and its acceleration is zero. State whether it is 1-D, 2-D or 3-D motion?*

Solution Since, acceleration of the particle is zero. Therefore, it is uniform motion or motion in a straight line. So, it is one dimensional motion.

Example 6.5 *Projectile motion is a two dimensional motion with constant acceleration. Is this statement true or false?*

Solution True. Projectile motion takes place in a plane. So, it is two dimensional. For small heights, its acceleration is constant (= acceleration due to gravity). Therefore, it is a two dimensional motion with constant acceleration.

INTRODUCTORY EXERCISE 6.2

1. Velocity and acceleration of a particle are

$$\mathbf{v} = (2\hat{\mathbf{i}} - 4\hat{\mathbf{j}})\ \text{m/s}$$

and

$$\mathbf{a} = (-2\hat{\mathbf{i}} + 4\hat{\mathbf{j}})\ \text{m/s}^2$$

Which type of motion is this ?

2. Velocity and acceleration of a particle are

$$\mathbf{v} = (2\hat{\mathbf{i}})\ \text{m/s}$$

and

$$\mathbf{a} = (4t\hat{\mathbf{i}} + t^2\hat{\mathbf{j}})\ \text{m/s}^2$$

where, t is the time. Which type of motion is this ?

3. In the above question, can we use $\mathbf{v} = \mathbf{u} + \mathbf{a}t$ equation directly?

6.4 Basic Definitions

Position Vector and Displacement Vector

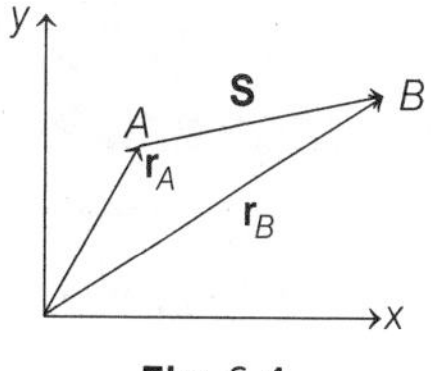

Fig. 6.4

If coordinates of point A are (x_1, y_1, z_1) and B are (x_2, y_2, z_2). Then, position vector of A

$$= \mathbf{r}_A = \mathbf{OA} = x_1\hat{\mathbf{i}} + y_1\hat{\mathbf{j}} + z_1\hat{\mathbf{k}}$$

Position vector of $B = \mathbf{r}_B = \mathbf{OB} = x_2\hat{\mathbf{i}} + y_2\hat{\mathbf{j}} + z_2\hat{\mathbf{k}}$

and

$$\mathbf{AB} = \mathbf{OB} - \mathbf{OA} = \mathbf{r}_B - \mathbf{r}_A$$
$$= (x_2 - x_1)\,\hat{\mathbf{i}} + (y_2 - y_1)\,\hat{\mathbf{j}} + (z_2 - z_1)\,\hat{\mathbf{k}}$$

Distance and Displacement

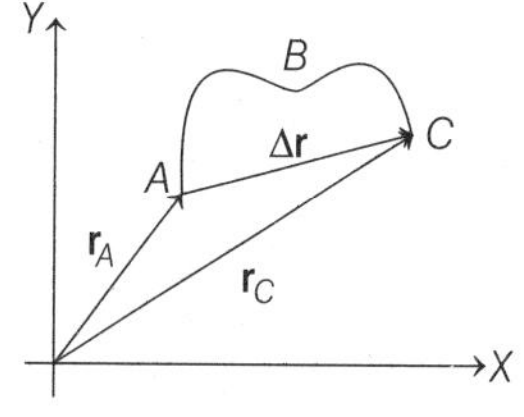

Fig. 6.5

Distance is the actual path length covered by a moving particle or body in a given time interval, while displacement is the change in position vector, i.e. a vector joining initial to final positions. If a particle moves from A to C (Fig. 6.5) through a path ABC. Then, distance travelled is the actual path length ABC, while the displacement is

$$\mathbf{s} = \Delta\mathbf{r} = \mathbf{r}_C - \mathbf{r}_A$$

If a particle moves in a straight line without change in direction, the magnitude of displacement is equal to the distance travelled, otherwise, it is always less than it. Thus,

$$|\text{displacement}| \le \text{distance}$$

Average Speed and Average Velocity

The average speed of a particle in a given time interval is defined as the ratio of total distance travelled to the total time take.

The average velocity is defined as the ratio of total displacement to the total time taken.

Thus, $$v_{av} = \text{average speed} = \frac{\text{total distance}}{\text{total time}}$$

and $$\mathbf{v}_{av} = \text{average velocity} = \frac{\text{total displacement}}{\text{total time}}$$

$$= \frac{\mathbf{S}}{\Delta t} \quad \text{or} \quad \frac{\mathbf{S}}{t} \quad \text{or} \quad \frac{\Delta\mathbf{r}}{\Delta t} = \frac{\mathbf{r}_f - \mathbf{r}_i}{\Delta t}$$

Here, $\mathbf{r}_f$ = final position vector and $\mathbf{r}_i$ = initial position vector

Instantaneous Velocity and Instantaneous Speed

Instantaneous velocity and instantaneous speed are defined at a particular instant and are given by

$$\mathbf{v}_i \text{ or simply } \mathbf{v} = \lim_{\Delta t \to 0} \frac{\Delta\mathbf{s}}{\Delta t} \quad \text{or} \quad \frac{d\mathbf{s}}{dt} \quad \text{or} \quad \frac{d\mathbf{r}}{dt}$$

Here, $\mathbf{r}$ is position vector of the body (or particle) at a general time t.

Magnitude of instantaneous velocity at any instant is called its instantaneous speed at that instant. Thus,

$$\text{Instantaneous speed} = v = |\mathbf{v}| = \left|\frac{ds}{dt} \text{ or } \frac{d\mathbf{r}}{dt}\right|$$

Average and Instantaneous Acceleration

Average acceleration is defined as the ratio of change in velocity, i.e. $\Delta\mathbf{v}$ to the time interval Δt in which this change occurs. Hence,

$$\mathbf{a}_{\text{av}} = \frac{\Delta\mathbf{v}}{\Delta t} = \frac{\mathbf{v}_f - \mathbf{v}_i}{\Delta t}$$

The instantaneous acceleration is defined at a particular instant and is given by

$$\mathbf{a} = \lim_{\Delta t \to 0} \frac{\Delta\mathbf{v}}{\Delta t} = \frac{d\mathbf{v}}{dt}$$

Here, $\mathbf{v}_f$ = final velocity and $\mathbf{v}_i$ = initial velocity vector

Extra Points to Remember

- If motion is one dimensional (let along x-axis) then all vector quantities (displacement, velocity and acceleration) can be treated like scalars by assuming one direction as positive and the other as negative. In this case, all vectors along positive direction are given positive sign and the vectors in negative direction are given negative sign.
- For example, displacement, instantaneous velocity, instantaneous acceleration, average velocity and average acceleration in this case be written as

$$s = \Delta r = r_f - r_i \quad \text{or} \quad x_f - x_i$$

$$v = \frac{ds}{dt} \quad \text{or} \quad \frac{dx}{dt} \quad \text{or} \quad a = \frac{dv}{dt}$$

$$v_{\text{av}} = \frac{\Delta s}{\Delta t} = \frac{r_f - r_i}{\Delta t} = \frac{x_f - x_i}{\Delta t} \quad \text{and} \quad a_{\text{av}} = \frac{\Delta v}{\Delta t} = \frac{v_f - v_i}{\Delta t}$$

Example 6.6 *In one second, a particle goes from point A to point B moving in a semicircle (Fig. 6.6). Find the magnitude of the average velocity.*

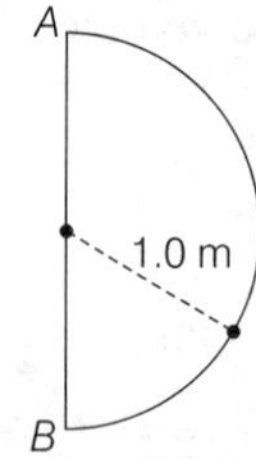

Fig. 6.6

Solution

$$|\mathbf{v}_{\text{av}}| = \frac{AB}{\Delta t} \text{ m/s}$$

$$= \frac{2.0}{1.0} \text{ m/s} = 2 \text{ m/s}$$

Example 6.7 *A table is given below of a particle moving along x-axis. In the table, speed of particle at different time intervals is shown.*

Table 6.1

Time interval (in sec)	**Speed of particle** (in m/s)
0 – 2	2
2 – 5	3
5 – 10	4
10 – 15	2

Find total distance travelled by the particle and its average speed.

Solution Distance = speed × time

$\therefore$ Total distance $= (2 \times 2) + (3)(3) + (5)(4) + (5)(2) = 43$ m

Total time taken is 15 s. Hence,

$$\text{Average speed} = \frac{\text{Total distance}}{\text{Total time}}$$

$$= \frac{43}{15} = 2.87 \text{ m/s}$$

Example 6.8 *A particle is moving along x-axis. Its X-coordinate varies with time as,*

$$X = 2t^2 + 4t - 6$$

Here, X is in metres and t in seconds. Find average velocity between the time interval $t = 0$ to $t = 2$ s.

Solution In 1-D motion, average velocity can be written as

$$v_{av} = \frac{\Delta s}{\Delta t} = \frac{X_f - X_i}{\Delta t} = \frac{X_{2\,\text{sec}} - X_{0\,\text{sec}}}{2 - 0}$$

$$= \frac{[2(2)^2 + 4(2) - 6] - [2(0)^2 + 4(0) - 6]}{2}$$

$$= 8 \text{ m/s}$$ **Ans.**

Example 6.9 *A particle is moving in x-y plane. Its x and y co-ordinates vary with time as*

$$x = 2t^2 \text{ and } y = t^3$$

Here, x and y are in metres and t in seconds. Find average acceleration between a time interval from $t = 0$ *to* $t = 2$ *s.*

Solution The position vector of the particle at any time t can be given as

$$\mathbf{r} = x\hat{\mathbf{i}} + y\hat{\mathbf{j}} = 2t^2\hat{\mathbf{i}} + t^3\hat{\mathbf{j}}$$

The instantaneous velocity is $\mathbf{v} = \frac{d\mathbf{r}}{dt} = (4t\hat{\mathbf{i}} + 3t^2\hat{\mathbf{j}})$

Now, $$\mathbf{a}_{av} = \frac{\Delta \mathbf{v}}{\Delta t} = \frac{\mathbf{v}_f - \mathbf{v}_i}{\Delta t} = \frac{\mathbf{v}_{2\,sec} - \mathbf{v}_{0\,sec}}{2-0}$$

$$= \frac{[(4)(2)\hat{\mathbf{i}} + (3)(2)^2\hat{\mathbf{j}}] - [(4)(0)\hat{\mathbf{i}} + (3)(0)^2\hat{\mathbf{j}}]}{2}$$

$$= (4\hat{\mathbf{i}} + 6\hat{\mathbf{j}})\ \text{m/s}^2$$ **Ans.**

INTRODUCTORY EXERCISE 6.3

1. Average speed is always equal to magnitude of average velocity. Is this statement true or false?
2. When a particle moves with constant velocity its average velocity, its instantaneous velocity and its speed all are equal. Is this statement true or false?
3. A stone is released from an elevator going up with an acceleration of $g/2$. What is the acceleration of the stone just after release?
4. A clock has its second hand 2.0 cm long. Find the average speed and modulus of average velocity of the tip of the second hand in 15 s.
5. (a) Is it possible to be accelerating if you are travelling at constant speed?
   (b) Is it possible to move on a curved path with zero acceleration, constant acceleration, variable acceleration?
6. A particle is moving in a circle of radius 4 cm with constant speed of 1 cm/s. Find
   (a) time period of the particle.
   (b) average speed, average velocity and average acceleration in a time interval from $t = 0$ to $t = T/4$. Here, T is the time period of the particle. Give only their magnitudes.

6.5 Uniform Motion

As we have discussed earlier also, in uniform motion velocity of the particle is constant and acceleration is zero. Velocity is constant means its magnitude (called speed) is constant and direction is fixed. Therefore, motion is 1-D in same direction. If velocity is along positive direction, then displacement is also along positive direction. Therefore, distance travelled (d) is equal to the displacement (s). If velocity is along negative direction then displacement is also negative and distance travelled in this case is the magnitude of displacement. Equations involved in this motion are

(i) Velocity (may be positive or negative) = constant
(ii) Speed, v = constant
(iii) Acceleration = 0
(iv) Displacement (may be positive or negative) = velocity × time
(v) Distance = speed × time or $\boxed{d = vt}$
(vi) Distance and speed are always positive, whereas displacement and velocity may be positive or negative.

Example 6.10 *A particle travels first half of the total distance with constant speed v_1 and second half with constant speed v_2. Find the average speed during the complete journey.*

Solution

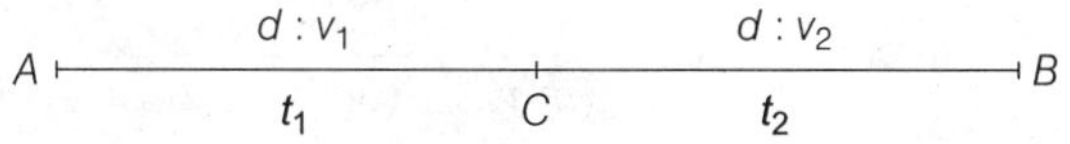

A — $d : v_1$, t_1 — C — $d : v_2$, t_2 — B

Fig. 6.7

$$t_1 = \frac{d}{v_1} \quad \text{and} \quad t_2 = \frac{d}{v_2}$$

$$\text{Average speed} = \frac{\text{total distance}}{\text{total time}} = \frac{d+d}{t_1+t_2} = \frac{2d}{(d/v_1)+(d/v_2)} = \frac{2v_1v_2}{v_1+v_2}$$ **Ans.**

Example 6.11 *A particle travels first half of the total time with speed v_1 and second half time with speed v_2. Find the average speed during the complete journey.*

Solution

A — $t : v_1$, d_1 — C — $t : v_2$, d_2 — B

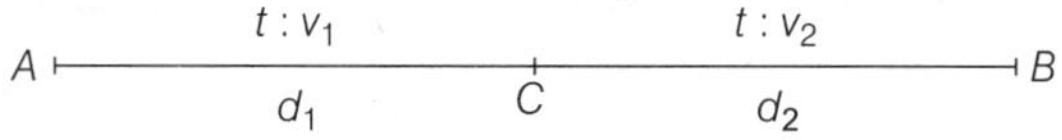

Fig. 6.8

$$d_1 = v_1 t \quad \text{and} \quad d_2 = v_2 t$$

$$\text{Average speed} = \frac{\text{total distance}}{\text{total time}} = \frac{d_1+d_2}{t+t} = \frac{v_1 t + v_2 t}{2t} = \frac{v_1+v_2}{2}$$ **Ans.**

Example 6.12 *A particle travels first half of the total distance with speed v_1. In second half distance, constant speed in $\frac{1}{3}$ rd time is v_2 and in remaining $\frac{2}{3}$ rd time constant speed is v_3. Find average speed during the complete journey.*

Solution

A — $d : v_1$ — C — $\frac{t}{3}, v_2$ — D — $\frac{2t}{3}, v_3$ — B; C to B: d

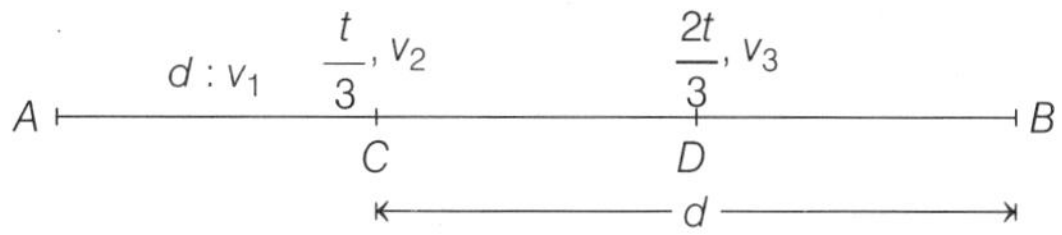

Fig. 6.9

$$CD + DB = d \quad \Rightarrow \quad v_2\left(\frac{t}{3}\right) + \left(\frac{2t}{3}\right)(v_3) = d$$

or $$t = \frac{3d}{v_2 + 2v_3} \qquad \text{...(i)}$$

Further, $$t_{AC} = \frac{d}{v_1}$$

Now, $$\text{average speed} = \frac{\text{total distance}}{\text{total time}} = \frac{d+d}{t_{AC}+t_{CD}+t_{DB}}$$

$$= \frac{2d}{\frac{d}{v_1} + \frac{t}{3} + \frac{2t}{3}} = \frac{2d}{\left(\frac{d}{v_1} + t\right)}$$

Substituting value of t from Eq. (i), we have

$$\text{average speed} = \frac{2d}{(d/v_1) + (3d/v_2 + 2v_3)}$$

$$= \frac{2v_1(v_2 + 2v_3)}{3v_1 + v_2 + 2v_3}$$ **Ans.**

INTRODUCTORY EXERCISE 6.4

1. A particle moves in a straight line with constant speed of 4 m/s for 2 s, then with 6 m/s for 3 s. Find the average speed of the particle in the given time interval.
2. A particle travels half of the time with constant speed 2 m/s. In remaining half of the time it travels, $\frac{1}{4}$ th distance with constant speed of 4 m/s and $\frac{3}{4}$ th distance with 6 m/s. Find average speed during the complete journey.

6.6 One Dimensional Motion with Uniform Acceleration

As we have discussed in article 6.3 that equations like $\mathbf{v} = \mathbf{u} + \mathbf{a}t$ etc. can be applied directly with constant (or uniform) acceleration. Further, in one dimensional motion, all vector quantities (displacement, velocity and acceleration) can be treated like scalars by using sign convention method. In this method, one direction is taken as positive and the other as the negative and then all vector quantities are written with paper signs. In most of the cases, we will take following sign convention.

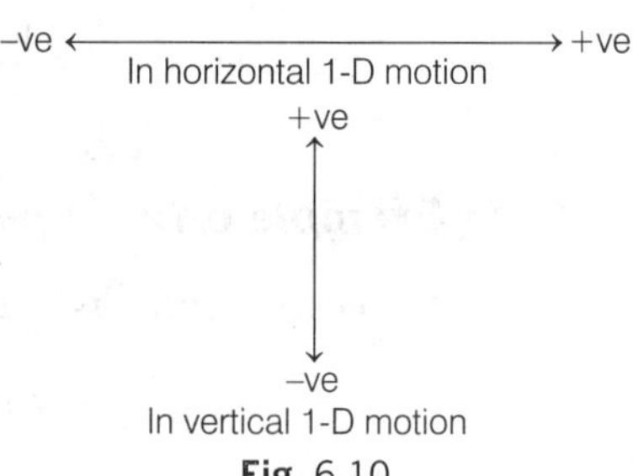

Fig. 6.10

The equations used in 1-D motion with uniform acceleration are

$$v = u + at \quad \text{...(i)}$$

$$v^2 = u^2 + 2as \quad \text{...(ii)}$$

$$s = ut + \frac{1}{2}at^2 \quad \text{...(iii)}$$

$$s_1 = s_0 + ut + \frac{1}{2}at^2 \quad \text{...(iv)}$$

$$s_t = u + at - \frac{1}{2}a \quad \text{...(v)}$$

In the above equations, u = initial velocity, v = velocity at time t, a = constant acceleration

s = displacement measured from the starting point

Here, starting point means the point where the particle was at $t = 0$. It is not the point where $u = 0$.

s_1 = displacement measured from any other point, say P, where P is not the starting point.

s_0 = displacement of the starting point from P.

s_t = displacement (not the distance in t^{th} second).

Extra Points to Remember

- In most of the cases, displacement is measured from the starting point, therefore Eq. (iii) or $s = ut + \frac{1}{2}at^2$ is used.
- For small heights, if the motion is taking place under gravity then acceleration is always constant (= acceleration due to gravity). This is 9.8 m/s^2 ($\approx 10 \text{ m/s}^2$) in downward direction. According to sign convention upwards positive downward direction is negative. Therefore,

$$a = g = 9.8 \text{ m/s}^2 \approx -10 \text{ m/s}^2$$

- One-dimensional motion (with constant acceleration) can be observed in following three cases:
  Case 1 Initial velocity is zero.
  Case 2 Initial velocity is parallel to constant acceleration.
  Case 3 Initial velocity is antiparallel to constant acceleration.
  In first two cases, motion is only accelerated and direction of motion does not change. In the third case, motion is first retarded (till the velocity becomes zero) and then accelerated in opposite direction.

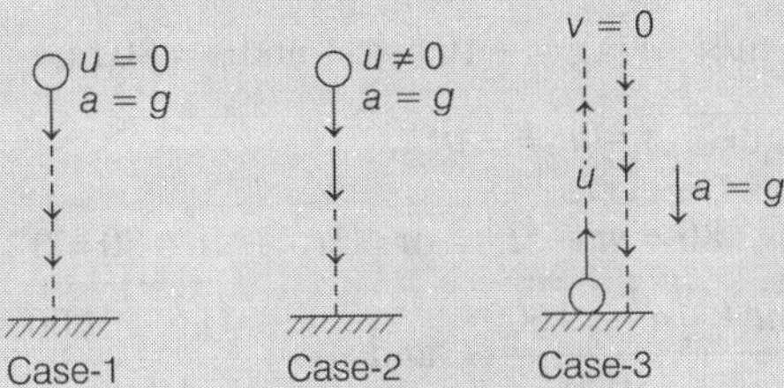

Fig. 6.11

- In most of the problems of time calculations, $s = ut + \frac{1}{2}at^2$ equation is useful. But s has to be measured from the starting point.
- In case 3 (of point 3), we need not to apply two separate equations, one for retarded motion (when motion is upwards) and other for accelerated motion (when motion is downwards). Problem can be solved by applying the equations only one time, provided s (in $s = ut + \frac{1}{2}at^2$) is measured from the starting point and all vector quantities are substituted with proper signs.

Example 6.13 *A ball is thrown upwards from the top of a tower 40 m high with a velocity of 10 m/s. Find the time when it strikes the ground. Take $g = 10 \text{ m/s}^2$.*

Solution In the problem, $u = +10 \text{ m/s}$, $a = -10 \text{ m/s}^2$

and $s = -40 \text{ m}$ (at the point where stone strikes the ground)

Substituting in $s = ut + \frac{1}{2}at^2$, we have

$$-40 = 10t - 5t^2$$

or $$5t^2 - 10t - 40 = 0$$

or $$t^2 - 2t - 8 = 0$$

Solving this, we have $t = 4$ s and -2 s.

Taking the positive value $t = 4$ s.

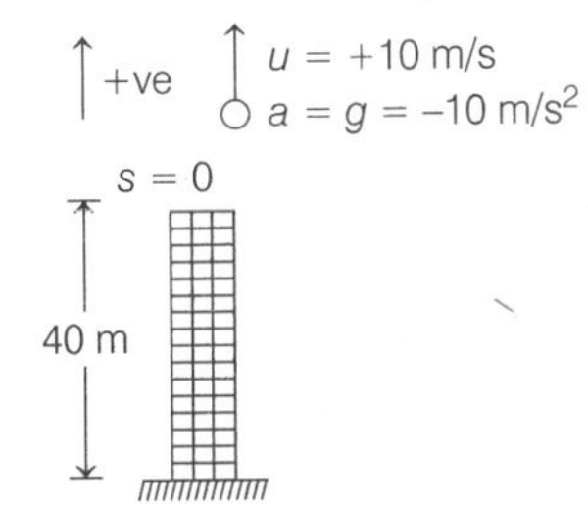

Fig. 6.12

$V_0 = U = 10$

$a = -10$

ft = –2 s can be understood by following figure

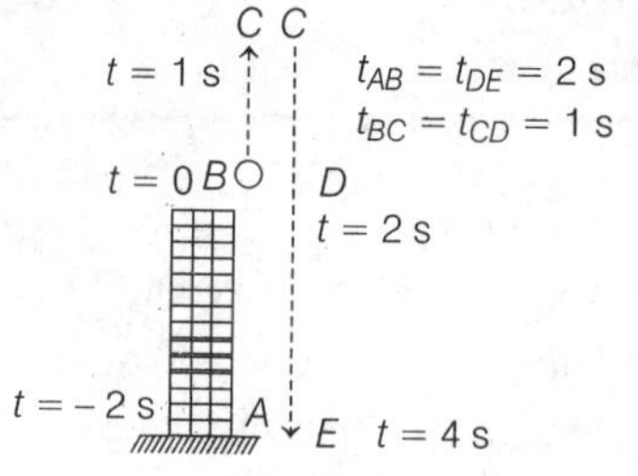

$t_{AB} = t_{DE} = 2$ s
$t_{BC} = t_{CD} = 1$ s

Fig. 6.13

Example 6.14 *A ball is thrown upwards from the ground with an initial speed of u. The ball is at a height of 80 m at two times, the time interval being 6 s. Find u. Take g = 10 m/s².*

Solution Here, $u = u$ m/s, $a = g = -10 \text{ m/s}^2$ and $s = 80$ m.

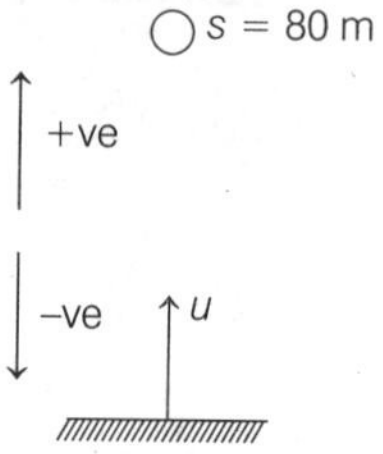

Substituting the values in $s = ut + \frac{1}{2}at^2$,

we have $80 = ut - 5t^2$ or $5t^2 - ut + 80 = 0$

or $t = \frac{u + \sqrt{u^2 - 1600}}{10}$ and $\frac{u - \sqrt{u^2 - 1600}}{10}$

Now, it is given that $\frac{u + \sqrt{u^2 - 1600}}{10} - \frac{u - \sqrt{u^2 - 1600}}{10} = 6$

or $\frac{\sqrt{u^2 - 1600}}{5} = 6$ or $\sqrt{u^2 - 1600} = 30$ or $u^2 - 1600 = 900$

$\therefore$ $u^2 = 2500$ or $u = \pm 50$ m/s

Ignoring the negative sign, we have $u = 50$ m/s

Fig. 6.14

Extra Points to Remember

- In motion under gravity, we can use the following results directly in objective problems:
  (a) If a particle is projected upwards with velocity u, then
  (i) maximum height attained by the particle, $h = \frac{u^2}{2g}$
  (ii) time of ascent = time of descent = $\frac{u}{g}$ $\Rightarrow$ $\therefore$ Total time of flight = $\frac{2u}{g}$

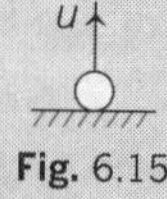

Fig. 6.15

  (b) If a particle is released from rest from a height h (also called free fall), then
  (i) velocity of particle at the time of striking with ground, $v = \sqrt{2gh}$
  (ii) time of descent (also called free fall time) $t = \sqrt{\frac{2h}{g}}$

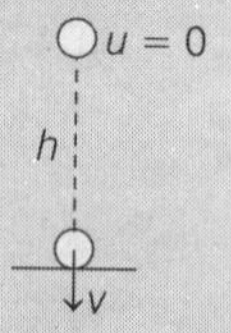

Fig. 6.16

Note *In the above results, air resistance has been neglected and we have already substituted the signs of u, g etc. So, you have to substitute only their magnitudes.*

- **Exercise** Derive the above results.

Difference between Distance (d) and Displacement (s)

The s in equations of motion ($s = ut + \frac{1}{2}at^2$ and $v^2 = u^2 + 2as$) is really the displacement not the distance. They have different values only when u and a are of opposite sign or $u \uparrow\downarrow a$.

Let us take the following two cases :

Case 1 When u is either zero or parallel to a, then motion is simply accelerated and in this case distance is equal to displacement. So, we can write

$$\boxed{d = s = ut + \frac{1}{2}at^2}$$

Case 2 When u is antiparallel to a, the motion is first retarded then accelerated in opposite direction. So, distance is either greater than or equal to displacement ($d \geq |s|$). In this case, first find the time when velocity becomes zero. Say it is t_0.

$$0 = u - at_0 \quad \Rightarrow \quad \therefore \quad t_0 = \left|\frac{u}{a}\right|$$

Now, if the given time $t \leq t_0$, distance and displacement are equal. So, $d = s = ut + \frac{1}{2}at^2$

For $t \leq t_0$, (with u positive and a negative)

For $t > t_0$, distance is greater than displacement. $d = d_1 + d_2$

Here, d_1 = distance travelled before coming to rest $= \left|\frac{u^2}{2a}\right|$

d_2 = distance travelled in remaining time $t - t_0 = \frac{1}{2}|a(t - t_0)^2|$

$$\therefore \quad \boxed{d = \left|\frac{u^2}{2a}\right| + \frac{1}{2}|a(t - t_0)^2|}$$

Note *The displacement is still $s = ut + \frac{1}{2}at^2$ with u positive and a negative.*

Example 6.15 *A particle is projected vertically upwards with velocity 40 m/s. Find the displacement and distance travelled by the particle in*

(a) 2 s *(b)* 4 s *(c)* 6 s

Take $g = 10\ m/s^2$.

Solution Here, u is positive (upwards) and a is negative (downwards). So, first we will find t_0, the time when velocity becomes zero.

$$t_0 = \left|\frac{u}{a}\right| = \frac{40}{10} = 4\ \text{s}$$

(a) $t < t_0$. Therefore, distance and displacement are equal.

$$d = s = ut + \frac{1}{2}at^2 = 40 \times 2 - \frac{1}{2} \times 10 \times 4 = 60\ \text{m}$$

(b) $t = t_0$. So, again distance and displacement are equal.

$$d = s = 40 \times 4 - \frac{1}{2} \times 10 \times 16 = 80 \text{ m}$$

(c) $t > t_0$. Hence, $d > s$, $$s = 40 \times 6 - \frac{1}{2} \times 10 \times 36 = 60 \text{ m}$$

While
$$d = \left|\frac{u^2}{2a}\right| + \frac{1}{2}|a(t - t_0)^2|$$

$$= \frac{(40)^2}{2 \times 10} + \frac{1}{2} \times 10 \times (6 - 4)^2$$

$$= 100 \text{ m}$$

INTRODUCTORY EXERCISE 6.5

1. Prove the relation, $s_t = u + at - \frac{1}{2}a$.
2. Equation $s_t = u + at - \frac{1}{2}a$ does not seem dimensionally correct, why?
3. A particle is projected vertically upwards. What is the value of acceleration
   (i) during upward journey,
   (ii) during downward journey and
   (iii) at highest point?
4. A ball is thrown vertically upwards. Which quantity remains constant among, speed, kinetic energy, velocity and acceleration?
5. A particle is projected vertically upwards with an initial velocity of 40 m/s. Find the displacement and distance covered by the particle in 6 s. Take $g = 10 \text{ m/s}^2$.
6. A particle moves rectilinearly with initial velocity u and constant acceleration a. Find the average velocity of the particle in a time interval from $t = 0$ to $t = t$ second of its motion.
7. A particle moves in a straight line with uniform acceleration. Its velocity at time $t = 0$ is v_1 and at time $t = t$ is v_2. The average velocity of the particle in this time interval is $\frac{v_1 + v_2}{2}$.
   Is this statement true or false?
8. Find the average velocity of a particle released from rest from a height of 125 m over a time interval till it strikes the ground. Take $g = 10 \text{ m/s}^2$.
9. A particle starts with an initial velocity 2.5 m/s along the positive x-direction and it accelerates uniformly at the rate 0.50 m/s^2.
   (a) Find the distance travelled by it in the first two seconds
   (b) How much time does it take to reach the velocity 7.5 m/s? (c) How much distance will it cover in reaching the velocity 7.5 m/s?
10. A ball is projected vertically upward with a speed of 50 m/s. Find (a) the maximum height, (b) the time to reach the maximum height, (c) the speed at half the maximum height. Take $g = 10 \text{ m/s}^2$.

6.7 One Dimensional Motion with Non-uniform Acceleration

When acceleration of a particle is not constant we take help of differentiation or integration.

Equations of Differentiation

(a)
$$v=\frac{ds}{dt} \quad \text{...(i)}$$

If the motion is taking place along x-axis, then this equation can be written as,

$$v=\frac{dx}{dt}$$

Here, v is the instantaneous velocity and x, the x co-ordinate at a general time t.

(b)
$$a=\frac{dv}{dt} \quad \text{...(ii)}$$

Here, a is the instantaneous acceleration of the particle. Further, a can also be written as

$$a=\frac{dv}{dt}=\left(\frac{ds}{dt}\right)\left(\frac{dv}{ds}\right)=v\left(\frac{dv}{ds}\right) \qquad \left[\text{as } \frac{ds}{dt}=v\right]$$

$\therefore$
$$a=v\left(\frac{dv}{ds}\right) \quad \text{...(iii)}$$

Equations of Integration

(c)
$$\int ds=\int v\,dt \quad \text{...(iv)}$$

or
$$s=\int v\,dt \quad \text{...(v)}$$

In the above equations, v should be either constant or function of t.

(d)
$$\int dv=\int a\,dt \quad \text{...(vi)}$$

or
$$\Delta v=v_f-v_i=\int a\,dt \quad \text{...(vii)}$$

In the above equations a should be either constant or function of time t.

(e)
$$\int v\,dv=\int a\,ds \quad \text{...(viii)}$$

In the above equation a should be either constant or function of s.

Note *(i) To convert s-t equation into v-t equation or v-t equation into a-t equation differentiation will be done.*

$$s\text{-}t \rightarrow v\text{-}t \rightarrow a\text{-}t \qquad \textit{(differentiation)}$$

(ii) To convert a-t equation into v-t equation or v-t equation into s-t equation, integration equations (with some limits) are required. By limit we mean the value of physical quantity which we will get after integration should be known at some given time.

For example, after integrating v (w.r.t time) we will get displacement s. Therefore, to get complete s function value of s should be known at some given time. Otherwise constant of integration remains as an unknown.

Thus, $$a\text{-}t \rightarrow v\text{-}t \rightarrow s\text{-}t \qquad \textit{(integration with limits)}$$

Derivation of Equation of Motion ($v = u + at$ etc.)

For one dimensional motion with $a =$ constant.

We can write, $$dv = a\,dt \qquad \left(\text{as } a = \frac{dv}{dt}\right)$$

Integrating both sides, we have $$\int dv = a \int dt \qquad (\text{as } a = \text{constant})$$

At $t = 0$, velocity is u and at $t = t$ velocity is v. Hence,

$$\int_u^v dv = a \int_0^t dt$$

$\therefore$ $$[v]_u^v = a\,[t]_0^t \text{ or } v - u = at$$

$\therefore$ $$\boxed{v = u + at}$$ **Hence proved.**

Further, we can write $$ds = v\,dt \qquad \left(\text{as } v = \frac{ds}{dt}\right)$$

$$= (u + at)\,dt \qquad (\text{as } v = u + at)$$

At time $t = 0$ suppose $s = 0$ and at $t = t$, displacement is s, then

$$\int_0^s ds = \int_0^t (u + at)\,dt \Rightarrow \therefore \quad [s]_0^s = \left[ut + \frac{1}{2}at^2\right]_0^t$$

or $$\boxed{s = ut + \frac{1}{2}at^2}$$ **Hence proved.**

We can also write, $$v \cdot dv = a \cdot ds \qquad \left(\text{as } a = v \cdot \frac{dv}{ds}\right)$$

When $s = 0$, v is u and at $s = s$, velocity is v. Therefore,

$$\int_u^v v \cdot dv = a \int_0^s ds \text{ or } \left[\frac{v^2}{2}\right]_u^v = a\,[s]_0^s \qquad (\text{as } a = \text{constant})$$

$\therefore$ $$\frac{v^2}{2} - \frac{u^2}{2} = as$$

or $$\boxed{v^2 = u^2 + 2as}$$ **Hence proved.**

Example 6.16 *Displacement-time equation of a particle moving along x-axis is*

$$x = 20 + t^3 - 12t \text{ (SI units)}$$

(a) Find, position and velocity of particle at time t = 0.

(b) State whether the motion is uniformly accelerated or not.

(c) Find position of particle when velocity of particle is zero.

Solution (a) $$x = 20 + t^3 - 12t \qquad \ldots\text{(i)}$$

At $t = 0$, $$x = 20 + 0 - 0 = 20\text{ m}$$

Velocity of particle at time t can be obtained by differentiating Eq. (i) w.r.t. time i.e.

$$v = \frac{dx}{dt} = 3t^2 - 12 \qquad \ldots\text{(ii)}$$

At $t = 0$, $$v = 0 - 12 = -12\text{ m/s}$$

(b) Differentiating Eq. (ii) w.r.t. time t, we get the acceleration $a = \frac{dv}{dt} = 6t$

As acceleration is a function of time, the motion is non-uniformly accelerated.

(c) Substituting $v = 0$ in Eq. (ii), we have $0 = 3t^2 - 12$

Positive value of t comes out to be 2 s from this equation. Substituting $t = 2$ s in Eq. (i), we have $x = 20 + (2)^3 - 12(2)$ or $x = 4$ m

Example 6.17 *Velocity-time equation of a particle moving in a straight line is,*

$$v = (10 + 2t + 3t^2) \quad (SI\ units)$$

Find

(a) displacement of particle from the mean position at time t = 1 s, if it is given that displacement is 20 m at time t = 0.

(b) acceleration-time equation.

Solution (a) The given equation can be written as,

$$v = \frac{ds}{dt} = (10 + 2t + 3t^2) \quad \text{or} \quad ds = (10 + 2t + 3t^2)\,dt$$

or $$\int_{20}^{s} ds = \int_0^1 (10 + 2t + 3t^2)\,dt \quad \text{or} \quad s - 20 = [10t + t^2 + t^3]_0^1$$

or $$s = 20 + 12 = 32 \text{ m}$$

(b) Acceleration-time equation can be obtained by differentiating the given equation w.r.t. time.

Thus, $$a = \frac{dv}{dt} = \frac{d}{dt}(10 + 2t + 3t^2) \quad \text{or} \quad a = 2 + 6t$$

INTRODUCTORY EXERCISE 6.6

1. Velocity (in m/s) of a particle moving along x-axis varies with time as, $v = (10 + 5t - t^2)$ At time $t = 0$, $x = 0$. Find
   (a) acceleration of particle at $t = 2$ s and
   (b) x-coordinate of particle at $t = 3$ s
2. A particle is moving with a velocity of $v = (3 + 6t + 9t^2)$ cm/s. Find out
   (a) the acceleration of the particle at $t = 3$ s.
   (b) the displacement of the particle in the interval $t = 5$ s to $t = 8$ s.
3. The motion of a particle along a straight line is described by the function $x = (2t - 3)^2$, where x is in metres and t is in seconds. Find
   (a) the position, velocity and acceleration at $t = 2$ s.
   (b) the velocity of the particle at origin.
4. x-coordinate of a particle moving along this axis is $x = (2 + t^2 + 2t^3)$. Here, x is in metres and t in seconds. Find (a) position of particle from where it started its journey, (b) initial velocity of particle and (c) acceleration of particle at $t = 2$ s.
5. The velocity of a particle moving in a straight line is directly proportional to 3/4th power of time elapsed. How does its displacement and acceleration depend on time?

6.8 Motion in Two and Three Dimensions

The motion of a particle thrown in a vertical plane at some angle with horizontal ($\neq 90°$) is an example of two dimensional motion. Similarly, a circular motion is also an example of 2-D motion. A two dimensional motion takes place in a plane. In most of the cases plane of circular motion is horizontal or vertical. According to nature of acceleration we can classify this motion in following two types.

Uniform Acceleration

Equations of motion for uniformly accelerated motion ($\mathbf{a}$ = constant) are as under

$$\mathbf{v} = \mathbf{u} + \mathbf{a}\,t,$$

$$\mathbf{s} = \mathbf{u}t + \frac{1}{2}\mathbf{a}\,t^2,$$

$$\mathbf{v} \cdot \mathbf{v} = \mathbf{u} \cdot \mathbf{u} + 2\,\mathbf{a} \cdot \mathbf{s}$$

Here, $\mathbf{u}$ = initial velocity of particle, $\mathbf{v}$ = velocity of particle at time t and $\mathbf{s}$ = displacement of particle in time t

Note *If initial position vector of a particle is* $\mathbf{r}_0$, *then position vector at time t can be written as*

$$\mathbf{r} = \mathbf{r}_0 + \mathbf{s} = \mathbf{r}_0 + \mathbf{u}t + \frac{1}{2}\mathbf{a}t^2$$

Non-Uniform Acceleration

When acceleration is not constant then we will have to go for differentiation or integration. The equations in differentiation are

(i) $\mathbf{v} = \dfrac{d\mathbf{s}}{dt}$ or $\dfrac{d\mathbf{r}}{dt}$ (ii) $\mathbf{a} = \dfrac{d\mathbf{v}}{dt}$

Here, $\mathbf{v}$ and $\mathbf{a}$ are instantaneous velocity, acceleration vectors. The equations of integration are

(iii) $\int d\mathbf{s} = \int \mathbf{v}dt$ and (iv) $\int d\mathbf{v} = \int \mathbf{a}\,dt$

Extra Points to Remember

A two or three dimensional motion can also be solved by component method.

For example, in two dimensional motion (in *x-y* plane) the motion can be resolved along *x* and *y* directions. Now, along these two directions we can use sign method, as we used in one-dimensional motion (but separately). By separately we mean, when we are looking the motion along *x*-axis we need not to bother about the motion along *y*-axis.

Example 6.18 *A particle of mass 1 kg has a velocity of 2 m/s. A constant force of 2 N acts on the particle for 1 s in a direction perpendicular to its initial velocity. Find the velocity and displacement of the particle at the end of 1 s.*

Solution Force acting on the particle is constant. Hence, acceleration of the particle will also remain constant.

$$a = \frac{F}{m} = \frac{2}{1} = 2\ \text{m/s}^2$$

Since, acceleration is constant. We can apply

$$\mathbf{v} = \mathbf{u} + \mathbf{a}t$$

and

$$\mathbf{s} = \mathbf{u}t + \frac{1}{2}\mathbf{a}t^2 \cdot$$

Refer Fig. 6.17 (a) $\mathbf{v} = \mathbf{u} + \mathbf{a}\,t$

Here, **u** and **a** t are two mutually perpendicular vectors. So,

$$|\mathbf{v}| = \sqrt{(|\mathbf{u}|)^2 + (|\mathbf{a}t|)^2}$$

$$= \sqrt{(2)^2 + (2)^2}$$

$$= 2\sqrt{2} \text{ m/s}$$

$$\alpha = \tan^{-1}\frac{|\mathbf{a}t|}{|\mathbf{u}|} = \tan^{-1}\left(\frac{2}{2}\right)$$

$$= \tan^{-1}(1) = 45°$$

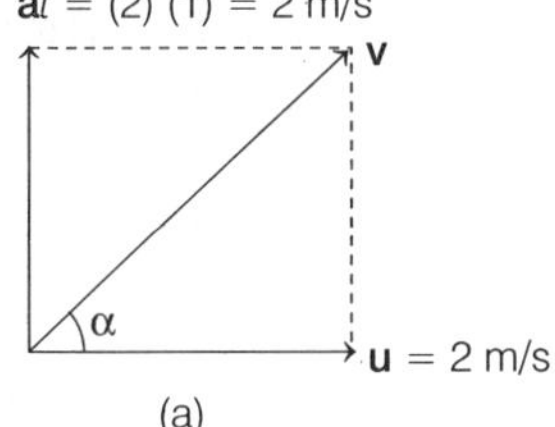

(a)

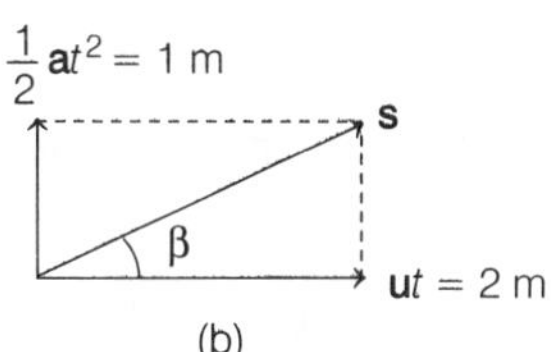

(b)

Fig. 6.17

Thus, velocity of the particle at the end of 1s is $2\sqrt{2}$ m/s at an angle of 45° with its initial velocity.

Refer Fig. 6.17 (b), $\mathbf{s} = \mathbf{u}\,t + \frac{1}{2}\,\mathbf{a}\,t^2$

Here, **u** t and $\frac{1}{2}$ **a** t^2 are also two mutually perpendicular vectors. So,

$$|\mathbf{s}| = \sqrt{(|\mathbf{u}t|)^2 + (|\tfrac{1}{2}\,\mathbf{a}\,t^2|)^2}$$

$$= \sqrt{(2)^2 + (1)^2}$$

$$= \sqrt{5} \text{ m}$$

and

$$\beta = \tan^{-1}\frac{\left|\frac{1}{2}\mathbf{a}t^2\right|}{|\mathbf{u}t|}$$

$$= \tan^{-1}\left(\frac{1}{2}\right)$$

Thus, displacement of the particle at the end of 1 s is $\sqrt{5}$ m at an angle of $\tan^{-1}\left(\frac{1}{2}\right)$ from its initial velocity.

Example 6.19 *Velocity and acceleration of a particle at time $t = 0$ are $\mathbf{u} = (2\hat{\mathbf{i}} + 3\hat{\mathbf{j}})$ m/s and $\mathbf{a} = (4\hat{\mathbf{i}} + 2\hat{\mathbf{j}})$ m/s^2 respectively. Find the velocity and displacement of particle at $t = 2$ s.*

Solution Here, acceleration $\mathbf{a} = (4\hat{\mathbf{i}} + 2\hat{\mathbf{j}})$ m/s^2 is constant.

So, we can apply

$$\mathbf{v} = \mathbf{u} + \mathbf{a}t \quad \text{and} \quad \mathbf{s} = \mathbf{u}t + \frac{1}{2}\mathbf{a}t^2$$

Substituting the proper values, we get

$$\mathbf{v} = (2\hat{\mathbf{i}} + 3\hat{\mathbf{j}}) + (2)(4\hat{\mathbf{i}} + 2\hat{\mathbf{j}})$$

$$= (10\hat{\mathbf{i}} + 7\hat{\mathbf{j}}) \text{ m/s}$$

and

$$\mathbf{s} = (2)(2\hat{\mathbf{i}} + 3\hat{\mathbf{j}}) + \frac{1}{2}(2)^2(4\hat{\mathbf{i}} + 2\hat{\mathbf{j}})$$

$$= (12\hat{\mathbf{i}} + 10\hat{\mathbf{j}}) \text{ m}$$

Therefore, velocity and displacement of particle at $t = 2$s are $(10\hat{\mathbf{i}} + 7\hat{\mathbf{j}})$ m/s and $(12\hat{\mathbf{i}} + 10\hat{\mathbf{j}})$ m respectively.

Example 6.20 *Velocity of a particle in x-y plane at any time t is*

$$\mathbf{v} = (2t\hat{\mathbf{i}} + 3t^2\hat{\mathbf{j}}) \text{ m/s}$$

At $t = 0$, particle starts from the co-ordinates (2 m, 4 m). Find

(a) acceleration of the particle at $t = 1$ s.

(b) position vector and co-ordinates of the particle at $t = 2$ s.

Solution (a) $\mathbf{a} = \dfrac{d\mathbf{v}}{dt} = \dfrac{d}{dt}(2t\,\hat{\mathbf{i}} + 3t^2\hat{\mathbf{j}})$

$$= (2\hat{\mathbf{i}} + 6t\,\hat{\mathbf{j}}) \text{ m/s}^2$$

At $t = 1$s,

$$\mathbf{a} = (2\hat{\mathbf{i}} + 6\hat{\mathbf{j}}) \text{ m/s}^2$$ **Ans.**

(b) $\int d\mathbf{s} = \int \mathbf{v}\,dt$

or

$$\mathbf{s} = \int \mathbf{v}\,dt = \int (2t\,\hat{\mathbf{i}} + 3t^2\hat{\mathbf{j}})\,dt$$

∴

$$\mathbf{r}_f - \mathbf{r}_i = \int_{\text{initial}}^{\text{final}} (2t\,\hat{\mathbf{i}} + 3t^2\hat{\mathbf{j}})\,dt$$

or

$$\mathbf{r}_{2\,\text{sec}} - \mathbf{r}_{0\,\text{sec}} = \int_0^2 (2t\hat{\mathbf{i}} + 3t^2\hat{\mathbf{j}})\,dt$$

∴

$$\mathbf{r}_{2\,\text{sec}} = \mathbf{r}_{0\,\text{sec}} + [t^2\hat{\mathbf{i}} + t^3\hat{\mathbf{j}}]_0^2$$

$$= (2\hat{\mathbf{i}} + 4\hat{\mathbf{j}}) + (4\hat{\mathbf{i}} + 8\hat{\mathbf{j}})$$

$$= (6\hat{\mathbf{i}} + 12\hat{\mathbf{j}}) \text{ m}$$ **Ans.**

Therefore, coordinates of the particle at $t = 2$s are (6 m, 12 m) **Ans.**

INTRODUCTORY EXERCISE 6.7

1. Velocity of a particle at time $t = 0$ is 2 m/s. A constant acceleration of 2 m/s^2 acts on the particle for 2 s at an angle of 60° with its initial velocity. Find the magnitude of velocity and displacement of particle at the end of $t = 2$s.
2. Velocity of a particle at any time t is $\mathbf{v} = (2\hat{\mathbf{i}} + 2t\hat{\mathbf{j}})$ m/s. Find acceleration and displacement of particle at $t = 1$s. Can we apply $\mathbf{v} = \mathbf{u} + \mathbf{a}t$ or not?
3. Acceleration of a particle in x-y plane varies with time as

$$\mathbf{a} = (2t\hat{\mathbf{i}} + 3t^2\hat{\mathbf{j}})\ \text{m/s}^2$$

At time $t = 0$, velocity of particle is 2 m/s along positive x-direction and particle starts from origin. Find velocity and coordinates of particle at $t = 1$s.

6.9 Graphs

Before studying graphs of kinematics, let us first discuss some general points :

(i) Mostly a graph is drawn between two variable quantities (say x and y). In kinematics, the frequently asked graphs are s-t, v-t, a-t or v-s.

(ii) Equation between x and y will decide the shape of graph whether it is straight line, circle, parabola or rectangular hyperbola etc. If the equation is linear, graph is a straight line. If equation is quadratic then graph is a parabola. In kinematics, most of the graphs are straight line or parabola.

(iii) By putting $x = 0$ in y-x equation if we get $y = 0$, then graph passes through origin, otherwise not.

(iv) If $z = \frac{dy}{dx}$, then the value of z at any point can be obtained by the slope of the graph at that point.

For example,

instantaneous velocity $v = \frac{ds}{dt}$ = slope of s-t graph.

instantaneous acceleration $a = \frac{dv}{dt}$ = slope of v-t graph.

(v) If $dz = y\,dx$. Then, $\int dz = \int y\,dx$

$\Rightarrow$ z or $z_f - z_i$ or Δz = area under y-x graph, with projection along x-axis.

For example,

$$ds = vdt$$

$\Rightarrow$ Displacement $s = \int vdt$ = area under v-t graph with projection along t-axis.

Further, $dv = adt$

$\Rightarrow$ $v_f - v_i$ or $\Delta v = \int adt$ = area under a-t graph with projection along t-axis.

These results have been summarized in following table :

Table 6.2

Name of Graph	Slope	Area
s-t	v	No physical quantity
v-t	a	s
a-t	Rate of change of acceleration	$v_f - v_i$ or Δv

For better understanding of three graphs (s-t, v-t and a-t) of kinematics, we have classified the one dimensional motion in following four types.

Uniform Motion

Equations

The three equations of uniform motion are as under

$a = 0$, $v =$ constant and $s = vt$ or $s = s_0 + vt$

Important Points

(i) s-t equation is linear. Therefore, s-t graph is straight line.

(ii) In $s = vt$, displacement is measured from the starting point ($t = 0$). Corresponding to this equation s-t graph passes through origin, as $s = 0$ when $t = 0$. In $s = s_0 + vt$, displacement is measured from any other point and s_0 is the initial displacement.

(iii) Slope of s-t graph $= v$. Now, since $v =$ constant, therefore slope of s-t graph = constant.

(iv) Slope of v-t graph $= a$. Now, since $a = 0$, therefore slope of v-t graph $= 0$.

The Corresponding Graphs

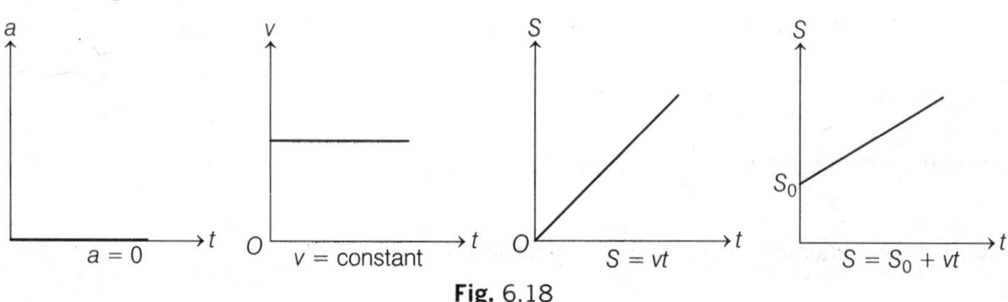

Fig. 6.18

Example 6.21 *s-t graph of a particle in motion is as shown below.*

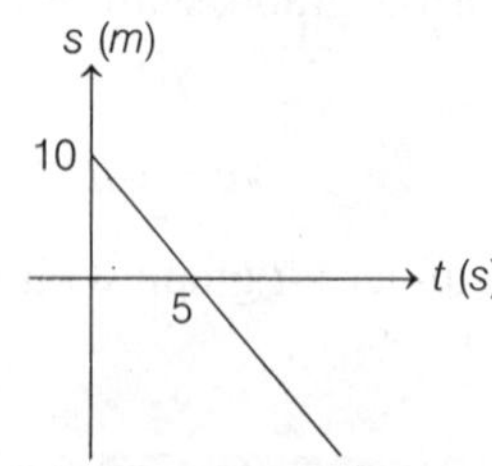

Fig. 6.19

(a) State, whether the given graph represents a uniform motion or not.

(b) Find velocity of the particle.

Solution (a) v = slope of s-t graph. Since, the given s-t graph is a straight line and slope of a straight line is always constant. Hence, velocity is constant. Therefore, the given graph represents a uniform motion.

(b) $v = \text{slope of } s\text{-}t \text{ graph} = -\frac{10}{5} = -2 \text{ m/s}$ **Ans.**

Example 6.22 *A particle is moving along x-axis. Its x-coordinate versus time graph is as shown below.*

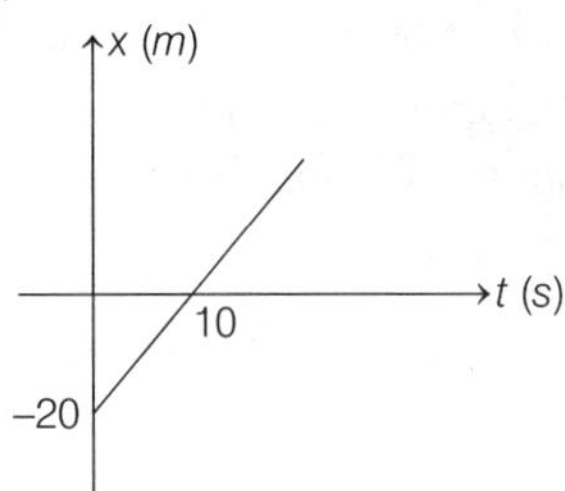

Fig. 6.20

Draw some conclusions from the given graph.

Solution The conclusions drawn from the graph are as under:

(i) x-t graph is a straight line, slope of which $\left(v = \frac{dx}{dt}\right)$ is positive and constant. Therefore, velocity is positive and constant.

(ii) $v = \frac{dx}{dt}$ = slope of x-t graph

$$= +\frac{20}{10} = +2 \text{ m/s}$$

Therefore, velocity is 2 m/s along positive x-direction.

(iii) At $t = 0, x = -20$ m and at $t = 10$ s, $x = 0$

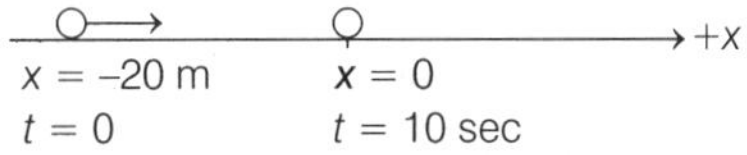

+x
x = –20 m, t = 0
x = 0, t = 10 sec

Fig. 6.21

Uniformly Accelerated Motion

Equations

$$a = \text{constant (and positive)}$$

$$v = u + at \text{ or } v = at, \text{ if } u = 0$$

$$s = ut + \frac{1}{2}at^2 \text{ or } s = \frac{1}{2}at^2 \text{ if } u = 0$$

or $$s = s_0 + ut + \frac{1}{2}at^2 \text{ if } s_0 \neq 0$$

or $$s = s_0 + \frac{1}{2}at^2 \text{ if } s_0 \neq 0 \text{ but } u = 0$$

Important Points

(i) v-t equation is linear. Therefore, v-t graph is a straight line. Further, $v = at$ is a straight line passing through origin (as $v = 0$ when $t = 0$)

(ii) All s-t equations are quadratic. Therefore, all s-t graphs should be parabolic.

(iii) Slope of s-t graph gives the instantaneous velocity. Therefore, initial slope of s-t graph gives initial velocity u. In this case, we are considering only accelerated motion (in which speed keeps on increasing in positive direction). Therefore, velocity is positive and continuously increasing. Hence, slope of s-t graph should be positive and should keep on increasing.

(iv) Slope of v-t graph gives instantaneous acceleration. Now, acceleration is positive and constant. Therefore, slope of v-t graph should be positive and constant.

Graphs

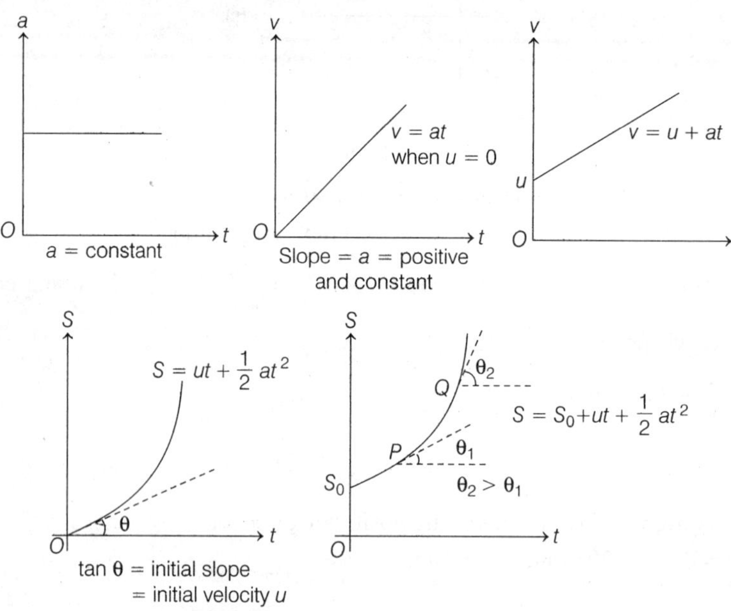

Fig. 6.22

From P to Q slope is increasing (positive at both points). Therefore, velocity is positive and increasing.

Uniformly Retarded Motion (till velocity becomes zero)

We are considering the case when initial velocity is positive and a constant acceleration acts in negative direction (till the velocity becomes zero).

Equations

$$a = \text{constant (and negative)}$$

$$v = u - at$$

$$s = ut - \frac{1}{2}at^2$$

Important Points

(i) In this case, u cannot be zero. Therefore, v-t straight line cannot pass through origin. Further, initial slope of s-t parabolic graph cannot be zero.

(ii) Velocity is positive but keeps on decreasing from u to zero.

(iii) Slope of v-t graph gives instantaneous acceleration. Acceleration is constant and negative. Therefore, slope of v-t graph should be negative and constant.

(iv) Initial slope of s-t graph will give us initial velocity u. Final slope of s-t graph will give us final velocity zero. In between these two times, velocity is positive and decreasing. Therefore, slope of s-t graph (= instantaneous velocity) should be positive and decreasing.

Graphs

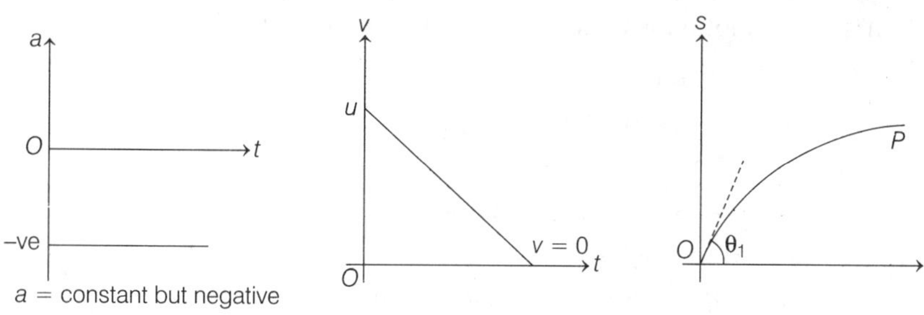

Fig. 6.23

$\tan\theta_1$ = initial slope = u

From O to P, slope or v is positive but decreasing.

At P, slope = 0, therefore $v = 0$

Uniformly Retarded and then Accelerated Motion in Opposite Direction

If a particle is projected upwards then first it is retarded in upward (say positive) direction. At highest point its velocity becomes zero and finally it is retarded in downward (or negative) direction. Throughout the motion, its acceleration is downwards and constant (= acceleration due to gravity). Therefore, it is negative and constant. If air resistance is neglected, then speed of the particle at the time of projection is equal to speed at the time of striking with the ground. But velocities are in opposite directions. So, their signs are different. During retardation, velocity is upwards (therefore positive) but decreasing.

During acceleration, velocity is downwards (therefore negative) and increasing. Upward journey time is equal to the downward journey time. Finally, the particle returns to the ground. Therefore final displacement is zero. In upward journey, displacement increases (parabolically) in positive direction. In downward journey, it decreases. But displacement from the starting point (ground) is still positive. Slope of s-t graphs gives the instantaneous velocity. In upward journey, velocity is positive and decreasing. Therefore, slope is positive and decreasing. At highest point velocity is zero. Therefore, slope is zero. In downward journey, velocity is negative and increasing. Therefore, slope is negative and increasing.

Graphs

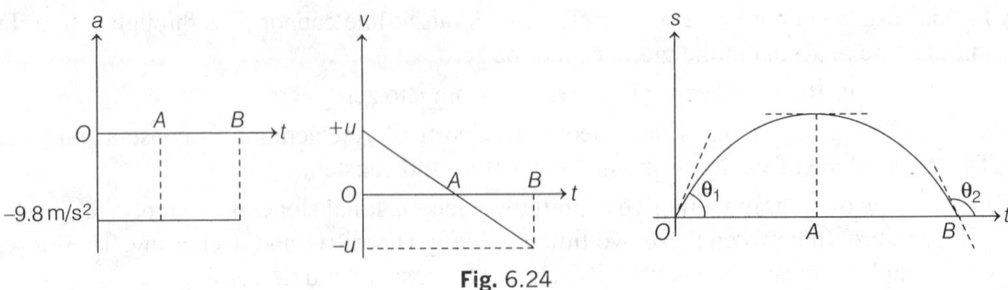

Fig. 6.24

In the above graphs,

(i) $a = -9.8 \text{ m/s}^2$ if the motion is taking place under gravity.

(ii) O is the starting point, where

$$v = +u \Rightarrow \text{slope of } s\text{-}t \text{ graph} = \tan\theta_1 = u$$

(iii) A is the highest point, where

$$v = 0 \Rightarrow \text{slope of } s\text{-}t \text{ graph} = 0$$

(iv) B is the point when particle again strikes the ground. At this point,

$$v = -u \Rightarrow \text{slope of } s\text{-}t \text{ graph} = \tan\theta_2 = -u$$

At this point,

$$s = 0$$

(v) Upwards journey time t_{OA} = downward journey time t_{AB}

(vi) In upward motion (from O to A), velocity is positive and decreasing. Therefore, slope of s-t graph is positive and decreasing.

(vii) In downward motion (from A to B), velocity is negative and increasing. Therefore, slope of s-t graph is negative and increasing.

Extra Points to Remember

- Slope of v-t or s-t graph can never be infinite at any point, because infinite slope of v-t graph means infinite acceleration. Similarly, infinite slope of s-t graph means infinite velocity. Hence, the following graphs are not possible :

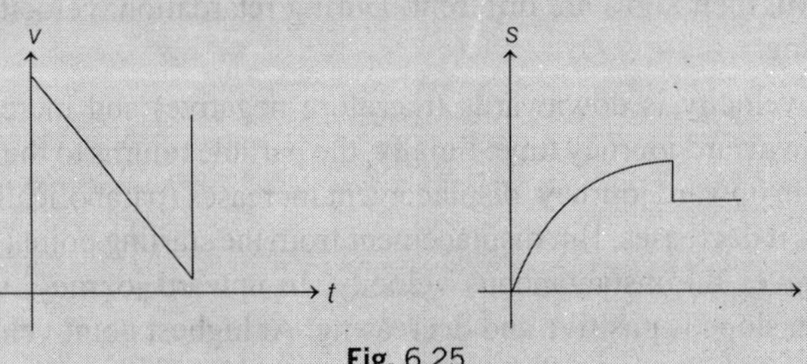

Fig. 6.25

- At one time (say t_0), two values of velocity or displacement are not possible. Hence, the following graphs are not acceptable :

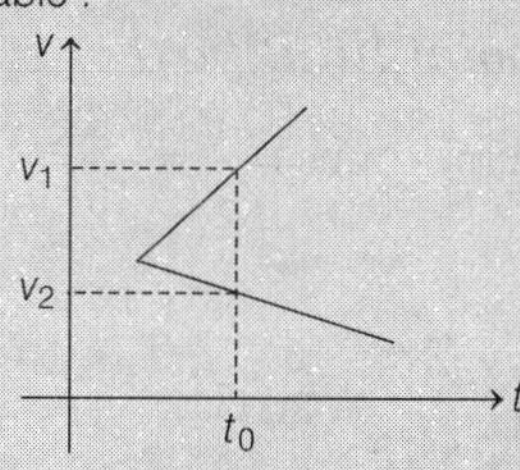

Fig. 6.26

- Time never returns. Therefore, on time axis we will always move ahead. On this ground, following graph cannot exist in real life :

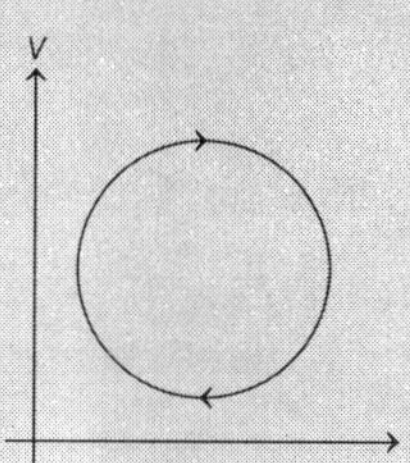

Fig. 6.27

- Different values of displacements in *s*-*t* graph corresponding to given *v*-*t* graph can be obtained just by calculating area under *v*-*t* graph. There is no need of using equations like $s = ut + \frac{1}{2}at^2$ etc.

Example 6.23 *Acceleration-time graph of a particle moving in a straight line is as shown in Fig. 6.28. Velocity of particle at time t = 0 is 2 m/s. Find the velocity at the end of fourth second.*

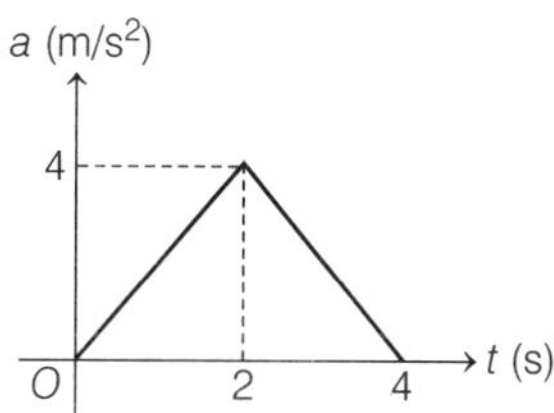

Fig. 6.28

Solution
$$\int dv = \int a\,dt$$

or change in velocity = area under *a*-*t* graph

Hence,
$$v_f - v_i = \frac{1}{2}(4)(4)$$
$$= 8 \text{ m/s}$$

∴
$$v_f = v_i + 8 = (2 + 8) \text{ m/s}$$
$$= 10 \text{ m/s}$$

Example 6.24 *A particle is projected upwards with velocity 40 m/s. Taking the value of g = 10 m/s² and upward direction as positive, plot a-t, v-t and s-t graphs of the particle from the starting point till it further strikes the ground.*

Solution Upward journey time = downward journey time $= \frac{u}{g} = \frac{40}{10} = 4\text{ s}$

$\therefore$ Total time of journey = 8 s

Maximum height attained by the particle $= \frac{u^2}{2g} = \frac{(40)^2}{2 \times 10} = 80\text{ m}$

***a-t* graph** During complete journey $a = g = -10\text{ m/s}^2$

Corresponding *a-t* graph is as shown below.

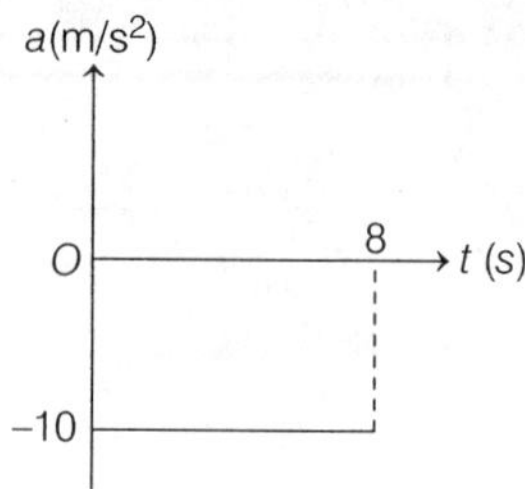

Fig. 6.29

***v-t* graph** In upward journey velocity first decreases from + 40 m/s to 0. Then, in downward journey it increases from 0 to – 40 m/s. Negative sign just signifies its downward direction. Corresponding *v-t* graph is as shown below.

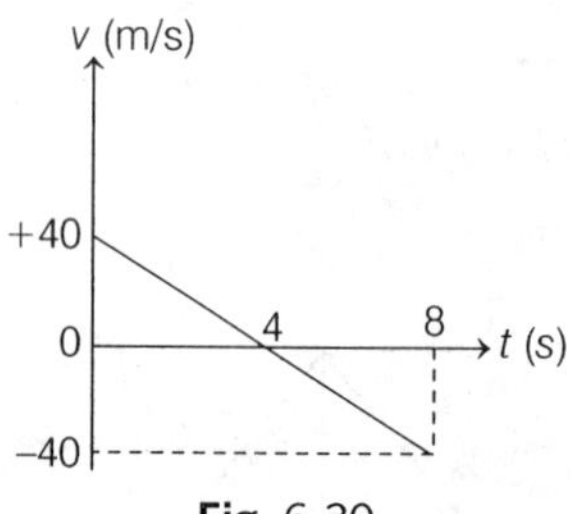

Fig. 6.30

***s-t* graph** In upward journey displacement first increases from 0 to + 80 m. Then, it decreases from + 80 m to 0. Corresponding *s-t* graph is as shown below.

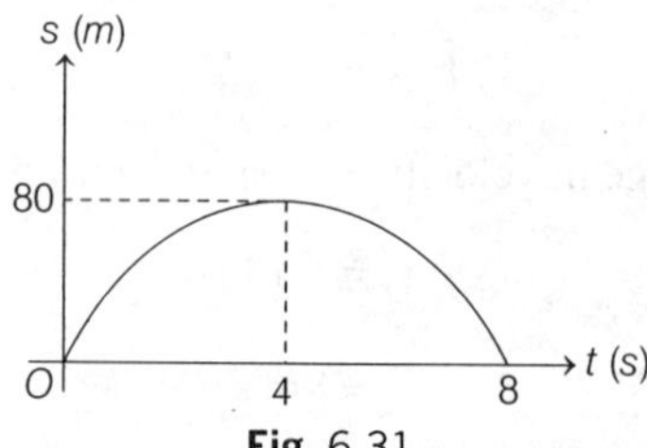

Fig. 6.31

Example 6.25 *A car accelerates from rest at a constant rate α for some time, after which it decelerates at a constant rate β, to come to rest. If the total time elapsed is t seconds, then evaluate (a) the maximum velocity reached and (b) the total distance travelled.*

Solution (a) Let the car accelerates for time t_1 and decelerates for time t_2. Then,

$$t = t_1 + t_2 \qquad \text{...(i)}$$

and corresponding velocity-time graph will be as shown in Fig. 6.32.

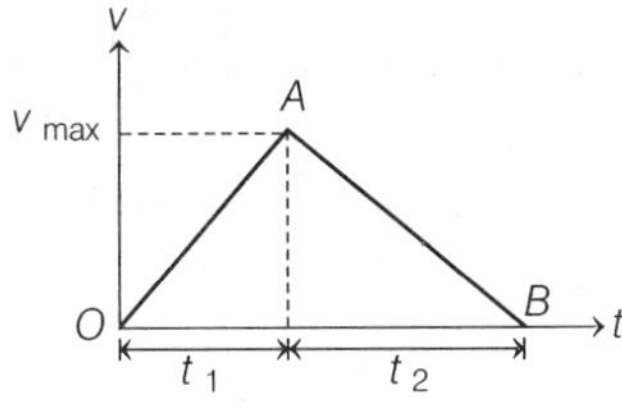

Fig. 6.32

From the graph,

$$\alpha = \text{slope of line } OA = \frac{v_{max}}{t_1}$$

or $$t_1 = \frac{v_{max}}{\alpha} \qquad \text{...(ii)}$$

and $$\beta = - \text{ slope of line } AB = \frac{v_{max}}{t_2}$$

or $$t_2 = \frac{v_{max}}{\beta} \qquad \text{...(iii)}$$

From Eqs. (i), (ii) and (iii), we get

$$\frac{v_{max}}{\alpha} + \frac{v_{max}}{\beta} = t$$

or $$v_{max}\left(\frac{\alpha + \beta}{\alpha\beta}\right) = t$$

or $$v_{max} = \frac{\alpha\beta t}{\alpha + \beta} \qquad \textbf{Ans.}$$

(b) Total distance = total displacement = area under v-t graph

$$= \frac{1}{2} \times t \times v_{max}$$

$$= \frac{1}{2} \times t \times \frac{\alpha\beta t}{\alpha + \beta}$$

or $$\text{Distance} = \frac{1}{2}\left(\frac{\alpha\beta t^2}{\alpha + \beta}\right) \qquad \textbf{Ans.}$$

Note *This problem can also be solved by using equations of motion ($v = u + at$ etc.). Try it yourself.*

Example 6.26 *The acceleration versus time graph of a particle moving along a straight line is shown in the figure. Draw the respective velocity-time graph. Given $v = 0$ at $t = 0$.*

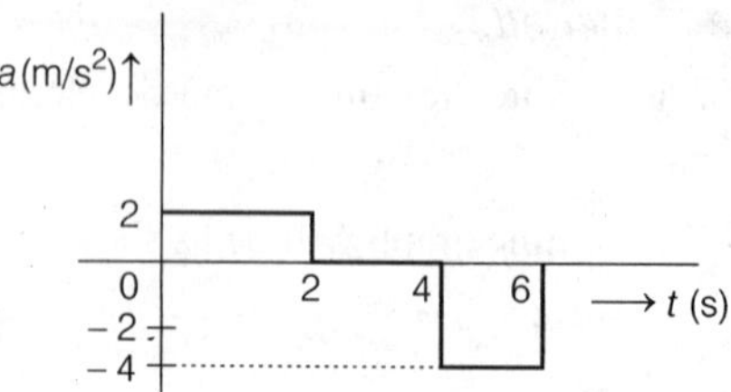

Fig. 6.33

Solution From $t = 0$ to $t = 2\,\text{s}$, $a = +2\ \text{m/s}^2$

$\therefore$ $$v = at = 2t$$

or v-t graph is a straight line passing through origin with slope $2\ \text{m/s}^2$.

At the end of 2 s,

$$v = 2 \times 2 = 4\ \text{m/s}$$

From $t = 2$ to 4 s, $a = 0$.

Hence, $v = 4$ m/s will remain constant.

From $t = 4$ to 6 s, $a = -4\ \text{m/s}^2$.

Hence, $$v = u - at = 4 - 4t \qquad \text{(with } t = 0 \text{ at 4 s)}$$

$v = 0$ at $t = 1$ s or at 5 s from origin.

At the end of 6 s (or $t = 2$ s) $v = -4$ m/s. Corresponding v-t graph is as shown in Fig. 6.34.

Fig. 6.34

INTRODUCTORY EXERCISE 6.8

1. Two particles A and B are moving along x-axis. Their x-coordinate *versus* time graphs are as shown below

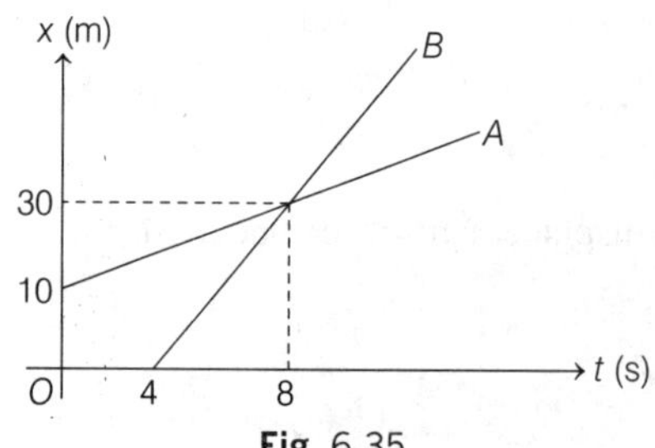

Fig. 6.35

(a) Find the time when the particles start their journey and the x-coordinate at that time.
(b) Find velocities of the two particles.
(c) When and where the particles strike with each other.

2. The velocity of a car as a function of time is shown in Fig. 6.36. Find the distance travelled by the car in 8 s and its acceleration.

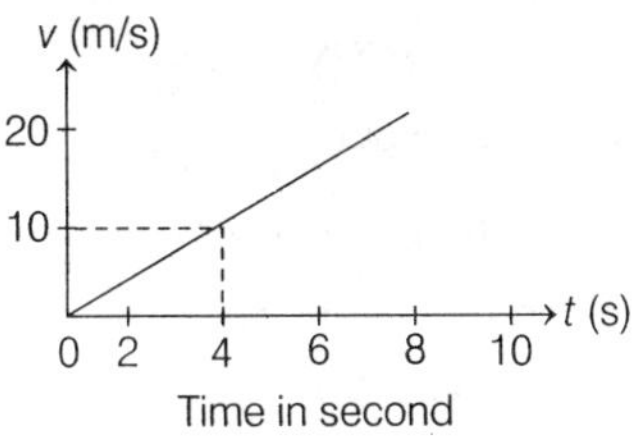

Fig. 6.36

3. Fig. 6.37 shows the graph of velocity versus time for a particle going along the *x*-axis. Find (a) acceleration, (b) the distance travelled in 0 to 10 s and (c) the displacement in 0 to 10 s.

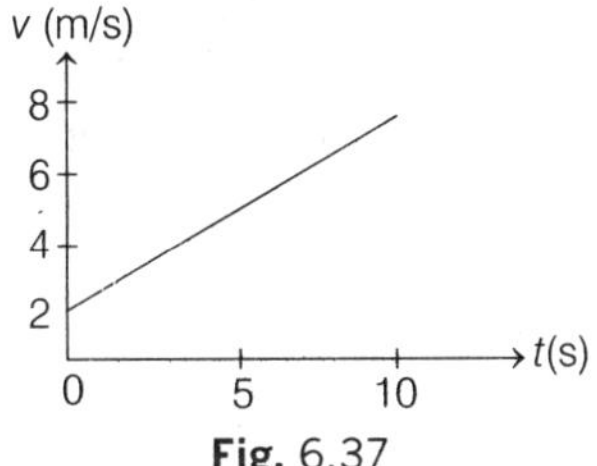

Fig. 6.37

4. Fig. 6.38 shows the graph of the *x*-coordinate of a particle going along the *x*-axis as a function of time. Find (a) the average velocity during 0 to 10 s, (b) instantaneous velocity at 2, 5, 8 and 12 s.

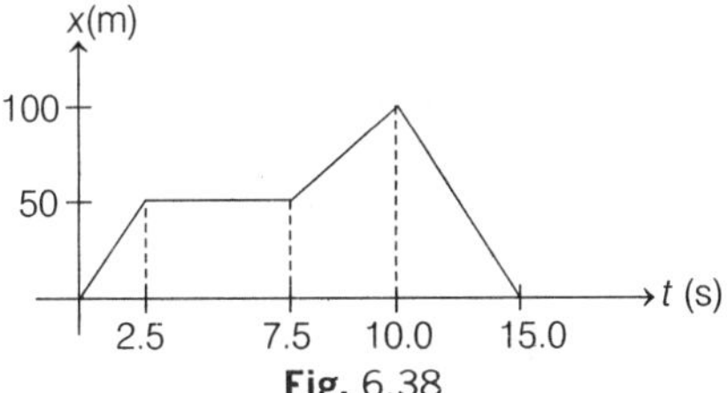

Fig. 6.38

5. From the velocity-time plot shown in Fig. 6.39, find the distance travelled by the particle during the first 40 s. Also find the average velocity during this period.

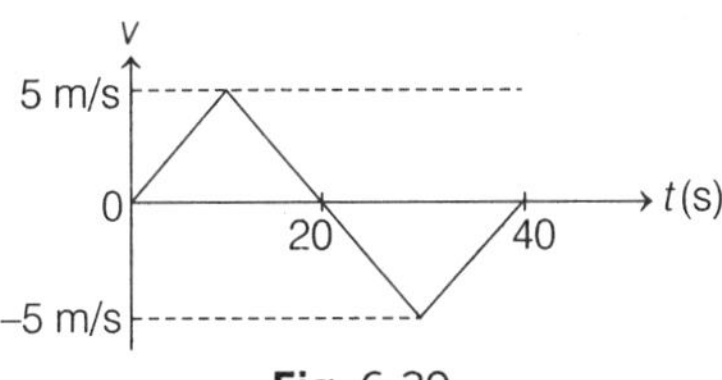

Fig. 6.39

6.10 Relative Motion

The word 'relative' is a very general term, which can be applied to physical, non-physical, scalar or vector quantities. For example, my height is 167 cm while my wife's height is 162 cm. If I ask you what is my height relative to my wife, your answer will be 5 cm. What did you do? You simply subtracted my wife's height from my height. The same concept is applied everywhere, whether it is a relative velocity, relative acceleration or anything else. So, from the above discussion we may now conclude that relative velocity of A with respect to B (written as $\mathbf{v}_{AB}$) is

$$\boxed{\mathbf{v}_{AB} = \mathbf{v}_A - \mathbf{v}_B}$$

Similarly, relative acceleration of A with respect to B is

$$\boxed{\mathbf{a}_{AB} = \mathbf{a}_A - \mathbf{a}_B}$$

If it is a one dimensional motion we can treat the vectors as scalars just by assigning the positive sign to one direction and negative to the other. So, in case of a one dimensional motion the above equations can be written as

$$v_{AB} = v_A - v_B$$

and $$a_{AB} = a_A - a_B$$

Further, we can see that

$$\boxed{\mathbf{v}_{AB} = -\mathbf{v}_{BA} \text{ or } \mathbf{a}_{BA} = -\mathbf{a}_{AB}}$$

Example 6.27 *Anoop is moving due east with a velocity of 1 m/s and Dhyani is moving due west with a velocity of 2 m/s. What is the velocity of Anoop with respect to Dhyani?*

Solution It is a one dimensional motion. So, let us choose the east direction as positive and the west as negative. Now, given that

$$v_A = \text{velocity of Anoop} = 1 \text{ m/s}$$

and $$v_D = \text{velocity of Dhyani} = -2 \text{ m/s}$$

Thus, $$v_{AD} = \text{velocity of Anoop with respect to Dhyani}$$

$$= v_A - v_D = 1 - (-2) = 3 \text{ m/s}$$

Hence, velocity of Anoop with respect to Dhyani is 3 m/s due east.

Example 6.28 *Car A has an acceleration of 2 m/s² due east and car B, 4 m/s² due north. What is the acceleration of car B with respect to car A?*

Solution It is a two dimensional motion. Therefore,

$$\mathbf{a}_{BA} = \text{acceleration of car } B \text{ with respect to car } A$$

$$= \mathbf{a}_B - \mathbf{a}_A$$

Here, $$\mathbf{a}_B = \text{acceleration of car } B$$

$$= 4 \text{ m/s}^2 \text{ (due north)}$$

and $$\mathbf{a}_A = \text{acceleration of car } A$$

$$= 2 \text{ m/s}^2 \text{ (due east)}$$

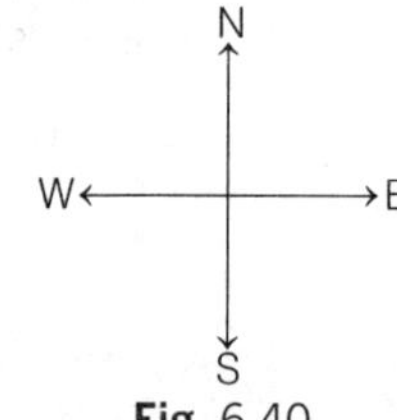

Fig. 6.40

$$|\mathbf{a}_{BA}| = \sqrt{(4)^2 + (2)^2} = 2\sqrt{5} \text{ m/s}^2$$

and $$\alpha = \tan^{-1}\left(\frac{4}{2}\right) = \tan^{-1}(2)$$

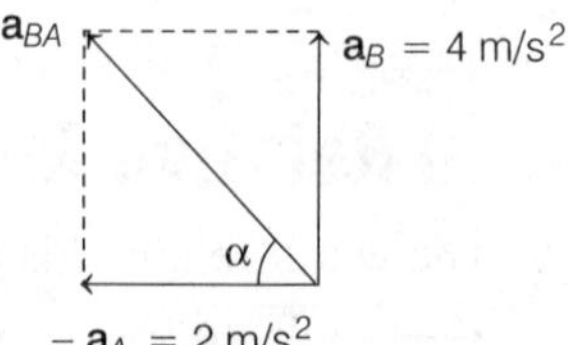

Fig. 6.41

Thus, $\mathbf{a}_{BA}$ is $2\sqrt{5}$ m/s² at an angle of $\alpha = \tan^{-1}(2)$ from west towards north.

The topic 'relative motion' is very useful in two and three dimensional motion. Questions based on relative motion are usually of following four types :

(a) Minimum distance or collision or overtaking problems
(b) River-boat problems
(c) Aircraft-wind problems
(d) Rain problems

Minimum Distance or Collision or Overtaking Problems

When two bodies are in motion, the questions like, the minimum distance between them or the time when one body overtakes the other can be solved easily by the principle of relative motion. In these type of problems, one body is assumed to be at rest and the relative motion of the other body is considered. By assuming so, two body problem is converted into one body problem and the solution becomes easy. Following example will illustrate the statement:

Example 6.29 *Car A and car B start moving simultaneously in the same direction along the line joining them. Car A moves with a constant acceleration $a = 4\ m/s^2$, while car B moves with a constant velocity $v = 1\ m/s$. At time $t = 0$, car A is 10 m behind car B. Find the time when car A overtakes car B.*

Solution Given, $u_A = 0$, $u_B = 1$ m/s, $a_A = 4$ m/s^2 and $a_B = 0$

Assuming car B to be at rest, we have

$$u_{AB} = u_A - u_B = 0 - 1 = -1\ \text{m/s}$$

$$a_{AB} = a_A - a_B = 4 - 0 = 4\ \text{m/s}^2$$

–ve ← → +ve

Fig. 6.42

Now, the problem can be assumed in simplified form as shown below.

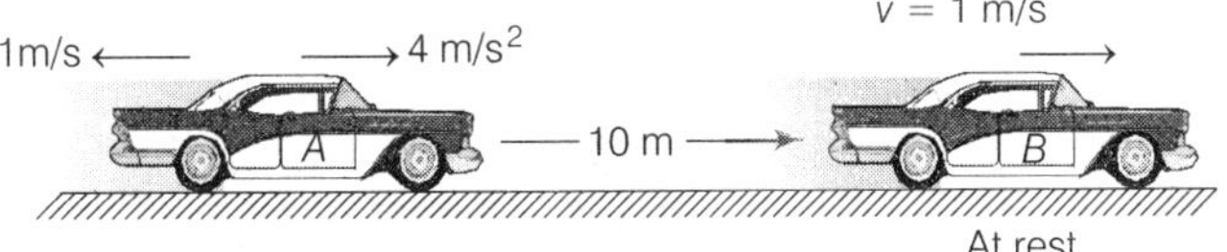

Fig. 6.43

Substituting the proper values in equation $s = ut + \frac{1}{2}at^2$,

we get $$10 = -t + \frac{1}{2}(4)(t^2)$$

or $$2t^2 - t - 10 = 0$$

or $$t = \frac{1 \pm \sqrt{1 + 80}}{4}$$

$$= \frac{1 \pm \sqrt{81}}{4}$$

$$= \frac{1 \pm 9}{4}$$

or $$t = 2.5\ \text{s} \quad \text{and} \quad -2\ \text{s}$$

Ignoring the negative value, the desired time is 2.5 s.

Example 6.30 *Two ships A and B are 10 km apart on a line running south to north. Ship A farther north is streaming west at 20 km/h and ship B is streaming north at 20 km/h. What is their distance of closest approach and how long do they take to reach it?*

Solution Ships A and B are moving with same speed 20 km/h in the directions shown in figure. It is a two dimensional, two body problem with zero acceleration.

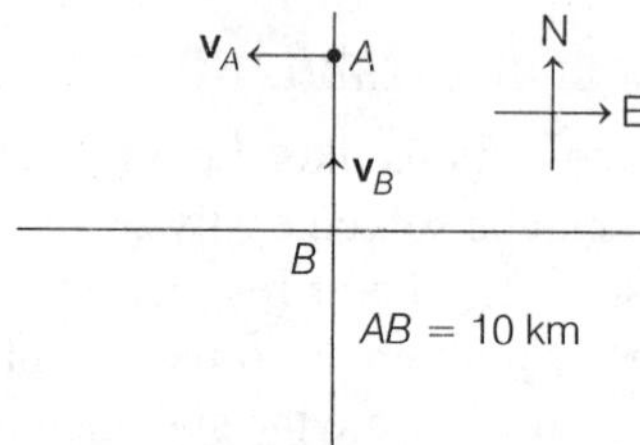

Fig. 6.44

Let us find $\mathbf{v}_{BA}$.

$\therefore$
$$\mathbf{v}_{BA} = \mathbf{v}_B - \mathbf{v}_A$$

Here,
$$|\mathbf{v}_{BA}| = \sqrt{(20)^2 + (20)^2}$$
$$= 20\sqrt{2} \text{ km/h}$$

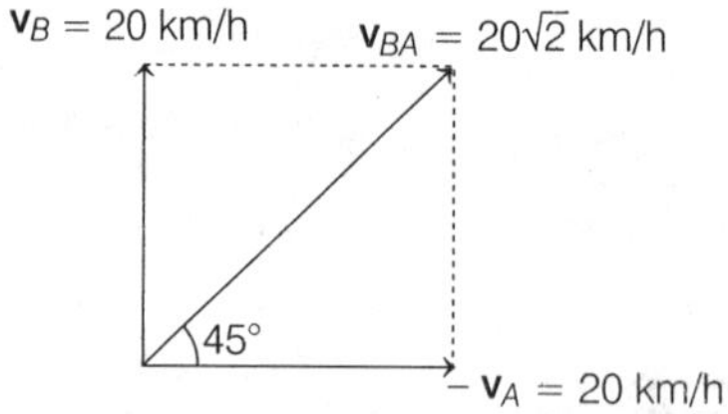

Fig. 6.45

i.e. $\mathbf{v}_{BA}$ is $20\sqrt{2}$ km/h at an angle of 45° from east towards north. Thus, the given problem can be simplified as A is at rest and B is moving with $\mathbf{v}_{BA}$ in the direction shown in Fig. 6.46.

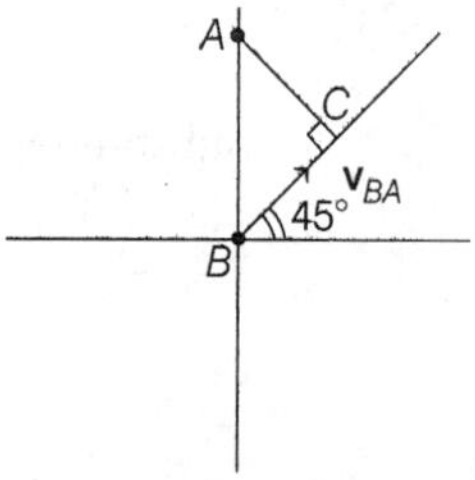

Therefore, the minimum distance between the two is

$$s_{\text{min}} = AC = AB \sin 45°$$
$$= 10\left(\frac{1}{\sqrt{2}}\right) \text{ km}$$
$$= 5\sqrt{2} \text{ km} \qquad \textbf{Ans.}$$

Fig. 6.46

and the desired time is

$$t = \frac{BC}{|\mathbf{v}_{BA}|} = \frac{5\sqrt{2}}{20\sqrt{2}} \qquad (BC = AC = 5\sqrt{2} \text{ km})$$
$$= \frac{1}{4} \text{ h} = 15 \text{ min} \qquad \textbf{Ans.}$$

River-Boat Problems

In river-boat problems, we come across the following three terms :

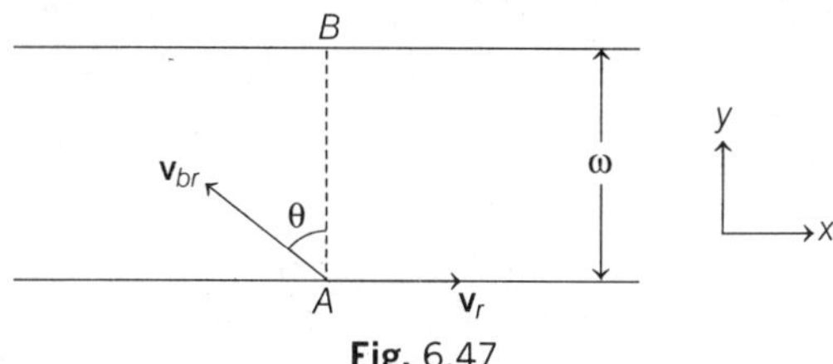

Fig. 6.47

$\mathbf{v}_r$ = absolute velocity of river

$\mathbf{v}_{br}$ = velocity of boatman with respect to river or velocity of boatman in still water

and $\mathbf{v}_b$ = absolute velocity of boatman.

Here, it is important to note that $\mathbf{v}_{br}$ is the velocity of boatman with which he steers and $\mathbf{v}_b$ is the actual velocity of boatman relative to ground.

Further, $$\mathbf{v}_b = \mathbf{v}_{br} + \mathbf{v}_r \qquad (\text{as } \mathbf{v}_{br} = \mathbf{v}_b - \mathbf{v}_r)$$

Now, let us derive some standard results and their special cases.

A boatman starts from point A on one bank of a river with velocity $\mathbf{v}_{br}$ in the direction shown in Fig. 6.47. River is flowing along positive x-direction with velocity $\mathbf{v}_r$. Width of the river is ω, then

$$\mathbf{v}_b = \mathbf{v}_r + \mathbf{v}_{br}$$

Therefore, $$v_{bx} = v_{rx} + v_{brx} = v_r - v_{br} \sin\theta$$

and $$v_{by} = v_{ry} + v_{bry}$$

$$= 0 + v_{br}\cos\theta = v_{br}\cos\theta$$

Now, time taken by the boatman to cross the river is

$$t = \frac{\omega}{v_{by}} = \frac{\omega}{v_{br}\cos\theta} \quad \text{or} \quad \boxed{t = \frac{\omega}{v_{br}\cos\theta}} \qquad \ldots\text{(i)}$$

Further, displacement along x-axis when he reaches the other bank (also called drift) is

$$x = v_{bx}\, t = (v_r - v_{br}\sin\theta)\frac{\omega}{v_{br}\cos\theta}$$

or $$\boxed{x = (v_r - v_{br}\sin\theta)\frac{\omega}{v_{br}\cos\theta}} \qquad \ldots\text{(ii)}$$

Three special cases are:

(i) **Condition when the boatman crosses the river in shortest interval of time** From Eq. (i) we can see that time (t) will be minimum when $\theta = 0°$, i.e. the boatman should steer his boat perpendicular to the river current.

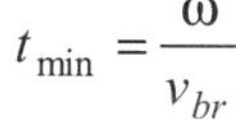

Also, $$t_{min} = \frac{\omega}{v_{br}}$$

as $$\cos\theta = 1$$

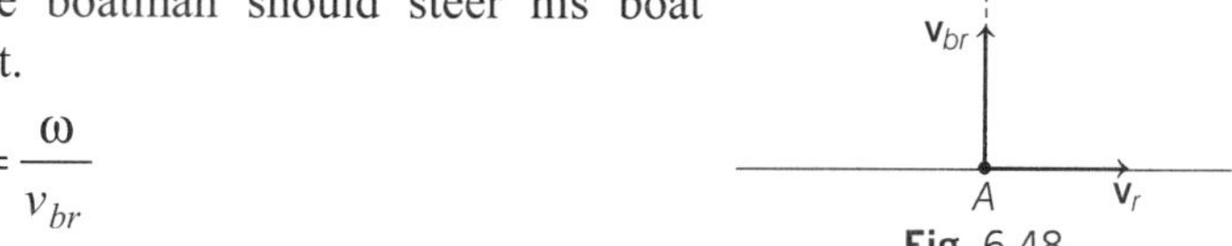

Fig. 6.48

(ii) Condition when the boatman wants to reach point *B*, i.e. **at a point just opposite from where he started**

In this case, the drift (x) should be zero.

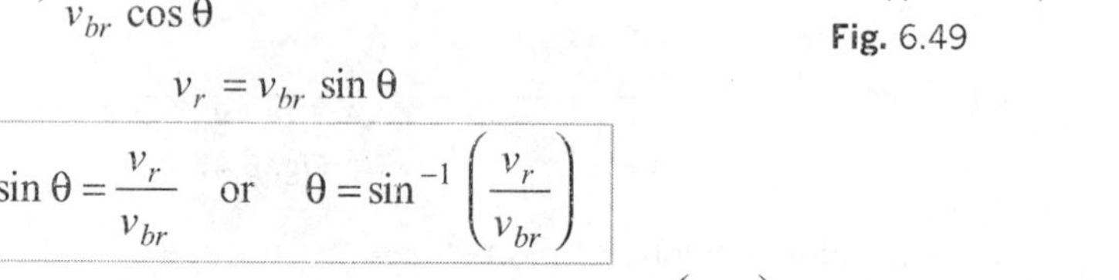

Fig. 6.49

$$\therefore \quad x = 0$$

or
$$(v_r - v_{br} \sin\theta)\frac{\omega}{v_{br}\cos\theta} = 0$$

or
$$v_r = v_{br}\sin\theta$$

or
$$\sin\theta = \frac{v_r}{v_{br}} \quad \text{or} \quad \theta = \sin^{-1}\left(\frac{v_r}{v_{br}}\right)$$

Hence, to reach point B the boatman should row at an angle $\theta = \sin^{-1}\left(\frac{v_r}{v_{br}}\right)$ upstream from AB.

Further, since $\sin\theta \not> 1$.

So, if $v_r \geq v_{br}$, the boatman can never reach at point B. Because if $v_r = v_{br}$, $\sin\theta = 1$ or $\theta = 90°$ and it is just impossible to reach at B if $\theta = 90°$. Moreover, it can be seen that $v_b = 0$ if $v_r = v_{br}$ and $\theta = 90°$. Similarly, if $v_r > v_{br}$, $\sin\theta > 1$, i.e. no such angle exists. Practically, it can be realized in this manner that it is not possible to reach at B if river velocity (v_r) is too high.

Extra Points to Remember

- In a general case, resolve $\mathbf{v}_{br}$ along the river and perpendicular to river as shown below.

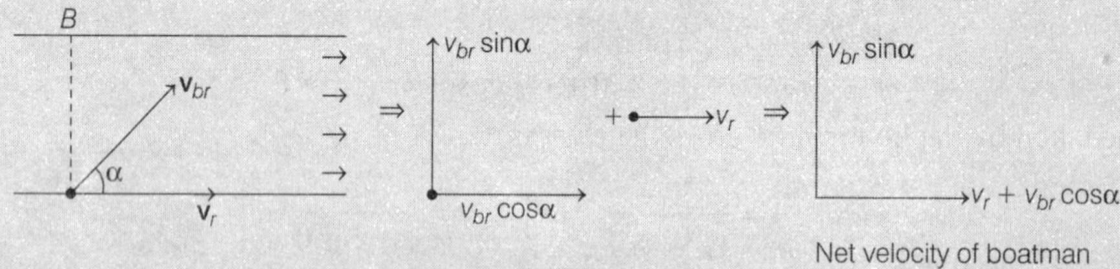

Fig. 6.50

Now, the boatman will cross the river with component of $\mathbf{v}_{br}$ perpendicular to river (= v_{br} sin α in above case)

$$\therefore \quad t = \frac{\omega}{v_{br}\sin\alpha}$$

To cross the river in minimum time, why to take help of component of $\mathbf{v}_{br}$ (which is always less that v_{br}), the complete vector $\mathbf{v}_{br}$ should be kept perpendicular to the river current. Due to the other component $v_r + v_{br}\cos\alpha$, boatman will drift along the river by a distance $x = (v_r + v_{br}\cos\alpha)$ (time)

- To reach a point B, which is just opposite to the starting point A, net velocity of boatman $\mathbf{v}_b$ or the vector sum of $\mathbf{v}_r$ and $\mathbf{v}_{br}$ should be along AB. The velocity diagram is as under

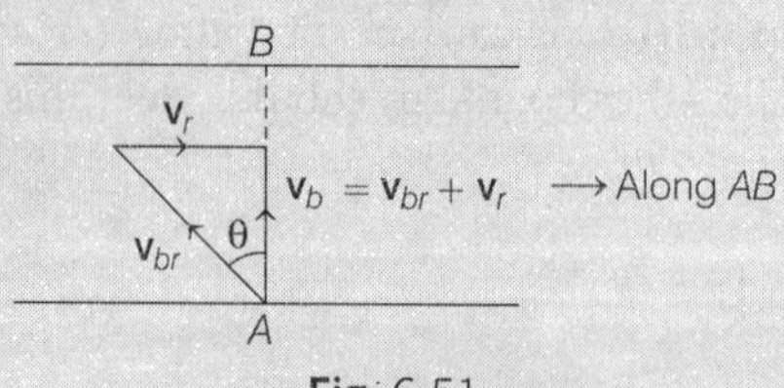

Fig. 6.51

From the diagram we can see that,

$$|\mathbf{v}_b| \text{ or } v_b = \sqrt{v_{br}^2 - v_r^2} \quad ...(i)$$

$$\text{Time, } t = \frac{\omega}{v_b} = \frac{\omega}{\sqrt{v_{br}^2 - v_r^2}}$$

$$\text{drift } x = 0 \text{ and } \sin\theta = \frac{v_r}{v_{br}} \text{ or } \theta = \sin^{-1}\left(\frac{v_r}{v_{br}}\right)$$

From Eq. (i), we can see that this case is possible if,

$$v_{br} > v_r$$

otherwise, v_b is either zero or imaginary.

- If the boatman rows his boat along the river (downstream), then net velocity of boatman will be $v_{br} + v_r$. If he rows along the river upstream then net velocity of boatman will be $v_{br} \sim v_r$.

Example 6.31 *Width of a river is 30 m, river velocity is 2 m/s and rowing velocity is 5 m/s at 37° from the direction of river current (a) find the time taken to cross the river, (b) drift of the boatman while reaching the other shore.*

Solution

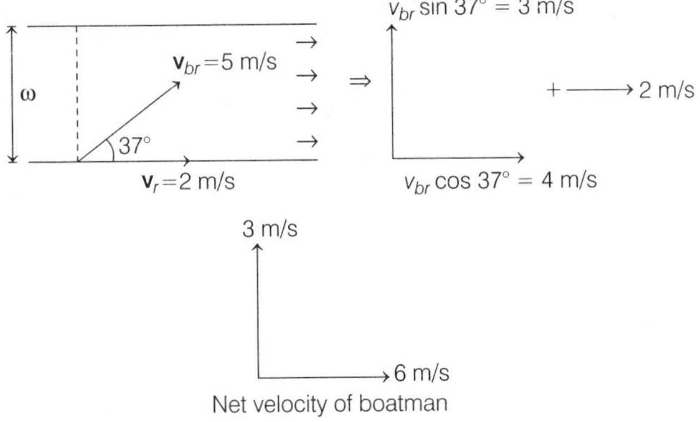

Fig. 6.52

(a) Time taken to cross the river,

$$t = \frac{\omega}{3} = \frac{30}{3} = 10\text{ s} \qquad \textbf{Ans.}$$

(b) Drift along the river

$$x = (6)(t) = 6 \times 10 = 60\text{ m} \qquad \textbf{Ans.}$$

Example 6.32 *Width of a river is 30 m, river velocity is 4 m/s and rowing velocity of boatman is 5 m/s*

(a) Make the velocity diagram for crossing the river in shortest time. Then, find this shortest time, net velocity of boatman and drift along the river.

(b) Can the boatman reach a point just opposite on the other shore? If yes then make the velocity diagram, the direction in which he should row his boat and the time taken to cross the river in this case.

(c) How long will it take him to row 10 m up the stream and then back to his starting point?

Solution (a) **Shortest time**

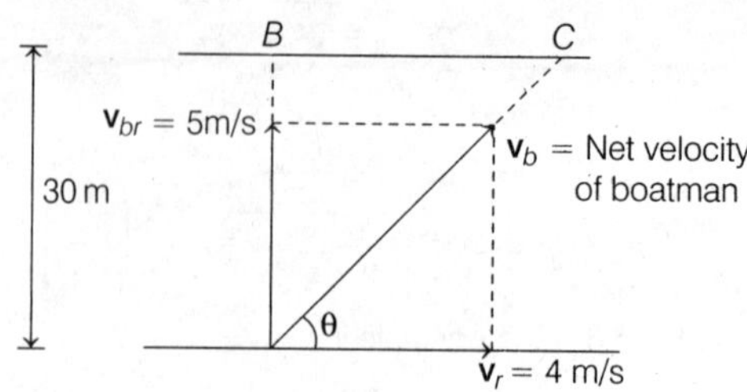

Fig. 6.53

$$t = \frac{30}{5} = 6\,\text{s} = t_{\text{min}}$$ **Ans.**

$$|\mathbf{v}_b| \text{ or } v_b = \sqrt{(5)^2 + (4)^2} = \sqrt{41}\text{ m/s}$$ **Ans.**

$$\tan\theta = \frac{5}{4} \Rightarrow \theta = \tan^{-1}\left(\frac{5}{4}\right)$$ **Ans.**

$$\text{Drift} = BC = (4)(t)$$
$$= 4 \times 6 = 24\text{ m}$$ **Ans.**

(b) Since, $v_{br} > v_r$, this case is possible. Velocity diagram is as under.

Net velocity $|\mathbf{v}_b|$ or $v_b = \sqrt{(5)^2 - (4)^2} = 3$ m/s along AB

$$\sin\theta = \frac{4}{5} \Rightarrow \theta = \sin^{-1}\frac{4}{5} = 53°$$ **Ans.**

$$t = \frac{AB}{v_b} = \frac{30}{3} = 10\,\text{sec}$$ **Ans.**

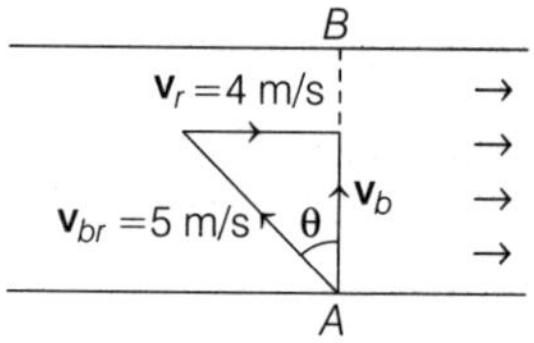

Fig. 6.54

Note *If the boatman wants to return to the same point A, then diagram is as under*

$$t_{BA} = \frac{BA}{3} = \frac{30}{3} = 10\text{ s}$$

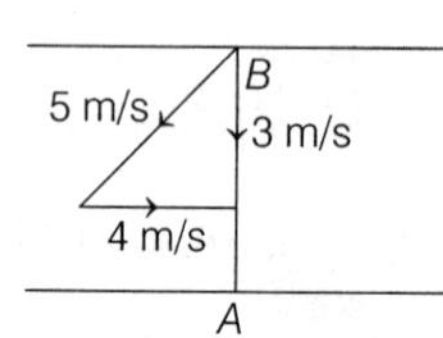

Fig. 6.55

(c)

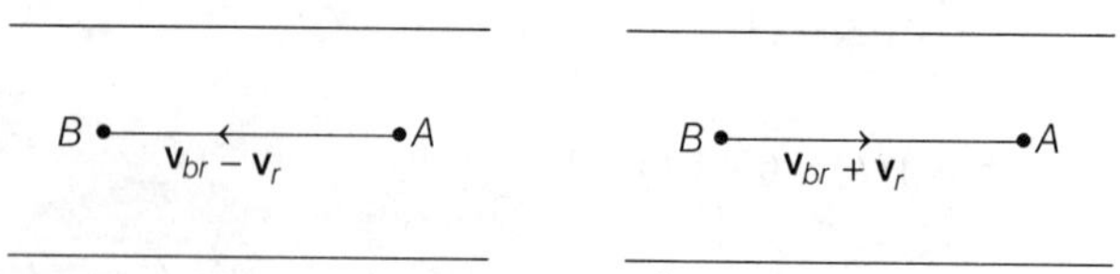

B • ← $v_{br} - v_r$ • A   B • → $v_{br} + v_r$ • A

Fig. 6.56

$$t = t_{AB} + t_{BA} = \frac{AB}{v_{br} - v_r} + \frac{BA}{v_{br} + v_r}$$

or
$$t = \frac{10}{5-4} + \frac{10}{5+4}$$
$$= \frac{100}{9}\text{ s}$$ **Ans.**

Aircraft Wind Problems

This is similar to river boat problems. The only difference is that $\mathbf{v}_{br}$ is replaced by $\mathbf{v}_{aw}$ (velocity of aircraft with respect to wind or velocity of aircraft in still air), $\mathbf{v}_r$ is replaced by $\mathbf{v}_w$ (velocity of wind) and $\mathbf{v}_b$ is replaced by $\mathbf{v}_a$ (absolute velocity of aircraft). Further, $\mathbf{v}_a = \mathbf{v}_{aw} + \mathbf{v}_w$.

In this case, problem is slightly different. The given variables are

(i) Complete wind velocity $\mathbf{v}_w$

(ii) Steering speed or $|\mathbf{v}_{aw}|$

(iii) Starting point (say A) and destination point (say B)

We have to find direction of $\mathbf{v}_{aw}$ (or steering velocity) and the time taken in moving from A to B. The concepts is : net velocity of aircraft $\mathbf{v}_a$ or vector sum of $\mathbf{v}_w$ and $\mathbf{v}_{aw}$ should be along AB.

To solve such problems, we can apply the following steps :

(i) Take starting point A as the origin.

(ii) Wind velocity vector is completely given. So, draw $\mathbf{v}_w$ from point A.

(iii) Draw another vector $\mathbf{v}_a$ starting from A in a direction from A to B.

(iv) In above two steps we have already made two sides of a triangle in vector form. Complete the third side. This represents $\mathbf{v}_{aw}$. While completing the triangle for finding direction of $\mathbf{v}_{aw}$, polygon law of vector addition is to be followed, so that,

$$\mathbf{v}_w + \mathbf{v}_{aw} = \mathbf{v}_a$$

(v) Applying, sine law in this triangle, we can find direction of $\mathbf{v}_{aw}$ and the net velocity of aircraft $\mathbf{v}_a$. Now,

time taken, $$t = \frac{AB}{|\mathbf{v}_a|} \quad \text{or} \quad \frac{AB}{v_a}$$

The following example will illustrate the above theory:

Example 6.33 *An aircraft flies at 400 km/h in still air. A wind of $200\sqrt{2}$ km/h is blowing from the south towards north. The pilot wishes to travel from A to a point B north east of A. Find the direction he must steer and time of his journey if AB = 1000 km.*

Solution Given that $v_w = 200\sqrt{2}$ km/h

$v_{aw} = 400$ km/h and $\mathbf{v}_a$ should be along AB or in north-east direction. Thus, the direction of $\mathbf{v}_{aw}$ should be such as the resultant of $\mathbf{v}_w$ and $\mathbf{v}_{aw}$ is along AB or in north-east direction.

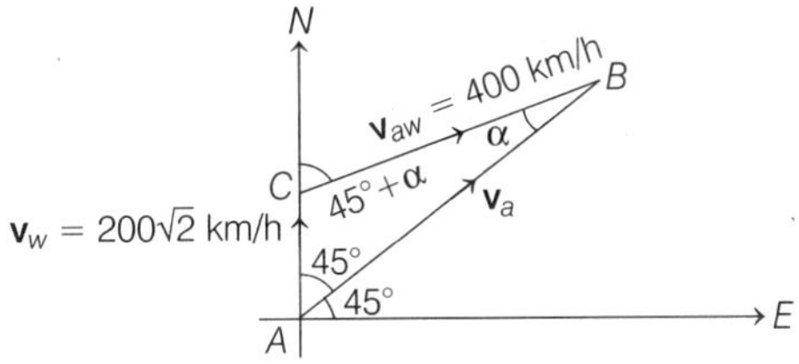

Let $\mathbf{v}_{aw}$ makes an angle α with AB as shown in Fig. 6.57. Applying sine law in triangle ABC, we get

Fig. 6.57

$$\frac{CB}{\sin 45^\circ} = \frac{AC}{\sin \alpha}$$

or $$\sin \alpha = \left(\frac{AC}{CB}\right) \sin 45^\circ$$

$$= \left(\frac{200\sqrt{2}}{400}\right)\frac{1}{\sqrt{2}} = \frac{1}{2}$$

$\therefore \qquad \alpha = 30°$

Therefore, the pilot should steer in a direction at an angle of $(45° + \alpha)$ or 75° from north towards east.

Further, $\dfrac{|\mathbf{v}_a|}{\sin(180° - 45° - 30°)} = \dfrac{400}{\sin 45°}$

or
$$|\mathbf{v}_a| = \frac{\sin 105°}{\sin 45°} \times (400) \text{ km/h}$$
$$= \left(\frac{\cos 15°}{\sin 45°}\right)(400) \text{ km/h}$$
$$= \left(\frac{0.9659}{0.707}\right)(400) \text{ km/h}$$
$$= 546.47 \text{ km/h}$$

$\therefore$ The time of journey from A to B is

$$t = \frac{AB}{|\mathbf{v}_a|} = \frac{1000}{546.47} \text{ h}$$

$$t = 1.83 \text{ h}$$ **Ans.**

Rain Problems

In these type of problems, we again come across three terms $\mathbf{v}_r$, $\mathbf{v}_m$ and $\mathbf{v}_{rm}$ Here,

$\mathbf{v}_r$ = velocity of rain

$\mathbf{v}_m$ = velocity of man (it may be velocity of cyclist or velocity of motorist also)

and $\mathbf{v}_{rm}$ = velocity of rain with respect to man.

Here, $\mathbf{v}_{rm}$ is the velocity of rain which appears to the man.

So, the man should hold his umbrella in the direction of $\mathbf{v}_{rm}$ or $\mathbf{v}_r - \mathbf{v}_m$, to save him from rain.

Example 6.34 *A man is walking with 3 m/s, due east. Rain is falling vertically downwards with speed 4 m/s. Find the direction in which man should hold his umbrella, so that rain does not wet him.*

Solution As we discussed above, he should hold his umbrella in the direction of $\mathbf{v}_{rm}$ or $\mathbf{v}_r - \mathbf{v}_m$

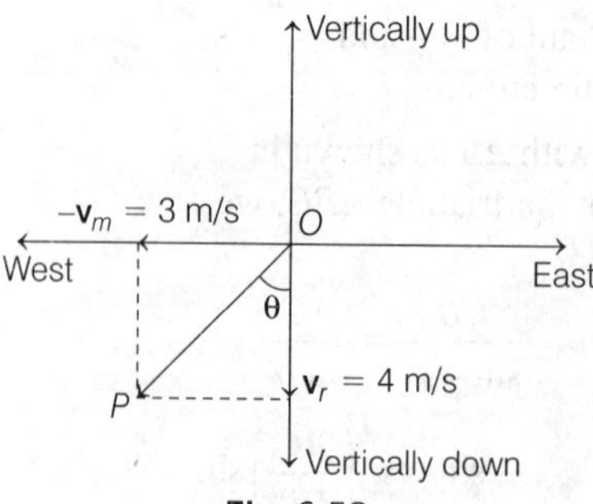

Fig. 6.58

$$\mathbf{OP} = \mathbf{v}_r + (-\mathbf{v}_m) = \mathbf{v}_r - \mathbf{v}_m = \mathbf{v}_{rm}$$

$$\Rightarrow \quad \tan\theta = \frac{3}{4}$$

$$\Rightarrow \quad \theta = \tan^{-1}\left(\frac{3}{4}\right) = 37°$$

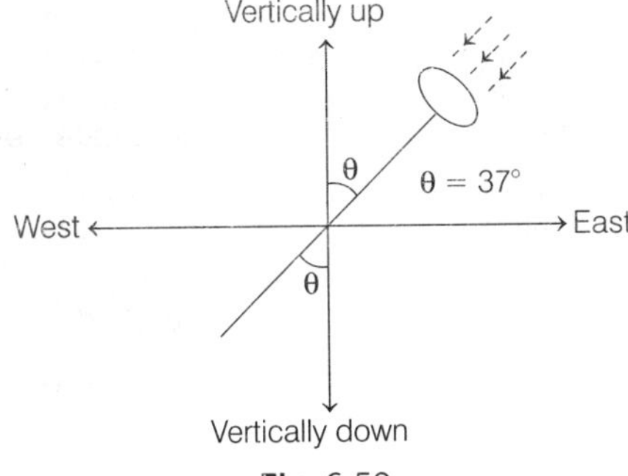

Fig. 6.59

Therefore, man should hold his umbrella at an angle of 37° east of vertical (or 37° from vertical towards east).

Example 6.35 *To a man walking at the rate of 3 km/h the rain appears to fall vertically downwards. When he increases his speed to 6 km/h it appears to meet him at an angle of 45° with vertical. Find the speed of rain.*

Solution Let $\hat{\mathbf{i}}$ and $\hat{\mathbf{j}}$ be the unit vectors in horizontal and vertical directions respectively.

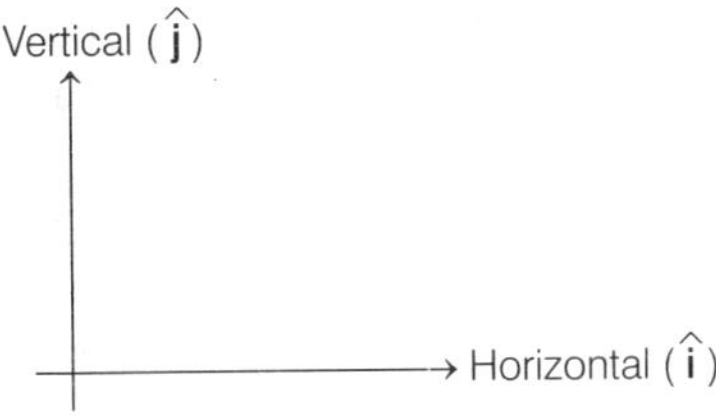

Fig. 6.60

Let velocity of rain $\quad \mathbf{v}_r = a\hat{\mathbf{i}} + b\hat{\mathbf{j}} \quad$ ...(i)

Then, speed of rain will be $\quad |\mathbf{v}_r| = \sqrt{a^2 + b^2} \quad$ ...(ii)

In the first case,

$$\mathbf{v}_m = \text{velocity of man} = 3\hat{\mathbf{i}}$$

$$\therefore \quad \mathbf{v}_{rm} = \mathbf{v}_r - \mathbf{v}_m = (a - 3)\,\hat{\mathbf{i}} + b\hat{\mathbf{j}}$$

It seems to be in vertical direction.

Hence, $\quad a - 3 = 0 \quad \text{or} \quad a = 3$

In the second case, $\quad \mathbf{v}_m = 6\,\hat{\mathbf{i}}$

$$\therefore \quad \mathbf{v}_{rm} = (a - 6)\hat{\mathbf{i}} + b\hat{\mathbf{j}} = -3\hat{\mathbf{i}} + b\hat{\mathbf{j}}$$

This seems to be at 45° with vertical. Hence, $|b| = 3$

Therefore, from Eq. (ii) speed of rain is

$$|\mathbf{v}_r| = \sqrt{(3)^2 + (3)^2}$$
$$= 3\sqrt{2} \text{ km/h}$$

Ans.

INTRODUCTORY EXERCISE 6.9

1. Two particles are moving along x-axis. Their x-coordinate *versus* time graph are as shown below.

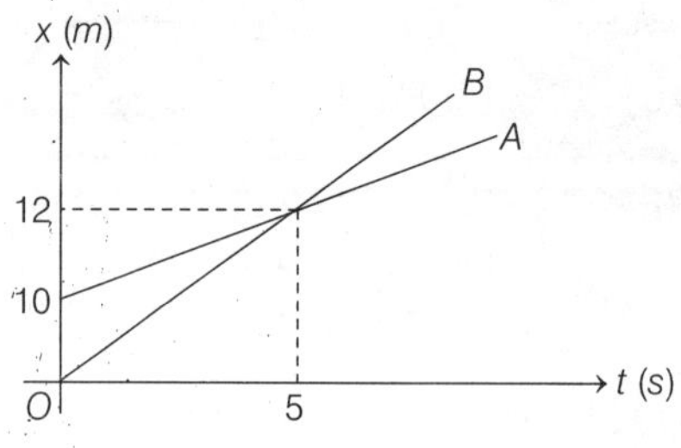

Fig. 6.61

Find velocity of A w.r.t. B.

2. Two balls A and B are projected vertically upwards with different velocities. What is the relative acceleration between them?
3. A river 400 m wide is flowing at a rate of 2.0 m/s. A boat is sailing at a velocity of 10.0 m/s with respect to the water in a direction perpendicular to the river.
   (a) Find the time taken by the boat to reach the opposite bank.
   (b) How far from the point directly opposite to the starting point does the boat reach the opposite bank?
4. An aeroplane has to go from a point A to another point B, 500 km away due 30° east of north. Wind is blowing due north at a speed of 20 m/s. The steering-speed of the plane is 150 m/s. (a) Find the direction in which the pilot should head the plane to reach the point B. (b) Find the time taken by the plane to go from A to B.
5. A man crosses a river in a boat. If he cross the river in minimum time he takes 10 min with a drift 120 m. If he crosses the river taking shortest path, he takes 12.5 min, find
   (a) width of the river
   (b) velocity of the boat with respect to water
   (c) speed of the current
6. A river is 20 m wide. River speed is 3 m/s. A boat starts with velocity $2\sqrt{2}$ m/s at angle 45° from the river current (relative to river)
   (a) Find the time taken by the boat to reach the opposite bank.
   (b) How far from the point directly opposite to the starting point does the boat reach the opposite bank?

Core Concepts

1. If a particle is just dropped from a moving body then just after dropping, velocity of the particle (not acceleration) is equal to the velocity of the moving body at that instant.

   For example, if a stone is dropped from a moving train with velocity 20 m/s, then initial velocity of the stone is 20 m/s horizontal in the direction of motion of train. But, after dropping it comes under gravity. Therefore, its acceleration is g downwards.

2. If y (may be velocity, acceleration etc.) is a function of time or $y = f(t)$ and we want to find the average value of y between a time interval of t_1 and t_2. Then,

$$< y >_{t_1 \text{ to } t_2} = \text{average value of } y \text{ between } t_1 \text{ and } t_2$$

$$= \frac{\int_{t_1}^{t_2} f(t)\, dt}{t_2 - t_1} \quad \text{or} \quad < y >_{t_1 \text{ to } t_2} = \frac{\int_{t_1}^{t_2} f(t)\, dt}{t_2 - t_1}$$

   If $f(t)$ is a linear function of t, then $$y_{av} = \frac{y_f + y_i}{2}$$

   Here, y_f = final value of y and y_i = initial value of y

   At the same time, we should not forget that

$$v_{av} = \frac{\text{total displacement}}{\text{total time}} \quad \text{and} \quad a_{av} = \frac{\text{change in velocity}}{\text{total time}}$$

   Example *In one dimensional uniformly accelerated motion, find average velocity between a time interval from $t = 0$ to $t = t$.*

   Solution We can solve this problem by three methods.

   Method 1. $v = u + at$

$$\therefore \quad < v >_{0-t} = \frac{\int_0^t (u + at)\, dt}{t - 0} = u + \frac{1}{2} at$$

   Method 2. Since, v is a linear function of time, we can write

$$v_{av} = \frac{v_f + v_i}{2} = \frac{(u + at) + u}{2} = u + \frac{1}{2} at$$

   Method 3. $$v_{av} = \frac{\text{Total displacement}}{\text{Total time}} = \frac{ut + \frac{1}{2} at^2}{t} = u + \frac{1}{2} at$$

3. A particle is thrown upwards with velocity u. Suppose it takes time t to reach its highest point, then distance travelled in last second is independent of u.

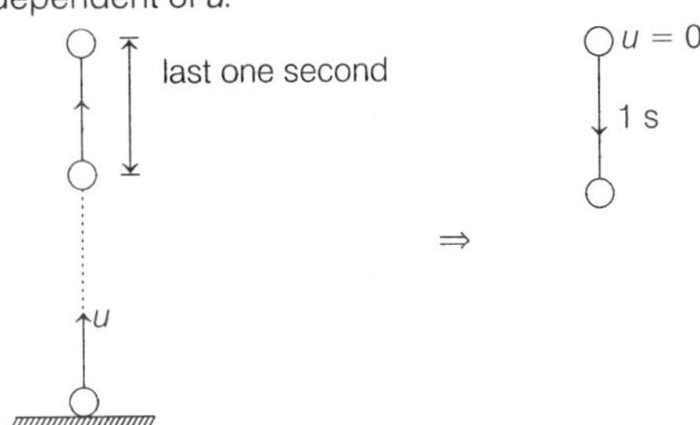

   This is because this distance is equal to the distance travelled in first second of a freely falling object. Thus,

$$s = \frac{1}{2} g \times (1)^2 = \frac{1}{2} \times 10 \times 1 = 5 \text{ m}$$

   Exercise: *A particle is thrown upwards with velocity u (> 20 m/s). Prove that distance travelled in last 2 s is 20 m.*

4. Angle between velocity vector **v** and acceleration vector **a** decides whether the speed of particle is increasing, decreasing or constant.

Speed increases, if $0° \le \theta < 90°$

Speed decreases, if $90° < \theta \le 180°$

Speed is constant, if $\theta = 90°$

The angle θ between **v** and **a** can be obtained by the relation,

$$\theta = \cos^{-1}\left(\frac{\mathbf{v}\cdot\mathbf{a}}{va}\right)$$

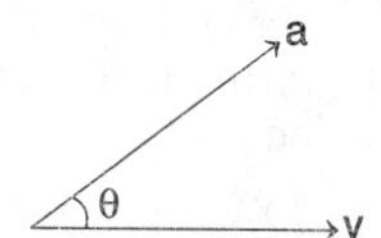

Exercise: *Prove that speed of a particle increases if dot product of* **v** *and* **a** *is positive, speed decreases, if the dot product is negative and speed remains constant if dot product is zero.*

5. The magnitude of instantaneous velocity is called the instantaneous speed, i.e.

$$v = |\mathbf{v}| = \left|\frac{d\mathbf{r}}{dt}\right|$$

Speed is not equal to $\frac{dr}{dt}$, i.e. $$v \ne \frac{dr}{dt}$$

where, r is the modulus of radius vector **r** because in general $|d\mathbf{r}| \ne dr$. For example, when **r** changes only in direction, i.e. if a point moves in a circle, then r = constant, $dr = 0$ but $|d\mathbf{r}| \ne 0$.

6. Suppose **C** is a vector sum of two vectors **A** and **B** and the direction of **C** is given to us (along PQ), then **A** + **B** should be along PQ or sum of components of **A** and **B** perpendicular to line PQ should be zero.

For instance, in example 6.33, $\mathbf{v}_a$ has to be along AB and we know that $\mathbf{v}_a = \mathbf{v}_{aw} + \mathbf{v}_w$. Therefore, sum of components of $\mathbf{v}_{aw}$ and $\mathbf{v}_w$ perpendicular to line AB (shown as dotted) should be zero.

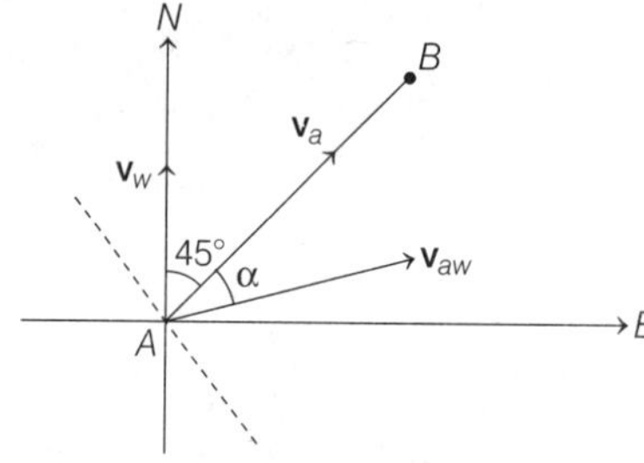

or $|\mathbf{v}_{aw}| \sin\alpha = |\mathbf{v}_w| \sin 45°$

or $$\sin\alpha = \frac{|\mathbf{v}_w|}{|\mathbf{v}_{aw}|}\sin 45°$$

$$= \left(\frac{200\sqrt{2}}{400}\right)\left(\frac{1}{\sqrt{2}}\right) = \frac{1}{2}$$

∴ $$\alpha = 30°$$

Now, $$|\mathbf{v}_a| = |\mathbf{v}_{aw}|\cos\alpha + |\mathbf{v}_w|\cos 45°$$

$$= (400)\cos 30° + (200\sqrt{2})\left(\frac{1}{\sqrt{2}}\right)$$

$$= (400)\frac{\sqrt{3}}{2} + 200 = 346.47 + 200$$

$$= 546.47 \text{ km/h}$$

∴ Time of journey from A to B will be

$$t = \frac{AB}{|\mathbf{v}_a|} = \frac{1000}{546.47} = 1.83 \text{ h}$$

7. From the given s-t graph, we can find sign of velocity and acceleration.

For example, in the given graph slope at t_1 and t_2 both are positive. Therefore, v_{t_1} and v_{t_2} are positive. Further, slope at $t_2 >$ Slope at t_1. Therefore $v_{t_2} > v_{t_1}$. Hence acceleration of the particle is also positive.

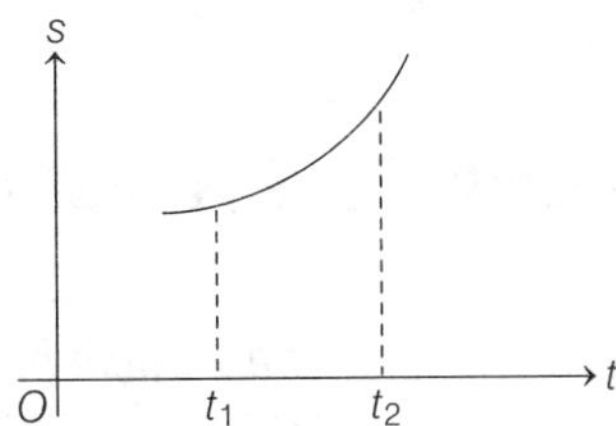

Exercise: *In the given s-t graph, find signs of v and a.*

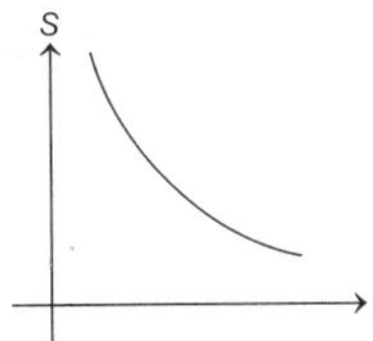

Ans. Negative, positive

8. **Shortest path in river boat problems**

Path length travelled by the boatman when he reaches the opposite shore is

$$s = \sqrt{\omega^2 + x^2}$$

Here, ω = width of river is constant. So, for s to be minimum modulus of x (drift) should be minimum. Now, two cases are possible.

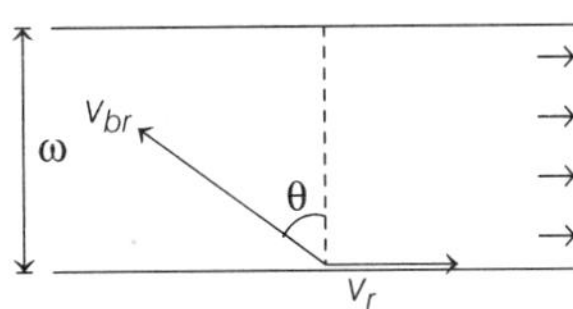

When $v_r < v_{br}$: In this case $x = 0$, when $\theta = \sin^{-1}\left(\frac{v_r}{v_{br}}\right)$

or
$$s_{min} = \omega \quad \text{at} \quad \theta = \sin^{-1}\left(\frac{v_r}{v_{br}}\right)$$

When $v_r > v_{br}$: In this case x is minimum, where $\frac{dx}{d\theta} = 0$

or
$$\frac{d}{d\theta}\left\{\frac{\omega}{v_{br}\cos\theta}(v_r - v_{br}\sin\theta)\right\} = 0$$

or
$$-v_{br}\cos^2\theta - (v_r - v_{br}\sin\theta)(-\sin\theta) = 0$$

or
$$-v_{br} + v_r\sin\theta = 0 \text{ or } \theta = \sin^{-1}\left(\frac{v_{br}}{v_r}\right)$$

Now, at this angle we can find x_{min} and then s_{min} which comes out to be

$$s_{min} = \omega\left(\frac{v_r}{v_{br}}\right) \quad \text{at} \quad \theta = \sin^{-1}\left(\frac{v_{br}}{v_r}\right)$$

Solved Examples

PATTERNED PROBLEMS

Type 1. *Collision of two particles or overtaking of one particle by the other particle*

Concept

(i) If two particles start from the same point and they collide, then their displacements are same or

$$S_1 = S_2$$

If they start from different points, then

$$S_1 \neq S_2$$

(ii) If they start their journeys simultaneously, then their time of journeys are same or

$$t_1 = t_2 = t \quad \text{(say)}$$

otherwise their time of journeys are different

$$t_1 \neq t_2$$

How to Solve? (In 1-D motion)

- Take one direction as positive and the other as negative.
- Without considering, the given directions of their initial velocities and accelerations assume that both particles are moving along positive direction.

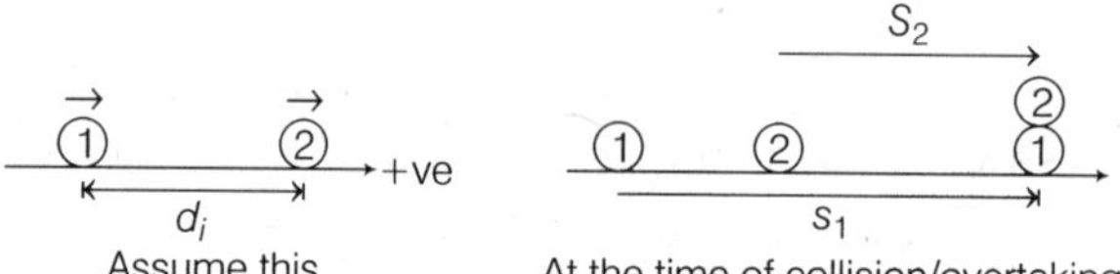

Assume this

At the time of collision/overtaking

From the second figure, we can see that particle-1 (which is behind the particle-2) will collide (or overtake) particle-2 if it travels an extra distance d_i (= initial distance between them) or

$$S_1 = S_2 + d_i \quad \text{...(i)}$$

If motion is uniformly accelerated, then for S we can write

$$S = ut + \frac{1}{2}at^2$$

Now, u and a are vector quantities so, in Eq. (i) we will substitute them with sign.

By putting proper values in Eq. (i) we can find their time of collision. Same method can be applied in vertical motion also.

Note *If two trains of length l_1 and l_2 cross each other or overtake each other (moving on two parallel tracks). Then, the equation will be,*

$$S_1 = S_2 + (l_1 + l_2)$$

Example 1 *Two particles are moving along x-axis. Particle-1 starts from $x = -10$ m with velocity 4 m/s along negative x-direction and acceleration 2 m/s^2 along positive x-direction. Particle-2 starts from $x = +2$ m with velocity 6 m/s along positive x-direction and acceleration 2 m/s^2 along negative x-direction.*

(a) Find the time when they collide.

(b) Find the x-coordinate where they collide. Both start simultaneously.

Solution (a)

4 m/s ← ① → 2 m/s^2 2 m/s^2 ← ② → 6 m/s +ve

x = −10m x = 0 x = +2m

Given values

① ② −ve

10m x = 0 2m

12 m

Assume this

Particle-1 is behind the particle-2 at a distance of 12 m. So particle-1 will collide particle-2, if

$$S_1 = S_2 + 12 \quad \rightarrow \quad \therefore \quad u_1 t + \frac{1}{2} a_1 t^2 = u_2 t + \frac{1}{2} a_2 t^2 + 12$$

But now we will substitute the values of u_1, u_2, a_1 and a_2 with sign

$$\therefore \qquad (-4)t + \frac{1}{2}(+2)t^2 = (+6)t + \frac{1}{2}(-2)t^2 + 12$$

Solving this equation, we get positive value of time,

$$t = 6 \text{ s}$$ **Ans.**

(b) At the time of collision, $S_1 = u_1 t + \frac{1}{2} a_1 t^2 = (-4)(6) + \frac{1}{2}(+2)(6)^2 = +12$ m

At the time of collision, x-coordinate of particle - 1 :

$$x_1 = (\text{Initial } x\text{-coordinate of particle-1}) + S_1$$
$$= -10 + 12 = +2 \text{ m}$$

Since, they collide at the same point. Hence,

$$x_2 = x_1 = +2 \text{ m}$$ **Ans.**

Note *This was also the starting x-coordinate of particle-2.*

Exercise: Find their velocities at the time of collision.

Ans. $v_1 = +8$ m/s, $v_2 = -6$ m/s

Type 2. *To find minimum distance between two particles moving in a straight line*

Concept

If two particles are moving along positive directions as shown in figure.

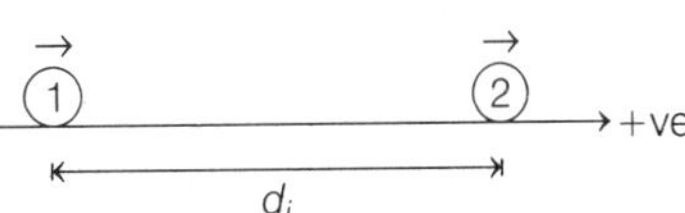

From the general experience, we can understand that distance between them will increase if $v_2 > v_1$ and distance between them will decrease if $v_1 > v_2$.

Therefore, in most of the cases at minimum distance, $v_1 = v_2$

How to Solve?

- By putting, $v_1 = v_2$ or,

$$u_1 + a_1 t = u_2 + a_2 t \qquad \text{(if } a = \text{constant)}$$

find the time when they are closest to each other.

- In this time, particle-1 should travel some extra distance and whatever is the extra displacement (of particle-1), that will be subtracted from the initial distance between them to get the minimum distance.

$$\therefore \qquad d_{min} = d_i - \Delta S = d_i - (S_1 - S_2)$$

For S, we can use $ut + \frac{1}{2}at^2$ if acceleration is constant.

Note *If $S_2 \geq S_1$, then $d_{min} = d_i$*

Example 2 *Two particles are moving along x-axis. Particle-1 is 40 m behind particle-2. Particle-1 starts with velocity 12 m/s and acceleration 4 m/s² both in positive x-direction. Particle-2 starts with velocity 4 m/s and acceleration 12 m/s² also in positive x-direction. Find*

(a) the time when distance between them is minimum.

(b) the minimum distance between them.

Solution

12 m/s, 4 m/s² (1)→   4 m/s, 12 m/s² (2)→   +ve

40 m

(a) As discussed above, distance between them is minimum, when

$$v_1 = v_2$$

or

$$u_1 + a_1 t = u_2 + a_2 t$$

Substituting the values with sign we have,

$$(+12) + (4)t = (+4) + (12)\,t$$

$$\therefore \qquad t = 1\text{ s}$$ **Ans.**

(b) **In 1 sec**

$$S_1 = u_1 t + \frac{1}{2}a_1 t^2$$

$$= 12 \times 1 + \frac{1}{2} \times 4 \times (1)^2 = 14\text{ m}$$

and

$$S_2 = u_2 t + \frac{1}{2}a_2 t^2$$

$$= 4 \times 1 + \frac{1}{2} \times 12 \times (1)^2$$

$$= 10\text{ m}$$

Extra displacement of particle-1 with respect to 2 is

$$\Delta S = S_1 - S_2 = 14 - 10 = 4\text{ m}$$

∴ Minimum distance between them

$$= d_i - \Delta S = 40 - 4$$

$$= 36\text{ m}$$ **Ans.**

Type 3. *To find trajectory of a particle*

In this type, a particle will be moving in x-y plane. Its x and y co-ordinates as function of time will be given in the question and we have to find trajectory (or x-y relation) of the particle.

How to Solve?

- From the given x and y co-ordinates (as function of time) just eliminate t and find x-y relation. This is a general method which can be applied anywhere in whole physics.

Example 3 *A particle is moving in x-y plane with its x and y co-ordinates varying with time as, $x = 2t$ and $y = 10t - 16\,t^2$. Find trajectory of the particle.*

Solution Given, $x = 2t$

$$\Rightarrow \qquad t = \frac{x}{2}$$

Now,
$$y = 10\,t - 16\,t^2$$

Substituting value of t in this equation we have,

$$y = 10\left(\frac{x}{2}\right) - 16\left(\frac{x}{2}\right)^2$$

or
$$y = 5x - 4x^2$$

This is the required equation of trajectory of the particle. This is a quadratic equation. Hence, the path of the particle is a parabola.

Type 4. *Two dimensional motion by component method.*

Concept

There are two methods of solving a two (or three) dimensional motion problems. In the first method, we use proper vector method. For example, we will use,

$\mathbf{v} = \mathbf{u} + \mathbf{a}t$ etc., if $\mathbf{a}$ = constant and, $\mathbf{v} = \dfrac{d\mathbf{s}}{dt}$ etc. if $\mathbf{a} \neq$ constant

In the second method, we find the components of all vector quantities along x, y and z-directions. Then, deal different axis separately as one dimension by assigning proper signs to all vector quantities. While dealing x-direction, we don't have to bother about y and z-directions.

Example 4 *A particle is moving in x-y plane. Its initial velocity and acceleration are $\mathbf{u} = (4\hat{\mathbf{i}} + 8\hat{\mathbf{j}})$ m/s and $\mathbf{a} = (2\hat{\mathbf{i}} - 4\hat{\mathbf{j}})$ m/s^2. Find*

(a) the time when the particle will cross the x-axis.

(b) x-coordinate of particle at this instant.

(c) velocity of the particle at this instant.

Initial coordinates of particle are (4m, 10m).

Solution

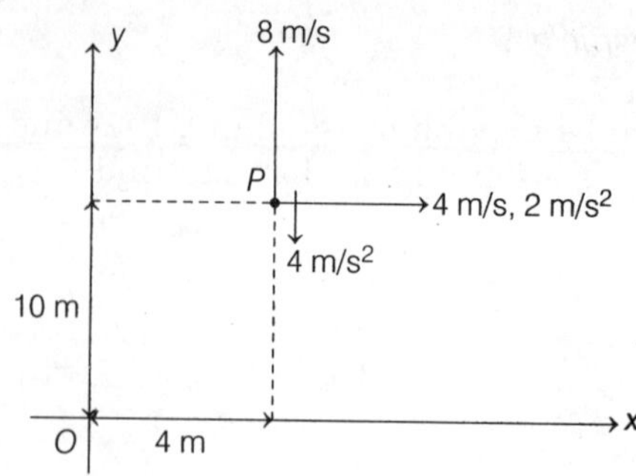

Particle starts from point P. Components of its initial velocity and acceleration are as shown in figure.

(a) At the time of crossing the x-axis, its y-coordinate should be zero or its y-displacement (w.r.t initial point P) is –10 m.

Using the equation,
$$s_y = u_y t + \frac{1}{2} a_y t^2$$
$$-10 = 8t - \frac{1}{2} \times 4 \times t^2$$

Solving this equation, we get positive value of time,
$$t = 5 \text{ s}$$

(b) x-coordinate of particle at time t :

x = initial x-coordinate + displacement along x-axis or $x = x_i + s_x$ (at time t)
$$= x_i + u_x t + \frac{1}{2} a_x t^2$$

Substituting the proper values, we have,
$$x = 4 + (4 \times 5) + \frac{1}{2} \times 2 \times (5)^2 = 49 \text{ m}$$ **Ans.**

(c) Since, given acceleration is constant, so we can use,
$$\mathbf{v} = \mathbf{u} + \mathbf{a}t$$
$$\therefore \quad \mathbf{v} = (4\hat{\mathbf{i}} + 8\hat{\mathbf{j}}) + (2\hat{\mathbf{i}} - 4\hat{\mathbf{j}})(5)$$
$$= (14\hat{\mathbf{i}} - 12\hat{\mathbf{j}}) \text{ m/s}$$

Type 5. *To convert given v-t graph into s-t graph (For a = 0 or a = constant)*

Concept

(i) If we integrate velocity, we get displacement. Therefore, the method discussed in this type is a general method, which can be applied in all those problems where we get the result after integration.

For example
$$v\text{-}t \longrightarrow s\text{-}t$$
$$a\text{-}t \longrightarrow v\text{-}t$$
$$F\text{-}t \longrightarrow P\text{-}t$$

Here, P = linear momentum and F is force ($F = \frac{dP}{dt}$ or $dP = Fdt$).

(ii) For zero or constant acceleration, we can classify the motion into six types. Corresponding v-t and s-t graphs are as shown below.

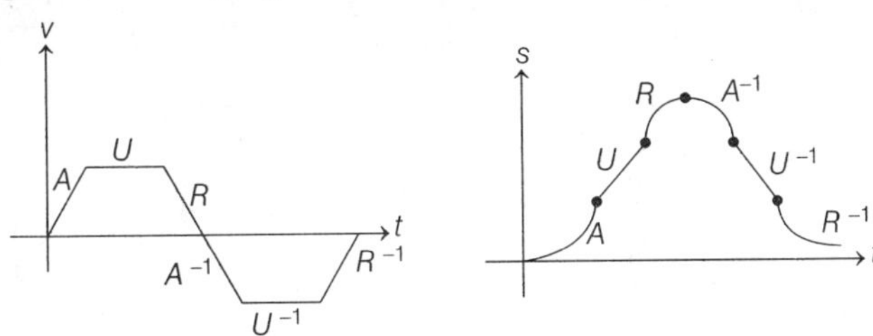

(iii) The explanation of these six motions is as under

Motion type	About the motion	Velocity or Slope of s-t graph ($v = ds/dt$)
A	Accelerated in positive direction	positive and increasing
U	Uniform in positive direction	positive and constant
R	Retarded in positive direction	positive and decreasing
A^{-1}	Accelerated in negative direction	negative and increasing
U^{-1}	Uniform in negative direction	negative and constant
R^{-1}	Retarded in negative direction	negative and decreasing

(iv) In A, U and R motions, velocity is positive (above t-axis). Therefore, body is moving along positive direction. In A^{-1}, U^{-1} and R^{-1} motions, velocity is negative (below t-axis). Therefore, body is moving along negative direction.

How to Solve?

- Mark A, U, R, A^{-1}, U^{-1} or R^{-1} in the given v-t graph for different time intervals.
- Calculate area (= displacement) under v-t graph for different time intervals.
- Plot s-t graph according to their shape of A, U, R etc. motions.
- Keep on adding area for further displacements.

Example 5 *Velocity-time graph* of a particle moving along x-axis is as shown below.

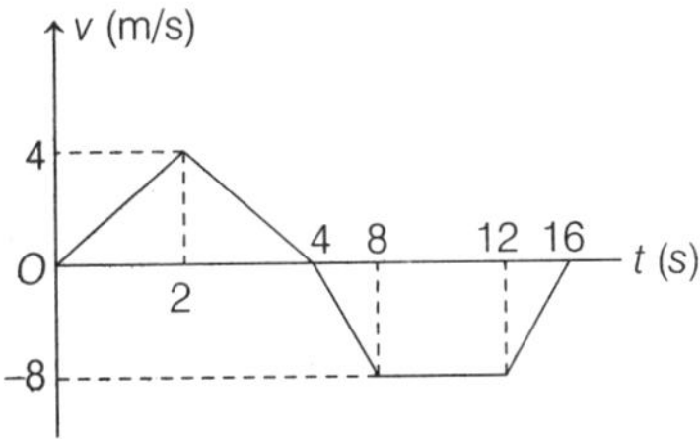

At time $t = 0$, x-coordinate of the particle is $x = 10\,m$.

(a) Plot x-coordinate versus time graph.

(b) Find average velocity and average speed of the particle during the complete journey.

(c) Find average acceleration of the particle between the time interval from $t = 2$ s to $t = 8$ s.

Solution (a) Let us first mark A, U, R etc. in the given v-t diagram and calculate their area (= displacement) in different time intervals.

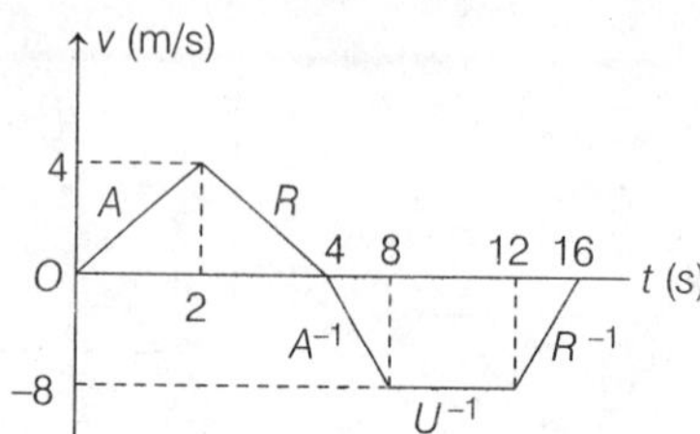

Time interval	Area or displacement	Final x-coordinate at the end of intervals $x = x_i + s$
0 – 2 s	+ 4 m	10 + 4 = 14 m
2 s – 4 s	+ 4 m	14 + 4 = 18 m
4 s – 8 s	– 16 m	18 – 16 = 2 m
8 s – 12 s	– 32 m	2 – 32 = – 30 m
12 s – 16 s	– 16 m	–30 – 16 = – 46 m

Corresponding x-t graph is as shown below.

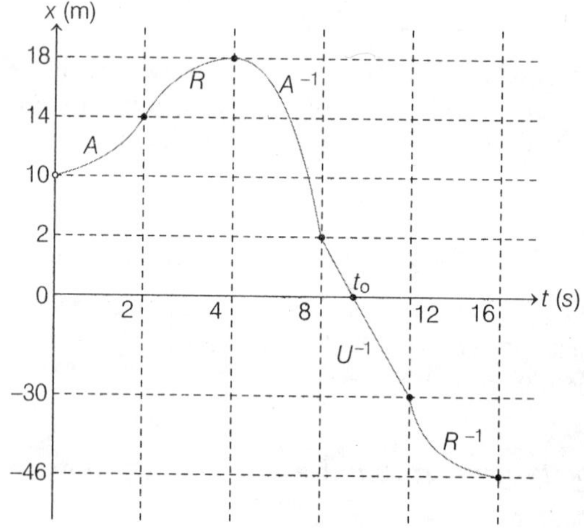

Exercise : *Find the time t_0 when x-coordinate of the particle is zero.*

Ans 8.25 s

(b) Total displacement $= 4 + 4 - 16 - 32 - 16 = -56$ m

This is also equal to $x_f - x_i = -46 - 10 = -56$ m

Total distance $= 4 + 4 + 16 + 32 + 16 = 72$ m

Total time = 16 s

Now, $$\text{average velocity} = \frac{\text{total diaplacement}}{\text{total time}}$$

$$= -\frac{56}{16} = -3.5 \text{ m/s}$$ **Ans.**

$$\text{average speed} = \frac{\text{total distance}}{\text{total time}}$$

$$= \frac{72}{16} = 4.5 \text{ m/s}$$ **Ans.**

(c) Average acceleration $= \dfrac{\Delta v}{\Delta t}$

$$= \frac{v_f - v_i}{\Delta t} = \frac{v_{8\,\text{sec}} - v_{2\text{sec}}}{8-2}$$

$$= \frac{-8-4}{6} = -2 \text{ m/s}^2$$ **Ans.**

Type 6. *General method of conversion of graph*

Concept

(i) In some cases, one graph can be converted into the other graph just by finding slope of the given graph. But this method is helpful when different segments of the given graph are straight lines.

For example,

(a) Given s-t graph can be converted into the v-t graph from the slope of s-t graph as

$$v = \frac{ds}{dt} = \text{slope of } s\text{-}t \text{ graph}$$

(b) Given v-t graph can be converted into the a-t graph from the slope of v-t graph, as

$$a = \frac{dv}{dt} = \text{slope of } v\text{-}t \text{ graph}$$

(ii) In few cases, we have to convert given y-x graph into z-x graph. For example, suppose we have to convert v-s graph into a-s graph.

In such cases, first you make v-s equation (if it is straight line graph) from the given v-s graph. Then, with the help of this v-s equation and some standard equations (like $a = v \cdot \dfrac{dv}{ds}$) make a-s equation and now draw a-s graph corresponding to this a-s equation.

Example 6 *A particle is moving along x-axis. Its x-coordinate versus time graph is as shown below.*

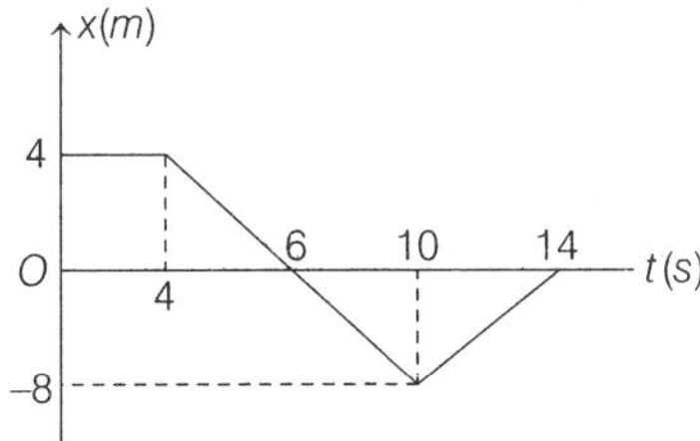

Plot v-t graph corresponding to this.

Solution $v = \frac{dx}{dt}$ = slope of x-t graph. Slope for different time intervals is given in following table.

Time interval	Slope of *x-t* graph (= v)
0 – 4 s	0
4 s – 10 s	– 2 m/s
10 s – 14 s	+ 2 m/s

v-t graph corresponding to this table is as shown below

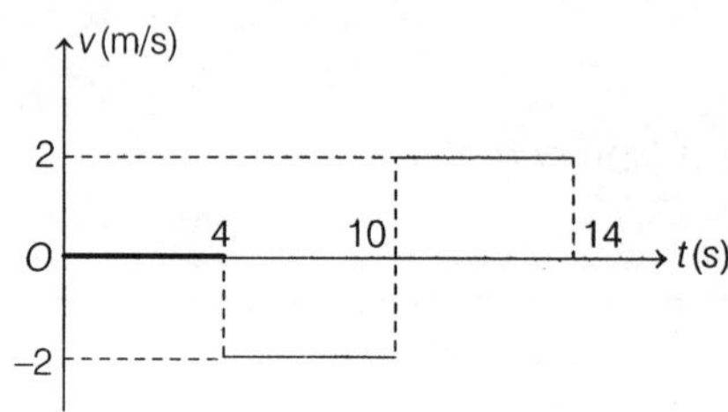

Example 7 *Corresponding to given v-s graph of a particle moving in a straight line, plot a-s graph.*

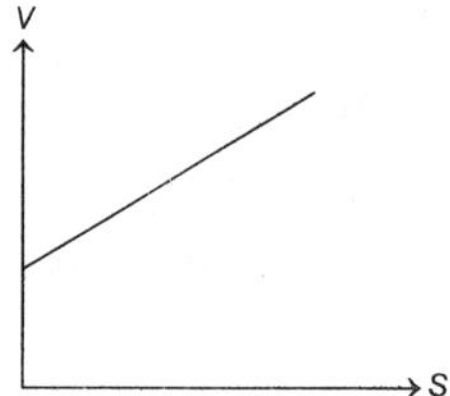

Solution The given v-s graph is a straight line with positive slope (say m) and positive intercept (say c). Therefore, v-s equation is

$$v = ms + c$$

$$\Rightarrow \qquad \frac{dv}{ds} = m$$

Now,
$$a = v \cdot \frac{dv}{ds} = (ms + c)(m)$$

$$a = m^2 s + mc$$

a-s equation is a linear equation. Therefore, a-s graph is also a straight line with positive slope $(= m^2)$ and positive intercept $(= mc)$. a-s graph is as shown below.

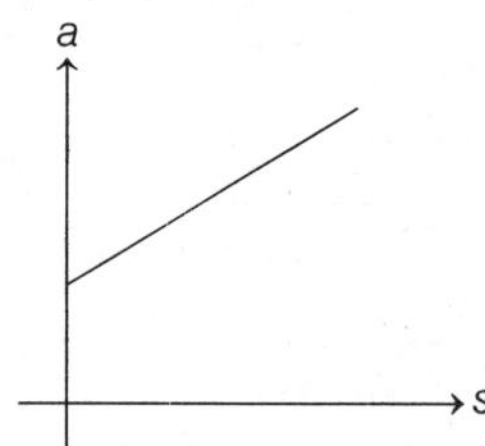

Type 7. *Based on difference between distance and displacement*

Concept

There is no direct formula for calculation of distance. In the formula,

$$s = ut + \frac{1}{2}at^2$$

s = displacement, not the distance

So, you will have to convert the given distance into proper displacement and then apply the above equation.

Example 8 *A particle is moving along x-axis. At time $t = 0$, its x-coordinate is $x = -4$ m. Its velocity-time equation is $v = 8 - 2t$ where, v is in m/s and t in seconds.*

(a) At how many times, particle is at a distance of 8 m from the origin?

(b) Find those times.

Solution (a) Comparing the given v-t equation with $v = u + at$. We have,

$$u = 8 \text{ m/s and}$$

$$a = -2 \text{ m/s}^2 = \text{constant}$$

Now, motion of the particle is as shown below.

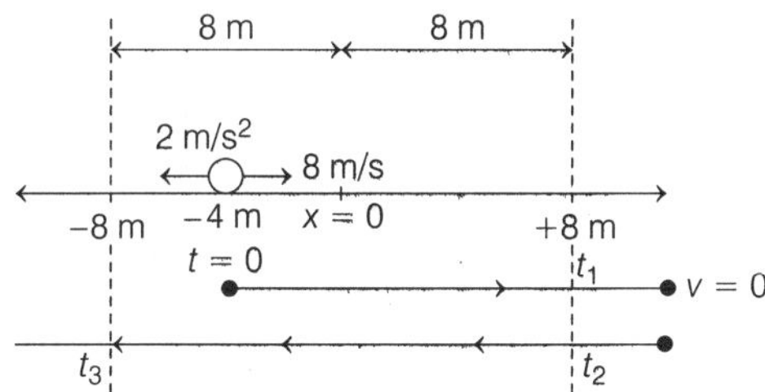

Now, 8 m distance from origin will be at two coordinates $x = 8$ m and $x = -8$ m. From the diagram, we can see that particle will cross these two points three times, t_1, t_2 and t_3.

(b) t_1 **and** t_2 **:** At $x = 8$ m, displacement from the starting point is

$$s = x_f - x_i = 8 - (-4) = 12 \text{ m}$$

Substituting in $s = ut + \frac{1}{2}at^2$, we have

$$12 = 8t - \frac{1}{2} \times 2 \times t^2$$

Solving this equation, we get

$$\text{smaller time } t_1 = 2 \text{ s} \qquad \textbf{Ans.}$$

$$\text{and larger time } t_2 = 6 \text{ s} \qquad \textbf{Ans.}$$

t_3 : At $x = -8$ m, displacement from the starting point is

$$s = x_f - x_i = -8 - (-4) = -4 \text{ m}$$

Substituting in $s = ut + \frac{1}{2}at^2$, we have $\quad -4 = 8t - \frac{1}{2} \times 2 \times t^2$

Solving this equation, we get the positive time,

$$t_3 = 8.47 \text{ s} \qquad \textbf{Ans.}$$

Miscellaneous Examples

Example 9 *A rocket is fired vertically upwards with a net acceleration of 4 m/s^2 and initial velocity zero. After 5 s its fuel is finished and it decelerates with g. At the highest point its velocity becomes zero. Then, it accelerates downwards with acceleration g and return back to ground. Plot velocity-time and displacement-time graphs for the complete journey. Take $g = 10\ m/s^2$.*

Solution In the graphs,

$$v_A = at_{OA} = (4)(5) = 20 \text{ m/s}$$

$$v_B = 0 = v_A - gt_{AB}$$

$$\therefore \quad t_{AB} = \frac{v_A}{g} = \frac{20}{10} = 2 \text{ s}$$

$$\therefore \quad t_{OAB} = (5 + 2) \text{ s} = 7 \text{ s}$$

Now, s_{OAB} = area under v-t graph between 0 to 7 s

$$= \frac{1}{2}(7)(20) = 70 \text{ m}$$

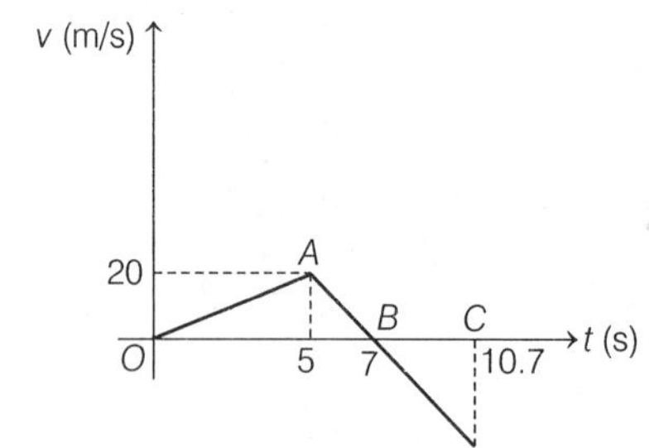

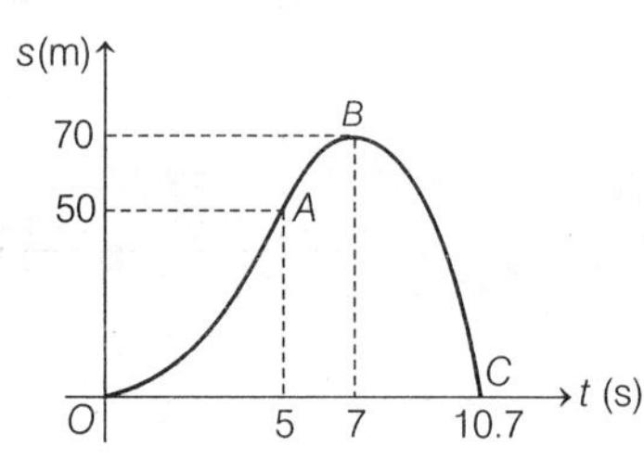

Further, $$|s_{OAB}| = |s_{BC}| = \frac{1}{2} g t_{BC}^2$$

$$\therefore \quad 70 = \frac{1}{2}(10)\, t_{BC}^2$$

$$\therefore \quad t_{BC} = \sqrt{14} = 3.7 \text{ s}$$

$$\therefore \quad t_{OABC} = 7 + 3.7 = 10.7 \text{ s}$$

Also, s_{OA} = area under v-t graph between OA

$$= \frac{1}{2}(5)(20) = 50 \text{ m}$$

Example 10 *An open lift is moving upwards with velocity 10 m/s. It has an upward acceleration of 2 m/s^2. A ball is projected upwards with velocity 20 m/s relative to ground. Find*

(a) time when ball again meets the lift

(b) displacement of lift and ball at that instant.

(c) distance travelled by the ball upto that instant.

Take $g = 10\ m/s^2$

Solution (a) At the time when ball again meets the lift,

$$s_L = s_B$$

$$\therefore \quad 10\,t + \frac{1}{2} \times 2 \times t^2 = 20\,t - \frac{1}{2} \times 10\,t^2$$

Solving this equation, we get

$$t = 0 \quad \text{and} \quad t = \frac{5}{3}\text{ s}$$

$\therefore$ Ball will again meet the lift after $\frac{5}{3}$ s.

(b) At this instant $s_L = s_B = 10 \times \frac{5}{3} + \frac{1}{2} \times 2 \times \left(\frac{5}{3}\right)^2 = \frac{175}{9}\text{ m} = 19.4\text{ m}$

(c) For the ball u is antiparallel to a. Therefore, we will first find t_0, the time when its velocity becomes zero.

$$t_0 = \left|\frac{u}{a}\right| = \frac{20}{10} = 2\text{ s}$$

As $t\left(= \frac{5}{3}\text{ s}\right) < t_0$, distance and displacement are equal

or $$d = 19.4\text{ m}$$

Example 11 *A particle starts with an initial velocity and passes successively over the two halves of a given distance with constant accelerations a_1 and a_2 respectively. Show that the final velocity is the same as if the whole distance is covered with a uniform acceleration $\frac{(a_1 + a_2)}{2}$.*

Solution

u → s, a_1 → v_1 → s, a_2 → v_2

First case

u → 2s, $\frac{a_1 + a_2}{2}$ → v

Second case

In the first case,

$$v_1^2 = u^2 + 2a_1 s \qquad \ldots \text{(i)}$$

$$v_2^2 = v_1^2 + 2a_2 s \qquad \ldots \text{(ii)}$$

Adding Eqs. (i) and (ii), we have

$$v_2^2 = u^2 + 2\left(\frac{a_1 + a_2}{2}\right)(2s) \qquad \ldots \text{(iii)}$$

In the second case,

$$v^2 = u^2 + 2\left(\frac{a_1 + a_2}{2}\right)(2s) \qquad \ldots \text{(iv)}$$

From Eqs. (iii) and (iv), we can see that

$$v_2 = v$$ **Hence proved.**

Example 12 *In a car race, car A takes a time t less than car B at the finish and passes the finishing point with speed v more than that of the car B. Assuming that both the cars start from rest and travel with constant acceleration a_1 and a_2 respectively. Show that $v = \sqrt{a_1 a_2}\, t$.*

Solution Let A takes t_1 second, then according to the given problem B will take $(t_1 + t)$ seconds. Further, let v_1 be the velocity of B at finishing point, then velocity of A will be $(v_1 + v)$. Writing equations of motion for A and B.

$$v_1 + v = a_1 t_1 \quad \text{...(i)}$$

and,

$$v_1 = a_2(t_1 + t) \quad \text{...(ii)}$$

From these two equations, we get

$$v = (a_1 - a_2)\, t_1 - a_2 t \quad \text{...(iii)}$$

Total distance travelled by both the cars is equal.

or

$$s_A = s_B$$

or

$$\frac{1}{2} a_1 t_1^2 = \frac{1}{2} a_2 (t_1 + t)^2$$

or

$$t_1 = \frac{\sqrt{a_2}\, t}{\sqrt{a_1} - \sqrt{a_2}}$$

Substituting this value of t_1 in Eq. (iii), we get the desired result

$$v = (\sqrt{a_1 a_2})\, t$$

Example 13 *An open elevator is ascending with constant speed $v = 10$ m/s. A ball is thrown vertically up by a boy on the lift when he is at a height $h = 10$ m from the ground. The velocity of projection is $v = 30$ m/s with respect to elevator. Find*

(a) the maximum height attained by the ball.
(b) the time taken by the ball to meet the elevator again.
(c) time taken by the ball to reach the ground after crossing the elevator.

Solution (a) Absolute velocity of ball = 40 m/s (upwards)

$\therefore$

$$h_{max} = h_i + h_f$$

Here, h_i = initial height = 10 m

and h_f = further height attained by ball

$$= \frac{u^2}{2g} = \frac{(40)^2}{2 \times 10} = 80 \text{ m}$$

$\therefore$

$$h_{max} = (10 + 80) \text{ m} = 90 \text{ m}$$ **Ans.**

(b) The ball will meet the elevator again when displacement of lift = displacement of ball

or

$$10 \times t = 40 \times t - \frac{1}{2} \times 10 \times t^2 \quad \text{or} \quad t = 6 \text{ s}$$ **Ans.**

(c) Let t_0 be the total time taken by the ball to reach the ground. Then,

$$-10 = 40 \times t_0 - \frac{1}{2} \times 10 \times t_0^2$$

Solving this equation we get, $t_0 = 8.24$ s

Therefore, time taken by the ball to reach the ground after crossing the elevator,

$$= (t_0 - t) = 2.24 \text{ s}$$

Example 14 *From an elevated point A, a stone is projected vertically upwards. When the stone reaches a distance h below A, its velocity is double of what it was at a height h above A. Show that the greatest height attained by the stone is* $\frac{5}{3}h$.

Solution Let u be the velocity with which the stone is projected vertically upwards.

Given that, $$v_{-h} = 2v_h$$

or $$(v_{-h})^2 = 4v_h^2$$

$\therefore$ $$u^2 - 2g(-h) = 4(u^2 - 2gh)$$

$\therefore$ $$u^2 = \frac{10gh}{3}$$

Now, $$h_{max} = \frac{u^2}{2g} = \frac{5h}{3}$$ **Hence proved.**

Example 15 *Velocity of a particle moving in a straight line varies with its displacement as* $v = (\sqrt{4 + 4s})$ *m/s. Displacement of particle at time* $t = 0$ *is* $s = 0$. *Find displacement of particle at time* $t = 2$ *s.*

Solution Squaring the given equation, we get

$$v^2 = 4 + 4s$$

Now, comparing it with $v^2 = u^2 + 2as$, we get

$$u = 2 \text{ m/s} \quad \text{and} \quad a = 2 \text{ m/s}^2$$

$\therefore$ Displacement at $t = 2$ s is

$$s = ut + \frac{1}{2}at^2 \quad \text{or} \quad s = (2)(2) + \frac{1}{2}(2)(2)^2 \quad \text{or} \quad s = 8 \text{ m}$$ **Ans.**

Example 16 *Figure shows a rod of length l resting on a wall and the floor. Its lower end A is pulled towards left with a constant velocity v. Find the velocity of the other end B downward when the rod makes an angle θ with the horizontal.*

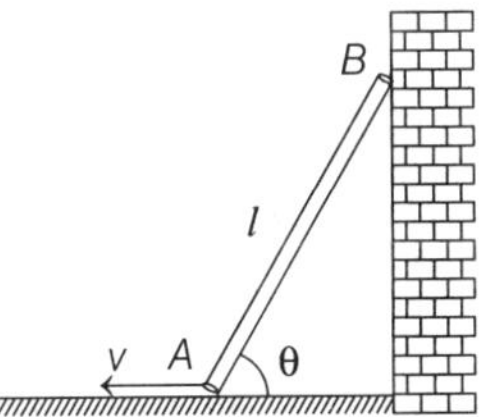

Solution In such type of problems, when velocity of one part of a body is given and that of other is required, we first find the relation between the two displacements, then differentiate them with respect to time. Here, if the distance from the corner to the point A is x and that up to B is y. Then,

$$v = \frac{dx}{dt}$$

and $$v_B = -\frac{dy}{dt}$$ (– sign denotes that y is decreasing)

Further, $$x^2 + y^2 = l^2$$

Differentiating with respect to time t

$$2x\frac{dx}{dt}+2y\frac{dy}{dt}=0$$

$$xv = yv_B$$

$$v_B = \frac{x}{y}v = v\cot\theta \qquad \textbf{Ans.}$$

Example 17 A particle is moving in a straight line with constant acceleration. If x, y and z be the distances described by a particle during the pth, qth and rth second respectively, prove that

$$(q-r)x+(r-p)y+(p-q)z=0$$

Solution As $\quad s_t = u + at - \frac{1}{2}a = u + \frac{a}{2}(2t-1)$

$\therefore$

$$x = u + \frac{a}{2}(2p-1) \qquad \text{...(i)}$$

$$y = u + \frac{a}{2}(2q-1) \qquad \text{...(ii)}$$

$$z = u + \frac{a}{2}(2r-1) \qquad \text{...(iii)}$$

Subtracting Eq. (iii) from Eq. (ii), $\quad y - z = \frac{a}{2}(2q-2r)$

or $\quad q - r = \frac{y-z}{a}$

or $\quad (q-r)x = \frac{1}{a}(yx - zx) \qquad \text{...(iv)}$

Similarly, we can show that

$$(r-p)y = \frac{1}{a}(zy - xy) \qquad \text{...(v)}$$

and $\quad (p-q)z = \frac{1}{a}(xz - yz) \qquad \text{...(vi)}$

Adding Eqs. (iv), (v) and (vi), we get $(q-r)x+(r-p)y+(p-q)z=0$

Example 18 *Three particles A, B and C are situated at the vertices of an equilateral triangle ABC of side d at time t = 0. Each of the particles moves with constant speed v. A always has its velocity along AB, B along BC and C along CA. At what time will the particles meet each other?*

Solution Velocity of A is v along AB. Velocity of B is along BC. Its component along BA is $v\cos 60° = v/2$. Thus, the separation AB decreases at the rate

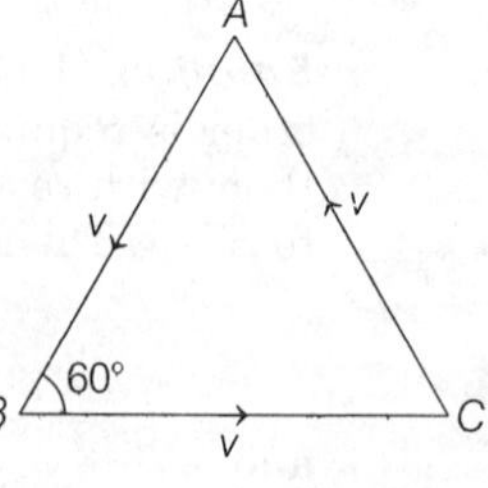

$$v + \frac{v}{2} = \frac{3v}{2}$$

Since, this rate is constant, the time taken in reducing the separation AB from d to zero is

$$t = \frac{d}{(3v/2)} = \frac{2d}{3v} \qquad \textbf{Ans.}$$

Example 19 *An elevator car whose floor to ceiling distance is equal to 2.7 m starts ascending with constant acceleration 1.2 m/s^2. 2 s after the start, a bolt begins falling from the ceiling of the car. Find*

(a) the time after which bolt hits the floor of the elevator.

(b) the net displacement and distance travelled by the bolt, with respect to earth. (Take $g = 9.8\ m/s^2$)

Solution (a) If we consider elevator at rest, then relative acceleration of the bolt is

$$a_r = 9.8 + 1.2$$
$$= 11\ \text{m/s}^2 \qquad \text{(downwards)}$$

After 2 s, velocity of lift is $v = at = (1.2)(2) = 2.4$ m/s. Therefore, initial velocity of the bolt is also 2.4 m/s and it gets accelerated with relative acceleration 11 m/s². With respect to elevator initial velocity of bolt is zero and it has to travel 2.7 m with 11 m/s². Thus, time taken can be directly given as

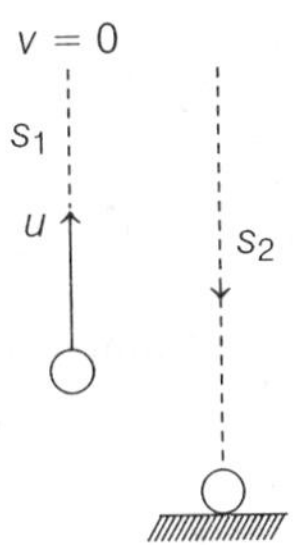

$$\sqrt{\frac{2s}{a}} = \sqrt{\frac{2 \times 2.7}{11}}$$
$$= 0.7\ \text{s}$$ **Ans.**

(b) Displacement of bolt relative to ground in 0.7 s.

$$s = ut + \frac{1}{2}at^2$$

or
$$s = (2.4)(0.7) + \frac{1}{2}(-9.8)(0.7)^2$$
$$s = -0.72\ \text{m}$$ **Ans.**

Velocity of bolt will become zero after a time

$$t_0 = \frac{u}{g} \qquad (v = u - gt)$$
$$= \frac{2.4}{9.8} = 0.245\ \text{s}$$

Therefore, distance travelled by the bolt $= s_1 + s_2 = \frac{u^2}{2g} + \frac{1}{2}g(t - t_0)^2$

$$= \frac{(2.4)^2}{2 \times 9.8} + \frac{1}{2} \times 9.8\,(0.7 - 0.245)^2$$
$$= 1.3\ \text{m}$$ **Ans.**

Example 20 *A man wants to reach point B on the opposite bank of a river flowing at a speed as shown in figure. What minimum speed relative to water should the man have so that he can reach point B? In which direction should he swim?*

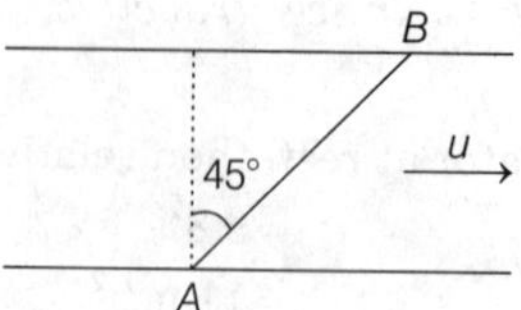

Solution Let v be the speed of boatman in still water.

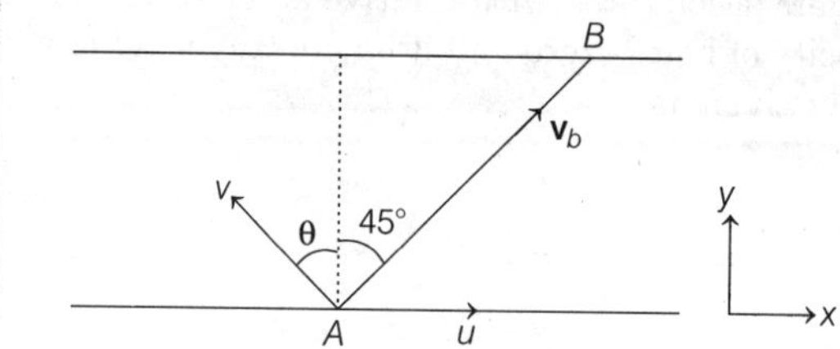

Resultant of v and u should be along AB. Components of $\mathbf{v}_b$ (absolute velocity of boatman) along x and y-directions are,

$$v_x = u - v \sin\theta$$

and

$$v_y = v\cos\theta$$

Further,

$$\tan 45° = \frac{v_y}{v_x}$$

or

$$1 = \frac{v\cos\theta}{u - v\sin\theta}$$

$\therefore$

$$v = \frac{u}{\sin\theta + \cos\theta} = \frac{u}{\sqrt{2}\sin(\theta + 45°)}$$

v is minimum at,

$$\theta + 45° = 90°$$

or

$$\theta = 45° \qquad \textbf{Ans.}$$

and

$$v_{min} = \frac{u}{\sqrt{2}} \qquad \textbf{Ans.}$$

Exercises

LEVEL 1

Assertion and Reason

Directions : *Choose the correct option.*

(a) *If both* ***Assertion*** *and* ***Reason*** *are true and the* ***Reason*** *is correct explanation of the* ***Assertion.***

(b) *If both* ***Assertion*** *and* ***Reason*** *are true but* ***Reason*** *is not the correct explanation of* ***Assertion.***

(c) *If* ***Assertion*** *is true, but the* ***Reason*** *is false.*

(d) *If* ***Assertion*** *is false but the* ***Reason*** *is true.*

(e) *If both* ***Assertion*** *and* ***Reason*** *are false.*

1. Assertion : In v-t graph shown in figure, average velocity in time interval from 0 to t_0 depends only on v_0. It is independent of t_0.

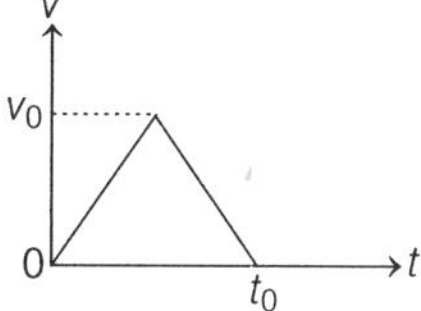

Reason : In the given time interval, average velocity is $\frac{v_0}{2}$.

2. Assertion : We know the relation $a = v \cdot \frac{dv}{ds}$. Therefore, if velocity of a particle is zero, then acceleration is also zero.

Reason : In the above equation, a is the instantaneous acceleration.

3. Assertion : Starting from rest with zero acceleration, if acceleration of particle increases at a constant rate of 2 ms^{-3}, then velocity should increase at constant rate of 1 ms^{-2}.

Reason : For the given condition,

$$\frac{da}{dt} = 2 \text{ ms}^{-3} \quad \therefore \quad a = 2t$$

4. Assertion : Average velocity can't be zero in case of uniform acceleration.

Reason : For average velocity to be zero, a non zero velocity should not remain constant.

5. Assertion : Displacement-time equation of two particles moving in a straight line are, $s_1 = 2t - 4t^2$ and $s_2 = -2t + 4t^2$. Relative velocity between the two will go on increasing.

Reason : If velocity and acceleration are of same sign, then speed will increase.

6. Assertion : Acceleration of a moving particle can change its direction without any change in direction of velocity.

Reason : If the direction of change in velocity vector changes, the direction of acceleration vector also changes.

7. **Assertion :** A body is dropped from height h and another body is thrown vertically upwards with a speed $\sqrt{gh}$. They meet at height $h/2$.

Reason : The time taken by both the blocks in reaching the height $h/2$ is same.

8. **Assertion :** Two bodies of unequal masses m_1 and m_2 are dropped from the same height. If the resistance offered by air to the motion of both bodies is the same, the bodies will reach the earth at the same time.

Reason : For equal air resistance, acceleration of fall of masses m_1 and m_2 will be different.

9. **Assertion :** In the x-t diagram shown in figure, the body starts in positive direction but not from $x = 0$.

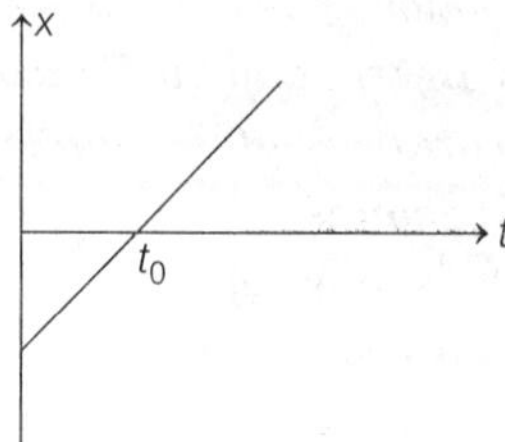

Reason : At $t = t_0$, velocity of body changes its direction of motion.

Objective Questions

Single Correct Option

1. A stone is released from a rising balloon accelerating upward with acceleration a. The acceleration of the stone just after the release is

(a) a upward (b) g downward
(c) $(g - a)$ downward (d) $(g + a)$ downward

2. A ball is thrown vertically upwards from the ground. If T_1 and T_2 are the respective time taken in going up and coming down, and the air resistance is not ignored, then

(a) $T_1 > T_2$ (b) $T_1 = T_2$
(c) $T_1 < T_2$ (d) nothing can be said

3. When a ball is thrown up vertically with velocity v_0, it reaches a maximum height of h. If one wishes to triple the maximum height then the ball should be thrown with velocity

(a) $\sqrt{3}\, v_0$ (b) $3\, v_0$ (c) $9\, v_0$ (d) $\frac{3}{2}\, v_0$

4. From the displacement-time graph, find out the velocity of a moving body

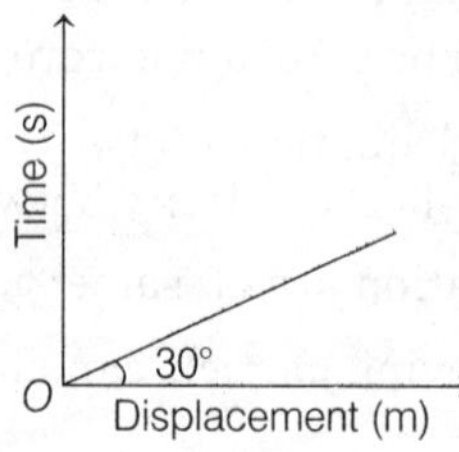

(a) $\frac{1}{\sqrt{3}}$ m/s (b) 3 m/s (c) $\sqrt{3}$ m/s (d) $\frac{1}{3}$ m/s

5. The displacement of a particle moving in a straight line depends on time as $x = \alpha t^3 + \beta t^2 + \gamma t = \delta$.

The ratio of initial acceleration to its initial velocity depends

(a) only on α and γ
(b) only on β and γ
(c) only on α and β
(d) only on α

6. The length of a seconds hand in watch is 1 cm. The change in velocity of its tip in 15 s is

(a) zero
(b) $\frac{\pi}{30\sqrt{2}}$ cm/s
(c) $\frac{\pi}{30}$ cm/s
(d) $\frac{\pi\sqrt{2}}{30}$ cm/s

7. The acceleration of a particle is increasing linearly with time t as bt. The particle starts from the origin with an initial velocity v_0. The distance travelled by the particle in time t will be

(a) $v_0 t + \frac{1}{6} bt^3$
(b) $v_0 t + \frac{1}{3} bt^3$
(c) $v_0 t + \frac{1}{3} bt^2$
(d) $v_0 t + \frac{1}{2} bt^2$

8. The acceleration-time (a-t) graph of a particle moving in a straight line is as shown in the figure. The velocity-time graph of the particle would be

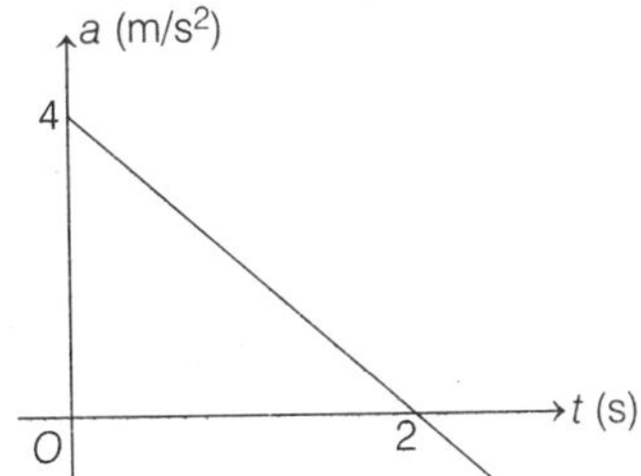

(a) a straight line
(b) a parabola
(c) a circle
(d) an ellipse

9. A 100 m long train crosses a man travelling at 5 km/h, in opposite direction , in 7.2 s then the velocity of train is

(a) 40 km/h
(b) 25 km/h
(c) 20 km/h
(d) 45 km/h

10. What are the speeds of two objects if, when they move uniformly towards each other, they get 4 m closer in each second and when they move uniformly in the same direction with the original speeds, they get 4.0 m closer each 10 s?

(a) 2.8 m/s and 1.2 m/s
(b) 5.2 m/s and 4.6 m/s
(c) 3.2 m/s and 2.1 m/s
(d) 2.2 m/s and 1.8 m/s

11. Four particles A, B, C and D are moving with constant speed v each. At the instant shown relative velocity of A with respect to B, C and D are in directions.

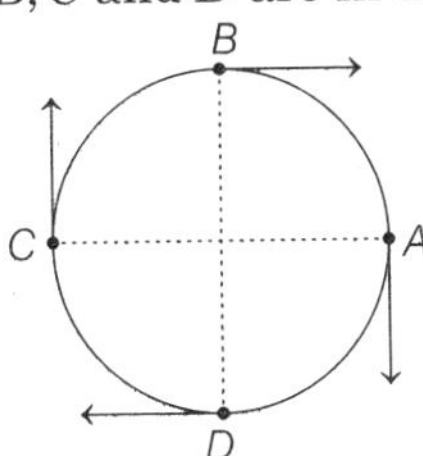

(a) 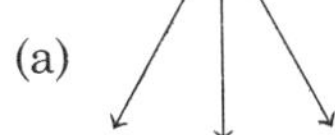
(b) 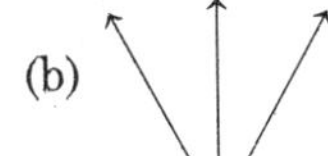
(c) 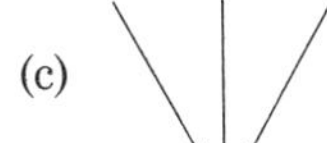
(d) 

12. A point traversed 3/4th of the circle of radius R in time t. The magnitude of the average velocity of the particle in this time interval is

(a) $\frac{\pi R}{t}$ (b) $\frac{3\pi R}{2t}$

(c) $\frac{R\sqrt{2}}{t}$ (d) $\frac{R}{\sqrt{2}t}$

13. If the displacement of a particle varies with time as $\sqrt{x} = t + 3$

(a) velocity of the particle is inversely proportional to t

(b) velocity of particle varies linearly with t

(c) velocity of particle is proportional to $\sqrt{t}$

(d) initial velocity of the particle is zero

14. A particle starting from rest with constant acceleration travels a distance x in first 2 s and a distance y in next 2 s, then

(a) $y = x$ (b) $y = 2x$

(c) $y = 3x$ (d) $y = 4x$

15. A particle moves along the curve $y = \frac{x^2}{2}$. Here x varies with time as $x = \frac{t^2}{2}$. Where x and y are measured in metres and t in seconds. At $t = 2$ s, the velocity of the particle (in ms^{-1}) is

(a) $4\hat{\mathbf{i}} + 6\hat{\mathbf{j}}$ (b) $2\hat{\mathbf{i}} + 4\hat{\mathbf{j}}$

(c) $4\hat{\mathbf{i}} + 2\hat{\mathbf{j}}$ (d) $4\hat{\mathbf{i}} + 4\hat{\mathbf{j}}$

16. The position vector of a particle is $\mathbf{r} = a \cos \omega t \hat{\mathbf{i}} + a \sin \omega t \hat{\mathbf{j}}$.
The velocity of the particle is

(a) parallel to position vector (b) perpendicular to position vector

(c) directed towards origin (d) directed away from the origin

17. An ant is at a corner of a cubical room of side a. The ant can move with a constant speed u. The minimum time taken to reach the farthest corner of the cube is

(a) $\frac{3a}{u}$ (b) $\frac{\sqrt{3}a}{u}$ (c) $\frac{\sqrt{5}a}{u}$ (d) $\frac{(\sqrt{2}+1)a}{u}$

18. A particle moving with uniform speed v, changes its direction by angle θ in time t. Magnitude of its average acceleration during this time is

(a) zero (b) $\frac{2v}{t} \sin \frac{\theta}{2}$ (c) $\frac{v\sqrt{2}}{t}$ (d) None of these

19. A particle moves along a straight line. Its position at any instant is given by $x = 32t - \frac{8t^3}{3}$ where x is in metres and t in seconds. Find the acceleration of the particle at the instant when particle is at rest.

(a) -16 ms^{-2} (b) -32 ms^{-2}

(c) 32 ms^{-2} (d) 16 ms^{-2}

20. A point traversed half of the distance with a velocity v_0. The remaining part of the distance was covered with velocity v_1 for half the time and with velocity v_2 for the other half of the time. The mean velocity of the point averaged over the whole time of motion is

(a) $\frac{v_0 + v_1 + v_2}{3}$ (b) $\frac{2v_0 + v_1 + v_2}{3}$ (c) $\frac{v_0 + 2v_1 + 2v_2}{3}$ (d) $\frac{2v_0 (v_1 + v_2)}{(2v_0 + v_1 + v_2)}$

21. A particle moving in a straight line has velocity-displacement equation as $v = 5\sqrt{1+s}$. Here v is in ms^{-1} and s in metres. Select the correct alternative.
(a) Particle is initially at rest
(b) Initially velocity of the particle is 5 m/s and the particle has a constant acceleration of 12.5 ms^{-2}
(c) Particle moves with a uniform velocity
(d) None of the above

22. A particle located at $x = 0$ at time $t = 0$, starts moving along the positive x-direction with a velocity 'v' which varies as $v = \alpha\sqrt{x}$, then velocity of particle varies with time as (α is a constant)
(a) $v \propto t$
(b) $v \propto t^2$
(c) $v \propto \sqrt{t}$
(d) $v \propto$ constant

23. Water drops fall at regular intervals from a tap 5 m above the ground. The third drop is leaving the tap, the instant the first drop touches the ground. How far above the ground is the second drop at that instant? ($g = 10\ ms^{-2}$)
(a) 1.25 m
(b) 2.50 m
(c) 3.75 m
(d) 4.00 m

24. A stone is dropped from the top of a tower and one second later, a second stone is thrown vertically downward with a velocity 20 ms^{-1}. The second stone will overtake the first after travelling a distance of ($g = 10\ ms^{-2}$)
(a) 13 m
(b) 15 m
(c) 11.25 m
(d) 19.5 m

25. A ball is released from the top of a tower of height h metre. It takes T second to reach the ground. What is the position of the ball in $T/3$ second?
(a) $\frac{h}{9}$ metre from the ground
(b) $(7h/9)$ metre from the ground
(c) $(8h/9)$ metre from the ground
(d) $(17h/18)$ metre from the ground

26. A ball is thrown vertically upwards from the ground and a student gazing out of the window sees it moving upward past him at 10 ms^{-1}. The window is at 15 m above the ground level. The velocity of ball 3 s after it was projected from the ground is [Take $g = 10\ ms^{-2}$]
(a) 10 m/s, up
(b) 20 ms^{-1}, up
(c) 20 ms^{-1}, down
(d) 10 ms^{-1}, down

27. A particle is projected vertically upwards and reaches the maximum height H in time T. The height of the particle at any time $t\ (< T)$ will be
(a) $g\,(t - T)^2$
(b) $H - g\,(t - T)^2$
(c) $\frac{1}{2}\,g\,(t - T)^2$
(d) $H - \frac{1}{2}\,g\,(T - t)^2$

28. A stone is thrown vertically upwards. When stone is at a height half of its maximum height, its speed is 10 ms^{-1}; then the maximum height attained by the stone is ($g = 10\ ms^{-2}$)
(a) 25 m
(b) 10 m
(c) 15 m
(d) 20 m

29. A body dropped from the top of a tower covers a distance $7x$ in the last second of its journey where x is the distance covered in first second. How much time does it take to reach the ground?
(a) 3 s
(b) 4 s
(c) 5 s
(d) 6 s

30. A stone is allowed to fall freely from rest. The ratio of the times taken to fall through the first metre and the second metre distance is
(a) $\sqrt{2} - 1$
(b) $\sqrt{2} + 1$
(c) $\sqrt{2}$
(d) None of these

31. A stone thrown upward with a speed u from the top of the tower reaches the ground with a speed $3u$. The height of the tower is

(a) $3u^2/g$ (b) $4u^2/g$
(c) $6u^2/g$ (d) $9u^2/g$

32. A particle is dropped under gravity from rest from a height h ($g = 9.8$ m/s^2) and it travels a distance $9h/25$ in the last second, the height h is

(a) 100 m (b) 122.5 m
(c) 145 m (d) 167.5 m

33. A stone is dropped from a height h. Simultaneously, another stone is thrown up from the ground which reaches a height $4h$. The two stones will cross each other after time

(a) $\sqrt{\frac{h}{8g}}$ (b) $\sqrt{8gh}$
(c) $\sqrt{2gh}$ (d) $\sqrt{\frac{h}{2g}}$

34. A ball is thrown vertically upward with a speed v from a height h metre above the ground. The time taken for the ball to hit ground is

(a) $\frac{v}{g}\sqrt{1 - \frac{2hg}{v^2}}$ (b) $\frac{v}{g}\sqrt{1 + \frac{2hg}{v^2}}$
(c) $\sqrt{1 + \frac{2hg}{v^2}}$ (d) $\frac{v}{g}\left[1 + \sqrt{1 + \frac{2hg}{v^2}}\right]$

35. A body thrown vertically up from the ground passes the height of 10.2 m twice in an interval of 10 s. What was its initial velocity?

(a) 52 m/s (b) 61 m/s
(c) 45 m/s (d) 26 m/s

36. A particle is thrown upwards from ground. It experiences a constant resistance force which can produce a retardation of 2 ms^{-2}. The ratio of time of ascent to time of descent is ($g = 10$ ms^{-2})

(a) 1 : 1 (b) $\sqrt{\frac{2}{3}}$
(c) $\frac{2}{3}$ (d) $\sqrt{\frac{3}{2}}$

37. Two bodies A and B start from rest from the same point with a uniform acceleration of 2 m/s^2. If B starts one second later, then the two bodies are separated, at the end of the next second, by

(a) 1 m (b) 2 m
(c) 3 m (d) 4 m

38. Two objects are moving along the same straight line. They cross a point A with an acceleration a, $2a$ and velocity $2u$, u at time $t = 0$. The distance moved by the object when one overtakes the other is

(a) $\frac{6u^2}{a}$ (b) $\frac{2u^2}{a}$ (c) $\frac{4u^2}{a}$ (d) $\frac{8u^2}{a}$

39. A body moving with a uniform acceleration crosses a distance of 15 m in the 3rd second and 23 m in the 5th second. The displacement in 10 s will be

(a) 150 m (b) 200 m
(c) 250 m (d) 300 m

40. A body is moving with uniform velocity of 8 ms^{-1}. When the body just crossed another body, the second one starts and moves with uniform acceleration of 4 m/s^2. The time after which two bodies meet, will be

(a) 2 s (b) 4 s (c) 6 s (d) 8 s

41. A car starts from rest and moves on straight line with constant acceleration a_0. After time t_0, brakes is applied which cause of deceleration of magnitude as initial acceleration. The distance travelled by car is

(a) $\frac{1}{2} a_0 t_0^2$ (b) $2a_0 t_0^2$ (c) $a_0 t_0^2$ (d) $\frac{2}{3} a_0 t_0^2$

42. A body starts moving with a velocity $v_0 = 10$ ms^{-1}. It experiences a retardation equal to $0.2v^2$. Its velocity after 2s is given by

(a) $+2$ ms^{-1} (b) $+4$ ms^{-1} (c) -2 ms^{-1} (d) $+6$ ms^{-1}

43. A body of mass 10 kg is being acted upon by a force $3t^2$ and an opposing constant force of 32 N. The initial speed is 10 ms^{-1}. The velocity of body after 5 s is

(a) 14.5 ms^{-1} (b) 6.5 ms^{-1} (c) 3.5 ms^{-1} (d) 4.5 ms^{-1}

44. The position of a particle along x-axis at time t is given by $x = 2 + t - 3t^2$. The displacement and the distance travelled in the interval $t = 0$ to $t = 1$ are respectively,

(a) 2, 2 (b) -2, 2.5 (c) 0, 2 (d) None of these

45. Acceleration-time graph for a particle moving in a straight line is as shown in figure. Change in velocity of the particle from $t = 0$ to $t = 6$ s is

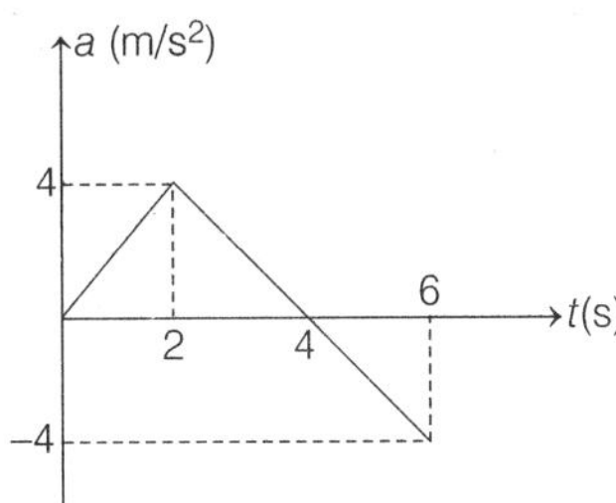

(a) 10 m/s (b) 4 m/s (c) 12 m/s (d) 8 m/s

46. The velocity-time graph for a particle moving along x-axis is shown in the figure. The corresponding displacement-time graph is correctly shown by

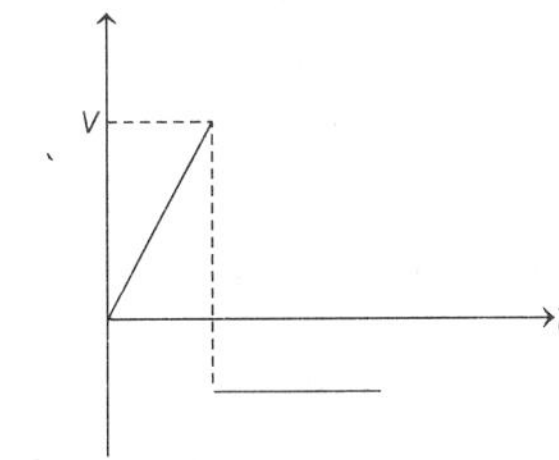

(a) (b) (c) 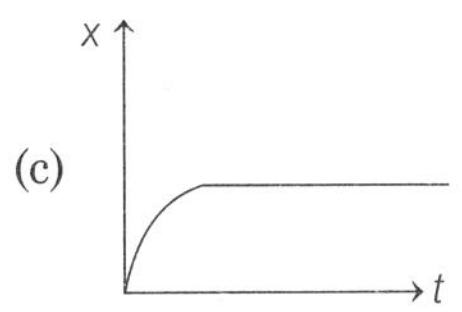

(d)

47. Acceleration *versus* time graph of a body starting from rest is shown in the figure. The velocity *versus* time graph of the body is given by

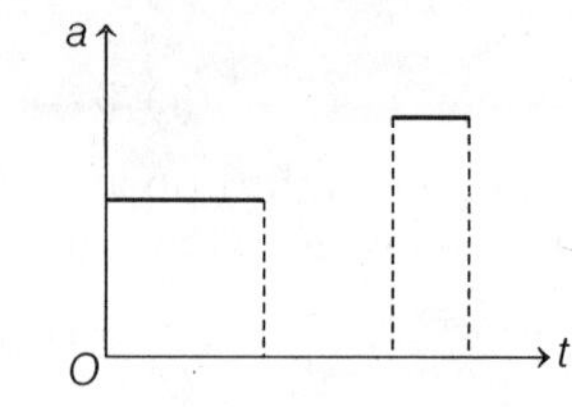

(a)
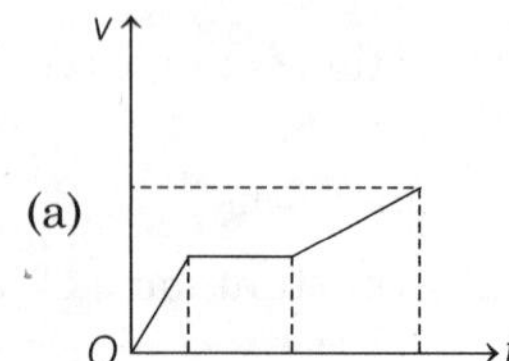

(b)
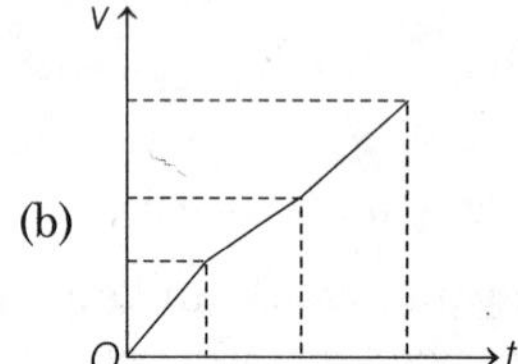

(c)
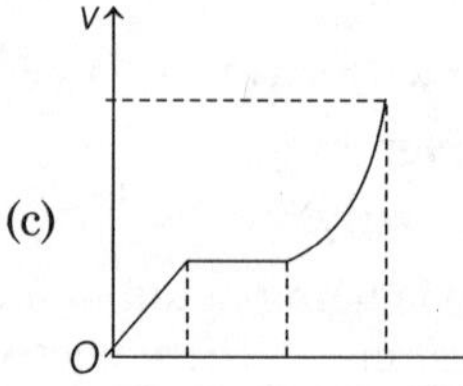

(d)
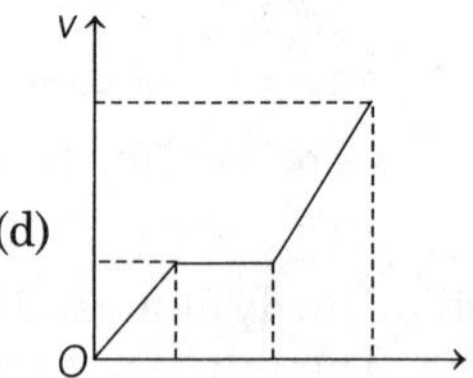

48. If the velocity v of a particle moving along a straight line decreases linearly with its displacement s from 20 ms^{-1} to a value approaching zero at $s = 30$ m, then acceleration of the particle at $s = 15$ m is

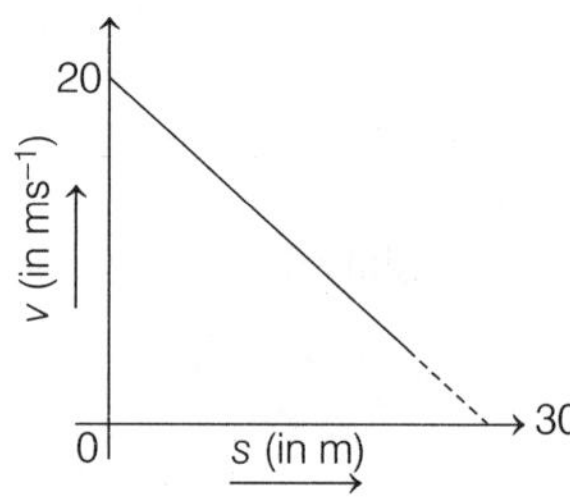

(a) $\frac{2}{3}\ \text{ms}^{-2}$ (b) $-\frac{2}{3}\ \text{ms}^{-2}$ (c) $\frac{20}{3}\ \text{ms}^{-2}$ (d) $-\frac{20}{3}\ \text{ms}^{-2}$

49. A point moves with uniform acceleration and v_1, v_2 and v_3 denote the average velocities in the three successive intervals of time t_1, t_2 and t_3. Which of the following relation is correct?

(a) $(v_1 - v_2) : (v_2 - v_3) = (t_1 - t_2) : (t_2 + t_3)$
(b) $(v_1 - v_2) : (v_2 - v_3) = (t_1 + t_2) : (t_2 + t_3)$
(c) $(v_1 - v_2) : (v_2 - v_3) = (t_1 - t_2) : (t_1 - t_3)$
(d) $(v_1 - v_2) : (v_2 - v_3) = (t_1 - t_2) : (t_2 - t_3)$

50. A particle moves in the x-y plane with velocity $v_x = 8t - 2$ and $v_y = 2$. If it passes through the point $x = 14$ and $y = 4$ at $t = 2$ s, the equation of the path is

(a) $x = y^2 - y + 2$
(b) $x = y^2 - 2$
(c) $x = y^2 + y - 6$
(d) None of these

51. A particle is moving with velocity $\mathbf{v} = k(y\hat{\mathbf{i}} + x\hat{\mathbf{j}})$, where k is a constant. The general equation for its path is

(a) $y = x^2$ + constant (b) $y^2 = x$+ constant (c) xy = constant (d) $y^2 = x^2$ + constant

52. A particle moves in the xy-plane according to the law $x = kt$, $y = kt\,(1 - \alpha t)$ where k and α are positive constants and t is time. The trajectory of the particle is

(a) $y = kx$
(b) $y = x - \frac{\alpha x^2}{k}$
(c) $y = -\frac{\alpha x^2}{k}$
(d) $y = \alpha x$

53. The equation of trajectory of a particle is $x = \sqrt{3}y - 5y^2$

The particle is at origin at $t = 0$. Its acceleration is $\mathbf{a} = -10\,\hat{\mathbf{i}}$. Its initial speed is

(a) $1\ ms^{-1}$
(b) $2\ ms^{-1}$
(c) $10\ ms^{-1}$
(d) cannot be determined

54. A particle moves on a straight line under deceleration of bv^2, initial velocity is v_0. The distance covered in time t is

(a) $bv_0 t$
(b) $\frac{1}{b}[\ln(1 + bv_0 t)]$
(c) $\frac{\ln bv_0 t}{b}$
(d) $b \ln bv_0 t$

55. A train starting from rest accelerates uniformly for 100 s, then comes to a stop with a uniform retardation in the next 200 s. During the motion, it covers a distance of 3 km. Choose the correct option.

(a) Its acceleration is $0.2\ m/s^2$
(b) Its retardation is $0.1\ m/s^2$
(c) The maximum velocity is 20 m/s
(d) All of these

56. A lift starts from rest. Its acceleration is plotted against time. When it comes to rest its height above its starting point is

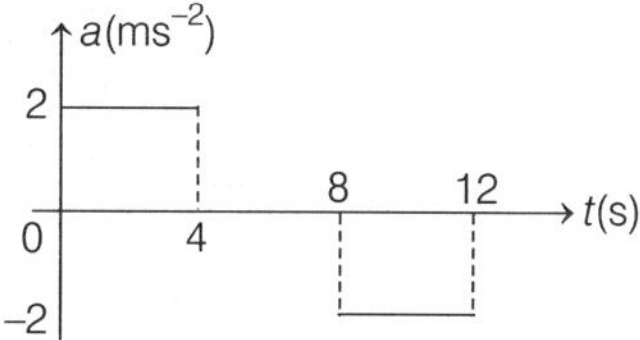

(a) 20 m
(b) 64 m
(c) 32 m
(d) 36 m

57. The figure shows velocity-time graph of a particle moving along a straight line. Identify the correct statement.

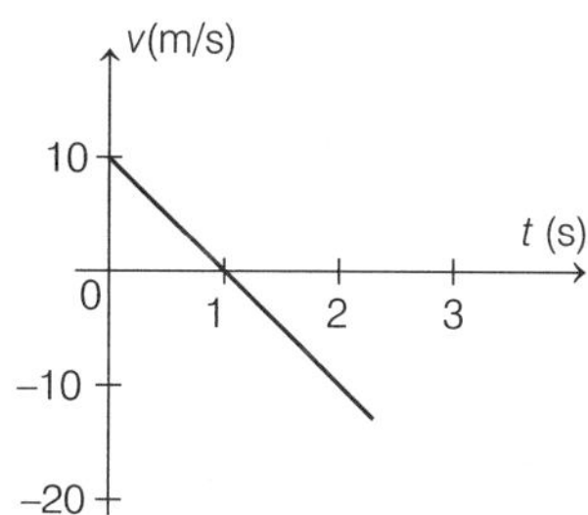

(a) The particle starts from the origin
(b) The particle crosses it initial position at $t = 2$ s
(c) The average speed of the particle in the time interval, $0 \le t \le 2$ s is zero
(d) All of the above

58. v^2 *versus* s graph of a particle moving in a straight line is as shown in figure. From the graph some conclusions are drawn. State which statement is **wrong**.

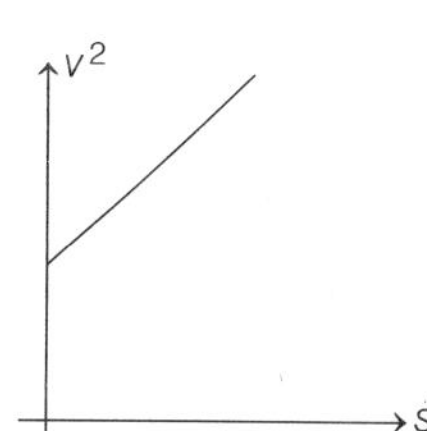

(a) The given graph shows a uniformly accelerated motion
(b) Initial velocity of particle is zero
(c) Corresponding s-t graph will be a parabola
(d) None of the above

59. A graph between the square of the velocity of a particle and the distance s moved by the particle is shown in the figure. The acceleration of the particle is

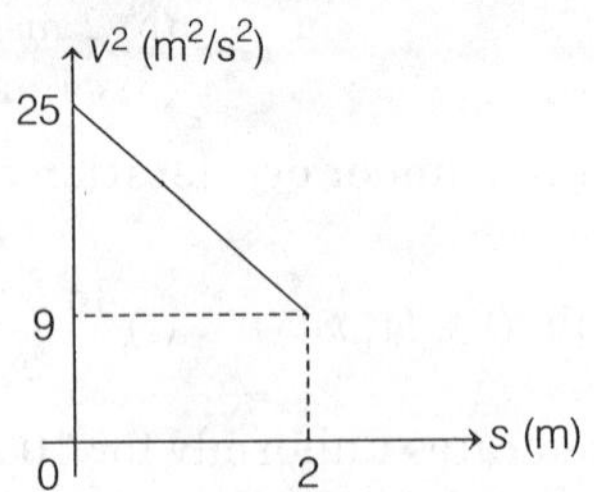

(a) $-8\ m/s^2$ (b) $4\ m/s^2$
(c) $-16\ m/s^2$ (d) None of these

60. Two balls are projected simultaneously with the same speed from the top of a tower, one vertically upwards and the other vertically downwards. They reach the ground in 9 s and 4 s, respectively. The height of the tower is ($g = 10\ m/s^2$)

(a) 90 m (b) 180 m
(c) 270 m (d) 360 m

61. The displacement x of a particle in a straight line motion is given by $x = 1 - t - t^2$. The correct representation of the motion is

(a)
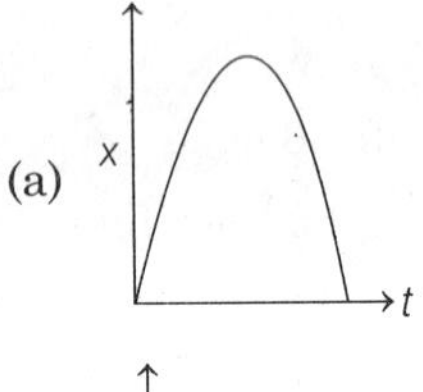

(b)
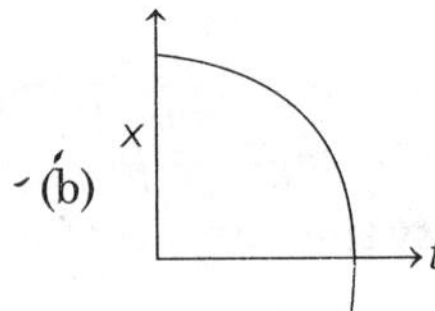

(c)
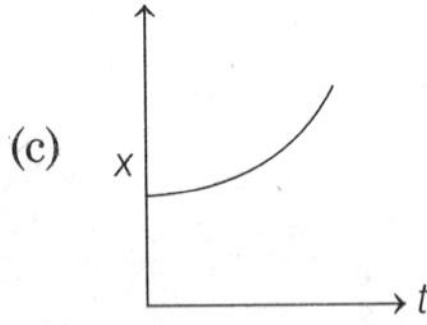

(d)
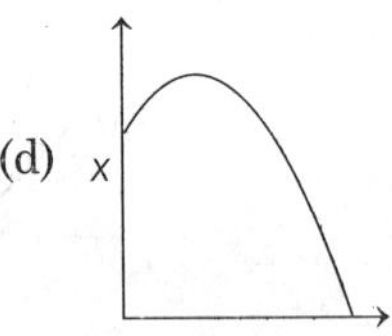

62. During the first 18 min of a 60 min trip, a car has an average speed of 11 ms^{-1}. What should be the average speed for remaining 42 min so that car is having an average speed of 21 ms^{-1} for the entire trip?

(a) 25.3 ms^{-1} (b) 29.2 ms^{-1}
(c) 31 ms^{-1} (d) 35.6 ms^{-1}

63. The horizontal and vertical displacements of a particle moving along a curved line are given by $x = 5t$ and $y = 2t^2 + t$. Time after which its velocity vector makes an angle of 45° with the horizontal is

(a) 0.5 s (b) 1 s (c) 2 s (d) 1.5 s

64. A cart is moving horizontally along a straight line with constant speed 30 ms^{-1}. A particle is to be fired vertically upwards from the moving cart in such a way that it returns to the cart at the same point from where it was projected after the cart has moved 80 m. At what speed (relative to the cart) must the projectile be fired? (Take $g = 10\ ms^{-2}$)

(a) 10 ms^{-1} (b) $10\sqrt{8}\ ms^{-1}$ (c) $\frac{40}{3}\ ms^{-1}$ (d) None of these

65. Two trains are moving with velocities $v_1 = 10\ \text{ms}^{-1}$ and $v_2 = 20\ \text{ms}^{-1}$ on the same track in opposite directions. After the application of brakes if their retarding rates are $a_1 = 2\ \text{ms}^{-2}$ and $a_2 = 1\ \text{ms}^{-2}$ respectively, then the minimum distance of separation between the trains to avoid collision is

(a) 150 m (b) 225 m (c) 450 m (d) 300 m

66. Two identical balls are shot upward one after another at an interval of 2 s along the same vertical line with same initial velocity of $40\ \text{ms}^{-1}$. The height at which the balls collide is

(a) 50 m (b) 75 m
(c) 100 m (d) 125 m

67. A body starts from rest with uniform acceleration a, its velocity after n seconds is v. The displacement of the body in last 3 s is (assume total time of journey from 0 to n second)

(a) $\frac{v(6n-9)}{2n}$ (b) $\frac{2v(6n-9)}{n}$
(c) $\frac{2v(2n+1)}{n}$ (d) $\frac{2v(n-1)}{n}$

68. A body is thrown vertically upwards from the top A of tower. It reaches the ground in t_1 s. If it is thrown vertically downwards from A with the same speed it reaches the ground in t_2 s. If it is allowed to fall freely from A, then the time it takes to reach the ground is given by

(a) $t = \frac{t_1 + t_2}{2}$ (b) $t = \frac{t_1 - t_2}{2}$
(c) $t = \sqrt{t_1 t_2}$ (d) $t = \sqrt{\frac{t_1}{t_2}}$

69. A lift performs the first part of its ascent with uniform acceleration a and the remaining with uniform retardation $2a$. If t is the time of ascent, find the depth of the shaft.

(a) $\frac{at^2}{4}$ (b) $\frac{at^2}{3}$ (c) $\frac{at^2}{2}$ (d) $\frac{at^2}{8}$

70. Two particles A and B start from rest and move for equal time on a straight line. Particle A has an acceleration of $2\ \text{m/s}^2$ for the first half of the total time and $4\ \text{m/s}^2$ for the second half. The particle B has acceleration $4\ \text{m/s}^2$ for the first half and $2\ \text{m/s}^2$ for the second half. Which particle has covered larger distance?

(a) A (b) B
(c) Both have covered the same distance (d) Data insufficient

71. A particle starts from rest and traverses a distance l with uniform acceleration, then moves uniformly over a further distance $2l$ and finally comes to rest after moving a further distance $3l$ under uniform retardation. Assuming entire motion to be rectilinear motion the ratio of average speed over the journey to the maximum speed on its ways is

(a) 1/5 (b) 2/5 (c) 3/5 (d) 4/5

72. A ball is dropped on the floor from a height of 80 m rebounds to a height of 20 m. If the ball is in contact with the floor for 0.1 s, the average acceleration during contact is

(a) $400\ \text{m/s}^2$ (b) $500\ \text{m/s}^2$
(c) $600\ \text{m/s}^2$ (d) $800\ \text{m/s}^2$

73. The speed of a boat is 5 km/h in still water. It crosses a river of width 1 km along the shortest possible path in 15 min. Then, velocity of the river will be

(a) 4.5 km/h (b) 4 km/h (c) 1.5 km/h (d) 3 km/h

74. The initial velocity of a particle of mass 2 kg is $(4\hat{i} + 4\hat{j})$ m/s. A constant force of $-20\hat{j}$ N is applied on the particle. Initially, the particle was at (0, 0). Find the x-coordinate of the point where its y-coordinate is again zero.

(a) 3.2 m (b) 6 m
(c) 4.8 m (d) 1.2 m

75. A man standing on a road has to hold his umbrella at 30° with the vertical to keep the rain away. He throws the umbrella and starts running at 10 km/h. He finds that raindrops are hitting his head vertically. What is the speed of rain with respect to ground?

(a) $10\sqrt{3}$ km/h (b) 20 km/h
(c) $\frac{20}{\sqrt{3}}$ km/h (d) $\frac{10}{\sqrt{3}}$ km/h

76. Two points move in the same straight line starting at the same moment from the same point in it. The first moves with constant velocity u and the second with constant acceleration f. During the time elapses before the second catches the first greatest distance between the particle is

(a) $\frac{u}{f}$ (b) $\frac{u^2}{2f}$
(c) $\frac{f}{2u^2}$ (d) $\frac{f}{u^2}$

77. Figure shows two ships moving in xy-plane with velocities v_A and v_B. The ships move such that B always remains north of A. The ratio $\frac{v_A}{v_B}$ is equal to

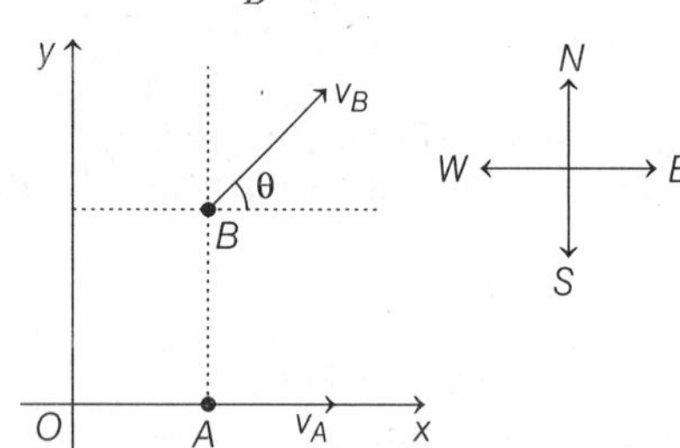

(a) cos θ (b) sin θ
(c) sec θ (d) cosec θ

78. A body is projected vertically upwards. If t_1 and t_2 be the times at which it is at height h above the point of projection while ascending and descending respectively, then h is

(a) $\frac{1}{2} g\, t_1 t_2$ (b) $g\, t_1 t_2$
(c) $2g\, t_1 t_2$ (d) $4g\, t_1 t_2$

79. In the previous problem, the velocity of projection is

(a) $\frac{1}{2} g(t_1 + t_2)$ (b) $g(t_1 + t_2)$
(c) $2g(t_1 + t_2)$ (d) $4g(t_1 + t_2)$

80. A ball is thrown vertically upwards with a speed u. It reaches a point B at a height h (lower than the maximum height) after time t_1. It returns to the ground after time t_2 from the instant it was at B during the upward journey. Then, $t_1\, t_2$ is equal to

(a) $2h/g$ (b) h/g
(c) $h/2g$ (d) $h/4g$

Subjective Questions

1. (a) What does $\left|\frac{d\mathbf{v}}{dt}\right|$ and $\frac{d|\mathbf{v}|}{dt}$ represent?

(b) Can these be equal?

2. A farmer has to go 500 m due north, 400 m due east and 200 m due south to reach his field. If he takes 20 min to reach the field.

(a) What distance he has to walk to reach the field ?
(b) What is the displacement from his house to the field ?
(c) What is the average speed of farmer during the walk ?
(d) What is the average velocity of farmer during the walk ?

3. A rocket is fired vertically up from the ground with a resultant vertical acceleration of 10 m/s^2. The fuel is finished in 1 min and it continues to move up.(a) What is the maximum height reached? (b) After how much time from then will the maximum height be reached? (Take $g = 10\ m/s^2$)

4. A block moves in a straight line with velocity v for time t_0. Then, its velocity becomes $2v$ for next t_0 time. Finally, its velocity becomes $3v$ for time T. If average velocity during the complete journey was 2.5 v, then find T in terms of t_0.

5. A particle starting from rest has a constant acceleration of 4 m/s^2 for 4 s. It then retards uniformly for next 8 s and comes to rest. Find during the motion of particle (a) average acceleration (b) average speed and (c) average velocity.

6. Two particles A and B start moving simultaneously along the line joining them in the same direction with acceleration of 1 m/s^2 and 2 m/s^2 and speeds 3 m/s and 1 m/s respectively. Initially, A is 10 m behind B. What is the minimum distance between them?

7. Displacement-time graph of a particle moving in a straight line is as shown in figure.

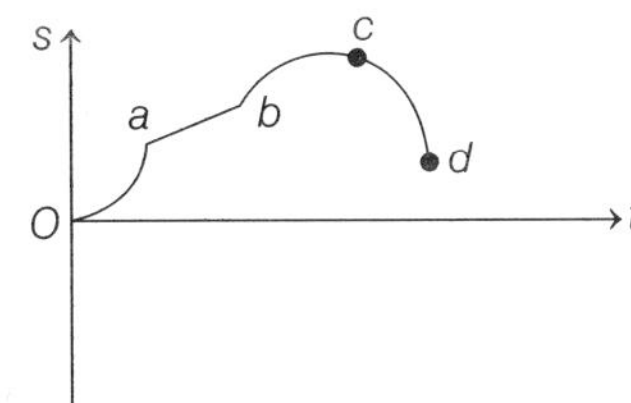

(a) Find the sign of velocity in regions *oa*, *ab*, *bc* and *cd*.
(b) Find the sign of acceleration in the above region.

8. Velocity-time graph of a particle moving in a straight line is shown in figure. In the time interval from $t = 0$ to $t = 14$ s, find

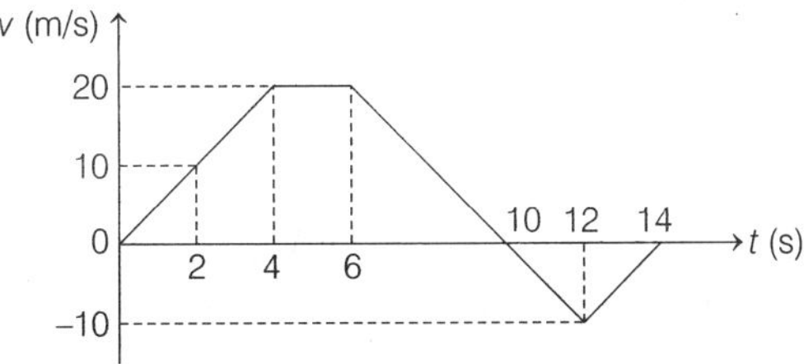

(a) average velocity and (b) average speed of the particle.

9. A person walks up a stalled 15 m long escalator in 90 s. When standing on the same escalator, now moving, the person is carried up in 60 s. How much time would it take that person to walk up the moving escalator? Does the answer depend on the length of the escalator?

10. Velocity of a particle moving along positive x-direction is $v = (40 - 10\,t)$ m/s. Here, t is in seconds. At time $t = 0$, the x-coordinate of particle is zero. Find the time when the particle is at a distance of 60 m from origin.

11. Acceleration-time graph of a particle moving in a straight line is as shown in figure. At time $t = 0$, velocity of the particle is zero. Find

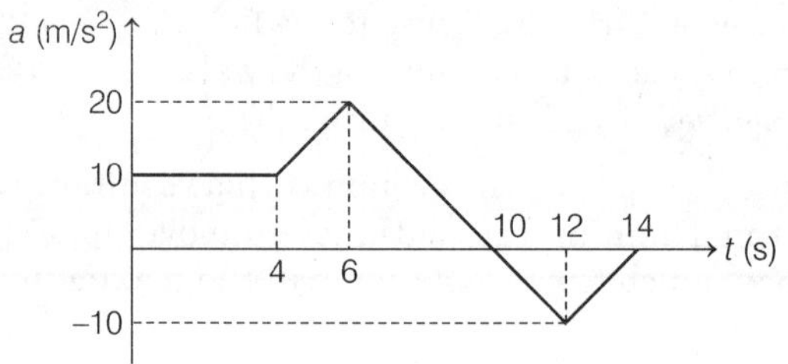

(a) average acceleration in a time interval from $t = 6$ s to $t = 12$ s,
(b) velocity of the particle at $t = 14$ s.

12. A particle is moving in x-y plane. At time $t = 0$, particle is at (1m, 2m) and has velocity $(4\hat{i} + 6\hat{j})$ m/s. At $t = 4$ s, particle reaches at (6m, 4m) and has velocity $(2\hat{i} + 10\hat{j})$ m/s. In the given time interval, find
(a) average velocity,
(b) average acceleration and
(c) from the given data, can you find average speed?

13. A point mass starts moving in a straight line with constant acceleration. After time t_0 the acceleration changes its sign, remaining the same in magnitude. Determine the time T from the beginning of motion in which the point mass returns to the initial position.

14. In one dimensional motion position of a particle from a fixed point is (say P) is $+\,2m$ at time $t = 0$ and the particle is at P at $t = 10$ s. If velocity of particle is zero at $t = 6$ s, determine the constant acceleration a and velocity at $t = 10$ s.

15. At time $t = 0$, a particle is at (2m, 4m). It starts moving towards positive x-axis with constant acceleration 2 m/s^2 (initial velocity = 0). After 2 s, an additional acceleration of 4 m/s^2 starts acting on the particle in negative y-direction also. Find after next 2 s.
(a) velocity and
(b) coordinates of particle.

16. A particle starts from the origin at $t = 0$ with a velocity of $8.0\hat{j}$ m/s and moves in the x-y plane with a constant acceleration of $(4.0\hat{i} + 2.0\hat{j})$ m/s^2. At the instant the particle's x-coordinate is 29 m, what are
(a) its y-coordinate and
(b) its speed ?

17. A particle moves along a horizontal path, such that its velocity is given by $v = (3t^2 - 6t)$ m/s, where t is the time in seconds. If it is initially located at the origin O, determine the distance travelled by the particle in time interval from $t = 0$ to $t = 3.5$ s and the particle's average velocity and average speed during the same time interval.

18. A particle travels in a straight line, such that for a short time $2\text{ s} \le t \le 6\text{ s}$, its motion is described by $v = (4/a)\text{ m/s}$, where a is in m/s^2. If $v = 6\text{ m/s}$ when $t = 2\text{ s}$, determine the particle's acceleration when $t = 3\text{ s}$.

19. Velocity-time graph of a particle moving in a straight line is shown in figure. At time $t = 0$, $s = -10\text{ m}$. Plot corresponding a-t and s-t graphs.

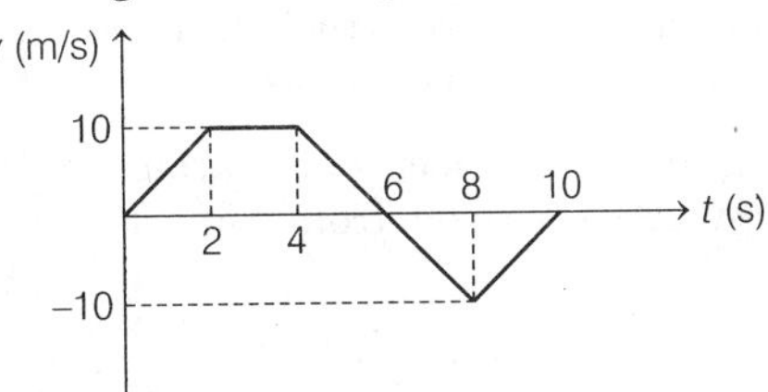

20. A particle of mass m is released from a certain height h with zero initial velocity. It strikes the ground elastically (direction of its velocity is reversed but magnitude remains the same). Plot the graph between its kinetic energy and time till it returns to its initial position.

21. A ball is dropped from a height of 80 m on a floor. At each collision, the ball loses half of its speed. Plot the speed-time graph and velocity-time graph of its motion till two collisions with the floor. (Take, $g = 10\text{ m/s}^2$)

22. Velocity-time graph of a particle moving in a straight line is shown in figure. At time $t = 0$, displacement of the particle from mean position is 10 m. Find

(a) acceleration of particle at $t = 1\text{ s}, 3\text{ s}$ and 9 s.

(b) position of particle from mean position at $t = 10\text{ s}$.

(c) write down s-t equation for time interval

(i) $0 \le t \le 2\text{ s}$,

(ii) $4\text{ s} \le t \le 8\text{ s}$

23. Two particles 1 and 2 are thrown in the directions shown in figure simultaneously with velocities 5 m/s and 20 m/s. Initially, particle 1 is at height 20 m from the ground. Taking upwards as the positive direction, find

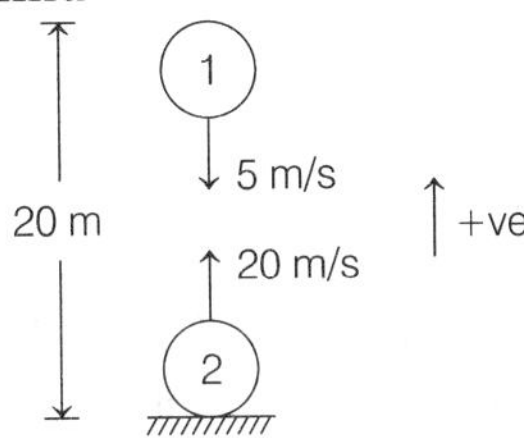

(a) acceleration of 1 with respect to 2

(b) initial velocity of 2 with respect to 1

(c) velocity of 1 with respect to 2 after time $t = \frac{1}{2}\text{ s}$

(d) time when the particles will collide.

24. A ball is thrown vertically upward from the 12 m level with an initial velocity of 18 m/s. At the same instant an open platform elevator passes the 5 m level, moving upward with a constant velocity of 2 m/s. Determine ($g = 9.8\text{ m/s}^2$)

(a) when and where the ball will meet the elevator,

(b) the relative velocity of the ball with respect to the elevator when the ball hits the elevator.

25. An automobile and a truck start from rest at the same instant, with the automobile initially at some distance behind the truck. The truck has a constant acceleration of 2.2 m/s^2 and the automobile has an acceleration of 3.5 m/s^2. The automobile overtakes the truck when it (truck) has moved 60 m.

(a) How much time does it take the automobile to overtake the truck ?

(b) How far was the automobile behind the truck initially ?

(c) What is the speed of each during overtaking ?

26. Given $|\mathbf{v}_{br}| = 4$ m/s = magnitude of velocity of boatman with respect to river, $\mathbf{v}_r = 2$ m/s in the direction shown. Boatman wants to reach from point A to point B. At what angle θ should he row his boat?

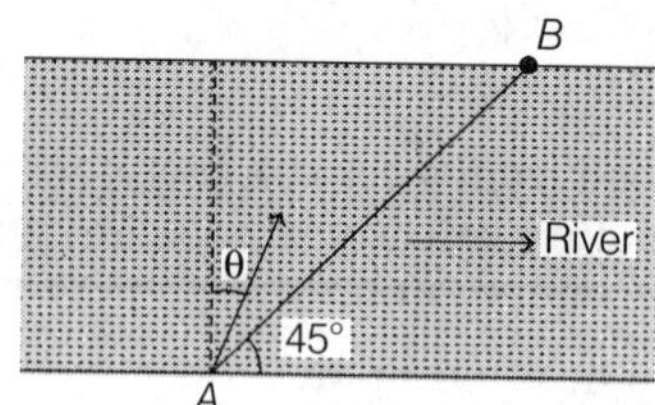

27. An aeroplane has to go from a point P to another point Q, 1000 km away due north. Wind is blowing due east at a speed of 200 km/h. The air speed of plane is 500 km/h.

(a) Find the direction in which the pilot should head the plane to reach the point Q.

(b) Find the time taken by the plane to go from P to Q.

28. A train stopping at two stations 4 km apart takes 4 min on the journey from one of the station to the other. Assuming that it first accelerates with a uniform acceleration x and then that of uniform retardation y, prove that $\frac{1}{x} + \frac{1}{y} = 2$.

LEVEL 2

Objective Questions

Single Correct Option

1. When a man moves down the inclined plane with a constant speed 5 ms^{-1} which makes an angle of 37° with the horizontal, he finds that the rain is falling vertically downward. When he moves up the same inclined plane with the same speed, he finds that the rain makes an angle $\theta = \tan^{-1}\left(\frac{7}{8}\right)$ with the horizontal. The speed of the rain is

(a) $\sqrt{116}$ ms^{-1} (b) $\sqrt{32}$ ms^{-1} (c) 5 ms^{-1} (d) $\sqrt{73}$ ms^{-1}

2. Equation of motion of a body is $\frac{dv}{dt} = -4v + 8$, where v is the velocity in ms^{-1} and t is the time in second. Initial velocity of the particle was zero. Then,

(a) the initial rate of change of acceleration of the particle is 8 ms^{-2}

(b) the terminal speed is 2 ms^{-1}

(c) Both (a) and (b) are correct

(d) Both (a) and (b) are wrong

3. Two particles A and B are placed in gravity free space at (0, 0, 0) m and (30, 0, 0) m respectively. Particle A is projected with a velocity $(5\hat{\mathbf{i}} + 10\hat{\mathbf{j}} + 5\hat{\mathbf{k}})\ \text{ms}^{-1}$, while particle B is projected with a velocity $(10\,\hat{\mathbf{i}} + 5\hat{\mathbf{j}} + 5\hat{\mathbf{k}})\ \text{ms}^{-1}$ simultaneously. Then,

(a) they will collide at (10, 20, 10) m
(b) they will collide at (10, 10, 10) m
(c) they will never collide
(d) they will collide at 2 s

4. Velocity of the river with respect to ground is given by v_0. Width of the river is d. A swimmer swims (with respect to water) perpendicular to the current with acceleration $a = 2t$ (where t is time) starting from rest from the origin O at $t = 0$. The equation of trajectory of the path followed by the swimmer is

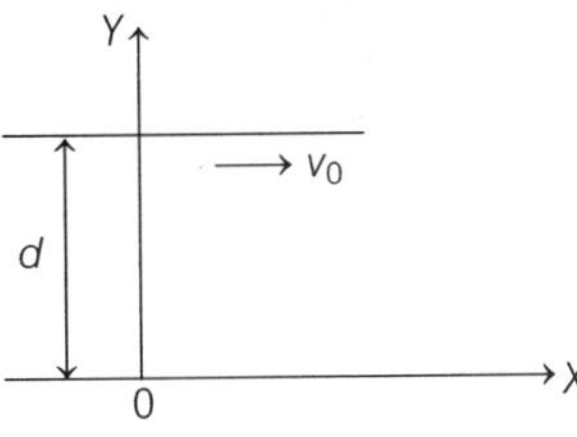

(a) $y = \dfrac{x^3}{3v_0^3}$
(b) $y = \dfrac{x^2}{2v_0^2}$
(c) $y = \dfrac{x}{v_0}$
(d) $y = \sqrt{\dfrac{x}{v_0}}$

5. The relation between time t and displacement x is $t = \alpha x^2 + \beta x$, where α and β are constants. The retardation is

(a) $2\,\alpha v^3$
(b) $2\,\beta v^3$
(c) $2\,\alpha\beta v^3$
(d) $2\,\beta^2 v^3$

6. A street car moves rectilinearly from station A to the next station B (from rest to rest) with an acceleration varying according to the law $f = a - bx$, where a and b are constants and x is the distance from station A. The distance between the two stations and the maximum velocity are

(a) $x = \dfrac{2a}{b},\ v_{max} = \dfrac{a}{\sqrt{b}}$
(b) $x = \dfrac{b}{2a},\ v_{max} = \dfrac{a}{b}$
(c) $x = \dfrac{a}{2b},\ v_{max} = \dfrac{b}{\sqrt{a}}$
(d) $x = \dfrac{a}{b},\ v_{max} = \dfrac{\sqrt{a}}{b}$

7. A particle of mass m moves on positive x-axis under the influence of force acting towards the origin given by $-kx^2\hat{\mathbf{i}}$. If the particle starts from rest at $x = a$, the speed it will attain when it crosses the origin is

(a) $\sqrt{\dfrac{k}{ma}}$
(b) $\sqrt{\dfrac{2k}{ma}}$
(c) $\sqrt{\dfrac{ma}{2k}}$
(d) None of these

8. A particle is moving along a straight line whose velocity-displacement graph is as shown in the figure. What is the magnitude of acceleration when displacement is 3 m ?

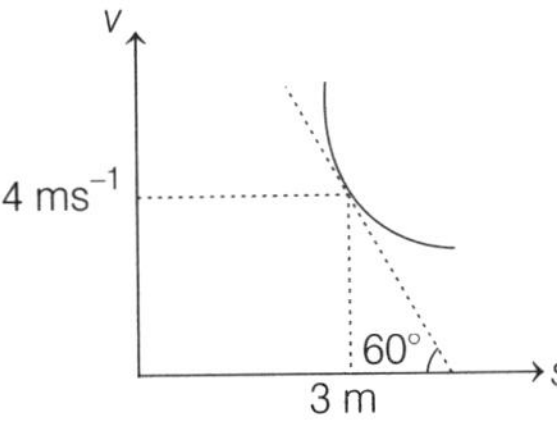

(a) $4\sqrt{3}\ \text{ms}^{-2}$
(b) $3\sqrt{3}\ \text{ms}^{-2}$
(c) $\sqrt{3}\ \text{ms}^{-2}$
(d) $\dfrac{4}{\sqrt{3}}\ \text{ms}^{-2}$

9. A thief in a stolen car passes through a police check post at his top speed of 90 kmh^{-1}. A motorcycle cop, reacting after 2 s, accelerates from rest at 5 ms^{-2}. His top speed being 108 kmh^{-1}. Find the maximum separation between policemen and thief.

(a) 112.5 m (b) 115 m
(c) 116.5 m (d) None of these

10. Anoop (A) hits a ball along the ground with a speed u in a direction which makes an angle 30° with the line joining him and the fielder Babul (B). Babul runs to intercept the ball with a speed $\frac{2u}{3}$. At what angle θ should he run to intercept the ball ?

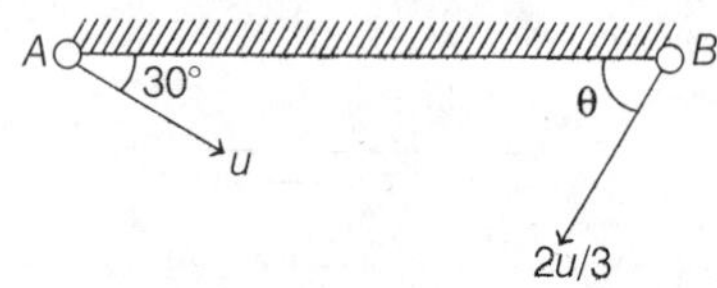

(a) $\sin^{-1}\left[\frac{\sqrt{3}}{2}\right]$ (b) $\sin^{-1}\left[\frac{2}{3}\right]$
(c) $\sin^{-1}\left[\frac{3}{4}\right]$ (d) $\sin^{-1}\left[\frac{4}{5}\right]$

11. A car is travelling on a straight road. The maximum velocity the car can attain is 24 ms^{-1}. The maximum acceleration and deceleration it can attain are 1 ms^{-2} and 4 ms^{-2} respectively. The shortest time the car takes from rest to rest in a distance of 200 m is,

(a) 22.4 s (b) 30 s
(c) 11.2 s (d) 5.6 s

12. A car is travelling on a road. The maximum velocity the car can attain is 24 ms^{-1} and the maximum deceleration is 4 ms^{-2}. If car starts from rest and comes to rest after travelling 1032 m in the shortest time of 56 s, the maximum acceleration that the car can attain is

(a) 6 ms^{-2} (b) 1.2 ms^{-2}
(c) 12 ms^{-2} (d) 3.6 ms^{-2}

13. Two particles are moving along two long straight lines, in the same plane with same speed equal to 20 cm/s. The angle between the two lines is 60° and their intersection point is O. At a certain moment, the two particles are located at distances 3m and 4m from O and are moving towards O. Subsequently, the shortest distance between them will be

(a) 50 cm (b) $40\sqrt{2}$ cm
(c) $50\sqrt{2}$ cm (d) $50\sqrt{3}$ cm

14. A particle starting from rest. Its acceleration at an instant t is $a = \frac{10}{v+1}$ ms^{-2}, where v is instantaneous velocity. The distance travelled after which the particle attain a velocity of 15 ms^{-1} is

(a) 123.75 m (b) 1237.5 m
(c) 200 m (d) 375 m

15. Two stones are thrown up simultaneously with initial speeds of u_1 and u_2 ($u_2 > u_1$). They hit the ground after 6 s and 10 s respectively. Which graph in figure correctly represents the time variation of $\Delta x = (x_2 - x_1)$, the relative position of the second stone with respect to the first upto $t = 10$ s?

Assume that the stones do not rebound after hitting the ground.

(a) 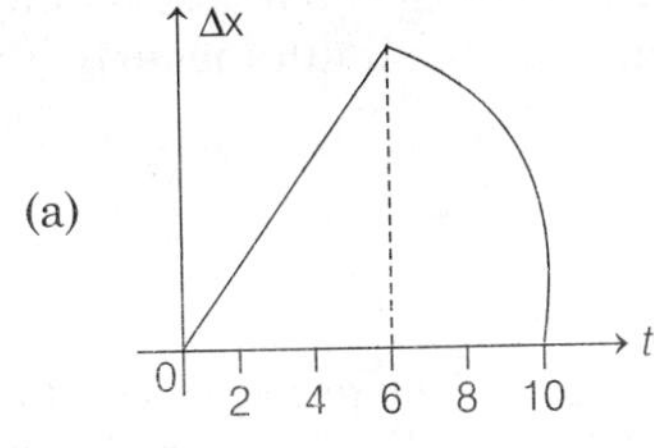

(b) 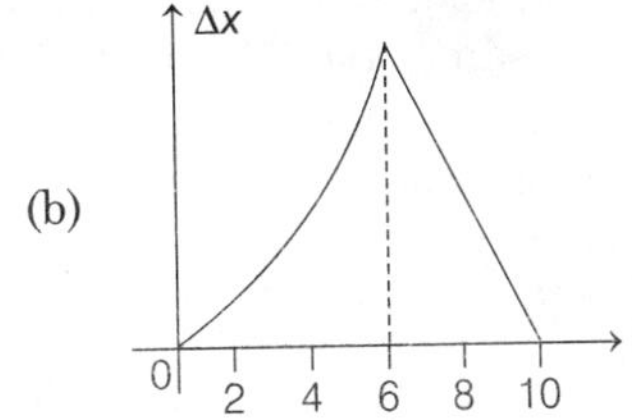

(c) 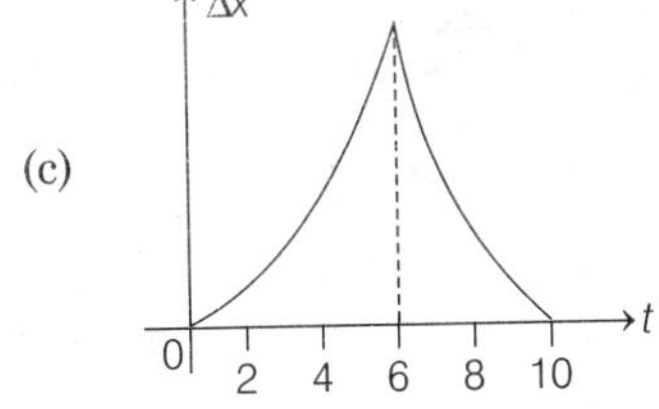

(d) 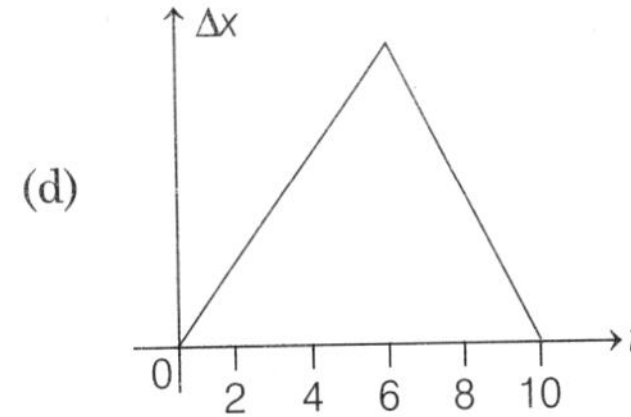

16. A body is at rest at $x = 0$. At $t = 0$, it starts moving in the positive X-direction with a constant acceleration. At the same instant, another body passes through $x = 0$ moving in the positive X-direction with a constant speed. The position of the first body is given by $x_1(t)$ after time t and that of the second body by $x_2(t)$ after the same time interval. Which of the following graphs correctly describes $(x_2 - x_1)$ as a function of time?

(a) 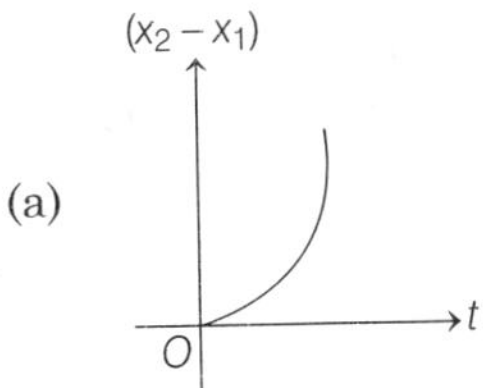

(b) 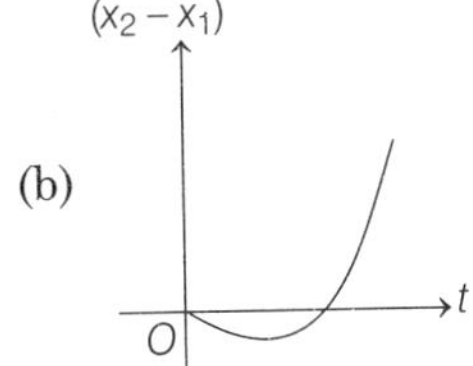

(c) 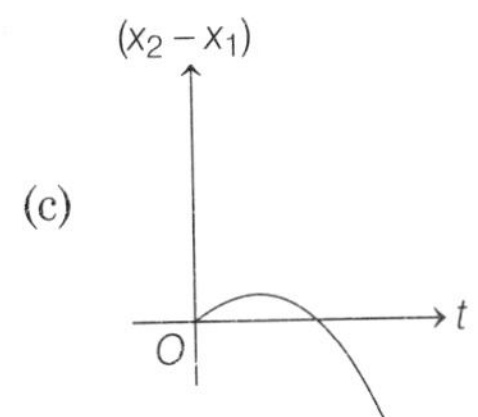

(d) 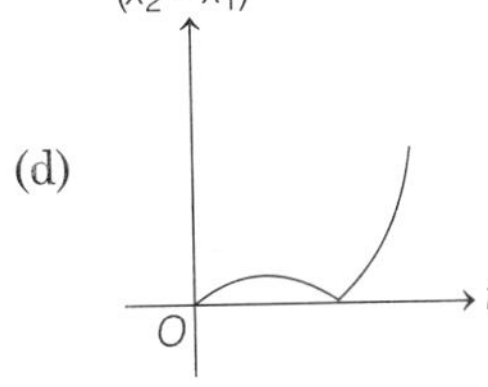

17. A particle of mass m is initially situated at point P inside a hemispherical surface of radius r as shown in the figure. A horizontal acceleration of magnitude a_0 is suddenly produced on the particle in the horizontal direction. If gravitational acceleration is neglected, then time taken by the particle to touch the sphere gain is

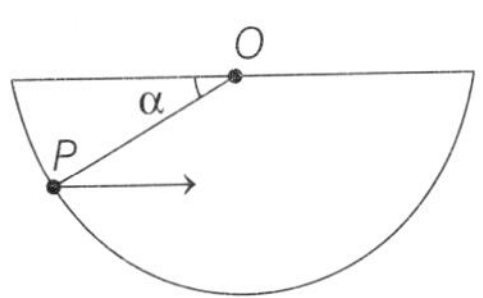

(a) $\sqrt{\dfrac{4r\sin\alpha}{a_0}}$ (b) $\sqrt{\dfrac{4r\tan\alpha}{a_0}}$ (c) $\sqrt{\dfrac{4r\cos\alpha}{a_0}}$ (d) None of these

18. The vertical height of point P above the ground is twice that of Q. A particle is projected downward with a speed of 5 m/s from P and at the same time another particle is projected upward with the same speed from Q. Both particles reach the ground simultaneously, then

(a) $PQ = 30$ m
(b) time of flight of stones = 3 s
(c) Both (a) and (b) are correct
(d) Both (a) and (b) are wrong

19. Three particles are initially at the verticle of an equilateral triangle. The particle A and B start to move with constant velocities $\mathbf{v}_A$ and $\mathbf{v}_B$ in any direction. Which of following relations satisfy the speed of the 3rd particle C such that all particles lie on equilateral triangle ?

(a) $v_C \le v_A + v_B$
(b) $v_C < v_A + v_B$
(c) $v_C \ge v_A + v_B$
(d) $v_C \le \frac{1}{2}(v_A + v_B)$

20. Three particles start simultaneously from a point on a horizontal smooth plane. First particle moves with speed v_1 towards east, second particle moves towards north with speed v_2 and third-one moves towards north east. The velocity of the third particle, so that the three always lie on a line, is

(a) $\dfrac{v_1 + v_2}{\sqrt{2}}$
(b) $\sqrt{v_1 v_2}$
(c) $\dfrac{v_1 v_2}{v_1 + v_2}$
(d) $\sqrt{2}\left(\dfrac{v_1 v_2}{v_1 + v_2}\right)$

21. Three particles start from the origin at the same time, one with a velocity $v_0 = 1\ \text{ms}^{-1}$ along X-axis. Second with $v_2 = 2\ \text{ms}^{-1}$ along Y-axis and third along $x = y$ line. Find the velocity of third particle, so that they are always on a straight line.

(a) $2\ \text{ms}^{-1}$
(b) $2\sqrt{2}\ \text{ms}^{-1}$
(c) $\dfrac{2\sqrt{2}}{3}\ \text{ms}^{-1}$
(d) $3\sqrt{2}\ \text{ms}^{-1}$

22. A target is made of two plates, one of wood and the other of iron. The thickness of the wooden plate is 4 cm and that of iron plate is 2 cm . A bullet fired goes through the wood first and then penetrates 1 cm into iron. A similar bullet fired with the same velocity from opposite direction goes through iron first and then penetrates 2 cm into wood. If a_1 and a_2 be the retardations offered to the bullet by wood and iron plates respectively, then

(a) $a_1 = 2a_2$
(b) $a_2 = 2a_1$
(c) $a_1 = a_2$
(d) Data insufficient

23. A body starts with an initial velocity of $10\ \text{ms}^{-1}$ and is moving along a straight line with constant acceleration. When the velocity of the particle is $50\ \text{ms}^{-1}$, the acceleration is reversed in direction. The velocity of the particle when it again reaches the starting point is

(a) $70\ \text{ms}^{-1}$
(b) $60\ \text{ms}^{-1}$
(c) $10\ \text{ms}^{-1}$
(d) $30\ \text{ms}^{-1}$

24. Two particles P and Q simultaneously start moving from point A with velocities 15 m/s and 20 m/s, respectively. The two particles move with accelerations equal in magnitude but opposite in direction. At some instant velocity of P is 30 m/s. The velocity of Q at this instant will be

(a) 30 m/s
(b) 5 m/s
(c) 20 m/s
(d) 15 m/s

25. Speed-time graph of two cars A and B approaching towards each other is shown in figure. Initial distance between them is 60 m . The two cars will cross each other after time

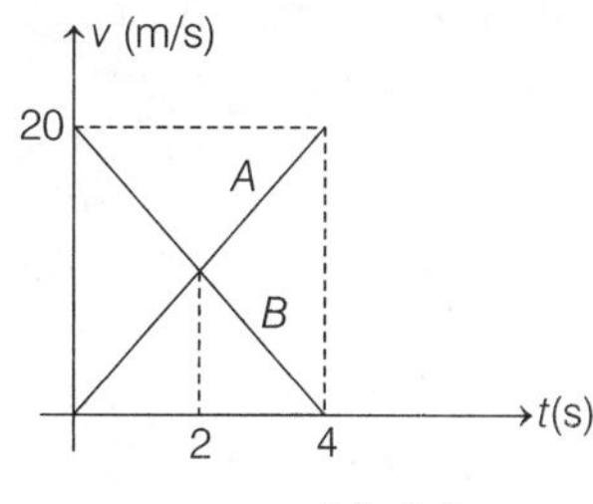

(a) 2 s (b) 3 s (c) 1.5 s (d) $\sqrt{2}$ s

26. The acceleration-time graph of a particle moving along a straight line is as shown in figure. At what time the particle acquires its initial velocity?

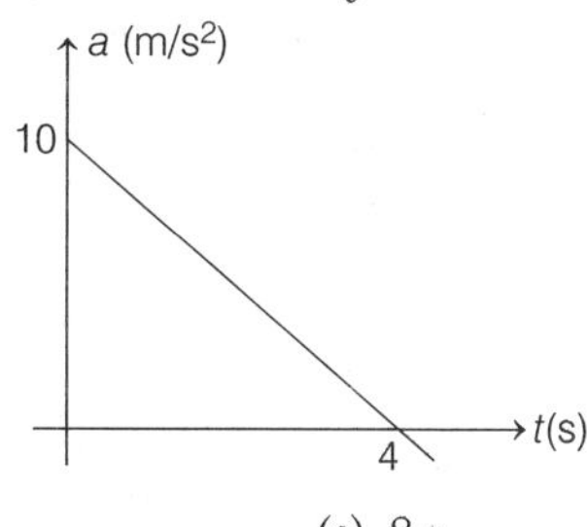

(a) 12 s (b) 5 s (c) 8 s (d) 16 s

27. From a tower of height H, a particle is thrown vertically upwards with a speed u. The time taken by the particle to hit the ground, is n times that taken by it to reach the highest point of its path. The relation between H, u and n is

(a) $2gH = n^2u^2$ (b) $gH = (n-2)^2u^2$

(c) $2gH = nu^2(n-2)$ (d) $gH = (n-2)^2u^2$

28. A particle starting from rest and moving with a uniform acceleration along a straight line covers distances a and b in first p and next q second. The acceleration of the particle is

(a) $\dfrac{a+b}{2\,(p+q)}$ (b) $\dfrac{2b}{(q+2p)\,q}$

(c) $\dfrac{2a}{p\,(p+2p)}$ (d) $\dfrac{a+b}{(p+q)^2}$

29. A swimmer crosses a river of width d flowing at velocity v. While swimming, he heads himself always at an angle of 120° with the river flow and on reaching the other end he finds a drift of $d/2$ in the direction of flow of river. The speed of the swimmer with respect to the river is

(a) $(2-\sqrt{3})\,v$ (b) $2\,(2-\sqrt{3})\,v$

(c) $4\,(2-\sqrt{3})\,v$ (d) $(2+\sqrt{3})\,v$

30. On a calm day a boat can go across a lake and return in time T_0 at a speed V. On a rough day there is a uniform current at speed v to help the onward journey and impede the return journey. If the time taken to go across and return on the rough day be T, then T/T_0 is

(a) $1 - v^2/V^2$ (b) $\dfrac{1}{1 - v^2/V^2}$

(c) $1 + v^2/V^2$ (d) $\dfrac{1}{1 + v^2/V^2}$

31. Two particles start simultaneously from the same point and move along two straight lines, one with uniform velocity v and other with a uniform acceleration a. If α is the angle between the lines of motion of two particles then the relative velocity will be perpendicular to the velocity of first particle at time given by

(a) $\frac{v}{a}\sin\alpha$ (b) $\frac{v}{a}\sec\alpha$
(c) $\frac{v}{a}\tan\alpha$ (d) $\frac{v}{a}\cot\alpha$

32. Six particles situated at the corners of a regular hexagon of side d move at a constant speed v. Each particle maintains a direction towards the particle at the next corner. The time of the particles will take to meet each other.

(a) $2d/3v$ (b) $2d/v$
(c) $3d/2v$ (d) $4d/3v$

33. Two towns A and B are connected by a regular bus service with a bus leaving in either direction every T minutes. A man cycling with a speed of 20 kmh^{-1} in the direction A to B notices that a bus goes past him every 18 min in the direction of his motion, and every 6 min in the opposite direction. What is the period T of the bus service and with what speed (assumed constant) do the buses ply on the road?

(a) $T = 9$ min, speed = 40 kmh^{-1} (b) $T = 10$ min, speed = 40 kmh^{-1}
(c) $T = 9$ min, speed = 20 kmh^{-1} (d) $T = 10$ min, speed = 20 kmh^{-1}

34. Two bodies move in a straight line towards each other at initial velocities v_1 and v_2 and with constant acceleration a_1 and a_2 directed against the corresponding velocities at the initial instant. The maximum initial separation d_{max} between the bodies for which they will meet during the motion is

(a) $\frac{v_1^2}{a_1}+\frac{v_2^2}{a_2}$ (b) $\frac{(v_1+v_2)^2}{2(a_1+a_2)}$
(c) $\frac{v_1 v_2}{\sqrt{a_1 a_2}}$ (d) $\frac{v_1^2-v_2^2}{2(a_1-a_2)}$

35. A long horizontal belt is moving from left to right with a uniform speed 2 m/s. There are two ink marks A and B on the belt 60 m apart. An insect runs on the belt to and fro between A and B such that its speed relative to belt is constant and equals 4 m/s. When the insect is moving on the belt in the direction of motion of the belt, its speed as observed by a person standing on ground will be

(a) 6 m/s (b) 2 m/s
(c) 1.5 m/s (d) 4 m/s

36. In Q. 35, if A lies to the left of B, then

(a) time taken by insect to travel from A to B and time taken by it to travel from B to A are equal
(b) time taken by insect to travel from A to B is less than taken by it to travel from B to A
(c) time taken by insect to travel from A to B is more than the time taken by it to travel from B to A
(d) None of the above

37. In Q. 35, if A lies to the left of B, time taken by the insect to travel from B to A will be

(a) 12 s (b) 15 s
(c) 18 s (d) 21 s

More than One Correct Options

1. A particle having a velocity $v = v_0$ at $t = 0$ is decelerated at the rate $|a| = \alpha\sqrt{v}$, where α is a positive constant.
(a) The particle comes to rest at $t = \frac{2\sqrt{v_0}}{\alpha}$
(b) The particle will come to rest at infinity
(c) The distance travelled by the particle before coming to rest is $\frac{2v_0^{3/2}}{\alpha}$
(d) The distance travelled by the particle before coming to rest is $\frac{2v_0^{3/2}}{3\alpha}$

2. At time $t = 0$, a car moving along a straight line has a velocity of 16 ms^{-1}. It slows down with an acceleration of $-0.5t$ ms^{-2}, where t is in second. Mark the correct statement (s).
(a) The direction of velocity changes at $t = 8$ s
(b) The distance travelled in 4 s is approximately 58.67 m
(c) The distance travelled by the particle in 10 s is 94 m
(d) The speed of particle at $t = 10$ s is 9 ms^{-1}

3. An object moves with constant acceleration **a**. Which of the following expressions are also constant ?
(a) $\frac{d|\mathbf{v}|}{dt}$
(b) $\left|\frac{d\mathbf{v}}{dt}\right|$
(c) $\frac{d(v^2)}{dt}$
(d) $\frac{d\left(\frac{\mathbf{v}}{|\mathbf{v}|}\right)}{dt}$

4. Ship A is located 4 km north and 3 km east of ship B. Ship A has a velocity of 20 kmh^{-1} towards the south and ship B is moving at 40 kmh^{-1} in a direction 37° north of east. X and Y-axes are along east and north directions, respectively
(a) Velocity of A relative to B is $(-32\hat{\mathbf{i}} - 44\hat{\mathbf{j}})$ km/h
(b) Position of A relative to B as a function of time is given by $\mathbf{r}_{AB} = [(3-32t)\hat{\mathbf{i}} + (4-44t)\hat{\mathbf{j}}]$ km
(c) Velocity of A relative to B is $(32\hat{\mathbf{i}} - 44\hat{\mathbf{j}})$ km/h
(d) Position of A relative to B as a function of time is given by $(32t\hat{\mathbf{i}} - 44t\hat{\mathbf{j}})$ km

5. Starting from rest a particle is first accelerated for time t_1 with constant acceleration a_1 and then stops in time t_2 with constant retardation a_2. Let v_1 be the average velocity in this case and s_1 the total displacement. In the second case it is accelerating for the same time t_1 with constant acceleration $2a_1$ and come to rest with constant retardation a_2 in time t_3. If v_2 is the average velocity in this case and s_2 the total displacement, then
(a) $v_2 = 2v_1$
(b) $2v_1 < v_2 < 4v_1$
(c) $s_2 = 2s_1$
(d) $2s_1 < s_2 < 4s_1$

6. A particle is moving along a straight line. The displacement of the particle becomes zero in a certain time ($t > 0$). The particle does not undergo any collision.
(a) The acceleration of the particle may be zero always
(b) The acceleration of the particle may be uniform
(c) The velocity of the particle must be zero at some instant
(d) The acceleration of the particle must change its direction

7. A particle is resting over a smooth horizontal floor. At $t = 0$, a horizontal force starts acting on it. Magnitude of the force increases with time according to law $F = \alpha t$, where α is a positive constant. From figure, which of the following statements are correct ?

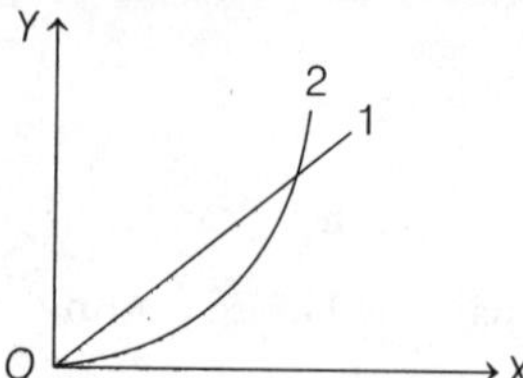

(a) Curve 1 can be the plot of acceleration against time
(b) Curve 2 can be the plot of velocity against time
(c) Curve 2 can be the plot of velocity against acceleration
(d) Curve 1 can be the plot of displacement against time

8. A train starts from rest at $S = 0$ and is subjected to an acceleration as shown in figure. Then,

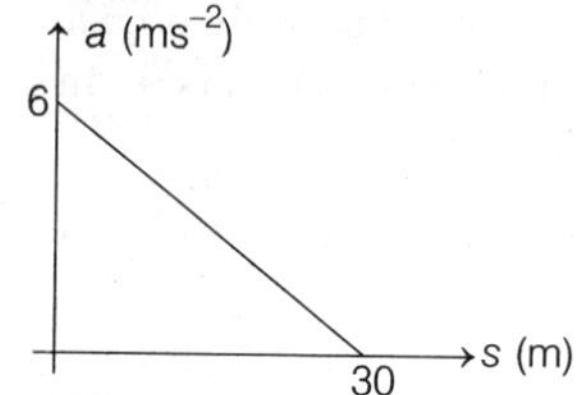

(a) velocity at the end of 10 m displacement is 20 ms^{-1}
(b) velocity of the train at $s = 10$ m is 10 ms^{-1}
(c) The maximum velocity attained by train is $\sqrt{180}$ ms^{-1}
(d) The maximum velocity attained by the train is 15 ms^{-1}

9. For a moving particle, which of the following options may be correct?

(a) $|\mathbf{v}_{av}| < v_{av}$
(b) $|\mathbf{v}_{av}| > v_{av}$
(c) $\mathbf{v}_{av} = 0$ but $v_{av} \neq 0$
(d) $\mathbf{v}_{av} \neq 0$ but $v_{av} = 0$

Here, $\mathbf{v}_{av}$ is average velocity and v_{av} the average speed.

10. Identify the correct graph representing the motion of a particle along a straight line with constant acceleration with zero initial velocity.

(a) 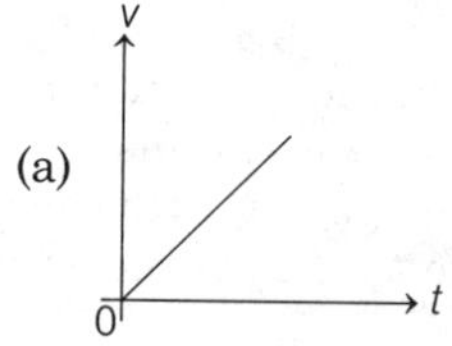

(b) 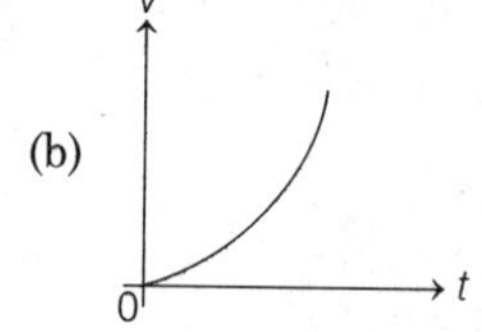

(c) 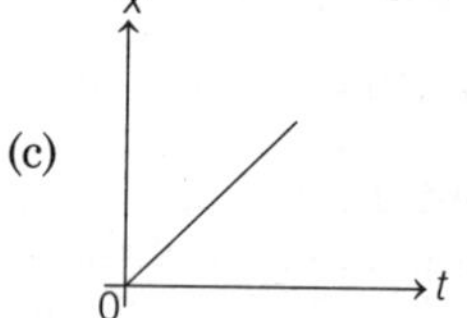

(d) 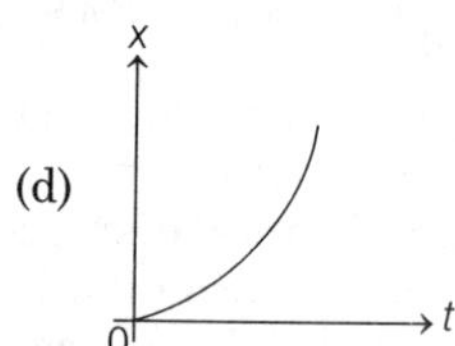

11. A man who can swim at a velocity v relative to water wants to cross a river of width b, flowing with a speed u.

(a) The minimum time in which he can cross the river is $\dfrac{b}{v}$
(b) He can reach a point exactly opposite on the bank in time $t = \dfrac{b}{\sqrt{v^2 - u^2}}$ if $v > u$
(c) He cannot reach the point exactly opposite on the bank if $u > v$
(d) He cannot reach the point exactly opposite on the bank if $v > u$

12. The figure shows the velocity (v) of a particle plotted against time (t).

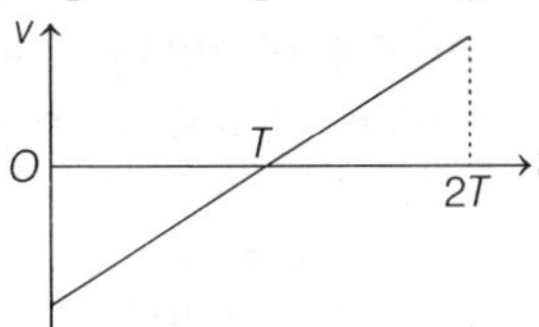

(a) The particle changes its direction of motion at some point
(b) The acceleration of the particle remains constant
(c) The displacement of the particle is zero
(d) The initial and final speeds of the particle are the same

13. The speed of a train increases at a constant rate α from zero to v and then remains constant for an interval and finally decreases to zero at a constant rate β. The total distance travelled by the train is l. The time taken to complete the journey is t. Then,

(a) $t = \frac{l(\alpha + \beta)}{\alpha\beta}$
(b) $t = \frac{l}{v} + \frac{v}{2}\left(\frac{1}{\alpha} + \frac{1}{\beta}\right)$
(c) t is minimum when $v = \sqrt{\frac{2l\alpha\beta}{(\alpha - \beta)}}$
(d) t is minimum when $v = \sqrt{\frac{2l\alpha\beta}{(\alpha + \beta)}}$

14. A particle moves in x-y plane and at time t is at the point $(t^2, t^3 - 2t)$, then which of the following is/are correct?

(a) At $t = 0$, particle is moving parallel to y-axis
(b) At $t = 0$, direction of velocity and acceleration are perpendicular
(c) At $t = \sqrt{\frac{2}{3}}$, particle is moving parallel to x-axis
(d) At $t = 0$, particle is at rest

15. A car is moving with uniform acceleration along a straight line between two stops X and Y. Its speed at X and Y are 2 ms^{-1} and 14 ms^{-1}, Then

(a) its speed at mid-point of XY is 10 ms^{-1}
(b) its speed at a point A such that $XA : AY = 1 : 3$ is 5 ms^{-1}
(c) the time to go from X to the mid-point of XY is double of that to go from mid-point to Y
(d) the distance travelled in first half of the total time is half of the distance travelled in the second half of the time

16. The displacement (x) of a particle depends on time t as $x = \alpha t^2 - \beta t^3$. Choose the **incorrect** statements from the following.

(a) The particle never returns to its starting point
(b) The particle comes to rest after time $\frac{2\alpha}{3\beta}$
(c) The initial velocity of the particle is zero
(d) The initial acceleration of the particle is zero

17. A body is projected from origin such that its position vector varies with time as $\mathbf{r} = [3t\hat{\mathbf{i}} + (4t - 5t^2)\hat{\mathbf{j}}]$ m and t is time in second. Then,

(a) x-coordinate of particle is 2.4 m when y-coordinate is zero
(b) speed of projection is 5 m/s^2
(c) angle of projection with x-axis is $\tan^{-1}$ (4/3)
(d) time when particle is again at x-axis is 0.8 s

18. A rocket is fired vertically up from the ground with a resultant acceleration of 10 m/s^2. The fuel is finished in 1 min and it continues to move up ($g = 10 \text{ m/s}^2$)

(a) the maximum height reached by rocket from ground is 18 km

(b) the maximum height reached by rocket from ground is 36 km

(c) the time from initial when rocket is again at ground is $(180 + 30\sqrt{2})$ s

(d) the time from initial when rocket is again at ground is $(120 + 60\sqrt{2})$ s

19. Two particles P and Q are moving along x-axis. Their position-time graph is shown in the figure.

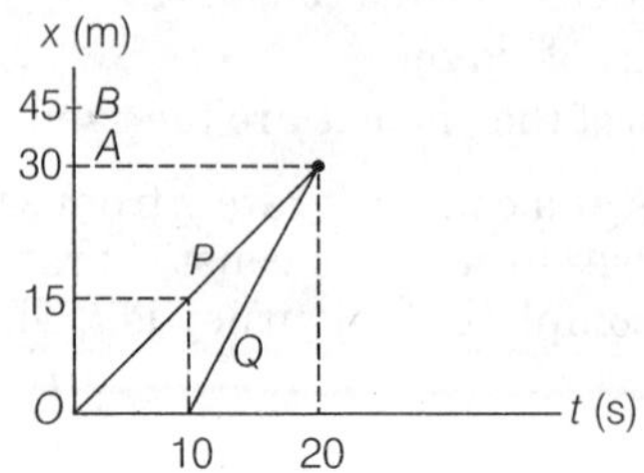

Choose the correct option(s).

(a) Particle P starts from point O at $t = 0$

(b) Particle Q starts from point O at $t = 10$ s

(c) Particle Q overtakes the particle P at $x = 30$ m and $t = 20$ s

(d) None of the above

Comprehension Based Questions

Passage 1 (Q.Nos. 1 to 4)

An elevator without a ceiling is ascending up with an acceleration of 5 ms^{-2}. A boy on the elevator shoots a ball in vertical upward direction from a height of 2 m above the floor of elevator. At this instant the elevator is moving up with a velocity of 10 ms^{-1} and floor of the elevator is at a height of 50 m from the ground. The initial speed of the ball is 15 ms^{-1} with respect to the elevator. Consider the duration for which the ball strikes the floor of elevator in answering following questions. ($g = 10 \text{ ms}^{-2}$)

1. The time in which the ball strikes the floor of elevator is given by

(a) 2.13 s (b) 2.0 s

(c) 1.0 s (d) 3.12 s

2. The maximum height reached by ball, as measured from the ground would be

(a) 73.65 m (b) 116.25 m

(c) 82.56 m (d) 63.25 m

3. Displacement of ball with respect to ground during its flight would be

(a) 16.25 m (b) 8.76 m

(c) 20.24 m (d) 30.56 m

4. The maximum separation between the floor of elevator and the ball during its flight would be

(a) 12 m (b) 15 m

(c) 9.5 m (d) 7.5 m

Passage 2 (Q.Nos. 5 to 7)

A situation is shown in which two objects A and B start their motion from same point in same direction. The graph of their velocities against time is drawn. u_A and u_B are the initial velocities of A and B respectively. T is the time at which their velocities become equal after start of motion. You cannot use the data of one question while solving another question of the same set. So all the questions are independent of each other.

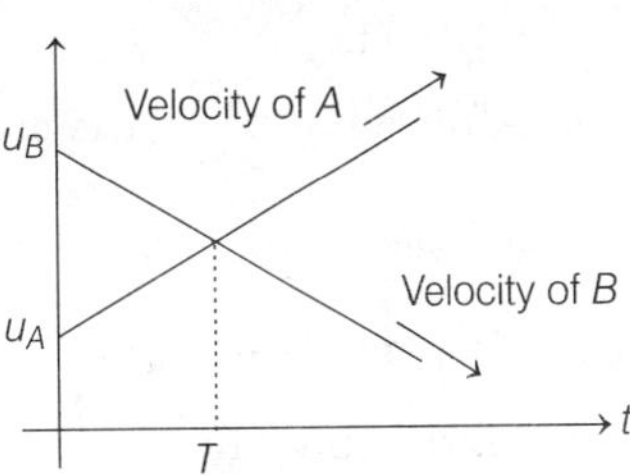

5. If the value of T is 4 s, then the time after which A will meet B is

(a) 12 s (b) 6 s

(c) 8 s (d) data insufficient

6. Let v_A and v_B be the velocities of the particles A and B respectively at the moment A and B meet after start of the motion. If $u_A = 5\text{ ms}^{-1}$ and $u_B = 15\text{ ms}^{-1}$, then the magnitude of the difference of velocities v_A and v_B is

(a) 5 ms^{-1} (b) 10 ms^{-1}

(c) 15 ms^{-1} (d) data insufficient

7. After 10 s of the start of motion of both objects A and B, find the value of velocity of A if $u_A = 6\text{ ms}^{-1}$, $u_B = 12\text{ ms}^{-1}$ and at T, velocity of A is 8 ms^{-1} and $T = 4$ s

(a) 12 ms^{-1} (b) 10 ms^{-1}

(c) 15 ms^{-1} (d) None of these

Passage 3 (Q.Nos. 8 to 9)

If particles A and B are moving with velocities $\mathbf{v}_A$ and $\mathbf{v}_B$, respectively. The relative velocity of A with respect to B is defined as $\mathbf{v}_{AB} = \mathbf{v}_A - \mathbf{v}_B$. The driver of a car travelling Southward at 30 kmh^{-1} observes that wind appears to be coming from the West. The driver of another car travelling Southward at 50 kmh^{-1} observes that wind appears to be coming from the South-West.

8. Mark the correct option.

(a) Wind is blowing in a direction $\tan^{-1}\left(\frac{3}{2}\right)$ South to East

(b) Wind is blowing in a direction $\tan^{-1}\left(\frac{3}{2}\right)$ North to West

(c) Wind is blowing towards West

(d) Wind is blowing towards North

9. The speed of wind is

(a) 10 kmh^{-1} (b) $10\sqrt{13}\text{ kmh}^{-1}$

(c) $5\sqrt{3}\text{ kmh}^{-1}$ (d) 25 kmh^{-1}

Passage 4 (Q.Nos. 10 to 12)

Two buses A and B are running over a two line bridge with the same speed 20 ms^{-1} in opposite direction. Both buses approaches a car C moving with a speed of 15 ms^{-1} in the same direction of bus A. To avoid accident the driver of bus A decides to over take car C just before the bus B does, at the instant when buses A and B are 500 m apart and provides atleast required acceleration 2 ms^{-2} to bus.

10. Find the distance of car C from the bus B when driver of bus A starts providing acceleration.

(a) 100 m (b) 200 m

(c) 350 m (d) 400 m

11. Find the distance of car C from the bus A. When driver of bus A starts providing acceleration.

(a) 100 m (b) 150 m (c) 200 m (d) 350 m

12. After what time, the crossing of bus A and B occur

(a) 10 s (b) 35 s
(c) 20 s (d) 15 s

Match the Columns

1. Match the following two columns :

Column I	Column II
(a)	(p) speed must be increasing
(b)	(q) speed must be decreasing
(c)	(r) speed may be increasing
(d)	(s) speed may be decreasing

2. Match the following two columns :

Column I	Column II
(a) $\mathbf{v} = -2\hat{\mathbf{i}}, \mathbf{a} = -4\hat{\mathbf{j}}$	(p) speed increasing
(b) $\mathbf{v} = 2\hat{\mathbf{i}}, \mathbf{a} = 2\hat{\mathbf{i}} + 2\hat{\mathbf{j}}$	(q) speed decreasing
(c) $\mathbf{v} = -2\hat{\mathbf{i}}, \mathbf{a} = +2\hat{\mathbf{i}}$	(r) speed constant
(d) $\mathbf{v} = 2\hat{\mathbf{i}}, \mathbf{a} = -2\hat{\mathbf{i}} + 2\hat{\mathbf{j}}$	(s) Nothing can be said

3. The velocity-time graph of a particle moving along X-axis is shown in figure. Match the entries of Column I with the entries of Column II.

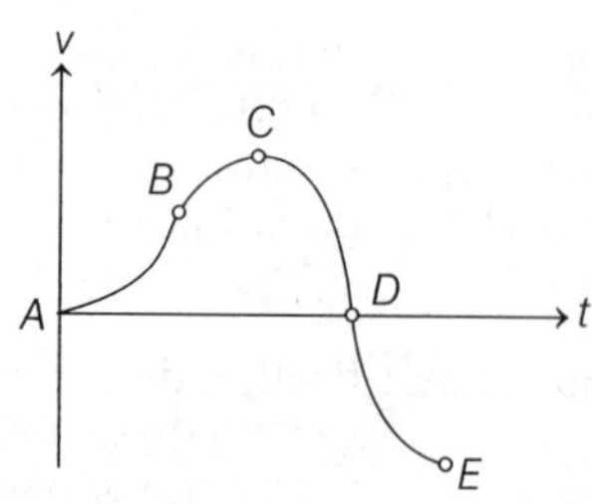

Column I	Column II
(a) For AB, particle is	(p) Moving in +ve X-direction with increasing speed
(b) For BC, particle is	(q) Moving in +ve X-direction with decreasing speed
(c) For CD, particle is	(r) Moving in –ve X-direction with increasing speed
(d) For DE, particle is	(s) Moving in –ve X-direction with decreasing speed

4. Corresponding to velocity-time graph in one dimensional motion of a particle as shown in figure, match the following two columns.

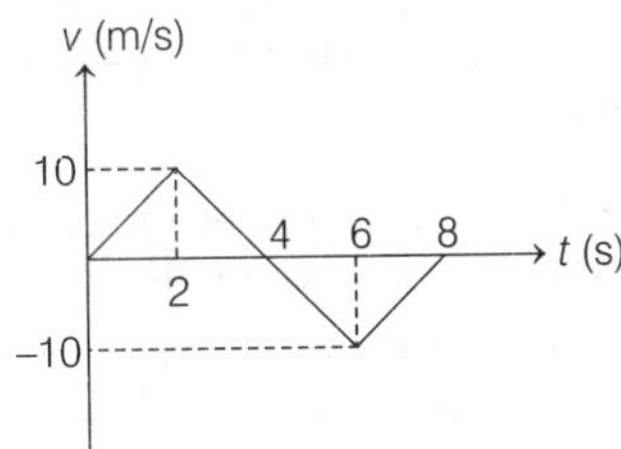

Column I	Column II
(a) Average velocity between zero second and 4 s	(p) 10 SI units
(b) Average acceleration between 1 s and 4 s	(q) 2.5 SI units
(c) Average speed between zero seccond and 6 s	(r) 5 SI units
(d) Rate of change of speed at 4 s	(s) None of the above

5. A particle is moving along x-axis. Its x-coordinate varies with time as :

$$x = -20 + 5t^2$$

For the given equation match the following two columns :

Column I	Column II
(a) Particle will cross the origin at	(p) zero second
(b) At what time velocity and acceleration are equal	(q) 1 s
(c) At what time particle changes its direction of motion	(r) 2 s
(d) At what time velocity is zero	(s) None of the above

6. x and y-coordinates of a particle moving in x -y plane are,

$$x = 1 - 2t + t^2 \text{ and } y = 4 - 4t + t^2$$

For the given situation match the following two columns :

Column I	Column II
(a) y-component of velocity when it crosses the y-axis	(p) + 2 SI unit
(b) x-component of velocity when it crosses the x-axis	(q) – 2 SI units
(c) Initial velocity of particle	(r) + 4 SI units
(d) Initial acceleration of particle	(s) None of the above

7. A car accelerates from rest at a constant rate 10 ms^{-2} for some time after which it decelerates at constant rate 5 ms^{-2} to come to rest. If total time elapsed is 15 s.
Match the following columns and select the correct option from the codes given below :

Column I	Column II
(a) Maximum velocity of car (in ms^{-1}).	(p) 10
(b) Distance (in m) travelled by car, at the instant when its velocity is half of its maximum velocity.	(q) 25
(c) Average velocity (in ms^{-1}) during total time of motion.	(r) 50
(d) The time (in s) during which the particle is in the condition of deceleration.	(s) None of the above

8. When a ball drops from a certain height, it experiences retardation due to air resistance which is equal to $(5\,v)$ ms^{-2}, where v is instantaneous velocity. A student drops three balls *A*, *B* and *C* one by one. He observes that ball *A* moves with constant velocity, but ball *B* moves with increasing speed for some time and then moves with constant velocity. He also observes that ball *C* moves with decreasing speed and after some time it moves with constant velocity.
In Column I, some results are given related to Column II. Match the following columns and select the correct option from the codes given below.

Column I	Column II
(a) Ball *A*	(p) Initial velocity is 2 ms^{-1}
(b) Ball *B*	(q) Initial velocity may be zero
(c) Ball *C*	(r) Initial velocity is greater than 2 ms^{-1}
	(s) Final velocity is 2 ms^{-1}

Subjective Questions

1. The acceleration-displacement graph of a particle moving in a straight line is as shown in figure, initial velocity of particle is zero. Find the velocity of the particle when displacement of the particle is $s = 12$ m.

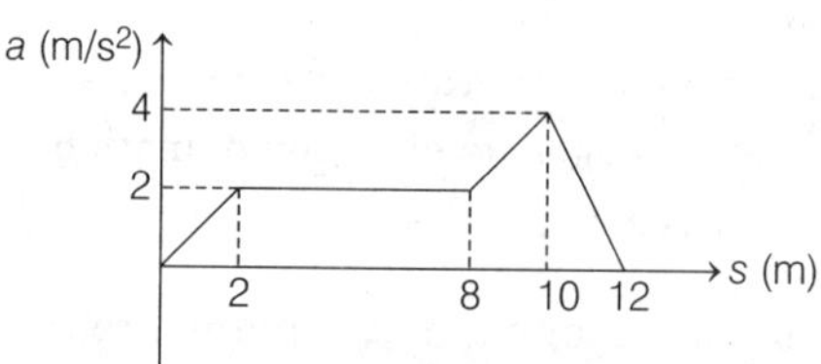

2. At the initial moment three points *A*, *B* and *C* are on a horizontal straight line at equal distances from one another. Point *A* begins to move vertically upward with a constant velocity v and point *C* vertically downward without any initial velocity but with a constant acceleration a. How should point *B* move vertically for all the three points to be constantly on one straight line. The points begin to move simultaneously.

3. A particle moves in a straight line with constant acceleration a. The displacements of particle from origin in times t_1, t_2 and t_3 are s_1, s_2 and s_3 respectively. If times are in AP with common difference d and displacements are in GP, then prove that $a = \dfrac{(\sqrt{s_1} - \sqrt{s_3})^2}{d^2}$.

4. A car is to be hoisted by elevator to the fourth floor of a parking garage, which is 14 m above the ground. If the elevator can have maximum acceleration of 0.2 m/s^2 and maximum deceleration of 0.1 m/s^2 and can reach a maximum speed of 2.5 m/s, determine the shortest time to make the lift, starting from rest and ending at rest.

5. To stop a car, first you require a certain reaction time to begin braking; then the car slows under the constant braking deceleration. Suppose that the total distance moved by your car during these two phases is 56.7 m when its initial speed is 80.5 km/h and 24.4 m when its initial speed is 48.3 km/h. What are
   (a) your reaction time and
   (b) the magnitude of the deceleration?

6. An elevator without a ceiling is ascending with a constant speed of 10 m/s. A boy on the elevator shoots a ball directly upward, from a height of 2.0 m above the elevator floor. At this time the elevator floor is 28 m above the ground. The initial speed of the ball with respect to the elevator is 20 m/s. (Take $g = 9.8\ m/s^2$)
   (a) What maximum height above the ground does the ball reach?
   (b) How long does the ball take to return to the elevator floor?

7. A man in a boat crosses a river from point A. If he rows perpendicular to the banks he reaches point C ($BC = 120$ m) in 10 min. If the man heads at a certain angle α to the straight line AB (AB is perpendicular to the banks) against the current he reaches point B in 12.5 min. Find the width of the river w, the rowing velocity u, the speed of the river current v and the angle α. Assume the velocity of the boat relative to water to be constant and the same magnitude in both cases.

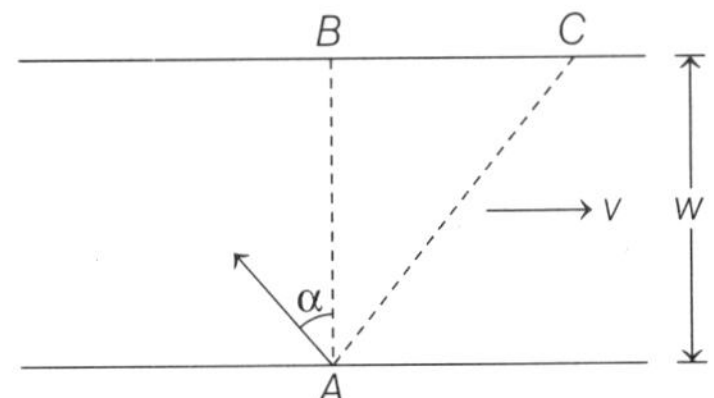

8. The acceleration of particle varies with time as shown.

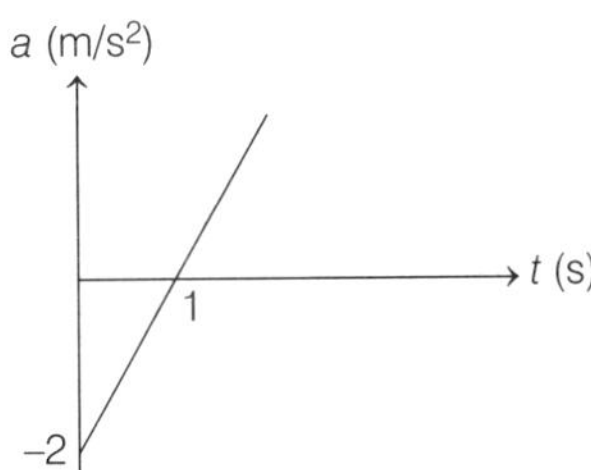

   (a) Find an expression for velocity in terms of t.
   (b) Calculate the displacement of the particle in the interval from $t = 2$ s to $t = 4$ s. Assume that $v = 0$ at $t = 0$.

9. A man wishes to cross a river of width 120 m by a motorboat. His rowing speed in still water is 3 m/s and his maximum walking speed is 1 m/s. The river flows with velocity of 4 m/s.
   (a) Find the path which he should take to get to the point directly opposite to his starting point in the shortest time.
   (b) Also, find the time which he takes to reach his destination.

10. The current velocity of river grows in proportion to the distance from its bank and reaches the maximum value v_0 in the middle. Near the banks the velocity is zero. A boat is moving along the river in such a manner that the boatman rows his boat always perpendicular to the current. The speed of the boat in still water is u. Find the distance through which the boat crossing the river will be carried away by the current, if the width of the river is c. Also determine the trajectory of the boat.

11. A river of width a with straight parallel banks flows due north with speed u. The points O and A are on opposite banks and A is due east of O. Coordinate axes Ox and Oy are taken in the east and north directions respectively. A boat, whose speed is v relative to water, starts from O and crosses the river. If the boat is steered due east and u varies with x as : $u = x(a - x)\dfrac{v}{a^2}$. Find

(a) equation of trajectory of the boat,
(b) time taken to cross the river,
(c) absolute velocity of boatman when he reaches the opposite bank,
(d) the displacement of boatman when he reaches the opposite bank from the initial position.

12. A river of width ω is flowing with a uniform velocity v. A boat starts moving from point P also with velocity v relative to the river. The direction of resultant velocity is always perpendicular to the line joining boat and the fixed point R. Point Q is on the opposite side of the river. P, Q and R are in a straight line. If $PQ = QR = \omega$, find (a) the trajectory of the boat, (b) the drifting of the boat and (c) the time taken by the boat to cross the river.

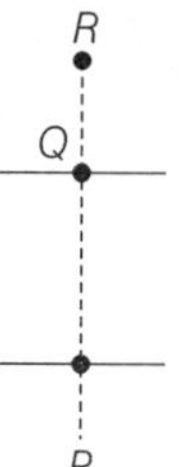

13. The v-s graph describing the motion of a motorcycle is shown in figure. Construct the a-s graph of the motion and determine the time needed for the motorcycle to reach the position $s = 120$ m. Given ln 5 = 1.6.

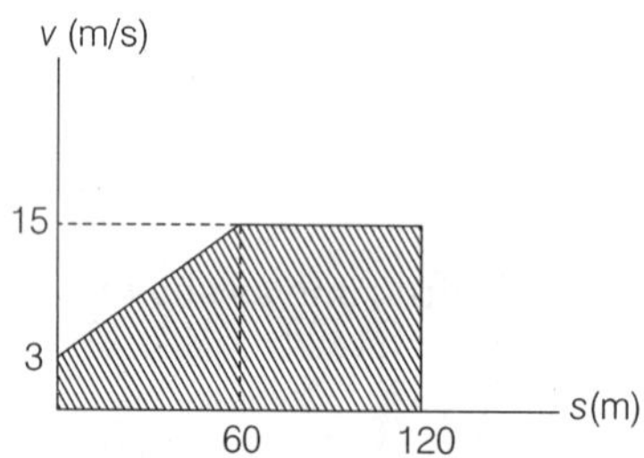

14. The jet plane starts from rest at $s = 0$ and is subjected to the acceleration shown. Determine the speed of the plane when it has travelled 60 m.

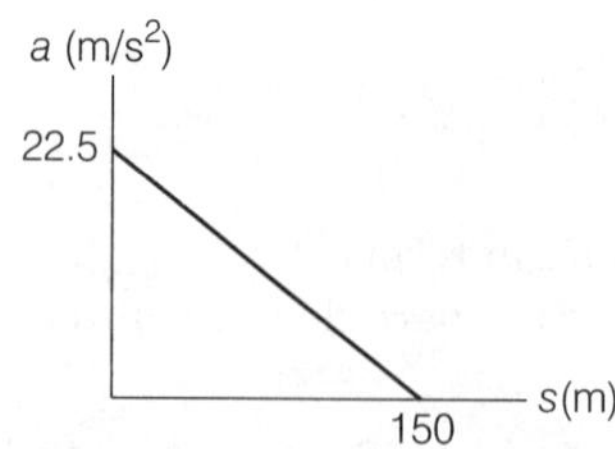

15. A particle leaves the origin with an initial velocity $\mathbf{v} = (3.00\hat{\mathbf{i}})$ m/s and a constant acceleration $\mathbf{a} = (-1.00\hat{\mathbf{i}} - 0.500\hat{\mathbf{j}})\,\text{m/s}^2$. When the particle reaches its maximum x coordinate, what are

(a) its velocity and
(b) its position vector?

16. The speed of a particle moving in a plane is equal to the magnitude of its instantaneous velocity, $v = |\mathbf{v}| = \sqrt{v_x^2 + v_y^2}$.

(a) Show that the rate of change of the speed is $\frac{dv}{dt} = (v_x a_x + v_y a_y)/\sqrt{v_x^2 + v_y^2}$.

(b) Show that the rate of change of speed can be expressed as $\frac{dv}{dt} = \mathbf{v} \cdot \mathbf{a}/v$, and use this result to explain why $\frac{dv}{dt}$ is equal to a_t the component of **a** that is parallel to **v**.

17. A man with some passengers in his boat, starts perpendicular to flow of river 200 m wide and flowing with 2 m/s. Speed of boat in still water is 4 m/s. When he reaches half the width of river the passengers asked him that they want to reach the just opposite end from where they have started.

(a) Find the direction due which he must row to reach the required end.

(b) How many times more time, it would take to that if he would have denied the passengers?

18. A child in danger of drowning in a river is being carried downstream by a current that flows uniformly at a speed of 2.5 km/h. The child is 0.6 km from shore and 0.8 km upstream of a boat landing when a rescue boat sets out. If the boat proceeds at its maximum speed of 20 km/h with respect to the water, what angle does the boat velocity v make with the shore? How long will it take boat to reach the child?

19. A launch plies between two points A and B on the opposite banks of a river always following the line AB. The distance S between points A and B is 1200 m. The velocity of the river current $v = 1.9$ m/s is constant over the entire width of the river. The line AB makes an angle $\alpha = 60°$ with the direction of the current. With what velocity u and at what angle β to the line AB should the launch move to cover the distance AB and back in a time $t = 5$ min? The angle β remains the same during the passage from A to B and from B to A.

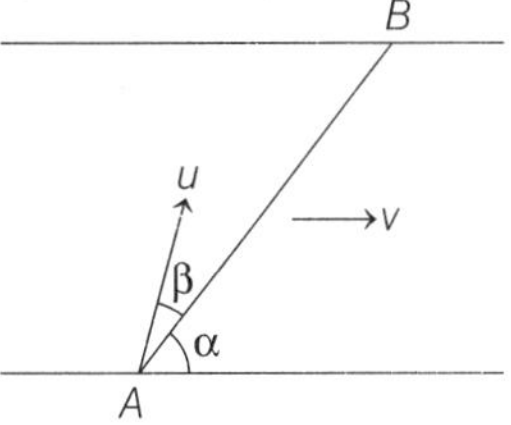

20. The slopes of wind screen of two cars are $\alpha_1 = 30°$ and $\alpha_2 = 15°$ respectively. At what ratio v_1/v_2 of the velocities of the cars will their drivers see the hail stones bounced back by the wind screen on their cars in vertical direction? Assume hail stones fall vertically downwards and collisions to be elastic.

21. A projectile of mass m is fired into a liquid at an angle θ_0 with an initial velocity v_0 as shown. If the liquid develops a frictional or drag resistance on the projectile which is proportional to its velocity, i.e. $F = -kv$ where k is a positive constant, determine the x and y components of its velocity at any instant. Also find the maximum distance x_{max} that it travels?

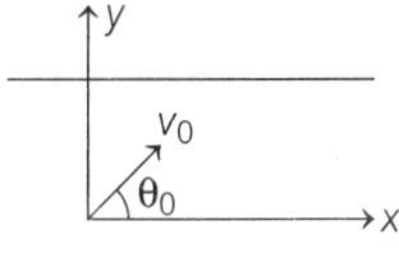

Integer Type Questions

22. A truck is moving at a speed of 72 kmh^{-1} on a straight road. The driver can produce deceleration of 2 ms^{-2} by applying brakes. The stopping distance of truck is $13x$ m, if the reaction time of the driver is 0.2 s. Find the value of x.

23. A student used to go to his coaching institute every evening and he takes 20 min. Once on his way, he realised that he had forgotten his book at home. He knew that if he continued walking to the coaching at the same speed, he would be there 8 min before the bell, so he went back home for the book and arrived the coaching 10 min late. If he had walked all the way with his usual speed, the fraction of the way to coaching institute had he covered at that moment when he turned back is $\frac{x}{20}$. Find the value of x.

24. A train is moving on straight track with velocity $v_0 = 13.5\ \text{ms}^{-1}$. To stop the train at a particular station, driver apply brakes at $t = 0$, which is caused of a retardation proportional to velocity of the train. The speed of train reduces 50% in the first $t_0 = 4 \ln 2$ s. Find velocity of train (in ms^{-1}) at $t = 4$ s. (Given, $e = 2.7$)

25. A ball is released from rest from top of a tower. The retardation due to air resistance is bv, where b is 10 per second and velocity v is in ms^{-1}. The velocity of ball at $t = \frac{1}{10}$ s is $\frac{n}{27}\ \text{ms}^{-1}$. Find the value of n. (Given, $e = 2.7$)

26. A ball is projected upward with initial velocity v_0. The retardation due to air resistance is bv, where b is positive constant. The time taken by particle to reach maximum height is t_0. If $\frac{bv_0}{g} = 2.$, then find the value of e^{bt_0}.

27. A particle starts from rest to move along X-axis. The acceleration of the particle is $a = (t - x)\ \text{ms}^{-2}$. During motion, maximum acceleration of the particle is $a_0 = 2\ \text{ms}^{-2}$.Find the velocity (in ms^{-1}) of the particle at $t = \frac{\pi}{3}$ s.

28. If a particle is moving on a straight line, then its velocity-time graph is sinusoidal as shown in the figure.

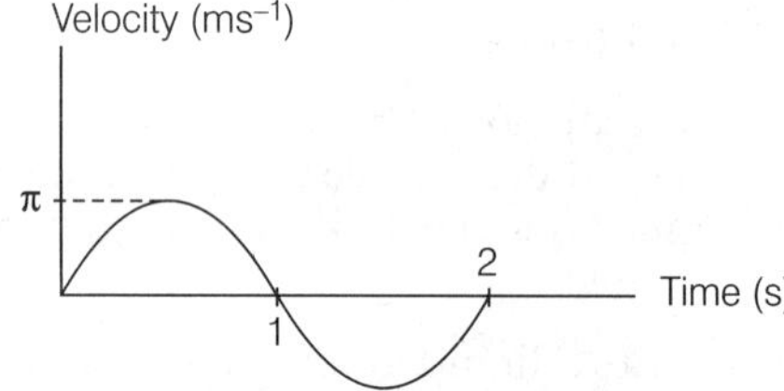

Find distance (in m) travelled by the particle in 2 s.

29. A vertical wind screen of a vehicle is made of two parts, the upper one is 25 cm vertically long and covers the top 5 cm of lower fixed part. The upper part is hinged at upper end, so that it can be opened outward. The car is running on the horizontal road at $20\sqrt{3}\ \text{kmh}^{-1}$ in the rain falling vertically with speed of $20\ \text{kmh}^{-1}$. The maximum angle through which the upper part can be opened outward is θ. If $\sin\left(\frac{\pi}{3} + \theta\right) = \frac{\sqrt{12}}{n}$, then find the value of n.

30. River stream velocity grows in proportion to the distance from the bank and reaches its maximum velocity $2\ \text{ms}^{-1}$ in the middle. Near the bank velocity is zero. The velocity of a swimmer in still water is $5\ \text{ms}^{-1}$and is directed perpendicular to river stream. The width of river is 100 m. The drifting in swimmer is $5\,n$ metre. Find the value of n.

Answers

Introductory Exercise 6.1

1. Both downwards 2. (a) $-2\,m^2/s^3$, (b) obtuse, (c) decreasing

Introductory Exercise 6.2

1. One dimensional with constant acceleration 2. Two dimensional with non-uniform acceleration
3. No

Introductory Exercise 6.3

1. False 2. True 3. g (downwards) 4. $\frac{\pi}{15}$ cm/s, $\frac{2\sqrt{2}}{15}$ cm/s
5. (a) Yes, in uniform circular motion (b) No, yes (projectile motion), yes
6. (a) 25.13 s (b) 1 cm/s, 0.9 cm/s, 0.23 cm/s^2

Introductory Exercise 6.4

1. 5.2 m/s 2. $\frac{11}{3}$ m/s

Introductory Exercise 6.5

2. See the hints
3. Always g 4. Acceleration 5. 60 m, 100 m
6. $u + \frac{1}{2}at$ 7. True 8. 25 m/s (downwards)
9. (a) 6.0 m, (b) 10 s, (c) 50 m
10. 125 m, (b) 5 s, (c) approximately 35 m/s

Introductory Exercise 6.6

1. (a) $1\,m/s^2$ (b) 43.5 m 2. (a) $60\,cm/s^2$, (b) 1287 cm
3. (a) $x = 1.0$ m, $v = 4$ m/s, $a = 8\,m/s^2$, (b) zero 4. (a) $x = 2.0$ m (b) zero (c) 26 ms^{-2}
5. $s \propto t^{7/4}$ and $a \propto t^{-1/4}$

Introductory Exercise 6.7

1. $2\sqrt{7}$ m/s, $4\sqrt{3}$ m 2. $(2\hat{j})\,m/s^2$, $(2\hat{i} + \hat{j})$ m, yes
3. $\mathbf{v} = (3\hat{i} + \hat{j})$ m/s, co-ordinates $= \left(\frac{7}{3}\text{m}, \frac{1}{4}\text{m}\right)$

Introductory Exercise 6.8

1. (a) Particle A starts at $t = 0$ from $x = 10$ m. Particle B starts at $t = 4$ s from $x = 0$.
   (b) $v_A = +2.5$ m/s, $v_B = +7.5$ m/s (c) They strike at $x = 30$ m and $t = 8$ s
2. 80 m, 2.5 m/s^2
3. (a) 0.6 m/s^2, (b) 50 m, (c) 50 m
4. (a) 10 m/s, (b) 20 m/s, zero, 20 m/s, −20 m/s
5. 100 m, zero

Introductory Exercise 6.9

1. $-2\,\text{m/s}$
2. zero
3. (a) 40 s (b) 80 m
4. (a) $\sin^{-1}\left(\frac{1}{15}\right)$ east of the line AB (b) 50 min
5. (a) 200 m, (b) 20 m/min, (c) 12 m/min
6. (a) 10 s, (b) 50 m

Exercises

LEVEL 1

Assertion and Reason

1. (a) 2. (d) 3. (d) 4. (d) 5. (d) 6. (a or b) 7. (a) 8. (d) 9. (c)

Single Correct Option

1. (b)	2. (c)	3. (a)	4. (c)	5. (b)	6. (d)	7. (a)	8. (b)	9. (d)	10. (d)
11. (a)	12. (c)	13. (b)	14. (c)	15. (b)	16. (b)	17. (c)	18. (b)	19. (b)	20. (d)
21. (b)	22. (a)	23. (c)	24. (c)	25. (c)	26. (d)	27. (d)	28. (b)	29. (b)	30. (b)
31. (b)	32. (b)	33. (a)	34. (d)	35. (a)	36. (b)	37. (c)	38. (a)	39. (c)	40. (b)
41. (c)	42. (a)	43. (b)	44. (d)	45. (b)	46. (d)	47. (d)	48. (d)	49. (b)	50. (a)
51. (d)	52. (b)	53. (b)	54. (b)	55. (d)	56. (b)	57. (b)	58. (b)	59. (d)	60. (b)
61. (b)	62. (a)	63. (b)	64. (c)	65. (b)	66. (b)	67. (a)	68. (c)	69. (b)	70. (b)
71. (c)	72. (c)	73. (d)	74. (a)	75. (b)	76. (b)	77. (a)	78. (a)	79. (a)	80. (a)

Subjective Questions

1. (a) Magnitude of total acceleration and tangential acceleration, (b) equal in 1-D motion
2. (a) 1100 m, (b) 500 m, (c) 55 m/min, (d) 25 m/min,
3. (a) 36 km (b) 1 min
4. $T = 4t_0$
5. (a) zero (b) 8 ms^{-1} (c) 8 ms^{-1}
6. 8 m
7. (a) positive, positive, positive, negative (b) positive, zero, negative, negative
8. (a) $\frac{50}{7}\,\text{ms}^{-1}$ (b) 10 ms^{-1}
9. 36 s, No
10. 2 s, 6 s, $2(2+\sqrt{7})$ s
11. (a) $-5\,\text{ms}^{-2}$ (b) 90 ms^{-1}
12. (a) $(1.25\hat{\mathbf{i}} + 0.5\hat{\mathbf{j}})\,\text{ms}^{-1}$ (b) $(-0.5\hat{\mathbf{i}} + \hat{\mathbf{j}})\,\text{ms}^{-2}$ (c) No
13. $(3.414)\,t_0$
14. 0.2 ms^{-2}, 0.8 ms^{-1}
15. (a) $(8\hat{\mathbf{i}} - 8\hat{\mathbf{j}})\,\text{ms}^{-1}$ (b) (18 m, − 4m)
16. (a) 45 m (b) 22 ms^{-1}
17. 14.125 m, 1.75 ms^{-1}, 4.03 ms^{-1}
18. 0.603 ms^{-2}
19.

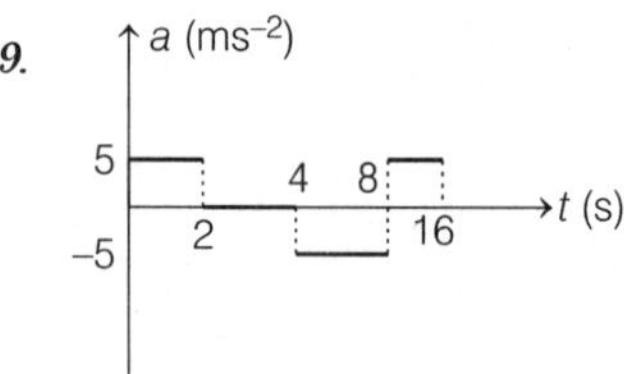

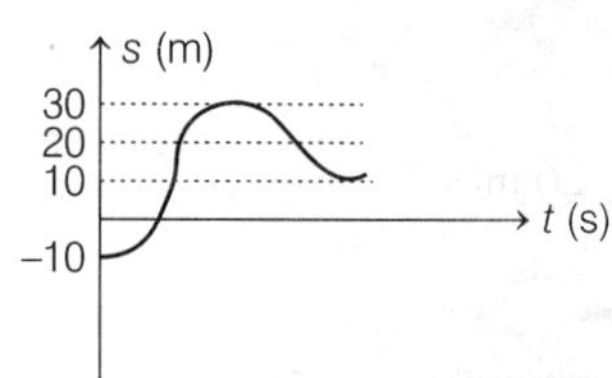

20.

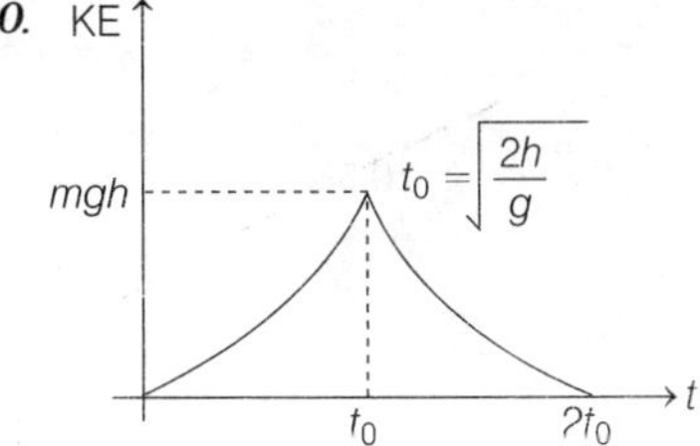

21.

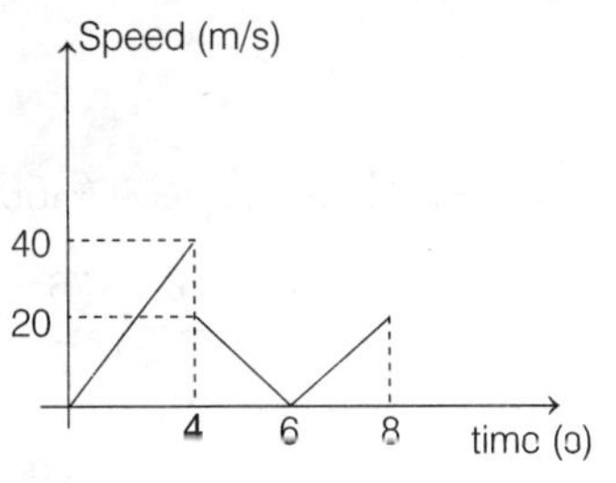

Velocity (m/s)
40
20
−20
4
6
8 time (s)

22 (a) 5 ms^{-2}, zero, 5 ms^{-2} (b) $s = 30$ m (c) (i) $s = 10 + 2.5t^2$ (ii) $s = 40 + 10(t-4) - 2.5(t-4)^2$

23. (a) zero (b) 25 ms^{-1} (c) -25 ms^{-1} (d) 0.8 s

24. (a) 3.65 s, at 12.30 m level (b) 19.8 ms^{-1} (downwards)

25. (a) 7.39 s (b) 35.5 m (c) automobile 25.9 ms^{-1}, truck 16.2 ms^{-1}

26. $45° - \sin^{-1}\left(\frac{1}{2\sqrt{2}}\right) \approx 24.3°$

27. (a) at an angle $\theta = \sin^{-1}(0.4)$ west of north (b) $\frac{10}{\sqrt{21}}h$

LEVEL 2

Single Correct Option

1. (b)	2. (b)	3. (c)	4. (a)	5. (a)	6. (a)	7. (d)	8. (a)	9. (a)	10. (c)
11. (a)	12. (b)	13. (d)	14. (a)	15. (a)	16. (c)	17. (c)	18. (c)	19. (a)	20. (d)
21. (c)	22. (b)	23. (a)	24. (b)	25. (b)	26. (c)	27. (c)	28. (b)	29. (c)	30. (b)
31. (b)	32. (b)	33. (a)	34. (b)	35. (a)	36. (a)	37. (b)			

More than One Correct Options

1. (a,d)	2. (all)	3. (b)	4. (a,b)	5. (a,d)	6. (b,c)	7. (a,b)	8. (b,c)	9. (a,c)	10. (a,d)
11. (a,b,c)	12. (all)	13. (b,d)	14. (a,b,c)	15. (a,c)	16. (a,d)	17. (all)	18. (b,d)	19. (a,b,c)	

Comprehension Based Questions

1. (a)	2. (c)	3. (d)	4. (c)	5. (c)	6. (b)	7. (d)	8. (a)	9. (b)	10. (c)
11. (b)	12. (a)								

Match thc Columns

1.	(a) → r,s	(b) → r,s	(c) → p	(d) → q
2.	(a) → r	(b) → p	(c) → q	(d) → q
3.	(a) → p	(b) → p	(c) → q	(d) → r
4.	(a) → r	(b) → s	(c) → r	(d) → r
5.	(a) → r	(b) → q	(c) → s	(d) → p
6.	(a) → q	(b) → p	(c) → s	(d) → s
7.	(a) → r	(b) → s	(c) → q	(d) → p
8.	(a) → p,s	(b) → q,s	(c) → r,s	

Subjective Questions

1. $4\sqrt{3}\ \text{ms}^{-1}$

2. B moves up with initial velocity $\frac{v}{2}$ and downward acceleration $-\frac{a}{2}$

4. 20.5 s

5. (a) 0.74 s (b) 6.2 ms^{-2}

6. (a) 76 m (b) 4.2 s

7. 200 m, 20 m/min, 12 m/min, 36°50.

8. (a) $v = t^2 - 2t$ (b) 6.67 m

9. (a) $90° + \sin^{-1}(3/5)$ from river current (b) 2 min 40 s

10. $\frac{cv_0}{2u}, y^2 = \frac{ucx}{v_0}$

11. (a) $y = \frac{x^2}{2a} - \frac{x^3}{3a^2}$ (b) $\frac{a}{v}$ (c) v (due east) (d) $a\hat{i} + \frac{a\hat{j}}{6}$

12. (a) circle (b) $\sqrt{3}\,\omega$ (c) $\frac{1.317\,\omega}{v}$

13. 12.0 s, For the graph see the hints

14. 46.47 ms^{-1}

15. (a) $(-1.5\hat{j})\ \text{ms}^{-1}$ (b) $(4.5\hat{i} - 2.25\hat{j})$ m

17. (a) At an angle $(90° + 2\theta)$ from river current (upstream). Here : $\theta = \tan^{-1}\left(\frac{1}{2}\right)$ (b) $\frac{4}{3}$

18. 37°, 3 min

19. $u = 8\ \text{ms}^{-1}, \beta = 12°$

20. $\frac{v_1}{v_2} = 3$

21. $v_x = v_0 \cos\theta_0\, e^{-kt/m}, v_y = \frac{m}{k}\left[\left(\frac{k}{m}v_0 \sin\theta_0 + g\right)e^{-\frac{kt}{m}} - g\right],\ x_m = \frac{mv\cos\theta_0}{k}$

22. 8

23. 9

24. 5

25. 7

26. 3

27. 1

28. 4

29. 5

30. 4

7

Projectile Motion

7.1 Introduction

Motion of a particle under constant acceleration is either a straight line (one-dimensional) or parabolic (two-dimensional). Motion is one dimensional under following three conditions :

(i) Initial velocity of the particle is zero.

(ii) Initial velocity of the particle is in the direction of constant acceleration (or parallel to it).

(iii) Initial velocity of the particle is in the opposite direction of constant acceleration (or antiparallel to it).

For small heights acceleration due to gravity (g) is almost constant. The three cases discussed about are as shown in the Fig. 7.1.

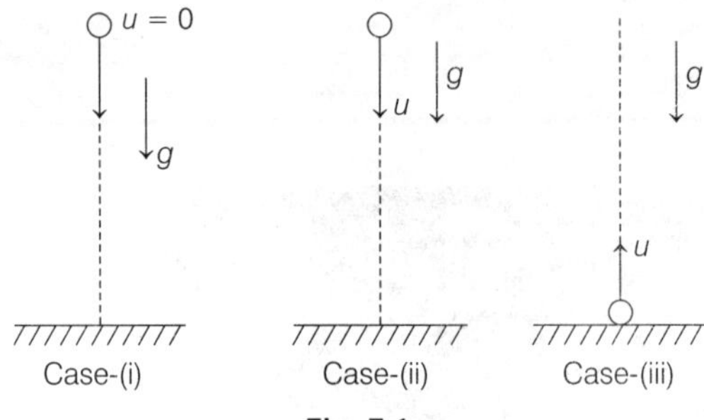

Fig. 7.1

In all other cases when initial velocity is at some angle ($\neq 0°$ or $180°$) with constant acceleration, motion is parabolic as shown below.

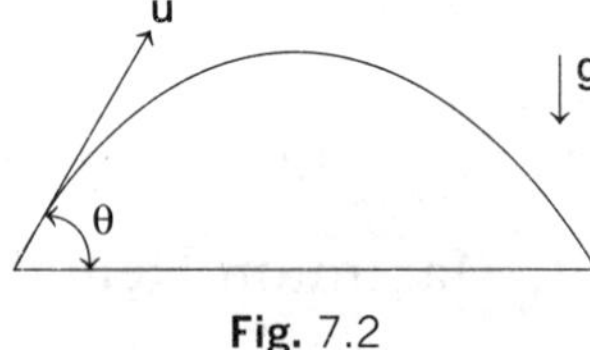

Fig. 7.2

This motion under acceleration due to gravity is called projectile motion.

7.2 Projectile Motion

As we have seen above, projectile motion is a two-dimensional motion (or motion in a plane) with constant acceleration (or acceleration due to gravity for small heights).

The different types of projectile motion are as shown below.

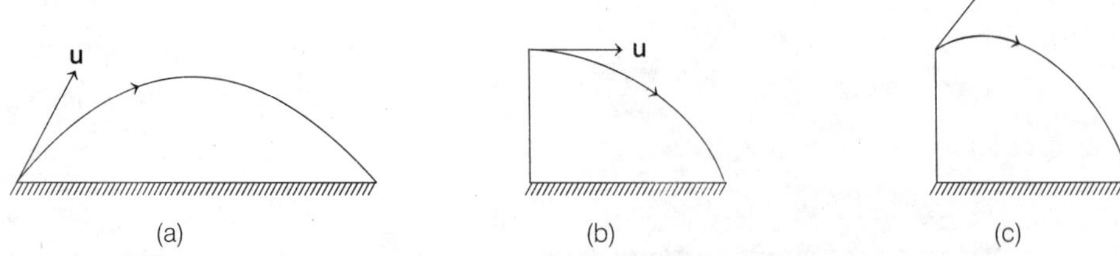

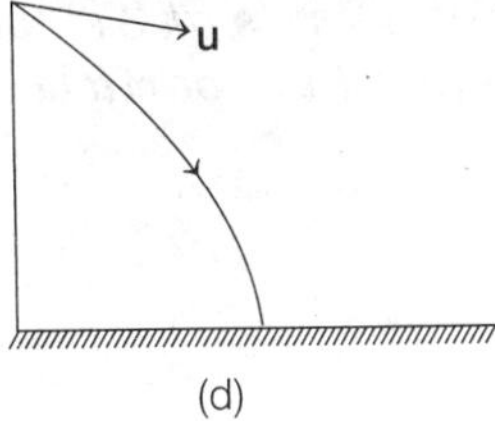

(d)

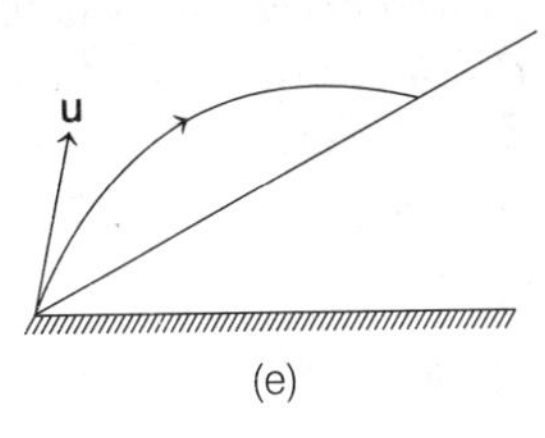

(e)

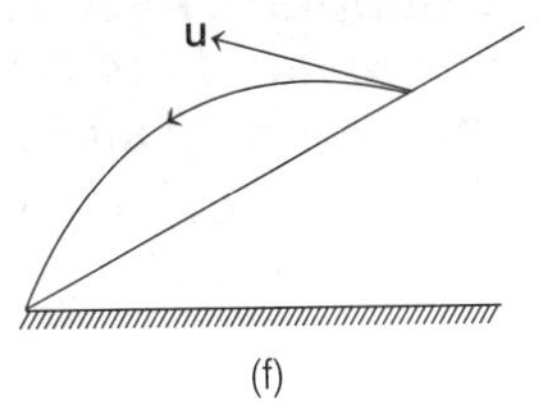

(f)

Fig. 7.3

The plane of the projectile motion is a vertical plane.

7.3 Two Methods of Solving a Projectile Motion

Every projectile motion can be solved by either of the following two methods:

Method 1 Projectile motion is a two dimensional motion with constant acceleration. Therefore, we can use the equations

$$\mathbf{v} = \mathbf{u} + \mathbf{a}t \text{ and } \mathbf{s} = \mathbf{u}t + \frac{1}{2}\mathbf{a}t^2$$

For example, in the shown figure

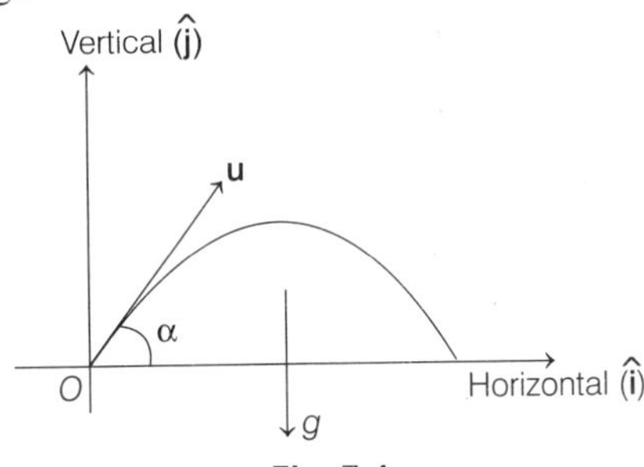

Fig. 7.4

$$\mathbf{u} = u\cos\alpha\hat{\mathbf{i}} + u\sin\alpha\hat{\mathbf{j}} \quad \text{and} \quad \mathbf{a} = -g\hat{\mathbf{j}}$$

Now, suppose we want to find velocity at time t.

$$\mathbf{v} = \mathbf{u} + \mathbf{a}t = (u\cos\alpha\hat{\mathbf{i}} + u\sin\alpha\hat{\mathbf{j}}) - gt\hat{\mathbf{j}}$$

or

$$\mathbf{v} = u\cos\alpha\hat{\mathbf{i}} + (u\sin\alpha - gt)\hat{\mathbf{j}}$$

Similarly, displacement at time t will be

$$\mathbf{s} = \mathbf{u}t + \frac{1}{2}\mathbf{a}t^2 = (u\cos\alpha\hat{\mathbf{i}} + u\sin\alpha\hat{\mathbf{j}})\,t - \frac{1}{2}gt^2\,\hat{\mathbf{j}}$$

$$= ut\cos\alpha\hat{\mathbf{i}} + \left(ut\sin\alpha - \frac{1}{2}gt^2\right)\hat{\mathbf{j}}$$

Note *In all problems, value of* $\mathbf{a}$ $(= \mathbf{g})$ *will be same only* $\mathbf{u}$ *will be different.*

Example 7.1 *A particle is projected with a velocity of 50 m/s at 37° with horizontal. Find velocity, displacement and co-ordinates of the particle (w.r.t. the starting point) after 2 s.*
Given, $g = 10\, m/s^2$, $\sin 37° = 0.6$ *and* $\cos 37° = 0.8$

Solution In the given problem,

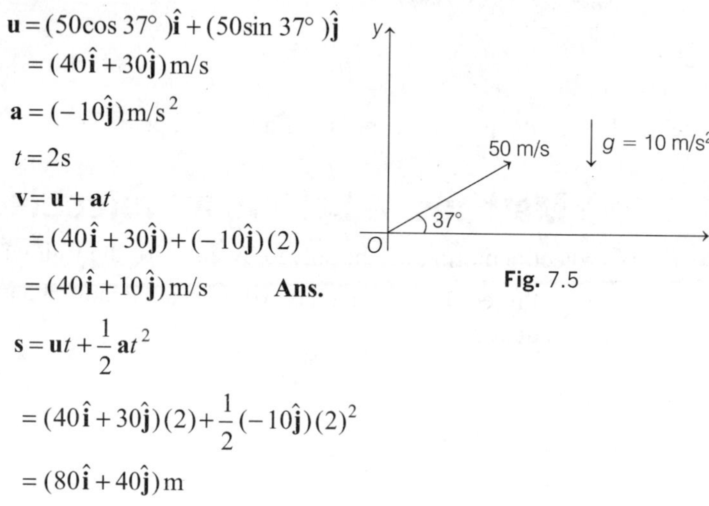

Fig. 7.5

$$\mathbf{u} = (50\cos 37°)\hat{\mathbf{i}} + (50\sin 37°)\hat{\mathbf{j}}$$
$$= (40\hat{\mathbf{i}} + 30\hat{\mathbf{j}})\, \text{m/s}$$
$$\mathbf{a} = (-10\hat{\mathbf{j}})\, \text{m/s}^2$$
$$t = 2\text{s}$$
$$\mathbf{v} = \mathbf{u} + \mathbf{a}t$$
$$= (40\hat{\mathbf{i}} + 30\hat{\mathbf{j}}) + (-10\hat{\mathbf{j}})(2)$$
$$= (40\hat{\mathbf{i}} + 10\hat{\mathbf{j}})\, \text{m/s} \qquad \textbf{Ans.}$$
$$\mathbf{s} = \mathbf{u}t + \frac{1}{2}\mathbf{a}t^2$$
$$= (40\hat{\mathbf{i}} + 30\hat{\mathbf{j}})(2) + \frac{1}{2}(-10\hat{\mathbf{j}})(2)^2$$
$$= (80\hat{\mathbf{i}} + 40\hat{\mathbf{j}})\, \text{m}$$

Coordinates of the particle are

$$x = 80 \text{ m} \quad \text{and} \quad y = 40 \text{ m} \qquad \textbf{Ans.}$$

Example 7.2 *A particle is projected with velocity u at angle θ with horizontal. Find the time when velocity vector is perpendicular to initial velocity vector.*

Solution

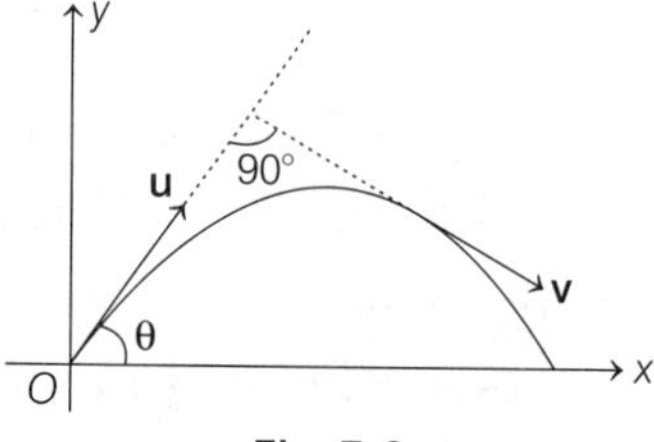

Fig. 7.6

Given, $\mathbf{v} \perp \mathbf{u}$

$$\Rightarrow \qquad \mathbf{v} \cdot \mathbf{u} = 0$$
$$\Rightarrow \qquad (\mathbf{u} + \mathbf{a}t) \cdot \mathbf{u} = 0 \qquad \text{.....(i)}$$

Substituting the proper values in Eq. (i), we have

$$[\{(u\cos\theta)\hat{\mathbf{i}} + (u\sin\theta)\hat{\mathbf{j}}\} + (-g\hat{\mathbf{j}})t] \cdot [(u\cos\theta)\hat{\mathbf{i}} + (u\sin\theta)\hat{\mathbf{j}}] = 0$$
$$\Rightarrow \qquad u^2\cos^2\theta + u^2\sin^2\theta - (ug\sin\theta)t = 0$$
$$\Rightarrow \qquad u^2(\sin^2\theta + \cos^2\theta) = (ug\sin\theta)t$$

Solving this equation, we get

$$t = \frac{u}{g\sin\theta} = \frac{u\operatorname{cosec}\theta}{g} \qquad \textbf{Ans.}$$

Alternate method

$$\mathbf{a} = \mathbf{g}$$

Angle between **u** and **a** is $\alpha = 90° + \theta$

Now, Eq. (i) can be written as

$$\mathbf{u}\cdot\mathbf{u} + \mathbf{u}\cdot\mathbf{a}t = 0$$

or $$u^2 + (ug\cos\alpha)t = 0$$

or $$u^2 + [ug\cos(90° + \theta)]t = 0$$

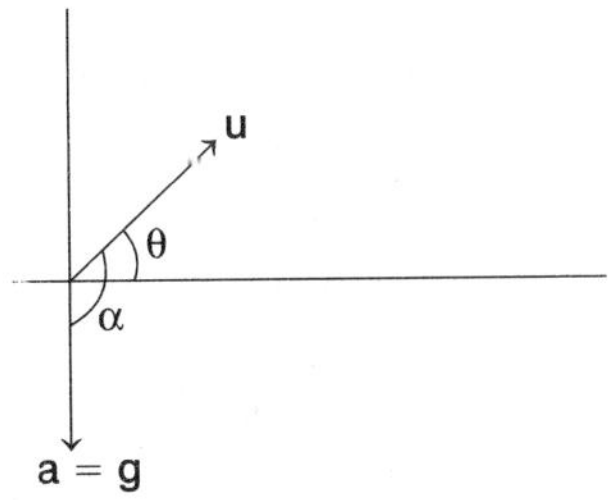

Solving this equation, we get

Fig. 7.7

$$t = \frac{u}{g\sin\theta} = \frac{u\operatorname{cosec}\theta}{g} \qquad \textbf{Ans.}$$

Method 2 In this method, select two mutually perpendicular directions x and y and find the two components of initial velocity and acceleration along these two directions, i.e. find u_x, u_y, a_x and a_y. Now apply the appropriate equation (s) of the following six equations :

$$\left.\begin{aligned} v_x &= u_x + a_x t \\ s_x &= u_x t + \frac{1}{2}a_x t^2 \\ v_x^2 &= u_x^2 + 2a_x s_x \end{aligned}\right] \rightarrow \text{Along } x\text{-axis}$$

and

$$\left.\begin{aligned} v_y &= u_y + a_y t \\ s_y &= u_y t + \frac{1}{2}a_y t^2 \\ v_y^2 &= u_y^2 + 2a_y s_y \end{aligned}\right] \rightarrow \text{Along } y\text{-axis}$$

Substitute $v_x, u_x, a_x, s_x, v_y, u_y, a_y$ and s_y with proper signs but choosing one direction as positive and other as the negative along both axes. In most of the problems $s = ut + \frac{1}{2}at^2$ equation is useful for time calculation. Under normal projectile motion, x-axis is taken along horizontal direction and y-axis along vertical direction. In projectile motion along an inclined plane, x-axis is normally taken along the plane and y-axis perpendicular to the plane. Two simple cases are shown below.

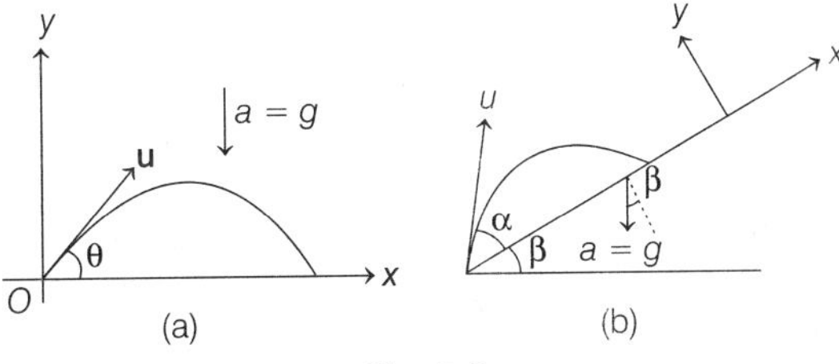

Fig. 7.8

In Fig. 7.8 (a)

$$u_x = u\cos\theta,\ u_y = u\sin\theta,\ a_x = 0,\ a_y = -g$$

In Fig. 7.8 (b)

$$u_x = u\cos\alpha,\ u_y = u\sin\alpha,\ a_x = -g\sin\beta,\ a_y = -g\cos\beta$$

Example 7.3 *A projectile is fired horizontally with velocity of 98 m/s from the top of a hill 490 m high. Find*

(a) the time taken by the projectile to reach the ground,

(b) the distance of the point where the particle hits the ground from foot of the hill and

(c) the velocity with which the projectile hits the ground. ($g = 9.8\ m/s^2$)

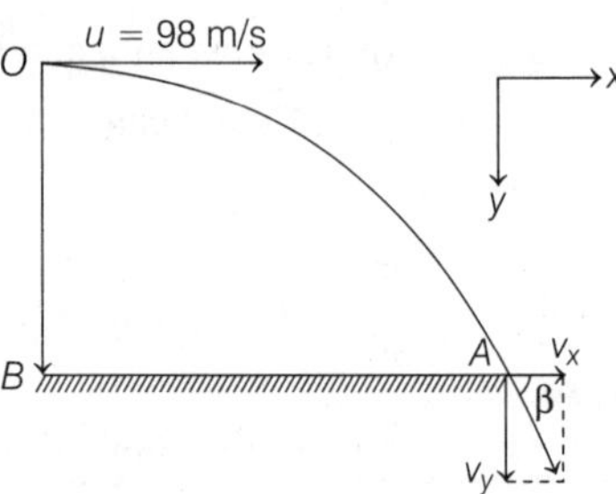

Fig. 7.9

Solution Here, it will be more convenient to choose x and y directions as shown in figure.

Here, $u_x = 98$ m/s, $a_x = 0$, $u_y = 0$ and $a_y = g$

(a) At A, $s_y = 490$ m. So, applying

$$s_y = u_y t + \frac{1}{2} a_y t^2$$

$$\therefore \quad 490 = 0 + \frac{1}{2}(9.8)t^2$$

$$\therefore \quad t = 10\,\text{s}$$ **Ans.**

(b) $BA = s_x = u_x t + \frac{1}{2} a_x t^2$

or $$BA = (98)(10) + 0$$

or $$BA = 980\ \text{m}$$ **Ans.**

(c) $v_x = u_x + a_x t = 98 + 0 = 98$ m/s

$$v_y = u_y + a_y t = 0 + (9.8)(10) = 98\ \text{m/s}$$

$$\therefore \quad v = \sqrt{v_x^2 + v_y^2} = \sqrt{(98)^2 + (98)^2} = 98\sqrt{2}\ \text{m/s}$$

and $$\tan\beta = \frac{v_y}{v_x} = \frac{98}{98} = 1$$

$$\therefore \quad \beta = 45°$$

Thus, the projectile hits the ground with velocity $98\sqrt{2}$ m/s at an angle of $\beta = 45°$ with horizontal as shown in Fig. 7.9.

Example 7.4 *A body is thrown horizontally from the top of a tower and strikes the ground after three seconds at an angle of 45° with the horizontal. Find the height of the tower and the speed with which the body was projected. Take $g = 9.8\ m/s^2$.*

Solution As shown in the figure of Example 7.3.

$$u_y = 0 \text{ and } a_y = g = 9.8 \text{ m/s}^2 ,$$

$$s_y = u_y t + \frac{1}{2} a_y t^2$$

$$s_y = 0 \times 3 + \frac{1}{2} \times 9.8 \times (3)^2$$

$$= 44.1 \text{ m}$$

Thus, height of the tower is 44.1 m.

Further, $v_y = u_y + a_y t = 0 + (9.8)(3) = 29.4$ m/s

As the resultant velocity v makes an angle of 45° with the horizontal, so

$$\tan 45° = \frac{v_y}{v_x} \quad \text{or} \quad 1 = \frac{29.4}{v_x}$$

$$v_x = 29.4 \text{ m/s}$$

$$v_x = u_x + a_x t$$

$\Rightarrow$ $$29.4 = u_x + 0$$

or $$u_x = 29.4 \text{ m/s}$$

Therefore, the speed with which the body was projected (horizontally) is 29.4 m/s.

INTRODUCTORY EXERCISE 7.1

1. Two particles are projected from a tower horizontally in opposite directions with velocities 10 m/s and 20 m/s. Find the time when their velocity vectors are mutually perpendicular. Take $g = 10 \text{ m/s}^2$.
2. Projectile motion is a 3-dimensional motion. Is this statement true or false?
3. Projectile motion (at low speed) is uniformly accelerated motion. Is this statement true or false?
4. A particle is projected from ground with velocity 50 m/s at 37° from horizontal. Find velocity and displacement after 2 s. $\sin 37° = \frac{3}{5}$.
5. A particle is projected from a tower of height 25 m with velocity $20\sqrt{2}$ m/s at 45°. Find the time when particle strikes with ground. The horizontal distance from the foot of tower where it strikes. Also find the velocity at the time of collision.

Note *In question numbers 4 and 5,* $\hat{\mathbf{i}}$ *is in horizontal direction and* $\hat{\mathbf{j}}$ *is vertically upwards.*

7.4 Time of Flight, Maximum Height and Horizontal Range of a Projectile

Fig. 7.10 shows a particle projected from the point O with an initial velocity u at an angle α with the horizontal. It goes through the highest point A and falls at B on the horizontal surface through O. The point O is called the **point of projection**, the angle α is called the **angle of projection**, the distance OB is called the **horizontal range (R)** or simply range and the vertical height AC is called the **maximum height (H).** The total time taken by the particle in describing the path OAB is called the **time of flight (T).**

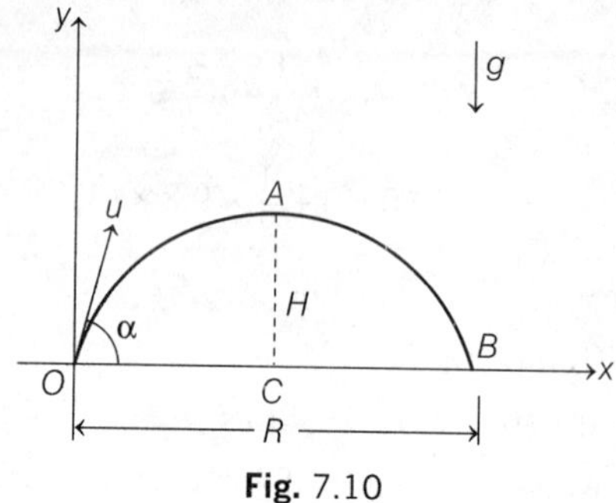

Fig. 7.10

Time of Flight (T)

Refer Fig. 7.10. Here, x and y-axes are in the directions shown in figure. Axis x is along horizontal direction and axis y is vertically upwards. Thus,

$$u_x = u\cos\alpha,$$

$$u_y = u\sin\alpha,\ a_x = 0$$

and

$$a_y = -g$$

At point B, $s_y = 0$. So, applying

$$s_y = u_y t + \frac{1}{2} a_y t^2, \text{ we have}$$

$$0 = (u\sin\alpha)t - \frac{1}{2} g t^2$$

$$\therefore \quad t = 0,\ \frac{2u\sin\alpha}{g}$$

Both $t = 0$ and $t = \frac{2u\sin\alpha}{g}$ correspond to the situation where $s_y = 0$. The time $t = 0$ corresponds to point O and time $t = \frac{2u\sin\alpha}{g}$ corresponds to point B. Thus, time of flight of the projectile is

$$T = t_{OAB} \quad \text{or} \quad \boxed{T = \frac{2u\sin\alpha}{g}}$$

Maximum Height (H)

At point A vertical component of velocity becomes zero, i.e. $v_y = 0$. Substituting the proper values in

$$v_y^2 = u_y^2 + 2a_y s_y$$

we have,

$$0 = (u\sin\alpha)^2 + 2(-g)(H)$$

$$\therefore \quad \boxed{H = \frac{u^2\sin^2\alpha}{2g}}$$

Horizontal Range (R)

Distance OB is the range R. This is also equal to the displacement of particle along x-axis in time $t = T$. Thus, applying $s_x = u_x t + \frac{1}{2} a_x t^2$, we get

$$R = (u \cos \alpha)\left(\frac{2u \sin \alpha}{g}\right) + 0$$

as $$a_x = 0 \quad \text{and} \quad t = T = \frac{2u \sin \alpha}{g}$$

$\therefore$ $$R = \frac{2u^2 \sin \alpha \cos \alpha}{g} = \frac{u^2 \sin 2\alpha}{g} \quad \text{or} \quad \boxed{R = \frac{u^2 \sin 2\alpha}{g}}$$

Following are given two important points regarding the range of a projectile

(i) Range is maximum where $\sin 2\alpha = 1$ or $\alpha = 45°$ and this maximum range is

$$R_{max} = \frac{u^2}{g} \qquad \text{(at } \alpha = 45°\text{)}$$

(ii) For given value of u range at α and range at $90° - \alpha$ are equal, although times of flight and maximum heights may be different. Because

$$R_{90° - \alpha} = \frac{u^2 \sin 2(90° - \alpha)}{g}$$

$$= \frac{u^2 \sin (180° - 2\alpha)}{g}$$

$$= \frac{u^2 \sin 2\alpha}{g} = R_\alpha$$

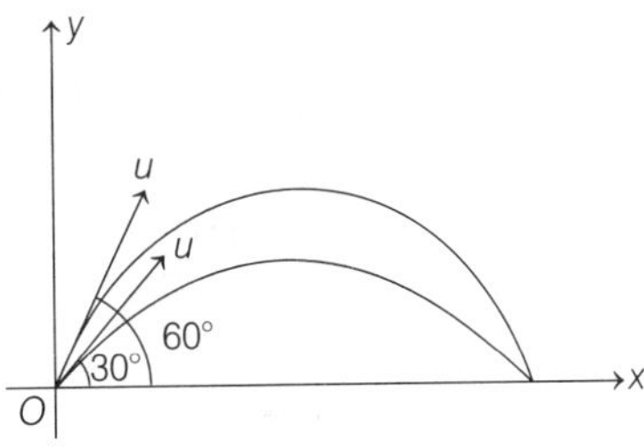

Fig. 7.11

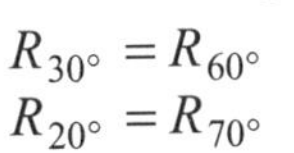

So, $$R_{30°} = R_{60°}$$
or $$R_{20°} = R_{70°}$$

This is shown in Fig. 7.11.

Extra Points to Remember

- Formulae of T, H and R can be applied directly between two points lying on same horizontal line.

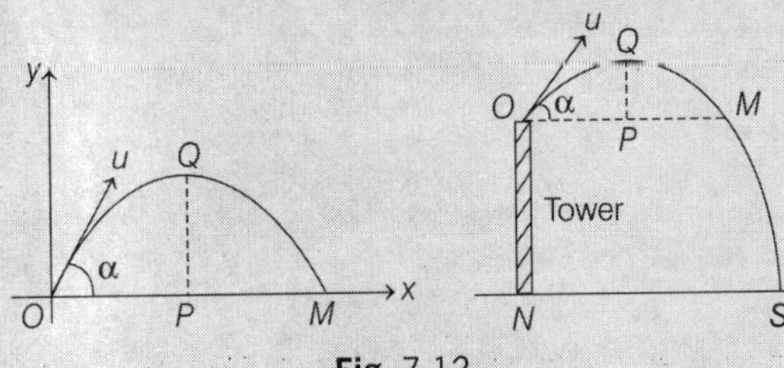

Fig. 7.12

For example, in the two projectile motions shown in figure,

$$t_{OQM} = T = \frac{2u \sin \alpha}{g}, \; PQ = H = \frac{u^2 \sin^2 \alpha}{2g} \text{ and } OM = R = \frac{u^2 \sin 2\alpha}{g}$$

For finding t_{OQMS} or distance NS method-2 discussed in article 7.3 is more useful.

- As we have seen in the above derivations that $a_x = 0$, i.e. motion of the projectile in horizontal direction is uniform. Hence, horizontal component of velocity $u \cos \alpha$ does not change during its motion.
- Motion in vertical direction is first retarded then accelerated in opposite direction. Because u_y is upwards and a_y is downwards. Hence, vertical component of its velocity first decreases from O to A and then increases from A to B. This can be shown as in Fig. 7.13.

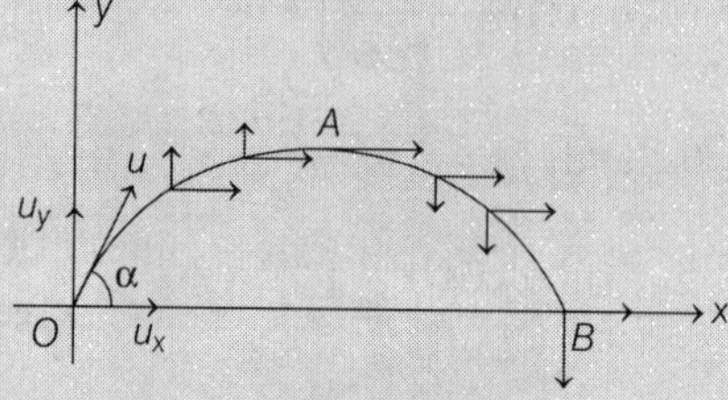

Fig. 7.13

- The coordinates and velocity components of the projectile at time t are

$$x = s_x = u_x t = (u \cos \alpha) t$$

$$y = s_y = u_y t + \frac{1}{2} a_y t^2$$

$$= (u \sin \alpha) t - \frac{1}{2} g t^2$$

$$v_x = u_x = u \cos \alpha$$

and

$$v_y = u_y + a_y t = u \sin \alpha - gt$$

Therefore, speed of projectile at time t is $v = \sqrt{v_x^2 + v_y^2}$ and the angle made by its velocity vector with positive x-axis is

$$\theta = \tan^{-1}\left(\frac{v_y}{v_x}\right)$$

- **Equation of trajectory of projectile**

$$x = (u \cos \alpha) t$$

$\therefore$

$$t = \frac{x}{u \cos \alpha}$$

Substituting this value of t in, $y = (u \sin \alpha) t - \frac{1}{2} g t^2$, we get

$$\boxed{y = x \tan \alpha - \frac{g x^2}{2 u^2 \cos^2 \alpha}}$$

or

$$y = x \tan \alpha - \frac{g x^2}{2 u^2} \sec^2 \alpha$$

$$\boxed{y = x \tan \alpha - \frac{g x^2}{2 u^2} (1 + \tan^2 \alpha)}$$

These are the standard equations of trajectory of a projectile. The equation is quadratic in x. This is why the path of a projectile is a parabola. The above equation can also be written in terms of range (R) of projectile as:

$$\boxed{y = x\left(1 - \frac{x}{R}\right) \tan \alpha}$$

Example 7.5 *Find the angle of projection of a projectile for which the horizontal range and maximum height are equal.*

Solution Given, $R = H$

$$\therefore \qquad \frac{u^2 \sin 2\alpha}{g} = \frac{u^2 \sin^2 \alpha}{2g} \quad \text{or} \quad 2\sin\alpha\cos\alpha = \frac{\sin^2\alpha}{2}$$

$$\text{or} \qquad \frac{\sin\alpha}{\cos\alpha} = 4 \quad \text{or} \quad \tan\alpha = 4$$

$$\therefore \qquad \alpha = \tan^{-1}(4)$$

Ans.

Example 7.6 *Prove that the maximum horizontal range is four times the maximum height attained by the projectile; when fired at an inclination so as to have maximum horizontal range.*

Solution For $\theta = 45°$, the horizontal range is maximum and is given by

$$R_{max} = \frac{u^2}{g}$$

Maximum height attained

$$H_{max} = \frac{u^2 \sin^2 45°}{2g} = \frac{u^2}{4g} = \frac{R_{max}}{4}$$

or

$$R_{max} = 4\,H_{max}$$

Proved.

Example 7.7 *For given value of u, there are two angles of projection for which the horizontal range is the same. Show that the sum of the maximum heights for these two angles is independent of the angle of projection.*

Solution There are two angles of projection α and $90° - \alpha$ for which the horizontal range R is same.

Now,

$$H_1 = \frac{u^2 \sin^2 \alpha}{2g} \quad \text{and} \quad H_2 = \frac{u^2 \sin^2(90° - \alpha)}{2g} = \frac{u^2 \cos^2 \alpha}{2g}$$

Therefore,

$$H_1 + H_2 = \frac{u^2}{2g}(\sin^2\alpha + \cos^2\alpha)$$

$$= \frac{u^2}{2g}$$

Clearly the sum of the heights for the two angles of projection is independent of the angles of projection.

Example 7.8 *Show that there are two values of time for which a projectile is at the same height. Also show mathematically that the sum of these two times is equal to the time of flight.*

Solution For vertically upward motion of a projectile,

$$y = (u\sin\alpha)t - \frac{1}{2}gt^2 \quad \text{or} \quad \frac{1}{2}gt^2 - (u\sin\alpha)t + y = 0$$

This is a quadratic equation in t. Its roots are

$$t_1 = \frac{u \sin \alpha - \sqrt{u^2 \sin^2 \alpha - 2gy}}{g}$$

and

$$t_2 = \frac{u \sin \alpha + \sqrt{u^2 \sin^2 \alpha - 2gy}}{g}$$

$\therefore$ $$t_1 + t_2 = \frac{2u \sin \alpha}{g} = T$$ (time of flight of the projectile)

INTRODUCTORY EXERCISE 7.2

1. A particle is projected from ground with velocity $40\sqrt{2}$ m/s at 45°. Find
   (a) velocity and
   (b) displacement of the particle after 2 s. ($g = 10 \text{ m/s}^2$)
2. Under what conditions the formulae of range, time of flight and maximum height can be applied directly in case of a projectile motion?
3. What is the average velocity of a particle projected from the ground with speed u at an angle α with the horizontal over a time interval from beginning till it strikes the ground again?
4. What is the change in velocity in the above question?
5. A particle is projected from ground with initial velocity $u = 20\sqrt{2}$ m/s at $\theta = 45°$. Find
   (a) R, H and T,
   (b) velocity of particle after 1 s
   (c) velocity of particle at the time of collision with the ground (x-axis).

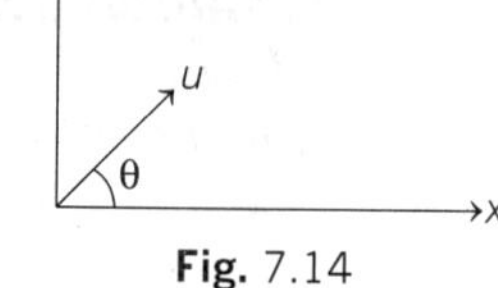

Fig. 7.14

6. A particle is projected from ground at angle 45° with initial velocity $20\sqrt{2}$ m/s. Find
   (a) change in velocity,
   (b) magnitude of average velocity in a time interval from $t = 0$ to $t = 3$ s.
7. The coach throws a baseball to a player with an initial speed of 20 m/s at an angle of 45° with the horizontal. At the moment the ball is thrown, the player is 50 m from the coach. At what speed and in what direction must the player run to catch the ball at the same height at which it was released? ($g = 10 \text{ m/s}^2$)
8. A ball is thrown horizontally from a point 100 m above the ground with a speed of 20 m/s. Find (a) the time it takes to reach the ground, (b) the horizontal distance it travels before reaching the ground, (c) the velocity (direction and magnitude) with which it strikes the ground.
9. A bullet fired at an angle of 30° with the horizontal hits the ground 3.0 km away. By adjusting its angle of projection, can one hope to hit a target 5.0 km away? Assume the muzzle speed to be fixed and neglect air resistance.
10. A particle moves in the xy-plane with constant acceleration a directed along the negative y-axis. The equation of path of the particle has the form $y = bx - cx^2$, where b and c are positive constants. Find the velocity of the particle at the origin of coordinates.

7.5 Projectile Motion along an Inclined Plane

Here, two cases arise. One is up the plane and the other is down the plane. Let us discuss both the cases separately.

Up the Plane

In this case direction x is chosen up the plane and direction y is chosen perpendicular to the plane. Hence,

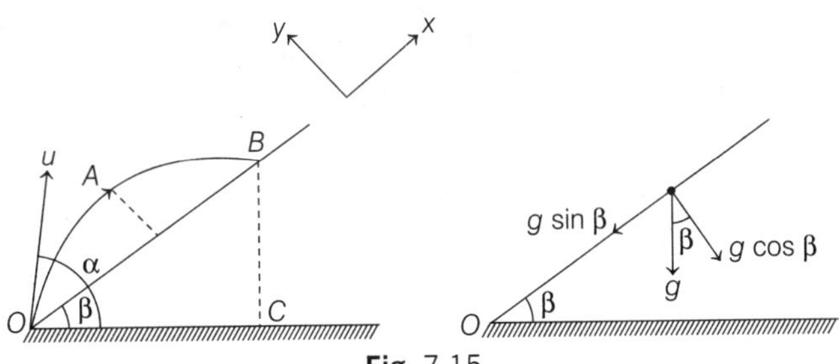

Fig. 7.15

$$u_x = u\cos(\alpha-\beta), \qquad a_x = -g\sin\beta$$
$$u_y = u\sin(\alpha-\beta) \quad \text{and} \quad a_y = -g\cos\beta$$

Now, let us derive the expressions for time of flight (T) and range (R) along the plane.

Time of Flight

At point B displacement along y-direction is zero. So, substituting the proper values in $s_y = u_y t + \frac{1}{2} a_y t^2$, we get

$$0 = ut\sin(\alpha-\beta) + \frac{1}{2}(-g\cos\beta)\,t^2 \;\Rightarrow\; \therefore\; t = 0 \text{ and } \frac{2u\sin(\alpha-\beta)}{g\cos\beta}$$

$t = 0$, corresponds to point O and $t = \dfrac{2u\sin(\alpha-\beta)}{g\cos\beta}$ corresponds to point B. Thus,

$$\boxed{T = \frac{2u\sin(\alpha-\beta)}{g\cos\beta}}$$

Note *Substituting $\beta = 0$, in the above expression, we get $T = \dfrac{2u\sin\alpha}{g}$ which is quite obvious because $\beta = 0$ is the situation shown in Fig. 7.16.*

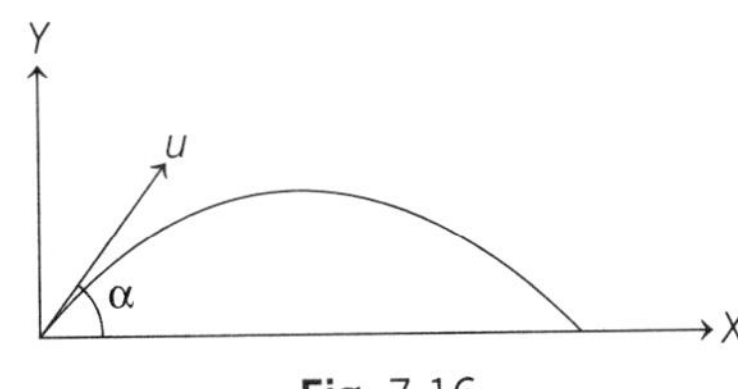

Fig. 7.16

Range

Range (R) or the distance OB can be found by following two methods:

Method 1 Horizontal component of initial velocity is

$$u_H = u\cos\alpha$$

$$\therefore \quad OC = u_H T \qquad (\text{as } a_H = 0)$$

$$= \frac{(u\cos\alpha)\,2u\sin(\alpha-\beta)}{g\cos\beta}$$

$$= \frac{2u^2\sin(\alpha-\beta)\cos\alpha}{g\cos\beta}$$

$$\therefore \quad R = OB = \frac{OC}{\cos\beta}$$

$$= \frac{2u^2\sin(\alpha-\beta)\cos\alpha}{g\cos^2\beta}$$

Using, $\sin C - \sin D = 2\sin\left(\frac{C-D}{2}\right)\cos\left(\frac{C+D}{2}\right)$,

Range can also be written as,

$$\boxed{R = \frac{u^2}{g\cos^2\beta}[\sin(2\alpha-\beta) - \sin\beta]}$$

This range will be maximum when

$$2\alpha - \beta = \frac{\pi}{2} \quad \text{or} \quad \alpha = \frac{\pi}{4} + \frac{\beta}{2}$$

and $$\boxed{R_{max} = \frac{u^2}{g\cos^2\beta}[1-\sin\beta]}$$

Here, also we can see that for $\beta = 0$, range is maximum at $\alpha = \frac{\pi}{4}$ or $\alpha = 45°$

and $$R_{max} = \frac{u^2}{g\cos^2 0°}(1-\sin 0°) = \frac{u^2}{g}$$

Method 2 Range (R) or the distance OB is also equal to the displacement of projectile along x-direction in time $t = T$. Therefore,

$$R = s_x = u_x T + \frac{1}{2}a_x T^2$$

Substituting the values of u_x, a_x and T, we get the same result.

(ii) **Down the Plane** Here, x and y-directions are down the plane and perpendicular to plane respectively as shown in Fig. 7.17. Hence,

$$u_x = u\cos(\alpha+\beta), \quad a_x = g\sin\beta$$

$$u_y = u\sin(\alpha+\beta), \quad a_y = -g\cos\beta$$

Proceeding in the similar manner, we get the following results :

$$T = \frac{2u \sin(\alpha + \beta)}{g \cos \beta}, \quad R = \frac{u^2}{g \cos^2 \beta}[\sin(2\alpha + \beta) + \sin \beta]$$

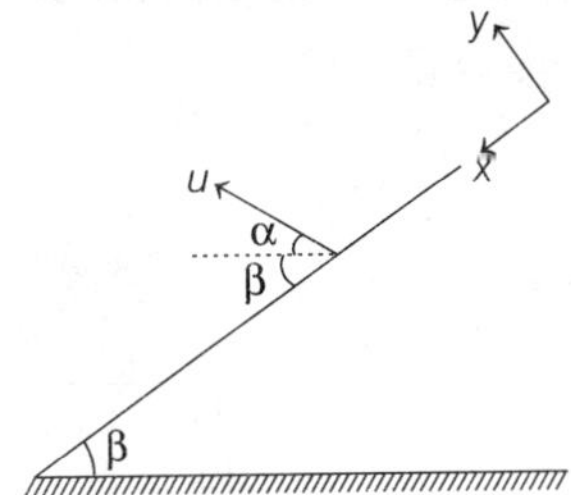

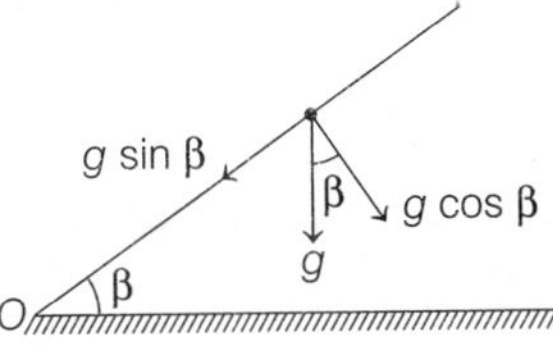

Fig. 7.17

From the above expressions, we can see that if we replace β by –β, the equations of T and R for up the plane and down the plane are interchanged provided α (angle of projection) in both the cases is measured from the horizontal not from the plane.

Example 7.9 *A man standing on a hill top projects a stone horizontally with speed v_0 as shown in figure. Taking the co-ordinate system as given in the figure. Find the co-ordinates of the point where the stone will hit the hill surface.*

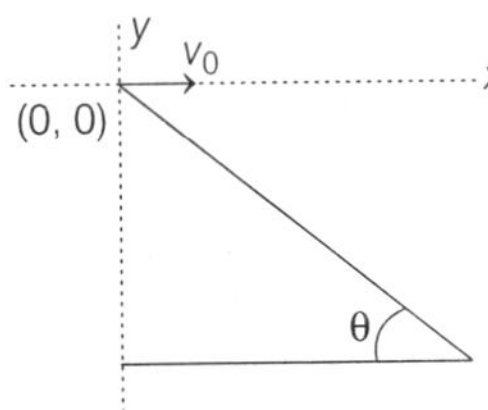

Fig. 7.18

Solution Range of the projectile on an inclined plane (down the plane) is,

$$R = \frac{u^2}{g \cos^2 \beta}[\sin(2\alpha + \beta) + \sin \beta]$$

Here, $u = v_0, \quad \alpha = 0 \quad \text{and} \quad \beta = \theta$

Fig. 7.19

$\therefore$
$$R = \frac{2v_0^2 \sin \theta}{g \cos^2 \theta}$$

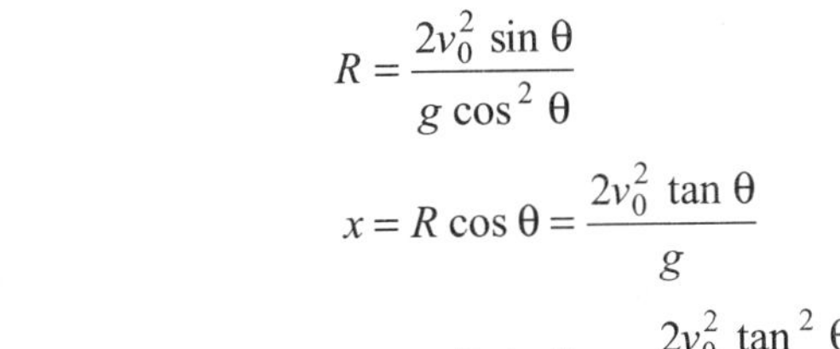
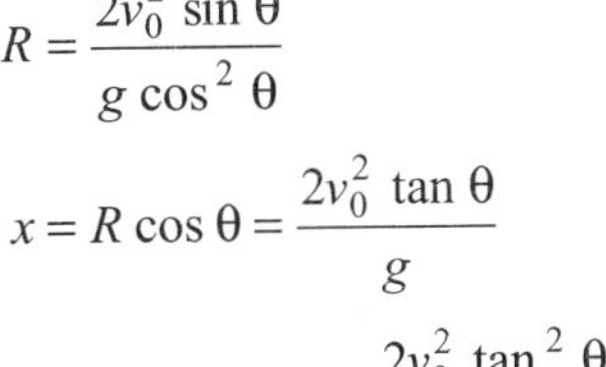

Now,
$$x = R \cos \theta = \frac{2v_0^2 \tan \theta}{g}$$

and
$$y = -R \sin \theta = -\frac{2v_0^2 \tan^2 \theta}{g}$$

7.6 Relative Motion between Two Projectiles

Let us now discuss the relative motion between two projectiles or the path observed by one projectile of the other. Suppose that two particles are projected from the ground with speeds u_1 and u_2 at angles α_1 and α_2 as shown in Fig. 7.20(a) and (b). Acceleration of both the particles is g downwards. So, relative acceleration between them is zero because

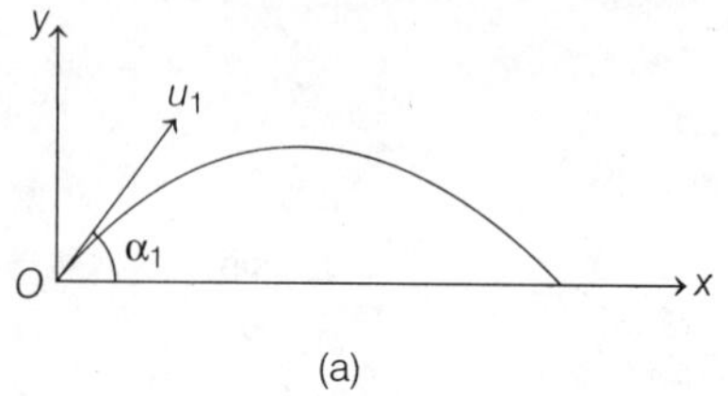

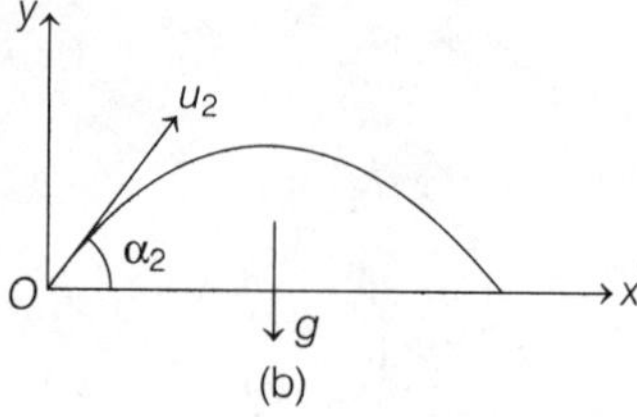

Fig. 7.20

$$\mathbf{a}_{12} = \mathbf{a}_1 - \mathbf{a}_2 = \mathbf{g} - \mathbf{g} = 0$$

i.e. the relative motion between the two particles is uniform.

Now, $\quad u_{1x} = u_1 \cos \alpha_1, \quad u_{2x} = u_2 \cos \alpha_2$

$\quad u_{1y} = u_1 \sin \alpha_1 \quad$ and $\quad u_{2y} = u_2 \sin \alpha_2$

Therefore, $\quad u_{12x} = u_{1x} - u_{2x} = u_1 \cos \alpha_1 - u_2 \cos \alpha_2$

and $\quad u_{12y} = u_{1y} - u_{2y} = u_1 \sin \alpha_1 - u_2 \sin \alpha_2$

u_{12x} and u_{12y} are the x and y components of relative velocity of 1 with respect to 2.

Hence, relative motion of 1 with respect to 2 is a straight line at an angle $\theta = \tan^{-1}\left(\dfrac{u_{12y}}{u_{12x}}\right)$ with positive x-axis.

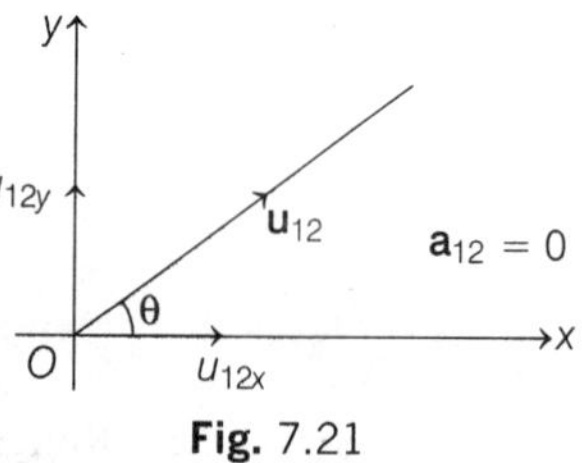

Fig. 7.21

Now, if $u_{12x} = 0$ or $u_1 \cos \alpha_1 = u_2 \cos \alpha_2$, the relative motion is along y-axis or in vertical direction (as $\theta = 90°$). Similarly, if $u_{12y} = 0$ or $u_1 \sin \alpha_1 = u_2 \sin \alpha_2$, the relative motion is along x-axis or in horizontal direction (as $\theta = 0°$).

Note *Relative acceleration between two projectiles is zero. Relative motion between them is uniform. Therefore, condition of collision of two particles in air is that relative velocity of one with respect to the other should be along line joining them, i.e., if two projectiles A and B collide in mid air, then $\mathbf{v}_{AB}$ should be along AB or $\mathbf{v}_{BA}$ along BA.*

Example 7.10 *A particle A is projected with an initial velocity of 60 m/s at an angle 30° to the horizontal. At the same time a second particle B is projected in opposite direction with initial speed of 50 m/s from a point at a distance of 100 m from A. If the particles collide in air, find (a) the angle of projection α of particle B, (b) time when the collision takes place and (c) the distance of P from A, where collision occurs.* ($g = 10\ m/s^2$)

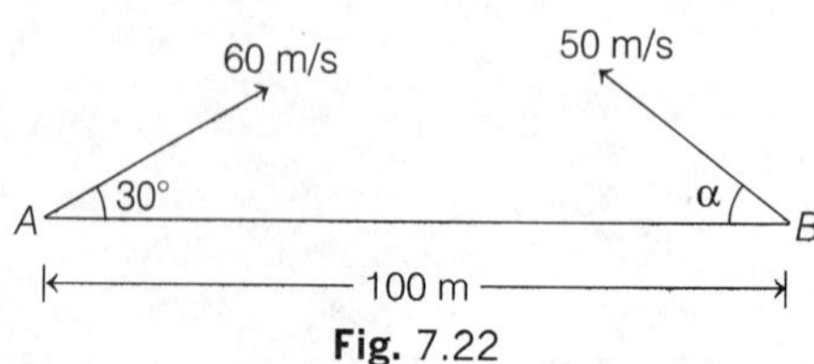

Fig. 7.22

Solution (a) Taking x and y-directions as shown in figure.

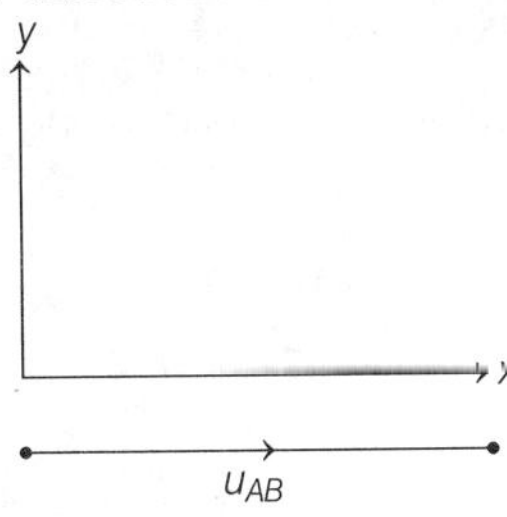

Fig. 7.23

Here,
$$\mathbf{a}_A = -g\hat{\mathbf{j}}$$
$$\mathbf{a}_B = -g\hat{\mathbf{j}}$$
$$u_{Ax} = 60\cos 30° = 30\sqrt{3} \text{ m/s}$$
$$u_{Ay} = 60\sin 30° = 30 \text{ m/s}$$
$$u_{Bx} = -50\cos\alpha$$
and
$$u_{By} = 50\sin\alpha$$

Relative acceleration between the two is zero as $\mathbf{a}_A = \mathbf{a}_B$. Hence, the relative motion between the two is uniform. It can be assumed that B is at rest and A is moving with $\mathbf{u}_{AB}$. Hence, the two particles will collide, if $\mathbf{u}_{AB}$ is along AB. This is possible only when

$$u_{Ay} = u_{By}$$

i.e. component of relative velocity along y-axis should be zero.

or
$$30 = 50\sin\alpha$$
$\therefore$
$$\alpha = \sin^{-1}(3/5) = 37°$$ **Ans.**

(b) Now,
$$|\mathbf{u}_{AB}| = u_{Ax} - u_{Bx} = (30\sqrt{3} + 50\cos\alpha) \text{ m/s}$$
$$= \left(30\sqrt{3} + 50 \times \frac{4}{5}\right) \text{ m/s}$$
$$= (30\sqrt{3} + 40) \text{ m/s}$$

Therefore, time of collision is
$$t = \frac{AB}{|\mathbf{u}_{AB}|} = \frac{100}{30\sqrt{3} + 40} \quad \text{or} \quad t = 1.09 \text{ s}$$ **Ans.**

(c) Distance of point P from A where collision takes place is
$$d = \sqrt{(u_{Ax}t)^2 + \left(u_{Ay}t - \frac{1}{2}gt^2\right)^2}$$
$$= \sqrt{(30\sqrt{3} \times 1.09)^2 + \left(30 \times 1.09 - \frac{1}{2} \times 10 \times 1.09 \times 1.09\right)^2}$$
or
$$d = 62.64 \text{ m}$$ **Ans.**

INTRODUCTORY EXERCISE 7.3

1. Find time of flight and range of the projectile along the inclined plane as shown in figure. ($g = 10 \text{ m/s}^2$)

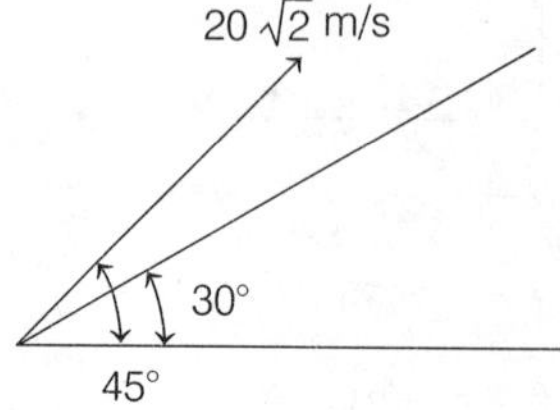

Fig. 7.24

2. Find time of flight and range of the projectile along the inclined plane as shown in figure. ($g = 10 \text{ m/s}^2$)

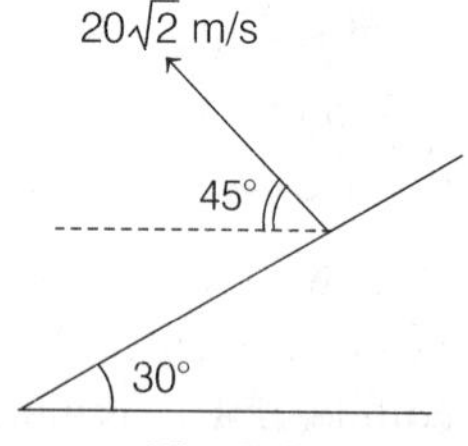

Fig. 7.25

3. Find time of flight and range of the projectile along the inclined plane as shown in figure. ($g = 10 \text{ m/s}^2$)

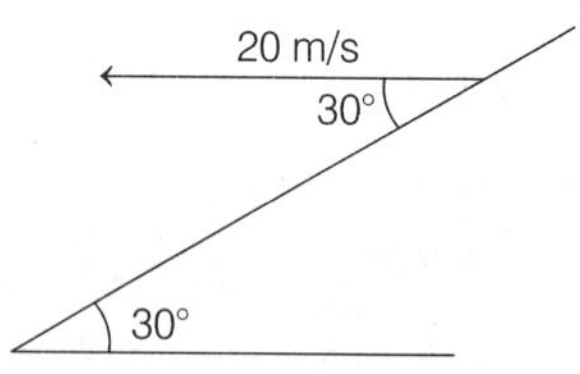

Fig. 7.26

4. Passenger of a train just drops a stone from it. The train was moving with constant velocity. What is path of the stone as observed by (a) the passenger itself, (b) a man standing on ground?
5. A particle is projected upwards with velocity 20 m/s. Simultaneously another particle is projected with velocity $20\sqrt{2}$ m/s at 45°. ($g = 10 \text{ m/s}^2$)
   (a) What is acceleration of first particle relative to the second?
   (b) What is initial velocity of first particle relative to the other?
   (c) What is distance between two particles after 2 s?
6. A particle is projected from the bottom of an inclined plane of inclination 30°. At what angle α (from the horizontal) should the particle be projected to get the maximum range on the inclined plane.

Core Concepts

1. In projectile motion speed (and hence kinetic energy) is minimum at highest point.

Speed = ($\cos\theta$) times the speed of projection

and kinetic energy = ($\cos^2\theta$) times the initial kinetic energy

Here, θ = angle of projection

2. In projectile motion it is sometimes better to write the equations of H, R and T in terms of u_x and u_y as

$$T = \frac{2u_y}{g}, \quad H = \frac{u_y^2}{2g} \quad \text{and} \quad R = \frac{2u_x u_y}{g}$$

3. If a particle is projected vertically upwards, then during upward journey gravity forces (weight) and air drag both are acting downwards. Hence, |retardation| > $|g|$. During its downward journey air drag is upwards while gravity is downwards. Hence, acceleration < g.. Therefore we may conclude that,

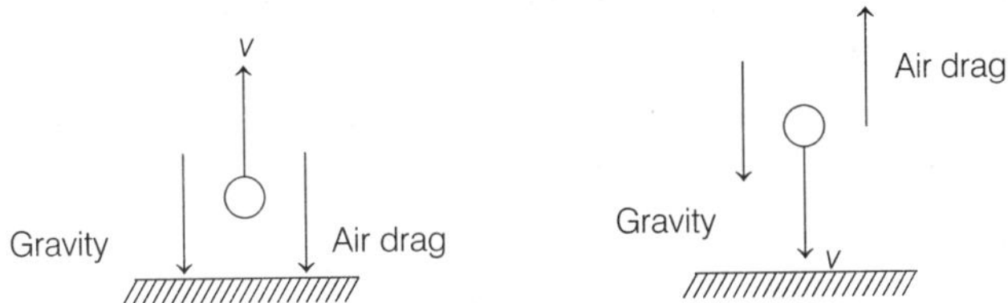

time of ascent < time of descent

Exercise : In projectile motion, if air drag is taken into consideration than state whether the H, R and T will increase, decrease or remain same.

Ans. T will increase, H will decrease and R may increase, decrease or remain same.

4. At the time of collision coordinates of particles should be same, i.e.

$x_1 = x_2$ and $y_1 = y_2$ (for a 2-D motion)

Similarly $x_1 = x_2$, $y_1 = y_2$ and $z_1 = z_2$ (for a 3-D motion)

Two particles collide at the same moment. Of course their time of journeys may be different, i.e. they may start at different times (t_1 and t_2 may be different). If they start together then $t_1 = t_2$.

Solved Examples

PATTERNED PROBLEMS

Type 1. *Based on the concept that horizontal component of velocity remains unchanged*

This type can be better understood by the following example.

Example 1 *A particle is projected from ground with velocity 40m/s at 60° from horizontal.*

(a) Find the speed when velocity of the particle makes an angle of 37° from horizontal.

(b) Find the time for the above situation.

(c) Find the vertical height and horizontal distance of the particle from the starting point in the above position. Take $g = 10\ m/s^2$.

Solution In the figure shown,

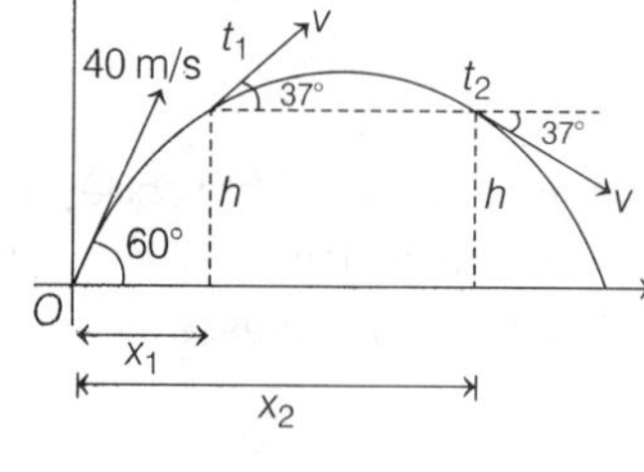

$$u_x = 40\cos 60° = 20\text{ m/s}$$
$$u_y = 40\sin 60° = 20\sqrt{3}\text{ m/s}$$
$$a_x = 0 \text{ and } a_y = -10\text{ m/s}^2$$

(a) Horizontal component of velocity remains unchanged.

$$v_x = u_x$$

or $$v\cos 37° = 20$$

$\Rightarrow$ $$v(0.8) = 20$$

$\therefore$ $$v = 25\text{ m/s}.$$

(b) Using, $v_y = u_y + a_y t \quad \Rightarrow \quad t = \dfrac{v_y - u_y}{a_y}$

For t_1, $$t_1 = \frac{v\sin 37° - 20\sqrt{3}}{-10} = \frac{(25)(0.6) - 20\sqrt{3}}{-10} = 1.96\text{ s}$$

For t_2, $$t_2 = \frac{-v\sin 37° - 20\sqrt{3}}{-10} = \frac{-(25)(0.6) - 20\sqrt{3}}{-10} = 4.96\text{ s}.$$

(c) Vertical height $$h = s_y \qquad \text{(at } t_1 \text{ or } t_2\text{)}$$

Let us calculate at t_1

$\therefore$ $$h = u_y t_1 + \frac{1}{2}a_y t_1^2 = (20\sqrt{3})(1.96) + \frac{1}{2}(-10)(1.96)^2$$
$$= 48.7\text{ m}.$$

Horizontal distances

$$x_1 = u_x t_1 \qquad \text{(as } a_x = 0\text{)}$$
$$= (20)(1.96) = 39.2\text{ m}$$

Similarly, $$x_2 = u_x t_2 = (20)(4.96)$$
$$= 99.2\text{ m}.$$

Type 2. *Situations where the formulae, H, R and T cannot be applied directly.*

Concept

As discussed earlier also, formulae of H, R and T can be applied directly between two points lying on the same horizontal line.

How to Solve?

- In any other situation apply component method (along x and y-axes). In most of the problems it is advisable to first find the time, using the equation, $s = ut + \frac{1}{2}at^2$ in vertical (or y) direction.

Example 2 *In the figures shown, three particles are thrown from a tower of height 40 m as shown in figure. In each case find the time when the particles strike the ground and the distance of this point from foot of the tower.*

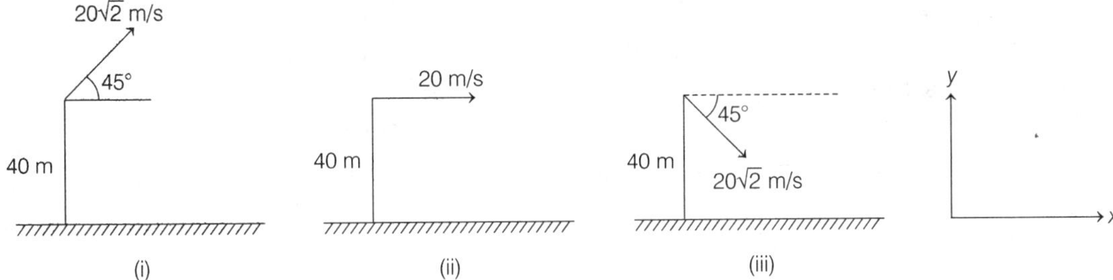

Solution For time calculation, apply

$$s_y = u_y t + \frac{1}{2} a_y t^2$$

in vertical direction.

In all figures, $s = -40 \text{ m}, a_y = -10 \text{ m/s}^2$

In first figure $u_y = +20\sqrt{2} \cos 45° = +20 \text{ m/s}$

In second figure, $u_y = 0$

In third figure, $u_y = -20\sqrt{2} \cos 45° = -20 \text{ m/s}$

For horizontal distance,

$$x = u_x t$$

$$u_x = 20 \text{ m/s} \quad \text{in all cases}$$

Substituting the proper values and then solving we get,

In first figure

Time $t_1 = 5.46$ s and horizontal distance $x_1 = 109.2$ m

In second figure

Time $t_2 = 2.83$ s and the horizontal distance $x_2 = 56.6$ m

In third figure

Time $t_3 = 1.46$ s and the horizontal distance $x_3 = 29.2$ m

Type 3. *Horizontal projection of a projectile from some height*

Concept

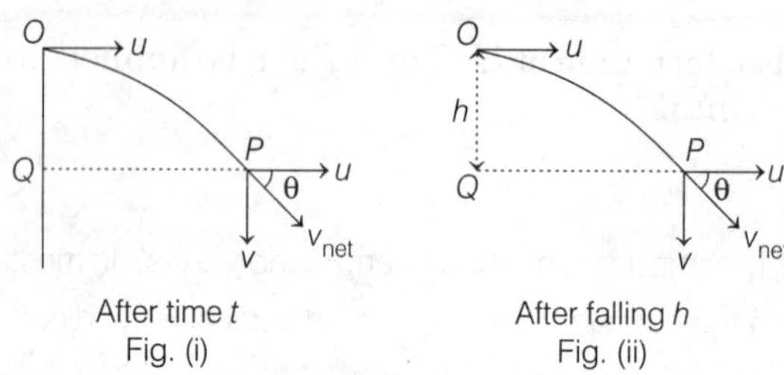

After time t
Fig. (i)

After falling h
Fig. (ii)

Suppose a particle is projected from point O with a horizontal velocity 'u' as shown in two figures. Then,

In Fig. (i) or after time t

Suppose the particle is at point P, then

$$\text{Horizontal component of velocity} = u$$

$$\text{Vertical component of velocity, } v = gt$$

If $g = 10\,\text{m/s}$, then

$$v = 10t \quad \text{(downwards)}$$

Horizontal distance $QP = ut$ and vertical height fallen $OQ = \frac{1}{2}gt^2$

If $g = 10\,\text{m/s}^2$, then

$$OQ = 5t^2$$

If Fig. (ii) or after falling a height 'h'

Suppose the particle is at point P, then

Horizontal component of velocity $= u$

Vertical component of velocity $v = \sqrt{2gh}$ (downwards)

Time taken in falling a height h is

$$t = \sqrt{\frac{2h}{g}} \qquad \left(\text{as } h = \frac{1}{2}gt^2\right)$$

The horizontal distance $QP = ut$

Note *In both figures, net velocity of the particle at point P is,*

$$v_{net} = \sqrt{v^2 + u^2}$$

and the angle θ of this net velocity with horizontal is

$$\tan\theta = \frac{v}{u} \quad \text{or} \quad \theta = \tan^{-1}\left(\frac{v}{u}\right)$$

Example 3 *A ball rolls off the edge of a horizontal table top 4 m high. If it strikes the floor at a point 5 m horizontally away from the edge of the table, what was its speed at the instant it left the table?*

Solution Using $h = \frac{1}{2} gt^2$, we have

$$h_{AB} = \frac{1}{2} gt_{AC}^2$$

or $$t_{AC} = \sqrt{\frac{2h_{AB}}{g}}$$

$$= \sqrt{\frac{2 \times 4}{9.8}} = 0.9 \text{ s}$$

Further, $$BC = vt_{AC}$$

or $$v = \frac{BC}{t_{AC}} = \frac{5.0}{0.9} = 5.55 \text{ m/s}$$ **Ans.**

Example 4 *An aeroplane is flying in a horizontal direction with a velocity 600 km/h at a height of 1960 m. When it is vertically above the point A on the ground, a body is dropped from it. The body strikes the ground at point B. Calculate the distance AB.*

Solution From $$h = \frac{1}{2} gt^2$$

we have, $$t_{OB} = \sqrt{\frac{2h_{OA}}{g}} = \sqrt{\frac{2 \times 1960}{9.8}} = 20 \text{ s}$$

Horizontal distance $$AB = vt_{OB}$$

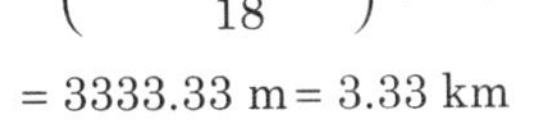

$$= \left(600 \times \frac{5}{18} \text{ m/s}\right) (20 \text{ s})$$

$$= 3333.33 \text{ m} = 3.33 \text{ km}$$ **Ans.**

Example 5 *In the figure shown, find*

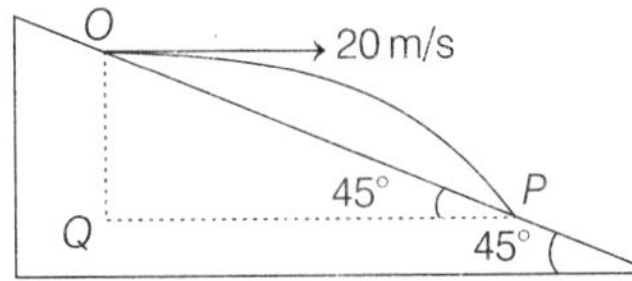

(a) the time of flight of the projectile over the inclined plane

(b) range OP

Solution (a) Let the particle strikes the plane at point P at time t, then

$$OQ = \frac{1}{2} g t^2 = 5t^2$$

$$QP = 20\,t$$

In ΔOPQ, angle OPQ is 45°.

$\therefore$ $$OQ = QP \quad \text{or} \quad 5t^2 = 20t$$

$\therefore$ $$t = 4 \text{ s}$$ **Ans.**

(b) $$OP = QP \sin 45° = (20t)(\sqrt{2})$$

Substituting $t = 4$ s, we have

$$OP = 80\sqrt{2} \text{ m}$$ **Ans.**

Example 6 *In the figure shown, find*

(a) the time when the particle strikes the ground at P
(b) the horizontal distance QP
(c) velocity of the particle at P
Take $g = 10\ m/s^2$

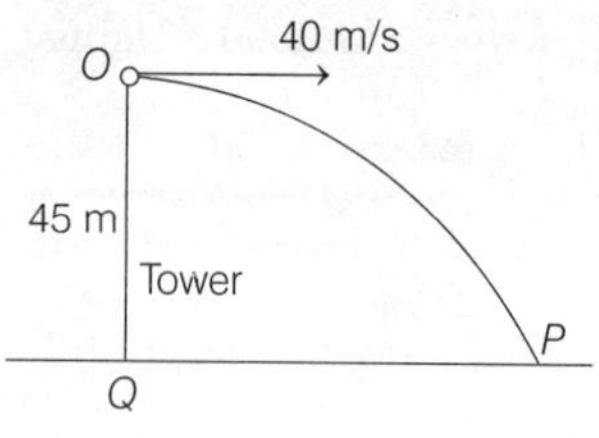

Solution (a) $t = \sqrt{\frac{2h}{g}} = \sqrt{\frac{2 \times 45}{10}} = 3\,\text{s}$

(b) Horizontal distance $QP = 40\,t$

$$= 40 \times 3 = 120\,\text{m}$$ **Ans.**

(c) Horizontal component of velocity at $P = 40$ m/s

Vertical compound of velocity $= gt = 10t = 10 \times 3 = 30$ m/s (downwards)

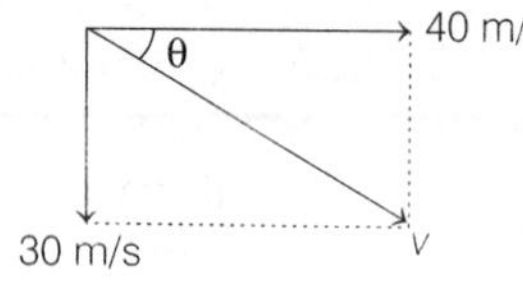

Net velocity $v = \sqrt{(40)^2 + (30)^2} = 50$ m/s **Ans.**

$$\tan\theta = \frac{30}{40} \text{ or } \frac{3}{4}$$

$\therefore$ $$\theta = \tan^{-1}\left(\frac{3}{4}\right) = 37°$$ **Ans.**

Type 4. *Based on trajectory of a projectile*

Concept

We have seen that equation of trajectory of projectile is

$$y = x\tan\theta - \frac{gx^2}{2u^2\cos^2\theta} = x\tan\theta - \frac{gx^2}{2u^2}(1 + \tan^2\theta)$$

In some problems, the given equation of a projectile is compared with this standard equation to find the unknowns.

Example 7 *A particle moves in the plane xy with constant acceleration 'a' directed along the negative y-axis. The equation of motion of the particle has the form $y = px - qx^2$ where p and q are positive constants. Find the velocity of the particle at the origin of co-ordinates.*

Solution Comparing the given equation with the equation of a projectile motion,

$$y = x\tan\theta - \frac{gx^2}{2u^2}(1 + \tan^2\theta)$$

We find that $$g = a, \tan\theta = p \text{ and } \frac{a}{2u^2}(1 + \tan^2\theta) = q$$

$\therefore$ u = velocity of particle at origin

Type 5. *Based on basic concepts of projectile motion.*

Concept

Following are given some basic concepts of any projectile motion :

(i) Horizontal component of velocity always remains constant.

(ii) Vertical component of velocity changes by 10 m/s or 9.8 m/s in every second in downward direction. For example, if vertical component of velocity at $t = 0$ is 30 m/s then change in vertical component in first five seconds is as given in following table:

Time (in sec)	**Vertical component** (in m/s)	**Direction**
0	30	upwards
1	20	upwards
2	10	upwards
3	0	-
4	10	downwards
5	20	downwards

In general we can use, $v_y = u_y + a_y t$

(iii) At a height difference 'h' between two points 1 and 2, the vertical components v_1 and v_2 are related as,

$$v_2 = \pm\sqrt{v_1^2 \pm 2gh}$$

In moving upwards, vertical component decreases. So, take $-2gh$ in the above equation if point 2 is higher than point 1.

(iv) Horizontal displacement is simply,

$$s_x = u_x t \qquad \text{(in the direction of } u_x\text{)}$$

(v) Vertical displacement has two components (say s_1 and s_2), one due to initial velocity u_y and the other due to gravity.

$s_1 = u_y t =$ displacement due to initial component of velocity u_y.

This s_1 is in the direction of u_y (upwards or downwards)

$$s_2 = \frac{1}{2} g t^2 = 5t^2 \qquad \text{(if } g = 10\,\text{m/s}^2\text{)}$$

This s_2 is always downwards.

Net vertical displacement is the resultant of s_1 and s_2.

Example 8 *In the figure shown, find*

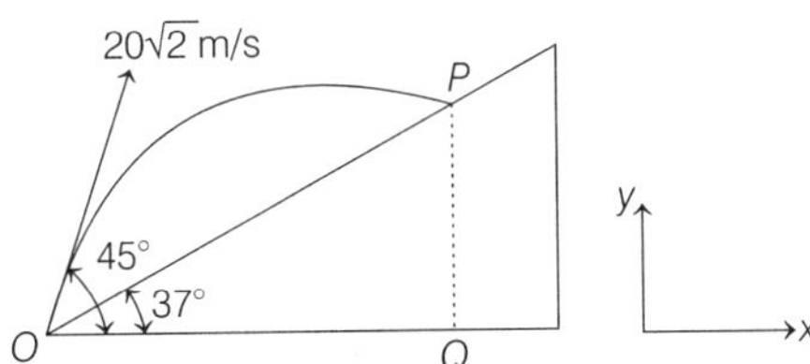

(a) time of flight of the projectile along the inclined plane.

(b) range OP

Solution (a) Horizontal component of initial velocity,

$$u_x = 20\sqrt{2}\cos 45° = 20 \text{ m/s}$$

Vertical component of initial velocity

$$u_y = 20\sqrt{2}\sin 45° = 20 \text{ m/s}$$

Let the particle strikes at P after time t, then

horizontal displacement $\quad OQ = u_x t = 20t$

In vertical displacement, $u_y t$ or $20t$ is upwards and $\frac{1}{2}gt^2$ or $5t^2$ is downwards. But net displacement is upwards, therefore $20t$ should be greater than $5t^2$ and

$$QP = 20t - 5t^2$$

In ΔOPQ,

$$\tan 37° = \frac{QP}{OQ}$$

or,

$$\frac{3}{4} = \frac{20t - 5t^2}{20t}$$

Solving this equation, we get

$$t = 1 \text{ s}$$ **Ans.**

(b) Range

$$OP = OQ \sec 37°$$

$$= (20t)\left(\frac{5}{4}\right)$$

Substituting $t = 1$ s, we have

$$OP = 25 \text{ m}$$ **Ans.**

Example 9 *In the shown figure, find*

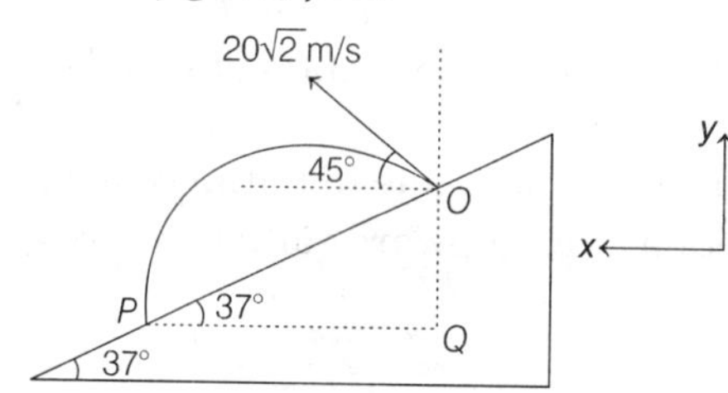

(a) time of flight of the projectile along the inclined plane

(b) range OP

Solution (a) Horizontal component of initial velocity, $u_x = 20\sqrt{2}\cos 45° = 20$ m/s

Vertical component of initial velocity,

$$u_y = 20\sqrt{2}\sin 45° = 20 \text{ m/s}$$

Let the particle, strikes the inclined plane at P after time t, then horizontal displacement

$$QP = u_x t = 20t$$

In vertical displacement, $u_y t$ or $20t$ is upwards and $\frac{1}{2}gt^2$ or $5t^2$ is downwards. But net vertical displacement is downwards. Hence $5t^2$ should be greater than $20t$ and therefore,

$$OQ = 5t^2 - 20t$$

In ΔOQP,

$$\tan 37° = \frac{OQ}{QP}$$

or $$\frac{3}{4} = \frac{5t^2 - 20t}{20t}$$

Solving this equation, we get

$$t = 7\text{ s}$$ **Ans.**

(b) Range, $OP = (PQ)\sec 37°$

$$= (20t)\left(\frac{5}{4}\right)$$

Substituting the value of t, we get

$$OP = 175\text{ m}$$ **Ans.**

Example 10 *At a height of 45 m from ground velocity of a projectile is,*

$$\mathbf{v} = (30\hat{\mathbf{i}} + 40\hat{\mathbf{j}})\text{ m/s}$$

Find initial velocity, time of flight, maximum height and horizontal range of this projectile. Here $\hat{\mathbf{i}}$ and $\hat{\mathbf{j}}$ are the unit vectors in horizontal and vertical directions.

Solution Given, $v_x = 30\text{ m/s}$ and $v_y = 40\text{ m/s}$

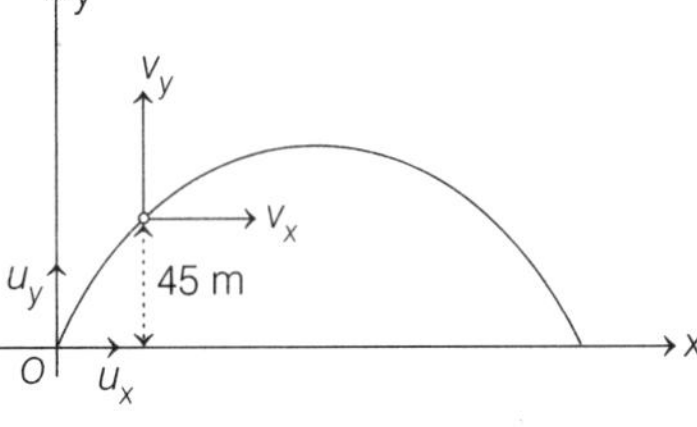

Horizontal component of velocity remains unchanged.

$\therefore$ $$u_x = v_x = 30\text{ m/s}$$

Vertical component of velocity is more at lesser heights. Therefore,

$$u_y > v_y$$

or $$u_y = \sqrt{v_y^2 + 2gh}$$

$$= \sqrt{(40)^2 + (2)(10)(45)}$$

$$= 50\text{ m/s}$$

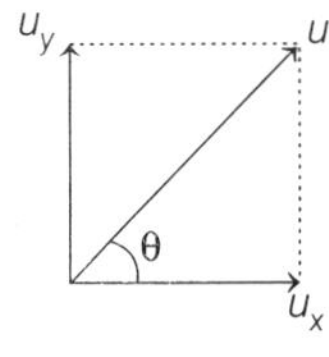

Initial velocity of projectile,

$$u = \sqrt{u_x^2 + u_y^2}$$

$$= \sqrt{(30)^2 + (50)^2}$$

$$= 10\sqrt{34}\text{ m/s}$$ **Ans.**

$$\tan\theta = \frac{u_y}{u_x} = \frac{50}{30} = \frac{5}{3}$$

$\therefore$ $$\theta = \tan^{-1}\left(\frac{5}{3}\right)$$ **Ans.**

Time of flight, $$T = \frac{2u\sin\theta}{g} = \frac{2u_y}{g}$$

$$= \frac{2 \times 50}{10}$$

$$= 10\text{ s}$$ **Ans.**

Maximum height,
$$H = \frac{u^2 \sin^2 \theta}{2g} = \frac{u_y^2}{2g}$$
$$= \frac{(50)^2}{2 \times 10} = 125 \text{ m}$$ **Ans.**

Horizontal range,
$$R = u_x T$$
$$= 30 \times 10$$
$$= 300 \text{ m}$$ **Ans.**

Miscellaneous Examples

Example 11 *A particle is thrown over a triangle from one end of a horizontal base and after grazing the vertex falls on the other end of the base. If α and β be the base angles and θ the angle of projection, prove that* $\tan\theta = \tan\alpha + \tan\beta$.

Solution The situation is shown in figure.

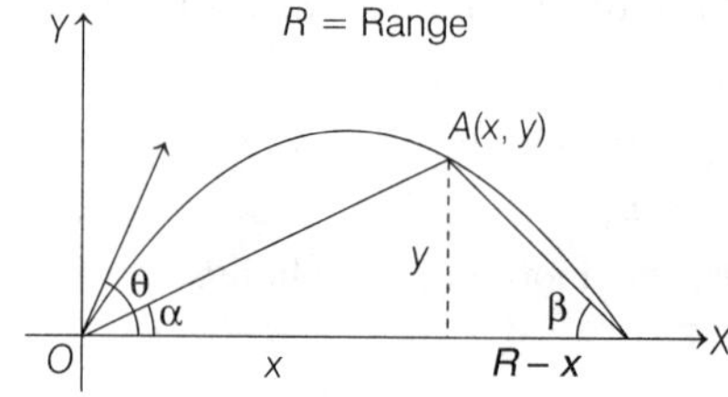

From figure, we have
$$\tan\alpha + \tan\beta = \frac{y}{x} + \frac{y}{R - x}$$
$$\tan\alpha + \tan\beta = \frac{yR}{x(R - x)} \quad \text{...(i)}$$

Equation of trajectory is
$$y = x \tan\theta \left[1 - \frac{x}{R}\right]$$

or,
$$\tan\theta = \frac{yR}{x(R - x)} \quad \text{...(ii)}$$

From Eqs. (i) and (ii), we have
$$\tan\theta = \tan\alpha + \tan\beta$$ **Hence Proved.**

Example 12 *The velocity of a projectile when it is at the greatest height is* $\sqrt{2/5}$ *times its velocity when it is at half of its greatest height. Determine its angle of projection.*

Solution Suppose the particle is projected with velocity u at an angle θ with the horizontal. Horizontal component of its velocity at all height will be $u \cos\theta$.

At the greatest height, the vertical component of velocity is zero, so the resultant velocity is

$$v_1 = u\cos\theta$$

At half the greatest height during upward motion,

$$y = h/2,\ a_y = -g,\ u_y = u\sin\theta$$

Using $$v_y^2 - u_y^2 = 2a_y y$$

we get, $$v_y^2 - u^2\sin^2\theta = 2(-g)\frac{h}{2}$$

or $$v_y^2 = u^2\sin^2\theta - g\times\frac{u^2\sin^2\theta}{2g} = \frac{u^2\sin^2\theta}{2} \qquad \left[\because\ h = \frac{u^2\sin^2\theta}{2g}\right]$$

or $$v_y = \frac{u\sin\theta}{\sqrt{2}}$$

Hence, resultant velocity at half of the greatest height is

$$v_2 = \sqrt{v_x^2 + v_y^2}$$

$$= \sqrt{u^2\cos^2\theta + \frac{u^2\sin^2\theta}{2}}$$

Given, $$\frac{v_1}{v_2} = \sqrt{\frac{2}{5}}$$

$\therefore$ $$\frac{v_1^2}{v_2^2} = \frac{u^2\cos^2\theta}{u^2\cos^2\theta + \frac{u^2\sin^2\theta}{2}} = \frac{2}{5}$$

or $$\frac{1}{1 + \frac{1}{2}\tan^2\theta} = \frac{2}{5}$$

or $$2 + \tan^2\theta = 5 \quad \text{or} \quad \tan^2\theta = 3$$

or $$\tan\theta = \sqrt{3}$$

$\therefore$ $$\theta = 60^\circ$$ **Ans.**

Example 13 *A car accelerating at the rate of $2\ m/s^2$ from rest from origin is carrying a man at the rear end who has a gun in his hand. The car is always moving along positive x-axis. At $t = 4$ s, the man fires a bullet from the gun and the bullet hits a bird at $t = 8$ s. The bird has a position vector $40\hat{\mathbf{i}} + 80\hat{\mathbf{j}} + 40\hat{\mathbf{k}}$. Find velocity of projection of the bullet. Take the y-axis in the horizontal plane. ($g = 10\ m/s^2$)*

Solution Let velocity of bullet be,

$$\mathbf{v} = v_x\hat{\mathbf{i}} + v_y\hat{\mathbf{j}} + v_z\hat{\mathbf{k}}$$

At $t = 4$ s, x-coordinate of car is $$x_c = \frac{1}{2}at^2 = \frac{1}{2}\times 2\times 16 = 16\text{ m}$$

x-coordinate of bird is $x_b = 40$ m

$\therefore$ $$x_b = x_c + v_x(8 - 4)$$

or $$40 = 16 + 4v_x$$

$\therefore$ $$v_x = 6\text{ m/s}$$

Similarly, $$y_b = y_c + v_y\,(8-4)$$

or $$80 = 0 + 4v_y$$

or $$v_y = 20 \text{ m/s}$$

and $$z_b = z_c + v_z\,(8-4) - \frac{1}{2}\,g\,(8-4)^2$$

or $$40 = 0 + 4v_z - \frac{1}{2} \times 10 \times 16$$

or $$v_z = 30 \text{ m/s}$$

∴ Velocity of projection of bullet

$$\mathbf{v} = (6\hat{\mathbf{i}} + 20\hat{\mathbf{j}} + 30\hat{\mathbf{k}}) \text{ m/s}$$

Example 14 *Two inclined planes OA and OB having inclinations 30° and 60° with the horizontal respectively intersect each other at O, as shown in figure. A particle is projected from point P with velocity $u = 10\sqrt{3}$ m/s along a direction perpendicular to plane OA. If the particle strikes plane OB perpendicular at Q. Calculate*

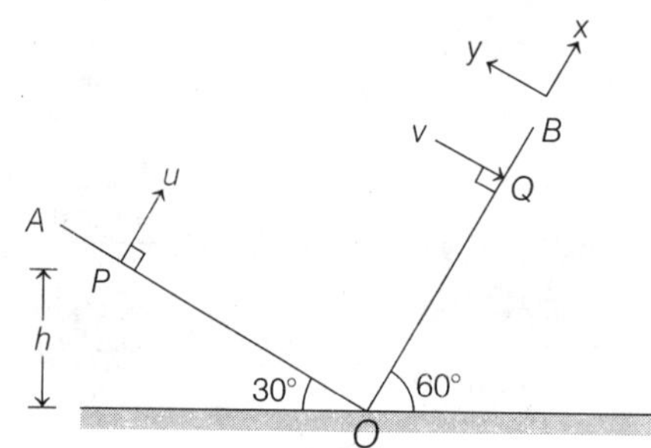

(a) time of flight,

(b) velocity with which the particle strikes the plane OB,

(c) height h of point P from point O,

(d) distance PQ. (Take $g = 10\ m/s^2$)

Solution Let us choose the x and y directions along OB and OA respectively. Then,

$$u_x = u = 10\sqrt{3} \text{ m/s}, \quad u_y = 0$$

$$a_x = -g \sin 60° = -5\sqrt{3} \text{ m/s}^2$$

and $$a_y = -g \cos 60° = -5 \text{ m/s}^2$$

(a) At point Q, x-component of velocity is zero. Hence, substituting in

$$v_x = u_x + a_x t$$

$$0 = 10\sqrt{3} - 5\sqrt{3}t$$

or $$t = \frac{10\sqrt{3}}{5\sqrt{3}} = 2\text{ s}$$ **Ans.**

(b) At point Q, $$v = v_y = u_y + a_y t$$

∴ $$v = 0 - (5)(2) = -10 \text{ m/s}$$ **Ans.**

Here, negative sign implies that velocity of particle at Q is along negative y-direction.

(c) Distance $PO = |$ displacement of particle along y-direction $| = |s_y|$

Here, $$s_y = u_y t + \frac{1}{2} a_y t^2$$

$$= 0 - \frac{1}{2}(5)(2)^2 = -10 \text{ m}$$

$\therefore$ $$PO = 10 \text{ m}$$

Therefore, $$h = PO \sin 30°$$

$$= (10)\left(\frac{1}{2}\right)$$

or $$h = 5 \text{ m}$$ **Ans.**

(d) Distance $OQ =$ displacement of particle along x-direction $= s_x$

Here, $$s_x = u_x t + \frac{1}{2} a_x t^2$$

$$= (10\sqrt{3})(2) - \frac{1}{2}(5\sqrt{3})(2)^2$$

$$= 10\sqrt{3} \text{ m}$$

or $$OQ = 10\sqrt{3} \text{ m}$$

$\therefore$ $$PQ = \sqrt{(PO)^2 + (OQ)^2}$$

$$= \sqrt{(10)^2 + (10\sqrt{3})^2}$$

$$= \sqrt{100 + 300} = \sqrt{400}$$

$\therefore$ $$PQ = 20 \text{ m}$$ **Ans.**

Exercises

LEVEL 1

Assertion and Reason

Directions : *Choose the correct option.*

(*a*) *If both **Assertion** and **Reason** are true and the **Reason** is correct explanation of the **Assertion.***

(*b*) *If both **Assertion** and **Reason** are true but **Reason** is not the correct explanation of **Assertion.***

(*c*) *If **Assertion** is true, but the **Reason** is false.*

(*d*) *If **Assertion** is false but the **Reason** is true.*

(*e*) *If both **Assertion** and **Reason** are false.*

1. Assertion : A particle follows only a parabolic path, if acceleration is constant.

Reason : In projectile motion, path is parabolic, as acceleration is assumed to be constant at low heights.

2. Assertion : If time of flight in a projectile motion is made two times, its maximum height will become four times.

Reason : In projectile motion $H \propto T^2$, where H is maximum height and T is time of flight.

3. Assertion : A particle is projected with velocity $\mathbf{u}$ at angle 45° with ground. Let $\mathbf{v}$ be the velocity of particle at time $t\,(\neq 0)$, then value of $\mathbf{u} \cdot \mathbf{v}$ can be zero.

Reason : Value of dot product is zero when angle between two vectors is 90°.

4. Assertion : In projectile motion at any two positions $\dfrac{\mathbf{v}_2 - \mathbf{v}_1}{t_2 - t_1}$ always remains constant.

Reason : The given quantity is average acceleration, which should remain constant as acceleration is constant.

5. Assertion : Particle A is projected upwards. Simultaneously particle B is projected as projectile as shown. Particle A returns to ground in 4 s. At the same time particle B collides with A. Maximum height H attained by B would be 20 m. ($g = 10 \text{ ms}^{-2}$)

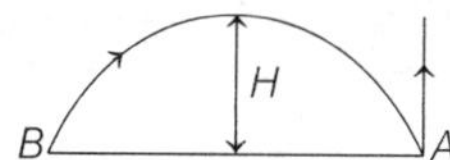

Reason : Speed of projection of both the particles should be same under the given condition.

6. Assertion : Two projectiles have maximum heights $4H$ and H, respectively. The ratio of their horizontal components of velocities should be 1 : 2 for their horizontal ranges to be same.

Reason : Horizontal range = horizontal component of velocity × time of flight.

7. Assertion : In projectile motion, if particle is projected with speed u, then speed of particle at height h would be $\sqrt{u^2 - 2gh}$.

Reason : If particle is projected with vertical component of velocity u_y, then vertical component at the height h would be $\pm\sqrt{u_y^2 - 2gh}$.

8. **Assertion :** If a particle is projected vertically upwards with velocity u, the maximum height attained by the particle is h_1. The same particle is projected at angle 30° from horizontal with the same speed u. Now, the maximum height is h_2. Then, $h_1 = 4h_2$.
Reason : In first case $v = 0$ at highest point and in second case $v \neq 0$ at highest point.

9. **Assertion :** At height 20 m from ground, velocity of a projectile is $\mathbf{v} = (20\hat{\mathbf{i}} + 20\hat{\mathbf{j}})$ m/s. Here, $\hat{\mathbf{i}}$ in horizontal direction and $\hat{\mathbf{j}}$ in vertical direction. Then, the particle is at the same height after 4 s.
Reason : Maximum height of particle from ground is 40 m. (Take $g = 10$ m/s^2)

Objective Questions

Single Correct Option

1. Two bodies were thrown simultaneously from the same point, one straight up, and the other, at an angle of $\theta = 30°$ to the horizontal. The initial velocity of each body is 20 ms^{-1}. Neglecting air resistance, the distance between the bodies at $t = 1.2$ later is
(a) 20 m (b) 30 m
(c) 24 m (d) 50 m

2. Two bodies are thrown with the same initial velocity at angles θ and $(90° - \theta)$ respectively with the horizontal, then their maximum heights are in the ratio
(a) 1 : 1 (b) $\sin\theta : \cos\theta$
(c) $\sin^2\theta : \cos^2\theta$ (d) $\cos\theta : \sin\theta$

3. The range of a projectile at an angle θ is equal to half of the maximum range, if thrown at the same speed. The angle of projection θ is given by
(a) 15° (b) 30°
(c) 60° (d) data insufficient

4. A ball is projected with a velocity 20 ms^{-1} at an angle to the horizontal. In order to have the maximum range. Its velocity at the highest position must be
(a) 10 ms^{-1} (b) 14 ms^{-1}
(c) 18 ms^{-1} (d) 16 ms^{-1}

5. A particle has initial velocity $\mathbf{v} = 3\hat{\mathbf{i}} + 4\hat{\mathbf{j}}$ and a constant force $\mathbf{F} = 4\hat{\mathbf{i}} - 3\hat{\mathbf{j}}$ acts on it. The path of the particle is
(a) straight line (b) parabolic
(c) circular (d) elliptical

6. A body is projected at an angle 60° with the horizontal with kinetic energy K. When the velocity makes an angle 30° with the horizontal, the kinetic energy of the body will be
(a) $K/2$ (b) $K/3$
(c) $2K/3$ (d) $3K/4$

7. If T_1 and T_2 are the times of flight for two complementary angles, then the range of projectile R is given by
(a) $R = 4gT_1T_2$ (b) $R = 2gT_1T_2$ (c) $R = \frac{1}{4}gT_1T_2$ (d) $R = \frac{1}{2}gT_1T_2$

8. A gun is firing bullets with velocity v_0 by rotating it through 360° in the horizontal plane. The maximum area covered by the bullets is
(a) $\frac{\pi v_0^2}{g}$ (b) $\frac{\pi^2 v_0^2}{g}$ (c) $\frac{\pi v_0^4}{g^2}$ (d) $\frac{\pi^2 v_0^4}{g}$

9. A grasshopper can jump maximum distance 1.6 m. It spends negligible time on ground. How far can it go in $10\sqrt{2}$ s ?
(a) 45 m
(b) 30 m
(c) 20 m
(d) 40 m

10. Two stones are projected with the same speed but making different angles with the horizontal. Their horizontal ranges are equal. The angle of projection of one is $\frac{\pi}{3}$ and the maximum height reached by it is 102 m. Then, the maximum height reached by the other (in metres) is
(a) 76
(b) 84
(c) 56
(d) 34

11. A ball is projected upwards from the top of a tower with a velocity 50 ms^{-1} making an angle 30° with the horizontal. The height of tower is 70 m. After how many seconds from the instant of throwing, will the ball reach the ground? ($g = 10\ ms^{-2}$)
(a) 2 s
(b) 5 s
(c) 7 s
(d) 9 s

12. Average velocity of a particle in projectile motion between its starting point and the highest point of its trajectory is (projection speed = u, angle of projection from horizontal = θ)
(a) $u \cos\theta$
(b) $\frac{u}{2}\sqrt{1 + 3\cos^2\theta}$
(c) $\frac{u}{2}\sqrt{2 + \cos^2\theta}$
(d) $\frac{u}{2}\sqrt{1 + \cos^2\theta}$

13. A train is moving on a track at 30 ms^{-1}. A ball is thrown from it perpendicular to the direction of motion with 30 ms^{-1} at 45° from horizontal. Find the distance of ball from the point of projection on train to the point, where it strikes the ground.
(a) 90 m
(b) $90\sqrt{3}$ m
(c) 60 m
(d) $60\sqrt{3}$ m

14. A body is projected at time $t = 0$ from a certain point on a planet's surface with a certain velocity at a certain angle with the planet's surface (assumed horizontal). The horizontal and vertical displacements x and y (in metre) respectively vary with time t in second as, $x = (10\sqrt{3})\,t$ and $y = 10t - t^2$. The maximum height attained by the body is
(a) 75 m (b) 100 m (c) 50 m (d) 25 m

15. A ground to ground projectile is at point A at $t = \frac{T}{3}$, is at point B at $t = \frac{5T}{6}$ and reaches the ground at $t = T$. The difference in heights between points A and B is
(a) $\frac{gT^2}{6}$
(b) $\frac{gT^2}{12}$
(c) $\frac{gT^2}{18}$
(d) None of these

16. A fixed mortar fires a bomb at an angle of 53° above the horizontal with a muzzle velocity of 80 ms^{-1}. A tank is advancing directly towards the mortar on level ground at a constant speed of 5 m/s. The initial separation (at the instant mortar is fired) between the mortar and tank, so that the tank would be hit is [Take $g = 10\ ms^{-2}$]
(a) 662.4 m
(b) 526.3 m
(c) 486.6 m
(d) None of these

17. The range of a projectile when launched at angle θ is same as when launched at angle 2θ. What is the value of θ?

(a) $15°$ (b) $30°$ (c) $45°$ (d) $60°$

18. A stone is projected in air. Its time of flight is 3 s and range is 150 m. Maximum height reached by the stone is (Take, $g = 10 \text{ ms}^{-2}$)

(a) 37.5 m (b) 22.5 m (c) 90 m (d) 11.25 m

19. A body of mass 1 kg is projected with velocity 50 m/s at an angle of 30° with the horizontal. At the highest point of its path, a force 10 N starts acting on body for 5 s vertically upward besides gravitational force, what is horizontal range of the body? (Take $g = 10 \text{ m/s}^2$)

(a) $125\sqrt{3}$ m (b) $200\sqrt{3}$ m
(c) 500 m (d) $250\sqrt{3}$ m

20. A projectile can have same range from two angles of projection with same initial speed. If h_1 and h_2 be the maximum heights, then

(a) $R = \sqrt{h_1 h_2}$ (b) $R = \sqrt{2 h_1 h_2}$ (c) $R = 2\sqrt{h_1 h_2}$ (d) $R = 4\sqrt{h_1 h_2}$

21. The equation of motion of a projectile are given by $x = 36\,t$ m and $2y = 96\,t - 9.8\,t^2$ m. The angle of projection from horizontal is

(a) $\sin^{-1}\left(\frac{4}{5}\right)$ (b) $\sin^{-1}\left(\frac{3}{5}\right)$ (c) $\sin^{-1}\left(\frac{4}{3}\right)$ (d) $\sin^{-1}\left(\frac{3}{4}\right)$

22. A projectile, thrown with velocity v_0 at an angle α to the horizontal, has a range R. It will strike a vertical wall at a distance $R/2$ from the point of projection with a speed of

(a) v_0 (b) $v_0 \sin\alpha$ (c) $v_0 \cos\alpha$ (d) $\sqrt{\frac{gR}{2}}$

23. The velocity at the maximum height of a projectile is half of its initial velocity of projection (u). Its range on horizontal plane is

(a) $\frac{3u^2}{g}$ (b) $\frac{3}{2}\cdot\frac{u^2}{g}$ (c) $\frac{u^2}{3g}$ (d) $\frac{\sqrt{3}}{2}\cdot\frac{u^2}{g}$

24. A boy throws a ball with a velocity u at an angle θ with the horizontal. At the same instant, he starts running with uniform velocity to catch the ball before it hits the ground. To achieve this, he should run with a velocity of

(a) $u\cos\theta$ (b) $u\sin\theta$ (c) $u\tan\theta$ (d) $u\sec\theta$

25. Two balls are thrown simultaneously from ground with same velocity of 10 m/s but different angles of projection with horizontal. Both balls fall at same distance $5\sqrt{3}$ m from point of projection. What is the time interval between balls striking the ground?

(a) $(\sqrt{3} - 1)$ s (b) $(\sqrt{3} + 1)$ s (c) $\sqrt{3}$ s (d) 1 s

26. The equation of projectile is $y = \sqrt{3}x - \frac{g}{2}x^2$, the angle of its projection is

(a) $90°$ (b) zero
(c) $60°$ (d) $30°$

27. The equation of motion of a projectile is

$$y = 12x - \frac{3}{4}x^2$$

What is the range of the projectile?

(a) 12 m (b) 16 m (c) 20 m (d) 24 m

28. The maximum height attained by a projectile is increased by 10% by increasing its speed of projection, without changing the angle of projection. The percentage increase in the horizontal range will be

(a) 20%
(b) 15%
(c) 10%
(d) 5%

29. A ball is thrown up with a certain velocity at an angle θ to the horizontal. The kinetic energy (KE) of the ball varies with horizontal displacement x as

(a) 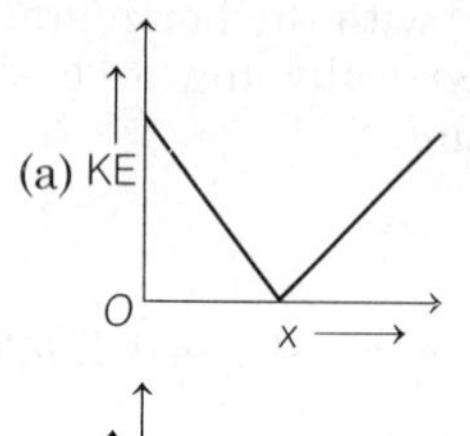

(b) 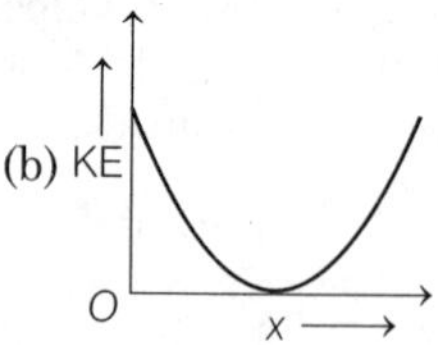

(c) 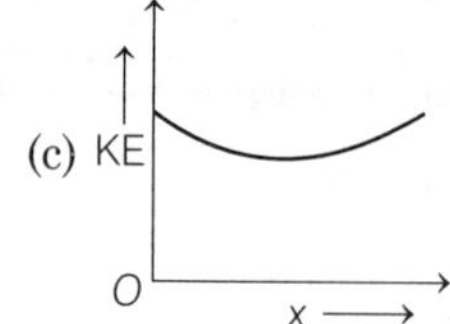

(d) 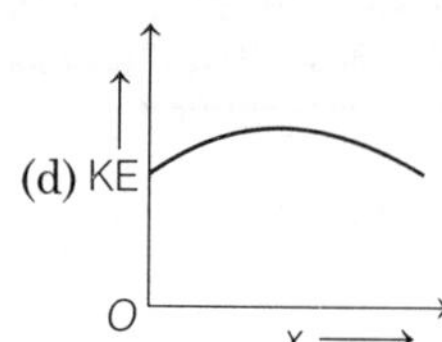

30. A ball is thrown up with a certain velocity at an angle θ to the horizontal. The kinetic energy (KE) of the ball varies with height h as

(a) 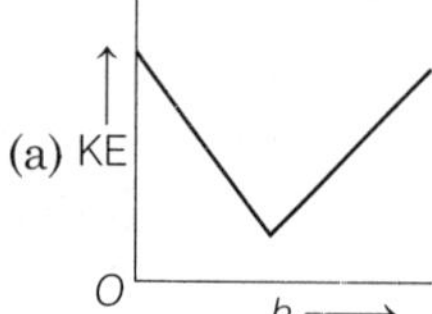

(b) 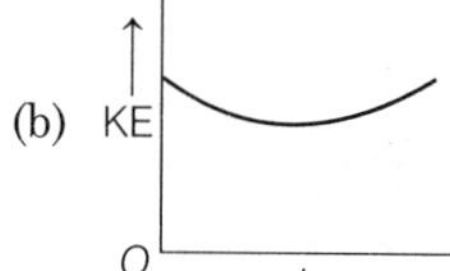

(c) 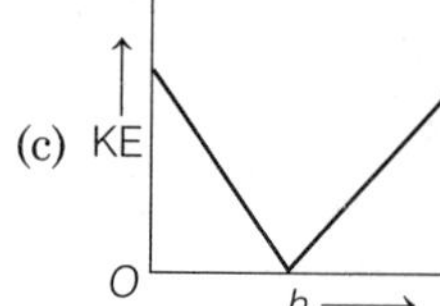

(d) 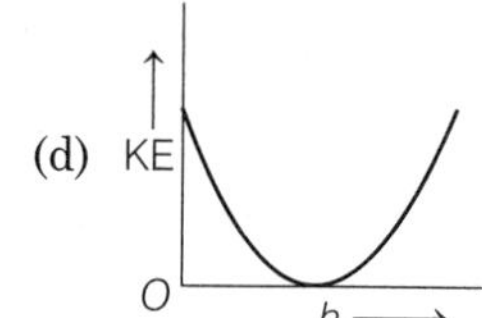

31. A ball is thrown at different angles with the same speed u and from the same point. It has the same range in both cases. If y_1 and y_2 be the heights attained in the two cases, then $y_1 + y_2$ equals to

(a) $\frac{u^2}{g}$
(b) $\frac{2u^2}{g}$
(c) $\frac{u^2}{2g}$
(d) $\frac{u^2}{4g}$

32. A ball is thrown from the ground to clear a wall 3 m high at a distance of 6 m and falls 18 m away from the wall, the angle of projection of ball is

(a) $\tan^{-1}\left(\frac{3}{2}\right)$
(b) $\tan^{-1}\left(\frac{2}{3}\right)$
(c) $\tan^{-1}\left(\frac{1}{2}\right)$
(d) $\tan^{-1}\left(\frac{3}{4}\right)$

33. A projectile is thrown with a velocity of 10 m/s at an angle of 60° with horizontal. The interval between the moments when speed is $5\sqrt{2}$ m/s is (Take, $g = 10 \text{ m/s}^2$)

(a) 1 s
(b) 3 s
(c) 2 s
(d) 4 s

34. A projectile is thrown with an initial velocity of $(a\hat{\mathbf{i}} + b\hat{\mathbf{j}})$ ms^{-1}. If the range of the projectile is twice the maximum height reached by it, then

(a) $a = 2b$
(b) $b = a$
(c) $b = 2a$
(d) $b = 4a$

35. A man standing on a hill top projects a stone horizontally with speed v_0 as shown in figure. Taking the coordinates system as given in the figure. The coordinates of the point, where the stone will hit the hill surface are

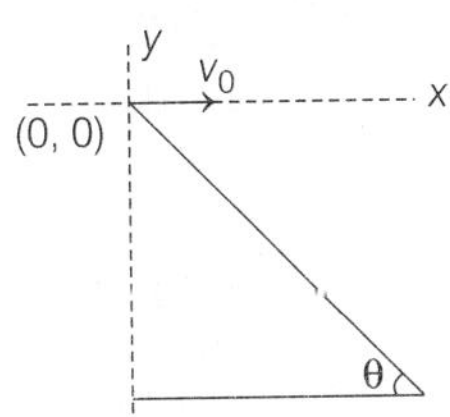

(a) $\left(\dfrac{2v_0^2 \tan\theta}{g}, -\dfrac{2v_0^2 \tan^2\theta}{g}\right)$ (b) $\left(\dfrac{2v_0^2}{g}, -\dfrac{2v_0^2 \tan^2\theta}{g}\right)$

(c) $\left(\dfrac{2v_0^2 \tan\theta}{g}, -\dfrac{2v_0^2}{g}\right)$ (d) $\left(\dfrac{2v_0^2 \tan^2\theta}{g}, -\dfrac{2v_0^2 \tan\theta}{g}\right)$

36. A body, projected horizontally with a speed u from the top of a tower of height h, reaches the ground at a horizontal distance R from the tower. Another body, projected horizontally from the top of a tower of height $4h$, reaches the ground at horizontal distance $2R$ from the tower. The initial speed of the second body is

(a) u (b) $2u$

(c) $3u$ (d) $4u$

37. A projectile is projected and it takes 9 s to reach in the horizontal plane through the point of projection. In its paths, it passes a point P after 4 s. The height of P above the horizontal plane is

(a) 10 m (b) 50 m

(c) 100 m (d) 200 m

38. The ceiling of a hall is 40 m. For maximum horizontal distance, the angle at which the ball can be thrown with a speed of 56 ms^{-1} without hitting the ceiling of the hall is (Take $g = 9.8$ ms^{-2})

(a) 60° (b) 30°

(c) 45° (d) data insufficient

39. A particle is projected on smooth inclined plane in a direction perpendicular to line of greatest slope with speed 8 ms^{-1}. Its speed at $t = 1$ s is

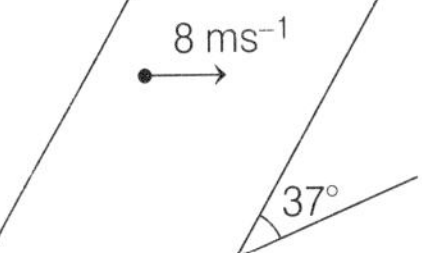

(a) 5 ms^{-1} (b) 8 ms^{-1}

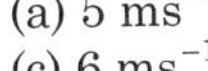

(c) 6 ms^{-1} (d) 10 ms^{-1}

40. A projectile is thrown with velocity u making angle θ with vertical. It just crosses the tops of two poles each of height h after 1s and 3s, respectively. The maximum height of projectile is

(a) 9.8 m (b) 19.6 m (c) 39.2 m (d) 4.9 m

41. Two particles A and B are projected from a building A is projected with speed $2v$ and angle 30° with horizontal and B with speed v and angle 60° with horizontal, which particle will hit the ground earlier

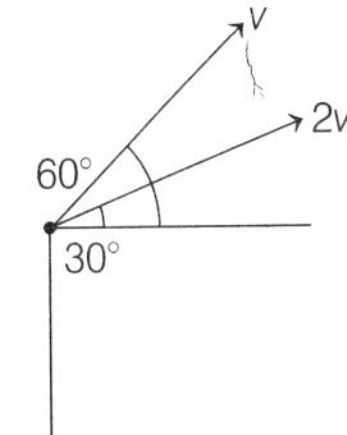

(a) Particle A

(b) Particle B

(c) Particle A and B will hit at same time

(d) Data insufficient

42. A projectile is thrown with velocity v at an angle θ with horizontal. When the projectile is at a height equal to half of the maximum height, the vertical component of the velocity of the projectile is

(a) $\frac{v\sin\theta}{4}$ (b) $\frac{v\sin\theta}{3}$

(c) $\frac{v\sin\theta}{\sqrt{2}}$ (d) $\frac{v\sin\theta}{\sqrt{3}}$

43. A projectile is given an initial velocity of $(\hat{\mathbf{i}} + 2\hat{\mathbf{j}})$ m/s, where $\hat{\mathbf{i}}$ is along the ground and $\hat{\mathbf{j}}$ is along the vertical. If $g = 10\,\text{m/s}^2$, then the equation of its trajectory is

(a) $y = x - 5x^2$ (b) $y = 2x - 5x^2$

(c) $4y = 2x - 5x^2$ (d) $4y = 2x - 25x^2$

Subjective Questions

1. At time $t = 0$, a small ball is projected from point A with a velocity of 60 m/s at 60° angle with horizontal. Neglect atmospheric resistance and determine the two times t_1 and t_2 when the velocity of the ball makes an angle of 45° with the horizontal x-axis.

2. A particle is projected from ground with velocity $20\sqrt{2}$ m/s at 45°. At what time, particle is at height 15 m from ground? (Take, $g = 10\,\text{m/s}^2$)

3. A particle is projected at an angle 60° with horizontal with a speed $v = 20$ m/s. Taking $g = 10\,\text{m/s}^2$. Find the time after which the speed of the particle remains half of its initial speed.

4. Two particles A and B are projected from ground towards each other with speeds 10 m/s and $5\sqrt{2}$ m/s at angles 30° and 45° with horizontal from two points separated by a distance of 15 m. Will they collide or not?

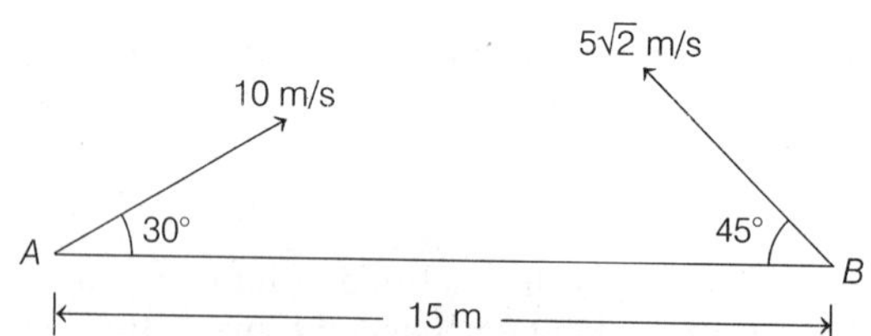

5. A body is projected up such that its position vector varies with time as $\mathbf{r} = \{3t\hat{\mathbf{i}} + (4t - 5t^2)\hat{\mathbf{j}}\}$ m. Here, t is in seconds. Find the time and x-coordinate of particle when its y-coordinate is zero.

6. A particle is projected along an inclined plane as shown in figure. What is the speed of the particle when it collides at point A? (Take, $g = 10\,\text{m/s}^2$)

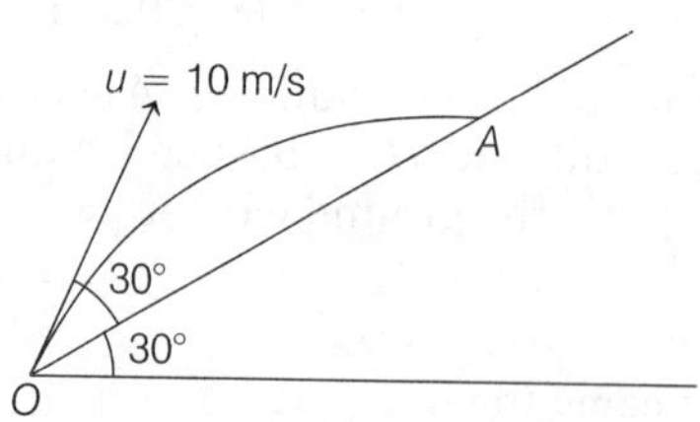

7. In the above problem, what is the component of its velocity perpendicular to the plane when it strikes at A ?

8. Two particles A and B are projected simultaneously from two towers of heights 10 m and 20 m respectively. Particle A is projected with an initial speed of $10\sqrt{2}$ m/s at an angle of 45° with horizontal, while particle B is projected horizontally with speed 10 m/s. If they collide in air, what is the distance d between the towers?

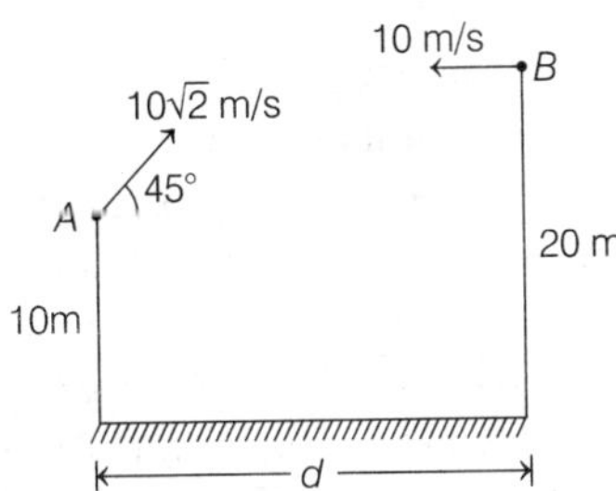

9. A particle is projected from the bottom of an inclined plane of inclination 30° with velocity of 40 m/s at an angle of 60° with horizontal. Find the speed of the particle when its velocity vector is parallel to the plane. (Take, $g = 10\ \text{m/s}^2$)

10. Two particles A and B are projected simultaneously in the directions shown in figure with velocities $v_A = 20\ \text{m/s}$ and $v_B = 10\ \text{m/s}$, respectively. They collide in air after $\frac{1}{2}$ s. Find

(a) the angle θ (b) the distance x.

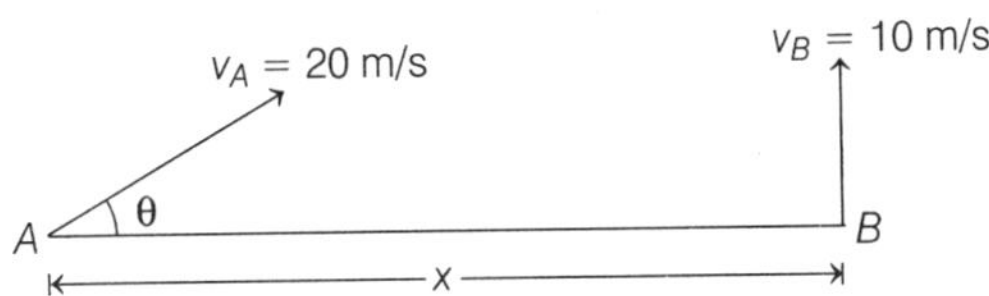

11. A ball is shot from the ground into the air. At a height of 9.1 m, its velocity is observed to be $\mathbf{v} = 7.6\hat{\mathbf{i}} + 6.1\hat{\mathbf{j}}$ in metre per second ($\hat{\mathbf{i}}$ is horizontal, $\hat{\mathbf{j}}$ is upward). Give the approximate answers.

(a) To what maximum height does the ball rise?
(b) What total horizontal distance does the ball travel?
(c) What is the magnitude and
(d) What is the direction of the ball's velocity just before it hits the ground?

12. A particle is projected with velocity $2\sqrt{gh}$, so that it just clears two walls of equal height h which are at a distance of $2h$ from each other. Show that the time of passing between the walls is $2\sqrt{\frac{h}{g}}$.

[**Hint :** First find velocity at height h. Treat it as initial velocity and $2h$ as the range.]

13. A particle is projected at an angle of elevation α and after t second, it appears to have an elevation of β as seen from the point of projection. Find the initial velocity of projection.

14. A projectile aimed at a mark, which is in the horizontal plane through the point of projection, falls a cm short of it when the elevation is α and goes b cm far when the elevation is β. Show that, if the speed of projection is same in all the cases the proper elevation is $\frac{1}{2}\sin^{-1}\left[\frac{b \sin 2\alpha + a \sin 2\beta}{a + b}\right]$

15. Two particles are simultaneously thrown in horizontal direction from two points on a riverbank, which are at certain height above the water surface. The initial velocities of the particles are $v_1 = 5$ m/s and $v_2 = 7.5$ m/s, respectively. Both particles fall into the water at the same time. First particle enters the water at a point $s = 10$ m from the bank. Determine

(a) the time of flight of the two particles,

(b) the height from which they are thrown,

(c) the point where the second particle falls in water.

16. A balloon is ascending at the rate $v = 12$ km/h and is being carried horizontally by the wind at $v_w = 20$ km/h. If a ballast bag is dropped from the balloon at the instant $h = 50$ m, determine the time needed for it to strike the ground. Assume that the bag was released from the balloon with the same velocity as the balloon. Also, find the speed with which the bag strikes the ground.

17. An elevator is going up with an upward acceleration of 1 m/s^2. At the instant, when its velocity is 2 m/s, a stone is projected upward from its floor with a speed of 2 m/s relative to the elevator, at an elevation of 30°.

(a) Calculate the time taken by the stone to return to the floor.

(b) Sketch the path of the projectile as observed by an observer outside the elevator.

(c) If the elevator was moving with a downward acceleration equal to g, how would the motion be altered?

18. Two particles A and B are projected simultaneously in a vertical plane as shown in figure. They collide at time t in air. Write down two necessary equations for collision to take place.

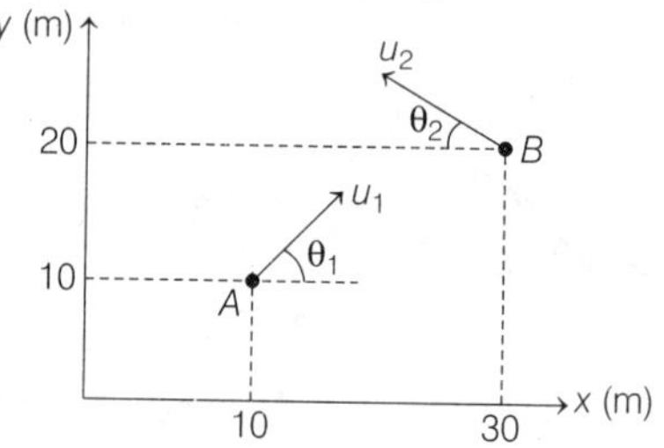

LEVEL 2

Objective Questions

Single Correct Option

1. A particle is dropped from a height h. Another particle which is initially at a horizontal distance d from the first is simultaneously projected with a horizontal velocity u and the two particles just collide on the ground. Then

(a) $d^2 = \frac{u^2h}{2h}$ (b) $d^2 = \frac{2u^2h}{g}$ (c) $d = h$ (d) $gd^2 = u^2h$

2. A ball is projected from point A with velocity 10 ms^{-1} perpendicular to the inclined plane as shown in figure. Range of the ball on the inclined plane is

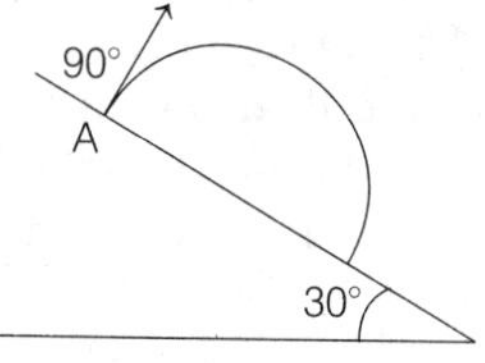

(a) $\frac{40}{3}$ m (b) $\frac{20}{3}$ m

(c) $\frac{12}{3}$ m (d) $\frac{60}{3}$ m

3. A heavy particle is projected with a velocity at an angle with the horizontal into the uniform gravitational field. The slope of the trajectory of the particle varies as

(a) 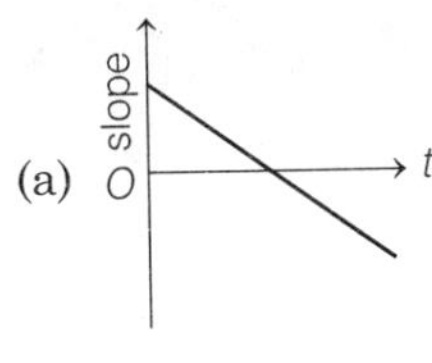

(b) 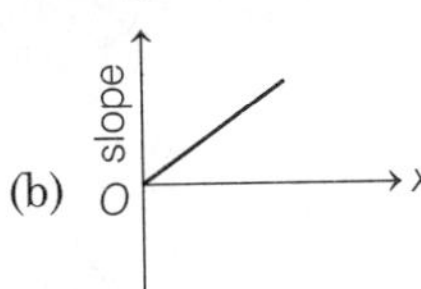

(c) 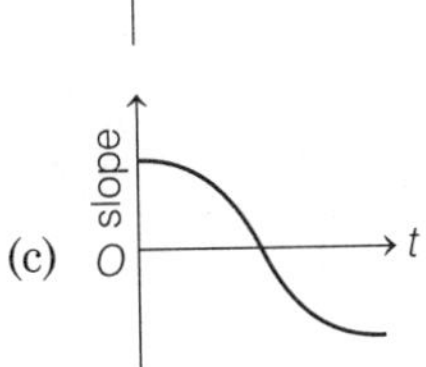

(d) 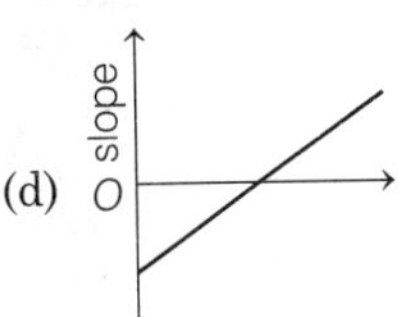

4. A particle starts from the origin of coordinates at time $t = 0$ and moves in the xy-plane with a constant acceleration α in the y-direction. Its equation of motion is $y = \beta x^2$. Its velocity component in the x-direction is

(a) variable
(b) $\sqrt{\frac{2\alpha}{\beta}}$
(c) $\frac{\alpha}{2\beta}$
(d) $\sqrt{\frac{\alpha}{2\beta}}$

5. A projectile is projected with speed u at an angle of 60° with horizontal from the foot of an inclined plane. If the projectile hits the inclined plane horizontally, the range on inclined plane will be

(a) $\frac{u^2\sqrt{21}}{2g}$
(b) $\frac{3u^2}{4g}$
(c) $\frac{u^2}{2\beta}$
(d) $\frac{\sqrt{21}\,u^2}{8g}$

6. A particle is projected at an angle 60° with speed $10\sqrt{3}$ m/s, from the point A, as shown in the figure. At the same time, the wedge is made to move with speed $10\sqrt{3}$ m/s towards right as shown in the figure. Then, the time after which particle will strike with wedge is

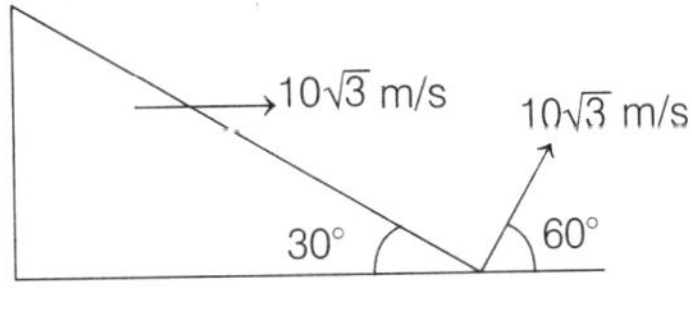

(a) 2 s
(b) $2\sqrt{3}$ s
(c) $\frac{4}{\sqrt{3}}$ s
(d) None of these

7. A particle moves along the parabolic path $x = y^2 + 2y + 2$ in such a way that Y-component of velocity vector remains 5 ms^{-1} during the motion. The magnitude of the acceleration of the particle is

(a) 50 ms^{-2}
(b) 100 ms^{-2}
(c) $10\sqrt{2}$ ms^{-2}
(d) 0.1 ms^{-2}

8. A shell fired from the base of a mountain just clears it. If α is the angle of projection, then the angular elevation of the summit β is

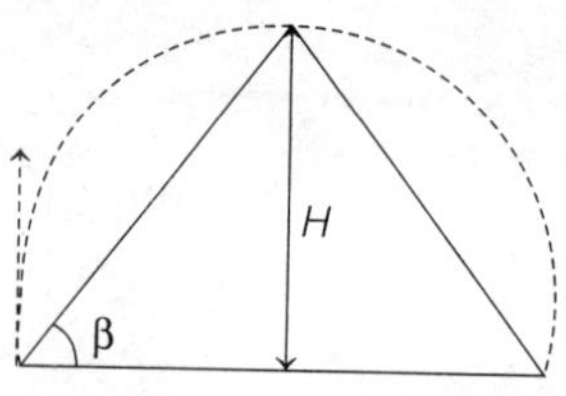

(a) $\frac{\alpha}{2}$

(b) $\tan^{-1}\left(\frac{1}{2}\right)$

(c) $\tan^{-1}\left(\frac{\tan\alpha}{2}\right)$

(d) $\tan^{-1}(2\tan\alpha)$

9. In the figure shown, the two projectiles are fired simultaneously. The minimum distance between them during their flight is

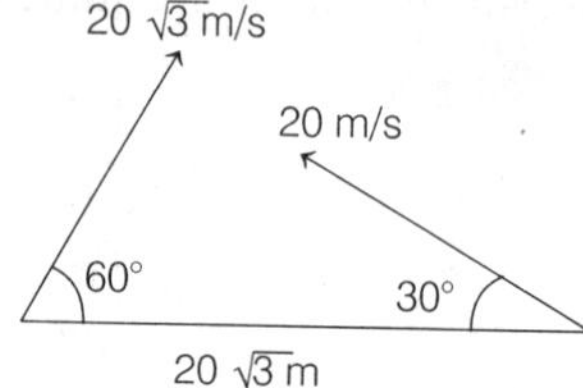

(a) 20 m

(b) $10\sqrt{3}$ m

(c) 10 m

(d) None of these

10. A very broad elevator is going up vertically with a constant acceleration of 2 m/s^2. At the instant, when its velocity is 4 m/s, a ball is projected from the floor of the lift with a speed of 4 m/s relative to the floor at an elevation of 30°. The time taken by the ball to return the floor is (Take, $g = 10$ m/s^2)

(a) $\frac{1}{2}$ s (b) $\frac{1}{3}$ s (c) $\frac{1}{4}$ s (d) 1 s

11. A particle moves along a parabolic path $y = -9x^2$ in such a way that the x-component of velocity remains constant and has a value $\frac{1}{3}$ m/s. The acceleration of the particle is

(a) $\frac{1}{3}$ m/s^2 (b) 3 m/s^2 (c) $\frac{2}{3}$ m/s^2 (d) 2 m/s^2

12. Two particles A and B are projected simultaneously from a fixed point of the ground. Particle A is projected on a smooth horizontal surface with speed v, while particle B is projected in air with speed $\frac{2v}{\sqrt{3}}$. If particle B hits the particle A, the angle of projection of B with the horizontal is

(a) 30°

(b) 60°

(c) 45°

(d) Both (a) and (b)

13. A projectile is thrown with some initial velocity at an angle α to the horizontal. Its velocity when it is at the highest point is $(2/5)^{1/2}$ times the velocity when it is at height half of the maximum height. Find the angle of projection α with the horizontal.

(a) 30°

(b) 45°

(c) 60°

(d) 37°

14. If the instantaneous velocity of a particle projected as shown in figure is given by $\mathbf{v} = a\hat{\mathbf{i}} + (b - ct)\hat{\mathbf{j}}$, where a, b and c are positive constants, the range on the horizontal plane will be

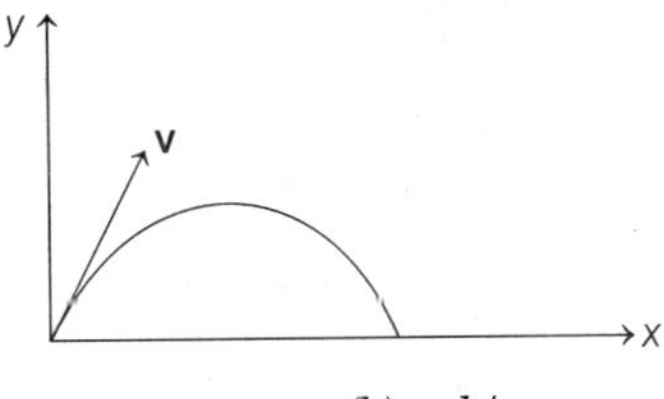

(a) $2ab/c$
(b) ab/c
(c) ac/b
(d) $a/2bc$

15. A stone is projected from a point on the ground so as to hit a bird on the top of a vertical pole of height h and then attain a maximum height $2h$ above the ground. If at the instant of projection the bird flies away horizontally with a uniform speed and if the stone hits the bird while descending, then the ratio of the speed of the bird to the horizontal speed of the stone is

(a) $\frac{\sqrt{2}}{\sqrt{2}+1}$
(b) $\frac{\sqrt{2}}{\sqrt{2}-1}$
(c) $\frac{1}{\sqrt{2}} + \frac{1}{2}$
(d) None of these

16. Two stones are thrown up simultaneously from the edge of a cliff 240 m high with initial speed of 10m/s and 40 m/s, respectively. Which of the following graph best represents the time variation of relative position of the second stone with respect to the first? (Assume stones do not rebound after hitting the ground and neglect air resistance (Take, $g = 10\text{ m/s}^2$)

(a)
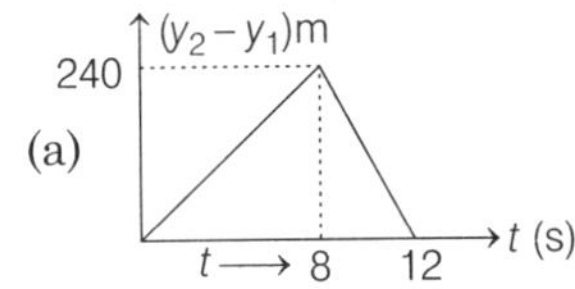

(b)
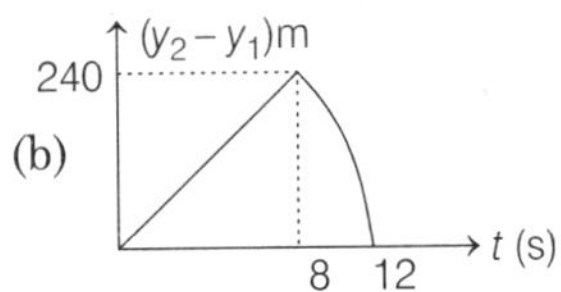

(c)
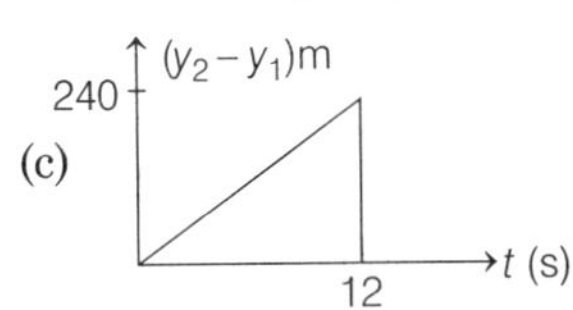

(d)
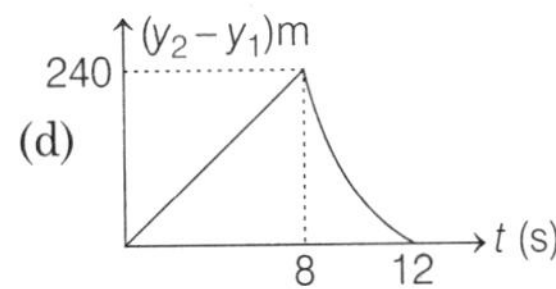

More than One Correct Options

1. Two particles projected from the same point with same speed u at angles of projection α and β strike the horizontal ground at the same point. If h_1 and h_2 are the maximum heights attained by the projectile, R is the range for both and t_1 and t_2 are their times of flights respectively, then

(a) $\alpha + \beta = \frac{\pi}{2}$
(b) $R = 4\sqrt{h_1 h_2}$
(c) $\frac{t_1}{t_2} = \tan\alpha$
(d) $\tan\alpha = \sqrt{\frac{h_1}{h_2}}$

2. A ball is dropped from a height of 49 m. The wind is blowing horizontally. Due to wind a constant horizontal acceleration is provided to the ball. Choose the correct statement (s). (Take, $g = 9.8\text{ ms}^{-2}$)

(a) Path of the ball is a straight line
(b) Path of the ball is a curved one
(c) The time taken by the ball to reach the ground is 3.16 s
(d) Actual distance travelled by the ball is more than 49 m

3. A particle is projected from a point P with a velocity v at an angle θ with horizontal. At a certain point Q, it moves at right angles to its initial direction. Then,

(a) velocity of particle at Q is $v \sin\theta$
(b) velocity of particle at Q is $v \cot\theta$
(c) time of flight from P to Q is (v/g) cosecθ
(d) time of flight from P to Q is $(v/g) \sec\theta$

4. At a height of 15 m from ground velocity of a projectile is $\mathbf{v} = (10\hat{\mathbf{i}} + 10\hat{\mathbf{j}})$. Here, $\hat{\mathbf{j}}$ is vertically upwards and $\hat{\mathbf{i}}$ is along horizontal direction, then (Take, $g = 10 \text{ ms}^{-2}$)

(a) particle was projected at an angle of 45° with horizontal
(b) time of flight of projectile is 4 s
(c) horizontal range of projectile is 100 m
(d) maximum height of projectile from ground is 20 m

5. Which of the following quantities remain constant during projectile motion?

(a) Average velocity between two points
(b) Average speed between two points
(c) $\dfrac{d\mathbf{v}}{dt}$
(d) $\dfrac{d^2\mathbf{v}}{dt^2}$

6. In the projectile motion shown is figure, given $t_{AB} = 2$ s, then (Take, $g = 10 \text{ ms}^{-2}$)

(a) particle is at point B at 3 s
(b) maximum height of projectile is 20 m
(c) initial vertical component of velocity is 20 ms^{-1}
(d) horizontal component of velocity is 20 ms^{-1}

7. The trajectory of a projectile is $y = x(1 - x)$, where y and x are in metres.

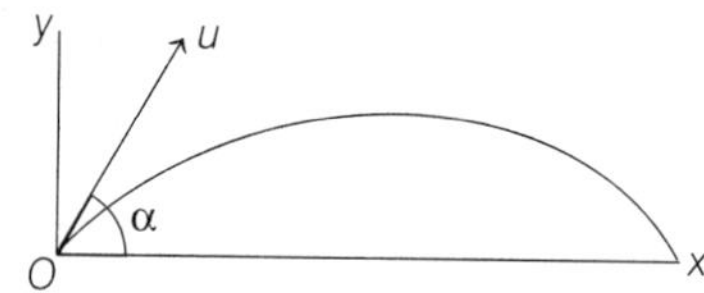

Choose the correct option(s).

(a) The horizontal range is 1 m
(b) The angle of projection is 45°
(c) The horizontal range is 2m
(d) The angle of projection is 30°

Match the Columns

1. Particle-1 is just dropped from a tower. 1 s later particle-2 is thrown from the same tower horizontally with velocity 10 ms^{-1}. Taking $g = 10 \text{ ms}^{-2}$, match the following two columns at $t = 2$ s.

Column I	Column II
(a) Horizontal displacement between two	(p) 10 SI units
(b) Vertical displacement between two	(q) 20 SI units
(c) Magnitude of relative horizontal component of velocity	(r) $10\sqrt{2}$ SI units
(d) Magnitude of relative vertical component of velocity	(s) None of the above

2. In a projectile motion, given $H = \frac{R}{2} = 20$ m. Here, H is maximum height and R the horizontal range. For the given condition, match the following two columns.

Column I	Column II
(a) Time of flight	(p) 1
(b) Ratio of vertical component of velocity and horizontal component of velocity	(q) 2
(c) Horizontal component of velocity (in m/s)	(r) 10
(d) Vertical component of velocity (in m/s)	(s) None of the above

3. A particle can be thrown at a constant speed at different angles. When it is thrown at 15° with horizontal, it falls at a distance of 10 m from point of projection. For this speed of particle, match the following two columns.

Column I	Column II
(a) Maximum horizontal range which can be taken with this speed	(p) 10 m
(b) Maximum height which can be taken with this speed	(q) 20 m
(c) Range at 75°	(r) 15 m
(d) Height at 30°	(s) None of the above

4. In projectile motion, if vertical component of velocity is increased to two times, keeping horizontal component unchanged, then

Column I	Column II
(a) Time of flight	(p) will remain same
(b) Maximum height	(q) will become two times
(c) Horizontal range	(r) will become four times
(d) Angle of projection with horizontal	(s) None of the above

5. In projectile motion shown in figure.

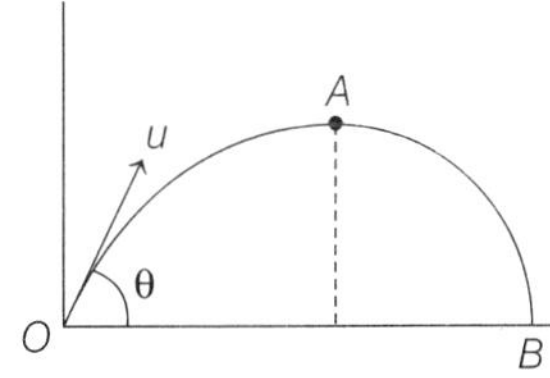

Column I	Column II
(a) Change in velocity between O and A	(p) $u \cos\theta$
(b) Average velocity between O and A	(q) $u \sin\theta$
(c) Change in velocity between O and B	(r) $2u \sin\theta$
(d) Average velocity between O and B	(s) None of the above

6. Particle-1 is projected from ground (take it origin) at time $t = 0$, with velocity $(30\hat{\mathbf{i}} + 30\hat{\mathbf{j}})\ \text{ms}^{-1}$. Particle-2 is projected from (130 m, 75 m) at time $t = 1$ s with velocity $(-20\,\hat{\mathbf{i}} + 20\,\hat{\mathbf{j}})\ \text{ms}^{-1}$. Assuming $\hat{\mathbf{j}}$ to be vertically upward and $\hat{\mathbf{i}}$ to be in horizontal direction, match the following two columns at $t = 2$ s.

Column I	Column II
(a) Horizontal distance between two	(p) 30 SI units
(b) Vertical distance between two	(q) 40 SI units
(c) Relative horizontal component of velocity between two	(r) 50 SI units
(d) Relative vertical component of velocity between two	(s) None of the above

7. The trajectories of the motion of three particles are shown in the figure. Match the entries of Column I with the entries of Column II. Neglect air resistance.

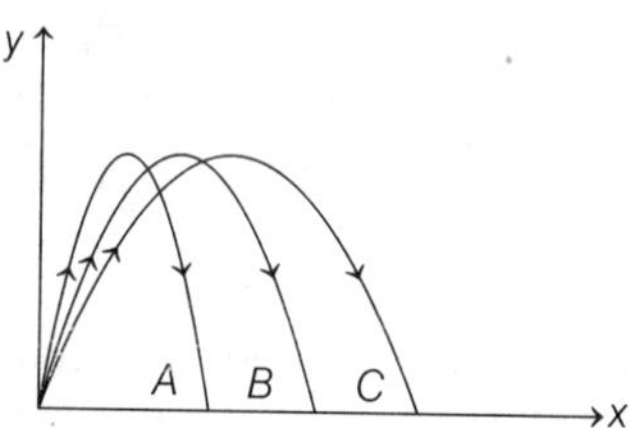

Column I	Column II
(a) Time of flight is least for	(p) A
(b) Vertical component of velocity is greatest for	(q) B
(c) Horizontal component of velocity is greatest for	(r) C
(d) Launch speed is least for	(s) same for all

Subjective Questions

1. Determine the horizontal velocity v_0 with which a stone must be projected horizontally from a point P, so that it may hit the inclined plane perpendicularly. The inclination of the plane with the horizontal is θ and point P is at a height h above the foot of the incline, as shown in the figure.

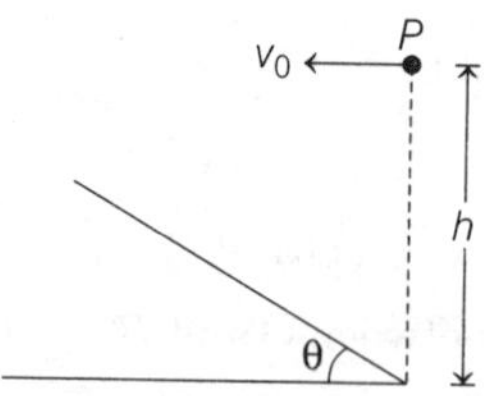

2. A particle is dropped from point P at time $t = 0$. At the same time another particle is thrown from point O as shown in the figure and it collides with the particle P. Acceleration due to gravity is along the negative y-axis. If the two particles collide 2 s after they start, find the initial velocity v_0 of the particle which was projected from O. Point O is not necessarily on ground.

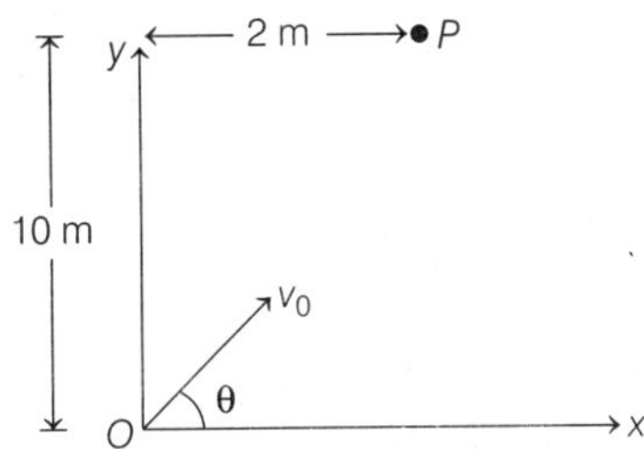

3. Two particles are simultaneously projected in the same vertical plane from the same point with velocities u and v at angles α and β with horizontal. Find the time that elapses when their velocities are parallel.

4. A projectile takes off with an initial velocity of 10 m/s at an angle of elevation of 45°. It is just able to clear two hurdles of height 2 m each, separated from each other by a distance d. Calculate d. At what distance from the point of projection is the first hurdle placed? (Take, $g = 10\text{ m/s}^2$)

5. A particle is released from a certain height $H = 400$ m. Due to the wind, the particle gathers the horizontal velocity component $v_x = ay$, where $a = \sqrt{5}\text{ s}^{-1}$ and y is the vertical displacement of the particle from the point of release, then find
   (a) the horizontal drift of the particle when it strikes the ground,
   (b) the speed with which particle strikes the ground. (Take $g = 10\text{ m/s}^2$)

6. A train is moving with a constant speed of 10 m/s in a circle of radius $\dfrac{16}{\pi}$ m. The plane of the circle lies in horizontal x-y plane. At time $t = 0$, train is at point P and moving in counter-clockwise direction. At this instant, a stone is thrown from the train with velocity 10 m/s relative to train towards negative x-axis at an angle of 37° with vertical z-axis.

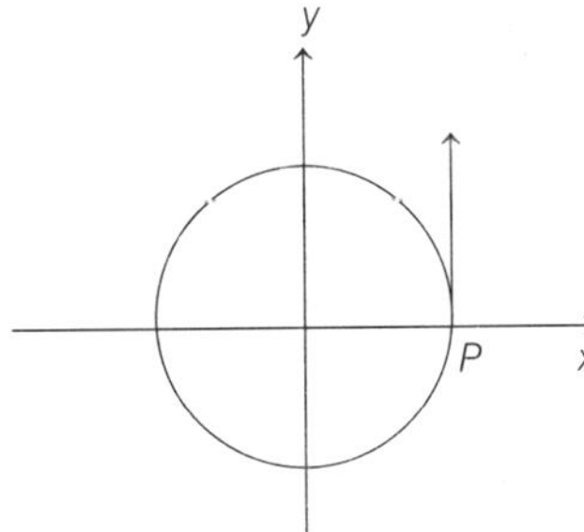

Find
   (a) the velocity of particle relative to ground at the highest point of its trajectory.
   (b) the coordinates of points on the ground, where it finally falls and that of the highest point of its trajectory. $\left(\text{Take, } g = 10\text{ m/s}^2, \sin 37° = \dfrac{3}{5}\right)$

7. A particle is projected from an inclined plane OP_1 from A with velocity $v_1 = 8\ \text{ms}^{-1}$ at an angle 60° with horizontal. An another particle is projected at the same instant from B with velocity $v_2 = 16\ \text{ms}^{-1}$ and perpendicular to the plane OP_2 as shown in figure. After time $10\sqrt{3}$ s, there separation was minimum and found to be 70 m. Then, find distance AB.

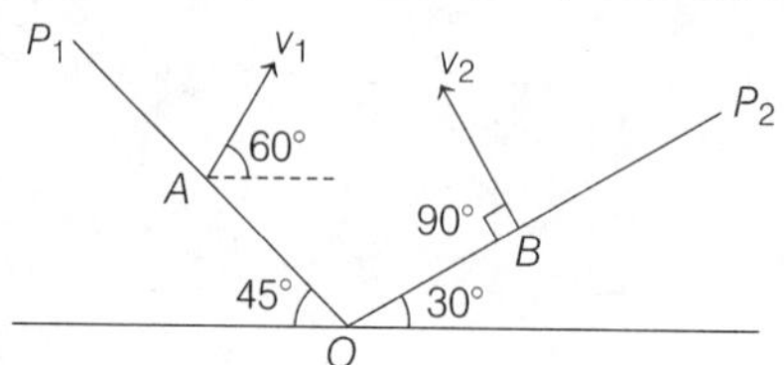

8. A particle is projected from point O on the ground with velocity $u = 5\sqrt{5}$ m/s at angle $\alpha = \tan^{-1}(0.5)$. It strikes at a point C on a fixed smooth plane AB having inclination of 37° with horizontal as shown in figure. If the particle does not rebound, calculate

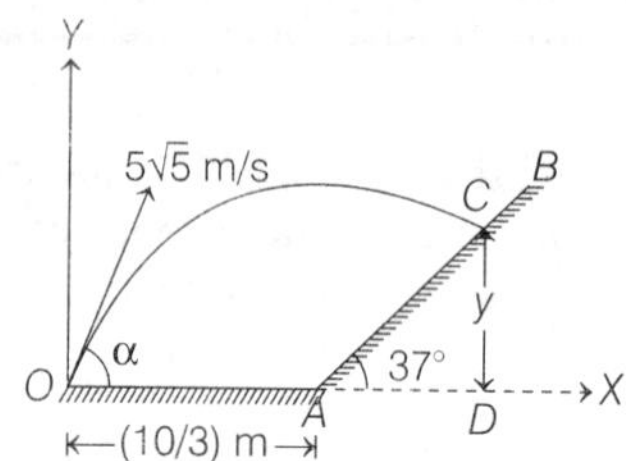

(a) coordinates of point C in reference to coordinate system as shown in the figure.
(b) maximum height from the ground to which the particle rises. (Take, $g = 10\ \text{m/s}^2$)

9. A plank fitted with a gun is moving on a horizontal surface with speed of 4 m/s along the positive x-axis. The z-axis is in vertically upward direction. The mass of the plank including the mass of the gun is 50 kg. When the plank reaches the origin, a shell of mass 10 kg is fired at an angle of 60° with the positive x-axis with a speed of $v = 20$ m/s with respect to the velocity of plank (and gun) just after shell is fired in x-z plane. Find the position vector of the shell at $t = 2$ s after firing it. (Take, $g = 9.8\ \text{m/s}^2$)

Integer Type Questions

10. A stone targeted at point P which is in the same horizontal plane through the point of projections, falls x_1 distance before the point P when angle of projection is 15°. It goes x_2 distance beyond when the angle of projection is 45°. The proper angle of projection is 30° to hit the point P. If the velocity of projection remains same, find the value of $\dfrac{(\sqrt{3}-1)x_1}{x_2}$.

11. A particle is projected from the base of a cone with a speed of u at an angle of projection α. The particle grazes the vertex of the cone and strikes again at the base. If θ is half angle of cone and h is its height. Find the value of $\left(\dfrac{u^2}{gh} - \dfrac{1}{2}\tan^2\theta\right)$.

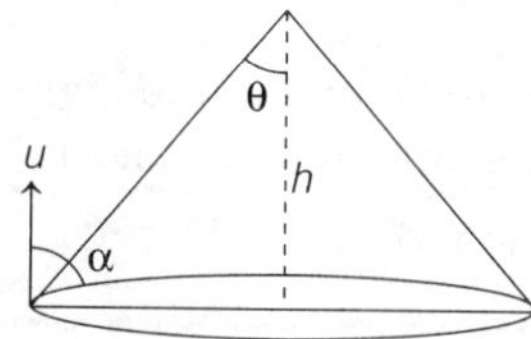

12. Three balls are thrown in the same vertical plane with different speeds and at different angles. The area of triangle formed by the balls at instant t is proportional to t^n. Find the value of n.

13. Two particles A and B are projected from point O with equal speeds. They both hit the point P of an inclined plane of inclination 15°. Particle A is projected at an angle 30° with inclined plane. If the ratio of time of flight of particles A and B is $1:\sqrt{n}$, find the value of n.

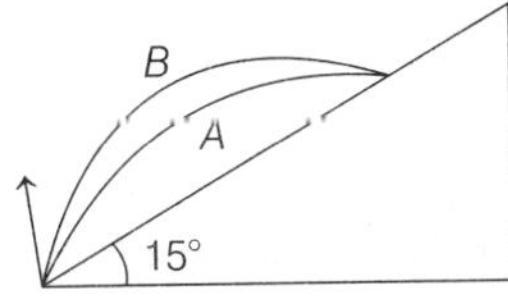

14. A projectile is projected from ground with least velocity to cross a wall 3.6 m high and 4.8 m away from the point of projection. The range of projectile is 8.4 m. If angle of projection is α and $\tan\alpha = \frac{n}{4}$, find the value of n.

15. A particle starts from point A and slides along smooth inclined with an acceleration 6 ms^{-2} and finally strikes at point P after travelling same distance in air. If $x_0 = \frac{36}{n}$ m, find the value of n.

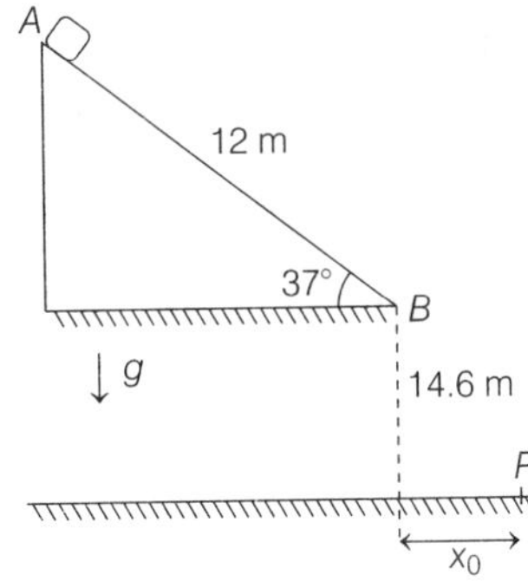

16. The length of inclined plane is 15 m. A stone is projected with speed v_0 from point A to cross through point B. If minimum value of v_0 is $3x$ ms^{-1}, find the value of x.

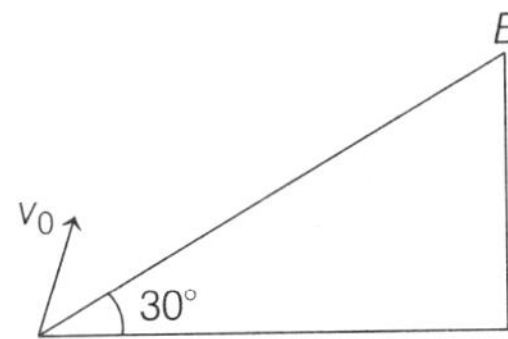

Answers

Introductory Exercise 7.1

1. $\sqrt{2}$ s 2. False 3. True 4. $\mathbf{v} = (40\hat{\mathbf{i}} + 10\hat{\mathbf{j}})$ m/s, $\mathbf{s} = (80\hat{\mathbf{i}} + 40\hat{\mathbf{j}})$ m
5. $t = 5$ s, $d = 100$ m, $\mathbf{v} = (20\hat{\mathbf{i}} - 30\hat{\mathbf{j}})$ ms^{-1}

Introductory Exercise 7.2

1. (a) $20\sqrt{5}$ m/s at angle $\tan^{-1}\left(\frac{1}{2}\right)$ with horizontal, (b) 100 m.
2. Between two points lying on the same horizontal line
3. $u \cos \alpha$
4. $2u \sin \alpha$, downwards
5. (a) 80 m, 20 m, 4s (b) $(20\hat{\mathbf{i}} + 10\hat{\mathbf{j}})$ ms^{-1} (c) $(20\hat{\mathbf{i}} - 20\hat{\mathbf{j}})$ ms^{-1}
6. (a) 30 ms^{-1} (vertically downwards) (b) 20.62 ms^{-1}
7. $\frac{5}{\sqrt{2}}$ ms^{-1}
8. (a) $\sqrt{20}$ s (b) $20\sqrt{20}$ m (c) 49 m/s, $\theta = \tan^{-1}(\sqrt{5})$ with horizontal
9. No
10. $\sqrt{\frac{a(1+b^2)}{2c}}$

Introductory Exercise 7.3

1. 1.69 s, 39 m 2. 6.31 s, 145.71 m
3. 2.31 s, 53.33 mm 4. (a) A vertical straight line (b) A parabola
5. (a) zero (b) 20 ms^{-1} in horizontal direction (c) 40 m
6. 60°

Exercises

LEVEL 1

Assertion and Reason

1. (d) 2. (a) 3. (b) 4. (a) 5. (c) 6. (a or b) 7. (b) 8. (b) 9. (b)

Single Correct Option

1. (c) 2. (c) 3. (a) 4. (b) 5. (b) 6. (b) 7. (d) 8. (c) 9. (d) 10. (d)
11. (c) 12. (b) 13. (a) 14. (d) 15. (d) 16. (d) 17. (b) 18. (d) 19. (d) 20. (d)
21. (a) 22. (c) 23. (d) 24. (a) 25. (a) 26. (c) 27. (b) 28. (c) 29. (c) 30. (a)
31. (c) 32. (b) 33. (a) 34. (c) 35. (a) 36. (a) 37. (c) 38. (b) 39. (d) 40. (b)
41. (b) 42. (c) 43. (b)

Subjective Questions

1. $t_1 = 2.19$ s, $t_2 = 8.20$ s
2. 3 s and 1 s
3. $\sqrt{3}$ s
4. No
5. time = zero, 0.8 s, x-coordinate = 0, 2.4 m
6. $\frac{10}{\sqrt{3}}$ m/s
7. 5 m/s
8. 20 m
9. $\frac{40}{\sqrt{3}}$ m/s
10. (a) 30° (b) $5\sqrt{3}$ m

11. (a) 11 m, (b) 23 m (c) 16.6 m/s (d) $\tan^{-1}(2)$, below horizontal

13. $u = \dfrac{gt\cos\beta}{\sin(\alpha-\beta)}$

15. (a) 2s (b) 19.6 m (c) 15 m

16. 3.55 s, 32.7 m/s

17. (a) 0.18 s (c) a straight line with respect to elevator and projectile with respect to ground

18. $(u_1\cos\theta_1 + u_2\cos\theta_2)t = 20$ ...(i) $(u_1\sin\theta_1 - u_2\sin\theta_2)t = 10$ ...(ii)

LEVEL 2

Single Correct Option

1. (b) 2. (a) 3. (a) 4. (d) 5. (d) 6. (a) 7. (a) 8. (c) 9. (b) 10. (b)
11. (d) 12. (a) 13. (c) 14. (a) 15. (d) 16. (b)

More than One Correct Options

1. (all) 2. (a,c,d) 3. (b,c) 4. (b,d) 5. (c,d) 6. (all) 7. (a,b)

Match the Columns

1. (a)→(p), (b)→(s), (c)→(p), (d)→(p)
2. (a)→(s), (b)→(q), (c)→(r), (d)→(s)
3. (a)→(q), (b)→(p), (c)→(p), (d)→(s)
4. (a)→(q), (b)→(r), (c)→(q), (d)→(s)
5. (a)→(q), (b)→(s), (c)→(r), (d)→(p)
6. (a)→(r), (b)→(r), (c)→(r), (d)→(s)
7. (a)→(s), (b)→(s), (c)→(r), (d)→(p)

Subjective Questions

1. $v_0 = \sqrt{\dfrac{2gh}{2+\cot^2\theta}}$

2. $\sqrt{26}\ \text{ms}^{-1}$ at angle $\theta = \tan^{-1}(5)$ with x-axis

3. $t = \dfrac{uv\sin(\alpha-\beta)}{g(v\cos\beta - u\cos\alpha)}$

4. 4.47 m, 2.75 m

5. (a) 2.67 km (b) 0.9 km/s

6. (a) $(-6\hat{\mathbf{i}} + 10\hat{\mathbf{j}})\ \text{ms}^{-1}$ (b) (−4.5 m, 16 m, 0), (0.3 m, 8.0 m, 3.2 m)

7. 250 m

8. (a) (5 m, 1.25 m) (b) 4.45 m

9. $(24\hat{\mathbf{i}} + 15\hat{\mathbf{k}})$ m

10. 2

11. 2

12. 2

13. 2

14. 7

15. 5

16. 5

8

Laws of Motion

8.1 Types of Forces

There are basically three forces which are commonly encountered in mechanics.

Field Forces

These are the forces in which contact between two objects is not necessary. Gravitational force between two bodies and electrostatic force between two charges are two examples of field forces. Weight ($w = mg$) of a body comes in this category.

Contact Forces

Two bodies in contact exert equal and opposite forces on each other. If the contact is frictionless, the contact force is perpendicular to the common surface and known as **normal reaction.**

If however, the objects are in rough contact and move (or have a tendency to move) relative to each other without losing contact then **frictional force** arise which oppose such motion. Again each object exerts a frictional force on the other and the two forces are equal and opposite. This force is perpendicular to normal reaction. Thus, the contact force (F) between two objects is made up of two forces.

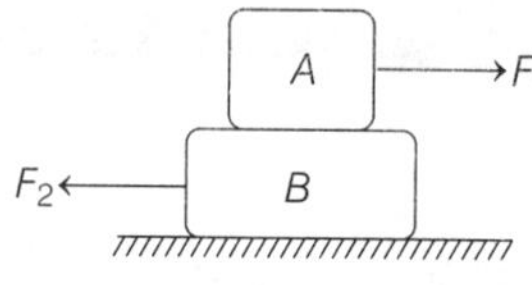

Fig. 8.1

(i) Normal reaction (N) (ii) Force of friction (f)

and since these two forces are mutually perpendicular,

$$F = \sqrt{N^2 + f^2}$$

Note *In this book normal reaction at most of the places has been represented by N. But at some places, it is also represented by R. This is because N is confused with the SI unit of force newton.*

Consider two wooden blocks A and B being rubbed against each other.

In Fig. 8.1, A is being moved to the right while B is being moved leftward. In order to see more clearly which forces act on A and which on B, a second diagram is drawn showing a space between the blocks but they are still supposed to be in contact.

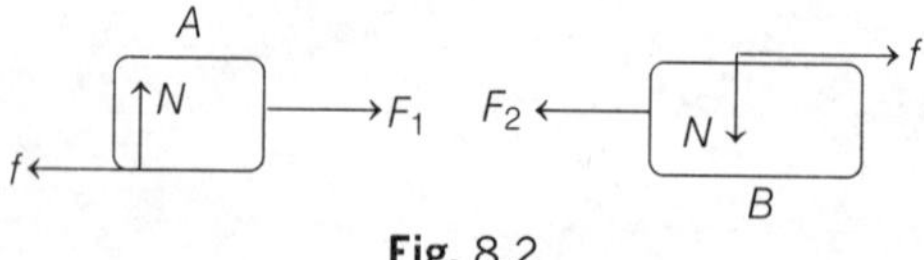

Fig. 8.2

In Fig. 8.2, the two normal reactions each of magnitude N are perpendicular to the surface of contact between the blocks and the two frictional forces each of magnitude f act along that surface, each in a direction opposing the motion of the block upon which it acts.

Note *Forces on block B from the ground are not shown in the figure.*

Attachment to Another Body

Tension (T) in a string and **spring force** ($F = kx$) come in this group. Regarding the tension and string, the following three points are important to remember:

1. If a string is inextensible the magnitude of acceleration of any number of masses connected through the string is always same.

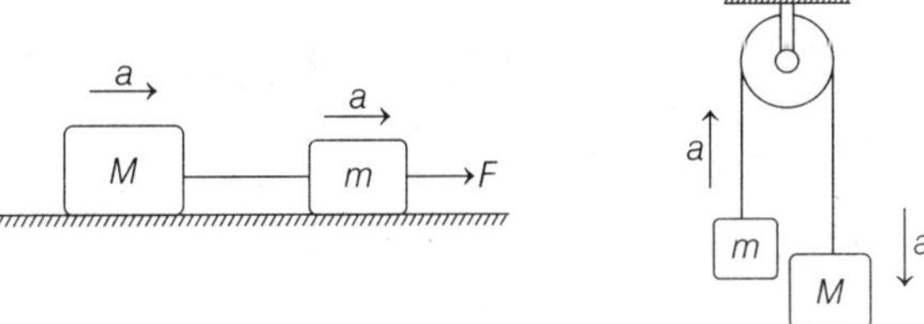

Fig. 8.3

2. If a string is massless, the tension in it is same everywhere. However, if a string has a mass and it is accelerated, tension at different points will be different.
3. If pulley is massless and frictionless, tension will be same on both sides of the pulley.

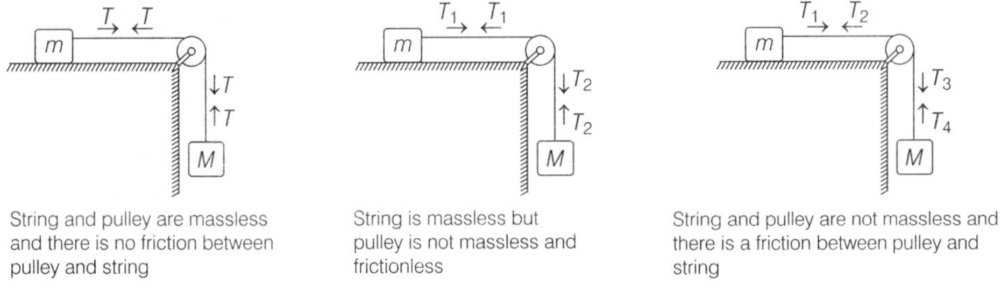

Fig. 8.4

Spring force ($F = kx$) has been discussed in detail in the chapter of work, energy and power.

Hinge Force

In the figure shown there is a hinge force on the rod (from the hinge). There are two methods of finding a hinge force :

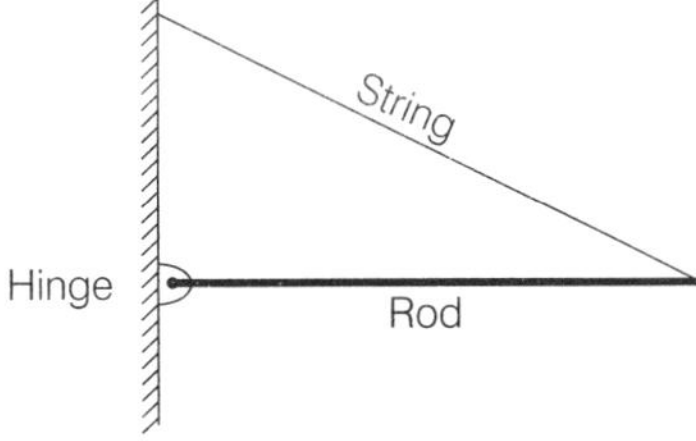

Fig. 8.5

(i) either you find its horizontal (H) and vertical (V) components

(ii) or you find its magnitude and direction.

Extra Points to Remember

- Normal reaction is perpendicular to the common tangent direction and always acts towards the body. It is just like a pressure force ($F = PA$) which is also perpendicular to a surface and acts towards it.

  For example

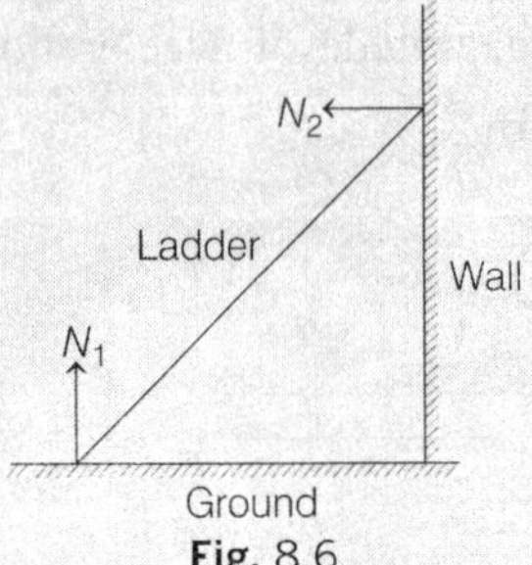

Fig. 8.6

Normal reaction on ladder from ground is N_1 and from wall is N_2.

- Tension in a string is as shown in Fig. 8.7.

  In the figure :

  T_1 goes to block A (force applied by string on block A).

  T_2 and T_3 to pulley P_1

  T_4, T_5 and T_7 to pulley P_2

  T_8 to block B and

  T_6 to roof

  If string and pullies are massless and there is no friction in the pullies, then

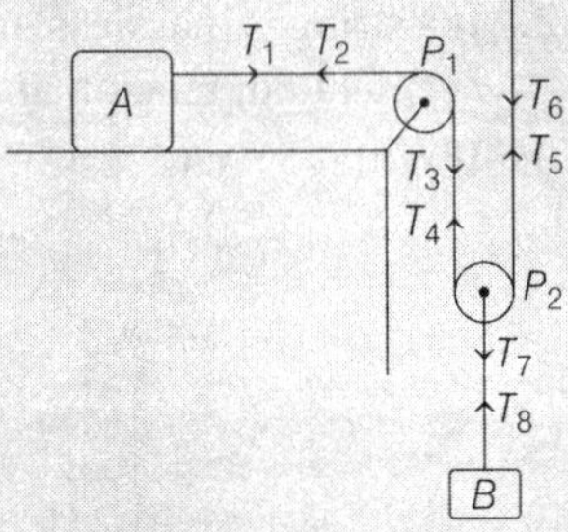

Fig. 8.7

$$T_1 = T_2 = T_3 = T_4 = T_5 = T_6 \quad \text{and} \quad T_7 = T_8$$

- If a string is attached with a block then it can apply force on the block only in a direction away from the block (in the form of tension).

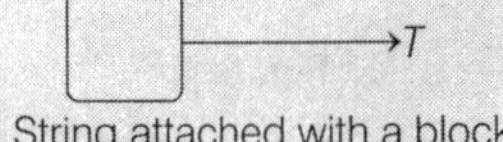

String attached with a block

Fig. 8.8

If the block is attached with a rod, then it can apply force on the block in both directions, towards the block (may be called push) or away from the block (called pull)

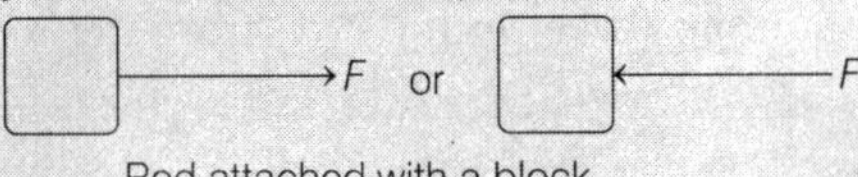

Rod attached with a block

Fig. 8.9

- All forces discussed above make a pair of equal and opposite forces acting on two different bodies (Newton's third law).

8.2 Free Body Diagram

No system, natural or man made, consists of a single body alone or is complete in itself. A single body or a part of the system can, however be isolated from the rest by appropriately accounting for its effect on the remaining system.

A free body diagram (FBD) consists of a diagrammatic representation of a single body or a sub-system of bodies isolated from its surroundings showing all the forces acting on it.

Consider, for example, a book lying on a horizontal surface.

A free body diagram of the book alone would consist of its weight ($w = mg$), acting through the centre of gravity and the reaction (N) exerted on the book by the surface.

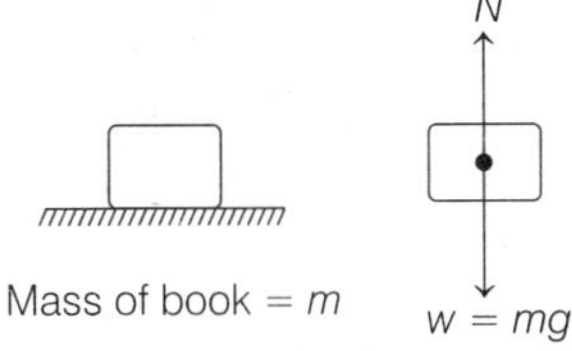

Fig. 8.10

Example 8.1 *A cylinder of weight W is resting on a V-groove as shown in figure. Draw its free body diagram.*

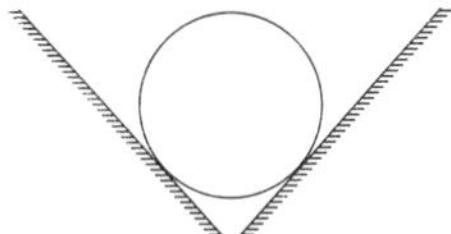

Fig. 8.11

Solution The free body diagram of the cylinder is as shown in Fig. 8.12.

Here, w = weight of cylinder and N_1 and N_2 are the normal reactions between the cylinder and the two inclined walls.

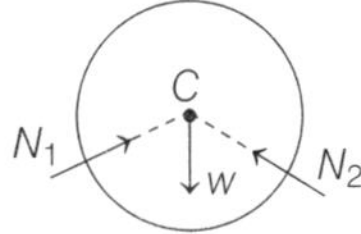

Fig. 8.12

Example 8.2 *Three blocks A, B and C are placed one over the other as shown in figure. Draw free body diagrams of all the three blocks.*

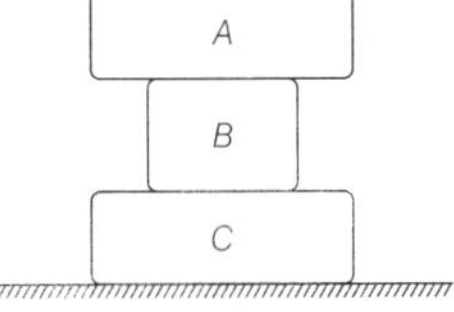

Fig. 8.13

Solution Free body diagrams of A, B and C are shown below.

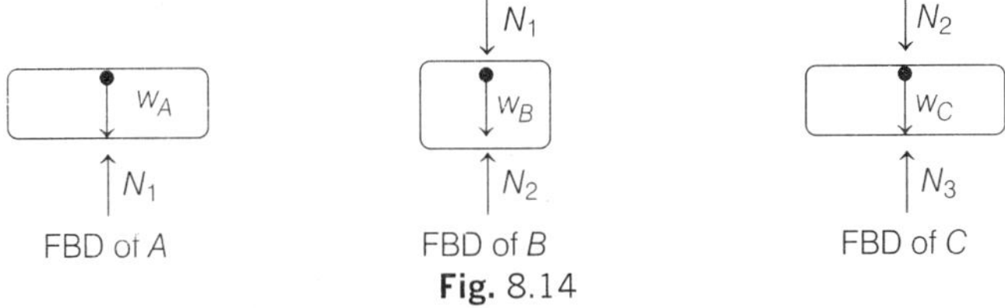

Fig. 8.14

Here, N_1 = normal reaction between A and B

N_2 = normal reaction between B and C

and N_3 = normal reaction between C and ground.

Example 8.3 *A block of mass m is attached with two strings as shown in figure. Draw the free body diagram of the block.*

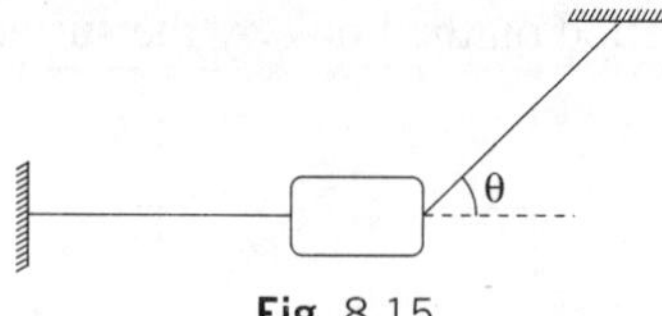

Fig. 8.15

Solution The free body diagram of the block is as shown in Fig. 8.16.

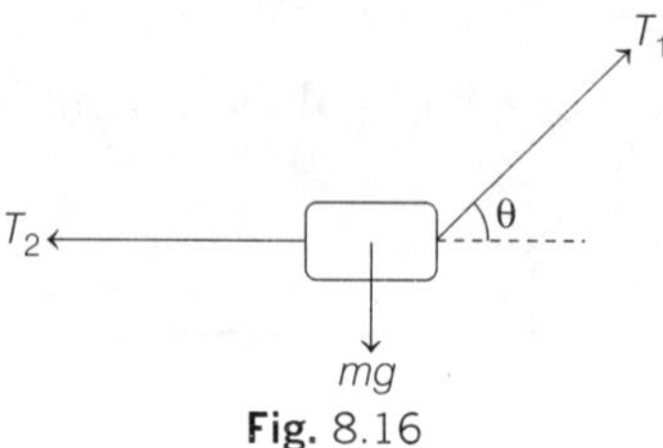

Fig. 8.16

8.3 Equilibrium

Forces which have zero resultant and zero turning effect will not cause any change in the motion of the object to which they are applied. Such forces (and the object) are said to be in equilibrium. For understanding the equilibrium of an object under two or more concurrent or coplanar forces let us first discuss the resolution of force and moment of a force about some point.

Resolution of a Force

When a force is replaced by an equivalent set of components, it is said to be resolved. One of the most useful ways in which to resolve a force is to choose only two components (although a force may be resolved in three or more components also) which are at right angles also. The magnitude of these components can be very easily found using trigonometry.

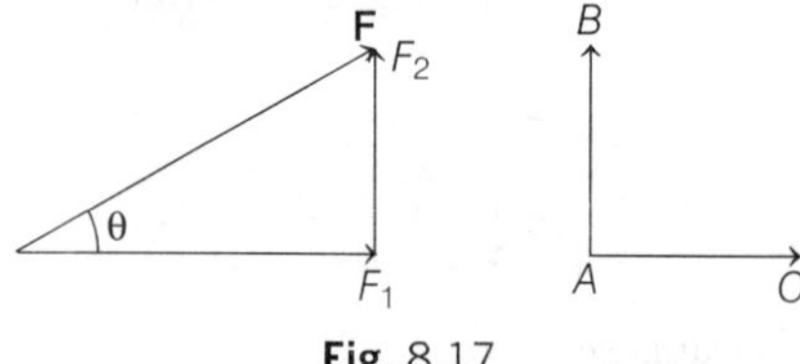

Fig. 8.17

In Fig. 8.17, $F_1 = F \cos\theta =$ component of **F** along AC

$F_2 = F \sin\theta =$ component of **F** perpendicular to AC or along AB

Finding such components is referred to as resolving a force in a pair of perpendicular directions. Note that the component of a force in a direction perpendicular to itself is zero. For example, if a force of 10 N is applied on an object in horizontal direction then its component along vertical is zero. Similarly, the component of a force in a direction parallel to the force is equal to the magnitude of the force. For example component of the above force in the direction of force (horizontal) will be 10 N. In the opposite direction the component is −10 N.

Example 8.4 *Resolve a weight of 10 N in two directions which are parallel and perpendicular to a slope inclined at 30° to the horizontal.*

Solution Component perpendicular to the plane

$$w_{\perp} = w\cos 30° = (10)\frac{\sqrt{3}}{2} = 5\sqrt{3}\text{ N}$$

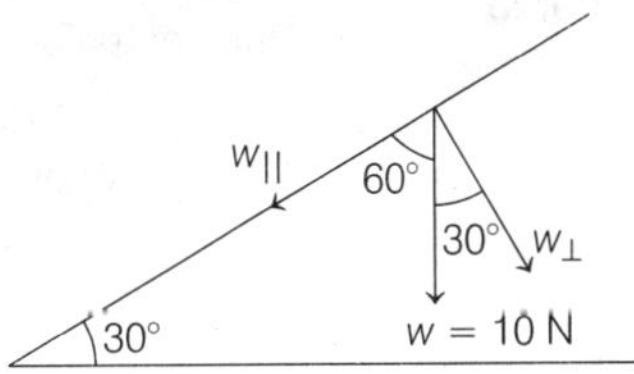

Fig. 8.18

and component parallel to the plane

$$w_{||} = w\sin 30° = (10)\left(\frac{1}{2}\right) = 5\text{ N}$$

Example 8.5 *Resolve horizontally and vertically a force F = 8 N which makes an angle of 45° with the horizontal.*

Solution Horizontal component of **F** is

$$F_H = F\cos 45° = (8)\left(\frac{1}{\sqrt{2}}\right) = 4\sqrt{2}\text{ N}$$

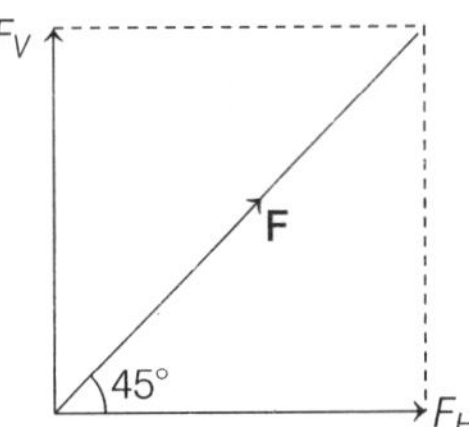

Fig. 8.19

and vertical component of **F** is $F_V = F\sin 45° = (8)\left(\frac{1}{\sqrt{2}}\right) = 4\sqrt{2}\text{ N}$

Example 8.6 *A body is supported on a rough plane inclined at 30° to the horizontal by a string attached to the body and held at an angle of 30° to the plane. Draw a diagram showing the forces acting on the body and resolve each of these forces*

(a) horizontally and vertically,

(b) parallel and perpendicular to the plane.

Solution The forces are

The tension in the string T

The normal reaction with the plane N

The weight of the body w and the friction f

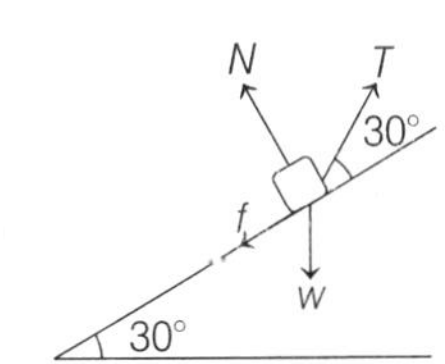

Fig. 8.20

(a) Resolving horizontally and vertically

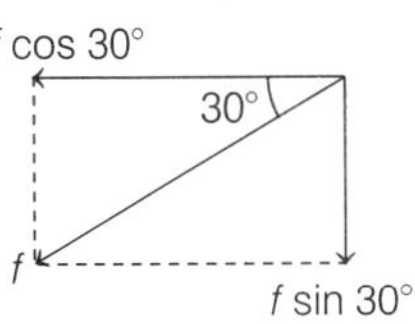

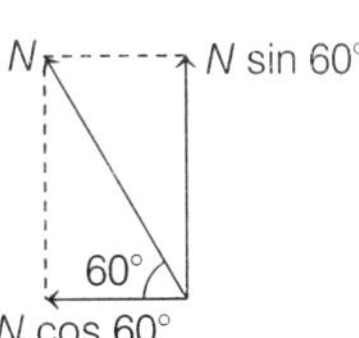

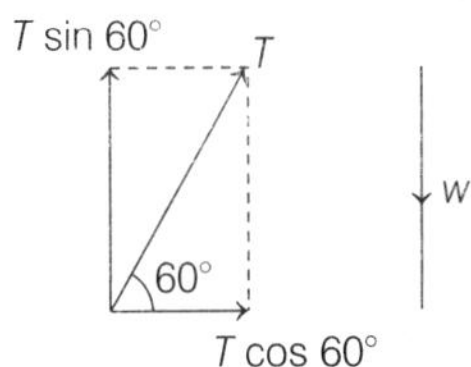

Fig. 8.21

Resolving horizontally and vertically in the senses OX and OY as shown, the components are

Force	Components	
	Parallel to *OX* (horizontal)	**Parallel to *OY*** (vertical)
f	$-f\cos 30°$	$-f\sin 30°$
N	$-N\cos 60°$	$N\sin 60°$
T	$T\cos 60°$	$T\sin 60°$
w	0	$-w$

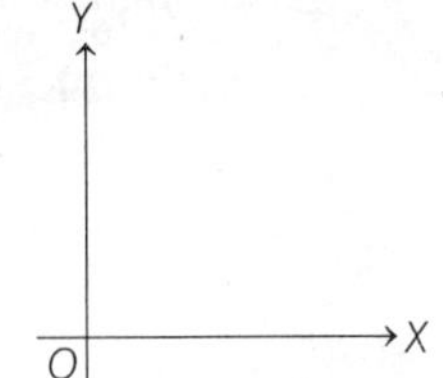

Fig. 8.22

(b) Resolving parallel and perpendicular to the plane

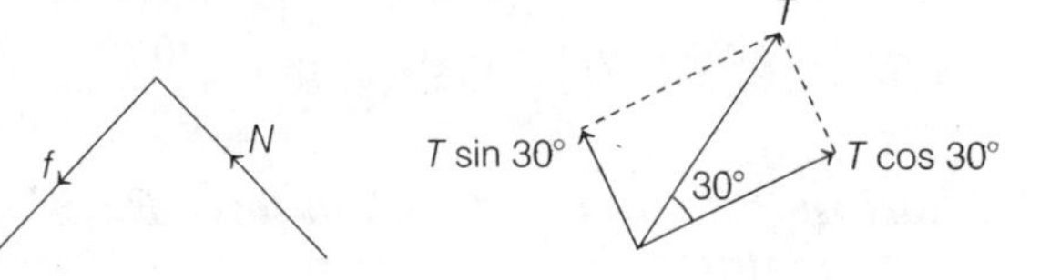

Fig. 8.23

Resolving parallel and perpendicular to the plane in the senses OX' and OY' as shown, the components are :

Force	Components	
	Parallel to *OX'* (parallel to plane)	**Parallel to *OY'*** (perpendicular to plane)
f	$-f$	0
N	0	N
T	$T\cos 30°$	$T\sin 30°$
w	$-w\sin 30°$	$-w\cos 30°$

Fig. 8.24

Moment of a Force

The general name given to any turning effect is **torque.** The magnitude of torque, also known as the moment of a force F is calculated by multiplying together the magnitude of the force and its perpendicular distance $r_\perp$ from the axis of rotation. This is denoted by C or τ (tau).

i.e. $$C = Fr_\perp \quad \text{or} \quad \tau = Fr_\perp$$

Direction of Torque

The angular direction of a torque is the sense of the rotation it would cause.

Consider a lamina that is free to rotate in its own plane about an axis perpendicular to the lamina and passing through a point A on the lamina. In the diagram, the moment about the axis of rotation of the force F_1 is F_1r_1 anticlock-wise and the moment of the force F_2 is F_2r_2 clockwise. A convenient way to differentiate between clockwise and anticlock-wise torques is to allocate a positive sign to one sense (usually, but not invariably, this is anticlockwise) and negative sign to the other. With this convention, the moments of F_1 and F_2 are $+F_1r_1$ and $-F_2r_2$ (when using a sign convention in any problem it is advisable to specify the chosen positive sense).

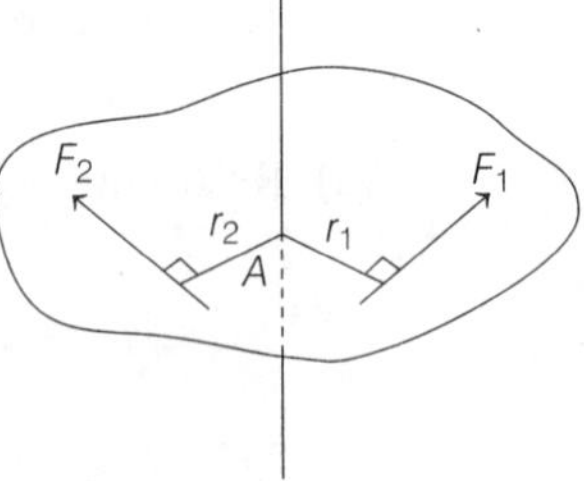

Fig. 8.25

Zero Moment

If the line of action of a force passes through the axis of rotation, its perpendicular distance from the axis is zero. Therefore, its moment about that axis is also zero.

Note *Later in the chapter of rotation we will see that torque is a vector quantity.*

Example 8.7 *ABCD is a square of side 2 m and O is its centre. Forces act along the sides as shown in the diagram. Calculate the moment of each force about*

(a) an axis through A and perpendicular to the plane of square.

(b) an axis through O and perpendicular to the plane of square.

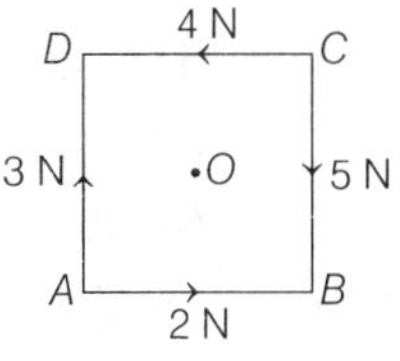

Fig. 8.26

Solution Taking anticlockwise moments as positive we have:

(a) Magnitude of force	2 N	5 N	4 N	3 N
Perpendicular distance from A	0	2 m	2 m	0
Moment about A	0	–10 N-m	+8 N-m	0

(b) Magnitude of force	2 N	5 N	4 N	3 N
Perpendicular distance from O	1 m	1 m	1 m	1 m
Moment about O	+2 N-m	–5 N-m	+4 N-m	–3 N-m

Example 8.8 *Forces act as indicated on a rod AB which is pivoted at A. Find the anticlockwise moment of each force about the pivot.*

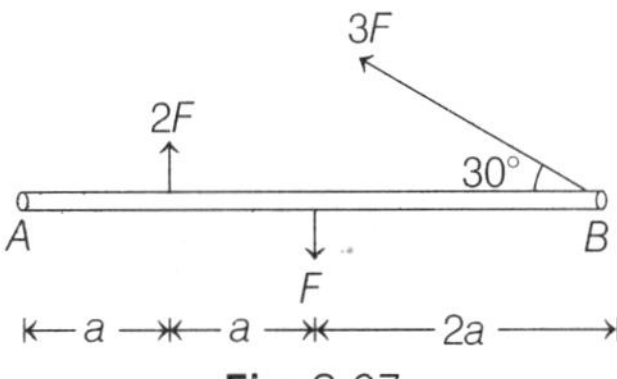

Fig. 8.27

Solution

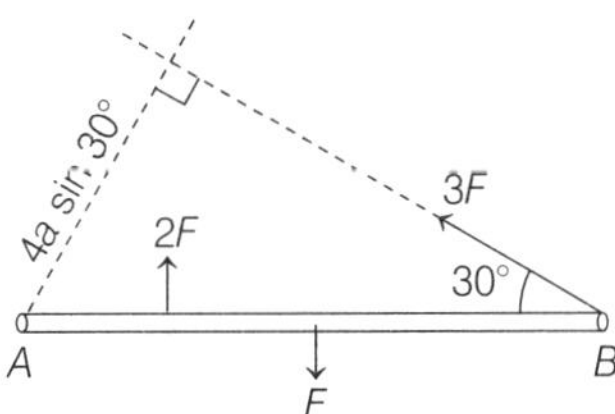

Fig. 8.28

Magnitude of force	2F	F	3F
Perpendicular distance from A	a	2a	$4a \sin 30° = 2a$
Anticlockwise moment about A	+2 Fa	–2 Fa	+6 Fa

Coplanar Forces in Equilibrium

When an object is in equilibrium under the action of a set of two or more coplanar forces, each of three factors which comprise the possible movement of the object must be zero, i.e. the object has

(i) no linear movement along any two mutually perpendicular directions OX and OY.

(ii) no rotation about any axis.

The set of forces must, therefore, be such that

(a) the algebraic sum of the components parallel to OX is zero or $\Sigma F_x = 0$

(b) the algebraic sum of the components parallel to OY is zero or $\Sigma F_y = 0$

(c) the resultant moment about any specified axis is zero or $\Sigma \tau_{\text{any axis}} = 0$

Thus, for the equilibrium of a set of two or more coplanar forces

$$\Sigma F_x = 0$$
$$\Sigma F_y = 0 \quad \text{and} \quad \Sigma \tau_{\text{any axis}} = 0$$

Using the above three conditions, we get only three set of equations. So, in a problem number of unknowns should not be more than three.

Example 8.9 *A rod AB rests with the end A on rough horizontal ground and the end B against a smooth vertical wall. The rod is uniform and of weight w. If the rod is in equilibrium in the position shown in figure. Find*

(a) frictional force at A

(b) normal reaction at A

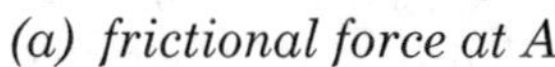

(c) normal reaction at B.

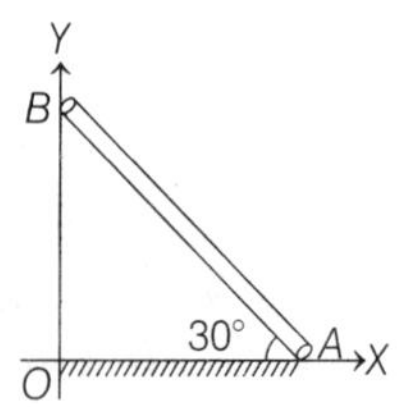

Fig. 8.29

Solution Let length of the rod be $2l$. Using the three conditions of equilibrium. Anticlockwise moment is taken as positive.

(i) $\Sigma F_X = 0 \Rightarrow \quad \therefore \quad N_B - f_A = 0$

or $\quad N_B = f_A \quad$ ...(i)

(ii) $\Sigma F_Y = 0 \Rightarrow \quad \therefore \quad N_A - w = 0$

or $\quad N_A = w \quad$ ...(ii)

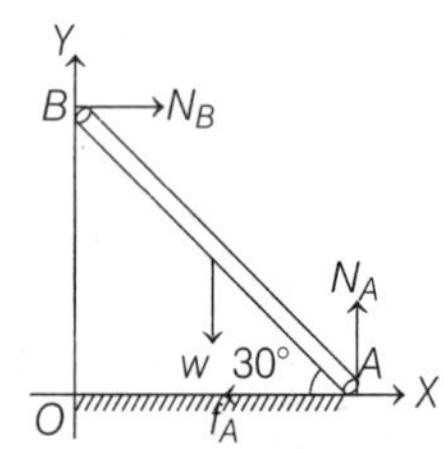

Fig. 8.30

(iii) $\Sigma \tau_O = 0$

$$\therefore \quad N_A (2l \cos 30°) - N_B (2l \sin 30°) - w(l \cos 30°) = 0$$

or
$$\sqrt{3} N_A - N_B - \frac{\sqrt{3}}{2} w = 0 \quad \text{...(iii)}$$

Solving these three equations, we get

(a) $f_A = \frac{\sqrt{3}}{2} w \quad$ (b) $N_A = w \quad$ (c) $N_B = \frac{\sqrt{3}}{2} w$

Exercise : What happens to N_A, N_B and f_A if (a) Angle $\theta = 30°$ is slightly increased, (b) A child starts moving on the ladder from A to B without changing the angle θ.

Ans (a) Unchanged, decrease, decrease, (b) Increase, increase, increase

Equilibrium of Concurrent Coplanar Forces

If an object is in equilibrium under two or more concurrent coplanar forces the algebraic sum of the components of forces in any two mutually perpendicular directions OX and OY should be zero, i.e. the set of forces must be such that

(i) the algebraic sum of the components parallel to OX is zero, i.e. $\Sigma F_x = 0$.

(ii) the algebraic sum of the components parallel to OY is zero, i.e. $\Sigma F_y = 0$.

Thus, for the equilibrium of two or more concurrent coplanar forces

$$\Sigma F_x = 0$$
$$\Sigma F_y = 0$$

The third condition of zero moment about any specified axis is automatically satisfied if the moment is taken about the point of intersection of the forces. So, here we get only two equations. Thus, number of unknown in any problem should not be more than two.

Example 8.10 *An object is in equilibrium under four concurrent forces in the directions shown in figure. Find the magnitudes of* $\mathbf{F}_1$ *and* $\mathbf{F}_2$.

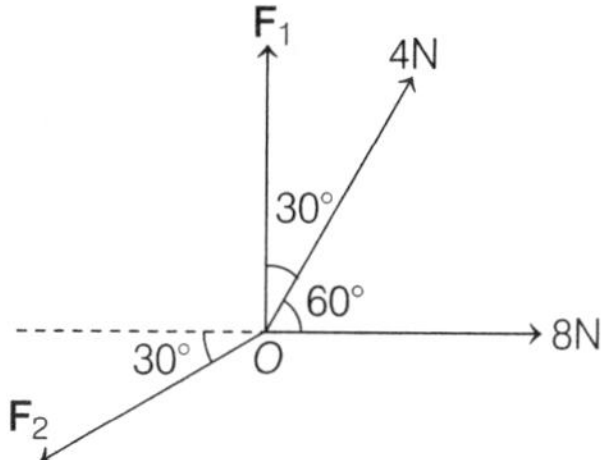

Fig. 8.31

Solution The object is in equilibrium. Hence,

(i) $\Sigma F_x = 0$

$$\therefore \quad 8 + 4\cos 60° - F_2 \cos 30° = 0$$

or $$8 + 2 - F_2 \frac{\sqrt{3}}{2} = 0$$

or $$F_2 = \frac{20}{\sqrt{3}} \text{ N}$$

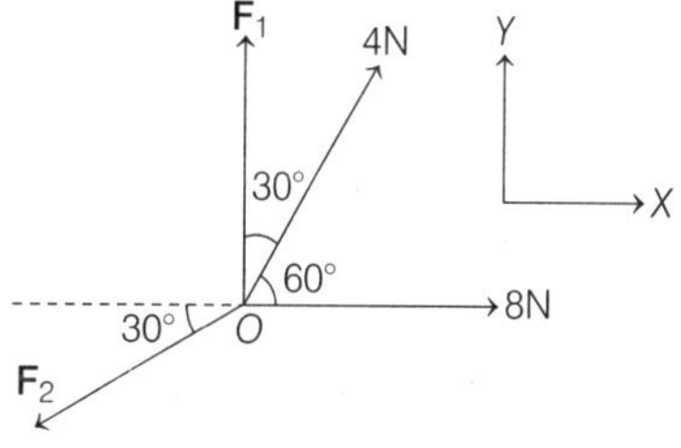

Fig. 8.32

(ii) $\Sigma F_y = 0$

$$\therefore \quad F_1 + 4\sin 60° - F_2 \sin 30° = 0$$

or $$F_1 + \frac{4\sqrt{3}}{2} - \frac{F_2}{2} = 0$$

or $$F_1 = \frac{F_2}{2} - 2\sqrt{3} = \frac{10}{\sqrt{3}} - 2\sqrt{3}$$

or $$F_1 = \frac{4}{\sqrt{3}} \text{ N}$$

Lami's Theorem

If an object O is in equilibrium under three concurrent forces $\mathbf{F}_1$, $\mathbf{F}_2$ and $\mathbf{F}_3$ as shown in figure. Then,

$$\frac{F_1}{\sin\alpha} = \frac{F_2}{\sin\beta} = \frac{F_3}{\sin\gamma}$$

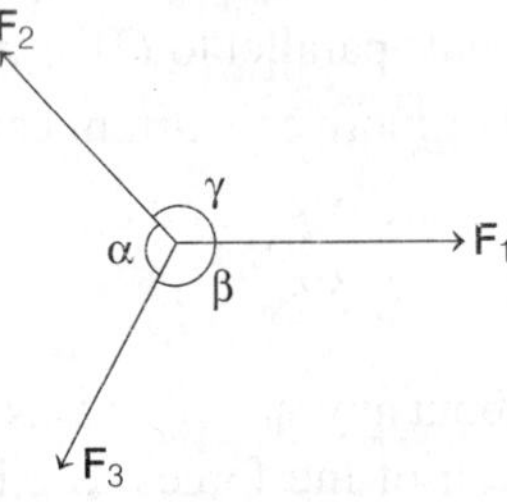

Fig. 8.33

This property of three concurrent forces in equilibrium is known as Lami's theorem and is very useful method of solving problems related to three concurrent forces in equilibrium.

Example 8.11 *One end of a string 0.5 m long is fixed to a point A and the other end is fastened to a small object of weight 8 N. The object is pulled aside by a horizontal force F, until it is 0.3 m from the vertical through A. Find the magnitudes of the tension T in the string and the force F.*

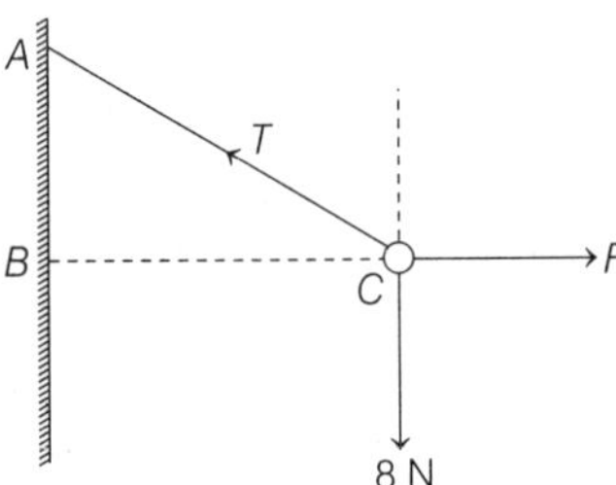

Fig. 8.34

Solution $AC = 0.5\text{ m}, \quad BC = 0.3\text{ m}$

$\therefore \qquad AB = 0.4\text{ m}$

and if $\qquad \angle BAC = \theta.$

Then $$\cos\theta = \frac{AB}{AC} = \frac{0.4}{0.5} = \frac{4}{5}$$

and $$\sin\theta = \frac{BC}{AC} = \frac{0.3}{0.5} = \frac{3}{5}$$

Here, the object is in equilibrium under three concurrent forces. So, we can apply Lami's theorem.

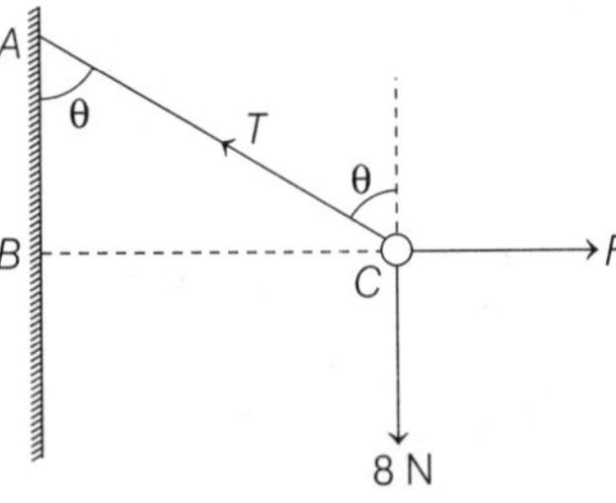

Fig. 8.35

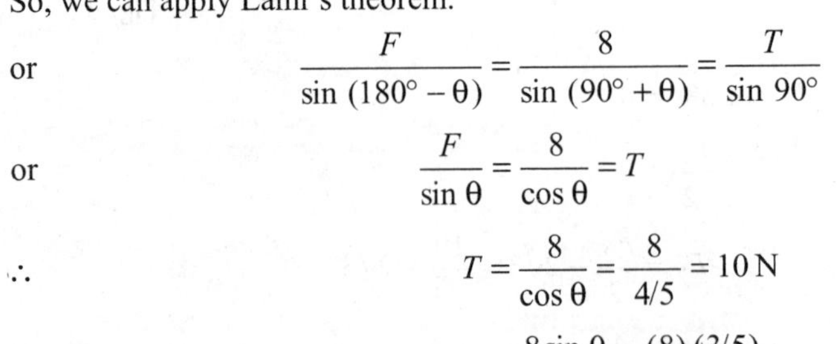

or $$\frac{F}{\sin(180^\circ - \theta)} = \frac{8}{\sin(90^\circ + \theta)} = \frac{T}{\sin 90^\circ}$$

or $$\frac{F}{\sin\theta} = \frac{8}{\cos\theta} = T$$

$\therefore$ $$T = \frac{8}{\cos\theta} = \frac{8}{4/5} = 10\text{ N}$$

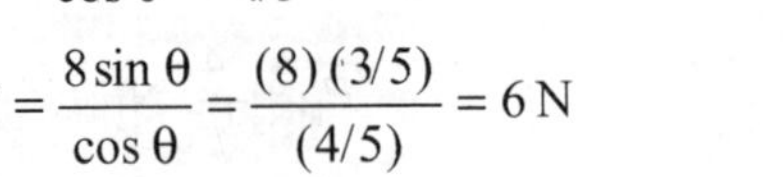

and $$F = \frac{8\sin\theta}{\cos\theta} = \frac{(8)(3/5)}{(4/5)} = 6\text{ N}$$ **Ans.**

Example 8.12 *The rod shown in figure has a mass of 2 kg and length 4 m. In equilibrium, find the hinge force (or its two components) acting on the rod and tension in the string. Take $g = 10\ m/s^2$, $\sin 37° = \frac{3}{5}$ and $\cos 37° = \frac{4}{5}$.*

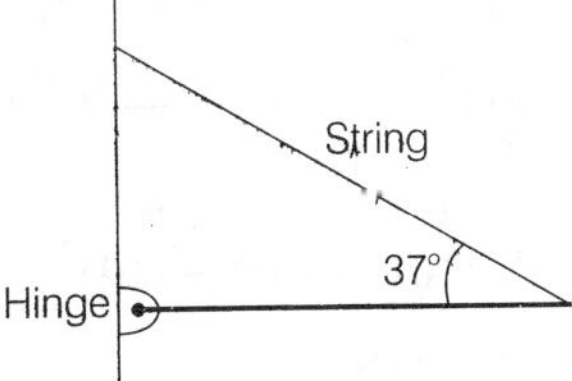

Fig. 8.36

Solution

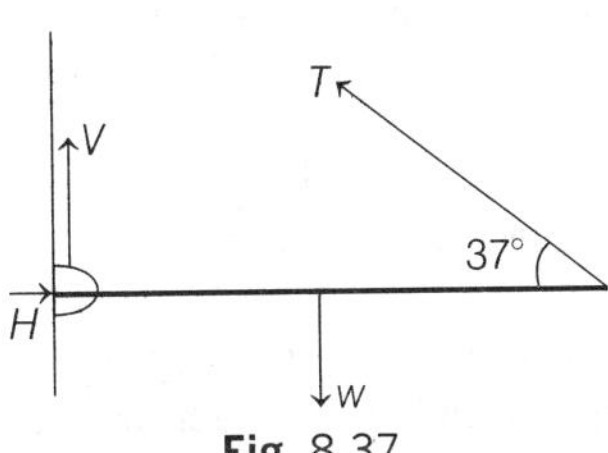

Fig. 8.37

In the figure, only those forces which are acting on the rod have been shown. Here H and V are horizontal and vertical components of the hinge force.

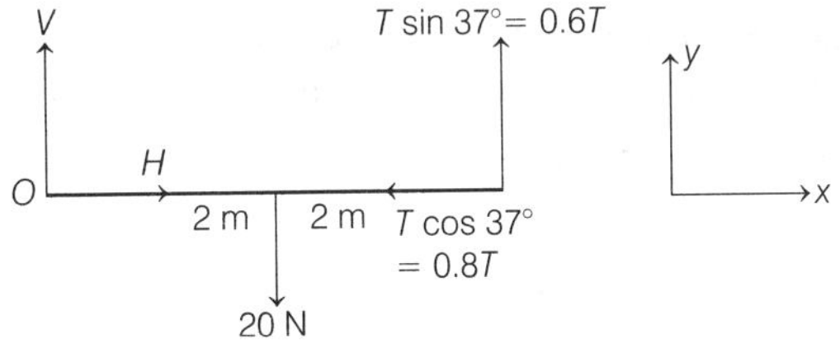

Fig. 8.38

$$\Sigma F_x = 0$$

$\Rightarrow$ $$H - 0.8T = 0 \qquad \text{...(i)}$$

$$\Sigma F_y = 0$$

$\Rightarrow$ $$V + 0.6T - 20 = 0 \qquad \text{...(ii)}$$

$$\Sigma \tau_O = 0$$

$\Rightarrow$ Clockwise torque of 20 N = anticlock-wise torque of 0.6 T.

All other forces (H, V and 0.8 T pass through O, hence their torques are zero).

$\therefore$ $$20 \times 2 = 0.6T \times 4 \qquad \text{...(iii)}$$

Solving these three equations, we get

$$T = 16.67 \text{ N},$$

$$H = 13.33 \text{ N}$$

and $$V = 10 \text{ N}$$ **Ans.**

Hinge force (F)

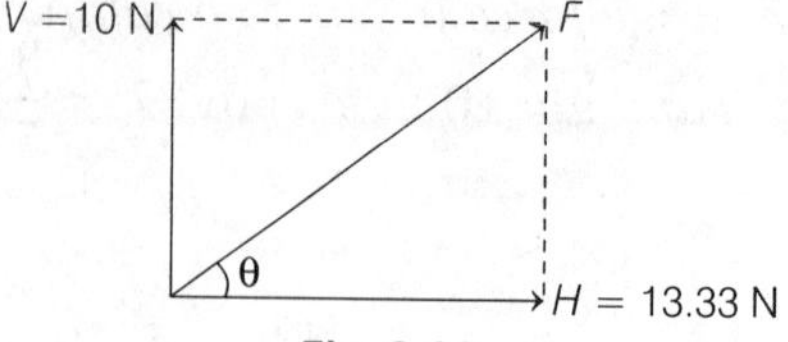

Fig. 8.39

$$F = \sqrt{(13.33)^2 + (10)^2} = 16.67 \text{ N}$$ **Ans.**

$$\tan\theta = \frac{10}{13.33}$$

$$\therefore \quad \theta = \tan^{-1}\left(\frac{10}{13.33}\right) = 37^\circ$$ **Ans.**

INTRODUCTORY EXERCISE 8.1

1. The diagram shows a rough plank resting on a cylinder with one end of the plank on rough ground. Neglect friction between plank and cylinder. Draw diagrams to show
   (a) the forces acting on the plank,
   (b) the forces acting on the cylinder.

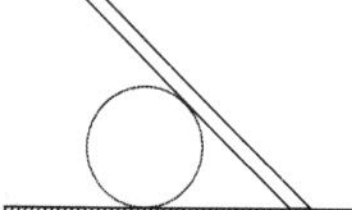

Fig. 8.40

2. Two spheres A and B are placed between two vertical walls as shown in figure. Friction is absent everywhere. Draw the free body diagrams of both the spheres.

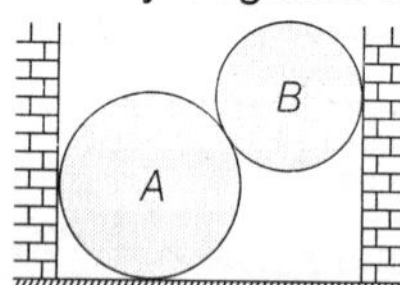

Fig. 8.41

3. A point A on a sphere of weight w rests in contact with a smooth vertical wall and is supported by a string joining a point B on the sphere to a point C on the wall. Draw free body diagram of the sphere.

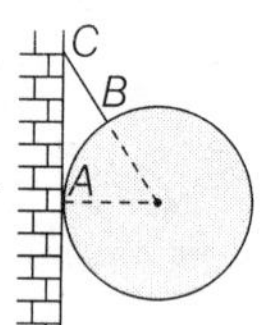

Fig. 8.42

4. A rod AB of weight w_1 is placed over a sphere of weight w_2 as shown in figure. Ground is rough and there is no friction between rod and sphere and sphere and wall. Draw free body diagrams of sphere and rod separately.

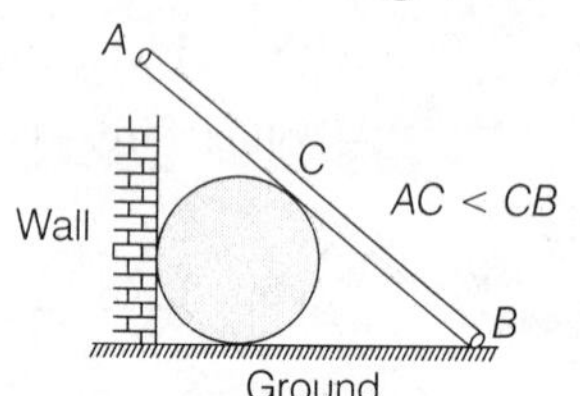

Fig. 8.43

Note *No friction will act between sphere and ground, think why ?*

5. A rod OA is suspended with the help of a massless string AB as shown in Fig. 8.44. Rod is hinged at point O. Draw free body diagram of the rod.

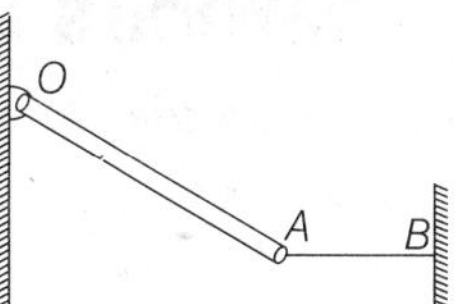
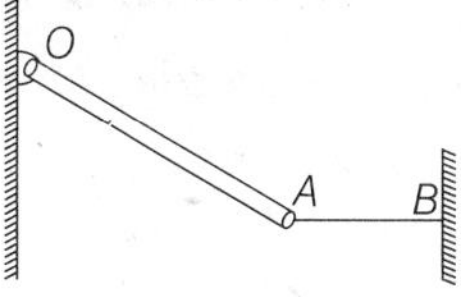

Fig. 8.44

6. A rod AB is placed inside a rough spherical shell as shown in Fig.8.45. Draw the free body diagram of the rod.

Fig. 8.45

7. Write down the components of four forces F_1, F_2, F_3 and F_4 along ox and oy directions as shown in Fig. 8.46.

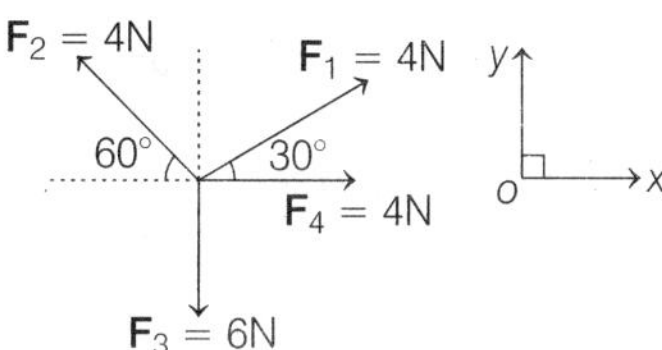

Fig. 8.46

8. All the strings shown in figure are massless. Tension in the horizontal string is 30 N. Find W.

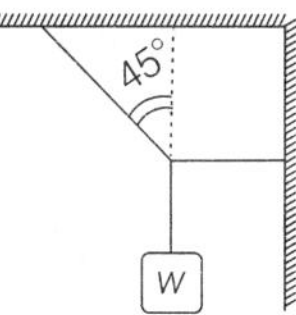

Fig. 8.47

9. The 50 kg homogeneous smooth sphere rests on the 30° incline A and against the smooth vertical wall B. Calculate the contact forces at A and B.

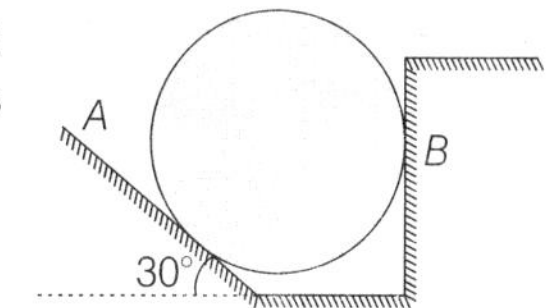

Fig. 8.48

10. In question 3 of the same exercise, the radius of the sphere is a. The length of the string is also a. Find tension in the string.

11. A sphere of weight $w = 100$ N is kept stationary on a rough inclined plane by a horizontal string AB as shown in figure. Find
(a) tension in the string,
(b) force of friction on the sphere and
(c) normal reaction on the sphere by the plane.

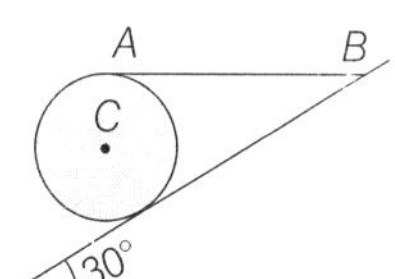

Fig. 8.49

8.4 Newton's Laws of Motion

It is interesting to read Newton's original version of the laws of motion.

Law I Every body continues in its state of rest or in uniform motion in a straight line unless it is compelled to change that state by forces impressed upon it.

Law II The change of motion is proportional to the magnitude of force impressed and is made in the direction of the straight line in which that force is impressed.

Law III To every action there is always an equal and opposite reaction or the mutual actions of two bodies upon each other are always directed to contrary parts.

The modern versions of these laws are:

1. A body continues in its initial state of rest or motion with uniform velocity unless acted on by an unbalanced external force.
2. The acceleration of a body is inversely proportional of its mass and directly proportional to the resultant external force acting on it, i.e.

$$\Sigma \mathbf{F} = \mathbf{F}_{\text{net}} = m\,\mathbf{a} \quad \text{or} \quad \mathbf{a} = \frac{\mathbf{F}_{\text{net}}}{m}$$

3. Forces always occur in pairs. If body A exerts a force on body B, an equal but opposite force is exerted by body B on body A.

Working with Newton's First and Second Laws

Normally any problem relating to Newton's laws is solved in following four steps:

1. First of all we decide the system on which the laws of motion are to be applied. The system may be a single particle, a block or a combination of two or more blocks, two blocks connected by a string, etc. The only restriction is that all parts of the system should have the same acceleration.
2. Once the system is decided, we make the list of all the forces acting on the system. Any force applied by the system on other bodies is not included in the list of the forces.
3. Then we make a free body diagram of the system and indicate the magnitude and directions of all the forces listed in step 2 in this diagram.
4. In the last step we choose any two mutually perpendicular axes say x and y in the plane of the forces in case of coplanar forces. Choose the x-axis along the direction in which the system is known to have or is likely to have the acceleration. A direction perpendicular to it may be chosen as the y-axis. If the system is in equilibrium any mutually perpendicular directions may be chosen. Write the components of all the forces along the x-axis and equate their sum to the product of the mass of the system and its acceleration, i.e.

$$\Sigma F_x = ma \qquad \text{...(i)}$$

This gives us one equation. Now, we write the components of the forces along the y-axis and equate the sum to zero. This gives us another equation, i.e.

$$\Sigma F_y = 0 \qquad \text{...(ii)}$$

Note *(i) If the system is in equilibrium we will write the two equations as*

$$\Sigma F_x = 0 \quad \textit{and} \quad \Sigma F_y = 0$$

(ii) If the forces are collinear, the second equation, i.e. $\Sigma F_y = 0$ is not needed.

Extra Points to Remember

- If **a** is the acceleration of a body, then $m\mathbf{a}$ force does not act on the body but this much force is required to provide **a** acceleration to the body. The different available forces acting on the body provide this $m\mathbf{a}$ force or, we can say that vector sum of all forces acting on the body is equal to $m\mathbf{a}$. The available forces may be weight, tension, normal reaction, friction or any externally applied force etc.
- If all bodies of a system has a common acceleration then that common acceleration can be given by

$$a = \frac{\text{Net pulling/pusing force}}{\text{Total mass}} = \frac{\text{NPF}}{\text{TM}}$$

Net pulling/pushing force (NPF) is actually the net force.

Example Suppose two unequal masses m and $2m$ are attached to the ends of a light inextensible string which passes over a smooth massless pulley. We have to find the acceleration of the system. We can assume that the mass $2m$ is pulled downwards by a force equal to its weight, i.e. $2mg$. Similarly, the mass m is being pulled by a force of mg downwards. Therefore, net pulling force on the system is $2mg - mg = mg$ and total mass being pulled is $2m + m = 3m$.

$\therefore$ Acceleration of the system is

$$a = \frac{\text{Net pulling force}}{\text{Total mass to be pulled}} = \frac{mg}{3m} = \frac{g}{3}$$

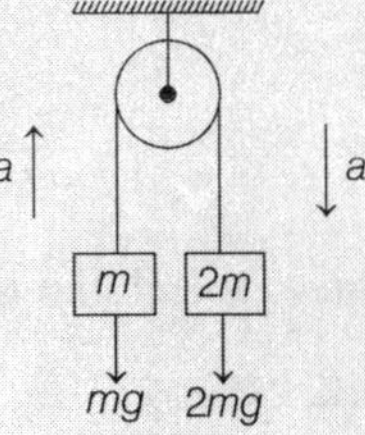

Fig. 8.50

Note *While finding net pulling force, take the forces (or their components) which are in the direction of motion (or opposite to it) and are single (i.e. they are not forming pair of equal and opposite forces). For example weight (mg) or some applied force F. Tension makes an equal and opposite pair. So, they are not to be included, unless the system in broken at some place and only one tension is considered on the system under consideration.*

- After finding that common acceleration, we will have to draw free body diagrams of different blocks to find normal reaction or tension etc.

Example 8.13 *Two blocks of masses 4 kg and 2 kg are placed side by side on a smooth horizontal surface as shown in the figure. A horizontal force of 20 N is applied on 4 kg block. Find*

(a) the acceleration of each block.

(b) the normal reaction between two blocks.

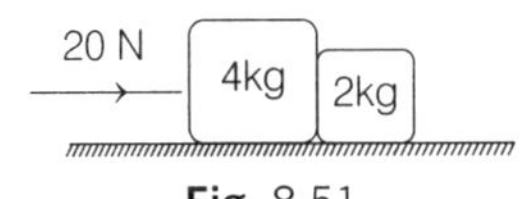

Fig. 8.51

Solution (a) Both the blocks will move with same acceleration (say a) in horizontal direction.

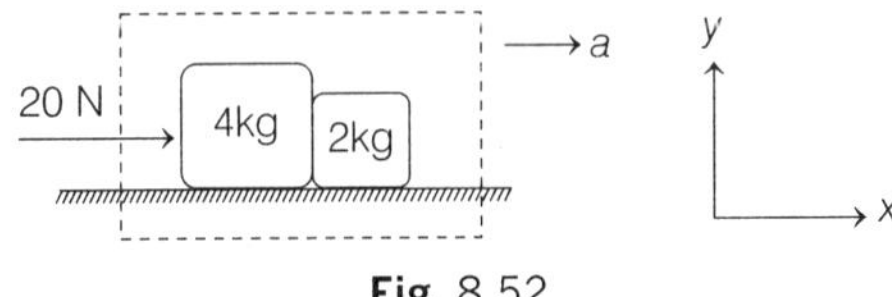

Fig. 8.52

Let us take both the blocks as a system. Net external force on the system is 20 N in horizontal direction.

Using $\Sigma F_x = ma_x$

$$20 = (4 + 2)a = 6a$$

or $a = \frac{10}{3}\ \text{m/s}^2$ **Ans.**

Alternate Method

$$a = \frac{\text{Net pushing force}}{\text{Total mass}}$$

$$= \frac{20}{4+2} = \frac{10}{3} \text{ m/s}^2$$

(b) The free body diagram of both the blocks are as shown in Fig. 8.53.

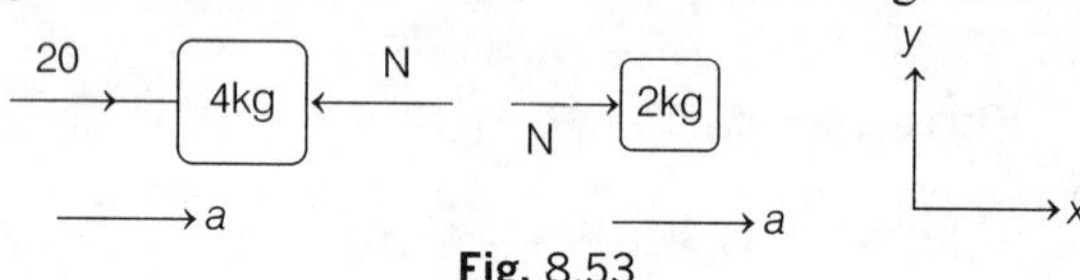

Fig. 8.53

Using $\qquad \Sigma F_x = ma_x$

For 4 kg block, $\qquad 20 - N = 4a = 4 \times \frac{10}{3}$

$$N = 20 - \frac{40}{3} = \frac{20}{3} \text{ newton} \qquad \textbf{Ans.}$$

This can also be solved as under

For 2 kg block, $\qquad N = 2a = 2 \times \frac{10}{3} = \frac{20}{3}$ newton

Here, N is the normal reaction between the two blocks.

Note *In free body diagram of the blocks we have not shown the forces acting on the blocks in vertical direction, because normal reaction between the blocks and acceleration of the system can be obtained without using* $\Sigma F_y = 0$.

Example 8.14 *Three blocks of masses 3 kg, 2 kg and 1 kg are placed side by side on a smooth surface as shown in figure. A horizontal force of 12 N is applied on 3 kg block. Find the net force on 2 kg block.*

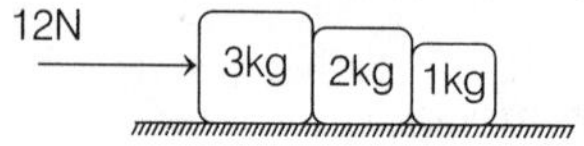

12N → 3kg | 2kg | 1kg

Fig. 8.54

Solution Since, all the blocks will move with same acceleration (say a) in horizontal direction. Let us take all the blocks as a single system.

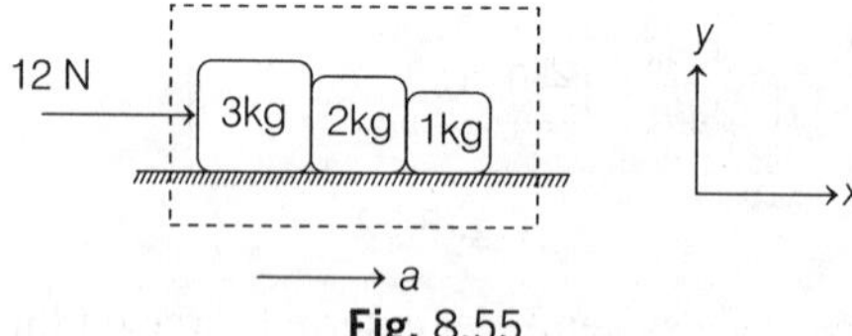

Fig. 8.55

Net external force on the system is 12 N in horizontal direction.

Using $\qquad \Sigma F_x = ma_x$

$$12 = (3 + 2 + 1)a = 6a$$

or $\qquad a = \frac{12}{6} = 2 \text{ m/s}^2$

Alternate Method

$$a = \frac{\text{Net pushing force}}{\text{Total mass}} = \frac{12}{3+2+1} = 2\ \text{m/s}^2$$

Now, let F be the net force on 2 kg block in x-direction, then using $\Sigma F_x = ma_x$ for 2 kg block, we get

$$F = (2)(2) = 4\ \text{N}$$ **Ans.**

Note *Here, net force F on 2 kg block is the resultant of N_1 and N_2 ($N_1 > N_2$)*
where, N_1 = normal reaction between 3 kg and 2 kg block,
and N_2 = normal reaction between 2 kg and 1 kg block.
Thus, $F = N_1 - N_2$

Example 8.15 *In the arrangement shown in figure. The strings are light and inextensible. The surface over which blocks are placed is smooth. Find*
(a) the acceleration of each block,
(b) the tension in each string.

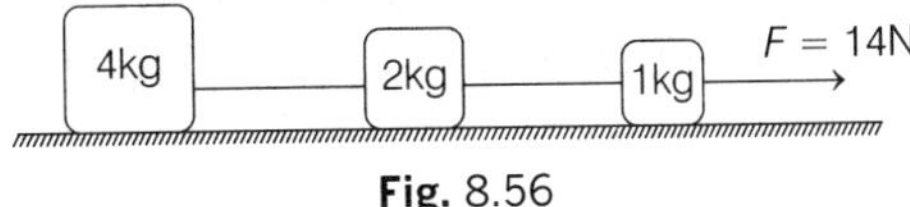

Fig. 8.56

Solution (a) Let a be the acceleration of each block and T_1 and T_2 be the tensions, in the two strings as shown in figure.

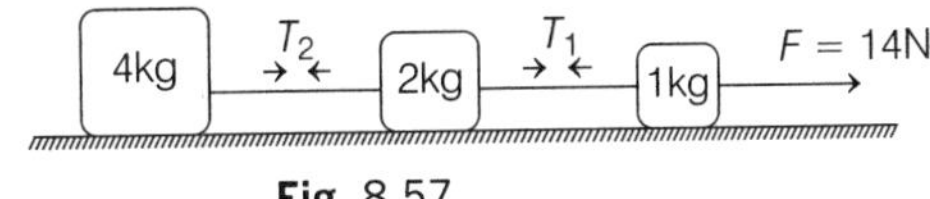

Fig. 8.57

Taking the three blocks and the two strings as the system.

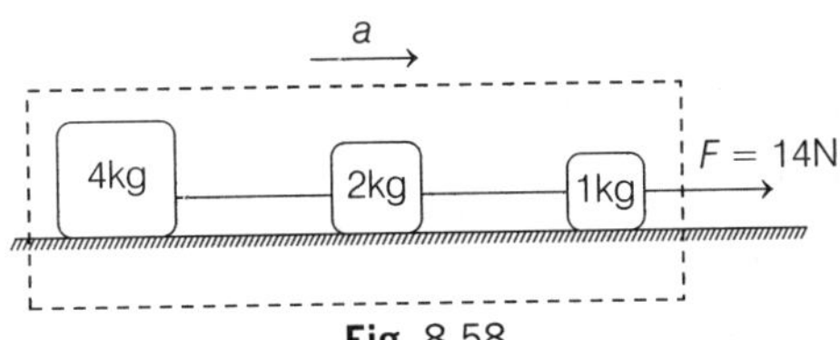

Fig. 8.58

Using $\Sigma F_x = ma_x$ or $14 = (4+2+1)a$ or $a = \frac{14}{7} = 2\ \text{m/s}^2$ **Ans.**

Alternate Method

$$a = \frac{\text{Net pulling force}}{\text{Total mass}} = \frac{14}{4+2+1} = 2\ \text{m/s}^2$$

(b) Free body diagram (showing the forces in x-direction only) of 4 kg block and 1kg block are shown in Fig. 8.59.

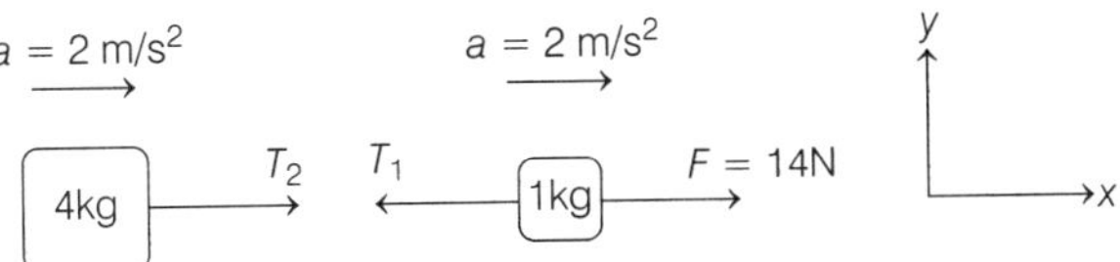

Fig. 8.59

Using $\Sigma F_x = ma_x$

For 1 kg block, $F - T_1 = (1)(a)$

or $14 - T_1 = (1)(2) = 2$

$\therefore$ $T_1 = 14 - 2 = 12\text{ N}$ **Ans.**

For 4 kg block, $T_2 = (4)(a)$

$\therefore$ $T_2 = (4)(2) = 8\text{ N}$ **Ans.**

Example 8.16 *Two blocks of masses 4 kg and 2 kg are attached by an inextensible light string as shown in figure. Both the blocks are pulled vertically upwards by a force F = 120 N. Find*
(a) the acceleration of the blocks,
(b) tension in the string. (Take g = 10 m/s²).

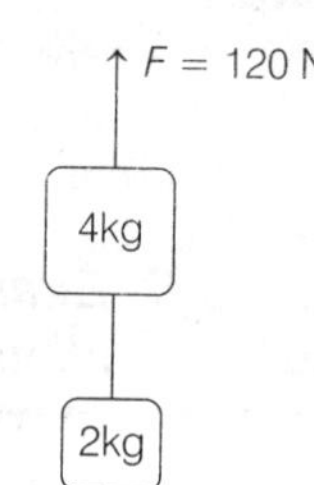

Fig. 8.60

Solution (a) Let a be the acceleration of the blocks and T the tension in the string as shown in figure.

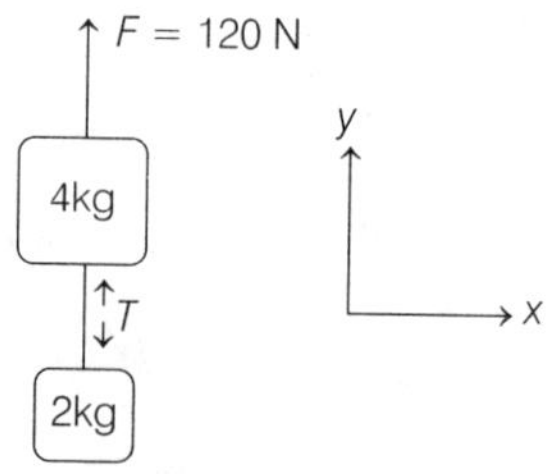

Fig. 8.61

Taking the two blocks and the string as the system shown in Fig. 8.62.

Using $\Sigma F_y = ma_y$, we get

$$F - 4g - 2g = (4 + 2)a$$

or $$120 - 40 - 20 = 6a \quad \text{or} \quad 60 = 6a$$

$\therefore$ $$a = 10\text{ m/s}^2$$ **Ans.**

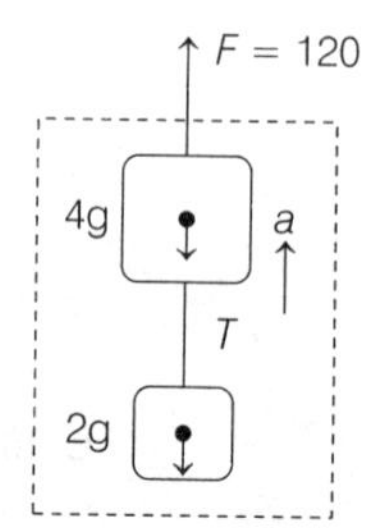

Fig. 8.62

Alternate Method

$$a = \frac{\text{Net pulling force}}{\text{Total mass}} = \frac{120 - 60}{4 + 2} = 10\text{ m/s}^2$$

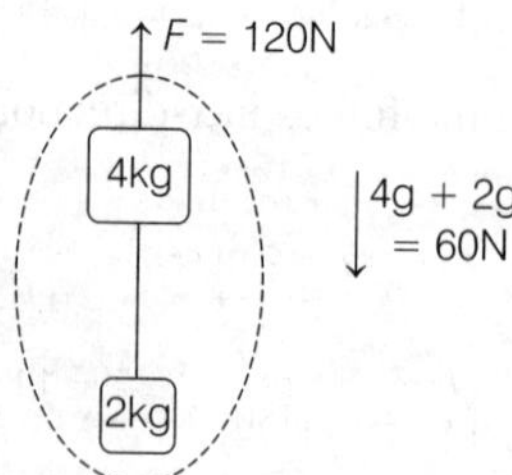

Fig. 8.63

(b) Free body diagram of 2 kg block is as shown in Fig. 8.64.

Using $\Sigma F_y = ma_y$

we get, $T - 2g = 2a$

or $T - 20 = (2)(10)$

$\therefore$ $T = 40\text{ N}$ **Ans.**

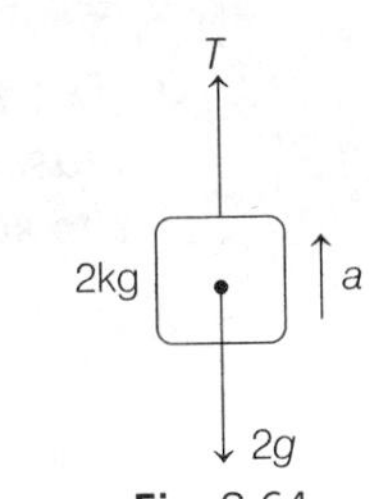

Fig. 8.64

Example 8.17 *In the system shown in figure pulley is smooth. String is massless and inextensible. Find acceleration of the system a, tensions T_1 and T_2. ($g = 10\ m/s^2$)*

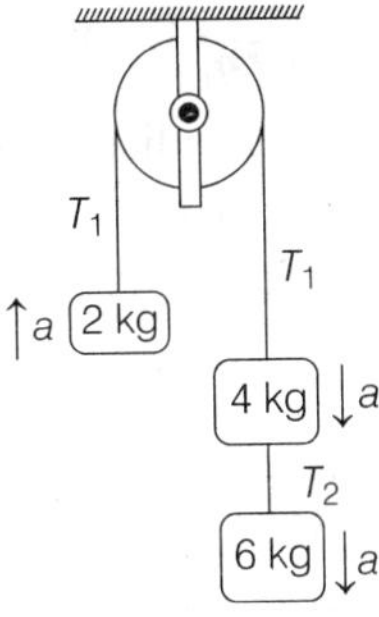

Fig. 8.65

Solution Here, net pulling force will be

Weight of 4 kg and 6 kg blocks on one side – weight of 2 kg block on the other side. Therefore,

$$a = \frac{\text{Net pulling force}}{\text{Total mass}}$$

$$= \frac{(6 \times 10) + (4 \times 10) - (2)(10)}{6 + 4 + 2}$$

$$= \frac{20}{3}\ \text{m/s}^2$$ **Ans.**

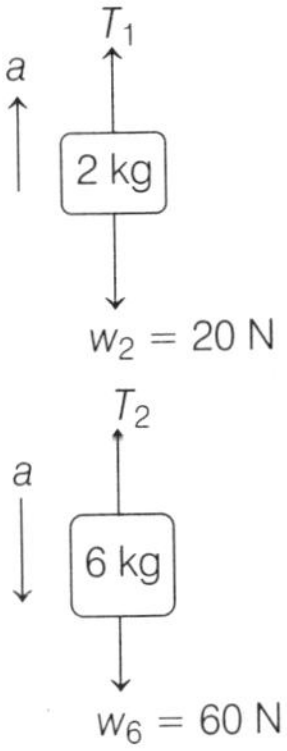

For T_1, let us consider FBD of 2 kg block. Writing equation of motion, we get

$$T_1 - 20 = 2a \quad \text{or} \quad T_1 = 20 + 2 \times \frac{20}{3} = \frac{100}{3}\ \text{N}$$ **Ans.**

For T_2, we may consider FBD of 6 kg block. Writing equation of motion, we get

$$60 - T_2 = 6a$$

$\therefore$
$$T_2 = 60 - 6a = 60 - 6\left(\frac{20}{3}\right)$$

$$= \frac{60}{3}\ \text{N}$$ **Ans.**

Fig. 8.66

Exercise: *Draw FBD of 4 kg block. Write down the equation of motion for it and check whether the values calculated above are correct or not.*

Example 8.18 *In the system shown in figure all surfaces are smooth. String is massless and inextensible. Find acceleration a of the system and tension T in the string.* ($g = 10\ m/s^2$)

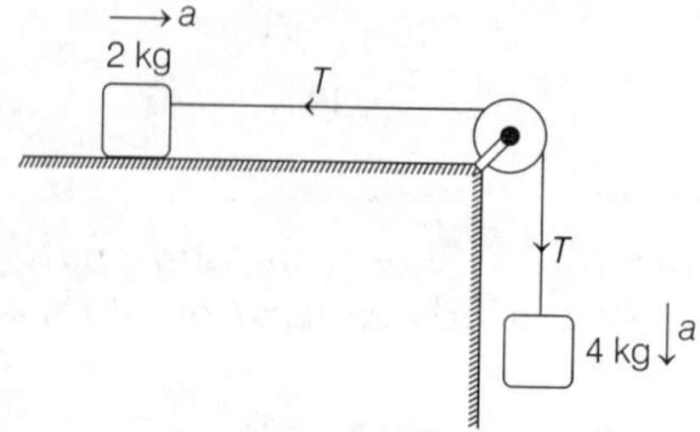

Fig. 8.67

Solution Here, weight of 2 kg is perpendicular to motion (or a). Hence, it will not contribute in net pulling force. Only weight of 4 kg block will be included.

$$\therefore \qquad a = \frac{\text{Net pulling force}}{\text{Total mass}}$$

$$= \frac{(4)(10)}{(4+2)} = \frac{20}{3}\ \text{m/s}^2 \qquad \textbf{Ans.}$$

For T, consider FBD of 4 kg block. Writing equation of motion.

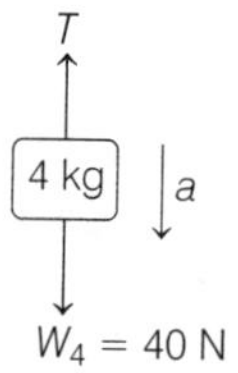

$$40 - T = 4a$$

$$\therefore \qquad T = 40 - 4a$$

$$= 40 - 4\left(\frac{20}{3}\right) = \frac{40}{3}\ \text{N} \qquad \textbf{Ans.}$$

T

4 kg a

$W_4 = 40$ N

Fig. 8.68

Exercise: *Draw FBD of 2 kg block and write down equation of motion for it. Check whether the values calculated above are correct or not.*

Example 8.19 *In the adjacent figure, masses of A, B and C are 1 kg, 3 kg and 2 kg respectively. Find*

(a) the acceleration of the system and

(b) tensions in the strings.

Neglect friction. ($g = 10\ m/s^2$)

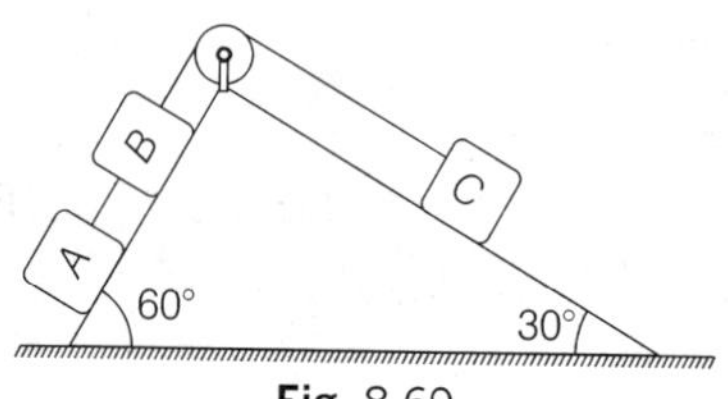

Fig. 8.69

Solution (a) In this case net pulling force

$$= m_A g \sin 60° + m_B g \sin 60° - m_C g \sin 30°$$

$$= (1)(10)\frac{\sqrt{3}}{2} + (3)(10)\left(\frac{\sqrt{3}}{2}\right) - (2)(10)\left(\frac{1}{2}\right)$$

$$= 21.17\ \text{N}$$

Total mass being pulled $= 1 + 3 + 2 = 6$ kg

$$\therefore \text{ Acceleration of the system } a = \frac{21.17}{6} = 4.1\ \text{m/s}^2 \qquad \textbf{Ans.}$$

(b) For the tension in the string between A and B.

FBD of A

$$m_A g \sin 60° - T_1 = (m_A)(a)$$

$$\therefore \quad T_1 = m_A\, g \sin 60° - m_A\, a$$

$$= m_A\, (g \sin 60° - a)$$

$$\therefore \quad T_1 = (1)\left(10 \times \frac{\sqrt{3}}{2} - 4.1\right)$$

$$= 4.56 \text{ N}$$

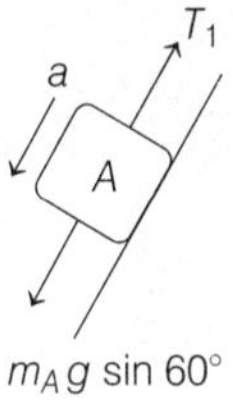

Ans.

Fig. 8.70

For the tension in the string between B and C.

FBD of C

$$T_2 - m_C g \sin 30° = m_C a$$

$$\therefore \quad T_2 = m_C\, (a + g \sin 30°)$$

$$\therefore \quad T_2 = 2\left[4.1 + 10\left(\frac{1}{2}\right)\right]$$

$$= 18.2 \text{ N}$$

Ans.

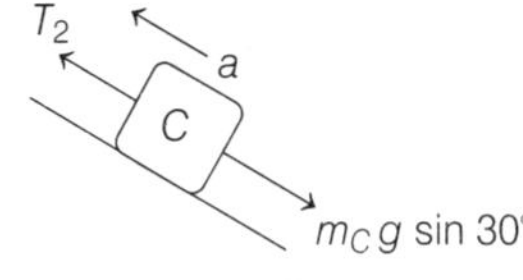

Fig. 8.71

INTRODUCTORY EXERCISE 8.2

1. Three blocks of masses 1 kg, 4 kg and 2 kg are placed on a smooth horizontal plane as shown in figure. Find
   (a) the acceleration of the system,
   (b) the normal force between 1 kg block and 4 kg block,
   (c) the net force on 2 kg block.

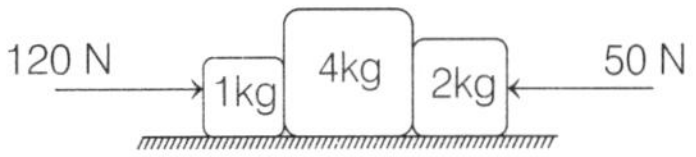

Fig. 8.72

2. In the arrangement shown in figure, find the ratio of tensions in the strings attached with 4 kg block and that with 1 kg block.

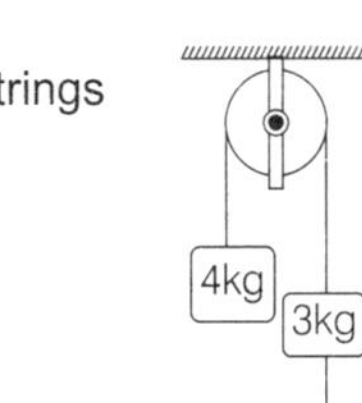

Fig. 8.73

3. Two unequal masses of 1 kg and 2 kg are connected by an inextensible light string passing over a smooth pulley as shown in figure. A force $F = 20$ N is applied on 1 kg block. Find the acceleration of either block. ($g = 10$ m/s^2).

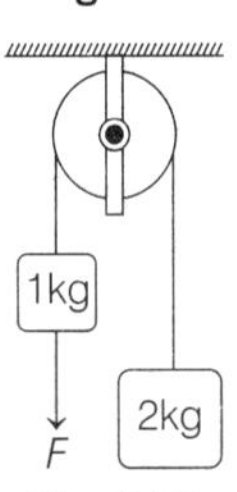

Fig. 8.74

4. In the arrangement shown in figure what should be the mass of block A, so that the system remains at rest? Neglect friction and mass of strings.

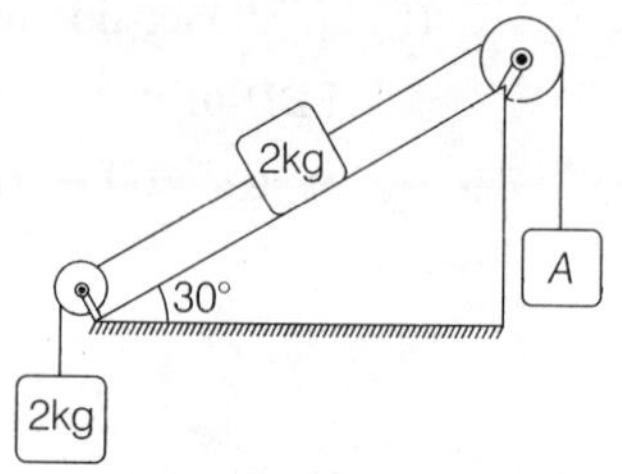

Fig. 8.75

5. Two blocks of masses 2 kg and 4 kg are released from rest over a smooth inclined plane of inclination 30° as shown in figure. What is the normal force between the two blocks?

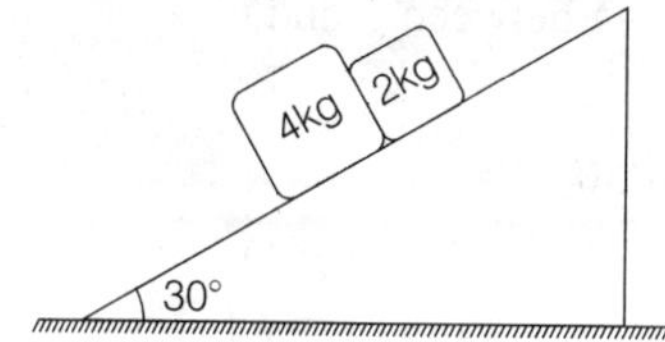

Fig. 8.76

6. What should be the acceleration a of the box shown in Fig. 8.77 so that the block of mass m exerts a force $\frac{mg}{4}$ on the floor of the box?

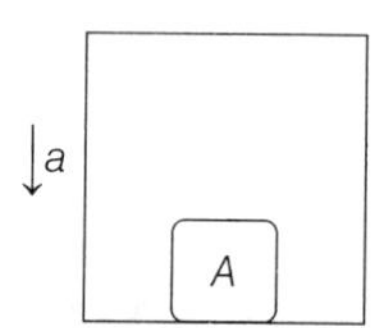

Fig. 8.77

7. In the figure shown, find acceleration of the system and tensions T_1, T_2 and T_3. (Take $g = 10\,m/s^2$)

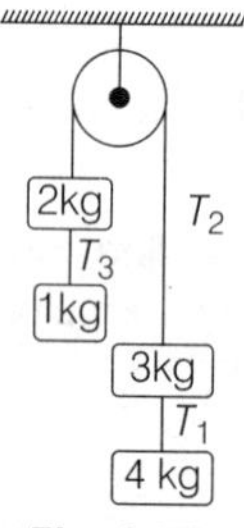

Fig. 8.78

8. In the figure shown, all surfaces are smooth. Find
(a) acceleration of all the three blocks,
(b) net force on 6 kg, 4 kg and 10 kg blocks and
(c) force acting between 4 kg and 10 kg blocks.

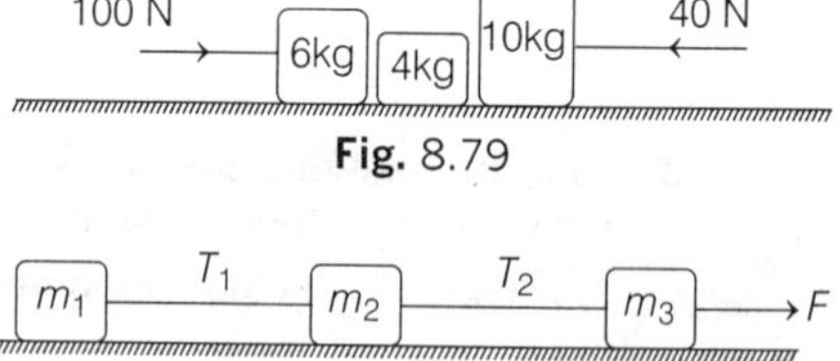

Fig. 8.79

9. Three blocks of masses $m_1 = 10$ kg, $m_2 = 20$ kg and $m_3 = 30$ kg are on a smooth horizontal table, connected to each other by light horizontal strings. A horizontal force $F = 60$ N is applied to m_3, towards right. Find
(a) tensions T_1 and T_2 and
(b) tension T_2 if all of a sudden the string between m_1 and m_2 snaps.

m_1 — T_1 — m_2 — T_2 — m_3 → F

Fig. 8.80

8.5 Constraint Equations

In the above article, we have discussed the cases where different blocks of the system had a common acceleration and that common acceleration was given by

$$a = \frac{\text{Net pulling / pushing force}}{\text{Total mass}}$$

Now, the question is, if different blocks have different accelerations then what? In those cases, we take help of constraint equations. These equations establish the relation between accelerations (or velocities) of different blocks of a system. Depending upon different kinds of problems we have divided the constraint equations in following two types. Most of them are directly explained with the help of some example(s) in their support.

Type 1

Example 8.20 *Using constraint method find the relation between accelerations of* 1 *and* 2.

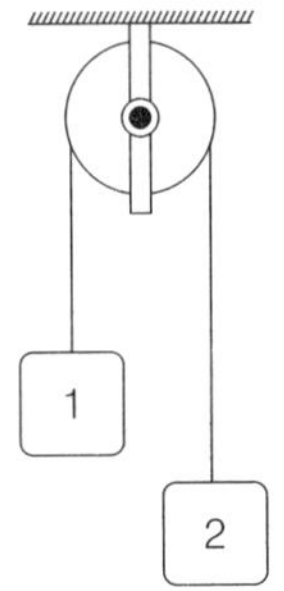

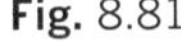

Fig. 8.81

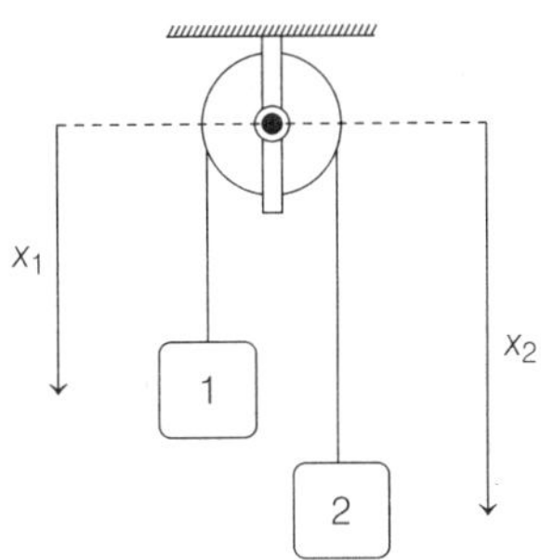

Fig. 8.82

Solution At any instant of time let x_1 and x_2 be the displacements of 1 and 2 from a fixed line (shown dotted). Here x_1 and x_2 are variables but,

$$x_1 + x_2 = \text{constant}$$

or $$x_1 + x_2 = l \quad \text{(length of string)}$$

Differentiating with respect to time, we have

$$v_1 + v_2 = 0$$

or $$v_1 = - v_2$$

Again differentiating with respect to time, we get

$$a_1 + a_2 = 0$$

or $$a_1 = - a_2$$

This is the required relation between a_1 and a_2, i.e. accelerations of 1 and 2 are equal but in opposite directions.

Note *(i) In the equation $x_1 + x_2 = l$, we have neglected the length of string over the pulley. But that length is also constant.*

(ii) In constraint equation if we get $a_1 = - a_2$, then negative sign does not always represent opposite directions of a_1 and a_2. The real significance of this sign is, x_2 decreases if x_1 increases and vice-versa.

Example 8.21 *Using constraint equations find the relation between a_1 and a_2.*

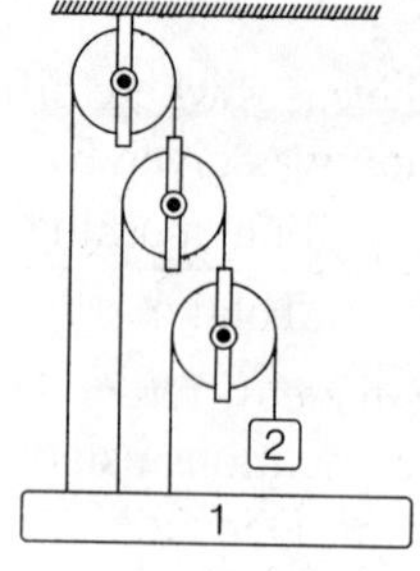

Fig. 8.83

Solution In Fig. 8.84, points 1, 2, 3 and 4 are movable. Let their displacements from a fixed dotted line be x_1, x_2, x_3 and x_4

$$x_1 + x_3 = l_1$$
$$(x_1 - x_3) + (x_4 - x_3) = l_2$$
$$(x_1 - x_4) + (x_2 - x_4) = l_3$$

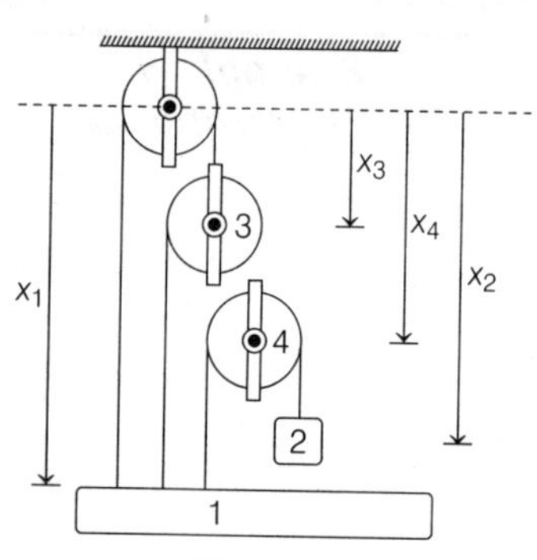

Fig. 8.84

On double differentiating with respect to time, we will get following three constraint relations

$$a_1 + a_3 = 0 \quad \text{...(i)}$$
$$a_1 + a_4 - 2a_3 = 0 \quad \text{...(ii)}$$
$$a_1 + a_2 - 2a_4 = 0 \quad \text{...(iii)}$$

Solving Eqs. (i), (ii) and (iii), we get

$$a_2 = -7a_1$$

Which is the desired relation between a_1 and a_2.

Example 8.22 *In the above example, if two blocks have masses 1 kg and 2 kg respectively then find their accelerations and tensions in different strings.*

Solution Pulleys 3 and 4 are massless. Hence net force on them should be zero. Therefore, if we take T tension in the shortest string, then tension in other two strings will be $2T$ and $4T$.

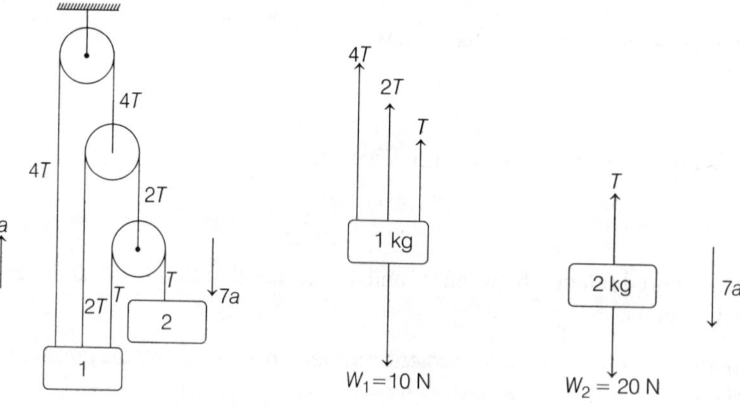

Fig. 8.85

Further, if a is the acceleration of 1 in upward direction, then from the constraint equation $a_2 = -7a_1$, acceleration of 2 will be $7a$ downwards.

Writing the equation, $F_{net} = ma$ for the two blocks we have

$$4T + 2T + T - 10 = 1 \times a$$

or $$7T - 10 = a \quad \text{...(i)}$$

$$20 - T = 2 \times (7a)$$

or $$20 - T = 14a \quad \text{...(ii)}$$

Solving these two equations we get,

$$T = 1.62 \text{ N}$$ **Ans.**

and $$a = 1.31 \text{ m/s}^2$$ **Ans.**

Note *In a problem if 'a' comes out to be negative after calculations then we will change the initially assumed directions of accelerations.*

Type 2

Example 8.23 *The system shown in figure is released from rest. Find acceleration of different blocks and tension in different strings.*

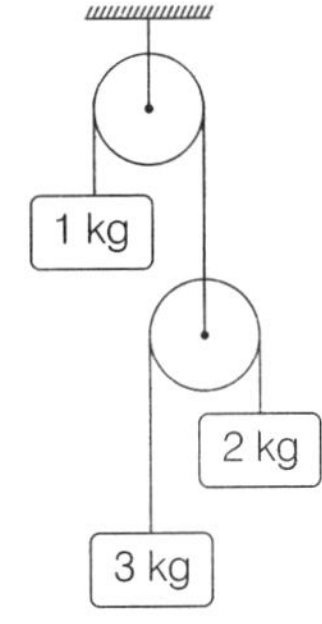

Fig. 8.86

Solution

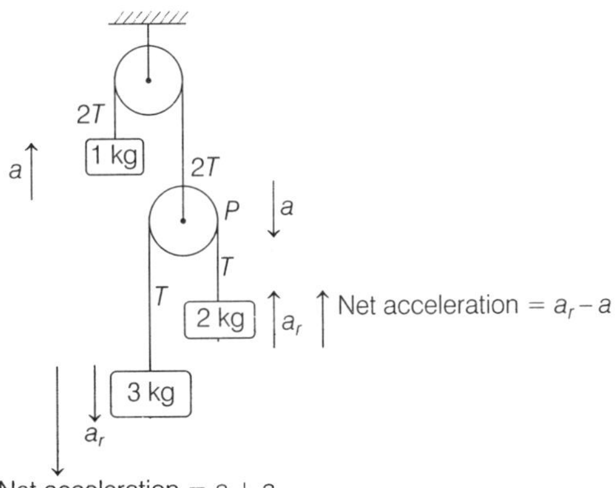

Fig. 8.87

(i) Pulley P and 1 kg mass are attached with the same string. Therefore, if 1 kg mass has an acceleration 'a' in upward direction, then pulley P will have an acceleration 'a' downwards.

(ii) 2 kg and 3 kg blocks are attached with the same string passing over a moveable pulley P. Therefore, their relative acceleration, a_r (relative to pulley) will be same. Their net accelerations (relative to ground) are as shown in figure.

(iii) Pulley P is massless. Hence net force on this pulley should be zero. If T is the tension in the string connecting 2 kg and 3 kg mass, then tension in the upper string will be $2T$.

Now writing the equation, $F_{net} = ma$ for three blocks, we have:

1 kg block:

Fig. 8.88

$$2T - 10 = 1 \times a \quad \text{...(i)}$$

2 kg block:

Fig. 8.89

$$T - 20 = 2(a_r - a) \quad \text{...(ii)}$$

3 kg block:

Fig. 8.90

$$30 - T = 3(a_r + a) \quad \text{...(iii)}$$

Solving Eqs. (i), (ii) and (iii) we get,

$$T = 8.28 \text{ N}, \; a = 6.55 \text{ m/s}^2 \quad \text{and} \quad a_r = 0.7 \text{ m/s}^2.$$

Now, acceleration of 3kg block is $(a + a_r)$ or 7.25 m/s^2 downwards and acceleration of 2kg is $(a_r - a)$ or -5.85 m/s^2 upwards. Since, this comes out to be negative, hence acceleration of 2 kg block is 5.85 m/s^2 downwards.

Extra Points to Remember

- In some cases, acceleration of a block is inversely proportional to tension force acting on the block (or its component in the direction of motion or acceleration). If tension is double (as compared to other block), then acceleration will be half.

  In Fig. (a): Tension force on block-1 is double ($=2T$) than the tension force on block-2 ($=T$). Therefore, acceleration of block-1 will be half. If block-1 has an acceleration 'a' in downward direction, then block -2 will have an acceleration '$2a$' towards right.

  In Fig. (b): Tension force on block-1 is three times ($2T+T=3T$) than the tension force on block-2 ($=T$). Therefore acceleration of block-2 will be three times. If block-1 has an acceleration 'a' in upwards direction, then acceleration of block-2 will be '$3a$' downwards.

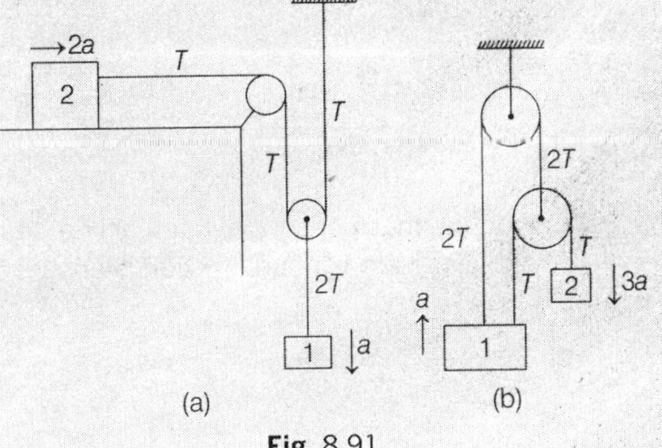

Fig. 8.91

INTRODUCTORY EXERCISE 8.3

1. Make the constraint relation between a_1, a_2 and a_3.

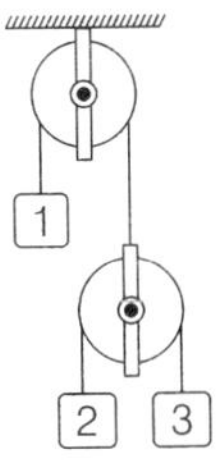

Fig. 8.92

2. At certain moment of time, velocities of 1 and 2 both are 1 m/s upwards. Find the velocity of 3 at that moment.

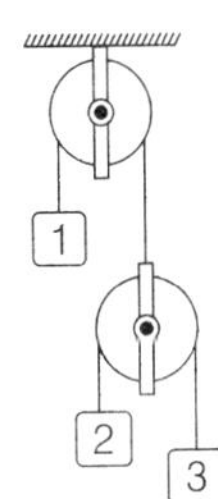

Fig. 8.93

3. Consider the situation shown in figure. Both the pulleys and the string are light and all the surfaces are smooth.
   (a) Find the acceleration of 1 kg block.
   (b) Find the tension in the string. ($g = 10\,\text{m/s}^2$).

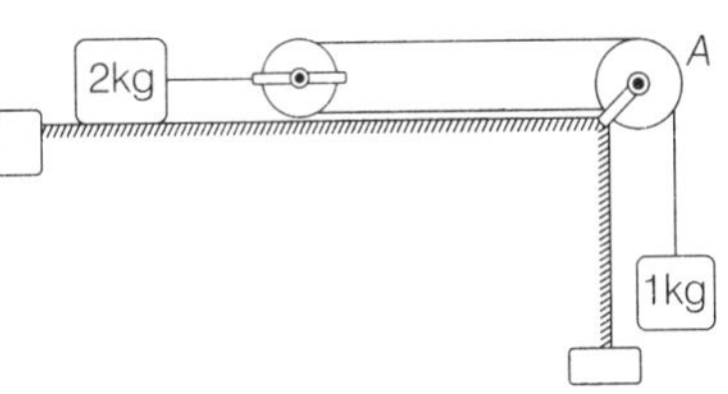

Fig. 8.94

4. Calculate the acceleration of either blocks and tension in the string shown in figure. The pulley and the string are light and all surfaces are smooth.

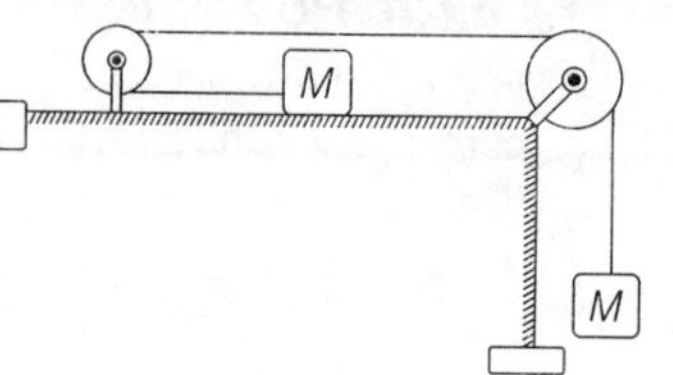

Fig. 8.95

5. Find the mass M so that it remains at rest in the adjoining figure. Both the pulley and string are light and friction is absent everywhere. ($g = 10$ m/s^2).

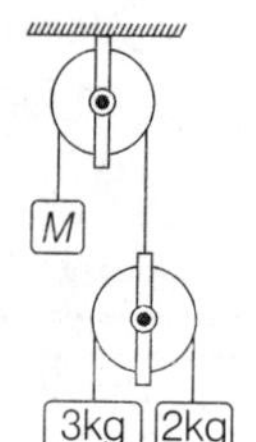

Fig. 8.96

6. In Fig. 8.97 assume that there is negligible friction between the blocks and table. Compute the tension in the cord connecting m_2 and the pulley and acceleration of m_2 if $m_1 = 300$ g, $m_2 = 200$ g and $F = 0.40$ N.

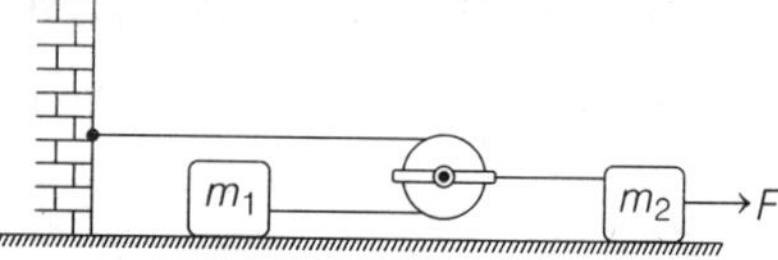

Fig. 8.97

7. In the figure shown, $a_3 = 6$ m/s^2 (downwards) and $a_2 = 4$ m/s^2 (upwards). Find acceleration of 1.

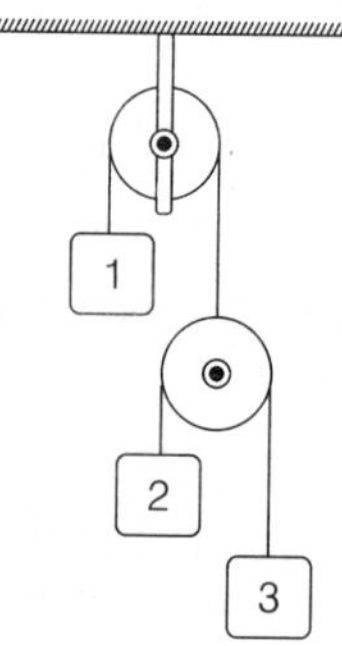

Fig. 8.98

8. Find the acceleration of the block of mass M in the situation shown in the figure. All the surfaces are frictionless.

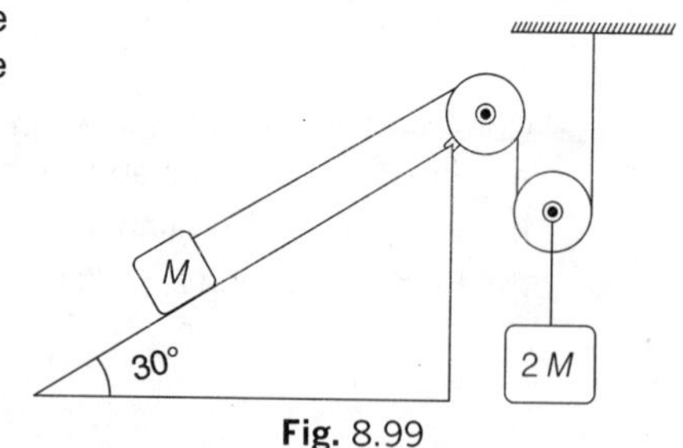

Fig. 8.99

8.6 Pseudo Force

Before studying the concept of pseudo force let us first discuss frame of reference.

Frame of reference is the way of observing the things.

Inertial Frame of Reference

A non-accelerating frame of reference is called an inertial frame of reference. A frame of reference moving with a constant velocity is an inertial frame of reference.

Non-inertial Frame of Reference

An accelerating frame of reference is called a non-inertial frame of reference.

Note *(i) A rotating frame of reference is a non-inertial frame of reference, because it is also an accelerating one.*
(ii) Earth is rotating about its axis of rotation and it is revolving around the centre of sun also. So, it is non-intertial frame of reference. But for most of the cases, we consider its as an inertial frame of reference.

Now let us come to the pseudo force. Instead of ground (or inertial frame of reference) when we start watching the objects from a non-inertial (accelerating) frame of reference its motion conditions are felt differently.

For example Suppose a child is standing inside an accelerating lift. From ground frame of reference this child appears to be accelerating but from lift (non-inertial) frame of reference child appears to be at rest. To justify this changed condition of motion, from equations point of view we have to apply a pseudo force. This pseudo force is given by

$$\mathbf{F}_p = -m\mathbf{a}$$

Here, 'm' is the mass of that body/object which is being observed from non-inertial frame of reference and $\mathbf{a}$ is the acceleration of frame of reference. Negative sign implies that direction of pseudo force $\mathbf{F}_p$ is opposite to $\mathbf{a}$. Hence whenever you make free body diagram of a body from a non-inertial frame, apply all real forces (actually acting) on the body plus one pseudo force. Magnitude of this pseudo force is 'ma' and the direction is opposite to $\mathbf{a}$.

Example Suppose a block A of mass m is placed on a lift ascending with an acceleration a_0. Let N be the normal reaction between the block and the floor of the lift. Free body diagram of A in ground frame of reference (inertial) is shown in Fig. 8.100.

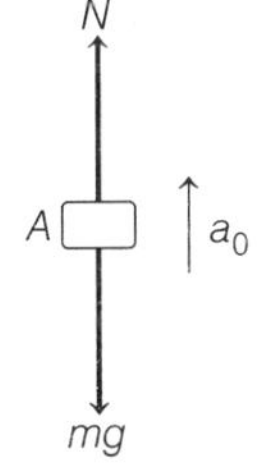

Fig. 8.100

$\therefore$ $$N - mg = ma_0$$

or $$N = m(g + a_0) \quad \text{...(i)}$$

But if we draw the free body diagram of A with respect to the elevator (a non-inertial frame of reference) without applying the pseudo force, as shown in Fig. 8.101, we get

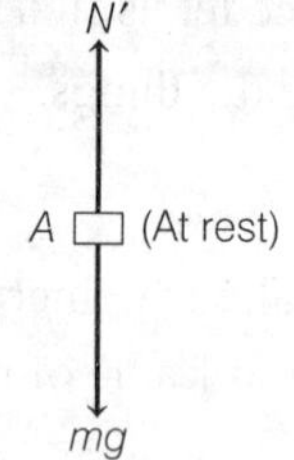

Fig. 8.101

$$N' - mg = 0$$

or
$$N' = mg \qquad \ldots\text{(ii)}$$

Since, $N' \neq N$, either of the equations is wrong. If we apply a pseudo force in non-inertial frame of reference, N' becomes equal to N as shown in Fig. 8.102. Acceleration of block with respect to elevator is zero.

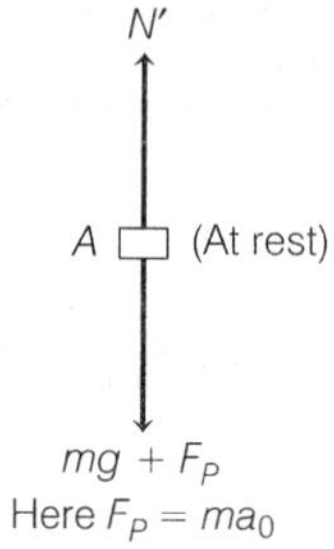

$\therefore$
$$N' - mg - ma_0 = 0$$

or
$$N' = m(g + a_0) \qquad \ldots\text{(iii)}$$

$\therefore$
$$N' = N$$

N′ A (At rest)

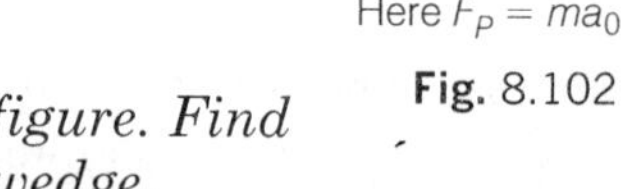

Fig. 8.102

Example 8.24 *All surfaces are smooth in following figure. Find F, such that block remains stationary with respect to wedge.*

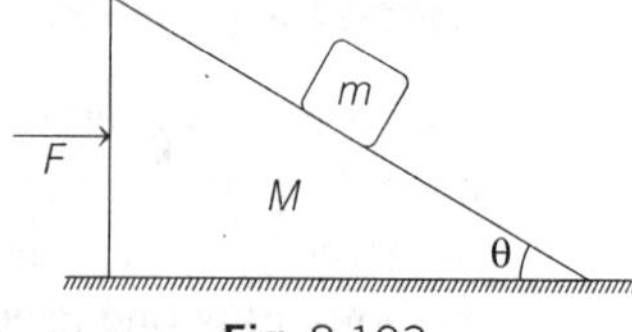

Fig. 8.103

Solution Acceleration of (block + wedge) $a = \dfrac{F}{(M + m)}$

Let us solve the problem by both the methods. Such problems can be solved with or without using the concept of pseudo force.

From Inertial Frame of Reference (Ground)

FBD of block w.r.t. ground (Apply real forces):

With respect to ground block is moving with an acceleration a.

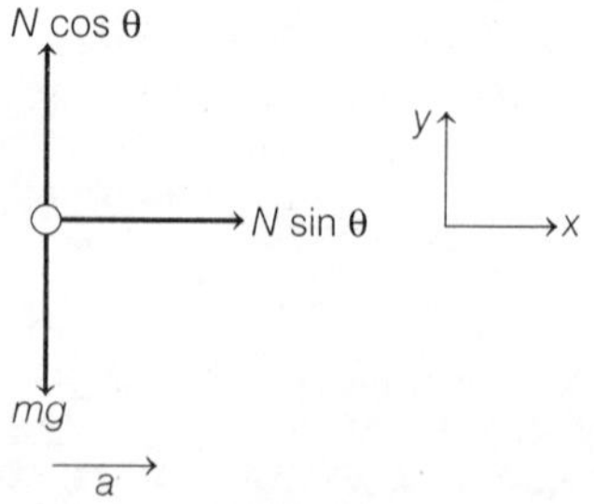

$\therefore$
$$\Sigma F_y = 0$$

$\Rightarrow$
$$N \cos\theta = mg \qquad \ldots\text{(i)}$$

and
$$\Sigma F_x = ma$$

$\Rightarrow$
$$N \sin\theta = ma \qquad \ldots\text{(ii)}$$

N cos θ, N sin θ, mg, a, y, x

Fig. 8.104

From Eqs. (i) and (ii), we get

$$a = g \tan \theta$$

$$\therefore \quad F = (M + m)a = (M + m)\, g \tan \theta$$

From Non-inertial Frame of Reference (Wedge)

FBD of block w.r.t. wedge (real forces + pseudo force)

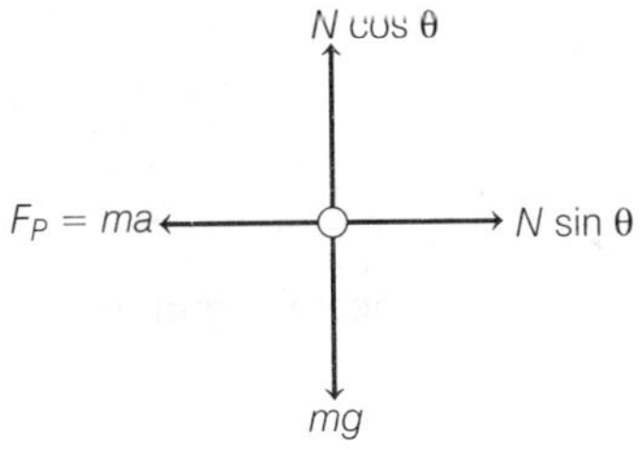

w.r.t. wedge, block is stationary

$$\therefore \quad \Sigma F_y = 0 \Rightarrow N \cos \theta = mg \qquad \text{...(iii)}$$

$$\Sigma F_x = 0 \Rightarrow N \sin \theta = ma \qquad \text{...(iv)}$$

From Eqs. (iii) and (iv), we will get the same result

i.e. $$F = (M + m)\, g \tan \theta.$$

Fig. 8.105

Example 8.25 *A bob of mass m is suspended from the ceiling of a train moving with an acceleration a as shown in figure. Find the angle θ in equilibrium position.*

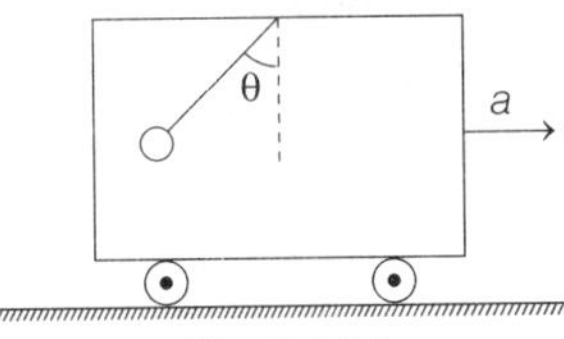

Fig. 8.106

Solution This problem can also be solved by both the methods.

Inertial Frame of Reference (Ground)

FBD of bob w.r.t. ground (only real forces)

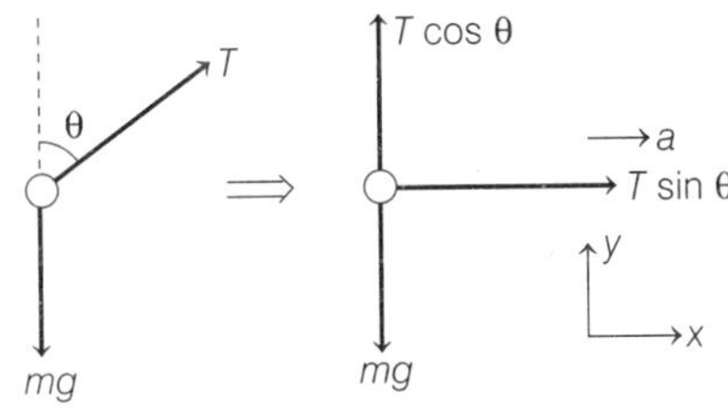

Fig. 8.107

With respect to ground, bob is also moving with an acceleration a.

$$\therefore \quad \Sigma F_x = ma \Rightarrow T \sin \theta = ma \qquad \text{...(i)}$$

and $$\Sigma F_y = 0 \Rightarrow T \cos \theta = mg \qquad \text{...(ii)}$$

From Eqs. (i) and (ii), we get

$$\tan \theta = \frac{a}{g} \quad \text{or} \quad \theta = \tan^{-1}\left(\frac{a}{g}\right)$$

Non-inertial Frame of Reference (Train)

FBD of bob w.r.t. train (real forces + pseudo force):

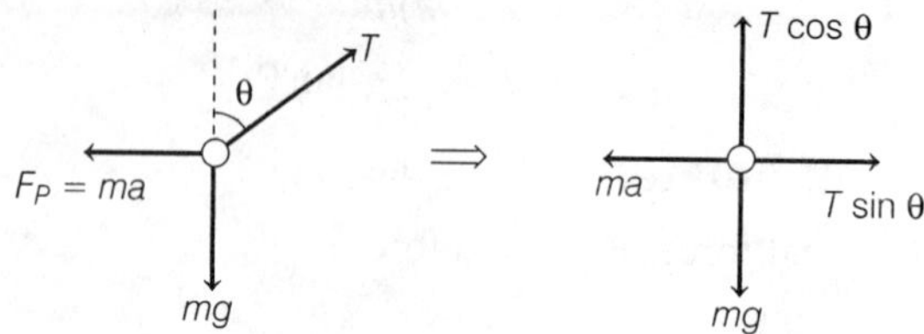

Fig. 8.108

with respect to train, bob is in equilibrium

$\therefore \quad \Sigma F_x = 0$

$\Rightarrow \quad T \sin\theta = ma \quad \text{...(iii)}$

$\therefore \quad \Sigma F_y = 0$

$\Rightarrow \quad T \cos\theta = mg \quad \text{...(iv)}$

From Eqs. (iii) and (iv), we get the same result, i.e.

$$\theta = \tan^{-1}\left(\frac{a}{g}\right)$$

INTRODUCTORY EXERCISE 8.4

1. Two blocks A and B of masses 1kg and 2 kg have accelerations $(2\hat{\mathbf{i}})\,\text{m/s}^2$ and $(-4\hat{\mathbf{j}})\,\text{m/s}^2$. Find
   (a) Pseudo force on block A as applied with respect to the block B.
   (b) Pseudo force on block B as applied with respect to the block A.
2. Pseudo force with respect to a frame moving with constant velocity is zero. Is this statement true or false?
3. Problems of non-intertial frames can be solved only with the concept of pseudo force. Is this statement true or false?

8.7 Friction

Regarding the frictional force (f) following points are worthnoting :

1. It is the tangential component of net contact force (F) acting between two bodies in contact.
2. It starts acting when there is tendency of relative motion (different velocities) between two bodies in contact or actual relative motion takes place. So, friction has a tendency to stop relative motion between two bodies in contact.
3. If there is only tendency of relative motion then static friction acts and if actual relative motion takes place, then kinetic friction acts.

4. Like any other force of nature friction force also makes a pair of equal and opposite forces acting on two different bodies.
5. Direction of friction force on a given body is opposite to the direction of relative motion (or its tendency) of this body.
6.

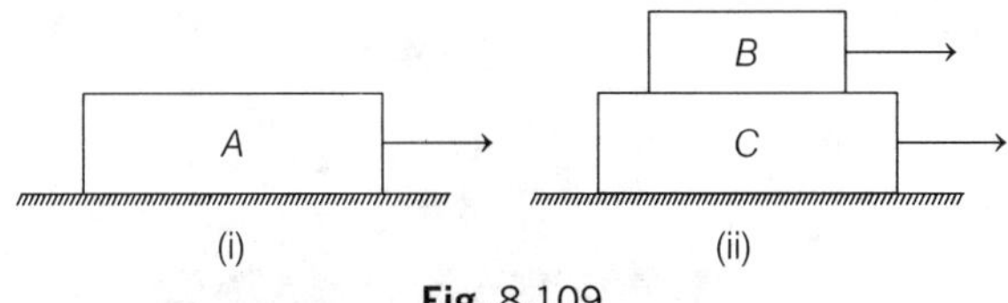

Fig. 8.109

In Fig. (i), motion of block A means its relative motion with respect to ground. So, in this case friction between block and ground has a tendency to stop its motion.

In Fig. (ii), relative motion between two blocks B and C means their different velocities. So, friction between these two blocks has a tendency to make their velocities same.

7. Static friction is self adjusting in nature. This varies from zero to a limiting value f_L. Only that much amount of friction will act which can stop the relative motion.
8. Kinetic friction is constant and it can be denoted by f_k.
9. It is found experimentally that limiting value of static friction f_L and constant value of kinetic friction f_k both are directly proportional to normal reaction N acting between the two bodies.

$\therefore$ $$f_L \text{ or } f_k \propto N$$

$\Rightarrow$ $$f_L = \mu_s N$$

and $$f_k = \mu_k N$$

Here, μ_s = coefficient of static friction

and μ_k = coefficient of kinetic friction.

Both μ_s and μ_k are dimensionless constants which depend on the nature of surfaces in contact. Value of μ_k is usually less than the value of μ_s i.e. constant value of kinetic friction is less than the limiting value of static friction.

Note *(i) In problems, if μ_s and μ_k are not given separately but only μ is given. Then use*

$$f_L = f_k = \mu N$$

(ii) If more than two blocks are placed one over the other on a horizontal ground then normal reaction between two blocks will be equal to the weight of the blocks over the common surface.

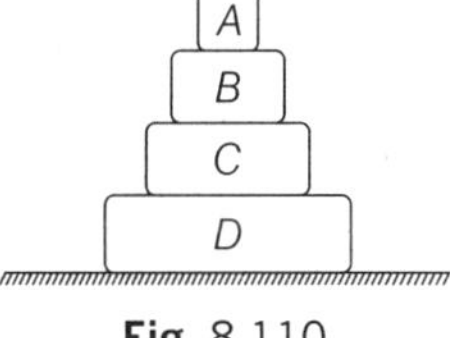

Fig. 8.110

For example, N_1 = *normal reaction between A and B*

$= m_A g$

N_2 = *normal reaction between B and C*

$= (m_A + m_B) g$ *and so on.*

Extra Points to Remember

- **Friction force is electromagnetic in nature.**

The surfaces in contact, however smooth they may appear, actually have imperfections called asperities. When one surface rests on the other the actual area of contact is very less than the surface area of the face of contact.

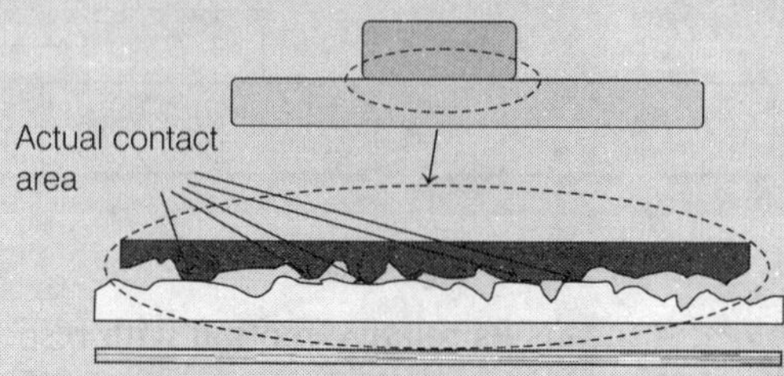

Fig. 8.111

The pressure due to the reaction force between the surfaces is very high as the true contact area is very small. Hence, these contact points deform a little and cold welds are formed at these points.
So, in order to start the relative sliding between these surfaces, enough force has to be applied to break these welds. But, once the welds break and the surfaces start sliding over each other, the further formation of these welds is relatively slow and weak and hence a smaller force is enough to keep the block moving with uniform velocity.
This is the reason why limiting value of static friction is greater than the kinetic friction.

Note *By making the surfaces extra smooth, frictional force increases as actual area of contact increases and the two bodies in contact act like a single body.*

Example 8.26 *Suppose a block of mass 1 kg is placed over a rough surface and a horizontal force F is applied on the block as shown in figure. Now, let us see what are the values of force of friction f and acceleration of the block a if the force F is gradually increased. Given that* $\mu_s = 0.5, \mu_k = 0.4$ *and* $g = 10\ m/s^2$.

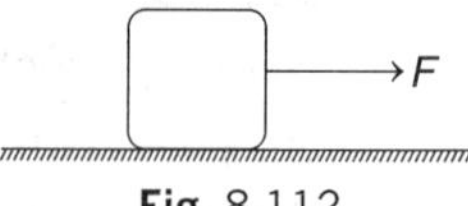

Fig. 8.112

Solution Free body diagram of the block is

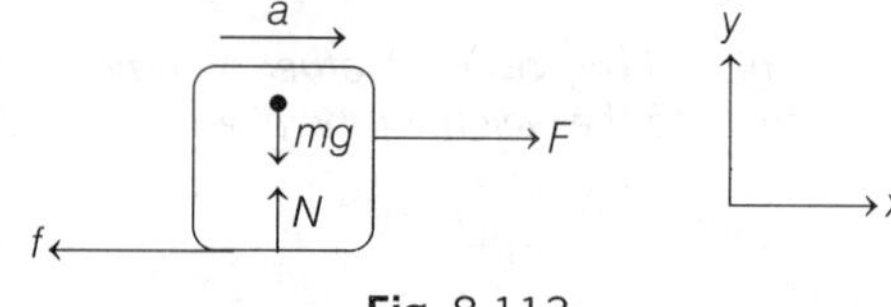

Fig. 8.113

$$\Sigma F_y = 0$$

$\therefore$ $$N - mg = 0$$

or $$N = mg = (1)(10) = 10\ N$$

$$f_L = \mu_s N = (0.5)(10) = 5\ N$$

and $$f_k = \mu_k N = (0.4)(10) = 4\ N$$

Below is explained in tabular form, how the force of friction f depends on the applied force F.

F	f	$F_{net} = F - f$	Static or kinetic friction	Relative motion or tendency of relative motion	Acceleration of block $a = \frac{F_{net}}{m}$	Diagram
0	0	0	static	Neither tendency nor actual relative motion	0	
2 N	2 N	0	static	Tendency	0	$f = 2$ N, $F = 2$ N
4 N	4 N	0	static	Tendency	0	$f = 4$ N, $F = 4$ N
5 N	5 N	0	static	Tendency	0	$f_L = 5$ N, $F = 5$ N
6 N	4 N	2 N	kinetic	Actual relative motion	2 m/s^2	$a = 2$ m/s^2, $f_k = 4$ N, $F = 6$ N
8 N	4 N	4 N	kinetic	Actual relative motion	4 m/s^2	$a = 4$ m/s^2, $f_k = 4$ N, $F = 8$ N

Graphically, this can be understood as under:

Note that $f = F$ till $F \leq f_L$. Therefore, slope of line OA will be 1 ($y = mx$) or angle of line OA with F-axis is 45°.

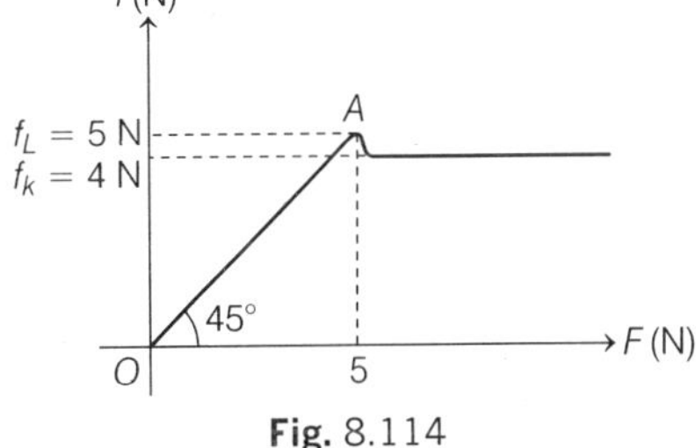

Fig. 8.114

Here, $a = 0$ for $F \leq 5$ N

and $$a = \frac{F - f_K}{m} = \frac{F - 4}{1} = F - 4 \text{ for } F > 5 \text{ N}$$

a-F graph is as shown in Fig. 8.115. When F is slightly increased from 5 N, acceleration of block increases from 0 to 1 m/s^2. Think why?

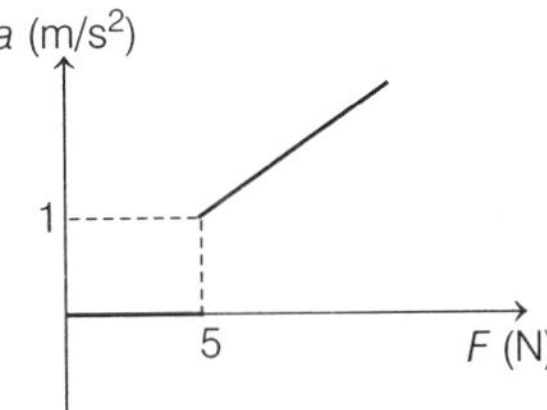

Fig. 8.115

Note *Henceforth, we will take coefficient of friction as μ unless and until specially mentioned in the question μ_s and μ_k separately.*

Angle of Friction (λ)

At a point of rough contact, where slipping is about to occur, the two forces acting on each object are the normal reaction N and frictional force μN.

The resultant of these two forces is F and it makes an angle λ with the normal reaction, where

$$\tan \lambda = \frac{\mu N}{N} = \mu \quad \text{or} \quad \lambda = \tan^{-1}(\mu) \qquad \ldots\text{(i)}$$

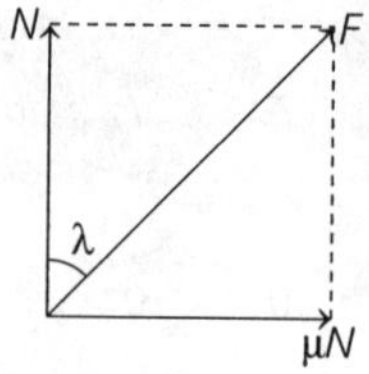

Fig. 8.116

This angle λ is called the angle of friction.

Angle of Repose (α)

Suppose a block of mass m is placed on an inclined plane whose inclination θ can be increased or decreased. Let μ be the coefficient of friction between the block and the plane. At a general angle θ,

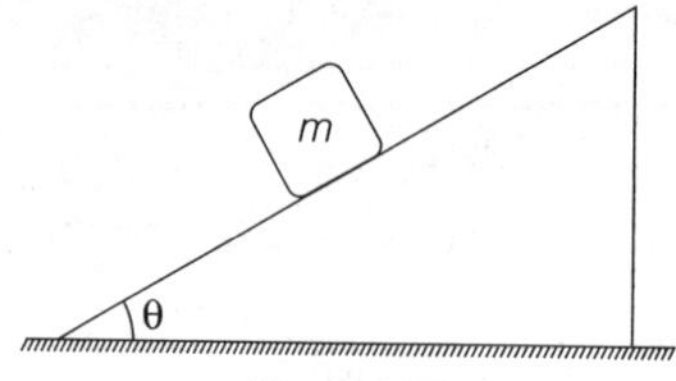

Fig. 8.117

Normal reaction $\quad N = mg \cos \theta$

Limiting friction $\quad f_L = \mu N = \mu mg \cos \theta$

and the driving force (or pulling force)

$$F = mg \sin \theta \qquad \text{(Down the plane)}$$

From these three equations we see that, when θ is increased from 0° to 90°, normal reaction N and hence, the limiting friction f_L is decreased while the driving force F is increased. There is a critical angle called angle of repose (α) at which these two forces are equal. Now, if θ is further increased, then the driving force F becomes more than the limiting friction f_L and the block starts sliding.

Thus,
$$f_L = F \quad \text{at} \quad \theta = \alpha$$

or
$$\mu\, mg \cos \alpha = mg \sin \alpha$$

or
$$\tan \alpha = \mu$$

or
$$\alpha = \tan^{-1}(\mu) \qquad \ldots\text{(ii)}$$

From Eqs. (i) and (ii), we see that angle of friction (λ) is numerically equal to the angle of repose.

or
$$\lambda = \alpha$$

From the above discussion we can conclude that

If $\theta < \alpha$, $F < f_L$ the block is stationary.

If $\theta = \alpha$, $F = f_L$ the block is on the verge of sliding.

and if $\theta > \alpha$, $F > f_L$ the block slides down with acceleration

$$a = \frac{F - f_L}{m} = g(\sin \theta - \mu \cos \theta)$$

Variation of N, f_L and F with θ, is shown graphically in Fig. 8.118.

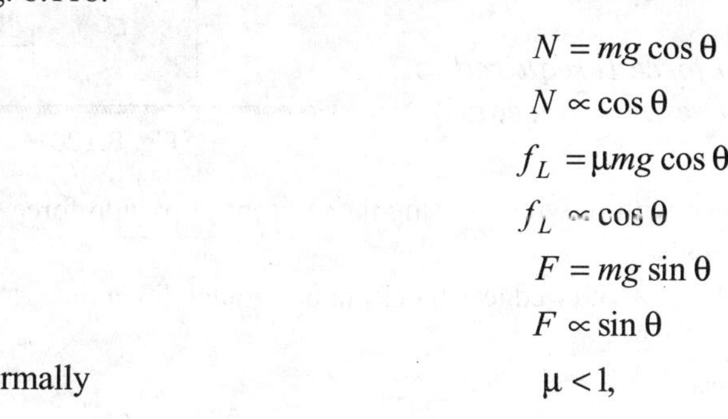

$$N = mg \cos\theta$$

or $$N \propto \cos\theta$$

$$f_L = \mu mg \cos\theta$$

or $$f_L \propto \cos\theta$$

$$F = mg \sin\theta$$

or $$F \propto \sin\theta$$

Normally $$\mu < 1,$$

So, $$f_L < N.$$

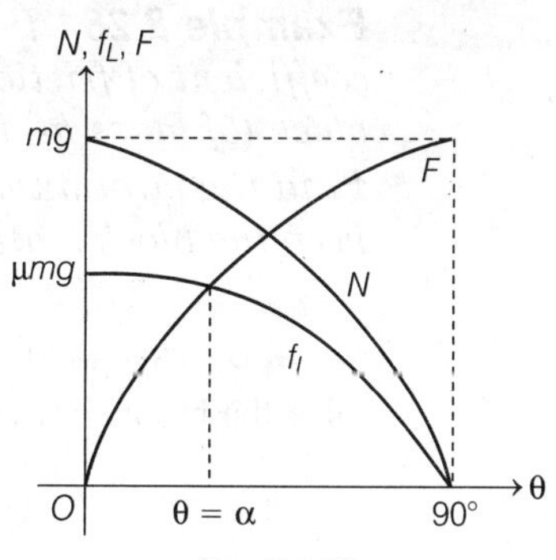

Fig. 8.118

Example 8.27 *A particle of mass 1 kg rests on rough contact with a plane inclined at 30° to the horizontal and is just about to slip. Find the coefficient of friction between the plane and the particle.*

Solution

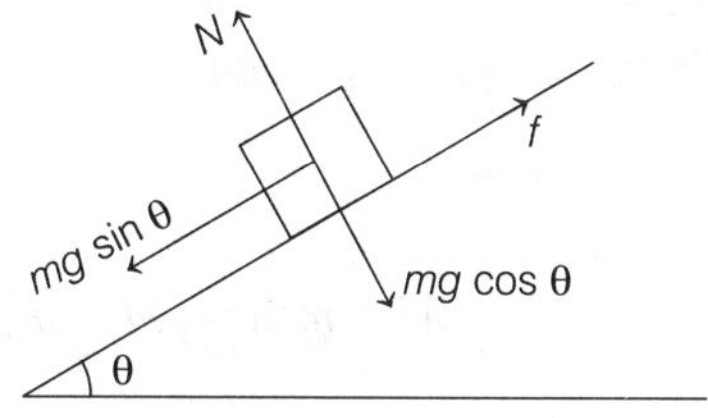

Fig. 8.119

Weight mg has two components $mg\sin\theta$ and $mg\cos\theta$. Block is at rest

$\therefore$ $$N = mg\cos\theta \quad \text{...(i)}$$

$$f = mg\sin\theta \quad \text{...(ii)}$$

Block is about to slip.

$\therefore$ $$f = f_L = \mu N \quad \text{...(iii)}$$

Here $$\mu_s = \mu$$

Solving these three equations, we get

$$\mu = \tan\theta = \tan 30°$$

$$= \frac{1}{\sqrt{3}} \quad \textbf{Ans.}$$

Note *The given angle is also angle of repose α.*

$\therefore$ $$\mu = \tan\theta = \tan\alpha = \tan 30° = \frac{1}{\sqrt{3}}$$

Example 8.28 *In the adjoining figure, the coefficient of friction between wedge (of mass M) and block (of mass m) is μ.*
Find the minimum horizontal force F required to keep the block stationary with respect to wedge.

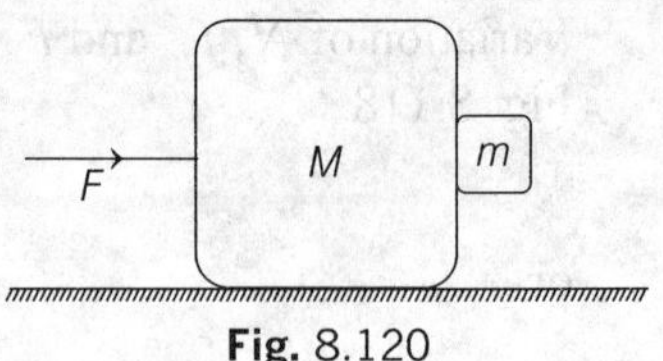

Fig. 8.120

Solution This problem can be solved with or without using the concept of pseudo force. Let us solve the problem by both the methods.

$$a = \text{acceleration of (wedge + block) in horizontal direction}$$
$$= \frac{F}{M + m}$$

Inertial Frame of Reference (Ground)

FBD of block with respect to ground (only real forces have to applied) is as shown in Fig. 8.121. With respect to ground block is moving with an acceleration a. Therefore,

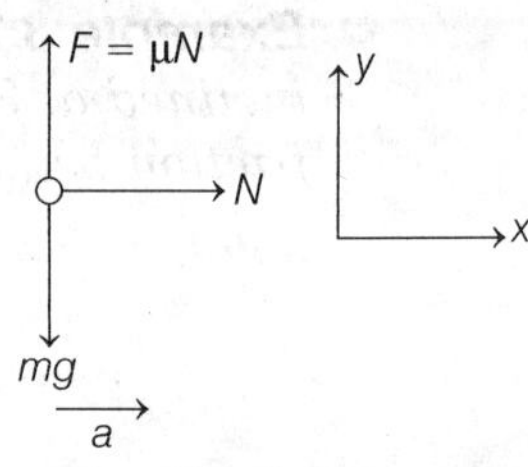

Fig. 8.121

$$\Sigma F_y = 0 \quad \text{and} \quad \Sigma F_x = ma$$
$$mg = \mu N \quad \text{and} \quad N = ma$$
$$\therefore \quad a = \frac{g}{\mu}$$
$$\therefore \quad F = (M + m)a = (M + m)\frac{g}{\mu}$$

Non-inertial Frame of Reference (Wedge)

FBD of m with respect to wedge (real + one pseudo force) is as shown in Fig. 8.122. With respect to wedge block is stationary.

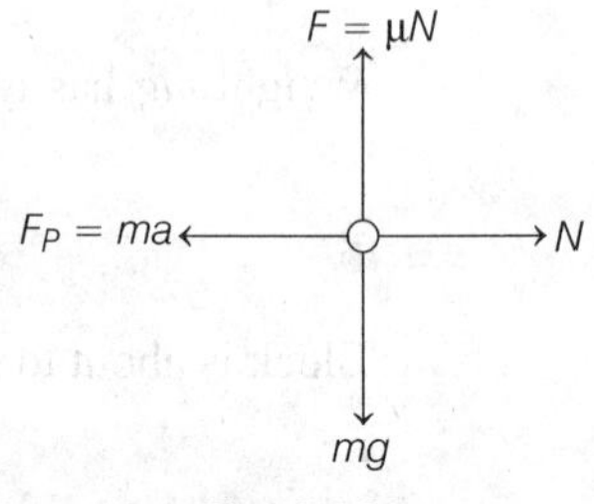

Fig. 8.122

$$\therefore \quad \Sigma F_x = 0 \text{ and } \Sigma F_y = 0$$
$$\therefore \quad mg = \mu N \quad \text{and} \quad N = ma$$
$$\therefore \quad a = \frac{g}{\mu} \quad \text{and} \quad F = (M + m)a$$
$$= (M + m)\frac{g}{\mu}$$

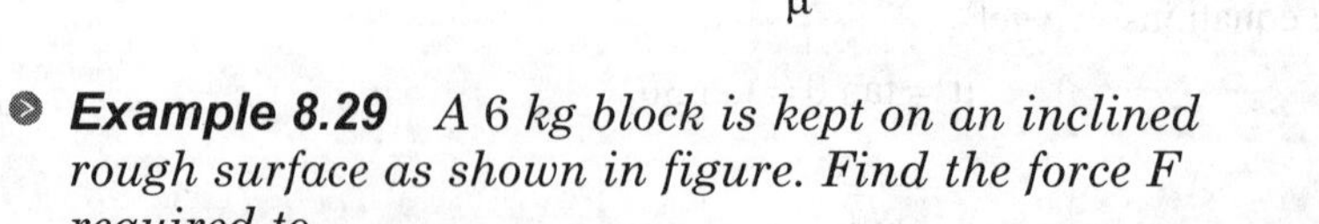

Example 8.29 *A 6 kg block is kept on an inclined rough surface as shown in figure. Find the force F required to*
(a) keep the block stationary,
(b) move the block downwards with constant velocity and
(c) move the block upwards with an acceleration of 4 m/s^2.
(Take $g = 10\, m/s^2$)

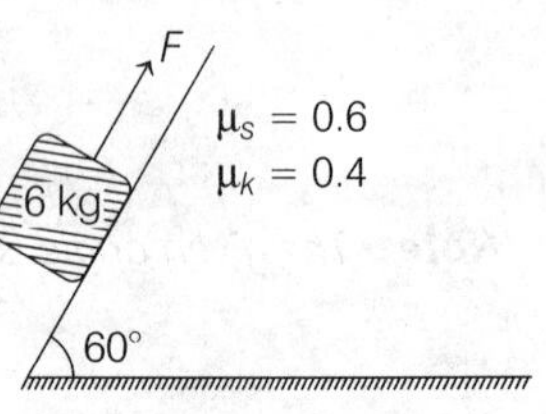

Fig. 8.123

Solution $N = mg \cos 60° = (6)(10)\left(\dfrac{1}{2}\right) = 30 \text{ N}$

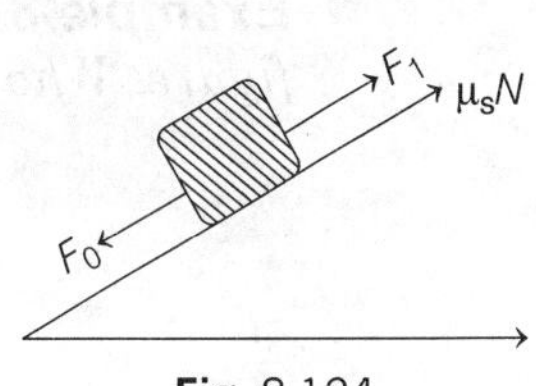

Fig. 8.124

$$\mu_S N = 18 \text{ N}$$
$$\mu_K N = 12 \text{ N}$$

Driving force $F_0 = mg \sin 60° = (6)(10)\left(\dfrac{\sqrt{3}}{2}\right) = 52 \text{ N}$

(a) Force needed to keep the block stationary is

$$F_1 = F_0 - \mu_S N \quad \text{(upwards)}$$
$$= 52 - 18$$
$$= 34 \text{ N} \quad \text{(upwards)}$$ **Ans.**

(b) If the block moves downwards with constant velocity ($a = 0, F_{net} = 0$), then kinetic friction will act in upward direction.

$\therefore$ Force needed,

$$F_2 = F_0 - \mu_K N \quad \text{(upwards)}$$
$$= 52 - 12$$
$$= 40 \text{ N} \quad \text{(upwards)}$$ **Ans.**

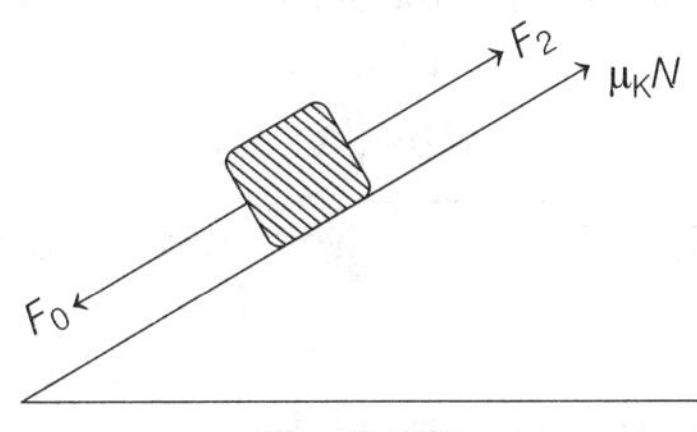

Fig. 8.125

(c) In this case, kinetic friction will act in downward direction

$$F_3 - F_0 - \mu_K N = ma$$

or $$F_3 - 52 - 12 = ma = (6)(4)$$

$\therefore$ $$F_3 = 88 \text{ N} \quad \text{(upwards)}$$ **Ans.**

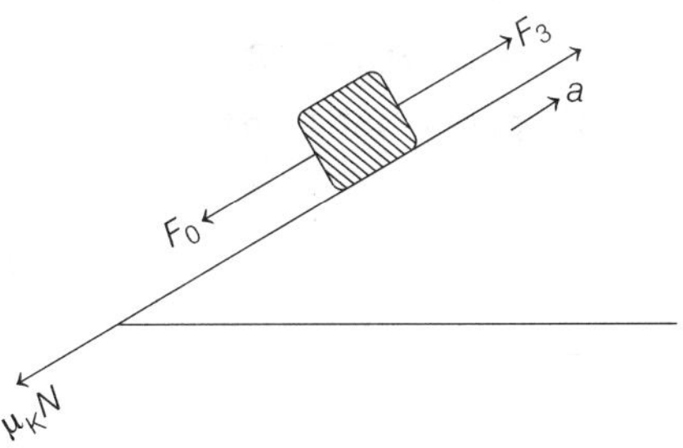

Fig. 8.126

Example 8.30 *A block of mass m is at rest on a rough wedge as shown in figure. What is the force exerted by the wedge on the block?*

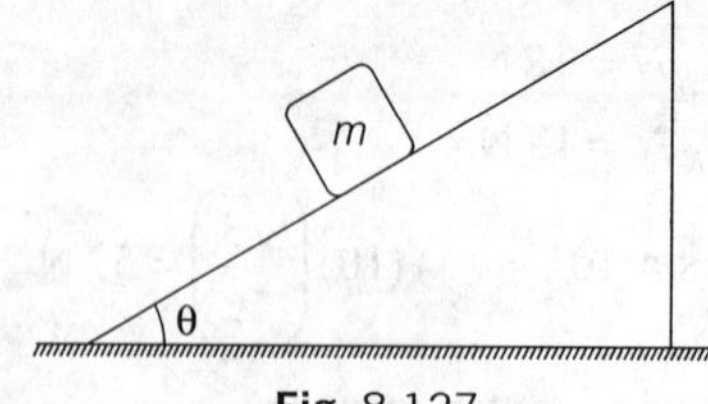

Fig. 8.127

Solution Since, the block is permanently at rest, it is in equilibrium. Net force on it should be zero. In this case, only two forces are acting on the block

(1) Weight = mg (downwards).

(2) Contact force (resultant of normal reaction and friction force) applied by the wedge on the block.

For the block to be in equilibrium, these two forces should be equal and opposite.

Therefore, force exerted by the wedge on the block is mg (upwards).

Note *(i) From Newton's third law of motion, force exerted by the block on the wedge is also mg but downwards.*

(ii) This result can also be obtained in a different manner. The normal force on the block is $N = mg\cos\theta$ and the friction force on the block is $f = mg\sin\theta$ (not $\mu\, mg\cos\theta$)

These two forces are mutually perpendicular.

$\therefore$ *Net contact force would be* $\sqrt{N^2 + f^2}$

or $\sqrt{(mg\cos\theta)^2 + (mg\sin\theta)^2}$ *which is equal to mg.*

INTRODUCTORY EXERCISE 8.5

1. In the three figures shown, find acceleration of block and force of friction on it in each case.

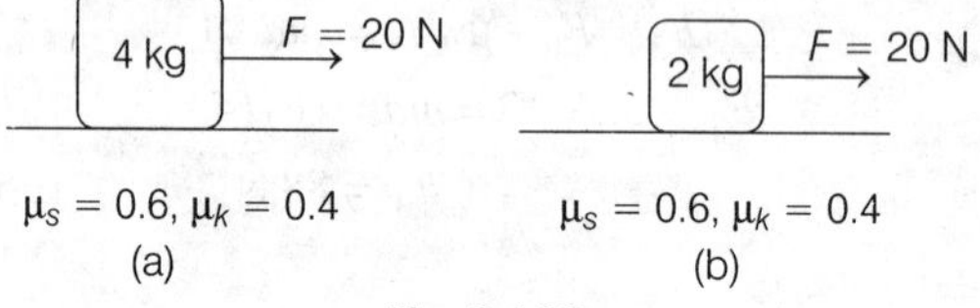

Fig. 8.128

2. In the figure shown, angle of repose is 45°. Find force of friction, net force and acceleration of the block when

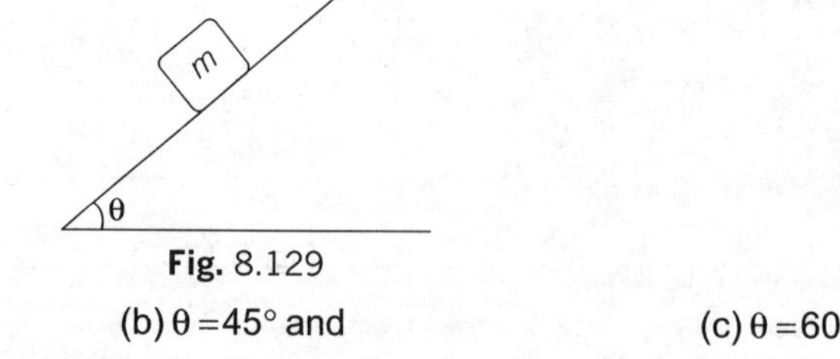

Fig. 8.129

(a) $\theta = 30°$ (b) $\theta = 45°$ and (c) $\theta = 60°$

Core Concepts

1. In Fig. (i), normal reaction at point P (between blocks C and D) is given by,

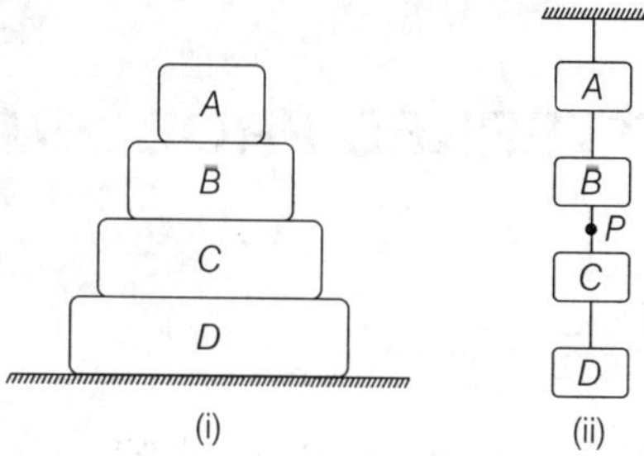

$$N = [\Sigma(\text{mass above } P)] \times g_{\text{eff}} = (m_A + m_B + m_C)\, g_{\text{eff}}$$

In Fig. (ii), tension at point P is given by,

$$T = \Sigma\,[(\text{mass below } P)] \times g_{\text{eff}}$$

If the strings are massless then, $T = (m_C + m_D) g_{\text{eff}}$

Here, $g_{\text{eff}} = g$ if acceleration of system is zero

$= (g + a)$ if acceleration a is upwards

$= (g - a)$ if acceleration a is downwards

2. Feeling of weight to a person is due to the normal reaction. Under normal conditions, $N = mg$. Therefore feeling of weight is the actual weight mg. If we are standing on a lift and the lift has an acceleration 'a' upwards then $N = m(g + a)$. Therefore feeling of weight is more than the actual weight mg. Similarly if 'a' is downwards then $N = m(g - a)$ and feeling of weight is less than the actual weight mg.

3. If $\mu_s = \mu_N = \mu$ then, limiting value of static friction = constant value of kinetic friction = μN.

Here, $N = mg$ on horizontal ground or $N = mg\cos\theta$ on inclined ground as long as the external forces (other than weight and normal reaction) are either zero or tangential to the surface. If the external force is inclined to the horizontal surface (or inclined plane), then normal reaction either increases or decreases depending on the direction of F.

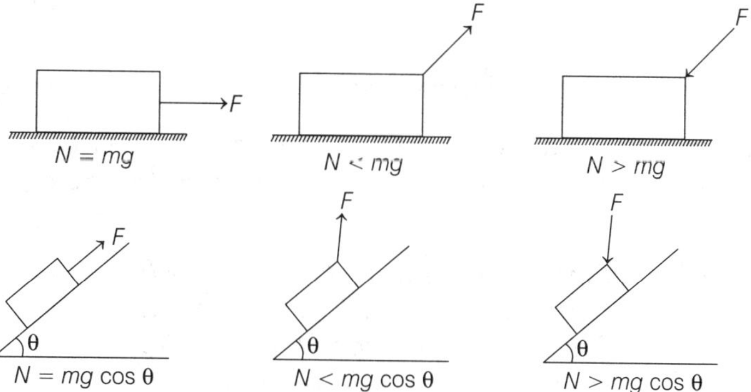

Solved Examples

PATTERNED PROBLEMS

Type 1. *Resolution of forces*

Concept

Different situations of this type can be classified in following two types:

(i) Permanent rest, body in equilibrium, net force equal to zero, net acceleration equal to zero or moving with constant velocity.

(ii) Accelerated and temporary rest.

How to Solve?

- In the first situation, forces can be resolved in any direction. Net force (or summation of components of different forces acting on the body) in any direction should be zero.
- In the second situation forces are normally resolved along acceleration and perpendicular to it. In a direction perpendicular to acceleration net force is zero and along acceleration net force is *ma*.
- In temporary rest situation velocity of the body is zero but acceleration is not zero. The direction of acceleration in this case is the direction in which the body is supposed to move just after few seconds. Three situations of temporary rest are shown below.

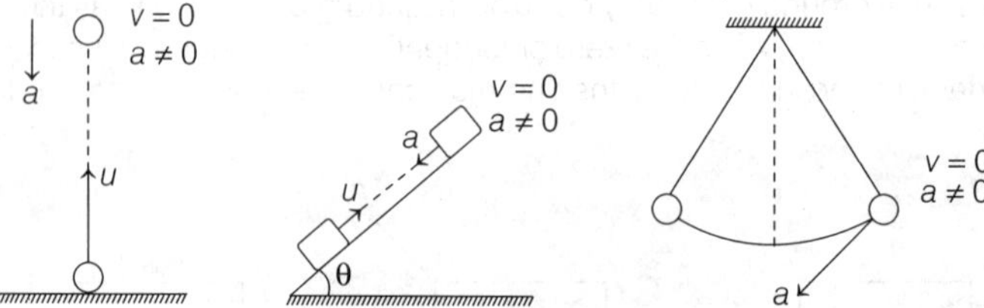

Note *In the second situation also, we can resolve the forces in any direction. In that case, net force along this direction = (mass) (component of acceleration in this direction)*

Example 1 *A ball of mass 1 kg is at rest in position P by means of two light strings OP and RP. The string RP is now cut and the ball swings to position Q. If $\theta = 45°$. Find the tensions in the strings in positions OP (when RP was not cut) and OQ (when RP was cut). (Take $g = 10\ m/s^2$).*

Solution In the first case, ball is in equilibrium (permanent rest). Therefore, net force on the ball in any direction should be zero.

$\therefore$ (ΣF) in vertical direction $= 0$

or $$T_1 \cos\theta = mg$$

or $$T_1 = \frac{mg}{\cos\theta}$$

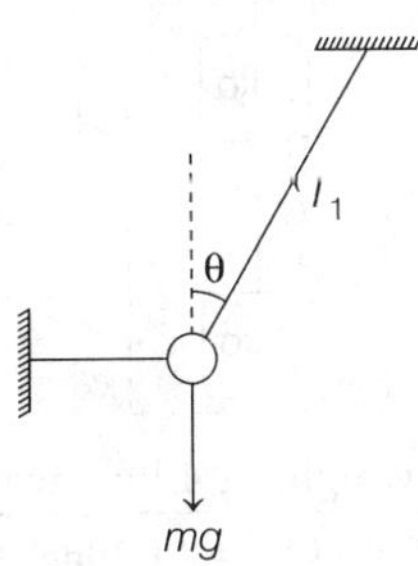

Substituting $m_1 = 1$ kg, $g = 10$ m/s^2 and $\theta = 45°$

we get, $$T_1 = 10\sqrt{2}\text{ N}$$

Note *Here, we deliberately resolved all the forces in vertical direction because component of the tension in RP in vertical direction is zero. In a direction other than vertical we will also have to consider component of tension in RP, which will unnecessarily increase our calculation.*

In the second case ball is not in equilibrium (temporary rest). After few seconds it will move in a direction perpendicular to OQ. Therefore, net force on the ball at Q is perpendicular to OQ or net force along $OQ = 0$.

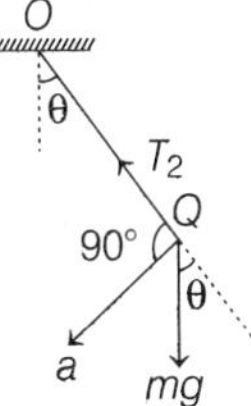

$\therefore$ $$T_2 = mg\cos\theta$$

Substituting the values, we get $$T_2 = 5\sqrt{2}\text{ N}$$

Here, we can see that $$T_1 \neq T_2$$

Type 2. *To find tension at some point (say at P) if it is variable*

How to Solve?

- Find acceleration (a common acceleration) of the system by using the equation
$$a = \frac{\text{net pulling or pushing force}}{\text{total mass}}$$
In some cases, 'a' will be given in the question.
- Cut the string at P and divide the system in two parts.
- Make free body diagram of any one part (preferably of the smaller one).
- In its FBD make one tension at point P in a direction away from the block with which this part of the string is attached.
- Write the equation,
$$F_{net} = ma$$
for this part. You will get tension at P. In this equation m is not the total mass. It is mass of this part only.

Example 2 *In the given figure mass of string AB is 2 kg. Find tensions at A, B and C, where C is the mid point of string.*

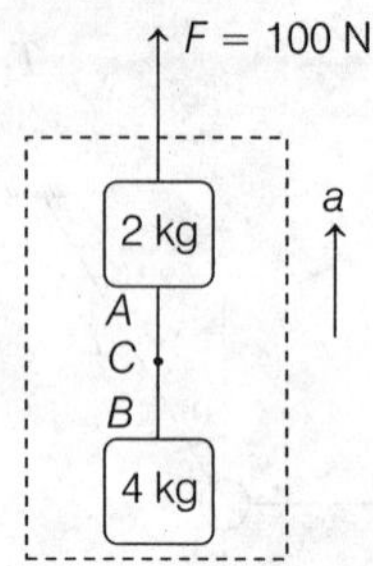

Solution $a = \dfrac{F - \text{weight of 2 kg} - \text{weight of 4 kg} - \text{weight of string}}{\text{mass of 2 kg} + \text{mass of 4 kg} + \text{mass of string}}$

$= \dfrac{100 - 20 - 40 - 20}{2 + 4 + 2}$ $\quad (g = 10 \text{ m/s}^2)$

$= \dfrac{20}{8} = 2.5 \text{ m/s}^2$

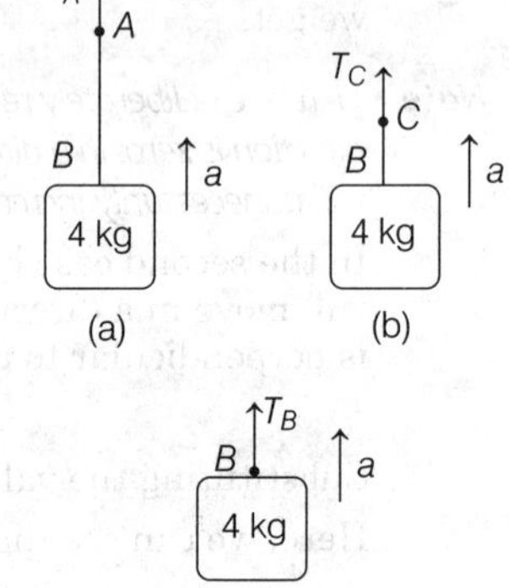

Refer Fig. (a) $\quad T_A - m_{AB}g - 40 = (m_{AB} + 4)a$

or $\quad T_A - 20 - 40 = (2 + 4)(2.5)$

$T_A = 75 \text{ N}$ **Ans.**

Refer Fig. (b) $\quad T_C - m_{BC}g - 40 = (m_{BC} + 4)a$

or $\quad T_C - 10 - 40 = (1 + 4)(2.5)$

or $\quad T_C = 62.5 \text{ N}$ **Ans.**

Refer Fig. (c) $\quad T_B - 40 = 4a$

or $\quad T_B = 40 + 4 \times 2.5$

or $\quad T_B = 50 \text{ N}$ **Ans.**

Note *Tension at a general point P can be given by :*

$$T_P = [(\Sigma \text{ mass below } P) \times g_{eff}]$$

Here $\quad g_{eff} = g + a = 12.5 \text{ m/s}^2$

Type 3. ***Based on constraint relation between a block (or a plank) and a wedge.***

These type of problems can be understood by following two examples:

Example 3 *In the figure shown find relation between magnitudes of* $\mathbf{a}_A$ *and* $\mathbf{a}_B$.

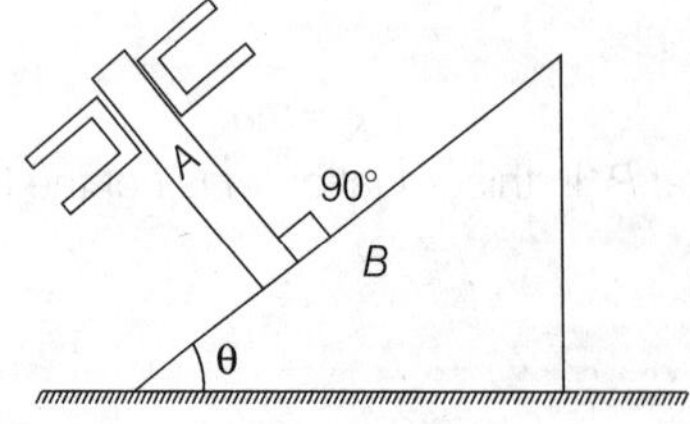

Solution $x_A = x_B \sin\theta$ ...(i)

Here, θ = constant

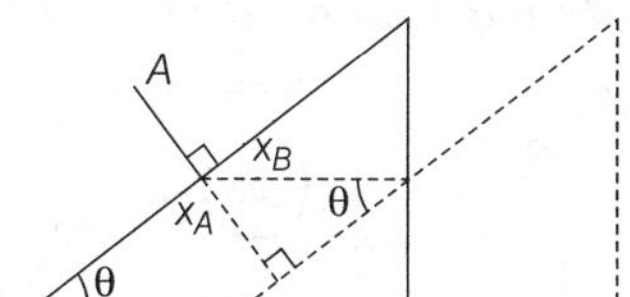

Double differentiating Eq. (i) with respect to time, we get

$$a_A = a_B \sin\theta$$ **Ans.**

Example 4 *In the arrangement shown in the figure, the rod of mass m held by two smooth walls, remains always perpendicular to the surface of the wedge of mass M. Assuming all the surfaces to be frictionless, find the acceleration of the rod and that of the wedge.*

Solution Let acceleration of m be a_1 (absolute) and that of M be a_2 (absolute).

Writing equations of motion only in the directions of a_1 or a_2.

For *m* $$mg\cos\alpha - N = ma_1$$ ...(i)

For *M*, $$N\sin\alpha = Ma_2$$ ...(ii)

Here, N = normal reaction between m and M

As discussed above, constraint equation can be written as,

$$a_1 = a_2 \sin\alpha$$ ...(iii)

Solving above three equations, we get

acceleration of rod, $$a_1 = \frac{mg\cos\alpha\sin\alpha}{\left(m\sin\alpha + \dfrac{M}{\sin\alpha}\right)}$$ **Ans.**

and acceleration of wedge $$a_2 = \frac{mg\cos\alpha}{m\sin\alpha + \dfrac{M}{\sin\alpha}}$$ **Ans.**

Type 4. *Based on constraint relation which keeps on changing.*

Concept

(i) In the constraint relations discussed so far the relation between different accelerations was fixed.

For example: In the two illustrations discussed above $a_A = a_B \sin\theta$ or $a_1 = a_2 \sin\alpha$ but these relations were fixed, as θ or α was constant.

(ii) In some cases, θ or α keeps on changing. Therefore, the constraint relation also keeps on changing.

(iii) In this case, constraint relation between different accelerations becomes very complex. So, normally constraint relation between velocities is only asked.

Example 5 *In the arrangement shown in the figure, the ends P and Q of an unstretchable string move downwards with uniform speed U. Pulleys A and B are fixed. Mass M moves upwards with a speed* **(JEE 1982)**

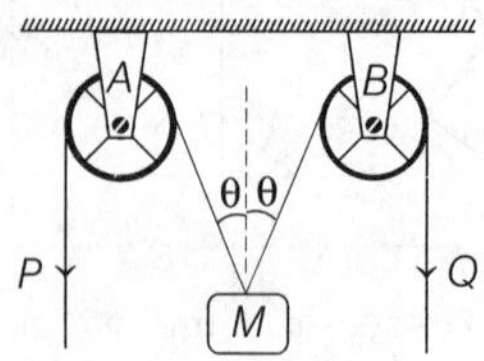

(a) $2U\cos\theta$ (b) $\dfrac{U}{\cos\theta}$ (c) $\dfrac{2U}{\cos\theta}$ (d) $U\cos\theta$

Solution In the right angle ΔPQR

$$l^2 = c^2 + y^2$$

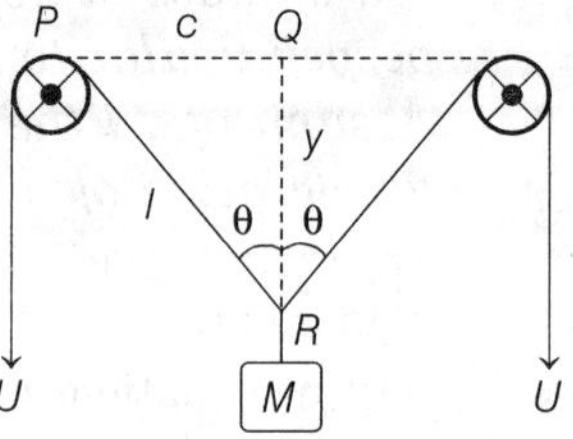

c = constant, l and y are variables

Differentiating this equation with respect to time, we get

$$2l\frac{dl}{dt} = 0 + 2y\frac{dy}{dt} \quad \text{or} \quad \left(-\frac{dy}{dt}\right) = \frac{l}{y}\left(-\frac{dl}{dt}\right)$$

Here, $-\dfrac{dy}{dt} = v_M,\ \dfrac{l}{y} = \dfrac{1}{\cos\theta}$ and $-dl/dt = U$

Hence, $$v_M = \frac{U}{\cos\theta}$$

∴ The correct option is (b).

Note *Here θ is variable. Therefore the constraint relation* $v_M = \dfrac{U}{\cos\theta}$ *is also variable.*

Example 6 *In the adjoining figure, wire PQ is smooth, ring A has a mass 1 kg and block B, 2 kg. If system is released from rest with θ=60°, find*

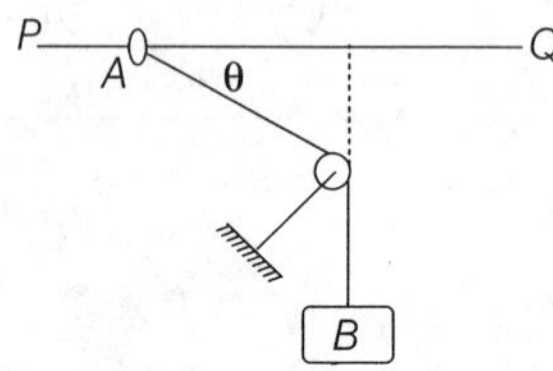

(a) constraint relation between their velocities as a function of θ.
(b) constraint relation between their accelerations just after the release at θ = 60°.
(c) tension in the string and the values of these accelerations at this instant.

Solution M and Q are two fixed fixed points. Therefore,

$$MQ = \text{constant} = c$$

$$l = \text{length of string} = \text{constant}.$$

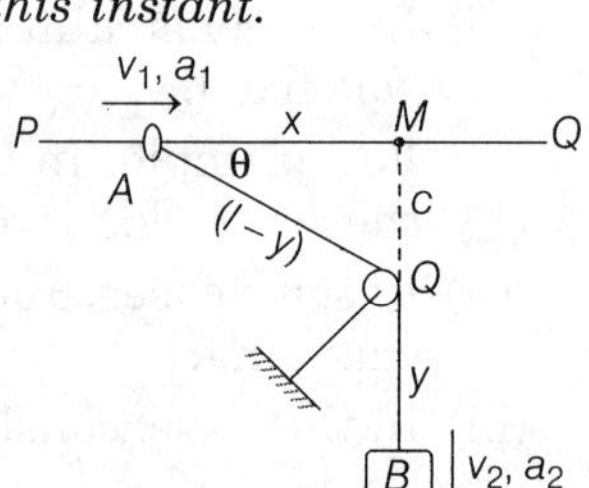

(a) In triangle MQA, $(l-y)^2 = x^2 + c^2$

Differentiating w.r.t time, we get

$$2(l-y)\left(-\frac{dy}{dt}\right) = 2x\left(+\frac{dx}{dt}\right) + 0$$

or $$(l-y)\left(+\frac{dy}{dt}\right)=x\left(-\frac{dx}{dt}\right) \quad \text{...(i)}$$

$\therefore$ $$\frac{dy}{dt}=\left(\frac{x}{l-y}\right)\left(-\frac{dx}{dt}\right) \quad \text{...(ii)}$$

y is increasing with time,

$\therefore$ $$+\frac{dy}{dt}=v_2$$

x is decreasing with time

$\therefore$ $$-\frac{dx}{dt}=v_1 \quad \text{and} \quad \frac{x}{l-y}=\cos\theta$$

Substituting these values in Eq. (ii), we have

$$v_2=v_1\cos\theta$$ **Ans.**

(b) Further differentiating Eq. (i), we have

$$\frac{d^2y}{dt^2}(l-y)-\left(\frac{dy}{dt}\right)^2=-\left[x\cdot\frac{d^2x}{dt^2}+\left(\frac{dx}{dt}\right)^2\right] \quad \text{...(iii)}$$

Just after the release, $v_1, v_2, \frac{dx}{dt}$ and $\frac{dy}{dt}$ all are zero. Substituting in Eq. (iii), we have,

$$\frac{d^2y}{dt^2}=\left(\frac{x}{l-y}\right)\left(-\frac{d^2x}{dt^2}\right) \quad \text{...(iv)}$$

Here, $$\frac{d^2y}{dt^2}=a_2 \text{ and } -\frac{d^2x}{dt^2}=a_1$$

$$\frac{x}{l-y}=\cos\theta=\cos 60°=\frac{1}{2}$$

Substituting in Eq. (iv), we have $$a_2=\frac{a_1}{2} \quad \text{...(v)}$$

(c) **For *A*** Equation is

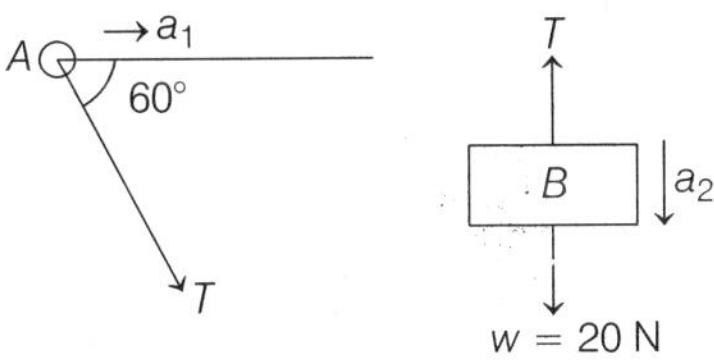

$$T\cos 60°=m_A a_1 \quad \text{or} \quad \frac{T}{2}=(1)a_1=a_1 \quad \text{...(vi)}$$

For *B*

$$20-T=m_B a_2$$

$$20-T=2a_2 \quad \text{...(vii)}$$

Solving Eqs. (v), (vi) and (vii), we get

$$T=\frac{40}{3}\text{ N} \Rightarrow a_1=\frac{20}{3}\text{ m/s}^2$$

and $$a_2=\frac{10}{3}\text{ m/s}^2$$

Note *Eq. (iii) converts into a simple Eq. (iv), just after the release when v_1, v_2, $\frac{dx}{dt}$ and $\frac{dy}{dt}$ all are zero.*

Type 5. *To find whether the block will move or not under different forces kept over a rough surface*

How to Solve?

- The rough surface may be horizontal, inclined or vertical.
- Resolve the forces along the surface and perpendicular to the surface.
- In most of the cases, acceleration perpendicular to the surface is zero.
- So net force perpendicular to the surface should be zero. By putting net force perpendicular to the surface equal to zero we will get normal reaction N.
- After finding, N, calculate $\mu_s N$, $\mu_k N$ or μN.
- Calculate net force along the plane and call it the driving force F.

Now, if $$F \le \mu_s N$$

Then $$f = F \qquad (f = \text{Force of friction})$$

and $$F_{net} = 0 \quad \text{or} \quad a = 0,$$

If $$F > \mu_s N$$

Then, $$f = \mu_k N \quad \text{and} \quad F_{net} = F - f \quad \text{or} \quad a = \frac{F_{net}}{m} \qquad \text{(in the direction of } F)$$

Example 7 *In the figure shown,*

(a) find the force of friction acting on the block.

(b) state whether the block will move or not. If yes then with what acceleration?

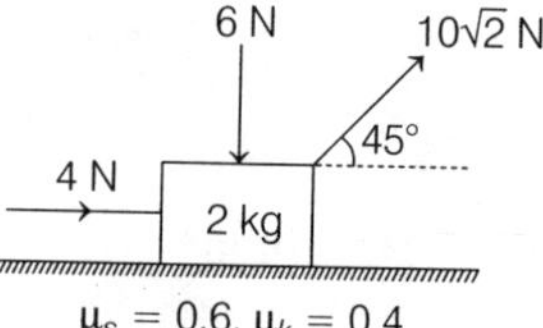

Solution Resolving the force in horizontal (along the plane) and in vertical (perpendicular to the plane) directions (except friction)

Here, R is the normal reaction.

$$\Sigma F_y = 0 \Rightarrow R = 16\,\text{N}$$

$$\mu_s R = 0.6 \times 16 = 9.6\,\text{N}$$

$$\mu_k R = 0.4 \times 16 = 6.4\,\text{N}$$

$$\Sigma F_x = \text{net driving force } F = 14\,\text{N}$$

(a) Since, $F > \mu_s R$

$\therefore$ Force of friction $f = \mu_x R$ or 6.4 N

This friction will act in the opposite direction of F.

(b) Since, $F > \mu_s R$, the block will move with an acceleration,

$$a = \frac{14 - 6.4}{2} = 3.8\,\text{m/s}^2$$

Example 8 *In the figure shown,*

(a) find the force of friction acting on the block.

(b) state whether the block will move or not. If yes then with what acceleration?

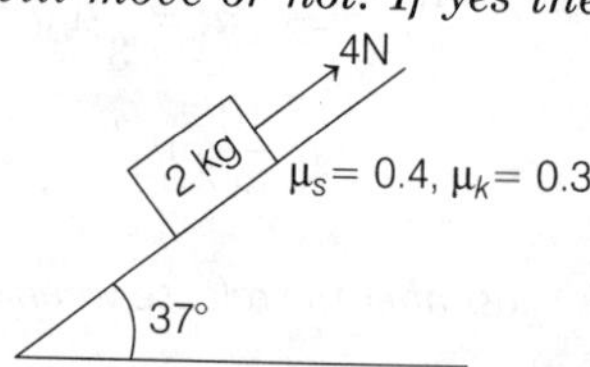

Solution Resolving the forces along the plane and perpendicular to ththe plane. (except friction)

Here, R is the normal reaction. $\Sigma F_y = 0 \Rightarrow R = 16\text{ N}$

$$\mu_s R = 0.4 \times 16 = 6.4\text{ N}$$

$$\mu_k R = 0.3 \times 16 = 4.8\text{ N}$$

$\Sigma F_x =$ net driving force $F = (12 - 4)\text{ N} = 8\text{ N}$

(a) Since, $F > \mu_s R$, therefore kinetic friction or 4.8 N will act in opposite direction of F.

(b) Since, $F > \mu_s R$, the block will move in the direction of F (or downwards) with an acceleration,

$$a = \frac{F_{\text{net}}}{m} = \frac{F - f}{m} = \frac{8 - 4.8}{2} = 1.6\text{ m/s}^2$$

This acceleration is in the direction of F (or downwards).

Example 9 *A block of mass 1 kg is pushed against a rough vertical wall with a force of 20 N, coefficient of static friction being $\frac{1}{4}$. Another horizontal force of*

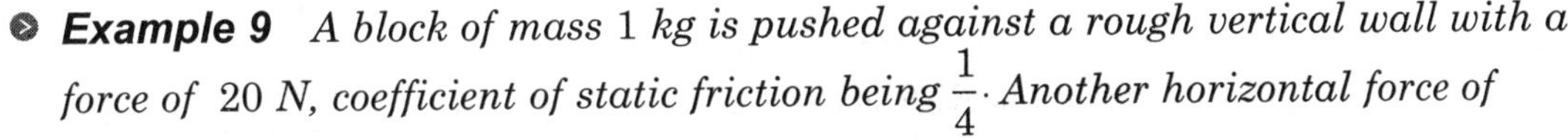

10 N is applied on the block in a direction parallel to the wall. Will the block move? If yes, in which direction? If no, find the frictional force exerted by the wall on the block. ($g = 10\ m/s^2$)

Solution Normal reaction on the block from the wall will be ($F_{\text{net}} = 0$, perpendicular to the wall)

$$R = F = 20\text{ N}$$

Therefore, limiting friction $f_L = \mu R = \left(\frac{1}{4}\right)(20) = 5\text{ N}$

Weight of the block is $w = mg = (1)(10) = 10\text{ N}$

A horizontal force of 10 N is applied to the block. Both weight and this force are along the wall. The resultant of these two forces will be $10\sqrt{2}$ N in the direction shown in figure. Since, this resultant is greater than the limiting friction. The block will move in the direction of $\mathbf{F}_{\text{net}}$ with acceleration

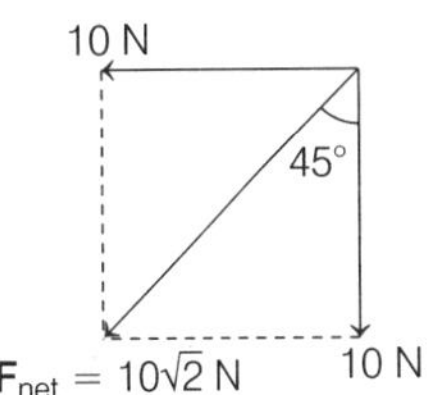

$$a = \frac{\mathbf{F}_{\text{net}} - f_L}{m} = \frac{10\sqrt{2} - 5}{1} = 9.14\text{ m/s}^2$$

Type 6. *To draw acceleration versus time graph. Following three examples will illustrate this type.*

Example 10 *In the figure shown, F is in newton and t in seconds. Take $g = 10\ m/s^2$.*

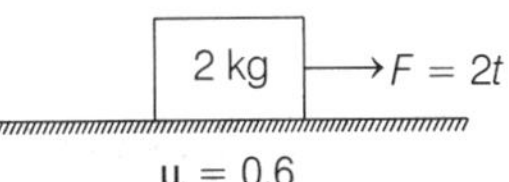

(a) Plot acceleration of the block versus time graph.

(b) Find force of friction at, $t = 2$ s and $t = 8$ s.

Solution (a) Normal reaction, $R = mg = 20\text{N}$. Limiting value of friction, $f_1 = \mu R = 0.6 \times 20 = 12\text{N}$

The applied force $F\ (=2t)$ crosses this limiting value of friction at 6 s. Therefore, upto 6 s block remains stationary and after 6 s it starts moving. After 6 s, friction becomes constant at 12 N but the applied force keeps on increasing. Therefore, acceleration keeps on increasing.

For $t \le 6$ s

$$f = F = 2t \quad \text{...(i)}$$

$$F_{\text{net}} = F - f = 0$$

$$\therefore \quad a = \frac{F_{\text{net}}}{m} = 0$$

For $t > 6$ s

$$F = 2t$$

$$f = 12\text{ N} = f_1 \quad \text{...(ii)}$$

$$F_{\text{net}} = F - f = 2t - 12$$

$$\therefore \quad a = \frac{F_{\text{net}}}{m} = \frac{2t - 12}{2} = (t - 6)$$

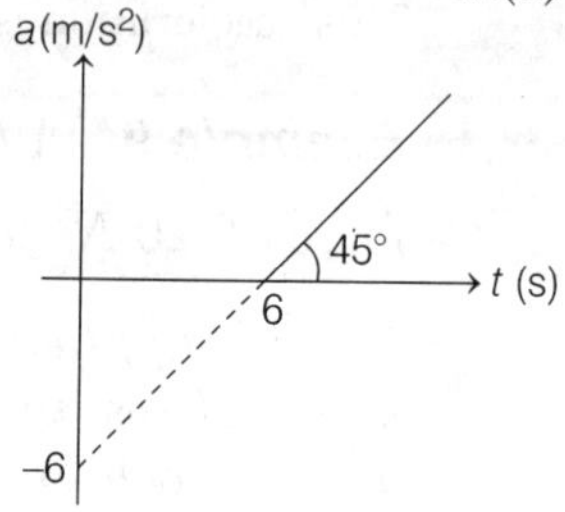

$\therefore$ a-t graph is a straight line with slope $=1$ and intercept $=-6$.

Corresponding a-t graph is as shown.

a(m/s²)
45°
t (s)
6
–6

(b) At $t = 2\text{s}$, $f = 4\text{ N}$ [from Eq. (i)]

At $t = 8\text{s}$, $f = 12\text{ N}$ [from Eq. (ii)]

Example 11 *Repeat the above problem, if instead of μ we are given μ_s and μ_k, where $\mu_s = 0.6$ and $\mu_k = 0.4$.*

Solution (a) $R = mg = 20\text{ N}$

$$\mu_s R = 0.6 \times 20 = 12\text{ N}$$

$$\mu_k R = 0.4 \times 20 = 8\text{ N}$$

Upto 6 s, situation is same but after 6 s, a constant kinetic friction of 8N will act. At 6 s, friction will suddenly change from 12 N $(=\mu_s R)$ to 8N $(=\mu_k R)$ and direction of friction is opposite to its motion. Therefore, at 6 s it will start with an initial acceleration.

$$a_i = \frac{\text{decrease in friction}}{\text{mass}} = \frac{12 - 8}{2} = 2\text{ m/s}^2$$

For $t \le 6$ s

$$f = F = 2t \quad \text{...(i)}$$

$$F_{\text{net}} = F - f = 0$$

$$\therefore \quad a = \frac{F_{\text{net}}}{m} = 0$$

For $t \ge 6$ s

$$F = 2t$$

$$f = \mu_k R = 8\text{N}$$

$$F_{\text{net}} = F - f = 2t - 8$$

$$\therefore \quad a = \frac{F_{\text{net}}}{m} = \frac{2t - 8}{2} = (t - 4)$$

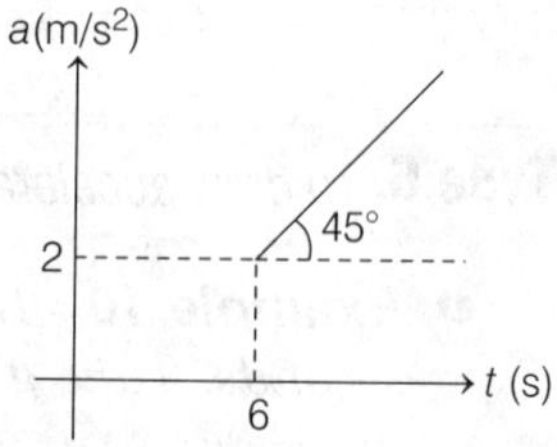

a(m/s²)
45°
2
t (s)
6

At $t = 6$ s, we can see that, $a_i = 2\text{ m/s}^2$

Further, a - t graph is a straight line of slope = 1 and intercept = –4. Corresponding a - t graph is as shown in figure.

Example 12 *Two blocks A and B of masses 2 kg and 4 kg are placed one over the other as shown in figure. A time varying horizontal force $F = 2t$ is applied on the upper block as shown in figure. Here t is in second and F is in newton. Draw a graph showing accelerations of A and B on y-axis and time on x-axis. Coefficient of friction between A and B is $\mu = \frac{1}{2}$ and the horizontal surface over which B is placed is smooth. ($g = 10\ m/s^2$)*

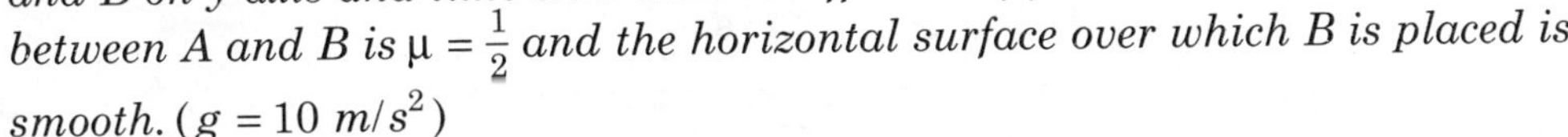

Concept

In the given example, block A will move due to the applied force but block B moves due to friction (between A and B). But there is a limiting value of friction between them. Therefore, there is a limiting value of acceleration (of block B). Up to this acceleration they move as a single block with a common acceleration, but after that acceleration of B will become constant (as friction acting on this block will become constant). But acceleration of A will keep on increasing as a time increasing force is acting on it.

Solution Limiting friction between A and B is

$$f_L = \mu m_A g = \left(\frac{1}{2}\right)(2)\ (10) = 10\ \text{N}$$

Block B moves due to friction only. Therefore, maximum acceleration of B can be

$$a_{\max} = \frac{f_L}{m_B} = \frac{10}{4} = 2.5\ \text{m/s}^2$$

Thus, both the blocks move together with same acceleration till the common acceleration becomes $2.5\ \text{m/s}^2$, after that acceleration of B will become constant while that of A will go on increasing. To find the time when the acceleration of both the blocks becomes $2.5\ \text{m/s}^2$ (or when slipping will start between A and B) we will write

For $t \geq 7.5$ s

$$2.5 = \frac{F}{(m_A + m_B)} = \frac{2t}{6}$$

$\therefore$ $\quad t = 7.5$ s

Hence, for $\quad t \leq 7.5$ s

$$a_A = a_B = \frac{F}{m_A + m_B} = \frac{2t}{6} = \frac{t}{3}$$

Thus, a_A *versus* t or a_B *versus* t graph is a straight line passing through origin of slope $\frac{1}{3}$.

For, $\quad t \geq 7.5$ s

$$a_B = 2.5\ \text{m/s}^2 = \text{constant}$$

and

$$a_A = \frac{F - f_L}{m_A}$$

or

$$a_A = \frac{2t - 10}{2} \quad \text{or} \quad a_A = t - 5$$

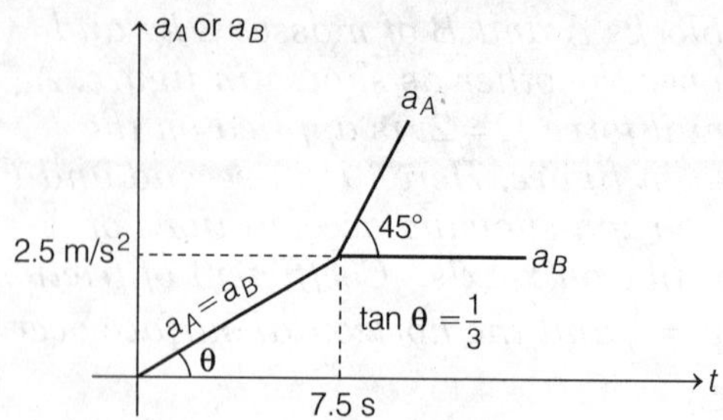

Thus, a_A *versus* t graph is a straight line of slope 1 and intercept –5. While a_B *versus* t graph is a straight line parallel to t-axis. The corresponding graph is as shown in above figure.

Type 7. *When two blocks in contact are given different velocities and after some time, due to friction their velocities become equal.*

Concept

In the figure shown, if $v_1 > v_2$ (or $v_1 \neq v_2$) then there is a relative motion between the two blocks.

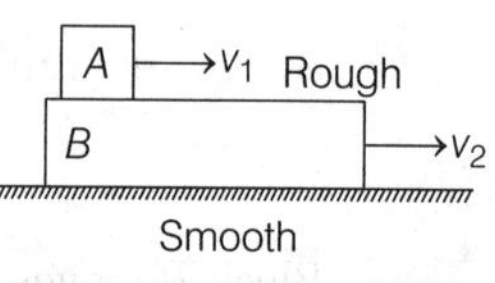

As $v_1 > v_2$, relative motion of A is towards right and relation motion of B is towards left. Since, relative motion is there, so kinetic friction (or limiting value of friction) will act in the opposite direction of relative motion. This friction (and acceleration due to this force) with decrease the velocity of A and increase the velocity of B. After some time when their velocities become equal, frictional force between them becomes zero and they continue to be moving with that common velocity (as the ground is smooth).

How to Solve?

- Find value of kinetic friction or limiting value of friction ($f = \mu_k N$ or μN) between the two blocks and then accelerations of these blocks $\left(= \frac{f}{m}\right)$. Then write $v_1 = v_2$, as their velocities become same when relatative motion is stopped.

  or
  $$u_1 + a_1 t = u_2 + a_2 t \quad \dots \text{(i)}$$
  Substituting the proper values of u_1, a_1, u_2 and a_2 in Eq. (i), we can find the time when the velocities become equal.

Example 13 *Coefficient of friction between two blocks shown in figure is $\mu = 0.6$. The blocks are given velocities in the directions shown in figure. Find*

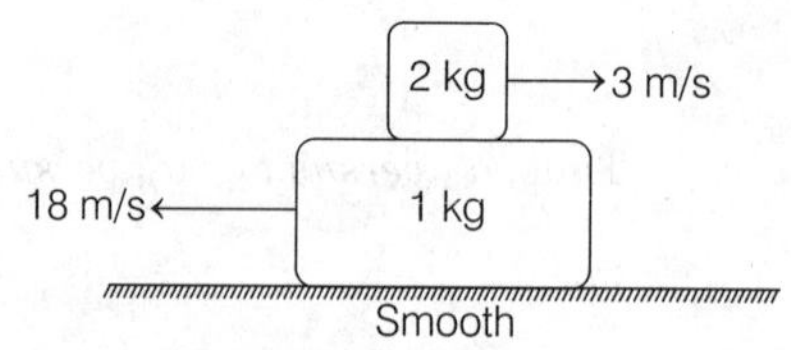

(a) the time when relative motion between them is stopped.

(b) the common velocity of the two blocks.

(c) the displacements of 1 kg and 2 kg blocks upto that instant. (Take $g = 10\ m/s^2$)

Note *Assume that lower block is sufficiently long and upper block does not fall from it.*

Solution Relative motion of 2 kg block is towards right. Therefore, maximum friction on this block will act towards left

2 kg → 3 m/s
12 N ←
← a_2
– ←→ +

→ 12 N
18 m/s ← 1 kg
→ a_1

$$f = \mu N = (0.6)\,(2)\,(10) = 12 \text{ N}$$

$$a_2 = -\frac{12}{2} = -6 \text{ m/s}^2$$

$$a_1 = \frac{12}{1} = 12 \text{ m/s}^2$$

(a) Relative motion between them will stop when,

$$v_1 = v_2 \quad \text{or} \quad u_1 + a_1 t = u_2 + a_2 t$$

or $$-18 + 12t = 3 - 6t \qquad \text{...(i)}$$

Solving we get, $$t = \frac{7}{6} \text{ s}$$ **Ans.**

(b) Substituting value of 't' in Eq. (i) either on RHS or on LHS we have,

common velocity $= -4$ m/s **Ans.**

(c)

$$s_1 = u_1\,t + \frac{1}{2}\,a_1 t^2$$

$$= (-18)\left(\frac{7}{6}\right) + \frac{1}{2}\,(12)\left(\frac{7}{6}\right)^2$$

$$= -12.83 \text{ m}$$ **Ans.**

$$s_2 = u_2 t + \frac{1}{2}\,a_2 t^2$$

$$= (3)\left(\frac{7}{6}\right) + \frac{1}{2}\,(-6)\left(\frac{7}{6}\right)^2$$

$$= -0.58 \text{ m}$$ **Ans.**

Type 8. *Acceleration or retardation of a car*

Concept

A car accelerates or retards due to friction. On a horizontal road maximum available friction is μN or $\mu\, mg$ (as $N = mg$). Therefore, maximum acceleration or retardation of a car on a horizontal road is

$$a_{\max} = \frac{f_{\max}}{m} = \frac{\mu\, mg}{m} = \mu\, g$$

On an inclined plane maximum value of friction is μN or $\mu\, mg\cos\theta$ (as $N = mg\cos\theta$). Now $mg\sin\theta$ is a force which is always downwards but the frictional force varying from 0 to $\mu\, mg\cos\theta$ can be applied in upward or downward direction by the application of brakes or accelerator.

Example 14 *On a horizontal rough road, value of coefficient of friction $\mu = 0.4$. Find the minimum time in which a distance of 400m can be covered. The car starts from rest and finally comes to rest.*

Solution Maximum friction on horizontal rough road, $f_{max} = \mu mg$

$\therefore$ Maximum acceleration or retardation of the car may be

$$a_{max} \text{ or } a = \frac{f_{max}}{m} = \frac{\mu mg}{m} = \mu g$$

$$= 0.4 \times 10 = 4 \text{ m/s}^2$$

Let, the car accelerates and retards for time 't' with 4 m/s^2.

Then, $$\frac{1}{2}at^2 + \frac{1}{2}at^2 = 400 \text{ m}$$

or $$at^2 = 400 \text{ m}$$

or $$4t^2 = 400$$

or $$t = 10 \text{ s}$$

Therefore, the minimum time is 20 s (10 s of acceleration and 10 s of retardation). **Ans.**

Example 15 *A car is moving up the plane. Angle of inclination is θ and coefficient of friction is μ.*

(a) What is the condition in which car can be accelerated?

If this condition is satisfied then find

(b) maximum acceleration of the car.

(c) minimum retardation of the car.

(d) maximum retardation of the car.

Solution (a) $mg \sin\theta$ in all conditions is downwards but direction of friction may be upwards or downwards. We will have to press accelerator for upward friction and brakes for downward friction.

To accelerate the car friction should be upwards. Therefore, car can be accelerated if maximum upward friction $> mg \sin\theta$

or $$\mu mg \cos\theta > mg \sin\theta \quad \text{or} \quad \mu > \tan\theta$$

(b) Maximum acceleration

$$= \frac{\text{maximum upwards force}}{\text{mass}}$$

$$= \frac{\mu mg \cos\theta - mg \sin\theta}{m} = (\mu g \cos\theta - g \sin\theta)$$

(c) Minimum retardation will be zero, when upward friction $= mg \sin\theta$

(d) Maximum retardation

$$= \frac{\text{maximum downward force}}{m}$$

$$= \frac{mg \sin\theta + \mu mg \cos\theta}{m}$$

$$= (g \sin\theta + \mu g \cos\theta)$$

This is the case, when maximum friction force acts in downward direction.

Miscellaneous Examples

Example 16 *In the adjoining figure, angle of plane θ is increased from 0° to 90°. Plot force of friction 'f' versus θ graph.*

Solution Normal reaction, $N = mg\cos\theta$

Limiting value of static friction, $f_L = \mu_s N = \mu_s mg\cos\theta$

Constant value of kinetic friction,

$$f_K = \mu_k N = \mu_k mg\cos\theta$$

Driving force down the plane,

$$F = mg\sin\theta$$

Now block remains stationary and $f = F$ until F becomes equal to f_L

or $$mg\sin\theta = \mu_s mg\cos\theta$$

or $$\tan\theta = \mu_s \quad \text{or} \quad \theta = \tan^{-1}(\mu_s) = \theta_r \text{ (say)}$$

After this, block starts moving and constant value of kinetic friction will act. Thus,

For $\theta \le \tan^{-1}(\mu_s)$ or θ_r

$$f = F = mg\sin\theta \quad \text{or} \quad f \propto \sin\theta$$

At, $\theta = 0°$, $f = 0$ and at $\theta = \tan^{-1}(\mu_s)$ or θ_r

or $$f = mg\sin\theta_r \quad \text{or} \quad \mu_s mg\cos\theta_r$$

For $\theta > \tan^{-1}(\mu_s)$ or θ_r

$$f = f_k = \mu_k mg\cos\theta \quad \text{or} \quad f \propto \cos\theta$$

At $\theta = \tan^{-1}(\mu_s)$ or θ_r

$$f = \mu_k mg\cos\theta_r \text{ and at } \theta = 90°$$

$$f = 0$$

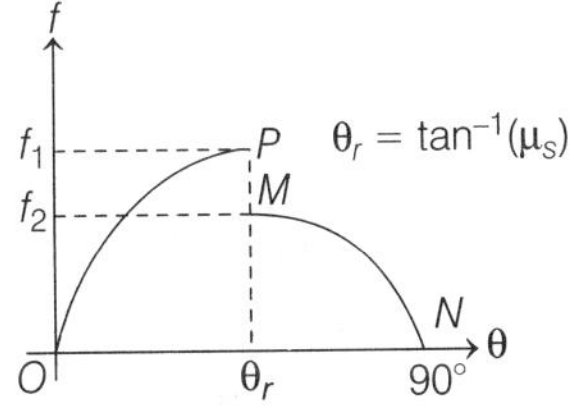

Corresponding f *versus* θ graph is as shown in figure

In the figure, OP is sine graph and MN is cos graph,

$$f_1 = mg\sin\theta_r = \mu_s mg\cos\theta_r$$

$$f_2 = \mu_k mg\cos\theta_r$$

Example 17 *Figure shows two blocks in contact sliding down an inclined surface of inclination 30°. The friction coefficient between the block of mass 2.0 kg and the incline is $\mu_1 = 0.20$ and that between the block of mass 4.0 kg and the incline is $\mu_2 = 0.30$. Find the acceleration of 2.0 kg block. ($g = 10\ m/s^2$).*

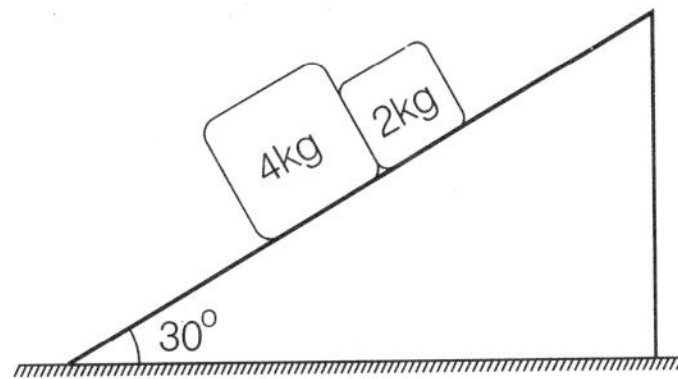

Solution Since, $\mu_1 < \mu_2$, acceleration of 2 kg block down the plane will be more than the acceleration of 4 kg block, if allowed to move separately. But, as the 2.0 kg block is behind the 4.0 kg block both of them will move with same acceleration say a. Taking both the blocks as a single system:

Force down the plane on the system = $(4 + 2)\, g \sin 30°$

$$= (6)(10)\left(\frac{1}{2}\right) = 30 \text{ N}$$

Force up the plane on the system

$$= \mu_1 (2)(g) \cos 30° + \mu_2 (4)(g) \cos 30°$$
$$= (2\mu_1 + 4\mu_2)\, g \cos 30°$$
$$= (2 \times 0.2 + 4 \times 0.3)\,(10)\,(0.86)$$
$$\approx 13.76 \text{ N}$$

$\therefore$ Net force down the plane is $F = 30 - 13.76 = 16.24$ N

$\therefore$ Acceleration of both the blocks down the plane will be a.

$$a = \frac{F}{4+2} = \frac{16.24}{6} = 2.7 \text{ m/s}^2$$ **Ans.**

Example 18 *Figure shows a man standing stationary with respect to a horizontal conveyor belt that is accelerating with 1 ms^{-2}. What is the net force on the man? If the coefficient of static friction between the man's shoes and the belt is 0.2, upto what maximum acceleration of the belt can the man continue to be stationary relative to the belt? Mass of the man = 65 kg. ($g = 9.8$ m/s^2)*

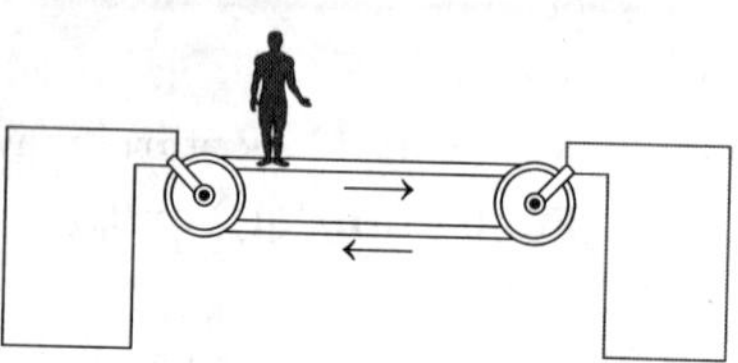

Solution As the man is standing stationary w.r.t. the belt,

$\therefore$ Acceleration of the man = Acceleration of the belt

$$= a = 1 \text{ ms}^{-2}$$

Mass of the man, $m = 65$ kg

Net force on the man $= ma = 65 \times 1 = 65$ N **Ans.**

Given coefficient of friction, $\mu = 0.2$

$\therefore$ Limiting friction, $f_L = \mu mg$

If the man remains stationary with respect to the maximum acceleration a_0 of the belt, then

$$m a_0 = f_L = \mu mg$$

$$\therefore \quad a_0 = \mu g = 0.2 \times 9.8 = 1.96 \text{ ms}^{-2}$$ **Ans.**

Example 19 *Two blocks of masses $m = 5$ kg and $M = 10$ kg are connected by a string passing over a pulley B as shown. Another string connects the centre of pulley B to the floor and passes over another pulley A as shown. An upward force F is applied at the centre of pulley A. Both the pulleys are massless.*

Find the acceleration of blocks m and M, if F is

(a) 100 N

(b) 300 N

(c) 500 N (Take $g = 10$ m/s^2)

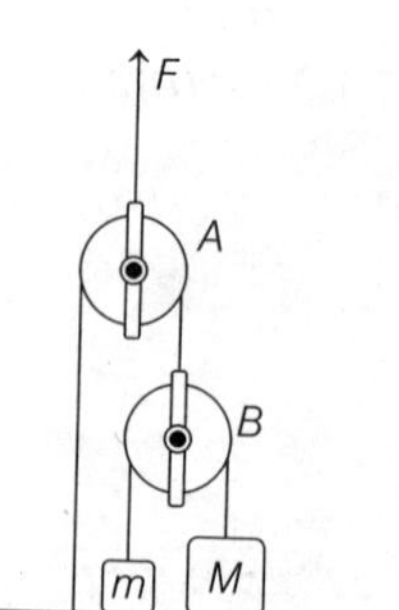

Solution Let T_0 = tension in the string passing over A

T = tension in the string passing over B

$$2T_0 = F \quad \text{and} \quad 2T = T_0$$

$$\therefore \qquad T = F/4$$

(a) $T = F/4 = 25$ N

weights of blocks are

$$mg = 50 \text{ N}$$
$$Mg = 100 \text{ N}$$

As $T < mg$ and Mg both, the blocks will remain stationary on the floor.

(b) $T = F/4 = 75$ N

As $T < Mg$ and $T > mg$, M will remain stationary on the floor, whereas m will move.

Acceleration of m,

$$a = \frac{T - mg}{m} = \frac{75 - 50}{5}$$
$$= 5 \text{ m/s}^2$$

Ans.

(c) $T = F/4 = 125$ N

As $T > mg$ and Mg both the blocks will accelerate upwards.

Acceleration of m,

$$a_1 = \frac{T - mg}{m} = \frac{125 - 50}{5} = 15 \text{ m/s}^2$$

Acceleration of M,

$$a_2 = \frac{T - Mg}{M} = \frac{125 - 100}{10} = 2.5 \text{ m/s}^2$$

Example 20 *Consider the situation shown in figure. The block B moves on a frictionless surface, while the coefficient of friction between A and the surface on which it moves is 0.2. Find the acceleration with which the masses move and also the tension in the strings. (Take $g = 10 \text{ m/s}^2$).*

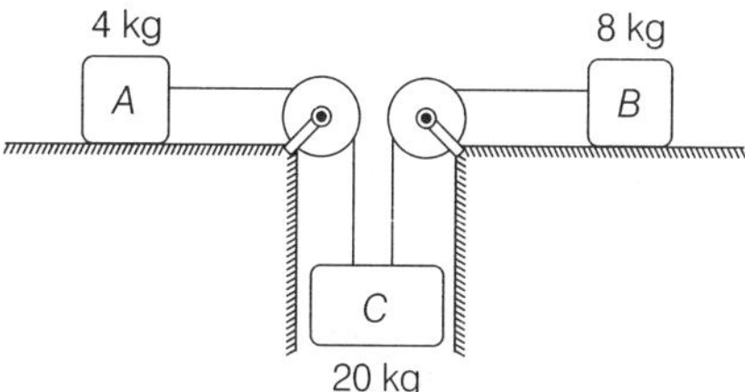

Solution Let a be the acceleration with which the masses move and T_1 and T_2 be the tensions in left and right strings. Friction on mass A is $\mu mg = 8$N. Then equations of motion of masses A, B and C are

For mass A $\qquad T_1 - 8 = 4a \qquad$ ...(i)

For mass B $\qquad T_2 = 8a \qquad$ ...(ii)

For mass C $\qquad 200 - T_1 - T_2 = 20a \qquad$ ...(iii)

Adding the above three equations, we get $32a = 192$

or $\qquad a = 6 \text{ m/s}^2$

From Eqs. (i) and (ii), we have $\qquad T_2 = 48$ N

and $\qquad T_1 = 32$ N

Example 21 *Two blocks A and B of masses 1 kg and 2 kg respectively are connected by a string, passing over a light frictionless pulley. Both the blocks are resting on a horizontal floor and the pulley is held such that string remains just taut. At moment $t = 0$, a force $F = 20\,t$ newton starts acting on the pulley along vertically upward direction as shown in figure. Calculate*

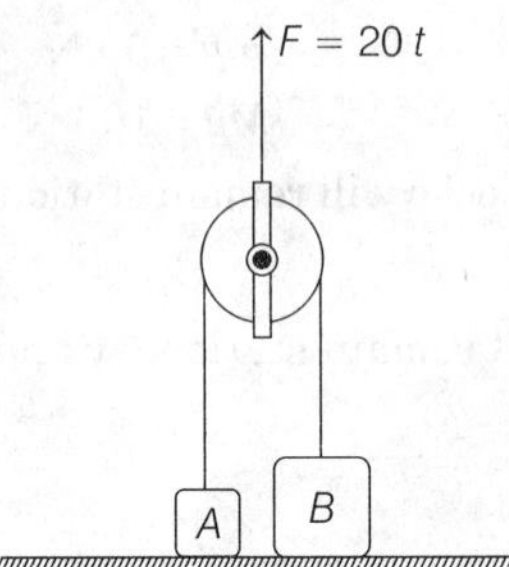

(a) velocity of A when B loses contact with the floor.

(b) height raised by the pulley upto that instant.

(Take, $g = 10\ m/s^2$)

Solution (a) Let T be the tension in the string. Then,

$$2T = 20\,t$$

or $$T = 10\,t \text{ newton}$$

Let the block A loses its contact with the floor at time $t = t_1$. This happens when the tension in string becomes equal to the weight of A. Thus,

$$T = mg$$

or $$10\,t_1 = 1 \times 10$$

or $$t_1 = 1 \text{ s} \quad \text{...(i)}$$

Similarly, for block B, we have

$$10t_2 = 2 \times 10$$

or $$t_2 = 2 \text{ s} \quad \text{...(ii)}$$

i.e. the block B loses contact at 2 s. For block A, at time t such that $t \geq t_1$ let a be its acceleration in upward direction. Then,

$$10t - 1 \times 10 = 1 \times a = (dv/dt)$$

or $$dv = 10(t - 1)\,dt \quad \text{...(iii)}$$

Integrating this expression, we get

$$\int_0^v dv = 10 \int_1^t (t - 1)\,dt$$

or $$v = 5t^2 - 10t + 5 \quad \text{...(iv)}$$

Substituting $t = t_2 = 2$ s

$$v = 20 - 20 + 5 = 5 \text{ m/s} \quad \text{...(v)}$$

(b) From Eq. (iv), $$dy = (5t^2 - 10t + 5)\,dt \quad \text{...(vi)}$$

where, y is the vertical displacement of block A at time t $(\geq t_1)$.

Integrating, we have

$$\int_{y=0}^{y=h} dy = \int_{t=1}^{t=2} (5t^2 - 10t + 5)\,dt$$

$$h = 5\left[\frac{t^3}{3}\right]_1^2 - 10\left[\frac{t^2}{2}\right]_1^2 + 5\,[t]_1^2 = \frac{5}{3}\text{ m}$$

$\therefore$ Height raised by pulley upto that instant $= \frac{h}{2} = \frac{5}{6}$ m **Ans.**

Example 22 *Find the acceleration of the body of mass m_2 in the arrangement shown in figure. If the mass m_2 is η times great as the mass m_1, and the angle that the inclined plane forms with the horizontal is equal to θ. The masses of the pulleys and threads, as well as the friction, are assumed to be negligible.*

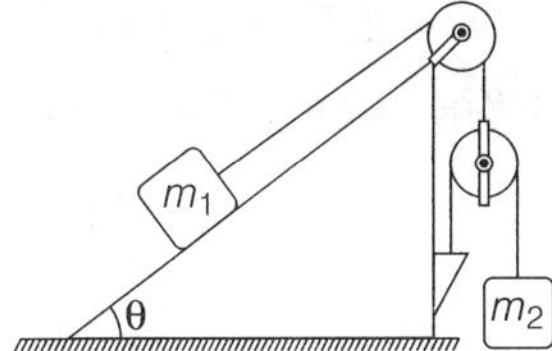

Solution Here, by constraint relation we can see that the acceleration of m_2 is two times that of m_1. So, we assume if m_1 is moving up the inclined plane with an acceleration a, the acceleration of mass m_2 going down is $2a$. The tensions in different strings are shown in figure.

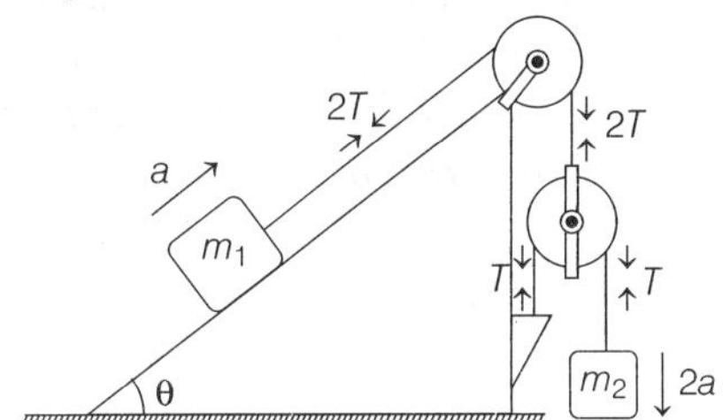

The dynamic equations can be written as

For mass m_1: $2T - m_1 g \sin\theta = m_1 a$ ...(i)

For mass m_2: $m_2 g - T = m_2(2a)$ ...(ii)

Substituting $m_2 = \eta m_1$ and solving Eqs. (i) and (ii), we get

Acceleration of $m_2 = 2a = \dfrac{2g(2\eta - \sin\theta)}{4\eta + 1}$ **Ans.**

Example 23 *In the arrangement shown in figure the mass of the ball is η times as great as that of the rod. The length of the rod is l, the masses of the pulleys and the threads, as well as the friction, are negligible. The ball is set on the same level as the lower end of the rod and then released. How soon will the ball be opposite the upper end of the rod ?*

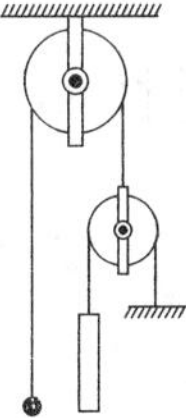

Solution From constraint relation we can see that the acceleration of the rod is double than that of the acceleration of the ball. If ball is going up with an acceleration a, rod will be coming down with the acceleration $2a$, thus, the relative acceleration of the ball with respect to rod is $3a$ in upward direction. If it takes time t seconds to reach the upper end of the rod, we have

$$t = \sqrt{\frac{2l}{3a}} \qquad \text{...(i)}$$

Let mass of ball be m and that of rod is M, the dynamic equations of these are

For rod $\qquad Mg - T = M(2a) \qquad$ ...(ii)

For ball $\qquad 2T - mg = ma \qquad$ ...(iii)

Substituting $m = \eta M$ and solving Eqs. (ii) and (iii), we get

$$a = \left(\frac{2-\eta}{\eta+4}\right) g$$

From Eq. (i), we have $\qquad t = \sqrt{\frac{2l(\eta+4)}{3g(2-\eta)}} \qquad$ **Ans.**

Example 24 *Figure shows a small block A of mass m kept at the left end of a plank B of mass M = 2m and length l. The system can slide on a horizontal road. The system is started towards right with the initial velocity v. The friction coefficients between the road and the plank is 1/2 and that between the plank and the block is 1/4. Find*

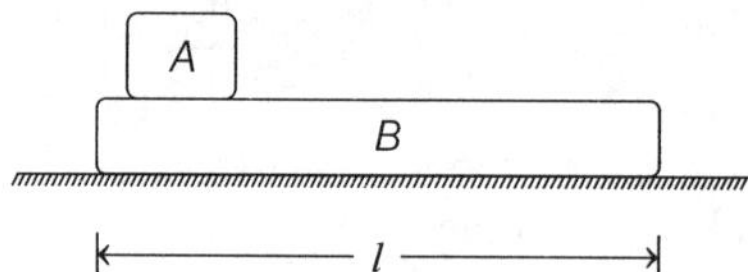

(a) the time elapsed before the block separates from the plank.
(b) displacement of block and plank relative to ground till that moment.

Solution There will be relative motion between block and plank and plank and road. So at each surface limiting friction will act. The direction of friction forces at different surfaces are as shown in figure.

Here, $\qquad f_1 = \left(\frac{1}{4}\right)(mg)$

and $\qquad f_2 = \left(\frac{1}{2}\right)(m + 2m)g = \left(\frac{3}{2}\right) mg$

Retardation of A is $\qquad a_1 = \frac{f_1}{m} = \frac{g}{4}$

and retardation of B is $\quad a_2 = \frac{f_2 - f_1}{2m} = \frac{5}{8} g$

Since, $\quad a_2 > a_1$

Relative acceleration of A with respect to B is

$$a_r = a_2 - a_1 = \frac{3}{8} g$$

Initial velocity of both A and B is v. So, there is no relative initial velocity. Hence,

(a) Applying $\quad s = \frac{1}{2} at^2$

or $\quad l = \frac{1}{2} a_r t^2 = \frac{3}{16} gt^2$

$\therefore \quad t = 4\sqrt{\frac{l}{3g}}$ **Ans.**

(b) Displacement of block $\quad s_A = u_A t - \frac{1}{2} a_A t^2$

or $\quad s_A = 4v\sqrt{\frac{l}{3g}} - \frac{1}{2} \cdot \frac{g}{4} \cdot \left(\frac{16l}{3g}\right) \qquad \left(a_A = a_1 = \frac{g}{4}\right)$

or $\quad s_A = 4v\sqrt{\frac{l}{3g}} - \frac{2}{3} l$

Displacement of plank $\quad s_B = u_B t - \frac{1}{2} a_B t^2$

or $\quad s_B = 4v\sqrt{\frac{l}{3g}} - \frac{1}{2}\left(\frac{5}{8} g\right)\left(\frac{16l}{3g}\right) \qquad \left(a_B = a_2 = \frac{5}{8} g\right)$

or $\quad s_B = 4v\sqrt{\frac{l}{3g}} - \frac{5}{3} l$ **Ans.**

Note *We can see that $s_A - s_B = l$. Which is quite obvious because block A has moved a distance l relative to plank.*

Exercises

LEVEL 1

Assertion and Reason

Directions : *Choose the correct option.*

(*a*) *If both* **Assertion** *and* **Reason** *are true and the* **Reason** *is correct explanation of the* **Assertion.**
(*b*) *If both* **Assertion** *and* **Reason** *are true but* **Reason** *is not the correct explanation of* **Assertion.**
(*c*) *If* **Assertion** *is true, but the* **Reason** *is false.*
(*d*) *If* **Assertion** *is false but the* **Reason** *is true.*
(*e*) *If both* **Assertion** *and* **Reason** *are false.*

1. Assertion : Two identical blocks are placed over a rough inclined plane. One block is given an upward velocity to the block and the other in downward direction. If $\mu = \frac{1}{3}$ and $\theta = 45°$ the ratio of magnitudes of accelerations of two is 2 : 1.

Reason : The desired ratio is $\frac{1+\mu}{1-\mu}$.

2. Assertion : A block A is just placed inside a smooth box B as shown in figure. Now, the box is given an acceleration $\mathbf{a} = (3\hat{\mathbf{j}} - 2\hat{\mathbf{i}})\ \text{ms}^{-2}$. Under this acceleration block A cannot remain in the position shown.

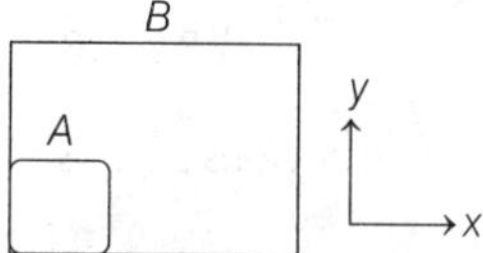

Reason : Block will require $m\mathbf{a}$ force for moving with acceleration **a**.

3. Assertion : A block is kept at rest on a rough ground as shown. Two forces F_1 and F_2 are acting on it. If we increase either of the two forces F_1 or F_2, force of friction acting on the block will increase.

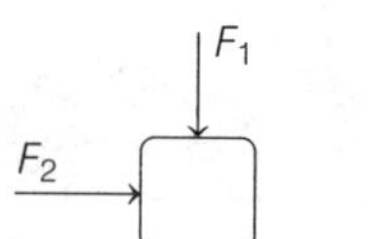

Reason : By increasing F_1, normal reaction from ground will increase.

4. Assertion : In the figure shown tension in string AB always lies between m_1g and m_2g. $(m_1 \neq m_2)$

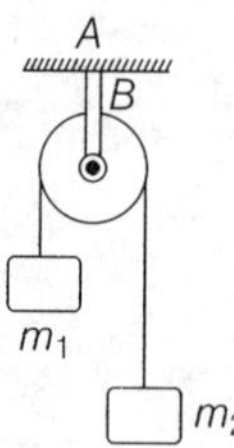

Reason : Tension in massless string is uniform throughout.

5. **Assertion :** Two frames S_1 and S_2 are non-inertial. Then frame S_2 when observed from S_1 is inertial.

Reason : A frame in motion is not necessarily a non-inertial frame.

6. **Assertion :** Moment of concurrent forces about any point is constant.

Reason : If vector sum of all the concurrent forces is zero, then moment of all the forces about any point is also zero.

7. **Assertion :** A block of weight 10 N is pushed against a vertical wall by a force of 15 N. The coefficient of friction between the wall and the block is 0.6. Then the magnitude of maximum frictional force is 9 N.

Reason : For given system block will remain stationary.

8. **Assertion :** In the system of two blocks of equal masses as shown, the coefficient of friction between the blocks (μ_2) is less than coefficient of friction (μ_1) between lower block and ground.

For all values of force F applied on upper block lower block remains at rest.

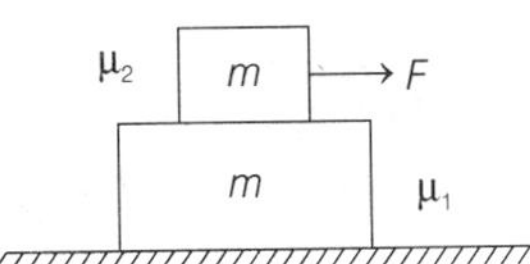

Reason : Frictional force on lower block due to upper block is not sufficient to overcome the frictional force on lower block due to ground.

9. **Assertion :** In the figure shown, block of mass m is stationary with respect to lift. Force of friction acting on the block is greater than $mg\sin\theta$.

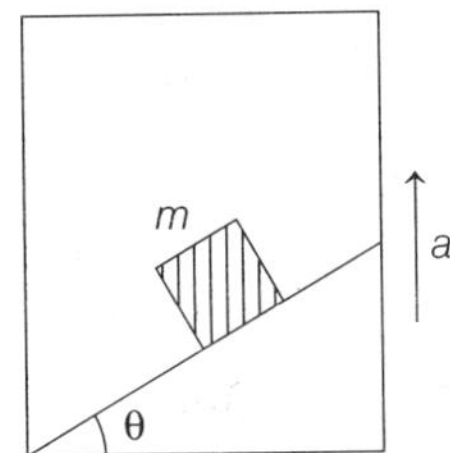

Reason : If lift moves with constant velocity then force of friction is equal to $mg\sin\theta$.

10. **Assertion :** A massless rod AB is suspended with the help of two strings as shown in figure. Tension on these two strings are T_1 and T_2. A force F is applied at distance x from end B. If x is decreased then T_1 will decrease and T_2 will increase.

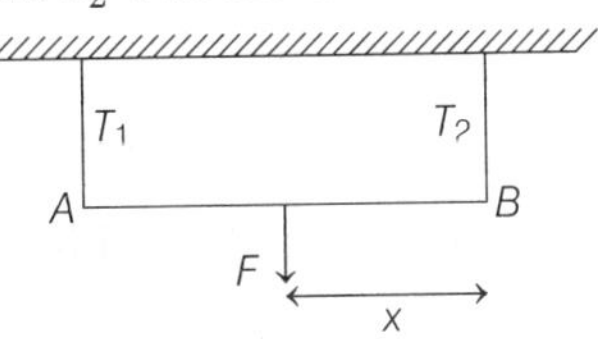

Reason : When $x = 0$, $T_1 = 0$ and $T_2 = F$.

11. **Assertion :** Normal reaction on a block does not accelerate the block.

Reason : Normal reaction always acts perpendicular to the surface of contact, no matter what the angle of that surface.

12. **Assertion :** Assume that earth consists of only neutrons. The normal reaction on a man standing on the surface of earth is zero.

Reason : Normal reaction is an electromagnetic force.

13. Assertion : If a man of 50 kg balances himself in a horizontal position by pushing his hands and back against two vertical walls, the frictional force on the man by each wall is 250 N.

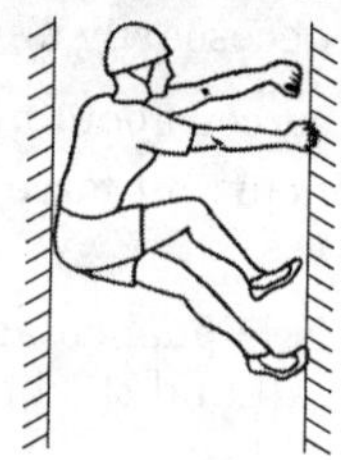

Reason : The weight of man is balanced by frictional forces by walls on the man.

Objective Questions

Single Correct Option

1. Two balls A and B of same size are dropped from the same point under gravity. The mass of A is greater than that of B. If the air resistance acting on each ball is same, then
(a) both the balls reach the ground simultaneously
(b) the ball A reaches earlier
(c) the ball B reaches earlier
(d) nothing can be said

2. A block of mass m is placed at rest on an inclined plane of inclination θ to the horizontal. If the coefficient of friction between the block and the plane is μ, then the total force, the inclined plane exerts on the block is
(a) mg
(b) $\mu\, mg \cos\theta$
(c) $mg \sin\theta$
(d) $\mu\, mg \tan\theta$

3. In the figure, a block of mass 10 kg is in equilibrium. Identify the string in which the tension is zero.

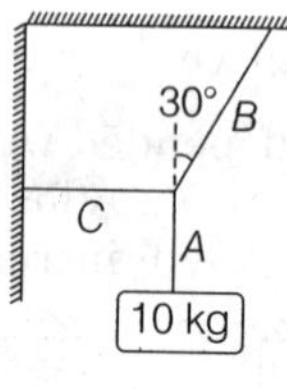

(a) B
(b) C
(c) A
(d) None of these

4. At what minimum acceleration should a monkey slide a rope whose breaking strength is $\frac{2}{3}$ rd of its weight ?
(a) $\frac{2g}{3}$
(b) g
(c) $\frac{g}{3}$
(d) zero

5. For the arrangement shown in the figure, the reading of spring balance is
(a) 50 N
(b) 100 N
(c) 150 N
(d) None of the above

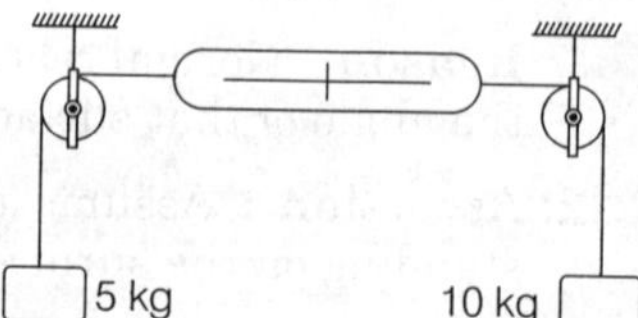

6. The time taken by a body to slide down a rough 45° inclined plane is twice that required to slide down a smooth 45° inclined plane. The coefficient of kinetic friction between the object and rough plane is given by

(a) $\frac{1}{3}$ (b) $\frac{3}{4}$

(c) $\sqrt{\frac{3}{4}}$ (d) $\sqrt{\frac{2}{3}}$

7. A force F_1 accelerates a particle from rest to a velocity v. Another force F_2 decelerates the same particle from v to rest, then

(a) F_1 is always equal to F_2

(b) F_2 is greater than F_1

(c) F_2 may be smaller than, greater than or equal to F_1

(d) F_2 cannot be equal to F_1

8. A particle is placed at rest inside a hollow hemisphere of radius R. The coefficient of friction between the particle and the hemisphere is $\mu = \frac{1}{\sqrt{3}}$. The maximum height up to which the particle can remain stationary is

(a) $\frac{R}{2}$ (b) $\left(1 - \frac{\sqrt{3}}{2}\right) R$

(c) $\frac{\sqrt{3}}{2} R$ (d) $\frac{3R}{8}$

9. In the figure shown, the frictional coefficient between table and block is 0.2. Find the ratio of tensions in the right and left strings.

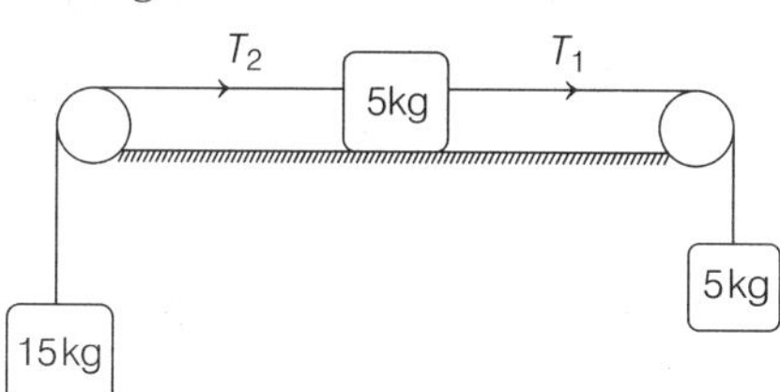

(a) 17 : 24 (b) 34 : 12

(c) 2 : 3 (d) 3 : 2

10. A smooth inclined plane of length L having inclination θ with the horizontal is inside a lift which is moving down with a retardation a. The time taken by a body to slide down the inclined plane from rest will be

(a) $\sqrt{\frac{2L}{(g + a)\sin\theta}}$ (b) $\sqrt{\frac{2L}{(g - a)\sin\theta}}$

(c) $\sqrt{\frac{2L}{a \sin\theta}}$ (d) $\sqrt{\frac{2L}{g \sin\theta}}$

11. A block rests on a rough inclined plane making an angle of 30° with horizontal. The coefficient of static friction between the block and inclined plane is 0.8. If the frictional force on the block is 10 N, the mass of the block (in kg) is (Take, $g = 10 \text{ m/s}^2$)

(a) 2.0 (b) 4.0

(c) 1.6 (d) 2.5

12. In figure, two identical particles each of mass m are tied together with an inextensible string. This is pulled at its centre with a constant force F. If the whole system lies on a smooth horizontal plane, then the acceleration of each particle towards each other is

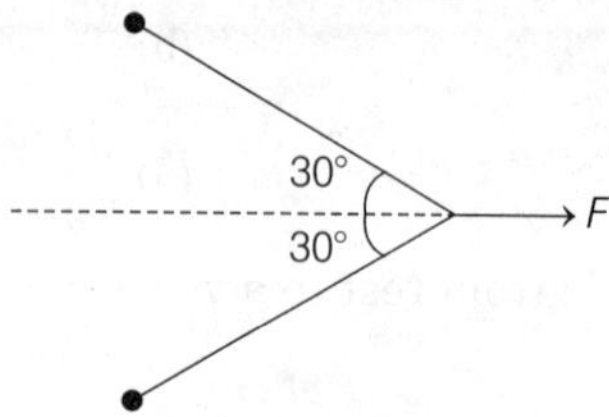

(a) $\frac{\sqrt{3}}{2}\frac{F}{m}$ (b) $\frac{1}{2\sqrt{3}}\frac{F}{m}$
(c) $\frac{2}{\sqrt{3}}\frac{F}{m}$ (d) $\sqrt{3}\frac{F}{m}$

13. A block of mass 4 kg is placed on a rough horizontal plane. A time dependent horizontal force $F = kt$ acts on the block. Here $k = 2\ \text{Ns}^{-1}$. The frictional force between the block and plane at time $t = 2$ s is ($\mu = 0.2$)

(a) 4 N (b) 8 N (c) 12 N (d) 10 N

14. A man of mass m slides down along a rope which is connected to the ceiling of an elevator with deceleration a relative to the rope. If the elevator is going upward with an acceleration a relative to the ground, then tension in the rope is

(a) mg (b) $m(g + 2a)$ (c) $m(g + a)$ (d) zero

15. A 50 kg person stands on a 25 kg platform. He pulls on the rope which is attached to the platform *via* the frictionless pulleys as shown in the figure. The platform moves upwards at a steady rate, if the force with which the person pulls the rope is

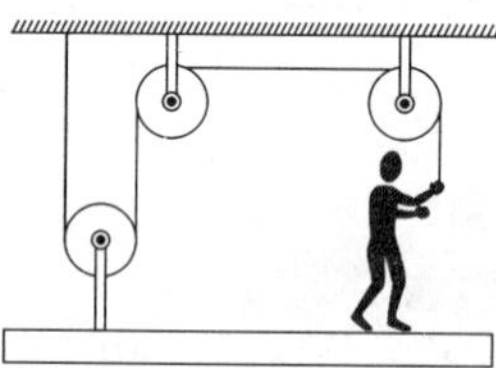

(a) 500 N (b) 250 N
(c) 25 N (d) None of these

16. If a ladder weighing 250 N is placed against a smooth vertical wall having coefficient of friction between it and floor 0.3, then what is the maximum force of friction available at the point of contact between the ladder and the floor?

(a) 75 N (b) 50 N (c) 35 N (d) 25 N

17. A rope of length L and mass M is being pulled on a rough horizontal floor by a constant horizontal force $F = Mg$. The force is acting at one end of the rope in the same direction as the length of the rope. The coefficient of kinetic friction between rope and floor is 1/2. Then, the tension at the mid-point of the rope is

(a) $\frac{Mg}{4}$ (b) $\frac{2Mg}{5}$
(c) $\frac{Mg}{8}$ (d) $\frac{Mg}{2}$

18. A block A of mass 4 kg is kept on ground. The coefficient of friction between the block and the ground is 0.8. The external force of magnitude 30 N is applied parallel to the ground. The resultant force exerted by the ground on the block is ($g = 10 \text{ m/s}^2$)

(a) 40 N
(b) 30 N
(c) zero
(d) 50 N

19. A block A of mass 2 kg rests on another block B of mass 8 kg which rests on a horizontal floor. The coefficient of friction between A and B is 0.2 while that between B and floor is 0.5. When a horizontal force F of 25 N is applied on the block B, the force of friction between A and B is

(a) 3 N
(b) 4 N
(c) 2 N
(d) zero

20. A body of mass 10 kg lies on a rough inclined plane of inclination $\theta = \sin^{-1}\left(\frac{3}{5}\right)$ with the horizontal. When the force of 30 N is applied on the block parallel to and upward the plane, the total force by the plane on the block is nearly along

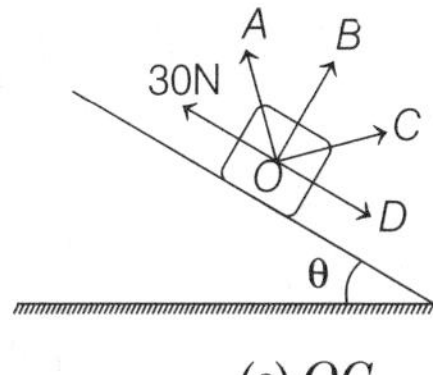

(a) OA
(b) OB
(c) OC
(d) OD

21. In the figure shown, a person wants to raise a block lying on the ground to a height h. In which case, he has to exert more force. Assume pulleys and strings are light

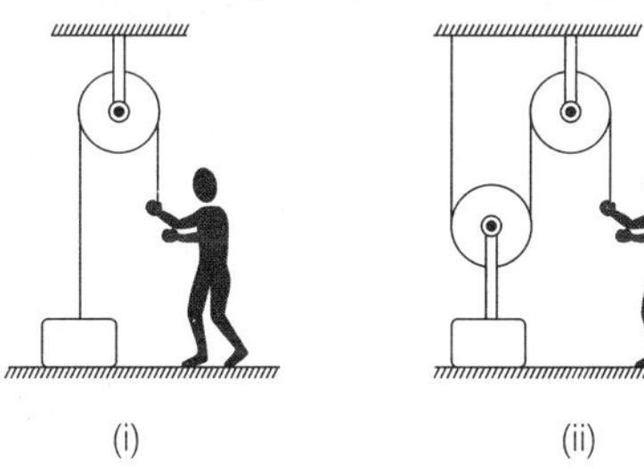

(a) Fig. (i)
(b) Fig. (ii)
(c) Same in both
(d) Cannot be determined

22. A man of mass m stands on a platform of equal mass m and pulls himself by two ropes passing over pulleys as shown in figure. If he pulls each rope with a force equal to half his weight, his upward acceleration would be

(a) $\frac{g}{2}$
(b) $\frac{g}{4}$
(c) g
(d) zero

23. A varying horizontal force $F = at$ acts on a block of mass m kept on a smooth horizontal surface. An identical block is kept on the first block. The coefficient of friction between the blocks is μ. The time after which the relative sliding between the blocks prevails is

(a) $\frac{2mg}{a}$ (b) $\frac{2\mu mg}{a}$ (c) $\frac{\mu mg}{a}$ (d) $2\mu\, mga$

24. Two particles start together from a point O and slide down along straight smooth wires inclined at 30° and 60° to the vertical plane and on the same side of vertical through O. The relative acceleration of second with respect to first will be of magnitude

(a) $\frac{g}{2}$ (b) $\frac{\sqrt{3}g}{2}$ (c) $\frac{g}{\sqrt{3}}$ (d) g

25. In the arrangement shown in the figure, the pulley has a mass $3m$. Neglecting friction on the contact surface, the force exerted by the supporting rope AB on the ceiling is

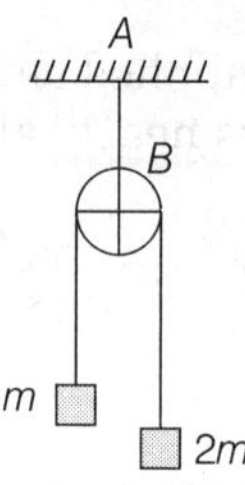

(a) 6 mg (b) 3 mg (c) 4 mg (d) None of these

26. If a body loses half of its velocity on penetrating 3 cm in a wooden block, then how much will it penetrate more before coming to rest?

(a) 1cm (b) 2 cm
(c) 3 cm (d) 4 cm

27. A weightless rod is acted upon by upward parallel forces of 4 N and 2 N magnitudes at ends A and B, respectively. The total length of the rod $AB = 3$ m. To keep the rod in equilibrium a force of 6 N should act in the following manner

(a) downward at any point between A and B
(b) downward at the mid-point of AB
(c) downward at a point C such that $AC = 1$ m
(d) downward at a point C such that $BC = 1$ m

28. A metal sphere is hung by a string fixed to a wall. The forces acting on the sphere are shown in figure. Which of the following statements is correct?

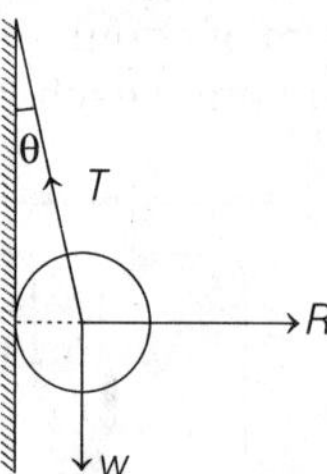

(i) $\mathbf{R} + \mathbf{T} + \mathbf{w} = 0$ (ii) $T^2 = R^2 + w^2$
(iii) $T = R + w$ (iv) $R = w \tan \theta$

(a) (i), (ii), (iii) (b) (ii), (iii), (iv)
(c) (i), (ii), (iv) (d) (i), (ii), (iii), (iv)

29. A box of mass 8 kg is placed on a rough inclined plane of inclination θ. Its downward motion can be prevented by applying an upward pull F. And it can be made to slide upwards by applying a force $2F$. The coefficient of friction between the box and the inclined plane is

(a) $\frac{1}{3}\tan\theta$
(b) $3\tan\theta$
(c) $\frac{1}{2}\tan\theta$
(d) $2\tan\theta$

30. A block of mass m is placed on a smooth plane inclined at an angle θ with the horizontal. The force exerted by the plane on the block has a magnitude

(a) mg
(b) $mg\sec\theta$
(c) $mg\cos\theta$
(d) $mg\sin\theta$

31. For the arrangement shown in the figure, the tension in the string is given by $\left(\sin 37° = \frac{3}{5}\right)$

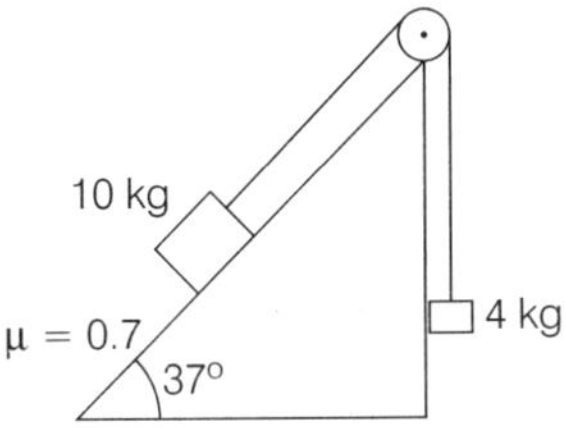

(a) 30 N
(b) 40 N
(c) 60 N
(d) 30 N

32. Consider the shown arrangement. Assume all surfaces to be smooth. If N represents magnitudes of normal reaction between block and wedge, then acceleration of M along horizontal is equal to

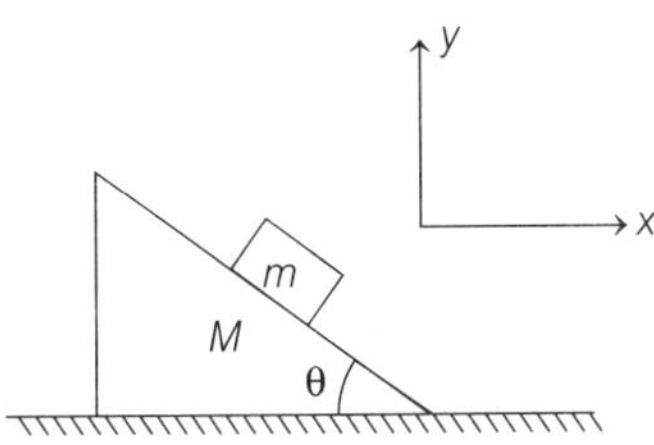

(a) $\frac{N\sin\theta}{M}$ along + ve x-axis
(b) $\frac{N\cos\theta}{M}$ along − ve x-axis
(c) $\frac{N\sin\theta}{M}$ along − ve x-axis
(d) $\frac{N\sin\theta}{m+M}$ along − ve x-axis

33. In the above problem, normal reaction between ground and wedge will have magnitude equal to

(a) $N\cos\theta + Mg$
(b) $N\cos\theta + Mg + mg$
(c) $N\cos\theta - Mg$
(d) $N\sin\theta + Mg + mg$

34. Ten coins are placed on top of each other on a horizontal table. If the mass of each coin is 10 g and acceleration due to gravity is 10 ms^{-2}, what is the magnitude and direction of the force on the 7th coin (counted from the bottom) due to all the coins above it?

(a) 0.3 N downwards
(b) 0.3 N upwards
(c) 0.7 N downwards
(d) 0.7 N upwards

35. A 50 kg boy stands on a platform spring scale in a lift that is going down with a constant speed 3 m/ s. If the lift is brought to rest by a constant deceleration in a distance of 9 m, what does the scale read during this period? (Take, $g = 9.8 \text{ m/s}^2$)

(a) 500 N
(b) 465 N
(c) 515 N
(d) Zero

36. The acceleration of the 2 kg block, if the free end of string is pulled with a force of 20 N as shown is

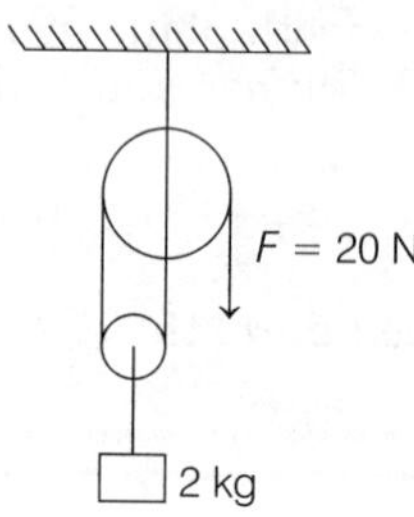

(a) zero
(b) 10 m/s^2
(c) 5 m/s^2 upward
(d) 5 m/s^2 downward

37. Two blocks, each having a mass M, rest on frictionless surfaces as shown in the figure. If the pulleys are light and frictionless and M on the incline is allowed to move down, then the tension in the string will be

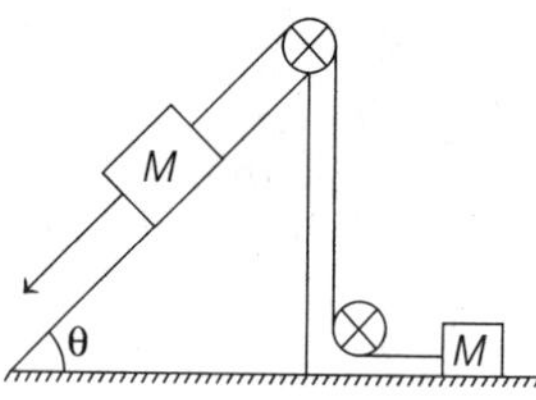

(a) $\frac{2}{3} Mg \sin\theta$
(b) $\frac{3}{2} Mg \sin\theta$
(c) $\frac{Mg \sin\theta}{2}$
(d) $2Mg \sin\theta$

38. A uniform rope of length l lies on a table. If the coefficient of friction is μ, then the maximum length l_1 of the hanging part of the rope which can overhang from the edge of the table without sliding down is

(a) l/μ
(b) $l/(\mu + 1)$
(c) $\mu l/(\mu + 1)$
(d) $\mu l/(\mu - 1)$

39. A man of mass 60 kg is standing on a horizontal conveyor belt. When the belt is given an acceleration of 1 ms^{-2}, the man remains stationary with respect to the moving belt. If $g = 10 \text{ ms}^{-2}$, the net force acting on the man is

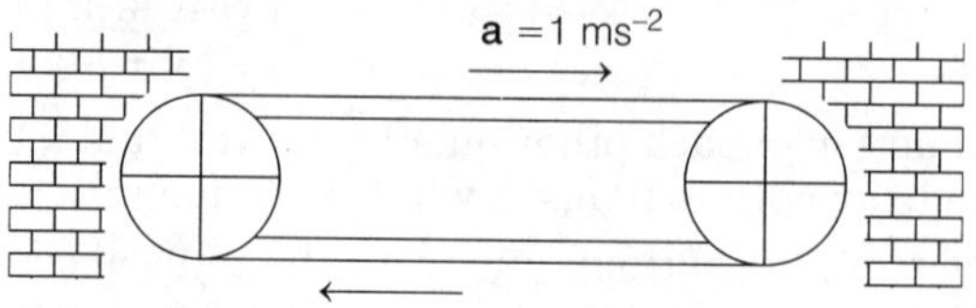

(a) Zero
(b) 120 N
(c) 60 N
(d) 600 N

40. Two masses are connected by a string which passes over a pulley accelerating upwards at a rate A as shown. If a_1 and a_2 be the accelerations of bodies 1 and 2 respectively, then

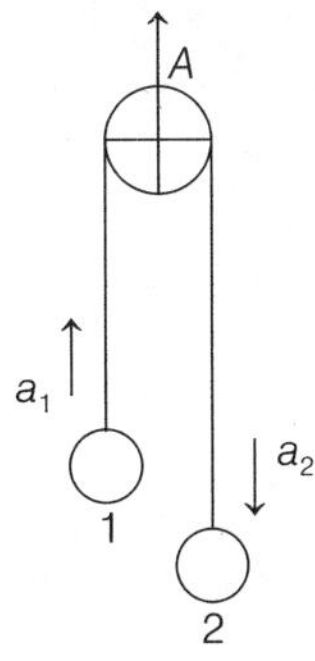

(a) $A = a_1 - a_2$ (b) $A = a_1 + a_2$

(c) $A = \frac{a_1 - a_2}{2}$ (d) $A = \frac{a_1 + a_2}{2}$

41. A smooth rod of mass 1 kg is in equilibrium inside a hollow fixed sphere such that $\angle ACB = 120°$. Find the normal reaction on the rod at end A.

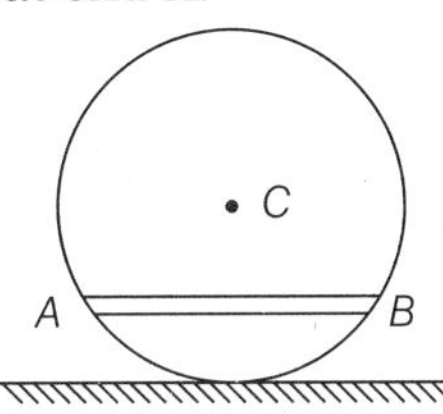

(a) 20 N (b) $10\sqrt{3}$ N (c) 10 N (d) $5\sqrt{3}$ N

42. A smooth light rod not reaching the rough floor is inserted between two identical blocks. A horizontal force F is applied to upper end of rod. The contact force between block A and rod is F_1 and contact force between block B and rod is F_2. Then,

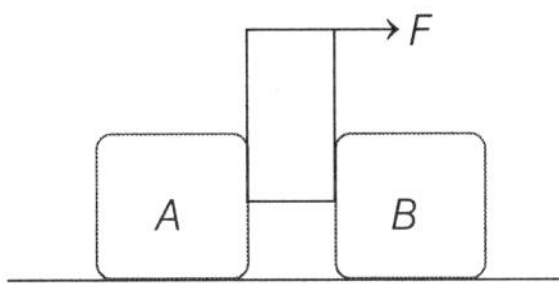

(a) $F_1 = F_2$ (b) $F_1 > F_2$

(c) $F_1 < F_2$ (d) $F_1 = 0$ and $F_2 > 0$

43. Three identical smooth cylinders each of mass $\sqrt{3}$ kg are placed as shown in the figure. Find normal reaction between cylinder A and cylinder B.

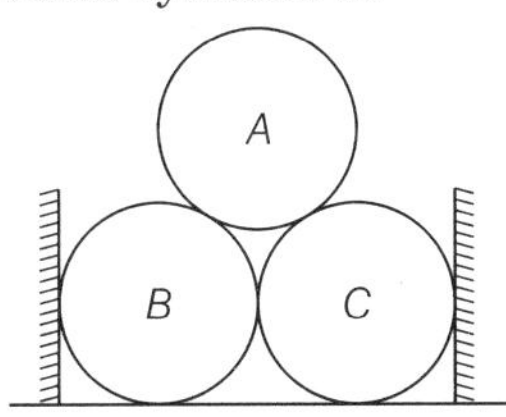

(a) 10 N (b) 20 N

(c) $10\sqrt{3}$ N (d) Cannot be calculated

44. A force of $5t$ N is applied on a block of mass 1 kg. The magnitude of normal reaction on the block by horizontal ground is N_1 and magnitude of normal reaction on block due to vertical wall is N_2. N_1 *versus* N_2 graph is

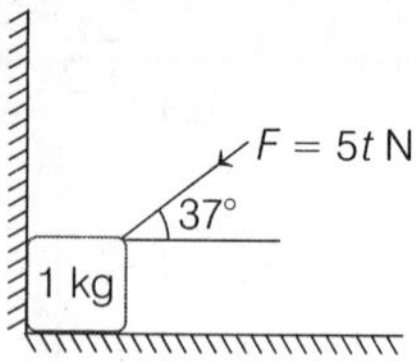

(a) 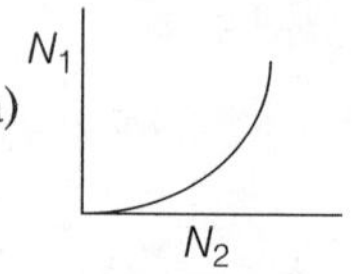

(b) 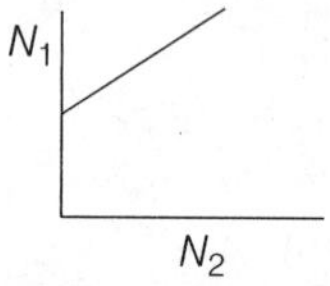

(c) 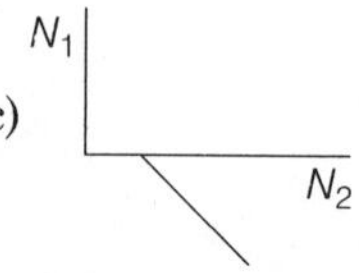

(d) None of these

45. If a force F is applied on a block of mass m_1, then it produces an acceleration a_1. The same force is applied to a second block of mass m_2, then it produces an acceleration a_2. If the same force is applied on a block of mass $(m_1 + m_2)$, then acceleration is

(a) $a_1 + a_2$ (b) $\frac{a_1 + a_2}{2}$ (c) $a_1 - a_2$ (d) $\frac{a_1 a_2}{a_1 + a_2}$

46. The force F which is applied to 1 kg block initially at rest varies linearly with time as shown in the figure. Find velocity of the block at $t = 4$ s.

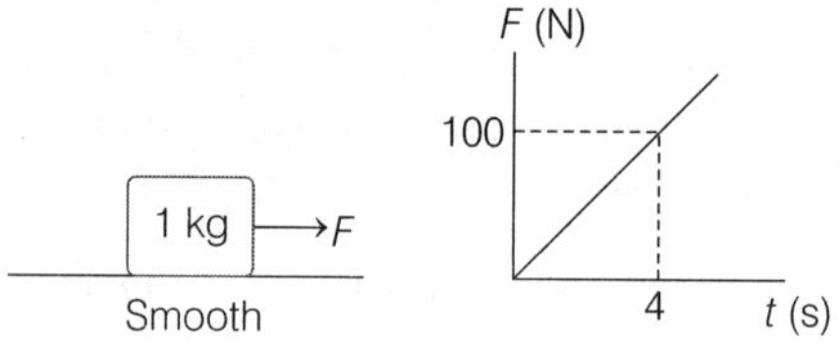

(a) 100 m/s (b) 200 m/s
(c) 20 m/s (d) 4 m/s

47. A massive rod of length 1 m placed straight on a smooth horizontal surface is pulled longitudinally by a force F of 10N as shown in the figure.

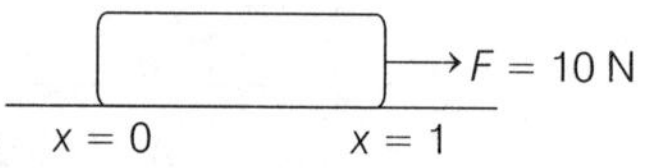

The tension in rod varies as $T = 10\sqrt{x}$. The linear mass density of rod is

(a) $\lambda \propto x$ (b) $\lambda \propto \frac{1}{\sqrt{x}}$
(c) $\lambda \propto \sqrt{x}$ (d) $\lambda \propto x^2$

48. If the acceleration of block A is 5 m/s^2, then acceleration of block B is

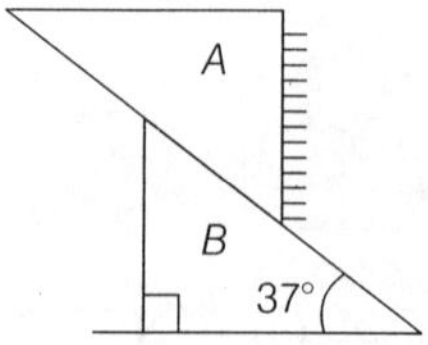

(a) 5 m/s^2
(b) 10 m/s^2
(c) zero
(d) 6.67 m/s^2

49. For the situation shown in the figure, find the speed of cylinder at the instant shown in figure.

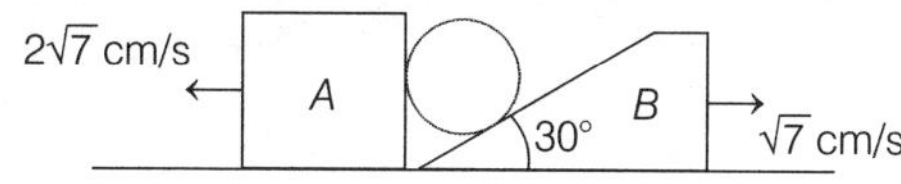

(a) $\sqrt{21}$ cm/s
(b) $\sqrt{17}$ cm/s
(c) 7 cm/s
(d) $2\sqrt{7}$ cm/s

50. A smooth plank of mass 1 kg and length 8 m is on smooth horizontal surface. The gap between fixed pulley P and plank is larger than the length of plank. A smooth block D is placed on the plank. The masses of blocks A and B are 1 kg and 3 kg, respectively.
Find the time elapsed before the block D separates from the plank.

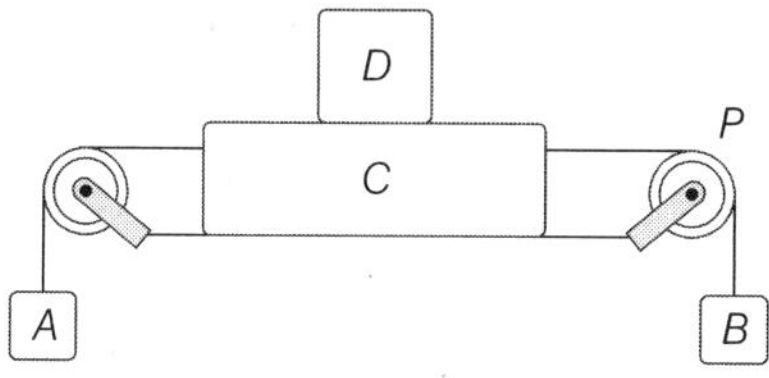

(a) 1 s
(b) 2 s
(c) 3 s
(d) Insufficient information

Note *Neglect size of block D and assume that initially it is at one end of plank C.*

51. One end of massless rope, which passes over a massless and frictionless pulley P is tied to a hook C while the other end is free. Maximum tension that the rope can bear is 360 N. With what value of maximum safe acceleration (in ms^{-2}) can a man of 60 kg climb up on the rope?

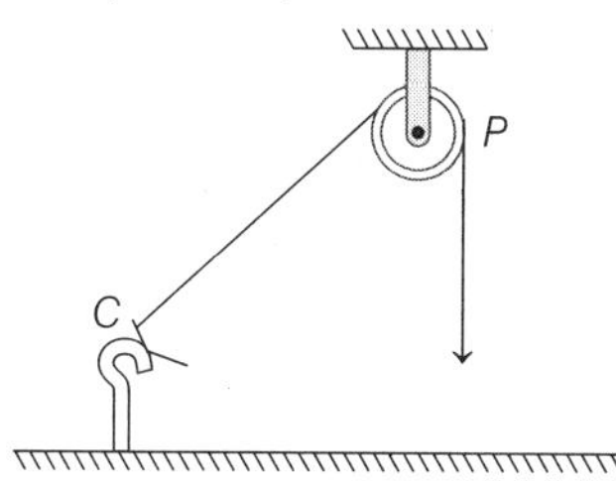

(a) 2
(b) 3
(c) 4
(d) None of these

52. Three identical billiard balls each of mass 1 kg are placed as shown in the figure. The upper ball is smooth. Find minimum coefficient of static friction between lower balls and ground, so that balls remain stationary.

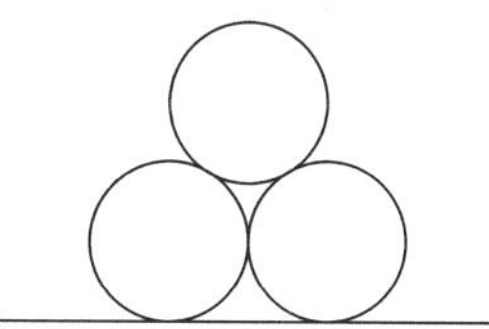

(a) $\frac{1}{\sqrt{3}}$
(b) $\frac{1}{3\sqrt{3}}$
(c) $\frac{2}{\sqrt{3}}$
(d) 0.5

53. In the situation shown in the figure, the coefficient of static friction for all surfaces of contact is 0.5. Find the maximum value of mass of block A, so that the blocks B, C and D move together.

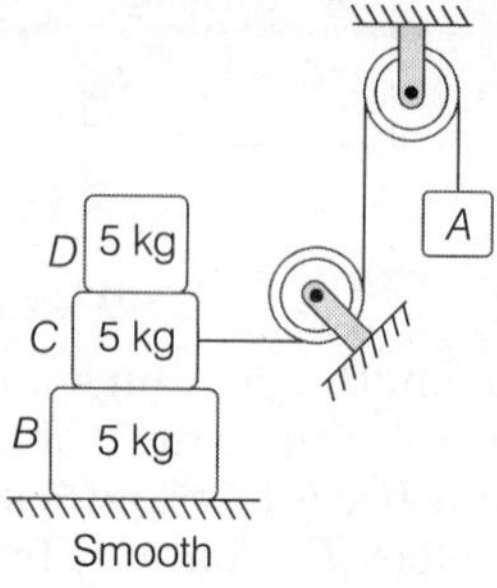

(a) 10 kg
(b) 15 kg
(c) 20 kg
(d) 25 kg

54. The situation shown in the figure, find the minimum value of coefficient of friction, so that all blocks move together.

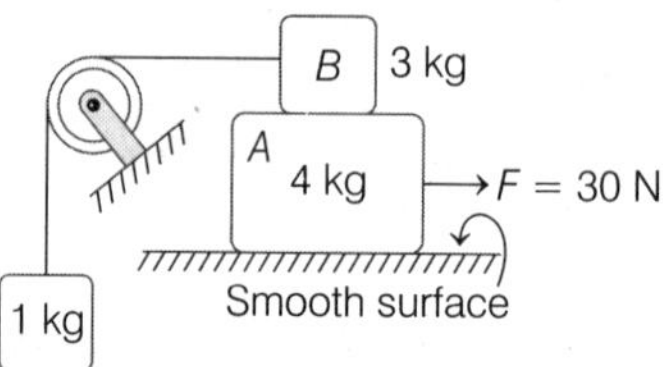

(a) 1
(b) $\frac{1}{2}$
(c) $\frac{1}{3}$
(d) $\frac{2}{3}$

55. A block of mass m is placed on surface with a vertical cross-section given by $y = \frac{x^3}{6}$. If the coefficient of friction is 0.5, the maximum height above the ground at which the block can be placed without slipping is

(a) $\frac{1}{6}$ m
(b) $\frac{2}{3}$ m
(c) $\frac{1}{3}$ m
(d) $\frac{1}{2}$ m

Subjective Questions

1. In figure, the tension in the diagonal string is 60 N.

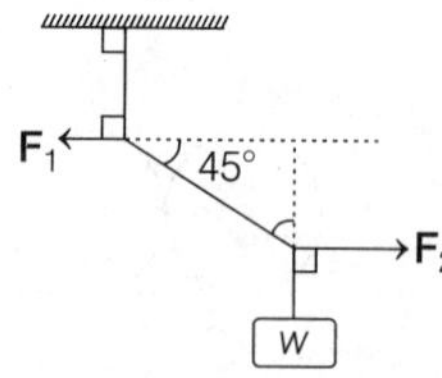

(a) Find the magnitude of the horizontal forces $\mathbf{F}_1$ and $\mathbf{F}_2$ that must be applied to hold the system in the position shown.

(b) What is the weight of the suspended block ?

2. Two beads of equal masses m are attached by a string of length $\sqrt{2}a$ and are free to move in a smooth circular ring lying in a vertical plane as shown in figure. Here, a is the radius of the ring. Find the tension and acceleration of B just after the beads are released to move.

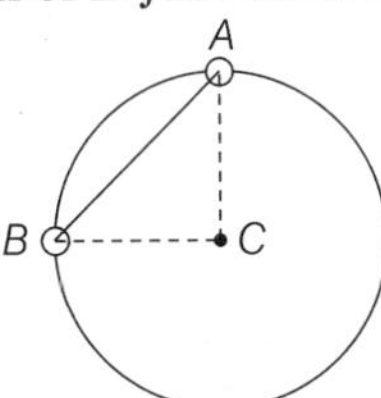

3. Two blocks of masses 2.9 kg and 1.9 kg are suspended from a rigid support S by two inextensible wires each of length 1 m, as shown in the figure. The upper wire has negligible mass and the lower wire has a uniformly distributed mass of 0.2 kg. The whole system of blocks, wires and support have an upward acceleration of 0.2 m/s^2. Acceleration due to gravity is 9.8 m/s^2.

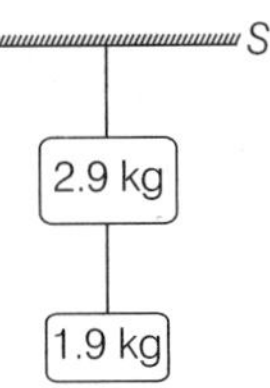

(a) Find the tension at the mid-point of the lower wire.
(b) Find the tension at the mid-point of the upper wire.

4. Two blocks shown in figure are connected by a heavy uniform rope of mass 4 kg. An upward force of 200 N is applied as shown. (Take, $g = 9.8 \text{ m/s}^2$)

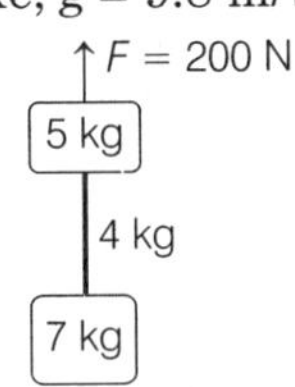

(a) What is the acceleration of the system ?
(b) What is the tension at the top of the rope ?
(c) What is the tension at the mid-point of the rope ?

5. A 4 m long ladder weighing 25 kg rests with its upper end against a smooth wall and lower end on rough ground. What should be the minimum coefficient of friction between the ground and the ladder for it to be inclined at 60° with the horizontal without slipping? (Take, $g = 10 \text{ m/s}^2$)

6. A plumb bob of mass 1 kg is hung from the ceiling of a train compartment. The train moves on an inclined plane with constant velocity. If the angle of incline is 30°. Find the angle made by the string with the normal to the ceiling. Also, find the tension in the string. (Take, $g = 10 \text{ m/s}^2$)

7. Repeat both parts of the above question, if the train moves with an acceleration $a = g/2$ up the plane.

8. Two unequal masses of 1 kg and 2 kg are connected by a string going over a clamped light smooth pulley as shown in figure. The system is released from rest. The larger mass is stopped for a moment 1.0 s after the system is set in motion. Find the time elapsed before the string is tight again.

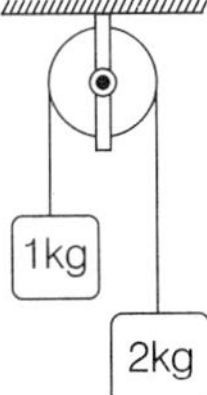

9. In figure $m_1 = 1$ kg and $m_2 = 4$ kg. Find the mass M of the hanging block which will prevent the smaller block from slipping over the triangular block. All the surfaces are frictionless and the strings and the pulleys are light.

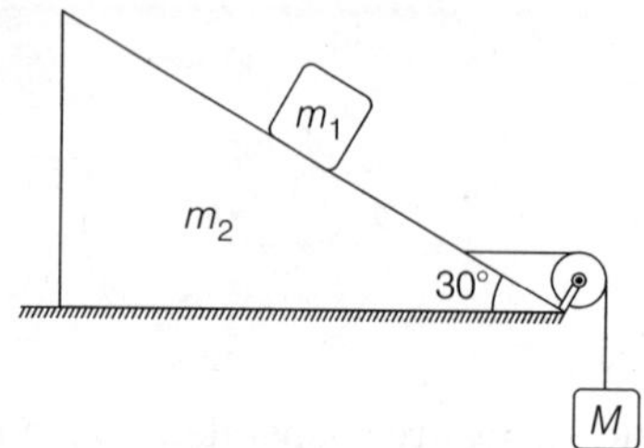

Note *In exercises 10 to 12, the situations described take place in a box car which has initial velocity v = 0 but acceleration* $\mathbf{a} = (5\ m/s^2)\ \hat{\mathbf{i}}$. *(Take, g = 10 m/s²)*

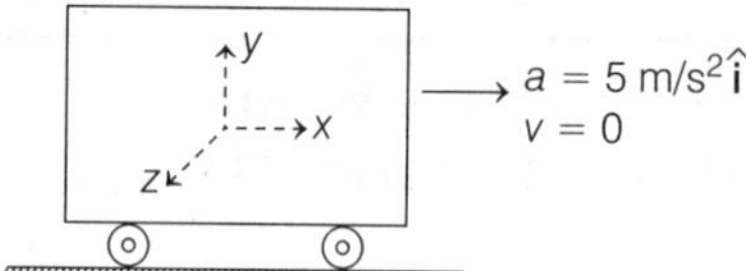

10. A 2 kg object slides along the frictionless floor with initial velocity $(10\ \text{m/s})\hat{\mathbf{i}}$ (a) Describe the motion of the object relative to car (b) when does the object reach its original position relative to the box car.

11. A 2 kg object slides along the frictionless floor with initial transverse velocity $(10\ \text{m/s})\ \hat{\mathbf{k}}$. Describe the motion (a) in car's frame and (b) in ground frame.

12. A 2 kg object slides along a rough floor (coefficient of sliding friction = 0.3) with initial velocity $(10\ \text{m/s})\ \hat{\mathbf{i}}$. Describe the motion of the object relative to car assuming that the coefficient of static friction is greater than 0.5.

13. A block is placed on an inclined plane as shown in figure. What must be the frictional force between block and incline, if the block is not to slide along the incline when the incline is accelerating to the right at $3\ \text{m/s}^2\left(\sin 37° = \frac{3}{5}\right)$? (Take, $g = 10\ \text{m/s}^2$)

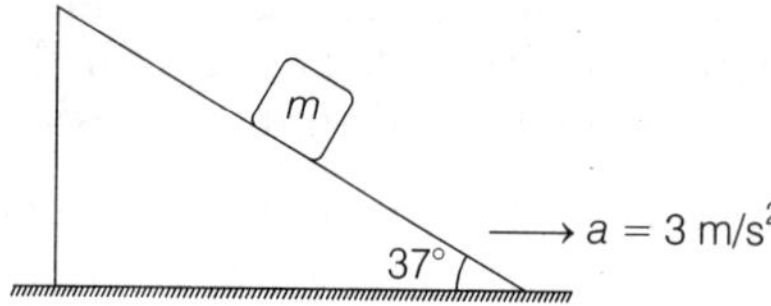

14. A block of mass 200 kg is set into motion on a frictionless horizontal surface with the help of frictionless pulley and a rope system as shown in figure. What horizontal force F should be applied to produce in the block an acceleration of $1\ \text{m/s}^2$?

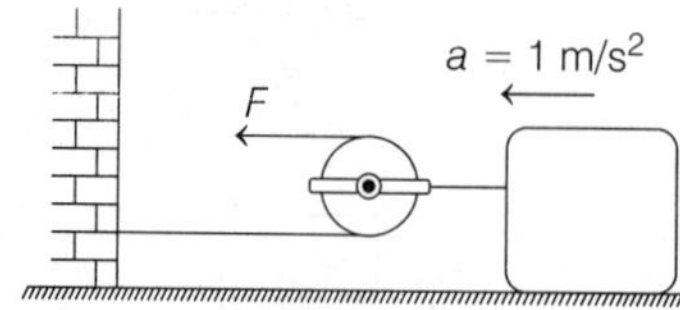

15. A cube of mass 2 kg is held stationary against a rough wall by a force $F = 40$ N passing through centre C. Find perpendicular distance of normal reaction between wall and cube from point C. Side of the cube is 20 cm. (Take, $g = 10 \text{ m/s}^2$)

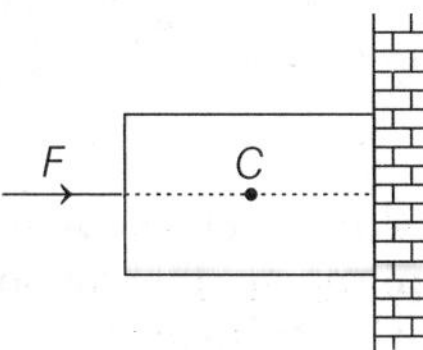

16. A 20 kg monkey has a firm hold on a light rope that passes over a frictionless pulley and is attached to a 20 kg bunch of bananas. The monkey looks upward, sees the bananas and starts to climb the rope to get them.

(a) As the monkey climbs, do the bananas move up, move down or remain at rest ?

(b) As the monkey climbs, does the distance between the monkey and the bananas decrease, increase or remain constant ?

(c) The monkey releases her hold on the rope. What happens to the distance between the monkey and the bananas while she is falling ?

(d) Before reaching the ground, the monkey grabs the rope to stop her fall. What do the bananas do?

17. In the pulley-block arrangement shown in figure, find the relation between a_A, a_B and a_C.

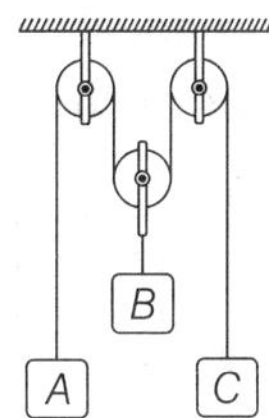

18. Find the acceleration of the blocks A and B in the situation shown in the figure.

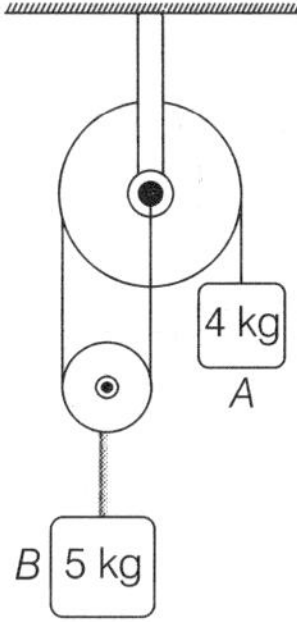

19. A conveyor belt is moving with constant speed of 6 m/s. A small block is just dropped on it. Coefficient of friction between the two is $\mu = 0.3$. Find

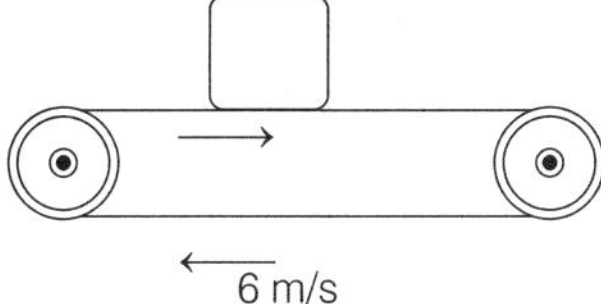

(a) the time when relative motion between them will stop.

(b) displacement of block upto that instant. (Take, $g = 10 \text{ m/s}^2$)

LEVEL 2

Objective Questions

Single Correct Option

1. What is the largest mass of C in kg that can be suspended without moving blocks A and B? The static coefficient of friction for all plane surface of contact is 0.3. Mass of block A is 50kg and block B is 70kg. Neglect friction in the pulleys.

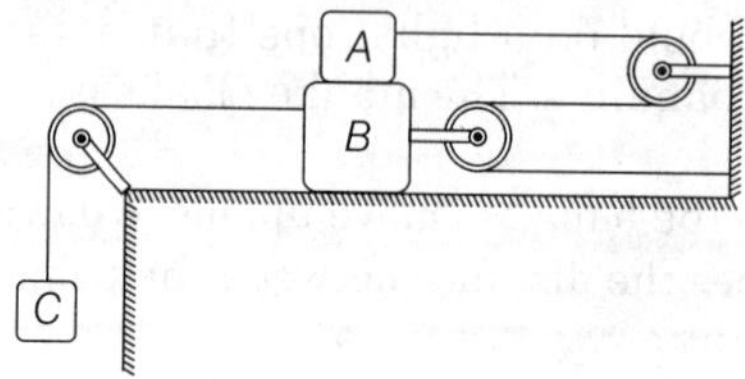

(a) 120 kg
(b) 92 kg
(c) 81 kg
(d) None of these

2. A sphere of mass 1 kg rests at one corner of a cube. The cube is moved with a velocity $\mathbf{v} = (8t\hat{\mathbf{i}} - 2t^2\hat{\mathbf{j}})$, where t is time in second. The force by sphere on the cube at $t = 1$ s is ($g = 10 \text{ ms}^{-2}$) [Figure shows vertical plane of the cube]

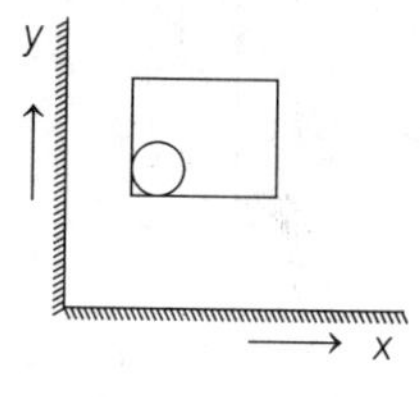

(a) 8 N
(b) 10 N
(c) 20 N
(d) 6 N

3. Two blocks of masses m_1 and m_2 are placed in contact with each other on a horizontal platform as shown in figure. The coefficient of friction between m_1 and platform is 2μ and that between block m_2 and platform is μ. The platform moves with an acceleration a. The normal reaction between the blocks is

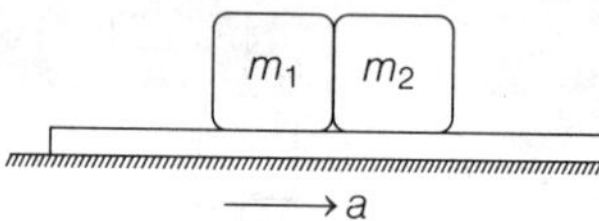

(a) zero in all cases
(b) zero only if $m_1 = m_2$
(c) non zero only if $a > 2\mu g$
(d) non zero only if $a > \mu g$

4. A block of mass m is resting on a wedge of angle θ as shown in the figure. With what minimum acceleration a should the wedge move, so that the mass m falls freely?

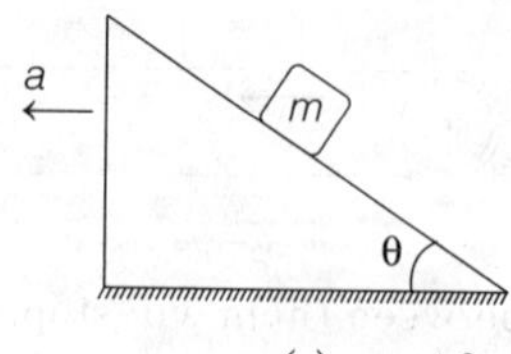

(a) g
(b) $g\cos\theta$
(c) $g\cot\theta$
(d) $g\tan\theta$

5. To a ground observer, the block C is moving with v_0 and the block A with v_1 and B is moving with v_2 relative to C as shown in the figure. Identify the correct statement.

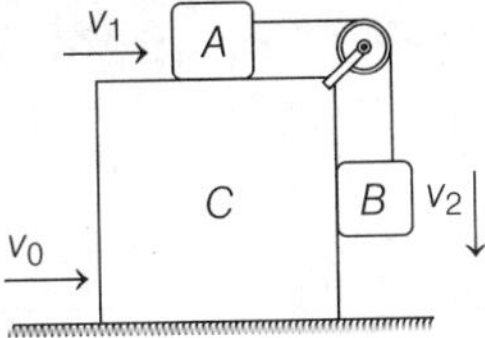

(a) $v_1 - v_2 = v_0$ (b) $v_1 = v_2$ (c) $v_1 + v_0 = v_2$ (d) None of these

6. In each case $m_1 = 4$ kg and $m_2 = 3$ kg. If a_1, a_2 and a_3 are the respective accelerations of the block m_1 in given situations, then

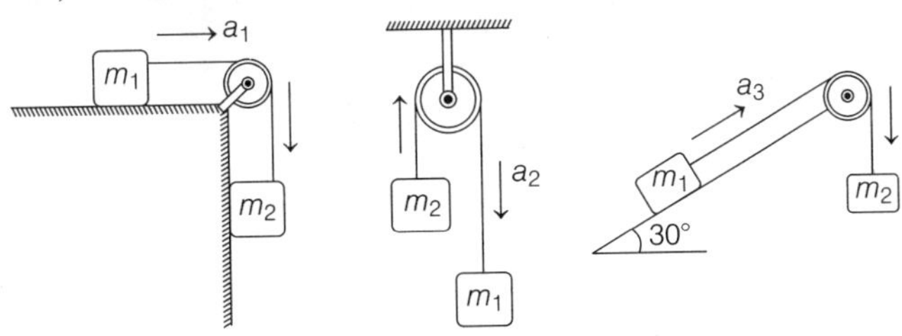

(a) $a_1 > a_2 > a_3$ (b) $a_1 > a_2 = a_3$
(c) $a_1 = a_2 = a_3$ (d) $a_1 > a_3 > a_2$

7. For the arrangement shown in figure, the coefficient of friction between the two blocks is μ. If both the blocks are identical and moving, then the acceleration of each block is

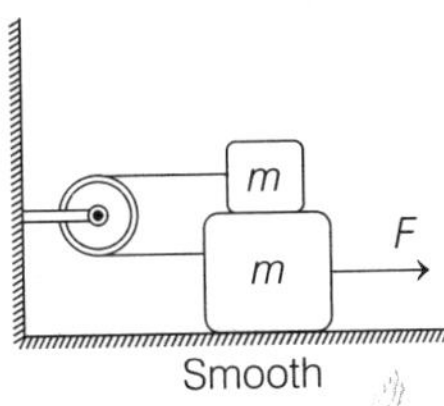

(a) $\frac{F}{2m} - 2\mu g$ (b) $\frac{F}{2m}$
(c) $\frac{F}{2m} - \mu g$ (d) zero

8. In the arrangement shown in the figure, the rod R is restricted to move in the vertical direction with acceleration a_1 and the block B can slide down the fixed wedge with acceleration a_2. The correct relation between a_1 and a_2 is given by

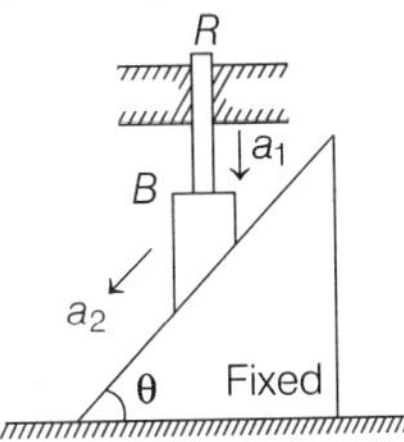

(a) $a_2 = a_1 \sin\theta$ (b) $a_2 \sin\theta = a_1$
(c) $a_2 \cos\theta = a_1$ (d) $a_2 = a_1 \cos\theta$

9. In the figure block moves downwards with velocity v_1, the wedge moves rightwards with velocity v_2. The correct relation between v_1 and v_2 is

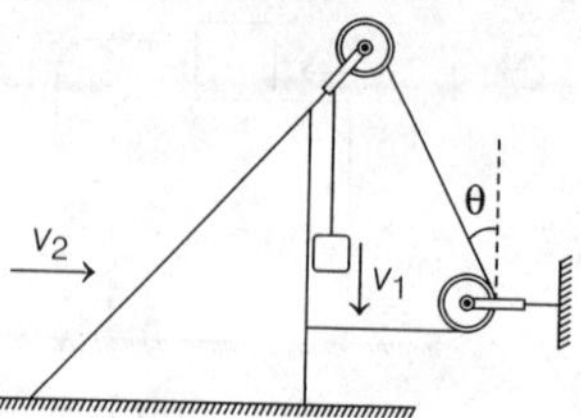

(a) $v_2 = v_1$ (b) $v_2 = v_1 \sin\theta$ (c) $2v_2 \sin\theta = v_1$ (d) $v_2 (1 + \sin\theta) = v_1$

10. In the figure, the minimum value of a at which the cylinder starts rising up the inclined surface is

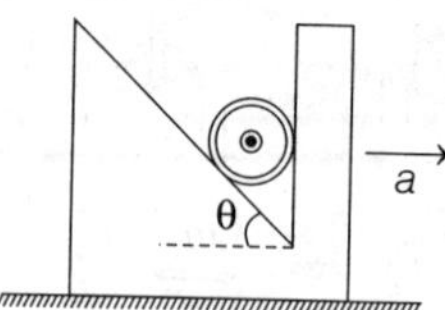

(a) $g \tan\theta$ (b) $g \cot\theta$ (c) $g \sin\theta$ (d) $g \cos\theta$

11. When the trolley shown in figure is given a horizontal acceleration a, the pendulum bob of mass m gets deflected to a maximum angle θ with the vertical. At the position of maximum deflection, the net acceleration of the bob with respect to trolley is

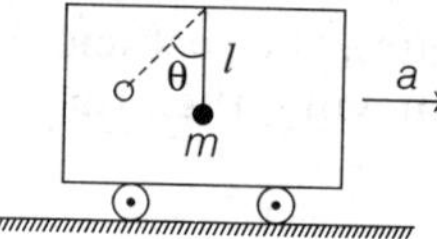

(a) $\sqrt{g^2 + a^2}$ (b) $a \cos\theta$ (c) $g \sin\theta - a \cos\theta$ (d) $a \sin\theta$

12. A block rests on a rough plane whose inclination θ to the horizontal can be varied. Which of the following graphs indicates how the frictional force F between the block and the plane varies as θ is increased ?

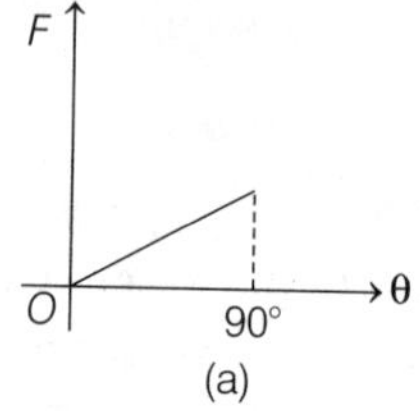

(a)

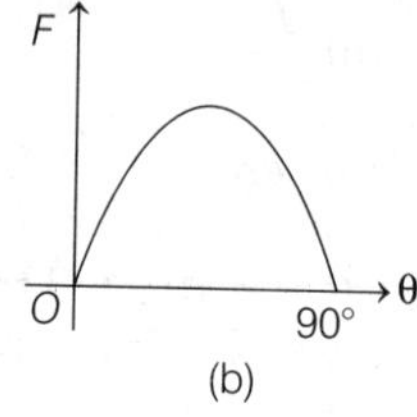

(b)

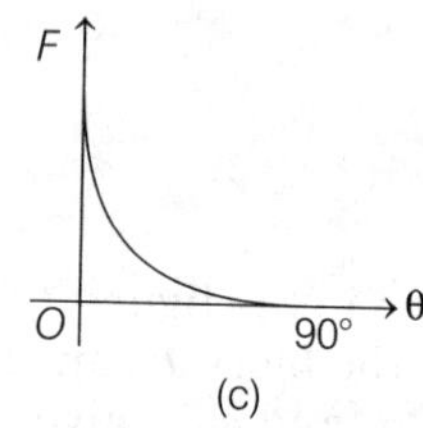

(c)

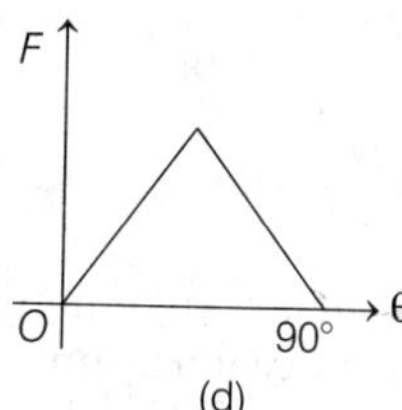

(d)

13. The minimum value of μ between the two blocks for no slipping is

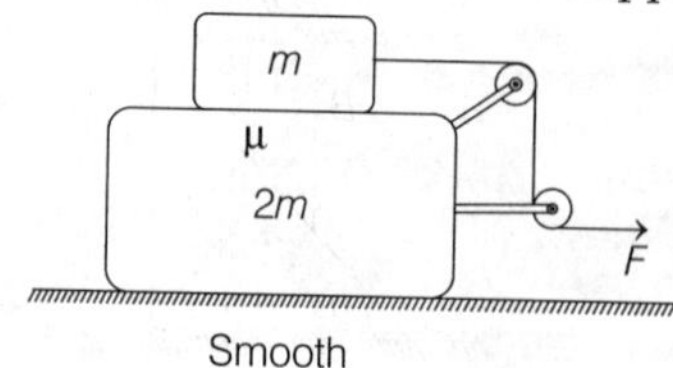

(a) $\frac{F}{mg}$ (b) $\frac{F}{3mg}$ (c) $\frac{2F}{3mg}$ (d) $\frac{4F}{3mg}$

14. A block is sliding along an inclined plane as shown in figure. If the acceleration of chamber is a as shown in the figure. The time required to cover a distance L along inclined is

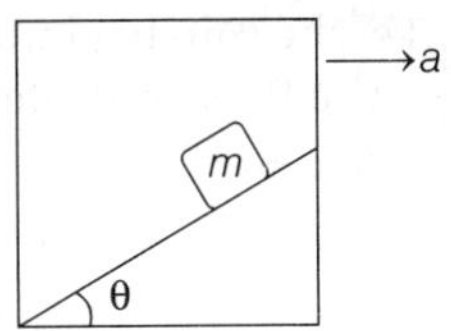

(a) $\sqrt{\dfrac{2L}{g\sin\theta - a\cos\theta}}$ (b) $\sqrt{\dfrac{2L}{g\sin\theta + a\sin\theta}}$ (c) $\sqrt{\dfrac{2L}{g\sin\theta + a\cos\theta}}$ (d) $\sqrt{\dfrac{2L}{g\sin\theta}}$

15. Two blocks A and B are separated by some distance and tied by a string as shown in the figure. The force of friction in both the blocks at $t = 2$ s is

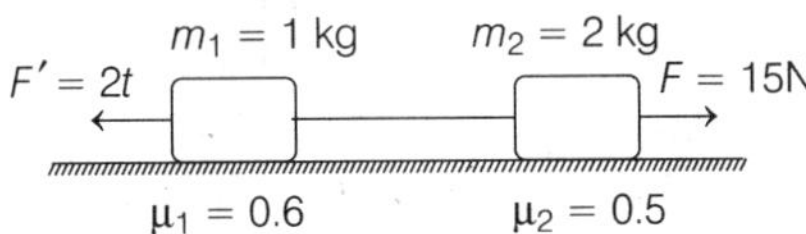

(a) 4 N (→), 5 N(←)
(b) 2 N(→), 5 N(←)
(c) 0 N(→), 10 N(←)
(d) 1 N(←), 10 N(←)

16. All the surfaces and pulleys are frictionless in the shown arrangement. Pulleys P and Q are massless. The force applied by clamp on pulley P is

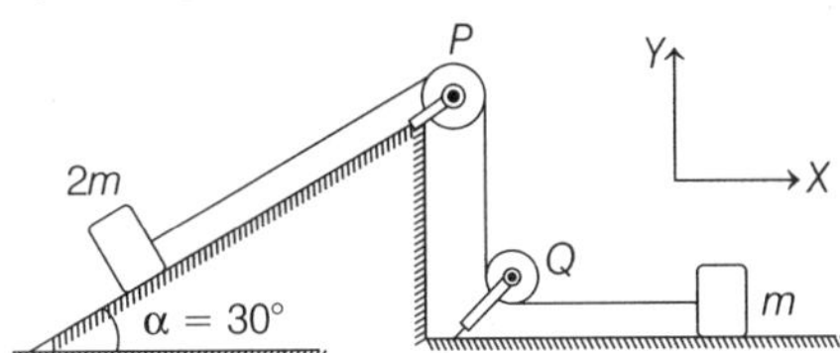

(a) $\dfrac{mg}{6}(-\sqrt{3}\,\hat{\mathbf{i}} - 3\,\hat{\mathbf{j}})$ (b) $\dfrac{mg}{6}(\sqrt{3}\,\hat{\mathbf{i}} + 3\,\hat{\mathbf{j}})$ (c) $\dfrac{mg}{6}\sqrt{2}$ (d) None of these

17. Two blocks of masses 2 kg and 4 kg are connected by a light string and kept on horizontal surface. A force of 16 N is acted on 4 kg block horizontally as shown in figure. Besides, it is given that coefficient of friction between 4 kg and ground is 0.3 and between 2 kg block and ground is 0.6. Then, frictional force between 2 kg block and ground is

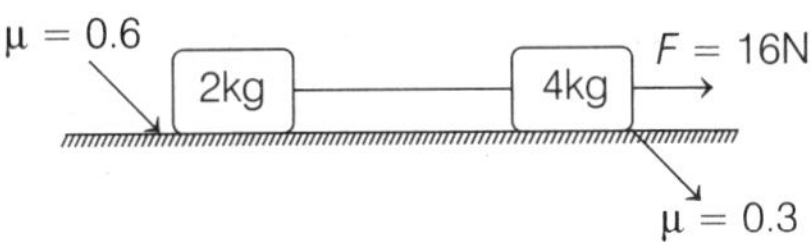

(a) 12 N
(b) 6 N
(c) 4 N
(d) zero

18. A smooth rod of length l is kept inside a trolley at an angle θ as shown in the figure. What should be the acceleration a of the trolley, so that the rod remains in equilibrium with respect to it?

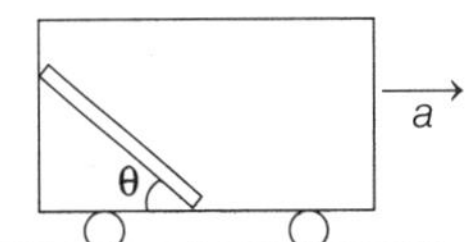

(a) $g\tan\theta$
(b) $g\cos\theta$
(c) $g\sin\theta$
(d) $g\cot\theta$

19. A car begins from rest at time $t = 0$, and then accelerates along a straight track during the interval $0 < t \leq 2$ s and thereafter with constant velocity as shown in the graph. A coin is initially at rest on the floor of the car. At $t = 1$ s, the coin begins to slip and its stops slipping at $t = 3$ s. The coefficient of static friction between the floor and the coin is (Take, $g = 10 \text{ m/s}^2$)

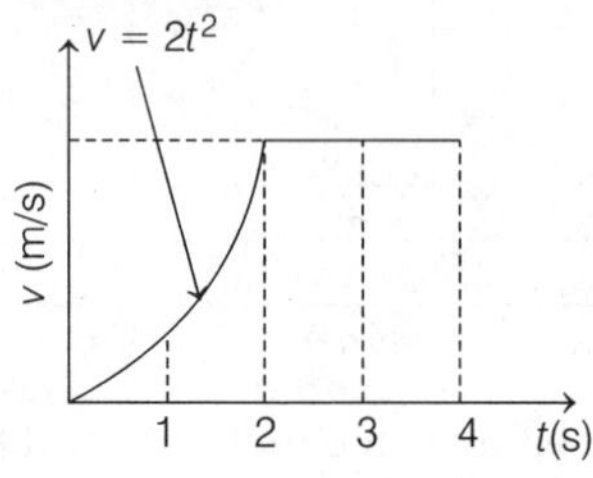

(a) 0.2
(b) 0.3
(c) 0.4
(d) 0.5

20. A horizontal plank is 10.0 m long with uniform density and mass 10 kg. It rests on two supports which are placed 1.0 m from each end as shown in the figure. A man of mass 80 kg can stand upto distance x on the plank without causing it to tip. The value of x is

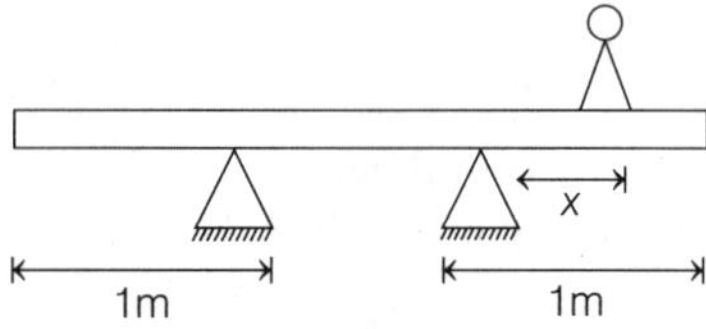

(a) $\frac{1}{2}$ m
(b) $\frac{1}{4}$ m
(c) $\frac{3}{4}$ m
(d) $\frac{1}{8}$ m

21. A block is kept on a smooth inclined plane of angle of inclination θ that moves with a constant acceleration, so that the block does not slide relative to the inclined plane. If the inclined plane stops, the normal contact force offered by the plane on the block changes by a factor

(a) $\tan\theta$
(b) $\tan^2\theta$
(c) $\cos^2\theta$
(d) $\cot\theta$

22. A horizontal force $F = \frac{mg}{3}$ is applied on the upper surface of a uniform cube of mass m and side a which is resting on a rough horizontal surface having $\mu = \frac{1}{2}$. The distance between lines of action of mg and normal reaction is

(a) $\frac{a}{2}$
(b) $\frac{a}{3}$
(c) $\frac{a}{4}$
(d) None of these

23. Two persons of equal heights are carrying a long uniform wooden plank of length l. They are at distance $\frac{l}{4}$ and $\frac{l}{6}$ from nearest end of the rod. The ratio of normal reaction at their heads is

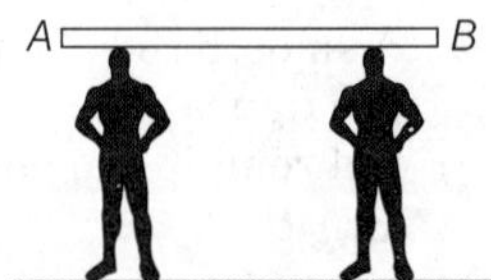

(a) 2 : 3
(b) 1 : 3
(c) 4 : 3
(d) 1 : 2

24. A ball connected with string is released at an angle 45° with the vertical as shown in the figure. Then, the acceleration of the box at this instant will be (mass of the box is equal to mass of ball)

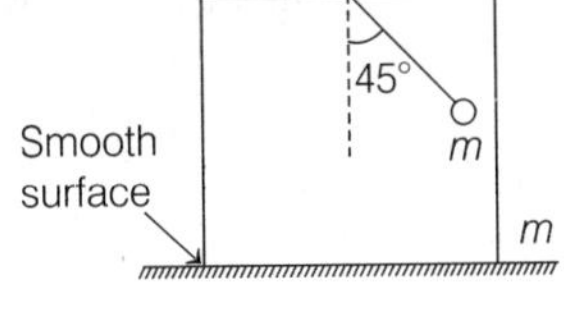

(a) 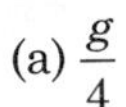 $\frac{g}{4}$ (b) $\frac{g}{3}$

(c) 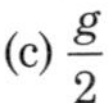 $\frac{g}{2}$ (d) g

25. In the system shown in figure all surfaces are smooth. Rod is moved by external agent with acceleration 9 ms^{-2} vertically downwards. Force exerted on the rod by the wedge will be

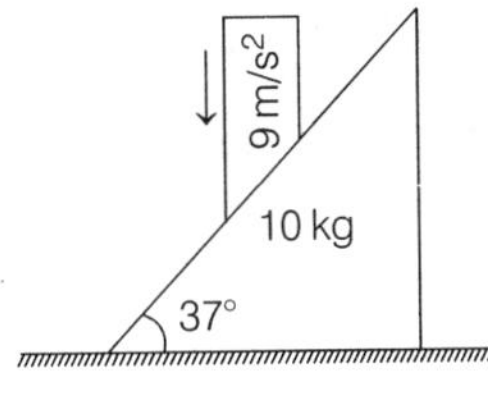

(a) 120 N (b) 200 N
(c) 160 N (d) 180 N

26. Mr. X of mass 80 kg enters a lift and selects the floor he wants. The lift now accelerates upwards at 2 ms^{-2} for 2 s and then moves with constant velocity. As the lift approaches his floor, it decelerates at the same rate as it previously accelerates. If the lift cables can safely withstand a tension of 2×10^4 N and the lift itself has a mass of 500 kg, how many Mr. X's could it safely carry at one time?

(a) 22 (b) 14
(c) 18 (d) 12

27. A particle when projected in vertical plane moves along smooth surface with initial velocity 20 ms^{-1} at an angle of 60°, so that its normal reaction on the surface remains zero throughout the motion. Then, the slope of the surface at height 5m from the point of projection will be

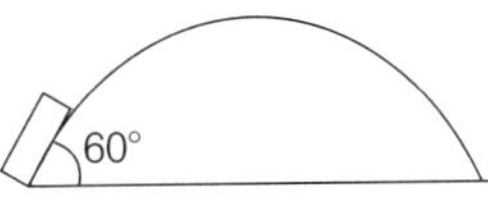

(a) $\sqrt{3}$ (b) 1
(c) 2 (d) None of these

28. Two blocks A and B, each of same mass are attached by a thin inextensible string through an ideal pulley. Initially block B is held in position as shown in figure. Now, the block B is released. Block A will slide to right and hit the pulley in time t_A. Block B will swing and hit the surface in time t_B. Assume the surface as frictionless, then

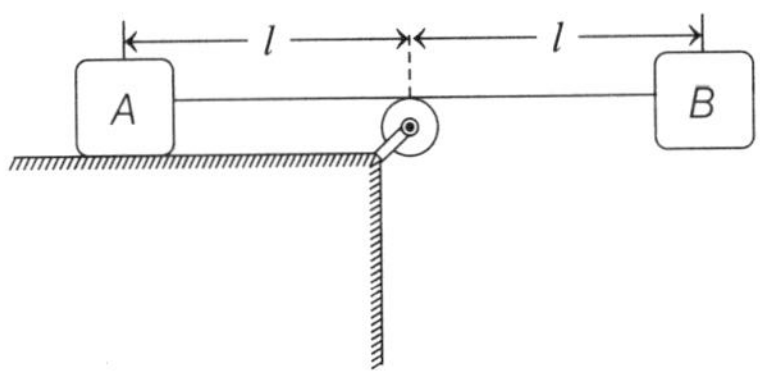

(a) $t_A > t_B$ (b) $t_A < t_B$
(c) $t_A = t_B$ (d) data insufficient

29. Three blocks are kept as shown in figure. Acceleration of 20 kg block with respect to ground is

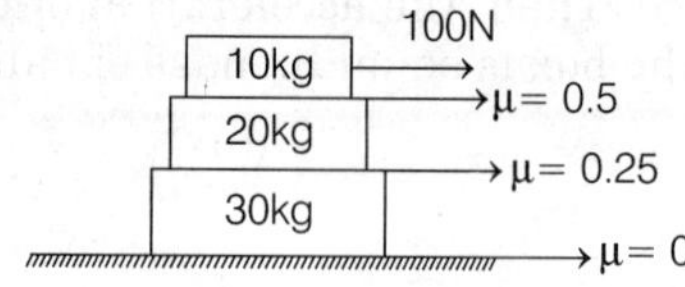

(a) 5 ms^{-2}
(b) 2 ms^{-2}
(c) 1 ms^{-2}
(d) None of these

30. A sphere of radius R is in contact with a wedge. The point of contact is $\frac{R}{5}$ from the ground as shown in the figure. Wedge is moving with velocity 20 ms^{-1} towards left, then the velocity of the sphere at this instant will be

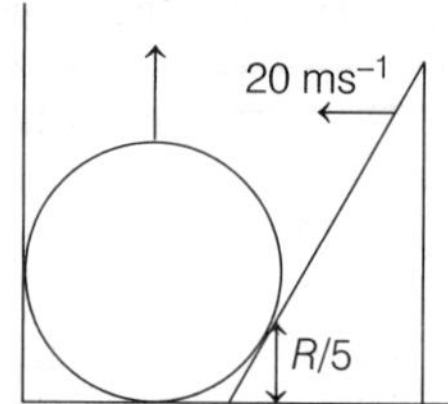

(a) 20 ms^{-1}
(b) 15 ms^{-1}
(c) 16 ms^{-1}
(d) 12 ms^{-1}

31. In the figure it is shown that the velocity of lift is 2 ms^{-1} while string is winding on the motor shaft with velocity 2 ms^{-1} and shaft A is moving downward with velocity 2 ms^{-1} with respect to lift, then find out the velocity of block B.

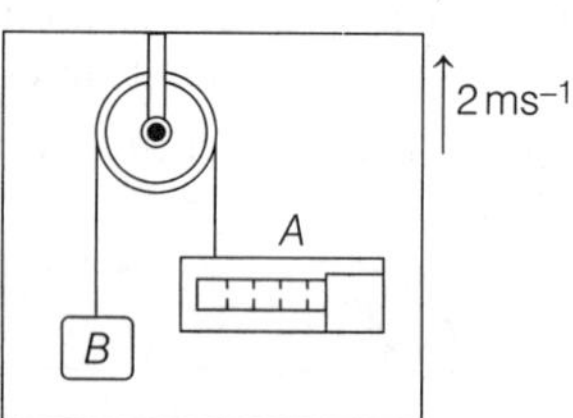

(a) 2 $ms^{-1}\uparrow$
(b) 2 $ms^{-1}\downarrow$
(c) 4 $ms^{-1}\uparrow$
(d) None of these

32. In the figure shown the block B moves with velocity 10 ms^{-1}. The velocity of A in the position shown is

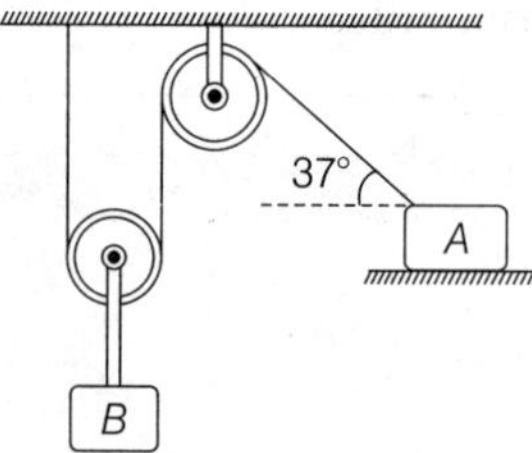

(a) 12.5 ms^{-1}
(b) 25 ms^{-1}
(c) 8 ms^{-1}
(d) 16 ms^{-1}

33. In the figure $m_A = m_B = m_c = 60$ kg. The coefficient of friction between C and ground is 0.5, B and ground is 0.3, A and B is 0.4. C is pulling the string with the maximum possible force without moving. Then, the tension in the string connected to A will be

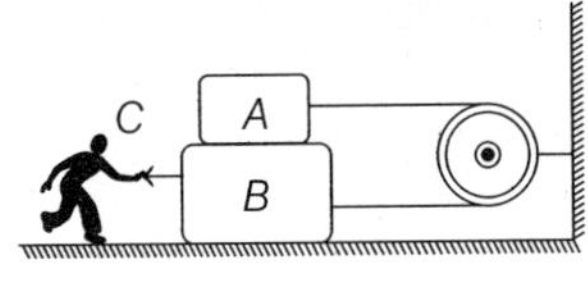

(a) 120 N (b) 60 N (c) 100 N (d) zero

34. In the figure shown the acceleration of A is $\mathbf{a}_A = (15\hat{\mathbf{i}} + 15\hat{\mathbf{j}})$. Then, the acceleration of B is (A remains in contact with B)

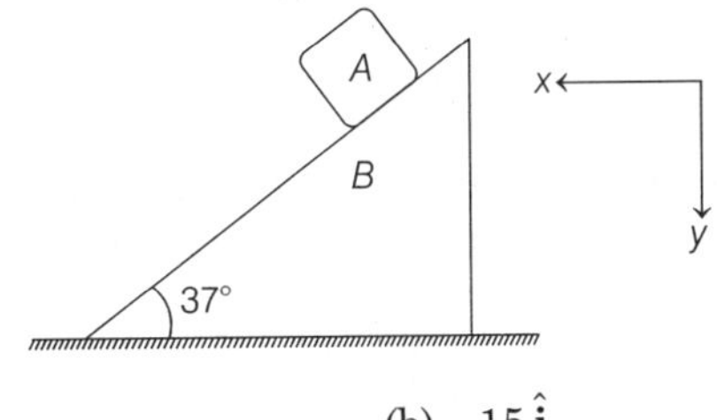

(a) $5\hat{\mathbf{i}}$ (b) $-15\hat{\mathbf{i}}$
(c) $-10\hat{\mathbf{i}}$ (d) $-5\hat{\mathbf{i}}$

35. Two blocks A and B each of mass m are placed on a smooth horizontal surface. Two horizontal forces F and $2F$ are applied on the blocks A and B respectively as shown in figure. The block A does not slide on block B. Then, the normal reaction acting between the two blocks is

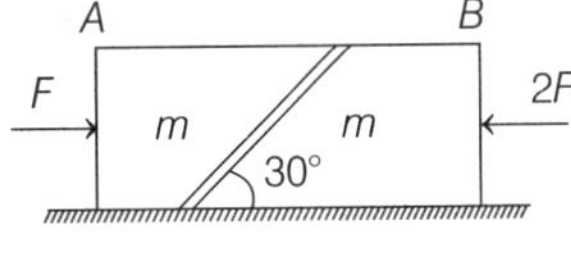

(a) F (b) $\frac{F}{2}$
(c) $\frac{F}{\sqrt{3}}$ (d) $3F$

36. Two beads A and B move along a semicircular wire frame as shown in figure. The beads are connected by an inelastic string which always remains tight. At an instant, the speed of A is u, $\angle BAC = 45°$ and $BOC = 75°$, where O is the centre of the semicircular arc. The speed of bead B at that instant is

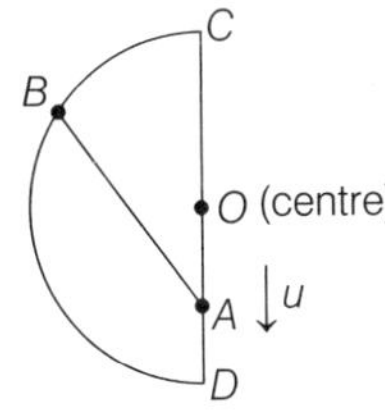

(a) $\sqrt{2}u$ (b) u
(c) $\frac{u}{2\sqrt{2}}$ (d) $\sqrt{\frac{2}{3}}u$

37. If the coefficient of friction between A and B is μ, the maximum acceleration of the wedge A for which B will remain at rest with respect to the wedge is

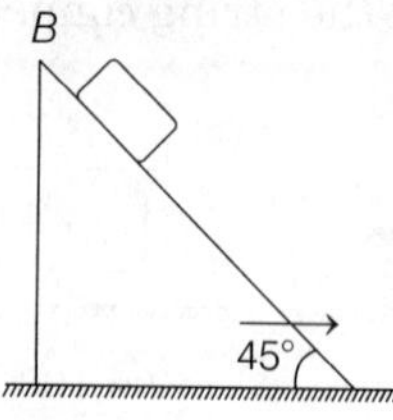

(a) μg

(b) $g\left(\frac{1+\mu}{1-\mu}\right)$

(c) $g\left(\frac{1-\mu}{1+\mu}\right)$

(d) $\frac{g}{\mu}$

38. A pivoted beam of negligible mass has a mass suspended from one end and an Atwood's machine suspended from the other. The frictionless pulley has negligible mass and dimension. Gravity is directed downward and $M_2 = 3M_3$, $l_2 = 3l_1$. Find the ratio M_1/M_2 which will ensure that the beam has no tendency to rotate just after the masses are released.

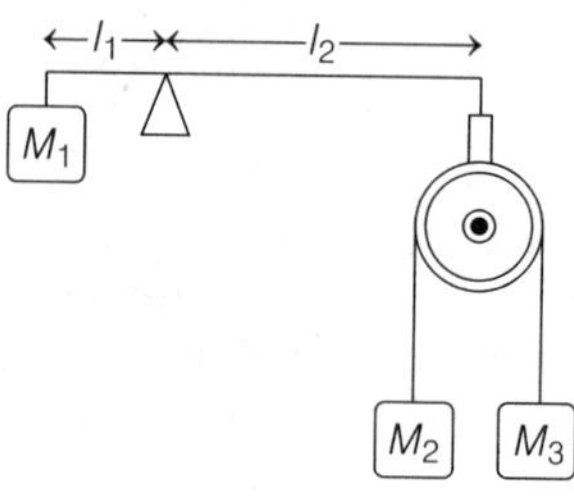

(a) $\frac{M_1}{M_2} = 2$

(b) $\frac{M_1}{M_2} = 3$

(c) $\frac{M_1}{M_2} = 4$

(d) None of these

39. If force F is increasing with time and at $t = 0$, $F = 0$, where will slipping first start?

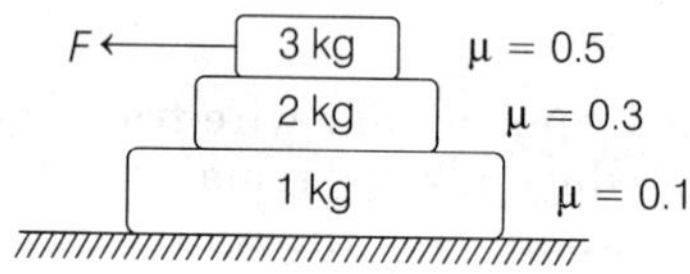

(a) Between 3 kg and 2 kg

(b) Between 2 kg and 1 kg

(c) Between 1 kg and ground

(d) Both (a) and (b)

40. A plank of mass 2 kg and length 1 m is placed on horizontal floor. A small block of mass 1 kg is placed on top of the plank, at its right extreme end. The coefficient of friction between plank and floor is 0.5 and that between plank and block is 0.2. If a horizontal force = 30 N starts acting on the plank to the right, the time after which the block will fall off the plank is (Take, $g = 10\,\text{ms}^{-2}$)

(a) $\left(\frac{2}{3}\right)$ s

(b) 1.5 s

(c) 0.75 s

(d) $\left(\frac{4}{3}\right)$ s

41. A block of mass m is placed on another block of mass M which itself is lying on a horizontal surface. The coefficient of friction between two blocks is μ_1 and that between the block of mass M and horizontal surface is μ_2. What maximum horizontal force can be applied to the lower block so that the two blocks move without separation?

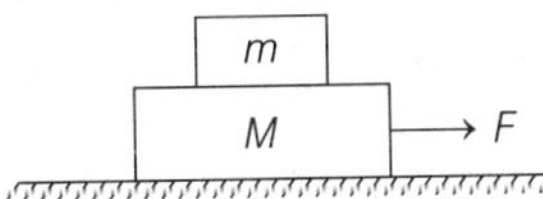

(a) $(M+m)(\mu_2-\mu_1)g$
(b) $(M-m)(\mu_2+\mu_1)g$
(c) $(M-m)(\mu_2+\mu_1)g$
(d) $(M+m)(\mu_2+\mu_1)g$

42. A balloon with mass m is descending down with an acceleration a (where $a<g$). How much mass should be removed from it, so that it starts moving up with an acceleration a?

(a) $\dfrac{2ma}{g+a}$
(b) $\dfrac{2ma}{g-a}$
(c) $\dfrac{ma}{g+a}$
(d) $\dfrac{ma}{g-a}$

43. If coefficient of friction between all surfaces is 0.4, then find the minimum force F to have equilibrium of the system. (Take, $g=10\,\text{m/s}^2$)

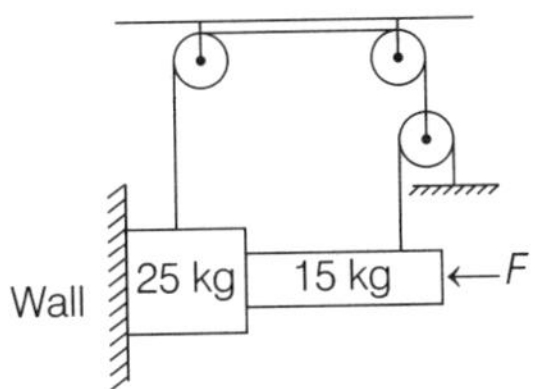

(a) 62.5 N
(b) 150 N
(c) 135 N
(d) 50 N

44. In the arrangement shown in figure, there is a friction force between the blocks of masses m and $2\,m$. The mass of the suspended block is m. The block of mass m is stationary with respect to block of mass $2\,m$. The minimum value of coefficient of friction between m and $2\,m$ is

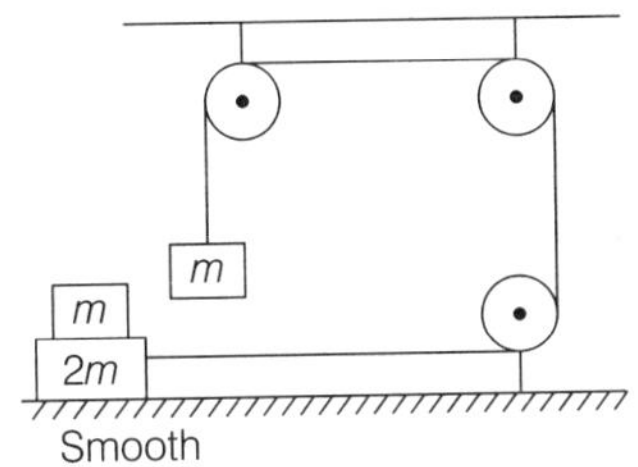

(a) $\dfrac{1}{2}$
(b) $\dfrac{1}{\sqrt{2}}$
(c) $\dfrac{1}{4}$
(d) $\dfrac{1}{3}$

45. Block B moves to the right with a constant velocity v_0. The velocity of body A relative to B is

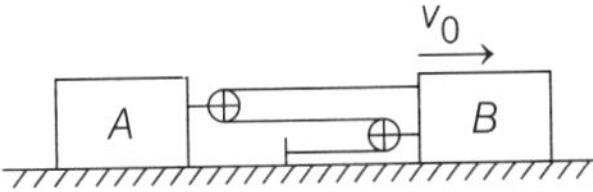

(a) $\dfrac{v_0}{2}$, towards left
(b) $\dfrac{v_0}{2}$, towards right
(c) $\dfrac{3v_0}{2}$, towards left
(d) $\dfrac{3v_0}{2}$, towards right

46. A mass of 3 kg descending vertically downwards supports a mass of 2 kg by means of a light string passing over a pulley. At the end of 5 s, the string breaks . How much high from now the 2 kg mass will go? (Take, $g = 9.8\,\text{m/s}^2$)

(a) 4.9 m (b) 9.8 m (c) 19.6 m (d) 2.45 m

47. The rear side of a truck is open and a box of mass 20 kg is placed on the truck 4 m away from the open end $\mu = 0.15$ and $g = 10\,\text{m/s}^2$. The truck starts from rest with an acceleration of $2\,\text{m/s}^2$ on a straight road. The box will fall off the truck when it is at a distance from the starting point equal to

(a) 4 m (b) 8 m (c) 16 m (d) 32 m

48. In the figure, pulleys are smooth and strings are massless, $m_1 = 1$ kg and $m_2 = \frac{1}{3}$ kg. To keep m_3 at rest, mass m_3 should be

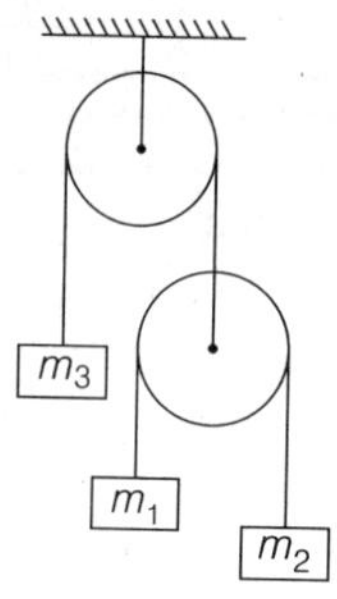

(a) 1 kg (b) $\frac{2}{3}$ kg (c) $\frac{1}{4}$ kg (d) 2 kg

49. A pendulum of mass m hangs from a support fixed to a trolley. The direction of the string (i.e. angle θ) when the trolley rolls up a plane of inclination α with acceleration a is

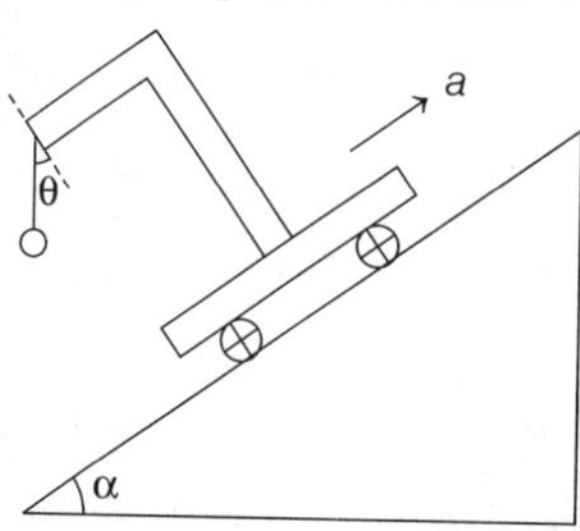

(a) 0 (b) $\tan^{-1}\alpha$ (c) $\tan^{-1}\left(\frac{a + g\sin\alpha}{g\cos\alpha}\right)$ (d) $\tan^{-1}\frac{a}{g}$

50. Two blocks of mass $m = 5$ kg and $M = 10$ kg are connected by a string passing over a pulley B as shown. Another string connects the centre of pulley B to the floor and passes over another pulley A as shown. An upward force F is applied at the centre of pulley A. Both the pulleys are massless. The accelerations of blocks m and M, if F is 300 N are (Take, $g = 10\,\text{m/s}^2$)

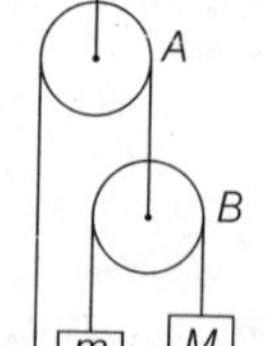

(a) $5\,\text{m/s}^2$, zero
(b) zero, $5\,\text{m/s}^2$
(c) zero, zero
(d) $5\,\text{m/s}^2$, $5\,\text{m/s}^2$

51. A body weighs 8 g when placed in one pan and 18 g when placed on the other pan of a false balance. If the beam is horizontal when both the pans are empty, the true weight of the body is

(a) 13 g (b) 12 g
(c) 15.5 g (d) 15 g

52. A man of mass m has fallen into a ditch of width d. Two of his friends are slowly pulling him out using a light rope and two fixed pulleys as shown in figure. Both the friends exert force of equal magnitudes F.

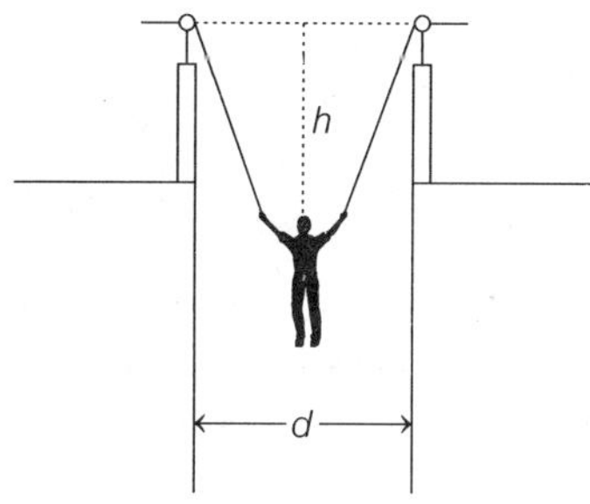

When the man is at a depth h, the value of F is

(a) $\frac{mg}{4h}\sqrt{d^2+4h^2}$ (b) hmg
(c) dmg (d) $\frac{mg}{2h}\sqrt{h^2+d^2}$

53. Two blocks of masses $M_1 = 4$ kg and $M_2 = 6$ kg are connected by a string of negligible mass passing over a frictionless pulley as shown in the figure below. The coefficient of friction between the block M_1 and the horizontal surface is 0.4. When the system is released, the masses M_1 and M_2 start accelerating. What additional mass m should be placed over M_1, so that the masses $(M_1 + m)$ slide with a uniform speed?

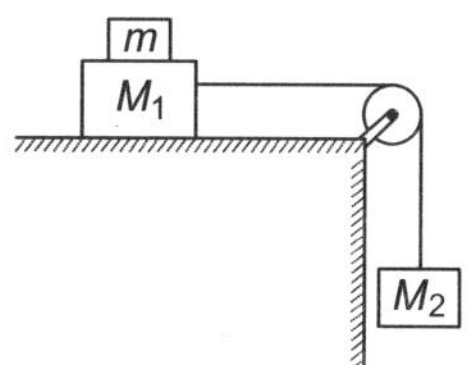

(a) 12 kg (b) 11 kg
(c) 10 kg (d) 15 kg

More than One Correct Options

1. Two blocks each of mass 1 kg are placed as shown. They are connected by a string which passes over a smooth (massless) pulley.

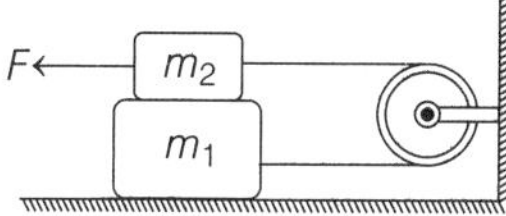

There is no friction between m_1 and the ground. The coefficient of friction between m_1 and m_2 is 0.2. A force F is applied to m_2. Which of the following statements is/are correct?

(a) The system will be in equilibrium if $F \le 4$ N
(b) If $F > 4$ N tension in the string will be 4 N
(c) If $F > 4$ N the frictional force between the blocks will be 2 N
(d) If $F = 6$ N tension in the string will be 3 N

2. Two particles A and B, each of mass m are kept stationary by applying a horizontal force $F = mg$ on particle B as shown in figure. Then,

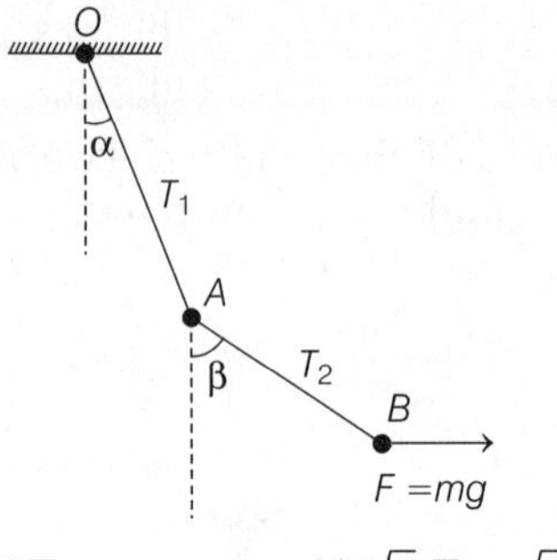

(a) $\tan\beta = 2\tan\alpha$ (b) $2T_1 = 5T_2$ (c) $\sqrt{2}\,T_1 = \sqrt{5}T_2$ (d) $\alpha = \beta$

3. The velocity-time graph of the figure shows the motion of a wooden block of mass 1 kg which is given an initial push at $t = 0$ along a horizontal table.

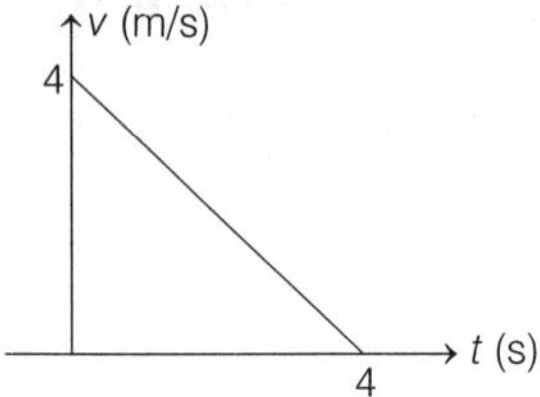

(a) The coefficient of friction between the block and the table is 0.1
(b) The coefficient of friction between the block and the table is 0.2
(c) If the table was half of its present roughness, the time taken by the block to complete the journey is 4 s
(d) If the table was half of its present roughness, the time taken by the block to complete the journey is 8 s

4. As shown in the figure, A is a man of mass 60 kg standing on a block B of mass 40 kg kept on ground. The coefficient of friction between the feet of the man and the block is 0.3 and that between B and the ground is 0.2. If the person pulls the string with 125 N force, then

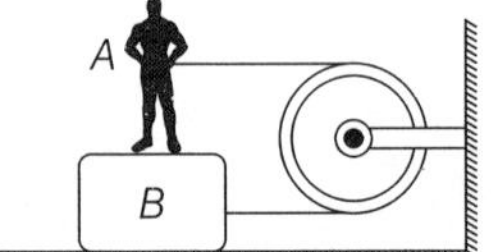

(a) B will slide on ground
(b) A and B will move with acceleration 0.5 ms^{-2}
(c) the force of friction acting between A and B will be 125 N
(d) the force of friction acting between B and ground will be 250 N

5. $M_A = 3$ kg, $M_B = 4$ kg, and $M_C = 8$ kg. Coefficient of friction between any two surfaces is 0.25. Pulley is frictionless and string is massless. A is connected to wall through a massless rigid rod. (Take, $g = 10\ ms^{-2}$)

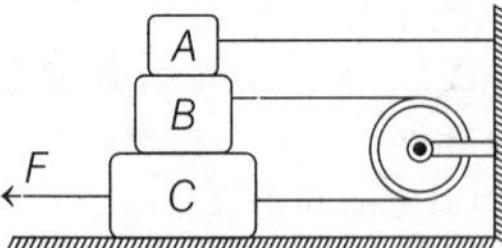

(a) value of F to keep C moving with constant speed is 80 N
(b) value of F to keep C moving with constant speed is 120 N
(c) if F is 200 N, then acceleration of B is 10 ms^{-2}
(d) to slide C towards left, F should be at least 50 N

6. A man pulls a block of mass equal to himself with a light string. The coefficient of friction between the man and the floor is greater than that between the block and the floor
(a) if the block does not move, then the man also does not move
(b) the block can move even when the man is stationary
(c) if both move, then the acceleration of the block is greater than the acceleration of man
(d) if both move, then the acceleration of man is greater than the acceleration of block

7. A block of mass 1 kg is at rest relative to a smooth wedge moving leftwards with constant acceleration $a = 5\ \text{ms}^{-2}$. Let N be the normal reaction between the block and the wedge. Then, $(g = 10\ \text{ms}^{-2})$

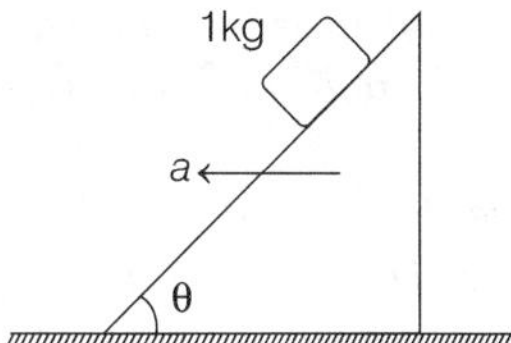

(a) $N = 5\sqrt{5}$ newton (b) $N = 15$ newton (c) $\tan\theta = \dfrac{1}{2}$ (d) $\tan\theta = 2$

8. For the given situation shown in figure, choose the correct options (Take, $g = 10\ \text{ms}^{-2}$)

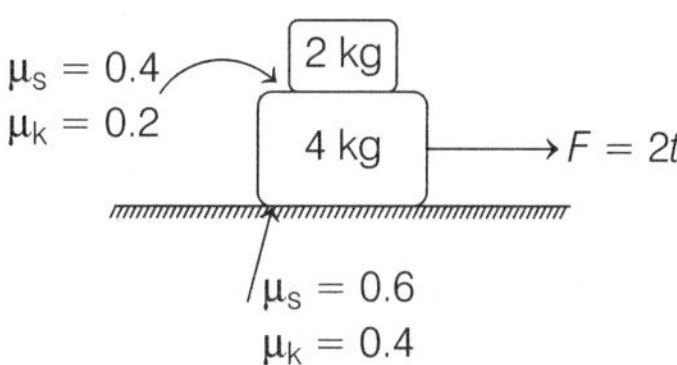

(a) At $t = 1$ s, force of friction between 2 kg and 4 kg is 2 N
(b) At $t = 1$ s, force of friction between 2 kg and 4 kg is zero
(c) At $t = 4$ s, force of friction between 4 kg and ground is 8 N
(d) At $t = 15$ s, acceleration of 2 kg is $1\ \text{ms}^{-2}$

9. Force acting on a block *versus* time graph is as shown in figure. Choose the correct options. (Take, $g = 10\ \text{ms}^{-2}$)

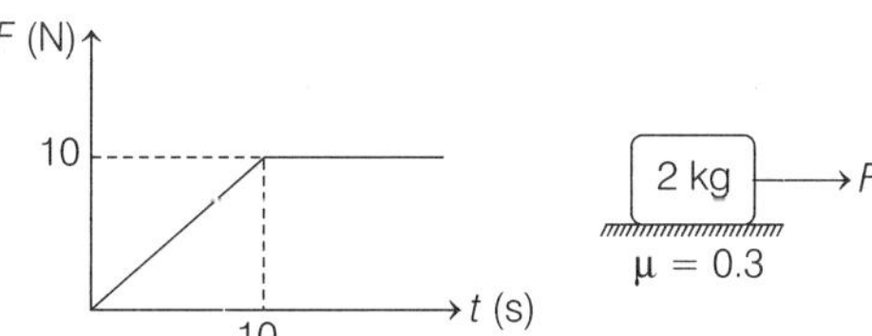

(a) At $t = 2$ s, force of friction is 2 N
(b) At $t = 8$ s, force of friction is 6 N
(c) At $t = 10$ s, acceleration of block is $2\ \text{ms}^{-2}$
(d) At $t = 12$ s, velocity of block is $8\ \text{ms}^{-1}$

10. For the situation shown in figure, mark the correct options.

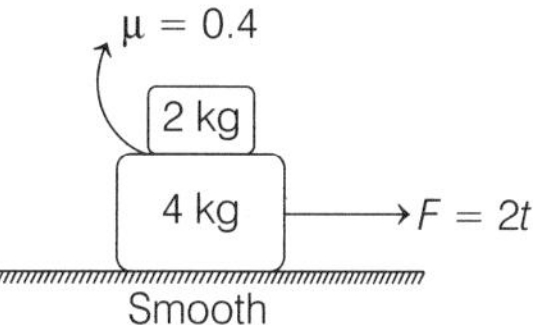

(a) At $t = 3$ s, pseudo force on 4 kg block applied from 2 kg is 4 N in forward direction
(b) At $t = 3$ s, pseudo force on 2 kg block applied from 4 kg is 2 N in backward direction
(c) Pseudo force does not make an equal and opposite pairs
(d) Pseudo force also makes a pair of equal and opposite forces

11. For the situation shown in figure, mark the correct options.

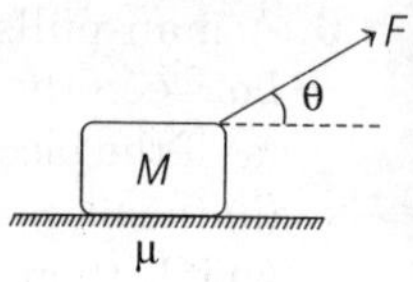

(a) Angle of friction is $\tan^{-1}(\mu)$

(b) Angle of repose is $\tan^{-1}(\mu)$

(c) At $\theta = \tan^{-1}(\mu)$, minimum force will be required to move the block

(d) Minimum force required to move the block is $\frac{\mu Mg}{\sqrt{1+\mu^2}}$.

Comprehension Based Questions

Passage 1 (Q. Nos. 1 to 5)

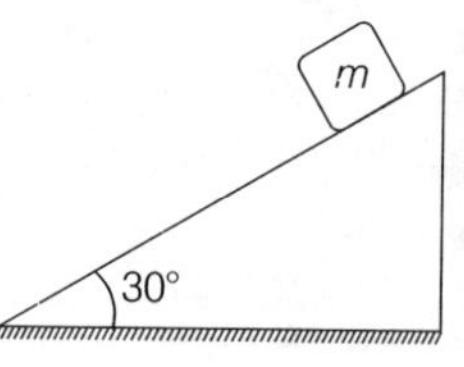

A man wants to slide down a block of mass m which is kept on a fixed inclined plane of inclination 30° as shown in the figure. Initially the block is not sliding.

To just start sliding the man pushes the block down the incline with a force F. Now, the block starts accelerating. To move it downwards with constant speed, the man starts pulling the block with same force. Surfaces are such that ratio of maximum static friction to kinetic friction is 2. Now, answer the following questions.

1. What is the value of F?

(a) $\frac{mg}{4}$ (b) $\frac{mg}{6}$ (c) $\frac{mg\sqrt{3}}{4}$ (d) $\frac{mg}{2\sqrt{3}}$

2. What is the value of μ_s, the coefficient of static friction?

(a) $\frac{4}{3\sqrt{3}}$ (b) $\frac{2}{3\sqrt{3}}$ (c) $\frac{3}{3\sqrt{3}}$ (d) $\frac{1}{2\sqrt{3}}$

3. If the man continues pushing the block by force F, its acceleration would be

(a) $\frac{g}{6}$ (b) $\frac{g}{4}$

(c) $\frac{g}{2}$ (d) $\frac{g}{3}$

4. If the man wants to move the block up the incline, what minimum force is required to start the motion?

(a) $\frac{2}{3}mg$ (b) $\frac{mg}{2}$ (c) $\frac{7mg}{6}$ (d) $\frac{5mg}{6}$

5. What minimum force is required to move it up the incline with constant speed?

(a) $\frac{2}{3}mg$ (b) $\frac{mg}{2}$ (c) $\frac{7mg}{6}$ (d) $\frac{5mg}{6}$

Passage 2 (Q. Nos. 6 to 7)

A lift with a mass 1200 kg is raised from rest by a cable with a tension 1350 kg-f. After sometime, the tension drops to 1000 kg-f and the lift comes to rest at a height of 25 m above its initial point. (Take, 1 kg-f = 9.8 N)

6. What is the height at which the tension changes?

(a) 10.8 m (b) 12.5 m

(c) 14.3 m (d) 16 m

7. What is the greatest speed of lift?

(a) 9.8 ms^{-1} (b) 7.5 ms^{-1} (c) 5.92 ms^{-1} (d) None of these

Passage 3 (Q. Nos. 8 to 9)

Blocks A and B shown in the figure are connected with a bar of negligible weight. A and B each has mass 170 kg, the coefficient of friction between A and the plane is 0.2 and that between B and the plane is 0.4 (Take, $g = 10\ ms^{-2}$)

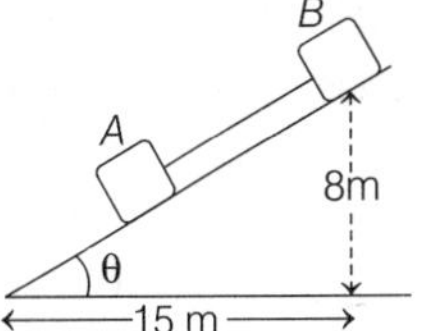

8. What is the total force of friction between the blocks and the plane?

(a) 900 N (b) 700 N
(c) 600 N (d) 300 N

9. What is the force acting on the connecting bar?

(a) 150 N (b) 100 N
(c) 75 N (d) 125 N

Passage 4 (Q. Nos. 10 to 12)

Two smooth blocks A of mass 1 kg and B of mass 2 kg are connected by a light string passing over a smooth pulley as shown. The block B is sliding down with a velocity 2 m/s. A force F is applied on the block A, so that the block B will reverse its direction of motion after 3 s.

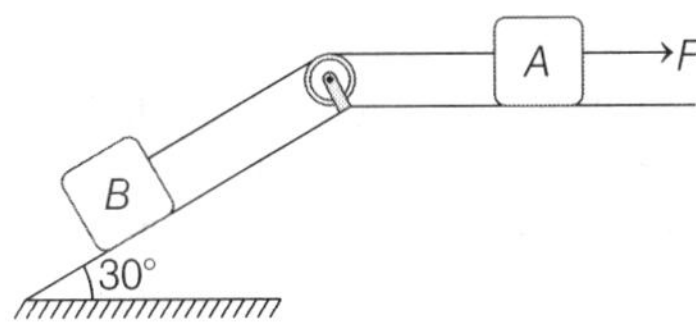

10. Find the acceleration of block A.

(a) $1\ m/s^2$ (b) $\frac{2}{3}\ m/s^2$
(c) $3\ m/s^2$ (d) $\frac{4}{9}\ m/s^2$

11. Find the tension in the string.

(a) 10 N (b) 11.33 N
(c) 13.67 N (d) 40 N

12. The value of F is

(a) 9 N (b) 10 N
(c) 11 N (d) 12 N

Match the Columns

1.

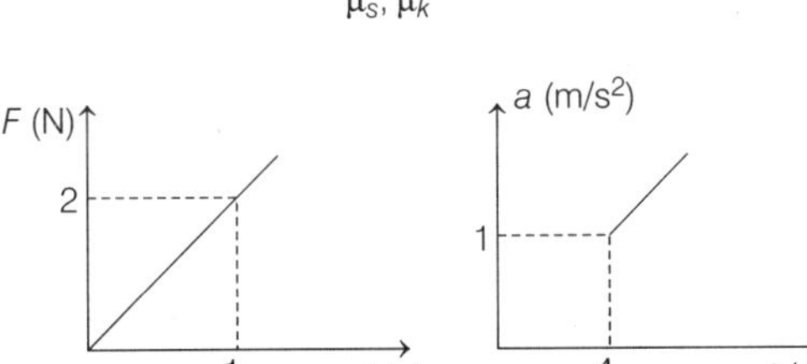

Force acting on a block *versus* time and acceleration *versus* time graph are as shown in figure. Taking value of $g = 10\ \text{ms}^{-2}$, match the following two columns.

Column I	Column II
(a) Coefficient of static friction	(p) 0.2
(b) Coefficient of kinetic friction	(q) 0.3
(c) Force of friction (in newton) at $t = 0.1$ s	(r) 0.4
(d) Value of $\frac{a}{10}$, where a is acceleration of block (in m/s^2) at $t = 8$ s	(s) 0.5

2. Angle θ is gradually increased as shown in figure. For the given situation, match the following two columns. (Take, $g = 10\ \text{ms}^{-2}$)

Column I	Column II
(a) Force of friction when $\theta = 0°$	(p) 10 N
(b) Force of friction when $\theta = 90°$	(q) $10\sqrt{3}$ N
(c) Force of friction when $\theta = 30°$	(r) $\frac{10}{\sqrt{3}}$ N
(d) Force of friction when $\theta = 60°$	(s) None of the above

3. Match the following two columns regarding fundamental forces of nature.

Column I	Column II
(a) Force of friction	(p) field force
(b) Normal reaction	(q) contact force
(c) Force between two neutrons	(r) electromagnetic force
(d) Force between two protons	(s) nuclear force

4. In the figure shown, match the following two columns. (Take, $g = 10\ \text{ms}^{-2}$)

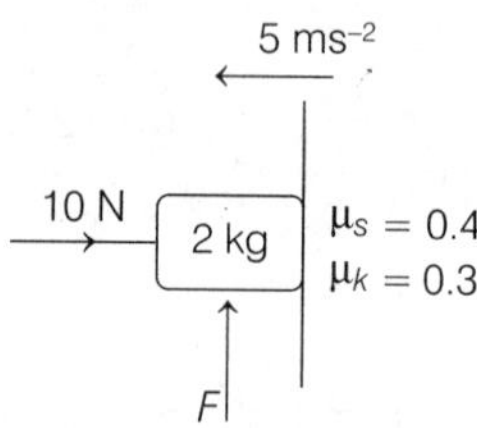

Column I	Column II
(a) Normal reaction	(p) 5 N
(b) Force of friction when $F = 15$ N	(q) 10 N
(c) Minimum value of F for stopping the block moving down	(r) 15 N
(d) Minimum value of F for stopping the block moving up	(s) None of the above

5. There is no friction between blocks B and C. But ground is rough. Pulleys are smooth and massless and strings are light. For $F = 10$ N, whole system remains stationary. Match the following two columns.($m_B = m_C = 1$ kg and $g = 10$ ms^{-2})

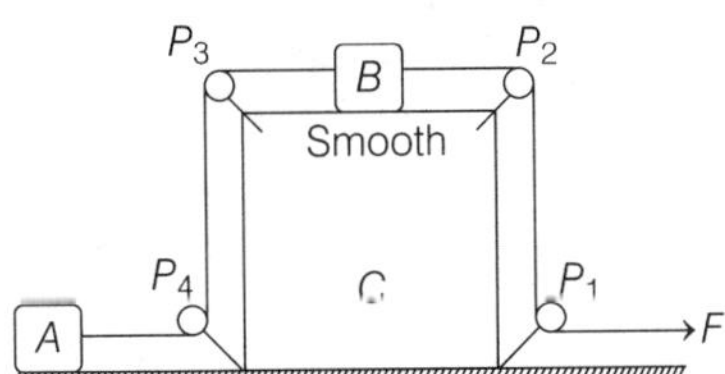

Column I	Column II
(a) Force of friction between A and ground	(p) 10 N
(b) Force of friction between C and ground	(q) 20 N
(c) Normal reaction on C from ground	(r) 5 N
(d) Tension in string between P_3 and P_4	(s) None of the above

6. Match the Column I with Column II.

Note *Applied force is parallel to plane.*

Column I	Column II
(a) If friction force is less than applied force, then friction may be	(p) static
(b) If friction force is equal to the force applied, then friction may be	(q) kinetic
(c) If a block is moving on ground, then friction is	(r) limiting
(d) If a block kept on ground is at rest, then friction may be	(s) no conclusion can be drawn

7. For the situation shown in figure in Column I, the statements regarding friction forces are mentioned, while in Column II some information related to friction forces are given. Match the entries of Column I with the entries of Column II. (Take, $g = 10$ ms^{-2})

$\mu = 0.2$ 2kg
$\mu = 0.1$ 3kg → $F = 100$N
5kg
Smooth

Column I	Column II
(a) Total friction force on 3 kg block is	(p) towards right
(b) Total friction force on 5 kg block is	(q) towards left
(c) Friction force on 2 kg block due to 3 kg block is	(r) zero
(d) Friction force on 3 kg block due to 5 kg block is	(s) non-zero

8. If the system is released from rest, then match the following two columns.

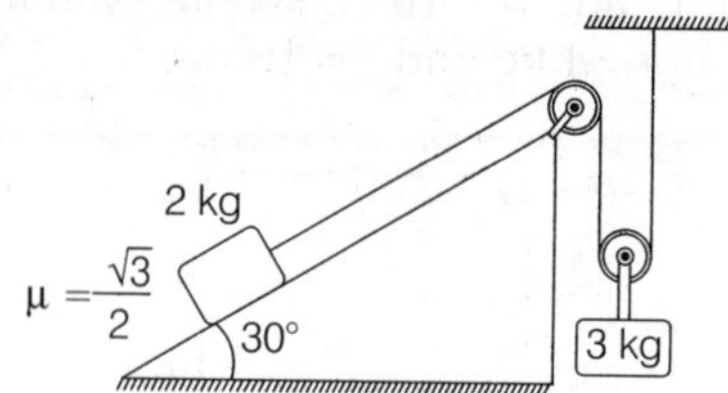

Column I	Column II
(a) Acceleration of 2 kg mass	(p) 2 SI unit
(b) Acceleration of 3 kg mass	(q) 5 SI unit
(c) Tension in the string connecting 2 kg mass	(r) Zero
(d) Frictional force on 2 kg mass	(s) None of these

9. Two blocks A and B of masses 2 kg and 3 kg are placed on horizontal surface. The coefficient of friction between block A and horizontal surface is 0.5 while the block B is smooth. A force $F = (\sqrt{2}\, t)$ N is applied on block A as shown in the figure.

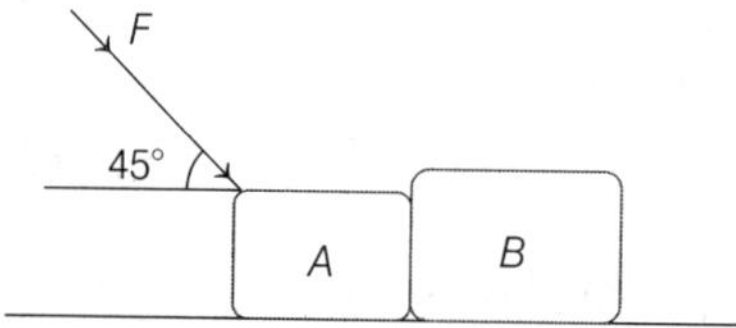

Match the Column I with Column II.

Column I	Column II
(a) $t = 4$ s	(p) The acceleration of block B is zero.
(b) $t = 20$ s	(q) Friction on block A is more than 20 N.
(c) $t = 40$ s	(r) The acceleration of block A is 2 m/s^2.
(d) $t = 60$ s	(s) Normal contact force between blocks A and B is non-zero.

Subjective Questions

1. A small marble is projected with a velocity of 10 m/s in a direction 45° from the y-direction on the smooth inclined plane. Calculate the magnitude v of its velocity after 2s. (Take, $g = 10\text{ m/s}^2$)

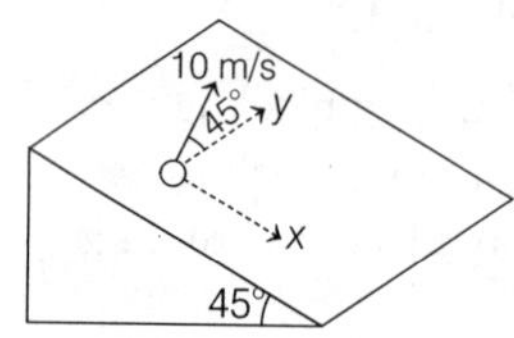

2. Determine the acceleration of the 5 kg block A. Neglect the mass of the pulley and cords. The block B has a mass of 10 kg. The coefficient of kinetic friction between block B and the surface is $\mu_k = 0.1$. (Take, $g = 10\,\text{m/s}^2$)

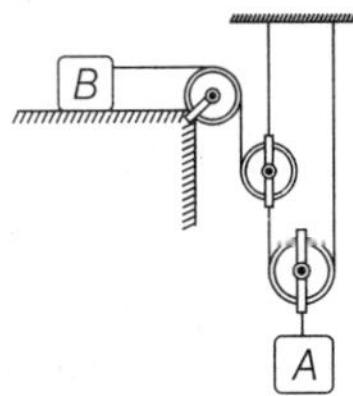

3. A 30 kg mass is initially at rest on the floor of a truck. The coefficient of static friction between the mass and the floor of truck in 0.3 and coefficient of kinetic friction is 0.2. Initially the truck is travelling due east at constant speed. Find the magnitude and direction of the friction force acting on the mass, if : (Take, $g = 10\ \text{m/s}^2$)

(a) The truck accelerates at $1.8\ \text{m/s}^2$ eastward

(b) The truck accelerates at $3.8\ \text{m/s}^2$ westward.

4. A 6 kg block B rests as shown on the upper surface of a 15 kg wedge A. Neglecting friction, determine immediately after the system is released from rest (a) the acceleration of A (b) the acceleration of B relative to A. (Take, $g = 10\ \text{m/s}^2$)

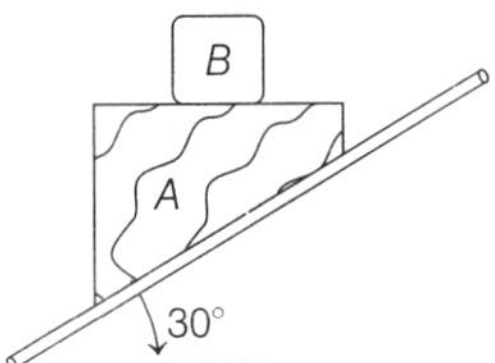

5. At the bottom edge of a smooth vertical wall, an inclined plane is kept at an angle of 45°. A uniform ladder of length l and mass M rests on the inclined plane against the wall such that it is perpendicular to the incline.

(a) If the plane is also smooth, which way will the ladder slide.

(b) What is the minimum coefficient of friction necessary so that the ladder does not slip on the incline?

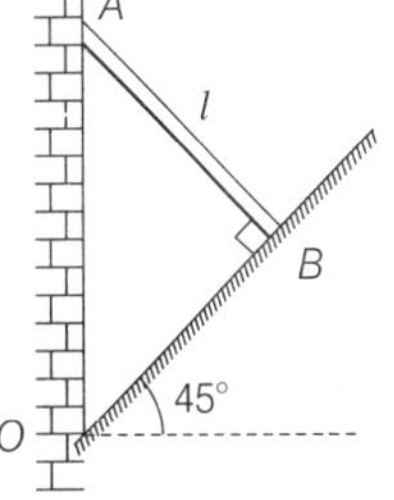

6. A plank of mass M is placed on a rough horizontal surface and a constant horizontal force F is applied on it. A man of mass m runs on the plank. Find the range of acceleration of the man so that the plank does not move on the surface. Coefficient of friction between the plank and the surface is μ. Assume that the man does not slip on the plank.

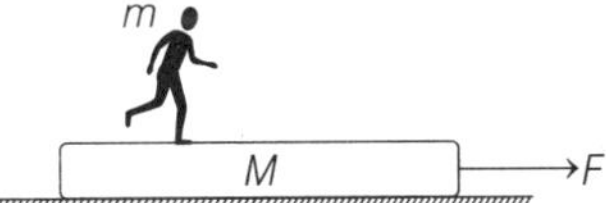

7. The upper portion of an inclined plane of inclination α is smooth and the lower portion is rough. A particle slides down from rest from the top and just comes to rest at the foot. If the ratio of smooth length to rough length is $m : n$, find the coefficient of friction.

8. Block B has a mass m and is released from rest when it is on top of wedge A, which has a mass $3m$. Determine the tension in cord CD while B is sliding down A. Neglect friction.

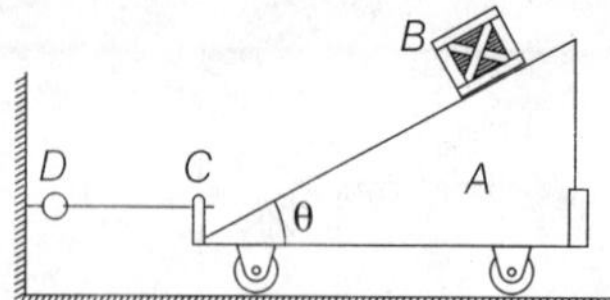

9. Coefficients of friction between the flat bed of the truck and crate are $\mu_s = 0.85$ and $\mu_k = 0.8$. The coefficient of kinetic friction between the truck tires and the road surface is 0.9. If the truck stops from an initial speed of 15 m/s with maximum braking (wheels skidding). Determine where on the bed the crate finally comes to rest. (Take, $g = 10\ \text{m/s}^2$)

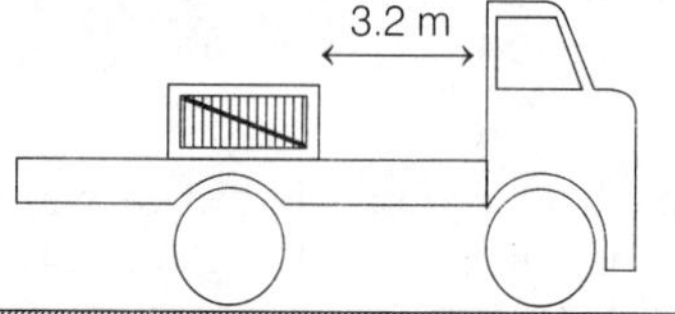

10. The 10 kg block is moving to the left with a speed of 1.2 m/s at time $t = 0$. A force F is applied as shown in the graph. After 0.2 s, the force continues at the 10 N level. If the coefficient of kinetic friction is $\mu_k = 0.2$. Determine the time t at which the block comes to a stop. (Take, $g = 10\ \text{m/s}^2$)

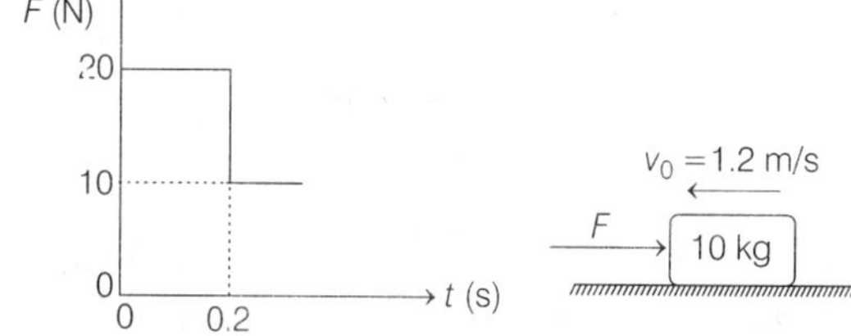

11. The 10 kg block is resting on the horizontal surface when the force F is applied to it for 7 s. The variation of F with time is shown. Calculate the maximum velocity reached by the block and the total time t during which the block is in motion. The coefficients of static and kinetic friction are both 0.50. (Take, $g = 9.8\ \text{m/s}^2$)

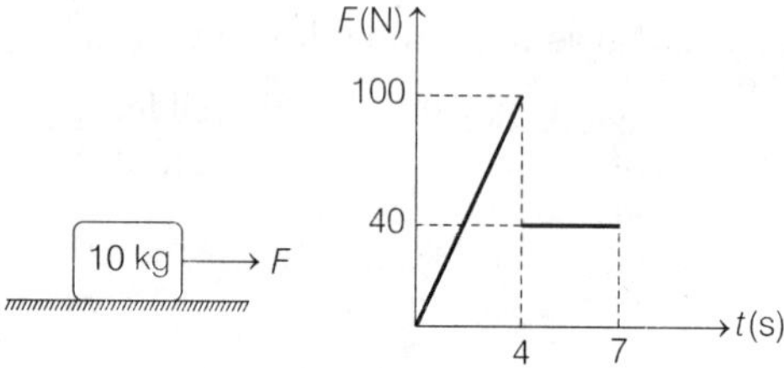

12. If block A of the pulley system is moving downward with a speed of 1 m/s while block C is moving up at 0.5 m/s, determine the speed of block B.

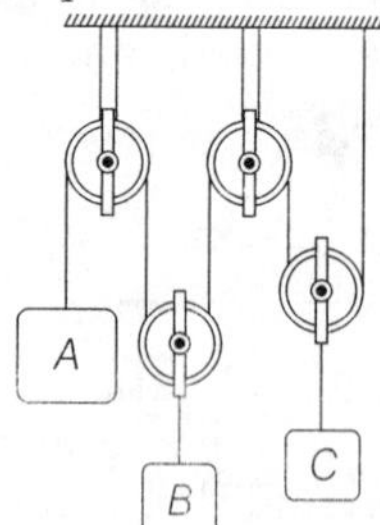

13. The collar A is free to slide along the smooth shaft B mounted in the frame. The plane of the frame is vertical. Determine the horizontal acceleration a of the frame necessary to maintain the collar in a fixed position on the shaft. (Take, $g = 9.8\ \text{m/s}^2$)

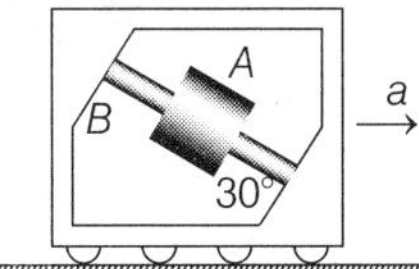

14. In the adjoining figure all surfaces are frictionless. What force F must by applied to M_1 to keep M_3 free from rising or falling?

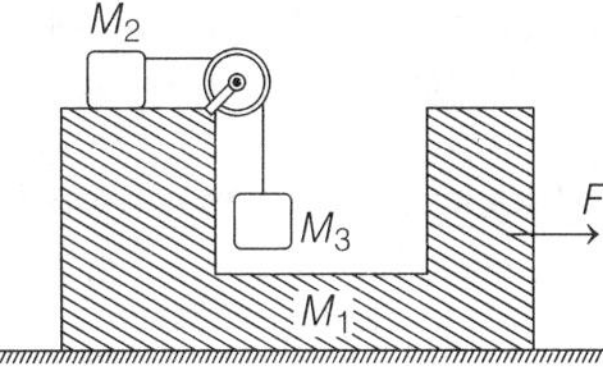

15. The conveyor belt is designed to transport packages of various weights. Each 10 kg package has a coefficient of kinetic friction $\mu_k = 0.15$. If the speed of the conveyor belt is 5 m/s, and then it suddenly stops, determine the distance the package will slide before coming to rest. (Take, $g = 9.8\ \text{m/s}^2$)

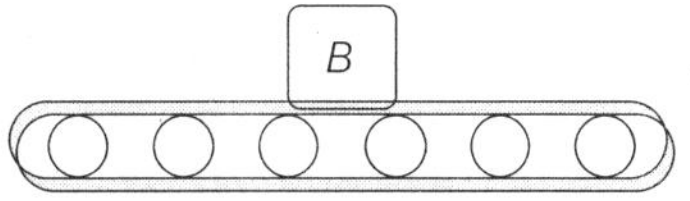

16. In figure, a crate slides down an inclined right-angled trough. The coefficient of kinetic friction between the crate and the trough is μ_k. What is the acceleration of the crate in terms of μ_k, θ and g?

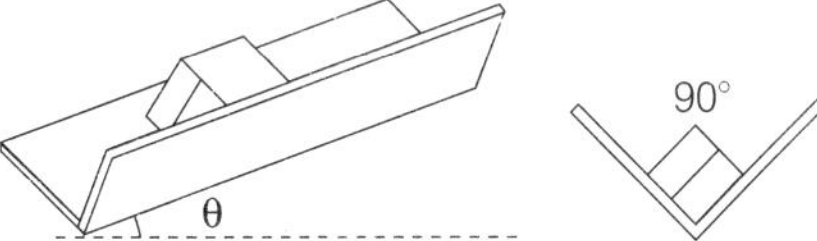

17. A heavy chain with a mass per unit length ρ is pulled by the constant force F along a horizontal surface consisting of a smooth section and a rough section. The chain is initially at rest on the rough surface with $x = 0$. If the coefficient of kinetic friction between the chain and the rough surface is μ_k, determine the velocity v of the chain when $x = L$. The force F is greater than $\mu_k \rho g L$ in order to initiate the motion.

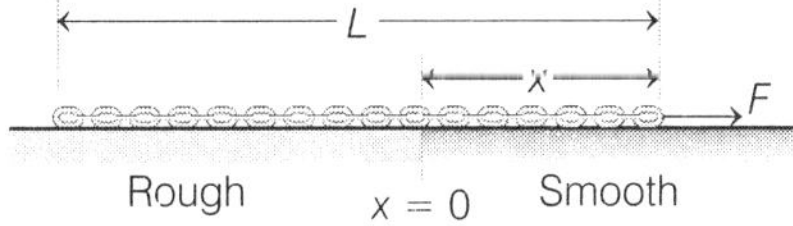

18. A package is at rest on a conveyor belt which is initially at rest. The belt is started and moves to the right for 1.3 s with a constant acceleration of 2 m/s². The belt then moves with a constant deceleration a_2 and comes to a stop after a total displacement of 2.2 m. Knowing that the coefficients of friction between the package and the belt are $\mu_s = 0.35$ and $\mu_k = 0.25$, determine (a) the deceleration a_2 of the belt, (b) the displacement of the package relative to the belt as the belt comes to a stop. (Take, $g = 10\ \text{m/s}^2$)

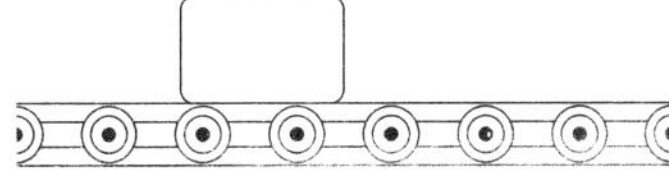

19. Determine the normal force the 10 kg crate A exerts on the smooth cart B, if the cart is given an acceleration of $a = 2\ \text{m/s}^2$ down the plane. Also, find the acceleration of the crate. Set $\theta = 30°$. (Take, $g = 10\ \text{m/s}^2$).

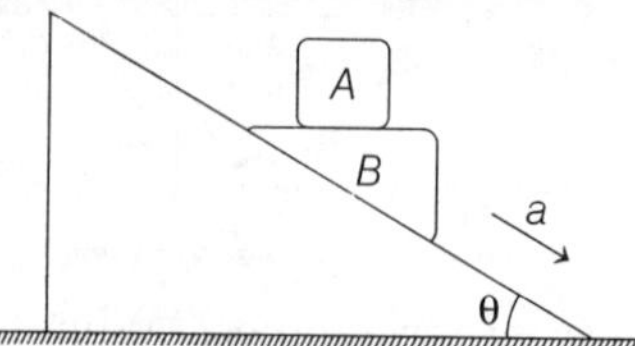

20. A small block of mass m is projected on a larger block of mass $10\,m$ and length l with a velocity v as shown in the figure. The coefficient of friction between the two blocks is μ_2 while that between the lower block and the ground is μ_1. Given that $\mu_2 > 11\mu_1$.

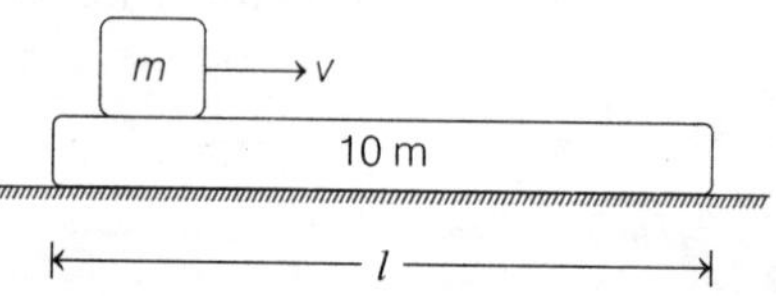

(a) Find the minimum value of v, such that the mass m falls off the block of mass $10\,m$.

(b) If v has this minimum value, find the time taken by block m to do so.

21. A particle of mass m and velocity v_1 in positive y direction is projected on to a belt that is moving with uniform velocity v_2 in x-direction as shown in figure. Coefficient of friction between particle and belt is μ. Assuming that the particle first touches the belt at the origin of fixed x-y coordinate system and remains on the belt, find the co-ordinates (x, y) of the point where sliding stops.

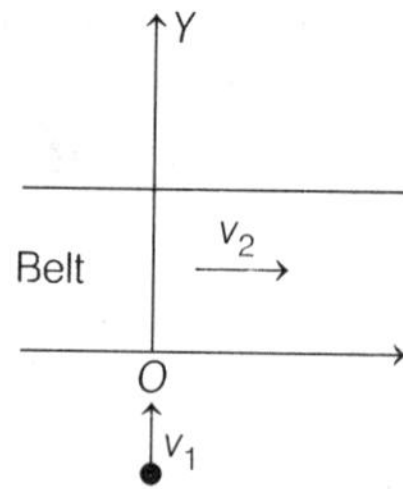

22. In the shown arrangement, both pulleys and the string are massless and all the surfaces are frictionless. Find the acceleration of the wedge.

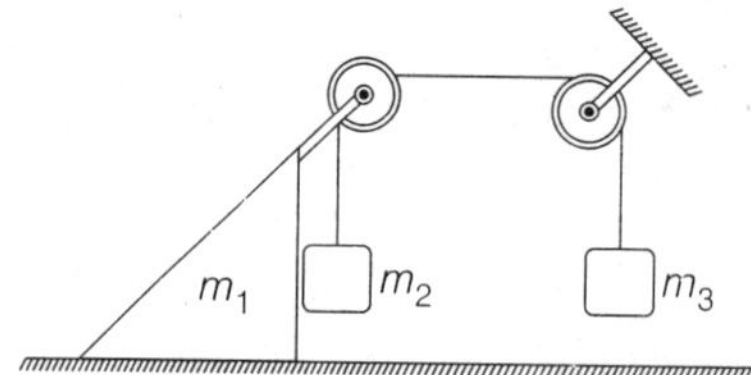

23. Neglect friction. Find accelerations of m, $2m$ and $3m$ as shown in the figure. The wedge is fixed.

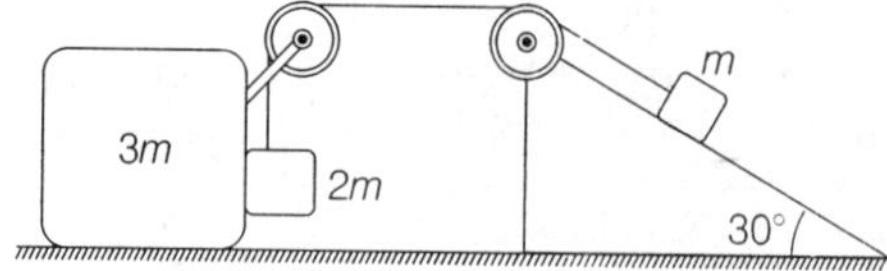

24. The figure shows an L shaped body of mass M placed on smooth horizontal surface. The block A is connected to the body by means of an inextensible string, which is passing over a smooth pulley of negligible mass. Another block B of mass m is placed against a vertical wall of the body. Find the minimum value of the mass of block A so that block B remains stationary relative to the wall. Coefficient of friction between the block B and the vertical wall is μ.

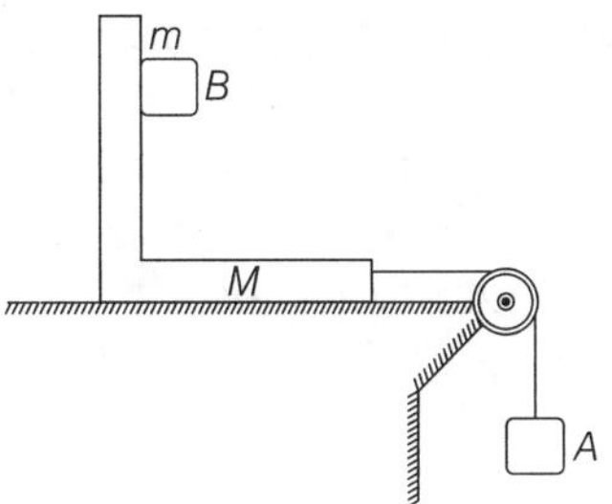

Integer Type Questions

25. Three smooth identical cylinders A, B and C are placed on smooth inclined plane shown in the figure. The minimum value of $\tan\theta$ that prevent the arrangement from collapse is $\frac{1}{3\sqrt{n}}$. Find the value of n.

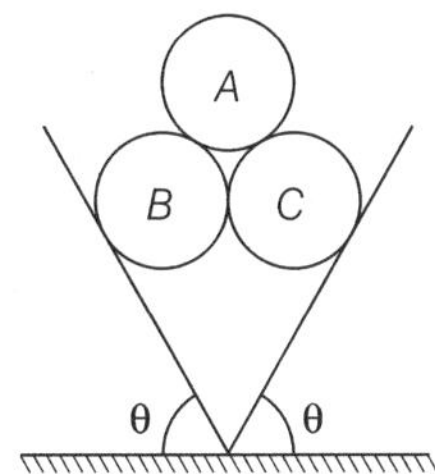

26. A block is at rest in gravity free space. It is acted by four forces, 3 N in East direction, 1 N in South direction, 1 N in downward direction and an unknown force $\mathbf{F}_0$. Due to these forces, the block starts to move in South-East direction. The minimum possible value of $\mathbf{F}_0$ is $\sqrt{n}$ newton. Find the value of n.

27. A force $\mathbf{F} = bt - cs$, (here $b = 1$ N/s and $c = 1$ N/m) is acting on a block of mass 1 kg placed on a smooth horizontal surface. During motion, the acceleration of the block is $a = a_0 \sin\omega t$. Find the value of ω.

Answers

Introductory Exercise 8.1

1. See the hints
2. See the hints
3. See the hints
4. See the hints
5. See the hints
6. See the hints
7. $F_{1x} = 2\sqrt{3}$ N, $F_2x = -2$ N, $F_3x = 0$, $F_4x = 4$ N, $F_1y = 2$ N, $F_{2y} = 2\sqrt{3}$ N, $F_{3y} = -6$ N, $F_{4y} = 0$
8. 30 N
9. $N_A = \frac{1000}{\sqrt{3}}$ N, $N_B = \frac{500}{\sqrt{3}}$ N
10. $\frac{2}{\sqrt{3}} W$
11. (a) 26.8 N (b) 26.8 N (c) 100 N

Introductory Exercise 8.2

1. (a) 10 ms^{-2} (b) 110 N (c) 20 N
2. 4
3. $\frac{10}{3}$ ms^{-2}
4. 3 kg
5. zero
6. $\frac{3g}{4}$
7. 4 ms^{-2}, 24 N, 42 N, 14 N
8. (a) 3 ms^{-2} (b) 18 N, 12 N, 30 N, (c) 70 N
9. (a) 10 N, 30 N (b) 24 N

Introductory Exercise 8.3

1. $2a_1 + a_2 + a_3 = 0$
2. 3 m/s downwards
3. (a) $\frac{2g}{3}$ (b) $\frac{10}{3}$ N
4. (a) $\frac{g}{2}, \frac{Mg}{2}$
5. 4.8 kg
6. $\frac{12}{35}$ N, $\frac{2}{7}$ ms^{-2}
7. 1 ms^{-2} (upwards)
8. $\frac{g}{3}$ (up the plane)

Introductory Exercise 8.4

1. (a) $(4\hat{j})$ N (b) $(-4\hat{i})$ N
2. True
3. False

Introductory Exercise 8.5

1. (a) zero, 20 N (b) 6 ms^{-2}, 8 N
2. (a) $\frac{mg}{2}, 0, 0$ (b) $\frac{mg}{\sqrt{2}}, 0, 0$ (c) $\frac{mg}{2}, \left(\frac{\sqrt{3}-1}{2}\right) mg, \left(\frac{\sqrt{3}-1}{2}\right) g$

Exercises

LEVEL 1

Assertion and Reason

1. (a)	2. (b)	3. (d)	4. (b)	5. (d)	6. (d)	7. (c)	8. (a)	9. (b)	10. (b)
11. (d)	12. (a)	13. (a)							

Single Correct Option

1. (b)	2. (a)	3. (d)	4. (c)	5. (d)	6. (b)	7. (c)	8. (b)	9. (a)	10. (a)
11. (a)	12. (b)	13. (a)	14. (b)	15. (b)	16. (a)	17. (d)	18. (d)	19. (d)	20. (a)
21. (a)	22. (d)	23. (b)	24. (a)	25. (d)	26. (a)	27. (c)	28. (c)	29. (a)	30. (c)
31. (b)	32. (c)	33. (a)	34. (a)	35. (c)	36. (b)	37. (c)	38. (c)	39. (c)	40. (c)
41. (c)	42. (c)	43. (a)	44. (b)	45. (d)	46. (b)	47. (b)	48. (d)	49. (c)	50. (b)
51. (d)	52. (b)	53. (b)	54. (d)	55. (a)					

Subjective Questions

1. $F_1 = F_2 = w = 30\sqrt{2}$ N 2. $\frac{mg}{\sqrt{2}}, \frac{g}{2}$ 3. (a) 20 N (b) 50 N
4. (a) 2.7 ms^{-2} (b) 137.5 N (c) 112.5 N 5. 0.288 6. $30°$, 10 N
7. $\tan^{-1}\left(\frac{2}{\sqrt{3}}\right), 5\sqrt{7}$ N 8. $\frac{1}{3}$ s 9. 6.83 kg
10. (a) $x = x_0 + 10t - 2.5t^2$ $v_x = 10 - 5t$ (b) $t = 4$ s
11. (a) $x = x_0 - 2.5t^2, z = z_0 + 10t, v_x = -5t, v_z = 10$ ms^{-1}
(b) $x = x_0, z = z_0 + 10t, v_x = 0, v_z = 10$ ms^{-1}
12. For $t \le 1.25$ s

$$x = x_0 + 10t - 4t^2$$
$$v_x = 10 - 8t$$

After 1.25 s Block remains stationary

13. $\frac{9}{25}mg$ 14. $F = 100$ N 15. 5 cm
16. (a) move up (b) constant (c) constant (d) stop 17. $a_A + 2a_B + a_C = 0$
18. $\frac{2}{7}g$ (downwards), $\frac{g}{7}$ (upwards) 19. (a) 2 s (b) 6 m

LEVEL 2

Single Correct Option

1. (c)	2. (b)	3. (d)	4. (c)	5. (a)	6. (b)	7. (c)	8. (b)	9. (d)	10. (a)
11. (c)	12. (b)	13. (c)	14. (c)	15. (d)	16. (b)	17. (c)	18. (d)	19. (c)	20. (a)
21. (c)	22. (b)	23. (c)	24. (b)	25. (b)	26. (b)	27. (d)	28. (b)	29. (c)	30. (b)
31. (d)	32. (b)	33. (d)	34. (d)	35. (d)	36. (a)	37. (b)	38. (b)	39. (c)	40. (a)
41. (d)	42. (a)	43. (a)	44. (c)	45. (b)	46. (a)	47. (c)	48. (a)	49. (c)	50. (a)
51. (b)	52. (a)	53. (b)							

More than One Correct Options

1. (a,c,d) 2. (a,c) 3. (a,d) 4. (c,d) 5. (a,c) 6. (a,b,c) 7. (a,c)
8. (b,c) 9. (all) 10. (b,c) 11. (all)

Comprehension Based Questions

1. (b) 2. (a) 3. (d) 4. (c) 5. (d) 6. (c) 7. (c) 8. (a) 9. (a) 10. (b)
11. (b) 12. (d)

Match the Columns

1. (a) → (r) (b) → (q) (c) → (p) (d) → (s)
2. (a) → (s) (b) → (s) (c) → (p) (d) → (p)
3. (a) → (q,r) (b) → (q,r) (c) → (s) (d) → (p, s)
4. (a) → (s) (b) → (p) (c) → (s) (d) → (s)
5. (a) → (p) (b) → (s) (c) → (q) (d) → (p)
6. (a) → (q) (b) → (p,q,r) (c) → (q) (d) → (p,r)
7. (a) → (q, s) (b) → (p,s) (c) → (p,s) (d) → (q,s)
8. (a) → (r) (b) → (r) (c) → (s) (d) → (q)
9. (a) → (p) (b) → (p) (c) → (q,r,s) (d) → (q,s)

Subjective Questions

1. $10\ ms^{-1}$

2. $\frac{2}{33}\ ms^{-2}$

3. (a) 54 N (due east) (b) 60 N (due west)

4. (a) $6.36\ ms^{-2}$ (b) $5.5\ ms^{-2}$

5. (a) Clockwise (b) $\frac{1}{3}$

6. $\frac{F}{m} - \frac{\mu(M+m)g}{m} \le a \le \frac{F}{m} + \frac{\mu(M+m)g}{m}$

7. $\mu = \left(\frac{m+n}{n}\right)\tan\alpha$

8. $\frac{mg}{2}\sin 2\theta$

9. Displacement of crate relative to truck is 1.56 m.

10. $t = 0.33$ s

11. 5.2 m/s, 5.55 s

12. zero

13. $5.66\ m/s^2$

14. $\frac{M_3}{M_2}(M_1 + M_2 + M_3)g$

15. 8.5 m

16. $g(\sin\theta - \sqrt{2}\mu_k\cos\theta)$

17. $\sqrt{\frac{2F}{\rho} - \mu_k gL}$

18. (a) $6.63\ m/s^2$ (b) 0.33 m

19. 90 N, $1\ ms^{-2}$

20. (a) $v_{min} = \sqrt{\frac{22(\mu_2 - \mu_1)gl}{10}}$ (b) $t = \sqrt{\frac{20l}{11g(\mu_2 - \mu_1)}}$

21. $x = v_2\frac{\sqrt{v_1^2 + v_2^2}}{2\mu g}, y = \frac{v_1\sqrt{v_1^2 + v_2^2}}{2\mu g}$

22. $\frac{2m_1m_3g}{(m_2 + m_3)(m_1 + m_2) + m_2m_3}$

23. $a_m = \frac{13}{34}g, a_{2m} = \frac{\sqrt{397}}{34}g, a_{3m} = \frac{3}{17}g$

24. $m_A = \frac{M+m}{\mu - 1}$ but $\mu > 1$

25. 3

26. 3

27. 1

9

Work, Energy and Power

9.1 Introduction to Work

9.2 Work Done

9.3 Conservative and Non-conservative Forces

9.4 Kinetic Energy

9.5 Work-Energy Theorem

9.6 Potential Energy

9.7 Three Types of Equilibrium

9.8 Power of a Force

9.9 Law of Conservation of Mechanical Energy

9.1 Introduction to Work

In our daily life, 'work' has many different meanings. For example, Ram is working in a factory. The machine is in working order. Let us work out a plan for the next year, etc. In physics however, the term 'work' has a special meaning. In physics, work is always associated with a force and a displacement. We note that for work to be done, the force must act through a distance. Consider a person holding a weight at a distance 'h' off the floor as shown in figure.

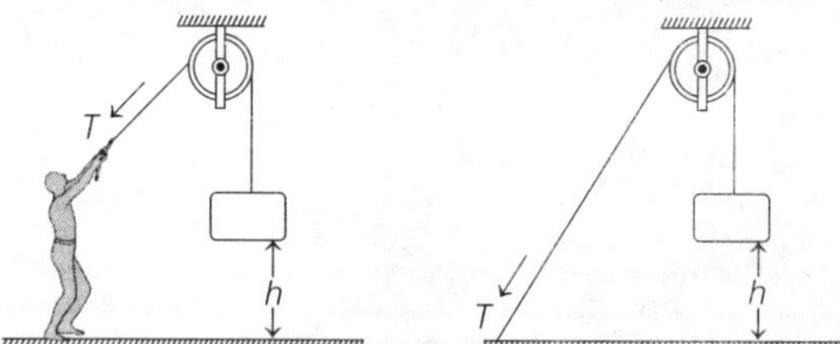

No work is done by the man holding the weight at a fixed position. The same task could be accomplished by tying the rope to a fixed point.

Fig. 9.1

In everyday usage, we might say that the man is doing work, but in our scientific definition, no work is done by a force acting on a stationary object. We could eliminate the effort of holding the weight by merely tying the string to some object and the weight could be supported with no help from us.

Let us now see what does 'work' mean in the language of physics.

9.2 Work Done

There are mainly three methods of finding work done by a force:

(i) Work done by a constant force.

(ii) Work done by a variable force.

(iii) Work done by the area under force and displacement graph.

Work done by a Constant Force

Work done by a constant force is given by

$$W = \mathbf{F} \cdot \mathbf{S} \qquad (\mathbf{F} = \text{force}, \mathbf{S} = \text{displacement})$$
$$= FS \cos\theta$$
$$= \text{(magnitude of force) (component of displacement in the direction of force)}$$
$$= \text{(magnitude of displacement) (component of force in the direction of displacement)}$$

Here, θ is the angle between **F** and **S**.

Thus, work done is the dot product of **F** and **S**.

Special Cases

(i) If $\theta = 0°$, $W = FS \cos 0° = FS$

(ii) If $\theta = 90°$, $W = FS \cos 90° = 0$

(iii) If $\theta = 180°$, $W = FS \cos 180° = -FS$

Extra Points to Remember

- Work done by a force may be positive, negative or even zero also, depending on the angle (θ) between the force vector **F** and displacement vector **S**. Work done by a force is zero when $\theta = 90°$, it is positive when $0° \le \theta < 90°$ and negative when $90° < \theta \le 180°$. For example, when a person lifts a body, the work done by the lifting force is positive (as $\theta = 0°$) but work done by the force of gravity is negative (as $\theta = 180°$).
- Work depends on frame of reference. With change of frame of reference, inertial force does not change while displacement may change. So, the work done by a force will be different in different frames. For example, if a person is pushing a box inside a moving train, then work done as seen from the frame of reference of train is $\mathbf{F} \cdot \mathbf{S}$ while as seen from the ground it is $\mathbf{F} \cdot (\mathbf{S} + \mathbf{S}_0)$. Here $\mathbf{S}_0$, is the displacement of train relative to ground.
- Suppose a body is displaced from point A to point B, then

$$\mathbf{S} = \mathbf{r}_B - \mathbf{r}_A = (x_B - x_A)\,\hat{\mathbf{i}} + (y_B - y_A)\,\hat{\mathbf{j}} + (z_B - z_A)\,\hat{\mathbf{k}}$$

Here, (x_A, y_A, z_A) and (x_B, y_B, z_B) are the co-ordinates of points A and B.

Example 9.1 *A body is displaced from $A = (2\ m, 4\ m, -6\ m)$ to $\mathbf{r}_B = (6\hat{\mathbf{i}} - 4\hat{\mathbf{j}} + 2\hat{\mathbf{k}})\ m$ under a constant force $\mathbf{F} = (2\hat{\mathbf{i}} + 3\hat{\mathbf{j}} - \hat{\mathbf{k}})\ N$. Find the work done.*

Solution $\quad \mathbf{r}_A = (2\hat{\mathbf{i}} + 4\hat{\mathbf{j}} - 6\hat{\mathbf{k}})\ \text{m}$

$$\therefore \quad \mathbf{S} = \mathbf{r}_B - \mathbf{r}_A$$

$$= (6\hat{\mathbf{i}} - 4\hat{\mathbf{j}} + 2\hat{\mathbf{k}}) - (2\hat{\mathbf{i}} + 4\hat{\mathbf{j}} - 6\hat{\mathbf{k}})$$

$$= 4\hat{\mathbf{i}} - 8\hat{\mathbf{j}} + 8\hat{\mathbf{k}}$$

$$W = \mathbf{F} \cdot \mathbf{S} = (2\hat{\mathbf{i}} + 3\hat{\mathbf{j}} - \hat{\mathbf{k}}) \cdot (4\hat{\mathbf{i}} - 8\hat{\mathbf{j}} + 8\hat{\mathbf{k}}) = 8 - 24 - 8 = -24\ \text{J}$$ **Ans.**

Note *Work done is negative. Therefore angle between* **F** *and* **S** *is obtuse.*

Example 9.2 *A block of mass $m = 2$ kg is pulled by a force $F = 40$ N upwards through a height $h = 2$ m. Find the work done on the block by the applied force F and its weight mg. ($g = 10\ m/s^2$)*

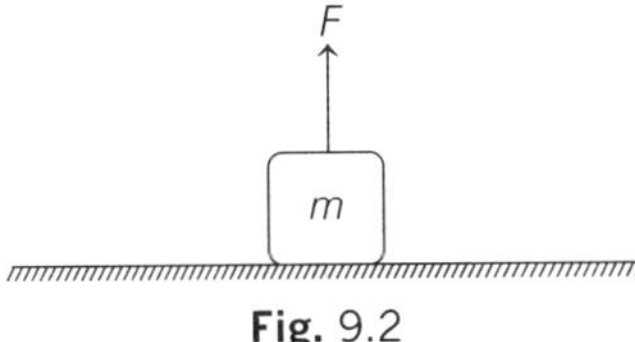

Fig. 9.2

Solution Weight $mg = (2)(10) = 20$ N

Work done by the applied force $W_F = Fh \cos 0°$.

As the angle between force and displacement is 0°

or $$W_F = (40)(2)(1) = 80\ \text{J}$$ **Ans.**

Similarly, work done by its weight

$$W_{mg} = (mg)(h) \cos 180°$$

or $$W_{mg} = (20)(2)(-1)$$

$$= -40\ \text{J}$$ **Ans.**

Example 9.3 *Two unequal masses of 1 kg and 2 kg are attached at the two ends of a light inextensible string passing over a smooth pulley as shown in Fig. 9.3. If the system is released from rest, find the work done by string on both the blocks in 1 s.*
(Take $g = 10\ m/s^2$).

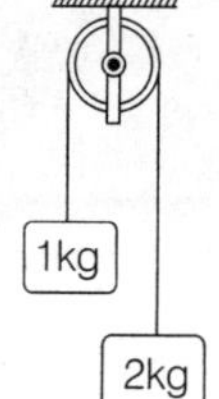

Fig. 9.3

Solution Net pulling force on the system is

$$F_{net} = 2g - 1g = 20 - 10 = 10\ \text{N}$$

Total mass being pulled $\quad m = (1 + 2) = 3\ \text{kg}$

Therefore, acceleration of the system will be

$$a = \frac{F_{net}}{m} = \frac{10}{3}\ \text{m/s}^2$$

Displacement of both the blocks in 1 s is

$$S = \frac{1}{2}at^2 = \frac{1}{2}\left(\frac{10}{3}\right)(1)^2 = \frac{5}{3}\ \text{m}$$

Free body diagram of 2 kg block is shown in Fig. 9.4 (b).

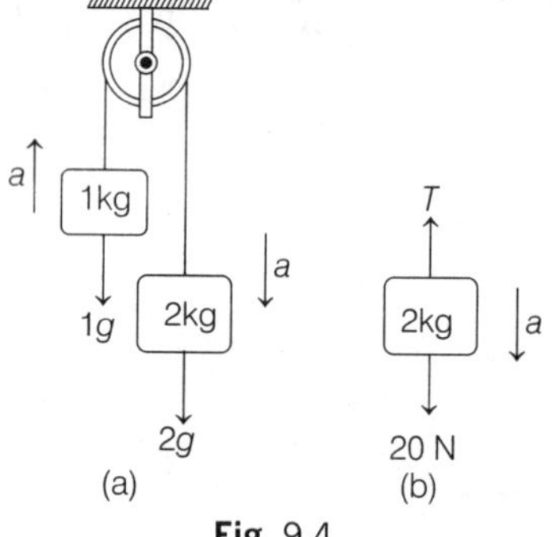

Fig. 9.4

Using $\Sigma F = ma$, we get

$$20 - T = 2a = 2\left(\frac{10}{3}\right) \quad \text{or} \quad T = 20 - \frac{20}{3} = \frac{40}{3}\ \text{N}$$

$\therefore$ Work done by string (tension) on 1 kg block in 1 s is

$$W_1 = (T)(S)\cos 0°$$

$$= \left(\frac{40}{3}\right)\left(\frac{5}{3}\right)(1) = \frac{200}{9}\ \text{J}$$ **Ans.**

Similarly, work done by string on 2 kg block in 1 s will be

$$W_2 = (T)(S)(\cos 180°)$$

$$= \left(\frac{40}{3}\right)\left(\frac{5}{3}\right)(-1) = -\frac{200}{9}\ \text{J}$$ **Ans.**

Work Done by a Variable Force

So far we have considered the work done by a force which is constant both in magnitude and direction. Let us now consider a force which acts always in one direction but whose magnitude may keep on varying. We can choose the direction of the force as x-axis. Further, let us assume that the magnitude of the force is also a function of x or say $F(x)$ is known to us. Now, we are interested in finding the work done by this force in moving a body from x_1 to x_2.

Work done in a small displacement from x to $x + dx$ will be

$$dW = F \cdot dx$$

Now, the total work can be obtained by integration of the above elemental work from x_1 to x_2 or

$$\boxed{W = \int_{x_1}^{x_2} dW = \int_{x_1}^{x_2} F \cdot dx}$$

Note *In this method of finding work done, you need not to worry for the sign of work done. If we put proper limits in integration then sign of work done automatically comes.*

It is important to note that $\int_{x_1}^{x_2} F\,dx$ is also the area under F-x graph between $x = x_1$ to $x = x_2$.

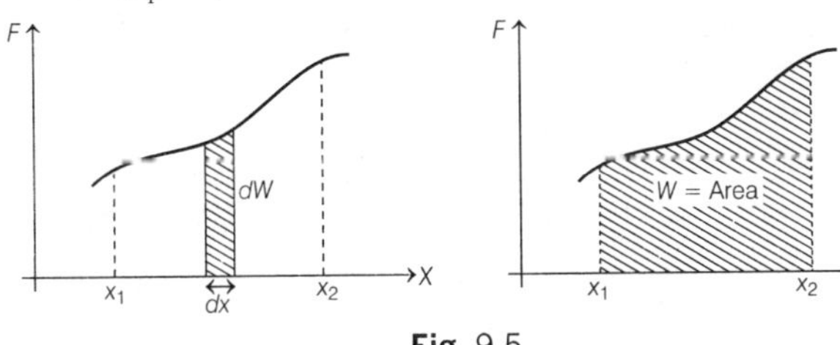

Fig. 9.5

Spring Force

An important example of the above idea is a spring that obeys Hooke's law. Consider the situation shown in figure. One end of a spring is attached to a fixed vertical support and the other end to a block which can move on a horizontal table. Let $x = 0$ denote the position of the block when the spring is in its natural length. When the block is displaced by an amount x (either compressed or elongated) a restoring force (F) is applied by the spring on the block. The direction of this force F is always towards its mean position ($x = 0$) and the magnitude is directly proportional to x or

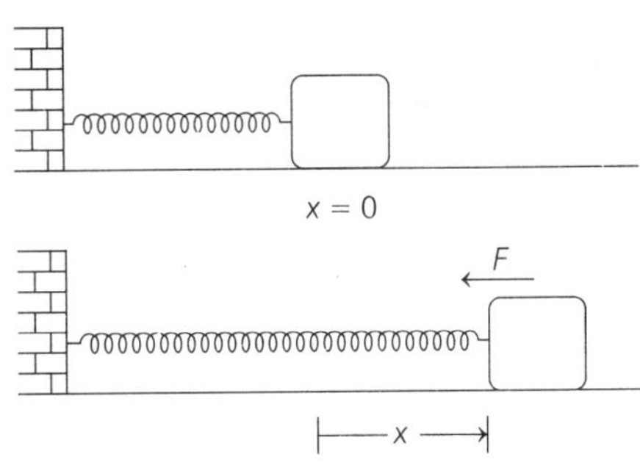

Fig. 9.6

$$F \propto x \qquad \text{(Hooke's law)}$$

$$\therefore \qquad F = -kx \qquad \ldots\text{(i)}$$

Here, k is a constant called force constant of spring and depends on the nature of spring. From Eq. (i) we see that F is a variable force and F-x graph is a straight line passing through origin with slope $= -k$. Negative sign in Eq. (i) implies that the spring force F is directed in a direction opposite to the displacement x of the block.

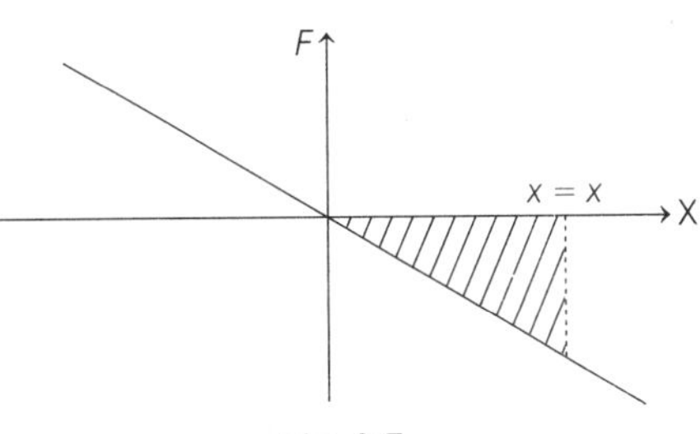

Fig. 9.7

Let us now find the work done by this force F when the block is displaced from $x = 0$ to $x = x$. This can be obtained either by integration or the area under F-x graph.

Thus, $$W = \int dW = \int_0^x F dx = \int_0^x -kx\,dx = -\frac{1}{2}kx^2$$

Here, work done is negative because force is in opposite direction of displacement.

Similarly, if the block moves from $x = x_1$ to $x = x_2$. The limits of integration are x_1 and x_2 and the work done is

$$W = \int_{x_1}^{x_2} -kx\,dx = \frac{1}{2}k\,(x_1^2 - x_2^2)$$

Example 9.4 *A force $F = (2 + x)$ acts on a particle in x-direction where F is in newton and x in metre. Find the work done by this force during a displacement from $x = 1.0$ m to $x = 2.0$ m.*

Solution As the force is variable, we shall find the work done in a small displacement from x to $x + dx$ and then integrate it to find the total work. The work done in this small displacement is

$$dW = F\,dx = (2 + x)\,dx$$

Thus,

$$W = \int_{1.0}^{2.0} dW = \int_{1.0}^{2.0} (2 + x)\,dx$$

$$= \left[2x + \frac{x^2}{2}\right]_{1.0}^{2.0} = 3.5 \text{ J}$$ **Ans.**

Example 9.5 *A force $F = -\frac{k}{x^2}$ $(x \neq 0)$ acts on a particle in x-direction. Find the work done by this force in displacing the particle from. $x = +a$ to $x = +2a$. Here, k is a positive constant.*

Solution

$$W = \int F\,dx = \int_{+a}^{+2a} \left(\frac{-k}{x^2}\right) dx = \left[\frac{k}{x}\right]_{+a}^{+2a}$$

$$= -\frac{k}{2a}$$ **Ans.**

Note *It is important to note that work comes out to be negative which is quite obvious as the force acting on the particle is in negative x-direction $\left(F = -\frac{k}{x^2}\right)$ while displacement is along positive x-direction. (from $x = a$ to $x = 2a$)*

Work Done by Area Under *F-S* or *F-x* Graph

This method is normally used when force and displacement are either parallel or antiparallel (or one dimensional). As we have discussed above

$$W = \int F dx = \text{area under } F\text{-}x \text{ graph}$$

So, work done by a force can be obtained from the area under F-x graph. Unlike the integration method of finding work done in which sign of work done automatically comes after integration, in this method area of the graph will only give us the magnitude of work done. If force and displacement have same sign, work done will be positive and if both have opposite signs, work done is negative. Let us take an example.

Example 9.6 *A force F acting on a particle varies with the position x as shown in figure. Find the work done by this force in displacing the particle from*

(a) $x = -2$ m to $x = 0$

(b) $x = 0$ to $x = 2$ m.

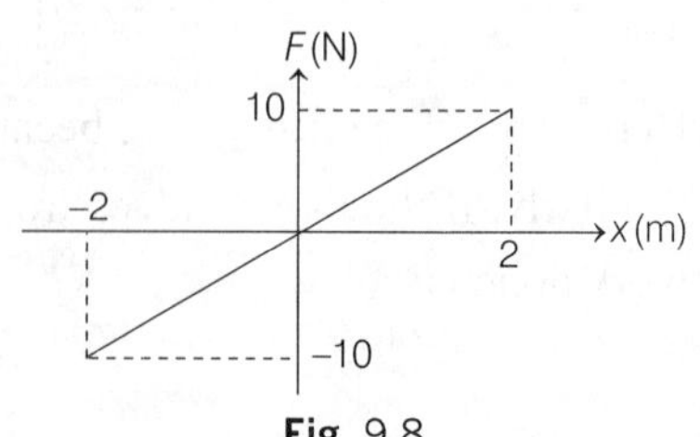

Fig. 9.8

Solution (a) From $x = -2$ m to $x = 0$, displacement of the particle is along positive x-direction while force acting on the particle is along negative x-direction. Therefore, work done is negative and given by the area under F-x graph with projection along x-axis.

$$\therefore \quad W = -\frac{1}{2}(2)(10) = -10 \text{ J} \qquad \textbf{Ans.}$$

(b) From $x = 0$ to $x = 2$ m, displacement of particle and force acting on the particle both are along positive x-direction. Therefore, work done is positive and given by the area under F-x graph,

$$\text{or} \quad W = \frac{1}{2}(2)(10) = 10 \text{ J} \qquad \textbf{Ans.}$$

INTRODUCTORY EXERCISE 9.1

1. A block is displaced from (1m, 4m, 6m) to $(2\hat{\mathbf{i}} + 3\hat{\mathbf{j}} - 4\hat{\mathbf{k}})$ m under a constant force $\mathbf{F} = (6\hat{\mathbf{i}} - 2\hat{\mathbf{j}} + \hat{\mathbf{k}})$ N. Find the work done by this force.
2. A block of mass 2.5 kg is pushed 2.20 m along a frictionless horizontal table by a constant force 16 N directed 45° above the horizontal. Determine the work done by
   (a) the applied force,
   (b) the normal force exerted by the table,
   (c) the force of gravity and
   (d) determine the total work done on the block
3. A block is pulled a distance x along a rough horizontal table by a horizontal string. If the tension in the string is T, the weight of the block is w, the normal reaction is N and frictional force is F. Write down expressions for the work done by each of these forces.
4. A bucket tied to a string is lowered at a constant acceleration of $g/4$. If mass of the bucket is m and it is lowered by a distance l then find the work done by the string on the bucket.
5. A 1.8 kg block is moved at constant speed over a surface for which coefficient of friction $\mu = \frac{1}{4}$. It is pulled by a force F acting at 45° with horizontal as shown in Fig. 9.9. The block is displaced by 2 m. Find the work done on the block by (a) the force F (b) friction (c) gravity.

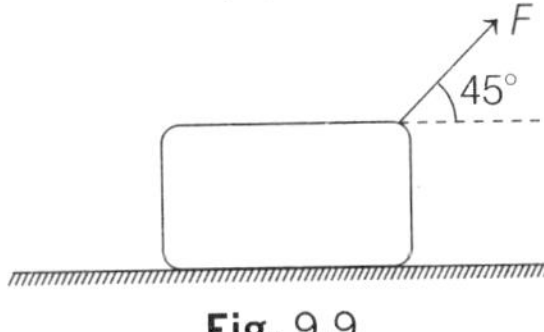

Fig. 9.9

6. A block is constrained to move along x-axis under a force $F = -2x$. Here, F is in newton and x in metre. Find the work done by this force when the block is displaced from $x = 2$ m to $x = -4$ m.
7. A block is constrained to move along x-axis under a force $F = \frac{4}{x^2}$ $(x \neq 0)$. Here, F is in newton and x in metre. Find the work done by this force when the block is displaced from $x = 4$ m to $x = 2$ m.

8. Force acting on a particle varies with displacement as shown in Fig. 9.10. Find the work done by this force on the particle from $x = -4$ m to $x = +4$ m.

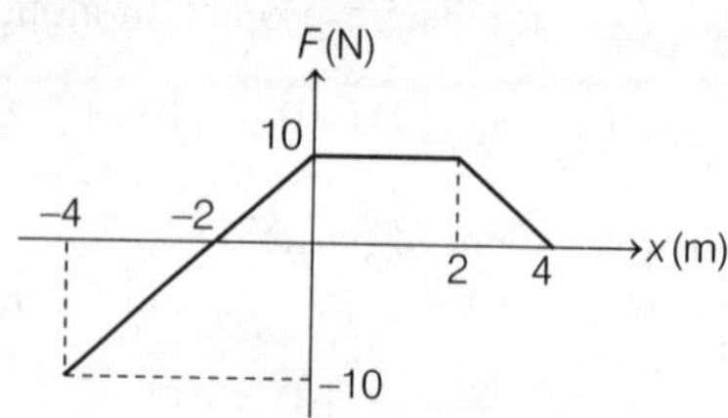

Fig. 9.10

9. A particle is subjected to a force F_x that varies with position as shown in figure. Find the work done by the force on the body as it moves

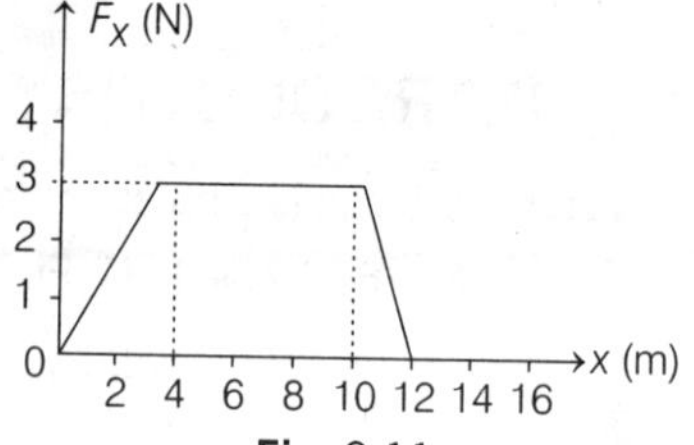

Fig. 9.11

(a) from $x = 10.0$ m to $x = 5.0$ m,

(b) from $x = 5.0$ m to $x = 10.0$ m,
(c) from $x = 10.0$ m to $x = 15.0$ m,
(d) what is the total work done by the force over the distance $x = 0$ to $x = 15.0$ m ?

10. A child applies a force **F** parallel to the x-axis to a block moving on a horizontal surface. As the child controls the speed of the block, the x-component of the force varies with the x-coordinate of the block as shown in figure. Calculate the work done by the force **F** when the block moves

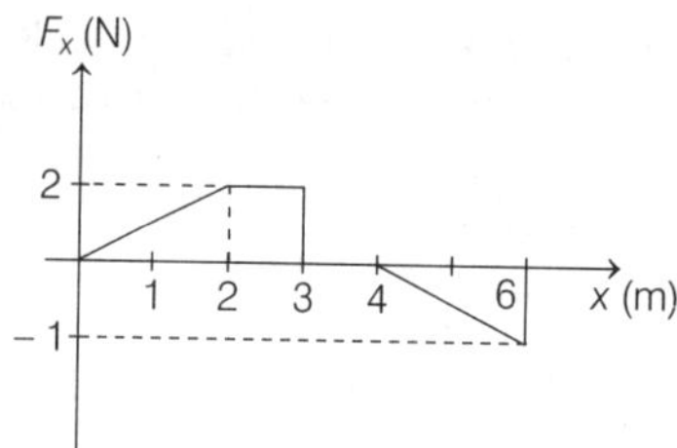

Fig. 9.12

(a) from $x = 0$ to $x = 3.0$ m
(b) from $x = 3.0$ m to $x = 4.0$ m
(c) from $x = 4.0$ m to $x = 7.0$ m
(d) from $x = 0$ to $x = 7.0$ m

9.3 Conservative and Non-Conservative Forces

In the above article, we considered the forces which were although variable but always directed in one direction. However, the most general expression for work done is

$$dW = \mathbf{F} \cdot d\mathbf{r}$$

and

$$W = \int_{\mathbf{r}_i}^{\mathbf{r}_f} dW = \int_{\mathbf{r}_i}^{\mathbf{r}_f} \mathbf{F} \cdot d\mathbf{r}$$

Here,

$$d\mathbf{r} = dx\hat{\mathbf{i}} + dy\hat{\mathbf{j}} + dz\hat{\mathbf{k}}$$

$\mathbf{r}_i =$ initial position vector and $\mathbf{r}_f =$ final position vector

Conservative and non-conservative forces can be better understood after going through the following two examples.

Example 9.7 *An object is displaced from point $A(2\ m, 3\ m, 4\ m)$ to a point $B(1\ m, 2\ m, 3\ m)$ under a constant force $\mathbf{F} = (2\hat{\mathbf{i}} + 3\hat{\mathbf{j}} + 4\hat{\mathbf{k}})\ N$. Find the work done by this force in this process.*

Solution

$$W = \int_{\mathbf{r}_i}^{\mathbf{r}_f} \mathbf{F}\cdot d\mathbf{r} = \int_{(2\text{ m}, 3\text{ m}, 4\text{ m})}^{(1\text{ m}, 2\text{ m}, 3\text{ m})} (2\hat{\mathbf{i}} + 3\hat{\mathbf{j}} + 4\hat{\mathbf{k}})\cdot(dx\hat{\mathbf{i}} + dy\hat{\mathbf{j}} + dz\hat{\mathbf{k}})$$

$$= [2x + 3y + 4z]_{(2\text{ m}, 3\text{ m}, 4\text{ m})}^{(1\text{ m}, 2\text{ m}, 3\text{ m})} = -9\text{ J}$$ **Ans.**

Alternate Solution

Since, **F** = constant, we can also use.

$$W = \mathbf{F}\cdot\mathbf{S}$$

Here,

$$\mathbf{S} = \mathbf{r}_f - \mathbf{r}_i = (\hat{\mathbf{i}} + 2\hat{\mathbf{j}} + 3\hat{\mathbf{k}}) - (2\hat{\mathbf{i}} + 3\hat{\mathbf{j}} + 4\hat{\mathbf{k}})$$

$$= (-\hat{\mathbf{i}} - \hat{\mathbf{j}} - \hat{\mathbf{k}})$$

∴

$$W = (2\hat{\mathbf{i}} + 3\hat{\mathbf{j}} + 4\hat{\mathbf{k}})\cdot(-\hat{\mathbf{i}} - \hat{\mathbf{j}} - \hat{\mathbf{k}})$$

$$= -2 - 3 - 4 = -9\text{J}$$ **Ans.**

Example 9.8 *An object is displaced from position vector $\mathbf{r}_1 = (2\hat{\mathbf{i}} + 3\hat{\mathbf{j}})\ m$ to $\mathbf{r}_2 = (4\hat{\mathbf{i}} + 6\hat{\mathbf{j}})\ m$ under a force $\mathbf{F} = (3x^2\hat{\mathbf{i}} + 2y\hat{\mathbf{j}})\ N$. Find the work done by this force.*

Solution

$$W = \int_{\mathbf{r}_1}^{\mathbf{r}_2} \mathbf{F}\cdot d\mathbf{r} = \int_{\mathbf{r}_1}^{\mathbf{r}_2} (3x^2\hat{\mathbf{i}} + 2y\hat{\mathbf{j}})\cdot(dx\hat{\mathbf{i}} + dy\hat{\mathbf{j}} + dz\hat{\mathbf{k}})$$

$$= \int_{\mathbf{r}_1}^{\mathbf{r}_2} (3x^2\,dx + 2y\,dy) = [x^3 + y^2]_{(2, 3)}^{(4, 6)}$$

$$= 83\text{ J}$$ **Ans.**

In the above two examples, we saw that while calculating the work done we did not mention the path along which the object was displaced. Only initial and final coordinates were required. It shows that in both the examples, the work done is path independent or work done will be same along all paths. The forces in which work is path independent are known as **conservative forces.**

Thus, if a particle or an object is displaced from position A to position B through three different paths under a conservative force field. Then,

$$W_1 = W_2 = W_3$$

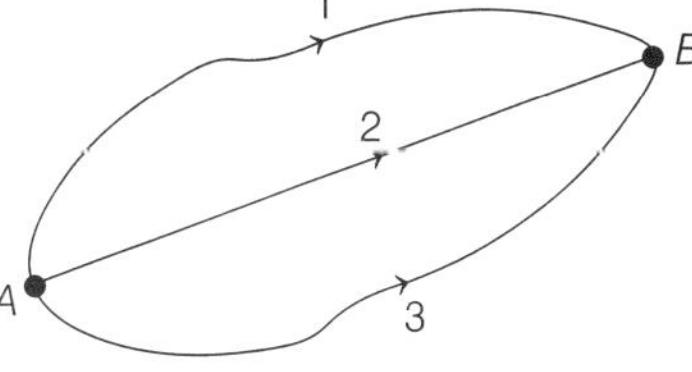

Fig. 9.13

Further, it can be shown that work done in a closed path is zero under a conservative force field. ($W_{AB} = -W_{BA}$ or $W_{AB} + W_{BA} = 0$). Gravitational force, Coulomb's force and spring force are few examples of conservative forces. On the other hand, if the work is path dependent or $W_1 \neq W_2 \neq W_3$, the force is called a **non-conservative.** Frictional force and viscous force are non-conservative in nature. Work done in a closed path is not zero in a non-conservative force field.

Note *The word potential energy is defined only for conservative forces like gravitational force, electrostatic force and spring force etc.*

We can differentiate the conservative and non-conservative forces in a better way by making a table as given below.

S.No	Conservative Forces	Non-conservative Forces
1.	Work done is path independent	Work done is path dependent
2.	Work done in a closed path is zero	Work done in a closed path is not zero
3.	The word potential energy is defined for conservative forces	The word potential energy is not defined for non-conservative forces.
4.	Examples are: gravitational force, electrostatic force, spring force etc.	Examples are: frictional force, viscous force etc.

Extra Points to Remember

- Gravitational force is a conservative force. Its work done is path independent. For small heights it only depends on the height difference 'h' between two points. Work done by gravitational force is ($\pm mgh$), in moving the mass 'm' from one point to another point. This is ($+mgh$) if the mass is moving downwards (as the force mg and displacement both are downwards, in the same direction) and ($-mgh$) if the mass is moving upwards.

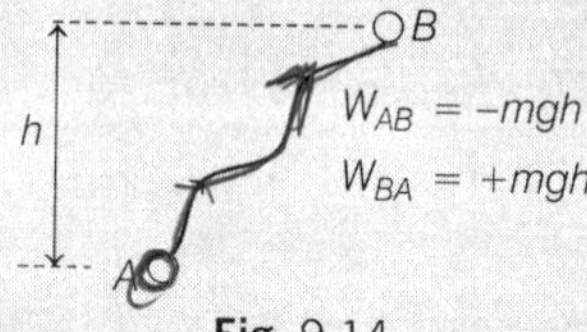

Fig. 9.14

- The magnetic field (and therefore the magnetic force) is neither conservative nor non-conservative.
- Electric field (and therefore electric force) is produced either by static charge or by time varying magnetic field. First is conservative and the other non-conservative.

9.4 Kinetic Energy

Kinetic energy (KE) is the capacity of a body to do work by virtue of its motion. If a body of mass m has a velocity v, its kinetic energy is equivalent to the work which an external force would have to do to bring the body from rest upto its velocity v. The numerical value of the kinetic energy can be calculated from the formula.

$$\text{KE} = \frac{1}{2} mv^2$$

This can be derived as follows:

Consider a constant force F which acting on a mass m initially at rest. This force provides the mass m a velocity v.

If in reaching this velocity, the particle has been moving with an acceleration a and has been given a displacement s, then

$$F = ma$$
$$v^2 = 2as$$

Work done by the constant force $= Fs$

or
$$W = (ma)\left(\frac{v^2}{2a}\right) = \frac{1}{2} mv^2$$

But the kinetic energy of the body is equivalent to the work done in giving the body this velocity.

Hence, $$\text{KE} = \frac{1}{2} mv^2$$

Regarding the kinetic energy the following two points are important to note:

1. Since, both m and v^2 are always positive. KE is always positive and does not depend on the direction of motion of the body.
2. Kinetic energy depends on the frame of reference. For example, the kinetic energy of a person of mass m sitting in a train moving with speed v is zero in the frame of train but $\frac{1}{2} mv^2$ in the frame of earth.

9.5 Work Energy Theorem

This theorem is a very important tool that relates work with kinetic energy. According to this theorem:

Work done by all the forces (conservative or non-conservative, external or internal) acting on a particle or an object is equal to the change in kinetic energy of it.

$$\therefore \quad W_{\text{net}} = \Delta\text{KE} = K_f - K_i$$

Let, $\mathbf{F}_1, \mathbf{F}_2 \ldots$ be the individual forces acting on a particle. The resultant force is $\mathbf{F} = \mathbf{F}_1 + \mathbf{F}_2 + \ldots$ and the work done by the resultant force is

$$W = \int \mathbf{F} \cdot \mathbf{dr} = \int (\mathbf{F}_1 + \mathbf{F}_2 + \ldots) \cdot \mathbf{dr}$$
$$= \int \mathbf{F}_1 \cdot \mathbf{dr} + \int \mathbf{F}_2 \cdot \mathbf{dr} + \ldots$$

where, $\int \mathbf{F}_1 \cdot \mathbf{dr}$ is the work done on the particle by $\mathbf{F}_1$ and so on. Thus, work energy theorem can also be written as: work done by the resultant force which is also equal to the sum of the work done by the individual forces is equal to change in kinetic energy.

Regarding the work-energy theorem it is worthnoting that :

(i) If W_{net} is positive then $K_f - K_i$ = positive,

i.e. $K_f > K_i$ or kinetic energy will increase and if W_{net} is negative then kinetic energy will decrease.

(ii) This theorem can be applied to non-inertial frames also. In a non-inertial frame it can be written as work done by all the forces (including the pseudo forces) = change in kinetic energy in non-inertial frame. Let us take an example.

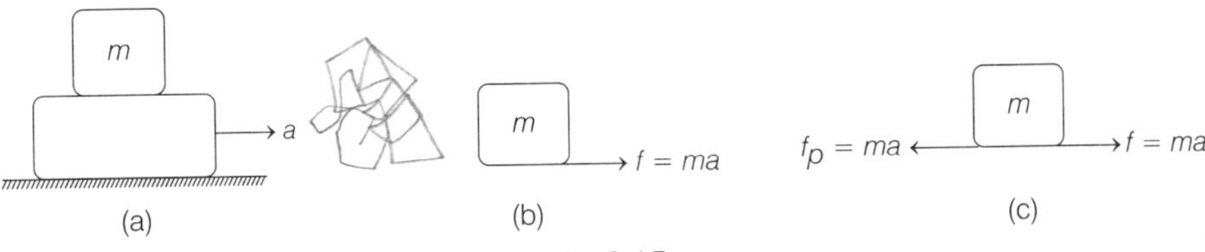

Fig. 9.15

Refer Figure (a)

A block of mass m is kept on a rough plank moving with an acceleration a. There is no relative motion between block and plank. Hence, force of friction on block is $f = ma$ in forward direction.

Refer Figure (b)

Horizontal force on the block has been shown from ground (inertial) frame of reference.

If the plank moves a distance s on the ground, the block will also move the same distance s (as there is no slipping between the two). Hence, work done by friction on the block (w.r.t. ground) is

$$W_f = fs = mas$$

From work-energy principle if v is the speed of block (w.r.t. ground), then

$$\text{KE} = W_f \quad \text{or} \quad \frac{1}{2}mv^2 = mas \quad \text{or} \quad v = \sqrt{2as}$$

Thus, velocity of block relative to ground is $\sqrt{2as}$.

Refer Figure (c)

Free body diagram of the block has been shown from accelerating frame (plank).

Here, $f_p = \text{pseudo force} = ma$

Work done by all the forces,

$$W = W_f + W_p = mas - mas = 0$$

From work-energy theorem,

$$\frac{1}{2}mv_r^2 = W = 0 \quad \text{or} \quad v_r = 0$$

Thus, velocity of block relative to plank is zero.

Note *Work-energy theorem is very useful in finding the work-done by a force whose exact nature is not known to us or to find the work done of a variable force whose exact variation is not known to us.*

Example 9.9 *An object of mass 5 kg falls from rest through a vertical distance of 20 m and attains a velocity of 10 m/s. How much work is done by the resistance of the air on the object ? ($g = 10\ m/s^2$)*

Solution Applying work-energy theorem,

work done by all the forces = change in kinetic energy

or $$W_{mg} + W_{\text{air}} = \frac{1}{2}mv^2$$

$\therefore$ $$W_{\text{air}} = \frac{1}{2}mv^2 - W_{mg} = \frac{1}{2}mv^2 - mgh$$

$$= \frac{1}{2} \times 5 \times (10)^2 - (5) \times (10) \times (20)$$

$$= -750\ \text{J}$$

Ans.

Example 9.10 *An object of mass m is tied to a string of length l and a variable force F is applied on it which brings the string gradually at angle θ with the vertical. Find the work done by the force F.*

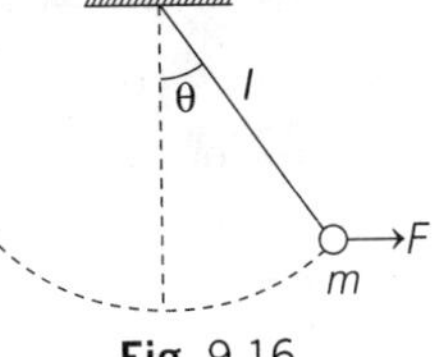

Fig. 9.16

Solution In this case, three forces are acting on the object:

1. tension (T)
2. weight (mg) and
3. applied force (F)

Using work-energy theorem

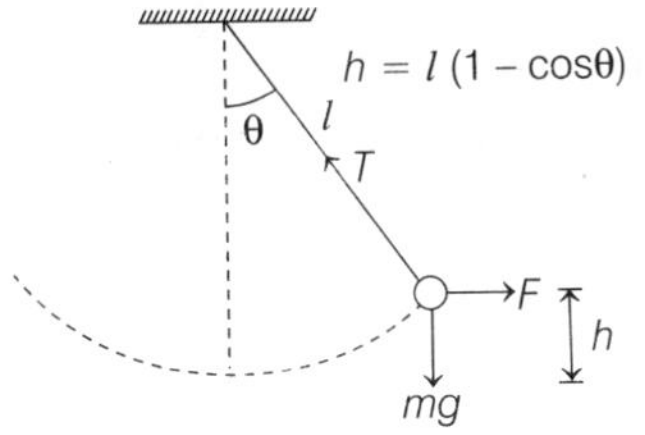

Fig. 9.17

$$W_{net} = \Delta KE$$

or $$W_T + W_{mg} + W_F = 0 \quad \ldots(i)$$

as $$\Delta KE = 0$$

because $$K_i = K_f = 0$$

Further, $W_T = 0$, as tension is always perpendicular to displacement.

$$W_{mg} = -mgh$$

or $$W_{mg} = -mgl(1 - \cos\theta)$$

Substituting these values in Eq. (i), we get

$$W_F = mgl(1 - \cos\theta)$$ **Ans.**

Note *Here, the applied force F is variable. So, if we do not apply the work energy theorem we will first find the magnitude of F at different locations and then integrate dW (= **F**·**dr**) with proper limits.*

Example 9.11 *A body of mass m was slowly hauled up the hill as shown in the Fig. 9.18 by a force F which at each point was directed along a tangent to the trajectory. Find the work performed by this force, if the height of the hill is h, the length of its base is l and the coefficient of friction is μ.*

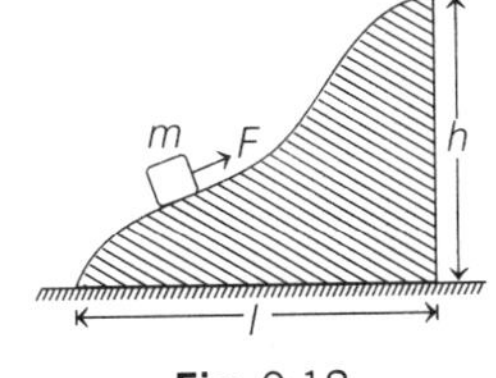

Fig. 9.18

Solution Four forces are acting on the body:

1. weight (mg)
2. normal reaction (N)
3. friction (f) and
4. the applied force (F)

Using work-energy theorem

$$W_{net} = \Delta KE$$

or $$W_{mg} + W_N + W_f + W_F = 0 \qquad \ldots(i)$$

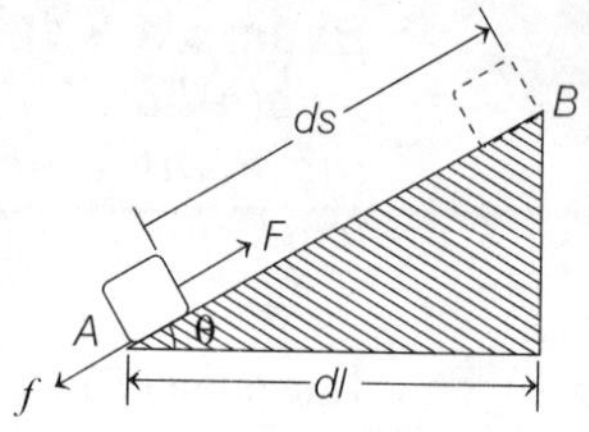

Here, $\Delta KE = 0$, because $K_i = 0 = K_f$

$$W_{mg} = -\ mgh$$

$$W_N = 0$$

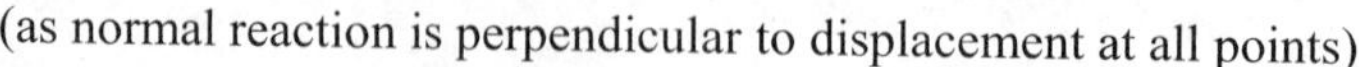

(as normal reaction is perpendicular to displacement at all points)

Fig. 9.19

W_f can be calculated as under

$$f = \mu\ mg \cos\theta$$

$\therefore$ $$(dW_{AB})_f = -\ f\,ds$$

$$= -\ (\mu\ mg \cos\theta)\,ds$$

$$= -\ \mu\ mg\ (dl) \qquad \text{(as } ds \cos\theta = dl\text{)}$$

$\therefore$ $$f = -\ \mu\ mg\ \Sigma\, dl = -\ \mu\ mgl$$

Substituting these values in Eq. (i), we get

$$W_F = mgh + \mu mgl$$ **Ans.**

Note *Here again, if we want to solve this problem without using work-energy theorem we will first find magnitude of applied force* **F** *at different locations and then integrate* $dW\ (= \mathbf{F} \cdot \mathbf{dr})$ *with proper limits.*

Example 9.12 *The displacement x of a particle moving in one dimension, under the action of a constant force is related to time t by the equation*

$$t = \sqrt{x} + 3$$

where, x is in metre and t in second. Calculate: (a) the displacement of the particle when its velocity is zero, (b) the work done by the force in the first 6 s.

Solution As $t = \sqrt{x} + 3$

i.e. $$x = (t - 3)^2 \qquad \ldots(i)$$

So, $$v = (dx/dt) = 2(t - 3) \qquad \ldots(ii)$$

(a) v will be zero when $2(t - 3) = 0$ i.e. $t = 3$

Substituting this value of t in Eq. (i),

$$x = (3 - 3)^2 = 0$$

i.e. when velocity is zero, displacement is also zero. **Ans.**

(b) From Eq. (ii), $$(v)_{t=0} = 2(0 - 3) = -\ 6\ \text{m/s}$$

and $$(v)_{t=6} = 2(6 - 3) = 6\ \text{m/s}$$

So, from work-energy theorem

$$w = \Delta KE = \frac{1}{2} m[v_f^2 - v_i^2]$$

$$= \frac{1}{2} m[6^2 - (-6)^2] = 0$$

i.e. work done by the force in the first 6 s is zero. **Ans.**

INTRODUCTORY EXERCISE 9.2

1. A ball of mass 100 gm is projected upwards with velocity 10 m/s. It returns back with 6 m/s. Find work done by air resistance.
2. Velocity-time graph of a particle of mass 2 kg moving in a straight line is as shown in Fig. 9.20. Find the work done by all the forces acting on the particle.

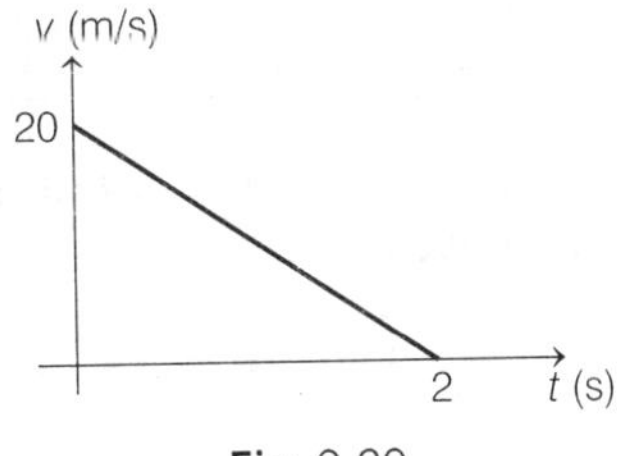

Fig. 9.20

3. Is work-energy theorem valid in a non-inertial frame?
4. A particle of mass m moves on a straight line with its velocity varying with the distance travelled according to the equation $v = \alpha\sqrt{x}$, where α is a constant. Find the total work done by all the forces during a displacement from $x = 0$ to $x = b$.
5. A 5 kg mass is raised a distance of 4 m by a vertical force of 80 N. Find the final kinetic energy of the mass if it was originally at rest. $g = 10\text{ m/s}^2$.
6. An object of mass m has a speed v_0 as it passes through the origin. It is subjected to a retarding force given by $F_x = -Ax$. Here, A is a positive constant. Find its x-coordinate when it stops.
7. A block of mass M is hanging over a smooth and light pulley through a light string. The other end of the string is pulled by a constant force F. The kinetic energy of the block increases by 40J in 1s. State whether the following statements are true or false:
   (a) The tension in the string is Mg
   (b) The work done by the tension on the block is 40 J
   (c) The tension in the string is F
   (d) The work done by the force of gravity is 40J in the above 1s
8. Displacement of a particle of mass 2 kg varies with time as $s = (2t^2 - 2t + 10)$ m. Find total work done on the particle in a time interval from $t = 0$ to $t = 2$ s.
9. A block of mass 30 kg is being brought down by a chain. If the block acquires a speed of 40 cm/s in dropping down 2 m. Find the work done by the chain during the process. $(g = 10\text{ m/s}^2)$

9.6 Potential Energy

The energy possessed by a body or system by virtue of its position or configuration is known as the potential energy. For example, a block attached to a compressed or elongated spring possesses some energy called elastic potential energy. This block has a capacity to do work. Similarly, a stone when released from a certain height also has energy in the form of gravitational potential energy. Two charged particles kept at certain distance have electrostatic potential energy.

Regarding the potential energy it is important to note that it is defined for a conservative force field only. For non-conservative forces it has no meaning. The change in potential energy (dU) of a system corresponding to a conservative force is given by

$$dU = -\mathbf{F}\cdot d\mathbf{r} = -dW$$

or

$$\int_i^f dU = -\int_{\mathbf{r}_i}^{\mathbf{r}_f} \mathbf{F}\cdot d\mathbf{r}$$

or

$$\Delta U = U_f - U_i = -\int_{\mathbf{r}_i}^{\mathbf{r}_f} \mathbf{F}\cdot d\mathbf{r}$$

We generally choose the reference point at infinity and assume potential energy to be zero there, i.e. if we take $r_i = \infty$ (infinite) and $U_i = 0$ then we can write

$$\boxed{U = -\int_{\infty}^{\mathbf{r}} \mathbf{F}\cdot d\mathbf{r} = -W}$$

or potential energy of a body or system is the negative of work done by the conservative forces in bringing it from infinity to the present position.

Regarding the potential energy it is worth noting that:

1. Potential energy can be defined only for conservative forces and it should be considered to be a property of the entire system rather than assigning it to any specific particle.
2. Potential energy depends on frame of reference.
3. If conservative force F and potential energy associated with this force U are functions of single variable r or x then :

$$F = -\frac{dU}{dr} \quad \text{or} \quad -\frac{dU}{dx}$$

Now, let us discuss three types of potential energies which we usually come across.

Elastic Potential Energy

In Article 9.2, we have discussed the spring force. We have seen there that the work done by the spring force (of course conservative for an ideal spring) is $-\frac{1}{2}kx^2$ when the spring is stretched or compressed by an amount x from its unstretched position. Thus,

$$U = -W = -\left(-\frac{1}{2}kx^2\right) \quad \text{or} \quad \boxed{U = \frac{1}{2}kx^2} \qquad (k = \text{spring constant})$$

Note that elastic potential energy is always positive.

Gravitational Potential Energy

The gravitational potential energy of two particles of masses m_1 and m_2 separated by a distance r is given by

$$\boxed{U = -G\frac{m_1 m_2}{r}}$$

Here, G = universal gravitation constant $= 6.67 \times 10^{-11} \dfrac{\text{N-m}^2}{\text{kg}^2}$

If a body of mass m is raised to a height h from the surface of earth, the change in potential energy of the system (earth + body) comes out to be

$$\Delta U = \frac{mgh}{\left(1+\frac{h}{R}\right)} \qquad (R = \text{radius of earth})$$

or $$\Delta U \approx mgh \quad \text{if} \quad h << R$$

Thus, the potential energy of a body at height h, i.e. mgh is really the change in potential energy of the system for $h << R$. So, be careful while using $U = mgh$, that h should not be too large. We will discuss this in detail in the chapter of Gravitation.

Electric Potential Energy

The electric potential energy of two point charges q_1 and q_2 separated by a distance r in vacuum is given by

$$U = \frac{1}{4\pi\varepsilon_0} \cdot \frac{q_1 q_2}{r}$$

Here, $$\frac{1}{4\pi\varepsilon_0} = 9.0 \times 10^9 \frac{\text{N-m}^2}{\text{C}^2} = \text{constant}$$

Extra Points to Remember

- Elastic potential energy is either zero or positive, but gravitational and electric potential energy may be zero, positive or negative.
- For increase or decrease in gravitational potential energy of a particle (for small heights) we write,

$$\Delta U = mgh$$

Here, h is the change in height of particle. In case of a rigid body, h of centre of mass of the rigid body is seen.

- Change in potential energy is equal to the negative of work done by the conservative force ($\Delta U = -\Delta W$). If work done by the conservative force is negative, change in potential energy will be positive or potential energy of the system will increase and *vice-versa*.

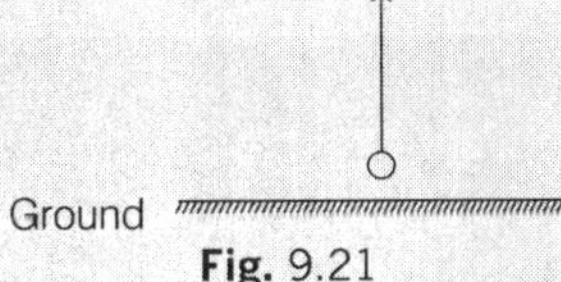

Fig. 9.21

This can be understood by a simple example. Suppose a ball is taken from the ground to some height, work done by gravity is negative, i.e. change in potential energy should increase or potential energy of the ball will increase.

$$\Delta W_{\text{gravity}} = -\text{ve}$$

$\therefore$ $$\Delta U = +\text{ve} \qquad (\Delta U = -\Delta W)$$

or $$U_f - U_i = +\text{ve}$$

- $F = -\frac{dU}{dr}$, i.e. conservative forces always act in a direction where potential energy of the system is decreased. This can also be shown as in Fig 9.22.

If a ball is dropped from a certain height. The force on it (its weight) acts in a direction in which its potential energy decreases.

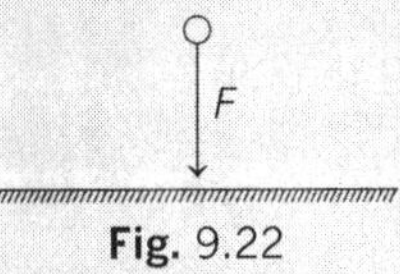

Fig. 9.22

Example 9.13 *A chain of mass 'm' and length 'l' is kept in three positions as shown below. Assuming h = 0 on the ground find potential energy of the chain in all three cases.*

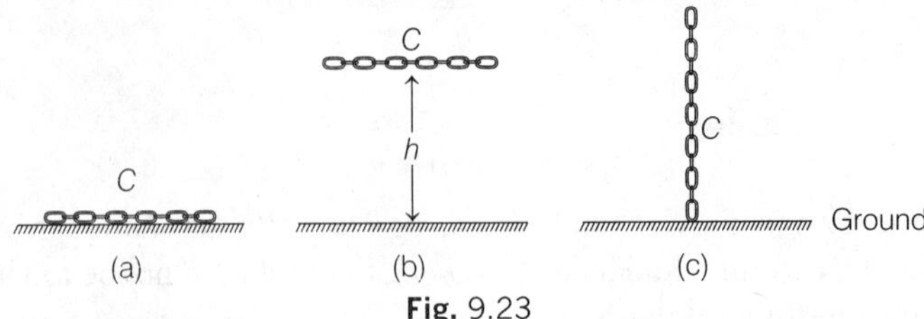

Fig. 9.23

Solution For finding potential energy of chain we will have to see its centre of mass height '*h*' from ground.

In figure (a): $h_c = 0 \Rightarrow$ Potential energy, $U = 0$

In figure (b): $h_c = h \Rightarrow$ Potential energy, $U = mgh$

In figure (c): $h_c = \frac{l}{2} \Rightarrow$ Potential energy, $U = mg\frac{l}{2}$

Example 9.14 *Potential energy of a body in position A is −40 J. Work done by conservative force in moving the body from A to B is −20 J. Find potential energy of the body in position B.*

Solution Work done by a conservative force is given by

$$W_{A \to B} = -\Delta U = -(U_B - U_A) = U_A - U_B$$

$\Rightarrow$
$$U_B = U_A - W_{A \to B} = (-40) - (-20) = -20 \text{ J}$$
Ans.

INTRODUCTORY EXERCISE 9.3

1. If work done by a conservative force is positive then select the correct option(s).
   (a) potential energy will decrease
   (b) potential energy may increase or decrease
   (c) kinetic energy will increase
   (d) kinetic energy may increase or decrease.
2. Work done by a conservative force in bringing a body from infinity to *A* is 60 J and to *B* is 20 J. What is the difference in potential energy between points *A* and *B*, i.e. $U_B - U_A$.

9.7 Three Types of Equilibrium

A body is said to be in translatory equilibrium, if net force acting on the body is zero, i.e.

$$\mathbf{F}_{\text{net}} = 0$$

If the forces are conservative
$$F = -\frac{dU}{dr}$$

and for equilibrium $F = 0$.

So,
$$-\frac{dU}{dr} = 0, \quad \text{or} \quad \frac{dU}{dr} = 0$$

i.e. at equilibrium position slope of U-r graph is zero or the potential energy is maximum, minimum or constant. Equilibrium are of three types, i.e. the situation where $F = 0$ and $\frac{dU}{dr} = 0$ can be obtained under three conditions. These are stable equilibrium, unstable equilibrium and neutral equilibrium. These three types of equilibrium can be better understood from the given three figures.

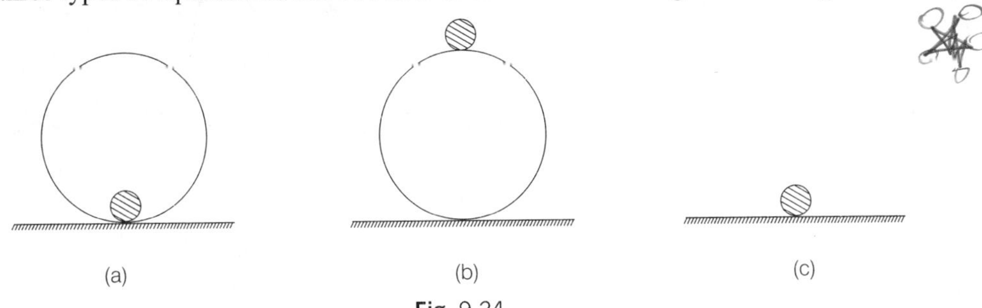

Fig. 9.24

Three identical balls are placed in equilibrium in positions as shown in figures (a), (b) and (c) respectively.

In Fig. (a), ball is placed inside a smooth spherical shell. This ball is in stable equilibrium position. In Fig. (b), the ball is placed over a smooth sphere. This is in unstable equilibrium position. In Fig. (c), the ball is placed on a smooth horizontal ground. This ball is in neutral equilibrium position.

The table given below explains what is the difference and what are the similarities between these three equilibrium positions in the language of physics.

Table 9.1

S. No.	Stable Equilibrium	Unstable Equilibrium	Neutral Equilibrium
1.	Net force is zero.	Net force is zero.	Net force is zero.
2.	$\frac{dU}{dr} = 0$ or slope of U-r graph is zero.	$\frac{dU}{dr} = 0$ or slope of U-r graph is zero.	$\frac{dU}{dr} = 0$ or slope of U-r graph is zero.
3.	When displaced from its equilibrium position a net restoring force starts acting on the body which has a tendency to bring the body back to its equilibrium position.	When displaced from its equilibrium position, a net force starts acting on the body which moves the body in the direction of displacement or away from the equilibrium position.	When displaced from its equilibrium position the body has neither the tendency to come back nor to move away from the original position. It is again in equilibrium.
4.	Potential energy in equilibrium position is minimum as compared to its neighbouring points. or $\frac{d^2U}{dr^2}$ = positive	Potential energy in equilibrium position is maximum as compared to its neighbouring points. or $\frac{d^2U}{dr^2}$ = negative	Potential energy remains constant even if the body is displaced from its equilibrium position. or $\frac{d^2U}{dr^2} = 0$
5.	When displaced from equilibrium position the centre of gravity of the body goes up.	When displaced from equilibrium position the centre of gravity of the body comes down.	When displaced from equilibrium position the centre of gravity of the body remains at the same level.

Extra Points to Remember

- If we plot graphs between F and r or U and r, F will be zero at equilibrium while U will be maximum, minimum or constant depending on the type of equilibrium. This all is shown in Fig. 9.24

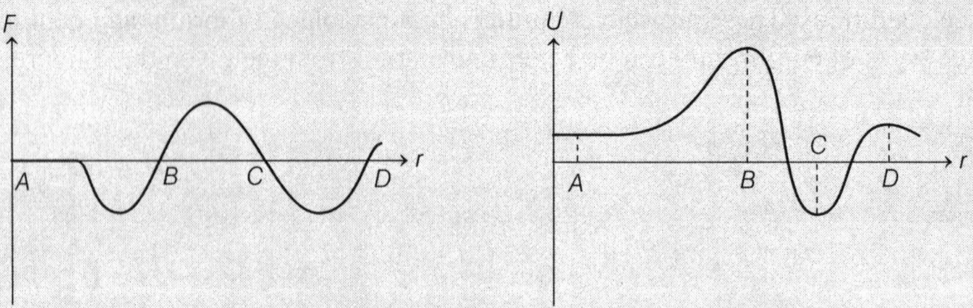

Fig. 9.25

At point A, $F=0$, $\frac{dU}{dr}=0$, but U is constant. Hence, A is neutral equilibrium position.

At points B and D, $F=0$, $\frac{dU}{dr}=0$ but U is maximum. Thus, these are the points of unstable equilibrium.

At point C, $F=0$, $\frac{dU}{dr}=0$, but U is minimum. Hence, point C is in stable equilibrium position.

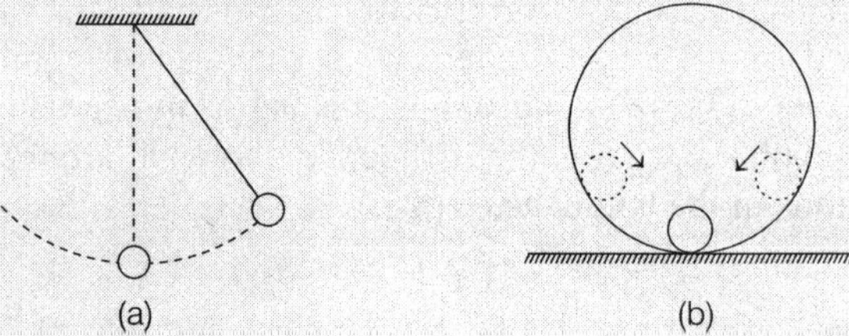

Fig. 9.26

- Oscillations of a body take place about stable equilibrium position. For example, bob of a pendulum oscillates about its lowest point which is also the stable equilibrium position of the bob. Similarly, in Fig. 9.26 (b), the ball will oscillate about its stable equilibrium position.
- If a graph between F and r is as shown in figure, then $F=0$, at $r=r_1$, $r=r_2$ and $r=r_3$. Therefore, at these three points, body is in equilibrium. But these three positions are three different types of equilibriums. For example :

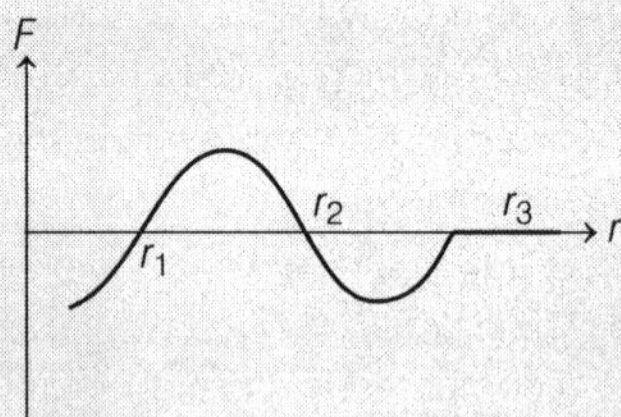

Fig. 9.27

at $r=r_1$, body is in unstable equilibrium. This is because, if we displace the body slightly rightwards (positive direction), force acting on the body is also positive, i.e. away from $r=r_1$ position.

At $r=r_2$, body is in stable equilibrium. Because if we displace the body rightwards (positive direction) force acting on the body is negative (or leftwards) or the force acting is restoring in nature.

At $r=r_3$, equilibrium is neutral in nature. Because if we displace the body rightwards or leftwards force is again zero.

Example 9.15 *For the potential energy curve shown in figure.*

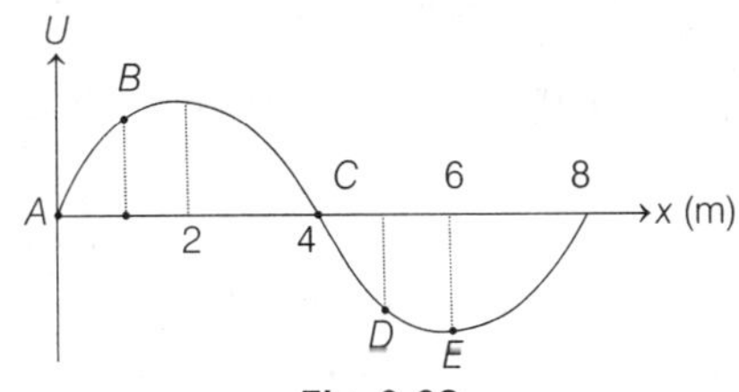

Fig. 9.28

(a) Find directions of force at points A, B, C, D and E.
(b) Find positions of stable, unstable and neutral equilibriums.

Solution (a) $F = -\dfrac{dU}{dr}$ or $-\dfrac{dU}{dx} = -$ (slope of U - x graph)

Point	Slope of U - x graph	F = (Slope of U - x graph)
A	Positive	Negative
B	Positive	Negative
C	Negative	Positive
D	Negative	Positive
E	Zero	Zero

(b) At point $x = 6\,\text{m}$, potential energy is minimum. So. it is stable equilibrium position.
At $x = 2\,\text{m}$, potential energy is maximum. So, it is unstable equilibrium position.
There is no point, where potential energy is constant. So, we don't have any point of neutral equilibrium position.

Example 9.16 *The potential energy of a conservative force field is given by*

$$U = ax^2 - bx$$

where, a and b are positive constants. Find the equilibrium position and discuss whether the equilibrium is stable, unstable or neutral.

Solution In a conservative field $F = -\dfrac{dU}{dx}$

$$\therefore \qquad F = -\frac{d}{dx}(ax^2 - bx) = b - 2ax$$

For equilibrium $F = 0$

$$\text{or} \qquad b - 2ax = 0 \quad \therefore \quad x = \frac{b}{2a}$$

From the given equation we can see that $\dfrac{d^2U}{dx^2} = 2a$ (positive), i.e. U is minimum.

Therefore, $x = \dfrac{b}{2a}$ is the stable equilibrium position. **Ans.**

INTRODUCTORY EXERCISE 9.4

1. Potential energy of a particle moving along x-axis is given by

$$U = \left(\frac{x^3}{3} - 4x + 6\right)$$

Here, U is in joule and x in metre. Find position of stable and unstable equilibrium.

2. A single force acting on a particle moving along x-axis is as shown in figure. Find points of stable and unstable equilibrium.

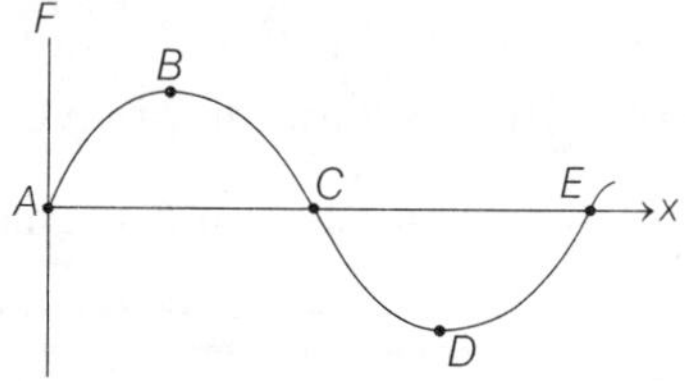

Fig. 9.29

3. Two point charges $+q$ and $+q$ are fixed at $(a, 0, 0)$ and $(-a, 0, 0)$. A third point charge $-q$ is at origin. State whether its equilibrium is stable, unstable or neutral if it is slightly displaced :
(a) along x-axis. (b) along y-axis.

4. Potential energy of a particle along x-axis, varies as, $U = -20 + (x - 2)^2$, where U is in joule and x in meter. Find the equilibrium position and state whether it is stable or unstable equilibrium.

5. Force acting on a particle constrained to move along x-axis is $F = (x - 4)$. Here, F is in newton and x in metre. Find the equilibrium position and state whether it is stable or unstable equilibrium.

9.8 Power of a Force

Power of a force is the rate of work done by this force. Now, power may be of two types:

(i) Instantaneous power (P_i or P) (ii) Average power (P_{av})

Instantaneous Power

The rate of doing work done by a force at a given instant is called instantaneous power of this force. Thus,

$$P = \frac{dW}{dt} = \frac{\mathbf{F} \cdot d\mathbf{r}}{dt} \qquad (\text{as } dW = \mathbf{F} \cdot d\mathbf{r})$$

$$= \mathbf{F} \cdot \mathbf{v} \qquad \left(\text{as } \frac{d\mathbf{r}}{dt} = \mathbf{v}\right)$$

$$= Fv\cos\theta$$

$$\therefore \qquad \boxed{P = \frac{dW}{dt} = \mathbf{F} \cdot \mathbf{v} = Fv\cos\theta}$$

Here, θ is the angle between $\mathbf{F}$ and $\mathbf{v}$. Hence power of a force is the dot product of this force and instantaneous velocity. If angle between $\mathbf{F}$ and $\mathbf{v}$ is acute then dot product is positive (or $\cos\theta$ is positive). So, power is positive. If angle is 90°, then dot product, $\cos\theta$ and hence power are zero. If θ is obtuse, then dot product, $\cos\theta$ and hence power are negative.

Average Power

The ratio of total work done and total time is defined as the average power.

Thus: $$P_{av} = \frac{W_{\text{Total}}}{t_{\text{total}}}$$

Example 9.17 *A ball of mass 1 kg is dropped from a tower. Find power of gravitational force at time t=2 s. Take g=10 m/s².*

Solution At $t = 2$s, velocity of the ball,

$$v = gt = 10 \times 2 = 20 \text{ m/s} \quad \text{(downwards)}$$

Gravitational force on the ball,

$$F = mg = 1 \times 10 = 10 \text{N} \quad \text{(downwards)}$$

∴ Instantaneous power, $P = \mathbf{F} \cdot \mathbf{v} = Fv\cos\theta$

$= (10)(20)\cos 0°$

$= 200 \text{ W}$ **Ans.**

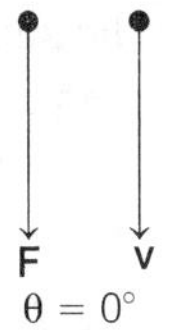

F V
θ = 0°

Fig. 9.30

Example 9.18 *A particle of mass m is lying on smooth horizontal table. A constant force F tangential to the surface is applied on it. Find*

(a) average power over a time interval from $t = 0$ to $t = t$,

(b) instantaneous power as function of time t.

Solution (a) $a = \dfrac{F}{m} = \text{constant}$

$$v = at = \frac{F}{m}t \Rightarrow P_{\text{av}} = \frac{W}{t} = \frac{\frac{1}{2}mv^2}{t} = \frac{\left(\frac{1}{2}\right)(m)\left(\frac{Ft}{m}\right)^2}{t}$$

$$= \frac{F^2 t}{2m}$$ **Ans.**

(b) $P_i = Fv\cos 0° = Fv = (F)\left(\dfrac{Ft}{m}\right) = \dfrac{F^2 t}{m}$ **Ans.**

INTRODUCTORY EXERCISE 9.5

1. A block of mass 1 kg starts moving with constant acceleration $a = 4 \text{ m/s}^2$. Find
   (a) average power of the net force in a time interval from $t = 0$ to $t = 2$ s,
   (b) instantaneous power of the net force at $t = 4$ s.
2. A constant power P is applied on a particle of mass m. Find kinetic energy, velocity and displacement of particle as function of time t.
3. A time varying power $P = 2t$ is applied on a particle of mass m. Find
   (a) kinetic energy and velocity of particle as function of time,
   (b) average power over a time interval from $t = 0$ to $t = t$.

9.9 Law of Conservation of Mechanical Energy

Suppose, only conservative forces are acting on a system of particles and potential energy U is defined corresponding to these forces. There are either no other forces or the work done by them is zero. We have

$$U_f - U_i = -W$$

and $$W = K_f - K_i \quad \text{(from work energy theorem)}$$

then $$U_f - U_i = -(K_f - K_i)$$

or $$U_f + K_f = U_i + K_i \quad \text{...(i)}$$

The sum of the potential energy and the kinetic energy is called the total mechanical energy. We see from Eq. (i), that the **total mechanical energy of a system remains constant, if only conservative forces are acting on a system of particles and the work done by all other forces is zero.** This is called the conservation of mechanical energy.

The total mechanical energy is not constant, if non-conservative forces such as friction is also acting on the system. However, the work energy theorem, is still valid. Thus, we can apply

$$W_c + W_{nc} + W_{\text{ext}} = K_f - K_i$$

Here, $$W_c = -(U_f - U_i)$$

So, we get $$W_{nc} + W_{\text{ext}} = (K_f + U_f) - (K_i + U_i)$$

or $$W_{nc} + W_{\text{ext}} = E_f - E_i = \Delta E$$

Here, $E = K + U$ is the total mechanical energy.

Extra Points to Remember

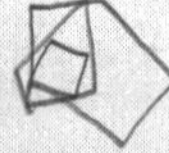

- Work done by conservative forces is equal to minus of change in potential energy

$$W_c = -\Delta U = -(U_f - U_i) = U_i - U_f$$

- Work done by all the forces is equal to change in kinetic energy.

$$W_{\text{all}} = \Delta K = K_f - K_i$$

- Work done by the forces other than the conservative forces (non-conservative + external forces) is equal to change in mechanical energy

$$W_{nc} + W_{\text{ext}} = \Delta E = E_f - E_i = (K_f + U_f) - (K_i + U_i)$$

- If there are no non-conservative forces, then

$$W_{\text{ext}} = \Delta E = E_f - E_i$$

Further, in this case if no information is given regarding the change in kinetic energy then we can take it zero. In that case,

$$W_{\text{ext}} = \Delta U = U_f - U_i$$

Example 9.19 *A body is displaced from position A to position B. Kinetic and potential energies of the body at positions A and B are*

$$K_A = 50\,J,\, U_A = -30\,J,\, K_B = 10\,J \text{ and } U_B = 20\,J.$$

Find work done by

(a) conservative forces (b) all forces (c) forces other than conservative forces.

Solution (a) $W_c = -\Delta U = -(U_f - U_i)$

$$= U_i - U_f = U_A - U_B$$

$$= -30 - 20 = -50 \text{ J}$$ **Ans.**

(b) $W_{all} = \Delta K = K_f - K_i$

$$= K_B - K_A$$

$$-10 - 50 - -40 \text{ J}$$ **Ans.**

(c) Work done by the forces other than conservative

$$= \Delta E = E_f - E_i$$

$$= (K_f + U_f) - (K_i + U_i)$$

$$= (K_B + U_B) - (K_A + U_A)$$

$$= (10 + 20) - (50 - 30) = 10 \text{ J}$$ **Ans.**

Note *Work done by conservative force is negative (= −50 J). Therefore potential energy should increase and we can see that,* $U_f > U_i$ *as* $U_B > U_A$

Core Concepts

1. Suppose a particle is released from point A with $u = 0$.

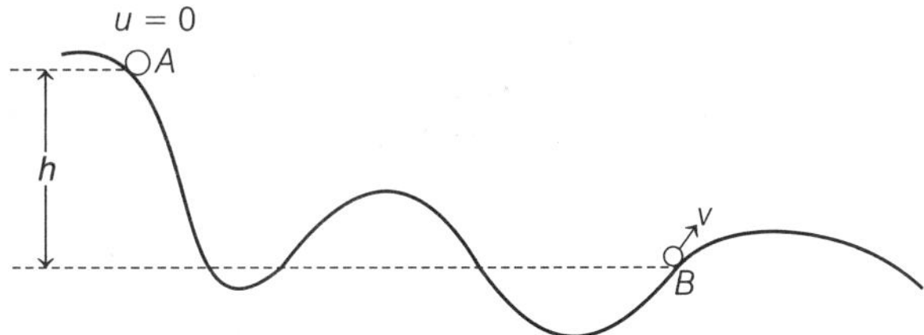

Friction is absent everywhere. Then velocity at B will be

$$v = \sqrt{2gh}$$ (irrespective of the track it follows from A to B)

Here, $h = h_A - h_B$

2. In circular motion, centripetal force acts towards the centre. This force is perpendicular to small displacement **dS** and velocity **v**. Hence, work done by it is zero and power of this force is also zero.

Solved Examples

PATTERNED PROBLEMS

Type 1. *Based on conservation of mechanical energy.*

Concept

If only conservative forces are acting on a system then its mechanical energy remains conserved. Otherwise, if all surfaces are given smooth, then also, mechanical energy will be conserved.

How to Solve?

- If mechanical energy is conserved then it is possible that some part of the energy may be decreasing while the other part may be increasing. Now the energy conservation equation can be written in following two ways :
- **First method** Magnitude of decrease of energy = magnitude of increase of energy.

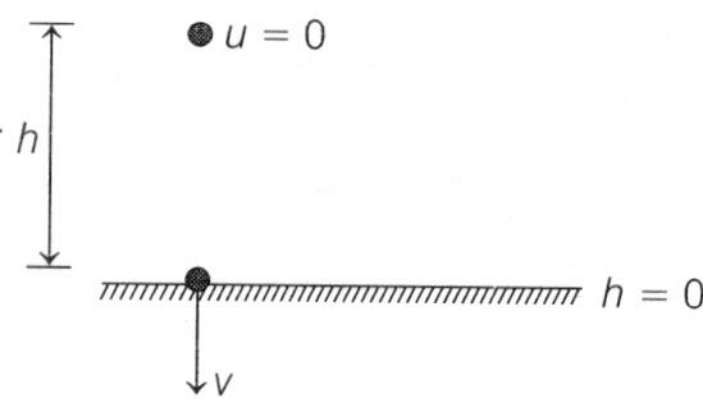

- **Second method** $E_i = E_f$ ($i \rightarrow$ initial and $f \rightarrow$ final)

  i.e. write down total initial mechanical energy on one side and total final mechanical energy on the other side. While writing gravitational potential energy we choose some reference point (where $h = 0$), but throughout the question this reference point should not change. Let us take a simple example.

  A ball of mass 'm' is released from a height h as shown in figure. The velocity of particle at the instant when it strikes the ground can be found using energy conservation principle by following two methods.

- **Method-1** Decrease in gravitational potential energy = increase in kinetic energy

$\therefore$
$$mgh = \frac{1}{2}mv^2$$

or
$$v = \sqrt{2gh}$$

- **Method-2**

$$E_i = E_f$$

or
$$K_i + U_i = K_f + U_f$$

or
$$0 + mgh = \frac{1}{2}mv^2 + 0$$

$\Rightarrow$
$$v = \sqrt{2gh}$$

Example 1 *In the figure shown, all surfaces are smooth and force constant of spring is $10 N/m$. Block of mass 2 kg is not attached with the spring. The spring is compressed by 2m and then released. Find the maximum distance 'd' travelled by the block over the inclined plane. Take $g = 10 m/s^2$.*

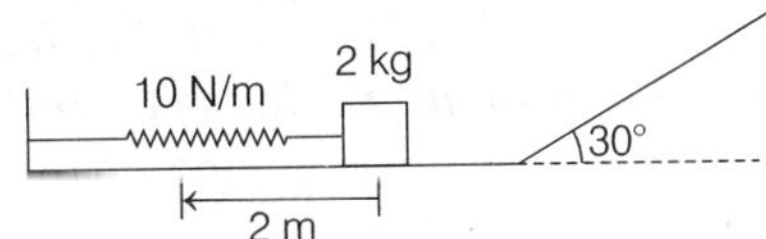

Solution In the final position, block will stop for a moment and then it will return back.

In the initial position system has only spring potential energy $\frac{1}{2}kx^2$ and in the final position it has only gravitational potential energy.

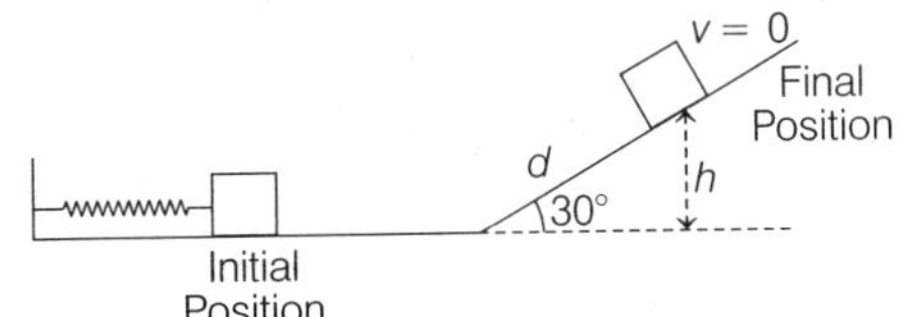

Since, all surfaces are smooth, therefore mechanical energy will remain conserved.

$$\Rightarrow \qquad E_i = E_f \quad \text{or} \quad \frac{1}{2}kx^2 = mgh = mg\left(\frac{d}{2}\right)$$

where
$$h = d \sin 30° = \frac{d}{2}$$

$$\Rightarrow \qquad d = \frac{kx^2}{mg}$$

Substituting the values we have,

$$d = \frac{(10)(2)^2}{(2)(10)}$$

$$= 2 \text{ m}$$

Ans.

Example 2 *A smooth narrow tube in the form of an arc AB of a circle of centre O and radius r is fixed so that A is vertically above O and OB is horizontal. Particles P of mass m and Q of mass 2 m with a light inextensible string of length $(\pi r/2)$ connecting them are placed inside the tube with P at A and Q at B and released from rest. Assuming the string remains taut during motion, find the speed of particles when P reaches B.*

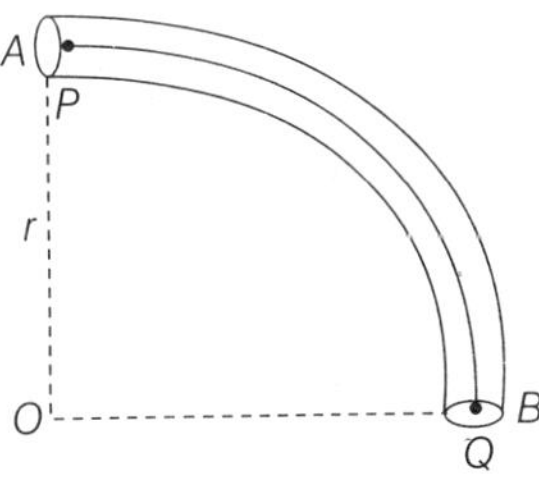

Solution All surfaces are smooth. Therefore, mechanical energy of the system will remain conserved.

$\therefore$ Decrease in PE of both the blocks = increase in KE of both the blocks

$$\therefore \qquad (mgr) + (2mg)\left(\frac{\pi r}{2}\right) = \frac{1}{2}(m + 2m)v^2$$

or
$$v = \sqrt{\frac{2}{3}(1 + \pi)gr}$$

Ans.

Example 3 *One end of a light spring of natural length d and spring constant k is fixed on a rigid wall and the other is attached to a smooth ring of mass m which can slide without friction on a vertical rod fixed at a distance d from the wall. Initially the spring makes an angle of 37° with the horizontal as shown in figure. When the system is released from rest, find the speed of the ring when the spring becomes horizontal.* ($\sin 37° = 3/5$)

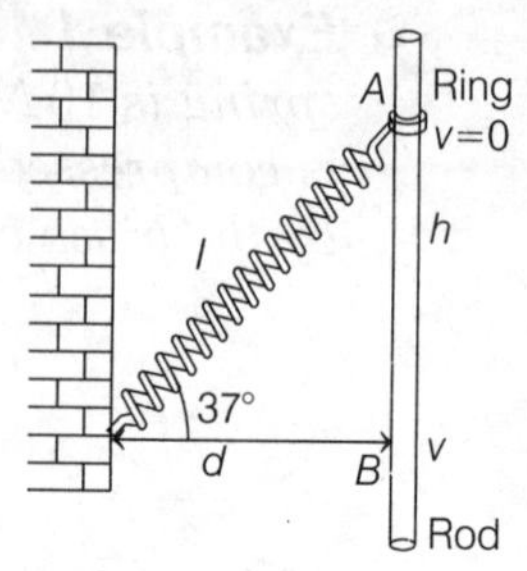

Solution If l is the stretched length of the spring, then from figure

$$\frac{d}{l} = \cos 37° = \frac{4}{5}, \quad \text{i.e.} \quad l = \frac{5}{4}d$$

So, the stretch
$$x = l - d = \frac{5}{4}d - d = \frac{d}{4}$$

and
$$h = l \sin 37° = \frac{5}{4}d \times \frac{3}{5} = \frac{3}{4}d$$

Now, taking point B as reference level and applying law of conservation of mechanical energy between A and B,

$$E_A = E_B$$

or
$$mgh + \frac{1}{2}kx^2 = \frac{1}{2}mv^2 \qquad \text{[At } B, h = 0 \text{ and } x = 0]$$

or
$$\frac{3}{4}mgd + \frac{1}{2}k\left(\frac{d}{4}\right)^2 = \frac{1}{2}mv^2 \qquad \left[\text{as for } A, h = \frac{3}{4}d \text{ and } y = \frac{1}{4}d\right]$$

or
$$v = d\sqrt{\frac{3g}{2d} + \frac{k}{16\,m}}$$

Ans.

Type 2. *Based on the position of equilibrium and momentary rest.*

Concept

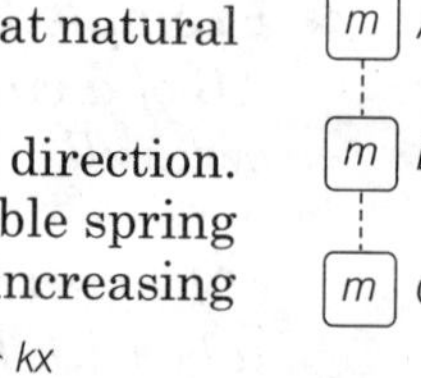

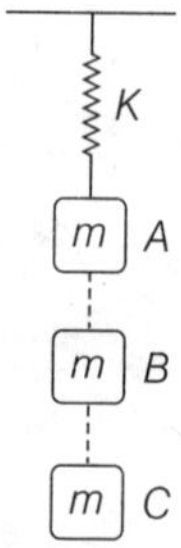

In the figure shown, block attached with the spring is released from rest at natural length of the spring at A.

At this position a constant force mg is acting on the block in downward direction. So, block starts moving downwards and spring is stretched. So, a variable spring force kx starts acting on the block in upward direction which keeps on increasing with extension 'x'. In position B, also called equilibrium position,

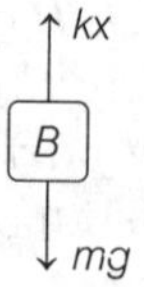

$$kx = mg$$

$\therefore$
$$F_{net} = 0$$

(Figure: block B with force kx upward and mg downward)

But the block does not stop here. Rather, it has maximum velocity in this position. After crossing B the block retards, as $kx > mg$ and net force is upwards. At point C (the maximum extension) block stops for a moment ($v = 0$) and then it returns back. The block starts oscillating between A and C.

Thus,

From	kx and mg	Direction of net force	Direction of velocity	Speed
A to B	$mg > kx$	Downwards	Downwards	Increasing
at B	$mg = kx$	$F_{net} = 0$	-	Maximum
B to C	$kx > mg$	Upwards	Downwards	Decreasing
C to B	$kx > mg$	Upwards	Upwards	Increasing
B to A	$mg > kx$	Downwards	Upwards	Decreasing

Note (i) *Points A and C are the points of momentary rest, where* $v = 0$ *but* $\mathbf{F}_{net} \neq 0$*. So the maximum extension (at point C) can be obtained by energy conservation principle but not by putting* $\mathbf{F}_{net} = 0$*.*

(ii) *Point B is the point of equilibrium where* $\mathbf{F}_{net} = 0$ *and speed is maximum. This point can be obtained by putting* $\mathbf{F}_{net} = 0$ *and after that, maximum speed can be obtained by energy conservation principle.*

Example 4 *In the figure shown in the concept, find*

(a) Equilibrium extension $x_0 (= AB)$

(b) Maximum extension $x_m (= AC)$

(c) Maximum speed at point B.

Solution (a) At point B,

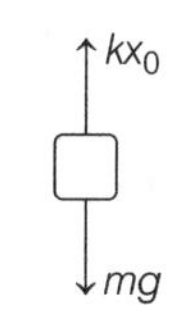

$$\mathbf{F}_{net} = 0$$

$$\Rightarrow \quad kx_0 = mg$$

$$\Rightarrow \quad x_0 = \frac{mg}{K}$$ **Ans.**

(b) **From A to C** $(v_A = v_C = 0)$

Decreasing in gravitational potential energy = increasing in spring potential energy.

$$\therefore \quad mgx_m = \frac{1}{2} Kx_m^2 \qquad (AC = x_m)$$

$$\Rightarrow \quad x_m = \frac{2mg}{K}$$ **Ans.**

(c) **From A to B**

Decreasing in gravitational potential energy = increasing in (spring potential energy + kinetic energy)

$$\Rightarrow \quad mg\,x_0 = \frac{1}{2} Kx_0^2 + \frac{1}{2} mv_{max}^2$$

Substituting the value of $x_0 = \dfrac{mg}{K}$ in the above equation, we get

$$v_{max} = \left(\sqrt{\frac{m}{K}}\right) g$$ **Ans.**

Example 5 *Consider the situation shown in figure. Mass of block A is m and that of block B is 2 m. The force constant of spring is K. Friction is absent everywhere. System is released from rest with the spring unstretched. Find*

(a) the maximum extension of the spring x_m

(b) the speed of block A when the extension in the spring is $x = \frac{x_m}{2}$

(c) net acceleration of block B when extension in the spring is $x = \frac{x_m}{4}$

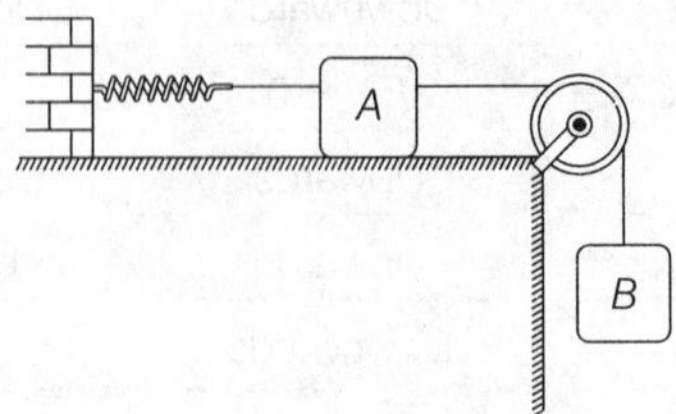

Solution (a) At maximum extension in the spring

$$v_A = v_B = 0 \quad \text{(momentarily)}$$

Therefore, applying conservation of mechanical energy:

decreasing in gravitational potential energy of block B = increasing in elastic potential energy of spring.

or $$m_B g x_m = \frac{1}{2} K x_m^2$$

or $$2\,mg x_m = \frac{1}{2} K x_m^2$$

$\therefore$ $$x_m = \frac{4\,mg}{K} \quad \textbf{Ans.}$$

(b) At $x = \frac{x_m}{2} = \frac{2\,mg}{K}$

Let $$v_A = v_B = v \text{ (say)}$$

Then, decrease in gravitational potential energy of block B = increase in elastic potential energy of spring + increase in kinetic energy of both the blocks.

$\therefore$ $$m_B g x = \frac{1}{2} K x^2 + \frac{1}{2}(m_A + m_B) v^2$$

or $$(2m)(g)\left(\frac{2\,mg}{K}\right) = \frac{1}{2} K \left(\frac{2\,mg}{K}\right)^2 + \frac{1}{2}(m + 2m) v^2$$

$\therefore$ $$v = 2g\sqrt{\frac{m}{3K}} \quad \textbf{Ans.}$$

(c) At $x = \frac{x_m}{4} = \frac{mg}{K}$

Kx = mg ← m → T
→ a

T
↑
2 m ↓ a
↓
2 mg

or $$Kx = mg$$

$$a = \frac{\text{Net pulling force}}{\text{Total mass}} = \frac{2\,mg - mg}{3\,m}$$

$$= \frac{g}{3} \text{ (downwards)} \quad \textbf{Ans.}$$

Type 3. *Problems with friction*

Concept

Mechanical energy does not remain constant if friction is there and work done by friction is not zero. So, initial mechanical energy is more than the final mechanical energy and the difference goes in the work done against friction.

How to Solve?

- The problem can be solved by the following simple equation:
  initial mechanical energy – final mechanical energy if work done against friction.
  Here, work done against friction is equal to ($\mu\, mg\, d$) if the block is moving on horizontal ground and this is equal to ($\mu d\, mg \cos\theta$) if the block is moving on an inclined plane. In these expressions 'd' is the distance travelled over the rough ground (not the displacement). If μ_s and μ_k two coefficients of friction are given, then we will have to take μ_k.

Example 6

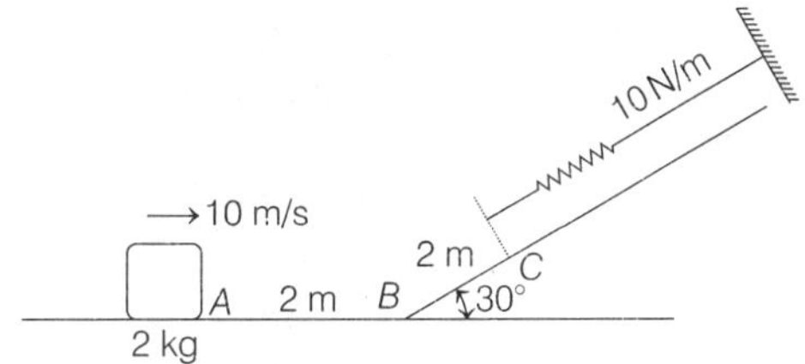

In the figure shown, AB = BC = 2 m. Friction coefficient everywhere is $\mu = 0.2$. Find the maximum compression of the spring.

Solution Let x be the maximum extension.

v = 0
→10 m/s
2 kg
2 m
(2 + x) m
30°
h
Final position
Initial position

$$h = (2 + x)\sin 30° = (1 + 0.5\,x)\,m$$

The block has travelled $d_1 = 2$ m on rough horizontal ground and $d_2 = (2 + x)$ m on rough inclined ground. In the initial position block has only kinetic energy and in the final position spring and gravitational potential energy. So, applying the equation.

$$E_i - E_f = \text{work done against friction}$$

$$\Rightarrow \quad \left(\frac{1}{2}mv^2\right) - \left(\frac{1}{2}kx^2 + mgh\right) = \mu\, mg\, d_1 + (\mu\, mg \cos\theta)\, d_2$$

$$\Rightarrow \frac{1}{2} \times 2 \times (10)^2 - \frac{1}{2} \times 10 \times x^2 - 2 \times 10 \times (1 + 0.5\,x) = 0.2 \times 2 \times 10 \times 2 + (0.2 \times 2 \times 10 \times \cos 30°)(2 + x)$$

Solving this equation we get,

$$x = 2.45\ \text{m}$$ **Ans.**

Example 7 *A small block slides along a track with elevated ends and a flat central part as shown in figure. The flat portion BC has a length $l = 3.0$ m. The curved portions of the track are frictionless. For the flat part, the coefficient of kinetic friction is $\mu_k = 0.20$, the particle is released at point A which is at height $h = 1.5$ m above the flat part of the track. Where does the block finally comes to rest?*

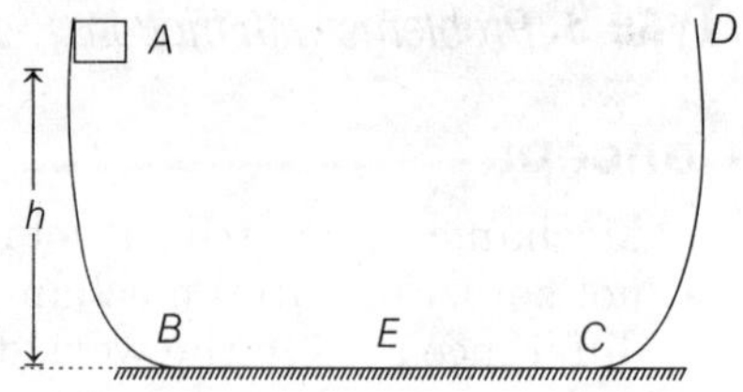

Solution As initial mechanical energy of the block is mgh and final is zero, so loss in mechanical energy = mgh. This mechanical energy is lost in doing work against friction in the flat part,

So, loss in mechanical energy = work done against friction

or $$mgh = \mu mgd$$

i.e. $$d = \frac{h}{\mu} = \frac{1.5}{0.2} = 7.5 \text{ m}$$

After starting from B, the block will reach C and then will rise up till the remaining KE at C is converted into potential energy. It will then again descend and at C will have the same value as it had when ascending, but now it will move from C to B. The same will be repeated and finally the block will come to rest at E such that

$$BC + CB + BE = 7.5$$

or $$3 + 3 + BE = 7.5$$

i.e. $$BE = 1.5$$

So, the block comes to rest at the centre of the flat part. **Ans.**

Example 8 *A 0.5 kg block slides from the point A on a horizontal track with an initial speed 3 m/s towards a weightless horizontal spring of length 1 m and force constant 2 N/m. The part AB of the track is frictionless and the part BC has the coefficient of static and kinetic friction as 0.22 and 0.20 respectively. If the distances AB and BD are 2 m and 2.14 m respectively, find the total distance through which the block moves before it comes to rest completely. ($g = 10$ m/s^2)*

(JEE 1983)

Solution As the track AB is frictionless, the block moves this distance without loss in its initial KE $= \frac{1}{2}mv^2 = \frac{1}{2} \times 0.5 \times 3^2 = 2.25$ J. In the path BD as friction is present, so work done against friction

$$= \mu_k mgd = 0.2 \times 0.5 \times 10 \times 2.14 = 2.14 \text{ J}$$

So, at D the KE of the block is $= 2.25 - 2.14 = 0.11$ J

Now, if the spring is compressed by x

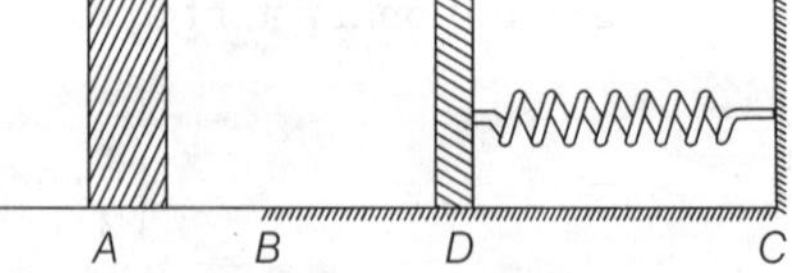

$$0.11 = \frac{1}{2} \times k \times x^2 + \mu_k mgx$$

i.e. $$0.11 = \frac{1}{2} \times 2 \times x^2 + 0.2 \times 0.5 \times 10x$$

or $$x^2 + x - 0.11 = 0$$

which on solving gives positive value of $x = 0.1$ m

After moving the distance $x = 0.1$ m the block comes to rest.

Now, the compressed spring exerts a force,

$$F = kx = 2 \times 0.1 = 0.2 \text{ N}$$

on the block while limiting frictional force between block and track is $f_L = \mu_s mg = 0.22 \times 0.5 \times 10 = 1.1 \text{ N}$. Since, $F < f_L$. The block will not move back. So, the total distance moved by the block

$$= AB + BD + 0.1 = 2 + 2.14 + 0.1$$

$$= 4.24 \text{ m}$$ **Ans.**

Type 4. *Dependent and path independent works*

Concept

$$W = \int \mathbf{F} \cdot d\mathbf{r}$$

Here, $d\mathbf{r} = dx\,\hat{\mathbf{i}} + dy\,\hat{\mathbf{j}} + dz\,\hat{\mathbf{k}}$

In the following three cases work done is path independent.

(i) **F** is a constant force.

(ii) **F** is of the type $\mathbf{F} = f_1(x)\,\hat{\mathbf{i}} + f_2(y)\,\hat{\mathbf{j}} + f_3(z)\,\hat{\mathbf{k}}$

(iii) $\mathbf{F} \cdot d\mathbf{r}$ is in the form d (function of x, y and z) e.g. $d(xy)$, so that,

$$W_{A \to B} = \int_A^B \mathbf{F} \cdot d\mathbf{r} = \int_A^B d(xy) = [xy]_A^B$$

In all other cases, we will have to mention the path. Along different paths work done will be different.

Example 9 *A body is displaced from origin to (2m, 4m) under the following two forces :*

(a) $\mathbf{F} = (2\,\hat{\mathbf{i}} + 6\,\hat{\mathbf{j}})\,N$, *a constant force*

(b) $\mathbf{F} = (2x\,\hat{\mathbf{i}} + 3y^2\,\hat{\mathbf{j}})\,N$

Find work done by the given forces in both cases.

Solution (a) $\mathbf{F} = (2\,\hat{\mathbf{i}} + 6\,\hat{\mathbf{j}})$ N

$$d\mathbf{r} = (dx\,\hat{\mathbf{i}} + dy\,\hat{\mathbf{j}})$$

$$\therefore \quad \mathbf{F} \cdot d\mathbf{r} = 2\,dx + 6\,dy$$

$$W = \int_{(0,0)}^{(2\text{m},4\text{m})} \mathbf{F} \cdot d\mathbf{r} = \int_{(0,0)}^{(2\text{m},4\text{m})} (2\,dx + 6\,dy)$$

$$= [2x + 6y]_{(0,0)}^{(2\text{m},4\text{m})} = (2 \times 2 + 6 \times 4)$$

$$= 28 \text{ J}$$ **Ans.**

Note *Here,* **F** *is constant, so the work done is path independent.*

(b) $\mathbf{F} = (2x\,\hat{\mathbf{i}} + 3y^2\,\hat{\mathbf{j}})$ N

$$d\mathbf{r} = (dx\,\hat{\mathbf{i}} + dy\,\hat{\mathbf{j}})$$

$$\therefore \quad \mathbf{F} \cdot d\mathbf{r} = (2x\,dx + 3y^2 dy)$$

$$W = \int_{(0,0)}^{(2m,\,4m)} \mathbf{F}\cdot d\mathbf{r} = \int_{(0,0)}^{(2m,\,4m)} (2x\,dx + 3y^2 dy)$$

$$= [x^2 + y^3]_{(0,0)}^{(2m,\,4m)} = (2)^2 + (4)^3$$

$$= 68\ \text{J}$$ **Ans.**

Note *Here the given force is of type* $\mathbf{F} = f_1(x)\,\hat{\mathbf{i}} + f_2(y)\,\hat{\mathbf{j}}$

So, the work done is path independent.

Example 10 *A force $\mathbf{F} = -k(y\hat{\mathbf{i}} + x\hat{\mathbf{j}})$ (where k is a positive constant) acts on a particle moving in the x-y plane. Starting from the origin, the particle is taken along the positive x-axis to the point $(a,0)$ and then parallel to the y-axis to the point (a,a). The total work done by the force $\mathbf{F}$ on the particle is* **(JEE 1998)**

(a) $-2ka^2$ (b) $2ka^2$ (c) $-ka^2$ (d) ka^2

Solution $dW = \mathbf{F}\cdot d\mathbf{r}$, where $d\mathbf{r} = dx\hat{\mathbf{i}} + dy\hat{\mathbf{j}} + dz\hat{\mathbf{k}}$

and $\mathbf{F} = -k\,(y\hat{\mathbf{i}} + x\hat{\mathbf{j}})$

$\therefore$ $dW = -k\,(ydx + xdy) = -kd(xy)$

$\therefore$ $W = \int_{(0,0)}^{(a,a)} dW = -k \int_{(0,0)}^{(a,a)} d\,(xy)$

$$= -k\,[xy]_{(0,\,0)}^{(a,\,a)}$$

$$W = -ka^2$$

$\therefore$ The correct option is (c).

Alternate Method

While moving from (0, 0) to $(a, 0)$ along positive x-axis, $y = 0$

$\therefore \mathbf{F} = -kx\hat{\mathbf{j}}$ i.e. force is in negative y-direction while the displacement is in positive x-direction. Therefore, $W_1 = 0$ (Force $\perp$ displacement).

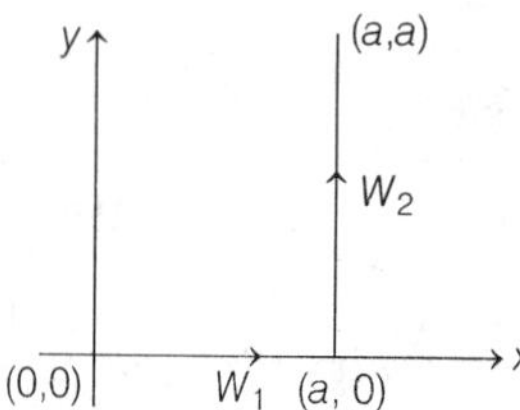

Then, it moves from $(a, 0)$ to (a, a) along a line parallel to y-axis $(x = +a)$. During this

$$\mathbf{F} = -k\,(y\hat{\mathbf{i}} + a\hat{\mathbf{j}})$$

The first component of force, $-ky\hat{\mathbf{i}}$ will not contribute any work, because this component is along negative x-direction $(-\hat{\mathbf{i}})$ while displacement is in positive y-direction $(a,0)$ to (a, a).

The second component of force i.e. $-ka\hat{\mathbf{j}}$ will perform negative work as :

$$\mathbf{F} = -ka\,\hat{\mathbf{j}} \text{ and } \mathbf{S} = a\,\hat{\mathbf{j}}$$

$\therefore$ $W_2 = \mathbf{F}\cdot\mathbf{S}$

or $W_2 = (-ka)\,(a) = -ka^2$

$\therefore$ $W = W_1 + W_2 = -ka^2$

Note *For the given force, work done is path independent. It depends only on initial and final positions.*

Example 11 *A body is displaced from origin to (1m, 1m) by a force $\mathbf{F} = (2y\hat{\mathbf{i}} + 3x^2\hat{\mathbf{j}})$ along two paths*

(a) $x = y$ *(b) $y = x^2$*

Find the work done along both paths.

Solution $\mathbf{F} = (2y\hat{\mathbf{i}} + 3x^2\hat{\mathbf{j}})$

$$d\mathbf{r} = (dx\,\hat{\mathbf{i}} + dy\,\hat{\mathbf{j}})$$

$$\mathbf{F} \cdot d\mathbf{r} = (2y\,dx + 3x^2\,dy)$$

We cannot integrate $\mathbf{F} \cdot d\mathbf{r}$ or $(2y\,dx + 3x^2\,dy)$ as such to find the work done. But along the given paths we can change this expression.

(a) Along the path $x = y$,

$$(2y\,dx + 3x^2dy) = (2x\,dx + 3y^2dy)$$

$$\therefore \quad W_1 = \int_{(0,0)}^{(1\text{m},1\text{m})} \mathbf{F} \cdot d\mathbf{r} = \int_{(0,0)}^{(1\text{m},1\text{m})} (2x\,dx + 3y^2dy)$$

$$= [x^2 + y^3]_{(0,0)}^{(1\text{m},1\text{m})}$$

$$= (1)^2 + (1)^3 = 2\text{ J} \qquad \textbf{Ans.}$$

(b) Along the path $y = x^2$

$$(2y\,dx + 3x^2dy) = (2x^2\,dx + 3y\,dy)$$

$$\therefore \quad W_2 = \int_{(0,0)}^{(1\text{m},1\text{m})} \mathbf{F} \cdot d\mathbf{r} = \int_{(0,0)}^{(1\text{m},1\text{m})} (2x^2dx + 3y\,dy)$$

$$= \left[\frac{2}{3}x^3 + \frac{3}{2}y^2\right]_{(0,0)}^{(1\text{m},1\text{m})}$$

$$= \frac{2}{3}(1)^3 + \frac{3}{2}(1)^2$$

$$= \frac{13}{6}\text{ J} \qquad \textbf{Ans.}$$

Note *We can see that $W_1 \neq W_2$ or work done is path dependent in this case.*

Type 5. *Based on relation between conservative force (F) and potential energy (U) associated with this force.*

Concept

$$F = -\frac{dU}{dx} \qquad \text{...(i)}$$

$$\therefore \quad \int dU = -\int F dx \qquad \text{...(ii)}$$

If U-x function is given, we can make F-x function by simple differentiation, using Eq. (i). If F-x function is given, then U-x function can be made by integration, using Eq. (ii). In this case, some limit of U (or value of U at some given value of x) should be known to us to make complete U-x function. Otherwise an unknown constant of integration will be there in U-x equation. If no limit is given in the question and we have to select the most appropriate answer then we can take $U = 0$ at $x = 0$.

Example 12 *A particle, which is constrained to move along x-axis, is subjected to a force in the same direction which varies with the distance x of the particle from the origin as $F(x) = -kx + ax^3$. Here, k and a are positive constants. For $x \geq 0$, the functional form of the potential energy U (x) of the particle is* **(JEE 2002)**

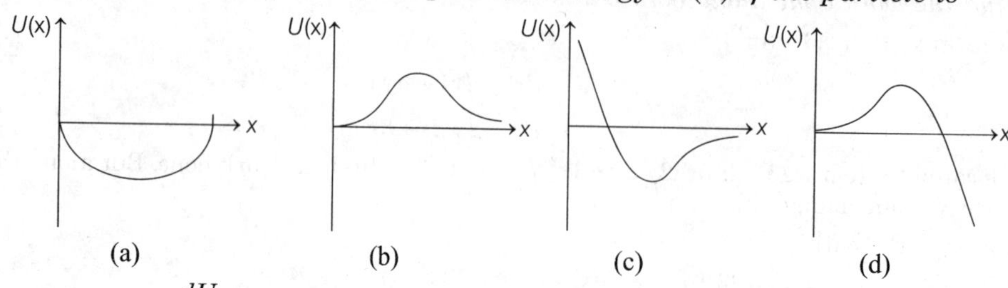

Solution $F = -\frac{dU}{dx}$

$\therefore$ $$dU = -F \cdot dx \quad \text{or} \quad U(x) = -\int_0^x (-kx + ax^3)\, dx$$

$$U(x) = \frac{kx^2}{2} - \frac{ax^4}{4}$$

$$U(x) = 0 \text{ at } x = 0 \text{ and } x = \sqrt{\frac{2k}{a}}$$

$$U(x) = \text{negative for } x > \sqrt{\frac{2k}{a}}$$

Further, $F = 0$ at $x = 0$. Therefore slope of U-x graph should be zero at $x = 0$.
Hence, the correct answer is (d).

Note *In this example, we have assumed a limit : $U = 0$ at $x = 0$.*

Example 13 *A particle is placed at the origin and a force $F = kx$ is acting on it (where k is a positive constant). If $U(0) = 0$, the graph of $U(x)$ versus x will be (where, U is the potential energy function)* **(JEE 2004)**

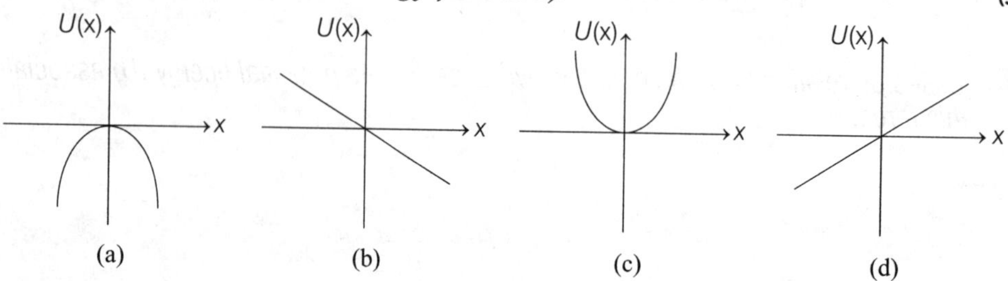

Solution From $F = -\frac{dU}{dx}$

$$\int_0^{U(x)} dU = -\int_0^x F dx = -\int_0^x (kx)\, dx$$

$\therefore$ $$U(x) = -\frac{kx^2}{2} \quad \text{as } U(0) = 0$$

Therefore, the correct option is (a).

Miscellaneous Examples

Example 14 *A small mass m starts from rest and slides down the smooth spherical surface of R. Assume zero potential energy at the top. Find*

(a) the change in potential energy,

(b) the kinetic energy,

(c) the speed of the mass as a function of the angle θ made by the radius through the mass with the vertical.

Solution In the figure, $h = R(1 - \cos\theta)$

(a) As the mass comes down, potential energy will decrease. Hence,

$$\Delta U = -mgh = -mgR(1-\cos\theta)$$

(b) Magnitude of decrease in potential energy = increase in kinetic energy

$\therefore$ Kinetic energy $= mgh$

$$= mgR(1-\cos\theta) \qquad \textbf{Ans.}$$

(c) $$\frac{1}{2}mv^2 = mgR(1-\cos\theta)$$

$\therefore$ $$v = \sqrt{2gR(1-\cos\theta)} \qquad \textbf{Ans.}$$

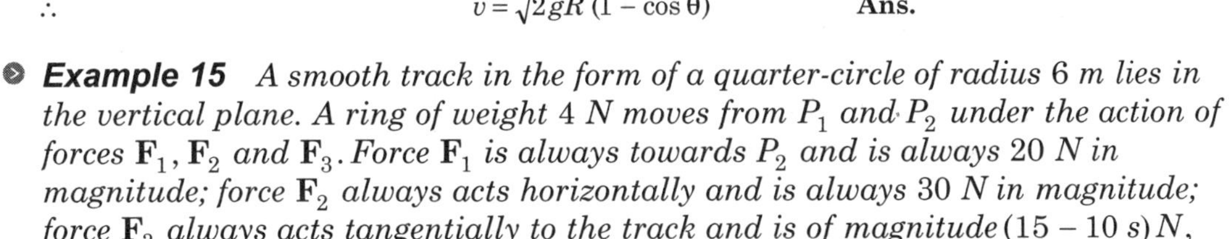

Example 15 *A smooth track in the form of a quarter-circle of radius 6 m lies in the vertical plane. A ring of weight 4 N moves from P_1 and P_2 under the action of forces $\mathbf{F}_1$, $\mathbf{F}_2$ and $\mathbf{F}_3$. Force $\mathbf{F}_1$ is always towards P_2 and is always 20 N in magnitude; force $\mathbf{F}_2$ always acts horizontally and is always 30 N in magnitude; force $\mathbf{F}_3$ always acts tangentially to the track and is of magnitude $(15 - 10\,s)$ N, where s is in metre. If the particle has speed 4 m/s at P_1, what will its speed be at P_2?*

Solution The work done by $\mathbf{F}_1$ is

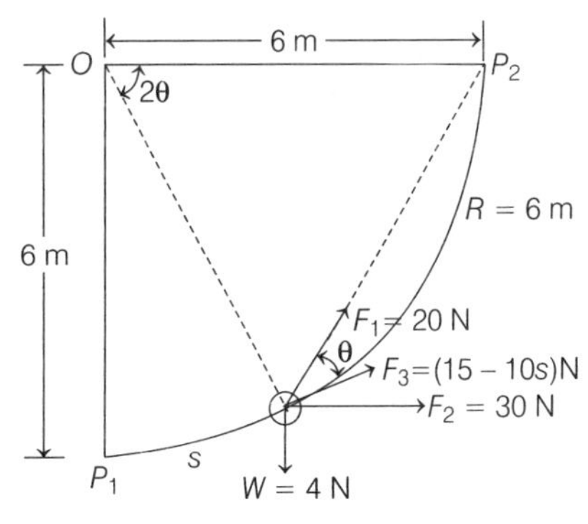

$$W_1 = \int_{P_1}^{P_2} F_1 \cos\theta\, ds$$

From figure, $$s = R\left(\frac{\pi}{2} - 2\theta\right)$$

or $$ds = (6\text{ m})\,d(-2\theta) = -12\,d\theta$$

and $$F_1 = 20.$$

At P_1, $$2\theta = \frac{\pi}{2} \Rightarrow \theta = \frac{\pi}{4}$$

At P_2, $$2\theta = 0 \Rightarrow \theta = 0$$

Hence, $$W_1 = -240\int_{\pi/4}^{0}\cos\theta\, d\theta$$

$$= 240\sin\frac{\pi}{4} = 120\sqrt{2}\text{ J}$$

The work done by $\mathbf{F}_3$ is

$$W_3 = \int F_3\, ds = \int_0^{6(\pi/2)}(15-10s)\,ds \qquad \left(P_1P_2 = R\frac{\pi}{2} = \frac{6\pi}{2}\right)$$

$$= [15s - 5s^2]_0^{3\pi} = 302.76\text{ J} = -302.8\text{ J}$$

To calculate the work done by $\mathbf{F}_2$ and by w, it is convenient to take the projection of the path in the direction of the force. Thus,

$$W_2 = F_2(OP_2) = 30(6) = 180 \text{ J}$$

$$W_4 = (-w)(P_1O) = (-4)(6) = -24 \text{ J} \qquad (w = \text{weight})$$

The total work done is
$$W_1 + W_3 + W_2 + W_4 = 23 \text{ J}$$

Then, by the work-energy principle.

$$K_{P_2} - K_{P_1} = 23 \text{ J}$$

$$= \frac{1}{2}\left(\frac{4}{9.8}\right) v_2^2 - \frac{1}{2}\left(\frac{4}{9.8}\right)(4)^2 = 23$$

$$v_2 = 11.3 \text{ m/s}$$ **Ans.**

Example 16 *A single conservative force $F(x)$ acts on a 1.0 kg particle that moves along the x-axis. The potential energy $U(x)$ is given by:*

$$U(x) = 20 + (x-2)^2$$

where, x is in meters. At $x = 5.0$ m the particle has a kinetic energy of 20 J.

(a) What is the mechanical energy of the system?

(b) Make a plot of $U(x)$ as a function of x for $-10 \text{ m} \le x \le 10$ m, and on the same graph draw the line that represents the mechanical energy of the system.
Use part (b) to determine.

(c) The least value of x and

(d) The greatest value of x between which the particle can move.

(e) The maximum kinetic energy of the particle and

(f) The value of x at which it occurs.

(g) Determine the equation for $F(x)$ as a function of x.

(h) For what (finite) value of x does $F(x) = 0$?

Solution (a) Potential energy at $x = 5.0$ m is

$$U = 20 + (5-2)^2 = 29 \text{ J}$$

∴ Mechanical energy

$$E = K + U = 20 + 29 = 49 \text{ J}$$

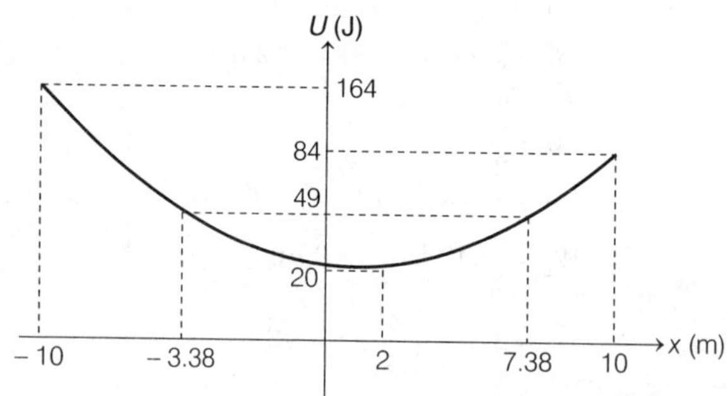

(b) At $x = 10$ m, $U = 84$ J at $x = -10$ m, $U = 164$ J
and at $x = 2$ m, $U = \text{minimum} = 20$ J

(c) and (d) Particle will move between the points where its kinetic energy becomes zero or its potential energy is equal to its mechanical energy.

Thus, $$49 = 20 + (x-2)^2$$

or $$(x-2)^2 = 29$$

or $$x - 2 = \pm\sqrt{29} = \pm 5.38 \text{ m}$$

$\therefore$ $$x = 7.38 \text{ m and } -3.38 \text{ m}$$

or the particle will move between $x = -3.38$ m and $x = 7.38$ m

(e) and (f) Maximum kinetic energy is at $x = 2$ m, where the potential energy is minimum and this maximum kinetic energy is,

$$K_{max} = E - U_{min} = 49 - 20$$
$$= 29 \text{ J}$$

(g) $F = -\dfrac{dU}{dx} = -2(x-2) = 2(2-x)$

(h) $F(x) = 0$, at $x = 2.0$ m

where potential energy is minimum (the position of stable equilibrium).

Example 17 *A small disc A slides down with initial velocity equal to zero from the top of a smooth hill of height H having a horizontal portion. What must be the height of the horizontal portion h to ensure the maximum distance s covered by the disc? What is it equal to?*

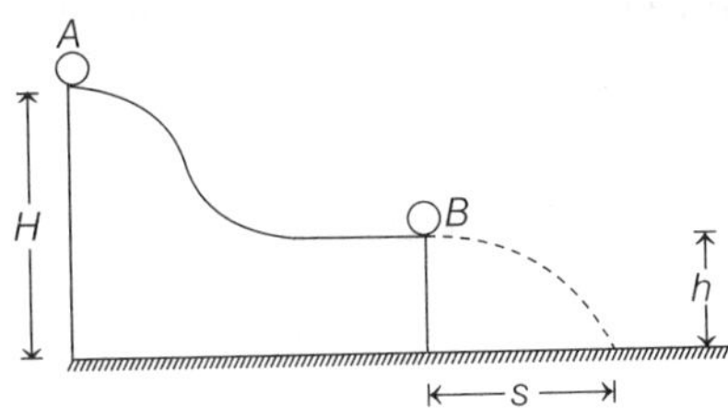

Solution In order to obtain the velocity at point B, we apply the law of conservation of energy. So,

$$\text{Loss in PE} = \text{Gain in KE}$$

$$m\, g\, (H-h) = \frac{1}{2} mv^2$$

$\therefore$ $$v = \sqrt{[2g\,(H-h)]}$$

Further $$h = \frac{1}{2} gt^2$$

$\therefore$ $$t = \sqrt{(2h/g)}$$

Now, $$s = v \times t = \sqrt{[2g(H-h)]} \times \sqrt{(2\,h/g)}$$

or $$s = \sqrt{[4\,h(H-h)]} \qquad \ldots\text{(i)}$$

For maximum value of s, $\dfrac{ds}{dh} = 0$

$\therefore$ $$\frac{1}{2\sqrt{[4\,h(H-h)]}} \times 4(H-2h) = 0 \quad \text{or} \quad h = \frac{H}{2}$$ **Ans.**

Substituting $h = H/2$, in Eq. (i), we get

$$s = \sqrt{[4(H/2)\,(H-H/2)]} = \sqrt{H^2} = H$$ **Ans.**

Example 18 *A small disc of mass m slides down a smooth hill of height h without initial velocity and gets onto a plank of mass M lying on a smooth horizontal plane at the base of hill figure. Due to friction between the disc and the plank, disc slows down and finally moves as one piece with the plank. (a) Find out total work performed by the friction forces in this process. (b) can it be stated that the result obtained does not depend on the choice of the reference frame.*

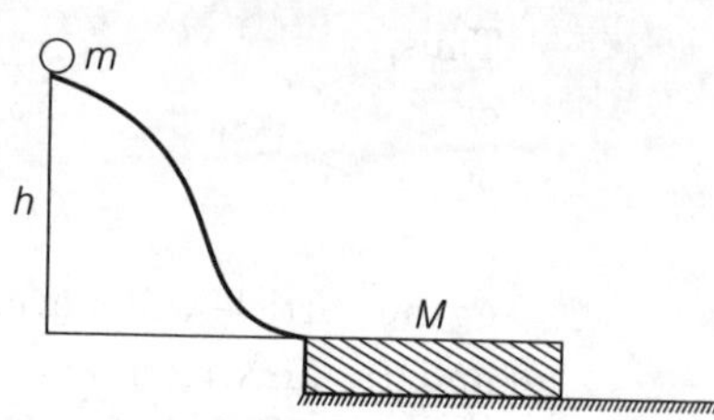

Solution (a) When the disc slides down and comes onto the plank, then

$$mgh = \frac{1}{2} mv^2$$

$$\therefore \quad v = \sqrt{(2 gh)} \qquad \text{...(i)}$$

Let v_1 be the common velocity of both, the disc and plank when they move together. From law of conservation of linear momentum,

$$mv = (M + m)\, v_1$$

$$\therefore \quad v_1 = \frac{mv}{(M + m)} \qquad \text{...(ii)}$$

Now, change in KE $= (K)_f - (K)_i = (\text{work done})_{\text{friction}}$

$$\therefore \quad \frac{1}{2}(M + m)v_1^2 - \frac{1}{2} mv^2 = (\text{work done})_{\text{friction}}$$

or
$$W_{\text{fr}} = \frac{1}{2}(M + m)\left[\frac{m\,v}{M + m}\right]^2 - \frac{1}{2} m\,v^2$$

$$= \frac{1}{2} mv^2 \left[\frac{m}{M + m} - 1\right]$$

as
$$\frac{1}{2} mv^2 = mgh$$

$$\therefore \quad W_{\text{fr}} = -mgh\left[\frac{M}{M + m}\right] \qquad \textbf{Ans.}$$

(b) In part (a), we have calculated work done from the ground frame of reference. Now, let us take plank as the reference frame.

$f = \mu mg \leftarrow$ m

M $\rightarrow f = \mu mg$

Acceleration of plank $a_0 = \dfrac{f}{M} = \dfrac{\mu\, mg}{M}$

Free body diagram of disc with respect to plank is shown in figure.

Here, ma_0 = pseudo force.

$\leftarrow f + ma_0$ ○ $\rightarrow v_r = v = \sqrt{2gh}$

$\therefore$ Retardation of disc w.r.t. plank,

$$a_r = \frac{f + ma_0}{m} = \frac{\mu mg + \dfrac{\mu m^2 g}{M}}{m} = \mu g + \frac{\mu mg}{M}$$

$$= \left(\frac{M + m}{M}\right)\mu g$$

The disc will stop after travelling a distance S_r relative to plank, where

$$S_r = \frac{v_r^2}{2a_r} = \frac{Mgh}{(M+m)\mu g} \qquad (0 = v_r^2 - 2a_r S_r)$$

$\therefore$ Work done by friction in this frame of reference

$$W_{fr} = -fS_r = -(\mu mg)\left[\frac{Mgh}{(M+m)\mu g}\right]$$

$$= -\frac{M\,mgh}{(M+m)}$$

which is same as part (a).

Note *Work done by friction in this problem does not depend upon the frame of reference, otherwise in general work depends upon reference frame.*

Example 19 *Two blocks A and B are connected to each other by a string and a spring. The string passes over a frictionless pulley as shown in figure. Block B slides over the horizontal top surface of a stationary block C and the block A slides along the vertical side of C, both with the same uniform speed. The coefficient of friction between the surfaces of the blocks is 0.2. The force constant of the spring is 1960 Nm^{-1}. If the mass of block A is 2 kg, calculate the mass of block B and the energy stored in the spring. ($g = 9.8\ m/s^2$)*

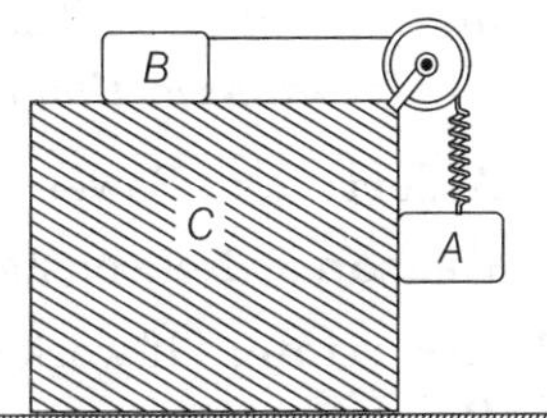

Solution Let m be the mass of B. From its free-body diagram

$$T - \mu N = m \times 0 = 0$$

where, T = tension of the string and $N = mg$

$\therefore \qquad T = \mu mg$

From the free-body diagram of the spring

$$T - T' = 0$$

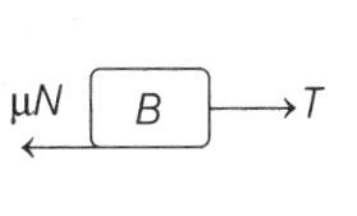

(a)

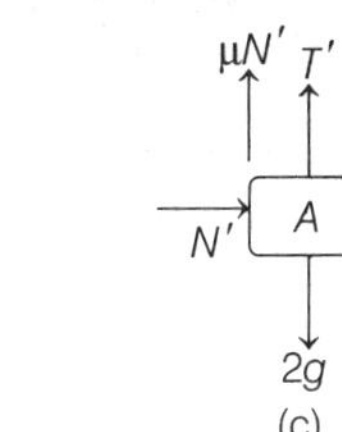

(b) (c)

where, T' is the force exerted by A on the spring or $T = T' = \mu mg$

From the free-body diagram of A $\qquad 2g - (T' + \mu N') = 2 \times 0 = 0$

where, N' is the normal reaction of the vertical wall of C on A and $N' = 2 \times 0$ (as there is no horizontal acceleration of A)

$$\therefore \qquad 2g = T' = \mu mg \quad \text{or} \quad m = \frac{2g}{\mu g} = \frac{2}{0.2} = 10\ \text{kg} \qquad \textbf{Ans.}$$

Tensile force on the spring $= T$ or $T' = \mu mg = 0.2 \times 10 \times 9.8 = 19.6$ N

Now, in a spring tensile force = force constant × extension

$$\therefore \qquad 19.6 = 1960\,x \quad \text{or} \quad x = \frac{1}{100}\ \text{m} \quad \text{or} \quad U\ (\text{energy of a spring}) = \frac{1}{2}kx^2$$

$$= \frac{1}{2} \times 1960 \times \left(\frac{1}{100}\right)^2 = 0.098\ \text{J} \qquad \textbf{Ans.}$$

Exercises

LEVEL 1

Assertion and Reason

Directions : *Choose the correct option.*

(a) *If both* **Assertion** *and* **Reason** *are true and the* **Reason** *is correct explanation of the* **Assertion.**
(b) *If both* **Assertion** *and* **Reason** *are true but* **Reason** *is not the correct explanation of* **Assertion.**
(c) *If* **Assertion** *is true, but the* **Reason** *is false.*
(d) *If* **Assertion** *is false but the* **Reason** *is true.*
(e) *If both* **Assertion** *and* **Reason** *are false.*

1. Assertion : Power of a constant force is also constant.

Reason : Net constant force will always produce a constant acceleration.

2. Assertion : If work done by conservative forces is positive, kinetic energy will increase.

Reason : Because potential energy will decrease.

3. Assertion : In projectile motion, the rate of change in magnitude of potential energy of a particle first decreases and then increases during motion.

Reason : In projectile motion, the rate of change in linear momentum of a particle remains constant during motion.

4. Assertion : Displacement-time graph of a particle moving in a straight line is shown in figure. Work done by all the forces between time interval t_1 and t_2 is definitely zero.

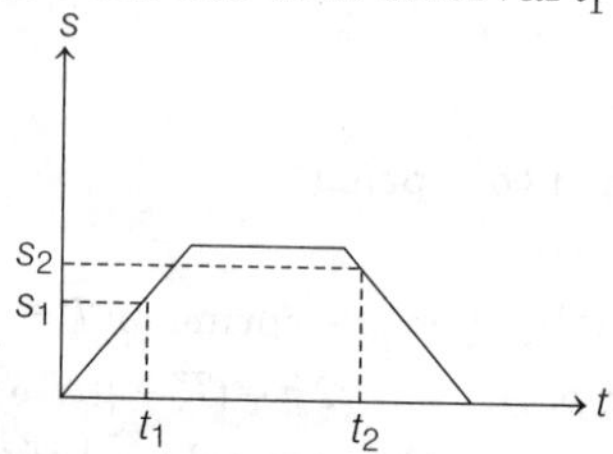

Reason : Work done by all the forces is equal to change in kinetic energy.

5. Assertion : All surfaces shown in figure are smooth. Block A comes down along the wedge B. Work done by normal reaction (between A and B) on B is positive while on A it is negative.

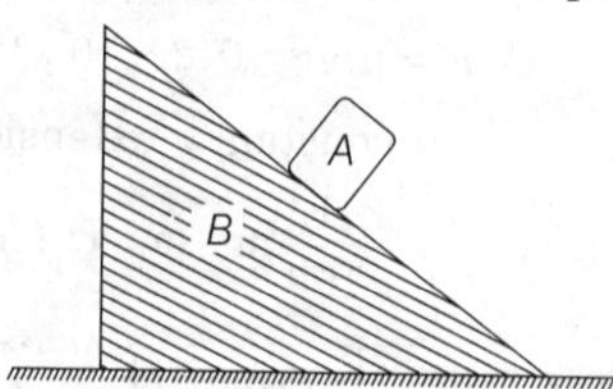

Reason : Angle between normal reaction and net displacement of A is greater than 90° while between normal reaction and net displacement of B is less than 90°.

6. **Assertion :** A plank A is placed on a rough surface over which a block B is placed. In the shown situation, elastic cord is unstretched. Now a gradually increasing force F is applied slowly on A until the relative motion between the block and plank starts.

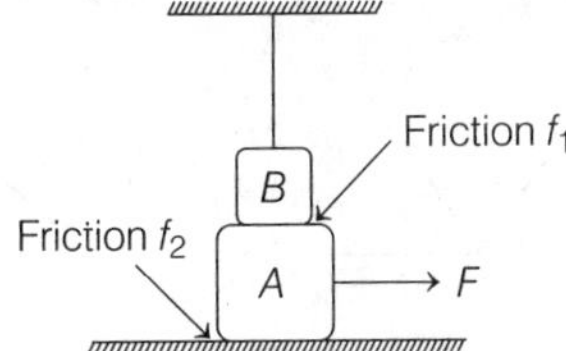

At this moment, cord is making an angle θ with the vertical. Work done by force F is equal to energy lost against friction f_2.

Reason : Work done by static friction f_1 on the system as a whole is zero.

7. **Assertion :** A block of mass m starts moving on a rough horizontal surface with a velocity v. It stops due to friction between the block and the surface after moving through a ceratin distance. The surface is now tilted to an angle of 30° with the horizontal and the same block is made to go up on the surface with the same initial velocity v. The block stops after moving certain distance. The decrease in the mechanical energy in the second situation is smaller than that in the first situation.

Reason : The coefficient of friction between the block and the surface decreases with the increase in the angle of inclination.

8. **Assertion :** Consider a person of mass 80 kg who is climbing a ladder. In climbing up a vertical distance of 5 m, the contact force exerted by ladder on person's feet does 4000 J of work. [Take, $g = 10\,\text{m/s}^2$]

Reason : Work done by a force F is defined as the dot product of force with the displacement of point of application of force.

9. **Assertion :** The work done in bringing a body down from the top to the base along a frictionless inclined plane is the same as the work done in bringing it down from the vertical side.

Reason : The gravitational force on the body along the inclined plane is the same as that along the vertical side.

Objective Questions

Single Correct Option

1. Initially the system shown in figure is in equilibrium. At the moment, the string is cut the downward acceleration of blocks A and B are respectively a_1 and a_2. The magnitudes of a_1 and a_2 are

A
k
B
m

(a) zero and zero

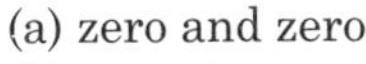

(b) $2g$ and zero

(c) g and zero

(d) None of the above

2. System shown in figure is in equilibrium. Find the magnitude of net change in the string tension between two masses just after, when one of the springs is cut. Mass of both the blocks is same and equal to m and spring constant of both the springs is k

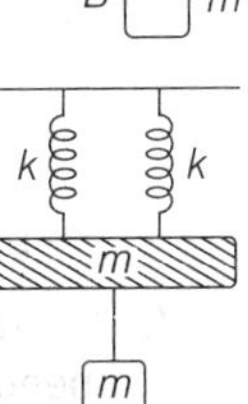

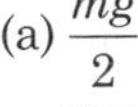

(a) $\frac{mg}{2}$ (b) $\frac{mg}{4}$

(c) $\frac{mg}{3}$ (d) $\frac{3mg}{2}$

3. A particle is projected at $t = 0$ from a point on the ground with certain velocity at an angle with the horizontal. The power of gravitation force is plotted against time. Which of the following is the best representation?

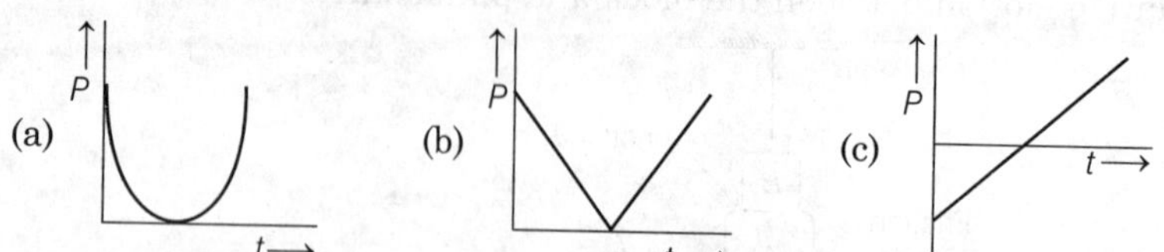

4. A block of mass m slides along the track with kinetic friction μ. A man pulls the block through a rope which makes an angle θ with the horizontal as shown in the figure. The block moves with constant speed v. Power delivered by man is

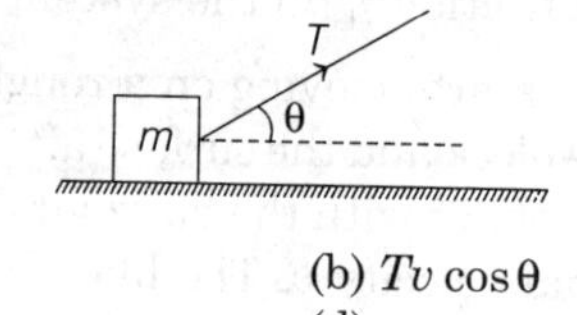

(a) Tv
(b) $Tv \cos\theta$
(c) $(T \cos\theta - \mu mg)\, v$
(d) zero

5. The force acting on a body moving along x-axis varies with the position of the particle shown in the figure. The body is in stable equilibrium at

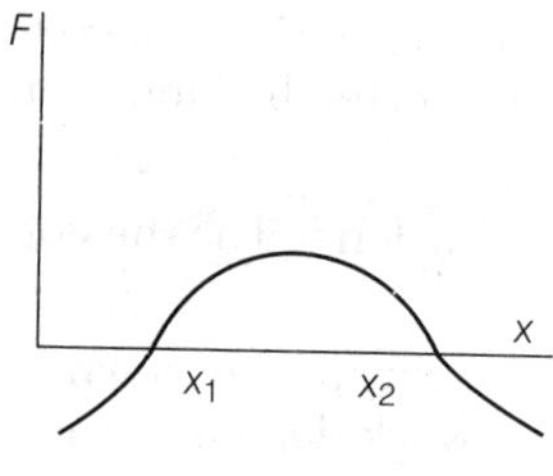

(a) $x = x_1$
(b) $x = x_2$
(c) both x_1 and x_2
(d) neither x_1 nor x_2

6. Two light vertical springs with spring constants k_1 and k_2 are separated by a distance l. Their upper ends are fixed to the ceiling and their lower ends to the ends A and B of a light horizontal rod AB. A vertical downward force F is applied at point C on the rod. AB will remain horizontal in equilibrium, if the distance AC is

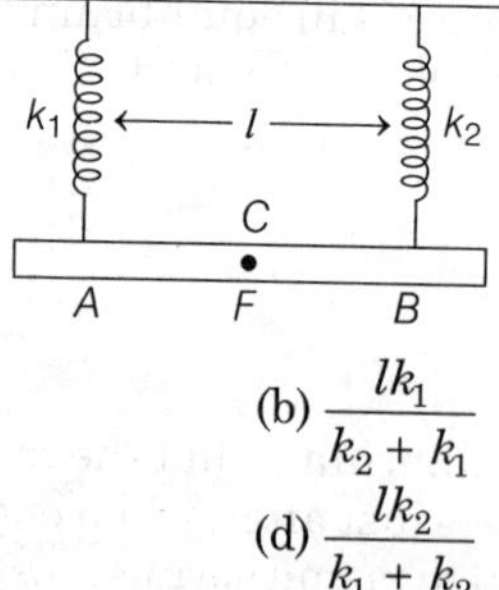

(a) $\dfrac{lk_1}{k_2}$
(b) $\dfrac{lk_1}{k_2 + k_1}$
(c) $\dfrac{lk_2}{k_1}$
(d) $\dfrac{lk_2}{k_1 + k_2}$

7. A pump is required to lift 800 kg of water per minute from a 10 m deep well and eject it with speed of 20 m/s. The required power (in watts) of the pump will be
(a) 6000
(b) 4000
(c) 5000
(d) 8000

8. A block of mass 1 kg slides down a curved track which forms one quadrant of a circle of radius 1 m as shown in figure. The speed of block at the bottom of the track is $v = 2\ \text{ms}^{-1}$. The work done by the force of friction is

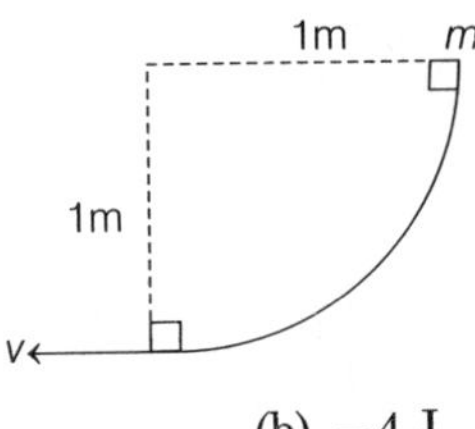

(a) + 4 J
(b) − 4 J
(c) − 8 J
(d) + 8 J

9. A body with mass 1 kg moves in one direction in the presence of a force which is described by the potential energy graph. If the body is released from rest at $x = 2$ m, than its speed when it crosses $x = 5$ m is (Neglect dissipative forces)

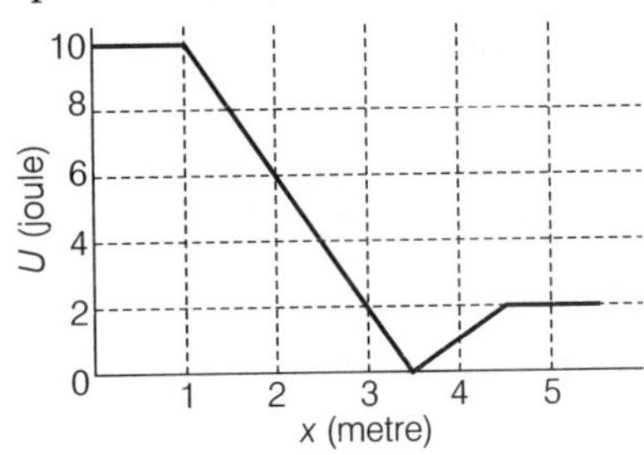

(a) $2\sqrt{2}\ \text{ms}^{-1}$
(b) $1\ \text{ms}^{-1}$
(c) $2\ \text{ms}^{-1}$
(d) $3\ \text{ms}^{-1}$

10. In the figure, m_1 and m_2 ($< m_1$) are joined together by a pulley. When the mass m_1 is released from the height h above the floor, it strikes the floor with a speed

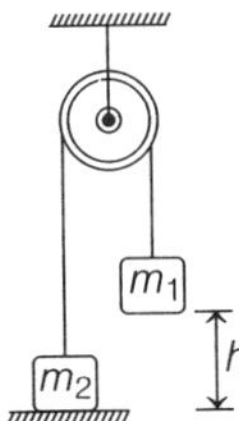

(a) $\sqrt{2gh\left(\frac{m_1 - m_2}{m_1 + m_2}\right)}$
(b) $\sqrt{2gh}$
(c) $\sqrt{\frac{2m_2gh}{m_1 + m_2}}$
(d) $\sqrt{\frac{2m_1gh}{m_1 + m_2}}$

11. A person pulls a bucket of water from a well of depth h. If the mass of uniform rope is m and that of the bucket full of water is M, then work done by the person is

(a) $\left(M + \frac{m}{2}\right)gh$
(b) $\frac{1}{2}(M + m)gh$
(c) $(M + m)\ gh$
(d) $\left(\frac{M}{2} + m\right)gh$

12. The velocity of a particle decreases uniformly from 20 ms^{-1} to zero in 10 s as shown in figure. If the mass of the particle is 2 kg, then identify the correct statement.

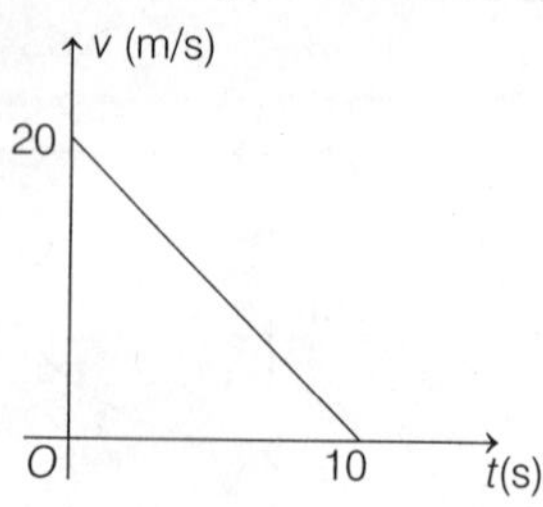

(a) The net force acting on the particle is opposite to the direction of motion
(b) The work done by friction force is –400 J
(c) The magnitude of friction force acting on the particle is 4 N
(d) All of the above

13. The minimum stopping distance of a car moving with velocity v is x. If the car is moving with velocity $2v$, then the minimum stopping distance will be

(a) $2x$ (b) $4x$ (c) $3x$ (d) $8x$

14. A projectile is fired from the origin with a velocity v_0 at an angle θ with the x-axis. The speed of the projectile at an altitude h is

(a) $v_0 \cos\theta$ (b) $\sqrt{v_0^2 - 2gh}$ (c) $\sqrt{v_0^2 \sin^2\theta - 2gh}$ (d) None of these

15. A particle of mass m moves from rest under the action of a constant force F which acts for two seconds. The maximum power attained is

(a) $2Fm$ (b) $\dfrac{F^2}{m}$ (c) $\dfrac{2F}{m}$ (d) $\dfrac{2F^2}{m}$

16. A body moves under the action of a constant force along a straight line. The instantaneous power developed by this force with time t is correctly represented by

(a) 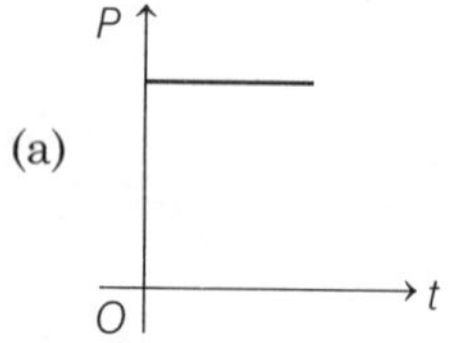

(b) 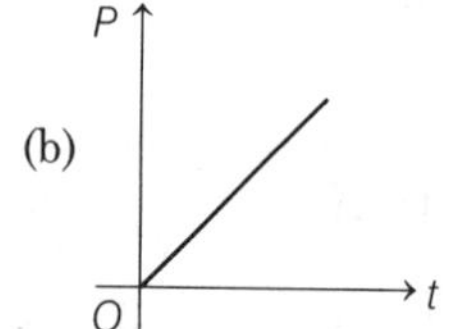

(c) 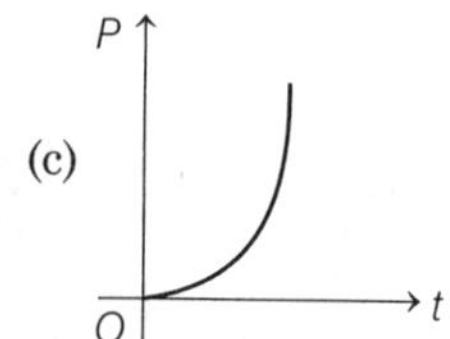

(d) 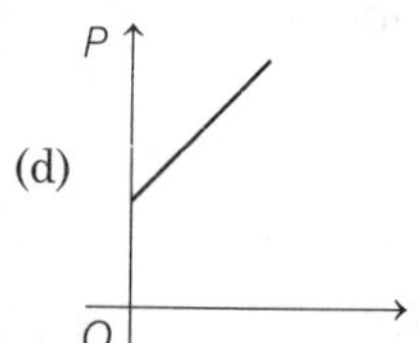

17. A ball is dropped at $t = 0$ from a height on a smooth elastic surface. Identify the graph which correctly represents the variation of kinetic energy K with time t.

(a) 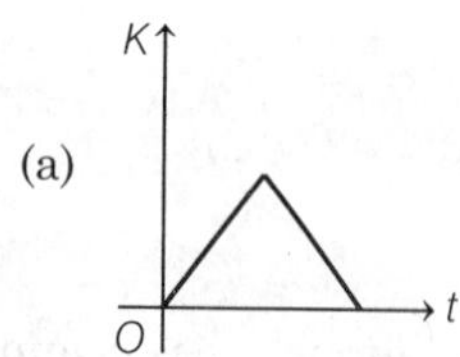

(b) 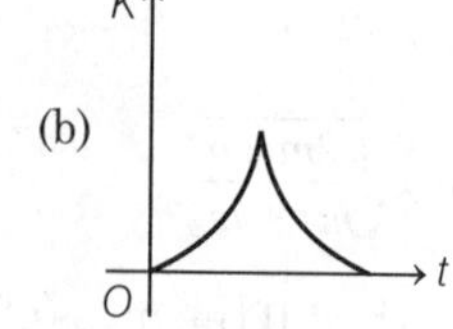

(c) 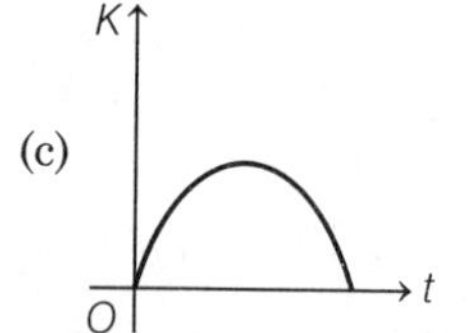

(d) 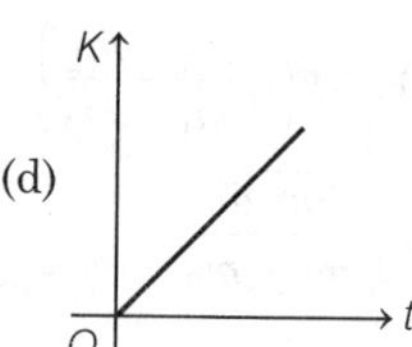

18. A block of mass 5 kg is raised from the bottom of the lake to a height of 3 m without change in kinetic energy at any instant. If the density of the block is 3000 kg m^{-3}, then the work done by the external force is equal to

(a) 100 J (b) 150 J (c) 50 J (d) 75 J

Note *Upthrust = (volume immersed) (density of liquid) (g)*

19. A body of mass m is projected at an angle θ with the horizontal with an initial velocity u. The average power of gravitational force over the whole time of flight is

(a) $mgu \cos\theta$ (b) $\frac{1}{2} mg \sqrt{u \cos\theta}$

(c) $\frac{1}{2} mgu \sin\theta$ (d) zero

20. A spring of force constant k is cut in two parts at its one-third length. When both the parts are stretched by same amount. The work done in the two parts will be

(a) equal in both (b) greater for the longer part

(c) greater for the shorter part (d) data insufficient

Note *Spring constant of a spring is inversely proportional to length of spring.*

21. A particle moves under the action of a force $\mathbf{F} = 20\hat{\mathbf{i}} + 15\hat{\mathbf{j}}$ along a straight line $3y + \alpha x = 5$, where, α is a constant. If the work done by the force F is zero, then the value of α is

(a) $\frac{4}{9}$ (b) $\frac{9}{4}$

(c) 3 (d) 4

22. A system of wedge and block as shown in figure, is released with the spring in its natural length. All surfaces are frictionless. Maximum elongation in the spring will be

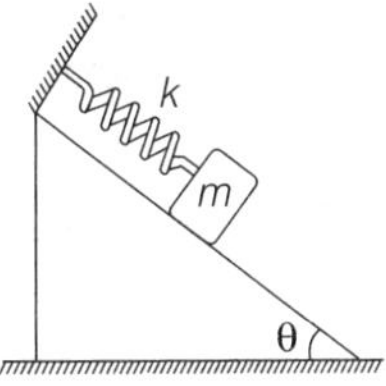

(a) $\frac{2\, mg \sin\theta}{k}$ (b) $\frac{mg \sin\theta}{k}$

(c) $\frac{4\, mg \sin\theta}{k}$ (d) $\frac{mg \sin\theta}{2k}$

23. A force $\mathbf{F} = (3t\,\hat{\mathbf{i}} + 5\,\hat{\mathbf{j}})\text{N}$ acts on a body due to which its displacement varies as $\mathbf{s} = (2t^2\,\hat{\mathbf{i}} - 5\hat{\mathbf{j}})\text{ m}$. Work done by this force in 2 second is

(a) 32 J (b) 24 J

(c) 46 J (d) 20 J

24. An open knife of mass m is dropped from a height h on a wooden floor. If the blade penetrates up to the depth d into the wood, the average resistance offered by the wood to the knife edge is

(a) $mg\left(1 + \frac{h}{d}\right)$ (b) $mg\left(1 + \frac{h}{d}\right)^2$

(c) $mg\left(1 - \frac{h}{d}\right)$ (d) $mg\left(1 + \frac{d}{h}\right)$

25. Two springs have force constants k_A and k_B such that $k_B = 2k_A$. The four ends of the springs are stretched by the same force. If energy stored in spring A is E, then energy stored in spring B is

(a) $\frac{E}{2}$ (b) $2E$

(c) E (d) $4E$

26. A block of mass m is connected with the wall of a toy car through a light spring of constant k. The toy car is moving with constant acceleration a_0 (neglect friction). The block is stationary with respect to car. Now, car is abruptly stopped. Then, maximum velocity of the block after stopping the car is

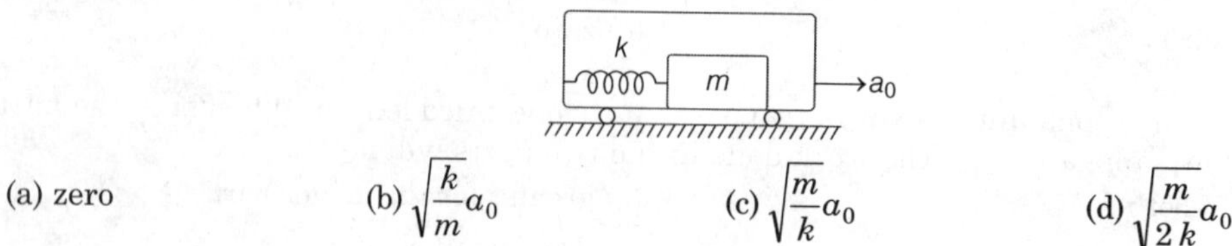

(a) zero (b) $\sqrt{\frac{k}{m}}a_0$ (c) $\sqrt{\frac{m}{k}}a_0$ (d) $\sqrt{\frac{m}{2k}}a_0$

27. A 2 kg block slides on a horizontal floor with a speed of 4 m/s. It strikes a uncompressed spring and compresses it till the block becomes motionless. The kinetic friction force is 15 N and spring constant is 10000 N/m. The spring compresses by

(a) 5.5 cm (b) 2.5 cm
(c) 11.0 cm (d) 8.5 cm

28. A body of mass 100 g is attached to a hanging spring whose force constant is 10 N/m. The body is lifted until the spring is in its unstretched state and then released. Calculate the speed of the body when it strikes the table 15 cm below the release point

(a) 1 m/s (b) 0.866 m/s (c) 0.225 m/s (d) 1.5 m/s

29. An ideal massless spring S can be compressed 1.0 m in equilibrium by a force of 100 N. This same spring is placed at the bottom of a friction less inclined plane which makes an angle $\theta = 30°$ with the horizontal. A 10 kg mass m is released from the rest at the top of the inclined plane and is brought to rest momentarily after compressing the spring by 2.0 m. The distance through which the mass moved before coming to rest is

(a) 8 m (b) 6 m (c) 4 m (d) 5 m

30. A body of mass m is released from a height h on a smooth inclined plane that is shown in the figure. The following can be true about the velocity of the block knowing that the wedge is fixed

(a) v is highest when it just touches the spring
(b) v is highest when it compresses the spring by some amount
(c) v is highest when the spring comes back to natural position
(d) v is highest at the maximum compression

31. A block of mass m is directly pulled up slowly on a smooth inclined plane of height h and inclination θ with the help of a string parallel to the incline. Which of the following statement is **incorrect** for the block when it moves up from the bottom to the top of the incline?

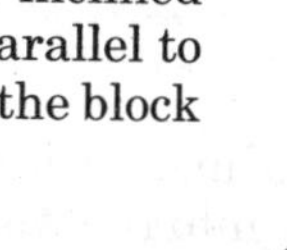

(a) Work done by the normal reaction force is zero
(b) Work done by the string is mgh
(c) Work done by gravity is mgh
(d) Net work done on the block is zero

32. A spring of natural length l is compressed vertically downward against the floor so that its compressed length becomes $\frac{l}{2}$. On releasing, the spring attains its natural length. If k is the stiffness constant of spring, then the work done by the spring on the floor is

(a) zero (b) $\frac{1}{2}kl^2$ (c) $\frac{1}{2}k\left(\frac{l}{2}\right)^2$ (d) kl^2

33. Two identical cylindrical vessels with their bases at the same level, each contains a liquid of density ρ. The height of the liquid in one vessel is h_1 and that in the other h_2. The area of either bases is A. The work done by the gravity in equalizing the levels when the vessels are interconnected is

(a) $A\rho g\left[\frac{(h_1-h_2)}{2}\right]$
(b) $A\rho g\left[\frac{(h_1+h_2)}{2}\right]^2$
(c) $A\rho g\left[\frac{(h_1-h_2)}{4}\right]$
(d) $A\rho g\left[\frac{(h_1-h_2)}{2}\right]^2$

34. The rate of doing work by force acting on a particle of mass m moving along x-axis depends on position x of particle and is equal to $2x$. The velocity of particle is given by expression

(a) $\left[\frac{3x^2}{m}\right]^{1/3}$
(b) $\left[\frac{3x^2}{2m}\right]^{1/3}$
(c) $\left(\frac{2mx}{9}\right)^{1/3}$
(d) $\left[\frac{mx^2}{3}\right]^{1/2}$

35. The kinetic energy of a projectile at its highest position is K. If the range of the projectile is four times the height of the projectile, then the initial kinetic energy of the projectile is

(a) $\sqrt{2}K$
(b) $2\,K$
(c) $4\,K$
(d) $2\sqrt{2}\,K$

36. A block of mass 10 kg is moving in x-direction with a constant speed of 10 m/s. It is subjected to a retarding force $F=-0.1x$ J/m during its travel from $x=20$ m to $x=30$ m. Its final kinetic energy will be

(a) 475 J (b) 450 J (c) 275 J (d) 250 J

37. A ball of mass 12 kg and another of mass 6 kg are dropped from a 60 feet tall building. After a fall of 30 feet each, towards earth, their kinetic energies will be in the ratio of

(a) $\sqrt{2}:1$
(b) $1:4$
(c) $2:1$
(d) $1:\sqrt{2}$

38. A spring of spring constant 5×10^3 N/m is stretched initially by 5 cm from the unstretched position. The work required to further stretch the spring by another 5 cm is

(a) 6.25 N-m
(b) 12.50 N-m
(c) 18.75 N-m
(d) 25.00 N-m

39. A uniform chain of length L and mass M is lying on a smooth table and one-third of its length is hanging vertically down over the edge of the table. If g is acceleration due to gravity, the work required to pull the hanging part on the table is

(a) MgL (b) $\frac{MgL}{3}$ (c) $\frac{MgL}{9}$ (d) $\frac{MgL}{18}$

40. A block of mass m moving with velocity v_0 on a smooth horizontal surface hits the spring of constant k as shown. The maximum compression in spring is

(a) 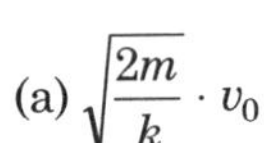 $\sqrt{\frac{2m}{k}}\cdot v_0$ (b) $\sqrt{\frac{m}{k}}\cdot v_0$ (c) $\sqrt{\frac{m}{2k}}\cdot v_0$ (d) $\frac{m}{2k}\cdot v_0$

41. A mass M is lowered with the help of a string by a distance x at a constant acceleration $\frac{g}{2}$. The magnitude of work done by the string will be

(a) Mgx (b) $\frac{1}{2}Mgx^2$ (c) $\frac{1}{2}Mgx$ (d) Mgx^2

42. A ball is released from the top of a tower. The ratio of work done by force of gravity in first, second and third second of the motion of ball is

(a) 1:2:3 (b) 1:4:9 (c) 1:3:5 (d) 1:9:25

43. An object of mass 5 kg is acted upon by a force that varies with position of the object as shown. If the object starts from rest at a point $x = 0$. What is its speed at $x = 50$ m ?

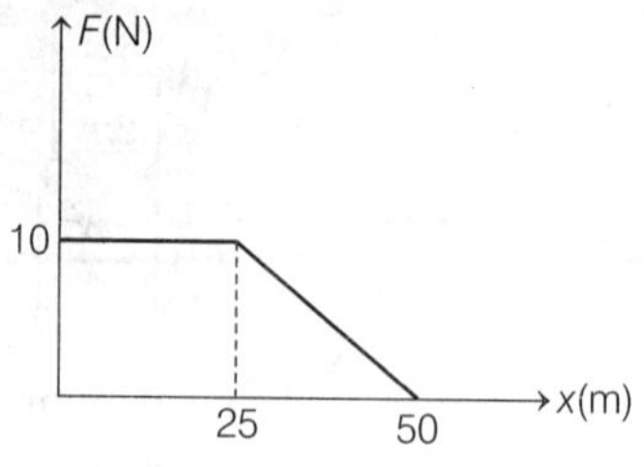

(a) 12.2 ms^{-1} (b) 18.2 ms^{-1} (c) 16.4 ms^{-1} (d) 20.4 ms^{-1}

44. A juggler keeps four balls in air. He throws each ball vertically upwards with the same speed at equal interval of time. The maximum height attained by each ball is 20 m. Find kinetic energy of first ball when fourth ball is in hand. Assume that the mass of each ball is 10 g.

(a) 0.5 J (b) 1 J
(c) 1.5 J (d) 2.5 J

45. A particle is moving in a conservative force field from point A to point B. U_A and U_B are the potential energies of the particle at points A and B and W_C is the work done by conservative forces in the process of taking the particle from A and B. Then,

(a) $W_C = U_B - U_A$ (b) $W_C = U_A - U_B$ (c) $U_A > U_B$ (d) $U_B > U_A$

46. A force $\left(\mathbf{F} = \frac{-ky}{\sqrt{x^2+y^2}}\hat{\mathbf{i}} + \frac{kx}{\sqrt{x^2+y^2}}\hat{\mathbf{j}}\right)$ N is applied on a block, whose position is $P(x, y)$. The block moves on a circular path of radius R. Find the work done by the force **F** in a complete rotation.

(a) $2\pi Rk$ (b) πRk (c) $4\pi Rk$ (d) Zero

47. If v be the instantaneous velocity of the body dropped from the top of a tower, when it is located at height h, then which of the following remains constant?

(a) $gh + v^2$ (b) $gh + \frac{v^2}{2}$ (c) $gh - \frac{v^2}{2}$ (d) $gh - v^2$

48. A pendulum of length 2 m is left from A. When it reaches B, it loses 10% of its total energy due to air resistance. The velocity at B is

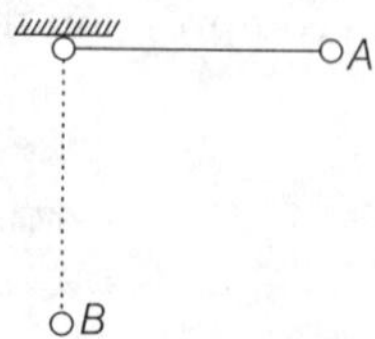

(a) 6 m/s (b) 1 m/s (c) 2 m/s (d) 8 m/s

49. A block of mass m is pulled along a horizontal surface by applying a force at an angle θ with the horizontal. If the block travels with a uniform velocity and has a displacement d and the coefficient of friction is μ, then the work done by the applied force is

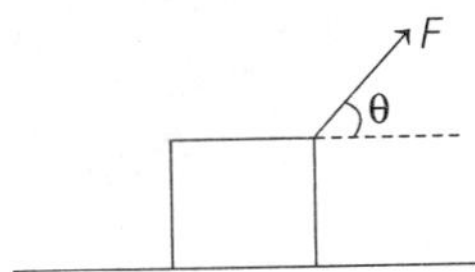

(a) $\dfrac{\mu mgd}{\cos\theta + \mu\sin\theta}$
(b) $\dfrac{\mu mgd\cos\theta}{\cos\theta + \mu\sin\theta}$
(c) $\dfrac{\mu mgd\sin\theta}{\cos\theta + \mu\sin\theta}$
(d) $\dfrac{\mu mgd\cos\theta}{\cos\theta - \mu\sin\theta}$

50. A plank of mass 10 kg and a block of mass 2 kg are placed on a horizontal plane as shown in the figure. There is no friction between plane and plank. The coefficient of friction between block and plank is 0.5. A force of 60 N is applied on plank horizontally. In first 2 s, the work done by friction on the block is

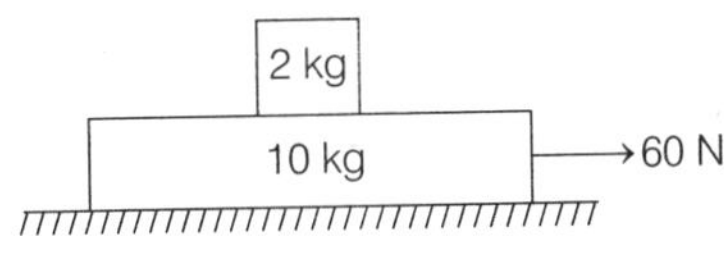

(a) – 100 J
(b) 100 J
(c) zero
(d) 200 J

51. A particle moves on a rough horizontal ground with some initial velocity say v_0. If $\left(\dfrac{3}{4}\right)$th of its kinetic energy is lost due to friction in time t_0, then coefficient of friction between the particle and the ground is

(a) $\dfrac{v_0}{2gt_0}$
(b) $\dfrac{v_0}{4gt_0}$
(c) $\dfrac{3v_0}{4gt_0}$
(d) $\dfrac{v_0}{gt_0}$

52. The net work done by the tension in the figure when the bigger block of mass M touches the ground is

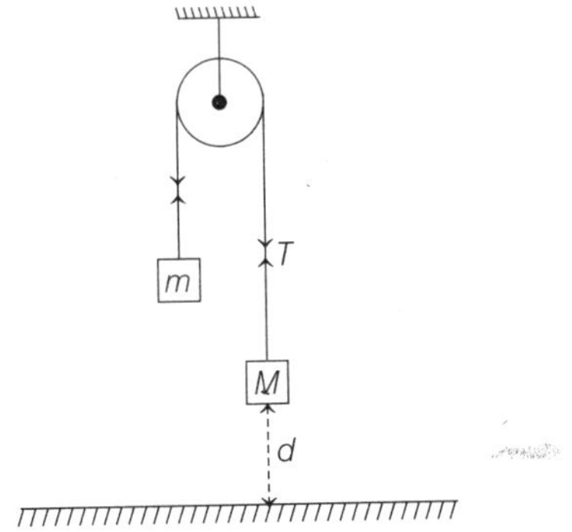

(a) $+ Mgd$
(b) $-(M+m)gd$
(c) $-mgd$
(d) zero

53. A particle at rest on a frictionless table is acted upon by a horizontal force which is constant in magnitude and direction. A graph is plotted of the work done on the particle W, against the speed of the particle v. If there are no frictional forces acting on the particle, the graph will look like

(a)
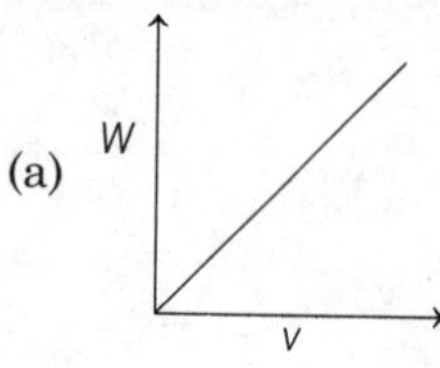

(b)
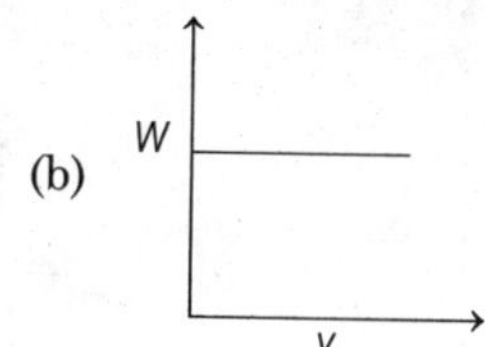

(c)
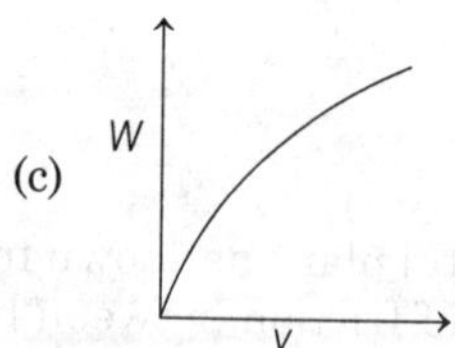

(d)
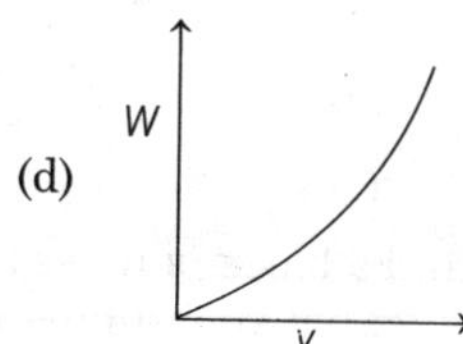

54. A body moves from rest with a constant acceleration. Which one of the following graphs represents the variation of its kinetic energy K with the distance travelled x?

(a)
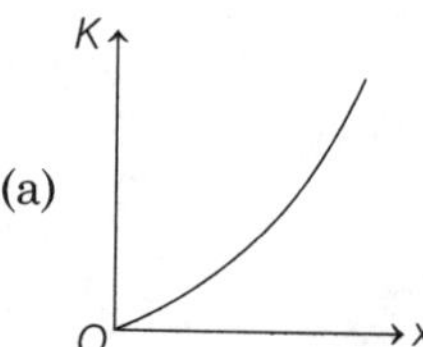

(b)
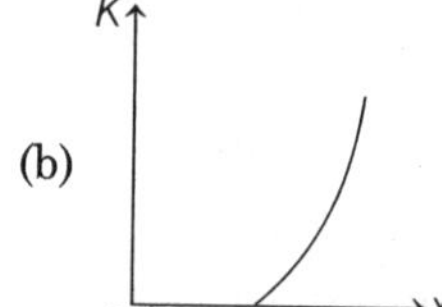

(c)
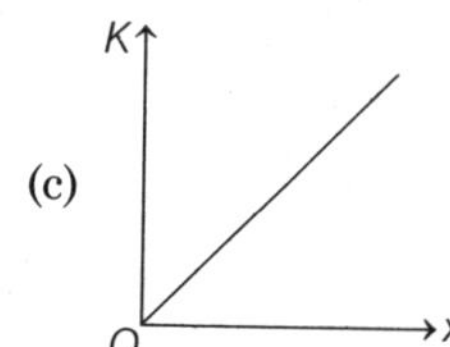

(d)
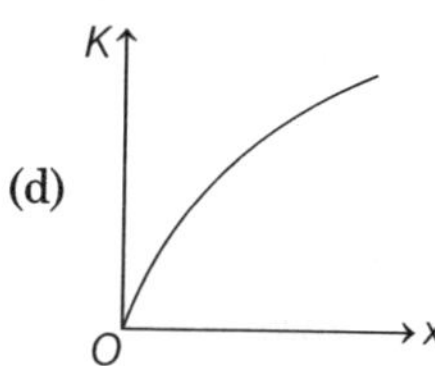

55. The pointer reading *versus* load graph for a spring balance is as shown

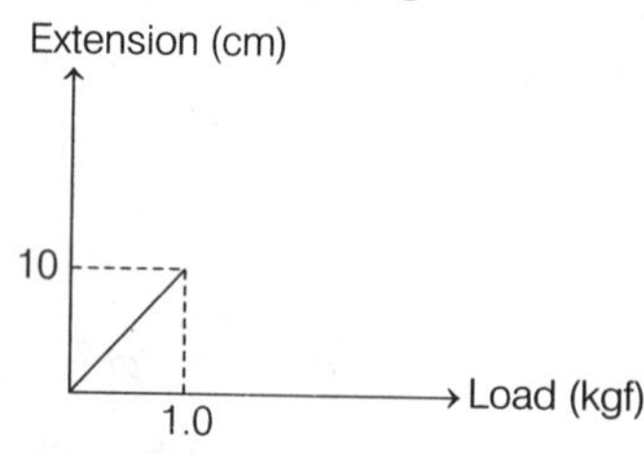

The spring constant is

(a) $\frac{15 \text{ kgf}}{\text{cm}}$
(b) $\frac{5 \text{ kgf}}{\text{cm}}$
(c) $\frac{0.1 \text{ kgf}}{\text{cm}}$
(d) $\frac{10 \text{ kgf}}{\text{cm}}$

56. v-t graph of an object of mass 1 kg is shown. Select the **wrong** statement.

(a) Work done on the object in 30 s is zero
(b) The average acceleration of the object is zero
(c) The average velocity of the object is zero
(d) The average force on the object is zero

57. If v, p and E denote velocity, linear momentum and KE of the particle, then

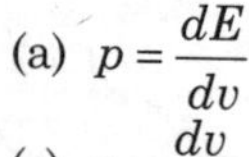
(a) $p = \frac{dE}{dv}$
(b) $p = \frac{dE}{dt}$
(c) $p = \frac{dv}{dt}$
(d) $p = \frac{dE}{dv} \times \frac{dE}{dt}$

58. The force required to stretch a spring varies with the distance as shown in the figure. If the experiment is performed with the above spring of half the length, the line OA will

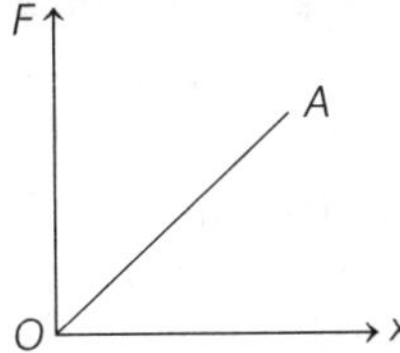

(a) shift towards F-axis
(b) shift towards x-axis
(c) remain as it is
(d) become double in length

59. Kinetic energy of a particle moving in a straight line varies with time t as $K = 4t^2$. The force acting on the particle

(a) is constant
(b) is increasing
(c) is decreasing
(d) first increases and then decreases

60. The figures shows a particle sliding on a frictionless track, which terminates in a straight horizontal section. If the particle starts slipping from the point A, how far away from the track will the particle hit the ground?

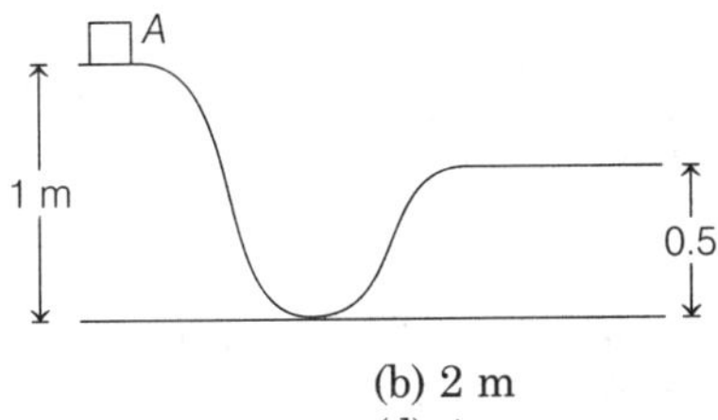

(a) 1 m
(b) 2 m
(c) 3 m
(d) 4 m

61. A block of mass m is attached to two unstretched springs of spring constants k each as shown. The block is displaced towards right through a distance x and is released. The speed of the block as it passes through the mean position will be

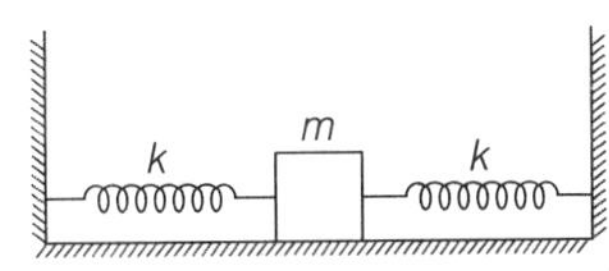

(a) $x\sqrt{\frac{m}{2k}}$
(b) $x\sqrt{\frac{2k}{m}}$
(c) $x\frac{m}{k}$
(d) $x\frac{2k}{m}$

62. The figure shows a smooth curved track terminating in a smooth horizontal part. A spring of spring constant 400 N/m is attached at one end to a wedge fixed rigidly with the horizontal part. A 40 g mass is released from rest at a height of 5 m on the curved track. The maximum compression of the spring will be

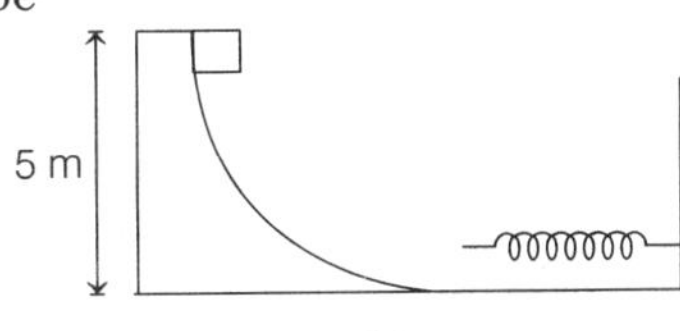

(a) 10 cm
(b) 2 cm
(c) 3 cm
(d) 4 cm

63. A bullet moving with a speed of 100 m/s can just penetrate two planks of equal thickness. Then, the number of such planks penetrated by the same bullet when the speed of bullet is doubled.

(a) 4 (b) 8
(c) 6 (d) 10

Hint : Assume same retardation.

64. A spring of force constant k is first stretched by distance a from its natural length and then further by distance b. The work done in stretching the part b is

(a) $\frac{1}{2}ka(a-b)$ (b) $\frac{1}{2}ka(a+b)$
(c) $\frac{1}{2}kb(a-b)$ (d) $\frac{1}{2}kb(2a+b)$

65. A block of mass 1 kg is projected from point A along irregular rough inclined surface and reaches at the point B as shown in the figure. The coefficient of friction between the block and the inclined plane is 0.5. Find work done by the friction on the block, if $AC = 1$ m.

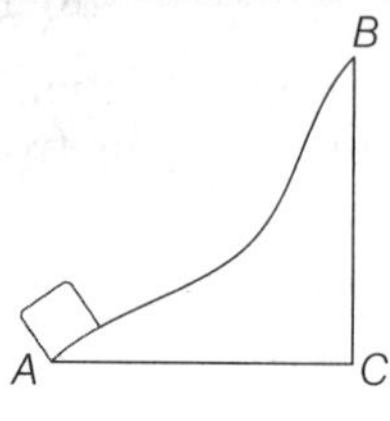

(a) −1 J (b) −2 J
(c) −4 J (d) −5 J

66. A block of mass 1 kg is connected with a fixed wall through a light spring of constant $k = 100$ N/m. The surfaces are frictionless. Initially, spring is in relaxed position. A horizontal force F of 50 N is applied on the block. Find the maximum elongation of the spring.

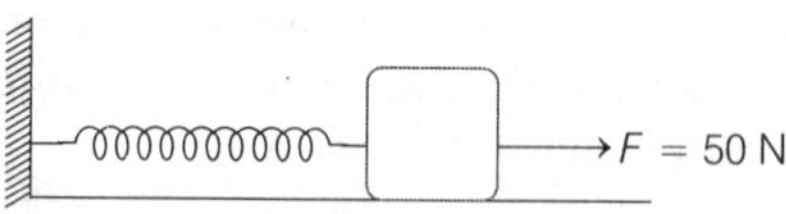

(a) 1 m (b) 0.5 m
(c) 0.25 m (d) 0.1 m

67. In previous problem, find maximum speed of the block during the motion of the block.

(a) 1 m/s (b) 2 m/s
(c) 5 m/s (d) 10 m/s

68. Two blocks each of mass 1 kg are connected by a light spring of spring constant $k = 100$ N/m. When spring is in natural length, each block is projected in opposite direction with speed of 10 m/s. The work done by spring on each block upto maximum compression is

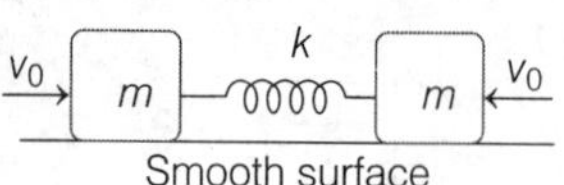

(a) 100 J (b) – 100 J
(c) 50 J (d) – 50 J

Subjective Questions

1. Momentum of a particle is increased by 50%. By how much percentage kinetic energy of particle will increase ?

2. Kinetic energy of a particle is increased by 1%. By how much percentage momentum of the particle will increase ?

3. Two equal masses are attached to the two ends of a spring of force constant k. The masses are pulled out symmetrically to stretch the spring by a length $2x_0$ over its natural length. Find the work done by the spring on each mass.

4. A particle is pulled a distance l up a rough plane inclined at an angle α to the horizontal by a string inclined at an angle β to the plane ($\alpha + \beta < 90°$). If the tension in the string is T, the normal reaction between the particle and the plane is N, the frictional force is F and the weight of the particle is w. Write down expressions for the work done by each of these forces.

5. A helicopter lifts a 72 kg astronaut 15 m vertically from the ocean by means of a cable. The acceleration of the astronaut is $\frac{g}{10}$. How much work is done on the astronaut by (Take, $g = 9.8 \text{ m/s}^2$)
   (a) the force from the helicopter and
   (b) the gravitational force on her ?
   (c) What are the kinetic energy and
   (d) the speed of the astronaut just before she reaches the helicopter ?

6. A 1.5 kg block is initially at rest on a horizontal frictionless surface when a horizontal force in the positive direction of x-axis is applied to the block. The force is given by $\mathbf{F}(x) = (2.5 - x^2)\hat{\mathbf{i}}$ N, where, x is in metre and the initial position of the block is $x = 0$.
   (a) What is the kinetic energy of the block as it passes through $x = 2.0$ m ?
   (b) What is the maximum kinetic energy of the block between $x = 0$ and $x = 2.0$ m ?

7. A small block of mass 1 kg is kept on a rough inclined wedge of inclination 45° fixed in an elevator. The elevator goes up with a uniform velocity $v = 2$ m/s and the block does not slide on the wedge. Find the work done by the force of friction on the block in 1 s. (Take, $g = 10 \text{ m/s}^2$)

8. Two masses $m_1 = 10$ kg and $m_2 = 5$ kg are connected by an ideal string as shown in the figure. The coefficient of friction between m_1 and the surface is $\mu = 0.2$. Assuming that the system is released from rest. Calculate the velocity of blocks when m_2 has descended by 4 m. (Take, $g = 10 \text{ m/s}^2$)

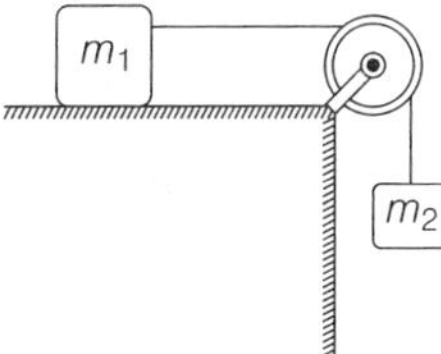

9. A smooth sphere of radius R is made to translate in a straight line with a constant acceleration $a = g$. A particle kept on the top of the sphere is released from there at zero velocity with respect to the sphere. Find the speed of the particle with respect to the sphere as a function of angle θ as it slides down.

10. In the arrangement shown in figure $m_A = 4.0$ kg and $m_B = 1.0$ kg. The system is released from rest and block B is found to have a speed 0.3 m/s after it has descended through a distance of 1 m. Find the coefficient of friction between the block and the table. Neglect friction elsewhere. (Take, $g = 10\ \text{m/s}^2$)

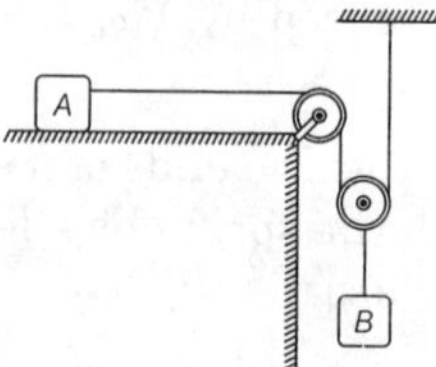

11. In the figure, block A is released from rest when the spring is in its natural length. For the block B of mass m to leave contact with the ground at some stage what should be the minimum mass of block A?

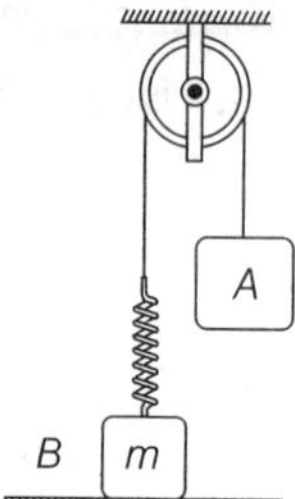

12. As shown in figure a smooth rod is mounted just above a table top. A 10 kg collar, which is able to slide on the rod with negligible friction is fastened to a spring whose other end is attached to a pivot at O. The spring has negligible mass, a relaxed length of 10 cm and a spring constant of 500 N/m. The collar is released from rest at point A. (a) What is its velocity as it passes point B? (b) Repeat for point C.

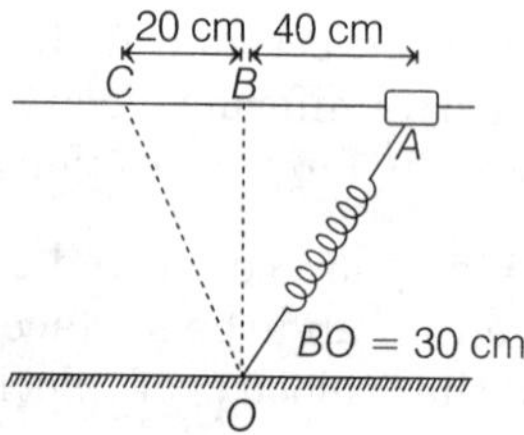

13. A block of mass m is attached with a massless spring of force constant K. The block is placed over a rough inclined surface for which the coefficient of friction is $\mu = \frac{3}{4}$. Find the minimum value of M required to move the block up the plane. (Neglect mass of string and pulley. Ignore friction in pulley).

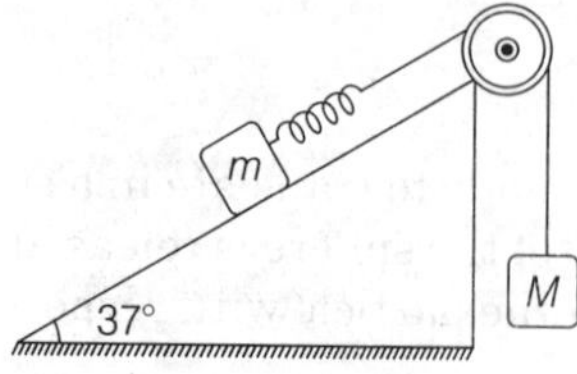

14. A block of mass 2 kg is released from rest on a rough inclined ground as shown in figure. Find the work done on the block by

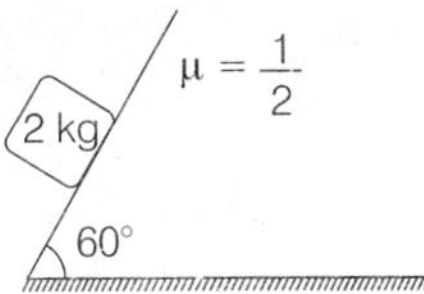

(a) gravity,
(b) force of friction

when the block is displaced downwards along the plane by 2 m. (Take, $g = 10 \text{ m/s}^2$)

15. The potential energy of a two particle system separated by a distance r is given by $U(r) = \frac{A}{r}$, where A is a constant. Find the radial force F_r, that each particle exerts on the other.

Integer Type Questions

16. A single conservative force F_x acts on a 2 kg particle that moves along the x-axis. The potential energy is given by $U = (x - 4)^2 - 16$.

Here, x is in metre and U in joule. At $x = 6.0$ m, kinetic energy of particle is 8 J. Find
(a) total mechanical energy
(b) maximum kinetic energy
(c) values of x between which particle moves
(d) the equation of F_x as a function of x
(e) the value of x at which F_x is zero

17. A 4 kg block is on a smooth horizontal table. The block is connected to a second block of mass 1 kg by a massless flexible taut cord that passes over a frictionless pulley. The 1 kg block is 1 m above the floor. The two blocks are released from rest. With what speed does the 1 kg block hit the ground ?

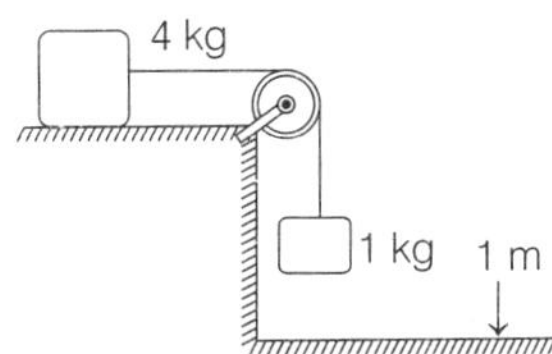

18. Block A has a weight of 300 N and block B has a weight of 50 N. Determine the distance that A must descend from rest before it obtains a speed of 2.5 m/s. Neglect the mass of the cord and pulleys. (Take $g = 9.8 \text{ m/s}^2$)

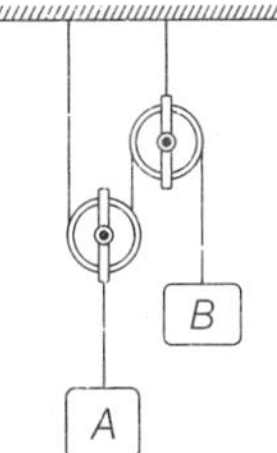

19. A sphere of mass m held at a height $2R$ between a wedge of same mass m and a rigid wall, is released from rest. Assuming that all the surfaces are frictionless. Find the speed of both the bodies when the sphere hits the ground.

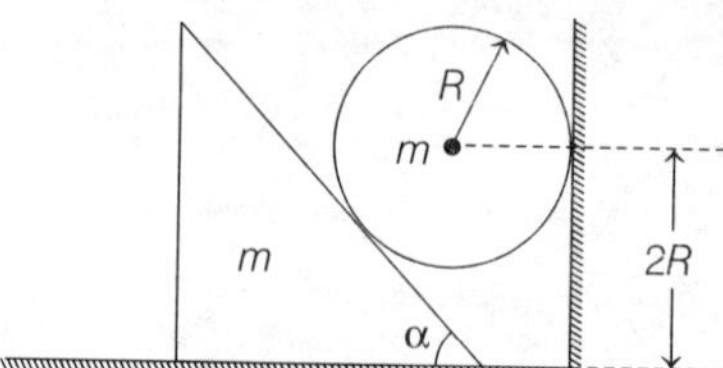

20. The system is released from rest with the spring initially stretched 75 mm. Calculate the velocity v of the block after it has dropped 12 mm. The spring has a stiffness of 1050 N/m. Neglect the mass of the small pulley.

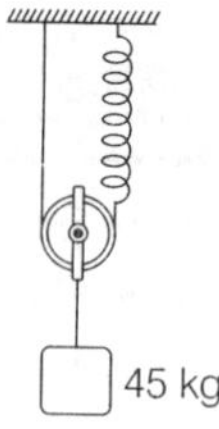

21. A disc of mass 50 g slides with zero initial velocity down an inclined plane set at an angle 30° to the horizontal. Having traversed a distance of 50 cm along the horizontal plane, the disc stops. Find the work performed by the friction forces over the whole distance, assuming the friction coefficient 0.15 for both inclined and horizontal planes. (Take, $g = 10\,\text{m/s}^2$)

22. Block A has a weight of 300 N and block B has a weight of 50 N. If the coefficient of kinetic friction between the incline and block A is $\mu_k = 0.2$. Determine the speed of block A after it moves 1 m down the plane, starting from rest. Neglect the mass of the cord and pulleys.

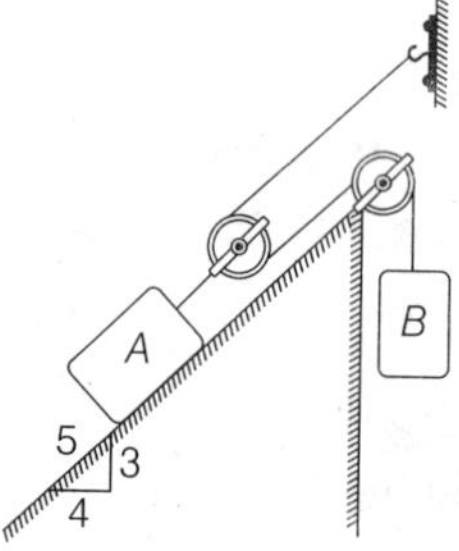

23. Figure shows a 3.5 kg block accelerated by a compressed spring whose spring constant is 640 N/m. After leaving the spring at the spring's relaxed length, the block travels over a horizontal surface, with a coefficient of kinetic friction of 0.25, for a distance of 7.8 m before stopping. (Take, $g = 9.8\,\text{m/s}^2$)

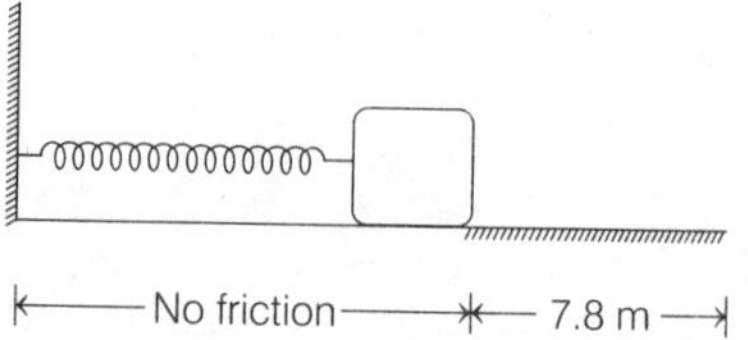

(a) What is the increase in the thermal energy of the block-floor system ?

(b) What is the maximum kinetic energy of the block ?

(c) Through what distance is the spring compressed before the block begins to move ?

LEVEL 2

Objective Questions

Single Correct Option

1. A bead of mass $\frac{1}{2}$ kg starts from rest from A to move in a vertical plane along a smooth fixed quarter ring of radius 5 m, under the action of a constant horizontal force $F = 5\,\text{N}$ as shown. The speed of bead as it reaches the point B is (Take, $g = 10\ \text{ms}^{-2}$)

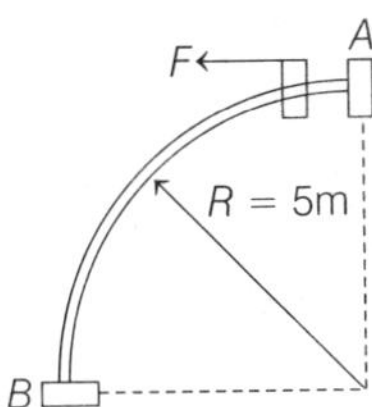

(a) $14.14\ \text{ms}^{-1}$
(b) $7.07\ \text{ms}^{-1}$
(c) $4\ \text{ms}^{-1}$
(d) $25\ \text{ms}^{-1}$

2. A car of mass m is accelerating on a level smooth road under the action of a single force F. The power delivered to the car is constant and equal to P. If the velocity of the car at an instant is v, then after travelling how much distance it becomes double?

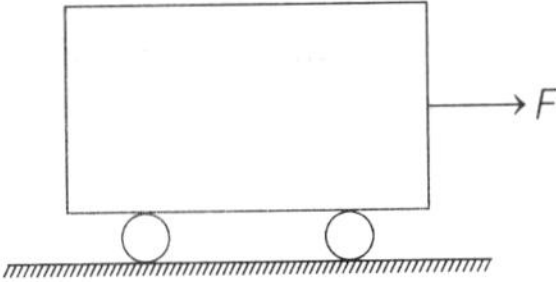

(a) $\frac{7mv^3}{3P}$
(b) $\frac{4mv^3}{3P}$
(c) $\frac{mv^3}{P}$
(d) $\frac{18mv^3}{7P}$

3. An ideal massless spring S can be compressed 1 m by a force of 100 N in equilibrium. The same spring is placed at the bottom of a frictionless inclined plane inclined at 30° to the horizontal. A 10 kg block M is released from rest at the top of the incline and is brought to rest momentarily after compressing the spring by 2 m. If $g = 10\ \text{ms}^{-2}$, what is the speed of mass just before it touches the spring?

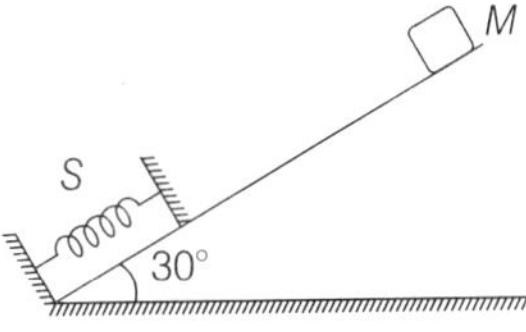

(a) $\sqrt{20}\ \text{ms}^{-1}$
(b) $\sqrt{30}\ \text{ms}^{-1}$
(c) $\sqrt{10}\ \text{ms}^{-1}$
(d) $\sqrt{40}\ \text{ms}^{-1}$

4. A smooth chain AB of mass m rests against a surface in the form of a quarter of a circle of radius R. If it is released from rest, the velocity of the chain after it comes over the horizontal part of the surface is

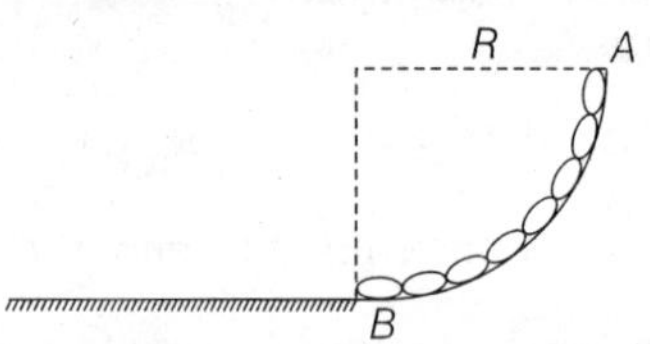

(a) $\sqrt{2gR}$ (b) $\sqrt{gR}$ (c) $\sqrt{2gR\left(1-\frac{2}{\pi}\right)}$ (d) $\sqrt{2gR\,(2-\pi)}$

5. In the diagram shown, the blocks A and B are of the same mass M and the mass of the block C is M_1. Friction is present only under the block A. The whole system is suddenly released from the state of rest. The minimum coefficient of friction to keep the block A in the state of rest is equal to

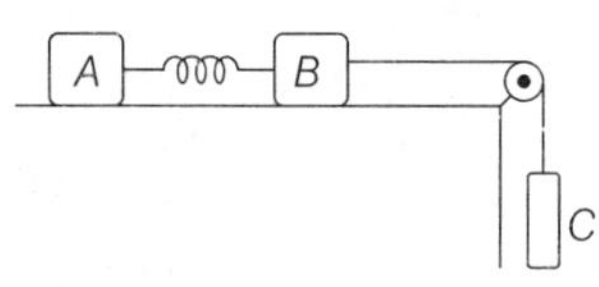

(a) $\frac{M_1}{M}$ (b) $\frac{2M_1}{M}$ (c) $\frac{M_1}{2M}$ (d) None of these

6. A body is moving down an inclined plane of slope 37°. The coefficient of friction between the body and the plane varies as $\mu = 0.3\,x$, where x is the distance traveled down the plane by the body. The body will have maximum speed. $\left(\text{Take, } \sin 37° = \frac{3}{5}\right)$

(a) at $x = 1.16$ m (b) at $x = 2$ m
(c) at bottommost point of the plane (d) at $x = 2.5$ m

7. The given plot shows the variation of U, the potential energy of interaction between two particles with the distance separating them r.

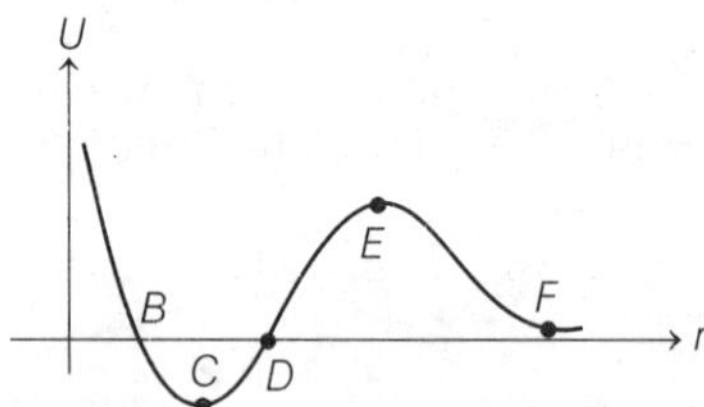

1. B and D are equilibrium points
2. C is a point of stable equilibrium
3. The force of interaction between the two particles is attractive between points C and D and repulsive between D and E
4. The force of interaction between particles is repulsive between points E and F.

Which of the above statements are correct?

(a) 1 and 2 (b) 1 and 4
(c) 2 and 4 (d) 2 and 3

8. A block of mass m is attached to one end of a mass less spring of spring constant k. The other end of spring is fixed to a wall. The block can move on a horizontal rough surface. The coefficient of friction between the block and the surface is μ. Then, the compression of the spring for which maximum extension of the spring becomes half of maximum compression is

(a) $\frac{2mg\mu}{k}$ (b) $\frac{mg\mu}{k}$

(c) $\frac{4\,mg\mu}{k}$ (d) None of these

9. The potential energy ϕ in joule of a particle of mass 1 kg moving in x-y plane obeys the law, $\phi = 3x + 4y$. Here, x and y are in metres. If the particle is at rest at (6m, 8m) at time 0, then the work done by conservative force on the particle from the initial position to the instant when it crosses the x-axis is

(a) 25 J (b) – 25 J

(c) 50 J (d) – 50 J

10. A small mass slides down an inclined plane of inclination θ with the horizontal. The coefficient of friction is $\mu = \mu_0 x$, where x is the distance through which the mass slides down and μ_0 a positive constant. Then, the distance covered by the mass before it stops is

(a) $\frac{2}{\mu_0}\tan\theta$ (b) $\frac{4}{\mu_0}\tan\theta$

(c) $\frac{1}{2\mu_0}\tan\theta$ (d) $\frac{1}{\mu_0}\tan\theta$

11. The potential energy function for a diatomic molecule is $U(x) = \frac{a}{x^{12}} - \frac{b}{x^6}$. In stable equilibrium, the distance between the particles is

(a) $\left(\frac{2a}{b}\right)^{1/6}$ (b) $\left(\frac{a}{b}\right)^{1/6}$ (c) $\left(\frac{b}{2a}\right)^{1/6}$ (d) $\left(\frac{b}{a}\right)^{1/6}$

12. A rod of mass M hinged at O is kept in equilibrium with a spring of stiffness k as shown in figure. The potential energy stored in the spring is

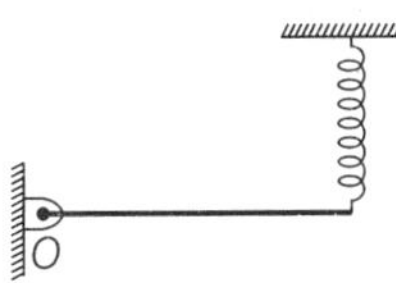

(a) $\frac{(mg)^2}{4k}$ (b) $\frac{(mg)^2}{2k}$

(c) $\frac{(mg)^2}{8k}$ (d) $\frac{(mg)^2}{k}$

13. Equal net forces act on two different blocks A and B of masses m and $4m$, respectively. For same displacement, identify the correct statement.

(a) Their kinetic energies are in the ratio $\frac{K_A}{K_B} = \frac{1}{4}$

(b) Their speeds are in the ratio $\frac{v_A}{v_B} = \frac{1}{1}$

(c) Work done on the blocks are in the ratio $\frac{W_A}{W_B} = \frac{1}{1}$

(d) All of the above

14. The potential energy function of a particle in the x-y plane is given by $U = k(x + y)$, where k is a constant. The work done by the conservative force in moving a particle from (1, 1) to (2, 3) is
(a) $-3k$ (b) $+3k$ (c) k (d) None of these

15. A vertical spring is fixed to one of its end and a massless plank fitted to the other end. A block is released from a height h as shown. Spring is in relaxed position. Then, choose the correct statement.

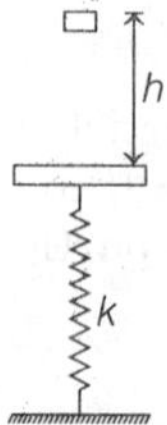

(a) The maximum compression of the spring does not depend on h
(b) The maximum kinetic energy of the block does not depend on h
(c) The compression of the spring at maximum KE of the block does not depend on h
(d) The maximum compression of the spring does not depend on k

16. A uniform chain of length πr lies inside a smooth semicircular tube AB of radius r. Assuming a slight disturbance to start the chain in motion, the velocity with which it will emerge from the end B of the tube will be

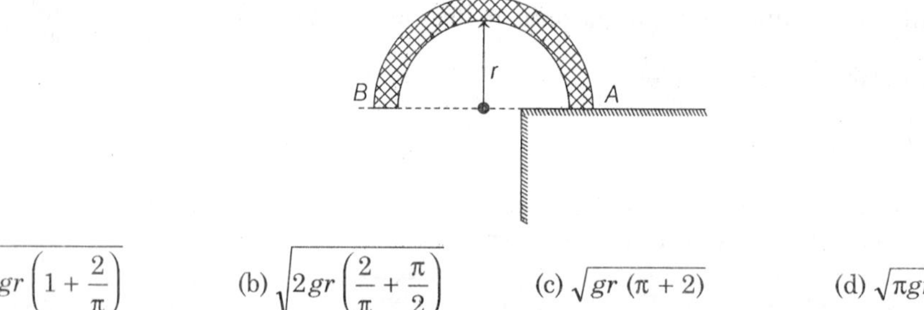

(a) $\sqrt{gr\left(1+\frac{2}{\pi}\right)}$ (b) $\sqrt{2gr\left(\frac{2}{\pi}+\frac{\pi}{2}\right)}$ (c) $\sqrt{gr(\pi+2)}$ (d) $\sqrt{\pi gr}$

17. Two blocks are connected to an ideal spring of stiffness 200 N/m. At a certain moment, the two blocks are moving in opposite directions with speeds 4 ms^{-1} and 6 ms^{-1}, and the instantaneous elongation of the spring is 10 cm. The rate at which the spring energy $\left(\frac{kx^2}{2}\right)$ is increasing is
(a) 500 J/s (b) 400 J/s (c) 200 J/s (d) 100 J/s

18. A block A of mass 45 kg is placed on another block B of mass 123 kg. Now, block B is displaced by external agent by 50 cm horizontally towards right. During the same time, block A just reaches to the left end of block B. Initial and final positions are shown in figures. The work done on block A in ground frame is

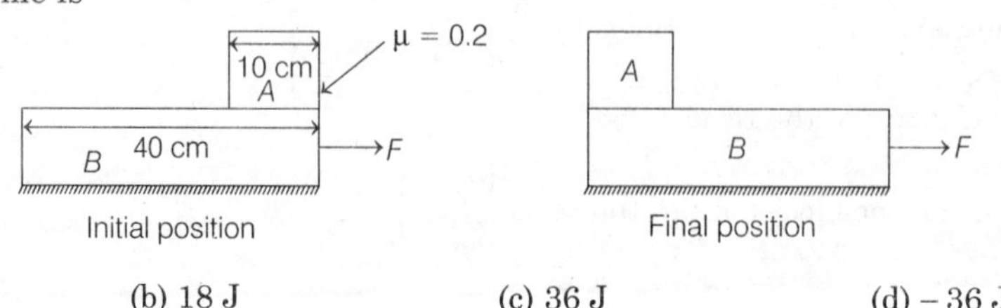

(a) -18 J (b) 18 J (c) 36 J (d) -36 J

19. A block of mass 10 kg is released on a fixed wedge inside a cart which is moving with constant velocity 10 ms^{-1} towards right. There is no relative motion between block and cart. Then, work done by normal reaction on block in two seconds from ground frame will be (Take, $g = 10\ ms^{-2}$)

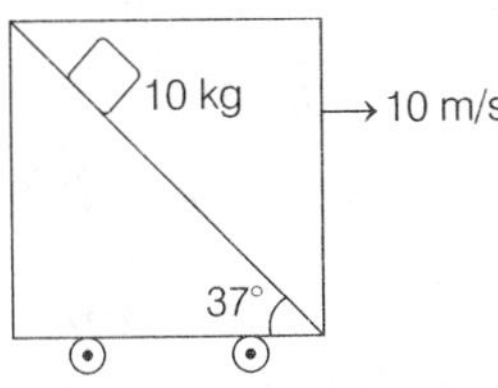

(a) 1320 J
(b) 960 J
(c) 1200 J
(d) 240 J

20. A block tied between two identical springs is in equilibrium. If upper spring is cut, then the acceleration of the block just after cut is 5 ms^{-2}. Now, if instead of upper spring lower spring is cut, then the acceleration of the block just after the cut will be (Take, $g = 10\ m/s^2$)

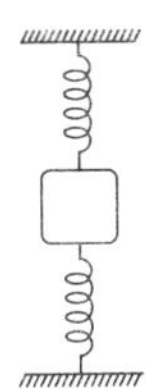

(a) 1.25 ms^{-2}
(b) 5 ms^{-2}
(c) 10 ms^{-2}
(d) 2.5 ms^{-2}

21. A particle of mass 1 g executes an oscillatory motion on the concave surface of a spherical dish of radius 2 m placed on a horizontal plane. If the motion of the particle begins from a point on the dish at a height of 1 cm from the horizontal plane and the coefficient of friction is 0.01, the total distance covered by the particle before it comes to rest, is approximately

(a) 2.0 m
(b) 10.0 m
(c) 1.0 m
(d) 20.0 m

22. A uniform flexible chain of mass m and length l hangs in equilibrium over a smooth horizontal pin of negligible diameter. One end of the chain is given a small vertical displacement so that the chain slips over the pin. The speed of chain when it leaves pin is

(a) $\sqrt{\frac{gl}{2}}$
(b) $\sqrt{gl}$
(c) $\sqrt{2gl}$
(d) $\sqrt{3gl}$

23. When a rubber band is stretched by a distance x, it exerts a restoring force of magnitude $F = ax + bx^2$, where a and b are constants. The work done in stretching the unstretched rubber band by L is

(a) $aL^2 + bL^3$
(b) $\frac{1}{2}(aL^2 + bL^3)$
(c) $\frac{aL^2}{2} + \frac{bL^3}{3}$
(d) $\frac{1}{2}\left(\frac{aL^2}{2} + \frac{bL^3}{3}\right)$

24. A pendulum of mass 1 kg and length $l = 1$ m is released from rest at angle $\theta = 60°$. The power delivered by all the forces acting on the bob at angle $\theta = 30°$ will be (Take, $g = 10\ m/s^2$).

(a) 13.4 W
(b) 20.4 W
(c) 24.6 W
(d) zero

25. A block A of mass M rests on a wedge B of mass $2M$ and inclination θ. There is sufficient friction between A and B so that A does not slip on B. If there is no friction between B and ground, the compression in spring is

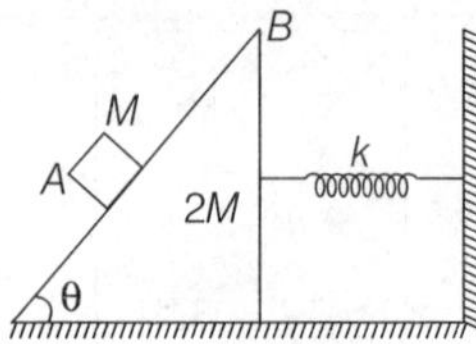

(a) $\dfrac{Mg\cos\theta}{k}$ (b) $\dfrac{Mg\cos\theta\sin\theta}{k}$

(c) $\dfrac{Mg\sin\theta}{k}$ (d) zero

26. A block of mass 10 kg is placed on a rough inclined plane of inclination 37° with horizontal. Now, the block is released. The work done by the gravitational force and friction force, when the block moves from A to B(Take, sin 37° = 0.6, cos 37° = 0.8)

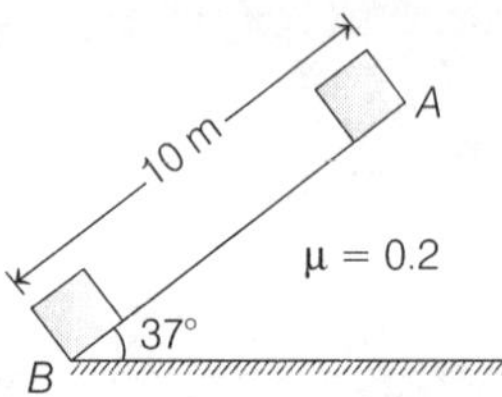

(a) 600 J, 160 J (b) −600 J, 160 J

(c) 600 J, −160 J (d) −600 J, −160 J

27. A particle moves in a straight line with retardation proportional to its displacement. Its loss of kinetic energy in any displacement x is proportional to

(a) x^2 (b) e^x (c) x (d) $\log_e x$

28. The potential energy of a 1 kg particle free to move along the x-axis is given by

$$V(x) = \left(\frac{x^4}{4} - \frac{x^2}{2}\right) \text{J}$$

The total mechanical energy of the particle is 2 J. Then, the maximum speed (in m/s) is

(a) $\sqrt{2}$ (b) $1/\sqrt{2}$ (c) 2 (d) $3/\sqrt{2}$

29. A block (B) is attached to two unstretched springs S_1 and S_2 with spring constants k and $4k$, respectively. The other ends are attached to two supports. M_1 and M_2 not attached to the walls. The springs and supports have negligible mass. There is no friction anywhere.

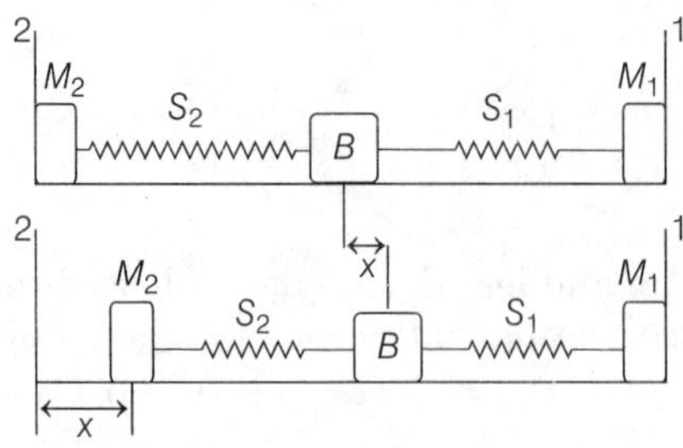

The block B is displaced towards wall 1 by a small distance x and released. The block returns and moves a maximum distance y towards wall 2. Displacements x and y are measured with respect to the equilibrium position of the block B. The ratio $\frac{y}{x}$ is

(a) 4 (b) 2 (c) $\frac{1}{2}$ (d) $\frac{1}{4}$

30. A block of mass 2 kg is free to move along the x-axis. Initiallly, it is at rest and from $t = 0$ onwards it is subjected to a time-dependent force $F(t)$ in the x-direction. The force $F(t)$ varies with t as shown in the figure. The kinetic energy of the block after 4.5 s is

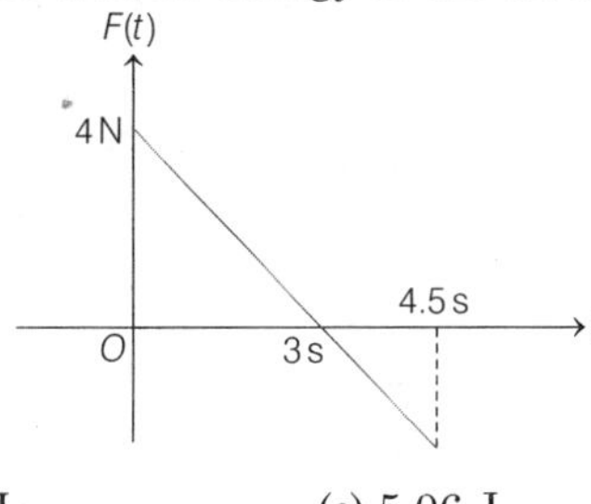

(a) 4.50 J (b) 7.50 J (c) 5.06 J (d) 14.06 J

More than One Correct Options

1. The potential energy of a particle of mass 5 kg moving in xy-plane is given as $U = (7x + 24y)$ joule, x and y being in metre. Initially at $t = 0$, the particle is at the origin (0, 0) moving with a velocity of $(8.6\hat{\mathbf{i}} + 23.2\,\hat{\mathbf{j}})\ \text{ms}^{-1}$. Then,

(a) the velocity of the particle at $t = 4$ s, is $5\ \text{ms}^{-1}$
(b) the acceleration of the particle is $5\ \text{ms}^{-2}$
(c) the direction of motion of the particle initially (at $t = 0$) is at right angles to the direction of acceleration
(d) the path of the particle is circle

2. The potential energy of a particle is given by formula $U = 100 - 5x + 100x^2$, where U and x are in SI units. If mass of the particle is 0.1 kg, then magnitude of it's acceleration

(a) At 0.05 m from the origin is $50\ \text{ms}^{-2}$
(b) At 0.05 m from the mean position is $100\ \text{ms}^{-2}$
(c) At 0.05 m from the origin is $150\ \text{ms}^{-2}$
(d) At 0.05 m from the mean position is $200\ \text{ms}^{-2}$

3. One end of a light spring of spring constant k is fixed to a wall and the other end is tied to a block placed on a smooth horizontal surface. In a displacement, the work done by the spring is $+\left(\frac{1}{2}\right)kx^2$. The possible cases are

(a) The spring was initially compressed by a distance x and was finally in its natural length
(b) It was initially stretched by a distance x and finally was in its natural length
(c) It was initially in its natural length and finally in a compressed position
(d) It was initially in its natural length and finally in a stretched position

4. Identify the correct statement about work-energy theorem.

(a) Work done by all the conservative forces is equal to the decrease in potential energy
(b) Work done by all the forces except, the conservative forces is equal to the change in mechanical energy
(c) Work done by all the forces is equal to the change in kinetic energy
(d) Work done by all the forces is equal to the change in potential energy

5. A disc of mass $3m$ and a disc of mass m are connected by a massless spring of stiffness k. The heavier disc is placed on the ground with the spring vertical and lighter disc on top. From its equilibrium position, the upper disc is pushed down by a distance δ and released. Then,

(a) if $\delta > \frac{3\,mg}{k}$, the lower disc will bounce up

(b) if $\delta = \frac{2\,mg}{k}$, maximum normal reaction from ground on lower disc $= 6\,mg$

(c) if $\delta = \frac{2\,mg}{k}$, maximum normal reaction from ground on lower disc $= 4\,mg$

(d) if $\delta > \frac{4\,mg}{k}$, the lower disc will bounce up

6. In the adjoining figure, block A is of mass m and block B is of mass $2\,m$. The spring has force constant k. All the surfaces are smooth and the system is released from rest with spring unstretched.

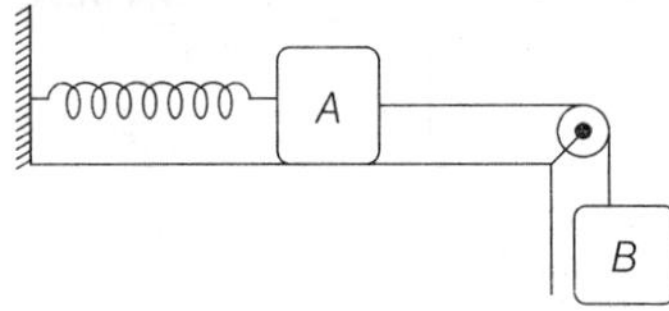

(a) The maximum extension of the spring is $\frac{4mg}{k}$

(b) The speed of block A when extension in spring is $\frac{2mg}{k}$, is $2g\sqrt{\frac{m}{3k}}$

(c) Net acceleration of block B when the extension in the spring is maximum, is $\frac{2}{3}g$

(d) Tension in the thread for extension of $\frac{2mg}{k}$ in spring is mg

7. If kinetic energy of a body is increasing then

(a) work done by conservative forces must be positive
(b) work done by conservative forces may be positive
(c) work done by conservative forces may be zero
(d) work done by non-conservative forces may be zero

8. Block A has no relative motion with respect to wedge fixed to the lift as shown in figure during motion 1 or motion 2. Then,

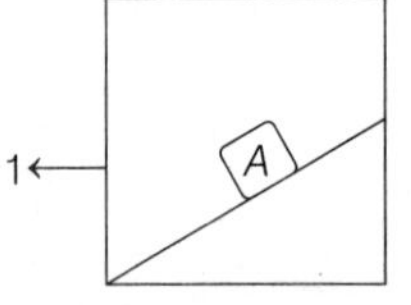

(a) work done by gravity on block A in motion 2 is less than in motion 1
(b) work done by normal reaction on block A in both the motions will be positive
(c) work done by force of friction in motion 1 may be positive
(d) work done by force of friction in motion 1 may be negative

9. In position A, kinetic energy of a particle is 60 J and potential energy is –20 J. In position B, kinetic energy is 100 J and potential energy is 40 J. Then, in moving the particle from A to B,

(a) work done by conservative forces is –60 J
(b) work done by external forces is 40 J
(c) net work done by all the forces is 40 J
(d) net work done by all the forces is 100 J

10. Two identical blocks each of mass m are connected by a light spring of constant $k = 100$ N/m. Initially, spring is compressed upto 0.2 m and then released. Which of the following statements is/are correct?

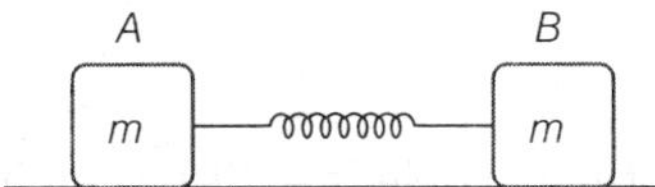

(a) The work done by the spring on the block A when the spring comes in natural length is 1 J
(b) The work done by the spring on the block B when the spring comes in natural length is 1 J
(c) The work done by the spring on the system (block A + block B) is 2 J
(d) The work done by the spring on the system (block A + block B) is −2 J

11. The acceleration of a particle with speed v is $\mathbf{a} = \mathbf{b} \times \mathbf{v}$, where $\mathbf{b}$ is a constant vector which neither parallel nor anti-parallel to velocity. Then,
(a) the velocity of the particle remains constant
(b) the work done on the particle is zero
(c) the speed of the particle remains constant
(d) the work done on the particle is non-zero

12. The force on a particle of mass m placed on smooth horizontal surface is $F = (2x^2 - 4)$ N directed along positive X-axis. The particle is projected with minimum speed from $x = 2$ m towards mean position along X-axis for crossing the origin, then the kinetic energy at
(a) the origin must be zero
(b) the origin is non-zero
(c) $x = \sqrt{2}$ must be zero
(d) $x = 2$ m may be zero

13. In previous problem, the particle is projected with minimum speed from $x = 2$ m towards mean position along X-axis for crossing the origin, then
(a) the minimum initial kinetic energy is $\frac{8}{3}(\sqrt{2} - 1)$
(b) the minimum kinetic energy at origin is just greater than $\frac{8\sqrt{2}}{3}$ J
(c) the minimum kinetic energy at $x = \sqrt{2}$ m is just greater than or equal to zero
(d) the minimum kinetic energy at origin is 4J

Comprehension Based Questions

Passage 1 (Q. Nos. 1 to 2)

The figure shows the variation of potential energy of a particle as a function of x, the x-coordinate of the region. It has been assumed that potential energy depends only on x. For all other values of x, U is zero, i.e. for $x < -10$ and $x > 15, U = 0$.

Based on above information answer the following questions:

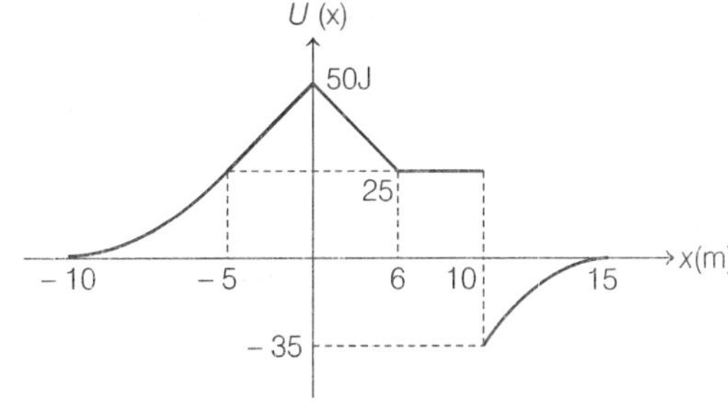

1. If total mechanical energy of the particle is 25 J, then it can be found in the region
   (a) $-10 < x < -5$ and $6 < x < 15$
   (b) $-10 < x < 0$ and $6 < x < 10$
   (c) $-5 < x < 6$
   (d) $-10 < x < 10$
2. If total mechanical energy of the particle is -40 J, then it can be found in region
   (a) $x < -10$ and $x > 15$
   (b) $-10 < x < -5$ and $6 < x < 15$
   (c) $10 < x < 15$
   (d) It is not possible

Passage 2 (Q. Nos. 3 to 5)

Consider the situation shown in the figure. The system is released from rest and the block A travels a distance 5 m in downward direction (Take, $g = 10\ m/s^2$).

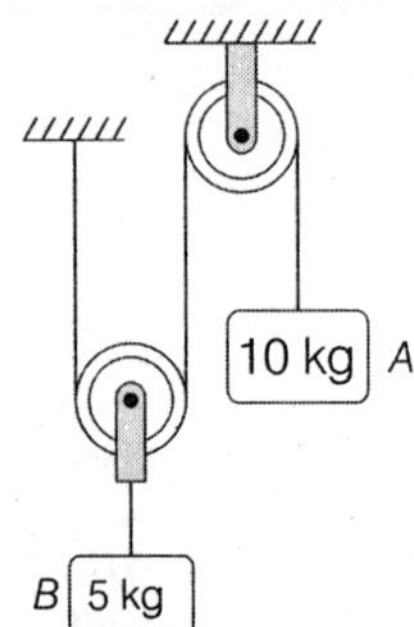

3. Find the work done by tension on the block *B*.
   (a) Zero
   (b) 116.67 J
   (c) 375 J
   (d) -116.67 J
4. Find the total work done by the tension on the system (block *A* + block *B*).
   (a) Zero
   (b) 116.67 J
   (c) 375 J
   (d) -375 J
5. Find net work done on the system.
   (a) Zero
   (b) 116.67 J
   (c) 375 J
   (d) -116.67 J

Match the Columns

1. A body is displaced from $x = 4$ m to $x = 2$ m along the x-axis. For the forces mentioned in Column I, match the corresponding work done is Column II.

Column I	Column II
(a) $\mathbf{F} = 4\hat{\mathbf{i}}$	(p) positive
(b) $\mathbf{F} = (4\hat{\mathbf{i}} - 4\hat{\mathbf{j}})$	(q) negative
(c) $\mathbf{F} = -4\hat{\mathbf{i}}$	(r) zero
(d) $\mathbf{F} = (-4\hat{\mathbf{i}} - 4\hat{\mathbf{j}})$	(s) $\lvert W \rvert = 8$ units

2. Two positive charges $+q$ each are fixed at points $(-a, 0)$ and $(a, 0)$. A third charge $+Q$ is placed at origin. Corresponding to small displacement of $+Q$ in the direction mentioned in Column I, match the corresponding equilibrium of Column II.

Column I	Column II
(a) Along positive x-axis	(p) stable equilibrium
(b) Along positive y-axis	(q) unstable equilibrium
(c) Along positive z-axis	(r) neutral equilibrium
(d) Along the line $x = y$	(s) no equilibrium

3. A block attached with a spring is released from A. Position B is the mean position and the block moves to point C. Match the following two columns.

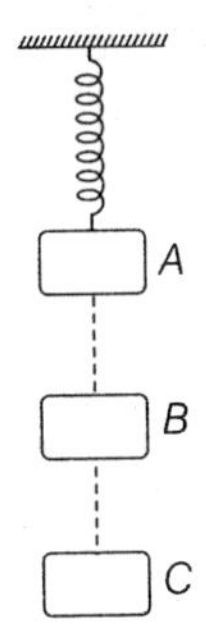

Column I	Column II
(a) From A to B decrease in gravitational potential energy is........, the increase in spring potential energy.	(p) less than
(b) From A to B increase in kinetic energy of block is........., the decrease in gravitational potential energy.	(q) more than
(c) From B to C decrease in kinetic energy of block is..... the increase in spring potential energy.	(r) equal to
(d) From B to C decrease in gravitational potential energy is ...., the increase in spring potential energy.	

4. In Column I, some statements are given related to work done by a force on an object while in Column II the sign and information about value of work done is given. Match the entries of Column I with the entries of Column II.

Column I	Column II
(a) Work done by friction force on the block as it slides down a rigid fixed incline with respect to ground.	(p) Positive
(b) In above case, work done by friction force on incline with respect to ground.	(q) Negative
(c) Work done by a man in lifting a bucket out of a well by means of a rope tied to the bucket with respect to ground.	(r) Zero
(d) Total work done by friction force in (a) with respect to ground.	(s) may be positive, negative or zero.

5. Two light springs S_1 and S_2 of spring constants $k_1 = 100$ N/m and $k_2 = 200$ N/m are connected in series. A man is keeping the springs stretched by applying a constant force of 50 N. Match the Column I with Column II.

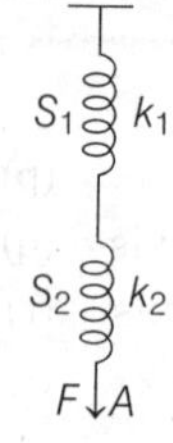

Column I	Column II
(a) How much work has been done by the spring S_1 on the spring S_2?	(p) 18.75 J
(b) How much work has been done by the spring S_2 on the spring S_1?	(q) −6.25 J
(c) How much total work has been done by the spring S_1 on both the spring S_2 and the man?	(r) 12.5 J
(d) How much work is done by the man on the spring S_2?	(s) −12.5 J

Subjective Questions

1. Two blocks of masses m_1 and m_2 connected by a light spring rest on a horizontal plane. The coefficient of friction between the blocks and the surface is equal to μ. What minimum constant force has to be applied in the horizontal direction to the block of mass m_1 in order to shift the other block?

2. The flexible bicycle type chain of length $\frac{\pi r}{2}$ and mass per unit length ρ is released from rest with $\theta = 0°$ in the smooth circular channel and falls through the hole in the supporting surface. Determine the velocity v of the chain as the last link leaves the slot.

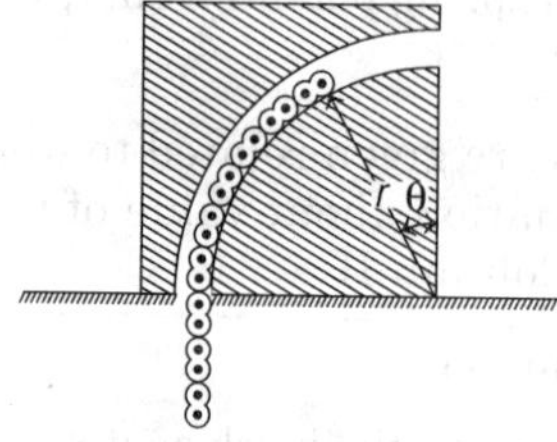

3. A baseball having a mass of 0.4 kg is thrown such that the force acting on it varies with time as shown in the first graph. The corresponding velocity-time graph is shown in the second graph. Determine the power applied as a function of time and the work done till $t = 0.3$ s.

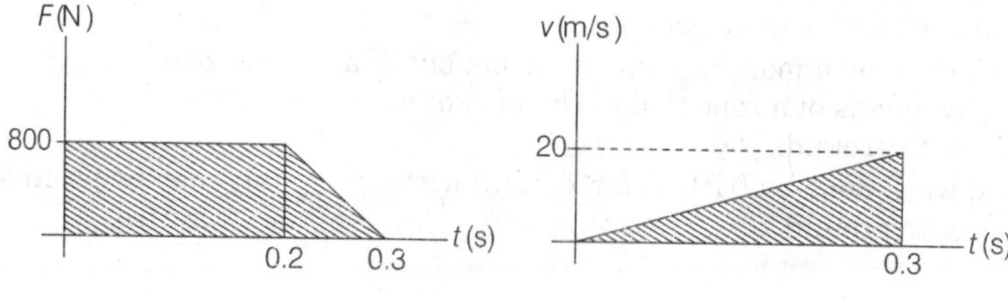

4. A body of mass 2 kg is being dragged with a uniform velocity of 2 m/s on a rough horizontal plane. The coefficient of friction between the body and the surface is 0.20, J = 4.2 J/cal and $g = 9.8 \text{ m/s}^2$. Calculate the amount of heat generated in 5 s.

5. The block shown in the figure is acted on by a spring with spring constant k and a weak frictional force of constant magnitude f. The block is pulled a distance x_0 from equilibrium position and then released. It oscillates many times and ultimately comes to rest.

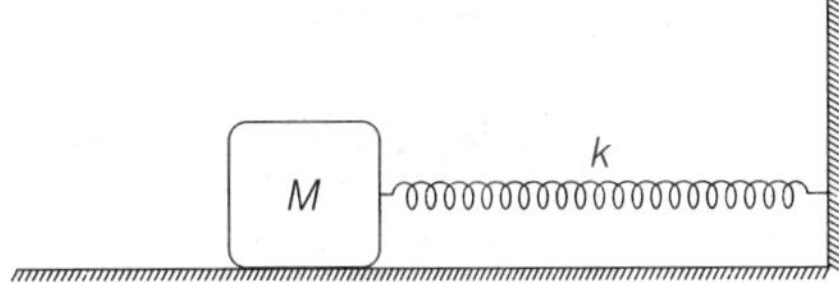

(a) Show that the decrease of amplitude is the same for each cycle of oscillation.

(b) Find the number of cycles the mass oscillates before coming to rest.

6. A spring mass system is held at rest with the spring relaxed at a height H above the ground. Determine the minimum value of H, so that the system has a tendency to rebound after hitting the ground. Given that the coefficient of restitution between m_2 and ground is zero.

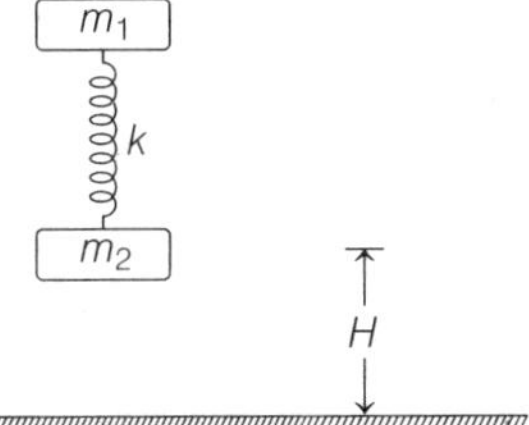

7. A block of mass m moving at a speed v compresses a spring through a distance x before its speed is halved. Find the spring constant of the spring.

8. In the figure shown masses of the blocks A, B and C are 6 kg, 2 kg and 1 kg, respectively. Mass of the spring is negligibly small and its stiffness is 1000 N/m. The coefficient of friction between the block A and the table is $\mu = 0.8$. Initially block C is held such that spring is in relaxed position. The block is released from rest. Find (Take, $g = 10 \text{ m/s}^2$)

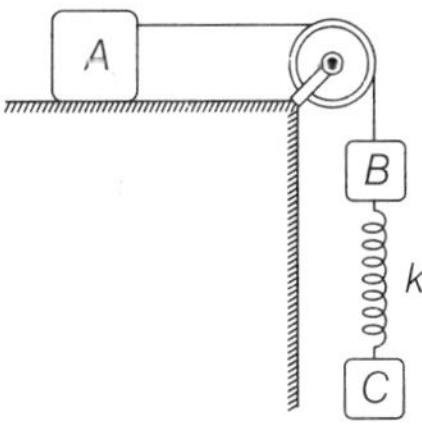

(a) the maximum distance moved by the block C.

(b) the acceleration of each block, when elongation in the spring is maximum.

9. A body of mass m slides down a plane inclined at an angle α. The coefficient of friction is μ. Find the rate at which kinetic plus gravitational potential energy is dissipated at any time t.

10. A particle moving in a straight line is acted upon by a force which works at a constant rate and changes its velocity from u and v over a distance x. Prove that the time taken in it is

$$\frac{3}{2}\frac{(u+v)\,x}{u^2+v^2+uv}$$

11. A chain of length l and mass m lies on the surface of a smooth sphere of radius $R > l$ with one end tied to the top of the sphere.

(a) Find the gravitational potential energy of the chain with reference level at the centre of the sphere.

(b) Suppose the chain is released and slides down the sphere. Find the kinetic energy of the chain, when it has slide through an angle θ.

(c) Find the tangential acceleration $\frac{dv}{dt}$ of the chain when the chain starts sliding down.

12. Find the speed of both the blocks at the moment of the block m_2 hits the wall AB, after the blocks are released from rest. Given that $m_1 = 0.5$ kg and $m_2 = 2$ kg, (Take, $g = 10 \text{ m/s}^2$)

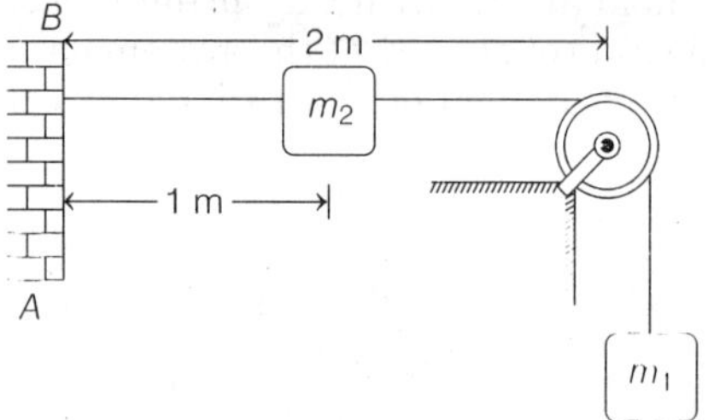

13. A block of mass M slides along a horizontal table with speed v_0. At $x = 0$, it hits a spring with spring constant k and begins to experience a friction force. The coefficient of friction is variable and is given by $\mu = bx$, where b is a positive constant. Find the loss in mechanical energy when the block has first come momentarily to rest.

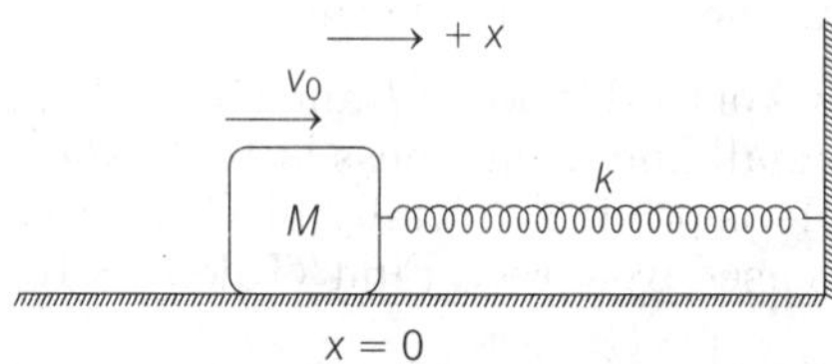

14. A small block of ice with mass 0.120 kg is placed against a horizontal compressed spring mounted on a horizontal table top that is 1.90 m above the floor. The spring has a force constant $k = 2300$ N/m and is initially compressed 0.045 m. The mass of the spring is negligible. The spring is released and the block slides along the table, goes off the edge and travels to the floor. If there is negligible friction between the ice and the table, what is the speed of the block of ice when it reaches the floor. (Take, $g = 9.8 \text{ m/s}^2$)

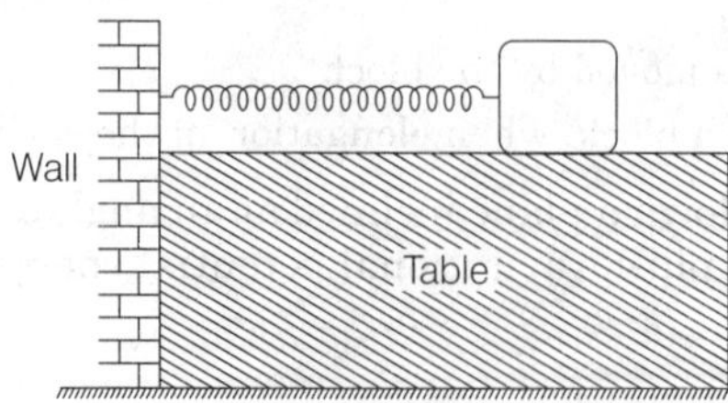

15. A 0.500 kg block is attached to a spring with length 0.60 m and force constant $k = 40.0$ N/m. The mass of the spring is negligible. You pull the block to the right along the surface with a constant horizontal force $F = 20.0$ N. (a) What is the block's speed when the block reaches point B, which is 0.25 m to the right of point A? (b) When the block reaches point B, you let go off the block. In the subsequent motion, how close does the block get to the wall, where the left end of the spring is attached? Neglect size of block and friction.

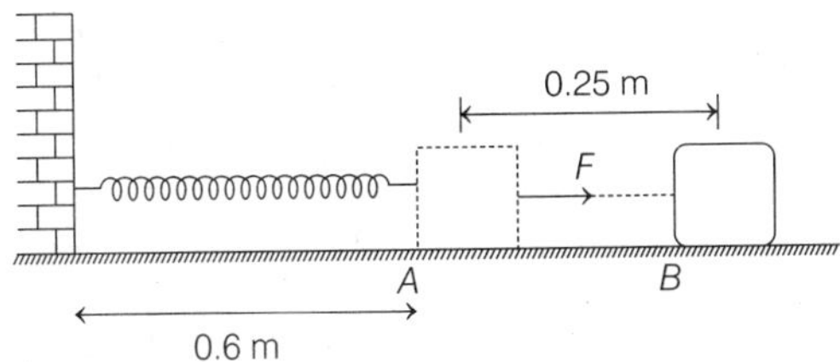

16. The situation shown in the figure, two blocks A and B, each having mass $m = \sqrt{2}$ kg are connected by a combination of light string and a light spring of constant k. The planes on which blocks A and B are placed are rough having coefficient of friction 0.5. Find the minimum value of constant force F required to move the block B up the inclined plane (Take, $g = 10\ \text{m/s}^2$). Assume that initially spring is relaxed.

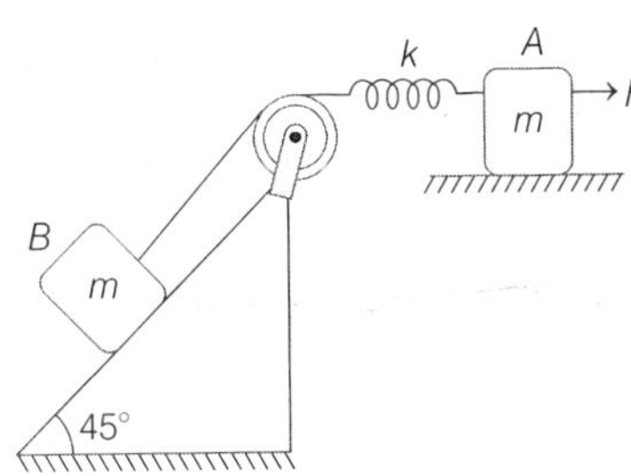

Integer Type Questions

17. A block of mass 1 kg is attached to three unstretched springs of spring constants $k_1 = 40\ \text{N/m}$, $k_2 = 15\ \text{N/m}$ and $k_3 = 45\ \text{N/m}$ as shown in the given figure.

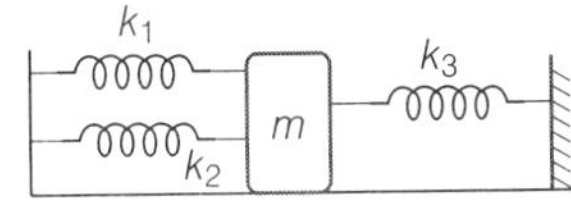

The block is displaced towards left on the horizontal smooth surface through a distance 10 cm and is released. Find maximum speed during its motion in m/s.

18. Two blocks A and B of equal masses ($m = 10$ kg) are connected by a light spring of spring constant $k = 150\ \text{N/m}$. The system is in equilibrium. The minimum value of initial downward velocity v_0 of the block B for which the block A bounce up is $\frac{20}{\sqrt{3n}}$ m/s. Find the value of n.

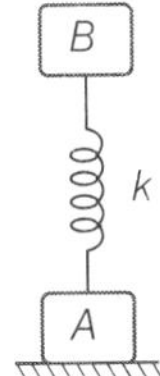

Answers

Introductory Exercise 9.1

1. -2 J 2. (a) 24.89 J (b) zero (c) zero (d) 24.9 J 3. $Tx, 0, 0, -Fx$ 4. $-\frac{3}{4}mgl$

5. (a) 7.2 J (b) -7.2 J (c) zero 6. -12 J 7. -1 J 8. 30 J

9. (a) -15 J (b) $+15$ J (c) 3 J (d) 27 J 10. (a) 4.0 J (b) zero (c) -1.0 J (d) 3.0 J

Introductory Exercise 9.2

1. -3.2 J 2. -400 J 3. Yes 4. $\frac{1}{2}m\alpha^2 b$

5. 120 J 6. $v_0\sqrt{\frac{m}{A}}$ 7. (a) False (b) False (c) True (d) False

8. 32 J 9. -597.6 J

Introductory Exercise 9.3

1. (a, d) 2. 40 J

Introductory Exercise 9.4

1. $x = 2$ m is position of stable equilibrium. $x = -2$ m is position of unstable equilibrium.
2. Points A and E are unstable equilibrium positions. Point C is stable equilibrium position.
3. (a) unstable (b) stable 4. $x = 2$ m, stable
5. $x = 4$ m, unstable

Introductory Exercise 9.5

1. (a) 16 W (b) 64 W 2. $K = Pt, v = \sqrt{\frac{2Pt}{m}}, S = \sqrt{\frac{8P}{9m}}t^{3/2}$

3. (a) $K = t^2, v = \sqrt{\frac{2}{m}}t$ (b) $P_{av} = t$

Exercises

LEVEL 1

Assertion and Reason

1. (d) 2. (d) 3. (b) 4. (d) 5. (a) 6. (d) 7. (c) 8. (d) 9. (b)

Single Correct Option

1. (b)	2. (a)	3. (c)	4. (b)	5. (b)	6. (d)	7. (b)	8. (c)	9. (a)	10. (a)
11. (a)	12. (a)	13. (b)	14. (b)	15. (d)	16. (b)	17. (b)	18. (a)	19. (d)	20. (c)
21. (d)	22. (a)	23. (a)	24. (a)	25. (a)	26. (c)	27. (a)	28. (b)	29. (c)	30. (b)
31. (c)	32. (a)	33. (d)	34. (a)	35. (b)	36. (a)	37. (c)	38. (c)	39. (d)	40. (b)
41. (c)	42. (c)	43. (a)	44. (a)	45. (b)	46. (a)	47. (b)	48. (a)	49. (b)	50. (b)
51. (a)	52. (d)	53. (d)	54. (c)	55. (c)	56. (c)	57. (a)	58. (a)	59. (a)	60. (a)
61. (b)	62. (a)	63. (b)	64. (d)	65. (d)	66. (a)	67. (c)	68. (d)		

Subjective Questions

1. 125 % 2. 0.5% 3. $-Kx_0^2$ 4. $TI\cos\beta, 0, -FI, -wI\sin\alpha$
5. (a) 11642 J (b) –10584 J (c) 1058 J (d) 5.42 m/s 6. (a) 2.33 J (b) 2.635 J
7. 10 J 8. 4 m/s 9. $\sqrt{2Rg(1+\sin\theta-\cos\theta)}$ 10. 0.115 11. $\frac{m}{2}$
12. (a) 2.45 m/s (b) 2.15 m/s 13. $\frac{3}{5}$ m 14. (a) 34.6 J (b) –10 J 15. $F_r = \frac{A}{r^2}$
16. (a) –4 J (b) 12 J (c) $x=(4-2\sqrt{3})$ m to $x=(4+2\sqrt{3})$ m (d) $F_x = 8-2x$ (e) $x = 4$ m 17. 2 m/s
18. 0.797 m 19. $v_w = \sqrt{2gR}\cos\alpha$, $v_s = \sqrt{2gR}\sin\alpha$ 20. $v = 0.37\ \text{ms}^{-1}$
21. – 0.05 J 22. 1.12 ms^{-1} 23. (a) 66.88 J (b) 66.88 J (c) 45.7 cm

LEVEL 2

Single Correct Option

1. (a)	2. (a)	3. (a)	4. (c)	5. (b)	6. (d)	7. (c)	8. (c)	9. (c)	10. (a)
11. (a)	12. (c)	13. (c)	14. (a)	15. (c)	16. (b)	17. (c)	18. (b)	19. (b)	20. (b)
21. (c)	22. (a)	23. (c)	24. (a)	25. (d)	26. (c)	27. (a)	28. (d)	29. (c)	30. (c)

More than One Correct Options

1. (a,b)	2. (a,b,c)	3. (a,b)	4. (b,c)	5. (b,d)	6. (a,b)	7. (b,c,d)
8. (all)	9. (a,c)	10. (a,b,c)	11. (b,c)	12. (b,c)	13. (a,b,c)	

Comprehension Based Questions

1. (a) 2. (d) 3. (b) 4. (a) 5. (c)

Match the Columns

1. (a)→ (q,s) (b)→ (q,s) (c)→ (p,s) (d)→ (p,s)
2. (a)→ (p) (b)→ (q) (c)→ (q) (d)→ (s)
3. (a)→ (q) (b)→ (p) (c)→ (p) (d)→ (p)
4. (a)→ (q) (b)→ (r) (c)→ (p) (d)→ (q)
5. (a)→ (s) (b)→ (r) (c)→ (q) (d)→ (p)

Subjective Questions

1. $\left(m_1 + \frac{m_2}{2}\right)\mu g$ 2. $\sqrt{gr\left(\frac{\pi}{2}+\frac{4}{\pi}\right)}$
3. For $t \le 0.2$ s, $P = (53.3t)$ kW, for $t > 0.2$ s, $P = (160t - 533t^2)$ kW, 1.69 kJ. 4. 9.33 cal
5. (b) $\frac{1}{4}\left[\frac{kx_0}{f} - 1\right]$ 6. $H_{\text{min}} = \frac{m_2 g}{k}\left[\frac{m_2 + 2m_1}{2m_1}\right]$ 7. $\frac{3mv^2}{4x^2}$
8. (a) 2×10^{-2}m (b) $a_A = a_B = 0$, $a_C = 10\ \text{m/s}^2$, upwards
9. $\mu mg^2\cos\alpha(\sin\alpha - \mu\cos\alpha)t$
11. (a) $\frac{mR^2g}{l}\sin\left(\frac{l}{R}\right)$ (b) $\frac{mR^2g}{l}\left[\sin\left(\frac{l}{R}\right) + \sin\theta - \sin\left(\theta + \frac{l}{R}\right)\right]$ (c) $\frac{Rg}{l}\left[1 - \cos\left(\frac{l}{R}\right)\right]$
12. $v_1 = 3.03\ \text{ms}^{-1}$, $v_2 = 3.39\ \text{ms}^{-1}$ 13. $\frac{bgv_0^2M^2}{2(k+bMg)}$ 14. 8.72 ms^{-1}
15. (a) 3.87 ms^{-1} (b) 0.10 m 16. 14.57 N 17. 1 18. 5

10
Circular Motion

10.1 Introduction

Circular motion is a two dimensional motion or motion in a plane. This plane may be horizontal, inclined or vertical. But in most of the cases, this plane is horizontal. In circular motion, direction of velocity continuously keeps on changing. Therefore, even though speed is constant and velocity keeps on changing. So body is accelerated. Later we will see that this is a variable acceleration. So, we cannot apply the equations $\mathbf{v} = \mathbf{u} + \mathbf{a}t$ etc. directly.

10.2 Kinematics of Circular Motion

Velocity

In circular motion, a particle has two velocities :

(i) Angular velocity

(ii) Linear velocity

Angular Velocity

Suppose a particle P is moving in a circle of radius r and centre O.

The position of the particle P at a given instant may be described by the angle θ between OP and OX. This angle θ is called the **angular position** of the particle. As the particle moves on the circle its angular position θ changes. Suppose the point rotates an angle $\Delta\theta$ in time Δt. The rate of change of angular position is known as the **angular velocity (ω)**. Thus,

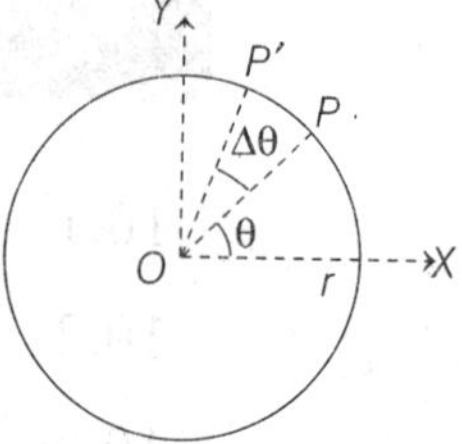

Fig. 10.1

$$\omega = \lim_{\Delta t \to 0} \frac{\Delta\theta}{\Delta t} = \frac{d\theta}{dt}$$

Here, ω is the angular speed or magnitude of angular velocity. Angular velocity is a vector quantity. Direction of ω is perpendicular to plane of circle and given by screw law.

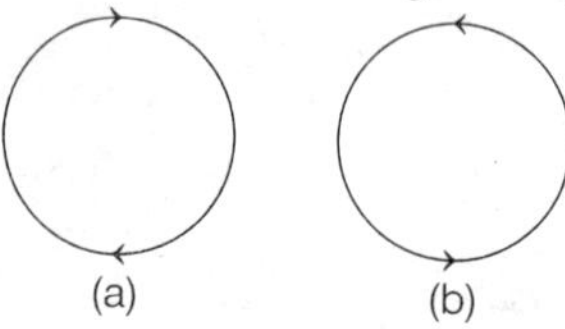

Fig. 10.2

In the Fig. 10.2 (a), when the particle is rotating clockwise, direction of ω is perpendicular to paper inwards or in ⊗ direction.

In Fig. 10.2 (b), when the particle is rotating in anticlockwise direction, direction of ω is perpendicular to paper outwards or in ʘ direction.

Linear velocity is as usual,

$$\mathbf{v} = \frac{d\mathbf{s}}{dt} \quad \text{or} \quad \frac{d\mathbf{r}}{dt}$$

Magnitude of linear velocity is called linear speed v. Thus,

$$v = |\mathbf{v}| = \left|\frac{d\mathbf{s}}{dt}\right| \quad \text{or} \quad \left|\frac{d\mathbf{r}}{dt}\right|$$

Relation between Linear Speed and Angular Speed

In the Fig. 10.1, linear distance PP' travelled by the particle in time Δt is

$$\Delta s = r\Delta\theta$$

or
$$\lim_{\Delta t \to 0} \frac{\Delta s}{\Delta t} = r \lim_{\Delta t \to 0} \frac{\Delta\theta}{\Delta t}$$

or
$$\frac{ds}{dt} = r\frac{d\theta}{dt} \quad \text{or} \quad \boxed{v = r\omega}$$

Acceleration

Like the velocity, a particle in circular motion has two accelerations:

(i) Angular acceleration

(ii) Linear acceleration

The rate of change of angular velocity is called the **angular acceleration** (α).

Thus,
$$\boxed{\alpha = \frac{d\omega}{dt} = \frac{d^2\theta}{dt^2}}$$

Angular acceleration is also a vector quantity. Direction of α is also perpendicular to plane of circle, either parallel or antiparallel to ω. If angular speed of the particle is increasing, then α is parallel to ω and if angular speed is decreasing, then α is antiparallel to ω. Angular acceleration is zero if angular speed (or angular velocity) is constant.

In circular motion, linear speed of the particle may or may not be constant but direction of linear velocity continuously keeps on changing. So, velocity is continuously changing. Therefore, acceleration cannot be zero. But of course we can resolve the linear acceleration into two components:

(i) tangential acceleration (a_t)

(ii) radial or centripetal acceleration (a_r)

Component of linear acceleration in tangential direction is called tangential acceleration (a_t). This component is responsible for change in linear speed. This is the rate of change of speed. Thus,

$$\boxed{a_t = \frac{dv}{dt} = \frac{d|\mathbf{v}|}{dt}}$$

If speed of the particle is constant, then a_t is zero. If speed is increasing, then this is positive and in the direction of linear velocity. If speed is decreasing, then this component is negative and in the opposite direction of linear velocity.

Tangential component of the linear acceleration and angular acceleration have following relation:

$$a_t = \frac{dv}{dt} = \frac{d(r\omega)}{dt} = r\frac{d\omega}{dt}$$

$$= r\alpha \qquad \left(\text{as } \frac{d\omega}{dt} = \alpha\right)$$

$\therefore$
$$\boxed{a_t = r\alpha}$$

Component of linear acceleration in radial direction (towards centre) is called radial or centripetal acceleration. This component is responsible for change in direction of linear velocity. So, this component can never be zero, as the direction continuously keeps on changing. Value of this component is

$$a_r = \frac{v^2}{r} = r\omega^2 \qquad \text{(as } v = r\omega\text{)}$$

These two components are mutually perpendicular. So, the net linear acceleration is the vector sum of these two, as shown in figure.

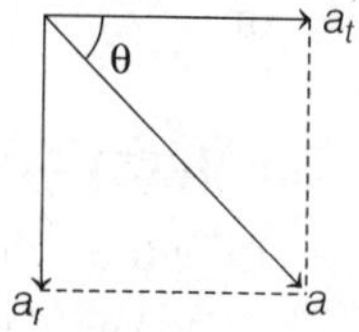

$$a = \sqrt{a_t^2 + a_r^2} = \sqrt{\left(\frac{dv}{dt}\right)^2 + \left(\frac{v^2}{r}\right)^2}$$

or

$$a = \sqrt{(r\alpha)^2 + (r\omega^2)^2}$$

and

$$\tan\theta = \frac{a_r}{a_t} \quad \text{or} \quad \theta = \tan^{-1}\left(\frac{a_r}{a_t}\right)$$

Fig. 10.3

Three Types of Circular Motion

For better understanding, we can classify the circular motion in following three types:

(i) **Uniform circular motion** in which v and ω are constant.

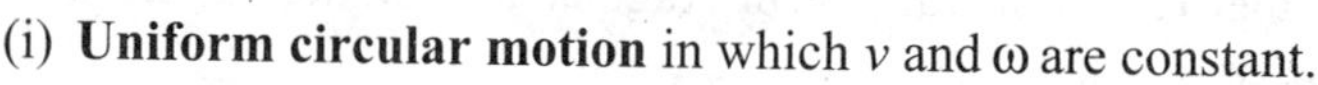

In this motion,

$$v \text{ or } |\mathbf{v}| = \text{constant} \Rightarrow a_t = 0 \Rightarrow \omega = \text{constant} \Rightarrow \alpha = 0$$

$$a = a_r = \frac{v^2}{r} = r\omega^2$$

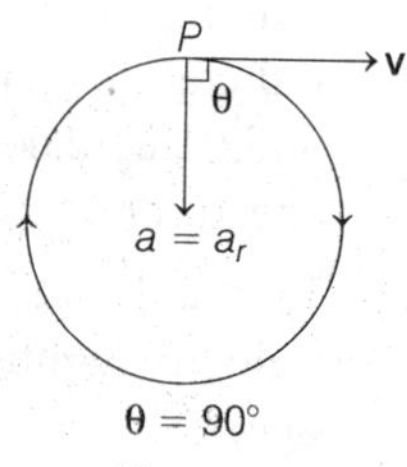

Fig. 10.4

a is towards centre, **v** is tangential and according to the shown figure, ω is perpendicular to paper inwards or in ⊗ direction.

(ii) **Accelerated circular motion** in which v and ω are increasing. So, a_t is in the direction of **v** and α is in the direction of ω.

In the figure shown, α and ω both are perpendicular to paper inwards. Further,

$$a = \sqrt{a_t^2 + a_r^2}$$

and

$$\tan\theta = \frac{a_r}{a_t}$$

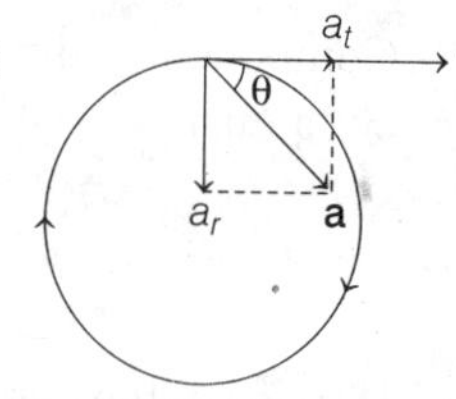

Fig. 10.5

(iii) **Retarded circular motion** in which v and ω are decreasing. So, a_t is in the opposite direction of **v** and α is in the opposite direction of ω.

In the figure shown, ω is perpendicular to paper inwards in ⊗ direction and α is perpendicular to paper outwards in ʘ direction.

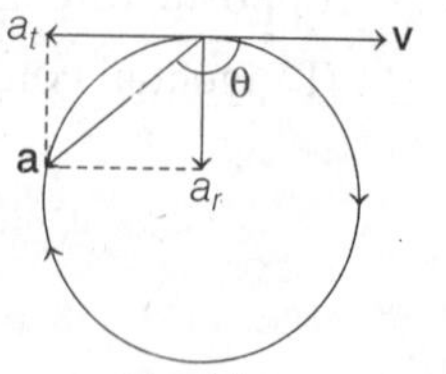

θ is obtuse

Fig. 10.6

Note *In the above figures, θ is the angle between* **v** *and* **a**.

Extra Points to Remember

- Relation between angular velocity vector ω, velocity vector $\mathbf{v}$ and position vector of the particle with respect to centre $\mathbf{r}$ is given by
$$\mathbf{v} = \boldsymbol{\omega} \times \mathbf{r}$$
- In circular motion, if angular acceleration α is constant then we can apply the following equations directly:
$$\omega = \omega_0 + \alpha t \quad \Rightarrow \quad \omega^2 = \omega_0^2 + 2\alpha\theta \text{ and } \theta = \omega_0 t + \frac{1}{2}\alpha t^2$$
Here, ω_0 is the initial angular velocity and ω, the angular velocity at time t. Similarly, θ is the angle rotated by position vector of the particle (with respect to centre).
- If angular acceleration is not constant, then we will have to take help of differentiation or integration. The basic equations are
$$\omega = \frac{d\theta}{dt} \quad \text{and} \quad \alpha = \frac{d\omega}{dt} = \omega\frac{d\omega}{d\theta}$$
$$\therefore \quad \int d\theta = \int \omega dt, \int d\omega = \int \alpha dt \text{ and } \int \omega d\omega = \int \alpha d\theta$$

Example 10.1 *A particle moves in a circle of radius 0.5 m at a speed that uniformly increases. Find the angular acceleration of particle if its speed changes from 2.0 m/s to 4.0 m/s in 4.0 s.*

Solution The tangential acceleration of the particle is
$$a_t = \frac{dv}{dt} = \frac{4.0 - 2.0}{4.0} = 0.5 \text{ m/s}^2$$
The angular acceleration is
$$\alpha = \frac{a_t}{r} = \frac{0.5}{0.5} = 1 \text{ rad/s}^2$$ **Ans.**

Example 10.2 *The speed of a particle moving in a circle of radius $r = 2$ m varies with time t as $v = t^2$, where t is in second and v in m/s. Find the radial, tangential and net acceleration at $t = 2$ s.*

Solution Linear speed of particle at $t = 2$ s is
$$v = (2)^2 = 4 \text{ m/s}$$
$\therefore$ Radial acceleration,
$$a_r = \frac{v^2}{r} = \frac{(4)^2}{2} = 8 \text{ m/s}^2$$
The tangential acceleration is $a_t = \frac{dv}{dt} = 2t$

$\therefore$ Tangential acceleration at $t = 2$ s is
$$a_t = (2)(2) = 4 \text{ m/s}^2$$
$\therefore$ Net acceleration of particle at $t = 2$s is
$$a = \sqrt{(a_r)^2 + (a_t)^2} = \sqrt{(8)^2 + (4)^2}$$
or
$$a = \sqrt{80} \text{ m/s}^2$$

Note *On any curved path (not necessarily a circular one) the acceleration of the particle has two components a_t and a_n in two mutually perpendicular directions. Component of* $\mathbf{a}$ *along* $\mathbf{v}$ *is a_t and perpendicular to* $\mathbf{v}$ *is a_n. Thus,*
$$|\mathbf{a}| = \sqrt{a_t^2 + a_n^2}$$

Example 10.3 *In circular motion, what are the possible values (zero, positive or negative) of the following :*

(a) $\boldsymbol{\omega} \cdot \mathbf{v}$ (b) $\mathbf{v} \cdot \mathbf{a}$ (c) $\boldsymbol{\omega} \cdot \boldsymbol{\alpha}$

Solution (a) **v** lies in the plane of circle and **ω** is always perpendicular to this plane.

$$\therefore \qquad \mathbf{v} \perp \boldsymbol{\omega} \qquad \text{(always)}$$

Hence, $\boldsymbol{\omega} \cdot \mathbf{v}$ is always zero.

(b) **v** and **a** both lie in the plane of circle and the angle between these two vectors may be acute (when speed is increasing) obtuse (when speed is decreasing) or 90° (when speed is constant). Hence, $\mathbf{v} \cdot \mathbf{a}$ may be positive, negative or zero.

(c) **ω** and **α** are either parallel ($\theta = 0°$ between **ω** and **α**) or antiparallel ($\theta = 180°$). In uniform circular motion, **α** has zero magnitude. Hence, $\boldsymbol{\omega} \cdot \boldsymbol{\alpha}$ may be positive, negative or zero.

INTRODUCTORY EXERCISE 10.1

1. Is the acceleration of a particle in uniform circular motion constant or variable?
2. Which of the following quantities may remain constant during the motion of an object along a curved path?
   (i) Velocity (ii) Speed (iii) Acceleration (iv) Magnitude of acceleration
3. A particle moves in a circle of radius 1.0 cm with a speed given by $v = 2t$, where v is in cm/s and t in seconds.
   (a) Find the radial acceleration of the particle at $t = 1$ s.
   (b) Find the tangential acceleration at $t = 1$ s.
   (c) Find the magnitude of net acceleration at $t = 1$ s.
4. A particle is moving with a constant speed in a circular path. Find the ratio of average velocity to its instantaneous velocity when the particle rotates an angle $\theta = \left(\frac{\pi}{2}\right)$.
5. A particle is moving with a constant angular acceleration of 4 rad/s^2 in a circular path. At time $t = 0$, particle was at rest. Find the time at which the magnitudes of centripetal acceleration and tangential acceleration are equal.
6. A particle rotates in a circular path of radius 54 m with varying speed $v = 4t^2$. Here v is in m/s and t in second. Find angle between velocity and acceleration at $t = 3$ s.
7. Figure shows the total acceleration and velocity of a particle moving clockwise in a circle of radius 2.5 m at a given instant of time. At this instant, find :

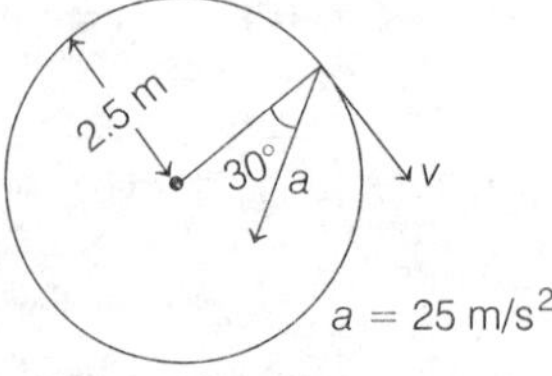

Fig. 10.7

   (a) the radial acceleration,
   (b) the speed of the particle and
   (c) its tangential acceleration.

10.3 Dynamics of Circular Motion

In the above article, we have learnt that linear acceleration of a particle in circular motion has two components, tangential and radial (or centripetal). So, normally we resolve the forces acting on the particle in two directions:

(i) tangential

(ii) radial

In tangential direction, net force on the particle is ma_t and in radial direction net force is ma_r.

In uniform circular motion, tangential acceleration is zero. Hence, net force in tangential direction is zero and in radial direction

$$F_{\text{net}} = ma_r = \frac{mv^2}{r} = mr\omega^2$$

as, $$a_r = \frac{v^2}{r} = r\omega^2$$

This net force (towards centre) is also called **centripetal force**.

In most of the cases plane of our uniform circular motion will be horizontal and one of the tangent is in vertical direction also. So, in this case we resolve the forces in:

(i) horizontal radial direction

(ii) vertical tangential direction

In vertical tangential direction net force is zero ($a_t = 0$) and in horizontal radial direction (towards centre) net force is $\frac{mv^2}{r}$ or $mr\omega^2$.

Note *Centripetal force $\frac{mv^2}{r}$ or $mr\omega^2$ (towards centre) does not act on the particle but this much force is required to the particle for rotating in a circle (as it is accelerated due to change in direction of velocity). The real forces acting on the particle provide this centripetal force or we can say that vector sum of all the forces acting on the particle is equal to $\frac{mv^2}{r}$ or $mr\omega^2$ (in case of uniform circular motion). The real forces acting on the particle may be, friction force, weight, normal reaction, tension etc.*

Conical Pendulum

If a small particle of mass m tied to a string is whirled in a horizontal circle, as shown in Fig.10.8. The arrangement is called the 'conical pendulum'. In case of conical pendulum, the vertical component of tension balances the weight in tangential direction, while its horizontal component provides the necessary centripetal force in radial direction (towards centre). Thus,

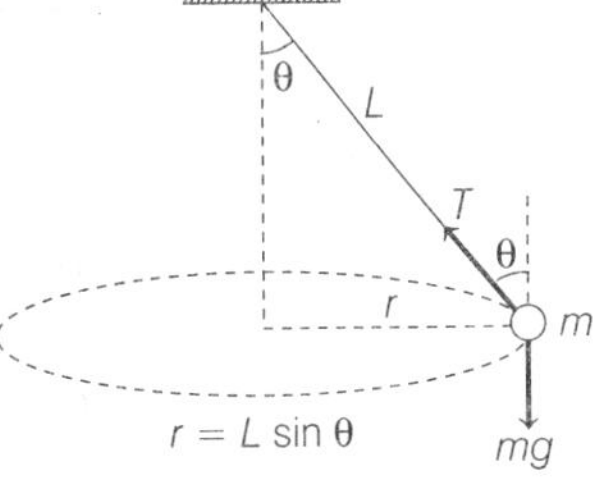

Fig. 10.8

$$T \sin \theta = \frac{mv^2}{r} \qquad \text{...(i)}$$

and $$T \cos \theta = mg \qquad \text{...(ii)}$$

From these two equations, we can find

$$v = \sqrt{rg \tan \theta}$$

$\therefore$ Angular speed

$$\omega = \frac{v}{r} = \sqrt{\frac{g \tan \theta}{r}}$$

So, the time period of pendulum is

$$T = \frac{2\pi}{\omega} = 2\pi \sqrt{\frac{r}{g \tan \theta}} = 2\pi \sqrt{\frac{L \cos \theta}{g}} \qquad (\text{as } r = L \sin \theta)$$

or

$$T = 2\pi \sqrt{\frac{L \cos \theta}{g}}$$

Motion of a Particle Inside a Smooth Cone

A particle of mass 'm' is rotating inside a smooth cone in horizontal circle of radius 'r' as shown in figure. constant speed of the particle is suppose 'v'.

Only two forces are acting on the particle in the shown directions:

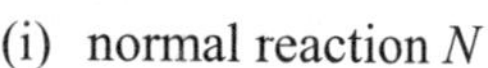

(i) normal reaction N

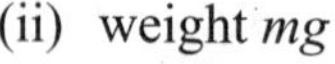

(ii) weight mg

Fig. 10.9

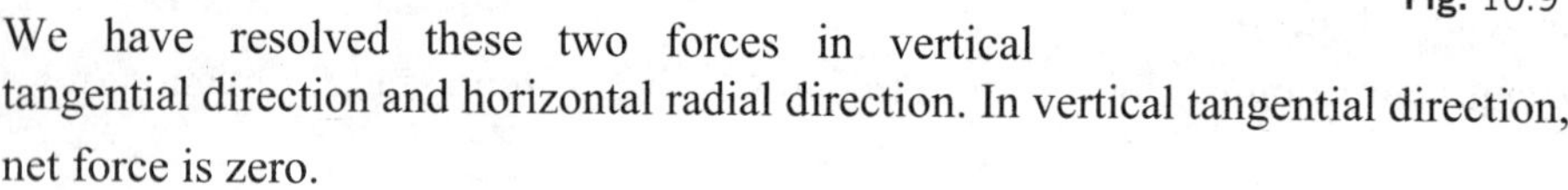

We have resolved these two forces in vertical tangential direction and horizontal radial direction. In vertical tangential direction, net force is zero.

$\therefore$

$$N \cos \theta = mg$$

In horizontal radial direction (towards centre), net force is $\frac{mv^2}{r}$.

$\therefore$

$$N \sin \theta = \frac{mv^2}{r}$$

'Death Well' or Rotor

In case of 'death well' a person drives a bicycle on a vertical surface of a large wooden well while in case of a rotor, at a certain angular speed of rotor a person hangs resting against the wall without any support from the bottom. In death well walls are at rest and person revolves while in case of rotor person is at rest and the walls rotate.

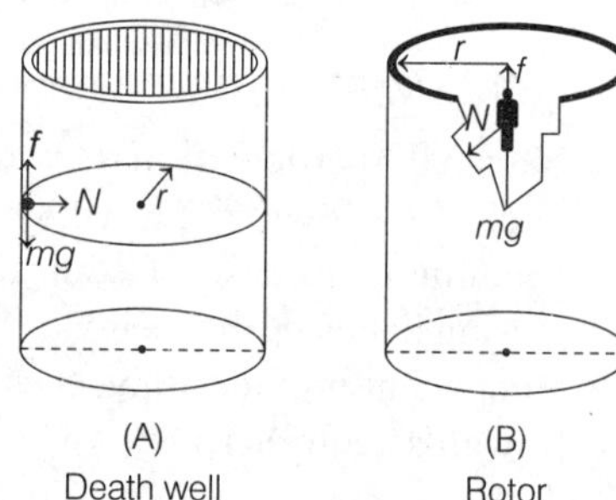

Fig. 10.10

In both cases, friction force balances the weight of person while reaction provides the centripetal force for circular motion, i.e.

$$f = mg$$

and

$$N = \frac{mv^2}{r} = mr\omega^2 \qquad (v = r\omega)$$

A Cyclist Bends Towards Centre on a Circular Path

In the figure, F is the resultant of N and f.

$\therefore \qquad F = \sqrt{N^2 + f^2}$

When the cyclist is inclined to the centre of the rounding of its path, the resultant of N, f and mg is directed horizontally to the centre of the circular path of the cycle. This resultant force imparts a centripetal acceleration to the cyclist.

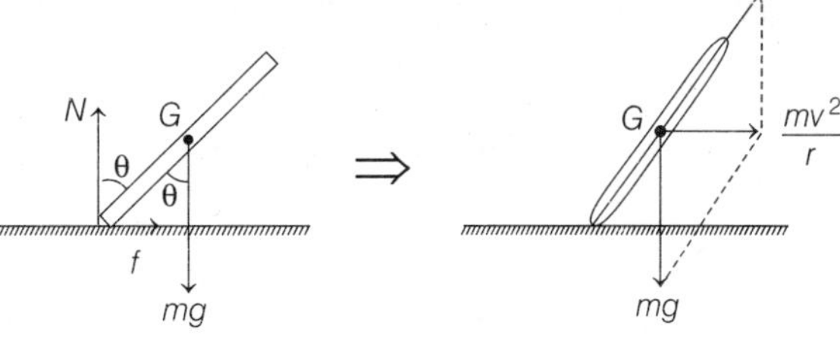

Fig. 10.11

Resultant of N and f, i.e. F should pass through G, the centre of gravity of cyclist (for complete equilibrium, rotational as well as translational). Hence,

$$\tan\theta = \frac{f}{N}, \text{ where } f = \frac{mv^2}{r} \text{ and } N = mg$$

$$\therefore \qquad \tan\theta = \frac{v^2}{rg}$$

Circular Turning of Roads

When vehicles go through turnings, they travel along a nearly circular arc. There must be some force which will provide the required centripetal acceleration. If the vehicles travel in a horizontal circular path, this resultant force is also horizontal. The necessary centripetal force is being provided to the vehicles by following three ways:

1. By friction only.
2. By banking of roads only.
3. By friction and banking of roads both.

In real life, the necessary centripetal force is provided by friction and banking of roads both. Now, let us write equations of motion in each of the three cases separately and see what are the constraints in each case.

1. By Friction Only

Suppose a car of mass m is moving at a speed v in a horizontal circular arc of radius r. In this case, the necessary centripetal force to the car will be provided by force of friction f acting towards centre.

Thus, $$f = \frac{mv^2}{r}$$

Further, limiting value of f is μN.

or $$f_L = \mu N = \mu mg \qquad (N = mg)$$

Therefore, for a safe turn without sliding

$$\frac{mv^2}{r} \le f_L \quad \text{or} \quad \frac{mv^2}{r} \le \mu mg$$

or $$\boxed{\mu \ge \frac{v^2}{rg} \quad \text{or} \quad v \le \sqrt{\mu rg}}$$

Here, two situations may arise. If μ and r are known to us, the speed of the vehicle should not exceed $\sqrt{\mu rg}$ and if v and r are known to us, the coefficient of friction should be greater than $\frac{v^2}{rg}$.

Note *You might have seen that if the speed of the car is too high, car starts skidding outwards. With this, radius of the circle increases or the necessary centripetal force is reduced (centripetal force* $\propto \frac{1}{r}$*).*

2. By Banking of Roads Only

Friction is not always reliable at circular turns if high speeds and sharp turns are involved. To avoid dependence on friction, the roads are banked at the turn so that the outer part of the road is some what lifted compared to the inner part.

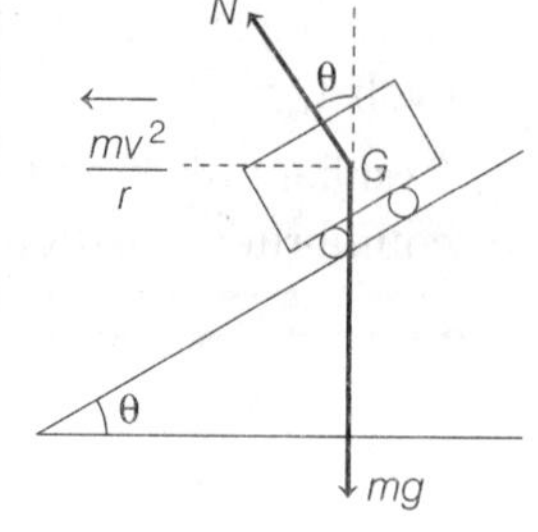

Fig. 10.12

Applying Newton's second law along the radius and the first law in the vertical direction.

$$N \sin \theta = \frac{mv^2}{r} \qquad \text{...(i)}$$

and

$$N \cos \theta = mg \qquad \text{...(ii)}$$

From these two equations, we get

$$\tan \theta = \frac{v^2}{rg} \quad \text{or} \quad \boxed{v = \sqrt{rg \tan \theta}}$$

Note *This is the speed at which car does not slide down even if track is smooth. If track is smooth and speed is less than* $\sqrt{rg \tan \theta}$, *vehicle will move down so that r gets decreased and if speed is more than this vehicle will move up.*

3. By Friction and Banking of Road Both

If a vehicle is moving on a circular road which is rough and banked also, then three forces may act on the vehicle of these the first force, i.e. weight (mg) is fixed both in magnitude and direction. The direction of second force, i.e. normal reaction N is also fixed (perpendicular to the road) while the direction of the third force, i.e. friction f can be either inwards or outwards, while its magnitude can be varied from zero to a maximum limit ($f_L = \mu N$). So, the magnitude of normal reaction N and direction plus magnitude of friction f are so adjusted that the resultant of the three forces mentioned above is $\frac{mv^2}{r}$ towards the centre. Of these m and r are also constant. Therefore, magnitude of N and direction plus magnitude of friction mainly depend on the speed of the vehicle v. Although situation varies from problem to problem yet, we can see that

(i) Friction f is upwards if the vehicle is at rest or $v = 0$.

Because in this case the component of weight $mg \sin \theta$ is balanced by f.

(ii) Friction f is downwards if $\quad v > \sqrt{rg \tan \theta}$

(iii) Friction f is upwards if $\quad v < \sqrt{rg \tan \theta}$

(iv) Friction f is zero if $\quad v = \sqrt{rg \tan \theta}$

Let us now see how the force of friction and normal reaction change as speed is gradually increased.

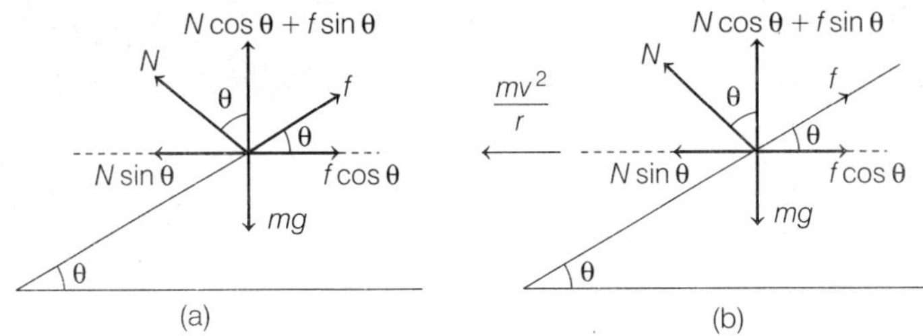

Fig. 10.13

In Fig. (a) When the car is at rest force of friction is upwards. We can resolve the forces in any two mutually perpendicular directions. Let us resolve them in horizontal and vertical directions.

$$\Sigma F_H = 0 \quad \therefore \quad N \sin\theta - f \cos\theta = 0 \qquad \text{...(i)}$$

$$\Sigma F_V = 0 \quad \therefore \quad N \cos\theta + f \sin\theta = mg \qquad \text{...(ii)}$$

In Fig. (b) Now, the car is given a small speed v, so that a centripetal force $\frac{mv^2}{r}$ is now required in horizontal direction towards centre. So, Eq. (i) will now become,

$$N \sin\theta - f \cos\theta = \frac{mv^2}{r}$$

or we can say that in first case $N \sin\theta$ and $f \cos\theta$ are equal while in second case their difference is $\frac{mv^2}{r}$.

This can occur in following three ways:

(i) N increases while f remains same.

(ii) N remains same while f decreases or

(iii) N increases and f decreases.

But only third case is possible, i.e. N will increase and f will decrease. This is because Eq. (ii), $N \cos\theta + f \sin\theta = mg =$ constant is still has to be valid.

So, to keep $N \cos\theta + f \sin\theta$ to be constant N should increase and f should decrease (as $\theta =$ constant).

Now, as speed goes on increasing, force of friction first decreases. Becomes zero at $v = \sqrt{rg \tan\theta}$ and then starts acting in downward direction, so that its horizontal component $f \cos\theta$ with $N \sin\theta$ now provides the required centripetal force.

Example 10.4 *A small block of mass 100 g moves with uniform speed in a horizontal circular groove, with vertical side walls of radius 25 cm. If the block takes 2.0 s to complete one round, find the normal constant force by the side wall of the groove.*

Solution The speed of the block is

$$v = \frac{2\pi \times (25\,\text{cm})}{2.0\text{ s}} = 0.785 \text{ m/s}$$

The acceleration of the block is

$$a = \frac{v^2}{r} = \frac{(0.785 \text{ m/s})^2}{0.25\text{m}} = 2.464 \text{ m/s}^2$$

towards the centre. The only force in this direction is the normal contact force due to the side walls. Thus, from Newton's second law, this force is

$$N = ma = (0.100 \text{ kg})(2.464 \text{ m/s}^2) = 0.246 \text{ N}$$ **Ans.**

Example 10.5 *A fighter plane is pulling out for a dive at a speed of 900 km/h. Assuming its path to be a vertical circle of radius 2000 m and its mass to be 16000 kg, find the force exerted by the air on it at the lowest point. Take, $g = 9.8 \text{ m/s}^2$.*

Solution At the lowest point in the path, the acceleration is vertically upward (towards the centre) and its magnitude is v^2/r.

The forces on the plane are :

(a) weight Mg downward and

(b) force F by the air upward.

Hence, Newton's second law of motion gives

$$F - Mg = Mv^2/r \quad \text{or} \quad F = M(g + v^2/r)$$

Here, $$v = 900 \text{ km/h} = \frac{9 \times 10^5}{3600} \text{ m/s} = 250 \text{ m/s}$$

$\therefore$ $$F = 16000\left(9.8 + \frac{62500}{2000}\right) \text{N} = 6.56 \times 10^5 \text{ N}$$ (upward).

Example 10.6 *Three particles, each of mass m are situated at the vertices of an equilateral triangle of side a. The only forces acting on the particles are their mutual gravitational forces. It is desired that each particle moves in a circle while maintaining the original mutual separation a. Find the initial velocity that should be given to each particle and also the time period of the circular motion.* $\left(F = \dfrac{Gm_1m_2}{r^2}\right)$.

Solution

$$r = \frac{a}{2}\sec 30° = \frac{a}{\sqrt{3}}$$

$$F = \frac{Gmm}{a^2}$$

$$F_{\text{net}} = \sqrt{3}F = \left(\frac{Gmm}{a^2}\right)(\sqrt{3})$$

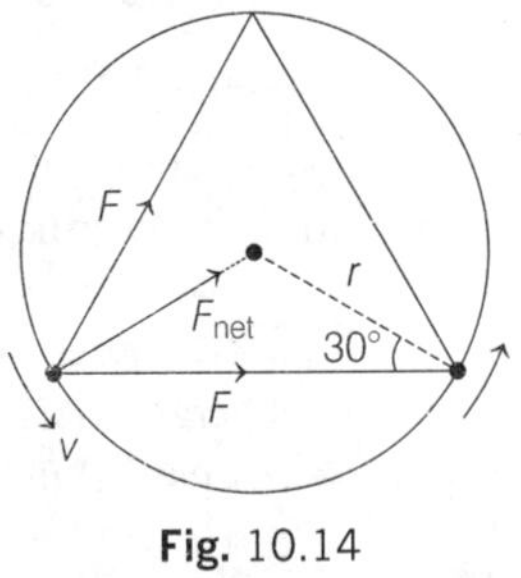

Fig. 10.14

This will provide the necessary centripetal force.

$\therefore$ $$\frac{mv^2}{r} = \frac{\sqrt{3}\,Gm^2}{a^2} \quad \text{or} \quad \frac{mv^2}{(a/\sqrt{3})} = \frac{\sqrt{3}\,Gm^2}{a^2}$$

$\Rightarrow$ $$v = \sqrt{\frac{Gm}{a}}$$ **Ans.**

$$T = \frac{2\pi r}{v} = \frac{2\pi\,(a/\sqrt{3})}{\sqrt{Gm/a}} = 2\pi\sqrt{\frac{a^3}{3Gm}}$$ **Ans.**

Example 10.7 *(a) How many revolutions per minute must the apparatus shown in figure make about a vertical axis so that the cord makes an angle of 45° with the vertical?*

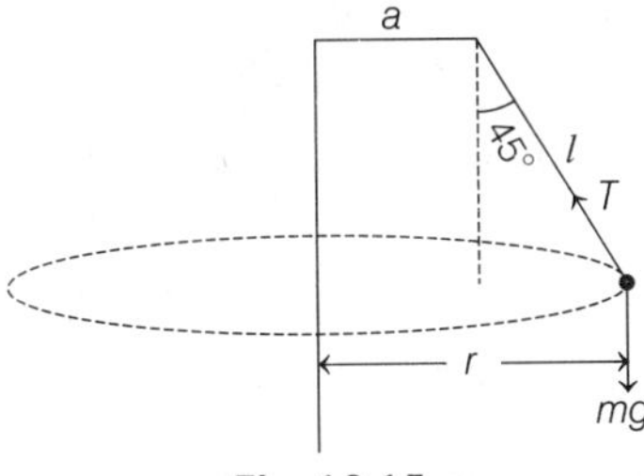

Fig. 10.15

(b) What is the tension in the cord then? Given, $l = \sqrt{2}\ m, a = 20\ cm$ and $m = 5.0\ kg$?

Solution (a) $r = a + l \sin 45° = (0.2) + (\sqrt{2})\left(\frac{1}{\sqrt{2}}\right) = 1.2 \text{ m}$

Now, $$T \cos 45° = mg \quad \text{...(i)}$$

and $$T \sin 45° = mr\omega^2 \quad \text{...(ii)}$$

From Eqs. (i) and (ii), we have $\omega = 2n\pi = \sqrt{\frac{g}{r}}$

$$\therefore \quad n = \frac{1}{2\pi}\sqrt{\frac{g}{r}} = \frac{60}{2\pi}\sqrt{\frac{9.8}{1.2}} \text{ rpm} = 27.3 \text{ rpm}$$ **Ans.**

(b) From Eq. (i), we have $T = \sqrt{2}\, mg = (\sqrt{2})(5.0)(9.8)$

$= 69.3$ N **Ans.**

Example 10.8 *A turn of radius 20 m is banked for the vehicle of mass 200 kg going at a speed of 10 m/s. Find the direction and magnitude of frictional force acting on a vehicle if it moves with a speed*

(a) 5 m/s

(b) 15 m/s.

Assume that friction is sufficient to prevent slipping. $(g = 10\ m/s^2)$

Solution (a) The turn is banked for speed $v = 10$ m/s

Therefore, $$\tan\theta = \frac{v^2}{rg} = \frac{(10)^2}{(20)(10)} = \frac{1}{2}$$

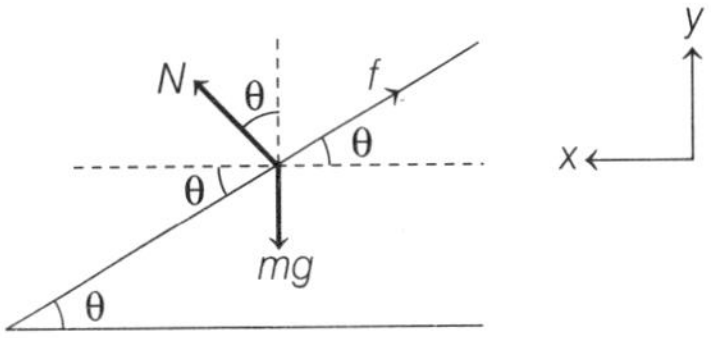

Now, as the speed is decreased, force of friction f acts upwards.

Fig. 10.16

Using the equations $$\Sigma F_x = \frac{mv^2}{r}$$

and $\Sigma F_y = 0$, we get

$$N \sin\theta - f \cos\theta = \frac{mv^2}{r} \quad \text{...(i)}$$

$$N \cos\theta + f \sin\theta = mg \qquad \text{...(ii)}$$

Substituting, $\theta = \tan^{-1}\left(\frac{1}{2}\right)$, $v = 5$ m/s, $m = 200$ kg and $r = 20$ m, in the above equations,

we get $$f = 300\sqrt{5}\ \text{N} \qquad \text{(upwards)}$$

(b) In the second case force of friction f will act downwards.

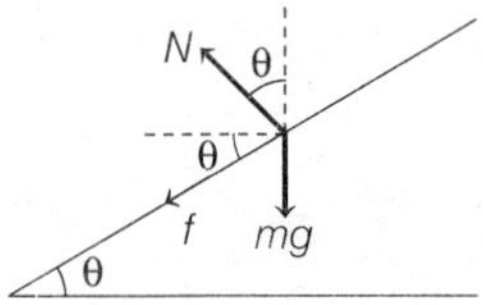

Using $$\Sigma F_x = \frac{mv^2}{r}$$

and $$\Sigma F_y = 0, \quad \text{we get}$$

$$N \sin\theta + f \cos\theta = \frac{mv^2}{r} \qquad \text{...(iii)}$$

$$N \cos\theta - f \sin\theta = mg \qquad \text{...(iv)}$$

Fig. 10.17

Substituting $\theta = \tan^{-1}\left(\frac{1}{2}\right)$, $v = 15$ m/s, $m = 200$ kg

and $r = 20$ m in the above equations, we get

$$f = 500\sqrt{5}\ \text{N} \qquad \text{(downwards)}$$

INTRODUCTORY EXERCISE 10.2

1. A turn has a radius of 10 m. If a vehicle goes round it at an average speed of 18 km/h, what should be the proper angle of banking?
2. If the road of the previous problem is horizontal (no banking), what should be the minimum friction coefficient so that a scooter going at 18 km/h does not skid?
3. A circular road of radius 50 m has the angle of banking equal to 30°. At what speed should a vehicle go on this road so that the friction is not used?
4. Is a body in uniform circular motion in equilibrium?
5. A car driver going at speed v suddenly finds a wide wall at a distance r. Should he apply brakes or turn the car in a circle of radius r to avoid hitting the wall.
6. A 4 kg block is attached to a vertical rod by means of two strings of equal length. When the system rotates about the axis of the rod, the strings are extended as shown in figure.
   (a) How many revolutions per minute must the system make in order for the tension in the upper string to be 200 N?
   (b) What is the tension in the lower string then?

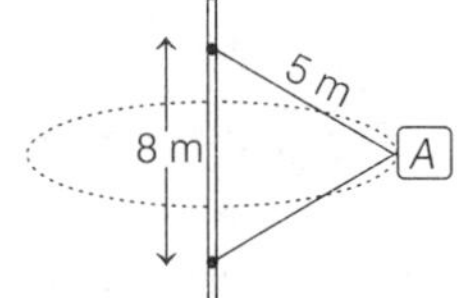

Fig. 10.18

7. A car moves at a constant speed on a straight but hilly road. One section has a crest and dip of the same 250 m radius.
   (a) As the car passes over the crest the normal force on the car is one half the 16 kN weight of the car. What will be the normal force on the car as its passes through the bottom of the dip?
   (b) What is the greatest speed at which the car can move without leaving the road at the top of the hill?
   (c) Moving at a speed found in part (b) what will be the normal force on the car as it moves through the bottom of the dip? (Take, $g = 10\ \text{m/s}^2$)

10.4 Centrifugal Force

Newton's laws are valid only in inertial frames. In non-inertial frames a pseudo force $-m\mathbf{a}$ has to be applied. ($\mathbf{a}$ = acceleration of frame of reference). After applying the pseudo force one can apply Newton's laws in their usual form. Now, suppose a frame of reference is rotating with constant angular velocity ω in a circle of radius 'r'. Then, it will become a non-inertial frame of acceleration $r\omega^2$ towards the centre. Now, if we observe an object of mass 'm' from this frame then a pseudo force of magnitude $mr\omega^2$ will have to be applied to this object in a direction away from the centre. This pseudo force is called the centrifugal force. After applying this force we can now apply Newton's laws in their usual form. Following examples will illustrate the concept more clearly:

Example 10.9 *A particle of mass m is placed over a horizontal circular table rotating with an angular velocity ω about a vertical axis passing through its centre. The distance of the object from the axis is r. Find the force of friction f between the particle and the table.*

Solution Let us solve this problem from both frames. The one is a frame fixed on ground and the other is a frame fixed on table itself.

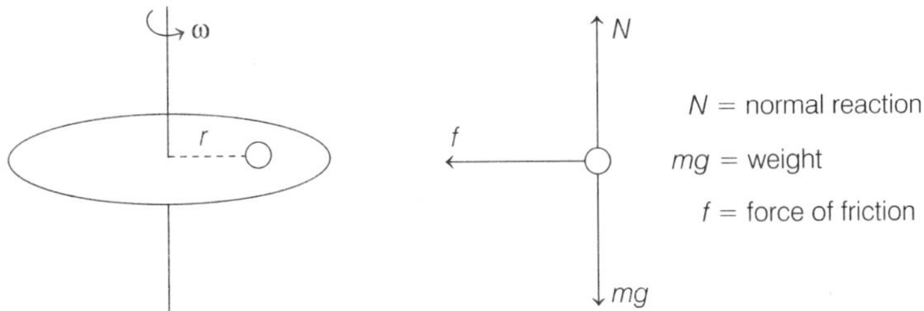

Fig. 10.19

From Frame of Reference Fixed on Ground (Inertial)

Here, N will balance its weight and the force of friction f will provide the necessary centripetal force.

Thus, $$f = mr\omega^2$$ **Ans.**

From Frame of Reference Fixed on Table Itself (Non-inertial)

In the free body diagram of particle with respect to table, in addition to above three forces (N, mg and f) a pseudo force of magnitude $mr\omega^2$ will have to be applied in a direction away from the centre. But one thing should be clear that in this frame the particle is in equilibrium, i.e. N will balance its weight in vertical direction while f will balance the pseudo force in horizontal direction.

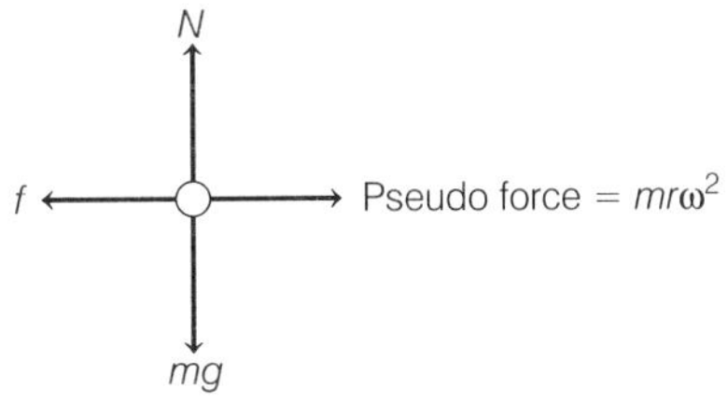

N

f — Pseudo force = $mr\omega^2$

mg

Fig. 10.20

or $$f = mr\omega^2$$ **Ans.**

Thus, we see that f comes out to be $mr\omega^2$ from both the frames.

Example 10.10 *Two blocks A and B of masses 1 kg and 3 kg are attached with two massless strings as shown in figure. The system is kept over a smooth table and it is rotated about the axis shown in figure with constant angular speed $\omega = 2 \, rad/s$.*

Find direction and magnitude of centrifugal force on
(a) A as observed by B
(b) B as observed by A

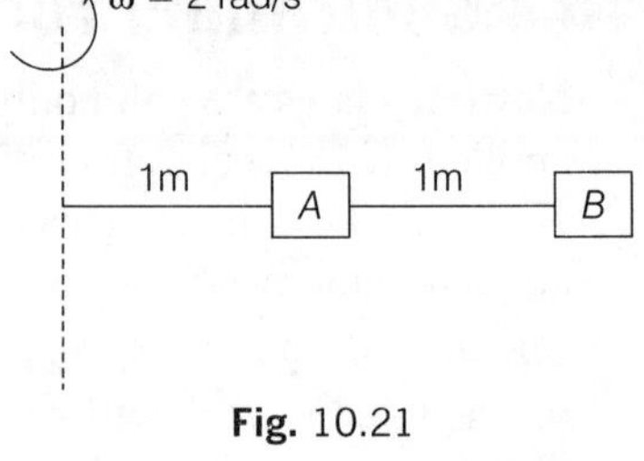

Fig. 10.21

Solution (a) Acceleration of B,

$$a_B = r_B \omega^2 = (2)(2)^2 = 8 \text{ m/s}^2 \quad \text{(towards centre)}$$

Mass of A $\quad m_A = 1$ kg .

$\therefore$ Centrifugal force (or pseudo force) on A,

$$F_A = m_A a_B = (1)(8) = 8 \text{N}$$ **Ans.**

Direction of this force is in the opposite direction of $\mathbf{a}_B$. Therefore, direction of $\mathbf{F}_A$ is radially outwards.

(b) Acceleration of A, $\quad a_A = r_A \omega^2 = (1)(2)^2 = 4 \text{ m/s}^2$ (towards centre)

Mass of B, $\quad m_B = 3$ kg

$\therefore$ Centrifugal force on B,

$$F_B = m_B a_A = (3)(4) = 12 \text{N}$$ **Ans.**

Direction of $\mathbf{F}_B$ is also radially outwards.

10.5 Motion in a Vertical Circle

Suppose a particle of mass m is attached to an inextensible light string of length R. The particle is moving in a vertical circle of radius R about a fixed point O. It is imparted a velocity u in horizontal direction at lowest point A. Let v be its velocity at point B of the circle as shown in figure. Here,

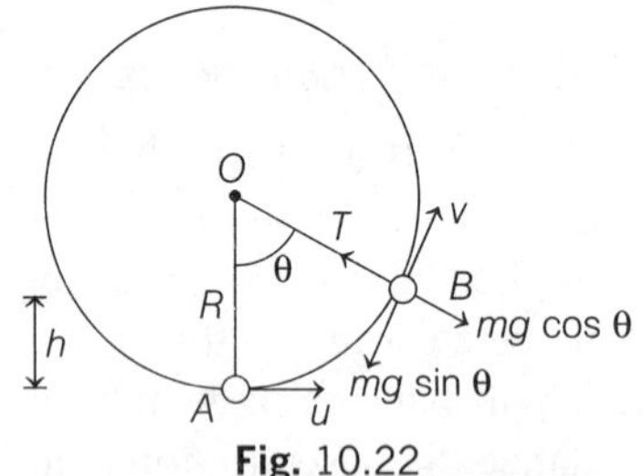

Fig. 10.22

$$h = R(1 - \cos\theta) \quad \text{...(i)}$$

From conservation of mechanical energy

$$\frac{1}{2} m(u^2 - v^2) = mgh$$

or

$$v^2 = u^2 - 2gh \quad \text{...(ii)}$$

The necessary centripetal force is provided by the resultant of tension T and $mg \cos\theta$

$$\therefore \qquad T - mg\cos\theta = \frac{mv^2}{R} \qquad \text{...(iii)}$$

Now, following three conditions arise depending on the value of u.

Condition of Looping the Loop ($u \geq \sqrt{5gR}$)

The particle will complete the circle if the string does not slack even at the highest point ($\theta = \pi$). Thus, tension in the string should be greater than or equal to zero ($T \geq 0$) at $\theta = \pi$. In critical case substituting $T = 0$ and $\theta = \pi$ in Eq. (iii), we get

$$mg = \frac{mv_{\min}^2}{R} \quad \text{or} \quad v_{\min}^2 = gR \quad \text{or} \quad v_{\min} = \sqrt{gR} \qquad \text{(at highest point)}$$

Substituting $\theta = \pi$ in Eq. (i), $\quad h = 2R$

Therefore, from Eq. (ii), we have

$$u_{\min}^2 = v_{\min}^2 + 2gh$$

or

$$u_{\min}^2 = gR + 2g(2R) = 5\,gR$$

or

$$u_{\min} = \sqrt{5\,gR}$$

Thus, if $u \geq \sqrt{5gR}$, the particle will complete the circle. At $u = \sqrt{5gR}$, velocity at highest point is $v = \sqrt{gR}$ and tension in the string is zero.

Substituting $\theta = 0°$ and $v = \sqrt{5gR}$ in Eq. (iii), we get $T = 6\,mg$ or in the critical condition tension in the string at lowest position is $6\,mg$. This is shown in Fig. 10.23.

If $u < \sqrt{5gR}$, following two cases are possible

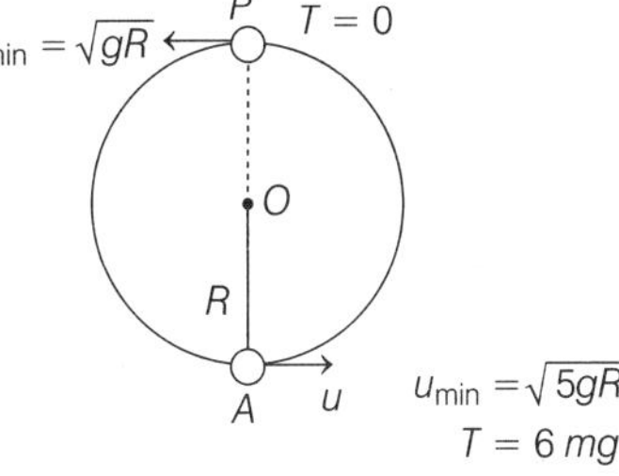

Fig. 10.23

Condition of Leaving the Circle ($\sqrt{2gR} < u < \sqrt{5gR}$)

If $u < \sqrt{5gR}$, the tension in the string will become zero before reaching the highest point. From Eq. (iii), tension in the string becomes zero ($T = 0$)

where,

$$\cos\theta = \frac{-v^2}{Rg} \quad \text{or} \quad \cos\theta = \frac{2gh - u^2}{Rg}$$

Substituting this value of $\cos\theta$ in Eq. (i), we get

$$\frac{2gh - u^2}{Rg} = 1 - \frac{h}{R} \quad \text{or} \quad h = \frac{u^2 + Rg}{3g} = h_1 \text{ (say)} \qquad \text{...(iv)}$$

or we can say that at height h_1 tension in the string becomes zero. Further, if $u < \sqrt{5gR}$, velocity of the particle becomes zero when

$$0 = u^2 - 2gh \quad \text{or} \quad h = \frac{u^2}{2g} = h_2 \text{ (say)} \qquad \text{...(v)}$$

i.e. at height h_2 velocity of particle becomes zero.

Now, the particle will leave the circle if tension in the string becomes zero but velocity is not zero or $T = 0$ but $v \neq 0$. This is possible only when

$$h_1 < h_2 \quad \text{or} \quad \frac{u^2 + Rg}{3g} < \frac{u^2}{2g}$$

or $$2u^2 + 2Rg < 3u^2 \quad \text{or} \quad u^2 > 2Rg \quad \text{or} \quad u > \sqrt{2Rg}$$

Therefore, if $\sqrt{2gR} < u < \sqrt{5gR}$, the particle leaves the circle.

From Eq. (iv), we can see that $h > R$ if $u^2 > 2gR$. Thus, the particle will leave the circle when $h > R$ or $90° < \theta < 180°$. This situation is shown in the Fig. 10.24.

$$\sqrt{2gR} < u < \sqrt{5gR} \quad \text{or} \quad 90° < \theta < 180°$$

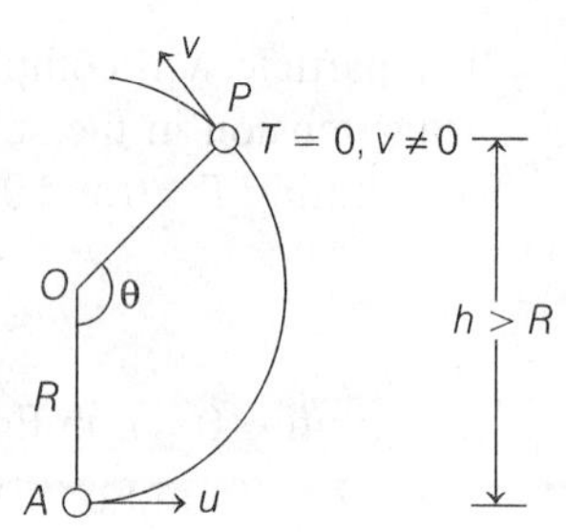

Fig. 10.24

Note *After leaving the circle, the particle will follow a parabolic path as the particle comes under gravity.*

Condition of Oscillation $(0 < u \leq \sqrt{2gR})$

The particle will oscillate, if velocity of the particle becomes zero but tension in the string is not zero. or $v = 0$, but $T \neq 0$. This is possible when

$$h_2 < h_1$$

or $$\frac{u^2}{2g} < \frac{u^2 + Rg}{3g}$$

or $$3u^2 < 2u^2 + 2Rg$$

or $$u^2 < 2Rg$$

or $$u < \sqrt{2Rg}$$

Moreover, if $h_1 = h_2$, $u = \sqrt{2Rg}$ and tension and velocity both becomes zero simultaneously.

Further, from Eq. (iv), we can see that $h \leq R$ if $u \leq \sqrt{2Rg}$. Thus, for $0 < u \leq \sqrt{2gR}$, particle oscillates in lower half of the circle $(0° < \theta \leq 90°)$.

This situation is shown in the figure.

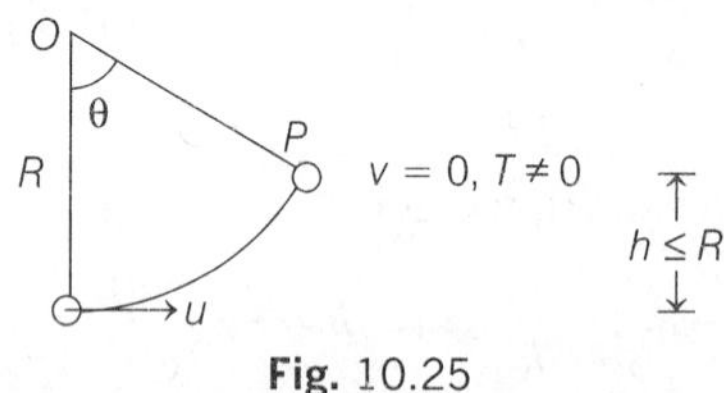

Fig. 10.25

$$0 < u \leq \sqrt{2gR} \quad \text{or} \quad 0° < \theta \leq 90°$$

Note *The above three conditions have been derived for a particle moving in a vertical circle attached to a string. The same conditions apply, if a particle moves inside a smooth spherical shell of radius R. The only difference is that the tension is replaced by the normal reaction N.*

Condition of Looping the Loop is $u \geq \sqrt{5gR}$

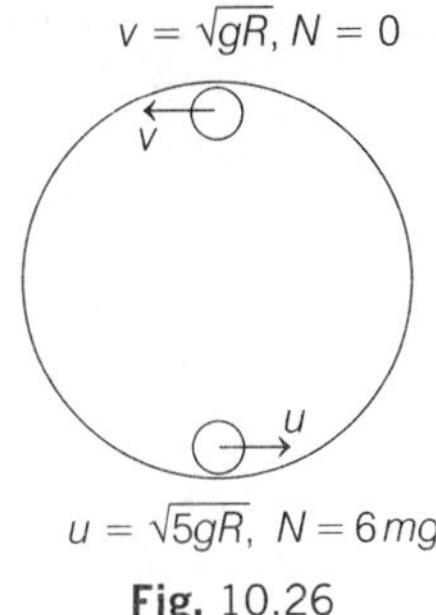

Fig. 10.26

Condition of Leaving the Circle is $\sqrt{2gR} < u < \sqrt{5gR}$

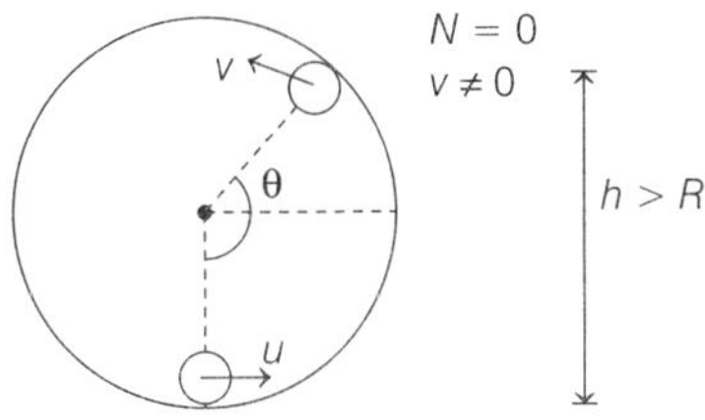

Fig. 10.27

Condition of Oscillation is $0 < u \leq \sqrt{2gR}$

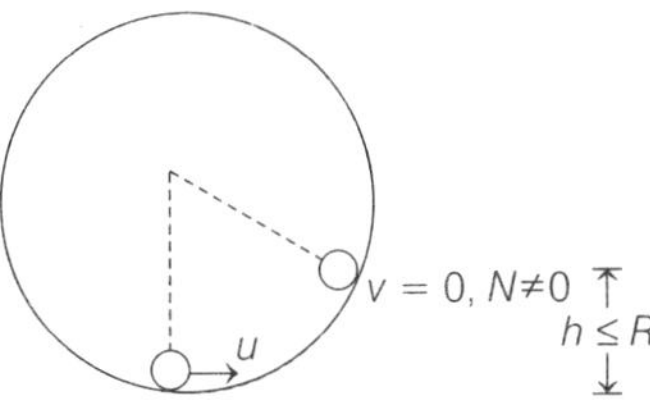

Fig. 10.28

Example 10.11 *A stone tied to a string of length L is whirled in a vertical circle with the other end of the string at the centre. At a certain instant of time the stone is at it lowest position and has a speed u. Find the magnitude of the change in its velocity as it reaches a position, where the string is horizontal.*

Solution $v = \sqrt{u^2 - 2gh} = \sqrt{u^2 - 2gL}$

$$|\Delta \mathbf{v}| = |\mathbf{v}_f - \mathbf{v}_i|$$

$$= \sqrt{v^2 + u^2 - 2v \cdot u \cos 90^\circ}$$

$$= \sqrt{(u^2 - 2gL) + u^2}$$

$$= \sqrt{2(u^2 - gL)}$$ **Ans.**

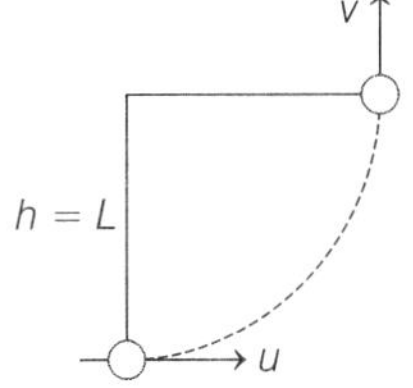

Fig. 10.29

Example 10.12 *With what minimum speed v must a small ball should be pushed inside a smooth vertical tube from a height h so that it may reach the top of the tube? Radius of the tube is R.*

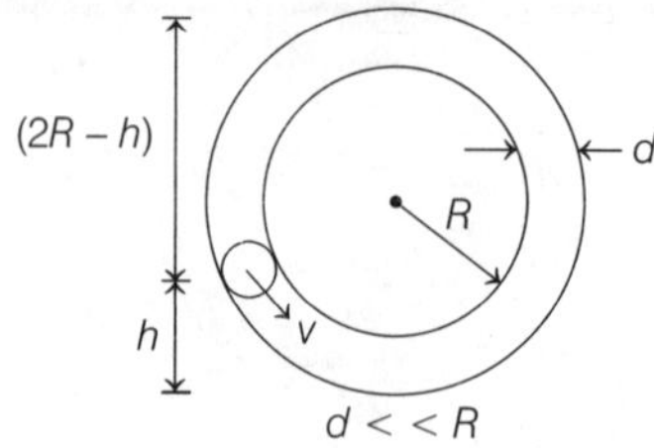

Fig. 10.30

Solution $v_{top} = \sqrt{v^2 - 2g(2R - h)}$

To just complete the vertical circle v_{top} may be zero.

$$\therefore \quad 0 = \sqrt{v^2 - 2g(2R - h)}$$

$$\text{or} \quad v = \sqrt{2g(2R - h)}$$ **Ans.**

Example 10.13 *A particle is suspended from a fixed point by a string of length 5 m. It is projected from the equilibrium position with such a velocity that the string slackens after the particle has reached a height 8 m above the lowest point. Find the velocity of the particle, just before the string slackens. Find also, to what height the particle can rise further?*

Solution At P,

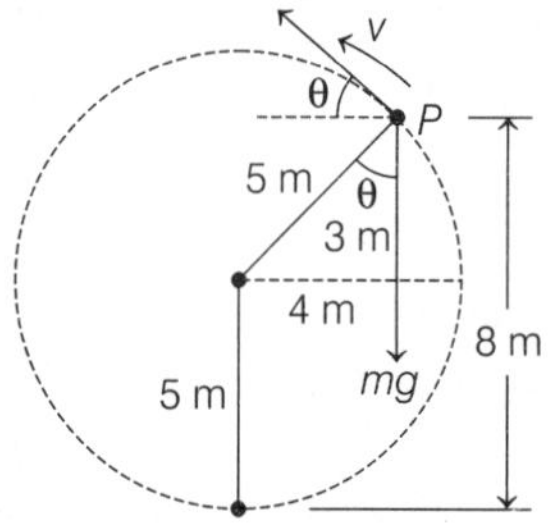

$$T = 0$$

$$\therefore \quad mg\cos\theta = \frac{mv^2}{R}$$

$$\text{or} \quad g\cos\theta = \frac{v^2}{R}$$

$$\text{or} \quad (9.8)\left(\frac{3}{5}\right) = \frac{v^2}{5}$$

Fig. 10.31

$$\therefore \quad v = 5.42 \text{ m/s}$$ **Ans.**

After point P motion is projectile

$$h = \frac{v^2 \sin^2\theta}{2g} = \frac{(5.42)^2 (4/5)^2}{2 \times 9.8}$$

$$= 0.96 \text{ m}$$ **Ans.**

Example 10.14 *A heavy particle hanging from a fixed point by a light inextensible string of length l is projected horizontally with speed $\sqrt{gl}$. Find the speed of the particle and the inclination of the string to the vertical at the instant of the motion when the tension in the string is equal to the weight of the particle.*

Solution Let $T = mg$ at angle θ as shown in figure.

$$h = l(1 - \cos\theta) \qquad \ldots(\text{i})$$

Applying conservation of mechanical energy between points A and B, we get

$$\frac{1}{2}m(u^2 - v^2) = mgh$$

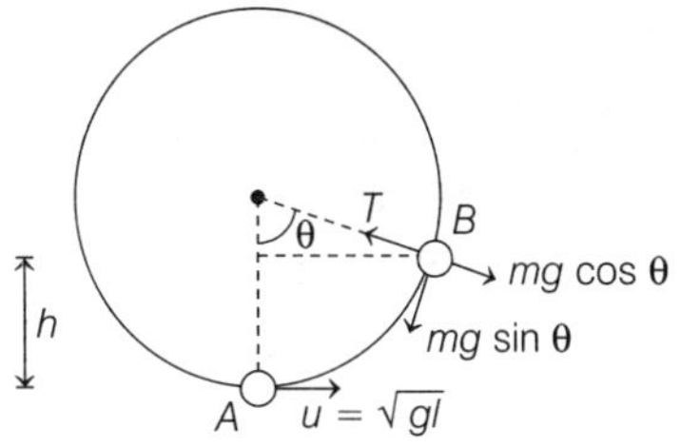

Fig. 10.32

Here, $$u^2 = gl \qquad \ldots(\text{ii})$$

and $v =$ speed of particle in position B

$\therefore$ $$v^2 = u^2 - 2gh \qquad \ldots(\text{iii})$$

Further, $$T - mg\cos\theta = \frac{mv^2}{l} \quad \text{or} \quad mg - mg\cos\theta = \frac{mv^2}{l} \qquad (T = mg)$$

or $$v^2 = gl(1 - \cos\theta) \qquad \ldots(\text{iv})$$

Substituting values of v^2, u^2 and h from Eqs. (iv), (ii) and (i) in Eq. (iii), we get

$$gl(1 - \cos\theta) = gl - 2gl(1 - \cos\theta) \quad \text{or} \quad \cos\theta = \frac{2}{3} \quad \text{or} \quad \theta = \cos^{-1}\left(\frac{2}{3}\right)$$

Substituting $\cos\theta = \frac{2}{3}$ in Eq. (iv), we get

$$v = \sqrt{\frac{gl}{3}}$$ **Ans.**

INTRODUCTORY EXERCISE 10.3

1. In the figure shown in Fig. 10.33, a bob attached with a light string of radius R is given an initial velocity $u = \sqrt{4\,gR}$ at the bottommost point.
   (a) At what height string will slack.
   (b) What is velocity of the bob just before slacking of string.

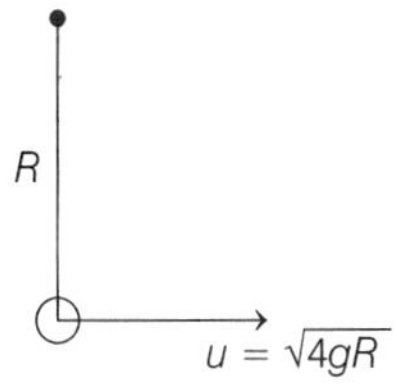

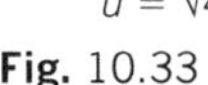

Fig. 10.33

2. In the above question, if $u = \sqrt{gR}$ then
   (a) after rotating an angle θ, velocity of the bob becomes zero. Find the value of θ.
   (b) If mass of the bob is 'm' then what is the tension in the string when velocity becomes zero?
3. In question number-1, if $u = \sqrt{7gR}$ then
   (a) What is the velocity at topmost point?
   (b) What is tension at the topmost point?
   (c) What is tension at the bottommost point?
4. A bob is suspended from a crane by a cable of length $l = 5$ m. The crane and load are moving at a constant speed v_0. The crane is stopped by a bumper and the bob on the cable swings out an angle of 60°. Find the initial speed v_0. ($g = 9.8$ m/s^2)

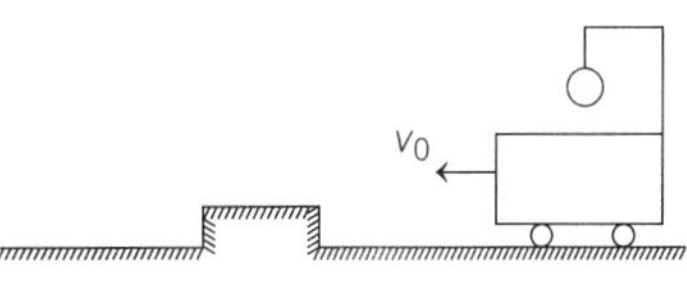

Fig. 10.34

Core Concepts

1. In general, in any curvilinear motion direction of instantaneous velocity is tangential to the path, while acceleration may have any direction. If we resolve the acceleration in two normal directions, one parallel to velocity and another perpendicular to velocity, the first component is a_t while the other is a_n

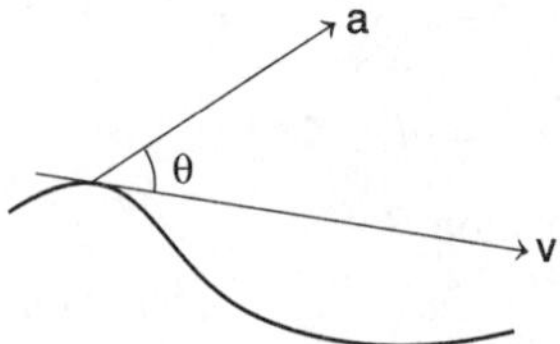

Thus, a_t = component of **a** along **v** $= a\cos\theta = \dfrac{\mathbf{a}\cdot\mathbf{v}}{v}$

$$= \frac{dv}{dt} = \frac{d|\mathbf{v}|}{dt} = \text{rate of change of speed}$$

and a_n = component of **a** perpendicular to **v** $= a\sin\theta = \sqrt{a^2 - a_t^2} = v^2/R$

Here, v is the speed of particle at that instant and R is called the radius of curvature to the curvilinear path at that point.

2. In $a_t = a\cos\theta$, if θ is acute, a_t will be positive and speed will increase. If θ is obtuse a_t will be negative and speed will decrease. If θ is 90°, a_t is zero and speed will remain constant.

3. If a particle of mass m is connected to a light rod and whirled in a vertical circle of radius R, then to complete the circle, the minimum velocity of the particle at the bottommost point is not $\sqrt{5gR}$. Because in this case, velocity of the particle at the topmost point can be zero also. Using conservation of mechanical energy between points A and B as shown in figure (a), we get

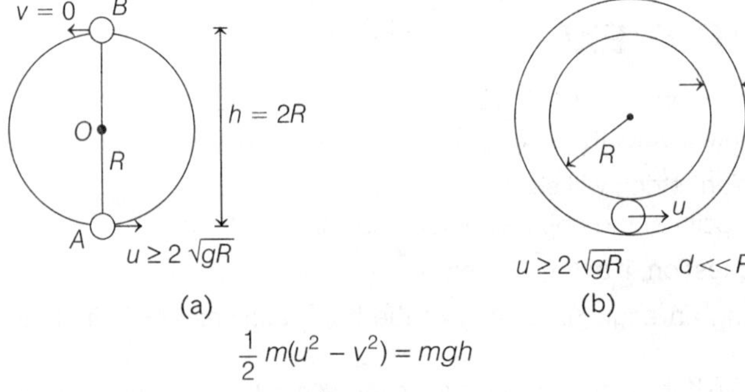

$$\frac{1}{2}m(u^2 - v^2) = mgh$$

or $$\frac{1}{2}mu^2 = mg\,(2R) \qquad (\text{as } v = 0)$$

$\therefore$ $$u = 2\sqrt{gR}$$

Therefore, the minimum value of u in this case is $2\sqrt{gR}$.

Same is the case when a particle is compelled to move inside a smooth vertical tube as shown in figure (b).

4. Oscillation of a pendulum is the part of a vertical circular motion. At point A and C since velocity is zero, net centripetal force will be zero. Only tangential force is present. From A to B or C to B speed of the bob increases. Therefore, tangential force is parallel to velocity. From B to A or B to C speed of the bob decreases. Hence, tangential force is antiparallel to velocity.

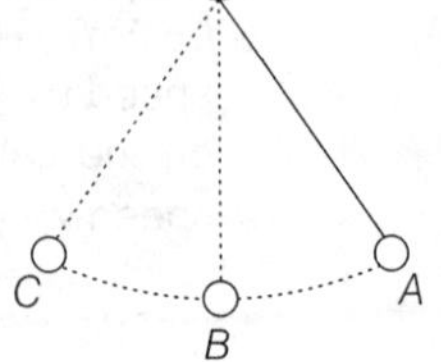

5. In circular motion, acceleration of the particle has two components

(i) tangential acceleration $a_t = \frac{dv}{dt} = R\alpha$

(ii) normal or radial acceleration $a_n = \frac{v^2}{R} = R\omega^2$

a_t and a_n are two perpendicular components of **a**. Hence, we can write $a = \sqrt{a_t^2 + a_n^2}$

Since, circular motion, is a 2-D motion we can write

$$a = \sqrt{a_x^2 + a_y^2} = \sqrt{\left(\frac{dv}{dt}\right)^2 + \left(\frac{v^2}{r}\right)^2}$$

Here, $$v = \sqrt{v_x^2 + v_y^2}$$

or $$v^2 = v_x^2 + v_y^2$$

6. Condition of toppling of a vehicle on circular tracks

While moving in a circular track normal reaction on the outer wheels (N_1) is more than the normal reaction on inner wheels (N_2).

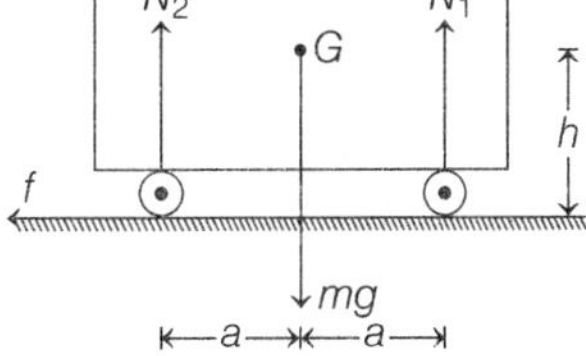

or $$N_1 > N_2$$

This can be proved as below.

Distance between two wheels = $2a$

Height of centre of gravity of car from road = h

For translational equilibrium of car

$$N_1 + N_2 = mg \quad \text{...(i)}$$

and $$f = \frac{mv^2}{r} \quad \text{...(ii)}$$

and for rotational equilibrium of car, net torque about centre of gravity should be zero.

or $$N_1(a) = N_2(a) + f(h) \quad \text{...(iii)}$$

From Eq. (iii), we can see that

$$N_2 = N_1 - \left(\frac{h}{a}\right)f = N_1 - \left(\frac{mv^2}{r}\right)\left(\frac{h}{a}\right) \quad \text{...(iv)}$$

or $$N_2 < N_1$$

From Eq. (iv), we see that N_2 decreases as v is increased.

In critical case, $$N_2 = 0$$

and $$N_1 = mg \quad \text{[From Eq. (i)]}$$

$\therefore$ $$N_1(a) = f(h) \quad \text{[From Eq. (iii)]}$$

or $$(mg)(a) = \left(\frac{mv^2}{r}\right)(h)$$

or $$v = \frac{gra}{h}$$

Now, if $v > \sqrt{\frac{gra}{h}}$, $N_2 < 0$, and the car topples outwards.

Therefore, for a safe turn without toppling $v \le \sqrt{\frac{gra}{h}}$.

7. From the above discussion, we can conclude that while taking a turn on a level road there are two critical speeds, one is the maximum speed for sliding ($= \sqrt{\mu rg}$) and another is maximum speed for toppling $\left(= \sqrt{\frac{gra}{h}}\right)$. One should keep ones car's speed less than both for neither to slide nor to overturn.

8. Motion of a ball over a smooth solid sphere

Suppose a small ball of mass m is given a velocity v over the top of a smooth sphere of radius R. The equation of motion for the ball at the topmost point will be

$$mg - N = \frac{mv^2}{R} \quad \text{or} \quad N = mg - \frac{mv^2}{R}$$

From this equation, we see that the value of N decreases as v increases. Minimum value of N can be zero. Hence,

$$0 = mg - \frac{mv_{max}^2}{R} \quad \text{or} \quad v_{max} = \sqrt{Rg}$$

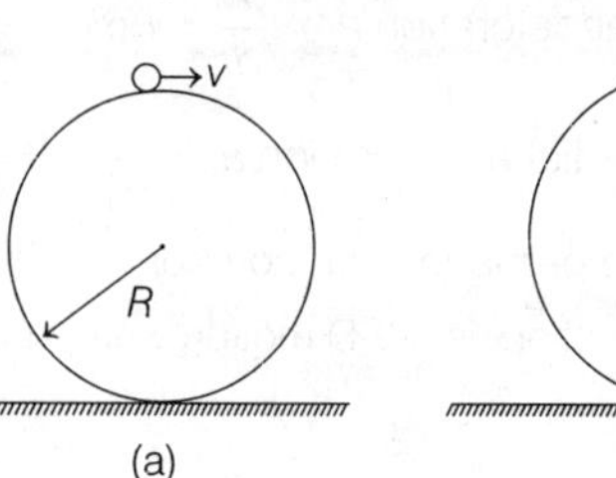

(a)

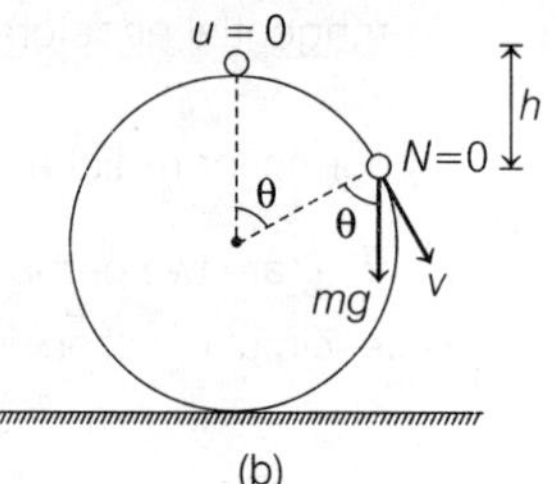

(b)

So, ball will lose contact with the sphere right from the beginning if velocity of the ball at topmost point $v > \sqrt{Rg}$. If $v < \sqrt{Rg}$ it will lose contact after moving certain distance over the sphere. Now, let us find the angle θ where the ball loses contact with the sphere if velocity at topmost point is just zero. Fig. (b)

$$h = R(1 - \cos\theta) \quad \text{...(i)}$$

$$v^2 = 2gh \quad \text{...(ii)}$$

$$mg\cos\theta = \frac{mv^2}{R} \quad (\text{as } N = 0) \quad \text{...(iii)}$$

Solving Eqs. (i), (ii) and (iii), we get

$$\theta = \cos^{-1}\left(\frac{2}{3}\right) = 48.2°$$

Thus, the ball can move on the sphere maximum upto $\theta = \cos^{-1}\left(\frac{2}{3}\right)$.

Exercise : Find angle θ where the ball will lose contact with the sphere, if velocity at topmost point is $u = \frac{v_{max}}{2} = \frac{\sqrt{gR}}{2}$.

Ans. $\theta = \cos^{-1}\left(\frac{3}{4}\right) = 41.4°$

Hint: Only Eq. (ii) will change as,

$$v^2 = u^2 + 2gh \quad (u \neq 0)$$

9. In the following two figures, surface is smooth. So, only two forces N and mg are acting. But direction of acceleration are different.

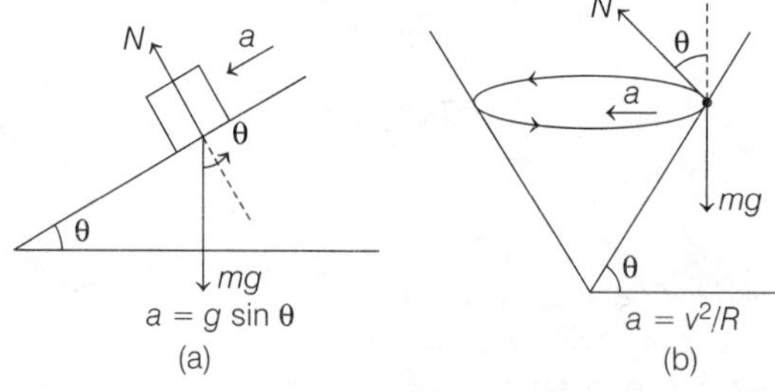

$a = g\sin\theta$ (a)

$a = v^2/R$ (b)

Net force perpendicular to acceleration should be zero. So, in the first figure.

$$N = mg\cos\theta$$

and in the second figure,

$$N\cos\theta = mg$$

Solved Examples

PATTERNED PROBLEMS

Type 1. *Based on vertical circular motion*

Concept

(i) Vertical circular motion is a non-uniform circular motion in which speed of the particle continuously keeps on changing. Therefore, a_t and a_r both are there. In moving upwards, speed decreases. So, a_t is in opposite direction of velocity. In moving downwards, speed increases. So, a_t is in the direction of velocity.

(ii) In circular motion normally, we resolve the forces in two directions, radial and tangential.
Here only two forces act on the particle, tension (T) and weight (mg). Tension is always in the radial direction (towards centre). So, resolve 'mg' along radial and tangential directions.

(iii) Weight (mg) is a constant force, while tension (T) is variable. It is maximum at the bottommost point and minimum at the topmost point.

Example 1 *In the figure shown,* $u = \sqrt{6\,gR}$ $(> \sqrt{5\,gR})$

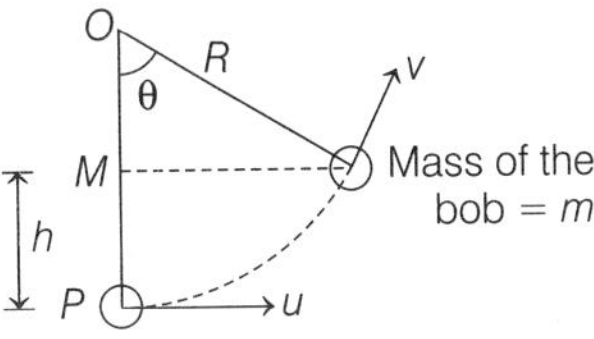

Find h, v, a_r, a_t, T *and* F_{net} *when*

(a) $\theta = 60°$

(b) $\theta = 90°$

(c) $\theta = 180°$

Solution (a) **When $\theta = 60°$**

In the figure, we can see that,

$$h = PM = OP - OM = R - R\cos\theta$$

$$= R - R\cos 60° = R - \frac{R}{2} \qquad \textbf{Ans.}$$

$$v = \sqrt{u^2 - 2\,gh} = \sqrt{6\,gR - 2\,g\left(\frac{R}{2}\right)} = \sqrt{5\,gR} \qquad \textbf{Ans.}$$

$$a_r = \frac{v^2}{R} = \frac{(\sqrt{5gR})^2}{R} = 5g$$ **Ans.**

$$a_t = \frac{F_t}{m} = \frac{\sqrt{3}\,mg}{2m} = \frac{\sqrt{3}g}{2}$$

$$a = \sqrt{a_r^2 + a_t^2} = \sqrt{(5g)^2 + \left(\frac{\sqrt{3}g}{2}\right)^2} = \frac{\sqrt{103}}{2}\,g$$

$$T - \frac{mg}{2} = ma_r = m\,(5g)$$

$\therefore$ $$T = 5.5\,mg$$ **Ans.**

$$F_{net} = ma = \frac{\sqrt{103}}{2}\,mg$$ **Ans.**

(b) **When $\theta = 90°$**

$$h = R$$ **Ans.**

$$v = \sqrt{u^2 - 2gh} = \sqrt{6gR - 2gR}$$

$$= 2\sqrt{gR}$$ **Ans.**

$$a_r = \frac{v^2}{R} = \frac{(2\sqrt{gR})^2}{R} = 4g$$

$$a_t = \frac{F_t}{m} = \frac{mg}{m} = g$$

$$a = \sqrt{a_r^2 + a_t^2} = \sqrt{(4g)^2 + (g)^2} = \sqrt{17}\,g$$

$$T = m\,a_r = m\,(4g)$$

$$= 4\,mg$$ **Ans.**

$$F_{net} = ma = m\,(\sqrt{17}\,g)$$

$$= \sqrt{17}\,mg$$ **Ans.**

(c) **When $\theta = 180°$**

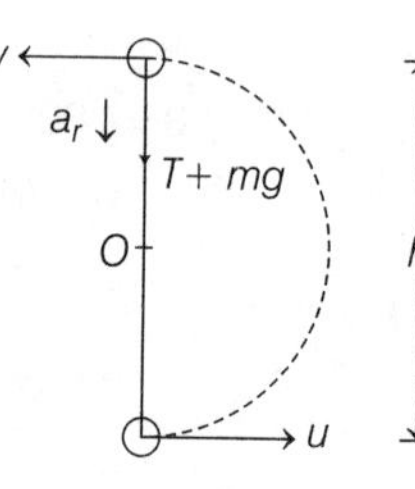

$$h = 2R$$ **Ans.**

$$v = \sqrt{u^2 - 2gh}$$

$$= \sqrt{6gR - 2g \times 2R}$$

$$= \sqrt{2gR}$$ **Ans.**

$$a_r = \frac{v^2}{R} = \frac{(\sqrt{2gR})^2}{R}$$

$$= 2g$$ **Ans.**

$$a_t = \frac{F_t}{m} = 0$$ (as $F_t = 0$, both forces are radial)

$$a = a_r$$ (as $a_t = 0$)

$$= 2g$$ **Ans.**

$$T + mg = ma_r = m\,(2g)$$

$\therefore$ $$T = mg$$

Note *This is the minimum tension during the motion.*

$$F_{net} = ma = m\,(2g) = 2\,mg$$ **Ans.**

Note Points

(i) $F_{net} (= ma)$ is also the vector sum of two forces. T and mg acting on the body.

(ii)

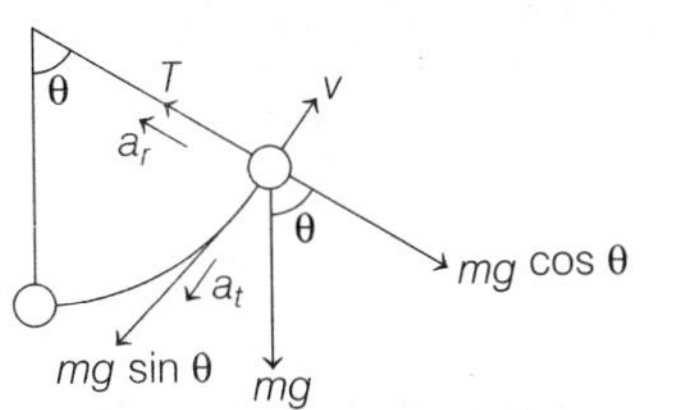

In general, $$a_t = \frac{F_t}{m} = \frac{mg\sin\theta}{m} = g\sin\theta$$

At $\theta = 60°$, $90°$ and $180°$, this value is $\frac{\sqrt{3}}{2}g, g$ and zero.

Similarly, $T - mg\cos\theta = ma_r = \frac{mv^2}{R} \Rightarrow T = mg\cos\theta + \frac{mv^2}{R}$

(iii) At topmost and bottommost points, both forces act in radial direction.

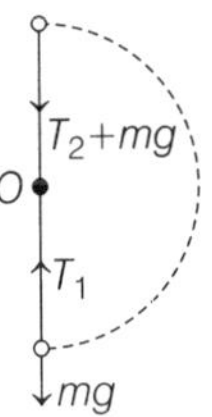

So, $$F_t = 0$$

$$\Rightarrow \qquad a_t = \frac{F_t}{m} = 0$$

Type 2. *Based on motion of a pendulum*

Concept

Motion of a pendulum is the part of a vertical circular motion. It is the case of oscillation in vertical circular motion.Therefore velocity at bottommost point C should be less than or equal to $\sqrt{2gl}$.

At extreme positions A and B where, $\theta = \pm\theta_0$, $v = 0$, $T \neq 0$, $a_r = 0 \cdot T$

Therefore, $a_t = g\sin\theta_0$ and $T = mg\cos\theta_0$

At the bottommost point C, where $\theta = 0°$

$$v = \text{maximum}$$
$$a_r = \text{maximum}$$
$$T = \text{maximum}$$

and $$a_t = 0$$

At some intermediate point P, where $\theta = \theta$, neither of the terms discussed above is zero,

$$h = l\cos\theta - l\cos\theta_0.$$
$$v = \sqrt{2gh}$$
$$a_r = \frac{v^2}{l},\ a_t = g\sin\theta,\ a = \sqrt{a_r^2 + a_t^2},$$

$F_{net} = ma$ and $T - mg\cos\theta = \frac{mv^2}{l} = ma_r$

Example 2 *A ball of mass 'm' is released from point A where, $\theta_0 = 53°$. Length of pendulum is 'l'. Find v, a_r, a_t, a, T and F_{net} at*

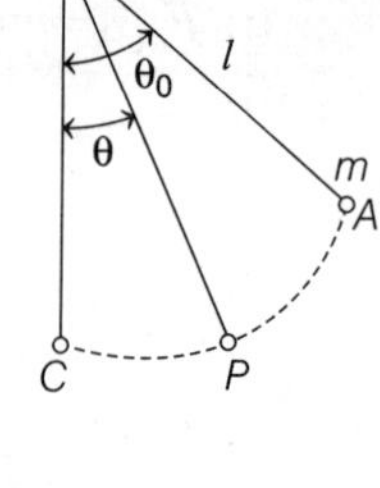

(a) point A

(b) point C

(c) pont P, where $\theta = 37°$

Solution (a) **At point A**

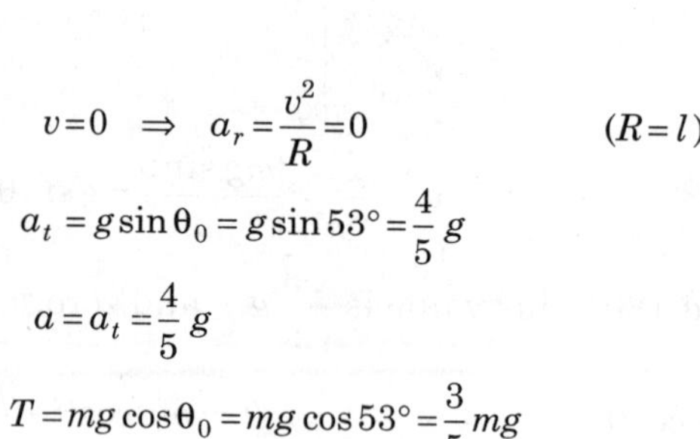

$$v = 0 \Rightarrow a_r = \frac{v^2}{R} = 0 \qquad (R = l)$$

$$a_t = g\sin\theta_0 = g\sin 53° = \frac{4}{5}g$$

$$a = a_t = \frac{4}{5}g$$

$$T = mg\cos\theta_0 = mg\cos 53° = \frac{3}{5}mg$$

$$F_{net} = ma = \frac{4}{5}mg$$

(b) **At point C**

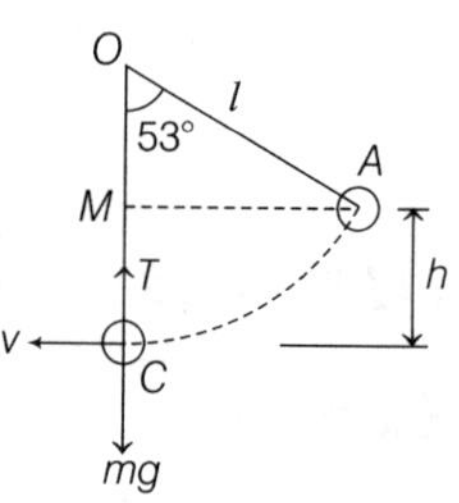

$$h = OC - OM = l - l\cos 53°$$

$$= l - \frac{3}{5}l = \frac{2}{5}l$$

$$v = \sqrt{2gh} = \sqrt{2g\left(\frac{2}{5}l\right)} = \sqrt{\frac{4}{5}gl}$$

$$a_r = \frac{v^2}{R} = \frac{\left(\sqrt{\frac{4}{5}gl}\right)^2}{l} = \frac{4}{5}g$$

$$a_t = 0$$

$$a = a_r = \frac{4}{5}g$$

$$T - mg = \frac{mv^2}{R} = \frac{4}{5}mg$$

$$\therefore \qquad T = \frac{9}{5}mg$$

$$F_{net} = ma = \frac{4}{5}mg$$

(c) At point P

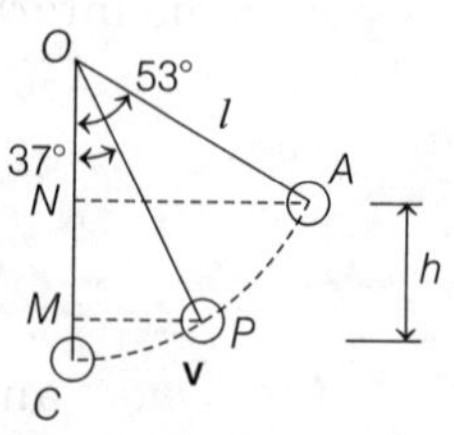

$$h = OM - ON = l\cos 37° - l\cos 53°$$

$$= \frac{4}{5}l - \frac{3}{5}l = \frac{l}{5}$$

$$v = \sqrt{2gh} = \sqrt{2g\left(\frac{l}{5}\right)} = \sqrt{\frac{2}{5}gl}$$

$$a_r = \frac{v^2}{R} = \frac{\left(\sqrt{\frac{2}{5}gl}\right)^2}{l} = \frac{2}{5}g$$

$$a_t = g\sin\theta = g\sin 37° = \frac{3}{5}g$$

$$a = \sqrt{a_r^2 + a_t^2} = \sqrt{\left(\frac{2}{5}g\right)^2 + \left(\frac{3}{5}g\right)^2} = \frac{\sqrt{13}}{5}g$$

$$T - mg\cos\theta = ma_r$$

or $$T - mg\cos 37° = m\left(\frac{2}{5}g\right)$$

$\therefore$ $$T = \frac{6}{5}mg$$

$$F_{\text{net}} = ma = \frac{\sqrt{13}}{5}mg$$

Miscellaneous Examples

Example 3 *A particle of mass m starts moving in a circular path of constant radius r, such that its centripetal acceleration a_c is varying with time t as $a_c = k^2rt^2$, where k is a constant. What is the power delivered to the particle by the forces acting on it ?*

[IIT JEE 1994]

Solution As $a_c = (v^2/r)$ so $(v^2/r) = k^2rt^2$

$\therefore$ Kinetic energy $K = \frac{1}{2}mv^2 = \frac{1}{2}mk^2r^2t^2$

Now, from work-energy theorem

$$W = \Delta K = \frac{1}{2}mk^2r^2t^2 - 0 \qquad \text{[as at } t = 0, K = 0]$$

So, $$P = \frac{dW}{dt} = \frac{d}{dt}\left(\frac{1}{2}mk^2r^2t^2\right) = mk^2r^2t$$ **Ans.**

Alternate solution : Given that $a_c = k^2rt^2$, so that

$$F_c = ma_c = mk^2rt^2$$

Now, as $$a_c = (v^2/r), \text{ so } (v^2/r) = k^2rt^2$$

or $$v = krt$$

So, that $$a_t = (dv/dt) = kr$$

i.e. $$F_t = ma_t = mkr$$

Now, as $$\mathbf{F} = \mathbf{F}_c + \mathbf{F}_t$$

So, $$P = \frac{dW}{dt} = \mathbf{F}\cdot\mathbf{v} = (\mathbf{F}_c + \mathbf{F}_t)\cdot\mathbf{v}$$

In circular motion, $\mathbf{F}_c$ is perpendicular to $\mathbf{v}$ while $\mathbf{F}_t$ parallel to it, so

$$P = F_t v \qquad [\text{as } \mathbf{F}_c \cdot \mathbf{v} = 0]$$

$$\therefore \quad P = mk^2r^2t$$ **Ans.**

Example 4 *If a point moves along a circle with constant speed, prove that its angular speed about any point on the circle is half of that about the centre.*

Solution Let, O be a point on a circle and P be the position of the particle at any time t, such that

$$\angle POA = \theta. \quad \text{Then,} \quad \angle PCA = 2\theta$$

Here, C is the centre of the circle.

Angular velocity of P about O is

$$\omega_O = \frac{d\theta}{dt}$$

and angular velocity of P about C is,

$$\omega_C = \frac{d}{dt}(2\theta) = 2\frac{d\theta}{dt}$$

or

$$\omega_C = 2\omega_O$$ **Proved.**

Example 5 *A particle is projected with a speed u at an angle θ with the horizontal. What is the radius of curvature of the parabola traced out by the projectile at a point where the particle velocity makes an angle $\frac{\theta}{2}$ with the horizontal.*

Solution Let v be the velocity at the desired point. Horizontal component of velocity remains unchanged. Hence,

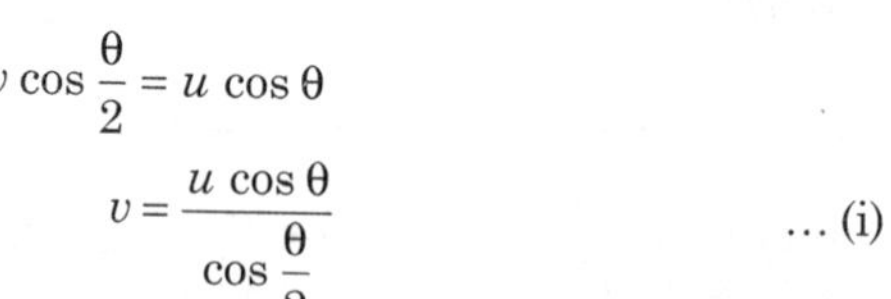

$$v \cos\frac{\theta}{2} = u \cos\theta$$

$$\therefore \quad v = \frac{u\cos\theta}{\cos\frac{\theta}{2}} \qquad \dots\text{(i)}$$

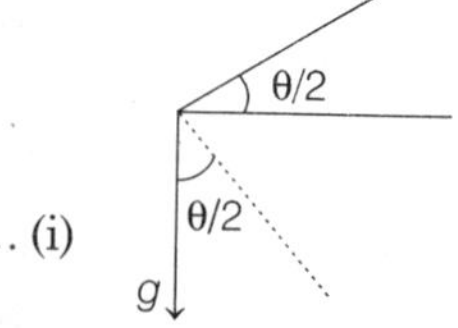

Radial acceleration is the component of acceleration perpendicular to velocity or

$$a_n = g\cos\left(\frac{\theta}{2}\right)$$

$$\therefore \quad \frac{v^2}{R} = g\cos\left(\frac{\theta}{2}\right) \qquad \dots\text{(ii)}$$

Substituting the value of v from Eq. (i) in Eq. (ii), we have radius of curvature

$$R = \frac{\left[\dfrac{u\cos\theta}{\cos\left(\dfrac{\theta}{2}\right)}\right]^2}{g\cos\left(\dfrac{\theta}{2}\right)} = \frac{u^2\cos^2\theta}{g\cos^3\left(\dfrac{\theta}{2}\right)}$$ **Ans.**

Example 6 *A point moves along a circle with a speed $v = kt$, where $k = 0.5\ m/s^2$. Find the total acceleration of the point at the moment when it has covered the nth fraction of the circle after the beginning of motion, where $n = \frac{1}{10}$.*

Solution $v = \frac{ds}{dt} = kt$ or $\int_0^s ds = k\int_0^t t\,dt \Rightarrow \therefore\ s = \frac{1}{2}kt^2$

For completion of nth fraction of circle,

$$s = 2\pi rn = \frac{1}{2}kt^2 \quad \text{or} \quad t^2 = (4\pi nr)/k \qquad \text{...(i)}$$

Tangential acceleration $= a_t = \frac{dv}{dt} = k$ ...(ii)

Normal acceleration $= a_n = \frac{v^2}{r} = \frac{k^2t^2}{r}$ ...(iii)

Substituting the value of t^2 from Eq. (i), we have

or $$a_n = 4\pi nk$$

$\therefore$
$$a = \sqrt{(a_t^2 + a_n^2)} = [k^2 + 16\pi^2 n^2 k^2]^{1/2}$$
$$= k\,[1 + 16\pi^2 n^2]^{1/2}$$
$$= 0.50\,[1 + 16 \times (3.14)^2 \times (0.10)^2]^{1/2}$$
$$= 0.8\ \text{m/s}^2$$

Ans.

Example 7 *In a two dimensional motion of a body, prove that tangential acceleration is nothing but component of acceleration along velocity.*

Solution Let velocity of the particle be,

$$\mathbf{v} = v_x\hat{\mathbf{i}} + v_y\hat{\mathbf{j}}$$

Acceleration
$$\mathbf{a} = \frac{dv_x}{dt}\hat{\mathbf{i}} + \frac{dv_y}{dt}\hat{\mathbf{j}}$$

Component of **a** along **v** will be,
$$\frac{\mathbf{a}\cdot\mathbf{v}}{|\mathbf{v}|} = \frac{v_x\frac{dv_x}{dt} + v_y\cdot\frac{dv_y}{dt}}{\sqrt{v_x^2 + v_y^2}} \qquad \text{... (i)}$$

Further, tangential acceleration of particle is rate of change of speed.

or
$$a_t = \frac{dv}{dt} = \frac{d}{dt}\left(\sqrt{v_x^2 + v_y^2}\right) \quad \text{or} \quad a_t = \frac{1}{2\sqrt{v_x^2 + v_y^2}}\left[2v_x\cdot\frac{dv_x}{dt} + 2v_y\,\frac{dv_y}{dt}\right]$$

or
$$a_t = \frac{v_x\cdot\frac{dv_x}{dt} + v_y\cdot\frac{dv_y}{dt}}{\sqrt{v_x^2 + v_y^2}} \qquad \text{... (ii)}$$

From Eqs. (i) and (ii), we can see that

$$a_t = \frac{\mathbf{a}\cdot\mathbf{v}}{|\mathbf{v}|}$$

or Tangential acceleration = component of acceleration along velocity. **Hence proved.**

Exercises

LEVEL 1

Assertion and Reason

Directions : *Choose the correct option.*

(a) *If both* ***Assertion*** *and* ***Reason*** *are true and the* ***Reason*** *is correct explanation of the* ***Assertion.***

(b) *If both* ***Assertion*** *and* ***Reason*** *are true but* ***Reason*** *is not the correct explanation of* ***Assertion.***

(c) *If* ***Assertion*** *is true, but the* ***Reason*** *is false.*

(d) *If* ***Assertion*** *is false but the* ***Reason*** *is true.*

(e) *If both* ***Assertion*** *and* ***Reason*** *are false.*

1. Assertion : A car moving on a horizontal rough road with velocity v can be stopped in a minimum distance d. If the same car, moving with same speed v takes a circular turn, then minimum safe radius can be $2d$.

Reason : $d = \dfrac{v^2}{2\mu g}$ and minimum safe radius $= \dfrac{v^2}{\mu g}$

2. Assertion : A particle is rotating in a circle with constant speed as shown. Between points A and B, ratio of average acceleration and average velocity is angular velocity of particle about point O.

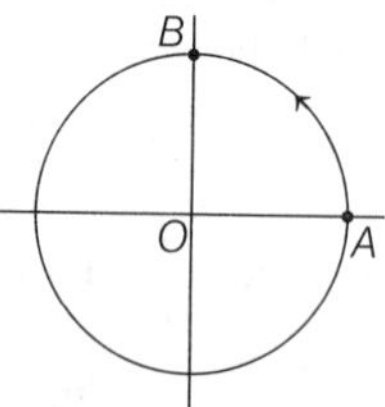

Reason : Since speed is constant, angular velocity is also constant.

3. Assertion : Velocity and acceleration of a particle in circular motion at some instant are: $\mathbf{v} = (2\hat{\mathbf{i}})\ \text{ms}^{-1}$ and $\mathbf{a} = (-\hat{\mathbf{i}} + 2\hat{\mathbf{j}})\ \text{ms}^{-2}$, then radius of circle is 2 m.

Reason : Speed of particle is decreasing at a rate of 1 ms^{-2}.

4. Assertion : In vertical circular motion, acceleration of bob at position A is greater than 'g'.

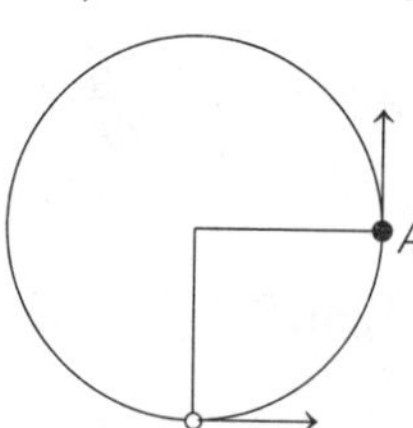

Reason : Net acceleration at A is resultant of tangential and radial components of acceleration.

5. **Assertion :** A particle of mass m takes uniform horizontal circular motion inside a smooth funnel as shown. Normal reaction in this case is not $mg\cos\theta$.

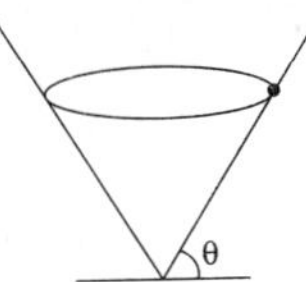

Reason : Acceleration of particle is not along the surface of funnel.

6. **Assertion :** When water in a bucket is whirled fast overhead, the water does not fall out at the top of the circular path.

Reason : The centripetal force in this position on water is more than the weight of water.

Objective Questions

Single Correct Option

1. In a clock, what is the time period of meeting of the minute hand and the second hand?

(a) 59 s (b) $\frac{60}{59}$ s (c) $\frac{59}{60}$ s (d) $\frac{3600}{59}$ s

2. A particle is moving in a circular path with a constant speed. If θ is the angular displacement, then starting from $\theta = 0$, the maximum and minimum change in the linear momentum will occur when value of θ is respectively

(a) 45° and 90° (b) 90° and 180°
(c) 180° and 360° (d) 90° and 270°

3. A simple pendulum of length l has maximum angular displacement θ. Then, maximum kinetic energy of a bob of mass m is

(a) $\frac{1}{2}mgl$ (b) $\frac{1}{2}mgl\cos\theta$ (c) $mgl(1-\cos\theta)$ (d) $\frac{1}{2}mgl\sin\theta$

4. A particle is given an initial speed u inside a smooth spherical shell of radius R so that it is just able to complete the circle. Acceleration of the particle, when its velocity is vertical, is

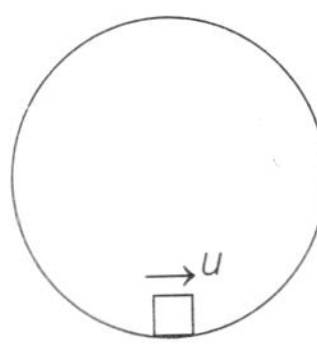

(a) $g\sqrt{10}$ (b) g
(c) $g\sqrt{2}$ (d) $g\sqrt{6}$

5. An insect of mass $m = 3$ kg is inside a vertical drum of radius 2 m that is rotating with an angular velocity of 5 rad s^{-1}. The insect doesn't fall off. Then, the minimum coefficient of friction required is

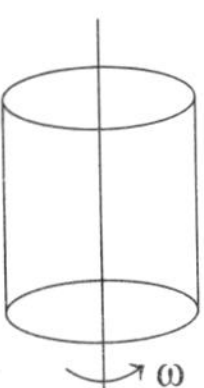

(a) 0.5
(b) 0.4
(c) 0.2
(d) None of the above

6. A point moves along a circle having a radius 20 cm with a constant tangential acceleration 5 cm/s^2. How much time is needed after motion begins for the normal acceleration of the point to be equal to tangential acceleration?
(a) 1 s
(b) 2 s
(c) 3 s
(d) 4 s

7. A ring of mass (2π) kg and of radius 0.25 m is making 300 rpm about an axis through its perpendicular to its plane. The tension (in newton) developed in ring is approximately
(a) 50
(b) 100
(c) 175
(d) 250

8. A car is moving on a circular level road of curvature 300 m. If the coefficient of friction is 0.3 and acceleration due to gravity is 10 m/s^2, the maximum speed of the car can be
(a) 90 km/h
(b) 81 km/h
(c) 108 km/h
(d) 162 km/h

9. A string of length 1 m is fixed at one end with a bob of mass 100 g and the string makes $\left(\frac{2}{\pi}\right)$ rev s^{-1} around a vertical axis through a fixed point. The angle of inclination of the string with vertical is
(a) $\tan^{-1}\left(\frac{5}{8}\right)$
(b) $\tan^{-1}\left(\frac{3}{5}\right)$
(c) $\cos^{-1}\left(\frac{3}{5}\right)$
(d) $\cos^{-1}\left(\frac{5}{8}\right)$

10. In the previous question, the tension in the string is
(a) $\frac{5}{8}$ N
(b) $\frac{8}{5}$ N
(c) $\frac{50}{8}$ N
(d) $\frac{80}{5}$ N

11. A small particle of mass 0.36 g rests on a horizontal turn-table at a distance 25 cm from the axis of spindle. The turn-table is accelerated at a rate of $\alpha = \frac{1}{3} \text{ rad s}^{-2}$. The frictional force that the table exerts on the particle 2 s after the startup is
(a) 40 μN
(b) 30 μN
(c) 50 μN
(d) 60 μN

12. A simple pendulum of length l and bob of mass m is displaced from its equilibrium position O to a position P, so that height of P above O is h. It is then released. What is the tension in the string when the bob passes through the equilibrium position O? Neglect friction, v is the velocity of the bob at O.
(a) $m\left(g - \frac{v^2}{l}\right)$
(b) $\frac{2\,mgh}{l}$
(c) $mg\left(1 + \frac{h}{l}\right)$
(d) $mg\left(1 + \frac{2h}{l}\right)$

13. Two particles revolve concentrically in a horizontal plane in the same direction. The time required to complete one revolution for particle A is 3 min, while for particle B is 1 min. The time required for A to complete one revolution relative to B is
(a) 2 min
(b) 1 min
(c) 1.5 min
(d) 1.25 min

14. Three particles A, B and C move in a circle in anti-clockwise direction with speeds 1 ms^{-1}, 2.5 ms^{-1} and 2 ms^{-1}, respectively. The initial positions of A, B and C are as shown in figure. The ratio of distance travelled by B and C by the instant A, B and C meet for the first time is

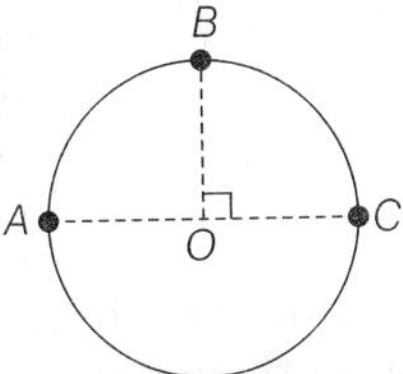

(a) 3 : 2 (b) 5 : 4
(c) 3 : 5 (d) data insufficient

15. The ratio of angular speeds of minute hand and hour hand of a watch is
(a) 1 : 12 (b) 6 : 1
(c) 12 : 1 (d) 1 : 6

16. A car moves along an uneven horizontal surface with a constant speed at all points. The normal reaction of the road on the car is

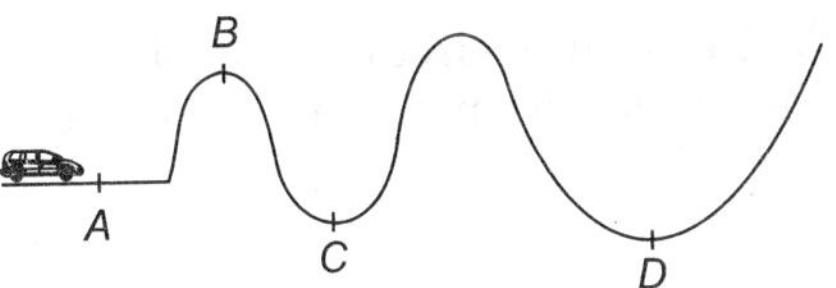

(a) $N_A = N_B = N_C = N_D$ (b) $N_C > N_D > N_A > N_B$
(c) $N_B > N_C > N_A > N_D$ (d) $N_C > N_D > N_B > N_A$

17. A particle moves in a circular path of radius R with an angular velocity $\omega = a - bt$, where a and b are positive constants and t is time. The magnitude of the acceleration of the particle after time $\frac{2a}{b}$ is
(a) $\frac{a}{R}$ (b) a^2R
(c) $R(a^2 + b)$ (d) $R\sqrt{a^4 + b^2}$

18. A coin, placed on a rotating turn-table slips, when it is placed at a distance of 9 cm from the centre. If the angular velocity of the turn-table is tripled, it will just slip, if its distance from the centre is
(a) 27 cm (b) 9 cm (c) 3 cm (d) 1 cm

19. A mass of 100 g is tied to one end of a string 2 m long. The body is revolving in a horizontal circle making a maximum of 200 rev per min. The other end of the string is fixed at the centre of the circle of revolution. The maximum tension that the string can bear is (approximately)
(a) 8.76 N (b) 8.94 N
(c) 89.42 N (d) 87.64 N

20. Toy cart tied to the end of an unstretched string of length a, when revolved moves in a horizontal circle of radius $2a$ with a time period T. Now, the toy cart is speeded up until it moves in a horizontal circle of radius $3a$ with a period T'. If Hooke's law ($F = kx$) holds, then
(a) $T' = \sqrt{\frac{3}{2}}\, T$ (b) $T' = \left(\frac{\sqrt{3}}{2}\right) T$ (c) $T' = \left(\frac{3}{2}\right) T$ (d) $T' = T$

21. A mass is attached to the end of a string of length l which is tied to a fixed point O. The mass is released from the initial horizontal position of the string. Below the point O, at what minimum distance a peg P should be fixed, so that the mass turns about P and can describe a complete circle in the vertical plane?

(a) $\left(\frac{3}{5}\right) l$
(b) $\left(\frac{2}{5}\right) l$
(c) $\frac{l}{3}$
(d) $\frac{2l}{3}$

22. A small body of mass m slides without friction from the top of a hemisphere of radius r. At what height will the body be detached from the centre of the hemisphere ?

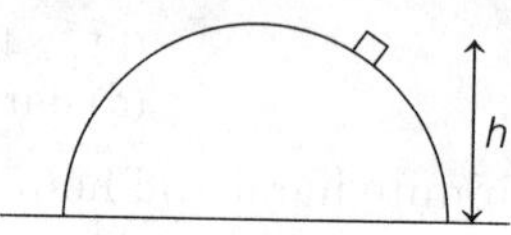

(a) $h = \frac{r}{2}$
(b) $h = \frac{r}{3}$
(c) $h = \frac{2r}{3}$
(d) $h = \frac{r}{4}$

23. A frictionless track $ABCDE$ ends in a circular loop of radius R. A body slides down the track from point A which is at height $h = 5$ cm. Maximum value of R for a body to complete the loop successfully is

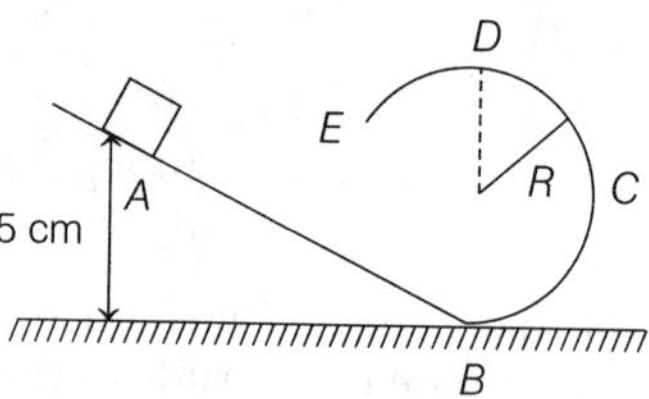

(a) 2 cm
(b) $\frac{10}{3}$ cm
(c) $\frac{15}{4}$ cm
(d) $\frac{18}{3}$ cm

24. A circular disc of radius R is rotating about its axis O with a uniform angular velocity ω as shown in the figure. The magnitude of the relative velocity of point A relative to point B on the disc is

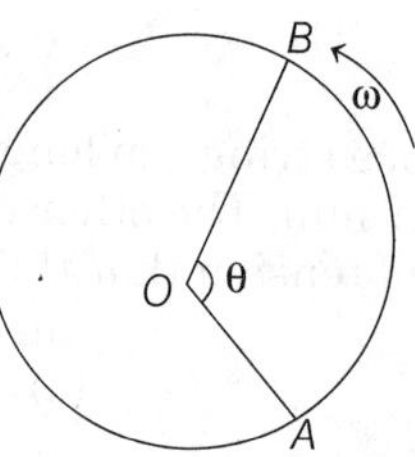

(a) zero
(b) $R\omega \sin\left(\frac{\theta}{2}\right)$
(c) $2R\omega \sin\left(\frac{\theta}{2}\right)$
(d) $\sqrt{3}\, R\omega \sin\left(\frac{\theta}{2}\right)$

25. A string of length l fixed at one end carries a mass m at the other end. The strings makes $\frac{2}{\pi}$ rev/s around the axis through the fixed end as shown in the figure, the tension in the string is

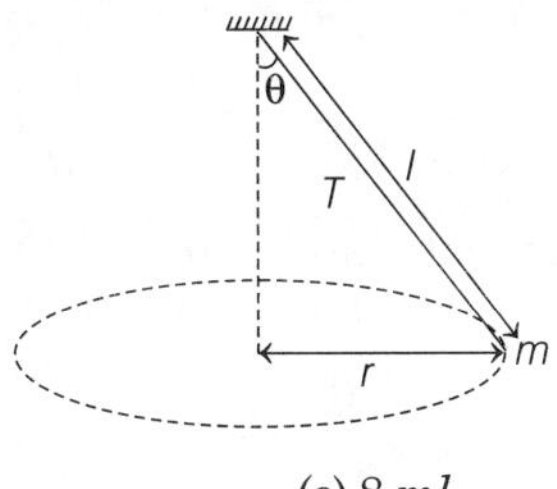

(a) 16 ml (b) 4 ml (c) 8 ml (d) 2 ml

26. A particle of mass m describes a circle of radius (r). The centripetal acceleration of the particle is $\frac{4}{r^2}$. The momentum of the particle is

(a) $\frac{2m}{r}$ (b) $\frac{2m}{\sqrt{r}}$

(c) $\frac{4m}{r}$ (d) $\frac{4m}{\sqrt{r}}$

27. Inside a smooth spherical cavity particle A can slide freely. The block having this cavity is moving horizontally with constant acceleration $a_0 = 10\ \text{m/s}^2$.

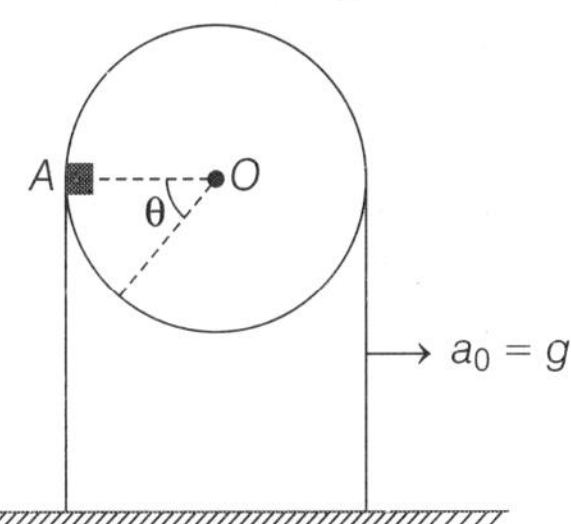

The particle is released from its initial position as shown in the figure. The angle θ with the vertical, when the particle will have maximum speed with respect to the block is

(a) 30° (b) 45° (c) 60° (d) 90°

28. A point P moves in a counter-clockwise direction on a circular path as shown in the figure. The movement of P is such that it sweeps out a length $s = t^3 + 5$, where s is in metre and t is in second. The radius of the path is 20 m. The acceleration of P when $t = 2$ s is nearly, is

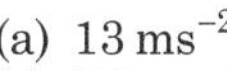

(a) 13 ms^{-2} (b) 12 ms^{-2}

(c) 7.2 ms^{-2} (d) 14 ms^{-2}

29. A mass m is fixed at $x = a$ on a parabolic wire with its axis vertical and vertex at the origin as shown in the figure. The equation of parabola is $x^2 = 4ay$. The wire frame is rotating with constant angular velocity ω about Y-axis. The acceleration of the bead is

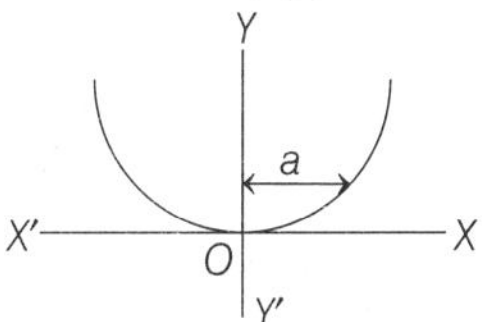

(a) $\frac{a}{4}\omega^2$ (b) $a\omega^2$

(c) zero (d) $\frac{\omega^2}{a}$

30. For a particle in a uniform circular motion, the acceleration **a** at a point $P(R, \theta)$ on the circle of radius R is (here, θ is measured from the X-axis)

(a) $-\frac{v^2}{R}\cos\theta\,\hat{\mathbf{i}} + \frac{v^2}{R}\sin\theta\,\hat{\mathbf{j}}$ (b) $-\frac{v^2}{R}\sin\theta\,\hat{\mathbf{i}} + \frac{v^2}{R}\cos\theta\,\hat{\mathbf{j}}$

(c) $-\frac{v^2}{R}\cos\theta\,\hat{\mathbf{i}} - \frac{v^2}{R}\sin\theta\,\hat{\mathbf{j}}$ (d) $\frac{v^2}{R}\hat{\mathbf{i}} + \frac{v^2}{R}\hat{\mathbf{j}}$

31. A particle suspended by a light inextensible thread of length l is projected horizontally from its lowest position with velocity $\sqrt{7gl/2}$. The string will slack after swinging through an angle equal to

(a) 30° (b) 90° (c) 120° (d) 150°

32. A conical pendulum of length L makes an angle θ with the vertical. The time period will be

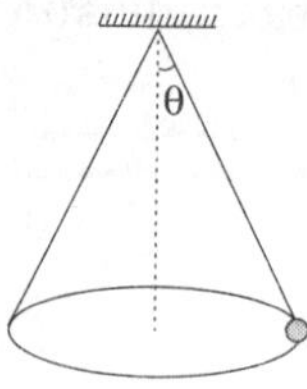

(a) $2\pi\sqrt{\frac{L\cos\theta}{g}}$ (b) $2\pi\sqrt{\frac{L}{g\cos\theta}}$

(c) $2\pi\sqrt{\frac{L\tan\theta}{g}}$ (d) $2\pi\sqrt{\frac{L}{g\tan\theta}}$

33. A particle starts travelling on a circle with constant tangential acceleration. The angle between velocity vector and acceleration vector, at the moment when particle completes half the circular track, is

(a) $\tan^{-1}(2\pi)$ (b) $\tan^{-1}(\pi)$ (c) $\tan^{-1}(3\pi)$ (d) zero

Subjective Questions

1. A particle is projected with a speed u at an angle θ with the horizontal. Consider a small part of its path near the highest position and take it approximately to be a circular arc. What is the radius of this circle? This radius is called the radius of curvature of the curve at the point.

2. Find the maximum speed at which a truck can safely travel without toppling over, on a curve of radius 250 m. The height of the centre of gravity of the truck above the ground is 1.5 m and the distance between the wheels is 1.5 m, the truck being horizontal.

3. A hemispherical bowl of radius R is rotating about its axis of symmetry which is kept vertical. A small ball kept in the bowl rotates with the bowl without slipping on its surface. If the surface of the bowl is smooth and the angle made by the radius through the ball with the vertical is α. Find the angular speed at which the bowl is rotating.

4. Show that the angle made by the string with the vertical in a conical pendulum is given by $\cos\theta = \frac{g}{L\omega^2}$, where L is the length of the string and ω is the angular speed.

5. A boy whirls a stone of small mass in a horizontal circle of radius 1.5 m and at height 2.9 m above level ground. The string breaks and the stone flies off horizontally and strikes the ground after travelling a horizontal distance of 10 m. What is the magnitude of the centripetal acceleration of the stone while in circular motion ?

6. A block of mass m is kept on a horizontal ruler. The friction coefficient between the ruler and the block is μ. The ruler is fixed at one end and the block is at a distance L from the fixed end. The ruler is rotated about the fixed end in the horizontal plane through the fixed end.
   (a) What can the maximum constant angular speed be for which the block does not slip ?
   (b) If the angular speed of the ruler is uniformly increased from zero at an angular acceleration α, at what angular speed will the block slip ?

7. A thin circular wire of radius R rotates about its vertical diameter with an angular frequency ω. Show that a small bead on the wire remains at its lowermost point for $\omega \le \sqrt{g/R}$. What is angle made by the radius vector joining the centre to the bead with the vertical downward direction for $\omega = \sqrt{2g/R}$? Neglect friction.

8. Two blocks tied with a massless string of length 3 m are placed on a rotating table as shown. The axis of rotation is 1 m from 1 kg mass and 2 m from 2 kg mass. The angular speed $\omega = 4$ rad/s. Ground below 2 kg block is smooth and below 1 kg block is rough. (Take, $g = 10\ \text{m/s}^2$)

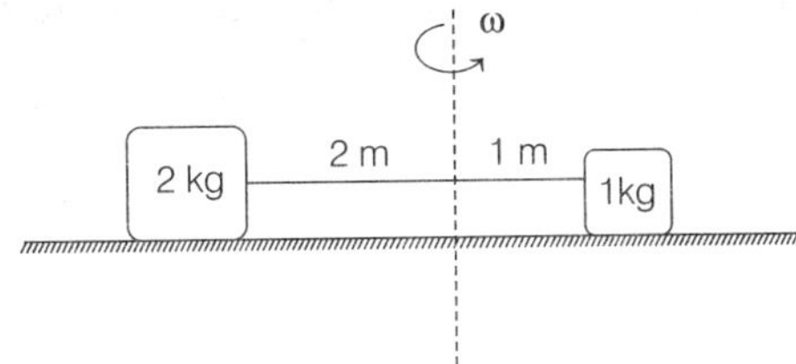

   (a) Find tension in the string, force of friction on 1 kg block and its direction.
   (b) If coefficient of friction between 1 kg block and ground is $\mu = 0.8$. Find maximum angular speed so that neither of the blocks slips.
   (c) If maximum tension in the string can be 100 N, then find maximum angular speed so that neither of the blocks slips.

Note *Assume that in part (b) tension can take any value and in parts (a) and (c) friction can take any value.*

9. A small block slides with velocity $0.5\sqrt{gr}$ on the horizontal frictionless surface as shown in the figure. The block leaves the surface at point C. Calculate angle θ in the figure.

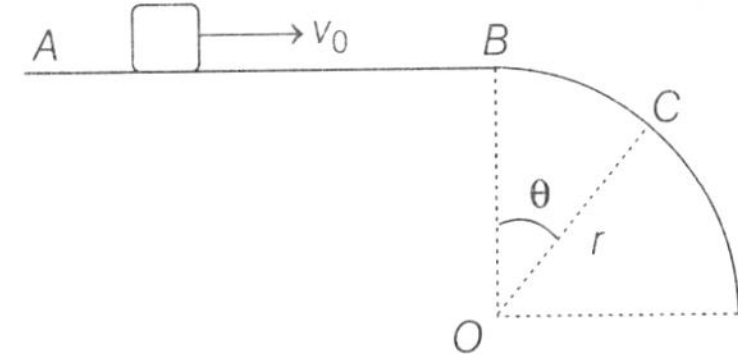

10. The bob of the pendulum shown in figure describes an arc of circle in a vertical plane. If the tension in the cord is 2.5 times the weight of the bob for the position shown. Find the velocity and the acceleration of the bob in that position.

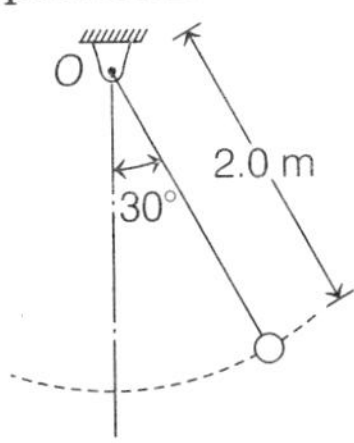

11. The sphere at A is given a downward velocity v_0 of magnitude 5 m/s and swings in a vertical plane at the end of a rope of length $l = 2$ m attached to a support at O. Determine the angle θ at which the rope will break, knowing that it can withstand a maximum tension equal to twice the weight of the sphere.

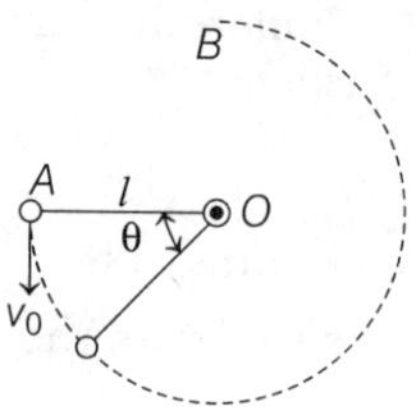

12. A toy car is moving on a circular path of radius 10 m on an inclined plane of inclination 30°. The coefficient of friction between the tyres and the inclined plane is $\mu = \frac{2}{\sqrt{3}}$. Find maximum constant speed of car such that car does not slip. Assume that the width of a car is negligible with respect to radius of circular path.

LEVEL 2

Objective Questions

Single Correct Option

1. A collar B of mass 2 kg is constrained to move along a horizontal smooth and fixed circular track of radius 5 m. The spring lying in the plane of the circular track and having spring constant 200 Nm^{-1} is undeformed when the collar is at A. If the collar starts from rest at B, the normal reaction exerted by the track on the collar when it passes through A is

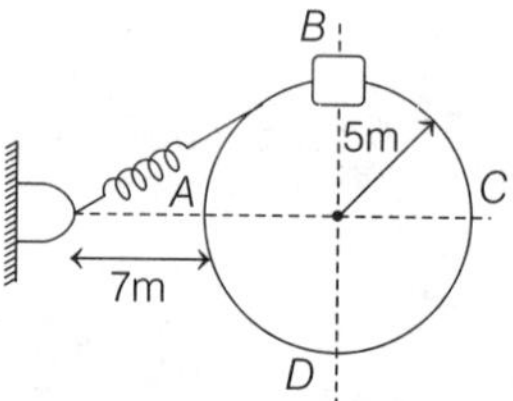

(a) 360 N
(b) 720 N
(c) 1440 N
(d) 2880 N

2. A particle is at rest with respect to the wall of an inverted cone rotating with uniform angular velocity ω about its central axis. The surface between the particle and the wall is smooth. Regarding the displacement of particle along the surface up or down, the equilibrium of particle is

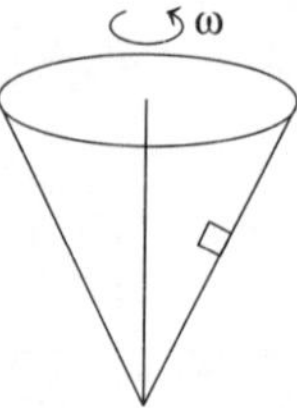

(a) stable
(b) unstable
(c) neutral
(d) None of these

3. A rough horizontal plate rotates with angular velocity ω about a fixed vertical axis. A particle of mass m lies on the plate at a distance $\frac{5a}{4}$ from this axis. The coefficient of friction between the plate and the particle is $\frac{1}{3}$. The largest value of ω^2 for which the particle will continue to be at rest on the revolving plate is

(a) $\frac{g}{3a}$ (b) $\frac{4g}{5a}$ (c) $\frac{4g}{9a}$ (d) $\frac{4g}{15a}$

4. A ball attached to one end of a string swings in a vertical plane such that its acceleration at point A (extreme position) is equal to its acceleration at point B (mean position). The angle θ is

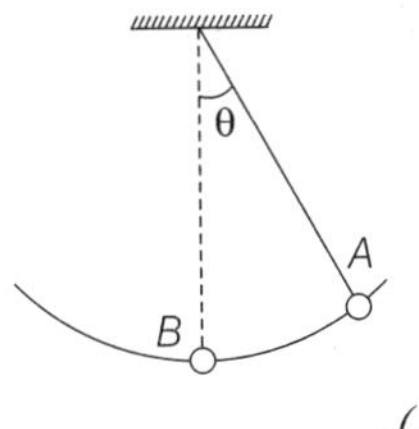

(a) $\cos^{-1}\left(\frac{2}{5}\right)$ (b) $\cos^{-1}\left(\frac{4}{5}\right)$

(c) $\cos^{-1}\left(\frac{3}{5}\right)$ (d) None of these

5. A skier plans to ski a smooth fixed hemisphere of radius R. He starts from rest from a curved smooth surfacé of height $\left(\frac{R}{4}\right)$. The angle θ at which he leaves the hemisphere is

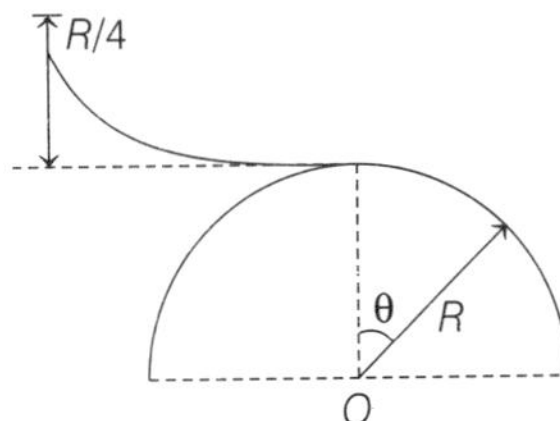

(a) $\cos^{-1}\left(\frac{2}{3}\right)$ (b) $\cos^{-1}\frac{5}{\sqrt{3}}$ (c) $\cos^{-1}\left(\frac{5}{6}\right)$ (d) $\cos^{-1}\left[\frac{5}{2\sqrt{3}}\right]$

6. A section of fixed smooth circular track of radius R in vertical plane is shown in the figure. A block is released from position A and leaves the track at B. The radius of curvature of its trajectory just after it leaves the track at B is

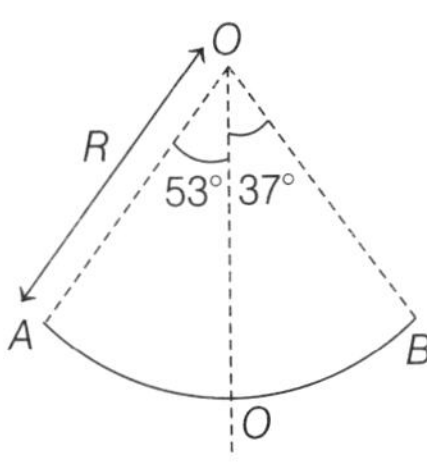

(a) R (b) $\frac{R}{4}$ (c) $\frac{R}{2}$ (d) $\frac{R}{3}$

7. A particle is projected with velocity u horizontally from the top of a smooth sphere of radius a, so that it slides down the outside of the sphere. If the particle leaves the sphere when it has fallen a height $\frac{a}{4}$, the value of u is

(a) $\sqrt{ag}$ (b) $\frac{\sqrt{ag}}{4}$

(c) $\frac{\sqrt{ag}}{2}$ (d) $\frac{\sqrt{ag}}{3}$

8. A 10 kg ball attached at the end of a rigid massless rod of length 1 m rotates at constant speed in a horizontal circle of radius 0.5 m and period of 1.58 s, as shown in the figure. The force exerted by the rod on the ball is (Take, $g = 10\ \text{ms}^{-2}$)

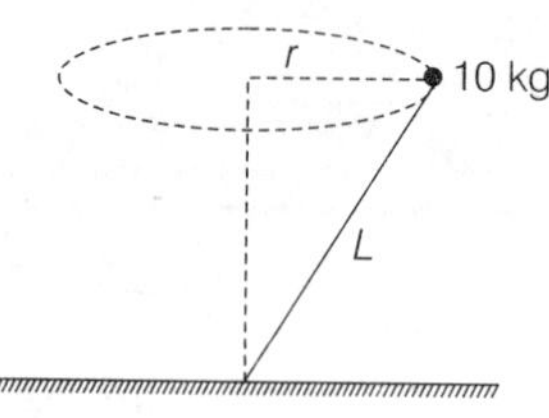

(a) 158 N (b) 128 N (c) 110 N (d) 98 N

9. A disc is rotating in a room. A boy standing near the rim of the disc of radius R finds the water droplet falling from the ceiling is always falling on his head. As one drop hits his head, other one starts from the ceiling. If height of the roof above his head is H, then angular velocity of the disc is

(a) $\pi\sqrt{\frac{2gR}{H^2}}$ (b) $\pi\sqrt{\frac{2gH}{R^2}}$

(c) $\pi\sqrt{\frac{2g}{H}}$ (d) None of these

10. A particle of mass m starts to slide down from the top of the fixed smooth sphere. What is the tangential acceleration when it breaks off the sphere ?

(a) $\frac{2g}{3}$ (b) $\frac{\sqrt{5}g}{3}$

(c) g (d) $\frac{g}{3}$

11. A simple pendulum is released from rest with the string in horizontal position. The vertical component of the velocity of the bob becomes maximum, when the string makes an angle θ with the vertical. The angle θ is equal to

(a) $\frac{\pi}{4}$ (b) $\cos^{-1}\left(\frac{1}{\sqrt{3}}\right)$ (c) $\sin^{-1}\left(\frac{1}{\sqrt{3}}\right)$ (d) $\frac{\pi}{3}$

12. A particle is moving in a circle of radius R in such a way that at any instant the normal and tangential component of its acceleration are equal. If its speed at $t = 0$ is v_0, the time taken to complete the first revolution is

(a) $\frac{R}{v_0}$ (b) $\frac{R}{v_0}e^{-2\pi}$

(c) $\frac{R}{v_0}(1 - e^{-2\pi})$ (d) $\frac{R}{v_0}(1 + e^{-2\pi})$

13. A particle is moving in a circular path in the vertical plane. It is attached at one end of a string of length l whose other end is fixed. The velocity at lowest point is u. The tension in the string is **T** and acceleration of the particle is **a** at any position. Then, $\mathbf{T} \cdot \mathbf{a}$ is zero at highest point, if

(a) $u > \sqrt{5\,gl}$ (b) $u = \sqrt{5\,gl}$
(c) Both (a) and (b) are correct (d) Both (a) and (b) are wrong

14. In the above question, $\mathbf{T} \cdot \mathbf{a}$ is positive at the lowest point for

(a) $u \le \sqrt{2\,gl}$ (b) $u = \sqrt{2\,gl}$ (c) $u < \sqrt{2\,gl}$ (d) any value of u

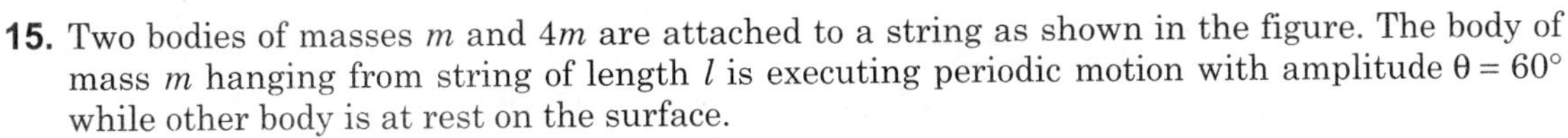

15. Two bodies of masses m and $4m$ are attached to a string as shown in the figure. The body of mass m hanging from string of length l is executing periodic motion with amplitude $\theta = 60°$ while other body is at rest on the surface.

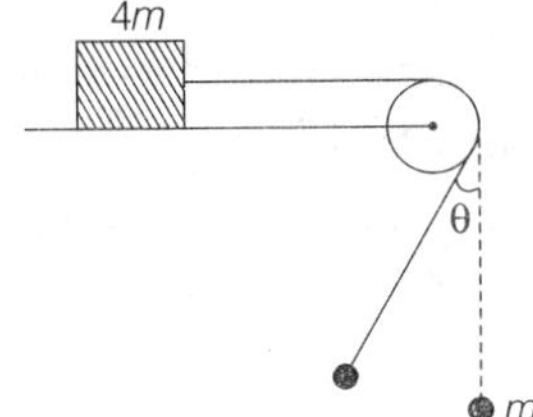

The minimum coefficient of friction between the mass $4m$ and the horizontal surface must be

(a) $\frac{1}{4}$ (b) $\frac{1}{3}$ (c) $\frac{1}{2}$ (d) $\frac{2}{3}$

16. The bob of a 0.2 m pendulum describes an arc of circle in a vertical plane. If the tension in the cord is $\sqrt{3}$ times the weight of the bob when the cord makes an angle 30° with the vertical, the acceleration of the bob in that position is

(a) g (b) $\frac{g}{2}$ (c) $\frac{\sqrt{3}\,g}{2}$ (d) $\frac{g}{4}$

17. An automobile enters a turn of radius r. If the road is banked at an angle of 45° and the coefficient of friction is $\frac{1}{2}$, the minimum speed with which the automobile can negotiate the turn without skidding is

(a) $\sqrt{\frac{rg}{2}}$ (b) $\frac{\sqrt{rg}}{2}$
(c) $\sqrt{rg}$ (d) $\sqrt{2\,rg}$

18. A stone of mass 1 kg tied to a light inextensible string of length $L = \frac{10}{3}$ m, whirling in a circular path in a vertical plane. The ratio of maximum tension to the minimum tension in the string is 4. If g is taken to be 10 m/s^2, the speed of the stone at the highest point of the circle is

(a) 10 m/s (b) $5\sqrt{2}$ m/s
(c) $10\sqrt{3}$ m/s (d) 20 m/s

19. A wet open umbrella is held vertical and whirled about the handle at a uniform rate of 21 rev in 44 s. If the rim of the umbrella is a circle of 1 m in diameter and the height of the rim above the floor is 4.9 m. The locus of the drop on floor is a circle of radius

(a) $\sqrt{2.5}$ m (b) 1 m (c) 3 m (d) 1.5 m

20. A 50 kg girl is swinging on a swing from rest. Then, the power delivered when moving with a velocity of 2 m/s upwards in a direction making an angle 60° (of string) with the vertical is

(a) 980 W (b) 490 W (c) $490\sqrt{3}$ W (d) 245 W

21. A particle of mass 1 g executes an oscillatory motion on the concave surface of a spherical dish of radius 2 m placed on a horizontal plane. If the motion of the particle begins from a point on the dish at a height of 1 cm from the horizontal plane and the coefficient of friction is 0.01, the total distance covered by the particle before it comes to rest, is approximately

(a) 2.0 m (b) 10.0 m (c) 1.0 m (d) 20.0 m

22. A particle moves from rest at A on the surface of a smooth circular cylinder of radius r as shown. At B it leaves the cylinder. The equation relating α and β is

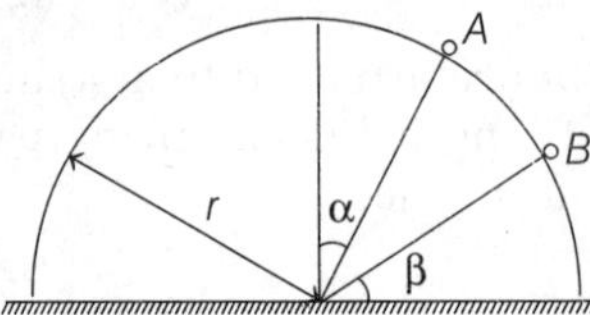

(a) $3 \sin \alpha = 2 \cos \beta$ (b) $2 \sin \alpha = 3 \cos \beta$ (c) $3 \sin \beta = 2 \cos \alpha$ (d) $2 \sin \beta = 3 \cos \alpha$

23. A ball suspended by a thread swings in a vertical plane, so that its acceleration in the extreme position and lowest position are equal. The angle θ of thread deflection in the extreme position will be

(a) $\tan^{-1}(2)$ (b) $\tan^{-1}(\sqrt{2})$ (c) $\tan^{-1}\left(\frac{1}{2}\right)$ (d) $2\tan^{-1}\left(\frac{1}{2}\right)$

24. A body of mass m hangs at one end of a string of length l, the other end of which is fixed. It is given a horizontal velocity, so that the string would just reach, where it makes an angle of 60° with the vertical. The tension in the string at bottommost point is

(a) $2mg$ (b) mg (c) $3mg$ (d) $\sqrt{3}\,mg$

25. The kinetic energy K of a particle moving along a circle of radius R depends on the distance covered s as $K = as^2$. The force acting on the particle is

(a) $\frac{2as^2}{R}$ (b) $2as\left(1+\frac{s^2}{R^2}\right)^{1/2}$ (c) $as\left(1+\frac{s^2}{R^2}\right)^{1/2}$ (d) None of these

26. A simple pendulum is vibrating with an angular amplitude of 90° as shown in the figure. For what value of α, is the acceleration directed?

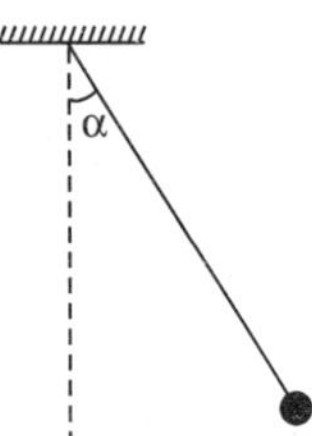

(i) Vertically upwards (ii) Horizontally (iii) Vertically downwards

(a) $0°, \cos^{-1}\left(\frac{1}{\sqrt{3}}\right), 90°$ (b) $90°, \cos^{-1}\left(\frac{1}{\sqrt{3}}\right), 0°$ (c) $0°, \cos^{-1}\frac{1}{\sqrt{2}}, 90°$ (d) $\cos^{-1}\left(\frac{1}{\sqrt{3}}\right), 90°, 0°$

27. The radius of the curved road on a national highway is R. The width of the road is b. The outer edge of the road is raised by h with respect to the inner edge, so that a car with velocity v can pass safe over it. The value of h is

(a) $\frac{v^2 b}{Rg}$ (b) $\frac{v}{Rgb}$ (c) $\frac{v^2 R}{g}$ (d) $\frac{v^2 b}{R}$

28. A particle A of mass m is attached to a vertical axis by two strings PA and QA of lengths $3L$ and $4L$, respectively. $PQ = 5L$. A rotates around the axis with an angular speed ω. The tensions in the two strings are T_1 and T_2. Then,

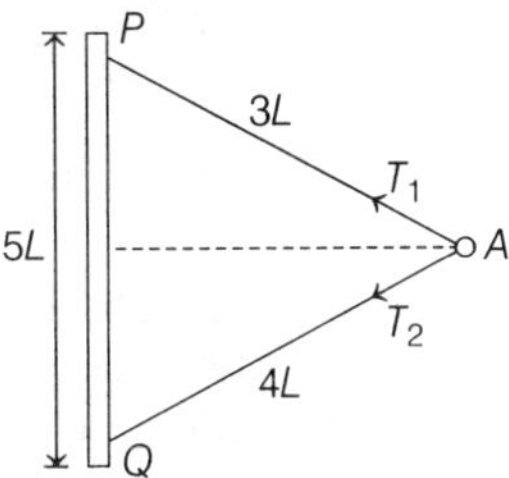

(i) $T_1 = T_2$ (ii) $3T_1 - 4T_2 = 5\,mg$ (iii) $4T_1 + 3T_2 = 12\,m\omega^2 L$

(a) (i) only
(b) (i), (ii)
(c) (i), (iii)
(d) (ii), (iii)

29. A tube of length L is filled completely with an incompressible liquid of mass M and closed at both the ends. The tube is then rotated in a horizontal plane about one of its ends with a uniform angular velocity ω. The force exerted by the liquid at the other end is

(a) $\frac{1}{2} M\omega^2 L^2$
(b) $M\omega^2 L$
(c) $\frac{1}{4} M\omega^2 L$
(d) $\frac{1}{2} M\omega^2 L$

30. A body moves on a horizontal circular road of radius r, with a tangential acceleration a_r. The coefficient of friction between the body and the road surface is μ. It begins to slip when its speed is v. Then,

(i) $v^2 = \mu rg$ (ii) $\mu g = \left(\frac{v^4}{r^2} + a_r\right)$ (iii) $\mu^2 g^2 = \left(\frac{v^4}{r^2} + a_t^2\right)$

(iv) The force of friction makes an angle $\tan^{-1}(v^2/a_t r)$ with the direction of motion at the point of slipping.

(a) (i), (ii)
(b) (ii), (iii)
(c) (i), (iv)
(d) (iii), (iv)

31. In a simple pendulum, the breaking strength of the string is double the weight of the bob. The bob is released from rest when the string is horizontal. The string breaks when it makes an angle θ with the vertical. Then,

(a) $\theta = \cos^{-1}(1/3)$
(b) $\theta = 60°$
(c) $\theta = \cos^{-1}(2/3)$
(d) $\theta = 0$

32. The figure shows a light rod of length L rigidly attached to a small heavy block at one end and a hook at the other end. The system is released from rest with the rod in a horizontal position. There is a fixed smooth ring at a depth h below the initial position of the hook and the hook gets into the ring as it reaches there. What should be the minimum value of h, so that the block moves in a complete circle about the ring?

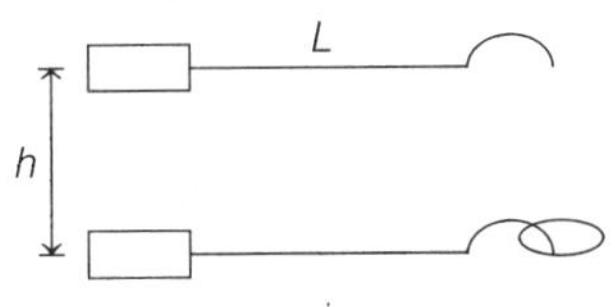

(a) $h = L$ (b) $h = 2L$ (c) $h = 3L$ (d) $h = 4L$

33. A boy holds a pendulum in his hand while standing at the edge of a circular platform of radius r rotating at an angular speed ω. The pendulum will hang at an angle θ with the vertical such that ($r >>$ length of pendulum)

(a) $\tan\theta = 0$
(b) $\tan\theta = \dfrac{\omega^2 r^2}{g}$
(c) $\tan\theta = \dfrac{r\omega^2}{g}$
(d) $\tan\theta = \dfrac{g}{\omega^2 r}$

34. A body tied to a string of length L is revolved in a vertical circle with minimum velocity, when the body reaches the uppermost point, the string breaks and the body moves under the influence of the gravitational field of earth along a parabolic path. The horizontal range AC of the body will be

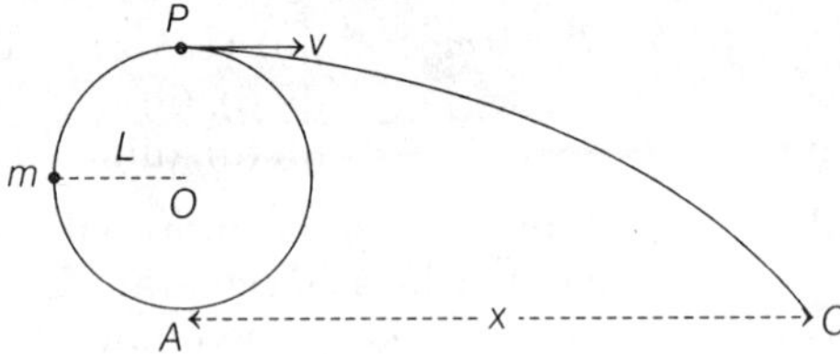

(a) $x = L$
(b) $x = 2L$
(c) $x = 2\sqrt{2}\,L$
(d) $x = \sqrt{2}\,L$

35. A mass tied to a string moves in a vertical circle with a uniform speed of 5 m/s as shown. At the point P, the string breaks. The mass will reach a height above P of nearly

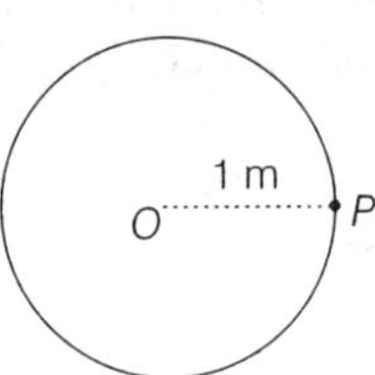

(a) 1 m
(b) 0.5 m
(c) 2.16 m
(d) 1.25 m

36. A bob of mass M is suspended by a massless string of length L. The horizontal velocity v at position A is just sufficient to make it reach the point B. The angle θ at which the speed of the bob is half of that at A, satisfies

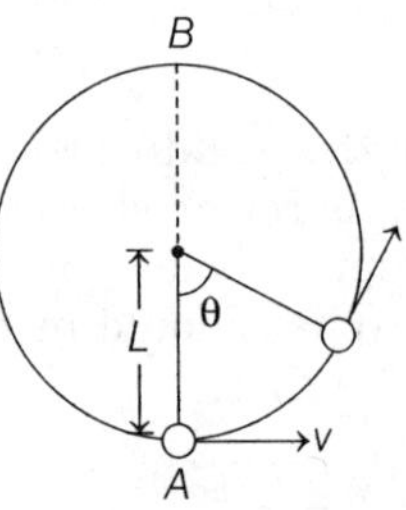

(a) $\theta = \dfrac{\pi}{4}$
(b) $\dfrac{\pi}{4} < \theta < \dfrac{\pi}{4}$
(c) $\dfrac{\pi}{2} < \theta < \dfrac{3\pi}{4}$
(d) $\dfrac{3\pi}{4} < \theta < \pi$

More than One Correct Options

1. A ball tied to the end of the string swings in a vertical circle under the influence of gravity.
   (a) When the string makes an angle 90° with the vertical, the tangential acceleration is zero and radial acceleration is somewhere between minimum and maximum
   (b) When the string makes an angle 90° with the vertical, the tangential acceleration is maximum and radial acceleration is somewhere between maximum and minimum
   (c) At no place in circular motion, tangential acceleration is equal to radial acceleration
   (d) When radial acceleration has its maximum value, the tangential acceleration is zero

2. A small spherical ball is suspended through a string of length l. The whole arrangement is placed in a vehicle which is moving with velocity v. Now, suddenly the vehicle stops and ball starts moving along a circular path. If tension in the string at the highest point is twice the weight of the ball, then (assume that the ball completes the vertical circle)
   (a) $v = \sqrt{5\,gl}$
   (b) $v = \sqrt{7\,gl}$
   (c) velocity of the ball at highest point is $\sqrt{gl}$
   (d) velocity of the ball at the highest point is $\sqrt{3\,gl}$

3. A particle is describing circular motion in a horizontal plane in contact with the smooth surface of a fixed right circular cone with its axis vertical and vertex down. The height of the plane of motion above the vertex is h and the semi-vertical angle of the cone is α. The period of revolution of the particle

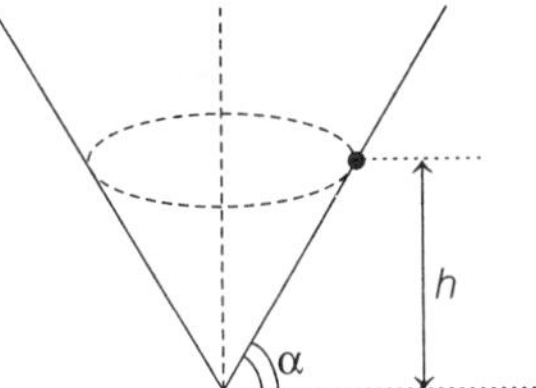

   (a) increases as h increases
   (b) decreases as h decreases
   (c) increases as α increases
   (d) decreases as α increases

4. In circular motion of a particle,
   (a) particle cannot have uniform motion
   (b) particle cannot have uniformly accelerated motion
   (c) particle cannot have net force equal to zero
   (d) particle cannot have any force in tangential direction

5. A smooth cone is rotated with an angular velocity ω as shown. A block A is placed at height h. Block has no motion relative to cone. Choose the correct options, when ω is increased

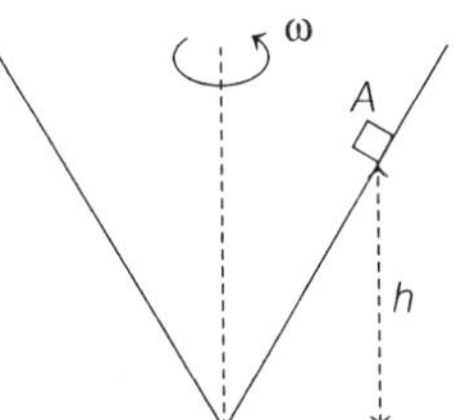

   (a) net force acting on block will increase
   (b) normal reaction acting on block will increase
   (c) h will increase
   (d) normal reaction will remain unchanged

6. A heavy particle is tied to the end A of a string of length 1.6 m. Its other end O is fixed. It revolves as a conical pendulum with the string making 60° with the horizontal. Then,

(a) its period of revolution is $\frac{4\pi}{7}$ s

(b) the tension in the string is $\frac{2}{\sqrt{3}}$ times the weight of the particle

(c) the speed of the particle is $2.8\sqrt{3}$ m /s

(d) the centripetal acceleration of the particle is $\frac{9.8}{\sqrt{3}}$ m/s^2

7. A jeep runs around a curve of radius 0.3 km at a constant speed of 60 ms^{-1}. The jeep covers a curve of 60° arc. Then,

(a) resultant change in velocity of jeep is 60 ms^{-1}

(b) instantaneous acceleration of jeep is 12 ms^{-2}

(c) average acceleration of jeep is approximately 11.5 ms^{-2}

(d) instantaneous and average acceleration are same in this case

8. A block of mass 10 kg is pulled along a smooth surface in the form of arc of radius 10 m. The applied force F is 200 N as shown in figure. If the block starts from point A, then

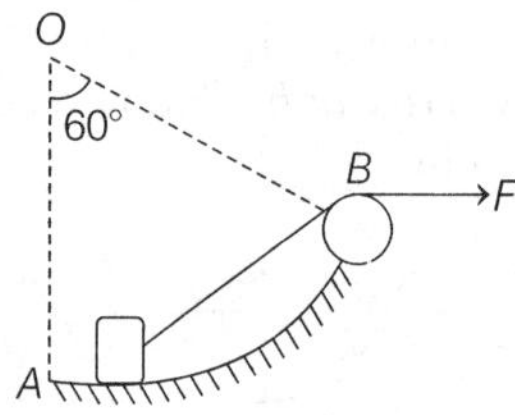

(a) the speed at point B is 15.7 m/s

(b) the speed at point B is 27 m/s

(c) the work done by gravity during moving from A to B is negative

(d) the work done by tension on block is zero

9. A small particle of mass m is given an initial velocity v_0 tangent to the horizontal rim of a smooth cone at a radius r_0 from the vertical centre line as shown in figure. As, the particle slides to point B, a vertical distance h below A and a distance r from vertical centre line, its velocity v is inclined at some angle with the horizontal tangent to the cone through the point B.

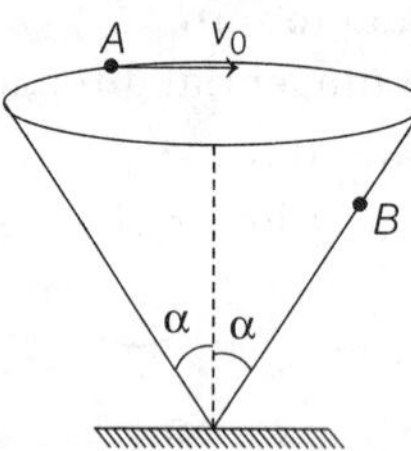

(a) The speed of particle at point B is $\sqrt{v_0^2 + 2gh}$

(b) The minimum value of v_0 for which particle will be moving in a horizontal circle of radius r_0 is $\sqrt{gr_0 \cot\alpha}$

(c) The speed of particle at point B is $\sqrt{v_0^2 - 2gh}$

(d) None of the above

Comprehension Based Questions

Passage 1 (Q.Nos. 1 to 2)

A ball with mass m is attached to the end of a rod of mass M and length l. The other end of the rod is pivoted, so that the ball can move in a vertical circle. The rod is held in the horizontal position as shown in the figure and then given just enough a downward push, so that the ball swings down and just reaches the vertical upward position having zero speed there. Now, answer the following questions.

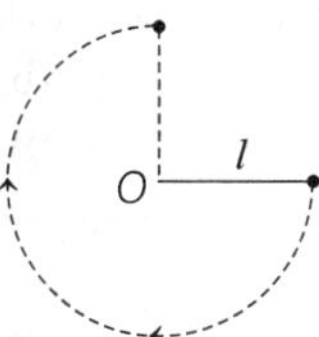

1. The change in potential energy of the system (ball + rod) is

(a) mgl (b) $(M + m) gl$

(c) $\left(\frac{M}{2} + m\right) gl$ (d) $\frac{(M + m)}{2} gl$

2. The initial speed given to the ball is

(a) $\sqrt{\frac{Mgl + 2mgl}{m}}$ (b) $\sqrt{2 gl}$

(c) $\sqrt{\frac{2Mgl + mgl}{m}}$ (d) None of these

Note *Attempt the above question after studying chapter of rotational motion.*

Passage 2 (Q.Nos. 3 to 5)

A small particle of mass m attached with a light inextensible thread of length L is moving in a vertical circle. In the given case particle is moving in complete vertical circle and ratio of its maximum to minimum velocity is 2 : 1.

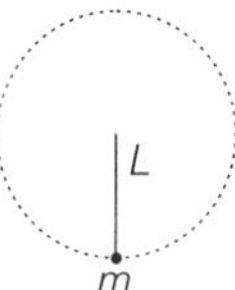

3. Minimum velocity of the particle is

(a) $4\sqrt{\frac{gL}{3}}$ (b) $2\sqrt{\frac{gL}{3}}$

(c) $\sqrt{\frac{gL}{3}}$ (d) $3\sqrt{\frac{gL}{3}}$

4. Kinetic energy of the particle at the lower most position is

(a) $\frac{4mgL}{3}$ (b) $2mgL$

(c) $\frac{8mgL}{3}$ (d) $\frac{2mgL}{3}$

5. Velocity of the particle when it is moving vertically downward is

(a) $\sqrt{\frac{10gL}{3}}$ (b) $2\sqrt{\frac{gL}{3}}$

(c) $\sqrt{\frac{8gL}{3}}$ (d) $\sqrt{\frac{13gL}{3}}$

Passage 3 (Q.Nos. 6 to 7)

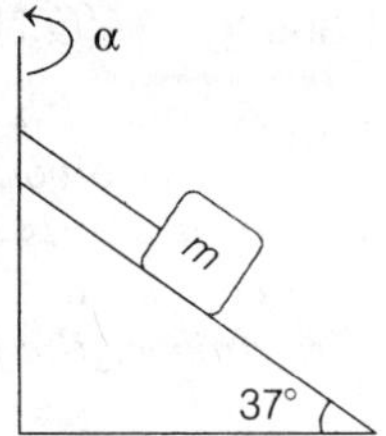

A block of mass 1 kg is attached to a 1.25 m long light string tied to the apex of a triangular smooth block as shown in the figure. At t = 0, the triangular block is imparted a constant angular acceleration $\sqrt{\frac{40}{3}}$ rad/ s^2 about an axis along its vertical side. Assume that the block is stationary with respect to triangular block.

6. At what time will the block leaves contact with the triangular block?
(a) 0.5 s (b) 1 s
(c) 2 s (d) 3 s

7. What would be tension in the string at the instant when the block leaves the contact of triangular block?
(a) 10 N (b) 16.67 N
(c) 30 N (d) 40 N

Passage 4 (Q.Nos. 8 to 9)

A small block of mass 1 kg is released from rest at the top of a rough track. The track is a circular arc of radius 40 m. The block slides along the track without toppling and a frictional force acts on it in the direction opposite to the instantaneous velocity. The work done in overcoming the friction up to the point Q as shown in the given figure, is 150 J. (Take, the acceleration due to gravity, $g = 10\ ms^{-2}$)

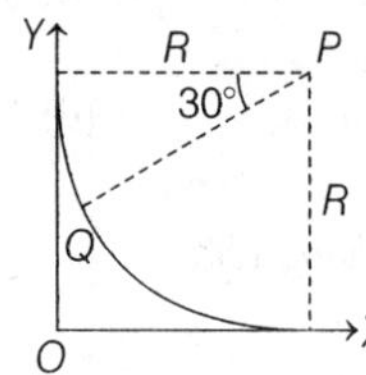

8. The speed of the block when it reaches the point Q is
(a) 5 ms^{-1} (b) 10 ms^{-1}
(c) $10\sqrt{3}$ ms^{-1} (d) 20 ms^{-1}

9. The magnitude of the normal reaction that acts on the block at the point Q is
(a) 7.5 N (b) 8.6 N
(c) 11.5 N (d) 22.5 N

Passage 5 (Q. Nos. 10 to 11)

A smooth rod AB is subjected to vertical up and down movement system, while resting on a hemisphere of radius R. The hemisphere moves to the right with a velocity v_0 and an acceleration of a_0.

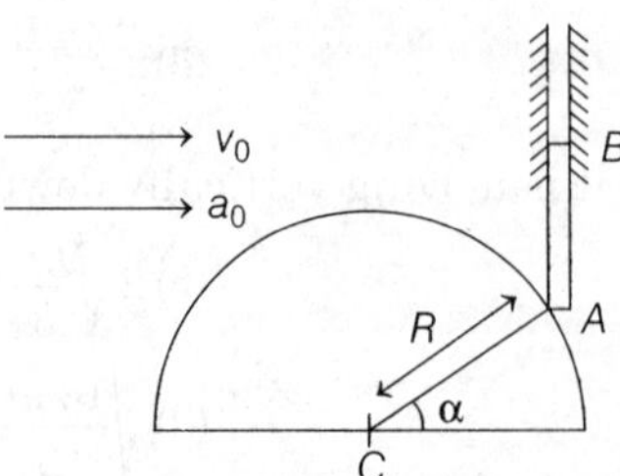

10. The velocity of the point B is

(a) $v_0 \tan \alpha$ (b) $v_0 \sin \alpha$

(c) $v_0 \cot \alpha$ (d) $v_0 \cos \alpha$

11. The acceleration of the point B is

(a) $a_0 \cot \alpha$ (b) $\dfrac{a_0 R \sin \alpha + v_0^2 + v_0^2 \tan^2 \alpha}{R \cos \alpha}$

(c) $\dfrac{a_0 R \cos \alpha + v_0^2 + \tan^2 \alpha}{R \cos \alpha}$ (d) None of these

Match the Columns

1. A bob of mass m is suspended from point O by a massless string of length l as shown. At the bottommost point, it is given a velocity $u = \sqrt{12gl}$ for $l = 1$ m and $m = 1$ kg, match the following two columns when string becomes horizontal (Take, $g = 10 \text{ ms}^{-2}$)

Column I	Column II (SI units)
(a) Speed of bob	(p) 10
(b) Acceleration of bob	(q) 20
(c) Tension in string	(r) 100
(d) Tangential acceleration of bob	(s) None

2. Speed of a particle moving in a circle of radius 2 m varies with time as $v = 2t$ (SI units). At $t = 1$ s match the following two columns.

Column I	Column II (SI units)
(a) $\mathbf{a} \cdot \mathbf{v}$	(p) $2\sqrt{2}$
(b) $\lvert \mathbf{a} \times \boldsymbol{\omega} \rvert$	(q) 2
(c) $\mathbf{v} \cdot \boldsymbol{\omega}$	(r) 4
(d) $\lvert \mathbf{v} \times \mathbf{a} \rvert$	(s) None

Here, symbols have their usual meanings.

3. A car is taking turn on a rough horizontal road without slipping as shown in figure. Let F is centripetal force, f the force of friction, N_1 and N_2 are two normal reactions. As the speed of car is increased, match the following two columns.

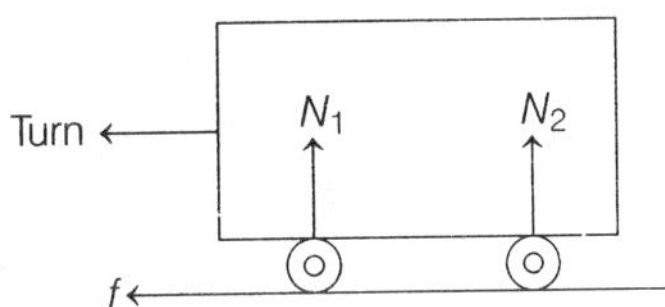

Column I	Column II
(a) N_1	(p) will increase
(b) N_2	(q) will decrease
(c) F/f	(r) will remain unchanged
(d) f	(s) cannot say anything

4. Position vector (with respect to centre) velocity vector and acceleration vector of a particle in circular motion are $\mathbf{r} = (3\hat{\mathbf{i}} - 4\hat{\mathbf{j}})$ m, $\mathbf{v} = (4\hat{\mathbf{i}} - a\hat{\mathbf{j}})$ ms^{-1} and $\mathbf{a} = (-6\hat{\mathbf{i}} + b\hat{\mathbf{j}})$ ms^{-2}. Speed of particle is constant. Match the following two columns.

Column I	Column II (SI units)
(a) Value of a	(p) 8
(b) Value of b	(q) 3
(c) Radius of circle	(r) 5
(d) $\mathbf{r} \cdot (\mathbf{v} \times \mathbf{a})$	(s) None

5. A particle is rotating in a circle of radius $R = \left(\frac{2}{\pi}\right)$ m, with constant speed 1 ms^{-1}. Match the following two columns for the time interval when it completes $\frac{1}{4}$th of the circle.

Column I	Column II (SI units)
(a) Average speed	(p) $\frac{\sqrt{2}}{\pi}$
(b) Average velocity	(q) $2\frac{\sqrt{2}}{\pi}$
(c) Average acceleration	(r) $\sqrt{2}$
(d) Displacement	(s) 1

Subjective Questions

1. A smooth circular tube of radius R is fixed in a vertical plane. A particle is projected from its lowest point with a velocity just sufficient to carry it to the highest point. Show that the time taken by the particle to reach the end of the horizontal diameter is $\sqrt{\frac{R}{g}} \ln(1 + \sqrt{2})$.

Hint : $\int \sec\theta \cdot d\theta = \ln(\sec\theta + \tan\theta)$

2. A heavy particle slides under gravity down the inside of a smooth vertical tube held in vertical plane. It starts from the highest point with velocity $\sqrt{2ag}$, where a is the radius of the circle. Find the angular position θ (as shown in figure) at which the vertical acceleration of the particle is maximum.

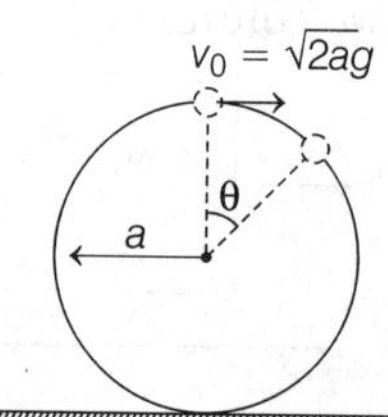

3. A particle of mass m is suspended by a string of length l from a fixed rigid support. A sufficient horizontal velocity $v_0 = \sqrt{3gl}$ is imparted to it suddenly. Calculate the angle made by the string with the vertical when the acceleration of the particle is inclined to the string by 45°.

4. A turn of radius 20 m is banked for the vehicles going at a speed of 36 km/h. If the coefficient of static friction between the road and the tyre is 0.4. What are the possible speeds of a vehicle, so that it neither slips down nor skids up ? (Take, $g = 9.8\ \text{m/s}^2$)

5. A particle is projected with a speed u at an angle θ with the horizontal. Find the radius of curvature of the parabola traced out by the projectile at a point, where the particle velocity makes an angle $\frac{\theta}{2}$ with the horizontal.

6. A particle is projected with velocity $20\sqrt{2}$ m/s at 45° with horizontal. After 1 s, find tangential and normal acceleration of the particle. Also, find radius of curvature of the trajectory at that point. (Take, $g = 10\ \text{m/s}^2$)

7. If the system shown in the figure is rotated in a horizontal circle with angular velocity ω . Find (Take, $g = 10\ \text{m/s}^2$)

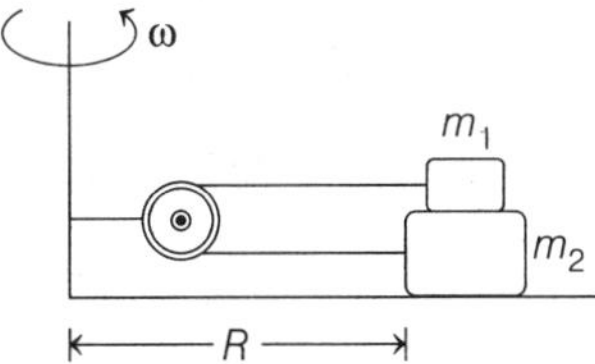

(a) the minimum value of ω to start relative motion between the two blocks.

(b) tension in the string connecting m_1 and m_2 when slipping just starts between the blocks.

The coefficient of friction between the two masses is 0.5 and there is no friction between m_2 and ground. The dimensions of the masses can be neglected.
(Take, $R = 0.5\ \text{m}$, $m_1 = 2\ \text{kg}$, $m_2 = 1\ \text{kg}$)

8. The simple 2 kg pendulum is released from rest in the horizontal position. As it reaches the bottom position, the cord wraps around the smooth fixed pin at B and continues in the smaller arc in the vertical plane. Calculate the magnitude of the force R supported by the pin at B when the pendulum passes the position $\theta = 30°$. (Take, $g = 9.8\ \text{m/s}^2$)

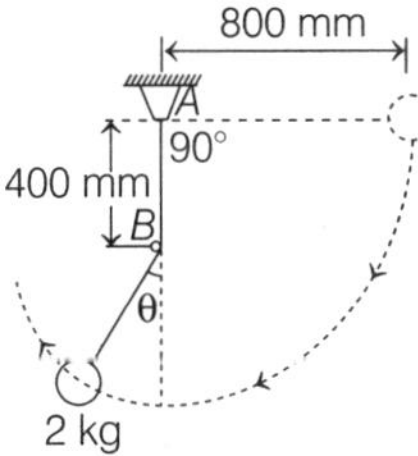

9. A circular tube of mass M is placed vertically on a horizontal surface as shown in the figure. Two small spheres, each of mass m, just fit in the tube, are released from the top. If θ gives the angle between radius vector of either ball with the vertical, obtain the value of the ratio M/m, if the tube breaks its contact with ground when $\theta = 60°$. Neglect any friction.

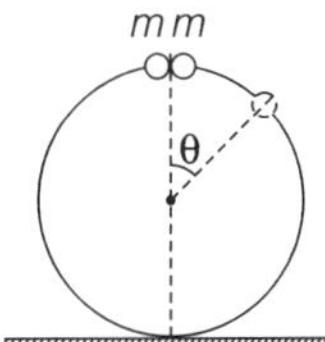

10. A table with smooth horizontal surface is turning at an angular speed ω about its axis. A groove is made on the surface along a radius and a particle is gently placed inside the groove at a distance a from the centre. Find the speed of the particle with respect to the table as its distance from the centre becomes L.

11. A block of mass m slides on a frictionless table. It is constrained to move inside a ring of radius R. At time $t = 0$, block is moving along the inside of the ring (i.e. in the tangential direction) with velocity v_0. The coefficient of friction between the block and the ring is μ. Find the speed of the block at time t.

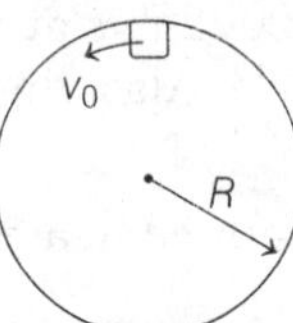

12. A ring of mass M hangs from a thread and two beads of mass m slides on it without friction. The beads are released simultaneously from the top of the ring and slides down in opposite sides. Show that the ring will start to rise, if $m > \frac{3M}{2}$.

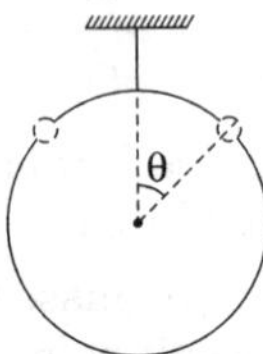

13. A vertical frictionless semicircular track of radius 1 m is fixed on the edge of a movable trolley (figure). Initially, the system is at rest and a mass m is kept at the top of the track. The trolley starts moving to the right with a uniform horizontal acceleration $a = 2g/9$. The mass slides down the track, eventually losing contact with it and dropping to the floor 1.3 m below the trolley. This 1.3 m is from the point, where mass loses contact. (Take, $g = 10 \text{ m/s}^2$)

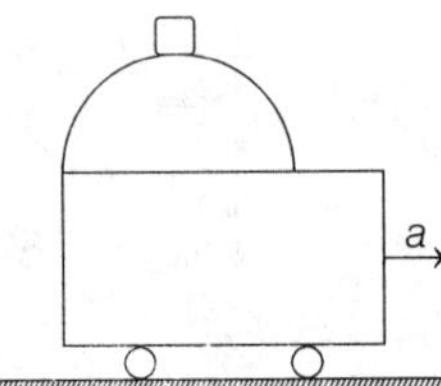

(a) Calculate the angle θ at which it loses contact with the trolley and
(b) the time taken by the mass to drop on the floor, after losing contact.

Answers

Introductory Exercise 10.1

1. Variable
2. speed, acceleration, magnitude of acceleration
3. (a) $4.0\ \text{cm/s}^2$ (b) $2.0\ \text{cm/s}^2$ (c) $2\sqrt{5}\ \text{cm/s}^2$
4. $\frac{2\sqrt{2}}{\pi}$
5. $\frac{1}{2}$ s
6. 45°
7. (a) $21.65\ \text{ms}^{-2}$ (b) $7.35\ \text{ms}^{-1}$ (c) $12.5\ \text{ms}^{-2}$

Introductory Exercise 10.2

1. $\tan^{-1}\left(\frac{1}{4}\right)$
2. 0.25
3. (a) $17\ \text{ms}^{-1}$
4. No
5. He should apply the brakes
6. (a) 39.6 rpm (b) 150 N
7. (a) 24 kN (b) $50\ \text{ms}^{-1}$ (c) 32 kN

Introductory Exercise 10.3

1. (a) $\frac{5}{3}R$ (b) $\sqrt{\frac{2}{3}gR}$
2. (a) 60° (b) $\frac{mg}{2}$
3. (a) $\sqrt{3gR}$ (b) 2 mg (c) 8 mg
4. $7\ \text{ms}^{-1}$

Exercises

LEVEL 1

Assertion and Reason

1. (a) 2. (b) 3. (b) 4. (a) 5. (a) 6. (a)

Single Correct Option

1. (d) 2. (c) 3. (c) 4. (a) 5. (c) 6. (b) 7. (d) 8. (c) 9. (d) 10. (b)
11. (c) 12. (d) 13. (c) 14. (b) 15. (c) 16. (b) 17. (d) 18. (d) 19. (d) 20. (b)
21. (a) 22. (c) 23. (a) 24. (c) 25. (a) 26. (b) 27. (b) 28. (d) 29. (b) 30. (c)
31. (c) 32. (a) 33. (a)

Subjective Questions

1. $\frac{u^2\cos^2\theta}{g}$
2. 35 m/s
3. $\sqrt{\frac{g}{R\cos\alpha}}$
5. $113\ \text{ms}^{-2}$
6. (a) $\sqrt{\frac{\mu g}{L}}$ (b) $\left[\left(\frac{\mu g}{L}\right)^2 - \alpha^2\right]^{\frac{1}{4}}$
7. 60°
8. (a) $T = 64$ N, $f = 48$ N (outwards) (b) 1.63 rad/s (c) 5 rad/s
9. $\theta = \cos^{-1}\left(\frac{3}{4}\right)$
10. $5.66\ \text{ms}^{-1}, 16.75\ \text{ms}^{-2}$
11. $\sin^{-1}\left(\frac{1}{4}\right)$
12. $5\sqrt{2}$ m/s

LEVEL 2

Single Correct Option

1. (c)	2. (b)	3. (d)	4. (c)	5. (c)	6. (c)	7. (c)	8. (b)	9. (c)	10. (b)
11. (b)	12. (c)	13. (b)	14. (d)	15. (c)	16. (a)	17. (d)	18. (a)	19. (a)	20. (c)
21. (c)	22. (c)	23. (d)	24. (a)	25. (b)	26. (a)	27. (a)	28. (d)	29. (d)	30. (d)
31. (c)	32. (a)	33. (c)	34. (b)	35. (d)	36. (c)				

More than One Correct Options

1. (b,d)	2. (b,d)	3. (a,d)	4. (a,b,c)	5. (d)	6. (b,d)	7. (a,b,c)	8. (a,c)
9. (a,b)							

Comprehension Based Questions

1. (c)	2. (d)	3. (b)	4. (c)	5. (a)	6. (b)	7. (b)	8. (b)	9. (a)	10. (c)
11. (d)									

Match the Columns

1. (a) → (p) (b) → (s) (c) → (r) (d) → (p)
2. (a) → (r) (b) → (p) (c) → (s) (d) → (r)
3. (a) → (q) (b) → (p) (c) → (r) (d) → (p)
4. (a) → (s) (b) → (s) (c) → (r) (d) → (s)
5. (a) → (s) (b) → (q) (c) → (r) (d) → (q)

Subjective Questions

2. $\theta = \cos^{-1}\left(\frac{2}{3}\right)$

3. $\theta = \frac{\pi}{2}$

4. $4.2 \text{ ms}^{-1} \le v \le 15 \text{ ms}^{-1}$

5. $\frac{u^2\cos^2\theta}{g\cos^3(\theta/2)}$

6. $a_t = -2\sqrt{5} \text{ ms}^{-2}$, $a_n = 4\sqrt{5} \text{ ms}^{-2}$, $R = 25\sqrt{5}$ m

7. (a) $\omega_{\min} = 6.32$ rad/s (b) $T = 30$ N

8. 45 N

9. $\frac{M}{m} = \frac{1}{2}$

10. $v = \omega\sqrt{L^2 - a^2}$

11. $\frac{v_0}{1 + \frac{\mu v_0 t}{R}}$

13. (a) 37° (b) 0.38 s

Hints & Solutions

1. Basic Mathematics

Subjective Questions

1. Angle $= \dfrac{\text{Arc}}{\text{Radius}}$

2. $x = \sqrt{(5)^2 - (2)^2} = \sqrt{21}$

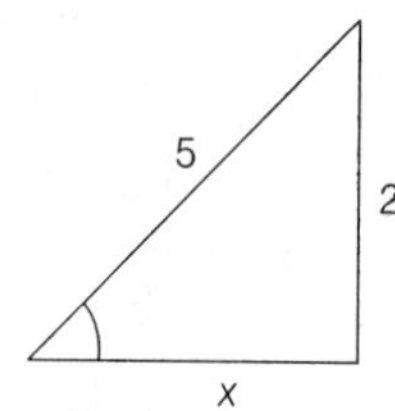

3. $\tan 3° = \tan\left(\dfrac{3 \times \pi}{180}\right)$ rad

$$\approx \frac{3 \times \pi}{180} = 0.052$$

4. 240° lies in 3rd quadrant and tan in 3rd quadrant is positive.

315° lies in 4th quadrant and cos in 4th quadrant is positive.

6. $\tan 105° = \tan(60° + 45°)$

$$= \frac{\tan 60° + \tan 45°}{1 - (\tan 60°)(\tan 45°)}$$

$$= \frac{\sqrt{3}+1}{1-\sqrt{3}}$$

7. $\cos 67° = \cos(30° + 37°)$

$$= (\cos 30°)(\cos 37°) - (\sin 30°)(\sin 37°)$$

$$= \left(\frac{\sqrt{3}}{2}\right)\left(\frac{4}{5}\right) - \left(\frac{1}{2}\right)\left(\frac{3}{5}\right)$$

$$= \left(\frac{4\sqrt{3}-3}{10}\right)$$

8. $\cos 105° + \cos 75° = 2\cos\left(\dfrac{105° + 75°}{2}\right)$

$$\cos\left(\frac{105° - 75°}{2}\right)$$

$$= 2(\cos 90°)(\cos 35°)$$

$$= 0 \text{ as } \cos 90° = 0$$

9. (c) 2 sin 45° cos 15°

$$\sin C + \sin D = 2\sin\left(\frac{C+D}{2}\right)\cos\left(\frac{C-D}{2}\right)$$

$$\therefore \quad \frac{C+D}{2} = 45°$$

or $\qquad C + D = 90° \qquad$ ...(i)

$$\frac{C-D}{2} = 15°$$

or $\qquad C - D = 30° \qquad$ ...(ii)

Solving these two equations, we get

$$C = 60°, \; D = 30°$$

$$\therefore \; 2\sin 45° \cos 15° = \sin 60° + \sin 30°$$

$$= \left(\frac{\sqrt{3}+1}{2}\right) \qquad \textbf{Ans.}$$

(d) Apply

$$\sin C - \sin D = 2\sin\left(\frac{C-D}{2}\right)\cos\left(\frac{C+D}{2}\right)$$

$$C = 60°$$

and $\qquad D = 30°$

$$\therefore \; 2\sin 15° \cos 45° = \sin 60° - \sin 30°$$

$$= \left(\frac{\sqrt{3}-1}{2}\right) \qquad \textbf{Ans.}$$

10. (a) $y_{max} = 5$, when $\cos\theta = -1$

(b) $y_{min} = -7$, when $\sin\theta = -1$

$y_{min} = -1$, when $\cos\theta = +1$

$y_{max} = +1$, when $\sin\theta = +1$

12. In (b) and (d) parts we get $y = 0$ by putting $x = 0$. Hence, graphs (b) and (d) pass through origin.

13. (a) For x = positive, y is negative. Hence, IV quadrant.

For x = negative, y is again negative. Hence, III quadrant.

(b) For x = positive, y is positive. Hence, I quadrant.

For x = negative, y is also negative. Hence, III quadrant.

14. For finding C_x, let us put $y = 0$, in the given equation. We find,

$$C_x = -\frac{5}{6}$$

For finding C_y, let us put $x = 0$, in the given equation. We find,

$$C_y = +2.5$$

28. (b) $y = (\sin 2x - x)$

$$\frac{dy}{dx} = 2\cos 2x - 1$$

and $\qquad \dfrac{d^2y}{dx^2} = -4\sin 2x$

Putting $\frac{dy}{dx} = 0$, we get

$$2 \cos 2x - 1 = 0$$

$\therefore$ $\cos 2x = \frac{1}{2}$

or $2x = \pm 60°$

$$= \pm \frac{\pi}{3}$$

At $2x = + 60°$, $\frac{d^2y}{dx^2}$ is –ve, so value of y is maximum. At $2x = - 60°$, $\frac{d^2y}{dx^2}$ is positive. So value of y is minimum.

$\therefore$ $y_{max} = \sin(+60°) - \frac{\pi}{6}$

$$= \left(\frac{\sqrt{3}}{2} - \frac{\pi}{6}\right) \text{ at } 2x = \frac{\pi}{3}$$

or $x = \pi/6$

and $y_{min} = \sin(-60°) + \frac{\pi}{6}$

at $x = -\frac{\pi}{6}$

$$= \left(\frac{\pi}{6} - \frac{\sqrt{3}}{2}\right)$$ **Ans.**

29. (c) and (d) parts : Refer (c) and (d) parts of example-1.16

31. $K = \frac{p^2}{2m}$

or $K \propto p^2$

$\therefore$ % change in K = 2 (% change in p)

$$= 2 \ (2\%)$$

$$= 4\%$$

32. $K = \frac{p^2}{2m}$ ...(i)

$$p' = 0.8\,p$$

$\therefore$ $K' = \frac{p'^2}{2m} = \frac{(0.8p)^2}{2m}$

$$= (0.64)\frac{p^2}{2m}$$

$$= 0.64\,K$$

Hence, kinetic energy has been decreased by 36%.

33. $p = \sqrt{2Km}$

or $p \propto K^{\frac{1}{2}}$

$\therefore$ (% change in p) $= \frac{1}{2}$ (% change in K)

$$= \frac{1}{2}(-3\%)$$

$$= -1.5\%$$

34. $p = \sqrt{2Km}$ ...(i)

$$K' = 1.5\,K$$

$\therefore$ $p' = \sqrt{2K'm}$

$= \sqrt{2\,(1.5K)\,m}$ ...(ii)

From Eqs. (i) and (ii), we get

$$p' \approx 1.22\,p$$

Therefore percentage change in momentum is approximately 22%.

2. Measurement and Errors

INTRODUCTORY EXERCISE 2.4

1. (a) $13.214 + 234.6 + 7.0350 + 6.38$

$$= 261.229$$
$$= 261.2$$

(rounding off to smallest one number of decimal place)

(b) $1247 + 134.5 + 450 + 78$

$$= 1909.5 = 1910$$

(rounding off to smallest one number of decimal place)

2. (a) $16.235 \times 0.217 \times 5$

$$= 17.614975$$
$$= 20$$

(rounding off to minimum one number of significant figure)

(b) 0.00435×4.6

$$= 0.02001$$
$$= 0.020$$

(rounding off to minimum two number of significant figures)

Exercises

Assertion and Reason

1. In 0.7 m, significant figure is only one.
In 0.70 m, significant figures are two.

2. Hour hand have least count 1 hour and the minute hand have the least count 1 min.

Objective Questions

3. The reliable digit plus the first uncertain digit is known as significant figures.

For the number 23.023, all the non-zero digits are significant, hence 5.

For the number 0.0003, number is less than 1, the zero(s) on the right of decimal point but to the left of the first non-zero digit are not significant, hence 1.

For the number 2.1×10^{-3}, significant figures are 2.

4. Measurement in (c) option has the maximum significant digits or three.

5. $525.5 + 10.81 - 53.15 = 525.5 + 10.8 - 53.2$

$$= 483.16 = 483.2$$

6. $\dfrac{3.008 \times 38.8}{2.8768} = 40.5695 = 40.6$

(least significant figure is 3)

7. $\therefore \quad A = l \times b = 3.124 \times 3.002$

$$= 9.378248 \text{ m}^2 = 9.378 \text{ m}^2$$ **Ans.**

(rounding off to four significant digits)

8. $\therefore V = lbt = 12 \times 6 \times 2.45 = 176.4 \text{ cm}^3$

$$= 2 \times 10^2 \text{ cm}^3$$

(rounding off to one significant digit of breadth) **Ans.**

9. If we add 1.76 kg, twenty five times

then, $\quad m_T = 44$ kg

From the law of significant figures for addition answer should be,

$$m_T = 44.00 \text{ kg}$$

10. Momentum, $p = mv = 3.513 \times 5.00$

$$= 17.565 \text{ kg-ms}^{-1}$$

As the number of significant digits in m is 4 and in v is 3, so p must have 3 (minimum) significant digits. Hence,

$$p = 17.6 \text{ kg-ms}^{-1}$$

11. According to Ohm's law,

$$V = IR \Rightarrow R = \frac{V}{I} = \frac{12.8}{0.30} = 42.667\ \Omega = 43\ \Omega$$

12. $\therefore \quad R = \dfrac{V}{I}$

$$\therefore \quad \frac{\Delta R}{R} = \frac{\Delta V}{V} + \frac{\Delta I}{I}$$

or $\quad \dfrac{\Delta R}{R} = \dfrac{0.1}{12.8} + \dfrac{0.01}{0.30} = 0.041$

Percentage error in resistance is

$$\frac{\Delta R}{R} \times 100 = 4.1\%$$

13. Magnification is 100. Hence, thickness of hair,

$$t = \frac{3.5}{100} = 0.035 \text{ mm}$$

14. Random error $\propto \dfrac{1}{\text{Number of observations}}$.

15. $V = \dfrac{4}{3}\pi R^3 \therefore$ (% error in V) = 3 (% error in R)

$$= 3\ (1\ \%) = 3\ \%$$ **Ans.**

16. $\rho = \frac{m}{V} = \frac{m}{l^3} = ml^{-3}$

$\therefore$ Maximum % error in ρ = (% error in m) + 3 (% error in l)

17. $K = \frac{1}{2} mv^2$

$\therefore$ % error in K = (% error in m) + 2 (% error in v)

18. $g = \frac{GM}{R^2}$ or $g \propto R^{-2}$

$\therefore$ % change in g = (−2) (% change in R)
$= (-2)(-2) = +4\%$

Rotational kinetic energy,

$$K = \frac{L^2}{2I} \quad \ldots(i)$$

L = angular momentum = constant

$$I = \frac{2}{5}mR^2 \quad \ldots(ii)$$

From Eqs. (i) and (ii),

$$K \propto R^{-2}$$

$\therefore$ % change in K = (−2) (% change in R)
$= (-2)(-2) = +4\%$ **Ans.**

19. $R = \frac{D}{2} \Rightarrow R \propto D$

or (% error in R) = (% error in D) = 4%

20. $l = l_1 + l_2 = 11.05 + 11.05 = 22.10\,\text{cm}$

$\Delta l = \Delta l_1 + \Delta l_2 = 0.2 + 0.2 = 0.4\,\text{cm}$

Hence, $(l \pm \Delta l) = (22.10 \pm 0.4 \text{ cm})$

21. Radius of ball = 5.2 cm

$$V = \frac{4}{3}\pi R^3 \Rightarrow \frac{\Delta V}{V} = 3\left(\frac{\Delta R}{R}\right)$$

$$\left(\frac{\Delta V}{V}\right) \times 100 = 3\left(\frac{0.2}{5.2}\right) \times 100 = 11\%$$

22. $v = \frac{d}{t} = \frac{13.8}{4.0} = 3.45\,\text{ms}^{-1}$

Further, $\frac{\Delta v}{v} = \frac{\Delta d}{d} + \frac{\Delta t}{t}$ or $\Delta v = \left[\frac{\Delta d}{d} + \frac{\Delta t}{t}\right]v$

$$= \left[\frac{0.2}{13.8} + \frac{0.3}{4}\right](3.45) = 0.3\,\text{m/s}$$

$\therefore$ $(v \pm \Delta v) = (3.45 \pm 0.3)\,\text{ms}^{-1}$

23. Since, error in measurement of momentum is + 100%.

$\therefore$ $p_1 = p,\ p_2 = 2p$

$$K_1 = \frac{p^2}{2m},\ K_2 = \frac{(2p)^2}{2m}$$

$$\%\text{ in } K = \left(\frac{K_2 - K_1}{K_1}\right) \times 100$$

$$= \left(\frac{4-1}{1}\right) \times 100 = 300\%$$

24. $2x - 2y$ is suppose z. Then,

$$z = 2 \times 10.0 - 2 \times 10.0 = 0.0$$

$$\Delta z = 2\Delta x + 2\Delta y = 2(0.1 + 0.1) = 0.4$$

$\therefore$ $(z \pm \Delta z) = (0.0 \pm 0.4)$

25. $\because$ Density, $\rho = \frac{\text{Mass}}{\text{Volume}} = \frac{m}{\pi r^2 l}$

$$= \frac{12}{3.14 \times (1.25 \times 10^{-1})^2 \times 25.0}$$

$$= 9.8 \text{ gcm}^{-3}$$

$\because$ $\rho = \frac{m}{\pi r^2 l}$

$\therefore$ $\frac{\Delta\rho}{\rho} = \frac{\Delta m}{m} + \frac{2\Delta r}{r} + \frac{\Delta l}{l}$

$$\Delta\rho = \left(\frac{1}{12} + \frac{2 \times 0.01}{1.25} + \frac{0.1}{25.0}\right) \times 9.8 = 1.0$$

$\therefore$ $\rho = (9.8 \pm 1.0) \text{ gcm}^{-1}$

26. $T = \frac{t}{n}$ and $\Delta T = \frac{\Delta t}{n}$

$\therefore$ $\frac{\Delta T}{T} \times 100 = \frac{\Delta t}{t} \times 100$

$$= \frac{0.1}{2 \times 100} \times 100 = 0.05\,\%$$

$$\frac{\Delta l}{l} \times 100 = \frac{0.1 \text{ cm}}{100 \text{ cm}} \times 100 = 0.1\,\%$$

Now, $T = 2\pi\sqrt{\frac{l}{g}}$

or $g = \frac{4\pi^2 l}{T^2} \propto \frac{l}{T^2}$

$\therefore$ % error in g = (% error in l) +2 (% error in T)
= 0.1 % + 2 (0.05 %)
= 0.2 % **Ans.**

27. $T = \frac{t}{n}$

$\Rightarrow$ $\Delta T = \frac{\Delta t}{n}$

$\therefore$ $\frac{\Delta T}{T} \times 100 = \frac{\Delta t}{t} \times 100$

$$= \frac{0.2}{25} \times 100$$

$= 0.8\%$ **Ans.**

Subjective Questions

1. (a) Here, mass of the box,

$$m = 2.3 \text{ kg}$$

Mass of one gold piece,

$$m = 20.15 \text{ g} = 0.02015 \text{ kg}$$

Mass of second gold piece,

$$m_2 = 20.17 \text{ g} = 0.02017 \text{ kg}$$

$\therefore$ Total mass $= 2.34032$ kg

After the decimal point there should be least or one significant figure. Therefore, answer should be 2.3 kg as we have to round off at one digit after decimal point.

(b) $m_1 - m_2 = 20.17 - 20.15 = 0.02$ g

In substraction, also the final result should retain as many decimal places as there are in the number with the least decimal places. Therefore, answer should be 0.02g.

2. $\therefore\ V = \pi r^2 l = (\pi)(0.046 \text{ cm})^2 (21.7 \text{ cm})$

$$= 0.1443112 \text{ cm}^3$$

$$= 0.14 \text{ cm}^3$$

(rounding off to two significant digits) **Ans.**

3. $V = a^3$

$$= (2.342 \text{ m})^3$$

$$= 12.84578569 \text{ m}^3$$

$$= 12.85 \text{ m}^3$$

(rounding off to four significant digits)

$S = a^2 = (2.342)^2 \text{ m}^2$

$= 5.484964 \text{ m}^2$

$= 5.485 \text{ m}^2$ (rounding off to four significant digits)

Ans.

4. $\rho = \dfrac{m}{V} = \dfrac{9.23}{1.1}$

$= 8.3909090 \text{ kg/m}^3$

$= 8.4 \text{ kg/m}^3$

(rounding off to two significant digits) **Ans.**

5. $S = 4\pi r^2 = 4\pi\,(2.1)^2 = 55.4 \text{ cm}^2$

$$\frac{\Delta S}{S} = 2 \times \frac{\Delta r}{r}$$

$$\Rightarrow \quad \Delta S = 2 \times \frac{\Delta r}{r} \times S$$

$$= 2 \times \frac{0.5}{2.1} \times 55.4$$

$$= 26.4 \text{ cm}^2$$

$$\therefore \quad (S \pm \Delta S) = (55.4 \pm 26.4) \text{ cm}^2$$ **Ans.**

6. $(50°\text{C} \pm 0.5°\text{C}) - (20°\text{C} \pm 0.5°\text{C})$

$$= (30 \pm 1)°\text{C}$$ **Ans.**

7. The percentage error in V is 5% and in I it is 2%. The total error in R would therefore be $5\% + 2\% = 7\%$

8. $\dfrac{\Delta\rho}{\rho} \times 100 = \left[2\left(\dfrac{\Delta r}{r}\right) + \left(\dfrac{\Delta R}{R}\right) + \left(\dfrac{\Delta l}{l}\right)\right] \times 100$

$$= \left[\frac{2 \times 0.02}{0.2} + \frac{2}{60} + \frac{0.1}{150}\right] \times 100$$

$$= 23.4\ \%$$ **Ans.**

9. % error in ρ = 3 (% error in α) +2 (% error in β)

$$+ \frac{1}{2}(\text{ \% error in } \gamma) + (\text{\% error in } \eta)$$

10. $g = 4\pi^2 L/T^2$

Here, $T = \dfrac{t}{n}$ and $\Delta T = \dfrac{\Delta t}{n}$.

Therefore, $\dfrac{\Delta T}{T} = \dfrac{\Delta t}{t}$.

The errors in both L and t are the least count errors. Therefore,

$$(\Delta g/g) = (\Delta L/L) + 2(\Delta T/T)$$

$$= (\Delta L/L) + 2(\Delta t/t)$$

$$= \frac{0.1}{20.0} + 2\left(\frac{1}{90}\right) = 0.027$$

Thus, the percentage error in g is

$$(\Delta g/g) \times 100 = 2.7\%$$ **Ans.**

3. Experiments

INTRODUCTORY EXERCISE 3.1

1. $LC = \dfrac{\text{Smallest division on main scale}}{\text{Number of divisions on vernier scale}}$

$= \dfrac{1 \text{ mm}}{10} = 0.1 \text{ mm} = 0.01 \text{ cm}$

Positive zero error $= N + x\,(\text{LC})$

$= 0 + 5 \times 0.01$

$= 0.05$ cm

Diameter $= 3.2 + 4 \times 0.01 = 3.24$ cm

Actual diameter $= 3.24 - 0.05 = 3.19$ cm

2. $(N + m)$ VSD $= (N)$ MSD

$\Rightarrow \quad 1 \text{ VSD} = \left(\dfrac{N}{N+m}\right) \text{MSD}$

$LC = 1 \text{ MSD} - 1 \text{ VSD} = 1 \text{ MSD} - \left(\dfrac{N}{N+m}\right) \text{MSD}$

$= \dfrac{m}{N+m} \text{ MSD} = \left(\dfrac{1}{1 + N/m}\right) \text{MSD}$

Now, least count will be minimum for $m = 1$.

INTRODUCTORY EXERCISE 3.2

1. $LC = \dfrac{\text{Pitch}}{\text{Number of divisions on circular scale}}$

$= \dfrac{1\text{mm}}{100} = 0.01$ mm

Linear scale reading = 10 (pitch) = 10 mm

Circular scale reading $= n\,(\text{LC}) = 65 \times 0.01$

$= 0.65$ mm

$\therefore$ Total reading $= (10 + 0.65)$ mm $= 10.65$ mm

2. $LC = \dfrac{\text{Pitch}}{\text{Number of divisions on circular scale}}$

$= \dfrac{1\text{mm}}{50} = 0.02$ mm

Positive zero error $= n_1\,(\text{LC})$

or $\qquad e = 6 \times 0.02 = 0.12$ mm

Linear scale reading = 3 (pitch) = 3 mm

Circular scale reading $= n_2\,(\text{LC}) = 31 \times 0.02$

$= 0.62$ mm

Measured diameter of wire $= (3 + 0.62)$ mm

$= 3.62$ mm

$\therefore$ Actual diameter of wire

$= 3.62 \text{ mm} - 0.12 \text{ mm} = 3.50$ mm

INTRODUCTORY EXERCISE 3.3

1. A pendulum which has a time period of two seconds is called a second's pendulum.

2. Because $T = 2\pi\sqrt{L/g}$ is based on the assumption that $\sin\theta \cong \theta$ which is true only for small amplitude.

3. $T = 2\pi\sqrt{\dfrac{L}{g}}$

and we can see that T does not depend upon the mass or material or bob.

4. $L = \left(\dfrac{g}{4\pi^2}\right) T^2$

5. The length of the pendulum used in clocks increases in summer and hence T increases whereas in winter, the length of the pendulum decreases, so T decreases. T increases means clock goes slow.

6. Invar is an alloy which has a very small coefficient of linear thermal expansion. Hence, the time period does not change appreciably with the change of temperature.

7. During the draining of the sand, the period first increases due to change in effective length, then decreases and finally attains a value that it had when the sphere was full of sand.

8. $g_{\text{moon}} = \dfrac{g_{\text{earth}}}{6} = \dfrac{g}{6} \quad \Rightarrow \quad T = \text{constant}$

$\therefore$ l should be made $\dfrac{l}{6}$ at moon

$\left(\text{because } T = 2\pi\sqrt{\dfrac{l}{g}} = 2\pi\sqrt{\dfrac{l/6}{g/6}}\right)$

INTRODUCTORY EXERCISE 3.4

1. $Y = \dfrac{4FL}{\pi d^2 l} = \dfrac{4 \times 1.0 \times 9.8 \times 2}{(\pi)\,(0.4 \times 10^{-3})^2\,(0.8 \times 10^{-3})}$

$= 1.94 \times 10^{11} \text{ N/m}^2$

Further, $Y = \dfrac{4MgL}{\pi d^2 l} \quad \Rightarrow \quad \dfrac{\Delta Y}{Y} = 2\left(\dfrac{\Delta d}{d}\right) + \dfrac{\Delta l}{l}$

or $\qquad \Delta Y = \left[2\left(\dfrac{\Delta d}{d}\right) + \left(\dfrac{\Delta l}{l}\right)\right] \times Y$

$= \left[2 \times \left(\dfrac{0.01}{0.4}\right) + \left(\dfrac{0.05}{0.8}\right)\right] \times 1.94 \times 10^{11}$

$= 0.22 \times 10^{11} \text{ N/m}^2$

INTRODUCTORY EXERCISE 3.5

1. Let Δl be the end correction.
Given that fundamental tone for a length 0.1m and first overtone for the length is 0.35 m.
$$f = \frac{v}{4(0.1 + \Delta l)}$$
$$= \frac{3v}{4(0.35 + \Delta l)}$$
Solving this equation, we get
$$\Delta l = 0.025\text{m}$$
2. With end correction,
$$f = n\left[\frac{v}{4\,(l + e)}\right] \quad (\text{where, } n = 1, 3, \ldots)$$
$$= n\left[\frac{v}{4\,(l + 0.6\,r)}\right]$$
Because $e = 0.6\,r$, where r is radius of pipe.
For first resonance, $n = 1$
$$\therefore \quad f = \frac{v}{4\,(l + 0.6\,r)}$$
or
$$l = \frac{v}{4f} - 0.6r$$
$$= \left[\left(\frac{336 \times 100}{4 \times 512}\right) - 0.6 \times 2\right]\text{cm}$$
$$= 15.2 \text{ cm}$$

INTRODUCTORY EXERCISE 3.6

1. $$\rho = \frac{\pi d^2 V}{4lI} = \frac{(3.14)(2.00 \times 10^{-3})^2(100.0)}{(4)(31.4)(10.0) \times 10^{-2}}$$
$$= 1.00 \times 10^{-4}\ \Omega\text{ - m (to three significant figures)}$$
2. $$\frac{\Delta\rho}{\rho} \times 100 = \left[2\frac{\Delta d}{d} + \frac{\Delta V}{V} + \frac{\Delta l}{l} + \frac{\Delta I}{I}\right] \times 100$$
$$= \left[2 \times \left(\frac{0.01}{2.00}\right) + \left(\frac{0.1}{100.0}\right) + \left(\frac{0.1}{31.4}\right) + \left(\frac{0.1}{10.0}\right)\right] \times 100$$
$$= 2.41\,\%$$
$$R = \frac{V}{I}$$
$$\Rightarrow \quad \frac{\Delta R}{R} \times 100 = \left[\left(\frac{\Delta V}{V}\right) + \left(\frac{\Delta I}{I}\right)\right] \times 100$$
$$= \left[\frac{0.1}{100} + \frac{0.1}{10}\right] \times 100 = 1.1\%$$

3. We will require a voltmeter, an ammeter, a test resistor and a variable battery to verify Ohm's law.
Voltmeter which is made by connecting a high resistance with a galvanometer is connected in parall‹ l with the test resistor.
Further, an ammeter which is formed by connecting a low resistance in parallel with galvanometer is required to measure the current through test resistor.

INTRODUCTORY EXERCISE 3.7

1. $R > 2\,\Omega \;\Rightarrow\; \therefore \quad 100 - x > x$

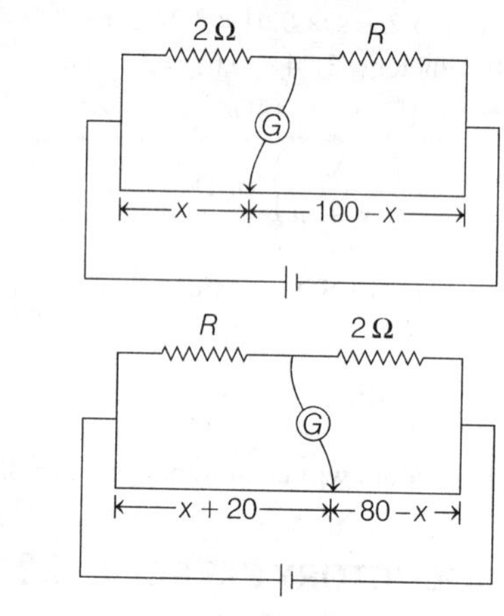

Applying $\quad \dfrac{P}{Q} = \dfrac{R}{S}$

We have $$\frac{2}{R} = \frac{x}{100 - x} \quad \ldots\text{(i)}$$
$$\frac{R}{2} = \frac{x + 20}{80 - x} \quad \ldots\text{(ii)}$$
Solving Eqs. (i) and (ii), we get
$$R = 3\,\Omega$$
$\therefore$ Correct option is (a).

2. Using the concept of balanced, Wheatstone bridge, we have
$$\frac{P}{Q} = \frac{R}{S}$$
$$\therefore \quad \frac{X}{(52 + 1)} = \frac{10}{(48 + 2)}$$
$$\therefore \quad X = \frac{10 \times 53}{50} = 10.6\,\Omega$$
$\therefore$ Correct option is (b).

3. Slide wire bridge is most sensitive when the resistance of all the four arms of bridge is same. Hence, B is the most accurate answer.

INTRODUCTORY EXERCISE 3.8

1. $\frac{P}{Q}=\frac{R}{X}$

$$\Rightarrow \quad X=\left(\frac{Q}{P}\right)R=\left(\frac{1}{10}\right)R$$

R lies between 14.2 Ω and 14.3 Ω.

Therefore, the unknown resistance X lies between 14.2 Ω and 14.3 Ω.

2. Experiment can be done in similar manner but now K_2 should be pressed first then K_1.

3. BC, CD and BA are known resistances.

The unknown resistance is connected between A and D.

Exercises

Assertion and Reason

1. Least count

$$=\frac{\text{Pitch}}{\text{Number of divisions on circular pitch}}$$

Objective Questions

2. Since, least count is 1 mm, so we cannot measure the length less than 1 mm. Hence, option (a) and (d) are correct.

3. (a) The least value of measurement in option (a) is one second. So, least count is one second.

(b) The least value of measurement in option (b) is one minute. So, least count is one minute.

6. $1\text{ MSD}=\frac{1}{10}(1\text{ cm})=1\text{ mm}$

$$10\text{ VSD}=8\text{ MSD}$$

$$1\text{ VSD}=\frac{8}{10}\text{ MSD}$$

Least count = 1 MSD − 1 VSD

$$\therefore \quad LC=1\text{ mm}-\frac{8}{10}\text{ mm}$$

$$\therefore \quad LC=\frac{2}{10}\text{ mm}$$

$$\therefore \quad LC=\frac{2}{100}\text{ cm}=0.02\text{ cm}$$ **Ans.**

7. 50 VSD = 49 MSD

$$1\text{ VSD}=\frac{49}{50}\text{ MSD}$$

$$\therefore \quad VC=1\text{ MSD}-1\text{ VSD}$$

$$\therefore \quad VC=1\text{ MSD}-\frac{49}{50}\text{MSD}$$

$$\therefore \quad VC=\frac{1}{50}\text{ MSD}$$

$$\therefore \quad 1\text{ MSD}=50\text{ (VC)}$$

$$=50\text{ (0.001 cm)}$$

$$\therefore \quad 1\text{ MSD}=0.5\text{ mm}$$ **Ans.**

8. $LC=\frac{1}{n}\text{ MSD}$

Here, n = number of vernier scale divisions

$$0.005\text{ cm}=\frac{1}{n}\left(\frac{1}{10}\text{ cm}\right)$$

$$n=\frac{0.1}{0.005}=\frac{1000}{50}$$

$$\therefore \quad n=20$$ **Ans.**

9. 100 VCD = 99 MSD

$$\therefore \quad 1\text{ VSD}=\frac{99}{100}\text{ MSD}$$

$$LC=1\text{ MSD}-1\text{ VSD}$$

$$\therefore \quad LC=1\text{ MSD}-\frac{99}{100}\text{ MSD}$$

$$\therefore \quad LC=0.01\text{ MSD}$$

$$\therefore \quad LC=0.01(1\text{ mm})=0.01\text{ mm}$$ **Ans.**

10. $1\text{ VSD}=\frac{0.8\text{ cm}}{10}=0.08\text{ cm}$

$$1\text{ MSD}=0.1\text{ cm}$$

$$\therefore \quad LC=1\text{ MSD}-1\text{ VSD}$$

$$=0.1\text{ cm}-0.08\text{ cm}$$

$$=0.02\text{ cm}$$

11. $A=l\times b=10\times 1.0=10\text{ cm}^2$

$$\frac{\Delta A}{A}=\frac{\Delta l}{l}+\frac{\Delta b}{b}$$

$$\therefore \quad \Delta A=\pm\left(\frac{\Delta l}{l}+\frac{\Delta b}{b}\right)\times A$$

$$=\pm\left(\frac{0.1}{10.0}-\frac{0.01}{1.00}\right)\times 10$$

$$=\pm 0.2\text{ cm}^2$$

13. $A=l\times\omega \quad \therefore \quad \frac{\Delta A}{A}\times 100=\frac{\Delta l}{l}\times 100+\frac{\Delta\omega}{\omega}\times 100$

$$=\frac{0.1}{10.0}\times 100+\frac{0.01}{1.0}\times 100=\pm 2\%$$

14. Volume of cylinder

$$V = \pi r^2 L,\ r = \left(\frac{D}{2}\right)$$

$$\therefore \left(\frac{\Delta V}{V}\right) \times 100 = 2\left(\frac{\Delta D}{D}\right) \times 100 + \left(\frac{\Delta L}{L}\right) \times 100$$

$$= 2\left(\frac{0.01}{4.0}\right) \times 100 + \left(\frac{0.1}{5.0}\right) \times 100$$

$$= 2.5\%$$

15. 1 MSD = 5.15 cm − 5.10 cm = 0.05 cm

$$1 \text{ VSD} = \frac{2.45 \text{ cm}}{50} = 0.049 \text{ cm}$$

$$\therefore \quad LC = 1 \text{ MSD} - 1 \text{ VSD} = 0.001 \text{ cm}$$

Hence, diameter of cylinder = (Main scale reading) + (Vernier scale reading) (LC)

$$= 5.10 + (24)(0.001) = 5.124 \text{ cm}$$

16. Least count = 1 Main scale division − 1 Vernier scale division

$$\Rightarrow \quad 0.02 = \frac{10}{100} - \frac{l}{n} = 0.1 - \frac{l}{n}$$

$$\Rightarrow \quad \frac{l}{n} = 0.1 - 0.02 = 0.08$$

$$\therefore \quad l = 0.08\, n$$

If $n = 10$, $l = 0.8$ cm

17. Least count = 1 mm − 0.9 mm = 0.1 mm

Reading = Main scale reading + Vernier scale reading − |zero error|

$$= 3.1 \text{ cm} + 4 \times 0.1 \text{ mm} - 0.8 \text{ mm}$$

$$= (3.1 + 0.04 - 0.08) \text{ cm}$$

$$= 3.06 \text{ cm}$$

21. Pitch $= \frac{2}{4} = 0.5$ mm

$\therefore$ Least count $= \frac{0.5}{50} = 0.01$ mm

22. Distance moved in one rotation = 0.5 mm

$$\text{Least count, LC} = \frac{0.5 \text{ mm}}{50 \text{ divisions}} = 0.01 \text{ mm}$$

Screw gauge has negative zero error.

This error is (50 − 20) 0.01 mm or (30) (0.01) mm.

Thickness of plate

$$= (2 \times 0.5 \text{ mm}) + (30 + 20)(0.01 \text{ mm})$$

$$= 1.5 \text{ mm}$$

23. Least count of screw gauge $= \frac{0.5}{50} = 0.01 \text{ mm} = \Delta r$

$$\text{Diameter, } r = 2.5 \text{ mm} + 20 \times \frac{0.5}{50} = 2.70 \text{ mm}$$

$$\frac{\Delta r}{r} = \frac{0.01}{2.70}$$

or

$$\frac{\Delta r}{r} \times 100 = \frac{1}{2.7}$$

Now, density $d = \frac{m}{V} = \frac{m}{\frac{4}{3}\pi\left(\frac{r}{2}\right)^3}$

Here, r is the diameter.

$$\therefore \quad \frac{\Delta d}{d} \times 100 = \left\{\frac{\Delta m}{m} + 3\left(\frac{\Delta r}{r}\right)\right\} \times 100$$

$$= \frac{\Delta m}{m} \times 100 + 3 \times \left(\frac{\Delta r}{r}\right) \times 100$$

$$= 2\% + 3 \times \frac{1}{2.7}$$

$$= 3.1\%$$

24. $LC = \frac{1}{100}$ mm = 0.01 mm

Diameter of wire = Reading of main scale + Reading of circular scale

$$= 1 \text{ mm} + 48 \times LC$$

$$= 1 \text{ mm} + 48 \times 0.01 \text{ mm}$$

$$= 1.48 \text{ mm}$$

$$\therefore \text{Volume of wire} = \pi \frac{d^2}{4} l$$

$$= 3.14 \times \frac{(1.48 \times 10^{-1})^2}{4} \times 5 \text{ cm}^3$$

$$= 0.0859732 \text{ cm}^3 = 0.086 \text{ cm}^3$$

$$= 0.086 \text{ cm}^3$$

25. $LC = \frac{1}{100} = 0.01$ mm

Zero error = + 8 × LC

$$= 8 \times 0.01 = 0.08 \text{ mm}$$

$\therefore$ Diameter of wire, d = Reading of main scale + Reading of circular scale − Zero error

$$\therefore \quad d = 1 \text{ mm} + 50 \times LC - 0.08 \text{ mm}$$

$$= 1 \text{ mm} + (50 \times 0.01 - 0.08) \text{ mm}$$

$$= 1.42 \text{ mm} = 1.42 \times 10^{-1} \text{ cm}$$

Curved surface area $= \pi\, ld$

$$= 3.14 \times 8.6 \times 1.42 \times 10^{-1}$$

$$= 3.8 \text{ cm}^2$$

26. Here, Pitch $= \frac{1\text{ cm}}{10} = \frac{10\text{ mm}}{10} = 1\text{ mm}$

Least count

$$(\text{LC}) = \frac{\text{Pitch}}{\text{Number of divisions on circular scale}}$$

$$= \frac{1}{100} = 0.01\text{ mm}$$

Zero error $= -(100-95)\times \text{LC}$

$= -5\times 0.01 = -0.05$ mm

The diameter of wire is

d = Reading of main scale + Reading of circular scale + (Zero error)

$= 2\text{mm} + (45\times 0.01 + 0.05)$ mm

$= 2.5$ mm

$\therefore$ Cross-sectional area $= \frac{\pi d^2}{4}$

$$= \frac{3.14\times(2.5\times10^{-1})^2}{4}\text{cm}^2$$

$$= 0.049\text{ cm}^2$$

27. Least count $= \frac{\text{Pitch}}{\text{Number of divisions on circular scale}}$

$$= \frac{\frac{0.5}{5}}{100} = \frac{0.1}{100}\text{ cm} = 0.001\text{ cm}$$

$\therefore$ Thickness $= 5\times 0.1 + 35\times 0.001$

$= 0.535$ cm

29. $\frac{R}{80} = \frac{20}{80}$

$\therefore \quad R = 20\ \Omega$ **Ans.**

30. Deflection is zero for $R = 324\ \Omega$

Now, $X = \left(\frac{Q}{P}\right)R = \left(\frac{1}{100}\right)(324)$

$= 3.24\ \Omega$

31. $\frac{R_1}{R_2} = \frac{50}{50} = 1$

$\therefore \quad R_1 = R_2 = R$ ...(i)

When 24 Ω is connected in parallel with R_2, then the balance point is 70 cm, so

$$\frac{R_P}{R} = \frac{\left(\frac{24R}{24+R}\right)}{R} = \frac{30}{70} \quad (\because\ R_P < R)$$

$\therefore \quad \frac{24}{24+R} = \frac{3}{7}$

$\therefore \quad 168 = 72 + 3R$

$\therefore \quad 96 = 3R$

$\therefore \quad R = 32\ \Omega$ **Ans.**

32. $\frac{R_1+10}{R_2} = \frac{50}{50} = 1$

$\therefore \quad R_1 + 10 = R_2$ ...(i)

Again, $\frac{R_1}{R_2} = \frac{40}{60} = \frac{2}{3}$

$\therefore \quad 3R_1 = 2R_2$

Substituting the value of R_2 from Eq. (i), we get

$3R_1 = 2(R_1+10)$

$\therefore \quad R_1 = 20\ \Omega$ **Ans.**

33. Battery is switched ON first to avoid large stopping and generated in galvanometer.

34. For balanced condition,

$R_2(1-x) = R_2(1)$ (here, $AB = 1$m)

For new balanced condition,

$R_2(x'-2) = R_1(2)$

$R_1(x'-2) = R_2(2)$

$R_1(x'-2) = R_1(x-1)2$

$x'-2 = 2x-2$

$x' = 2x$

35. $\frac{R_1}{R_2} = \frac{20}{80} = \frac{1}{4}$

$\therefore \quad R_2 = 4R_1$

$\therefore \quad \frac{R_1+15}{R_2} = \frac{40}{60} = \frac{2}{3}$

$\therefore \quad \frac{R_1+15}{4R_1} = \frac{2}{3}$

$\therefore \quad R_1 = 9\ \Omega$ **Ans.**

36. $\frac{X}{Y} = \frac{20}{80} = \frac{1}{4}$

$\therefore \quad Y = 4X$

Since, $\frac{4X}{Y} = \frac{l}{100-l}$

$\therefore \quad \frac{4X}{4X} = \frac{l}{100-l}$

$\therefore \quad 2l = 100$

$\therefore \quad l = 50$ cm **Ans.**

37. For meter bridge to be balanced

$\frac{P}{Q} = \frac{40}{60} = \frac{2}{3}$

$\therefore \quad P = \frac{2}{3}Q$

When Q is shunted, i.e. a resistance of 10 Ω is connected in parallel across Q, the net resistance becomes $\frac{10Q}{10+Q}$.

Now, the balance point shifts to 50 cm, i.e.

$$\frac{P}{\left(\frac{10Q}{10+Q}\right)} = 1$$

$$\therefore \quad \frac{2}{3} = \frac{10}{10+Q}$$

$$\therefore \quad 20 + 2Q = 30$$

$$\therefore \quad Q = 5\,\Omega$$

and $\quad P = \frac{10}{3}\,\Omega$ **Ans.**

38.

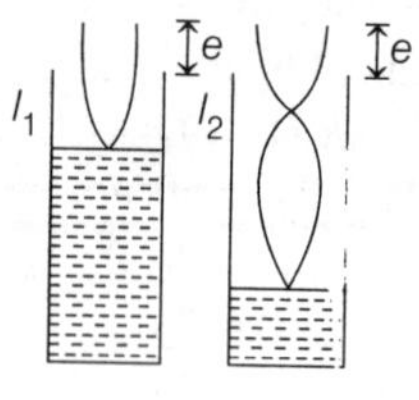

$$l_1 + e = \frac{\lambda}{4}$$

$$l_2 + e = \frac{3\lambda}{4}$$

Solving these two equations, we get

$$e = \frac{l_2 - 3l_1}{2}$$

39. $e = \frac{l_2 - 3l_1}{2}$

$$\therefore \quad e = 1\text{ cm} = \frac{1}{100}\text{ m}$$

$$\therefore \quad \frac{1}{100} = \frac{l_2 - 3\,(0.15)}{2}$$

$$\therefore \quad l_2 = 0.47\text{ m}$$

$$\therefore \quad l = 47\text{ cm}$$ **Ans.**

40. $\lambda = \frac{v}{f} = \frac{340}{340} = 1\text{ m} = 100\text{ cm}$

Length of air columns may be,

$\frac{\lambda}{4}, \frac{3\lambda}{4}, \frac{5\lambda}{4}$ ... or 25 cm, 75 cm 125 cm ...

Minimum height of water column

= 120 – maximum height of air column

= 120 – 75 = 45 cm

41. $f = \frac{v}{\lambda}$ ...(i)

Now, $\quad l_1 = \frac{\lambda}{4}, l_2 = \frac{3\lambda}{4}$

$$\Rightarrow \quad l_2 - l_1 = \frac{\lambda}{2}$$

or $\quad \lambda = 2\,(l_2 - l_1)$

Substituting in Eq. (i), we have

$$f = \frac{v}{2\,(l_2 - l_1)}$$

$$\Rightarrow \quad f \propto \frac{1}{l_2 - l_1}$$

$$\therefore \quad \frac{f_1}{f_2} = \frac{l_2' - l_1'}{l_2 - l_1}$$

$$= \frac{90 - 30}{30 - 10} = \frac{3}{1}$$

42. $\Delta l_1 = 0.1$ cm and $\Delta l_2 = 0.1$ cm

$$\because \quad v = 2f\,(l_2 - l_1) = 2 \times 300\,(75 - 25) \times 10^{-2}$$

$$= 300\text{ ms}^{-1}$$

$$\therefore \quad \Delta v = 2f\,(\Delta l_2 + \Delta l_1)$$

$$= 2 \times 300\,(0.1 \times 10^{-2} + 0.1 \times 10^{-2})\text{ ms}^{-1}$$

$$= 600 \times 0.2 \times 10^{-2} = 1.2\text{ ms}^{-1}$$

$$\therefore \quad v = (300 \pm 1.2)\text{ ms}^{-1}$$

43. $\because v = 2f\,(l_2 - l_1)$

or $\quad \frac{\Delta v}{v} = \frac{\Delta f}{f} + \frac{\Delta(l_2 - l_1)}{l_2 - l_1} = \frac{\Delta f}{f} + \frac{\Delta l_2}{l_2 - l_1} + \frac{\Delta l_1}{l_2 - l_1}$

or $\quad \frac{\Delta v}{v} = \frac{0.5}{400} + \frac{0.1}{40} + \frac{0.1}{40}$

$$= \frac{0.5}{400} + \frac{0.2}{40}$$

$$= 0.00625$$

$\therefore$ Percentage error $= \frac{\Delta v}{v} \times 100$

$$= 0.00625 \times 100$$

$$= 0.625\%$$

46. Intercept $= \frac{1}{f}$

Therefore, $\quad f = \frac{1}{\text{Intercept}} = \frac{1}{0.5}$

$$= 2\text{ m}$$

47. $\because \quad \frac{1}{f} = \frac{1}{v} - \frac{1}{u}$

or $\quad -\frac{1}{f^2}\frac{df}{dx} = -\frac{1}{v^2}\frac{dv}{dx} + \frac{1}{u^2}\frac{du}{dx}$

or $\quad \frac{\Delta f}{f^2} = \frac{\Delta v}{v^2} + \frac{\Delta u}{u^2}$

Given, $u = -30$ cm, $v = +60$ cm

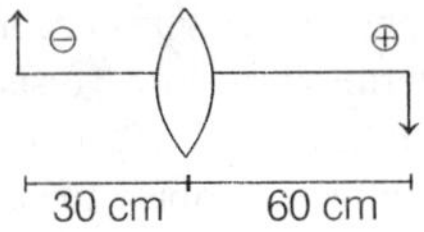

$$\frac{1}{v} - \frac{1}{u} = \frac{1}{f}$$

$$\Rightarrow \quad \frac{1}{60} + \frac{1}{30} = \frac{1}{f}$$

$$\therefore \quad f = 20 \text{ cm}$$

$$\therefore \quad \Delta f = \left(\frac{\Delta v}{v^2} + \frac{\Delta u}{u^2}\right) f^2$$

$$= \left(\frac{0.1}{60^2} + \frac{0.1}{30^2}\right) 20^2$$

$$= 0.06 \text{ cm}$$

$$\therefore \quad f = (20 \pm 0.06) \text{ cm}$$

48. Thermal capacity $= ms$

$$= (0.04 \text{ kg}) (4.2 \times 10^2 \text{ J kg}^{-1}\ {}^\circ\text{C}^{-1})$$

$$= 16.8 \text{ J}/{}^\circ\text{C}$$ **Ans.**

49. Heat lost = Heat gained

$$\therefore \quad m_1 s_1 \Delta T_1 = m_2 s_2 \Delta T_2$$

$$\therefore \quad s_1 = \frac{m_2 s_2 \Delta T_2}{m_1 \Delta T_1}$$

$$= \frac{0.5 \times 4.2 \times 10^3 \times 3}{0.2 \times 77} \text{ J kg}^{-1}\ {}^\circ\text{C}^{-1}$$

$$\therefore \quad s_1 = 0.41 \times 10^3 \text{ J kg}^{-1}\ {}^\circ\text{C}^{-1}$$ **Ans.**

50. Heat lost = Heat gained

$$0.20 \times 10^3 \times s(150 - 40)$$

$$= 150 \times 1 \times (40 - 27) + 0.025 \times 10^3 \times (40 - 27)$$

$$\{\because s_{water} = 1 \text{ cal g}^{-1} ({}^\circ\text{C})^{-1}\}$$

$$\therefore \quad 22000\, s = 1950 + 325$$

$$\therefore \quad 22000\, s = 2275$$

$$\therefore \quad s = 0.1 \text{ cal g}^{-1}\ {}^\circ\text{C}^{-1}$$ **Ans.**

51. Heat lost by aluminium $= 500 \times s \times (100 - 46.8)$ cal

$$\therefore \quad \text{Heat lost} = 26600\, s$$

Heat gained by water and calorimeter

$$= 300 \times 1 \times (46.8 - 30) + 500 \times 0.093 \times (46.8 - 30)$$

$$\therefore \quad \text{Heat gained} = 5040 + 781.2 = 5821.2$$

Now, heat lost = heat gained

$$\therefore \quad 26600\, s = 5821.2$$

$$\therefore \quad s \approx 0.22 \text{ cal g}^{-1}\ {}^\circ\text{C}^{-1}$$

53. $T = 2\pi \sqrt{\dfrac{l}{g}}$

$$\text{or} \quad g = \frac{4\pi^2 l}{T^2}$$

$$\therefore \quad \frac{\Delta g}{g} = \frac{\Delta l}{l} + 2\frac{\Delta T}{T}$$

$$= \frac{0.01}{1.00} + \frac{2 \times 0.01}{2.00}$$

$$= 0.01 + 0.01 = 0.02$$

Percentage error in $g = \dfrac{\Delta g}{g} \times 100$

$$= 0.02 \times 100 = 2\%$$

$$\because \quad g = \frac{4\pi^2 l}{T^2} = \frac{4 \times 10 \times 1.00}{(2.00)^2}$$

$$= \frac{40}{4} = 10 \text{ ms}^{-2}$$

$$\therefore \quad g = (10 \pm 2\%) \text{ ms}^{-2}$$

Comprehension Based Questions

1. $\because V = IR$

$$\text{or} \quad V = \frac{I\rho l}{A} = \frac{I\rho l}{\frac{\pi D^2}{4}}$$

$$\text{or} \quad \rho = \frac{V\pi D^2}{4Il}$$

$$\Rightarrow \quad \ln\rho = \ln\frac{\pi}{4} + \ln V + 2\ln D - \ln I - \ln l$$

$$\Rightarrow \quad \frac{1}{\rho}\frac{d\rho}{dx} = \frac{1}{V}\frac{dV}{dx} + \frac{2}{D}\frac{dD}{dx} - \frac{1}{I}\frac{dI}{dx} - \frac{1}{l}\frac{dl}{dx}$$

For maximum error

$$\left(\frac{\Delta\rho}{\rho}\right)_{max} = \frac{\Delta V}{V} + \frac{2\Delta D}{D} + \frac{\Delta I}{I} + \frac{\Delta l}{l}$$

$$\Rightarrow \quad \frac{\Delta\rho}{\rho} = \frac{0.1}{100.0} + \frac{2 \times 0.001}{5.000} + \frac{0.01}{1.00} + \frac{0.1}{100.0}$$

$$= 0.0124$$

$$\therefore \quad \text{Percentage error} = \frac{\Delta\rho}{\rho} \times 100 = 1.24\,\%$$

2. $\because V = IR$

$$\therefore \quad R = \frac{V}{I} = \frac{100.0}{1.00}\,\Omega = 1.00 \times 10^2\,\Omega$$

$$\because \quad R = \frac{V}{I}$$

$$\therefore \quad \frac{\Delta R}{R} = \frac{\Delta V}{V} + \frac{\Delta I}{I}$$

$$\Rightarrow \quad \frac{\Delta R}{R} = \frac{0.1}{100.0} + \frac{0.01}{1.00} = 0.011$$

$$\therefore \quad \Delta R = 0.011 \times 1.00 \times 10^2 = 1.1\ \Omega$$

$$\therefore \quad R = (1.00 \times 10^2 \pm 1.1)\ \Omega$$

3. $\because \; X = \dfrac{QR}{P}$

$$\therefore \quad X_{min} = \frac{Q_{min}\ R_{min}}{P_{max}} = \frac{10 \times 1}{1000} = 0.01\ \Omega$$

But $\quad X_{max} = \dfrac{Q_{max}\ R_{max}}{P_{min}} = \left(\dfrac{1000}{10}\right)(R_{max})$

$$R_{max} = 1 + 2 + 2 + 5 + 10 + 20 + 20 + 50 + 100 + 200 + 200 + 500 + 1000 + 2000 + 2000 + 5000 = 11110\ \Omega$$

$$\therefore \quad X_{max} = \left(\frac{1000}{10}\right)(11110) = 1111 \times 10^3\ \Omega$$

4. $\because \quad X = \dfrac{Q}{P} \times R = \dfrac{10}{1000} \times 999 = 9.99\ \Omega$

Subjective Questions

1. The bridge method is better because it is the null point method which is superior to all other methods.
2. Because the graph in this case is a straight line.
3. In the case of second resonance, energy gets distributed over a larger region and as such second resonance becomes feebler.
4. The bridge becomes insensitive for too high or too low values and the readings become undependable. When determining low resistance, the end resistance of the meter bridge wire and resistance of connecting wires contribute towards the major part of error.
5. No, the resistance of the connecting wires is itself of the order of the resistance to be measured. It would create uncertainty in the measurement of low resistance.
6. We have,

Least count of vernier callipers

$$= \frac{1\text{mm}}{10} = 0.1\text{ mm}$$

$$= 0.01\text{ cm}$$

Side of cube = (10) (1mm) + (1) (LC)

or $\quad a = 10\text{ mm} + 0.1\text{ mm}$

or $\quad a = 10.1\text{ mm}$

or $\quad a = 1.01\text{ cm}$

$$\rho = \frac{\text{mass}}{\text{volume}} = \frac{m}{a^3}$$

$$= \frac{2.736}{(1.01)^3}$$

$$= 2.65553\ \text{g/cm}^3$$

$$= 2.66\ \text{g/cm}^3 \qquad \textbf{Ans.}$$

4. Units and Dimensions

Exercises

Assertion and Reason

4. 1 cm = 10 mm. Here, mm is smaller unit.
But its numerical value is more.

Single Correct Option

1. $L = mvR = \frac{nh}{2\pi}$

$\therefore \quad [L] = [h] = [mvR]$

2. Velocity gradient is change in velocity per unit depth.

3. Coefficient of friction is unitless and dimensionless.

4. Dipole moment = (charge) × (distance)

Electric flux = (electric field) × (area)

Hence, the correct option is (d).

5. $[\eta] = \left[\frac{F}{av}\right] = \left[\frac{MLT^{-2}}{L^2T^{-1}}\right] L = ML^{-1}T^{-1}$

6. $a = \frac{F}{t}$

$b = \frac{F}{t^2}$

7. $R = \frac{l}{\sigma A}$

$\Rightarrow \quad \sigma = \frac{l}{RA}$

From $\quad H = I^2Rt$, we have

$R = \frac{H}{I^2 t}$

$\therefore \quad [\sigma] = \left[\frac{lI^2t}{HA}\right]$

$= \left[\frac{LA^2T}{ML^2T^{-2}L^2}\right]$

$= [M^{-1}L^{-3}T^3A^2]$

8. $\phi = BA = \frac{F}{IL} \cdot A = \left[\frac{MLT^{-2}}{AL}\right][L^2]$

$= [ML^2T^{-2}A^{-1}]$

10. $B = \frac{\mu_0}{2\pi}\frac{i}{r}$

But $\quad B = \frac{F}{il} \quad (\therefore F = ilB)$

$\therefore \quad \frac{F}{il} = \frac{\mu_0}{2\pi}\frac{i}{r}$

$\therefore \quad [\mu_0] = \left[\frac{F}{i^2}\right]$ **Ans.**

11. Let $E^a v^b F^c \propto m$

Then,

$[ML^2T^{-2}]^a [LT^{-1}]^b [MLT^{-2}]^c = [M]$

Equating the powers, we get

$a = 1, b = -2$

and $\quad c = 0$ **Ans..**

12. $L = I\omega = \frac{nh}{2\pi}$

$\therefore \quad \frac{h}{I} = [\omega]$

13. $\because \frac{2\pi x}{\lambda}$ is dimensionless.

$\therefore \quad [\lambda] = [x] = [L] = [A]$

14. In option (b), mass does not come anywhere.

15. $[Y] = \left[\frac{X}{Z^2}\right] = \left[\frac{\text{Capacitance}}{(\text{Magnetic induction})^2}\right]$

$= \left[\frac{M^{-1}L^{-2}Q^2T^2}{M^2Q^{-2}T^{-2}}\right]$

$= [M^{-3}L^{-2}T^4Q^4]$

16. $C = \frac{\Delta q}{\Delta V} = \frac{\varepsilon_0 A}{d}$

or $\quad \varepsilon_0 \frac{A}{L} = \frac{\Delta q}{\Delta V}$

or $\quad \varepsilon_0 = \frac{(\Delta q)\, L}{A \cdot (\Delta V)}$

$X = \varepsilon_0 L \frac{\Delta V}{\Delta t}$

$$= \frac{(\Delta q)L}{A\,(\Delta V)} L \frac{\Delta V}{\Delta t}$$

But $[A] = [L^2]$

$\therefore \quad X = \frac{\Delta q}{\Delta t} = \text{current}$

17. $\left[\frac{\alpha Z}{k\theta}\right] = [M^0L^0T^0]$

$$[\alpha] = \left[\frac{k\theta}{Z}\right]$$

Further $\quad [p] = \left[\frac{\alpha}{\beta}\right]$

$\therefore \quad [\beta] = \left[\frac{\alpha}{p}\right] = \left[\frac{k\theta}{Zp}\right]$

Dimensions of $k\theta$ are that to energy. Hence,

$$[\beta] = \left[\frac{ML^2T^{-2}}{LML^{-1}T^{-2}}\right]$$

$$= [M^0L^2T^0]$$

18. Since, $mvr = n \cdot \frac{h}{2\pi}$ and $E = h\nu$

So, unit of h = joule second = angular momentum

19. Power, $p = i^2R = Vi = \frac{V^2}{R}$

20. $[N/m] = [J/m^2] = \left[\frac{MLT^{-2}}{L}\right]$

$$= [MT^{-2}] = [kg/s^2]$$

21. Eight minutes and twenty second means 500 s.

$\therefore \quad d = 500c$

where, c = speed of light in vacuum which is taken as unity.

Hence, d = 500 units.

22. Heat current $= \frac{dQ}{dt} = \frac{TD}{R}$

Here, TD = temperature difference

and $\quad R$ = thermal resistance $= \frac{TD}{dQ/dt}$

$\therefore \quad [R] = [TD]\left[\frac{dt}{dQ}\right] = [K]\left[\frac{T}{ML^2T^{-2}}\right]$

$$= [M^{-1}L^{-2}T^3K]$$

23. Power, $P = Vi$

$\therefore \quad [V] = \left[\frac{P}{i}\right] = \left[\frac{ML^2T^{-3}}{A}\right] = [ML^2T^{-3}A^{-1}]$

24. Since, $p^xQ^yc^z$ is dimensionless. Therefore,

$$[ML^{-1}T^{-2}]^x[MT^{-3}]^y[LT^{-1}]^z = [M^0L^0T^0]$$

Only option (b) satisfies this expression.

So, $\quad x = 1,\ y = -1,\ z = 1$

25. Since, units of length, velocity and force are doubled.

Hence, $[m] = \frac{[\text{force}][\text{time}]}{[\text{velocity}]}$, $[\text{time}] = \frac{[\text{length}]}{[\text{velocity}]}$

Hence, unit of mass and time remain same. Momentum is doubled.

26. Since, $R = \frac{\rho l}{A}$, where ρ is a specific resistance.

$\therefore \quad [\rho] = \left[\frac{RA}{l}\right], R = \frac{V}{i}, V = \frac{W}{Q}$

$$[\rho] = [ML^3T^{-1}Q^{-2}]$$

27. Dimension of (ohm) $R = \frac{h}{e^2}$;

(e = charge = current × time)

$$= \frac{[Et]}{[it]^2} = \frac{P}{i^2} = R \text{ as } P = \frac{E}{t}$$

28. $\left[\frac{GIM^2}{E^2}\right] = \frac{[M^{-1}L^3T^{-2}][MLT^{-1}][M^2]}{[ML^2T^{-2}]^2} = [T]$

29. As $\frac{d^2s}{dt^2}$ is acceleration or $\frac{m}{s^2}$ or $[LT^{-2}]$.

In the similar way,

$$\left[\frac{d^2y}{dx^2}\right] = \left[\frac{y}{x^2}\right] = \frac{[ML^{-1}T^{-2}]}{[T^{-1}]^2} = [ML^{-1}T^0]$$

30. $4\frac{g}{cm^3} = \frac{4\left(\frac{1}{100}\right)}{\left(\frac{1}{10}\right)^3}$ units = 40 units

31. In Bohr's model, $\frac{1}{\lambda} = \frac{me^4}{\varepsilon_0^2h^3c}\left(\frac{1}{n_1^2} - \frac{1}{n_2^2}\right)$

where, λ = wavelength, n_1 and n_2 are principal quantum numbers.

$\therefore \quad \left[\frac{me^4}{\varepsilon_0^2h^3c}\right] = [L^{-1}] = [M^0L^{-1}T^0]$

32. The energy of electron in first orbit of H-atom is

$$E = \frac{-me^4}{8\,\varepsilon_0^2h^2}$$

$\Rightarrow \quad \left[\frac{me^4}{\varepsilon_0^2h^2}\right] = [E] =$ energy

More than One Correct Options

1. (a) Torque and work both have the dimensions $[ML^2T^{-2}]$.

(d) Light year and wavelength both have the dimensions of length, i.e. [L].

2. Reynold's number and coefficient of friction are dimensionless quantities.

Curie is the number of atoms decaying per unit time and frequency is the number of oscillations per unit time. Latent heat and gravitational potential both have the same dimension corresponding to energy per unit mass.

3. (a) $L = \frac{\phi}{i}$ or henry $= \frac{\text{weber}}{\text{ampere}}$

(b) $$e = -L\left(\frac{di}{dt}\right)$$

$$\therefore \quad L = -\frac{e}{(di/dt)}$$

or henry $= \frac{\text{volt-second}}{\text{ampere}}$

(c) $$U = \frac{1}{2}Li^2$$

$$\therefore \quad L = \frac{2U}{i^2}$$

or henry $= \frac{\text{joule}}{(\text{ampere})^2}$

(d) $$U = \frac{1}{2}Li^2 = i^2Rt$$

$\therefore$ $L = Rt$ or henry = ohm-second

4. $$F = \frac{1}{4\pi\varepsilon_0}\cdot\frac{q_1q_2}{r^2}$$

$$[\varepsilon_0] = \frac{[q_1][q_2]}{[F][r^2]} = \frac{[IT]^2}{[MLT^{-2}][L^2]}$$

$$= [M^{-1}L^{-3}T^4I^2]$$

Speed of light, $c = \frac{1}{\sqrt{\varepsilon_0\mu_0}}$

$$\therefore \quad [\mu_0] = \frac{1}{[\varepsilon_0][c]^2}$$

$$= \frac{1}{[M^{-1}L^{-3}T^4I^2][LT^{-1}]^2}$$

$$= [MLT^{-2}I^{-2}]$$

5. CR and $\frac{L}{R}$ both are time constants Their units is second.

$\therefore$ $\frac{1}{CR}$ and $\frac{R}{L}$ have the SI unit $(\text{second})^{-1}$. Further, resonance frequency $\omega = \frac{1}{\sqrt{LC}}$

Match the Columns

1. (a) $U = \frac{1}{2}kT$

$$\Rightarrow \quad [ML^2T^{-2}] = [k][K]$$

$$\Rightarrow \quad [K] = [ML^2T^{-2}K^{-1}]$$

(b) $F = \eta A\frac{dv}{dx}$

$$\Rightarrow \quad [\eta] = \frac{[MLT^{-2}]}{[L^2LT^{-1}L^{-1}]}$$

$$= [ML^{-1}T^{-1}]$$

(c) $E = h\nu$

$$\Rightarrow \quad [ML^2T^2] = [h][T^{-1}]$$

$$\Rightarrow \quad [h] = [ML^2T^{-1}]$$

(d) $$\frac{dQ}{dt} = \frac{kA\Delta\theta}{l}$$

$$\Rightarrow [k] = \frac{[ML^2T^{-3}L]}{[L^2K]} = [MLT^{-3}K^{-1}]$$

2. Angular momentum $L = I\omega$

$$\therefore \quad [L] = [I\omega] = [ML^2][T^{-1}] = [ML^2T^{-1}]$$

Latent heat, $L = \frac{Q}{m}$ (as $Q = mL$)

$$\Rightarrow \quad [L] = \left[\frac{Q}{m}\right] = \left[\frac{ML^2T^{-2}}{M}\right] = [L^2T^{-2}]$$

Torque $\tau = F \times r_\perp$

$$\therefore \quad [\tau] = [F \times r_\perp] = [MLT^{-2}][L]$$

$$= [ML^2T^{-2}]$$

Capacitance $C = \frac{1}{2}\frac{q^2}{U}$ $\left(\text{as } U = \frac{1}{2}\frac{q^2}{C}\right)$

$$\therefore \quad [C] = \left[\frac{q^2}{U}\right] = \left[\frac{Q^2}{ML^2T^{-2}}\right] = [M^{-1}L^{-2}T^2Q^2]$$

Inductance $L = \frac{2U}{i^2}$ $\left(\text{as } U = \frac{1}{2}Li^2\right)$

$\therefore$ $[L] = \left[\frac{U}{i^2}\right] = \left[\frac{Ut^2}{Q^2}\right]$ $\left(\text{as } i = \frac{Q}{t}\right)$

$= \left[\frac{ML^2T^{-2}T^2}{Q^2}\right] = [ML^2Q^{-2}]$

Resistivity $\rho = \frac{RA}{l}$ $\left(\text{as } R = \rho\frac{l}{A}\right)$

$= \left[\frac{H}{i^2t}\right]\left[\frac{A}{l}\right]$ (as $H = i^2Rt$)

$= \left[\frac{Ht}{Q^2}\right]\left[\frac{A}{l}\right]$ $\left(\text{as } i = \frac{Q}{t}\right)$

$= \left[\frac{ML^2T^{-2}TL^2}{Q^2L}\right] = [ML^3T^{-1}Q^{-2}]$

The correct table is as under

Column I	Column II
Angular momentum	$[ML^2T^{-1}]$
Latent heat	$[L^2T^{-2}]$
Torque	$[ML^2T^{-2}]$
Capacitance	$[M^{-1}L^{-2}T^2Q^2]$
Inductance	$[ML^2Q^{-2}]$
Resistivity	$[ML^3T^{-1}Q^{-2}]$

3. $t \equiv \frac{L}{R}$

$\therefore$ $L \equiv tR \equiv$ ohm-second

$U \equiv \frac{q^2}{2C}$

$\therefore$ $C \equiv \frac{q^2}{U} \equiv$ coulomb^2/joule

$q \equiv CV$

$\therefore$ $C \equiv \frac{q}{V} \equiv$ coulomb /volt

$L \equiv \frac{-e}{di/dt}$

$\therefore$ $L \equiv \frac{e\,(dt)}{(di)} \equiv$ volt-second/ampere

$F = ilB$

$\therefore$ $B \equiv \frac{F}{il} \equiv$ newton/ampere-metre

Column I	Column II
Capacitance	coulomb/(volt)$^{-1}$ (coulomb)^2 joule^{-1}
Inductance	ohm-second, volt-second/ampere^{-1}
Magnetic induction	newton (ampere-metre)$^{-1}$

4. (a) $F = \frac{GM_eM_s}{r^2}$

= Gravitational force between sun and earth

$\Rightarrow$ $GM_eM_s = Fr^2$

$\therefore$ $[GM_eM_s] = [Fr^2]$

$= [MLT^{-2}][L^2] = [ML^3T^{-2}]$

(b) $v_{rms} = \sqrt{\frac{3RT}{M}}$ = rms speed of gas molecules

$\therefore$ $\frac{3RT}{M} = v_{rms}^2$

or $\left[\frac{3RT}{M}\right] = [v_{rms}^2] = [LT^{-1}]^2 = [L^2T^{-2}]$

(c) $F = Bqv$ = magnetic force on a charged particle

$\therefore$ $\frac{F}{Bq} = v$

or $\left[\frac{F^2}{B^2q^2}\right] = [v]^2 = [L^2T^{-2}]$

(d) $v_o = \sqrt{\frac{GM_e}{R_e}}$ = orbital velocity of earth's satellite

$\therefore$ $\frac{GM_e}{R_e} = v_o^2$

or $\left[\frac{GM_e}{R_e}\right] = [v_o^2] = [L^2T^{-2}]$

(p) $W = qV$

$\Rightarrow$ (Coulomb) (Volt) = Joule

or [(Volt) (Coulomb) (Metre)] = [(Joule) (Metre)]

$= [ML^2T^{-2}][L] = [ML^3T^{-2}]$

(q) [(kilogram) (metre)^3 (second)$^{-2}$] $= [ML^3T^{-2}]$

(r) [(metre)^2 (second)$^{-2}$] $= [L^2T^{-2}]$

(s) $U = \frac{1}{2}CV^2$

$\Rightarrow$ (farad) $(\text{volt})^2$ = Joule

or $[(\text{farad})(\text{volt})^2(\text{kg})^{-1}] = [(\text{Joule})(\text{kg})^{-1}]$

$= [ML^2T^{-2}][M^{-1}] = [L^2T^{-2}]$

5. (a) $\dfrac{\text{Electric dipole moment}}{\text{Magnetic dipole moment}} = \dfrac{ql}{ml}$

where, q = charge = [AT],

m = pole strength = [AL],

l = length = [L]

$\therefore \dfrac{\text{Electric dipole moment}}{\text{Magnetic dipole moment}} = \dfrac{q}{m}$

$= \dfrac{[AT]}{[AL]} = [L^{-1}T]$

Thus, **(a) → (s)**

(b) (Electric flux) × (Magnetic flux) = $(EA)(BA)$

where, E = electric field, A = area,
B = magnetic field.

$\therefore$ Electric flux × Magnetic flux = EBA^2

$= [A^{-1}MLT^{-3}][A^{-1}MT^{-2}][L^4]$

$= [A^{-2}M^2L^5T^{-5}]$

Thus, **(b) → (r)**

(c) $\dfrac{G}{R} = \dfrac{[M^{-1}M^3T^{-2}]}{[\text{mol}^{-1}M][L^2T^{-2}K^{-1}]}$

$= [K\,\text{mol}\,M^{-2}L]$

Thus, **(c) → (q)**

(d) $\dfrac{\text{Inductance} \times \text{Electric permittivity}}{\text{Heat capacity}}$

$= [A^{-2}ML^2T^{-2}] \times \dfrac{[A^2M^{-1}L^{-3}T^4]}{[K^{-1}ML^2T^{-2}]}$

$= [KM^{-1}L^{-3}T^4]$

Thus, **(d) → (p)**

6. (a) $\because \dfrac{GMm}{R^2} = F$

$\therefore \dfrac{GM}{R} = \dfrac{FR}{m} = \dfrac{[MLT^{-2}L]}{[M]}$

$= [M^2T^{-2}]$

$\therefore \sqrt{\dfrac{GM}{R}} = [LT^{-1}]$

Thus, **(a) → (s)**

(b) $\lambda v^2 = [ML^{-1}][LT^{-1}]^2 = [MLT^{-2}]$

Thus, **(b) → (r)**

(c) Magnetic field, $B = \mu_0 Jr$

$\therefore [\mu_0 Jr] = \theta[B] = [A^{-1}MT^{-2}]$

Thus, **(c) → (q)**

(d) $\left[\dfrac{m}{qB}\right] = \dfrac{[M]}{[ATA^{-1}MT^{-2}]} = [T] = [M^0L^0T]$

Thus, **(d) → (p)**

Subjective Questions

1. $1\,N = 10^5$ dyne

$1\,m^2 = 10^4\,cm^2$

$\therefore 2.0 \times 10^{11}\dfrac{N}{m^2}$

$= \dfrac{2.0 \times 10^{11} \times 10^5}{10^4}\dfrac{\text{dyne}}{\text{cm}^2}$

$= 2.0 \times 10^{12}\,\text{dyne/cm}^2$

2. 1 dyne $= 10^{-5}$ N

1 cm $= 10^{-2}$ m

$\therefore$ 72 dyne/cm $= \dfrac{72 \times 10^{-5}}{10^{-2}}\dfrac{N}{m}$

$= 0.072\dfrac{N}{m}$

3. $[T] = [p^a d^b E^c] = [ML^{-1}T^{-2}]^a\,[ML^{-3}]^b[ML^2T^{-2}]^c$

Equating the powers of both sides, we have

$a + b + c = 0$ ... (i)

$-a - 3b + 2c = 0$ ... (ii)

$-2a - 2c = 1$ ... (iii)

Solving these three equations, we have

$a = -\dfrac{5}{6}, b = \dfrac{1}{2}$ and $c = \dfrac{1}{3}$

4. $[Y] = [ML^{-1}T^{-2}]$

$\left[\dfrac{MgL}{\pi r^2 l}\right] = \left[\dfrac{MLT^{-2}L}{L^2L}\right]$

$= [ML^{-1}T^{-2}]$

Dimensions of RHS and LHS are same. Therefore, the given equation is dimensionally correct.

5. $[E] = k[m]^x[n]^y[a]^z$

where, k is a dimensionless constant.

$\therefore \quad [ML^2T^{-2}] = k[M]^x[T^{-1}]^y[L]^z$

Solving, we get

$$x = 1, \; y = 2$$

and $\quad z = 2$

$\therefore \quad E = kmn^2a^2$

6. Since, dimension of Fv

$$= [Fv] = [MLT^{-2}][LT^{-1}] = [ML^2T^{-3}]$$

So, $\left[\dfrac{\beta}{x^2}\right]$ should also be $[ML^2T^{-3}]$

$$\frac{[\beta]}{[x^2]} = [ML^2T^{-3}]$$

$$[\beta] = [ML^4T^{-3}] \qquad \textbf{Ans.}$$

and $\left[Fv + \dfrac{\beta}{x^2}\right]$ will also have dimension $[ML^2T^{-3}]$, so LHS should also have the same dimension $[ML^2T^{-3}]$.

So, $\dfrac{[\alpha]}{[t^2]} = [ML^2T^{-3}]$

$$[\alpha] = [ML^2T^{-1}] \qquad \textbf{Ans.}$$

7. $[b] = [V] = [L^3]$

$$\frac{[a]}{[V]^2} = [P] = [ML^{-1}T^{-2}]$$

$\Rightarrow \quad [a] = [ML^5T^{-2}]$

8. $\left[\dfrac{a}{RTV}\right] = [M^0L^0T^0]$

$\therefore \quad [a] = [RTV] = \left[\dfrac{pV^2}{n}\right]$

$$= [ML^5T^{-2}mol^{-1}]$$

$$[b] = [L^3]$$

9. $\left[\dfrac{dx}{\sqrt{a^2 - x^2}}\right]$ is dimensionless.

$\left[\dfrac{1}{a}\sin^{-1}\left(\dfrac{a}{x}\right)\right]$ has the dimension of $[L^{-1}]$.

10. $\left[\dfrac{dx}{\sqrt{2ax - x^2}}\right]$ is dimensionless.

Therefore, $\left[a^n \sin^{-1}\left(\dfrac{x}{a} - 1\right)\right]$ should also be dimensionless.

Hence, $n = 0$

11. (a) $[\text{density}] = [F]^x[L]^y[T]^z$

$\therefore \quad [ML^{-3}] = [MLT^{-2}]^x[L]^y[T]^z$

Equating the powers, we get

$$x = 1, \; y = -4$$

and $\quad z = 2$

$\therefore \quad [\text{density}] = [FL^{-4}T^2]$

In the similar manner, other parts can be solved.

5. Vectors

INTRODUCTORY EXERCISE 5.1

3. Apply $R = \sqrt{A^2 + B^2 + 2AB\cos\theta}$

4. Apply $S = \sqrt{A^2 + B^2 - 2AB\cos\theta}$

5. $R = S \Rightarrow \sqrt{A^2 + B^2 + 2AB\cos\theta}$

$$= \sqrt{A^2 + B^2 - 2AB\cos\theta}$$

Solving, we get $\cos\theta = 0$ or $\theta = 90^\circ$

INTRODUCTORY EXERCISE 5.2

1. A or $|\mathbf{A}| = \sqrt{(3)^2 + (-4)^2 + (5)^2} = 5\sqrt{2}$ units

Directions of cosines are,

$$\cos\alpha = \frac{A_x}{A} = \frac{3}{5\sqrt{2}}$$

$$\cos\beta = \frac{A_y}{A} = \frac{-4}{5\sqrt{2}}$$

and $$\cos\gamma = \frac{A_z}{A} = \frac{1}{\sqrt{2}}$$

2.

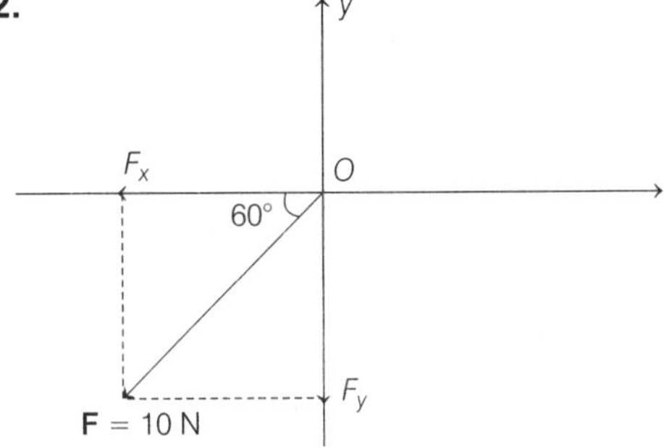

$F_x = 10\cos 60^\circ = 5$ N (along negative x-direction)

$F_y = 10\sin 60^\circ = 5\sqrt{3}$ N (along negative y-direction)

3. $\mathbf{A} - 2\mathbf{B} + 3\mathbf{C} = (2\hat{\mathbf{i}} + 3\hat{\mathbf{j}}) - 2(\hat{\mathbf{i}} + \hat{\mathbf{j}}) + 3\hat{\mathbf{k}}$

$$= (\hat{\mathbf{j}} + 3\hat{\mathbf{k}})$$

$\therefore \quad |\mathbf{A} - 2\mathbf{B} + 3\mathbf{C}| = \sqrt{(1)^2 + (3)^2}$

$$= \sqrt{10} \text{ units}$$

4. (a) Antiparallel vectors

(b) Perpendicular vectors

(c) **A** lies in xy-plane and **B** is along positive z-direction. So, they are mutually perpendicular vectors

(d)

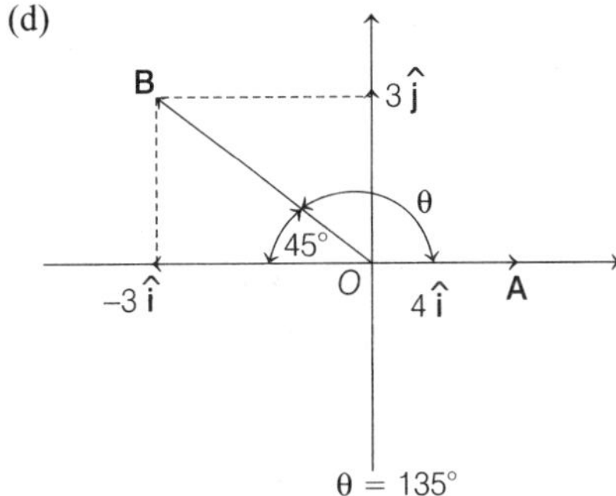

INTRODUCTORY EXERCISE 5.3

3. $\mathbf{A} \cdot \mathbf{B} = AB\cos\theta$

4. $2\mathbf{A} = 4\hat{\mathbf{i}} - 2\hat{\mathbf{j}}$

$-3\mathbf{B} = -3\hat{\mathbf{j}} - 3\hat{\mathbf{k}}$

$$\Rightarrow \quad (2\mathbf{A}) \times (-3\mathbf{B}) = \begin{vmatrix} \hat{\mathbf{i}} & \hat{\mathbf{j}} & \hat{\mathbf{k}} \\ 4 & -2 & 0 \\ 0 & -3 & -3 \end{vmatrix}$$

$$= \hat{\mathbf{i}}(6 - 0) + \hat{\mathbf{j}}(0 + 12) + \hat{\mathbf{k}}(-12 - 0) = 6\hat{\mathbf{i}} + 12\hat{\mathbf{j}} - 12\hat{\mathbf{k}}$$

Exercises

Single Correct Option

7. (a) is correct option according to question,

(b) $\hat{\mathbf{k}} \cdot \hat{\mathbf{i}} = 0$ as $\theta = 90^\circ$

(c) $\hat{\mathbf{i}} \cdot \hat{\mathbf{i}} = 1$

(d) $\hat{\mathbf{j}} \times \hat{\mathbf{j}} = 0$

8. $\mathbf{A} \cdot \mathbf{B} = AB\cos\theta = (3)(5)\cos 60^\circ = 7.5$

11. $|\mathbf{A} \times \mathbf{B}| = AB\sin\theta$

$$0 \le \sin\theta \le 1$$

$\therefore \quad 0 \le |\mathbf{A} \times \mathbf{B}| \le AB$

12. $\sqrt{(0.5)^2 + (0.8)^2 + c^2} = 1$ **Ans.**

13. $R = \sqrt{A^2 + A^2 + 2\,AA\cos\theta}$

$R = A$ at $\theta = 120^\circ$ **Ans.**

14. $(2\hat{\mathbf{i}} + 3\hat{\mathbf{j}} + 8\hat{\mathbf{k}}) \cdot (4\hat{\mathbf{i}} - 4\hat{\mathbf{j}} + \alpha\hat{\mathbf{k}}) = 0$

$\therefore \quad 8 - 12 + 8\alpha = 0$

$\therefore \quad \alpha = \frac{1}{2}$ **Ans.**

15. $(\mathbf{a} + \mathbf{b}) \times (\mathbf{a} - \mathbf{b})$

$= \mathbf{a} \times \mathbf{a} - \mathbf{a} \times \mathbf{b} + \mathbf{b} \times \mathbf{a} - \mathbf{b} \times \mathbf{b}$

$= 2\,(\mathbf{b} \times \mathbf{a})$

As $\mathbf{a} \times \mathbf{a}$ and $\mathbf{b} \times \mathbf{b}$ are two null vectors and $-\mathbf{a} \times \mathbf{b} = \mathbf{b} \times \mathbf{a}$

16.

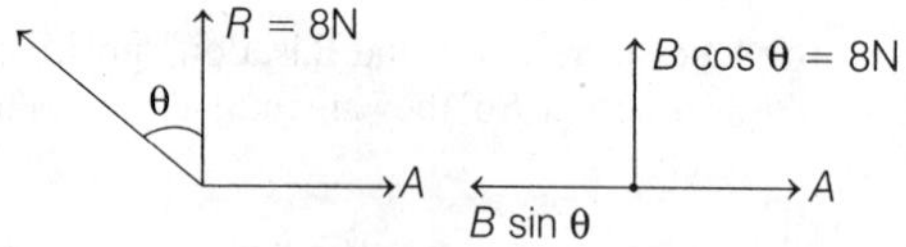

$R = 8\text{N}$, θ, A; $B\cos\theta = 8\text{N}$, $B\sin\theta$, A

$A + B = 16 \quad \text{...(i)}$

$B\sin\theta = A$

and $B\cos\theta = 8$

Squaring and adding these two equations, we get

$B^2 = A^2 + 64 \quad \text{...(ii)}$

Solving Eqs. (i) and (ii), we get

$A = 6\text{ N}$

and $B = 10\text{ N}$ **Ans.**

17. For given condition, $\theta = \frac{360°}{n} = 30°$

18. $\mathbf{a} - \mathbf{b}$ is nothing but addition of $\mathbf{a}$ and $-\mathbf{b}$.

So, the magnitude of $\mathbf{a} - \mathbf{b}$ will lie between $|\mathbf{a}| + |\mathbf{b}|$ and $|\mathbf{a}| - |\mathbf{b}|$.

19. Let $\mathbf{a} = a_1\hat{\mathbf{i}} + a_2\hat{\mathbf{j}} + a_3\hat{\mathbf{k}}$, Then,

$\hat{\mathbf{i}} \times \mathbf{a} = \hat{\mathbf{i}} \times (a_1\hat{\mathbf{i}} + a_2\hat{\mathbf{j}} + a_3\hat{\mathbf{k}})$

$= a_2\hat{\mathbf{k}} - a_3\hat{\mathbf{j}}$

$\hat{\mathbf{j}} \times \mathbf{a} = \hat{\mathbf{j}} \times (a_1\hat{\mathbf{i}} + a_2\hat{\mathbf{j}} + a_3\hat{\mathbf{k}})$

$= -a_1\hat{\mathbf{k}} + a_3\hat{\mathbf{i}} = a_3\hat{\mathbf{i}} - a_1\hat{\mathbf{k}}$

$\hat{\mathbf{k}} \times \mathbf{a} = \hat{\mathbf{k}} \times (a_1\hat{\mathbf{i}} + a_2\hat{\mathbf{j}} + a_3\hat{\mathbf{k}})$

$= a_1\hat{\mathbf{j}} - a_2\hat{\mathbf{i}}$

Now, $\hat{\mathbf{i}} \times (\hat{\mathbf{i}} \times \mathbf{a}) + \hat{\mathbf{j}} \times (\hat{\mathbf{j}} \times \mathbf{a}) + \hat{\mathbf{k}} \times (\hat{\mathbf{k}} \times \mathbf{a})$

$= \hat{\mathbf{i}} \times (a_2\hat{\mathbf{k}} - a_3\hat{\mathbf{j}}) + \hat{\mathbf{j}} \times (a_3\hat{\mathbf{i}} - a_1\hat{\mathbf{k}}) + \hat{\mathbf{k}} \times (a_1\hat{\mathbf{j}} - a_2\hat{\mathbf{i}})$

$= -a_2\hat{\mathbf{j}} - a_3\hat{\mathbf{k}} - a_3\hat{\mathbf{k}} - a_1\hat{\mathbf{i}} - a_1\hat{\mathbf{i}} - a_2\hat{\mathbf{j}}$

$= -2(a_1\hat{\mathbf{i}} + a_2\hat{\mathbf{j}} + a_3\hat{\mathbf{k}})$

$= -2\mathbf{a}$

20. $\mathbf{A} + \mathbf{B} + \mathbf{C} = 0$

$\Rightarrow \quad \mathbf{C} = -(\mathbf{A} + \mathbf{B}) \quad \text{or} \quad |\mathbf{C}| = |-(\mathbf{A} + \mathbf{B})|$

or $\quad A \sim B \le C \le A + B$

21. Resultant is always inclined towards a vector of larger magnitude.

22. $A = |\mathbf{A}| = \sqrt{(3)^2 + (6)^2 + (2)^2}$

$= 7$

$\alpha = \cos^{-1}\left(\frac{A_x}{A}\right) = \cos^{-1}\left(\frac{3}{7}\right)$

= angle of **A** with positive x-axis.

Similarly, β and γ angles.

23. $\mathbf{R} = \mathbf{A} + \mathbf{B} = 12\hat{\mathbf{i}} + 5\hat{\mathbf{j}}$

$R = |\mathbf{R}| = \sqrt{(12)^2 + (5)^2}$

$= 13$

$\hat{\mathbf{R}} = \frac{\mathbf{R}}{R} = \frac{12\hat{\mathbf{i}} + 5\hat{\mathbf{j}}}{13}$

24. $\cos^2\alpha + \cos^2\beta + \cos^2\gamma = 1$ (a standard result)

or $(1 - \sin^2\alpha) + (1 - \sin^2\beta) + (1 - \sin^2\gamma) = 1$

$\therefore \quad \sin^2\alpha + \sin^2\beta + \sin^2\gamma = 2$

25. $C^2 = A^2 + B^2 + 2AB\cos\theta$

At $\theta = 90°$; $C^2 = A^2 + B^2$

26. $|\mathbf{A} \times \mathbf{B}| = \sqrt{3}\, \mathbf{A} \cdot \mathbf{B}$

$\Rightarrow \quad AB\sin\theta = \sqrt{3}\, AB\cos\theta$

or $\quad \tan\theta = \sqrt{3}$

$\Rightarrow \quad \theta = 60°$

$|\mathbf{A} + \mathbf{B}| = \sqrt{A^2 + B^2 + 2AB\cos 60°}$

$= \sqrt{A^2 + B^2 + AB}$

27. $(\mathbf{B} \times \mathbf{A})$ is $\perp$ to both **A** and **B**

$\therefore \quad (\mathbf{B} \times \mathbf{A}) \cdot \mathbf{A} = 0$

28. $R = \sqrt{P^2 + Q^2 + 2PQ\cos\theta}$

Substituting the values of P, Q and R, we get

$\cos\theta = 0$

$\Rightarrow \quad \theta = 90°$

29.

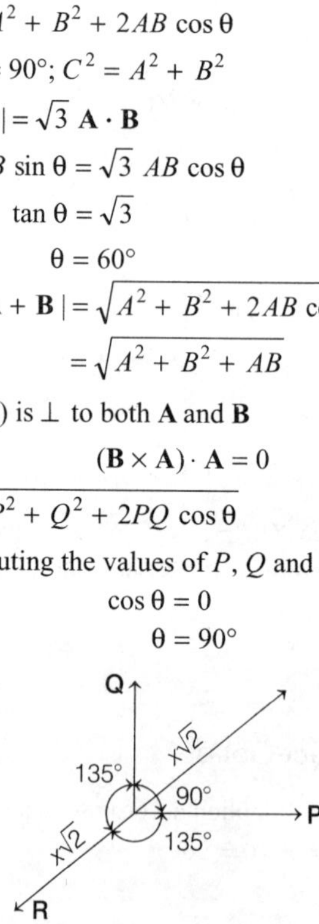

Q, P, R, $x\sqrt{2}$, $x\sqrt{2}$, 135°, 90°, 135°

$|\mathbf{P}| = |\mathbf{Q}| = x$

$|\mathbf{R}| = \sqrt{2}\, x$

30. $(\mathbf{P}+\mathbf{Q})\cdot(\mathbf{P}-\mathbf{Q})$

$$= P^2 + PQ\cos\theta - PQ\cos\theta - Q^2$$
$$= P^2 - Q^2$$

Since, dot product may be positive (if $P > Q$), negative (if $Q > P$) or zero (if $P = Q$). Therefore, angle between $(\mathbf{P}+\mathbf{Q})$ and $(\mathbf{P}-\mathbf{Q})$ may be acute, obtuse or 90°.

31. $R = \sqrt{(3P)^2 + (2P)^2 + 2\,(3P)\,(2P)\cos\theta}$ ...(i)

$2R = \sqrt{(6P)^2 + (2P)^2 + 2\,(6P)\,(2P)\cos\theta}$ ...(ii)

Solving these two equations, we get

$$\cos\theta = -\frac{1}{2}$$

or $\theta = 120°$

32.

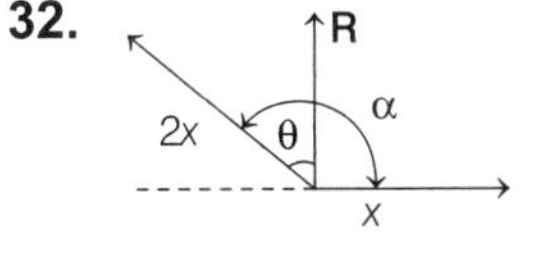

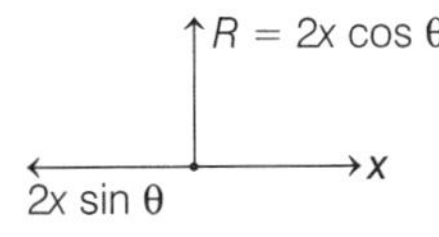

$$2x\sin\theta = x$$

$\therefore$ $\theta = 30°$

or $\alpha = 120°$ **Ans.**

33. $\mathbf{A}\cdot\mathbf{B} = 0$

$\therefore$ $\mathbf{A}\perp\mathbf{B}$

$\mathbf{A}\cdot\mathbf{C} = 0$

$\therefore$ $\mathbf{A}\perp\mathbf{C}$

A is perpendicular to both **B** and **C** and $\mathbf{B}\times\mathbf{C}$ is also perpendicular to both **B** and **C**. Therefore, **A** is parallel to $\mathbf{B}\times\mathbf{C}$.

34. $(\mathbf{A}+\mathbf{B})\perp(\mathbf{A}-\mathbf{B})$

$\therefore$ $(\mathbf{A}+\mathbf{B})\cdot(\mathbf{A}-\mathbf{B}) = 0$

$\therefore$ $A^2 + BA\cos\theta - AB\cos\theta - B^2 = 0$

or $A = B$ **Ans.**

35. $A \sim B \le C \le A + B$

36. $A \sim B \le C \le A + B$

37. Area of triangle $= \dfrac{1}{2}AB\sin\theta = \dfrac{|\mathbf{A}\times\mathbf{B}|}{2}$

$$\mathbf{A}\times\mathbf{B} = (\hat{\mathbf{i}}+\hat{\mathbf{j}}+\hat{\mathbf{k}})\times 3\hat{\mathbf{i}}$$
$$= -3\hat{\mathbf{k}} + 3\hat{\mathbf{j}}$$
$$|\mathbf{A}\times\mathbf{B}| = \sqrt{(-3)^2 + (3)^2}$$
$$= 3\sqrt{2}$$

$\therefore$ Area $= \dfrac{3\sqrt{2}}{2} = \dfrac{3}{\sqrt{2}}$ unit

38. $|\Delta\mathbf{r}| = |\mathbf{r}_f - \mathbf{r}_i|$

$$= \sqrt{l^2 + l^2 - 2(l)(l)\cos\theta}$$
$$= 2l\sin\frac{\theta}{2}$$

39. $|\Delta\mathbf{v}| = |\mathbf{v}_f - \mathbf{v}_i|$

$$= \sqrt{v^2 + v^2 - 2(v)(v)\cos 30°}$$
$$= (\sqrt{2-\sqrt{3}})v$$

40. $3 = \sqrt{(\sqrt{3})^2 + (\sqrt{3})^2 + 2\,(\sqrt{3})\,(\sqrt{3})\cos\theta}$

$\Rightarrow \theta = 60°$.

41. $|\mathbf{A}| = \sqrt{9+16} = 5$

and $|\mathbf{B}| = \sqrt{36+64} = 10$.

$\mathbf{B} = 2\mathbf{A}$ or **B** is parallel to **A**. Ratio of their coefficients are equal, so they are parallel. Or their cross product is zero.

42. Diagonal vector, $\mathbf{A} = b\hat{\mathbf{i}} + b\hat{\mathbf{j}} + b\hat{\mathbf{k}}$

or $A = \sqrt{b^2 + b^2 + b^2} = \sqrt{3}b$

$\therefore$ $\hat{\mathbf{A}} = \dfrac{\mathbf{A}}{A} = \dfrac{\hat{\mathbf{i}}+\hat{\mathbf{j}}+\hat{\mathbf{k}}}{\sqrt{3}}$

43. A vector parallel to **A** will be $n\mathbf{A}$ or $(3n\hat{\mathbf{i}} + 4n\hat{\mathbf{j}})$

Now, $|n\mathbf{A}| = |\mathbf{B}|$ is given.

Hence, $n\sqrt{9+16} = \sqrt{49+576}$

or $n = 5$

$\therefore$ $n\mathbf{A} = 15\hat{\mathbf{i}} + 20\hat{\mathbf{j}}$

44. $\dfrac{|\mathbf{a}+\mathbf{b}|}{|\mathbf{a}-\mathbf{b}|} = 1$

i.e. $|\mathbf{a}+\mathbf{b}| = |\mathbf{a}-\mathbf{b}|$

or $a^2 + b^2 + 2ab\cos\theta = a^2 + b^2 - 2ab\cos\theta$

$\therefore$ $\cos\theta = 0°$

or $\theta = 90°$

45. $(\mathbf{A}\times\mathbf{B})$ is perpendicular to both **A** and **B** or $(\mathbf{A}+\mathbf{B})$ and dot product of two perpendicular vectors is zero.

46. From polygon law of vector addition, $\mathbf{C}+\mathbf{A} = \mathbf{B}$.

47. $|\mathbf{a}+\mathbf{b}| = 2A\cos\dfrac{\theta}{2} = (2)\,(1)\cos 30° = \sqrt{3}$

$|\mathbf{a}-\mathbf{b}| = 2A\cos\dfrac{\theta}{2} = (2)\,(1)\cos 30° = 1$

48. $\sqrt{A^2 + B^2 + 2AB\cos\theta} = 2\sqrt{A^2 + B^2 - 2AB\cos\theta}$

From this equation, we can not find θ.

49. $\mathbf{P} + \mathbf{Q} = \mathbf{R}$ and $P = Q = R$

$\Rightarrow \qquad R = \sqrt{P^2 + Q^2 + 2PQ\cos\theta}$

Substituting $P = Q = R$, we get $\theta = 120°$

If $P = Q$, then **R** will pass through the centre of **P** and **Q**. Hence, angle between **P** and **R** will be

$$\theta_1 = \frac{\theta}{2} = 60°$$

In the second condition, given that $P = Q = R$ and $\mathbf{P} + \mathbf{Q} + \mathbf{R} = 0$. Then, angle between **P** and **R** will be $\theta_2 = 120°$

$$\therefore \qquad \theta_1 = \frac{\theta_2}{2}$$

50. Let θ be the angle between **A** and **B**,

$$|\mathbf{A} + \mathbf{B}| = n|\mathbf{A} - \mathbf{B}|$$

$$\Rightarrow \sqrt{A^2 + B^2 + 2AB\cos\theta} = n\sqrt{A^2 + B^2 + 2AB\cos(180° - \theta)}$$

$$|\mathbf{A}| = |\mathbf{B}| = A = B = x$$

$$2x^2(1 + \cos\theta) = n^2 \cdot 2x^2(1 - \cos\theta)$$

$$1 + \cos\theta = n^2 - n^2\cos\theta$$

$$(1 + n^2)\cos\theta = n^2 - 1$$

$$\cos\theta = \frac{n^2 - 1}{n^2 + 1}$$

$$\theta = \cos^{-1}\left(\frac{n^2 - 1}{n^2 + 1}\right)$$

51.

$$R_1^2 = A^2 + B^2 + 2AB\cos\theta$$

$$R_2^2 = A^2 + B^2 - 2AB\cos\theta$$

$$\therefore \qquad R_1^2 + R_2^2 = 2(A^2 + B^2)$$

52.

$$\mathbf{AB} + \mathbf{AC} + \mathbf{AD} + \mathbf{AE} + \mathbf{AF}$$

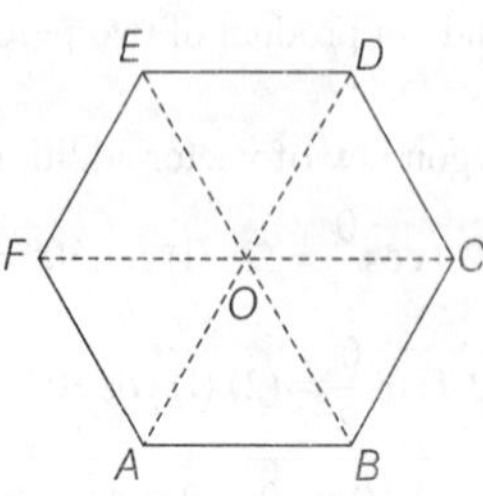

$$= \mathbf{AB} + (\mathbf{AB} + \mathbf{BC}) + (\mathbf{AB} + \mathbf{BC} + \mathbf{CD}) + (\mathbf{AF} + \mathbf{FE}) + \mathbf{AF}$$

$$= (\mathbf{AB} + \mathbf{CD}) + (\mathbf{BC}) + (\mathbf{BC}) + 2(\mathbf{AB} + \mathbf{AF}) + (\mathbf{FE})$$

$$= \mathbf{AO} + \mathbf{AO} + \mathbf{AO} + 2\,\mathbf{AO} + \mathbf{AO}$$

$$= 6\mathbf{AO}$$

53. Since, **A** is a unit vector in a given direction. It should be a constant unit vector.

or $\qquad \dfrac{d\hat{\mathbf{A}}}{dt} = 0$

54. $\qquad \mathbf{OB} + \mathbf{BC} = \mathbf{r}$

or $\qquad \mathbf{q} + \mathbf{BC} = \mathbf{r} \qquad$ ...(i)

$\qquad \mathbf{OA} + \mathbf{AC} = \mathbf{r}$

or $\qquad \mathbf{p} + \mathbf{AC} = \mathbf{r} \qquad$ ...(ii)

Adding these two equations, we get $\mathbf{p} + \mathbf{q} = 2\mathbf{r}$, as **AC** and **BC** are equal and opposite vectors

55. $|\Delta\mathbf{a}| = \sqrt{a^2 + a^2 - 2 \cdot a \cdot a \cdot \cos(\Delta\theta)}$

$$= 2a\sin\left(\frac{\Delta\theta}{2}\right)$$

For small angles, $\sin\dfrac{\Delta\theta}{2} \approx \dfrac{\Delta\theta}{2}$

$$\therefore \qquad |\Delta\mathbf{a}| = 2a \times \frac{\Delta\theta}{2} = a \cdot \Delta\theta$$

56. Apply polygon law.

57.

C is perpendicular to **A**. Therefore,

$$B\sin\alpha = A \qquad \text{...(i)}$$

Further, $\qquad C = B\cos\alpha = A \qquad$ ...(ii)

Dividing Eq. (i) by Eq. (ii), we get

$$\tan\alpha = 1 \quad \text{or} \quad \alpha = 45°$$

Therefore, angle between **A** and **B** is

$$\theta = 90° + \alpha = 135° \quad \text{or} \quad \frac{3\pi}{4}$$

58. Since, $\mathbf{a}_1$ and $\mathbf{a}_2$ are non-collinear.

$\therefore \qquad a_1 = a_2 = 1$

and $\qquad |\mathbf{a}_1 + \mathbf{a}_2| = \sqrt{3}$

$\Rightarrow \qquad a_1^2 + a_2^2 + 2a_1 a_2\cos\theta = (\sqrt{3})^2$

$\Rightarrow \qquad 1 + 1 + 2\cos\theta = 3$

$\Rightarrow \qquad \cos\theta = \dfrac{1}{2}$

Now, $(\mathbf{a}_1 - \mathbf{a}_2)\cdot(2\mathbf{a}_1 + \mathbf{a}_2)$

$$= 2a_1^2 - a_2^2 - a_1a_2\cos\theta$$

$$= 2 - 1 - \frac{1}{2} = \frac{1}{2}$$

59. According to Lami's theorem,

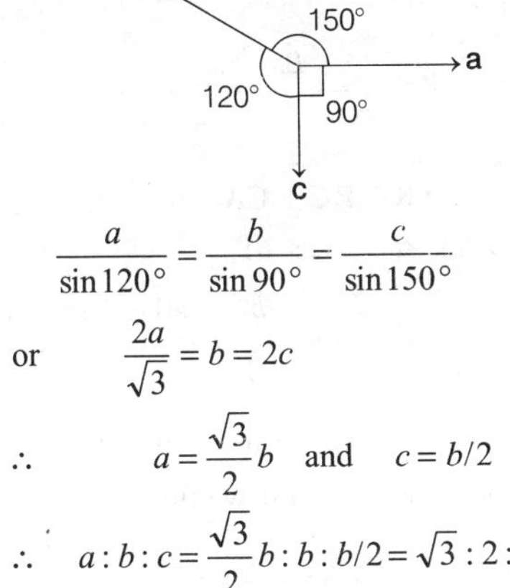

$$\frac{a}{\sin 120^\circ} = \frac{b}{\sin 90^\circ} = \frac{c}{\sin 150^\circ}$$

or $$\frac{2a}{\sqrt{3}} = b = 2c$$

$\therefore$ $$a = \frac{\sqrt{3}}{2}b \quad \text{and} \quad c = b/2$$

$\therefore$ $$a : b : c = \frac{\sqrt{3}}{2}b : b : b/2 = \sqrt{3} : 2 : 1$$

Match the Columns

1. (a) $AB\sin\theta = |AB\cos\theta|$

$\therefore$ $\tan\theta = \pm 1$

$\Rightarrow$ $\theta = 45^\circ$ or 135° **Ans.**

(b) If **A** and **B** are parallel or antiparallel to each other, then their cross product is a null vector and they may be said to be equal otherwise for any other angle,

$$\mathbf{A}\times\mathbf{B} = -\mathbf{B}\times\mathbf{A}$$

(c) $\sqrt{A^2 + B^2 + 2AB\cos\theta}$

$$= \sqrt{A^2 + B^2 - 2AB\cos\theta}$$

$\therefore$ $\cos\theta = 0$

or $\theta = 90^\circ$ **Ans.**

(d) $A + B = C$ only at $\theta = 0^\circ$

Subjective Questions

2. The angle between the force **F** and the displacement **r** is 180°. Thus, the work done is

$$W = \mathbf{F}\cdot\mathbf{r} = Fr\cos\theta$$

$$= (12\text{ N})(2.0\text{ m})(\cos 180^\circ)$$

$$= -24\text{ N-m} = -24\text{ J}$$

3. $\mathbf{A}\times\mathbf{B}$ is perpendicular to both **A** and **B**. So, this is parallel or antiparallel to **C**. Now, cross product of two parallel or antiparallel vectors is zero. Hence,

$$\mathbf{C}\times(\mathbf{A}\times\mathbf{B}) = 0.$$

4. $\mathbf{A}\times\mathbf{B}$ is perpendicular to **A**. Now, dot product of two perpendicular vectors is zero. Hence,

$$\mathbf{A}\cdot(\mathbf{A}\times\mathbf{B}) = 0$$

5. $\mathbf{S} = \mathbf{S}_1 + \mathbf{S}_2 + \mathbf{S}_3$

$$= [(5\cos 37^\circ)\hat{\mathbf{i}} + (5\sin 37^\circ)\hat{\mathbf{j}}] + 3\hat{\mathbf{i}} + 2\hat{\mathbf{j}}$$

$$= (4\hat{\mathbf{i}} + 3\hat{\mathbf{j}}) + 3\hat{\mathbf{i}} + 2\hat{\mathbf{j}}$$

$$= (7\hat{\mathbf{i}} + 5\hat{\mathbf{j}})\text{ m}$$

5 m, S, 7 m

$$S = \sqrt{(7)^2 + (5)^2}$$

$$= \sqrt{74}\text{ m}$$

$$\tan\theta = \frac{5}{7} \quad \text{or} \quad \theta = \tan^{-1}\left(\frac{5}{7}\right)$$

6. Suppose α is the angle between **A** and **B** and β the angle between **C** and **B**. But $\alpha \neq \beta$.

Given that,

$$\mathbf{A}\cdot\mathbf{B} = \mathbf{C}\cdot\mathbf{B}$$

$\Rightarrow$ $$AB\cos\alpha = CB\cos\beta$$

$\Rightarrow$ $$A\cos\alpha = C\cos\beta$$

or $$A \neq C \text{ as } \alpha \neq \beta$$

7. $\mathbf{A} + \mathbf{B} = \mathbf{R} = 3\hat{\mathbf{i}} + \hat{\mathbf{j}}$,

$\mathbf{A} - \mathbf{B} = \mathbf{S} = \hat{\mathbf{i}} + 5\hat{\mathbf{j}}$

Now, angle between **R** and **S** is

$$\theta = \cos^{-1}\left(\frac{\mathbf{R}\cdot\mathbf{S}}{RS}\right)$$

8. Ratio of their coefficients should be same.

$\therefore$ $$\frac{2}{3} = \frac{3}{-a} = \frac{-4}{b}$$

$\therefore$ $$a = -4.5 \quad \text{and} \quad b = -6$$

9. $$\mathbf{A}\times\mathbf{B} = \begin{vmatrix} \hat{\mathbf{i}} & \hat{\mathbf{j}} & \hat{\mathbf{k}} \\ 2 & 4 & -6 \\ 1 & 0 & 2 \end{vmatrix}$$

$$= \hat{\mathbf{i}}(8-0) + \hat{\mathbf{j}}(-6-4) + \hat{\mathbf{k}}(0-4)$$

$$= 8\hat{\mathbf{i}} - 10\hat{\mathbf{j}} - 4\hat{\mathbf{k}}$$

Area of parallelogram $= |\mathbf{A}\times\mathbf{B}|$

$$= \sqrt{(8)^2 + (10)^2 + (4)^2}$$

$= 13.4$ units **Ans.**

10. $$\mathbf{A}\cdot(\mathbf{B}\times\mathbf{C}) = \begin{vmatrix} 2 & -3 & 7 \\ 1 & 0 & 2 \\ 0 & 1 & -1 \end{vmatrix}$$

$$= 2(0-2) - 3(0+1) + 7(1-0)$$

$$= -4 - 3 + 7 = 0$$

11. (a) $\mathbf{A} + \mathbf{B} = \mathbf{R}$

$$R_x = A_x + B_x$$

$\therefore \quad B_x = R_x - A_x = 10 - 4 = 6 \text{ m}$

Similarly,

$$B_y = R_y - A_y = 9 - 6 = 3 \text{ m}$$

(b) $B = \sqrt{B_x^2 + B_y^2} = \sqrt{(6)^2 + (3)^2} = 3\sqrt{5} \text{ m}$

$$\tan\theta = \frac{B_y}{B_x} = \frac{3}{6} = \frac{1}{2}$$

$\therefore \quad \theta = \tan^{-1}\left(\frac{1}{2}\right)$

12. (a) $\mathbf{a} + \mathbf{b} + \mathbf{c} = \mathbf{P} = \hat{\mathbf{i}} - 2\hat{\mathbf{j}}$

(b) $\mathbf{a} + \mathbf{b} - \mathbf{c} = \hat{\mathbf{i}} + 4\hat{\mathbf{j}} = \mathbf{Q}$

(c) Angle between **P** and **Q** is, $\theta = \cos^{-1}\left(\frac{\mathbf{P}\cdot\mathbf{Q}}{PQ}\right)$

13. $\mathbf{R} = [(10\cos 30°)\hat{\mathbf{i}} + (10\cos 60°)\hat{\mathbf{j}}] + [(10\cos 60°)\hat{\mathbf{i}} + (10\cos 30°)\hat{\mathbf{j}}]$

$= 10(\cos 30° + \cos 60°)\hat{\mathbf{i}} + 10(\cos 60° + \cos 30°)\hat{\mathbf{j}}$

$= 10(2\cos 45° \cos 15°)\hat{\mathbf{i}} + 10(\cos 45° \cos 15°)\hat{\mathbf{j}}$

$= 20\cos 45° \cos 15°\hat{\mathbf{i}} + 20\cos 45° \cos 15°\hat{\mathbf{j}}$

$= R_x\hat{\mathbf{i}} + R_y\hat{\mathbf{j}}$

Here, $\quad R_x = R_y = 10\sqrt{2}\cos 15°$

$\therefore \quad |\mathbf{R}| = \sqrt{R_x^2 + R_y^2} = 20\cos 15°$

Since, $\quad R_x = R_y$, therefore $\theta = 45°$

14. Their x components should be equal and opposite.

$\therefore \quad 6\cos\theta = -4 \quad \text{or} \quad \theta = \cos^{-1}\left(-\frac{2}{3}\right)$

15. Find $\mathbf{A} \times \mathbf{B}$ and then prove that $(\mathbf{A} \times \mathbf{B}) \cdot \mathbf{A} = 0$ and $(\mathbf{A} \times \mathbf{B}) \cdot \mathbf{B} = 0$.

It means $(\mathbf{A} \times \mathbf{B}) \perp$ to both **A** and **B**.

16.

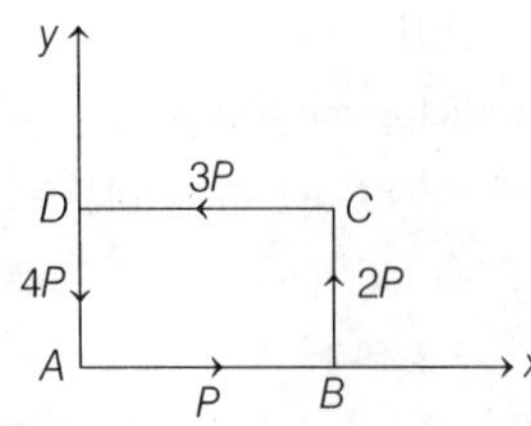

$$\mathbf{R} = (P\hat{\mathbf{i}} + 2P\hat{\mathbf{j}} - 3P\hat{\mathbf{i}} - 4P\hat{\mathbf{j}})$$

$$= (-2P\hat{\mathbf{i}} - 2P\hat{\mathbf{j}})$$

$|\mathbf{R}| = \sqrt{(2P)^2 + (2P)^2} = 2\sqrt{2}\,P$ **Ans.**

17. From polygon law of vector addition we can see that,

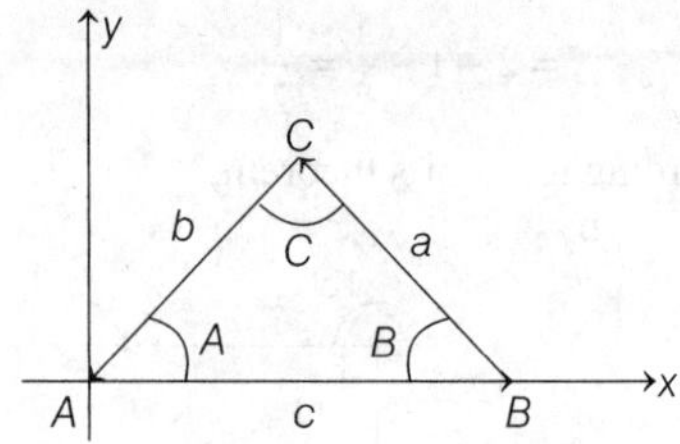

$$\mathbf{AB} + \mathbf{BC} + \mathbf{CA} = 0$$

$\therefore \quad c\hat{\mathbf{i}} + (a\sin B\hat{\mathbf{j}} - a\cos B\hat{\mathbf{i}}) + (-b\cos A\hat{\mathbf{i}} - b\sin A\hat{\mathbf{j}}) = 0$

$\therefore \quad (c - a\cos B - b\cos A)\,\hat{\mathbf{i}} + (a\sin B - b\sin A)\,\hat{\mathbf{j}} = 0$

Putting coefficient of $\hat{\mathbf{j}} = 0$, we find that

$$\frac{a}{\sin A} = \frac{b}{\sin P}$$

Now, taking B as origin and BC as the x-axis, we can prove other relation.

18. If **a** and **b** are perpendicular to each other.

$$R = \sqrt{a^2 + b^2}$$

If a and b are opposite to each other,

$$\frac{R}{\sqrt{2}} = a - b$$

$\Rightarrow \quad \frac{R^2}{2} = a^2 + b^2 - 2ab$

$\Rightarrow \quad a^2 + b^2 = 2a^2 + 2b^2 - 4ab$

$\Rightarrow \quad a^2 + b^2 - 4ab = 0$

$\Rightarrow \quad \frac{a^2 + b^2}{ab} = 4$

or $\quad \frac{a}{b} + \frac{b}{a} = 4$

19. $\because \quad \mathbf{R} = \mathbf{a} + \mathbf{b}$

$\therefore \quad \mathbf{b} = \mathbf{R} - \mathbf{a}$

$\Rightarrow \quad b^2 = R^2 + a^2 - 2Ra\cos 30°$

$\Rightarrow \quad b^2 = 4 + 12 - 2 \times 2 \times 2\sqrt{3} \times \frac{\sqrt{3}}{2}$

$\Rightarrow \quad b^2 = 16 - 12 = 4$

$\therefore \quad b = 2 \text{ N}$

6. Kinematics

INTRODUCTORY EXERCISE 6.1

2. (a) $\mathbf{v}\cdot\mathbf{a} = 6-4-4 = -2\ \text{m}^2/\text{s}^3$

(b) Since dot product is negative. So angle between **v** and **a** is obtuse.

(c) As angle between **v** and **a** at this instant is obtuse, speed is decreasing.

INTRODUCTORY EXERCISE 6.2

1. **v** and **a** both are constant vectors. Further, these two vectors are antiparallel.

2. **a** is function of time and **v** and **a** are neither parallel nor antiparallel.

INTRODUCTORY EXERCISE 6.3

1. Distance may be greater than or equal to magnitude of displacement.

2. Constant velocity means constant speed in same direction. Further if any physical quantity has a constant value (here, the velocity) then its average value in any interval of time is equal to that constant value

3. Stone comes under gravity

$\therefore \quad F = mg$

or $\quad a = \dfrac{F}{m} = g$ **Ans.**

4. In 15 s, it will rotate 90° or $\dfrac{1}{4}$ th circle.

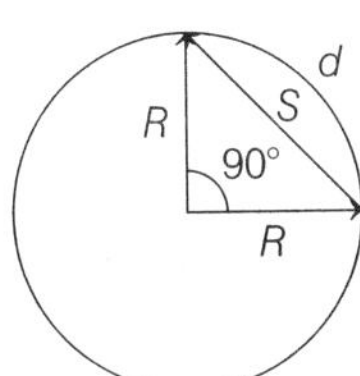

$$\therefore \quad \text{Average speed} = \frac{\text{Total distance}}{\text{Total time}} = \frac{d}{t}$$

$$= \frac{(2\pi R/4)}{15} = \frac{\pi R}{30} = \frac{\pi(2.0)}{30}$$

$$= \left(\frac{\pi}{15}\right) \text{cm/s} \qquad \textbf{Ans.}$$

$$\text{Average velocity} = \frac{\text{Total displacement}}{\text{Total time}} = \frac{s}{t}$$

$$= \frac{\sqrt{2}\,R}{t} = \frac{(\sqrt{2})(2.0)}{15} = \frac{2\sqrt{2}}{15}\ \text{cm/s} \qquad \textbf{Ans.}$$

5. (a) On a curvilinear path (a path which is not straight line), even if speed is constant, velocity will change due to change in direction.

$\therefore \quad \mathbf{a} \neq 0$

(b) (i) On a curved path velocity will definitely change (at least due to change in direction).

$\therefore \quad \mathbf{a} \neq 0$

(ii) In projectile motion, path is curved, but acceleration is constant $(= g)$.

(iii) Variable acceleration on curved path is definitely possible.

6. (a) $T = \dfrac{2\pi R}{v} = 25.13$ s **Ans.**

(b) (i) Since speed is constant. Therefore,

average speed = constant speed

= 1.0 cm/s **Ans.**

(ii) Average velocity $= \dfrac{s}{t} = \dfrac{\sqrt{2}R}{(T/4)} = \dfrac{4\sqrt{2}R}{T}$

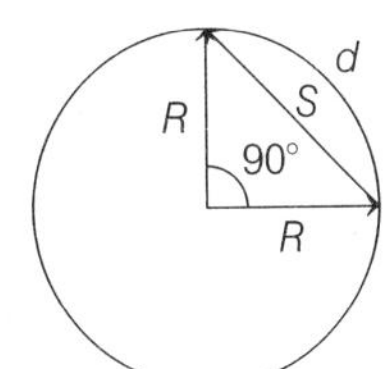

$$= \frac{(4)(\sqrt{2})(4.0)}{25.13} = 0.9\ \text{cm/s} \qquad \textbf{Ans.}$$

(iii) Velocity vector will rotate 90°

$$\therefore \quad |\Delta \mathbf{v}| = \sqrt{v^2 + v^2 - 2vv\cos 90°}$$

$$= \sqrt{2}\ v$$

$$\therefore \quad |\mathbf{a}_{av}| = \frac{|\Delta \mathbf{v}|}{\Delta t} = \frac{\sqrt{2}\ v}{(T/4)} = \frac{4\sqrt{2}\ v}{T}$$

$$= \frac{(4\sqrt{2})(1.0)}{25.13} = 0.23\ \text{cm/s}^2 \qquad \textbf{Ans.}$$

INTRODUCTORY EXERCISE 6.4

1. Average speed $= \dfrac{d}{t} = \dfrac{d_1 + d_2}{t_1 + t_2}$

$$= \frac{v_1 t_1 + v_2 t_2}{t_1 + t_2}$$

$$= \frac{(4 \times 2) + (6 \times 3)}{2 + 3}$$

$$= 5.2\ \text{m/s} \qquad \textbf{Ans.}$$

2. A —— 2 m/s, d_1 —— C —— d/4, 4 m/s —— D —— 3d/4, 6 m/s —— B; time t for AC, t for CB

$$2t = d_1 \quad ...(i)$$

$$\frac{(d/4)}{4} + \frac{(3d/4)}{6} = t$$

$$\Rightarrow \quad \frac{3d}{16} = t \quad ...(ii)$$

$$\text{Average speed} = \frac{\text{total distance}}{\text{total time}}$$

$$= \frac{d_1 + d}{2t} = \frac{2t + \frac{16t}{3}}{2t}$$

$$= \frac{11}{3}\ \text{m/s}$$

INTRODUCTORY EXERCISE 6.5

1. S_t = (displacement upto t second) − [displacement upto $(t-1)$ sec]

$$= (ut + \frac{1}{2}at^2) - [u(t-1) + \frac{1}{2}a(t-1)^2]$$

$$= u + at - \frac{1}{2}a$$

2. $s_t = \left[ut + \frac{1}{2}at^2\right] - \left[u(t-1) + \frac{1}{2}a(t-1)^2\right]$

$$= (u)(1) + \frac{1}{2}(a)(2t) - \frac{1}{2}(a)(1)^2$$

The first term is $(u)(1)$, which we are writing only u. Dimensions of u are $[LT^{-1}]$ and dimensions of 1 (which is actually 1 second) are $[T]$

$$\therefore \quad [(u)(1)] = [LT^{-1}][T]$$

$$= [L] = s_t$$

Therefore, dimension of (u) (1) are same as the dimensions of s_t. Same logic can be applied with other terms too.

5. In 4s, it reaches upto the highest point and then changes its direction of motion.

$$s = ut + \frac{1}{2}at^2 = (40)(6) + \frac{1}{2}(-10)(6)^2$$

$$= 60\ \text{m} \quad \textbf{Ans.}$$

$$d = |s|_{0-4} + |s|_{4-6} = \left|\frac{u^2}{2g}\right| + \left|\frac{1}{2}g(t-t_0)^2\right|$$

$$= \frac{(40)^2}{2\times 10} + \frac{1}{2}\times 10 \times (6-4)^2 = 100\text{m} \quad \textbf{Ans.}$$

6. $u_{av} = \frac{s}{t} = \frac{ut + \frac{1}{2}at^2}{t} = u + \frac{1}{2}at$ **Ans.**

7. $v = u + at$

i.e. v-t function is linear. In linear function,

$$\text{average value} = \frac{(\text{final value} + \text{initial value})}{2}$$

$$\therefore \quad v_{av} = \frac{v_f + v_i}{2} = \frac{v_1 + v_2}{2} \quad \textbf{Ans.}$$

8. $t = \sqrt{\frac{2h}{g}} = \sqrt{\frac{2\times 125}{10}} = 5\ \text{s}$

$$v_{av} = \frac{s}{t} = \frac{125}{5} = 25\ \text{m/s} \quad \text{(downwards)} \quad \textbf{Ans.}$$

9. (a) $s = ut + \frac{1}{2}at^2$

$$= (2.5\times 2) + \frac{1}{2}(0.5)(2)^2$$

$$= 6\ \text{m} = \text{distance}$$

(b) $v = u + at$

$$7.5 = 2.5 + 0.5\times t \Rightarrow t = 10\ s$$

(c) $v^2 = u^2 + 2as$

$$\therefore \quad (7.5)^2 = (2.5)^2 + (2)(0.5)s$$

$$\Rightarrow \quad s = 50\ \text{m} = \text{distance}$$

10. (a) $h = \frac{u^2}{2g} = \frac{(50)^2}{2\times 10} = 125\ \text{m}$

(b) Time of ascent $= \frac{u}{g} = \frac{50}{10} = 5\ \text{s}$

(c) $v^2 = u^2 + 2as = (50)^2 + 2(-10)\left(\frac{125}{2}\right)$

Solving, we get speed $v \approx 35\ \text{m/s}$

INTRODUCTORY EXERCISE 6.6

1. (a) $a = \frac{dv}{dt} = 5 - 2t$

At $t = 2\ \text{s}$

$$a = 1\ \text{m/s}^2 \quad \textbf{Ans.}$$

(b) $x = \int_0^3 v\,dt = \int_0^3 (10 + 5t - t^2)\,dt$

$$= \left[10t + 2.5t^2 - \frac{t^3}{3}\right]_0^3$$

$$= (10\times 3) + (2.5)(3)^2 - \frac{(3)^3}{3}$$

$$= 43.5\ \text{m} \quad \textbf{Ans.}$$

2. (a) Acceleration of particle,

$$a = \frac{dv}{dt} = (6 + 18t)\ \text{cm/s}^2$$

At $t = 3$ s,

$$a = (6 + 18 \times 3)\,\text{cm/s}^2$$
$$= 60\,\text{cm/s}^2$$

(b) Given, $v = (3 + 6t + 9t^2)\,\text{cm/s}$

or $\frac{ds}{dt} = (3 + 6t + 9t^2)$

or $ds = (3 + 6t + 9t^2)\,dt$

$\therefore$ $\int_0^s ds = \int_5^8 (3 + 6t + 9t^2)\,dt$

$\therefore$ $s = [3t + 3t^2 + 3t^3]_5^8$

or $s = 1287$ cm

3. (a) Position, $x = (2t - 3)^2$

Velocity, $v = \frac{dx}{dt} = 4\,(2t - 3)\text{m/s}$

and acceleration, $a = \frac{dv}{dt} = 8\ \text{m/s}^2$

At $t = 2$ s,

$$x = (2 \times 2 - 3)^2$$
$$= 1.0\ \text{m}$$
$$v = 4\,(2 \times 2 - 3)$$
$$= 4\ \text{m/s}$$

and $a = 8\,\text{m/s}^2$

(b) At origin, $x = 0$

or $(2t - 3) = 0$

$\therefore$ $v = 4 \times 0 = 0$

4. (a) At $t = 0$, $x = 2.0$ m **Ans.**

(b) $v = \frac{dx}{dt} = 2t + 6t^2$

At $t = 0$, $v = 0$ **Ans.**

(c) $a = \frac{dv}{dt} = 2 + 12t$

At $t = 2$ s

$a = 26\ \text{m/s}^2$ **Ans.**

5. $v \propto t^{3/4}$

$$a = \frac{dv}{dt} \Rightarrow a \propto t^{-1/4}$$
$$s = \int v\,dt \Rightarrow s \propto t^{7/4}$$

INTRODUCTORY EXERCISE 6.7

1. $\mathbf{u} = 2\hat{\mathbf{i}}$

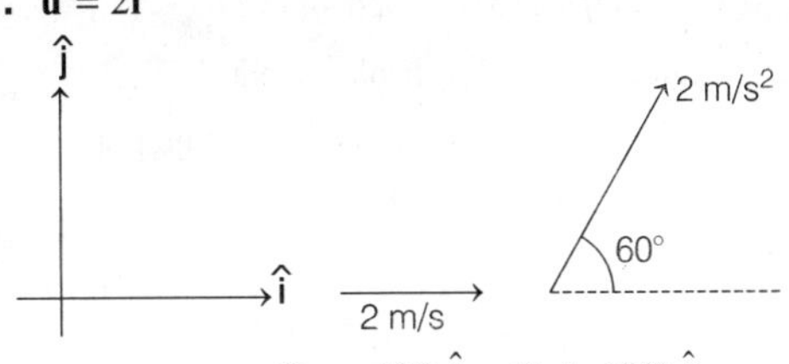

$$\mathbf{a} = (2\cos 60°)\,\hat{\mathbf{i}} + (2\sin 60°)\,\hat{\mathbf{j}}$$
$$= (\hat{\mathbf{i}} + \sqrt{3}\,\hat{\mathbf{j}})$$
$$t = 2\ \text{s}$$

(i) $\mathbf{v} = \mathbf{u} + \mathbf{a}t = (2\hat{\mathbf{i}}) + (\hat{\mathbf{i}} + \sqrt{3}\,\hat{\mathbf{j}})\,(2)$

$= 4\hat{\mathbf{i}} + 2\sqrt{3}\,\hat{\mathbf{j}}$

$\therefore$ $|\mathbf{v}| = \sqrt{(4)^2 + (2\sqrt{3})^2}$

$= 2\sqrt{7}\ \text{m/s}$ **Ans.**

(ii) $\mathbf{s} = \mathbf{u}\,t + \frac{1}{2}\,\mathbf{a}\,t^2 = (2\hat{\mathbf{i}})\,(2) + \frac{1}{2}\,(\hat{\mathbf{i}} + \sqrt{3}\,\hat{\mathbf{j}})\,(2)^2$

$= (6\hat{\mathbf{i}} + 2\sqrt{3}\,\hat{\mathbf{j}})$

$\therefore$ $|\mathbf{s}| = \sqrt{(6)^2 + (2\sqrt{3})^2}$

$= 4\sqrt{3}\ \text{m}$ **Ans.**

2. $\mathbf{v} = (2\hat{\mathbf{i}} + 2t\,\hat{\mathbf{j}})$

(i) $\mathbf{a} = \frac{d\mathbf{v}}{dt} = (2\hat{\mathbf{j}})\ \text{m/s}^2 = \text{constant}$

$\therefore$ $\mathbf{v} = \mathbf{u} + \mathbf{a}t$ can be applied.

(ii) $\mathbf{s} = \int_0^1 \mathbf{v}dt = \int_0^1 (2\hat{\mathbf{i}} + 2t\hat{\mathbf{j}})\,dt = [2t\hat{\mathbf{i}} + t^2\hat{\mathbf{j}}\,]_0^1$

$= (2\hat{\mathbf{i}} + \hat{\mathbf{j}})\ \text{m}$ **Ans.**

3. $\int_{2\hat{\mathbf{i}}}^{\mathbf{v}} d\mathbf{v} = \int \mathbf{a}dt = \int_0^t (2t\hat{\mathbf{i}} + 3t^2\hat{\mathbf{j}})\,dt$

Solving we get $\mathbf{v} = 2\hat{\mathbf{i}} + t^2\hat{\mathbf{i}} + t^3\hat{\mathbf{j}}$

At $t = 1$ s, $\mathbf{v} = (3\hat{\mathbf{i}} + \hat{\mathbf{j}}\,)\ \text{m/s}$

$$\int_0^t d\mathbf{r} = \int_0^t \mathbf{v}dt = \int_0^t [(2 + t^2)\hat{\mathbf{i}} + t^3\hat{\mathbf{j}}]\,dt$$

$\Rightarrow$ $\mathbf{r} = \left(2t + \frac{t^3}{3}\right)\hat{\mathbf{i}} + \frac{t^4}{4}\hat{\mathbf{j}}$

At $t = 1$ s, $\mathbf{r} = \frac{7}{3}\hat{\mathbf{i}} + \frac{1}{4}\,\hat{\mathbf{j}}$

Therefore, the co-ordinates are $\left(\frac{7}{3}, \frac{1}{4}\right)$ m

INTRODUCTORY EXERCISE 6.8

1. (b) v = Slope of x - t graph
2. Distance travelled = displacement

   = area under v - t graph

   Acceleration = Slope of v - t graph
3. Acceleration = Slope of v - t graph

   Distance travelled = displacement

   = area under v - t graph
4. (a) Average velocity $= \frac{s}{t} = \frac{x_f - x_i}{t}$

   $$= \frac{x_{10\,\text{sec}} - x_{0\,\text{sec}}}{10} = \frac{100}{10} = 10\text{ m/s}$$

   (b) Instantaneous velocity = Slope of x - t graph
5. From 0 to 20 s,

   displacement s_1 = area under v - t graph

   $= +50$ m (as v is positive)

   From 20 to 40 s,

   displacement s_2 = area under v - t graph

   $= -50$m (as v is negative)

   Total distance travelled $= s_1 + |s_2| = 100$ m

   Average velocity $= \frac{s}{t} = \frac{s_1 + s_2}{t}$

   $$= \frac{50 - 50}{40} = 0$$

INTRODUCTORY EXERCISE 6.9

1. v_A = Slope of $A = \frac{2}{5} = 0.4$ m/s

   v_B = Slope of $B = \frac{12}{5} = 2.4$ m/s

   $\therefore v_{AB} = v_A - v_B = -2$ m/s
2. $a_A = a_B = g$ (downwards)

   $\therefore \quad a_{AB} = a_A - a_B = 0$ **Ans.**
3. (a) $t = \frac{400}{10} = 40$ s **Ans.**

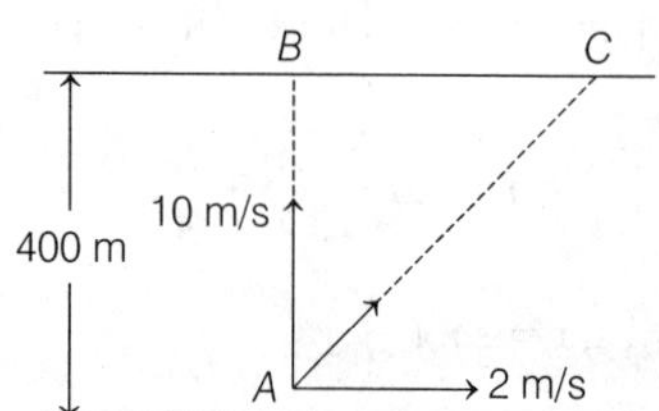

   (b) $BC = (2\text{ m/s})(t)$

   $= 2 \times 40 = 80$ m **Ans.**

4. Applying sine law in ΔABC, we have

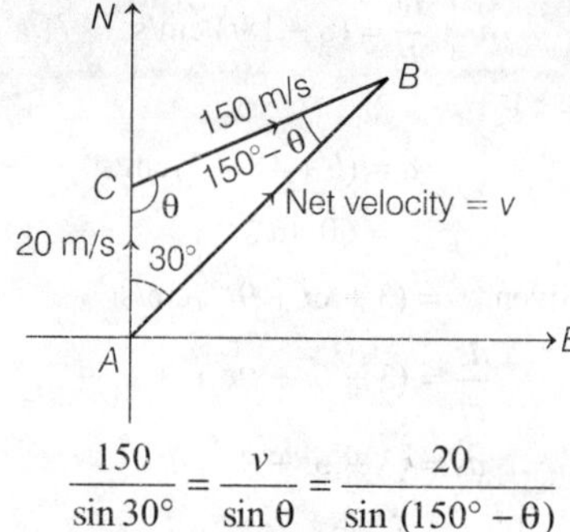

$$\frac{150}{\sin 30°} = \frac{v}{\sin \theta} = \frac{20}{\sin (150° - \theta)}$$

From first and third we have,

$$\sin (150° - \theta) = \frac{20 \sin 30°}{150} = \frac{1}{15}$$

$$\therefore \quad 150° - \theta = \sin^{-1}\left(\frac{1}{15}\right)$$ **Ans.**

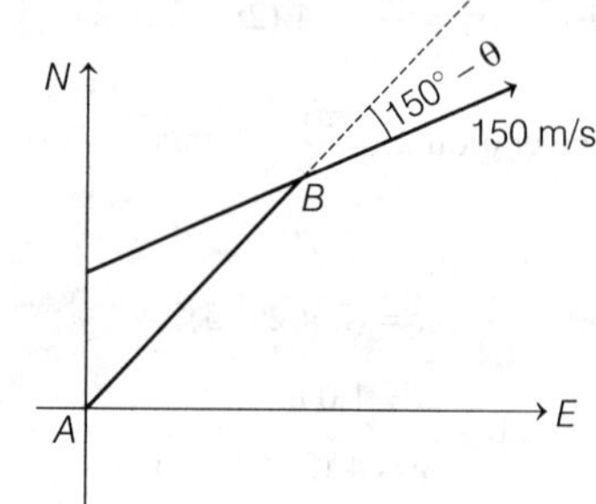

Hence, we can see that direction of 150 m/s is $150° - \theta \left[\text{or } \sin^{-1}\left(\frac{1}{15}\right)\right]$, east of the line AB

(b) $150° - \theta = \sin^{-1}\left(\frac{1}{15}\right) = 3.8°$

$\therefore \quad \theta = 146.2°$

From first and second relation,

$$v = \frac{150 \sin \theta}{\sin 30°}$$

Substituting the values we get,

$$v = 167\text{ m/s}$$

$$\therefore \quad t = \frac{AB}{v}$$

$$= \frac{500 \times 1000}{167 \times 60}\text{ min} = 49.9\text{ min}$$

≈ 50 min **Ans.**

5. Let v_r = velocity of river

v_{br} = velocity of river in still water and

ω = width of river

Given, $t_{min} = 10$ min or $\frac{\omega}{v_{br}} = 10$ ... (i)

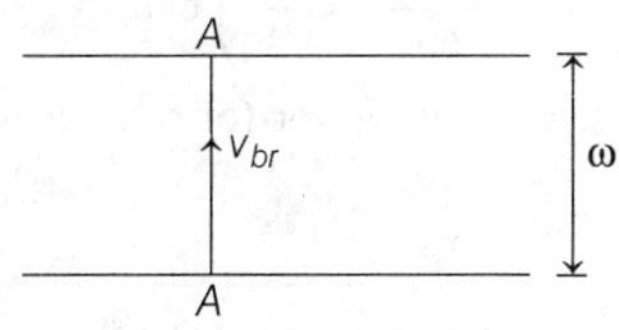

For minimum time

Drift in this case will be,

$$x = v_r t$$

$\therefore$ $120 = 10 v_r$ ... (ii)

Shortest path is taken when v_b is along AB. In this case,

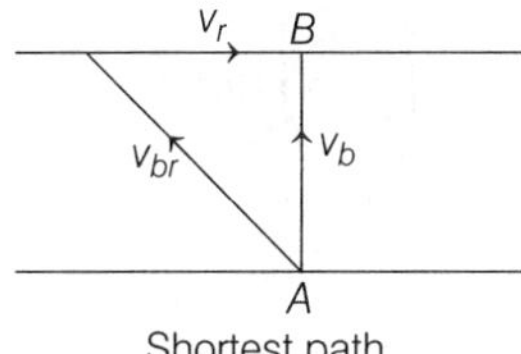

Shortest path

$$v_b = \sqrt{v_{br}^2 - v_r^2}$$

Now, $12.5 = \frac{\omega}{v_b} = \frac{\omega}{\sqrt{v_{br}^2 - v_r^2}}$ ... (iii)

Solving these three equations, we get

$v_{br} = 20$ m/min,

$v_r = 12$ m/min

and $\omega = 200$ m

6.

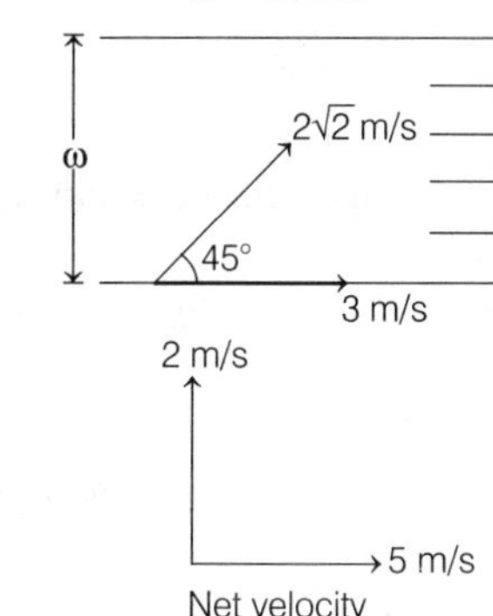

(a) $t = \frac{\omega}{2} = \frac{20}{2} = 10$ s

(b) Drift $= 5t = 50$ m

Exercises

LEVEL 1

Assertion and Reason

1. Average velocity $= \frac{s}{t}$

$$= \frac{\text{area of } v\text{-}t \text{ graph}}{t} = \frac{\left(\frac{1}{2} v_0 t_0\right)}{t_0}$$

$$= \frac{v_0}{2}$$

2. It is not necessary that if $v = 0$, then acceleration is also zero. If a particle is thrown upwards, then at highest point $v = 0$ but $a \neq 0$.

3. $a = 2t \neq$ constant

Therefore, velocity will not increase at a constant rate.

4. If a particle is projected upwards, then $s = 0$ when it returns back to its initial position.

$\therefore$ Average velocity $= \frac{s}{t} = 0$

But its acceleration is constant $= g$

5. $v_1 = \frac{ds_1}{dt} = (2 - 8t)$

$$v_2 = \frac{ds_2}{dt} = (-2 + 8t)$$

$\therefore$ $v_{12} = v_1 - v_2 = (4 - 16t)$

v_{12} does not keep on increasing.

6. $\mathbf{a} = \frac{d\mathbf{v}}{dt}$. So, direction of $\mathbf{a}$ and $d\mathbf{v}$ is same.

7. $t_1 = \sqrt{\frac{2(h/2)}{g}} = \sqrt{\frac{h}{g}}$

Velocity of second particle at height $\frac{h}{2}$ is,

$$v = \sqrt{u^2 - 2g(h/2)}$$

$$= \sqrt{gh - gh} = 0$$

or $\frac{h}{2}$ is its highest point.

$\therefore$ $t_2 = \frac{u}{g} = \frac{\sqrt{gh}}{g} = \sqrt{\frac{h}{g}}$

$\Rightarrow$ $t_1 = t_2$

8. $a = \dfrac{mg - F}{m} = g - \dfrac{F}{m} =$ depends on m

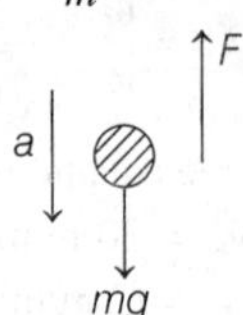

Since $m_1 \neq m_2$

$\therefore \quad a_1 \neq a_2$

or $\quad t_1 \neq t_2$

9. Slope of s-t graph = velocity = positive

At $t = 0$, $s \neq 0$

Further at $t = t_0 : s = 0, v \neq 0$.

Single Correct Option

1. Packet comes under gravity. Therefore only force is mg.

$$a = \frac{F}{m} = \frac{mg}{m} = g \qquad \text{(downwards)}$$

2. Air resistance (let F) is always opposite to motion (or velocity)

Retardation in upward journey

$$a_1 = \frac{F_1 + mg}{m} = g + \frac{F_1}{m}$$

Upward journey — Downward journey

Acceleration in downward journey

$$a_2 = \frac{mg - F_2}{m} = g - \frac{F_2}{m}$$

Since, $\quad a_1 > a_2 \Rightarrow T_1 < T_2$

3. $h = \dfrac{u^2}{2g}$ or $u \propto \sqrt{h}$

4. In first instant you will apply $v = \tan\theta$ and say

$$v = \tan 30° = \frac{1}{\sqrt{3}} \text{ m/s}$$

But it is wrong because formula $v = \tan\theta$ is valid when angle is measured with time axis.

Here, angle is taken from displacement axis. So, angle from time axis = 90° – 30° = 60°

Now, $\quad v = \tan 60° = \sqrt{3}$ m/s

5. $v = 3\alpha t^2 + 2\beta t + \gamma : v_{t=0} = v_i = \gamma$

$a = 6\alpha t + 2\beta : a_{t=0} = a_i = 2\beta$

$\therefore \quad \dfrac{v_i}{a_i} = \dfrac{\gamma}{2\beta}$

6. $v = \dfrac{2\pi R}{T} = \dfrac{(2\pi)(1)}{60} = \left(\dfrac{\pi}{30}\right)$ cm/s

In 15 s, velocity vector (of same magnitude) will rotate 90°.

$$\therefore \quad |\Delta \mathbf{v}| = |\mathbf{v}_f - \mathbf{v}_i|$$

$$= \sqrt{v^2 + v^2 - 2vv\cos 90°}$$

$$= \sqrt{2}\, v = \frac{\pi\sqrt{2}}{30} \text{ cm/s} \qquad \textbf{Ans.}$$

7. $a = bt$

$$\therefore \quad \frac{dv}{dt} = bt$$

or $$\int_{v_0}^{v} dv = \int_0^t (bt)\, dt$$

$$\therefore \quad v = v_0 + \frac{bt^2}{2}$$

$$s = \int_0^t v dt = \int_0^t \left(v_0 + \frac{bt^2}{2}\right) dt$$

$$= v_0 t + \frac{bt^3}{6}$$

8. a-t equation from the given graph can be written as

$$a = -2t + 4$$

or $\quad dv = a \cdot dt = (-2t + 4)\, dt$

Integrating we get, $v = -t^2 + 4t$

v-t equation is quadratic. Hence, v-t graph is a parabola.

9. $7.2 = \dfrac{100}{(v + 5)(5/18)}$ or $v = 45$ km/h

10. $v_A + v_B = 4$ m/s

and $v_A - v_B = \dfrac{4.0}{10} = 0.4$ m/s

11.

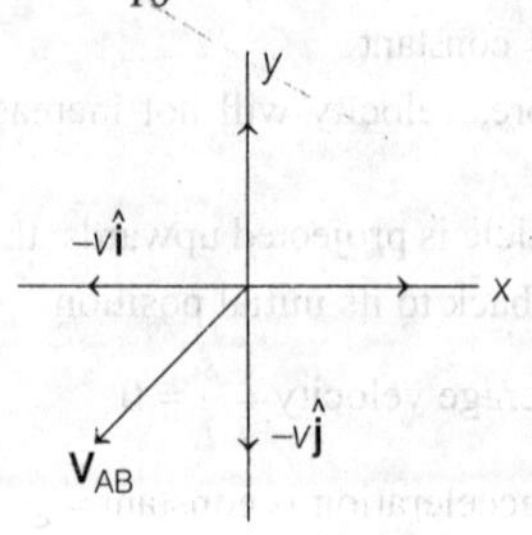

$$\mathbf{V}_{AB} = \mathbf{V}_A - \mathbf{V}_B = -v\hat{\mathbf{j}} - v\hat{\mathbf{i}}$$
$$\mathbf{V}_{AC} = \mathbf{V}_A - \mathbf{V}_C = -v\hat{\mathbf{j}} - v\hat{\mathbf{j}} = -2v\hat{\mathbf{j}}$$

Hence, $\mathbf{V}_{AC}$ is towards negative y-direction.

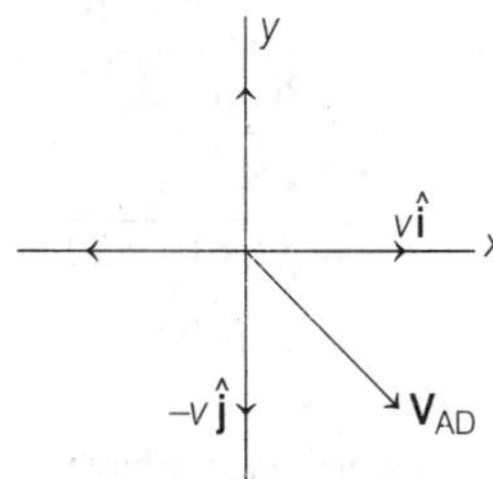

$$\mathbf{V}_{AD} = \mathbf{V}_A - \mathbf{V}_D = -v\hat{\mathbf{j}} - (-v\hat{\mathbf{i}}) = v\hat{\mathbf{i}} - v\hat{\mathbf{j}}$$

12. $v_{av} = \dfrac{\text{Displacement}}{\text{Time}} = \dfrac{\sqrt{2}R}{t}$

13. $\sqrt{x} = t + 3$

$\therefore \quad x = (t+3)^2$

or $\quad v = \dfrac{dx}{dt} = 2(t+3)$

$\therefore$ v-t equation is linear **Ans.**

14. $\dfrac{1}{2} \times (a)(2)^2 = x$

or $\quad 2a = x$

Now, $\dfrac{1}{2}(a)(4)^2 - \dfrac{1}{2}(a)(2)^2 = 6a = 3x$

15. $x = \dfrac{t^2}{2}$

$\therefore \quad v_x = \dfrac{dx}{dt} = t$

$$y = \frac{x^2}{2} = \frac{t^4}{8}$$

$\therefore \quad v_y = \dfrac{dy}{dt} = \dfrac{t^3}{2}$

At $t = 2$ s

$$v_x = 2 \text{ m/s}$$

and $\quad v_y = 4 \text{ m/s}$

$\therefore \quad \mathbf{v} = v_x\hat{\mathbf{i}} + v_y\hat{\mathbf{j}}$

$$= (2\hat{\mathbf{i}} + 4\hat{\mathbf{j}}) \text{ m/s}$$

16. $\mathbf{r} = (a\cos\omega t)\,\hat{\mathbf{i}} + (a\sin\omega t)\,\hat{\mathbf{j}}$

$\therefore \quad \mathbf{v} = \dfrac{d\mathbf{r}}{dt} = (-a\omega\sin\omega t)\,\hat{\mathbf{i}} + (a\omega\cos\omega t)\hat{\mathbf{j}}$

$$\mathbf{r}\cdot\mathbf{v} = 0$$

$\therefore \quad \mathbf{r} \perp \mathbf{v}$

17. It should follow the path PQR.

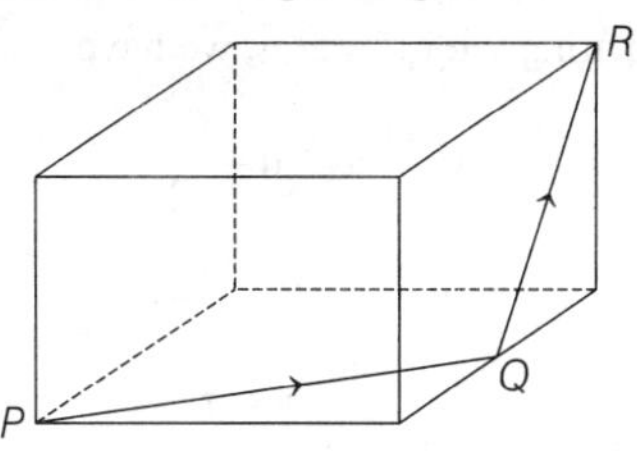

$$PQR = \sqrt{5}\,a$$

$\therefore \quad t = \dfrac{\sqrt{5}\,a}{u}$ **Ans.**

18. $a_{av} = \left|\dfrac{\Delta \mathbf{v}}{\Delta t}\right| = \dfrac{|\mathbf{v}_f - \mathbf{v}_i|}{t}$

$$= \frac{\sqrt{v^2 + v^2 - 2v.v.\cos\theta}}{t}$$

$$= \frac{2v(\sin\theta/2)}{t}$$

19. $v = \dfrac{dx}{dt} = 32 - 8t^2$

$v = 0$ at $t = 2$ s

$$a = \frac{dv}{dt} = -16\,t$$

at $\quad t = 2\text{s}, \; a = -32 \text{ m/s}^2$ **Ans.**

20. $v_1 t + v_2 t = s$

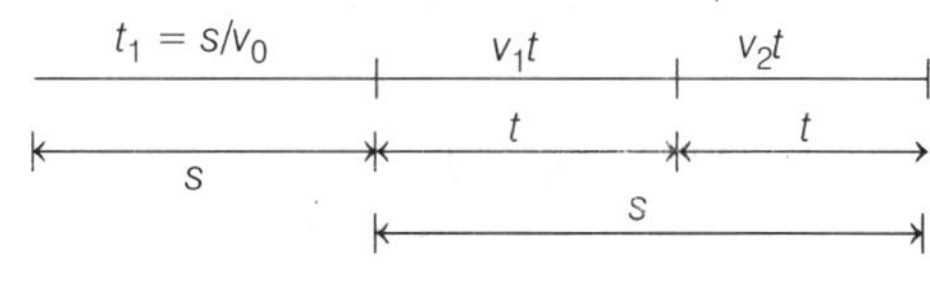

$$t = \frac{s}{v_1 + v_2}$$

Total time $= t_1 + 2t$

and total displacement $= 2s$

Mean velocity $= \dfrac{\text{Total displacement}}{\text{Total time}}$

$$= \frac{2s}{(s/v_0) + (2s/v_1 + v_2)}$$

$$= \frac{2}{(1/v_0) + (2/v_1 + v_2)}$$

$$= \frac{2v_0(v_1 + v_2)}{(2v_0 + v_1 + v_2)}$$

21. $v^2 = 25 + 25\,s$

or $\quad v^2 = (5)^2 + 2\,(12.5)\,s$

Now compare with $v^2 = u^2 + 2as$

22. $v^2 = \alpha^2 x$

Comparing with $v^2 = 2as$, we have

$$2a = \alpha^2 \quad \text{or} \quad a = \frac{\alpha^2}{2}$$

$$v = at \quad \text{or} \quad v = \frac{\alpha^2}{2} t$$

$$\Rightarrow \qquad v \propto t$$

23. $t = \sqrt{\frac{2h}{g}} = \sqrt{\frac{2 \times 5}{10}} = 1 \text{ s}$

Let t_0 is the interval between two drops. Then

$$2\,t_0 = t$$

$$\therefore \qquad t_0 = 0.5 \text{ s}$$

2nd drop has taken t_0 time to fall. Therefore distance fallen,

$$d = \frac{1}{2} g t_0^2$$

$$= \left(\frac{1}{2}\right)(10)\,(0.5)^2$$

$$= 1.25 \text{ m}$$

$\therefore$ Height from ground $= h - d$

$$= 5 - 1.25$$

$$= 3.75 \text{ m} \qquad \textbf{Ans.}$$

24. $\frac{1}{2} g t^2 = 20\,(t-1) + \frac{1}{2} g (t-1)^2$

Solving this equation, we get

$$\therefore \qquad t = 1.5 \text{ s}$$

Now, $\quad d = 20\,(t-1) + \frac{1}{2} g (t-1)^2$

$$= 11.25 \text{ cm} \qquad \textbf{Ans.}$$

25. $h = \frac{1}{2} g T^2$

At $\frac{T}{3}$ second, distance fallen

$$d = \frac{1}{2} g \left(\frac{T}{3}\right) = \frac{h}{9}$$

$\therefore$ Height from ground $= h - d = \frac{8h}{9}$ **Ans.**

26. Total height $= 15 + \frac{u^2}{2g}$

$$= 15 + \frac{(10)^2}{2 \times 10}$$

$$\Rightarrow \qquad h = 20 \text{ m}$$

Initial velocity $u = \sqrt{2gh}$

$$= \sqrt{2 \times 10 \times 20}$$

$$= 20 \text{ m/s}$$

Now applying

$$v = u + at, \text{ we have}$$

$$v = (+\,20) + (-10)\,(3)$$

$$= -\,10 \text{ m/s}$$

$\therefore$ Velocity is 10 m/s, downwards.

27. $d = \frac{1}{2} g\,(T - t)^2$

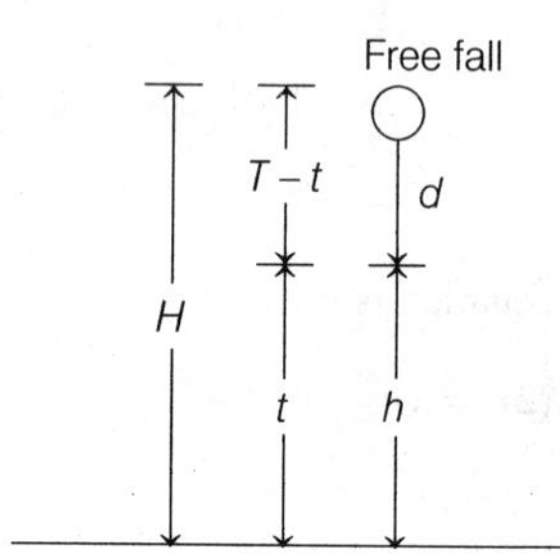

$$\therefore \qquad h = H - d = H - \frac{1}{2} g\,(T - t)^2$$

28.

$$v^2 = u^2 - 2g\left(\frac{h}{2}\right)$$

$$\therefore \qquad (10)^2 = u^2 - gh$$

$$\therefore \qquad u^2 = (100 + gh)$$

Now, $\quad h = \frac{u^2}{2g} = \frac{100 + gh}{2g}$

$$h = 5 + \frac{h}{2} \qquad (\text{as } 2g = 20 \text{ m/s}^2)$$

$$\therefore \qquad h = 10 \text{ m} \qquad \textbf{Ans.}$$

29. In first second distance travelled

$$x = \frac{1}{2} \times g \times t^2 = 5 \text{ m}$$

(for $g = 10 \text{ m/s}^2$) in last second $7x = 35$ m

Now, $\quad s_{t\text{th}} = u + at - \frac{1}{2} a$

or $\quad 35 = 0 + 10 \times t - \frac{1}{2} \times 10$

or $\quad t = 4 \text{ s}$

30. $1 = \frac{1}{2} g t_1^2$ or $t_1 = \sqrt{\frac{2}{g}}$

$2 = \frac{1}{2} g t^2$ or $t = \sqrt{\frac{4}{g}}$

But, $t_2 = t - t_1 = \sqrt{\frac{4}{g}} - \sqrt{\frac{2}{g}}$

$\therefore \quad \frac{t_1}{t_2} = \frac{\sqrt{2/g}}{\sqrt{4/g} - \sqrt{2/g}}$

$= \frac{\sqrt{2}}{2 - \sqrt{2}} = \frac{\sqrt{2}\,(2 + \sqrt{2})}{2}$

$= (\sqrt{2} + 1)$

31. $v^2 = u^2 + 2gh$

$\Rightarrow \quad (3u)^2 = (-u)^2 + 2gh \quad \Rightarrow \quad h = \frac{4u^2}{g}$

32. Let h distance is covered in t second,

$\Rightarrow \quad h = \frac{1}{2} gt^2$

Distance covered in t^{th} second $= \frac{1}{2} g\,(2t - 1)$

$\Rightarrow \quad \frac{9h}{25} = \frac{g}{2}(2t - 1)$

From above two equations, $h = 122.5$ m

33. $u = \sqrt{2g(4h)} = \sqrt{8gh}$

When they cross each other,

$d_1 + d_2 = h$

$\therefore \quad \left(\frac{1}{2}gt^2\right) + \left(ut - \frac{1}{2}gt^2\right) = h$

or $\quad t = \frac{h}{u} = \frac{h}{\sqrt{8gh}} = \sqrt{\frac{h}{8g}}$

34. $-h = vt - \frac{1}{2} gt^2$

or $\quad gt^2 - 2vt - 2h = 0$

$\therefore \quad t = \frac{2v + \sqrt{4v^2 + 8\,gh}}{2g}$

$= \frac{v}{g}\left[1 + \sqrt{1 + \frac{2hg}{v^2}}\right]$

35. $t_{ABC} = 10$ s

$\therefore \quad t_{AB} = 5$ s

At B, velocity becomes zero. Hence, at A velocity should be 50 m/s.

Now, $\quad (50)^2 = (u^2) - 2 \times 10 \times 10.2$

$\therefore \quad u = 52$ m/s

36. Retardation during upward motion

$a_1 = 10 + 2$

$= 12\ \text{m/s}^2$

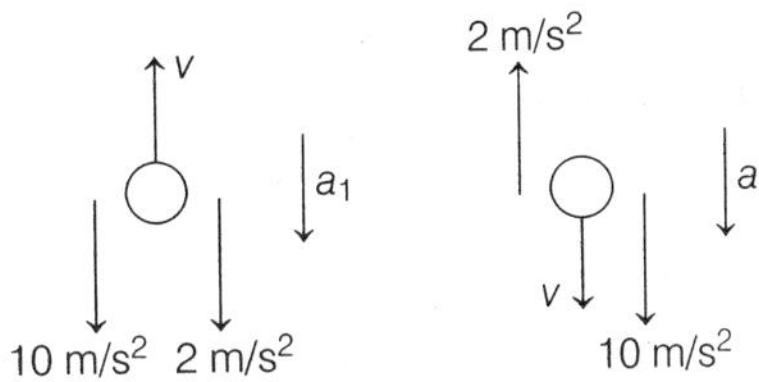

Acceleration during downward motion,

$a_2 = 10 - 2 = 8\ \text{m/s}^2$

$t = \sqrt{\frac{2s}{a}}$ or $t \propto \frac{1}{\sqrt{a}}$

$\therefore \quad \frac{t_1}{t_2} = \sqrt{\frac{a_2}{a_1}} = \sqrt{\frac{8}{12}} = \sqrt{\frac{2}{3}}$ **Ans.**

37. $s_B = \frac{1}{2} \times 2 \times (1)^2 = 1$ m

$s_A = \frac{1}{2} \times 2 \times (2)^2 = 4$ m

$\therefore \quad s_A - s_B = 3$ m

38. At the time of overtaking,

$s_1 = s_2$

$\therefore \quad 2ut + \frac{1}{2} at^2 = ut + \frac{1}{2}(2a)t^2$

$\therefore \quad t = \frac{2u}{a}$

$\therefore \quad s_1 (\text{or } s_2) = (2u)\left(\frac{2u}{a}\right) + \frac{1}{2}(a)\left(\frac{2u}{a}\right)^2$

$= \frac{6u^2}{a}$ **Ans.**

39. $15 = u + \frac{1}{2}a(2\times 3-1) = u + \frac{5a}{2}$ ...(i)

$23 = u + \frac{1}{2}a(2\times 5-1) = u + \frac{9a}{2}$ ...(ii)

Solving Eqs. (i) and (ii), $a = 4\ \text{ms}^2$, $u = 5$ m/s

Displacement in 10 s,

$$s = ut + \frac{1}{2}at^2 = 5\times 10 + \frac{1}{2}\times 4\times 10^2 = 250 \text{ m}$$

40. Displacements of both should be equal.

Or $8t = \frac{1}{2}\times 4\times t^2$ or $t = 4$ s

41. $s_1 = \frac{1}{2}a_0 t_0^2$

$$v_0 = a_0 t_0$$

$$v^2 = u^2 - 2as$$

$$0^2 = v_0^2 - 2a_0 s_2$$

$$s_2 = \frac{v_0^2}{2a_0} = \frac{(a_0 t_0)^2}{2a_0} = \frac{a_0^2 t_0^2}{2a_0} = \frac{1}{2}a_0 t_0^2$$

∴ Total distance travelled,

$$s = s_1 + s_2 = a_0 t_0^2$$

42. $a = \frac{dv}{dt} = 0.2\ v^2$

∴ $$\int_{10}^{v} -5v^{-2} = \int_0^2 dt$$

∴ $$\left[\frac{5}{v}\right]_{10}^{v} = 2$$

∴ $$\frac{5}{v} - \frac{5}{10} = 2$$

or $v = 2.0$ m/s **Ans.**

43. $F = 3t^2 - 32$

$$a = \frac{F}{m} = (0.3\ t^2 - 3.2)$$

$$\int_{10}^{v} dv = \int_0^5 a dt = \int_0^5 (0.3\ t^2 - 3.2)\ dt$$

$$v - 10 = -3.5$$

∴ $v = 6.5$ m/s **Ans.**

44. $x = 2 + t - 3t^2$, $v = \frac{dx}{dt} = 1 - 6t$, velocity will become zero at time, $0 = 1 - 6t_0$ or $t_0 = \frac{1}{6}$ s,

Since the given time $t = 1$ s is greater than $t_0 = \frac{1}{6}$ s,

Distance > | Displacement |

Displacement, $s = x_f - x_i$

$$= (2 + 1 - 3) - (2 + 0 - 0)$$

$$= -2 \text{ m}$$

Distance, $d = |s_{0-t_0}| + |s_{t-t_0}|$

$$= \frac{u^2}{2|a|} + \frac{1}{2}|a|(t - t_0)^2$$

Comparing $v = 1 - 6t$ with $v = u + ut$, we have $u = 1$ m/s and $a = -6$ m/s^2

∴ $$\text{Distance} = \frac{(1)^2}{2\times 6} + \frac{1}{2}\times 6\times\left(1 - \frac{1}{6}\right)^2$$

$$= 2.1 \text{ m}$$

45. Change in velocity = net area under a - t graph.

46. Motion is first accelerated in positive direction, then uniform in negative direction.

47. Acceleration in second case is more. Hence, slope is more.

48. $a = v\left(\frac{dv}{ds}\right) = (10)\left(-\frac{20}{30}\right) = -\frac{20}{3}$ m/s^2

Note *At s = 15 m, v = 10* $\frac{m}{s}$

49. Average velocity in uniformly accelerated motion is given by

$$v_{av} = \frac{s}{t} = \frac{ut + \frac{1}{2}at^2}{t} = u + \frac{1}{2}at$$

Now, $$v_1 = u + \frac{1}{2}at_1$$

$$v_2 = (u + at_1) + \frac{1}{2}at_2$$

and $$v_3 = u + a(t_1 + t_2) + \frac{1}{2}at_3$$

∴ $(v_1 - v_2) : (v_2 - v_3) = (t_1 + t_2) : (t_2 + t_3)$

50. $v_x = \frac{dx}{dt} = (8t - 2)$

∴ $$\int_{14}^{x} dx = \int_2^t (8t - 2)\ dt$$

$$x - 14 = (4t^2 - 2t) - (12)$$

∴ $x = 4t^2 - 2t + 2$ ...(i)

$$v_y = \frac{dy}{dt} = 2$$

∴ $$\int_4^y dy = \int_2^t 2dt$$

∴ $y - 4 = 2t - 4$

or $\quad y = 2t$

$\therefore \quad t = \dfrac{y}{2}$

Substituting this value of t in Eq. (i) we have,

$$x = y^2 - y + 2 \qquad \textbf{Ans.}$$

51. Given, $\quad \mathbf{v} = ky\mathbf{i} + kx\mathbf{j}$

$\Rightarrow \quad \dfrac{dx}{dt} = ky, \dfrac{dy}{dt} = kx$

$$\frac{dy}{dx} = \frac{dy}{dt} \times \frac{dt}{dx} = \frac{kx}{ky}$$

$$ydy = x\,dx$$

Integrating and using $\int x^n\,dx = \dfrac{x^{n+1}}{n+1}$, we have

$$y^2 = x^2 + c$$

52. $\quad x = kt, \quad t = \dfrac{x}{k}$

Now, $\quad y = k\left(\dfrac{x}{k}\right)\left(1 - \alpha \cdot \dfrac{x}{k}\right)$

or $\quad y = x - \dfrac{\alpha x^2}{k}$

53. $\quad y - y_0 = u_y t$

or $\quad y - 0 = u_y t$

or $\quad y = u_y t \qquad \ldots$(i)

and $\quad x - x_0 = u_x t + \dfrac{1}{2} a_x t^2$

or $\quad x - 0 = u_x \times \dfrac{y}{u_y} - \dfrac{1}{2} \times 10 \times \left(\dfrac{y}{u_y}\right)^2$

or $\quad x = \dfrac{u_x}{u_y} y - \dfrac{5}{u_y^2} y^2$

or $\quad \sqrt{3}y - 5y^2 = \dfrac{u_x}{u_y} y - \dfrac{5}{u_y^2} y^2$

or $\quad \dfrac{u_x}{u_y} = \sqrt{3}$

and $\quad 5 = \dfrac{5}{u_Y^2}$

$\therefore \quad u_y = 1$

$\therefore \quad u_x = \sqrt{3}\, u_y = \sqrt{3}$

$\therefore \quad u = \sqrt{u_x^2 + u_y^2} = 2 \text{ ms}^{-1}$

54. $\because \; a = -bv^2$

or $\quad \dfrac{dv}{dt} = -bv^2$

or $\quad \displaystyle\int_{v_0}^{v} \frac{dv}{v^2} = -b \int_0^t dt$

or $\quad \left[\dfrac{v^{-2+1}}{-2+1}\right]_{v_0}^{v} = -bt$

or $\quad \left[-\dfrac{1}{v}\right]_{v_0}^{v} = -bt$

or $\quad \left[\dfrac{1}{v_0} - \dfrac{1}{v}\right] = -bt \quad$ or $\quad \dfrac{1}{v} = \dfrac{1}{v_0} + bt$

or $\quad \dfrac{1}{v} = \dfrac{1 + v_0 bt}{v_0} \quad$ or $\quad v = \dfrac{v_0}{1 + v_0 bt}$

or $\quad \dfrac{ds}{dt} = \dfrac{v_0}{1 + v_0 bt} \quad$ or $\quad \displaystyle\int_0^s ds = \int_0^t \left(\frac{v_0}{1 + v_0 bt}\right) dt$

or $\quad s = \dfrac{v_0}{v_0 b} [\ln (1 + v_0 bt)]_0^t$

$$= \frac{1}{b} [\ln (1 + v_0 bt) - \ln (1)]$$

$$= \frac{1}{b} [\ln (1 + v_0 bt)]$$

55. $\rightarrow u = 0 \qquad v \qquad \rightarrow v' = 0$

$t_1 = 100$ s $\quad t_2 = 200$ s

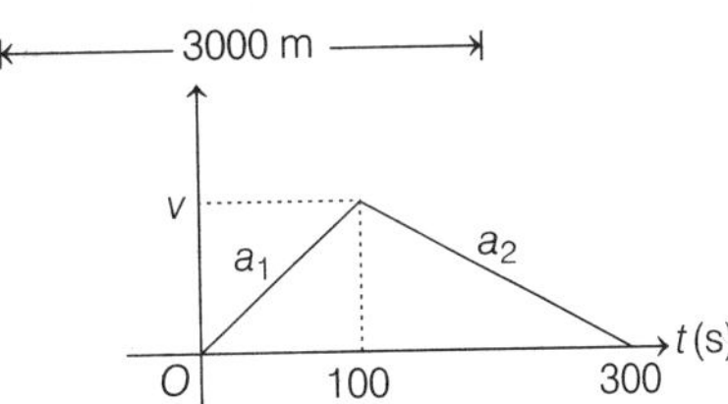

Area of v - t graph = displacement

$$\frac{1}{2} v \times 300 = 3000$$

$\Rightarrow \quad v = 20$ m/s

Maximum velocity = 20 m/s

Acceleration, $a_1 = \dfrac{v}{100} = \dfrac{20}{100} = 0.2 \text{ m/s}^2$

Retardation, $a_2 = \dfrac{v}{200} = \dfrac{20}{200} = 0.1 \text{ m/s}^2$

56. **At 4 s**

$$u = at = 8 \text{ m/s}$$

$$s_1 = \frac{1}{2} at^2 = \frac{1}{2} \times 2 \times 4^2$$

$$= 16 \text{ m}$$

From 4 s to 8 s

$$a = 0,\; v = \text{constant} = 8 \text{ m/s}$$

$\therefore \quad s_2 = vt = (8)(4) = 32$ m

From 8 s to 12 s

$$s_3 = s_1 = 16 \text{ m}$$

$\therefore \quad s_{\text{Total}} = s_1 + s_2 + s_3 = 64$ m **Ans.**

57. s = net area of v-t graph

At 2 s, net area = 0

$\therefore \quad s = 0$

and the particle crosses its initial position.

58. For uniformly accelerated motion, $v^2 = u^2 + 2as$,

i.e. v^2 *versus* s graph is a straight line with intercept u^2 and slope $2a$. Since, intercept is non-zero, so initial velocity is non-zero.

59. $v^2 = u^2 + 2as$,

$$\text{slope} = 2a = -\frac{16}{2} = -8 \text{ m/s}^2$$

or $\quad a = -4 \text{ m/s}^2$.

60.

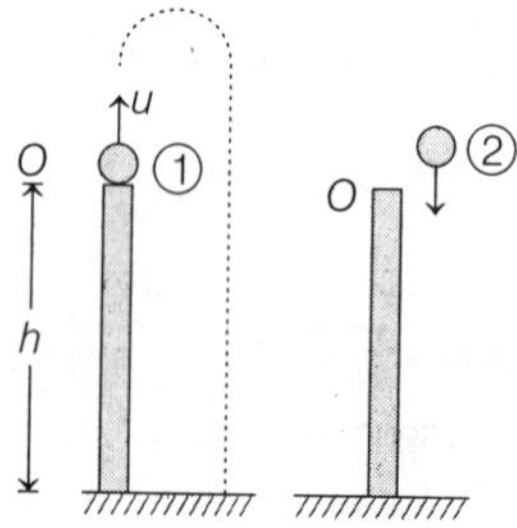

Ball 1 : $\quad -h = u \times 9 - \frac{1}{2} g(9)^2 \quad$ ...(i)

Ball 2 : $\quad h = u \times 4 + \frac{1}{2} g \times (4)^2 \quad$ ...(ii)

Solving, $\quad h = 180$ m

61. $\frac{dx}{dt} = v = -1 - 2t$

Comparing with $v = u + at$,

we have $u = -1$ m/s and $a = -2 \text{ m/s}^2$

At $t = 0, x = 1$ m. Then, u and a both are negative. Hence, x-coordinate of particle will go on decreasing.

62. $v_{\text{av}} = \frac{d}{t} = \frac{d_1 + d_2}{t_1 + t_2}$

$$21 = \frac{(18)(11) + (42)(v)}{60}$$

$\Rightarrow \quad v = 25.3$ m/s **Ans.**

63. $v_x = \frac{dx}{dt} = 5$

$$v_y = \frac{dy}{dt}$$

$$= (4t + 1)$$

At 45°, $\quad v_x = v_y$

$\Rightarrow \quad t = 1$ s **Ans.**

64. $t = \frac{80 \text{ m}}{30 \text{ m/s}} = \frac{8}{3}$ s.

Now in vertical direction,

$$t = \frac{2u_r}{a_r}$$

or $\quad u_r = \frac{ta_r}{2} \quad (a_r = g = 10 \text{ m/s}^2)$

$$= \frac{(8/3)(10)}{2}$$

$= \frac{40}{3}$ m/s **Ans.**

65. $d = d_1 + d_2$

$$= \frac{v_1^2}{2a_1} + \frac{v_2^2}{2a_2}$$

$$= \frac{(10)^2}{2 \times 2} + \frac{(20)^2}{(2 \times 1)}$$

$= 225$ m **Ans.**

66. $s_1 = s_2$

$$\therefore \quad (40)\,t - \frac{1}{2} \times 10 \times t^2 = (40)(t - 2) - \frac{1}{2} \times 10 \times (t-2)^2$$

Solving this equation, we get

$$t = 5 \text{ s}$$

Then $\quad s_1 = (40)(5) - \frac{1}{2} \times 10 \times (5)^2$

$= 75$ m **Ans.**

67. $\quad v = an \quad \Rightarrow \quad a = \left(\frac{v}{n}\right)$

Now, $\quad s_n = \frac{1}{2} an^2 = \frac{1}{2}\left(\frac{v}{n}\right)(n^2) = \frac{vn}{2}$

and $\quad s_{n-3} = \frac{1}{2} a (n-3)^3 = \frac{1}{2}\left(\frac{v}{n}\right)(n-3)^2$

$\therefore$ Displacement in last 3 s will be,

$$s = s_n - s_{n-3}$$

$$= \frac{v}{2}\left[n - \frac{(n-3)^2}{n}\right]$$

$$= \left(\frac{6n-9}{n}\right)\frac{v}{2}$$

68. Taking downward direction as the positive direction,

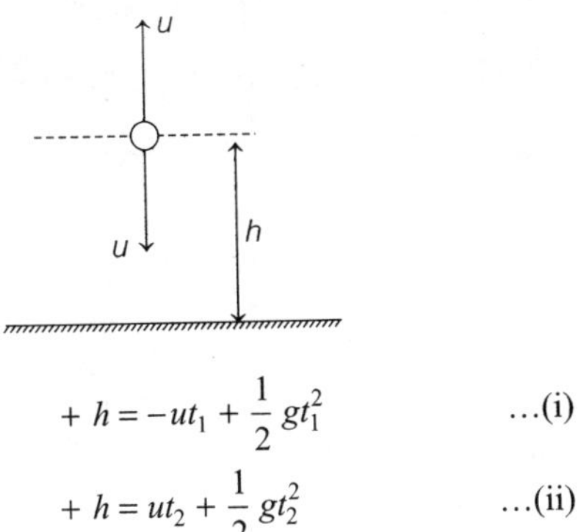

$$+h = -ut_1 + \frac{1}{2}gt_1^2 \quad \ldots\text{(i)}$$

$$+h = ut_2 + \frac{1}{2}gt_2^2 \quad \ldots\text{(ii)}$$

Multiplying Eq. (i) by t_2 and Eq. (ii) by t_1 and adding, we get

$$h(t_1 + t_2) = \frac{1}{2}gt_1t_2(t_1 + t_2)$$

or $$h = \frac{1}{2}gt_1t_2$$

For free fall from rest, $h = \frac{1}{2}gt^2$

$\therefore$ $$t^2 = t_1t_2$$

$$t = \sqrt{t_1t_2}$$

69. Retardation is double. Therefore, retardation time will be half.

Let t_0 = acceleration time

Then, $\frac{t_0}{2}$ = retardation time

$$t_0 + \frac{t_0}{2} = t$$

$\therefore$ $$t_0 = \frac{2t}{3}$$

Now, $$s = s_1 + s_2$$

$$= \left(\frac{1}{2}\right)(a)(t_0)^2 + \left(\frac{1}{2}\right)(2a)\left(\frac{t_0}{2}\right)^2$$

$$= \frac{3}{4}at_0^2 = \left(\frac{3}{4}\right)(a)\left(\frac{2t}{3}\right)^2$$

$$= \frac{at^2}{3} \quad \textbf{Ans.}$$

70. Area under v-t graph gives displacement. We can see that area for B is greater than area for A. Hence, B has covered larger distance.

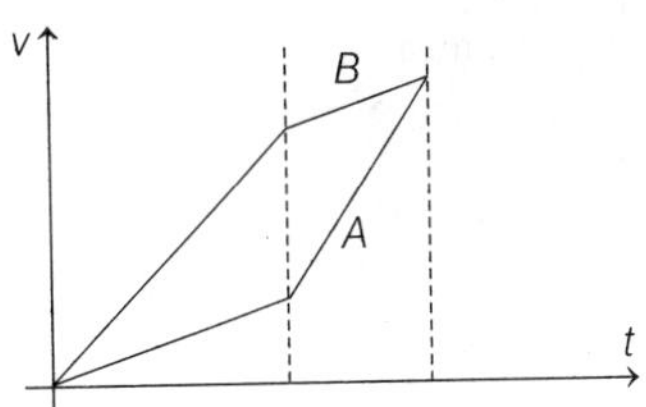

71. Let v_m be the maximum speed,

$$v_m = a_1t_1$$

and $$v_m = \sqrt{2a_1l}$$

$$t_2 = \frac{2l}{v_m}$$

and $$v_m = a_2t_3 = \sqrt{2a_2(3l)}$$

Now, average speed

$$v_{av} = \frac{l + 2l + 3l}{t_1 + t_2 + t_3}$$

$$v_{av} = \frac{6l}{(v_m/a_1) + (2l/v_m) + (v_m/a_2)}$$

$$= \frac{6l}{\left(\frac{v_m}{v_m^2/2l}\right) + \left(\frac{2l}{v_m}\right) + \left(\frac{v_m}{v_m^2/6l}\right)}$$

$$= \frac{6l}{(10l/v_m)} = \frac{3v_m}{5}$$

$$\frac{v_{av}}{v_m} = \frac{3}{5}$$

72.

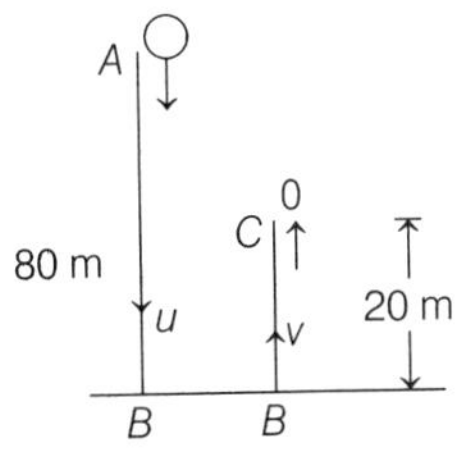

A to B : $u^2 = 0 + 2g \times 80$

$\Rightarrow$ $u = 40$ m/s

B to C : $v^2 - 2g \times 20 = 0$

$\Rightarrow$ $v = 20$ m/s

$$\bar{a} = \frac{\Delta v}{\Delta t} = \frac{v + u}{\Delta t}$$

$$= \frac{40 + 20}{0.1}$$

$$= 600 \text{ m/s}^2$$

73. $v_b = \frac{1}{1/4} = 4$ km/h

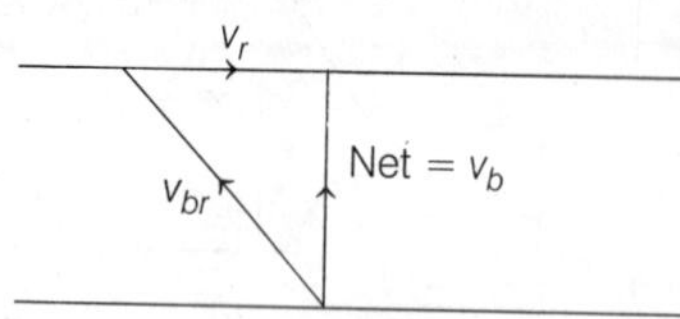

$v_{br} = 5$ km/h $\Rightarrow$ $v_r = 3$ km/h

74. Comparing with projectile motion we can see that it is like a projectile motion, with $u_x = 4$ m/s, $u_y = 4$ m/s and $a_y = 10$ m/s^2.

$$x\text{-coordinate} = \text{range} = \frac{2u_x u_y}{a_y}$$

$$= \frac{2 \times 4 \times 4}{10} = 3.2 \text{ m}$$

75. Velocity of rain is at 30° with vertical. So, its horizontal component is $v_R \sin 30° = \frac{v_R}{2}$. When man starts walking with 10 km/h, rain appears vertical. So, horizontal component $\frac{v_R}{2}$ is balanced by his speed of 10 km/h. Thus,

$$\frac{v_R}{2} = 10$$

or $$v_R = 20 \text{ km/h}$$

76. The greatest distance is, when velocities of both are equal.

or $$ft = u$$

$\Rightarrow$ $$t = \frac{u}{f}$$

$$s_1 = ut = \frac{u^2}{f}$$

and $$s_2 = \frac{1}{2} ft^2 = \frac{u^2}{2f}$$

$\therefore$ $$s_{max} = s_1 - s_2 = \frac{u^2}{2f}$$

77. $\mathbf{V}_{BA} = \mathbf{V}_B - \mathbf{V}_A = (V_B \cos\theta\ \hat{\mathbf{i}} + V_B \sin\theta)\hat{\mathbf{j}} - \mathbf{V}_A \hat{\mathbf{i}}$

$$= (V_B \cos\theta - V_A)\ \hat{\mathbf{i}} + V_B \sin\theta\ \hat{\mathbf{j}}$$

Ship B always remains north of A if $\mathbf{V}_{BA}$ is along north. Or its component along x-axis is zero.

$\therefore$ $$V_B \cos\theta - V_A = 0$$

or $$\frac{V_A}{V_B} = \cos\theta$$

78.

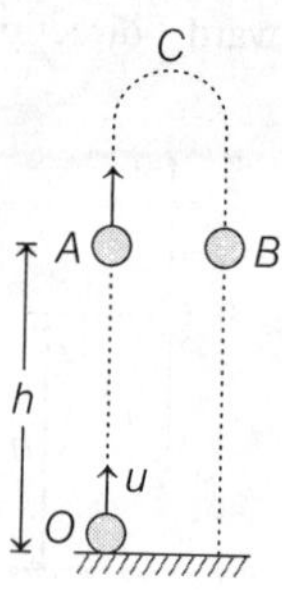

***O* to *A* :**

$$h = ut_1 - \frac{1}{2} gt_1^2 \quad \text{...(i)}$$

***O* to *B* :**

$$h = ut_2 - \frac{1}{2} gt_2^2 \quad \text{...(ii)}$$

Solving $u = \frac{g}{2}(t_1 + t_2)$

$$h = \frac{1}{2} gt_1 t_2$$

79. $t_{AB} = t_1,\ t_{ACB} = t_2$

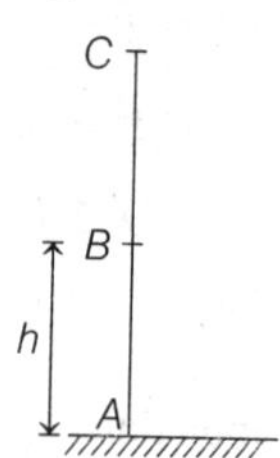

(a) $\therefore$ Total time of flight,

$$T = \frac{2u}{g} = t_1 + t_2$$

or $$u = \frac{g}{2}(t_1 + t_2).$$

80. Total time of journey is $(t_1 + t_2)$.

Therefore, $$\frac{2u}{g} = t_1 + t_2 \quad \text{...(i)}$$

Further,

$$h = ut_1 - \frac{1}{2} gt_1^2$$

or $$h = g\frac{(t_1 + t_2)\,t_1}{2} - \frac{1}{2} gt_1^2$$

or $$gt_1 t_2 = 2h$$

$\therefore$ $$t_1 t_2 = \frac{2h}{g}$$

Subjective Questions

1. (a) $\left|\frac{d\mathbf{v}}{dt}\right|$ is the magnitude of total acceleration.

While $\frac{d|\mathbf{v}|}{dt}$ represents the time rate of change of speed (called the tangential acceleration, a component of total acceleration) as $|\mathbf{v}| = v$.

(b) These two are equal in case of one dimensional motion.

2.

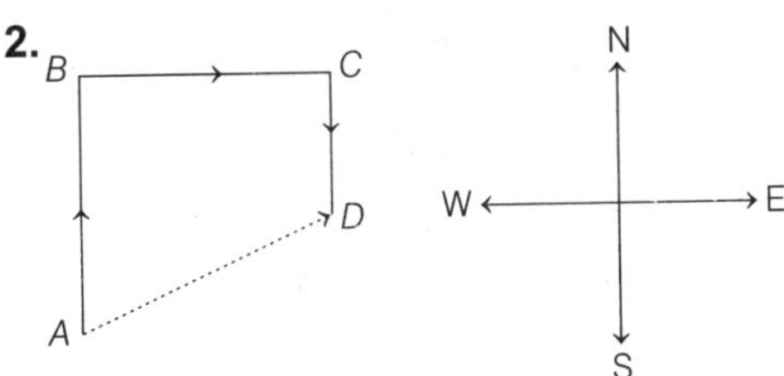

(a) Distance $= AB + BC + CD$

$= (500 + 400 + 200) = 1100$ m

(b) Displacement $= AD = \sqrt{(AB - CD)^2 + BC^2}$

$= \sqrt{(500 - 200)^2 + (400)^2}$

$= 500$ m

(c) Average speed $= \frac{\text{Total distance}}{\text{Total time}}$

$= \frac{1100}{20} = 55$ m/min

(d) Average velocity $= \frac{AD}{t}$

$= \frac{500}{20} = 25$ m/min (along AD)

3. (a) The distance travelled by the rocket in 1 min (= 60 s) in which resultant acceleration is vertically upwards and 10 m/s^2 will be

$h_1 = (1/2) \times 10 \times 60^2 = 18000 \text{ m} = 18 \text{ km}$ ...(i)

and velocity acquired by it will be

$v = 10 \times 60 = 600$ m/s ...(ii)

Now, after 1 min the rocket moves vertically up with velocity of 600 m/s and acceleration due to gravity opposes its motion. So, it will go to a height h_2 till its velocity becomes zero such that

$0 = (600)^2 - 2gh_2$

or $h_2 = 18000$ m [as $g = 10$ m/s^2] ...(iii)

$= 18$ km

So, from Eqs. (i) and (iii) the maximum height reached by the rocket from the ground

$h = h_1 + h_2 = 18 + 18 = 36$ km **Ans.**

(b) As after burning of fuel the initial velocity from Eq. (ii) is 600 m/s and gravity opposes the motion of rocket, so the time taken by it to reach the maximum height (for which $v = 0$),

$0 = 600 - gt$

or $t = 60$ s

i.e. after finishing fuel the rocket further goes up for 60 s, or 1 min. **Ans.**

4. Average velocity $= \frac{\text{Total displacement}}{\text{Total time}}$

$\therefore \quad 2.5\,v = \frac{vt_0 + 2vt_0 + 3vT}{t_0 + t_0 + T}$

Solving, we get

$T = 4\,t_0$ **Ans.**

5. Retardation time is 8s (double). Therefore, retardation should be half or 2 m/s^2.

s_1 = acceleration displacement

$= \frac{1}{2}\,a_1\,t_1^2 = \frac{1}{2} \times 4 \times (4)^2 = 32$ m

s_2 = retardation displacement

$= \frac{1}{2}\,a_2 t_2^2$

$= \frac{1}{2} \times 2 \times (8)^2 = 64$m

(a) $a_{av} = \frac{v_f - v_i}{t} = \frac{0 - 0}{12} = 0$ **Ans.**

(b) and (c) $d = s = s_1 + s_2 = 96$ m

$\therefore$ Average speed = Average velocity

$= \frac{d}{t}$

or $\frac{s}{t} = \frac{96}{12} = 8$ m/s **Ans.**

6. At minimum distance, their velocities are same,

$\therefore \quad v_A = v_B$ or $u_A + a_A t = u_B + a_B t$

or $(3 + t) = (1 + 2t)$ or $t = 2$ s

Minimum distance, d_{min} = Initial distance − extra displacement of A upto this instant due to its greater speed

$= 10 - (s_A - s_B)$

$= 10 + s_B - s_A$

$= 10 + \left(u_B t + \frac{1}{2}\,a_B t^2\right) - \left(u_A t + \frac{1}{2}\,a_A t^2\right)$

$= 10 + \left[(1)\,(2) + \frac{1}{2}\,(2)\,(2)^2\right] - \left[(3)\,(2) + \frac{1}{2}\,(1)\,(2)^2\right]$

$= 8$ m **Ans.**

7. (a) Velocity = slope of s-t graph

$\therefore$ Sign of velocity = sign of slope of s-t graph

(b) Let us discuss any one of them, let the portion cd, slope of s-t graph (= velocity) of this region is negative but increasing in magnitude. Therefore velocity is negative but increasing. Therefore sign of velocity and acceleration both are negative.

8. Displacement s = net area of v-t graph

$$= 40 + 40 + 40 - 20 = 100 \text{ m}$$

Distance d = |Total area|

$$= 40 + 40 + 40 + 20 = 140 \text{ m}$$

(a) Average velocity $= \frac{s}{t} = \frac{100}{14} = \frac{50}{7}$ m/s **Ans.**

(b) Average speed $= \frac{d}{t} = \frac{140}{14} = 10$ m/s **Ans.**

9. v_1 = speed of person

v_2 = speed of escalator

$$v_1 = \frac{l}{t_1} \quad \text{and} \quad v_2 = \frac{l}{t_2}$$

$$\therefore \quad t = \frac{l}{v_1 + v_2} = \frac{l}{\frac{l}{t_1} + \frac{l}{t_2}}$$

$$= \frac{t_1 t_2}{t_1 + t_2} = \frac{90 \times 60}{90 + 60} = 36 \text{ s}$$ **Ans.**

10. Comparing with $v = u + at$, we have

$$u = 40 \text{ m/s} \quad \text{and} \quad a = -10 \text{ m/s}^2$$

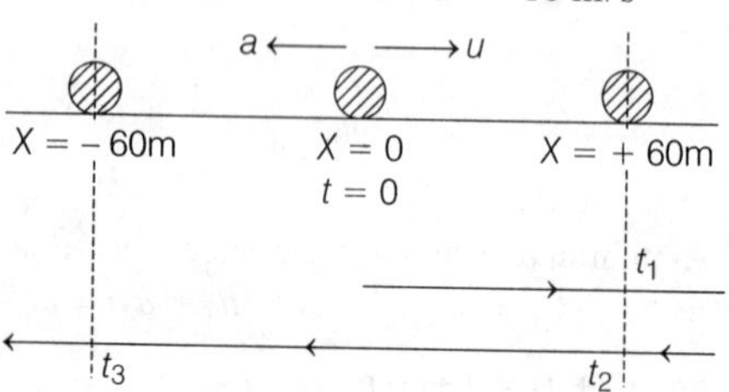

Distance of 60 m from origin may be at $x = +60$ m and $x = -60$ m.

From the figure, we can see that at these two points particle is at three times, t_1, t_2 and t_3.

For $X = +60$ m or t_1 and t_2

$$s = ut + \frac{1}{2}at^2$$

$$\Rightarrow \quad 60 = (+40)\,t + \frac{1}{2}(-10)\,t^2$$

Solving this equation, we get

$$t_1 = 2 \text{ s and } t_2 = 6 \text{ s}$$ **Ans.**

For $X = -60$ m or t_3

$$s = ut + \frac{1}{2}at^2$$

$$\therefore \quad -60 = (+40)\,t + \frac{1}{2}(-10)\,t^2$$

Solving this equation, we get positive value of t as

$$t_3 = 2\,(2 + \sqrt{7}) \text{ s}$$ **Ans.**

11. (a) $a_{av} = \frac{v_f - v_i}{t} = \frac{v_{12} - v_6}{12 - 6}$

$$= \frac{(-10) - (20)}{6}$$

$$= -5 \text{ m/s}^2$$ **Ans.**

(b) $\Delta v = v_f - v_i$ = net area of a-t graph

$\therefore \quad v_{14} - v_0 = 40 + 30 + 40 - 20 = 90$

But $\quad v_0 = 0$

$\therefore \quad v_{14} = 90$ m/s **Ans.**

12. (a) $\mathbf{v}_{av} = \frac{\mathbf{s}}{t} = \frac{\mathbf{r}_f - \mathbf{r}_i}{t}$

$$= \frac{(6\hat{\mathbf{i}} + 4\hat{\mathbf{j}}) - (\hat{\mathbf{i}} + 2\hat{\mathbf{j}})}{4}$$

$$= (1.25\hat{\mathbf{i}} + 0.5\hat{\mathbf{j}}) \text{ m/s}$$ **Ans.**

(b) $\mathbf{a}_{av} = \frac{\Delta \mathbf{v}}{t} = \frac{\mathbf{v}_f - \mathbf{v}_i}{t}$

$$= \frac{(2\hat{\mathbf{i}} + 10\hat{\mathbf{j}}) - (4\hat{\mathbf{i}} + 6\hat{\mathbf{j}})}{4}$$

$$= (-0.5\hat{\mathbf{i}} + \hat{\mathbf{j}}) \text{ m/s}^2$$ **Ans.**

(c) We cannot calculate the distance travelled from the given data.

13. If we start time calculations from point P and apply the equation,

a
a
+ve
u = 0
v = at_0
P
$\frac{1}{2}at_0^2$

$$s = ut + \frac{1}{2}at^2$$

$$\left(-\frac{1}{2}at_0^2\right) = (+at_0)\,t + \frac{1}{2}(-a)\,t^2$$

Solving we get, $t = (\sqrt{2} + 1)\,t_0$

$$= 2.414\,t_0$$

$\therefore$ Total time, $T = t + t_0$

$$= (3.414)\,t_0$$ **Ans.**

14. $s = s_0 + ut + \frac{1}{2}at^2$

at $t = 0, s = s_0 = 2$ m ...(i)

at $t = 10$ s,

$$s = 0 = s_0 + ut + \frac{1}{2}at^2$$

or $0 = 2 + 10u + 50a$

or $10u + 50a = -2$ ...(ii)

$$v = u + at$$

$\therefore$ $0 = u + 6a$ (at $t = 6$ s)

$\therefore$ $u + 6a = 0$ ...(iii)

Solving Eqs. (ii) and (iii), we get

$$u = -1.2 \text{ m/s}$$

and $a = 0.2 \text{ m/s}^2$ **Ans.**

Now, $v = u + at$

$\therefore$ $v = (-1.2) + (0.2)(10)$

$= 0.8$ m/s **Ans.**

15. After 2 s

$$\mathbf{v}_1 = \mathbf{u} + \mathbf{a}_1 t_1$$

$$= 0 + (2\hat{\mathbf{i}})(2) = (4\hat{\mathbf{i}}) \text{ m/s}$$

$$\mathbf{r}_1 = \mathbf{r}_i + \frac{1}{2}\mathbf{a}_1 t_1^2$$

$$= (2\hat{\mathbf{i}} + 4\hat{\mathbf{j}}) + \frac{1}{2}(2\hat{\mathbf{i}})(2)^2$$

$$= (6\hat{\mathbf{i}} + 4\hat{\mathbf{j}}) \text{ m}$$

After next 2 s

(a) $\mathbf{v}_2 = \mathbf{v}_1 + \mathbf{a}_2 t_2$

$$= (4\hat{\mathbf{i}}) + (2\hat{\mathbf{i}} - 4\hat{\mathbf{j}})(2)$$

$$= (8\hat{\mathbf{i}} - 8\hat{\mathbf{j}}) \text{ m/s}$$

(b) $\mathbf{r}_2 = \mathbf{r}_1 + \mathbf{v}_1 t_2 + \frac{1}{2}\mathbf{a}_2 t_2^2$

$$= (6\hat{\mathbf{i}} + 4\hat{\mathbf{j}}) + (4\hat{\mathbf{i}})(2) + \frac{1}{2}(2\hat{\mathbf{i}} - 4\hat{\mathbf{j}})(2)^2$$

$$= (18\hat{\mathbf{i}} - 4\hat{\mathbf{j}}) \text{ m}$$

$\therefore$ Co-ordinates are,

$x = 18$ m and $y = -4$ m

16. $x = u_x t + \frac{1}{2}a_x t^2$

$\therefore$ $29 = (0)(t) + \frac{1}{2} \times (4.0)\, t^2$

$\therefore$ $t^2 = \sqrt{14.5} \text{ s}^2$ or $t = 3.8$ s

(a) $y = u_y t + \frac{1}{2}a_y t^2$

$$= (8)(3.8) + \frac{1}{2} \times 2 \times 14.5$$

$= 44.9 \text{ m} \approx 45$ m **Ans.**

(b) $\mathbf{v} = \mathbf{u} + \mathbf{a}t$

$$= (8\hat{\mathbf{j}}) + (4.0\hat{\mathbf{i}} + 2.0\hat{\mathbf{j}})(3.8)$$

$$= (15.2\hat{\mathbf{i}} + 15.6\hat{\mathbf{j}})$$

$\therefore$ Speed $= |\mathbf{v}| = \sqrt{(15.2)^2 + (15.6)^2}$

$= 22$ m/s **Ans.**

17. $v = 3t^2 - 6t$

$\Rightarrow$ $v = 0$ at $t = 2$ s

For $t < 2$ s, velocity is negative. At $t = 2$ s, velocity is zero and for $t > 2$ s velocity is positive.

$\therefore$ $s_1 = \int_0^{3.5} v\,dt = \int_0^{3.5} (3t^2 - 6t)\,dt$

$= 6.125$ m

$=$ displacement upto 3.5 s

$s_2 = \int_0^{2} v\,dt = \int_0^{2} (3t^2 - 6t)\,dt$

$= -4$ m

$=$ displacement upto 2 s

– 4 m   O   6.125 m

$\therefore$ $d =$ distance travelled in 3.5 s

$= 4 + 4 + 6.125$

$= 14.125$ m **Ans.**

Average speed $= \frac{d}{t} = \frac{14.125}{3.5}$

$= 4.03$ m/s **Ans.**

Average velocity $= \frac{s_1}{t} = \frac{6.125}{3.5}$

$= 1.75$ m/s **Ans.**

18. $a = \frac{4}{v}$ or $\frac{dv}{dt} = \frac{4}{v}$

$\therefore$ $\int_6^v v\,dv = \int_2^t 4\,dt$

$\therefore$ $\frac{v^2}{2} - 18 = 4t - 8$

$\therefore$ $v = \sqrt{8t + 20}$

$$a = \frac{dv}{dt} = \frac{4}{\sqrt{8t + 20}}$$

At $t = 3$ s

$a = 0.603 \text{ m/s}^2$ **Ans.**

19. a = slope of v-t graph and s = area under v-t graph.

Further, for $t \le 2$s, velocity (i.e. slope of s-t graph) is positive but increasing. Therefore, s-t graph is as under.

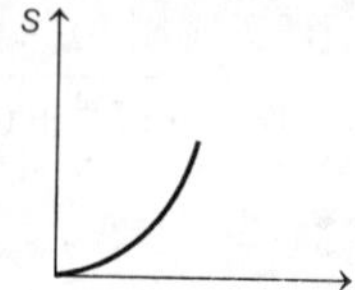

Same logic can be applied with other portions too.

20. Kinetic energy will first increase and then decrease.

$$v = gt \quad \text{(in downward journey)}$$

$$\therefore \quad KE = \frac{1}{2} mv^2 = \frac{1}{2} mg^2t^2$$

Hence, KE *versus* t graph is a parabola.

21. Speed first increases. Then just after collision, it becomes half and now it decreases.

Pattern of velocity is same (with sign). In the answer, downward direction is taken as positive.

Further, $\quad v = gt$

Hence, v-t graph is straight line.

22. (a) a = slope of v-t graph

(b) $s = r_f - r_i$ = net area of v-t graph

$$\therefore \quad r_f = r_i + \text{net area}$$
$$= 10 + 10 + 20 + 10 - 10 - 10$$
$$= 30 \text{ m}$$

(c) (i) **For $0 \le t \le 2$ s**

u = initial velocity = 0

s_0 = initial displacement = 10 m

a = slope of v-t graph = + 5 m/s^2

$$\therefore \quad s = s_0 + ut + \frac{1}{2}at^2 = 10 + 2.5\, t^2$$

(ii) **For 4 s $\le t \le$ 8 s**

u = initial velocity = 10 m/s = velocity at 4 s

s_0 = (10 m) + area of v-t graph upto 4 s = 10 + 10 + 20 = 40 m

a = slope of v-t graph = −5 m/s^2

$$\therefore \quad s = s_0 + u\,(t-4) + \frac{1}{2}a\,(t-4)^2$$
$$= 40 + 10\,(t-4) - 2.5\,(t-4)^2 \quad \textbf{Ans.}$$

23. (a) $a_1 = a_2 = -g$

$$\therefore \quad a_{12} = a_1 - a_2 = 0 \quad \textbf{Ans.}$$

(b) $u_{21} = u_2 - u_1 = 20 - (-5)$
$= +\,25$ m/s **Ans.**

(c) $u_{12} = -u_{21} = -25$ m/s

Since, $\quad a_{12} = 0$

$\therefore \quad u_{12}$ = constant $= -25$ m/s **Ans.**

(d) $a_{12} = 0$. Therefore, relative motion between them is uniform with constant velocity 25 m/s.

$$\therefore \quad t = \frac{d}{v} = \frac{20}{25} = 0.8 \text{ s} \quad \textbf{Ans.}$$

24. (a) When the two meet,

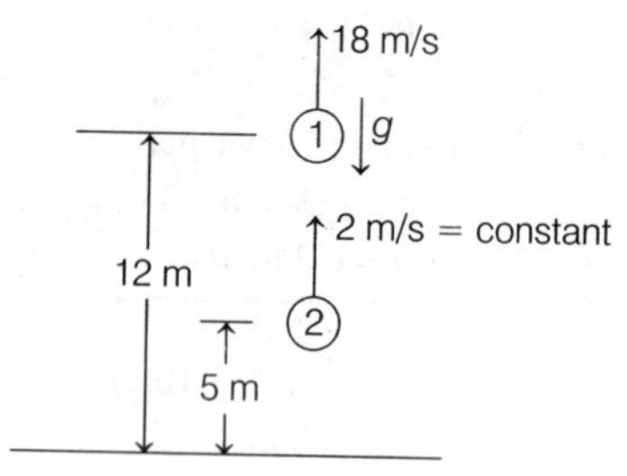

$$s_2 = s_1 + 7$$

or $\quad (2t) = (18t) - (4.9t^2) + 7$

Solving, we get

$$t = 3.65 \text{ s} \quad \textbf{Ans.}$$

$$s_2 = 2 \times 3.65 = 7.3 \text{ m}$$

$\therefore \quad$ Height $= 5 + 7.3 = 12.30$ mt **Ans.**

(b) $v_{ball} = u - gt = 18 - 9.8 \times 3.65$
$= -17.77$ m/s

$\therefore$ Velocity of ball with respect to elevator
= velocity of ball − velocity of elevator
= (−17.77) − (2)
= −19.77 m/s
≈ −19.8 m/s **Ans.**

Negative sign indicates the downward direction.

25. (a) For truck

$$s_1 = \frac{1}{2}a_1t^2$$

$$60 = \frac{1}{2} \times 2.2 \times t^2$$

$$\therefore \quad t = 7.39 \text{ s} \quad \textbf{Ans.}$$

(b) For automobile

$$s_2 = \frac{1}{2}a_2t^2 = \frac{1}{2} \times 3.5 \times (7.39)^2$$
$$= 95.5 \text{ m}$$

$\therefore$ Initial distance between them,

$$= s_2 - s_1$$
$$= 35.5 \text{ m} \quad \textbf{Ans.}$$

(c) $v_1 = a_1 t = (2.2)(7.39) = 16.2 \text{ m/s}$

and $v_2 = a_2 t = (3.5)(7.39) = 25.9 \text{ m/s}$

26. Net velocity is along AB or at 45° if,

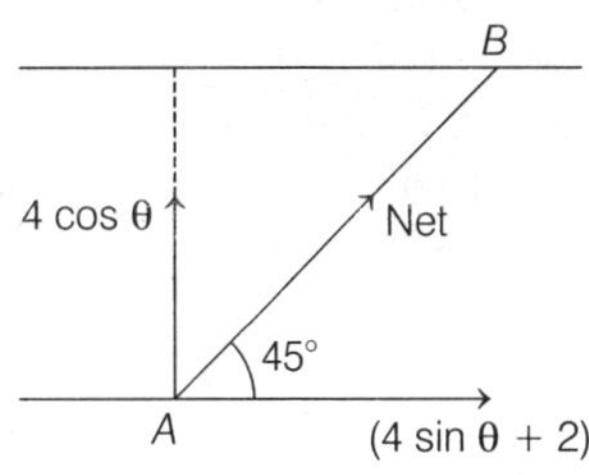

$$4\cos\theta = 4\sin\theta + 2$$

Solving this equation, we get

$$\theta \approx 24.3° \quad \textbf{Ans.}$$

27. (a) $\sin\theta = \frac{200}{500} = 0.4$

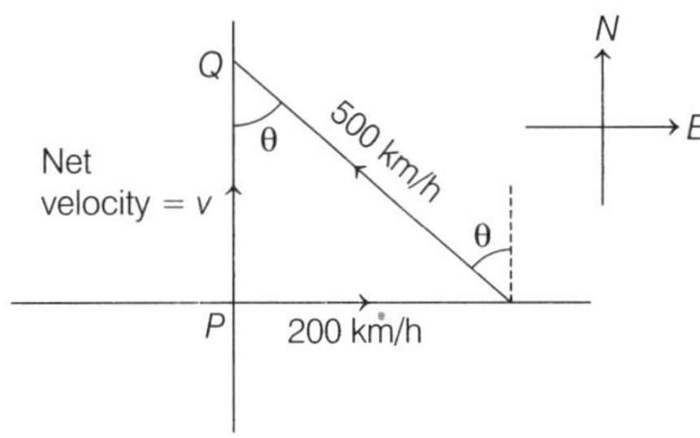

$\therefore$ $\theta = \sin^{-1}(0.4)$, west of north

(b) $v = \sqrt{(500)^2 - (200)^2}$

$= 100\sqrt{21}$ km/h

$\therefore$ $t = \frac{PQ}{v} = \frac{1000}{100\sqrt{21}} = \frac{10}{\sqrt{21}}$ h **Ans.**

28.

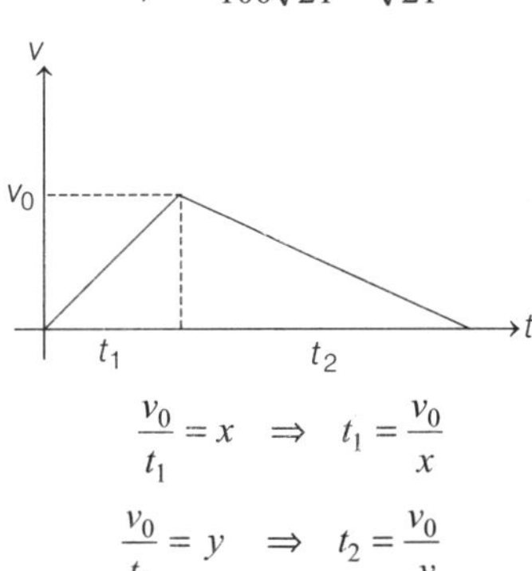

$$\frac{v_0}{t_1} = x \Rightarrow t_1 = \frac{v_0}{x}$$

$$\frac{v_0}{t_2} = y \Rightarrow t_2 = \frac{v_0}{y}$$

$$t_1 + t_2 = v_0\left(\frac{1}{x} + \frac{1}{y}\right) = 4 \quad \text{...(i)}$$

Further,

area = displacement

$\therefore$ $\frac{1}{2}v_0 \times t = s$

But numerically, $t = s = 4$ units

$\therefore$ $v_0 = 2$ units

Substituting in Eq. (i) we get,

$$\frac{1}{x} + \frac{1}{y} = 2.$$

LEVEL 2

Single Correct Option

1. Let velocity of rain is

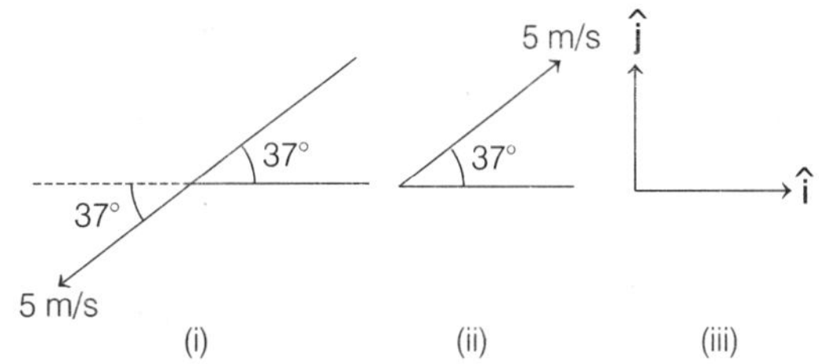

$$\mathbf{v}_R = a\hat{\mathbf{i}} - b\hat{\mathbf{j}}$$

In first case, $\mathbf{v}_M = (-4\hat{\mathbf{i}} - 3\hat{\mathbf{j}})$

$\therefore$ $\mathbf{v}_{RM} = \mathbf{v}_R - \mathbf{v}_M = (a+4)\hat{\mathbf{i}} + (-b+3)\hat{\mathbf{j}}$

It appears vertical

$\therefore$ $a + 4 = 0$ or $a = -4$

In second case, $\mathbf{v}_M = (4\hat{\mathbf{i}} + 3\hat{\mathbf{j}})$

$\therefore$ $\mathbf{v}_{RM} = \mathbf{v}_R - \mathbf{v}_M = (a-4)\hat{\mathbf{i}} + (-b-3\hat{\mathbf{j}})$

$= -8\hat{\mathbf{i}} + (-b-3\hat{\mathbf{j}})$

It appears at $\theta = \tan^{-1}\left(\frac{7}{8}\right)$

$\therefore$ $-b - 3 = -7$

$\therefore$ $b = 4$

and speed of rain $= \sqrt{a^2 + b^2}$

$= \sqrt{32}$ m/s **Ans.**

2. $\frac{dv}{dt} = a = -4v + 8$

$\therefore$ $\frac{da}{dt} = -4\frac{dv}{dt} = -4(-4v + 8)$

$= 16v - 32$

$\therefore \quad \left(\frac{da}{dt}\right)_i = 16\, v_i - 32$

$= (16)(0) - 32$

$= -32 \text{ m/s}^2$

Further, $\quad \int_0^v \frac{dv}{8-4v} = \int_0^t dt$

Solving this equation we get,

$v = 2\,(1 - e^{-4t})$

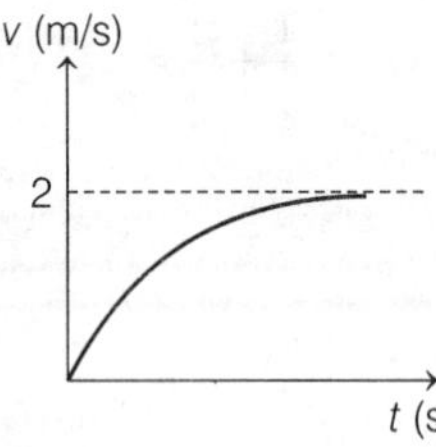

Hence, v-t graph is exponentially increasing graph, terminating at 2 m/s.

3. For collision,

$\mathbf{r}_A = \mathbf{r}_B$ (at same instant)

$\therefore \quad (\mathbf{r}_i + \mathbf{v})_A = (\mathbf{r}_i + \mathbf{v})_B$

$\Rightarrow (5\hat{\mathbf{i}} + 10\hat{\mathbf{j}} + 5\hat{\mathbf{k}})\,t = 30\hat{\mathbf{i}} + (10\hat{\mathbf{i}} + 5\hat{\mathbf{j}} + 5\hat{\mathbf{k}})\,t$

Equating the coefficients of x

$5t = 30 + 10t \quad \Rightarrow \quad t = -\text{ ve}$

So, they will never collide.

4. $\frac{dv_y}{dt} = 2t$

$\therefore \quad v_y = t^2 \quad \text{or} \quad \frac{dy}{dt} = t^2$

or $\quad y = \frac{t^3}{3} \quad$ ...(i)

and $\quad x = v_0 t \Rightarrow t = \frac{x}{v}$

Substituting in Eq. (i) we have,

$y = \frac{x^3}{3v_0^3}$ **Ans.**

5. $\frac{dt}{dx} = (2\alpha x + \beta)$

$\therefore \quad \frac{dx}{dt} = v = \left(\frac{1}{2\alpha x + \beta}\right)$

$a = \frac{dv}{dt} = -2\alpha\left(\frac{1}{2\alpha x + \beta}\right)^2 \cdot \frac{dx}{dt}$

$= -2\alpha\,(v^2)(v) = -2\alpha v^3$ **Ans.**

6. $f = v \cdot \frac{dv}{dx} = a - bx$

or $\quad \int_0^v v\,dv = \int_0^x (a - bx)\,dx$

$\therefore \quad v = \sqrt{2ax - bx^2} \quad$ ...(i)

At other station, $v = 0$

$\Rightarrow \quad x = \frac{2a}{b}$ **Ans.**

Further acceleration will change its direction when,

$f = 0$

or $\quad a - bx = 0$

or $\quad x = \frac{a}{b}$

At this x, velocity is maximum.

Using Eq. (i),

$v_{max} = \sqrt{2a\left(\frac{a}{b}\right) - b\left(\frac{a}{b}\right)^2}$

$= \frac{a}{\sqrt{b}}$ **Ans.**

7. $a = \frac{F}{m} = \frac{-kx^2}{m}$

$\therefore \quad v \cdot \frac{dv}{dx} = -\frac{kx^2}{m}$

or $\quad \int_0^v v\,dv = \int_a^0 -\frac{kx^2}{m}\,dx$

$\frac{v^2}{2} = \frac{ka^3}{3m}$

$\therefore \quad v = \sqrt{\frac{2ka^3}{3m}}$ **Ans.**

8. $a = v \cdot \frac{dv}{ds} = (4)(-\tan 60°)$

$= -4\sqrt{3} \text{ m/s}^2$

9. $90 \text{ km/h} = 90 \times \frac{5}{18} = 25 \text{ m/s}$

$180 \text{ km/h} = 108 \times \frac{5}{18} = 30 \text{ m/s}$

At maximum separation their velocities are same.

$\therefore$ Velocity of motorcycle = 25 m/s

or $\quad at = 25$

or $\quad t = 5$ s

But thief has travelled up to 7s.

s_1 = displacement of thief

$= v_1 t_1 = 25 \times 7 = 175$ m

s_2 = displacement of motorcycle

$$= \frac{1}{2} \times a_2 t_2^2$$

$$= \frac{1}{2} \times 5 \times (5)^2$$

$$= 62.5 \text{ m}$$

∴ Maximum separation

$$= s_1 - s_2 = 112.5 \text{ m}$$ **Ans.**

10. Relative velocity of A with respect to B should be along AB or absolute velocity components perpendicular to AB should be same.

∴ $$\frac{2u}{3} \sin \theta = u \sin 30°$$

∴ $$\theta = \sin^{-1}\left(\frac{3}{4}\right)$$ **Ans.**

11. Deceleration is four times. Therefore, deceleration time should be $\frac{1}{4}$ th.

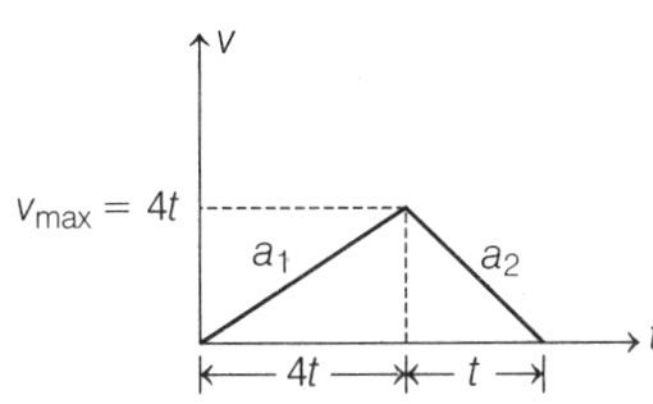

$$v_{max} = (a_1)(4t) = (1)(4t) = 4t$$

Area of v-t graph = displacement

∴ $$200 = \frac{1}{2}(5t)(4t)$$

or $$t = \sqrt{20} \text{ s}$$

Total journey time = $5t$ = 22.4 s **Ans.**

12. Area of v-t graph = displacement

∴ $$1032 = \frac{1}{2}(56 + t_0)(24)$$

or $$t_0 = 30 \text{ s}$$

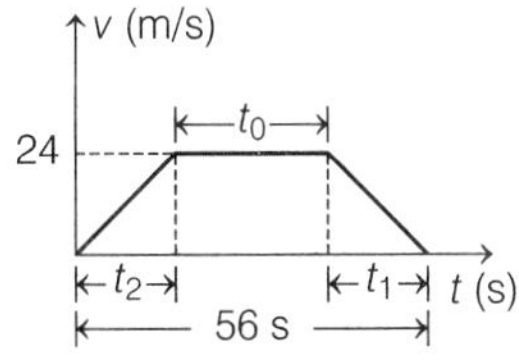

Deceleration time $t_1 = \frac{24}{4} = 6$ s

∴ Acceleration time $t_2 = 56 - t_0 - t_1 = 20$ s

∴ Acceleration $= \frac{24}{20} = 1.2 \text{ m/s}^2$ **Ans.**

13. $\mathbf{v}_Q = -20\hat{\mathbf{i}}$

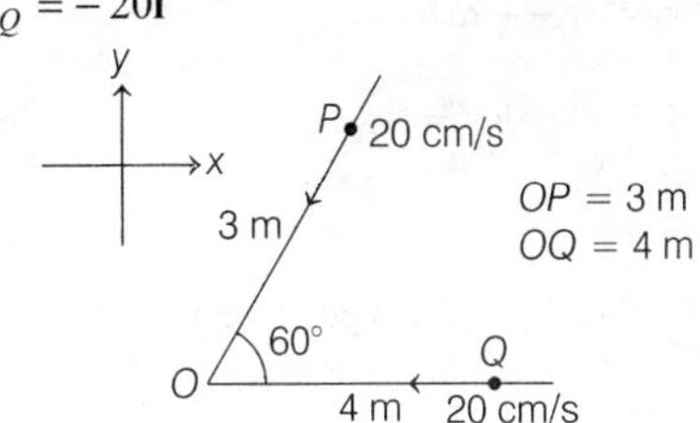

$$\mathbf{v}_P = -20 \cos 60\hat{\mathbf{i}} - 20 \sin 60° \hat{\mathbf{j}}$$
$$= -10\hat{\mathbf{i}} - 10\sqrt{3}\,\hat{\mathbf{j}}$$

Assuming P to be at rest,

$$\mathbf{v}_{QP} = \mathbf{v}_Q - \mathbf{v}_P$$
$$= -10\hat{\mathbf{i}} + 10\sqrt{3}\,\hat{\mathbf{j}}$$

Now, $$\tan \theta = \frac{10\sqrt{3}}{10} = \sqrt{3}$$

or $$\theta = 60°$$

where, θ is the angle of $\mathbf{v}_{QP}$ from x-axis towards positive y-axis.

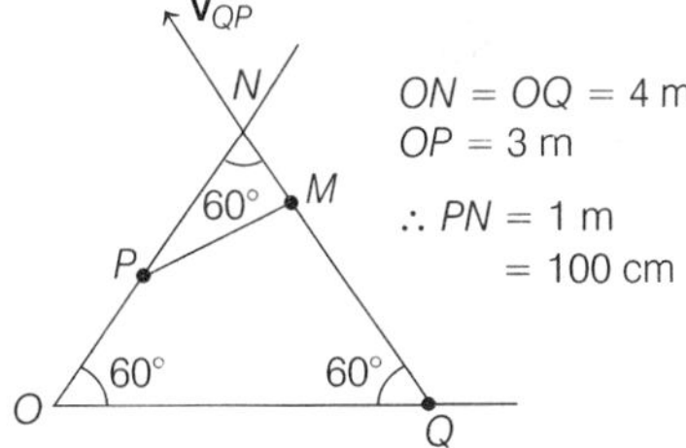

Shortest distance = $PM = PN \sin 60°$

$$= (100)\frac{\sqrt{3}}{2} = 50\sqrt{3} \text{ cm}$$

14. ∵ $a = \frac{vdv}{dx}$ or $v\,dv = adx$

or $$vdv = \frac{10}{v+1} dx$$

or $$\int_0^{15} v(v+1)\,dv = 10\int_0^x dx$$

or $$\left[\frac{v^3}{3} + \frac{v^2}{2}\right]_0^{15} = 10x$$

or $$\frac{1}{10}\left[\frac{15^3}{3} + \frac{15^2}{2}\right] = x$$

∴ $$x = 123.75 \text{ m}$$

15. Initially, relative acceleration between them is zero, so distance between them will increase linearly. Later when one stone strikes the ground, relative acceleration is g, so distance will decrease parabolically.

16. $x_2 - x_1 = vt - \frac{1}{2}at^2$

$x_2 - x_1$ is zero at $t = 0$

and $t = \frac{2v}{a}$.

For $t < \frac{2v}{a}$, $(x_2 - x_1)$ is positive and after that it is negative.

Further, $(x_2 - x_1)$ *versus* t graph is a parabola.

17.

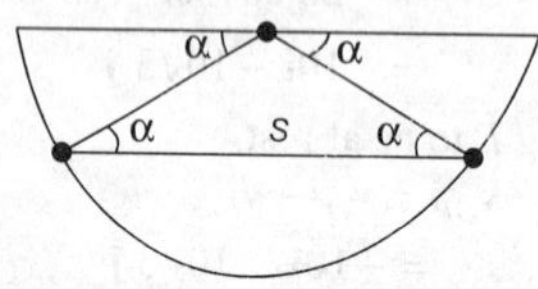

$$s = 2r\cos\alpha$$

$$\therefore \quad s = \frac{1}{2}a_0 t^2$$

$$\text{or} \quad 2r\cos\alpha = \frac{1}{2}a_0 t^2$$

$$\therefore \quad t = \sqrt{\frac{4r\cos\alpha}{a_0}}$$

18.

$$-h = 5t - 5t^2$$

and

$$-2h = -5t - 5t^2$$

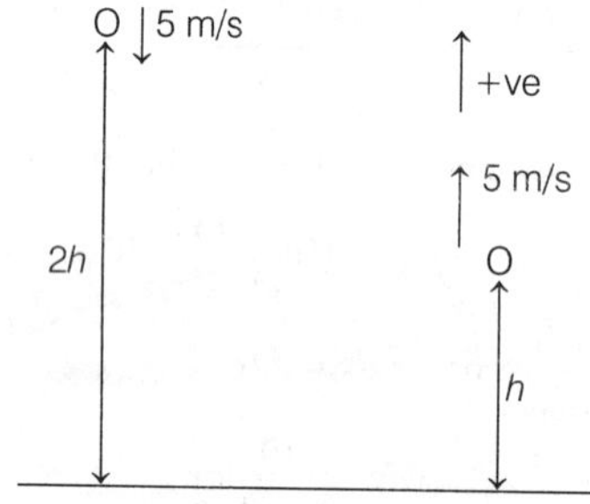

From these two equations,

we get $t = 3$ s

and h = distance between P

and $Q = 30$ m

19. According to addition law of vector,

$$\mathbf{v}_A + \mathbf{v}_C = \mathbf{v}_B$$

$$\mathbf{v}_C = \mathbf{v}_B - \mathbf{v}_A$$

Squaring on both sides, we get

$$v_C^2 = (\mathbf{v}_B - \mathbf{v}_A)^2$$

or

$$v_C^2 = v_B^2 + v_A^2 - 2v_Av_B\cos 60°$$

$$v_C \le v_A + v_B$$

20. Equation of line RS is $y = -mx + C$

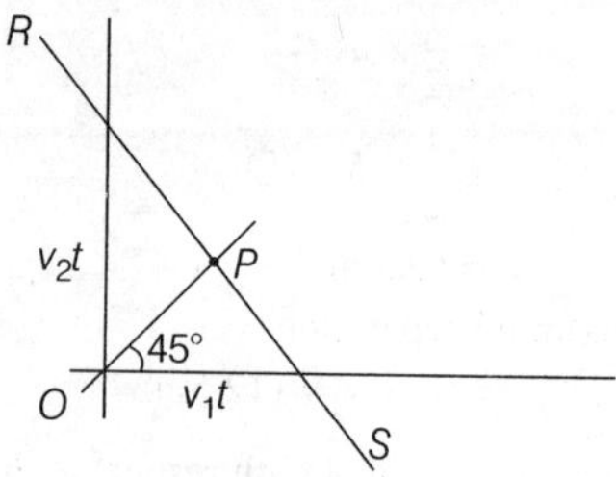

or $\quad y = -\left(\frac{v_2}{v_1}\right)x + v_2 t$

or $\quad v_1 y = -v_2 x + v_1 v_2 t \quad$ ...(i)

Equation of line OP is

$$y = x \quad \text{...(ii)}$$

Point P is the point of intersection. So, we get

$$x_P = y_P = \frac{v_1 v_2 t}{v_1 + v_2}$$

$$\therefore \quad OP = \sqrt{x_P^2 + y_P^2} = \frac{\sqrt{2}\, v_1 v_2 t}{v_1 + v_2}$$

or $\quad v_3 = \frac{OP}{t} = \frac{\sqrt{2}\, v_1 v_2}{v_1 + v_2}$

21. Here, $OA = t$, $OB = 2t$ and $OC = v_3 t$

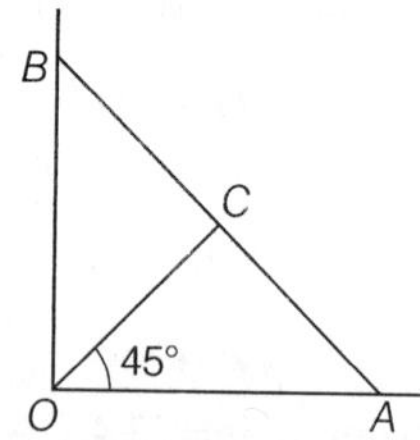

The equation of straight line AB is

$$y - 2t = -2x$$

$$\therefore \quad y = 2t - 2x$$

At point c,

$$x = v_3 t\cos 45° \quad \text{and} \quad y = v_3 t\sin 45°$$

$$\therefore \quad v_3 t\sin 45° = 2t - 2v_3 t\cos 45°$$

$$\frac{v_3}{\sqrt{2}} = 2 - \sqrt{2}\, v_3$$

or $\quad v_3 \cdot \left(\frac{1}{\sqrt{2}} + \sqrt{2}\right) = 2$

or $\quad v_3 = \frac{2\sqrt{2}}{3}\ \text{ms}^{-1}$

22.

$$0 = u^2 - 2a_1(4) - 2a_2(1) \quad \text{...(i)}$$

$$0 = u^2 - 2a_2(2) - 2a_1(2) \quad \text{...(ii)}$$

From these two equations, we get $a_2 = 2a_1$

23. $$(50)^2 = (10)^2 + 2as \quad \ldots\text{(i)}$$

→ a ← a
○→10 m/s ○→ 50 m/s
← s →

$$v^2 = (50)^2 + 2(-a)(-s) = (50)^2 + 2as \quad \ldots\text{(ii)}$$

Solving these two equations, we get

$$v = 70 \text{ m/s}$$

24. For P, $30 = 15 + at$ or $at = 15$ m/s

For Q, $v = 20 - at$ or $v = 20 - 15 = 5$ m/s

25. Slope of v-t graph gives acceleration/retardation. $|a| = 5$ m/s^2 for both of them. A has acceleration while B has retardation.

$$|s_A| + |s_B| = 60$$

or $$\left\{\frac{1}{2} \times 5 \times t^2\right\} + \left\{20\,t - \frac{1}{2} \times 5 \times t^2\right\} = 60$$

or $$t = 3 \text{ s}$$

26. Area of a - t graph gives change in velocity. When net area will become zero, particle will acquire its initial velocity.

27. Time taken to reach the maximum height, $t_1 = \dfrac{u}{g}$

If t_2 is the time taken to hit the ground, then

i.e. $$-H = ut_2 - \frac{1}{2}gt_2^2$$

But $$t_2 = nt_1 \quad \text{[Given]}$$

So, $$-H = u\frac{nu}{g} - \frac{1}{2}g\frac{n^2u^2}{g^2}$$

$$-H = \frac{nu^2}{g} - \frac{1}{2}\frac{n^2u^2}{g}$$

$$\Rightarrow \quad 2gH = nu^2(n-2)$$

28. Let x be the acceleration. Then,

$$a = \frac{1}{2}xp^2 \quad \ldots\text{(i)}$$

$$a + b = +\frac{1}{2}x(p+q)^2 \quad \ldots\text{(ii)}$$

Solving these two equations, we get

$$x = \frac{2b}{(q+2p)\,q}$$

29. $$t = \frac{d}{v_r \cos 30°} = \frac{2d}{\sqrt{3}\,v_r}$$

V_r 30° v

Now drift,

$$\frac{d}{2} = (v - v_r \sin 30°)\,t = (v - v_r/2)\left(\frac{2d}{\sqrt{3}\,v_r}\right)$$

$$\therefore \quad \sqrt{3}\,v_r = 4v - 2v_r$$

$$\therefore \quad v_r = \left(\frac{4}{2+\sqrt{3}}\right)v$$

$$= 4(2-\sqrt{3})\,v$$

30. $$T_0 = \frac{2s}{V}$$

and $$T = \frac{s}{V+v} + \frac{s}{V-v} = \frac{2sV}{V^2 - v^2}$$

$$\therefore \quad T/T_0 = \frac{(2sV/V^2 - v^2)}{2s/V}$$

$$= \frac{V^2}{V^2 - v^2} = \frac{1}{1 - v^2/V^2}$$

31.

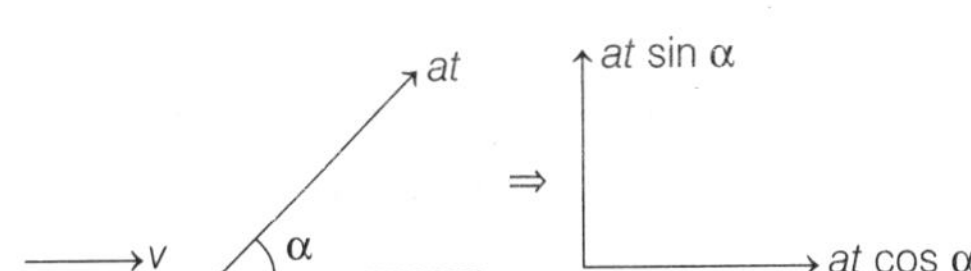

Relative velocity is perpendicular when

$$v = at\cos\alpha$$

$$\Rightarrow \quad t = \frac{v}{a\cos\alpha} = \frac{v}{a}\sec\alpha$$

32.

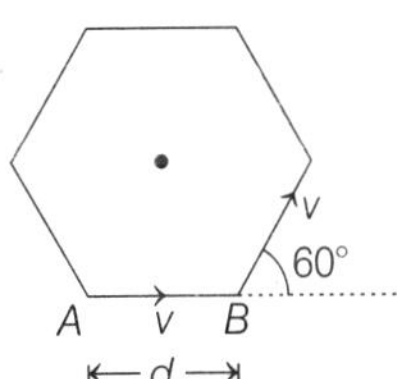

$$(v_{AB})_x = v - v\cos 60° = \frac{v}{2}$$

$$t = \frac{d}{v/2} = \frac{2d}{v}$$

33. Let v be the speed of buses. Distance between two buses $= vT = d$

In the same direction relative velocity is $(v - 20)$ kmh^{-1}.

$$d = v_r t$$

$$\Rightarrow \quad vT = (v-20)(18) \quad \ldots\text{(i)}$$

In the opposite direction, relative velocity is $(v + 20)$ kmh^{-1}.

Again using,

$$d = v_r t$$

We get, $vT = (v + 20)6$ ...(ii)

Solving Eqs. (i) and (ii), we get

$$T = 9 \text{ min} \quad \text{and} \quad v = 40 \text{ kmh}^{-1}$$

34. Relative velocity $= v_1 + v_2$

Relative retardation $= a_1 + a_2$

$$0 = u^2 - 2as$$

or $$s = d_{max} = \frac{u^2}{2a}$$

$$= \frac{(v_1 + v_2)^2}{2(a_1 + a_2)}$$

35. v_{IB} = velocity of insect w.r.t. belt $= v_I - v_B$

$\therefore$ $$v_I = v_{IB} + v_B = 4 + 2 = 6 \text{ms}^{-1}$$

36. & 37. A and B both are the marks on belt and relative to belt. Relative speed is constant in moving from A to B or B to A. This time is,

$$t = \frac{d}{\text{relative speed}}$$

$$= \frac{60}{4} = 15 \text{ s}$$

More than One Correct Options

1. (a) $a = -\alpha\sqrt{v}$

$\therefore$ $$\frac{dv}{dt} = -\alpha\sqrt{v}$$

or $$\int_0^t dt = -\frac{1}{\alpha}\int_{v_0}^0 v^{-1/2} \cdot dv$$

$\therefore$ $$t = \frac{2\sqrt{v_0}}{\alpha}$$ **Ans.**

(d) $a = -\alpha\sqrt{v}$

$\therefore$ $$v \cdot \frac{dv}{ds} = -\alpha\sqrt{v}$$

$\therefore$ $$\int_0^s ds = -\frac{1}{\alpha}\int_{v_0}^0 v^{1/2}\, dv$$

$\therefore$ $$s = \frac{2v_0^{3/2}}{3\alpha}$$ **Ans.**

2. $a = -0.5t = \dfrac{dv}{dt}$

$\therefore$ $$\int_{16}^v dv = \int_0^t -0.5t\, dt$$

$\therefore$ $$v = 16 - 0.25t^2$$

$$s = \int v dt = 16t - \frac{0.25t^3}{3}$$

$v = 0$ when $16 - 0.25t^2 = 0$

or $t = 8$ s **Ans.**

So direction of velocity changes at 8 s. Up to 8 s distance = displacement

$\therefore$ **At 4 s**

$$d = 16 \times 4 - \frac{0.25 \times (4)^3}{3} = 58.67 \text{ m}$$ **Ans.**

$$S_{8\,s} = 16 \times 8 - \frac{(0.25)(8)^3}{3}$$

$$= 85.33 \text{ m}$$

$$S_{10\,s} = 16 \times 10 - \frac{(0.25)(10)^3}{3}$$

$$= 76.67 \text{ cm}$$

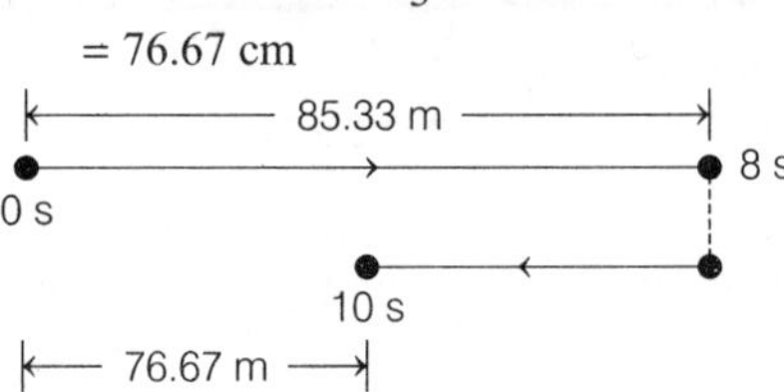

Distance travelled in 10 s,

$$d = (85.33) + (85.33 - 76.67)$$

$$= 94 \text{ m}$$ **Ans.**

At 10 s

$$v = 16 - 0.25\,(10)^2 = -9 \text{ m/s}$$

$\therefore$ Speed = 9 m/s **Ans.**

3. If **a** = constant

Then $|\mathbf{a}|$ is also constant or $\left|\dfrac{d\mathbf{v}}{dt}\right|$ = constant

4. $\mathbf{r}_B = 0$ at $t = 0$

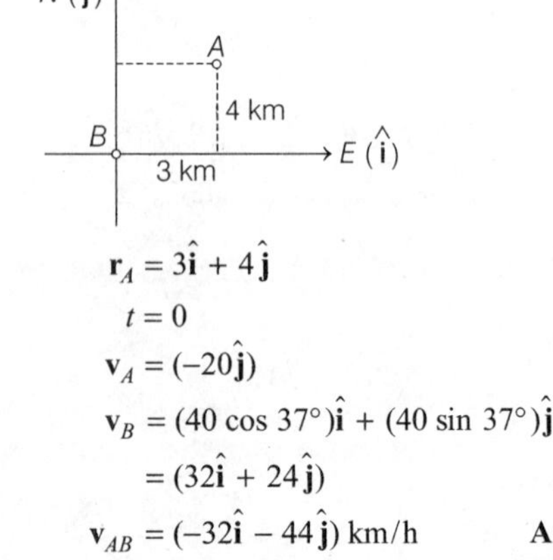

$$\mathbf{r}_A = 3\hat{\mathbf{i}} + 4\hat{\mathbf{j}}$$

at $$t = 0$$

$$\mathbf{v}_A = (-20\hat{\mathbf{j}})$$

$$\mathbf{v}_B = (40 \cos 37°)\hat{\mathbf{i}} + (40 \sin 37°)\hat{\mathbf{j}}$$

$$= (32\hat{\mathbf{i}} + 24\hat{\mathbf{j}})$$

$$\mathbf{v}_{AB} = (-32\hat{\mathbf{i}} - 44\hat{\mathbf{j}}) \text{ km/h}$$ **Ans.**

At time $t = 0$,

$$\mathbf{r}_{AB} = \mathbf{r}_A - \mathbf{r}_B = (3\hat{\mathbf{i}} + 4\hat{\mathbf{j}})$$

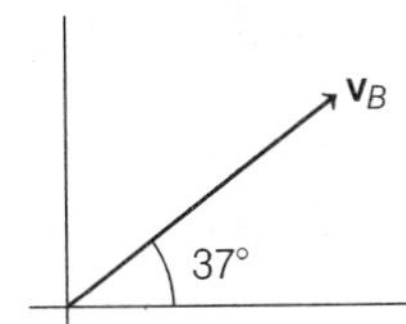

$\therefore$ At time $t = t$,

$$\mathbf{r}_{AB} = (\mathbf{r}_{AB} \text{ at } t = 0) + \mathbf{v}_{AB}\, t$$
$$= (3 - 32t)\hat{\mathbf{i}} + (4 - 44\,t)\hat{\mathbf{j}}$$ **Ans.**

5. $a_1 t_1 = a_2 t_2$

$$v_{\max} = a_1 t_1 = a_2 t_2$$
$$s_1 = \text{Area of } v\text{-}t \text{ graph}$$
$$= \frac{1}{2}(t_1 + t_2)(a_1 t_1)$$

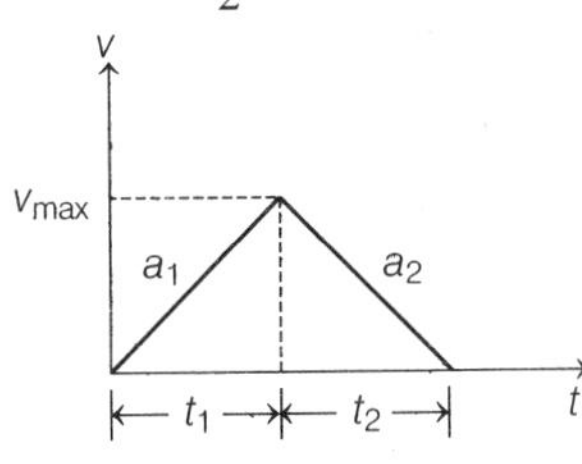

$$v_1 = \frac{s_1}{t_1 + t_2} = \frac{1}{2} a_1 t_1$$
$$s_2 = \frac{1}{2}(t_1 + t_3)\, v_{\max}$$
$$= \frac{1}{2}(t_1 + 2t_2)(2a_1 t_1)$$
$$v_2 = \frac{s_2}{(t_1 + t_3)} = a_1 t_1$$

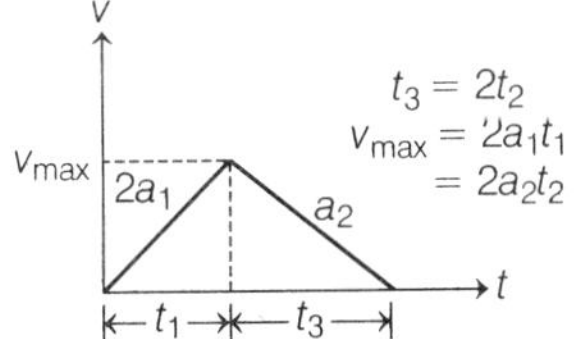

From the four relations we can see that

$$v_2 = 2v_1 \quad \text{and} \quad 2s_1 < s_2 < 4s_1$$ **Ans.**

6. In the complete journey,

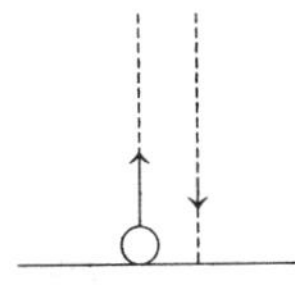

$s = 0$ and $a = \text{constant} = g$ (downwards)

7. $a = \dfrac{F}{m} = \dfrac{\alpha}{m} t$ ...(i)

or $a \propto t$

i.e. a-t graph is a straight line passing through origin.

If $u = 0$, then integration of Eq. (i) gives,

$$v = \frac{\alpha t^2}{2m}$$

or $v \propto t^2$

Hence in this situation (when $u = 0$) v-t graph is a parabola passing through origin.

8. a-s equation corresponding to given graph is,

$$a = 6 - \frac{s}{5}$$

$\therefore$ $$v \cdot \frac{dv}{ds} = \left(6 - \frac{s}{5}\right)$$

or $$\int_0^v v\,dv = \int_0^s \left(6 - \frac{s}{5}\right) ds$$

or $$v = \sqrt{12s - \frac{s^2}{5}}$$

At $s = 10\text{m}$, $v = 10 \text{ m/s}$ **Ans.**

Maximum values of v is obtained when

$$\frac{dv}{ds} = 0 \quad \text{which gives} \quad s = 30 \text{ m}$$

$\therefore$ $$v_{\max} = \sqrt{12 \times 30 - \frac{(30)^2}{5}}$$
$$= \sqrt{180} \text{ m/s}$$ **Ans.**

9. $\mathbf{v}_{av} = \dfrac{\mathbf{s}}{t}$

and $v_{av} = \dfrac{d}{t}$

Now, $d \geq |\mathbf{s}|$

$\therefore$ $v_{av} \geq |\mathbf{v}_{av}|$

10. $v = at$ and $x = \dfrac{1}{2}at^2$ $(u = 0)$, i.e. v-t graph is a straight line passing through origin and x-t graph a parabola passing through origin.

11. For minimum time

$\therefore$ $$t_{\min} = \frac{b}{v}$$

For reaching a point exactly opposite

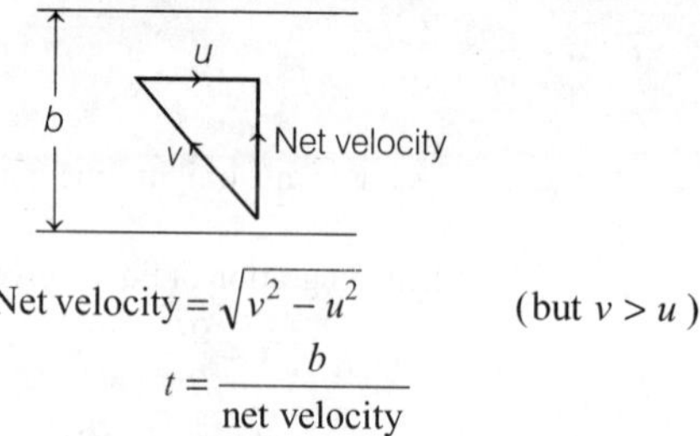

Net velocity $= \sqrt{v^2 - u^2}$ (but $v > u$)

$\therefore \quad t = \dfrac{b}{\text{net velocity}}$

12. For $t < T$, $v = -$ve

For $t > T$, $v = +$ve

At $t = T$, $v = 0$

$\therefore$ Particle changes direction of velocity at $t = T$

$s =$ Net area of v-t graph $= 0$

$a =$ Slope of v-t graph $=$ constant

13. $v = \alpha t_1 \Rightarrow t_1 = \dfrac{v}{\alpha}$

$v = \beta t_2 \Rightarrow t_2 = \dfrac{v}{\beta}$

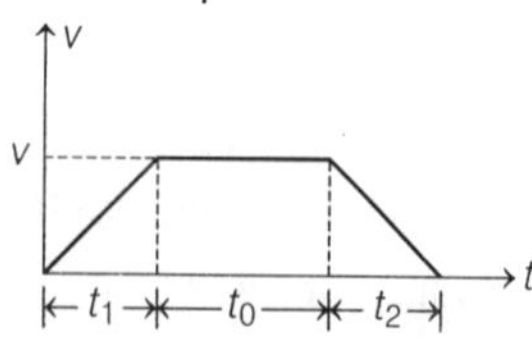

$\therefore \quad t_0 = t - t_1 - t_2 = \left(t - \dfrac{v}{\alpha} - \dfrac{v}{\beta}\right)$

Now, $\quad l = \dfrac{1}{2}\alpha t_1^2 + v t_0 + \dfrac{1}{2}\beta t_2^2$

$= \dfrac{1}{2}(\alpha)\left(\dfrac{v}{\alpha}\right)^2 + v\left(t - \dfrac{v}{\alpha} - \dfrac{v}{\beta}\right) + \dfrac{1}{2}(\beta)\left(\dfrac{v}{\beta}\right)^2$

$= vt - \dfrac{v^2}{2\alpha} - \dfrac{v^2}{2\beta}$

$\therefore \quad t = \dfrac{l}{v} + \dfrac{v}{2}\left(\dfrac{1}{\alpha} + \dfrac{1}{\beta}\right)$

For t to be minimum its first derivation with respect to velocity be zero, i.e.

$$0 = -\frac{l}{v^2} + \frac{\alpha + \beta}{2\alpha\beta}$$

$\therefore \quad v = \sqrt{\dfrac{2l\alpha\beta}{\alpha + \beta}}$

14. $x = t^2 \Rightarrow v_x = \dfrac{dx}{dt} = 2t$

$\Rightarrow \quad a_x = \dfrac{dv_x}{dt} = 2$

$\Rightarrow \quad y = t^3 - 2t$

$\Rightarrow \quad v_y = \dfrac{dy}{dt} = 3t^2 - 2$

$\Rightarrow \quad a_y = \dfrac{dv_y}{dt} = 6t$

At $t = 0$, $\quad v_x = 0,\ v_y = -2,\ a_x = 2$ and $a_y = 0$

$\therefore \quad \mathbf{v} = -2\hat{\mathbf{j}}$ and $\mathbf{a} = 2\hat{\mathbf{i}}$ or $\mathbf{v} \perp \mathbf{a}$

At $t = \sqrt{\dfrac{2}{3}}$, $\quad v_y = 0,\ v_x \neq 0$.

Hence, the particle is moving parallel to x-axis.

15. $(14)^2 = (2)^2 + 2\,as$

$\therefore \quad 2\,as = 192$ units

At mid point, $v^2 = (2)^2 + 2a\left(\dfrac{s}{2}\right)$

$= 4 + \dfrac{192}{2} = 100$

$\therefore \quad v = 10$ m/s **Ans.**

$XA : AY = 1 : 3$

$\therefore \quad XA = \dfrac{1}{4}s$ and $AY = \dfrac{3}{4}s$

$v_1^2 = (2)^2 + 2a\left(\dfrac{s}{4}\right)$

$= 4 + \dfrac{192}{4} = 52$

$\therefore \quad v_1 = \sqrt{52} \neq 5$ m/s **Ans.**

$10 = 2 + at_1$ $\quad (v = u + at)$

$\therefore \quad t_1 = \dfrac{8}{a} \quad 14 = 10 + at_2$

$\therefore \quad t_2 = \dfrac{4}{a}$ or $t_1 = 2\,t_2$ **Ans.**

$S_1 = (2t) + \dfrac{1}{2}a\,(t^2) =$ distance travelled in first half

$S_2 = 2\,(2t) + \dfrac{1}{2}a\,(2t)^2$

$S_3 = S_2 - S_1 =$ distance travelled in second half

We can see that,

$$S_1 \neq \frac{S_3}{2}$$

16. $x = 0$ at $t = 0$ and $t = \alpha/\beta$. So, the particle returns to starting point at $t = \alpha/\beta$.

$$v = \frac{dx}{dt} = 2\alpha t - 3\beta t^2$$

At $t = 0$, $v = 0$ i.e. initial velocity of particle is zero.

$v = 0$ at $t = 0$ and $t = \dfrac{2\alpha}{3\beta}$

Thus, the particle comes to rest after time.

$$t = 2\alpha/3\beta$$

$$a = \frac{dv}{dt} = 2\alpha - 6\beta t$$

At $t = 0$, $a = 2\alpha \neq 0$

17. Comparing with projectile motion,

$$\mathbf{r} = (u_x t)\,\hat{\mathbf{i}} + \left(u_y t - \frac{1}{2} g t^2\right)\hat{\mathbf{j}}$$

We have, $u_x = 3$ m/s, $u_y = 4$ m/s

and $g = 10$ m/s^2

$$T = \frac{2u_y}{g} = 0.8 \text{ s}$$

(a) $R = u_x\, T = 2.4$ m

(b) $u = \sqrt{u_x^2 + u_y^2} = 5$ m/s

(c) $\theta = \tan^{-1}\left(\frac{u_y}{u_x}\right) = \tan^{-1}\left(\frac{4}{3}\right)$

(d) $T = 0.8$ s

18. At 60 s,

$$h_1 = \frac{1}{2} \times 10 \times (60)^2 = 18000 \text{ m}$$

$$v_1 = 10 \times 60 = 600 \text{ m/s}$$

After that

$$h_2 = \frac{v_1^2}{2g} = 18000 \text{ m}$$

$\therefore$ $H_{\max} = h_1 + h_2$

$= 36000$ m $= 36$ km

Further, $-18000 = 600t - 5t^2$

or $t^2 - 120\,t - 3600 = 0$

or $t = \frac{120 + \sqrt{14400 + 14400}}{2}$

$= \frac{120 + 120\sqrt{2}}{2}$

$= 60 + 60\sqrt{2}$

$\therefore$ Total time $= 60 + (60 + 60\sqrt{2})$

$= (120 + 60\sqrt{2})$ s

19. (a) Graph is passing through origin. Hence, option (a) is correct.

(b) From graph, Q starts at $t = 10$ s.

(c) From the given graph, it is clear that particle Q will overtake the particle P at the distance of 30 m and the time difference of 30 s.

Comprehension Based Questions

1. Velocity of ball with respect to elevator is 15 m/s (up) and elevator has a velocity of 10 m/s (up). Therefore, absolute velocity of ball is 25 m/s (upwards). Ball strikes the floor of elevator if,

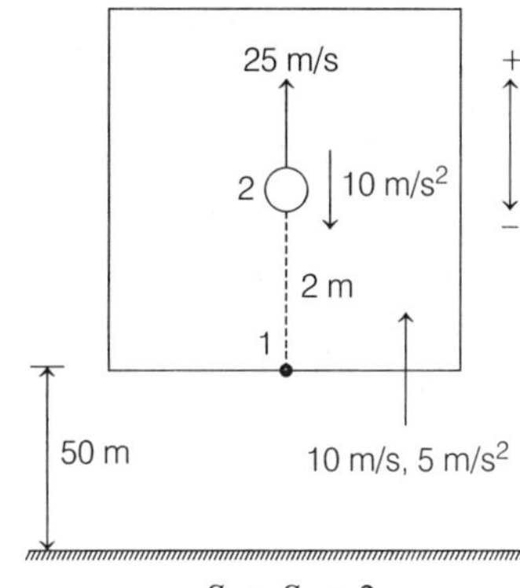

$$S_1 = S_2 + 2$$

$\therefore$ $10t + 2.5t^2 = 25t - 5t^2 + 2$

Solving this equation we get,

$t = 2.13$ s **Ans.**

2. If the ball does not collide, then it will reach its maximum height in time,

$$t_0 = \frac{u}{g} = \frac{25}{10} = 2.5 \text{ s}$$

Since, $t < t_0$, therefore as per the question ball is at its maximum height at 2.13 s.

$h_{\max} = 50 + 2 + 25 \times 2.13 - 5 \times (2.13)^2$

$= 82.56$ m **Ans.**

3. $S = 25 \times 2.13 - 5 \times (2.13)^2$

$= 30.56$ m **Ans.**

4. At maximum separation, their velocities are same

$\therefore$ $25 - 10t = 10 + 5t$ or $t = 1$ s

Maximum separation $= 2 + S_2 - S_1$

$= 2 + [25 \times 1 - 5 \times (1)^2] - [10 \times 1 + 2.5\,(1)^2]$

$= 9.5$ m **Ans.**

5. $u_A + a_A T = u_B - a_B T$

Putting $T = 4$ s

we get $4\,(a_A + a_B) = u_B - u_A$ ....(i)

Now, $S_A = S_B$

$\therefore$ $u_A t + \frac{1}{2} a_A t^2 = u_B\, t - \frac{1}{2} a_B\, t^2$

$\therefore$ $t = 2\frac{(u_B - u_A)}{(a_A + a_B)} = 2 \times 4 = 8$ s **Ans.**

6. $S_A = S_B$

$$5t + \frac{1}{2}a_At^2 = 15t - \frac{1}{2}a_Bt^2$$

or $\quad 10 + a_At = 30 - a_Bt$

$\therefore (5 + a_At) - (15 - a_Bt) = 10$

or $\quad v_A - v_B = 10$ m/s **Ans.**

7. $8 = 6 + a_AT = 6 + 4a_A$

$\therefore \quad a_A = 0.5$ m/s

At 10 s,

$$v_A = u_A + a_At$$
$$= (6) + (0.5)(10)$$
$$= 11 \text{ m/s}$$ **Ans.**

8. & 9.

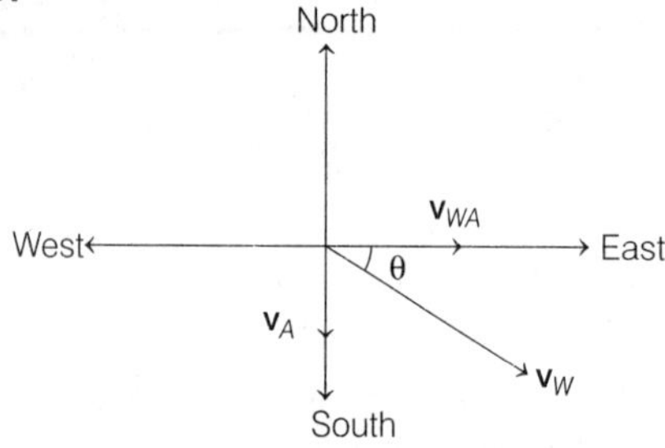

$\mathbf{v}_W$ = velocity of wind, $\mathbf{v}_A$ = velocity of car A

$\mathbf{v}_B$ = velocity of car B

$\mathbf{v}_{WA}$ = velocity of wind with respect to car A

$\mathbf{v}_{WB}$ = velocity of wind with respect to car B

For car *A*

$\because \quad \mathbf{v}_{WA} = \mathbf{v}_W - \mathbf{v}_A$

$\therefore \quad \tan\theta = \dfrac{v_A \sin(90° - \theta)}{v_W - v_A\cos(90° - \theta)}$

or $\quad \dfrac{\sin\theta}{\cos\theta} = \dfrac{30\cos\theta}{v_W - 30\sin\theta}$

or $\quad v_W\sin\theta - 30\sin^2\theta = 30\cos^2\theta$

or $\quad v_W\sin\theta = 30$

For car *B*

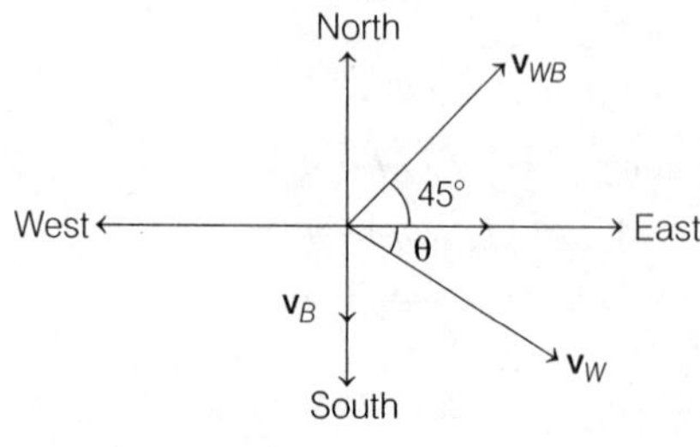

$\because \quad \mathbf{v}_{WB} = \mathbf{v}_W - \mathbf{v}_B$

$\therefore \quad \tan(45° + \theta) = \dfrac{v_B\sin(90° - \theta)}{v_W - v_B\cos(90° - \theta)}$

$\Rightarrow \quad \dfrac{\tan 45° + \tan\theta}{1 - (\tan 45° \times \tan\theta)} = \dfrac{50\cos\theta}{v_W - 50\sin\theta}$

$\Rightarrow \quad \dfrac{1 + \dfrac{\sin\theta}{\cos\theta}}{1 - \dfrac{\sin\theta}{\cos\theta}} = \dfrac{50\cos\theta}{v_W - 50\sin\theta}$

$\Rightarrow \quad \dfrac{\cos\theta + \sin\theta}{\cos\theta - \sin\theta} = \dfrac{50\cos\theta}{v_W - 50\sin\theta}$

$\Rightarrow (v_W - 50\sin\theta)(\cos\theta + \sin\theta)$
$= 50\cos\theta(\cos\theta - \sin\theta)$

$\Rightarrow v_W\cos\theta + v_W\sin\theta - 50\cos\theta\sin\theta$
$- 50\sin^2\theta = 50\cos^2\theta - 50\sin\theta\cos\theta$

$\Rightarrow \quad v_W\cos\theta + v_W\sin\theta = 50$

$\Rightarrow \quad v_W\cos\theta + 30 = 50$

$\Rightarrow \quad v_W\cos\theta = 20$

$\Rightarrow \quad \tan\theta = \dfrac{v_W\sin\theta}{v_W\cos\theta} = \dfrac{30}{20} = \dfrac{3}{2}$

$\Rightarrow \quad v_W\cos\theta = 20$

$\Rightarrow \quad v_W = \dfrac{20}{\cos\theta} = 20$

$= \dfrac{20}{2/\sqrt{9 + 4}} = 10\sqrt{13}$ kmh^{-1}

10. Initial position of buses A and B and car C are as shown in the figure.

Let A and B cross each other at D.

C
D
A •→ ←• B
|← 500 m →|

$v_{AC} = v_A - v_C = 20 - 15 = 5$ ms^{-1}

and $\quad v_{BC} = v_B - v_C = 20 - (-15) = 35$ ms^{-1}

Let the time taken by bus B to cover distance BC is t.

$\therefore \quad t = \dfrac{BC}{v_{BC}} = \dfrac{BC}{35}$

For bus A, $AC = v_{AC}t + \dfrac{1}{2}at^2$

$\Rightarrow 500 - BC = 5\left(\dfrac{BC}{35}\right) + \dfrac{1}{2} \times 2\left(\dfrac{BC}{35}\right)^2$

$\Rightarrow \quad (BC)^2 + 1400\,BC - 612500 = 0$

$\therefore \quad BC = \dfrac{-1400 \pm \sqrt{(1400)^2 + 4 \times 612500}}{2}$

Neglecting negative value, we get

$$BC = 350 \text{ m}$$

11. $AC = 500 - 350 = 150$ m

12. $\because$ Time, $t = \dfrac{BC}{35} = \dfrac{350}{35} = 10$ s

Match the Columns

1. In (a) and (b), if velocity is in the direction of acceleration (or of the same sign as that of acceleration) then speed increases. And if velocity is in opposite direction, then speed decreases.

In (c) slope of s-t graph (velocity) is increasing. Therefore speed is increasing. In (d) slope of s-t graph is decreasing. Therefore, speed is decreasing.

2. If $\mathbf{v} \cdot \mathbf{a} = 0$, speed is constant because angle between $\mathbf{v}$ and $\mathbf{a}$ in this case is 90°.

If $\mathbf{v} \cdot \mathbf{a}$ = positive then speed is increasing because angle between $\mathbf{v}$ and $\mathbf{a}$ in this case is acute.

If $\mathbf{v} \cdot \mathbf{a}$ = negative then speed is increasing because angle between $\mathbf{v}$ and $\mathbf{a}$ in this case is obtuse.

3. In portion AB, we can see that velocity is positive and increasing. Similarly for other parts we can draw the conclusions.

4. (a) Average velocity $= \dfrac{S}{t} = \dfrac{\text{Area of } v\text{-}t \text{ graph}}{\text{Time}}$

$$= \frac{20}{4} = 5 \text{ m/s}$$

(b) Average acceleration $= \dfrac{v_f - v_i}{\text{time}}$

$$= \frac{v_{4\,\text{s}} - v_{1\,\text{s}}}{4-1} = \frac{0-5}{3} = -\frac{5}{3} \text{ m/s}^2$$

(c) Average speed $= \dfrac{d}{t} = \dfrac{|\text{Total area}|}{\text{Time}}$

$$= \frac{20+10}{6} = 5 \text{ m/s}$$

(d) Rate of change of speed at 4 s $= |\mathbf{a}|$

$= |\text{slope of } v\text{-}t \text{ graph}| = 5 \text{ m/s}^2$

5. (a) $x = 0$ at $t = 2$s

(b) $v = \dfrac{dx}{dt} = 10\,t$

and $a = \dfrac{dv}{dt} = 10$

$v = a$ at 1s

(c) $v = 10\,t$

$\therefore$ Velocity is positive all the time.

(d) $v = 0$ at $t = 0$ s

6. $v_x = \dfrac{dx}{dt} = 2t - 2$

$$a_x = \frac{dv_x}{dt} = 2$$

$$v_y = \frac{dy}{dt} = 2t - 4$$

$$a_y = \frac{dv_y}{dt} = 2$$

(a) It crosses y-axis when, $x = 0$

$\Rightarrow$ $t = 1$ s

At this instant v_y is -2 m/s.

(b) It crosses x-axis when, $y = 0$

$\Rightarrow$ $t = 2$ s

At this instant v_x is $+2$ m/s

(c) At $t = 0$, $v_x = -2$ m/s and $v_y = -4$ m/s

$\therefore$ Speed $= \sqrt{v_x^2 + v_y^2} = 2\sqrt{5}$ m/s

(d) At $t = 0$, $a_x = 2 \text{ m/s}^2$

and $a_y = 2 \text{ m/s}^2$

$\therefore$ $a = \sqrt{a_x^2 + a_y^2}$

$= 2\sqrt{2}$ m/s

7.

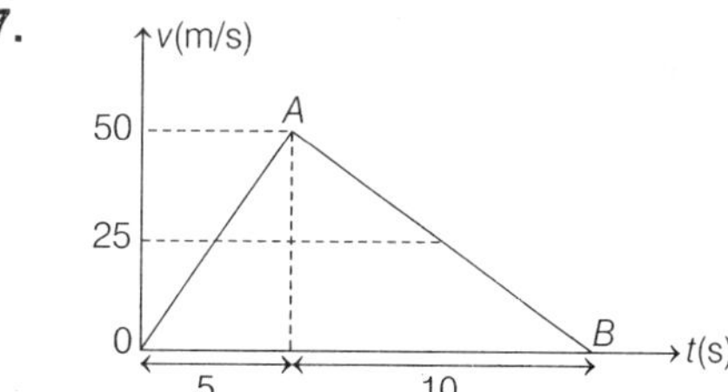

Slope of OA = acceleration

$= +10 \text{ m/s}^2$

Slope of AB = retardation

$= -5 \text{ m/s}^2$

Since the particle is not changing the direction. Hence,

distance = displacement = area under v-t graph.

8. (a) Since, ball A is moving with constant velocity, so its net acceleration is zero.

Let its initial velocity is v_0.

$\therefore$ $a = g - 5\,v_0$

or $0 = 10 - 5\,v_0$

$\therefore$ $v_0 = 2 \text{ ms}^{-1}$

(b) Ball B is moving with increasing speed.

$\therefore$ $a > 0$

or $g - 5v > 0$

or $10 - 5v > 0$

or $5v < 10$

or $v < 2\ \text{ms}^{-1}$

$\therefore$ During acceleration, its velocity is lying in the range of $0 \le v \le 2$.

When it gains constant velocity, $a = 0$

$\therefore$ $g - 5v_0 = 0$

$\therefore$ $v_0 = 2\ \text{ms}^{-1}$, this is its final velocity.

(c) Initially ball C is moving with decreasing speed. Let its initial velocity is u.

$\therefore$ $a < 0$

$\therefore$ $5v > 10$

or $g - 5v < 0$

or $v > 2\ \text{ms}^{-1}$

$\therefore$ $v_0 > 2\ \text{ms}^{-1}$

When it gains constant velocity,

$a = 0$

$\therefore$ $g - 5v_0 = 0$

$\therefore$ $v_0 = 2\ \text{ms}^{-1}$

Hence, (a) $\rightarrow$ (p,s), (b) $\rightarrow$ (q,s), (c) $\rightarrow$ (r,s)

Subjective Questions

1. $v\,dv = a\,ds$

$$\therefore \quad \int_0^v v\,dv = \int_0^{12\text{ m}} a\,ds$$

$\therefore$ $\dfrac{v^2}{2}$ = area under a-s graph from $s = 0$ to $s = 12$ m.

$$= 2 + 12 + 6 + 4$$
$$= 24\ \text{m}^2/\text{s}^2$$

or $v = \sqrt{48}$ m/s

$= 4\sqrt{3}$ m/s **Ans.**

2. Let $AB = BC = d$

$$BD = x$$

and $BB' = s$ = displacement of point B.

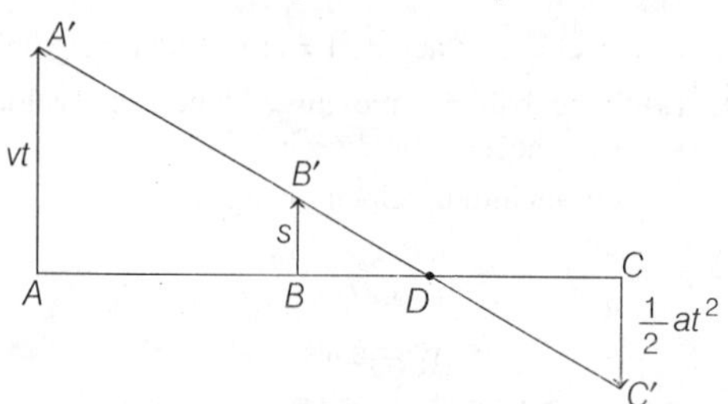

From similar triangles we can write,

$$\frac{vt}{d + x} = \frac{s}{x} = \frac{\frac{1}{2}at^2}{d - x}$$

From first two equations we have,

$$1 + \frac{d}{x} = \frac{vt}{s}$$

or $$\frac{d}{x} = \frac{vt}{s} - 1 \quad \text{...(i)}$$

From last two equations we have,

$$\frac{d}{x} - 1 = \frac{\frac{1}{2}at^2}{s}$$

or $$\frac{d}{x} = \frac{\frac{1}{2}at^2}{s} + 1 \quad \text{...(ii)}$$

Equating Eqs. (i) and (ii), we have

$$\frac{vt}{s} - 1 = \frac{\frac{1}{2}at^2}{s} + 1$$

or $$\frac{vt - \frac{1}{2}at^2}{s} = 2$$

$$\therefore \quad s = \left(\frac{v}{2}\right)t - \frac{1}{2}\left(\frac{a}{2}\right)t^2$$

Comparing with $s = ut + \frac{1}{2}at^2$ we have,

Initial velocity of B is $+\dfrac{v}{2}$ and acceleration $-\dfrac{a}{2}$.

3. Let us draw v - t graph of the given situation, area of which will give the displacement and slope the acceleration.

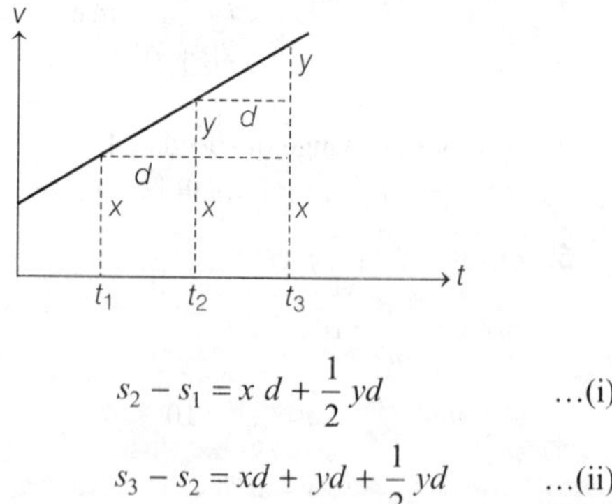

$$s_2 - s_1 = x\,d + \frac{1}{2}yd \quad \text{...(i)}$$

$$s_3 - s_2 = xd + yd + \frac{1}{2}yd \quad \text{...(ii)}$$

Subtracting Eq. (i) from Eq. (ii), we have

$$s_3 + s_1 - 2s_2 = yd$$

or $$s_3 + s_1 - 2\sqrt{s_1 s_3} = yd \qquad (s_2 = \sqrt{s_1 s_3})$$

Dividing by d^2 both sides we have,

$$\frac{(\sqrt{s_1} - \sqrt{s_3})^2}{d^2} = \frac{y}{d}$$

= slope of v - t graph = a. **Hence proved.**

4. Area of v-t graph = displacement

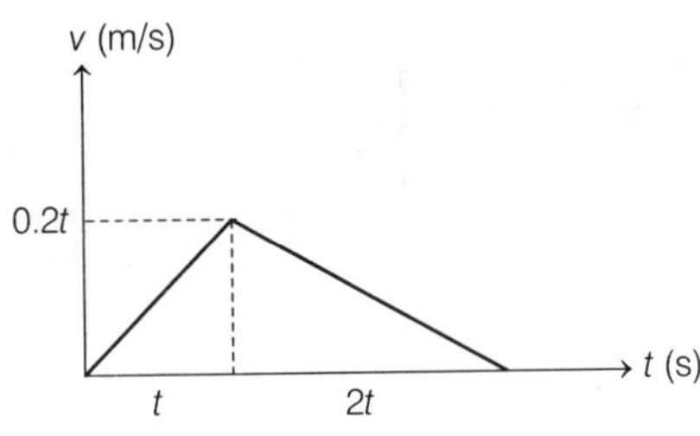

$\therefore$ $$\frac{1}{2}(3t)(0.2\,t) = 14 \qquad \textbf{Ans.}$$

Solving this equation, we get

$$3t = 20.5\text{ s}$$

Note *Maximum speed 0.2 t is less than 2.5 m/s.*

5. Let t_0 be the breaking time and a the magnitude of deceleration.

80.5 km/h = 22.36 m/s, 48.3 km/h = 13.42 m/s.

In the first case,

$$56.7 = (22.36 \times t_0) + \frac{(22.36)^2}{2a} \qquad \text{...(i)}$$

and $$24.4 = (13.42\, t_0) + \frac{(13.42)^2}{2a} \qquad \text{...(ii)}$$

Solving these two equations, we get

$$t_0 = 0.74\text{ s}$$

and $$a = 6.2\text{ m/s}^2 \qquad \textbf{Ans.}$$

6. Absolute velocity of ball = 30 m/s

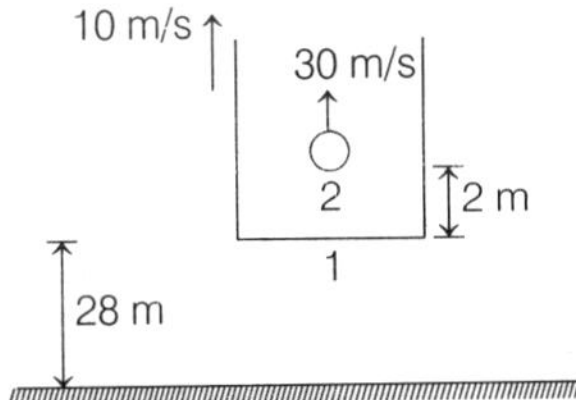

(a) Maximum height of ball from ground

$$= 28 + 2 + \frac{(30)^2}{2 \times 9.8} = 76\text{ m}$$

(b) Ball will return to the elevator floor when,

$s_1 = s_2 + 2$

or $$10t = (30t - 4.9\,t^2) + 2$$

Solving, we get

$$t = 4.2\text{ s} \qquad \textbf{Ans.}$$

7. In the first case,

$$BC = vt_1$$

and $$w = ut_1$$

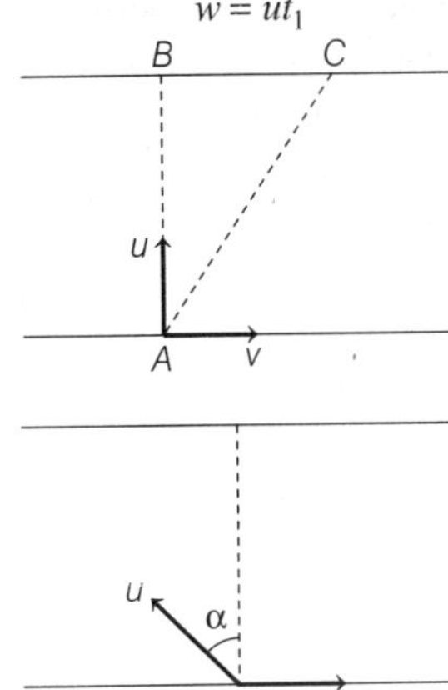

In the second case,

$u \sin \alpha = v$ and $w = (u \cos \alpha)\, t_2$

Solving these four equations with proper substitution, we get

$$w = 200\text{ m},$$
$$u = 20\text{ m/min},$$
$$v = 12\text{ m/min}$$

and $$\alpha = 36°50' \qquad \textbf{Ans.}$$

8. (a) $a = 2t - 2$ (from the graph)

Now, $$\int_0^v dv = \int_0^t a\, dt = \int_0^t (2t - 2)\, dt$$

$\therefore$ $$v = t^2 - 2t$$

(b) $$s = \int_2^4 v\, dt = \int_2^4 (t^2 - 2t)\, dt = 6.67\text{ m}$$

9. (a)

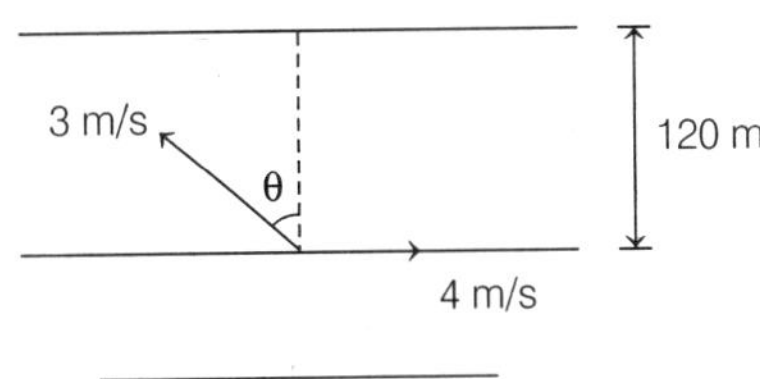

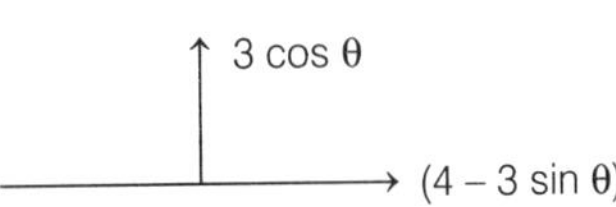

Time to cross the river

$$t_1 = \frac{120}{3\cos\theta} = \frac{40}{\cos\theta} = 40\sec\theta$$

Drift along the river $x = (4 - 3\sin\theta)\left(\frac{40}{\cos\theta}\right)$

$$= (160\sec\theta - 120\tan\theta)$$

To reach directly opposite, this drift will be covered by walking speed.

Time taken in this,

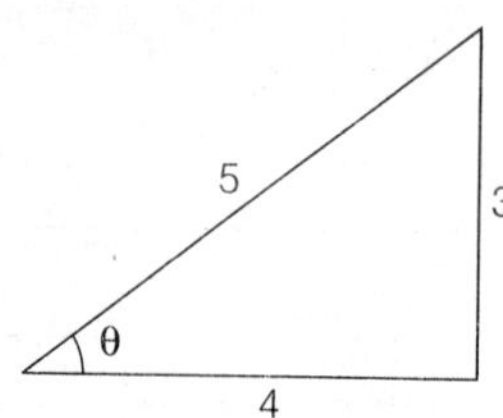

$$t_2 = \frac{160\sec\theta - 120\tan\theta}{1}$$

$$= 160\sec\theta - 120\tan\theta$$

∴ Total time taken

$$t = t_1 + t_2 = (200\sec\theta - 120\tan\theta)$$

For t to be minimum, $\frac{dt}{d\theta} = 0$

or $200\sec\theta\tan\theta - 120\sec^2\theta = 0$

or $\theta = \sin^{-1}(3/5)$

(b) $t_{\min} = 200\sec\theta - 120\tan\theta$ (where, $\sin\theta = \frac{3}{5}$)

$$= 200 \times \frac{5}{4} - 120 \times \frac{3}{4}$$

$= 250 - 90 = 160$ s $= 2$ min 40 s **Ans.**

10. Given that $|\mathbf{v}_{br}| = v_y = \frac{dy}{dt} = u$ ...(i)

$$|\mathbf{v}_r| = v_x = \frac{dx}{dt} = \left(\frac{2v_0}{c}\right)y \quad ...(ii)$$

From Eqs. (i) and (ii) we have, $\frac{dy}{dx} = \frac{uc}{2v_0 y}$

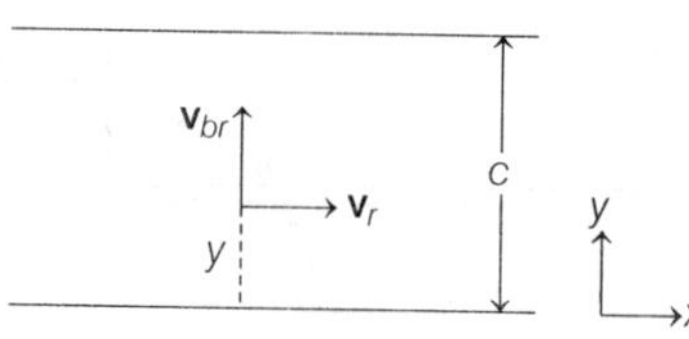

or $\int_0^y y\,dy = \frac{uc}{2v_0}\int_0^x dx$

or $y^2 = \frac{ucx}{v_0}$ **Ans.**

At $y = \frac{c}{2}$, $x = \frac{cv_0}{4u}$

or $x_{\text{net}} = 2x = \frac{cv_0}{2u}$ **Ans.**

11. (a) Let $\mathbf{v}_{br}$ be the velocity of boatman relative to river, $\mathbf{v}_r$ the velocity of river and $\mathbf{v}_b$ is the absolute velocity of boatman. Then,

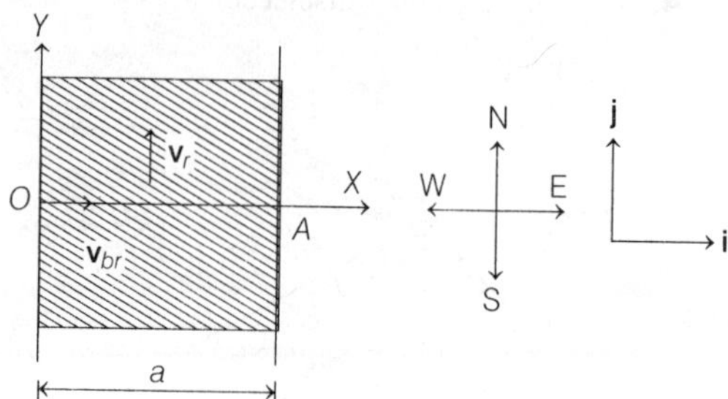

$$\mathbf{v}_b = \mathbf{v}_{br} + \mathbf{v}_r$$

Given, $|\mathbf{v}_{br}| = v$

and $|\mathbf{v}_r| = u$

Now $u = v_y = \frac{dy}{dt} = x(a - x)\frac{v}{a^2}$ ...(i)

and $v = v_x = \frac{dx}{dt} = v$ ...(ii)

Dividing Eq. (i) by Eq. (ii), we get

$$\frac{dy}{dx} = \frac{x(a-x)}{a^2}$$

or $dy = \frac{x(a-x)}{a^2}dx$

or $\int_0^y dy = \int_0^x \frac{x(a-x)}{a^2}dx$

or $y = \frac{x^2}{2a} - \frac{x^3}{3a^2}$ ...(iii)

This is the desired equation of trajectory.

(b) Time taken to cross the river is

$$t = \frac{a}{v_x} = \frac{a}{v}$$

(c) When the boatman reaches the opposite side, $x = a$ or $v_y = 0$ [from Eq. (i)]

Hence, resultant velocity of boatman is v along positive x-axis or due east.

(d) From Eq. (iii)

$$y = \frac{a^2}{2a} - \frac{a^3}{3a^2} = \frac{a}{6}$$

At $x = a$ (at opposite bank)

Hence, displacement of boatman will be

$$\mathbf{s} = x\,\hat{\mathbf{i}} + y\,\hat{\mathbf{j}}$$

or $\qquad \mathbf{s} = a\hat{\mathbf{i}} + \frac{a}{6}\hat{\mathbf{j}}$

12. (a) Since, the resultant velocity is always perpendicular to the line joining boat and R, the boat is moving in a circle of radius 2ω and centre at R.

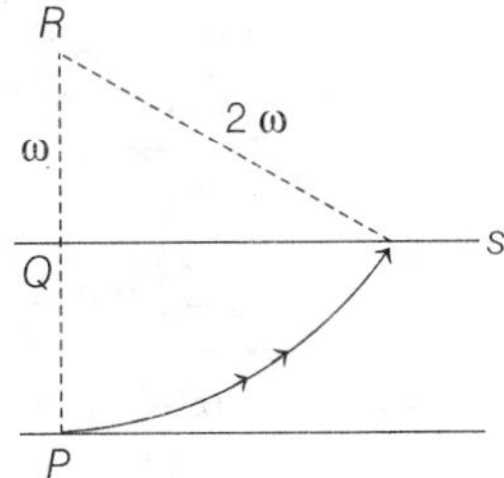

(b) Drifting $= Qs = \sqrt{4\omega^2 - \omega^2} = \sqrt{3}\omega$.

(c) Suppose at any arbitrary time, the boat is at point B.

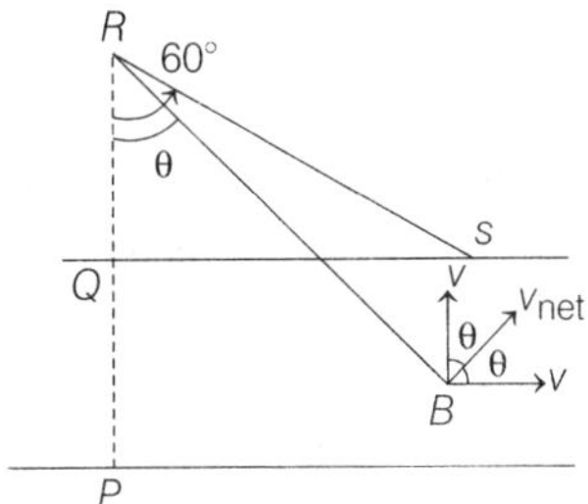

$$V_{net} = 2v\cos\theta$$

$$\frac{d\theta}{dt} = \frac{V_{net}}{2\omega} = \frac{v\cos\theta}{\omega}$$

or $\qquad \frac{\omega}{v}\sec\theta\, d\theta = dt$

$\therefore \qquad \int_0^t dt = \frac{\omega}{v}\int_0^{60^\circ}\sec\theta\, d\theta$

$\therefore \qquad t = \frac{\omega}{v}[\ln(\sec\theta + \tan\theta)]_0^{60^\circ}$

or $\qquad t = \frac{1.317\omega}{v}$ **Ans.**

13. For $0 < s \le 60$ m

$$v = \frac{12}{60}s + 3 = 3 + \frac{s}{5}$$

$$\frac{dv}{dt} = \left(\frac{1}{5}\right)\cdot\frac{ds}{dt}$$

$$= \frac{1}{5}(v) = \frac{1}{5}\left(3 + \frac{s}{5}\right) = \frac{3}{5} + \frac{s}{25} \qquad \ldots(i)$$

or $\qquad a = \frac{3}{5} + \frac{s}{25}$

i.e. a-s graph is a straight line.

At $s = 0$,

$$a = \frac{3}{5}\text{ m/s}^2 = 0.6\text{ m/s}^2$$

and at $\quad s = 60$ m, $\quad a = 3.0\text{ m/s}^2$

For $\qquad s > 60$ m

$\qquad v = $ constant

$\therefore \qquad a = 0$

Therefore, the corresponding a-s graph is shown in figure.

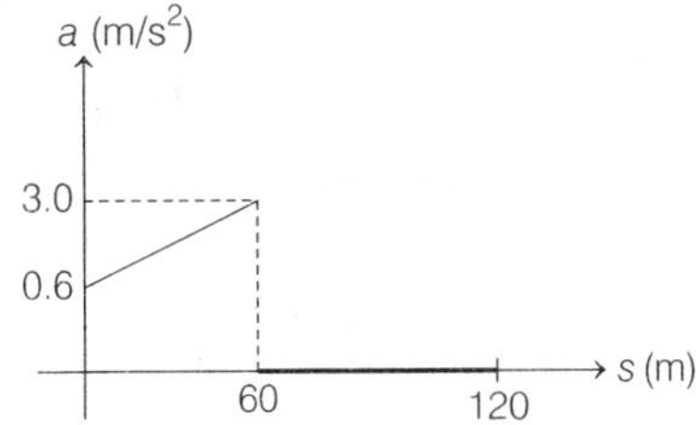

From Eq. (i), $\frac{dv}{dt} = \frac{v}{5}$

or $\qquad \int_3^v \frac{dv}{v} = \frac{1}{5}\int_0^t dt$

$$\ln\left(\frac{v}{3}\right) = \frac{t}{5}$$

$\therefore \qquad v = 3e^{t/5}$

or $\qquad \int_0^{60} ds = 3\int_0^{t_1} e^{t/5}\, dt$

$$60 = 15(e^{t_1/5} - 1)$$

or $\qquad t_1 = 8.0$ s

Time taken to travel next 60 m with speed 15m/s will be $\frac{60}{15} = 4$ s

$\therefore$ Total time $= 12.0$ s **Ans.**

14. From the graph,

$$a = 22.5 - \frac{22.5}{150}\cdot s$$

or $\qquad \int_0^v v\cdot dv = \int_0^{60}\left(22.5 - \frac{22.5}{150}\times s\right)ds$

$\therefore \qquad \frac{v^2}{2} = 22.5\times 60 - \frac{22.5}{150}\times\frac{(60)^2}{2}$

$\therefore \qquad v = 46.47$ m/s **Ans.**

15. (a) $u_x = 3$ m/s

$$a_x = -1.0\text{ m/s}^2$$

Maximum x-coordinate is attained after time

$$t = \left|\frac{u_x}{a_x}\right| = 3\text{ s}$$

At this instant $v_x = 0$ and

$v_y = u_y + a_y t = 0 - 0.5 \times 3 = -1.5$ m/s

$\therefore \quad \mathbf{v} = (-1.5\,\hat{\mathbf{j}})$ m/s **Ans.**

(b) $x = u_x t + \frac{1}{2} a_x t^2$

$= 3 \times 3 + \frac{1}{2}(-1.0)(3)^2 = 4.5$ m

$y = u_y t + \frac{1}{2} a_y t^2$

$= 0 - \frac{1}{2}(0.5)(3)^2 = -2.25$ m

$\therefore \quad \mathbf{r} = (4.5\,\hat{\mathbf{i}} - 2.25\,\hat{\mathbf{j}})$ m **Ans.**

16. (b) $\mathbf{v} = v_x\,\hat{\mathbf{i}} + v_y\,\hat{\mathbf{j}}$ and $\mathbf{a} = a_x\,\hat{\mathbf{i}} + a_y\,\hat{\mathbf{j}}$

$\mathbf{v} \cdot \mathbf{a} = v_x a_x + v_y a_y$

Further $v = \sqrt{v_x^2 + v_y^2}$

$\therefore \quad \frac{\mathbf{v} \cdot \mathbf{a}}{v} = \frac{v_x a_x + v_y a_y}{\sqrt{v_x^2 + v_y^2}}$

$= \frac{dv}{dt} = a_t$

or component of **a** parallel to **v**

= tangential acceleration.

17. (a) $v_{br} = 4$ m/s, $v_r = 2$ m/s

$\tan\theta = \frac{BC}{AB} = \frac{|\mathbf{v}_r|}{|\mathbf{v}_{br}|} = \frac{2}{4} = \frac{1}{2}$

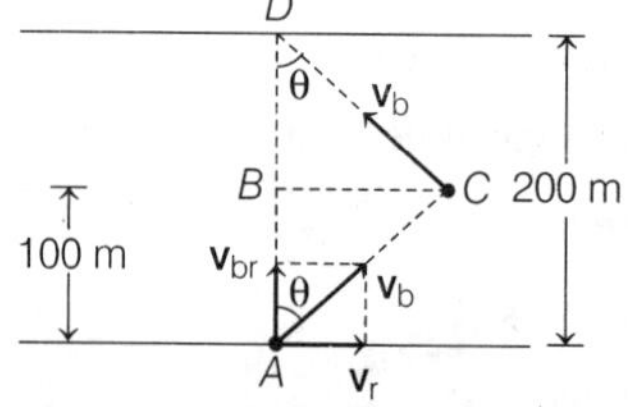

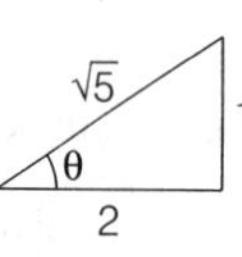

In this case, $\mathbf{v}_b$ should be along CD.

$\therefore \quad v_r \cos\theta = v_{br} \sin\alpha$

$2\left(\frac{2}{\sqrt{5}}\right) = 4 \sin\alpha$

or $\quad \sin\alpha = \frac{1}{\sqrt{5}}$

$\therefore \quad \alpha = \theta = \tan^{-1}\left(\frac{1}{2}\right)$

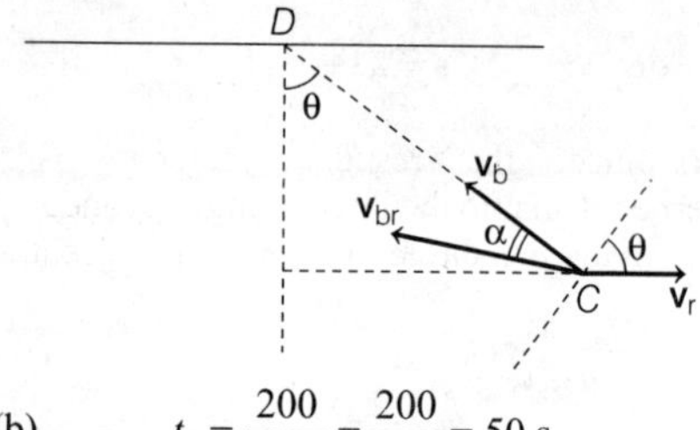

(b) $t_1 = \frac{200}{|\mathbf{v}_{br}|} = \frac{200}{4} = 50$ s

$DC = DB \sec\theta = (100)\frac{\sqrt{5}}{2} = 50\sqrt{5}$ m

$|\mathbf{v}_b| = |\mathbf{v}_{br}| \cos\alpha - |\mathbf{v}_r| \sin\theta$

$= 4\left(\frac{2}{\sqrt{5}}\right) - 2\left(\frac{1}{\sqrt{5}}\right) = \frac{6}{\sqrt{5}}$ m/s

$\therefore \quad t_2 = \frac{t_1}{2} + \frac{DC}{|\mathbf{v}_b|} = 25 + \frac{50\sqrt{5}}{\frac{6}{\sqrt{5}}} = \frac{200}{3}$ s

or $\quad \frac{t_2}{t_1} = \frac{4}{3}$ **Ans.**

18. $\mathbf{v}_b$ = velocity of boatman = $\mathbf{v}_{br} + \mathbf{v}_r$

and $\quad \mathbf{v}_c$ = velocity of child = $\mathbf{v}_r$

$\therefore \quad \mathbf{v}_{bc} = \mathbf{v}_b - \mathbf{v}_c = \mathbf{v}_{br}$

$\mathbf{v}_{bc}$ should be along BC.

i.e. $\mathbf{v}_{br}$ should be along BC,

where, $\quad \tan\alpha = \frac{0.6}{0.8} = \frac{3}{4}$

or $\quad \alpha = 37°$ **Ans.**

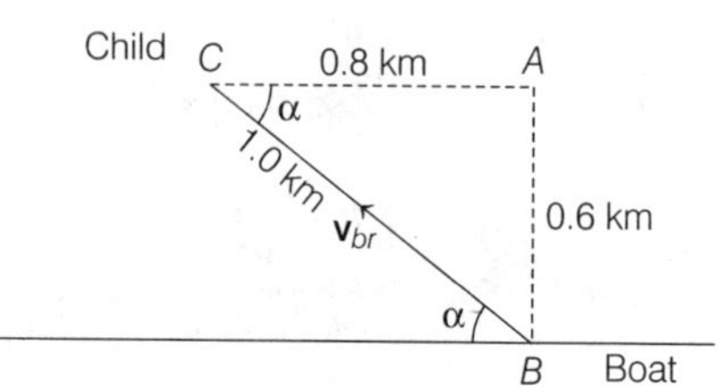

Further $\quad t = \frac{BC}{|\mathbf{v}_{br}|} = \frac{1}{20}$ h

$= 3$ min **Ans.**

19. In order that the moving launch is always on the straight line AB, the components of velocity of the current and of the launch in the direction perpendicular to AB should be equal, i.e.

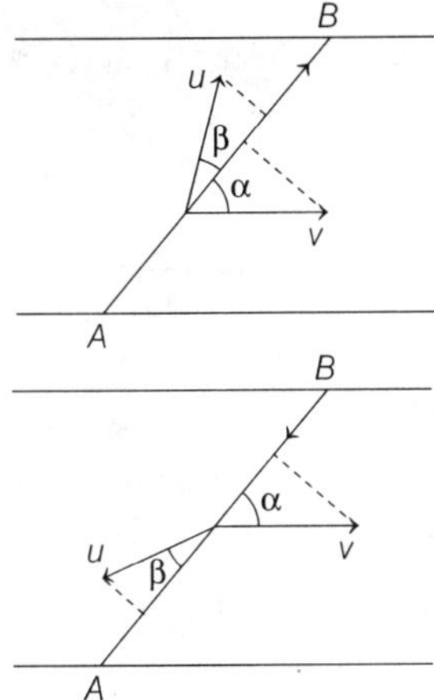

$$u \sin \beta = v \sin \alpha \qquad \ldots(\text{i})$$

$$S = AB = (u \cos \beta + v \cos \alpha) t_1 \qquad \ldots(\text{ii})$$

Further $\quad BA = (u \cos \beta - v \cos \alpha) t_2 \qquad \ldots(\text{iii})$

$$t_1 + t_2 = t \qquad \ldots(\text{iv})$$

Solving these equations after proper substitution, we get

$$u = 8 \text{ m/s} \quad \text{and} \quad \beta = 12° \qquad \textbf{Ans.}$$

20. Here, absolute velocity of hail stones **v** before colliding with wind screens is vertically downwards and velocity of hail stones with respect to cars after collision $\mathbf{v}'_{HC}$ is vertically upwards. Collision is elastic, hence, velocity of hail stones with respect to cars before collision $\mathbf{v}_{HC}$ and after collision $\mathbf{v}'_{HC}$ will make equal angles with the normal to the wind screen.

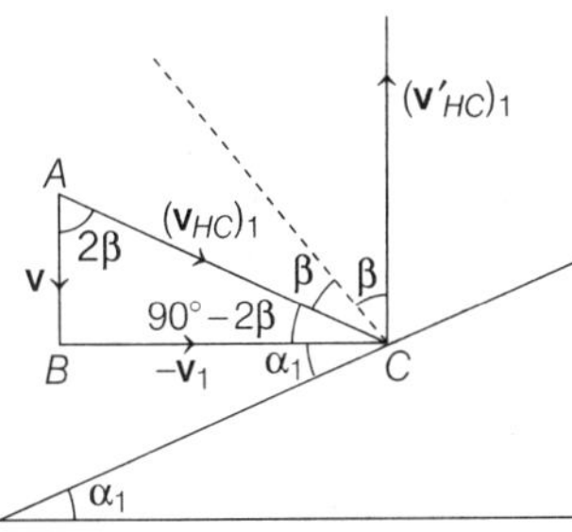

$(\mathbf{v}_{HC})_1 =$ velocity of hail stones – velocity of car 1

$= \mathbf{v} - \mathbf{v}_1$

From the figure, we can see that

$$\beta + 90° - 2\beta + \alpha_1 = 90°$$

or $\quad \alpha_1 = \beta \quad$ or $\quad 2\beta = 2\alpha_1$

In ΔABC, $\tan 2\beta = \tan 2\alpha_1 = \dfrac{v_1}{v} \qquad \ldots(\text{i})$

Similarly, we can show that

$$\tan 2\alpha_2 = \frac{v_2}{v} \qquad \ldots(\text{ii})$$

From Eqs. (i) and (ii), we get

$$\frac{v_1}{v_2} = \frac{\tan 2\alpha_1}{\tan 2\alpha_2} = \frac{\tan 60°}{\tan 30°} = \frac{\sqrt{3}}{1/\sqrt{3}} = 3$$

$\therefore \quad \dfrac{v_1}{v_2} = 3 \qquad$ **Ans.**

21. $a_x = \dfrac{dv_x}{dt} = -\dfrac{kv \cos \theta}{m} = -\dfrac{k}{m} v_x$

$\therefore \quad \dfrac{dv_x}{v_x} = -\dfrac{k}{m} dt$

or $\quad \displaystyle\int_{v_0 \cos \theta_0}^{v_x} \frac{dv_x}{v_x} = -\frac{k}{m} \int_0^t dt$

or $\quad v_x = v_0 \cos \theta_0 \, e^{-\frac{k}{m} t} \qquad \ldots(\text{i})$

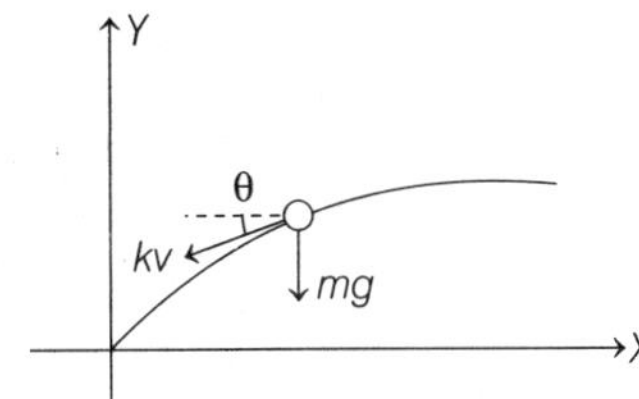

Similarly,

$$a_y = \frac{dv_y}{dt} = -\frac{kv \sin \theta}{m} - g = -\left(\frac{k}{m} v_y + g\right)$$

or $\quad \displaystyle\int_{v_0 \sin \theta_0}^{v_y} \frac{dv_y}{\frac{k}{m} v_y + g} = -\int_0^t dt$

or $\quad \dfrac{m}{k} \left[\ln \left(\dfrac{k}{m} v_y + g \right) \right]_{v_0 \sin \theta_0}^{v_y} = -t$

or $\quad \dfrac{\left(\dfrac{k}{m} v_y + g\right)}{\left(\dfrac{k}{m} v_0 \sin \theta_0 + g\right)} = e^{-\frac{k}{m} t}$

or $\quad v_y = \dfrac{m}{k} \left[\left(\dfrac{k}{m} v_0 \sin \theta_0 + g \right) e^{-\frac{k}{m} t} - g \right] \qquad \ldots(\text{ii})$

(b) Eq. (i) can be written as

$$\frac{dx}{dt} = v_0 \cos \theta_0 \, e^{-\frac{k}{m} t}$$

or $\quad \displaystyle\int_0^x dx = v_0 \cos \theta_0 \int_0^t e^{-\frac{k}{m} t} dt$

or $\quad x = \dfrac{m v_0 \cos \theta_0}{k} [1 - e^{-\frac{k}{m} t}]$

$$x_m = \frac{m v_0 \cos \theta_0}{k}$$

at $\quad t = \infty \qquad$ **Ans.**

Integer Type Questions

22. $\because v^2 = u^2 + 2as$

$$\Rightarrow \quad 0^2 = \left(72 \times \frac{5}{18}\right)^2 - 2 \times 2 s_0$$

$$\therefore \quad s_0 = \frac{400}{4} = 100 \text{ m}$$

Thus, stopping distance

$$= \left(72 \times \frac{5}{18}\right) \times 0.2 + s_0$$

$$= 4 + 100 = 104 \text{ m} = 13x$$

$$\therefore \quad x = \frac{104}{13} = 8$$

23. If he starts from home at 6 pm, he reaches at coaching at 6:20 pm. According to the question, he reaches at coaching 8 min before his daily routine. It means he starts at 5:52 pm. and will reach at the coaching at 6:12 pm. Let the distance between home and turning point 'C' is l. The distance between the coaching and home is $L = 20\,v$.

According to the problem,

$$\frac{l}{v} + \frac{l}{v} + \frac{l}{v} + \frac{L-l}{v} = (6:20 - 5:52) + 10 \text{ min}$$

or $$\frac{2l}{v} + \frac{L}{v} = 38 \text{ min}$$

or $$\frac{2l}{v} + \frac{20v}{v} = 38 \text{ min}$$

or $$\frac{2l}{v} = 18 \text{ min} \quad \text{or} \quad \frac{l}{v} = 9 \text{ min}$$

The fraction is $\frac{l}{L} = \frac{9v}{20v} = \frac{9}{20} = \frac{x}{20}$

$$\therefore \quad x = 9$$

24. $\because \quad a = -kv \quad \text{or} \quad \frac{dv}{dt} = -kv$

or $$\int_{v_0}^{v} \frac{dv}{v} = -k \int_0^t dt$$

or $$[\ln v]_{v_0}^{v} = -kt$$

or $$\ln v - \ln v_0 = -kt \quad \text{or} \quad \ln \frac{v}{v_0} = -kt$$

or $$\frac{v}{v_0} = e^{-kt}$$

For $t = t_0,\ v = v_0 - v_0 \times \frac{50}{100} = \frac{v_0}{2}$

$$\therefore \quad \frac{v_0}{2} = v_0 e^{-kt_0}$$

or $\frac{1}{2} = e^{-kt_0}$ or $\ln \frac{1}{2} = -kt_0$ or $k = \frac{\ln 2}{t_0}$

$$\therefore \quad v = v_0 e^{-kt} \quad \text{or} \quad v = v_0 e^{-\frac{\ln 2}{t_0} t}$$

or $\ln v = \ln v_0 - \frac{\ln 2}{t_0} t$ or $\ln \frac{v}{v_0} = -\frac{\ln 2}{4 \ln 2} t$

or $\ln \frac{v}{v_0} = -\frac{t}{4}$ or $\frac{v}{v_0} = e^{-\frac{t}{4}}$

$$\therefore \quad v = v_0 e^{-\frac{t}{4}} = 13.5\, e^{-\frac{4}{4}} = \frac{13.5}{e} = \frac{13.5}{2.7} = 5 \text{ ms}^{-1}$$

25. The acceleration of ball at instant t is

$$a = g - bv \quad \because \quad a = g - bv$$

or $\frac{dv}{dt} = g - bv$ or $\int_0^v \frac{dv}{g - bv} = \int_0^t dt$

or $$-\frac{1}{b} [\ln (g - bv)]_0^v = [t]_0^t$$

or $$[\ln (g - bv) - \ln g] = -bt$$

or $$\ln \frac{g - bv}{g} = -bt$$

or $1 - \frac{bv}{g} = e^{-bt}$ or $\frac{bv}{g} = 1 - e^{-bt}$

or $$v = \frac{g}{b}(1 - e^{-bt}) = \frac{10}{10}\left(1 - \frac{1}{e}\right)$$

$$= \left(\frac{e-1}{e}\right) = \frac{2.7 - 1}{2.7} = \frac{7}{27} = \frac{n}{27}$$

$$\therefore \quad n = 7$$

26. Here, $a = -g - bv$ or $\frac{dv}{dt} = -g - bv$

or $$\int_{v_0}^{0} \frac{dv}{g + bv} = -\int_0^{t_0} dt$$

or $$\frac{1}{b} [\ln (g + bv)]_{v_0}^{0} = -t_0$$

or $$\frac{1}{b} [\ln g - \ln (g + bv_0)] = -t_0$$

or $-\frac{1}{b} \ln \frac{g + bv_0}{g} = -t_0$ or $\ln \left(1 + \frac{bv_0}{g}\right) = bt_0$

$$\therefore \quad 1 + \frac{bv_0}{g} = e^{bt_0} \quad \Rightarrow \quad \therefore \quad e^{bt_0} = 1 + 2 = 3$$

27. $\because a = t - x$ or $\frac{da}{dt} = 1 - \frac{dx}{dt}$

or $\frac{da}{dt} = 1 - v$ or $\frac{d^2 a}{dt^2} = -\frac{dv}{dt} = -a$

The solution of this differential equation is $a = a_0 \sin (\omega t + \phi)$ where, $\omega = 1$ unit

At $t = 0, n = 0 \Rightarrow a = 0$

$$\therefore \quad 0 = a_0 \sin (\omega \times 0 + \phi)$$

$\therefore \quad \phi = 0$

$\therefore \quad a = a_0 \sin t \quad \text{or} \quad \frac{dv}{dt} = a_0 \sin t$

or $\int_0^v dv = a_0 \int_0^t \sin t \, dt$

or $v = a_0[-\cos t]_0^t = -a_0[\cos t - 1]$

$$v = a_0(1 - \cos t) = 2\left(1 - \cos\frac{\pi}{3}\right)$$

$$= \left(2 \times \frac{1}{2}\right) = 1 \text{ ms}^{-1}$$

28. $\because v = a \sin \omega t$

or $v = \pi \sin \frac{2\pi}{2} t$ or $v = \pi \sin \pi t$

The speed-time graph is

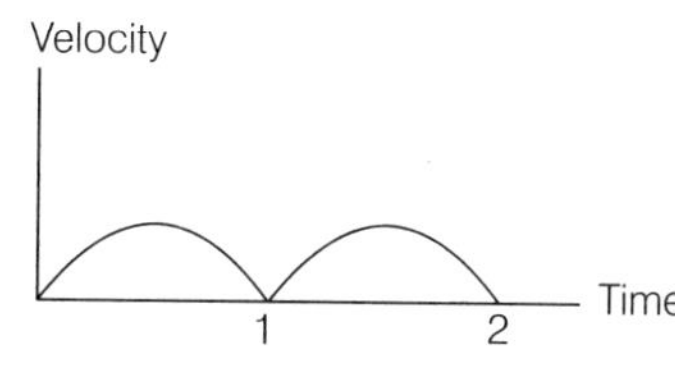

$\because \quad \text{Speed} = |v|$

$\therefore$ Distance $= \int_0^2 |v| \, dt = 2\int_0^1 |v| \, dt$

$$= \frac{2\pi}{\pi}[-\cos \pi t]_0^t = \frac{2\pi}{\pi} \times 2 = 4 \text{ m}$$

29. Here, $OA = 25$ cm and $OB = 20$ cm

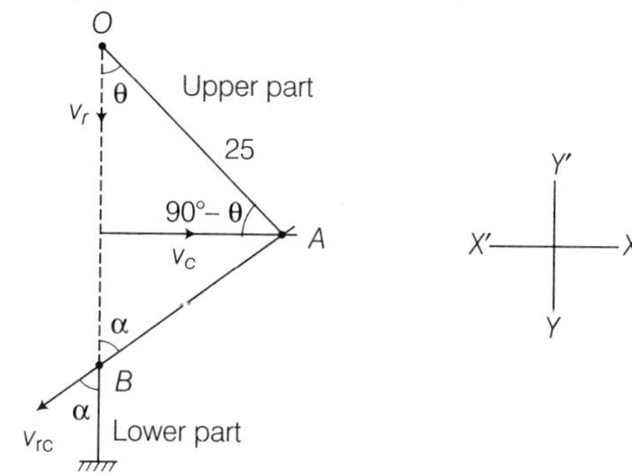

Here, $\mathbf{v}_{rc} = \mathbf{v}_r - \mathbf{v}_c$

$v_{rc} \cos \alpha \hat{\mathbf{j}} - v_{rc} \sin \alpha \hat{\mathbf{i}} = 20\hat{\mathbf{j}} - 20\sqrt{3}\hat{\mathbf{i}}$

$\Rightarrow \quad \tan \alpha = \frac{20\sqrt{3}}{20}$

$\Rightarrow \quad \alpha = 60°$

$\therefore \quad \frac{25}{\sin \alpha} = \frac{20}{\sin(90° - \theta + 90° - \alpha)}$

$\Rightarrow \quad \frac{25}{\sin 60°} = \frac{20}{\sin(60° + \theta)}$

$\Rightarrow \quad \sin(60° + \theta) = \frac{10\sqrt{3}}{25}$

$$= \frac{2\sqrt{3}}{5} = \frac{\sqrt{12}}{5}$$

$\therefore \quad \sin\left(\frac{\pi}{3} + \theta\right) = \frac{\sqrt{12}}{5} = \frac{\sqrt{12}}{n}$

$\therefore \quad n = 5$

30. $\therefore v_x = ky$ and $v_y = 5$

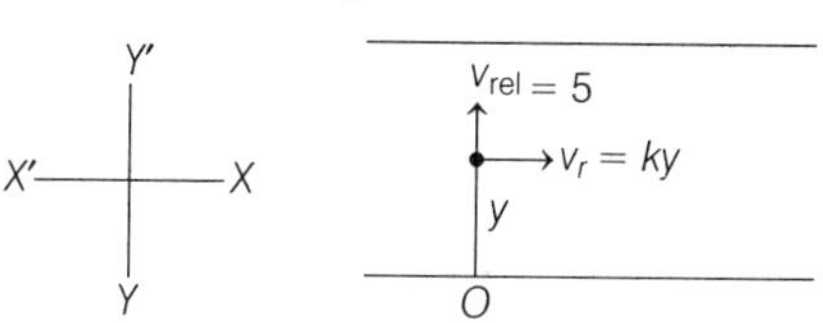

$\therefore \quad y = 5t$, At middle point, $50 = 5t$

$\therefore \quad t = 10$ s

$\because \quad v_x = ky$

At middle, $v_x = 2$

$\therefore \quad k = \frac{2}{50}$

$\therefore \quad v_x = \frac{2}{50} y = \frac{y}{25} = \frac{5t}{25} = \frac{t}{5}$

$\Rightarrow \quad \frac{dx}{dt} = \frac{t}{5}$

$\Rightarrow \quad \int_0^{x_0} dx = \int_0^{10} \frac{t}{5} dt$

$\therefore \quad x_0 = 10$ m upto middle

$\therefore$ Total drifting $= 2 \times 10 = 20$ m

$\therefore \quad 5n = 20, \quad n = 4$

7. Projectile Motion

INTRODUCTORY EXERCISE 7.1

1. $\mathbf{v}_1 \cdot \mathbf{v}_2 = 0$

$\Rightarrow \quad (\mathbf{u}_1 + \mathbf{a}_1 t)\cdot(\mathbf{u}_2 + \mathbf{a}_2 t) = 0$

$\Rightarrow \quad (10\hat{\mathbf{i}} - 10t\hat{\mathbf{j}})\cdot(-20\hat{\mathbf{i}} - 10t\hat{\mathbf{j}}) = 0$

$\Rightarrow \quad -200 + 100t^2 = 0$

$\Rightarrow \quad t = \sqrt{2}\ \text{s}$

2. It is two dimensional motion.

3. The uniform acceleration is **g**.

4. $\mathbf{u} = (40\hat{\mathbf{i}} + 30\hat{\mathbf{j}})$ m/s, $\mathbf{a} = (-10\hat{\mathbf{j}})$ m/s^2, $t = 2$ s

Now, $\mathbf{v} = \mathbf{u} + \mathbf{a}t$ and $\mathbf{s} = \mathbf{u}t + \frac{1}{2}\mathbf{a}t^2$

5. $u_x = u_y = 20$ m/s, $a_y = -10$ m/s^2

$$s_y = u_y t + \frac{1}{2} a_y t^2$$

$\Rightarrow \quad -25 = 20t - \frac{1}{2} \times 10 \times t^2$

Solving this equation, we get the positive value of,

$$t = 5\ \text{s}$$

Now apply, $\mathbf{v} = \mathbf{u} + \mathbf{a}t$ and $s_x = u_x t$

INTRODUCTORY EXERCISE 7.2

1. $\mathbf{u} = 40\hat{\mathbf{i}} + 40\hat{\mathbf{j}}$

$$\mathbf{a} = -10\hat{\mathbf{j}}$$

$$t = 2\ \text{s}$$

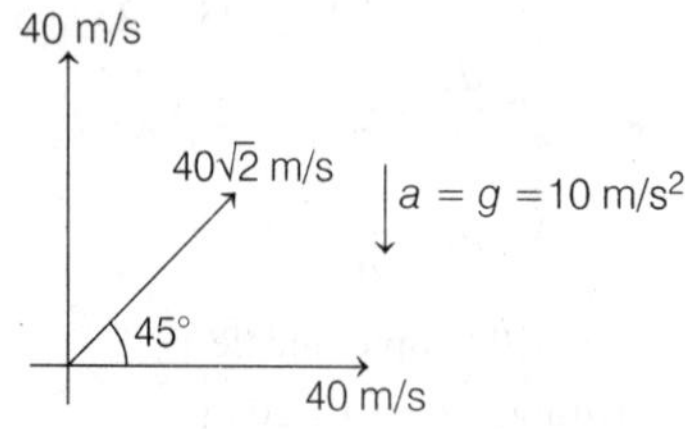

(a) Apply $\mathbf{v} = \mathbf{u} + \mathbf{a}t$ as $\mathbf{a}$ = constant

(b) Apply $\mathbf{s} = \mathbf{u}t + \frac{1}{2}\mathbf{a}t^2$

3. Average velocity

$$= \frac{s}{t} = \frac{R}{T} = \frac{(u_x T)}{T} = u_x$$

$= u \cos\alpha$

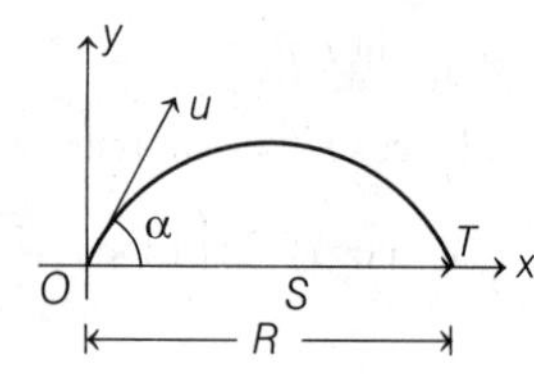

4. $\Delta\mathbf{v} = \mathbf{v}_f - \mathbf{v}_i$

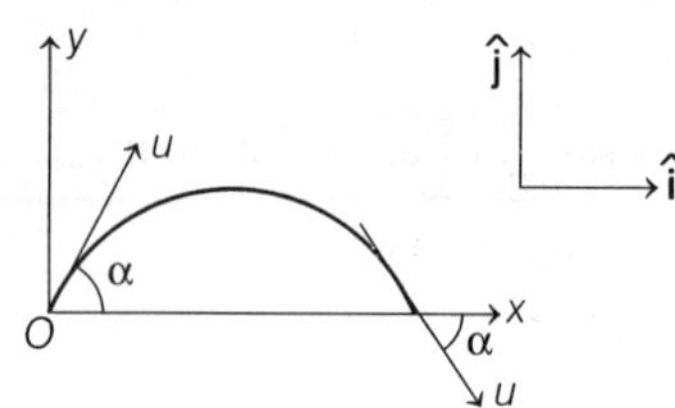

$= (u\cos\alpha\,\hat{\mathbf{i}} - u\sin\alpha\,\hat{\mathbf{j}}) - (u\cos\alpha\,\hat{\mathbf{i}} + u\sin\alpha\,\hat{\mathbf{j}})$

$= (-2u\sin\alpha)\,\hat{\mathbf{j}}$

Therefore, change in velocity is $2u\sin\alpha$ in downward direction.

5. (a) $R = \dfrac{u^2 \sin 2\theta}{g}$, $\quad H = \dfrac{u^2\sin^2\theta}{2g}$

and $\quad T = \dfrac{2u\sin\theta}{g}$

Here, $\quad u = 20\sqrt{2}$ m/s and $\theta = 45°$

(b) $\mathbf{v} = \mathbf{u} + \mathbf{a}t$

where, $\quad \mathbf{u} = (20\hat{\mathbf{i}} + 20\hat{\mathbf{j}})$ m/s

and $\quad \mathbf{a} = (-10\hat{\mathbf{j}})$ m/s^2

(c) Horizontal component remains unchanged $(= 20\hat{\mathbf{i}})$ and vertical component is reversed in direction $(= -20\hat{\mathbf{j}})$

$$\mathbf{v} = (20\hat{\mathbf{i}} - 20\hat{\mathbf{j}})\ \text{m/s}$$ **Ans.**

6. (a) Since, acceleration is constant. Therefore,

$$\mathbf{a}_{av} = \mathbf{a} = \mathbf{g} = (-10\hat{\mathbf{j}}) = \frac{\Delta\mathbf{v}}{\Delta t}$$

$\therefore \quad \Delta\mathbf{v} = (-10\hat{\mathbf{j}})(\Delta t) = (-10\hat{\mathbf{j}})(3)$

$= (-10\hat{\mathbf{j}})(3) = (-30\hat{\mathbf{j}})$ m/s

$\therefore$ Change in velocity is 30 m/s, vertically downwards. **Ans.**

(b) $\mathbf{v}_{av} = \dfrac{\mathbf{s}}{t} = \dfrac{\mathbf{u}t + \frac{1}{2}\mathbf{a}t^2}{t} = \mathbf{u} + \dfrac{1}{2}\mathbf{a}t$

$$= (20\hat{i} + 20\hat{j}) + \frac{1}{2}(-10\hat{j})(3)$$

$$= (20\hat{i} + 5\hat{j}) \text{ m/s}$$

$$\therefore |v_{av}| = \sqrt{(20)^2 + (5)^2}$$

$$= 20.62 \text{ m/s}$$ **Ans.**

7. $T = \frac{2u \sin\theta}{g} = \frac{2 \times 20 \times \frac{1}{\sqrt{2}}}{10} = 2\sqrt{2}$ s

$$R = \frac{u^2 \sin 2\theta}{g} = \frac{(20)^2 \sin 90^\circ}{10}$$

$$= 40 \text{ m}$$

Now, the remaining horizontal distance is $(50 - 40)$ m $= 10$ m. Let v is the speed of player, then

$$vT = 10$$

or $$v = \frac{10}{T} = \frac{10}{2\sqrt{2}} = \frac{5}{\sqrt{2}} \text{ m/s}$$ **Ans.**

8. (a) Initial velocity is horizontal. So, in vertical direction it is a case of free fall.

$$t = \sqrt{\frac{2h}{g}} = \sqrt{\frac{2 \times 100}{10}}$$

$$= \sqrt{20} \text{ s}$$

(b) $x = u_x t = 20\sqrt{20}$ m

(c) $v_x = u_x = 20$ m/s

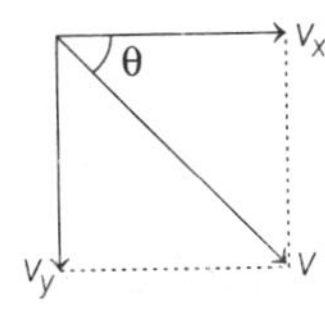

$$v_y = u_y + a_y t$$

$$= 0 - 10\sqrt{20}$$

$$= -10\sqrt{20} \text{ m/s}$$

$$v = \sqrt{v_x^2 + v_y^2} = 49 \text{ m/s}$$

$$\theta = \tan^{-1}\left(\frac{v_y}{v_x}\right) = \tan^{-1}(\sqrt{5})$$

9. $R = \frac{u^2 \sin 60^\circ}{g} = 3$ km

$$\Rightarrow \quad \frac{u^2}{g} = R_{max} = \frac{3}{\sin 60^\circ}$$

$$= 2\sqrt{3} \text{ km}$$

Since, $R_{max} < 5$ km

So, it can't hit the target at 5 km.

10. Comparing with,

$$y = x\tan\theta - \frac{gx^2}{2u^2}(1 + \tan^2\theta)$$

$$\tan\theta = b, g = a$$

and $$\frac{g}{2u^2}(1 + \tan^2\theta) = c$$

$$\therefore \quad \frac{a(1 + b^2)}{2u^2} = c$$

$$\therefore \quad u = \sqrt{\frac{a(1 + b^2)}{2c}}$$

INTRODUCTORY EXERCISE 7.3

1. $T = \frac{2u \sin(\alpha - \beta)}{g \cos\beta}$

$$= \frac{(2)(20\sqrt{2})\sin(45^\circ - 30^\circ)}{(10)(\cos 30^\circ)} = 1.69 \text{ s}$$

$$R = \frac{u^2}{g\cos^2\beta}[\sin(2\alpha - \beta) - \sin\beta]$$

$$= \frac{(20\sqrt{2})^2}{(10)\cos^2 30^\circ}[\sin(2 \times 45^\circ - 30^\circ) - \sin 30^\circ]$$

$$= 39 \text{m}$$

2. $T = \frac{2u \sin(\alpha + \beta)}{g\cos\beta}$

$$= \frac{2 \times 20\sqrt{2}\sin(45^\circ + 30^\circ)}{(10)\cos 30^\circ} \approx 6.31 \text{ s}$$

$$R = \frac{u^2}{g\cos^2\beta}[\sin(2\alpha + \beta) + \sin\beta]$$

$$= \frac{(20\sqrt{2})^2}{(10)\cos^2 30^\circ}[\sin(2 \times 45^\circ + 30^\circ) + \sin 30^\circ]$$

$$= 145.71 \text{ m}$$

3. Using the above equations with $\alpha = 0^\circ$

$$T = \frac{2(20)\sin 30^\circ}{(10)\cos 30^\circ} = 2.31 \text{ s}$$

$$R = \frac{(20)^2}{(10)\cos^2 30^\circ}[\sin 30^\circ + \sin 30^\circ]$$

$$= 53.33 \text{ m}$$

4. (a) Horizontal component of velocities of passenger and stone are same. Therefore relative velocity in horizontal direction is zero. Hence the relative motion is only in vertical direction.

(b) With respect to the man, stone has both velocity components, horizontal and vertical. Therefore, path of the stone is a projectile.

5. (a) $a_1 = a_2 = g$ (downwards)

$\therefore$ Relative acceleration = 0

(b) $\mathbf{u}_{12} = \mathbf{u}_1 - \mathbf{u}_2$

$= (20\hat{\mathbf{j}}) - (20\hat{\mathbf{i}} + 20\hat{\mathbf{j}})$

$= (-20\hat{\mathbf{i}})$ m/s

or 20 m/s in horizontal direction

(c) $\mathbf{u}_{12} = (-20\hat{\mathbf{i}})$ m/s is constant.

Therefore, relative motion is uniform.

$$\therefore \quad d = |\mathbf{u}_{12}|\, t = 20 \times 2 = 40\,\text{m}$$

6. The range is maximum at,

$$\alpha = \frac{\pi}{4} + \frac{\beta}{2} \quad \text{(given in the theory)}$$

$$= 45° + \frac{30°}{2} = 60°$$ **Ans.**

Exercises

LEVEL 1

Assertion and Reason

1. In the cases shown below path is straight line, even if **a** is constant

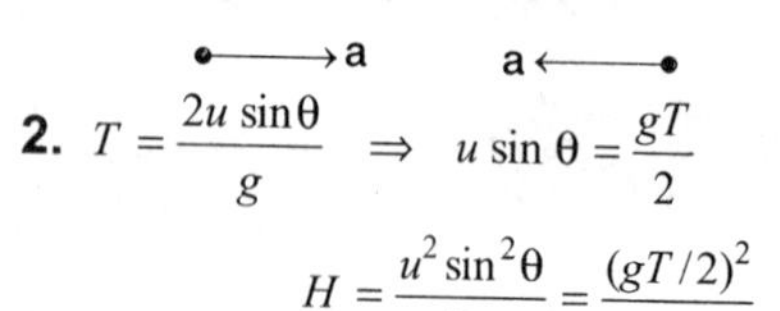

2. $T = \dfrac{2u\sin\theta}{g} \Rightarrow u\sin\theta = \dfrac{gT}{2}$

$$H = \frac{u^2\sin^2\theta}{2g} = \frac{(gT/2)^2}{2g}$$

or $H \propto T^2$

3.

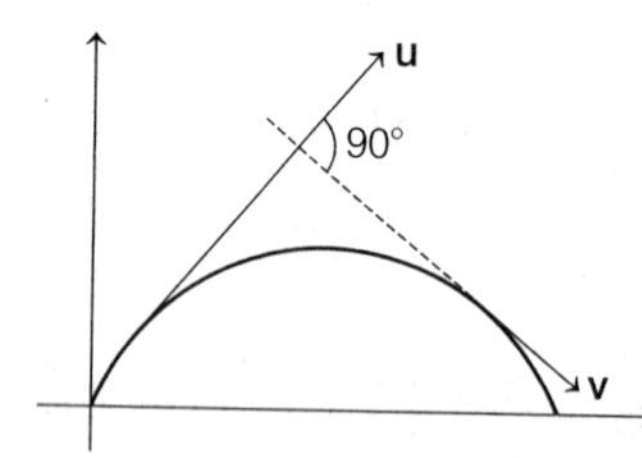

5. $T = \dfrac{2u\sin\theta}{g} = 4$

$\therefore \quad (u\sin\theta) = 20$ m/s

$$\therefore \quad H = \frac{u^2\sin^2\theta}{2g} = \frac{(20)^2}{20} = 20\text{ m}$$ **Ans.**

6. $H = \dfrac{u^2\sin^2\theta}{2g}$

or $u\sin\theta \propto \sqrt{H}$

$$\frac{(u\sin\theta)_1}{(u\sin\theta)_2} = \sqrt{\frac{4H}{H}} = 2$$

$$T = \frac{2u\sin\theta}{g} \Rightarrow T \propto u\sin\theta$$

$$\frac{T_1}{T_2} = \frac{(u\sin\theta)_1}{(u\sin\theta)_2} = \frac{2}{1}$$

$$R = u_x T$$

$$\therefore \quad \frac{R_1}{R_2} = \frac{(u_x)_1}{(u_x)_2}\cdot\frac{T_1}{T_2} = \left(\frac{1}{2}\right)\left(\frac{2}{1}\right) = 1$$

$$\therefore \quad R_1 = R_2$$

7. $v_x = u_x$

$$v_y = \pm\sqrt{u_y^2 - 2gh}$$

and $v = \sqrt{v_x^2 + v_y^2}$

and $u^2 = u_x^2 + u_y^2$

8. $h_1 = \dfrac{u^2}{2g},\ h_2 = \dfrac{u^2\sin^2 30°}{2g} = \dfrac{u^2}{8g}$

9. $t = \dfrac{2u_y}{g} = \dfrac{2\times 20}{10} = 4$ s

$$H = 20 + \frac{u_y^2}{2g} = 20 + \frac{(20)^2}{2\times 10}$$

$= 40$ m

Single Correct Option

1. Relative acceleration between two is zero. Therefore, relative motion is uniform.

$$\mathbf{u}_{12} = \mathbf{u}_1 + \mathbf{u}_2$$

$$= (20\hat{\mathbf{j}}) - (20\cos 30°\,\hat{\mathbf{i}} + 20\sin 30°\,\hat{\mathbf{j}})$$

$$= (10\hat{\mathbf{j}} - 10\sqrt{3}\,\hat{\mathbf{i}})$$

$$|\mathbf{u}_{12}| = \sqrt{(10)^2 + (10\sqrt{3})^2} = 20\text{ m/s}$$

$$\therefore \quad d = |\mathbf{u}_{12}|\, t = 24\text{ m}$$ **Ans.**

2. $H_\theta = \dfrac{u^2\sin^2\theta}{2g}$

$$H_{90-\theta} = \frac{u^2\sin^2(90-\theta)}{2g} = \frac{u^2\cos^2\theta}{2g}$$

$$\therefore \quad \frac{H_\theta}{H_{90-\theta}} = \frac{\sin^2\theta}{\cos^2\theta}$$

3. $R_\theta = \frac{R_{45°}}{2}$

$\therefore \quad \frac{u^2 \sin 2\theta}{g} = \frac{1}{2}\left(\frac{u^2}{g}\right)$

or $\quad \sin 2\theta = \frac{1}{2}$

$\therefore \quad 2\theta = 30°$

or $\quad \theta = 15°$

4. At 45°, range is maximum. At highest point, it has only horizontal component of velocity or 20 cos 45° ≈ 14 m/s.

5. $\mathbf{F} \cdot \mathbf{v} = 0 \Rightarrow \mathbf{F} \perp \mathbf{v}$

Hence path is parabola.

6. $v_x = u_x$

$\therefore \quad v \cos 30° = u \cos 60°$

or $\quad v = \frac{u}{\sqrt{3}}$

Velocity has become $\frac{1}{\sqrt{3}}$ times. Therefore, kinetic energy will become 1/3 times.

7. $T_1 = \frac{2u \sin\theta}{g}, \; T_2 = \frac{2u \cos\theta}{g}$

$$R = \frac{2(u \sin\theta)(u \cos\theta)}{g} = \frac{2\left(\frac{gT_1}{2}\right)\left(\frac{gT_2}{2}\right)}{g} = \frac{1}{2} g T_1 T_2 \qquad \textbf{Ans.}$$

8. $R_{max} = \frac{v_0^2}{g}$ at $\theta = 45°$

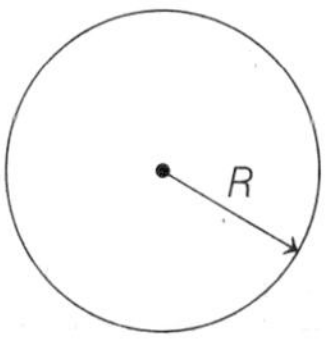

$\therefore \quad A_{max} = \pi R_{max}^2$

9. Maximum range is obtained at 45°

$\frac{u^2}{g} = 1.6$ or $u = 4$ m/s

$$T = \frac{2u \sin 45°}{g} = \frac{2 \times 4 \times (1/\sqrt{2})}{10} = 0.4\sqrt{2} \text{ s}$$

Number of jumps in given time,

$$n = \frac{t}{T} = \frac{10\sqrt{2}}{0.4\sqrt{2}} = 25$$

$\therefore$ Total distance travelled = 1.6 × 25 = 40 m **Ans.**

10. $H_1 = \frac{u^2 \sin^2\theta}{2g}$

$\therefore \quad 102 = \frac{(u^2)\sin^2 60°}{20}$

$\therefore \quad u = 52.2$ m/s

Other stone should be projected at 90° − θ or 30° from horizontal.

$$\therefore \quad H_2 = \frac{u^2 \sin^2 30°}{2g} = \frac{(52.2)^2 (1/4)}{20} = 34 \text{ m} \qquad \textbf{Ans.}$$

11. Using $s = ut + \frac{1}{2}at^2$ in vertical direction

$\therefore \quad -70 = (50 \sin 30°)\,t + \frac{1}{2}(-10)\,t^2$

On solving this equation, we get

$t = 7$ s **Ans.**

12. $S = \sqrt{H^2 + R^2/4}$

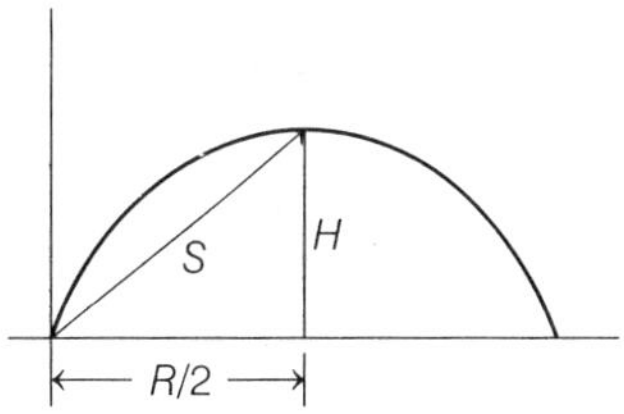

Average velocity $= \frac{S}{t} = \frac{S}{T/2} = \frac{2S}{T}$

13. Velocity of ball in the direction of train is also 30 m/s. So there is no relative motion in this direction. In perpendicular direction,

$$d = R = \frac{u^2 \sin 2\theta}{g} = \frac{(30)^2 \sin 90°}{10} = 90 \text{ m} \qquad \textbf{Ans.}$$

14. For maximum value of y

$\frac{dy}{dt} = 10 - 2t = 0$

$\Rightarrow \quad t = 5$ s

$y_{max} = (10)(5) - (5)^2$

$= 25$ m **Ans.**

15. $T = \dfrac{2u_y}{g}$

$\therefore \quad u_y = \dfrac{gT}{2} \Rightarrow h_A = u_y t_A - \dfrac{1}{2} g t_A^2$

$= u_y\left(\dfrac{2u_y}{3g}\right) - \dfrac{1}{2} g \left(\dfrac{2u_y}{3g}\right)^2$

$= \dfrac{4}{9}\dfrac{u_y^2}{g} = \left(\dfrac{4}{9g}\right)\left(\dfrac{gT}{2}\right)^2 = \dfrac{gT^2}{9}$

$h_B = u_y\left(\dfrac{5}{6} \times \dfrac{2u_y}{g}\right) - \dfrac{1}{2} \times g \times \left(\dfrac{5}{6} \times \dfrac{2u_y}{g}\right)^2$

$= \dfrac{5}{18}\dfrac{u_y^2}{g} = \dfrac{5}{18g}\left(\dfrac{gT}{2}\right)^2 = \dfrac{5}{12} gT^2$

$\therefore \quad h_A - h_B = \dfrac{11}{36} gT^2$

16. $T = \dfrac{2u\sin\theta}{g} = \dfrac{(2)(80)\sin 53°}{10} = 12.8 \text{ s}$

$R = \dfrac{u^2 \sin 2\theta}{g} = \dfrac{(80)^2 \sin(106°)}{10} = 615.2 \text{ m}$

Distance travelled by tank,

$d = (5)T = (5)(12.8) = 64 \text{ m}$

$\therefore$ Total distance $= (615.2 + 64)$ m

$= 679.2$ m **Ans.**

17. $2\theta = 90° - \theta$ or $3\theta = 90°$ or $\theta = 30°$

18. $T = \dfrac{2u_y}{g} = 3$

$\therefore \quad u_y = 15 \text{ m/s}$

Now, $\quad H = \dfrac{u_y^2}{2g} = \dfrac{(15)^2}{20} = 11.25 \text{ m}$

19. For 5 s weight of the body is balanced by the given force. Hence, it will move in a straight line as shown.

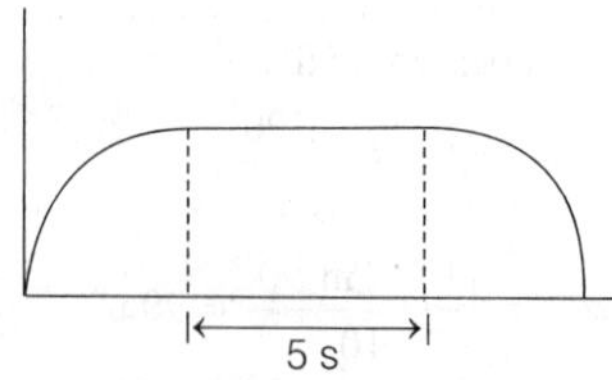

$R = \dfrac{u^2 \sin 2\theta}{g} + (u\cos\theta)(5)$

$= \dfrac{(50)^2 \cdot \sin 60°}{10} + (50 \times \cos 30°)(5)$

$= 250\sqrt{3}$ m

20. $R = \dfrac{u^2 \sin\theta}{g}$ at angles θ and $90° - \theta$

Now, $\quad h_1 = \dfrac{u^2 \sin^2\theta}{2g}$

and $\quad h_2 = \dfrac{u^2 \sin^2(90° - \theta)}{2g} = \dfrac{u^2 \cos^2\theta}{2g}$

$h_1 h_2 = \left(\dfrac{u^2 \sin 2\theta}{g}\right)^2 \cdot \dfrac{1}{16} = \dfrac{R^2}{16}$

$\therefore \quad R = 4\sqrt{h_1 h_2}$

21. $x = 36\,t$

$\therefore \quad v_x = \dfrac{dx}{dt} = 36 \text{ m/s}$

$y = 48t - 4.9\,t^2$

$\therefore \quad v_y = \dfrac{dy}{dt} = 48 - 9.8t$

At $t = 0$, $v_x = 36$ m/s and $v_y = 48$ m/s

So, angle of projection, $\theta = \tan^{-1}\left(\dfrac{v_y}{v_x}\right)$

$= \tan^{-1}\left(\dfrac{4}{3}\right)$

or $\quad \theta = \sin^{-1}\left(\dfrac{4}{5}\right)$

22. Projectile will strike at highest point of its path with velocity $v_0 \cos\alpha$.

23. $u\cos\theta = \dfrac{u}{2} \Rightarrow \theta = 60°$

Now, $\quad R = \dfrac{u^2 \sin 2\theta}{g} = \dfrac{u^2 \sin 120°}{g}$

$= \dfrac{\sqrt{3}\,u^2}{2g}$

24. Velocity of boy should be equal to the horizontal component of velocity of ball.

25. $5\sqrt{3} = \dfrac{(10)^2 \sin 2\theta}{g}$ or $\sin 2\theta = \dfrac{\sqrt{3}}{2}$

$\therefore \quad 2\theta = 60°$ or $\theta = 30°$

Two different angles of projection are therefore θ and $90° - \theta$ or $30°$ and $60°$.

$T_1 = \dfrac{2u\sin 30°}{g} = 1 \text{ s}$

$T_2 = 2\dfrac{u\sin 60°}{g} = \sqrt{3} \text{ s}$

$\therefore \quad \Delta t = T_2 - T_1 = (\sqrt{3} - 1) \text{ s}$

26. Compare with $y = x\tan\theta - \dfrac{gx^2}{2u^2\cos^2\theta}$

$$\tan\theta = \sqrt{3}$$

$$\therefore \quad \theta = 60^\circ$$

27. Put $y = 0$,

$$0 = 12x - \frac{3}{4}x^2$$

$$\Rightarrow \quad x = 16 \text{ m}$$

28. H and R both are proportional to u^2. Hence, percentage increases in horizontal range would also be 10%.

29. At highest point, kinetic energy will be minimum but not zero.

30. $K = K_0 - mgh$, here K = kinetic energy at height h, K_0 = initial kinetic energy. Variation of K with h is linear. At highest point, kinetic energy is not zero.

31. $y_1 + y_2 = \dfrac{u^2\sin^2\theta}{2g} + \dfrac{u^2\sin^2(90^\circ - \theta)}{2g} = \dfrac{u^2}{2g}$

32. $R = \dfrac{u^2\sin 2\theta}{g} = 24$ ...(i)

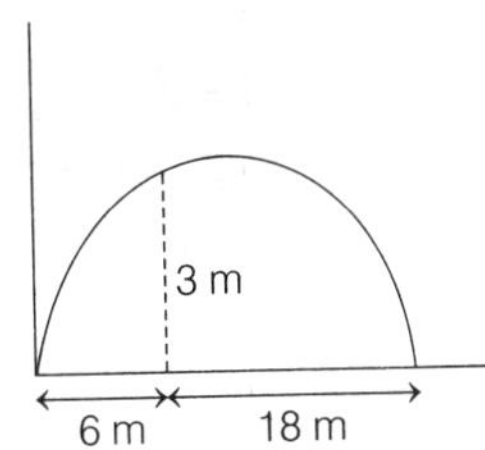

In $\quad y = x\tan\theta - \dfrac{gx^2}{2u^2\cos^2\theta}$

$$3 = 6\tan\theta - \frac{36g}{2u^2\cos^2\theta} \quad \text{...(ii)}$$

From Eq. (i), $\dfrac{g}{u^2} = \dfrac{\sin 2\theta}{24} = \dfrac{\sin\theta\cos\theta}{12}$

Substituting in Eq. (ii), we have

$$3 = 6\tan\theta - \frac{3}{2}\tan\theta = \frac{9}{2}\tan\theta$$

$$\therefore \quad \theta = \tan^{-1}\left(\frac{2}{3}\right)$$

33. $v^2 = v_y^2 + v_x^2$ or $(5\sqrt{2})^2 = (u_y - gt)^2 + u_x^2$

or $\quad 50 = (5\sqrt{3} - 10t)^2 + (5)^2$

$\therefore \quad (5\sqrt{3} - 10t) = \pm 5$

$$t_1 = \frac{5\sqrt{3} + 5}{10} \text{ and } t_2 = \frac{5\sqrt{3} - 5}{10}$$

$$\therefore \quad t_1 - t_2 = 1 \text{ s}$$

34. $R = 2H$ or $\dfrac{2u_x u_y}{g} = \dfrac{2u_y^2}{2g}$

or $2u_x = u_y$ or $2a = b$

35. $\dfrac{AB}{BC} = \dfrac{\frac{1}{2}gt^2}{v_0 t} = \tan\theta$

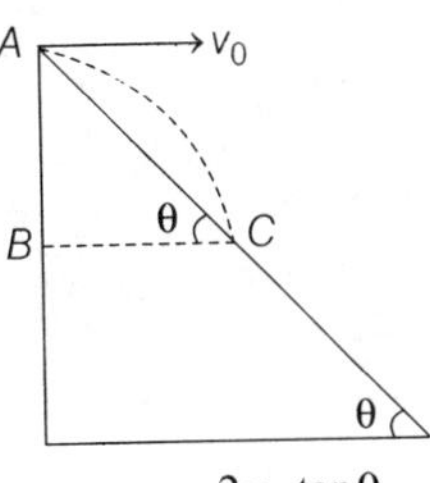

$$\therefore \quad t = \frac{2v_0\tan\theta}{g}$$

Now, x-coordinate $= v_0 t = \dfrac{2v_0^2\tan\theta}{g}$

and $\quad y$-coordinate $= -\dfrac{1}{2}gt^2 = -\dfrac{2v_0^2\tan^2\theta}{g}$

36. $y = \dfrac{gx^2}{2u^2} \Rightarrow h = \dfrac{gR^2}{2u^2}, 4h = \dfrac{g(2R)^2}{2u_1^2}$

$$u_1 = u$$

37. $\dfrac{2u\sin\theta}{g} = 9 \Rightarrow u\sin\theta = \dfrac{9g}{2}$

$(u\cos\theta)_4 = x_p \quad \therefore \quad y_p = x_p\tan\theta - g\dfrac{x_p^2}{2u^2\cos^2\theta}$

On solving, we get

$$y_p = 10g = 100 \text{ m}$$

38. $H = \dfrac{u^2\sin^2\theta}{2g}$

$$\sin\theta = \frac{\sqrt{2gH}}{u} = \frac{\sqrt{2 \times 9.8 \times 40}}{56} = \frac{1}{2}$$

$$\theta = 30^\circ$$

From 0° to 45°, horizontal range increases. Therefore, the appropriate angle is 30°.

39.

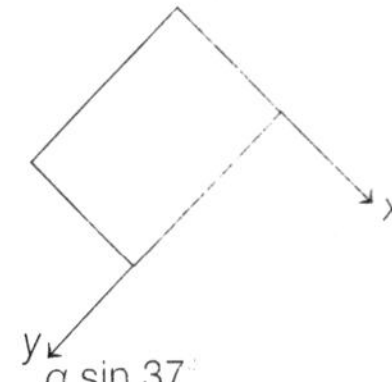

Here, $u_x = 8 \text{ ms}^{-1}$

$$a_x = 0$$

$\therefore \quad v_x = u_x$

$a_y = g \sin 37°, a_y = 10 \times \frac{3}{5} = 6 \text{ ms}^{-2}$

$\therefore \quad v_y = u_y + a_y t = 0 + 6 \times 1 = 6 \text{ ms}^{-1}$

$\therefore \quad v = \sqrt{v_x^2 + v_y^2} = \sqrt{8^2 + 6^2} = 10 \text{ ms}^{-1}$

40. $T = t_1 + t_2 = 4 \text{ s} = \frac{2u}{g}$

$\therefore \quad u = 2g$

$H = \frac{u^2}{2g} = 2g = 19.6 \text{ m}$

41. Vertical component of initial velocity of A

$= 2v \sin 30° = v = v_1$ (say)

Vertical component of initial velocity of B

$= v \sin 60° = \frac{\sqrt{3}v}{2} = v_2$ (say)

Since $v_2 < v_1$. Therefore, B will hit earlier.

42. $H = \frac{(v \sin\theta)^2}{2g}$

At height $h = \frac{H}{2}$ or $\frac{v^2 \sin^2\theta}{4g}$ vertical component of velocity is,

$$v_y = \sqrt{u_y^2 - 2gh}$$

$$= \sqrt{v^2 \sin^2\theta - 2g\left(\frac{v^2 \sin^2\theta}{4g}\right)}$$

$$= \frac{v \sin\theta}{\sqrt{2}}$$

43. Initial velocity $= (\hat{\mathbf{i}} + 2\hat{\mathbf{j}})$ m/s

Magnitude of initial velocity,

$$u = \sqrt{(1)^2 + (2)^2}$$

$$= \sqrt{5} \text{ m/s}$$

Equation of trajectory of projectile is

$$y = x \tan\theta - \frac{gx^2}{2u^2}(1 + \tan^2\theta)$$

$$\left[\tan\theta = \frac{y}{x} = \frac{2}{1} = 2\right]$$

$\therefore \quad y = x \times 2 - \frac{10(x)^2}{2(\sqrt{5})^2}[1 + (2)^2]$

$$= 2x - \frac{10(x^2)}{2 \times 5}(1 + 4)$$

$$= 2x - 5x^2$$

Subjective Questions

1. **At 45°**

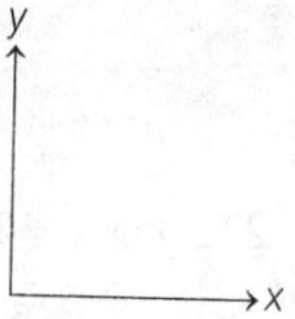

$v_y = \pm v_x = \pm u_x = \pm 60 \cos 60°$

$= \pm 30 \text{ m/s}$

Now, $v_y = u_y + a_y t$

$\therefore \quad t = \frac{v_y - u_y}{a_y}$

$$= \frac{(\pm 30) - 60 \sin 60°}{-10}$$

$\therefore \quad t_1 = 2.19 \text{ s}$ and $t_2 = 8.20 \text{ s}$ **Ans.**

2. Vertical component of initial velocity

$u = 20\sqrt{2} \sin 45° = 20 \text{ m/s}$

Now, apply $s = ut + \frac{1}{2}at^2$ (to find t) in vertical direction, with

$s = 15\text{m}, u = 20 \text{ m/s}$ and $a = -10 \text{ m/s}^2$ **Ans.**

3. $v_x = u_x = 20 \cos 60° = 10 \text{ m/s}$

Given, $v = \frac{u}{2}$

$\therefore \quad 4v^2 = u^2$

or $\quad 4(v_x^2 + v_y^2) = u^2$

$\therefore \quad 4[(10)^2 + v_y^2] = (20)^2$

or $\quad v_y = 0$

Hence, it is the highest point.

$\therefore \quad t = \frac{T}{2} = \frac{u \sin\theta}{g}$

$= \frac{(20) \sin 60°}{10} = \sqrt{3} \text{ s}$ **Ans.**

4. For collision to take place, relative velocity of A with respect to B should be along AB or their vertical components should be same.

Vertical components of A

$v_1 = 10 \sin 30° = 5 \text{ m/s}$

and vertical component of B

$v_2 = 5\sqrt{2} \cos 45° = 5 \text{ m/s}$

Since, $v_1 = v_2$, so they may collide.

Now, the second condition is,

$R_1 + R_2 \geq d \quad (\because d = 15 \text{ m})$

$\therefore \quad R_1 = \frac{(10)^2 \sin 60°}{10} = 8.66 \text{ m}$

$R_2 = \frac{(5\sqrt{2})^2 \sin 90°}{10} = 5 \text{ m}$

Since, $R_1 + R_2 < d$, so they will not collide.

5. y-coordinate of particle is zero when

$$4t - 5t^2 = 0$$

$\therefore$ $t = 0$ and 0.8 s

$$x = 3t$$

at $t = 0, x = 0$

and at $t = 0.8$ s, $x = 2.4$ m **Ans.**

6. $T = \dfrac{2u \sin(\alpha - \beta)}{g \cos \beta}$ $(\because \alpha = 60°, \beta = 30°)$

$$= \frac{2 \times 10 \times \sin 30°}{(10) \cos 30°} = \frac{2}{\sqrt{3}} \text{ s}$$

$$v_x = u_x = 10 \cos 60° = 5 \text{ m/s}$$

$$v_y = u_y + a_y t$$

$$= (10 \sin 60°) + (-10)(2/\sqrt{3})$$

$$= 5\sqrt{3} - \frac{20}{\sqrt{3}} = -\frac{5}{\sqrt{3}} \text{ m/s}$$

$\therefore$ $v = \sqrt{v_x^2 + v_y^2} = \sqrt{25 + \dfrac{25}{3}}$

$$= \frac{10}{\sqrt{3}} \text{ m/s}$$

7. $v_y = u_y + a_y t$

$$= (10 \sin 30°) + (-g \cos 30°)\, T$$

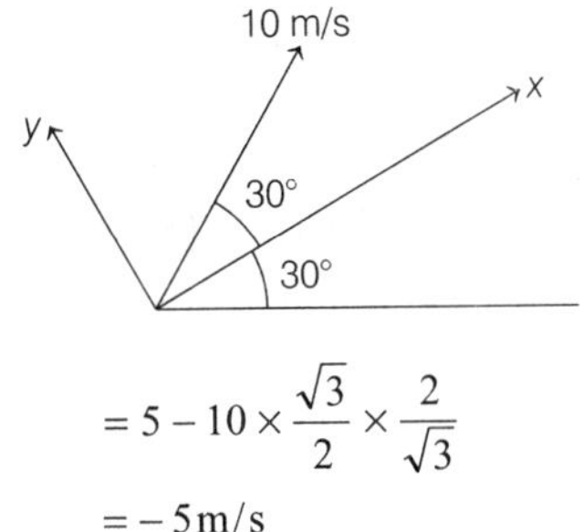

$$= 5 - 10 \times \frac{\sqrt{3}}{2} \times \frac{2}{\sqrt{3}}$$

$$= -5 \text{ m/s}$$

8. In vertical direction,

$$s_A = s_B + 10$$

$\therefore$ $(10)\, t - \dfrac{1}{2} gt^2 = -\dfrac{1}{2} gt^2 + 10$

$\therefore$ $t = 1$ s

In horizontal direction,

$$d = |s_A| + |s_B|$$

$$= (10)\, t + 10\, t = 20t$$

$$= 20 \text{ m} \quad (\text{as } t = 1 \text{ s})$$

9. Horizontal component of velocity always remains constant

$\therefore$ $40 \cos 60° = v \cos 30°$

or $v = \dfrac{40}{\sqrt{3}}$ m/s **Ans.**

10. (a) If they collide in air, then relative velocity of A with respect to B should be along AB or their vertical components should be same.

$\therefore$ $20 \sin \theta = 10$

or $\theta = 30°$ **Ans.**

(b) $x = |s_A| + |s_B|$

$$= (20 \cos 30°)(t) + 0$$

$$= 20 \times \frac{\sqrt{3}}{2} \times \frac{1}{2}$$

$$= 5\sqrt{3} \text{ m}$$ **Ans.**

11. $v_x = u_x = 7.6$ m/s

$$v_y = \sqrt{u_y^2 - 2gh}$$

$\therefore$ $u_y = \sqrt{v_y^2 + 2gh}$

$$= \sqrt{(6.1)^2 + 2 \times 10 \times 9.1}$$

$$= 14.8 \text{ m/s}$$

(a) $H = \dfrac{u_y^2}{2g} = \dfrac{(14.8)^2}{2 \times 10} \approx 11$ m

(b) $R = \dfrac{2u_x u_y}{g} = \dfrac{2 \times 7.6 \times 14.8}{10} \approx 23$ m **Ans.**

(c) $u = \sqrt{u_x^2 + u_y^2}$

$$= \sqrt{(7.6)^2 + (14.8)^2}$$

$$= 16.6 \text{ m/s}$$ **Ans.**

(d) $\theta = \tan^{-1}\left(\dfrac{u_y}{u_x}\right)$

$= \tan^{-1}\left(\dfrac{14.8}{7.6}\right) \approx \tan^{-1}(2)$, (below horizontal)

Ans.

12. $u_x^2 + u_y^2 = (2\sqrt{gh})^2 = 4gh$ ...(i)

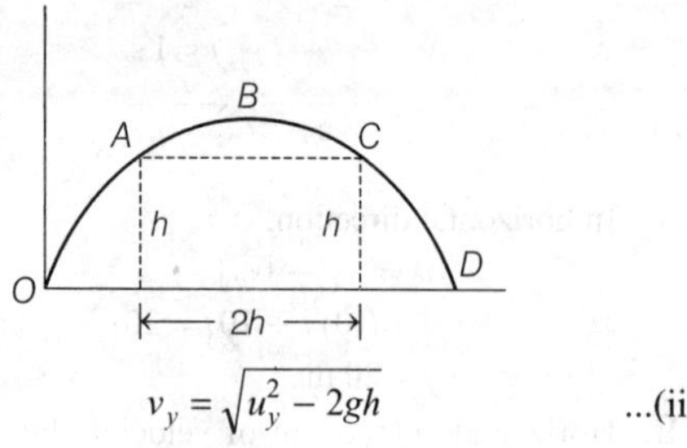

$$v_y = \sqrt{u_y^2 - 2gh} \quad \text{...(ii)}$$

$$v_x = u_x \quad \text{...(iii)}$$

Now for the projectile ABC, v_x and v_y are the initial components of velocity.

$$\therefore \quad 2h = \text{range} = \frac{2v_x v_y}{g} = \frac{2u_x v_y}{g}$$

or $$u_x = \frac{gh}{v_y} \quad \text{...(iv)}$$

Using Eqs. (ii) and (iv) for rewriting Eq. (i), we have

$$\left(\frac{gh}{v_y}\right)^2 + (v_y^2 + 2gh) = 4gh$$

$$\therefore \quad v_y^4 - (2gh)\, v_y^2 + g^2h^2 = 0$$

$$\therefore \quad v_y^2 = \frac{2gh \pm \sqrt{4g^2h^2 - 4g^2h^2}}{2} = gh$$

$$\therefore \quad v_y = \sqrt{gh}$$

Now, t_{AC} = time of projectile ABC

$$= \frac{2v_y}{g} = 2\sqrt{\frac{h}{g}}$$ **Ans.**

13. Let v is the velocity at time t,

Using $$v_y = u_y + a_y t$$

$$\therefore \quad v \sin\beta = u \sin\alpha - gt \quad \text{...(i)}$$

$$v_x = u_x$$

$$\therefore \quad v \cos\beta = u \cos\alpha \quad \text{...(ii)}$$

From Eqs. (i) and (ii), we get

$$\left(\frac{u\cos\alpha}{\cos\beta}\right)\sin\beta = u\sin\alpha - gt$$

On solving, we get

$$u = \frac{gt\cos\beta}{\sin(\alpha - \beta)}$$

14. $$R - a = \frac{u^2 \sin 2\alpha}{g}$$

Multiplying with b, we have

$$bR - ab = \frac{bu^2 \sin 2\alpha}{g} \quad \text{...(i)}$$

$$R + b = \frac{u^2 \sin 2\beta}{g}$$

Multiplying with a, we have

$$aR + ab = \frac{au^2 \sin 2\beta}{g} \quad \text{...(ii)}$$

Adding Eqs. (i) and (ii) and by putting

$$R = \frac{u^2 \sin 2\theta}{g},$$

we get the result.

15. (a) $t = \frac{s_x}{u_x} = \frac{10}{5}$

$= 2$ s

(b) Vertical components of velocities are zero.

$$\therefore \quad h = \frac{1}{2}gt^2 = \frac{1}{2} \times 9.8 \times (2)^2$$

$= 19.6$ m

(c) $s_x = u_x t = 7.5 \times 2 = 15$ m

16. $u_x = 20$ km/h $= 20 \times \frac{5}{18} = 5.6$ m/s

$u_y = 12$ km/h

$= 12 \times \frac{5}{18} = 3.3$ m/s

Using $s = ut + \frac{1}{2}at^2$ in vertical direction, we have

$$-50 = (3.3)\,t + \frac{1}{2}(-10)\,t^2$$

Solving this equation, we get

$$t \approx 3.55 \text{ s}$$

At the time of striking with ground,

$$v_x = u_x = 5.6 \text{ m/s}$$

$$v_y = u_y + a_y t$$

$$= (3.3) + (-10)(3.55)$$

$$= 32.2 \text{ m/s}$$

$$\therefore \quad \text{Speed} = \sqrt{(32.2)^2 + (5.6)^2}$$

$$\approx 32.7 \text{ m/s}$$

17. (a) Acceleration of stone is g or 10 m/s^2 in downward direction. Acceleration of elevator is 1 m/s^2 upwards. Therefore, relative acceleration of stone (with respect to elevator) is 11 m/s^2 downwards. Initial velocity is already given relative .

$$T = \frac{2u_r \sin\theta_r}{a_r} = \frac{(2)(2)\sin 30°}{11}$$

$= 0.18$ s **Ans.**

(b) $\mathbf{v}_S = \mathbf{v}_{SE} + \mathbf{v}_E$

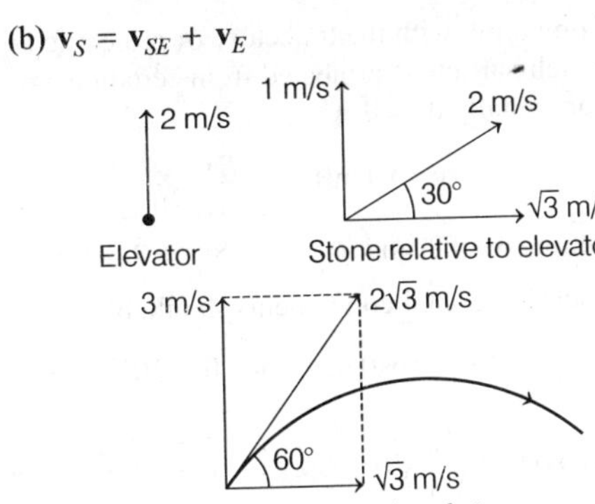

(c) In that case, relative acceleration between stone and elevator will be zero. So, with respect to elevator, path is a straight line (uniform) with constant velocity of 20 m/s at 30°. But path, with respect to man on ground will remain unchanged.

18. (i) $x_A = x_B$

$\therefore \quad 10 + (u_1 \cos\theta_1)t = 30 - (u_2 \cos\theta_2)t$

$\therefore \quad (u_1 \cos\theta_1 + u_2 \cos\theta_2)t = 20$

(ii) $y_A = y_B$

$\therefore \quad 10 + (u_1 \sin\theta_1)t - \frac{1}{2}gt^2 = 20 + (u_2 \sin\theta_2)t - \frac{1}{2}gt^2$

or $\quad (u_1 \sin\theta_1 - u_2 \sin\theta_2)t = 10$

LEVEL 2

Single Correct Option

1. $T = \sqrt{\frac{2h}{g}}$

$$d = (u)T = u\sqrt{\frac{2h}{g}}$$

$\therefore \quad d^2 = \frac{2hu^2}{g}$ **Ans.**

2. $R = \frac{u^2}{g\cos^2\beta}[\sin(2\alpha + \beta) + \sin\beta]$

$u = 10$ m/s, $g = 10$ m/s^2, $\beta = 30°$ and $\alpha = 60°$

3. $y = x\tan\theta - \frac{gx^2}{2u^2\cos^2\theta}$

$\therefore \quad \frac{dy}{dx} = (\tan\theta) - \left(\frac{g}{u^2\cos^2\theta}\right)x$

$\therefore \quad \frac{dy}{dx}$ *versus* x graph is a straight line with negative slope and positive intercept.

4. $\frac{dy}{dt} = (2\beta x)\cdot\frac{dx}{dt}$ and $\frac{d^2y}{dt^2} = 2\beta\left[\frac{d^2x}{dt^2} + \left(\frac{dx}{dt}\right)^2\right]$

$$\frac{d^2y}{dt^2} = \alpha = a_y$$

$$\frac{d^2x}{dt^2} = a_x = 0 \text{ and } \frac{dx}{dt} = v_x$$

$\therefore \quad \alpha = 2\beta\cdot v_x^2 \quad$ or $\quad v_x = \sqrt{\frac{\alpha}{2\beta}}$ **Ans.**

5.

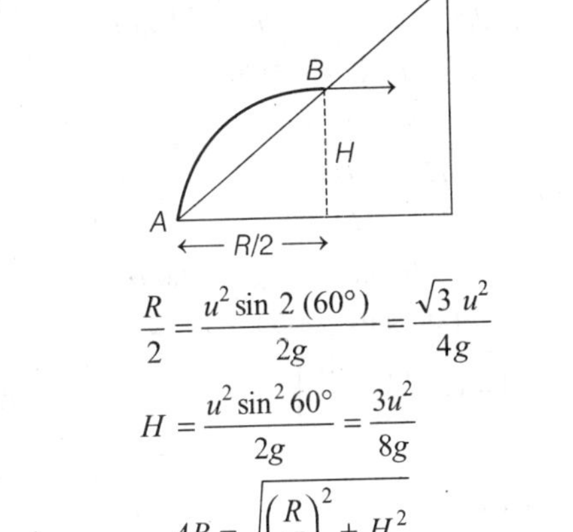

$$\frac{R}{2} = \frac{u^2\sin 2(60°)}{2g} = \frac{\sqrt{3}u^2}{4g}$$

$$H = \frac{u^2\sin^2 60°}{2g} = \frac{3u^2}{8g}$$

$\therefore \quad AB = \sqrt{\left(\frac{R}{2}\right)^2 + H^2}$

$$= \frac{\sqrt{21}u^2}{8g}$$ **Ans.**

6.

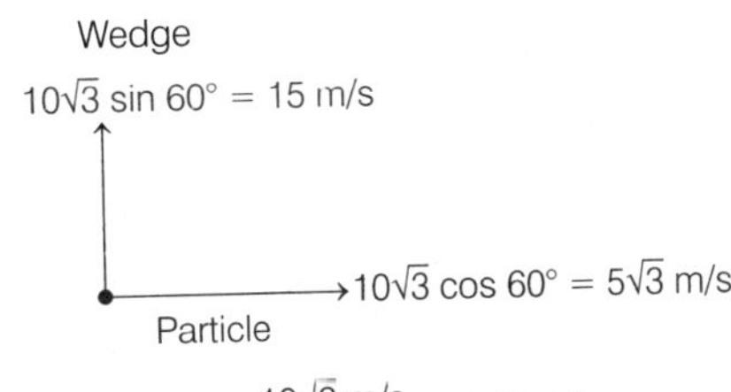

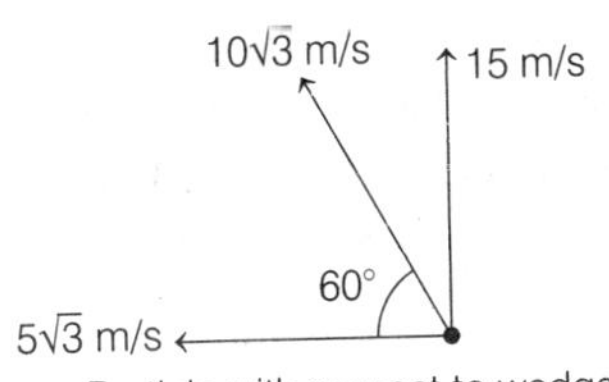

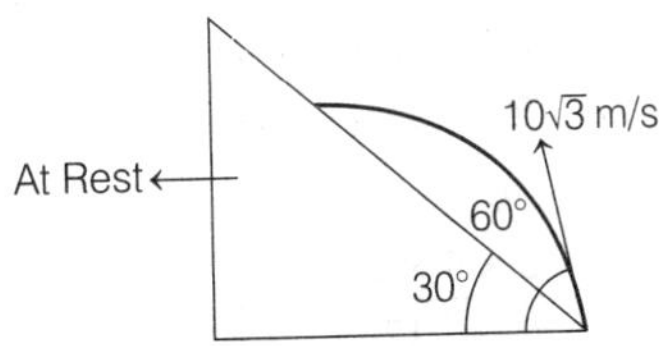

$$T = \frac{2u \sin (\alpha - \beta)}{g \cos \beta}$$

$$= \frac{2(10\sqrt{3}) \cdot \sin (60° - 30°)}{10 \cos 30°} = 2 \text{ s}$$

7. $a_y = 0 = \dfrac{d^2y}{dt^2}$

$$\frac{dx}{dt} = (2y + 2) \cdot \frac{dy}{dt}$$

$$\frac{d^2x}{dt^2} = (2y + 2) \cdot \frac{d^2y}{dt^2} + 2\left(\frac{dy}{dt}\right)^2$$

$\therefore$ $a_x = a = (2y + 2)(0) + 2(5)^2$

$= 50 \text{ m/s}^2$ **Ans.**

8. $\tan\beta = \dfrac{H}{R/2} = \dfrac{2H}{R}$

$$= \frac{(2u^2 \sin^2 \alpha)/2g}{(2u^2 \sin\alpha \cos \alpha)/g} = \frac{\tan\alpha}{2}$$

$\therefore$ $\beta = \tan^{-1}\left(\dfrac{\tan\alpha}{2}\right)$ **Ans.**

9. $a_1 = a_2 = g$ (downwards)

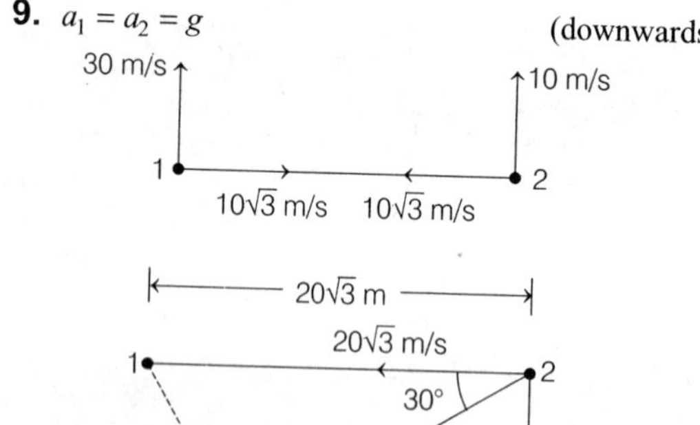

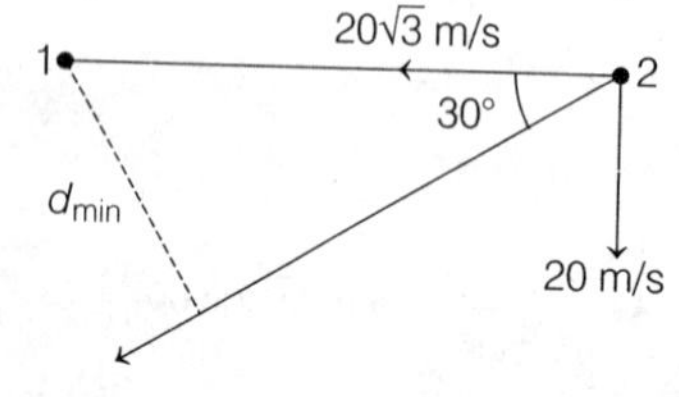

$\therefore$ $a_{12} = 0$

$\therefore$ Relative motion between them is uniform.

Relative velocity $v_{21} = 20\sqrt{3}$ m/s

$$d_{min} = 20\sqrt{3} \sin 30°$$

$= 10\sqrt{3}$ m **Ans.**

10. Let us see the motion relative to elevator,

$$a_r = a_b - a_e = (-10) - (+2) = -12 \text{ m/s}^2$$

Now, $T = \dfrac{2u_y}{a_r} = \dfrac{2 \times u\sin\theta}{a_r}$

$$= \frac{2 \times 4 \times \sin 30°}{12} = \frac{1}{3} \text{ s}$$

11. Comparing with the trajectory of projectile in which particle is projected from certain height horizontally ($\theta = 0°$).

$$y = x \tan\theta - \frac{gx^2}{2u^2 \cos^2\theta}$$

Putting $\theta = 0°$ and $g = a = 18u^2 = 2 \text{ m/s}^2$

12. Their horizontal components should be same.

$\therefore$ $\dfrac{2v}{\sqrt{3}} \cdot \cos\theta = v$ or $\theta = 30°$

13. $(u\cos \alpha) = \sqrt{\dfrac{2}{5}}\sqrt{(u\cos\alpha)^2 + \{(u\sin \alpha)^2 - 2gh\}}$

Here, $h = \dfrac{H}{2} = \dfrac{u^2 \sin^2\alpha}{4g}$

Solving this equation, we get $\alpha = 60°$

14. $u_x = a, u_y = b, g = c$

$\Rightarrow$ $R = \dfrac{2u_xu_y}{g} = \dfrac{2ab}{c}$

15.

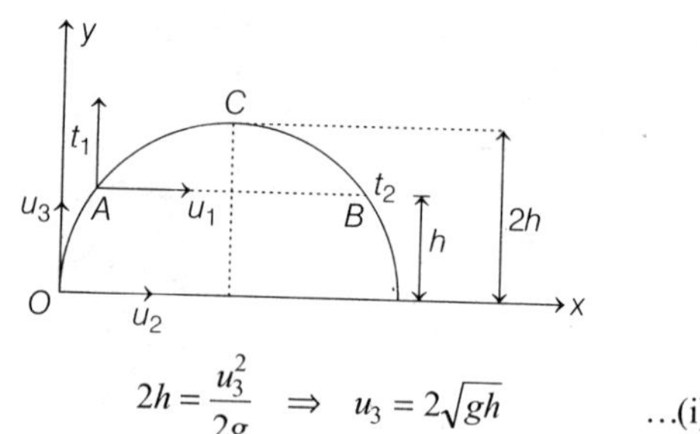

$$2h = \frac{u_3^2}{2g} \Rightarrow u_3 = 2\sqrt{gh} \quad \text{...(i)}$$

By the time, bird reaches from A to B, stone reaches from $\boldsymbol{O}$ **to** $\boldsymbol{B}$.

$\Rightarrow$ $u_1(t_2 - t_1) = u_2t_2$

$\Rightarrow$ $\dfrac{u_1}{u_2} = \dfrac{t_2}{t_2 - t_1}$ ...(ii)

Total time of flight,

$$T = t_1 + t_2 = \frac{2u_3}{g} = 4\sqrt{\frac{h}{g}} \quad \text{...(iii)}$$

At A, vertical component of velocity,

$$u_4 = \sqrt{u_3^2 - 2gh} = \sqrt{4gh - 2gh} = \sqrt{2gh}$$

From A to C, in time $\dfrac{t_2 - t_1}{2}$ this vertical component u_4 also becomes zero.

$\therefore$ $0 = u_4 - gt$

or $0 = \sqrt{2gh} - g\left(\dfrac{t_2 - t_1}{2}\right)$

$\therefore$ $t_2 - t_1 = 2\sqrt{2}\left(\sqrt{\dfrac{g}{h}}\right)$ ...(iv)

Solving Eqs. (iii) and (iv), we have

$$\frac{(t_1/t_2)+1}{1-(t_1/t_2)}=\sqrt{2}$$

$$\therefore \quad \frac{t_1}{t_2}=\frac{\sqrt{2}-1}{\sqrt{2}+1}$$

Now, from Eq. (ii), we have

$$\frac{u_1}{u_2}=\frac{1}{1-\frac{t_1}{t_2}}=\frac{1}{1-\left(\frac{\sqrt{2}-1}{\sqrt{2}+1}\right)}=\frac{\sqrt{2}+1}{2}$$

16. Let us first find, time of collision of two particles with ground by putting proper values in the equation

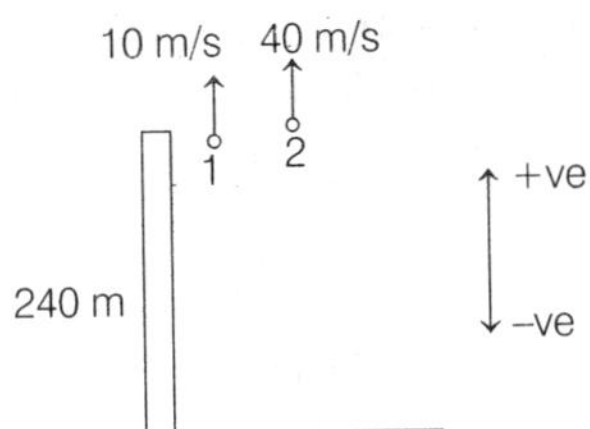

$$s=ut+\frac{1}{2}at^2$$

$$-240=10t_1-\frac{1}{2}\times 10\times t_1^2$$

Solving, we get the positive value of $t_1=8$ s

Therefore, the first particle will strike the ground at 8 s.

Similarly,

$$-240=40t_2-\frac{1}{2}\times 10\times t_2^2$$

Solving this equation, we get positive value of $t_2=12$ s.

Therefore, second particle strikes the ground at 12 s.

If y is measured from ground. Then,

from 0 to 8 s,

$$y_1=240+s_1=240+u_1t+\frac{1}{2}a_1t^2$$

or $\quad y_1=240+10t-\frac{1}{2}\times 10\times t^2$

Similarly, $y_2=240+40t-\frac{1}{2}\times 10\times t^2$

$\Rightarrow \quad y_2-y_1=30t$

$\therefore$ (y_2-y_1) *versus* t graph is a straight line passing through origin.

At $t=8$ s, $y_2-y_1=240$ m

From 8 s to 12 s,

$$y_1=0$$

$$\Rightarrow \quad y_2=240+40t-\frac{1}{2}\times 10\times t^2$$

$$=240+40t-5t$$

$$\therefore \quad (y_2-y_1)=240+40t-5t^2$$

Therefore, (y_2-y_1) *versus* t graph is parabolic. Substituting the values we can check that at $t=8$ s, y_2-y_1 is 240 m and at $t=12$ s, y_2-y_1 is zero. Hence, the correct graph is (b).

More than One Correct Options

1. $\alpha+\beta=90°$ or $\beta=90°-\alpha$

$$h_1=\frac{u^2\sin^2\alpha}{2g} \quad \text{and} \quad h_2=\frac{u^2\cos^2\alpha}{2g}$$

$$t_1=\frac{2u\sin\alpha}{g} \quad \text{and} \quad t_2=\frac{2u\cos\alpha}{g}$$

$$R_1=R_2=\frac{2u^2\sin\alpha\cos\alpha}{g}=R$$

2. Since $u=0$, motion of particle is a straight line in the direction of a_{net}.

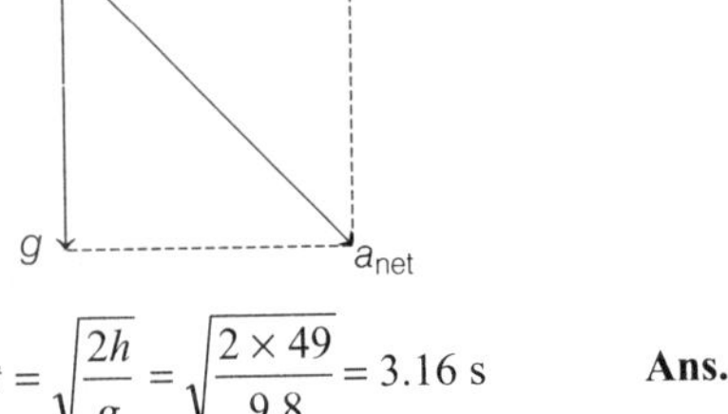

$$t=\sqrt{\frac{2h}{g}}=\sqrt{\frac{2\times 49}{9.8}}=3.16 \text{ s} \qquad \textbf{Ans.}$$

3. Horizontal component of velocity remains unchanged.

$$\therefore \quad v\cos\theta=v'\cos(90-\theta)$$

or $\quad v'=v\cot\theta$

In vertical (y) direction,

$$v_y=u_y+a_yt$$

$$\therefore \quad t=\frac{v_y-u_y}{a_y}$$

$$=\frac{-v^1\sin(90-\theta)-v\sin\theta}{-g}$$

$$=\frac{(v\cot\theta)\cdot\cos\theta+v\sin\theta}{g}$$

$$=\frac{v\,\text{cosec}\,\theta}{g} \qquad \textbf{Ans.}$$

4. $u_x = v_x = 10 \text{ m/s}$

$$u_y = \sqrt{v_y^2 + 2gh} = \sqrt{(10)^2 + (2)(10)(15)}$$

$= 20 \text{ m/s}$ **Ans.**

Angle of projection,

$$\theta = \tan^{-1}\left(\frac{u_y}{u_x}\right) = \tan^{-1}(2)$$

$$T = \frac{2u_y}{g} = \frac{(2)(20)}{10} = 4 \text{ s}$$

$$R = u_x T = (10)(4) = 40 \text{ m}$$

$$H = \frac{u_y^2}{2g} = \frac{(20)^2}{2 \times 10} = 20 \text{m}$$

5. $\frac{d\mathbf{v}}{dt} = \mathbf{a} = \text{constant} = \mathbf{g}$

$$\frac{d^2\mathbf{v}}{dt^2} = \frac{d\mathbf{a}}{dt} = 0 = \text{constant}$$

6. Horizontal component of velocity remains unchanged

$$X_{OA} = 20 \text{ m} = \frac{X_{AB}}{2}$$

$$\therefore \quad t_{OA} = \frac{t_{AB}}{2} = 1 \text{ s}$$

For *AB* projectile

$$T = 2 \text{ s} = \frac{2u_y}{g}$$

$$\therefore \quad u_y = 10 \text{ m/s}$$

$$H = \frac{u_y^2}{2g} = \frac{(10)^2}{2 \times 10} = 5 \text{ m}$$

$\therefore$ Maximum height of total projectile,

$$= 15 + 5 = 20 \text{ m}$$

$$t_{OB} = t_{OA} + t_{AB} = 1 + 2 = 3 \text{ s}$$

For complete projectile

$$T = 2(t_{OA}) + t_{AB}$$

$$= 4 \text{ s} = \frac{2u_y}{g}$$

$$\therefore \quad u_y = 20 \text{ m/s}$$

$$u_x = \frac{AB}{t_{AB}} = \frac{40}{2} = 20 \text{ m/s}$$

7. The equation of trajectory is $y = x \tan\alpha \left(1 - \frac{x}{R}\right)$

$\therefore$ Comparing the equation $y = x(1 - x)$

We see that,

$\tan\alpha = 1$ and $R = 1 \text{ m}$

$$\therefore \quad \alpha = \frac{\pi}{4}$$

Match the Columns

1. (a)

$$\Delta x = (u_x)_2 (t - 1)$$
$$= (10)(2 - 1)$$
$$= 10 \text{ m}$$

(b) $y_1 = \frac{1}{2} gt^2 = \frac{1}{2} \times 10 \times (2)^2 = 20\text{m}$

$$y_2 = \frac{1}{2} g (t - 1)^2 = 5 \text{ m}$$

$$\therefore \quad \Delta y = y_1 - y_2 = 15 \text{ m}$$

(c) $v_{x_1} = 0$, $v_{x_2} = 10 \text{ m/s}$

$$\therefore \ v_{x_2} - v_{x_1} = 10 \text{ m/s}$$

(d) $v_{y_1} = gt = 10 \times 2 = 20 \text{ m/s}$

$$v_{y_2} = g(t - 1) = 10 \times 1 = 10 \text{ m/s}$$

$$\therefore \quad v_{y_1} - v_{y_2} = 10 \text{ m/s}$$

2. $H = \frac{u_y^2}{2g} = 20 \text{ m}$

$$\therefore \quad u_y = 20 \text{ m/s}$$

$$T = \frac{2u_y}{g} = 4 \text{ s}$$

$$R = u_x T = 40\text{m}$$

$$\therefore \quad u_x = \frac{40}{T} = 10 \text{ m/s}$$

3. $10 = \frac{u^2 \sin 2(15°)}{g} \Rightarrow \frac{u^2}{g} = 20 \text{ m}$

(a) $R_{max} = \frac{u^2}{g} = 20 \text{ m}$

(b) $H_{max} = \frac{u^2}{2g}$ (when thrown vertically)

$$= 10 \text{ m}$$

(c) $R_{75°} = R_{15°} = 10 \text{ m}$

(d) $H_{30°} = \frac{u^2 \sin^2 30°}{2g}$

$$= \frac{u^2}{8g} = \frac{20}{8} = 2.5 \text{ m}$$

4. $T = \frac{2u_y}{g} \Rightarrow T \propto u_y$

$$H = \frac{u_y^2}{2g}$$

$$\Rightarrow \quad H \propto u_y^2$$

$$R = u_x T$$

$$\Rightarrow \quad R \propto T$$

$$\Rightarrow \quad R \propto u_x$$

$$\Rightarrow \quad \tan\theta = \frac{u_y}{u_x}$$

$$\Rightarrow \quad \tan\theta \propto u_y$$

By doubling u_y, $\tan\theta$ will become two times, not θ.

5. (a) $\mathbf{a}_{av} = \mathbf{a} = (-g\hat{\mathbf{j}}) = \frac{\Delta \mathbf{v}}{\Delta t}$

$$\therefore \quad \Delta\mathbf{v} = (-g\hat{\mathbf{j}})\,\Delta t$$

$$= (-g\hat{\mathbf{j}})\left(\frac{T}{2}\right)$$

$$= (-g\hat{\mathbf{j}})\left(\frac{u\sin\theta}{g}\right)$$

$$= (-u\sin\theta)\,\hat{\mathbf{j}}$$

(b) $v_{av} = \frac{s}{t}$

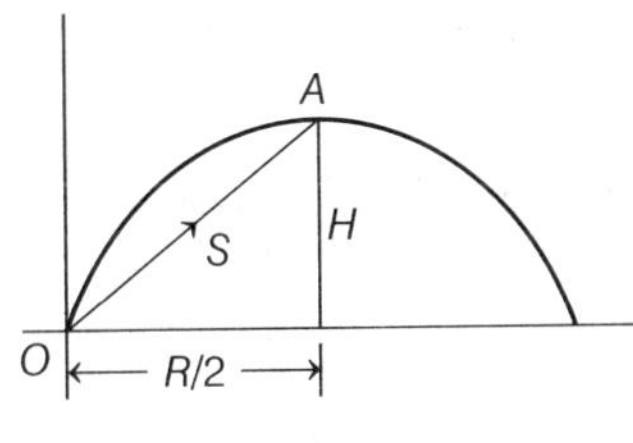

$$= \frac{\sqrt{(R/2)^2 + H^2}}{T/2}$$

(c) $\Delta\mathbf{v} = (-g\hat{\mathbf{j}})\,(\Delta t)$

$$= (-g\hat{\mathbf{j}})\,T$$

$$= (-g\hat{\mathbf{j}})\left(\frac{2u\sin\theta}{g}\right)$$

$$= (-2u\sin\theta)\,\hat{\mathbf{j}}$$

(d) $v_{av} = \frac{S}{t} = \frac{R}{T}$

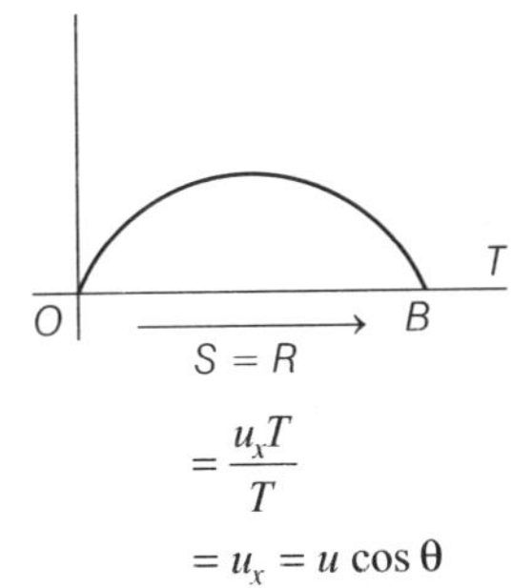

$$= \frac{u_x T}{T}$$

$$= u_x = u\cos\theta$$

6. (a) $x_1 = (u_{x1})\,t = (30)\,(2) = 60$ m

$$x_2 = (130) + (u_{x2})\,(t-1)$$

$$= 130 + (-20)\,(1)$$

$$= 110 \text{ m}$$

$$\therefore \quad \Delta x = 50 \text{ m}$$

(b) $y_1 = u_{y1}t - \frac{1}{2}gt^2$

$$= (30)\,(2) - \frac{1}{2}(10)\,(2)^2$$

$$= 40 \text{ m}$$

$$y_2 = 75 + u_{y2}\,(t-1) - \frac{1}{2}g\,(t-1)^2$$

$$= 75 + 20\times 1 - \frac{1}{2}\times 10\times (1)^2$$

$$= 90 \text{ m}$$

$$\therefore \quad \Delta y = 50 \text{ m}$$

(c) $v_{x1} = 30$ m/s

$$v_{x2} = -20 \text{ m/s}$$

$$\therefore \quad v_{x1} - v_{x2} = 50 \text{ m/s}$$

(d) $v_{y1} = u_{y1} + a_y t$

$$= (30) + (-10)\,(2)$$

$$= 10 \text{ m/s}$$

$$v_{y2} = u_{y2} + a_y\,(t-1)$$

$$= 20 + (-10)\,(1)$$

$$= 10 \text{ m/s}$$

$$\therefore \quad v_{y1} - v_{y2} = 0$$

7. $$H = \frac{u_y^2}{2g}$$

or $$H \propto u_y^2$$

Since H is same. Therefore, u_y is same for all three.

$$\therefore \quad T = \frac{2u_y}{g}$$

or $$t \propto u_y$$

Since u_y is same. Therefore, T is same for all.

$$R = u_x T$$

or $$R \propto u_x \qquad (\text{as } T \rightarrow \text{same})$$

R for C is maximum. Therefore u_x is greatest for C.

$$u = \sqrt{u_y^2 + u_x^2} \qquad (u_y \rightarrow \text{same})$$

R is least for A. Therefore u_x and hence u is least for A.

Subjective Questions

1. $u_x = v_0 \cos\theta, u_y = v_0 \sin\theta, a_x = -g \sin\theta,$
$a_y = g\cos\theta$

At Q, $v_x = 0$

$\therefore \quad u_x + a_x t = 0$

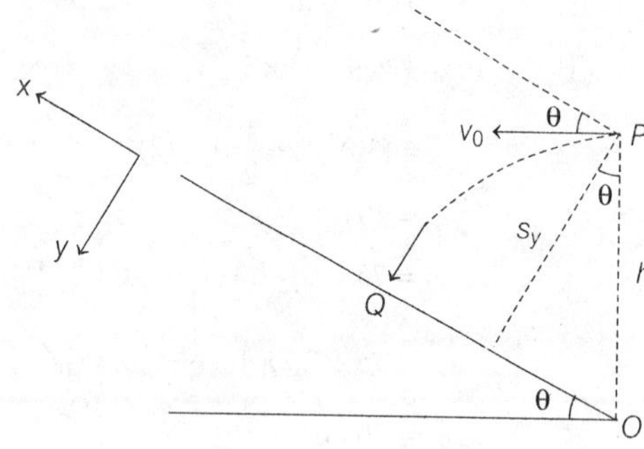

or $$t = \frac{v_0 \cos\theta}{g\sin\theta} \quad \ldots(i)$$

$$s_y = h\cos\theta$$

$$\therefore \quad u_y t + \frac{1}{2} a_y t^2 = h\cos\theta$$

$$\therefore \quad (v_0 \sin\theta)\left(\frac{v_0\cos\theta}{g\sin\theta}\right) + \frac{1}{2}(g\cos\theta)\left(\frac{v_0\cos\theta}{g\sin\theta}\right)^2 = h\cos\theta$$

Solving this equation, we get

$$v_0 = \sqrt{\frac{2gh}{2+\cot^2\theta}} \quad \textbf{Ans.}$$

2. Let v_x and v_y be the components of v_0 along x and y directions.

$$(v_x)(2) = 2$$

$$\therefore \quad v_x = 1 \text{ m/s}$$

$$v_y(2) = 10$$

or $$v_y = 5 \text{ m/s}$$

$$v_0 = \sqrt{v_x^2 + v_y^2}$$

$$= \sqrt{26} \text{ m/s}$$

$$\tan\theta = v_y/v_x = 5/1$$

$$\therefore \quad \theta = \tan^{-1}(5) \quad \textbf{Ans.}$$

Note *We have seen relative motion between two particles. Relative acceleration between them is zero.*

3. $\mathbf{v}_1 = (u\cos\alpha)\,\hat{\mathbf{i}} + (u\sin\alpha - gt)\,\hat{\mathbf{j}}$

$\mathbf{v}_2 = (v\cos\beta)\,\hat{\mathbf{i}} + (v\sin\beta - gt)\,\hat{\mathbf{j}}$

These two velocity vectors will be parallel when the ratio of coefficients of $\hat{\mathbf{i}}$ and $\hat{\mathbf{j}}$ are equal.

$$\therefore \quad \frac{u\cos\alpha}{v\cos\beta} = \frac{u\sin\alpha - gt}{v\sin\beta - gt}$$

Solving, we get

$$t = \frac{uv\sin(\alpha-\beta)}{g(v\cos\beta - u\cos\alpha)} \quad \textbf{Ans.}$$

4. At height 2 m, projectile will be at two times, which are obtained from the equation,

$$2 = (10\sin 45°)t + \frac{1}{2}(-10)t^2$$

or $$2 = 5\sqrt{2}t - 5t^2$$

or $$5t^2 - 5\sqrt{2}t + 2 = 0$$

or $$t_1 = \frac{5\sqrt{2} - \sqrt{50-40}}{10} = \frac{5\sqrt{2}-\sqrt{10}}{10}$$

and $$t_2 = \frac{5\sqrt{2}+\sqrt{10}}{10}$$

Now $$d = (10\cos 45°)(t_2 - t_1)$$

$$= \frac{10}{\sqrt{2}}\left(\frac{2\sqrt{10}}{10}\right) = 4.47 \text{ m}$$

Distance of point of projection from first hurdle

$$= (10\cos 45°)t_1$$

$$= \frac{10}{\sqrt{2}}\left(\frac{5\sqrt{2}-\sqrt{10}}{10}\right)$$

$$= 5 - \sqrt{5}$$

$$= 2.75 \text{ m} \quad \textbf{Ans.}$$

5. (a) Time of descent, $t = \sqrt{\frac{2H}{g}} = \sqrt{\frac{2\times 400}{10}}$

$$= 8.94 \text{ s}$$

Now $$v_x = ay = \sqrt{5}y$$

or $$\frac{dx}{dt} = \sqrt{5}\left(\frac{1}{2}gt^2\right) = 5\sqrt{5}t^2$$

$$\therefore \quad \int_0^x dx = 5\sqrt{5}\int_0^t t^2\,dt$$

or horizontal drift

$$x = \frac{5\sqrt{5}}{3}(8.94)^3 = 2663 \text{ m} \approx 2.67 \text{ km.}$$

(b) When particle strikes the ground

$$v_x = \sqrt{5}y = (\sqrt{5})(400) = 400\sqrt{5} \text{ m/s}$$

$$v_y = gt = 89.4 \text{ m/s}$$

$\therefore \quad \text{Speed} = \sqrt{v_x^2 + v_y^2} = 899 \text{ m/s}$

$\approx 0.9 \text{ km/s}$ **Ans.**

6. At $t = 0$, $\mathbf{v}_T = (10\hat{\mathbf{j}})$ m/s

$\mathbf{v}_{ST} = 10 \cos 37° \hat{\mathbf{k}} - 10 \sin 37° \hat{\mathbf{i}} = (8\hat{\mathbf{k}} - 6\hat{\mathbf{i}})$ m/s

$\therefore \quad \mathbf{v}_S = \mathbf{v}_{ST} + \mathbf{v}_T = (-6\hat{\mathbf{i}} + 10\hat{\mathbf{j}} + 8\hat{\mathbf{k}})$ m/s

(a) At highest point, vertical component $(\hat{\mathbf{k}})$ of $\mathbf{v}_S$ will become zero. Hence, velocity of particle at highest point will become $(-6\hat{\mathbf{i}} + 10\hat{\mathbf{j}})$ m/s.

(b) Time of flight, $T = \frac{2v_Z}{g} = \frac{2 \times 8}{10} = 1.6$ s

$$x = x_i + v_x T$$
$$= \frac{16}{\pi} - 6 \times 1.6 = -4.5 \text{ m}$$

$y = (10)(1.6) = 16$ m and $z = 0$

Therefore, coordinates of particle where it finally lands on the ground are (– 4.5 m, 16 m , 0).

At highest point, $t = \frac{T}{2} = 0.8$ s

$$\therefore \quad x = \frac{16}{\pi} - (6)(0.8) = 0.3 \text{ m}$$
$$y = (10)(0.8) = 8.0 \text{ m}$$

and $$z = \frac{v_Z^2}{2g} = \frac{(8)^2}{20} = 3.2 \text{ m}$$

Therefore, coordinates at highest point are (0.3 m, 8.0 m, 3.2 m). **Ans.**

7. $|v_{21x}| = (v_1 + v_2) \cos 60° = 12$ m/s

$|v_{21y}| = (v_2 - v_1) \sin 60° = 4\sqrt{3}$ m/s

$\therefore v_{21} = \sqrt{(12)^2 + (4\sqrt{3})^2} = \sqrt{192}$ m/s

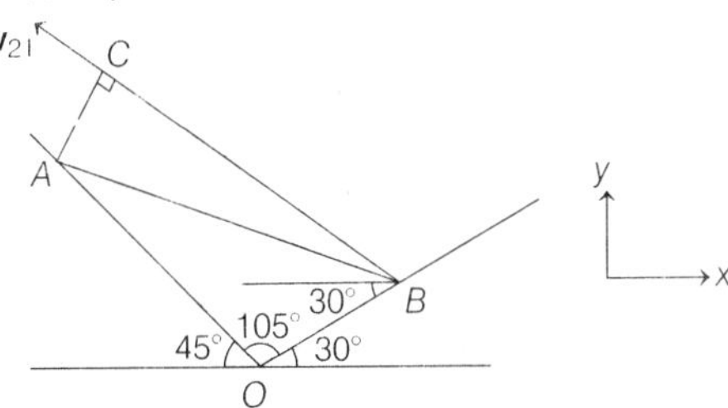

$$BC = (v_{21})\, t = 240 \text{ m}$$
$$AC = 70 \text{ m} \quad \text{(Given)}$$

Hence, $AB = \sqrt{(240)^2 + (70)^2} = 250$ m **Ans.**

8. (a) Let (x, y) be the coordinates of point C

$$x = OD = OA + AD$$
$$\therefore \quad x = \frac{10}{3} + y \cot 37° = \frac{10 + 4y}{3} \quad \ldots\text{(i)}$$

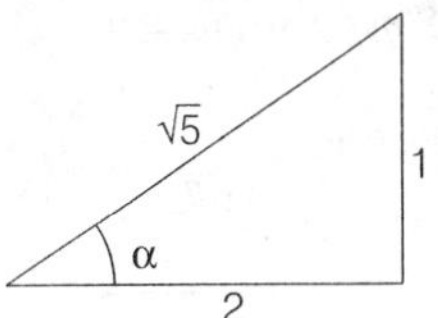

As point C lies on the trajectory of a parabola, we have

$$y = x \tan \alpha - \frac{gx^2}{2u^2}(1 + \tan^2 \alpha) \quad \ldots\text{(ii)}$$

Given that, $\tan \alpha = 0.5 = \frac{1}{2}$

Solving Eqs. (i) and (ii), we get $x = 5$ m and $y = 1.25$ m.

Hence, the coordinates of point C are (5 m, 1.25 m). **Ans.**

(b) Let v_y be the vertical component of velocity of the particle just before collision at C.

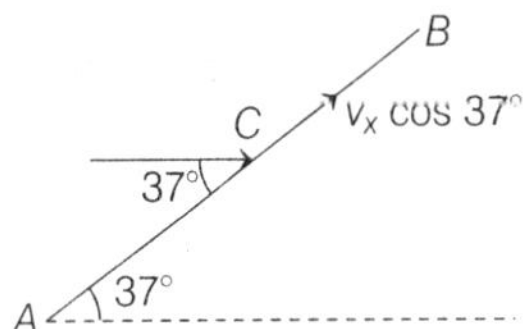

Using $v_y = u_y + a_y t$, we have

$v_y = u \sin \alpha - g\,(x/u \cos \alpha)\ (\because\ t = x/u \cos \alpha)$

$$= \frac{5\sqrt{5}}{\sqrt{5}} - \frac{10 \times 5}{(5\sqrt{5} \times 2/\sqrt{5})} = 0$$

Thus, at C, the particle has only horizontal component of velocity

$$v_x = u \cos \alpha = 5\sqrt{5} \times (2/\sqrt{5}) = 10 \text{m/s}$$

Given that, the particle does not rebound after collision. So, the normal component of velocity (normal to the plane AB) becomes zero. Now, the particle slides up the plane due to tangential component $v_x \cos 37° = (10)\left(\frac{4}{5}\right) = 8$ m/s

Let h be the further height raised by the particle. Then,

$$mgh = \frac{1}{2} m (8)^2$$

or $$h = 3.2 \text{ m}$$

Height of the particle from the ground $= y + h$

$\therefore \quad H = 1.25 + 3.2 = 4.45$ m **Ans.**

9. For shell $u_z = 20 \sin 60° = 17.32$ m/s

$$\therefore \quad z = u_z t - \frac{1}{2} gt^2 = (17.32 \times 2) - \left(\frac{1}{2} \times 9.8 \times 4\right)$$

or $z = 15$ m $\Rightarrow$ $u_y = 0$

$\therefore$ $y = 0$

For u_x conservation of linear momentum gives,

$$50 \times 4 = (40)(v) + 10(20\cos 60° + v)$$

or $v = 2$ m/s

$\therefore$ $u_x = (20\cos 60°) + 2 = 12$ m/s

$\therefore$ $x = u_x t = (12)(2) = 24$ m

$\therefore$ $\mathbf{r} = (24\hat{\mathbf{i}} + 15\hat{\mathbf{k}})$ m **Ans.**

10. $\because$ $R = \dfrac{u^2 \sin 60°}{g}$ ...(i)

and $R - x_1 = \dfrac{u^2 \sin 30°}{g}$ ...(ii)

and $R + x_2 = \dfrac{u^2 \sin 90°}{g}$ ...(iii)

From Eqs. (i), (ii) and (iii), we get

$$\frac{x_1}{x_2} = \frac{(\sqrt{3} - 1)}{(2 - \sqrt{3})}$$

$$\therefore \quad (\sqrt{3} - 1)\frac{x_1}{x_2} = \frac{(3 + 1 - 2\sqrt{3})}{(2 - \sqrt{3})} = \frac{2(2 - \sqrt{3})}{(2 - \sqrt{3})} = 2$$

11. Here, range is $OB = 2h \tan\theta = \dfrac{u^2 \sin 2\alpha}{g}$

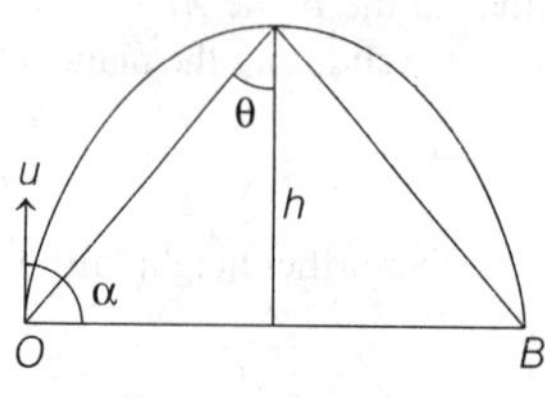

and $h = \dfrac{u^2 \sin^2\alpha}{2g}$

$$\therefore \quad \frac{2h\tan\theta}{h} = \frac{\dfrac{u^2 \sin 2\alpha}{g}}{\dfrac{u^2 \sin^2\alpha}{2g}}$$

$\therefore$ $\tan\alpha = 2\cot\theta$

or $\sin\alpha = \dfrac{2\cos\theta}{\sqrt{1 + 4\cot^2\theta}}$

$\because$ $h = \dfrac{u^2 \sin^2\alpha}{2g}$

or $\dfrac{u^2}{2g} = \dfrac{h}{\sin^2\alpha} = \dfrac{h}{4\cot^2\theta}(1 + 4\cot^2\theta)$

or $\dfrac{u^2}{2gh} = \dfrac{1}{4\cot^2\theta}(1 + 4\cot^2\theta)$

$= \dfrac{1}{4}\tan^2\theta + 1$

or $\dfrac{u^2}{gh} = \dfrac{1}{2}\tan^2\theta + 2$

$\therefore$ $\dfrac{u^2}{gh} - \dfrac{1}{2}\tan^2\theta = 2$

12. Let position vectors of balls are A, B and C at instant t.

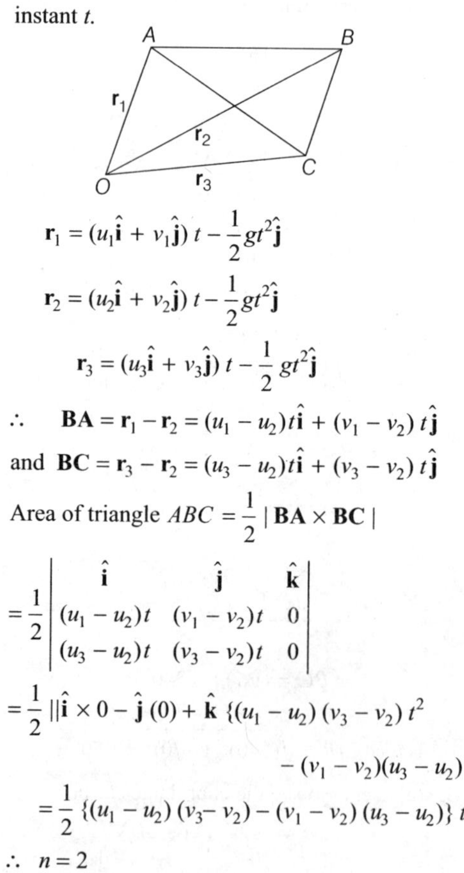

$$\mathbf{r}_1 = (u_1\hat{\mathbf{i}} + v_1\hat{\mathbf{j}})t - \frac{1}{2}gt^2\hat{\mathbf{j}}$$

$$\mathbf{r}_2 = (u_2\hat{\mathbf{i}} + v_2\hat{\mathbf{j}})t - \frac{1}{2}gt^2\hat{\mathbf{j}}$$

$$\mathbf{r}_3 = (u_3\hat{\mathbf{i}} + v_3\hat{\mathbf{j}})t - \frac{1}{2}gt^2\hat{\mathbf{j}}$$

$\therefore$ $\mathbf{BA} = \mathbf{r}_1 - \mathbf{r}_2 = (u_1 - u_2)t\hat{\mathbf{i}} + (v_1 - v_2)t\hat{\mathbf{j}}$

and $\mathbf{BC} = \mathbf{r}_3 - \mathbf{r}_2 = (u_3 - u_2)t\hat{\mathbf{i}} + (v_3 - v_2)t\hat{\mathbf{j}}$

Area of triangle $ABC = \dfrac{1}{2}|\mathbf{BA} \times \mathbf{BC}|$

$$= \frac{1}{2}\begin{vmatrix} \hat{\mathbf{i}} & \hat{\mathbf{j}} & \hat{\mathbf{k}} \\ (u_1 - u_2)t & (v_1 - v_2)t & 0 \\ (u_3 - u_2)t & (v_3 - v_2)t & 0 \end{vmatrix}$$

$$= \frac{1}{2}||\hat{\mathbf{i}} \times 0 - \hat{\mathbf{j}}(0) + \hat{\mathbf{k}}\{(u_1 - u_2)(v_3 - v_2)t^2 - (v_1 - v_2)(u_3 - u_2)t^2|$$

$$= \frac{1}{2}\{(u_1 - u_2)(v_3 - v_2) - (v_1 - v_2)(u_3 - u_2)\}t^2$$

$\therefore$ $n = 2$

13. $\because \; y = u_y t + \frac{1}{2} a_y t^2$

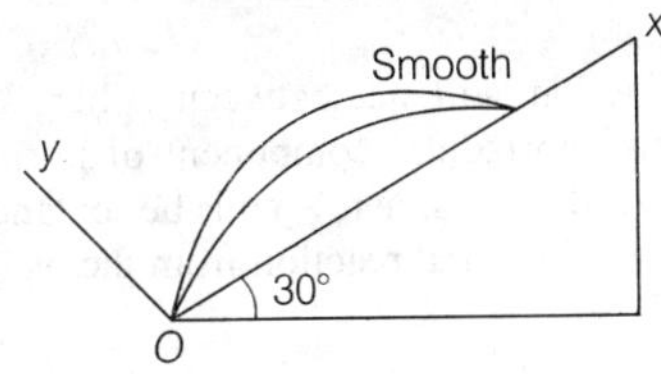

or $0 = u_y T - \frac{1}{2}(g \cos 30°) T^2$

$\therefore \; T = \frac{2u_y}{g \cos 30°} = \frac{4u_y}{10\sqrt{3}}$

$$\therefore \qquad T_A = \frac{4u \sin 15°}{10\sqrt{3}} \qquad \text{...(i)}$$

$$\text{and} \qquad T_B = \frac{4u \sin \alpha}{10\sqrt{3}}$$

where, α is angle of projection of particle B.

$\because \; R = u_x T + \frac{1}{2} a_x T^2$ ...(ii)

or $R = (u \cos 60°) T_A - \frac{1}{2} g \sin 30° T_A^2$

$= (u \cos \alpha) T_B - \frac{1}{2} g \sin 30° T_B^2$ ...(iii)

or $u \cos 60° \times \frac{4u \sin 60°}{10\sqrt{3}} - \frac{1}{2} g \sin 30° T_A^2$

$= (u \cos \alpha) T_B - \frac{1}{2} g \sin 30° T_B^2$

Putting the value of T_A and T_B,

$\alpha = 90° - 15° - 30° = 45°$

$$\therefore \qquad \frac{T_A}{T_B} = \frac{\frac{4u \sin 30°}{10\sqrt{3}}}{\frac{4u \sin \alpha}{10\sqrt{3}}} = \frac{\sin 30°}{\sin \alpha}$$

$$= \sqrt{2} \times \frac{1}{2} = \frac{1}{\sqrt{2}} = 1 : \sqrt{n}$$

$\therefore \qquad n = 2$

14. $R = \frac{v_0^2 \sin 2\alpha}{g}$ or $8.4 = \frac{v_0^2 \sin 2\alpha}{10}$

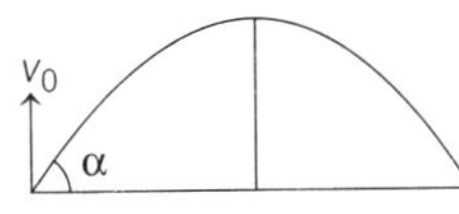

$\Rightarrow \qquad v_0^2 \sin 2\alpha = 84$

$$\Rightarrow \qquad v_0^2 = \frac{42}{\sin \alpha \cos \alpha}$$

The equation of trajectory is

$$y = x \tan \alpha - \frac{gx^2}{2v_0^2 \cos^2 \alpha}$$

$$\Rightarrow 3.6 = 4.8 \tan \alpha - \frac{10\,x^2}{2 \times \frac{42}{\sin\alpha \cos \alpha} \cos^2 \alpha}$$

$$\Rightarrow \qquad 3.6 = 4.8 \tan \alpha - \frac{5}{42}(4.8)^2 \tan \alpha$$

$$\therefore \qquad \tan \alpha = 1.75 = \frac{7}{4} = \frac{n}{4}$$

$\therefore \qquad n = 7$

15. $v_0^2 = 2as = 2 \times 6 \times 12$

$\therefore \qquad v_0 = 12 \text{ ms}^{-1}$

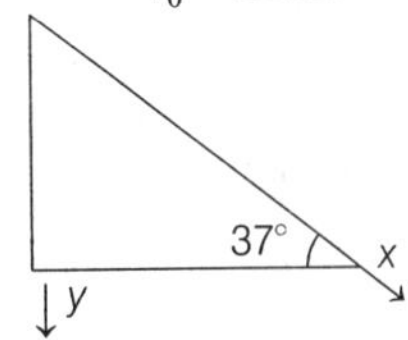

After point B,

$u_x = 12 \cos 37° = 12 \times \frac{4}{5} = 9.6 \text{ ms}^{-1}$

and $u_y = 12 \sin 37° = 12 \times \frac{3}{5} = 7.2 \text{ ms}^{-1}$

$\therefore \qquad y = u_y t + \frac{1}{2} g t^2 = 9.6\,t + \frac{1}{2} \times 10 \times t^2$

or $\qquad 14.6 = 9.6\,t + 5\,t^2$

$\therefore \qquad t = 1 \text{ s}$

$\therefore \qquad x_0 = u_x\, t = 7.2 \times 1 = 7.2 \text{ m} = \frac{36}{5}$

$\therefore \qquad n = 5$

16. For minimum value of v_0, the maximum range on inclined plane should be $AB = 15$ m.

The maximum range will be

$$R_{\max} = \frac{v_0^2}{g\,(1 + \sin 30°)}$$

or $\qquad v_0^2 = 15 \times 10 \times \frac{3}{2}$

$v_0^2 = 15^2$

$\therefore \qquad v_0 = 15 \text{ ms}^{-1} = 3x$

$\therefore \qquad x = 5$

8. Laws of Motion

INTRODUCTORY EXERCISE 8.1

1. w_1 = weight of cylinder

w_2 = weight of plank

N_1 = normal reaction between cylinder and plank

N_2 = normal reaction on cylinder from ground

N_3 = normal reaction on plank from ground

f_1 = force of friction on cylinder from ground

f_2 = force of friction on plank from ground

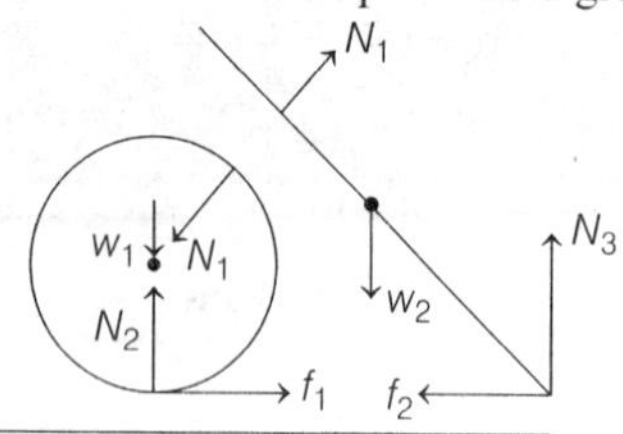

2. N = normal reactions

w = weights

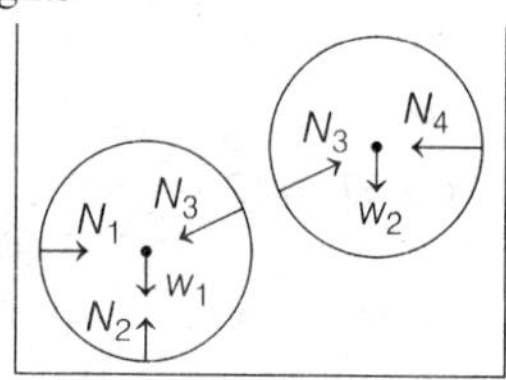

3.

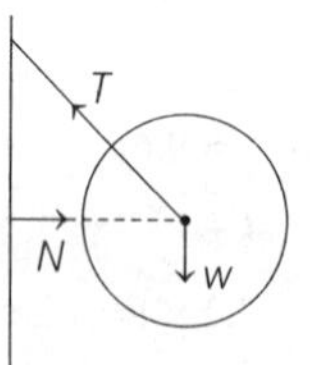

4.

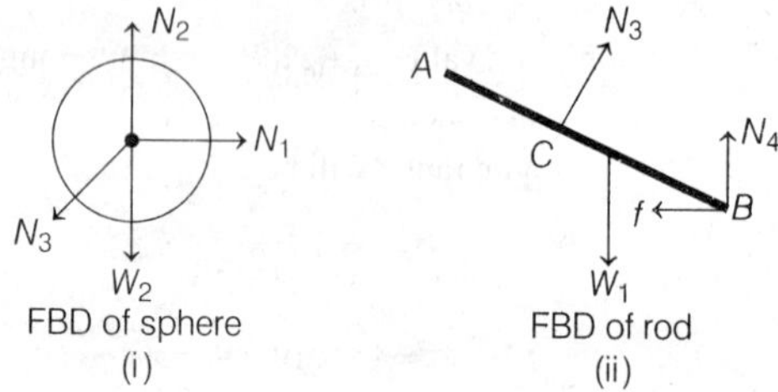

In the figure

N_1 = normal reaction between sphere and wall,

N_2 = normal reaction between sphere and ground

N_3 = normal reaction between sphere and rod and

N_4 = normal reaction between rod and ground

f = force of friction between rod and ground

No friction will act between sphere and ground because horizontal component of normal reaction from rod (on sphere) will be balanced by the horizontal normal reaction from the wall.

5.

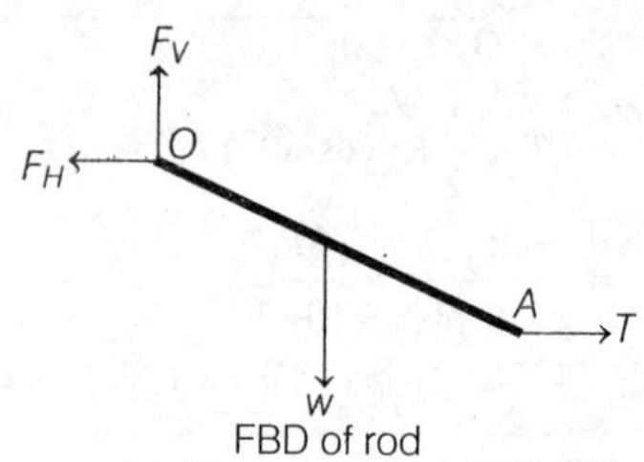

FBD of rod

In the figure

T = tension in the string, w = weight of the rod,

F_V = vertical force exerted by hinge on the rod

F_H = horizontal force exerted by hinge on the rod

6. In the figure

N_1 = Normal reaction at B,

f_1 = force of friction at B,

N_2 = normal reaction at A, f_2 = force of friction at A

w = weight of the rod.

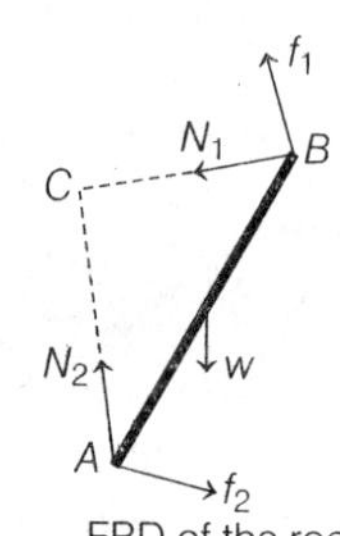

FBD of the rod

7.

Force	F_x	F_y
F_1	$4 \cos 30° = 2\sqrt{3}$ N	$4 \sin 30° = 2$ N
F_2	$-4 \cos 60° = -2$ N	$4 \sin 60° = 2\sqrt{3}$ N
F_3	0	-6 N
F_4	4 N	0

8. $T_1 \cos 45° = w$

and $\quad T_1 \sin 45° = 30$ N

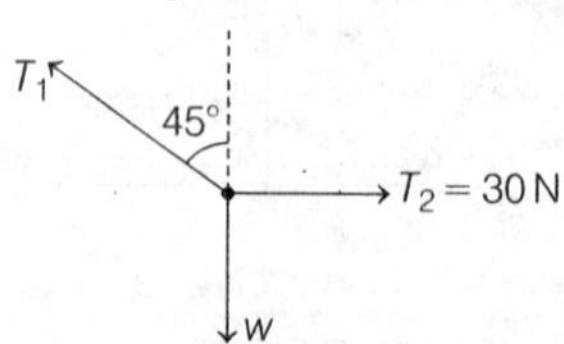

$\therefore \quad w = 30$ N **Ans.**

9. $N_A \cos 30° = 500 \text{ N}$ ...(i)

$N_A \sin 30° = N_B$ ...(ii)

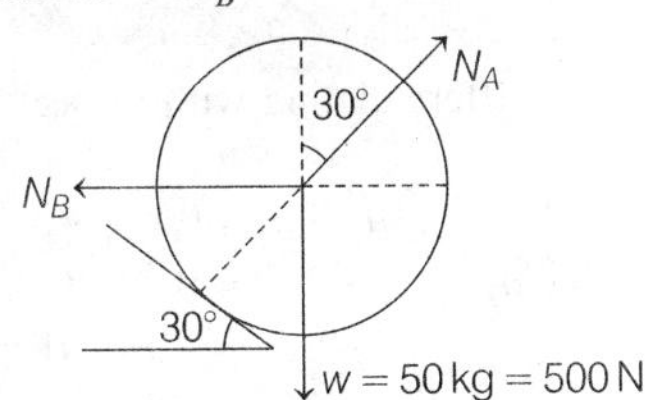

On solving these two equations, we get

$$N_A = \frac{1000}{\sqrt{3}} \text{ N}$$

and $$N_B = \frac{500}{\sqrt{3}} \text{N}$$ **Ans.**

10. Net force in vertical direction = 0

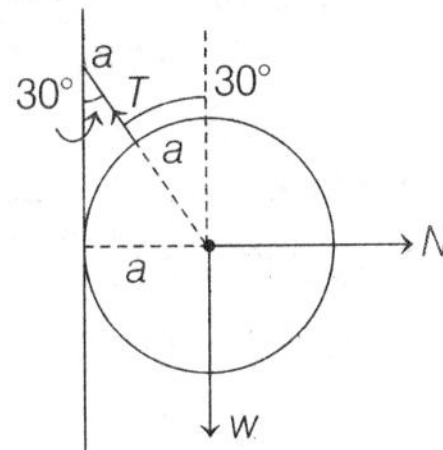

$\therefore \quad T \cos 30° = w \quad \text{or} \quad T = \dfrac{2w}{\sqrt{3}}$ **Ans.**

11. $w = 100 \text{ N}$

Σ(forces in horizontal direction) = 0

$\therefore \quad T + f \cos 30° = N \sin 30°$ ...(i)

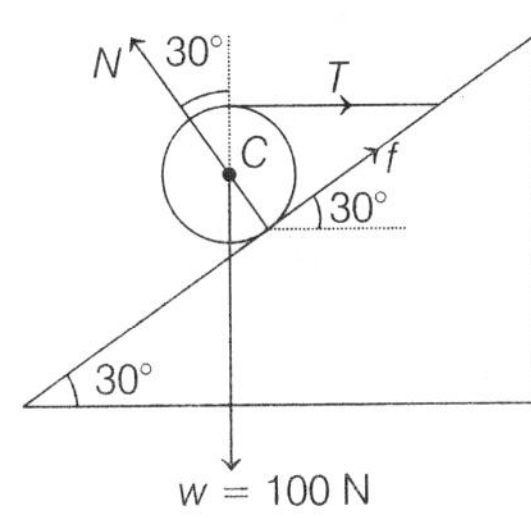

Σ(Forces in vertical direction) = 0

$\therefore \quad N \cos 30° + f \sin 30° = 100$ ...(ii)

Σ (moment of all forces about C) = 0

$\therefore \quad (T)(R) = f\,(R)$

or $\quad T = f$ ...(iii)

On solving these three equations, we get

$T = f = 26.8 \text{N}$

and $\quad N = 100 \text{ N}$ **Ans.**

INTRODUCTORY EXERCISE 8.2

1. (a)
$$a = \frac{\text{Net pushing force}}{\text{Total mass}} = \frac{120 - 50}{1 + 4 + 2} = 10 \text{ m/s}^2$$

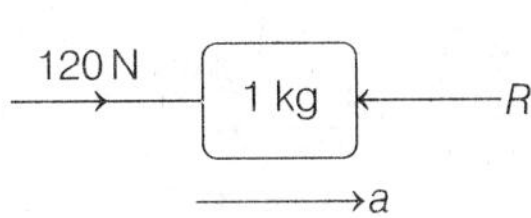

(b) $120 - R = 1 \times a = 10$

$\therefore \quad R = 110 \text{ N}$

(c) $F_{\text{net}} = ma = (2)(10)$

$= 20 \text{ N}$

2. $T_4 = 4g \quad \text{and} \quad T_1 = (1)\,g$ as $a = 0$

$\therefore \quad \dfrac{T_4}{T_1} = 4$ **Ans.**

3. $$a = \frac{\text{Net pulling force}}{\text{Total mass}} = \frac{F + 10 - 20}{1 + 2} \quad (F = 20 \text{ N})$$

$$= \frac{10}{3} \text{ m/s}^2$$ **Ans.**

4. $m_A g = (2)(g) + (2)g \sin 30°$ as $a = 0$

$\therefore \quad m_A = 3 \text{ kg}$ **Ans.**

5. Since surface is smooth, acceleration of both is $g \sin \theta = 10 \sin 30° = 5 \text{ m/s}^2$, down the plane.

The component of mg down the plane ($= mg \sin \theta$) provides this acceleration. So, normal reaction will be zero.

6. $N = \dfrac{mg}{4}$ is given

$$mg - \frac{mg}{4} = ma$$

$\therefore \quad a = \dfrac{3g}{4}$

7. $$a = \frac{\text{Net pulling force}}{\text{Total mass}} = \frac{(3 + 4 - 2 - 1)\,g}{3 + 4 + 2 + 1} = 4 \text{ m/s}^2$$ **Ans.**

4 kg $\quad 40 - T_1 = 4a \quad \therefore \quad T_1 = 24 \text{ N}$ **Ans.**

3 kg $\quad T_1 + 30 - T_2 = 3a \quad \therefore \quad T_2 = 42 \text{ N}$ **Ans.**

1 kg $\quad T_3 - 10 = (1)(a) \quad \therefore \quad T_3 = 14 \text{ N}$ **Ans.**

8. (a) $a = \dfrac{\text{Net pushing force}}{\text{Total mass}}$

$= \dfrac{100 - 40}{6 + 4 + 10} = 3\ \text{m/s}^2$

(b) Net force on any block $= ma$

(c) $N - 40 = 10\,a = 30$

$N \rightarrow$ 10 kg $\leftarrow$ 40 N, $\rightarrow a$

$\therefore \quad N = 70\ \text{N}$ **Ans.**

9. (a) $T_1 = 10a,\ T_2 - T_1 = 20a,\ 60 - T_2 = 30a$

10 kg $\rightarrow T_1$, $\rightarrow a$

$T_1 \leftarrow$ 20 kg $\rightarrow T_2$, $\rightarrow a$

$T_2 \leftarrow$ 30 kg $\rightarrow$ 60 N, $\rightarrow a$

$a = \dfrac{\text{Net pulling force}}{\text{Total mass}} = \dfrac{60}{10 + 20 + 30}$

$= 1\ \text{m/s}^2$

On solving, we get $T_1 = 10\ \text{N},\ T_2 = 30\ \text{N}$ **Ans.**

(b) $T_1 = 0,\ T_2 = 20a,\ 60 - T_2 = 30a$

$a = \dfrac{\text{Net pulling force}}{\text{Total mass}} = \dfrac{60}{20 + 30}$

$= 1.2\ \text{m/s}^2$

On solving, we get

$T_2 = 24\ \text{N}$ **Ans.**

INTRODUCTORY EXERCISE 8.3

1. Points 1, 2, 3 and 4 are movable. Let their displacements from the fixed dotted line be x_1, x_2, x_3 and x_4 (ignoring the length over the pulley)

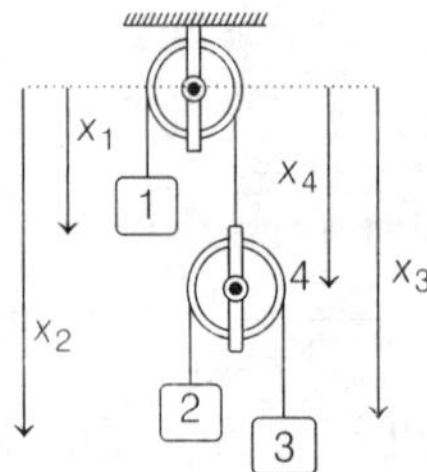

We have,

$x_1 + x_4 = l_1$ (length of first string) ...(i)

and $(x_2 - x_4) + (x_3 - x_4) = l_2$ (length of second string)

or $x_2 + x_3 - 2x_4 = l_2$ ...(ii)

On double differentiating with respect to time, we get

$a_1 + a_4 = 0$ ...(iii)

and $a_2 + a_3 - 2a_4 = 0$ ...(iv)

But $a_4 = -a_1$ [From Eq. (iii)]

We have, $a_2 + a_3 + 2a_1 = 0$

This is the required constraint relation between a_1, a_2 and a_3.

2. In above solution, we have found that

$a_2 + a_3 + 2a_1 = 0$

Similarly, we can find

$v_2 + v_3 + 2v_1 = 0$

Taking, upward direction as positive we are given

$v_1 = v_2 = 1\ \text{m/s}$

$\therefore \quad v_3 = -3\ \text{m/s}$

i.e. velocity of block 3 is 3 m/s (downwards).

3. **2 kg** $\quad 2T = 2\,(a)$ ...(i)

1 kg $\quad 10 - T = 1\,(2a)$ ...(ii)

On solving these two equations, we get

$T = \dfrac{10}{3}\ \text{N}$

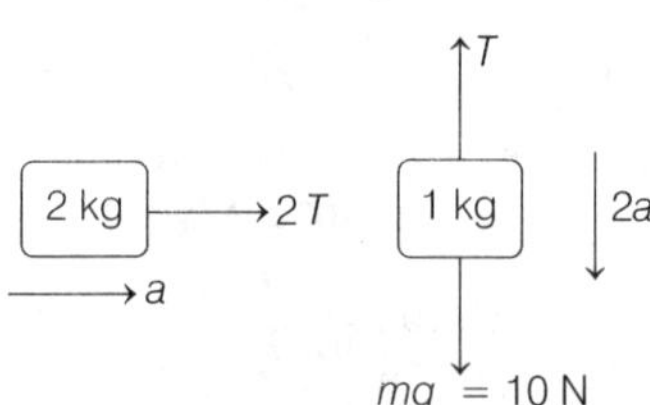

and $\quad 2a = 2T = \dfrac{20}{3}\ \text{m/s}^2$

= acceleration of 1 kg block

4.

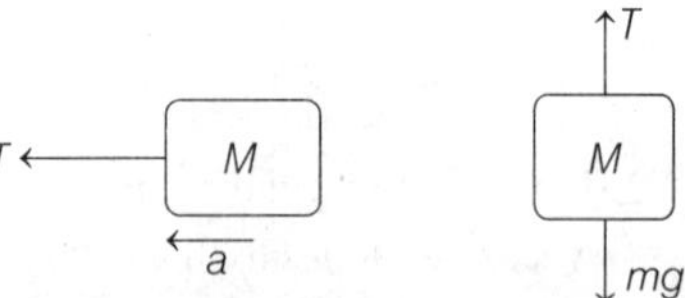

$T = Ma$ ...(i)

$Mg - T = Ma$ ...(ii)

On solving these two equations, we get

$a = \dfrac{g}{2}$

and $\quad T = \dfrac{Mg}{2}$ **Ans.**

5. In the figure shown,

$$a = \frac{\text{Net pulling force}}{\text{Total mass}} = \frac{30 - 20}{3 + 2}$$

$$= 2 \text{ m/s}^2$$

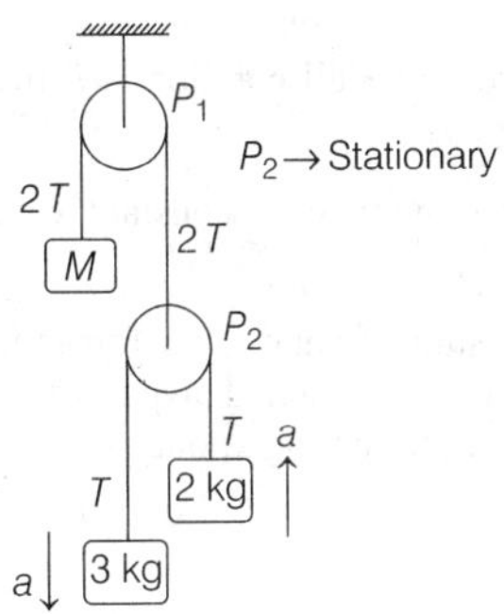

2 kg $\quad T - 20 = 2 \times a = 4$

$\therefore \quad T = 24$ N

Now, $\quad Mg = 2T$

$\therefore \quad M = \frac{2T}{g} = \frac{48}{10}$

$= 4.8$ kg **Ans.**

6. $T = m_1 (2a) = (0.3)(2a) = 0.6a$ ...(i)

$F - 2T = m_2 a$

$\therefore \quad 2T = 0.4 - 0.2a$ ...(ii)

On solving these two equations, we get

$$a = \frac{2}{7} \text{ m/s}^2$$ **Ans.**

and $\quad 2T = \frac{12}{35}$ N **Ans.**

7. $a_3 = a + a_r = 6$ ...(i)

$a_2 = a_r - a = 4$ ...(ii)

On solving these two equations, we get

$$a = 1 \text{ m/s}^2$$

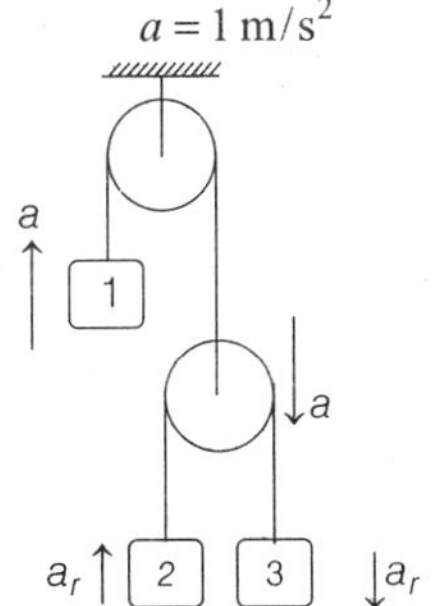

8. $T - Mg \sin 30° = Ma$ ...(i)

$2Mg - 2T = 2M\left(\frac{a}{2}\right)$ ...(ii)

Solving these equations, we get

$$a = \frac{g}{3}$$ **Ans.**

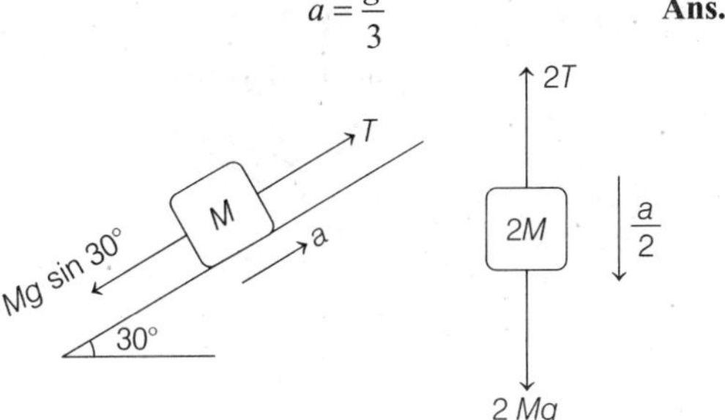

INTRODUCTORY EXERCISE 8.4

1. (a) $\mathbf{F}_A = -m_A \mathbf{a}_B = (4\hat{\mathbf{j}})$ N

(b) $\mathbf{F}_B = -m_B \mathbf{a}_A = (-4\hat{\mathbf{i}})$ N

2. Constant velocity means acceleration of frame is zero.

INTRODUCTORY EXERCISE 8.5

1. **Figure (a)** $\quad N = mg = 40$ N

$\mu_s N = 24$ N

Since, $\quad F < \mu_s N$

Block will remain stationary and

$f = F = 20$ N

Figure (b) $\quad N = mg = 20$ N

$\mu_S N = 12$ N

and $\quad \mu_K N = 8$ N

Since, $F > \mu_S N$, block will slide and kinetic friction (= 8 N) will act.

$$a = \frac{F - f}{m} = \frac{20 - 8}{2} = 6 \text{ m/s}^2$$

2. If $\theta \leq$ angle of repose, the block is stationary, $a = 0$, $F_{net} = 0$ and $f = mg \sin \theta$.

If $\theta >$ angle of repose, the block will move,

$f = \mu mg \cos \theta$

$$a = \frac{mg \sin \theta - \mu mg \cos \theta}{m}$$

$= g \sin \theta - \mu g \cos \theta$ and $F_{net} = ma$

Further, $\quad \mu = \tan \alpha \quad$ (α = angle of repose = 45°)

$= \tan 45° = 1$

Exercises

LEVEL 1

Assertion and Reason

1. $a_1 = g \sin\theta + \mu g \cos\theta$

$$a_2 = g \sin\theta - \mu g \cos\theta$$

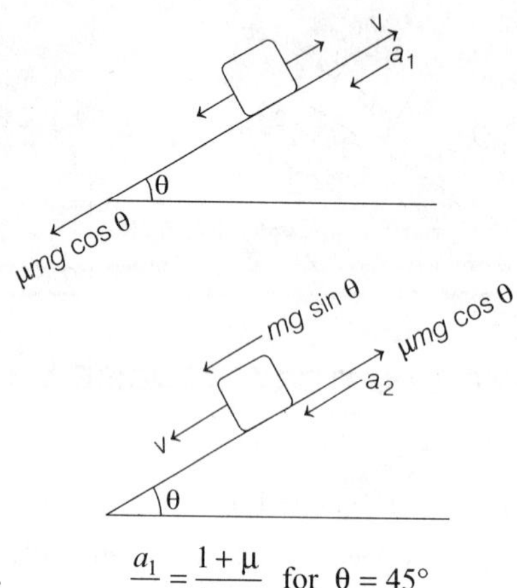

$$\therefore \quad \frac{a_1}{a_2} = \frac{1+\mu}{1-\mu} \quad \text{for } \theta = 45^\circ$$

2. For $(-2\hat{i})\,\text{m/s}^2$ component of acceleration, a horizontal force in $-$ve x- direction is required which can be provided only by the right vertical wall of the box.

3. By increasing F_1 limiting value of friction will increase. But it is not necessary that actual value of friction acting on block will increase.

4. **If $m_1 > m_2$**

$$a = \frac{\text{Net pulling force}}{\text{Total mass}} = \frac{(m_1 - m_2)\,g}{m_1 + m_2}$$

FBD of m_1

$$m_1 g - T = m_1 a = \frac{m_1 (m_1 - m_2)\,g}{m_1 + m_2}$$

$$\therefore \quad T = \frac{2\,m_1\,m_2}{(m_1 + m_2)}\,g$$

$$= m_1\,g\left[\frac{2m_2}{m_1 + m_2}\right] = m_2 g\left[\frac{2m_1}{m_1 + m_2}\right]$$

$$= m_1\,g\left[\frac{m_2 + m_2}{m_1 + m_2}\right] = m_2 g\left[\frac{m_1 + m_1}{m_1 + m_2}\right]$$

Since $m_1 > m_2$, $T < m_1 g$ but $T > m_2 g$

Similarly,

we can prove that

$$T < m_2 g$$

and $\quad T > m_1 g$

if $\quad m_2 > m_1$.

Therefore under all conditions T lies between $m_1 g$ and $m_2 g$.

5. A frame moving with constant velocity $(a = 0)$ is inertial.

6. If vector sum of concurrent forces is zero, then all forces can be assumed a pair of two equal and opposite forces acting at one point.

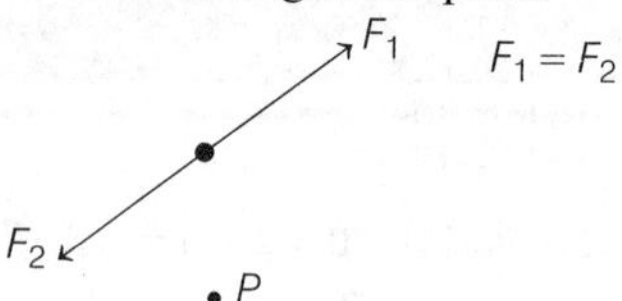

Now, if we take moment about any general point P, then moment of F_1 is clockwise and moment of F_2 (of same magnitude) is anti-clockwise. Therefore net moment is zero.

7. Normal reaction = 15 N

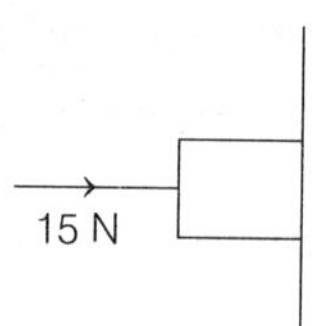

$$f_{max} = \mu N = 9\text{ N}$$

weight = 10 N

Since, weight $> f_{max}$

$\therefore$ 9 N friction will act and block will move downwards.

8. $(f_2)_{max} = \mu_2 mg$

$$(f_1)_{max} = \mu_1 (2m) g$$

Since $\quad (f_1)_{max} > (f_2)_{max}$

Lower block will not move at all.

9. $f - mg\sin\theta = ma\sin\theta$

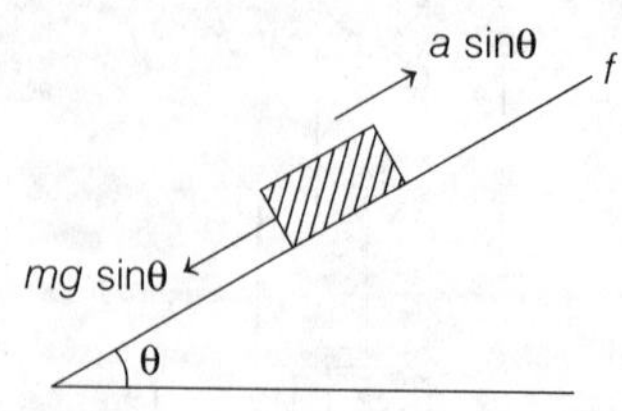

$$\therefore \quad f = m(g + a)\sin\theta > mg\sin\theta$$

10. Consider moment of forces about the point of application of force.

11. Suppose a block is placed inside an elevator moving upward with an acceleration a_0

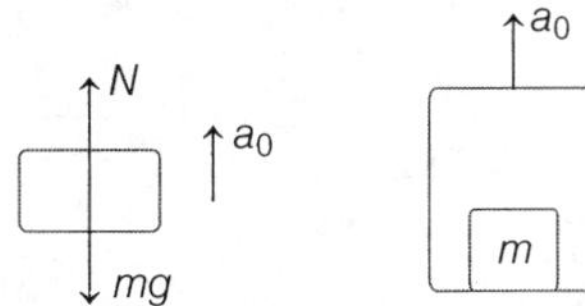

From free body diagram of block,

$$N - mg = ma_0$$

$$\therefore \quad N = mg + ma_0$$

Thus, normal reaction may accelerate a block. Hence, Statement I is wrong.

Normal reaction is +ve component of net contact force perpendicular to the surface of contact. Hence, Statement II is the correct.

13. Free body diagram of man,

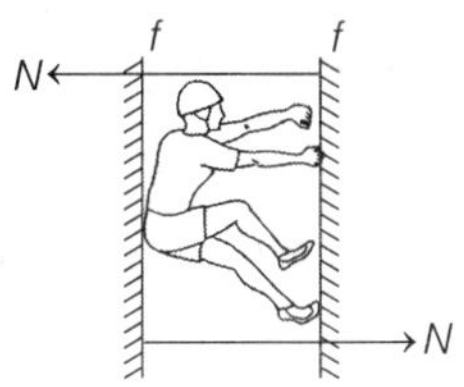

$$f + f = mg$$

$$2f = 50 \times 10$$

$$\Rightarrow \quad f = 250 \text{ N}$$

Single Correct Option

1. $a = \dfrac{mg - F}{m} = g - \dfrac{F}{m}$

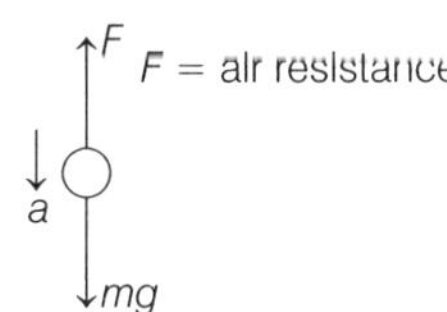

$$m_A > m_B$$

$\therefore \; a_A > a_B$ and A will reach earlier

2. Only two forces are acting, mg and net contact force (resultant of friction and normal reaction) from the inclined plane. Since, the body is at rest. Therefore, these two forces should be equal and opposite.

$\therefore$ Net contact force $= mg$ (upwards)

3. $T_A = 10\,g = 100$ N

$$T_B \cos 30° = T_A$$

$$\therefore \quad T_B = \frac{200}{\sqrt{3}} \text{ N}$$

$$T_B \sin 30° = T_C$$

$$\therefore \quad T_C = \frac{100}{\sqrt{3}} \text{ N}$$

4. $a = \dfrac{mg - T}{m} = g - \dfrac{T}{m}$

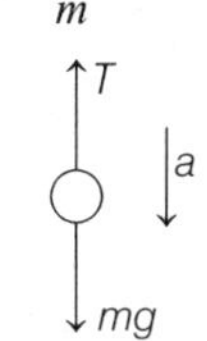

$$a_{\min} = g - \frac{T_{\max}}{m}$$

$$= g - \frac{\frac{2}{3}mg}{m} = \frac{g}{3}$$

5. $a = \dfrac{\text{Net pulling force}}{\text{Total mass}} = \dfrac{10 \times 10 - 5 \times 10}{10 + 5} = \dfrac{10}{3} \text{ m/s}^2$

For **5 kg**, $T - 5 \times 10 = 5 \times a = \dfrac{50}{3}$

$$\therefore \quad T = \frac{200}{3} \text{ N}$$

This is also the reading of spring balance.

6. $t = \sqrt{\dfrac{2S}{a}} \propto \dfrac{1}{\sqrt{a}}$

$$\therefore \quad \frac{t_1}{t_2} = \sqrt{\frac{a_2}{a_1}}$$

$$\frac{2}{1} = \sqrt{\frac{g \sin \theta}{g \sin\theta - \mu_K \, g \cos \theta}} = \sqrt{\frac{1}{1 - \mu_K}}$$

As, $\sin \theta = \cos \theta$ at 45°

On solving the above equation, we get

$$\mu_K = \frac{3}{4}$$

7. During acceleration,

$$v = a_1 t_1 = \frac{F_1}{m} t_1$$

$$\therefore \quad F_1 = \frac{mv}{t_1} \qquad \text{...(i)}$$

During retardation,

$$0 = v - a_2 \, t_2 = v - \frac{F_2}{m} t_2$$

$$\therefore \quad F_2 = \frac{mv}{t_2} \qquad \text{...(ii)}$$

If. $t_1 = t_2$ then $F_1 = F_2$
$t_1 < t_2$ then $F_1 > F_2$
and $t_1 > t_2$ then $F_1 < F_2$

8. Angle of repose $\theta = \tan^{-1}(\mu)$

$$= \tan^{-1}\left(\frac{1}{\sqrt{3}}\right) = 30°$$

So, particle may be placed maximum upto 30°, as shown in figure

$$h = R - R\cos 30° = \left(1 - \frac{\sqrt{3}}{2}\right)R$$

9. Net pulling force $F_1 = 15g - 5g$

$$F_1 = 10g = 100\text{ N}$$

Net stopping force $F_2 = 0.2 \times 5 \times 10 = 10\text{ N}$

Since $F_1 > F_2$, therefore the system will move (anti-clockwise) with an acceleration,

$$a = \frac{F_1 - F_2}{15 + 5 + 5} = \frac{90}{25}$$

$$= 3.6\text{ m/s}^2$$

15 kg block

$$15 \times 10 - T_2 = 15 \times a = 15 \times 3.6$$

$\therefore$ $T_2 = 96\text{ N}$

5 kg block

$$T_1 - 5 \times 10 = 5 \times a = 5 \times 3.6$$

$\therefore$ $T_1 = 68\text{ N}$

$\therefore$ $\frac{T_1}{T_2} = \frac{68}{96} = \frac{17}{24}$

10. Acceleration of block with respect to lift

Pseudo force = (downward)

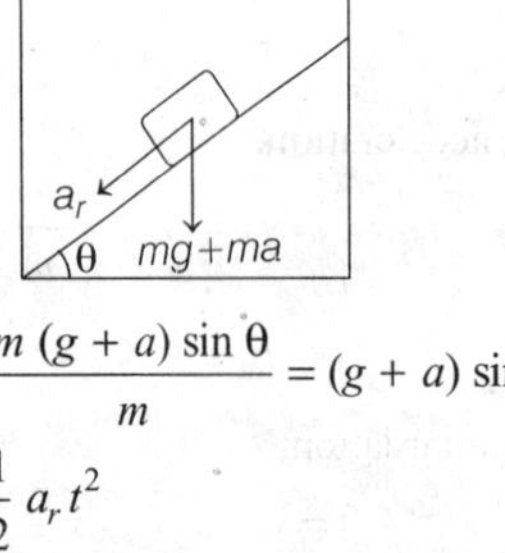

$$a_r = \frac{m(g + a)\sin\theta}{m} = (g + a)\sin\theta$$

$$S = \frac{1}{2}a_r t^2$$

$\therefore$ $t = \sqrt{\frac{2S}{a_r}} = \sqrt{\frac{2L}{(g + a)\sin\theta}}$

11. Since, the block is resting (not moving)

$\therefore$ $f = mg\sin\theta \neq \mu_S\, mg\cos\theta$

or $m = \frac{f}{g\sin\theta}$

$$= \frac{10}{10 \times \sin 30°}$$

$$= 2\text{ kg}$$ **Ans.**

12. At point P,

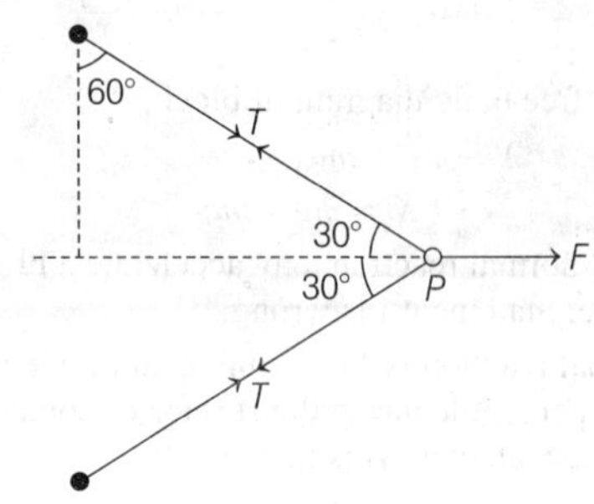

$$F = 2T\cos 30°$$

$\therefore$ $T = \frac{F}{\sqrt{3}}$

Acceleration of particle towards each other

$$= \frac{\text{component of } T \text{ towards each other particle}}{m}$$

$$= \frac{T\cos 60°}{m}$$

$$= \frac{(F/\sqrt{3})(1/2)}{m}$$

$$= \frac{F}{2\sqrt{3}\,m}$$

13. $N = mg = 40\text{ N}$

$$\mu N = 0.2 \times 40 = 8\text{ N}$$

At $t = 2\text{ s}, F = 4\text{ N}$

Since, $F < \mu N$

$\therefore$ $f = F = 4\text{ N}$

14. a_{mr} = acceleration of man relative to rope

$$= a_m - a_r$$

$\therefore$ $a_m = a_{mr} + a_r$

$$= (a) + (a)$$

$$= 2a$$

Now, $T - mg = m(a_m)$

$$= m(2a)$$

$\therefore$ $T = m(g + 2a)$ **Ans.**

Note *Man slides down with a deceleration a relative to the rope. So, $a_{mr} = +a$ not $-a$.*

15. Steady rate means, net force = 0

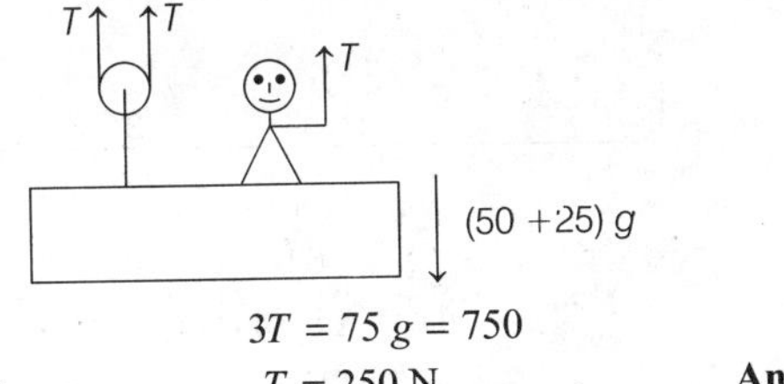

$\therefore \quad 3T = 75\,g = 750$

or $\quad T = 250$ N **Ans.**

16. In the figure, N_2 is always equal to w or 250 N

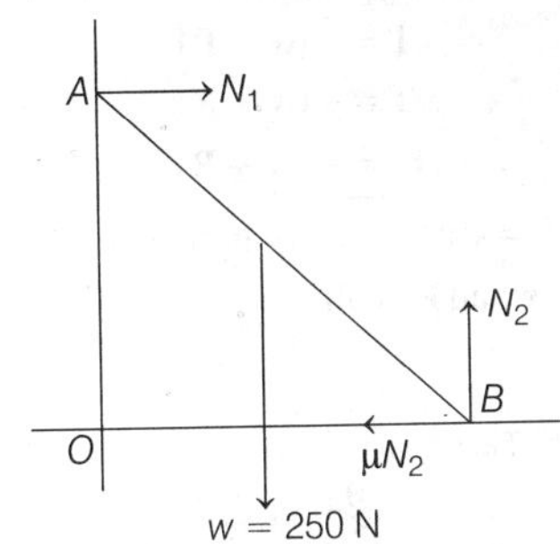

$\therefore$ Maximum value of friction available at B is μN_2 or 75 N.

17. $a = \dfrac{F - f}{M}$

$$= \frac{Mg - \mu mg}{M} = \frac{g}{2}$$

Now, at the mid-point,

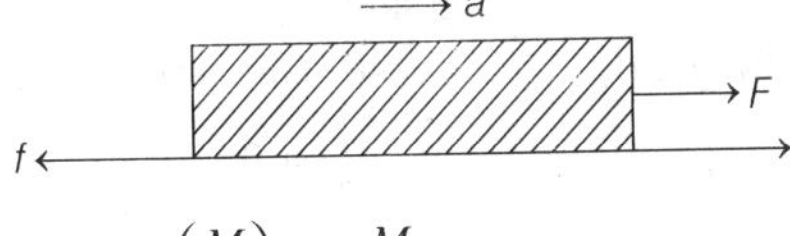

$$T - \mu\left(\frac{M}{2}\right)g = \frac{M}{2}$$

$$a = \left(\frac{M}{2}\right)\left(\frac{g}{2}\right)$$

Putting $\mu = \dfrac{1}{2}$, we get

$$T = \frac{Mg}{2}$$ **Ans.**

18. $N = mg = 40$ N

$$\mu N = 32 \text{ N}$$

Applied force $F = 30 \text{ N} < \mu N$

Therefore, friction force,

$$f = F = 30 \text{ N}$$

$\therefore$ Net contact force from ground on block

$$= \sqrt{N^2 + f^2} = 50 \text{ N}$$ **Ans.**

19. Maximum value of friction between B and ground

$$= \mu N = \mu\,(m_A + m_B)\,g$$
$$= (0.5)\,(2 + 8)\,(10) = 50 \text{ N}$$

Since, applied force $F = 25$ N is less than 50 N. Therefore, system will not move and force of friction between A and B is zero.

20. $mg \sin\theta = (10)\,(10)\,(3/5) = 60$ N

This 60 N > 30 N. Therefore, friction force f will act in upward direction.

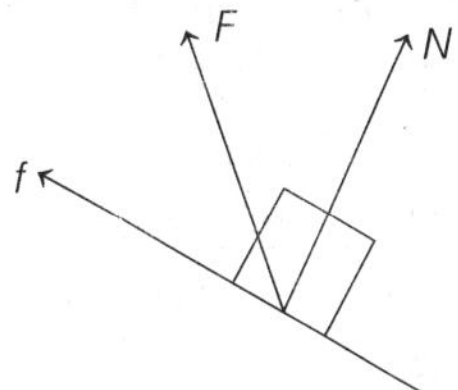

$F = \sqrt{N^2 + f^2}$ = net force by plane on the block.

21. If force applied by man is F, then in first figure, force transferred to the block is F, while in second figure force transferred to the block is $2F$.

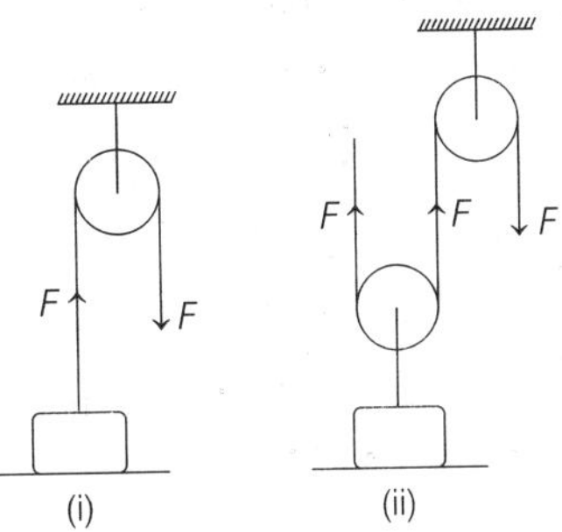

22. Total upward force $= 4\left(\dfrac{mg}{2}\right) = 2\,mg$

Total downward force $= (m + m)\,g = 2\,mg$

$\therefore \quad$ Net force = 0

$$F = \frac{mg}{2}$$

23. Maximum friction between two,

$$f_{max} = \mu N = \mu mg$$

upper block moves only due to friction. Therefore, its maximum acceleration may be

$$a_{max} = \frac{f_{max}}{m} = \mu g$$

Relative motion between them will start when common acceleration becomes μg.

$$\therefore \quad \mu g = \frac{\text{Net force}}{\text{Total mass}} = \frac{at}{2m}$$

$$\therefore \quad t = \frac{2\mu\, mg}{a}$$ **Ans.**

24. $a_1 = g \sin 30° = g/2$

$$a_2 = g \sin 60° = \sqrt{3}\, g/2$$

$$a_r = |\mathbf{a}_1 - \mathbf{a}_2|$$

Angle between $\mathbf{a}_1$ and $\mathbf{a}_2$ is 30°

$$\therefore \quad a_r = \sqrt{a_1^2 + a_2^2 - 2a_1 a_2 \cos 30°} = \frac{g}{2}$$

25. Acceleration of system,

$$a = \frac{\text{Net pulling force}}{\text{Total mass}} = \frac{2mg - mg}{3m} = \frac{g}{3}$$

Now, from equation of motion of m

$$T - mg = ma = \frac{mg}{3}$$

$$\therefore \quad T = \frac{4mg}{3}$$

For equilibrium of pulley,

$$T_{AB} = 2T + \text{weight of pulley} = \frac{8mg}{3} + 3mg = \frac{17mg}{3}$$

26. Assuming the resistance force or retardation to be constant.

$$\left(\frac{v}{2}\right)^2 = v^2 - 2as_1 \quad \text{... (i)}$$

$$0 = \left(\frac{v}{2}\right)^2 - 2as_2 \quad \text{... (ii)}$$

Solving these two equations, we get

$$s_2 = \frac{s_1}{3} = 1\,\text{cm}$$

27. Net moment about point C should be zero. Or

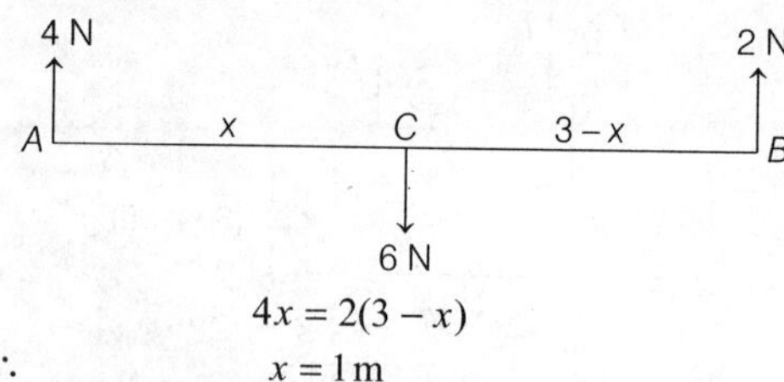

$$4x = 2(3 - x)$$

$$\therefore \quad x = 1\,\text{m}$$

28. (i) Sphere is in equilibrium, therefore vector sum of all three forces acting on sphere will be zero.

$$\therefore \quad \mathbf{T} = -(\mathbf{w} + \mathbf{R})$$

(ii) $\mathbf{T} = -(\mathbf{w} + \mathbf{R})$

or $|\mathbf{T}| = -|(\mathbf{w} + \mathbf{R})|$

$\therefore \quad T = \sqrt{w^2 + R^2}$ as angle between $\mathbf{w}$ and $\mathbf{R}$ is 90°.

(iv)

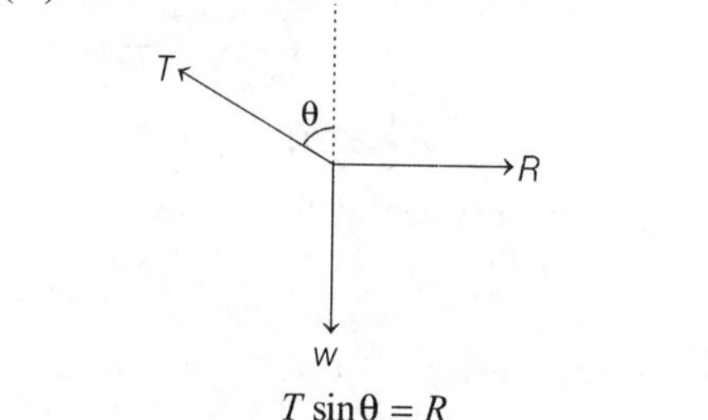

$$T \sin\theta = R \quad \text{...(i)}$$

$$T \cos\theta = w \quad \text{...(ii)}$$

Dividing Eq. (i) by Eq. (ii), we get

$$\tan\theta = \frac{R}{w}$$

or $R = w \tan\theta$

29.

$$F = mg\sin\theta - \mu mg\cos\theta \quad \text{... (i)}$$

$$2F = mg\sin\theta + \mu mg\cos\theta \quad \text{... (ii)}$$

or $2mg\sin\theta - 2\mu mg\cos\theta = mg\sin\theta + \mu mg\cos\theta$

or $\mu = \frac{1}{3}\tan\theta$

30. Force of friction is zero. Contact force is only normal reaction which is $mg\cos\theta$.

31. Net pulling force on the system,

$$F = 10g\sin 37° - 4g = 20\,\text{N}$$

Maximum force of friction

$$f_{max} = \mu mg\cos 37° = 0.7 \times 10 \times 10 \times \frac{4}{5} = 56\,\text{N}$$

Since, $F < f_{max}$, system will not move.

Equilibrium of 4 kg gives $T = 40\text{N}$.

32. Wedge moves due to horizontal component of normal reaction.

Thus, $a = \frac{N_H}{M} = \frac{N \sin\theta}{M}$ (along − ve x-axis)

33. Net force on M in vertical direction should be zero.

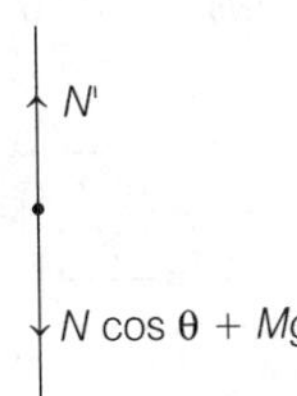

In vertically downwards direction, two forces $N \cos\theta$ and Mg are acting. Therefore N', the normal reaction from ground should be equal to $N \cos\theta + Mg$.

34. Three coins are above the 7th coin. Therefore, force from 3 coins above it will be

$3mg = 3(10 \times 10^{-3})(10) = 0.3$ N (in downward direction)

35. $0 = (3)^2 - 2(a)(9)$

$\therefore \quad a = \frac{1}{2} = 0.5 \text{ m/s}^2$ (upwards)

$N = m(g + a)$

$= 50(9.8 + 0.5) = 515 \text{ N}$

36. Upward force on 2 kg block in upward direction will be 40 N ($= 2F$) in the form of tension.

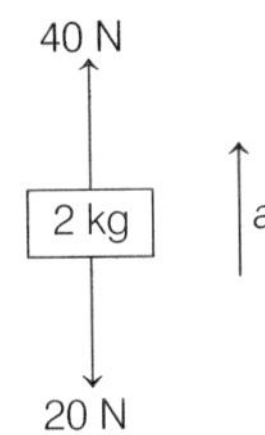

$\therefore \quad a = \frac{40 - 20}{2} = 10 \text{ m/s}^2$

37. Acceleration of system, $a = \frac{\text{Net pulling force}}{\text{Total mass}}$

$= \frac{Mg \sin\theta}{2M}$

$a = \frac{1}{2} g \sin\theta$

Now, the block on ground is moving due to tension.

Hence, $\quad T = Ma = \frac{Mg \sin\theta}{2}$

38. In critical case, weight of hanging part = force of friction on the part of rope lying on table.

$\therefore \quad \frac{m}{l} \cdot l_1 g = \mu \frac{m}{l}(l - l_1) g$

Solving this, we get

$$l_1 = \left(\frac{\mu}{1 + \mu}\right) l$$

39. F_{net} = mass × acceleration

40. $(x_P - x_1) + (x_P - x_2)$ = length of string = constant

Differentiating twice with respect to time, we get

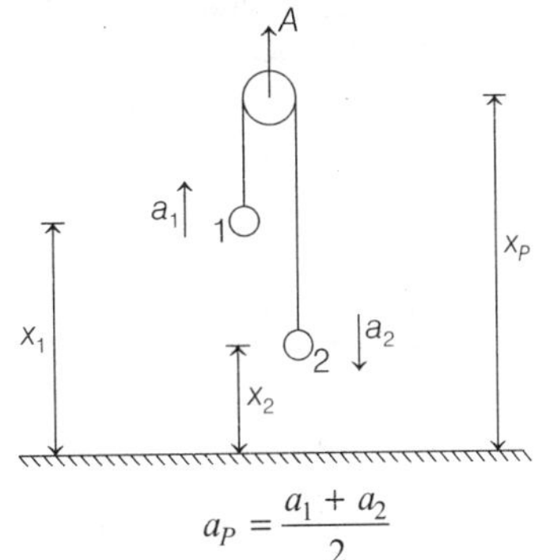

$$a_P = \frac{a_1 + a_2}{2}$$

Here $a_P = A, a_1$ is positive and a_2 is negative. Hence,

$$A = \frac{a_1 - a_2}{2}$$

41. From free body diagram of rod,

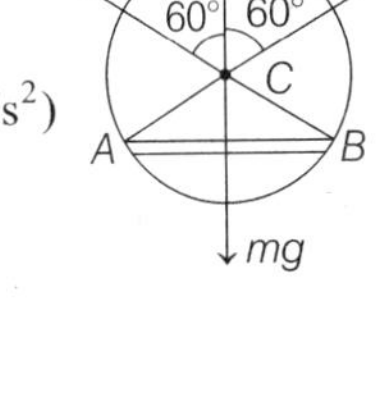

$2N \cos 60° = mg$

$(\because g = 10 \text{ m/s}^2)$

$\therefore \; N = \frac{mg}{2 \cos 60°} = 10 \text{ N}$

$\Rightarrow N = \frac{1 \times 10}{2 \times \frac{1}{2}} = 10 \text{ N}$

42. From free body diagram of light rod,

$\rightarrow F$

$\leftarrow F_2$

$\rightarrow F_1$

$\therefore \quad F + F_1 = F_2$

$\therefore \quad F_1 < F_2$

43. mg can be resolved into two forces of equal magnitude F inclined at an angle 60° with each other.

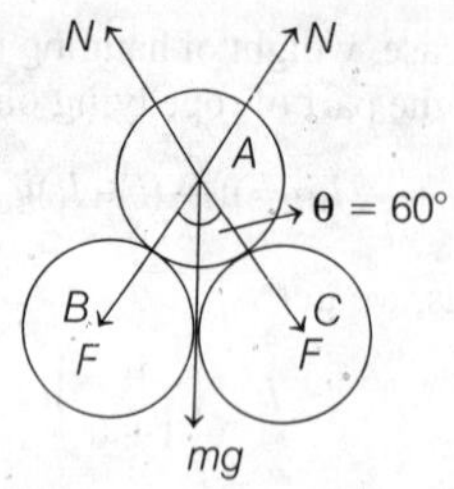

$$\therefore \quad \sqrt{F^2 + F^2 + 2F^2 \cos 60^\circ} = \sqrt{3}g$$

$$\Rightarrow \quad 3F^2 = 3g^2$$

$$F = g \text{ or } F = 10 \text{ N}$$

Hence, reaction of B on $A = 10$ N.

44. From free body diagram of the block,

$$N_2 = 5t \cos 37^\circ = 4t$$

$$N_1 = mg + 5t \sin 37^\circ = 10 + 3t$$

$$\therefore \quad N_1 = 10 + \frac{3}{4} N_2$$

45. $a_1 = \dfrac{F}{m_1}$ and $a_2 = \dfrac{F}{m_2}$

and $a = \dfrac{F}{m_1 + m_2} = \dfrac{F}{\dfrac{F}{a_1} + \dfrac{F}{a_2}} = \dfrac{a_1 a_2}{a_1 + a_2}$

46. The area of force – Time graph = Change in momentum

= Impulse

$$\therefore \quad p_f - p_i = \frac{1}{2} \times 100 \times 4 = 200$$

or $\quad mv - 0 = 200$

$\therefore \quad v = 200$ m/s

47. Here, $T = ma$, $10\sqrt{x} = ma$

$$\Rightarrow \quad m = \frac{10}{a}\sqrt{x}$$

or $\quad \dfrac{dm}{dx} = \dfrac{10}{a} \dfrac{d(\sqrt{x})}{dx}$

or $\quad \dfrac{dm}{dx} = \dfrac{10}{a} \dfrac{1}{2\sqrt{x}}$

or $\quad \dfrac{dm}{dx} = \dfrac{5}{a\sqrt{x}}$

or $\quad dm = \dfrac{5}{a\sqrt{x}} dx$

or $\quad \lambda \, dx = \dfrac{5}{a\sqrt{x}} dx$

$\Rightarrow \quad \lambda = \dfrac{5}{a\sqrt{x}}$

$\Rightarrow \quad \lambda \propto \dfrac{1}{\sqrt{x}}$

48. Here, $a_B \cos 53^\circ = a_A \cos 37^\circ$

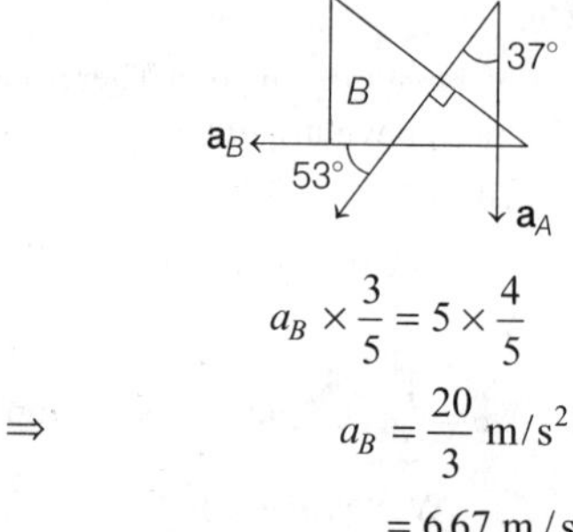

$$a_B \times \frac{3}{5} = 5 \times \frac{4}{5}$$

$$\Rightarrow \quad a_B = \frac{20}{3} \text{ m/s}^2$$

$$= 6.67 \text{ m/s}^2$$

49. For maintaining contact of cylinder with block A,

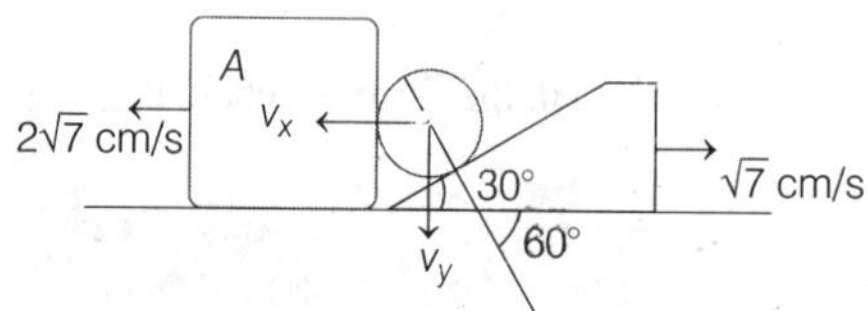

For maintaining contact of cylinder with block B,

$$\sqrt{7} \cos 60^\circ = v_y \cos 30^\circ - v_x \sin 30^\circ$$

$$\frac{\sqrt{7}}{2} = \frac{\sqrt{3}}{2} v_y - \sqrt{7}$$

$$\therefore \quad v_y = \sqrt{21}$$

$\therefore$ The speed of cylinder is

$$v = \sqrt{v_x^2 + v_y^2} = \sqrt{(2\sqrt{7})^2 + (\sqrt{21})^2}$$

$$= 7 \text{ cm/s}$$

50. $\quad a = \dfrac{m_B g - m_A g}{m_A + m_B + m_C} = \dfrac{20}{5} = 4$ m/s

$\therefore \quad s = \dfrac{1}{2} a t^2$ or $\sqrt{\dfrac{8 \times 2}{4}} = t$

$\therefore \quad t = 2$ s

51. For Climbing up $T > mg$

$$T_{max} = 360 \text{ N} \quad \text{(Given)}$$

and $$mg = 600 \text{ N}$$

So, it's not possible to climb up safely with some acceleration.

52. For equilibrium of upper ball,

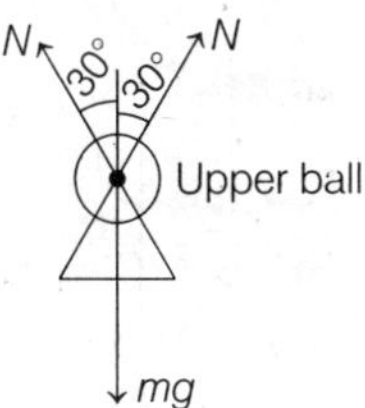

$$2N \cos 30° = mg$$

$$\therefore \quad N = \frac{mg}{2\cos 30°} = \frac{mg}{\sqrt{3}}$$

From free body diagram of leftward ball,

$$N_0 = N \sin 60° + mg$$

(resolving the forces vertically)

$$N \cos 60° = f \le \mu N_0$$

(resolving the forces horizontally)

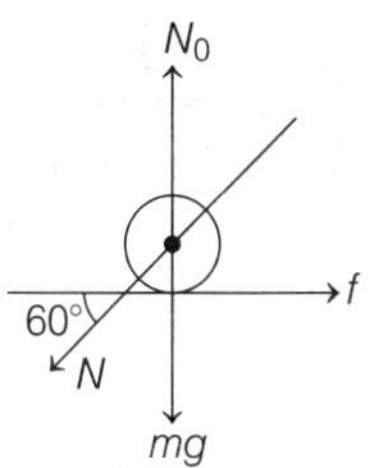

or $$\frac{N}{2} \le \mu\left(\frac{\sqrt{3}}{2}N + mg\right)$$

or $$\frac{mg}{2\sqrt{3}} \le \mu\frac{\sqrt{3}}{2} \times \frac{mg}{\sqrt{3}} + \mu mg$$

or $$\mu \ge \frac{1}{3\sqrt{3}}$$

$$\Rightarrow \quad \mu_{min} = \frac{1}{3\sqrt{3}}$$

53. Free body diagram of block A is as shown below,

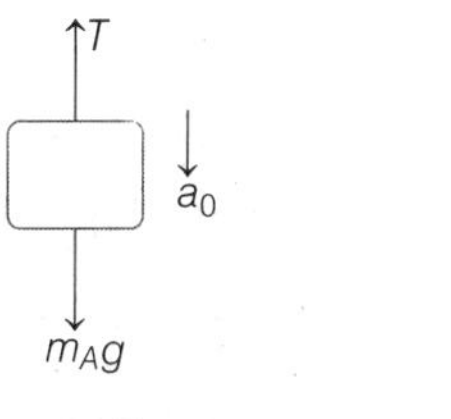

$$m_A g - T = m_A a_0 \quad \text{...(i)}$$

For all the blocks moving together, common acceleration is a_0

$$\Rightarrow \quad T = 15a_0 \quad \text{...(ii)}$$

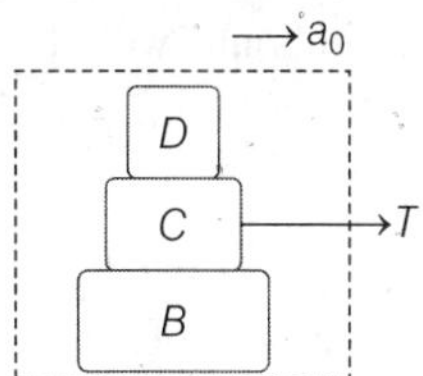

From Eqs. (i) and (ii), we get

$$m_A g - 15a_0 = m_A a_0$$

or $$a_0 = \frac{m_A g}{(15 + m_A)}$$

Free body diagram of block D in the frame of reference of block C.

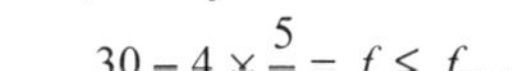

For all blocks moving together,

$$f_1 \le (f_1)_{max} \quad \text{or} \quad m_D a_0 \le \mu m_D g$$

or $$a_0 \le \mu g \Rightarrow \frac{m_A g}{(15 + m_A)} \le \mu g$$

$$m_A \le (0.5)(15 + m_A)$$

$$m_A - 0.5m_A \le 0.5 \times 15$$

$$\therefore \quad m_A \le 15$$

$$\therefore \quad m_{A\,max} = 15 \text{ kg}$$

54. Here, $F - 10 = 8a$ (where, a is the acceleration of the system)

or $30 - 10 = 8a$ or $a = \frac{20}{8} = \frac{5}{2}$ m/s^2

Since, blocks are moving together,

Free body diagram of A,

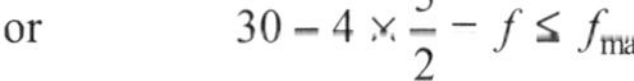

For block A, $F - f = 4a$

or $$30 - 4 \times \frac{5}{2} - f \le f_{max}$$

or $$20 \le 30\mu \quad \text{or} \quad 30\mu \ge 20$$

$$\Rightarrow \quad \mu \ge \frac{2}{3} \Rightarrow \mu_{min} = \frac{2}{3}$$

55. A block of mass m is placed on a surface with a vertical cross-section, then

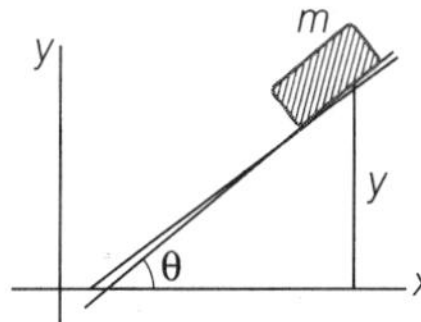

$$\tan\theta = \frac{dy}{dx} = \frac{d\left(\frac{x^3}{6}\right)}{dx} = \frac{x^2}{2}$$

At limiting equilibrium, we get

$$\mu = \tan\theta,\ 0.5 = x^2/2$$

$$\Rightarrow \quad x^2 = 1$$

$$\Rightarrow \quad x = \pm 1$$

Now, putting the value of x in $y = x^3/6$, we get

When $x = 1$ When $x = -1$

$$\therefore \quad y = \frac{(1)^3}{6} = \frac{1}{6} \qquad y = \frac{(-1)^3}{6} = \frac{-1}{6}$$

So, the maximum height above the ground at which the block can be placed without slipping is $\frac{1}{6}$ m.

Subjective Questions

1. (a) **At P**

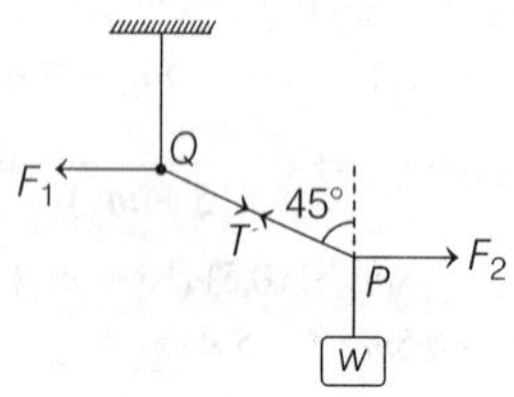

$$F_2 = T\cos 45° = \frac{T}{\sqrt{2}} \quad \text{...(i)}$$

$$w = T\cos 45° = \frac{T}{\sqrt{2}} \quad \text{...(ii)}$$

At Q, $$F_1 = \frac{T}{\sqrt{2}} \quad \text{...(iii)}$$

From these three equations, we can see that

$$F_1 = F_2 = w = \frac{T}{\sqrt{2}}$$

$$= \frac{60}{\sqrt{2}} = 30\sqrt{2}\ \text{N} \quad \textbf{Ans.}$$

2.

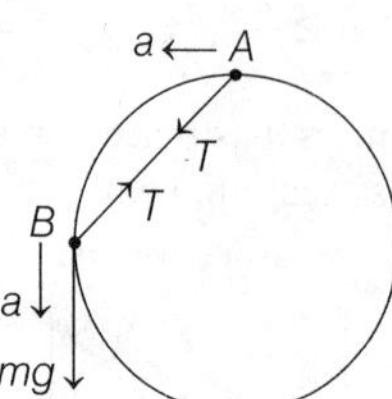

For A $\quad T\cos 45° = ma$

or $\quad T = \sqrt{2}\,ma \quad$ ...(i)

For B $\quad mg - T\cos 45° = ma$

$\therefore \quad mg - ma = ma$

or $\quad a = \frac{g}{2}$

Substituting in Eq. (i), we get

$$T = \frac{mg}{\sqrt{2}}$$

3. (a) $T_1 - 2g = 2a$

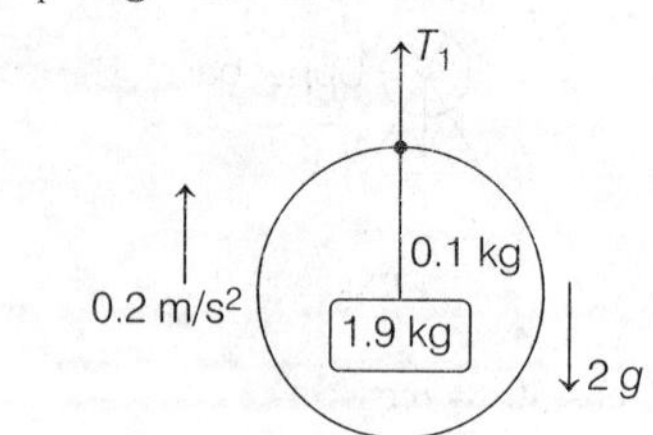

$$\therefore \quad T_1 = 2(g + a)$$
$$= 2(9.8 + 0.2)$$
$$= 20\ \text{N}$$

(b) $T_2 - 5g = 5a$

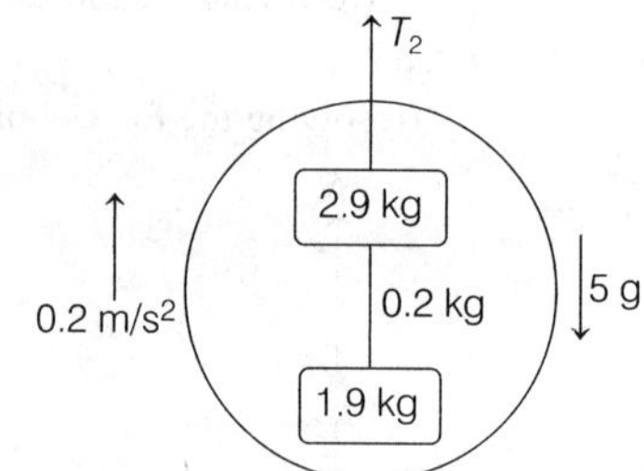

$$\therefore \quad T_2 = 5(g + a)$$
$$= 5(9.8 + 0.2)$$
$$= 50\ \text{N}$$

4. (a) $a = \frac{\text{Net pulling force}}{\text{Total mass}} = \frac{200 - 16 \times 9.8}{16}$

$= 2.7\ \text{m/s}^2$

(b) $200 - 49 - T_1 = 5a$

$\therefore \quad T_1 = 200 - 5 \times 2.7 - 49$

$= 137.5\ \text{N}$

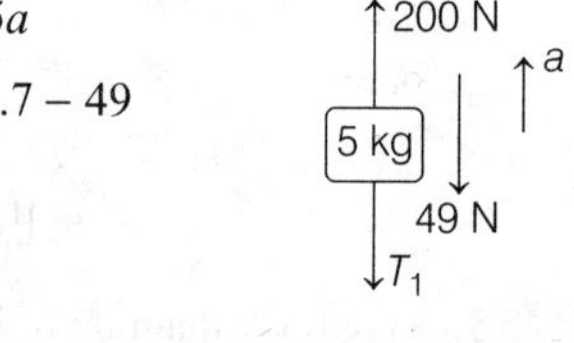

(c) $T_2 - 9g = 9a$

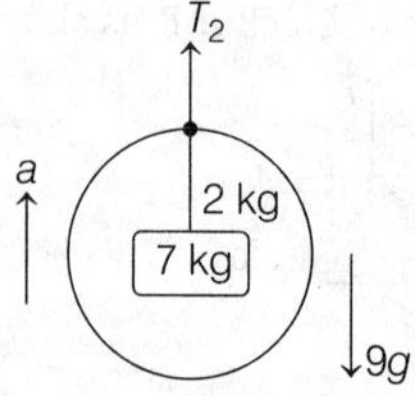

$$\therefore \quad T_2 = 9(g + a)$$

$= 9\,(9.8 + 2.7)$

$= 112.5$ N

5. In figure, AB is a ladder of weight w which acts at its centre of gravity G.

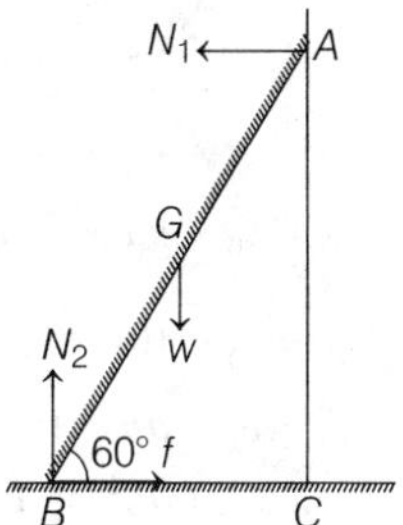

$$\angle ABC = 60°$$

$$\therefore \quad \angle BAC = 30°$$

Let N_1 be the reaction of the wall and N_2 the reaction of the ground.

Force of friction f between the ladder and the ground acts along BC.

For horizontal equilibrium,

$$f = N_1 \quad \text{...(i)}$$

For vertical equilibrium,

$$N_2 = w \quad \text{...(ii)}$$

Taking moments about B, we get for equilibrium,

$$N_1(4 \cos 30°) - w(2 \cos 60°) = 0 \quad \text{...(iii)}$$

Here, $w = 250$ N

Solving these three equations, we get

$$f = 72.17 \text{ N}$$

and $N_2 = 250$ N

$$\therefore \quad \mu = \frac{f}{N_2} = \frac{72.17}{250} = 0.288$$ **Ans.**

6. Constant velocity means net acceleration = 0. Therefore, net force should be zero. Only two forces T and mg are acting on the bob. So they should be equal and opposite.

Asked angle $\theta = 30°$

$$T = mg = (1)\,(10) = 10 \text{ N}$$

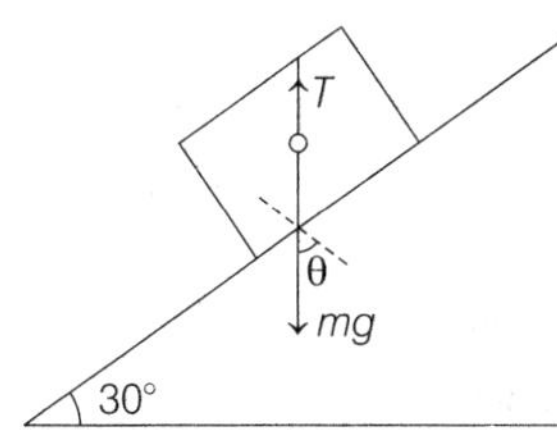

7. $T \sin\theta - mg \sin 30° = ma = \dfrac{mg}{2}$

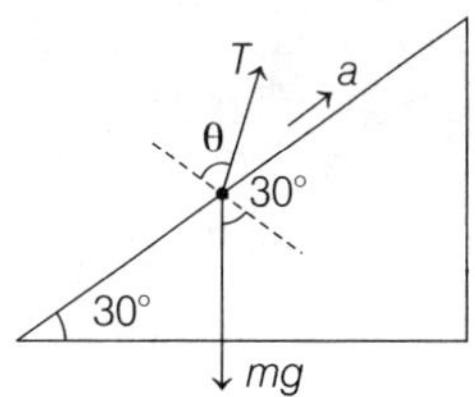

$$\therefore \quad T \sin\theta = mg \quad \text{...(i)}$$

$$T \cos\theta = mg \cos 30°$$

or
$$T \cos\theta = \frac{\sqrt{3}\, mg}{2} \quad \text{...(ii)}$$

Solving Eqs. (i) and (ii), we get

$$\theta = \tan^{-1}\left(\frac{2}{\sqrt{3}}\right)$$ **Ans.**

and
$$T = \frac{\sqrt{7}}{2}\, mg = 5\sqrt{7} \text{ N}$$ **Ans.**

8. $a = \dfrac{\text{Net pulling force}}{\text{Total mass}}$

$$= \frac{2g - (1)\,g}{2+1} = \frac{g}{3} = \frac{10}{3} \text{ m/s}^2$$

After 1 s, $v = at = \dfrac{10}{3}$ m/s

At this moment string slacks ($T = 0$)

String is again tight when,

$$s_1 = s_2$$

$$\therefore \quad \frac{10}{3}t - \frac{1}{2}gt^2 = \frac{1}{2}gt^2 \qquad (g = 10 \text{ m/s}^2)$$

On solving, we get

$$t = \frac{1}{3} \text{ s}$$ **Ans.**

9. $a = \dfrac{\text{Net pulling force}}{\text{Total mass}}$

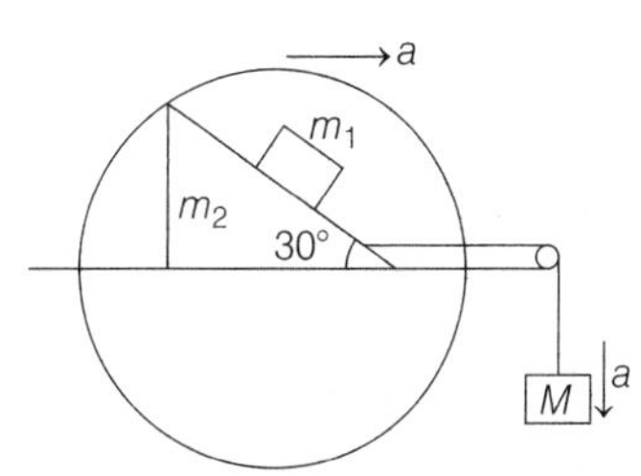

$$a = \frac{Mg}{m_1 + m_2 + M} \quad \text{...(i)}$$

For m_1 $\quad N \cos 30° = m_1 g \quad$ ...(ii)

$N \sin 30° = m_1 a \quad$ ...(iii)

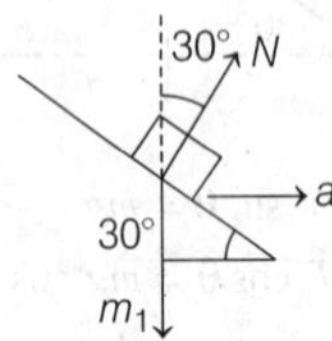

From Eqs. (ii) and (iii), we get

$$a = g \tan 30° = \frac{g}{\sqrt{3}}$$

Substituting this value in Eq. (i), we get

$$M = 6.83 \text{ kg} \quad \textbf{Ans.}$$

10. (a) **With respect to box** (Non-inertial)

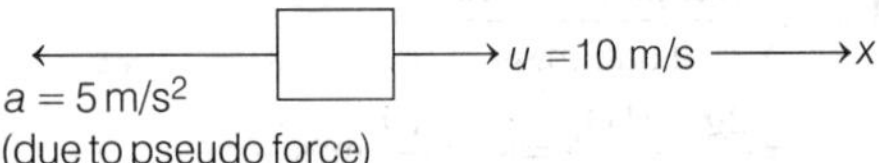

$$x = x_0 + u_x t + \frac{1}{2} a_x t^2$$

$$= x_0 + 10t - 2.5t^2 \quad \textbf{Ans.}$$

$$v_x = u_x + a_x t = 10 - 5t \quad \textbf{Ans.}$$

(b) $v_x = 0$ at $2\text{s} = t_0$ (say)

$\therefore$ To return to the original position,

time taken $= 2t_0 = 4$ s **Ans.**

11. (a) **In car's frame** (non-inertial)

$a_x = -5 \text{ m/s}^2$ (due to pseudo force)

$u_x = 0$

$a_z = 0$

$u_z = 10$ m/s

Now apply, $v = u + at$

and $\quad s = s_0 + ut + \frac{1}{2} at^2$

in x and z-directions.

(b) **In ground frame** (inertial)

$a_x = 0, u_x = 0, a_z = 0$ and $u_z = 10$ m/s

12. Relative to car (non-inertial)

$a_1 = 5 \text{ m/s}^2$ ← [box] → $u_x = 10$ m/s

$a_2 = \mu_x = 3 \text{ m/s}^2$

← a_x

a_1 is due to pseudo force

$$a_x = -(5 + 3) = -8 \text{ m/s}^2$$

Block will stop when

$$v_x = 0 = u_x + a_x t = 10 - 8t$$

or at $\quad t = 1.25$ s

So, for $t \le 1.25$ s

$$x = x_0 + u_x t + \frac{1}{2} a_x t^2$$

$$= x_0 + 10t - 4t^2$$

$$v_x = u_x + a_x t = 10 - 8t$$

After this $\mu_s g > 5 \text{ m/s}^2$ as $\mu_s > 0.5$

Therefore, now the block remains stationary with respect to car.

13.

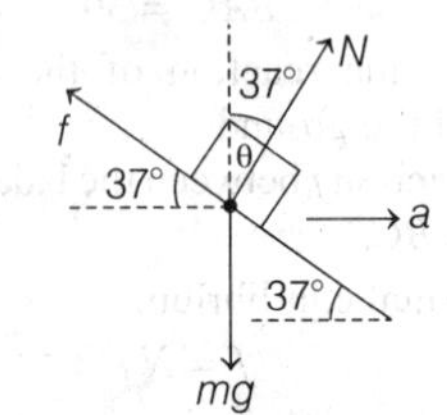

$N \cos 37° + f \sin 37° = mg \quad$ ...(i)

$N \sin 37° - f \cos 37° = ma \quad$ ...(ii)

On solving these two equations, we get

$$f = 3.6 \text{ m}$$

$$= \frac{9}{25} mg \quad \textbf{Ans.}$$

14. As shown in figure, when force F is applied at the end of the string, the tension in the lower part of the string is also F.

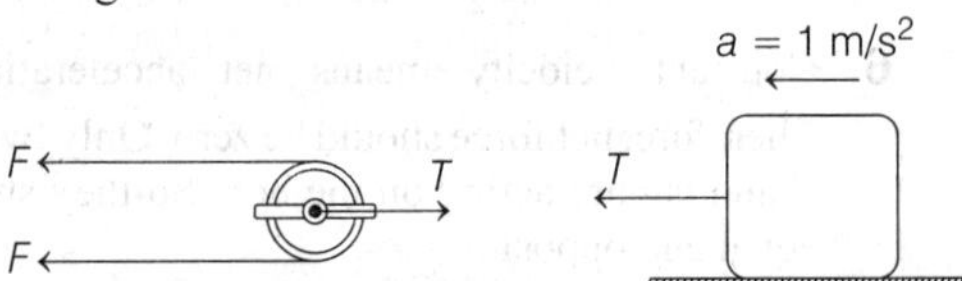

If T is the tension in string connecting the pulley and the block, then

$$T = 2F$$

But $\quad T = ma = (200)(1) = 200$ N

$\therefore \quad 2F = 200$ N

or $\quad F = 100$ N

15. $N = F = 40$ N

Net moment about $C = 0$

$\therefore$ Anti-clockwise moment of f = clockwise moment of N

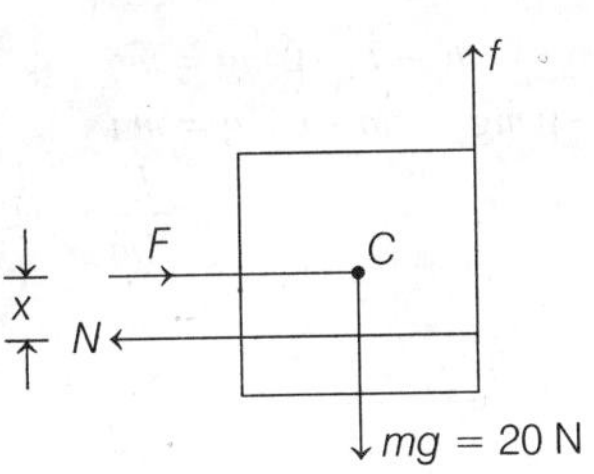

$$\therefore \quad (20)\left(\frac{20}{2}\right) = (40) \cdot x$$

or $\quad x = 5$ cm **Ans.**

16. Force diagram on both sides is always similar. Therefore motion of both sides is always similar. For example, if monkey accelerates upwards, then $T > 20\,g$. But same T is on RHS also.

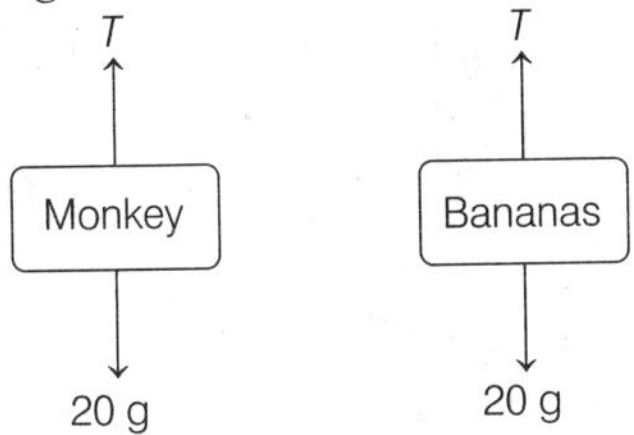

Therefore, bananas also accelerate upwards.

17. $X_A + 2X_B + X_C$

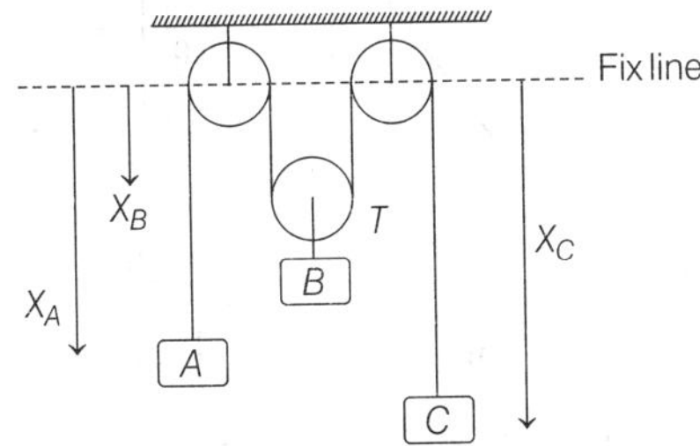

= constant on double differentiating with respect to time, we get

$$a_A + 2a_B + a_C = 0$$ **Ans.**

18. $2T - 50 = 5a$ ...(i)

$40 - T = 4\,(2a)$ ...(ii)

On solving these equations, we get

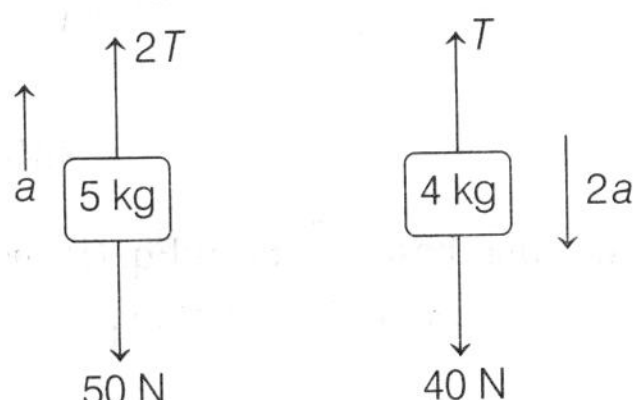

$$a = \frac{10}{7}\ \text{m/s}^2 \quad \text{or} \quad \frac{g}{7}$$ **Ans.**

and $$2a = \frac{20}{7}\ \text{m/s}^2 \quad \text{or} \quad \frac{2g}{7}$$ **Ans.**

19. $a = \dfrac{f}{m} = \mu g = 3\ \text{m/s}^2$

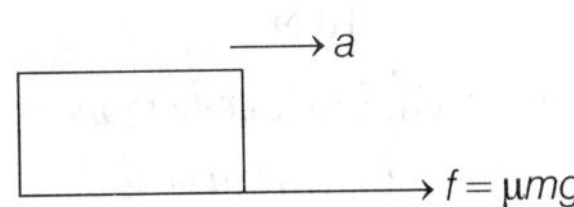

(a) Relative motion will stop when velocity of block also becomes 6 m/s by the above acceleration.

$$v = at$$

$$\therefore \quad t = \frac{v}{a} = \frac{6}{3} = 2\ \text{s}$$ **Ans.**

(b) $s = \dfrac{1}{2}at^2 = \dfrac{1}{2}(3)(2)^2 = 6$ m **Ans.**

LEVEL 2

Single Correct Option

1. Maximum value of friction between A and B

$$(f_1)_{max} = \mu N_1 = \mu m_A g = 0.3 \times 50 \times 10 = 150\ \text{N}$$

Maximum value of friction between B and ground

$$(f_2)_{max} = \mu N_2 = \mu\,(m_A + m_B)\,g = (0.3)(120)(10) = 360\ \text{N}$$

Force diagram is as shown below

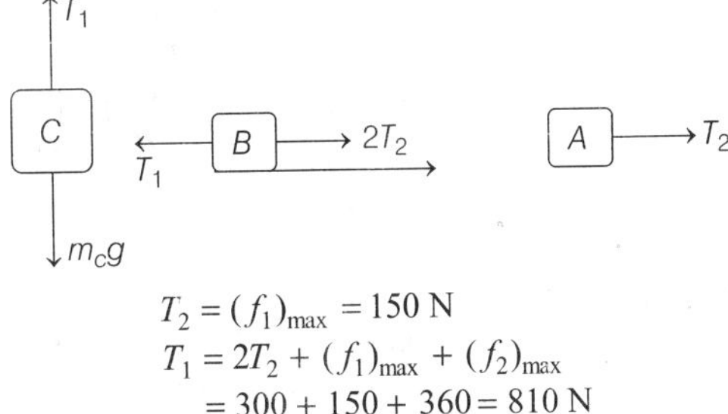

$$T_2 = (f_1)_{max} = 150\ \text{N}$$

$$T_1 = 2T_2 + (f_1)_{max} + (f_2)_{max} = 300 + 150 + 360 = 810\ \text{N}$$

$$T_1 = m_c g$$

$$\therefore \quad m_c = \frac{T_1}{g} = \frac{810}{10} = 81\ \text{kg}$$ **Ans.**

2. $\mathbf{a} = \dfrac{d\mathbf{v}}{dt} = (8\hat{\mathbf{i}} - 4t\hat{\mathbf{j}})$

At 1 s $\quad \mathbf{F}_{net} = m\mathbf{a} = (1)(8\hat{\mathbf{i}} - 4\hat{\mathbf{j}}) = (8\hat{\mathbf{i}} - 4\hat{\mathbf{j}}) = \mathbf{W} + \mathbf{F}$

where, $\mathbf{F}$ = force on cube

$\therefore \quad \mathbf{F} = (8\hat{\mathbf{i}} - 4\hat{\mathbf{j}}) - \mathbf{w}$

$= (8\hat{\mathbf{i}} - 4\hat{\mathbf{j}}) - (-10\hat{\mathbf{j}})$

$= (8\hat{\mathbf{i}} + 6\hat{\mathbf{j}})$

or $\quad |\mathbf{F}| = \sqrt{(8)^2 + (6)^2}$

$= 10$ N **Ans.**

3. Maximum friction available to m_2 is

$$(f_{\max}) = \mu m_2 g$$

Therefore, maximum acceleration which can be provided to m_2 by friction, (without the help of normal reaction from m_1) is

$$a_{\max} = \frac{f_{\max}}{m_2} = \mu g$$

If $a > \mu g$, normal reaction from m_1 (on m_2) is non zero.

4. $\dfrac{a}{g} = \cot \theta$

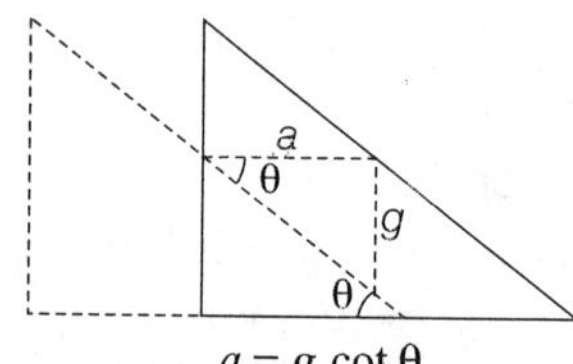

$\therefore \quad a = g \cot \theta$ **Ans.**

5. $x + y =$ constant

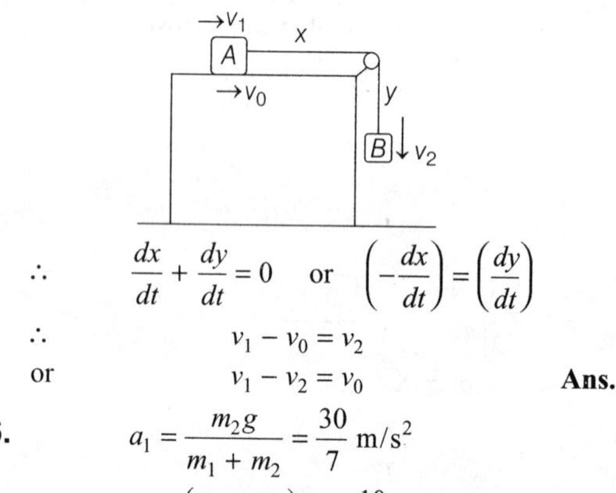

$\therefore \quad \dfrac{dx}{dt} + \dfrac{dy}{dt} = 0 \quad$ or $\quad \left(-\dfrac{dx}{dt}\right) = \left(\dfrac{dy}{dt}\right)$

$\therefore \quad v_1 - v_0 = v_2$

or $\quad v_1 - v_2 = v_0$ **Ans.**

6. $a_1 = \dfrac{m_2 g}{m_1 + m_2} = \dfrac{30}{7}$ m/s^2

$a_2 = \dfrac{(m_1 - m_2)\, g}{m_1 + m_2} = \dfrac{10}{7}$ m/s^2

$a_3 = \dfrac{m_2 g - m_1 g \sin 30°}{m_1 + m_2} = \dfrac{10}{7}$ m/s^2

$\therefore \quad a_1 > a_2 = a_3$ **Ans.**

7. $T - \mu mg = ma$

$\therefore \quad T = \mu mg + ma$

$F - T - \mu mg = ma$

$\therefore F - \mu mg - ma - \mu mg = ma$

or $\quad a = \dfrac{F}{2m} - \mu g$ **Ans.**

8. $\dfrac{a_1}{a_2} = \sin \theta$

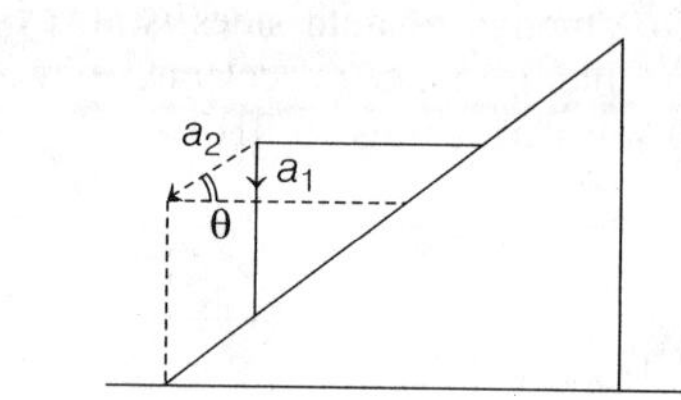

$\therefore \quad a_1 = a_2 \sin \theta$

9. $z = \sqrt{x^2 + c^2}$

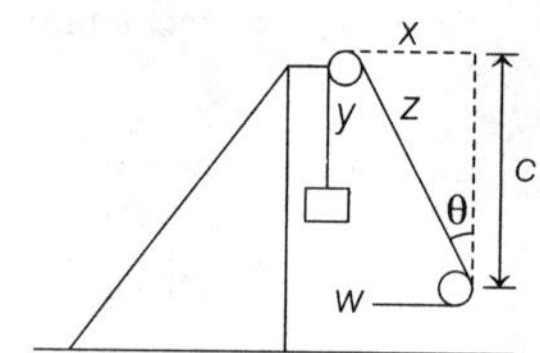

Now, $\quad w + y + z = l$

or $\quad w + y + \sqrt{x^2 + c^2} = l$

$\therefore \quad \dfrac{dw}{dt} + \dfrac{dy}{dt} + \dfrac{x}{\sqrt{x^2 + c^2}} \cdot \dfrac{dx}{dt} = 0$

or $\quad \left(-\dfrac{dw}{dt}\right) + \dfrac{x}{z}\left(-\dfrac{dx}{dt}\right) = \dfrac{dy}{dt} \quad$ ...(i)

$-\dfrac{dw}{dt} = -\dfrac{dx}{dt} = v_2$

$\dfrac{dy}{dt} = v_1$

and $\quad \dfrac{x}{z} = \sin\theta$

Substituting these values in Eq. (i), we have

$v_2\,(1 + \sin \theta) = v_1$ **Ans.**

10. On the cylinder

If N = normal reaction between cylinder and inclined plane

$N \sin\theta$ = horizontal component of N

$= ma$ ....(i)

$N \cos\theta$ = vertical component of N

$= mg$ ...(ii)

Dividing Eq. (i) by (ii), we get

$$\tan\theta = \frac{a}{g}$$

$\therefore$ $a = g \tan\theta$ **Ans.**

11. With respect to trolley means, assume trolley at rest and apply a pseudo force (= ma, towards left) on the bob.

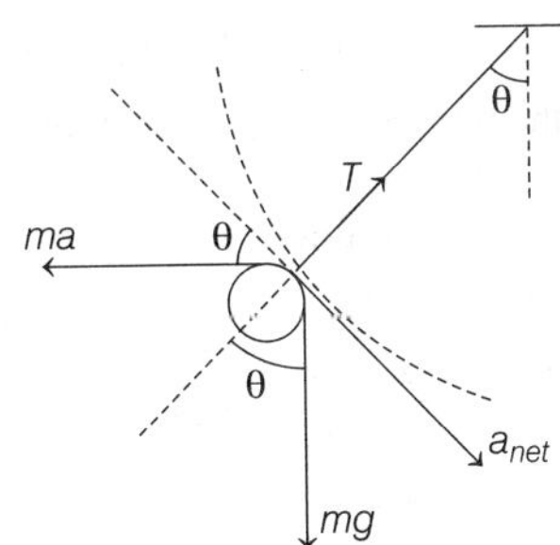

$$a_{\text{net}} = \frac{mg \sin\theta - ma\cos\theta}{m}$$

$= g\sin\theta - a\cos\theta$ **Ans**

12. Let α = angle of repose

For $\theta \le \alpha$ Block is stationary and force of friction,

$f = mg \sin\theta$ or $f \propto \sin\theta$

i.e. it is sine graph

For $\theta \ge \alpha$ Block slides downwards

$\therefore$ $f = \mu mg \cos\theta$ or $f \propto \cos\theta$

i.e. now it is cosine graph

The correct alternative is therefore (b).

13. If they do not slip, then net force on system = F

$\therefore$ Acceleration of system $a = \dfrac{F}{3m}$

$T = F$

FBD of m $F - \mu mg = ma = \dfrac{F}{3}$

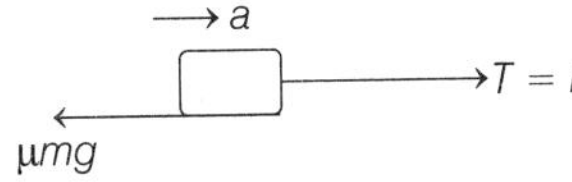

$\therefore$ $\mu mg = \dfrac{2F}{3}$ or $\mu = \dfrac{2F}{3mg}$ **Ans.**

14. FBD of m w.r.t. chamber

Relative acceleration along the inclined plane

$$a_r = \frac{ma\cos\theta + mg\sin\theta}{m}$$

$= (a\cos\theta + g\sin\theta)$

$$t = \sqrt{\frac{2s}{a_r}} = \sqrt{\frac{2L}{a\cos\theta + g\sin\theta}}$$ **Ans.**

N
ma (pseudo force)
θ
θ
a_2
mg

15. $(f_1)_{\max} = \mu_1 m_1 g = 6$ N

$(f_2)_{\max} = \mu_2 m_2 g = 10$ N

At $t = 2$ s, $F' = 4$ N

Net pulling force,

$F_1 = F - F' = 11$ N

T = 5N
f_1 = 1N
T = 5N
15N
f_2 = 10N

Total maximum resisting force,

$F_2 = (f_1)_{\max} + (f_2)_{\max} = 16$ N

Since $F_1 < F_2$, system will not move and free body diagrams of the two block are as shown in figure.

16. $a = \dfrac{\text{Net pulling force}}{\text{Total mass}}$

$= \dfrac{2mg \sin 30^\circ}{2m + m} = \dfrac{g}{3}$

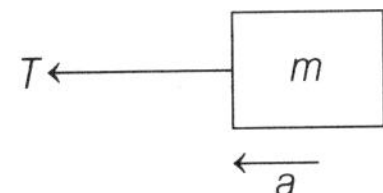

FBD of m

$T = ma = mg/3$

30°
P
T
T

Resultant of tensions

$$\mathbf{R} = -(T\cos 30°)\,\hat{\mathbf{i}} - (T\sin 30° + T)\,\hat{\mathbf{j}}$$

Putting $T = mg/3$

$$\mathbf{R} = -\frac{\sqrt{3}}{6}mg\,\hat{\mathbf{i}} - \frac{mg}{2}\,\hat{\mathbf{j}}$$

Since, pulley P is in equilibrium. Therefore,

$$\mathbf{F} + \mathbf{R} = 0$$

where, $\mathbf{F}$ = force applied by clamp on pulley

$$\therefore \quad \mathbf{F} = -\mathbf{R} = \frac{mg}{6}(\sqrt{3}\,\hat{\mathbf{i}} + 3\,\hat{\mathbf{j}}) \qquad \textbf{Ans.}$$

17. $(f_{2\,\text{kg}})_{\max} = \mu_2 m_2 g$

$= 0.6 \times 2 \times 10 = 12$ N

$(f_{4\,\text{kg}})_{\max} = \mu_4 m_4 g$

$= 0.3 \times 4 \times 10 = 12$ N

Net pulling force $F = 16$ N and

Net resistive force

$$F' = (f_{2\,\text{kg}})_{\max} + (f_{4\,\text{kg}})_{\max} = 24 \text{ N}$$

Since, $F < F'$, system will not move and free body diagrams of two blocks are as shown below.

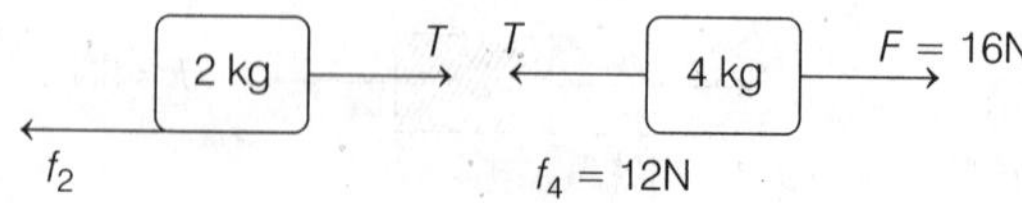

4 kg $\quad T + 12 = 16$

$\Rightarrow \quad T = 4$ N

2 kg $\quad f_2 = T = 4$ N **Ans.**

18. **FBD of rod w.r.t. trolley**

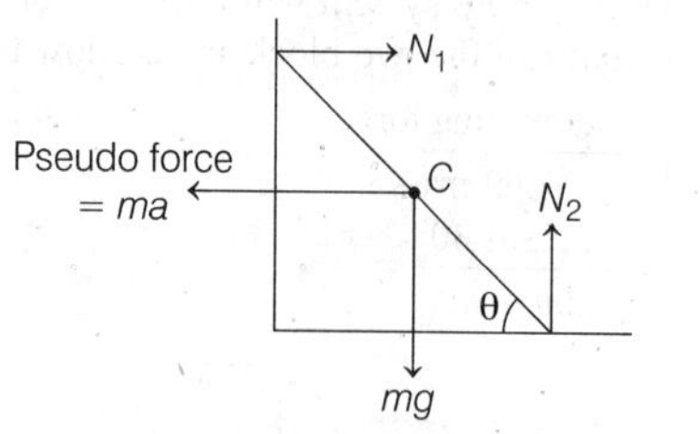

$$N_1 = ma \qquad \text{...(i)}$$

$$N_2 = mg \qquad \text{...(ii)}$$

Net torque about point $C = 0$

$$\therefore \quad N_1\left(\frac{l}{2}\sin\theta\right) = N_2\left(\frac{l}{2}\cos\theta\right)$$

or $\quad (ma)(\sin\theta) = (mg)(\cos\theta)$

$\Rightarrow \quad a = g\cot\theta$ **Ans.**

19. $v = 2t^2$

$$\therefore \quad a = \frac{dv}{dt} = 4t$$

At $\quad t = 1$ s,

$$a = 4 \text{ m/s}^2 \qquad \text{...(i)}$$

Limiting value of static friction,

$$f_L = \mu_S mg$$

$\therefore$ Maximum value of acceleration of coin which can be provided by the friction,

$$a_{\max} = \frac{f_L}{m} = \mu_S g \qquad \text{...(ii)}$$

Equating Eqs. (i) and (ii), we get

$$4 = \mu_S (10)$$

$\therefore \quad \mu_S = 0.4$ **Ans.**

20. Just at the time of tipping, normal reaction at 1 will become zero.

Σ (moments of all forces about point 2) = 0

$\therefore \quad w_1(4) = w_2(x)$

or $\quad x = \dfrac{4w_1}{w_2} = \dfrac{4(10\,g)}{80\,g} = \dfrac{1}{2}$ m **Ans.**

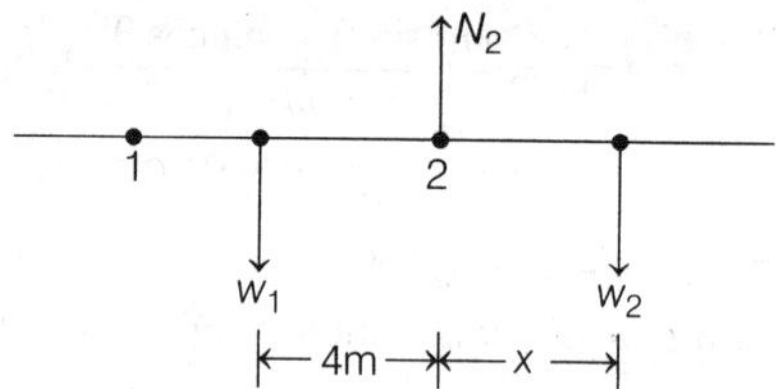

21. In vertical direction, net force = 0

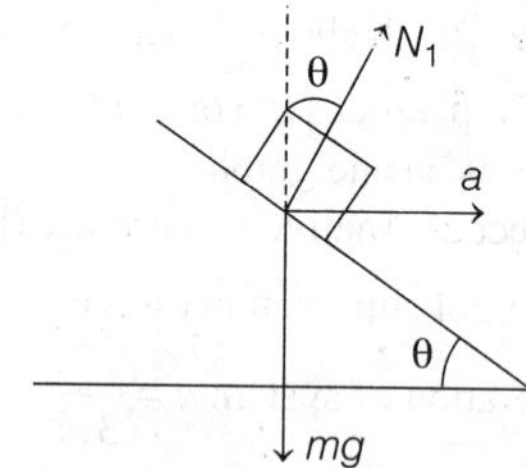

$$\therefore \quad N_1\cos\theta = mg \quad \text{or} \quad N_1 = \frac{mg}{\cos\theta} \qquad \text{...(i)}$$

Under normal condition, normal reaction is,

$$N_2 = mg\cos\theta \qquad \text{...(ii)}$$

$$\therefore \quad \frac{N_2}{N_1} = \cos^2\theta \qquad \textbf{Ans.}$$

22. Σ (moments of all forces about point C) = 0

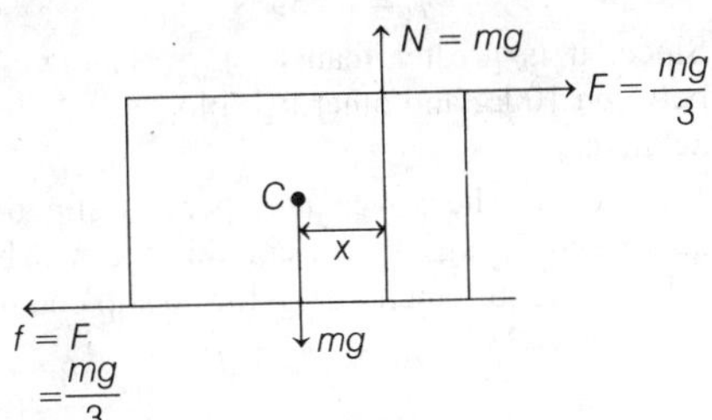

$$\therefore \quad Nx = F \cdot \frac{a}{2} + f \cdot \frac{a}{2}$$

or $$(mg)\,x = \frac{mg}{3}\left(\frac{a}{2}\right) + \frac{mg}{3}\left(\frac{a}{2}\right)$$

or $$x = \frac{a}{3}$$ **Ans.**

23. $x = \frac{l}{2} - \frac{l}{4} = \frac{l}{4}$

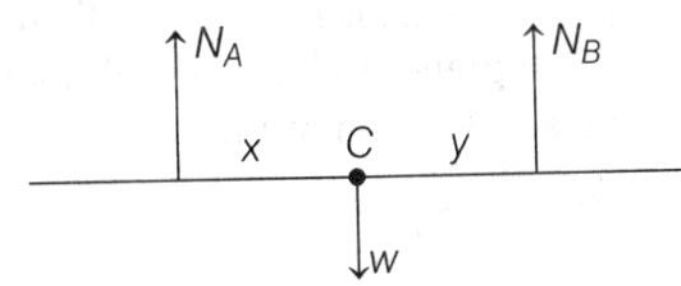

$$y = \frac{l}{2} - \frac{l}{6} = \frac{l}{3}$$

Σ (moments of all forces about point C) = 0

$$\therefore \quad N_A x = N_B\, y$$

or $$\frac{N_A}{N_B} = \frac{y}{x} = \frac{4}{3}$$ **Ans.**

24. Let acceleration of box at this instant is 'a' (towards right).

FBD of ball w.r.t. box

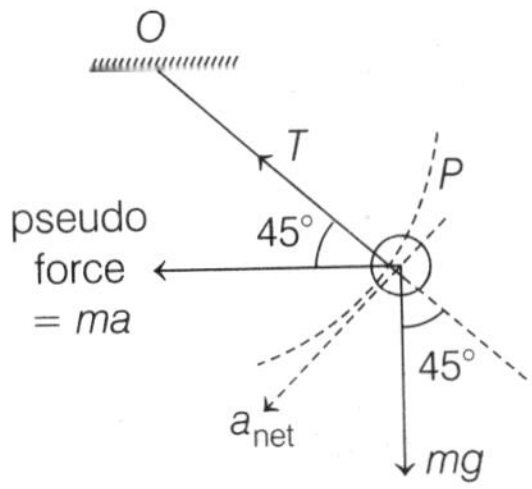

Net force in OP direction is zero

$$\therefore \quad T + \frac{ma}{\sqrt{2}} = \frac{mg}{\sqrt{2}} \qquad \text{...(i)}$$

FBD of box w.r. t. ground

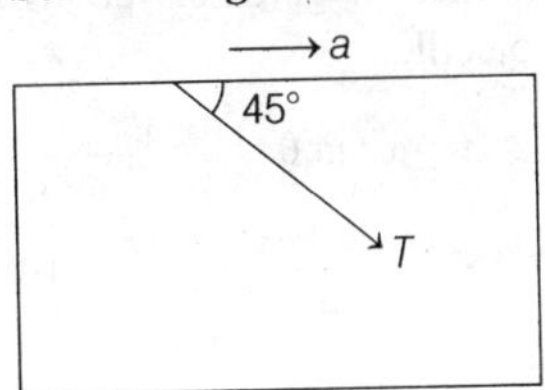

$$T \cos 45° = ma$$

or $$T = \sqrt{2}\, ma$$

Substituting in Eq. (i), we get

$$a = \frac{g}{3}$$ **Ans.**

25. $\frac{9}{a} = \tan 37° = \frac{3}{4} \quad \Rightarrow \quad a = 12\ \text{m/s}^2$

Let N = normal reaction between rod and wedge. Then $N \sin 37°$ will provide the necessary ma force to the wedge

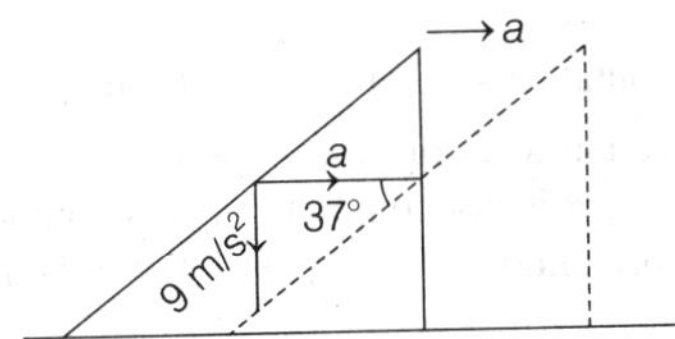

$$\therefore \quad N \sin 37° = ma = (10)\,(12) = 120$$

$$\therefore \quad N = \frac{120}{\sin 37°} = \frac{120}{0.6}$$

$$= 200\ \text{N}$$ **Ans.**

26. $T - (nm + M)\,g = (nm + M)\,a$

$\therefore \quad n\,(mg + ma) = T - Mg - Ma$

T
a
(nm + M)

or $$n = \frac{T - M\,(g + a)}{m\,(g + a)}$$

$$n_{\text{max}} = \frac{T_{\text{max}} - M\,(g + a)}{m\,(g + a)}$$

$$= \frac{2 \times 10^4 - 500\,(10 + 2)}{80\,(10 + 2)}$$

$$= 14.58$$

But answer will be 14. **Ans.**

27. It implies that the given surface is the path of the given projectile

$$y = x \tan \theta - \frac{gx^2}{2u^2 \cos^2 \theta}$$

$$= x \tan 60° - \frac{(10)\, x^2}{(2)\,(20)^2 \cos^2 60°}$$

$$y = \sqrt{3}\, x - 0.05\, x^2 \qquad \text{...(i)}$$

Slope, $\frac{dy}{dx} = \sqrt{3} - 0.1\, x$ ...(ii)

At $y = 5\text{m}$

$$5 = \sqrt{3}\, x - 0.05\, x^2$$

or $0.05\, x^2 - \sqrt{3}\, x + 5 = 0$

$$x = \frac{\sqrt{3} \pm \sqrt{3-1}}{0.1} = \frac{\sqrt{3} \pm \sqrt{2}}{0.1}$$

From Eq. (ii) slope at these two points are, $-\sqrt{2}$ and $\sqrt{2}$.

28. Horizontal displacement of both is same ($= l$). Horizontal force on A is complete T. But horizontal force on B is not complete T. It is component of T. So, horizontal acceleration of B will be less.

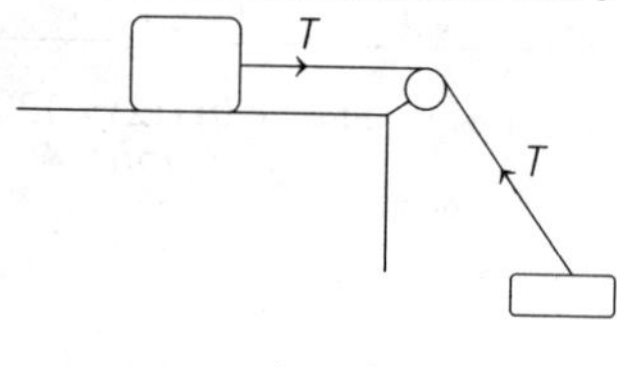

$\therefore \qquad t_B > t_A$

29. Maximum value of friction between 10 kg and 20 kg is

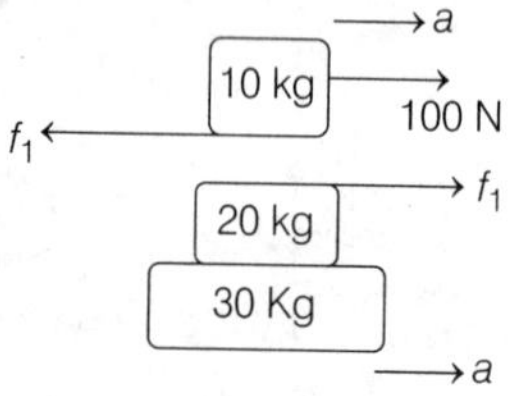

$$(f_1)_{max} = 0.5 \times 10 \times 10 = 50 \text{ N}$$

Maximum value of friction between 20 kg and 30 kg is

$$(f_2)_{max} = (0.25)\,(10 + 20)\,(10) = 75 \text{ N}$$

Now, let us first assume that 20 kg and 30 kg move as a single block with 10 kg block. So, let us first calculate the requirement of f_1 for this

$$100 - f_1 = 10\,a$$

$$f_1 = 50\,a$$

On solving these two equations, we get

$$f_1 = 83.33 \text{ N}$$

Since, it is greater than $(f_1)_{max}$, so there is slip between 10 kg and other two blocks and 50 N will act here.

Now let us check whether there is slip between 20 kg and 30 kg or not. For this we will have to calculate requirement of f_2 for no slip condition.

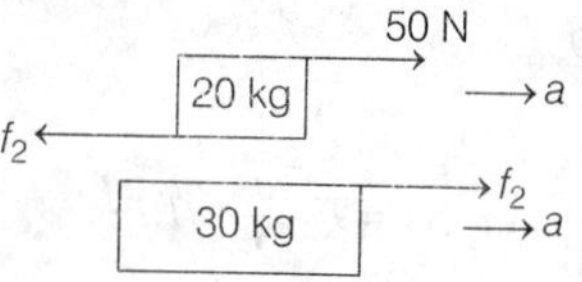

$$50 - f_2 = 20\,a$$

and $\qquad f_2 = 30\,a$

On solving these two equations, we get

$$f_2 = 30 \text{ N}$$

and $\qquad a = 1 \text{ m/s}^2$

Since, f_2 is less than $(f_2)_{max}$, so there is no slip between 20 kg and 30 kg and both move together with same acceleration of 1 m/s^2.

30. $\cos \theta = \frac{4R/5}{R} = 0.8$

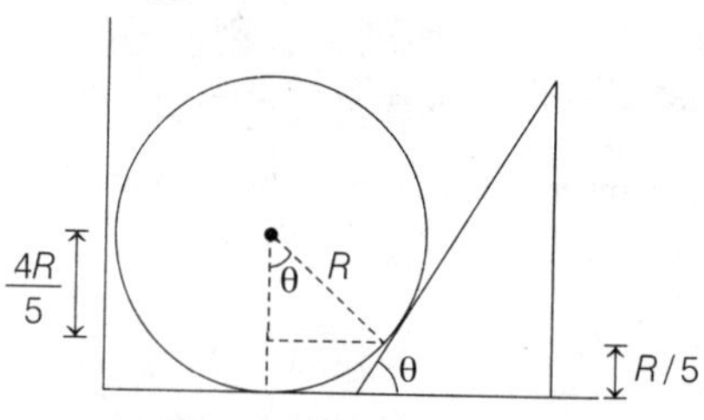

$\therefore \qquad \theta = 37°$

$$\frac{v_1}{v_2} = \tan \theta = \tan 37° = \frac{3}{4}$$

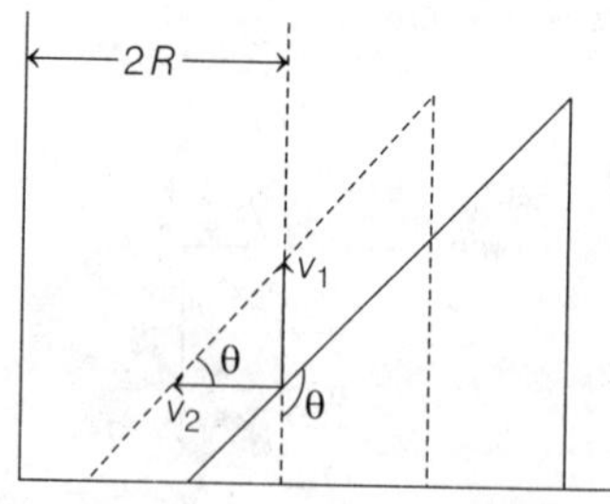

$\therefore \qquad v_1 = \frac{3}{4} v_2 = \frac{3}{4} \times 20$

$$= 15 \text{ m/s}$$

Ans.

31. $v_{AL} = v_A - v_L$

$\therefore \quad v_A = v_{AL} + v_L$

$= (-2) + 2 = 0$

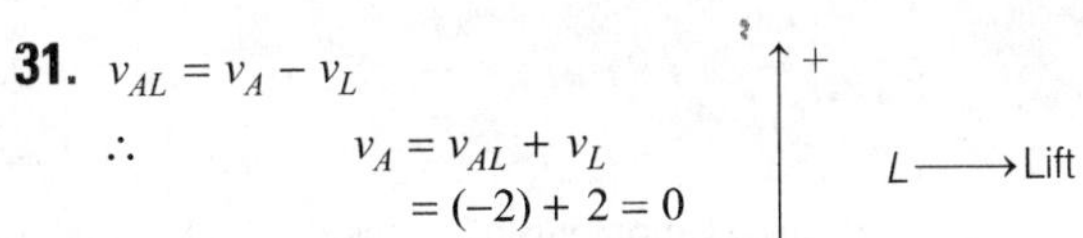

Let z = length of string at some instant. Then,

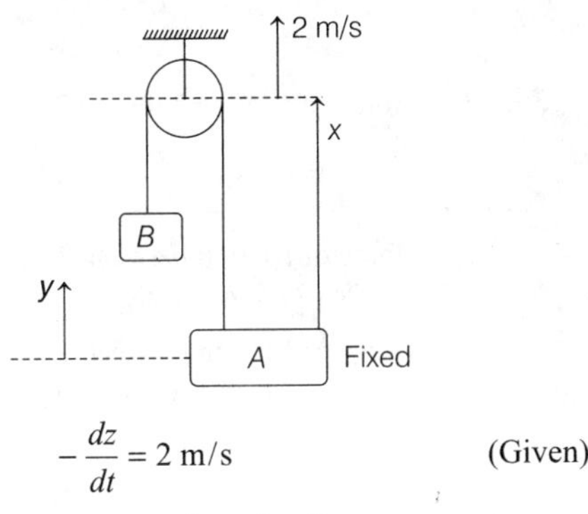

$$-\frac{dz}{dt} = 2 \text{ m/s} \qquad \text{(Given)}$$

Now, $\quad y = x - (z - x) = 2x - z$

$$\therefore \quad \frac{dy}{dt} = 2\frac{dx}{dt} + \left(-\frac{dz}{dt}\right)$$

$$= 2\,(2 \text{ m/s}) + 2 \text{ m/s}$$

$$= 6 \text{ m/s} = v_B \qquad \textbf{Ans.}$$

32. $x + x + \sqrt{y^2 + c^2} = l$ = length of string

Differentiating w.r.t. time, we get

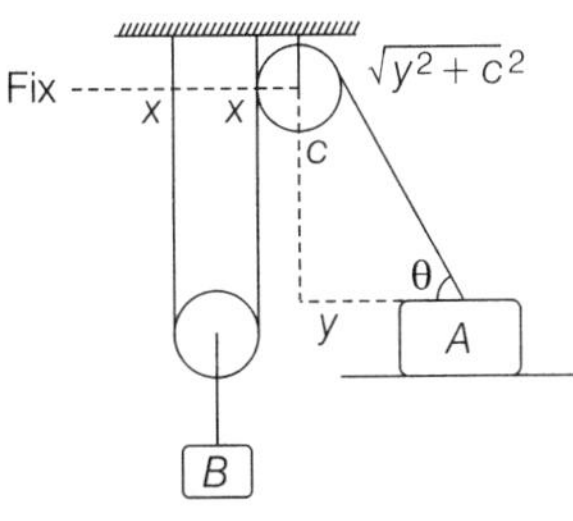

$$2\frac{dx}{dt} = \frac{y}{\sqrt{y^2 + c^2}}\left(-\frac{dy}{dt}\right)$$

or $\quad 2\,v_B = \cos\theta\, v_A$

$$\therefore \quad v_A = \frac{2\,v_B}{\cos\theta}$$

$$= \frac{2 \times 10}{0.8}$$

$$= 25 \text{ m/s} \qquad \textbf{Ans.}$$

33. Maximum force of friction between C and ground is

$$(f_C)_{\max} = (0.5)\,(60)\,(10) = 300 \text{ N}$$

Since, it is pulling the blocks by the maximum force (without moving). Therefore, the applied force is $F = 300$ N

A
B
F = 300 N

$$(f_{AB})_{\max} = 0.4 \times 60 \times 120 \times 10 = 240 \text{ N}$$

$$(f_{BG})_{\max} = 0.3 \times 120 \times 10 = 360 \text{ N}$$

Since, $(f_{BG})_{\max}$ is greater than 300 N, blocks will not move. Free body diagrams of block are as shown below.

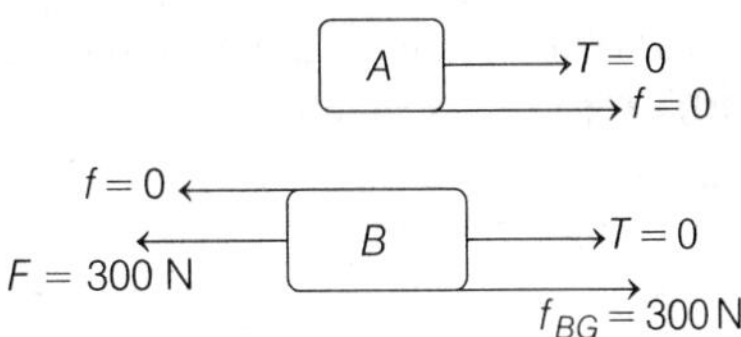

34. Let $\mathbf{a}_B = a\hat{\mathbf{i}}$

Then, $\quad \mathbf{a}_{AB} = \mathbf{a}_A - \mathbf{a}_B$

$= (15 - a)\,\hat{\mathbf{i}} + 15\hat{\mathbf{j}}$

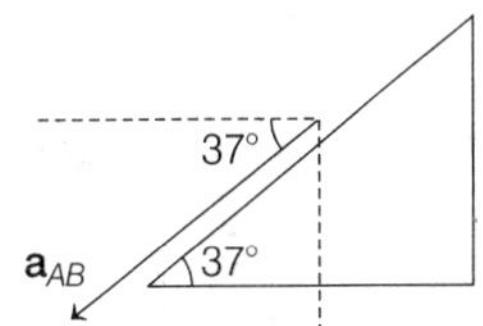

Since, $\mathbf{a}_{AB}$ is along the plane as shown in figure.

$$\therefore \quad \tan 37° = \frac{3}{4} = \frac{15}{15 - a}$$

Solving this equation, we get $a = -5$

or $\quad \mathbf{a}_B = (-5\hat{\mathbf{i}})$

35. Acceleration,

$$a = \frac{2F - F}{m + m} = \frac{F}{2m} \qquad \text{(towards left)}$$

Horizontal forces on B gives the equation,

$$2F - N \sin 30° = m \cdot a$$

or $$2F - \frac{N}{2} = m\left(\frac{F}{2m}\right)$$

$$\therefore \quad N = 3F \qquad \textbf{Ans.}$$

36. Distance AB = constant

$\therefore$ Component of v along BA = component of u along BA

or $\quad v \cos 60° = u \cdot \cos 45°$

or $\qquad v = \sqrt{2}\, u$ **Ans.**

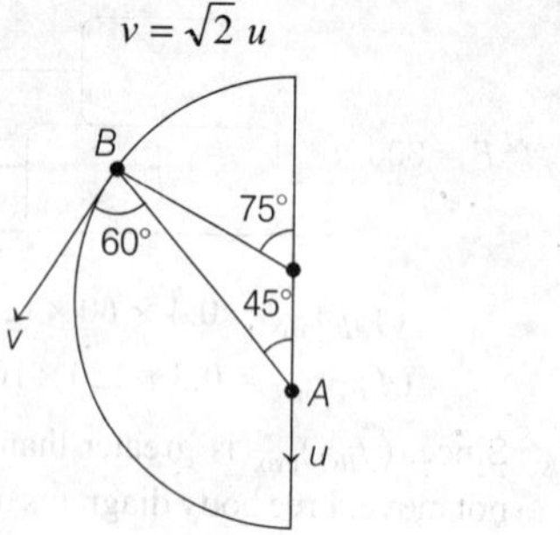

37. Let a = maximum acceleration of A.

Under no slip condition acceleration of B is also a

FBD of A w.r.t. ground

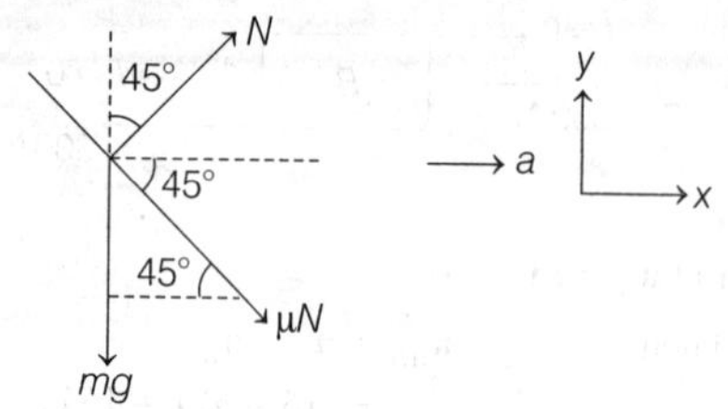

$$\Sigma F_y = 0$$

$$\therefore \quad \frac{N}{\sqrt{2}} = mg + \frac{\mu N}{\sqrt{2}} \qquad \text{...(i)}$$

$$\Sigma F_x = ma$$

$$\therefore \quad \frac{N}{\sqrt{2}} + \frac{\mu N}{\sqrt{2}} = ma \qquad \text{...(ii)}$$

Solving these two equations, we get

$$a = g\left(\frac{1+\mu}{1-\mu}\right) \qquad \textbf{Ans.}$$

38. For M_2 and M_3

$$a = \frac{M_2 g - M_3 g}{M_2 + M_3} = \frac{3M_3 g - M_3 g}{3M_3 + M_3}$$

$$= \frac{g}{2}$$

Now, FBD of M_2 gives the equation,

$$M_2 g - T = M_2 \cdot a = \frac{M_2 g}{2}$$

$$\therefore \quad T = \frac{M_2 g}{2}$$

or $\quad 2T = M_2 g$

Now, taking moments of forces about support point

$$M_1 g\,(l_1) = (2T)\, l_2 = (M_2 g)\,(3l_1)$$

$$\therefore \quad \frac{M_1}{M_2} = 3 \qquad \textbf{Ans.}$$

39. $f_1 \rightarrow$ force of friction between 2 kg and 3 kg

$$(f_1)_{max} = 0.5 \times 3 \times 10$$

$$= 15 \text{ N}$$

$f_2 \rightarrow$ force of friction between 2 kg and 1 kg

$$(f_2)_{max} = 0.3 \times 5 \times 10 = 15 \text{ N}$$

$f_3 \rightarrow$ force of friction between 1 kg and ground

$$(f_3)_{max} = 0.1 \times 6 \times 10$$

$$= 6 \text{ N}$$

When $F > 6$ N system will start moving with a common acceleration

$$a = \frac{F - 6}{3 + 2 + 1} = \left(\frac{F}{6} - 1\right) \text{m/s}^2$$

$$f_1 - 6 = (3)\, a = \frac{F}{2} - 3$$

$$\therefore \quad f_1 = \left(6 + \frac{F}{2} - 3\right)$$

$$= \left(\frac{F}{2} + 3\right)$$

Since, F is slightly greater than 6 N

$\therefore \quad f_1 < 15$ N

or $\quad < (f_1)_{max}$

$\therefore$ No slipping will occur here

$$f_2 - 6 = (1)\,(a) = \frac{F}{6} - 1$$

$$\therefore \quad f_2 = \frac{F}{6} + 5$$

Again $f_2 < (f_2)_{max}$. So no slip will take place here also.

40. $(f_1)_{max}$ = between 1 kg and 2 kg

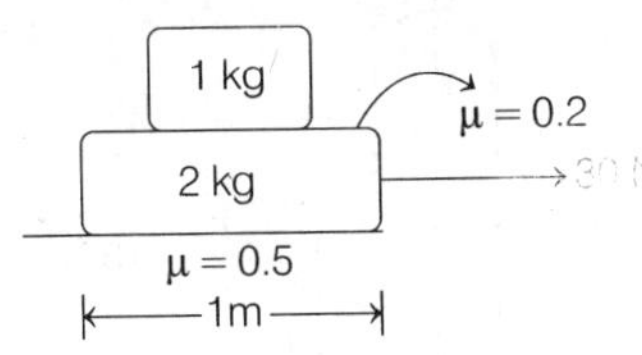

$$= 0.2 \times 1 \times 10 = 2 \text{ N}$$

$(f_2)_{max}$ = between 2 kg and ground

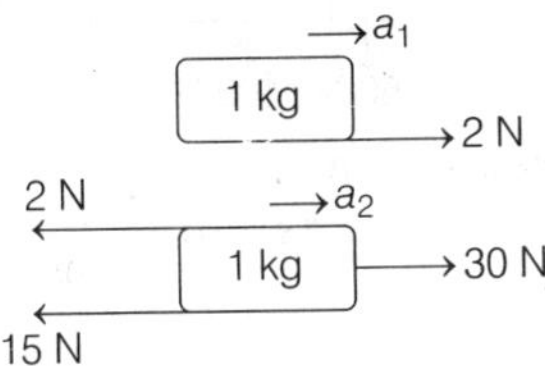

$$= 0.5 \times 3 \times 10 = 15 \text{ N}$$

$$a_1 = \frac{2}{1} = 2 \text{ m/s}^2$$

$$a_2 = \frac{30 - 15 - 2}{2} = 6.5 \text{ m/s}^2$$

$$a_r = a_2 - a_1 = 4.5 \text{ m/s}^2$$

$$t = \sqrt{\frac{2S_r}{a_r}} = \sqrt{\frac{2 \times 1}{4.5}} = \frac{2}{3} \text{ s}$$ **Ans.**

41. Maximum acceleration of m by friction = their maximum common acceleration

$$\therefore \quad \frac{\mu_1 mg}{m_2} = \frac{F - \mu_2(M + m)g}{(M + m)}$$

m will move by friction,

$$\therefore \quad F = (\mu_1 + \mu_2)(M + m)g$$

$$f_{max} = \mu_1 mg$$

$$\therefore \quad (a_m)_{max} = \frac{\mu_1 mg}{m} = \mu_1 g$$

42. The buoyant force (F) due to air is same in both cases. This buoyant force is always upwards.

In the first case,

$$mg - F = ma$$

$$\therefore \quad F = m(g - a) \quad \ldots\text{(i)}$$

In the second case,

$$F - m'g = m'a$$

$$\text{or} \quad F = m'(g + a) \quad \ldots\text{(ii)}$$

Equating Eqs. (i) and (ii), we get

$$m' = m\left(\frac{g - a}{g + a}\right)$$

$\therefore$ Mass removed,

$$\Delta m = m - m' = m - m\left(\frac{g - a}{g + a}\right) = \frac{2ma}{g + a}$$

Note *In this question, we have ignored the viscous forces.*

43. $2T = 250$

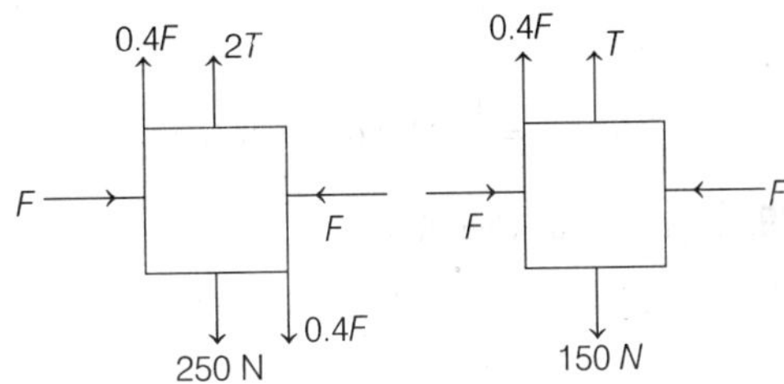

$$\therefore \quad T = 125 \text{ N}$$

$$T + 0.4F = 150$$

$$\therefore \quad F = 62.5 \text{ N}$$

44. Maximum acceleration due to friction of mass m over mass $2m$ can be μg. Now, for the whole system

$$a = \frac{\text{Net pulling force}}{\text{Total mass}}$$

$$\therefore \quad \mu g = \frac{mg}{4m} \text{ or } \mu = \frac{1}{4}$$

45. $T_B = 3T$ and $T_A = 2T$

$$\therefore \quad v_A = \frac{T_B}{T_A} \cdot v_B = \frac{3}{2} v_0 \quad \text{(towards right)}$$

$$\therefore \quad v_{AB} = \frac{3v_0}{2} - v_0 = \frac{v_0}{2} \quad \text{(towards right)}$$

In such cases, velocity and acceleration are in inverse ratio of tensions.

46. Acceleration of system before breaking the string

$$a = \frac{\text{Net pulling force}}{\text{Total mass}} = \frac{3g - 2g}{5} = \frac{g}{5}$$

After 5 s velocity of system,

$$v = at = \frac{g}{5} \times 5 = g \text{ m/s}$$

Now, $$h = \frac{v^2}{2g} = \frac{g^2}{2g} = \frac{g}{2} = 4.9 \text{ m}$$

47. Maximum acceleration of the box can be μg or 1.5 m/s^2, while acceleration of truck is 2 m/s^2. Therefore, relative acceleration of the box will be $a_r = 0.5 \text{ m/s}^2$ (backward). It will fall off the truck in a time.

$$t = \sqrt{\frac{2l}{a_r}} \qquad \left(s = \frac{1}{2}at^2\right)$$

$$= \sqrt{\frac{2 \times 4}{0.5}} = 4\text{s}$$

Displacement of truck upto this instant is

$$s_t = \frac{1}{2}a_r t^2$$

$$= \frac{1}{2} \times 2 \times (4)^2 = 16\text{m}$$

48. m_3 is at rest. Therefore,

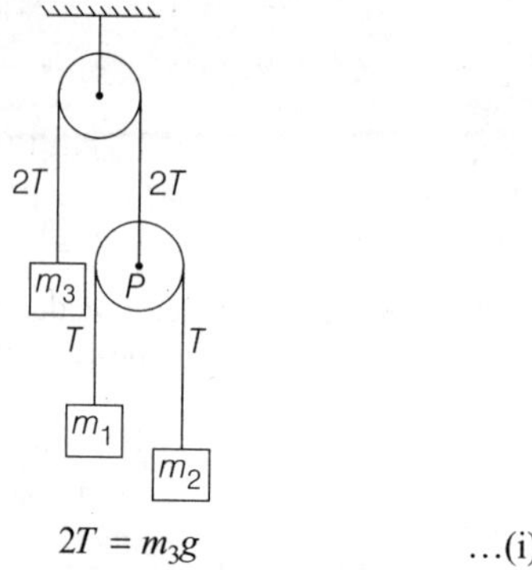

$$2T = m_3 g \qquad \text{...(i)}$$

Further if m_3 is at rest, then pulley P is also at rest. Writing equations of motion,

$$m_1 g - T = m_1 a \qquad \text{...(ii)}$$

$$T - m_2 g = m_2 a \qquad \text{...(iii)}$$

Solving Eqs. (ii) and (iii), we get

$$m_3 = 1\text{kg}$$

49. $T \sin\theta - mg \sin\alpha = ma$

$T \cos\theta = mg \cos\alpha$

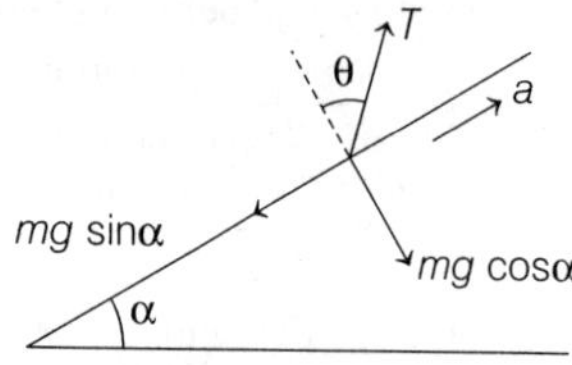

From these two equations, we get

$$\tan\theta = \frac{a + g\sin\alpha}{g\cos\alpha}$$

$$\theta = \tan^{-1}\left(\frac{a + g\sin\alpha}{g\cos\alpha}\right)$$

50. $$\frac{F}{4} = 75\text{N}$$

or $$\frac{F}{4} < 100\text{N}$$

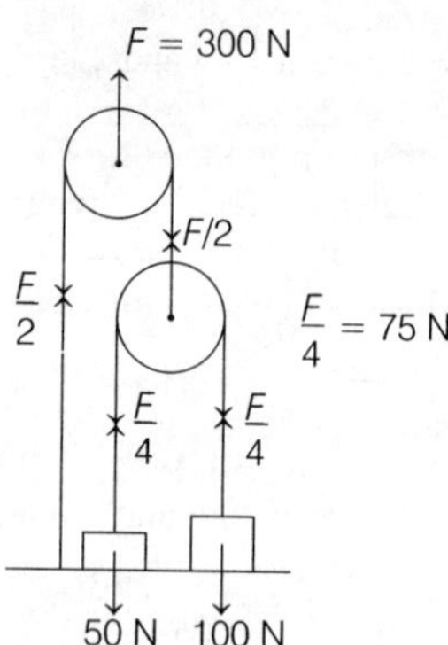

Therefore, $a_M = 0$

$$a_m = \frac{75 - 50}{5} = 5\text{m/s}^2$$

51. In false balance $l_1 \neq l_2$

Moments about O should be zero.

$\therefore$ $$w_1 l_1 = w \cdot l_2$$

$$w l_1 = w_2 l_2$$

Dividing two equations, we get

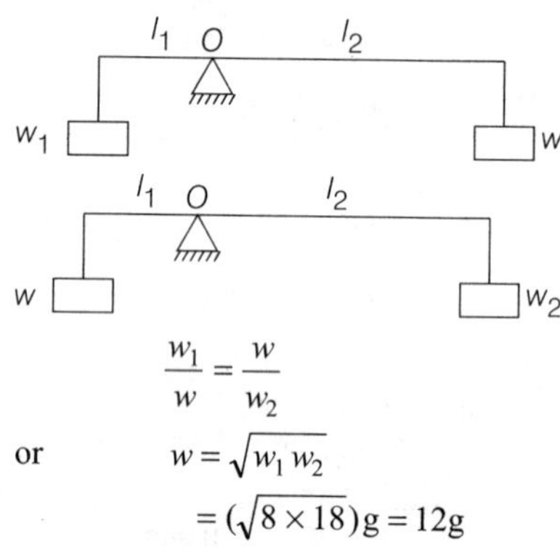

$$\frac{w_1}{w} = \frac{w}{w_2}$$

or $$w = \sqrt{w_1 w_2}$$

$$= (\sqrt{8 \times 18})\text{g} = 12\text{g}$$

52. $$2F\cos\theta = mg$$

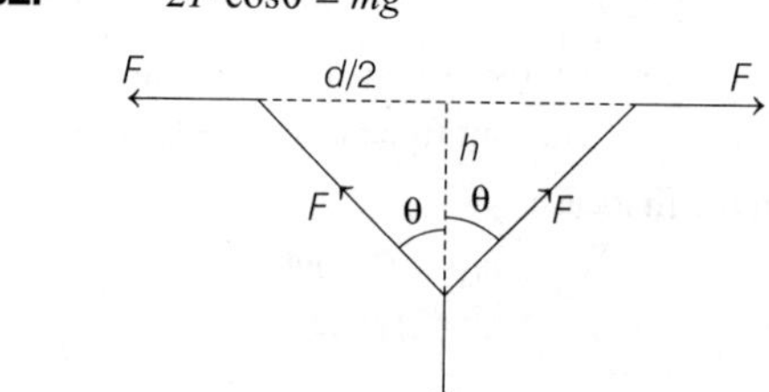

$\therefore$ $$F = \frac{mg}{2\cos\theta} = \frac{mg\sqrt{h^2 + \frac{d^2}{4}}}{2h}$$

$$= \frac{mg}{4h}\sqrt{d^2 + 4h^2}$$

53. Constant velocity means net acceleration or net force is zero. Hence,

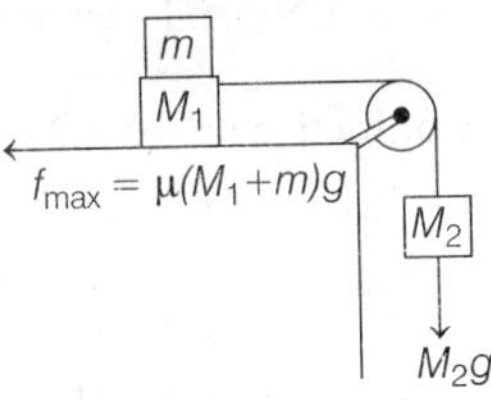

$$\mu(M_1 + m)g = M_2 g$$

or $$0.4(4 + m) = 6$$

$\therefore$ $$m = 11 \text{ kg}$$

More than One Correct Options

1. Maximum value of friction between two blocks

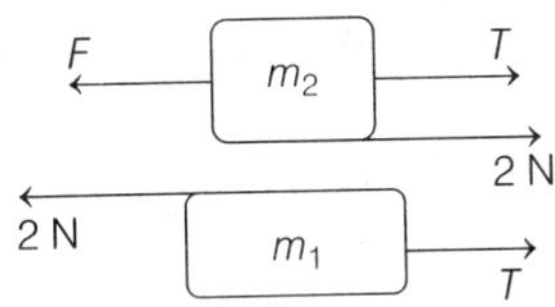

$$f_{max} = 0.2 \times 1 \times 10 = 2\text{N}$$

In critical case,

$$T = 2\text{ N}$$
$$F = T + 2 = 4\text{ N}$$

$\therefore$ System is in equilibrium, if $f \le 4$ N **Ans.**

For $F > 4$ N

$$F - (T + 2) = m_2 a = (1)(a) \quad \text{...(i)}$$
$$T - 2 = m_1 a = (1)(a) \quad \text{...(ii)}$$

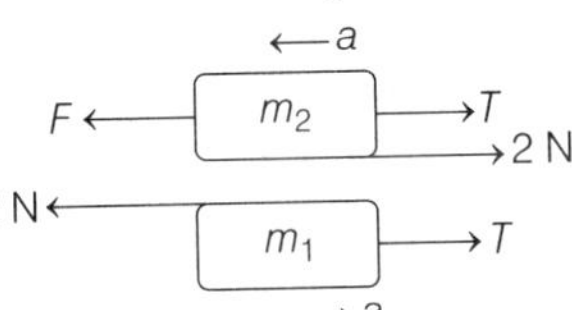

On solving these two equations, we get

$$T = \frac{F}{2}$$

When, $F = 6$ N, $T = 3$ N **Ans.**

2. Resultant of mg and mg is $\sqrt{2}\,mg$.

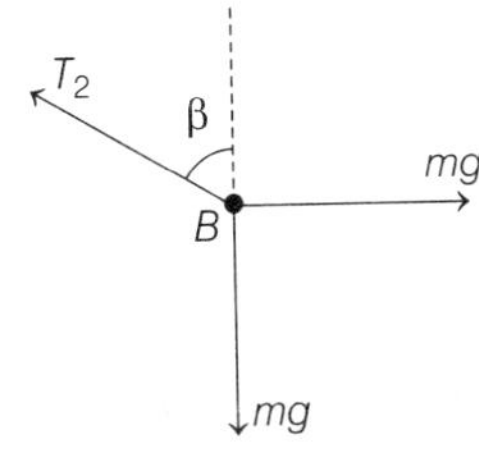

Therefore, T_2 should be equal and opposite of this.

or $$T_2 = \sqrt{2}\,mg \quad \text{...(i)}$$

Further, $$T_2 \cos\beta = mg \quad \text{...(ii)}$$

and $$T_2 \sin\beta = mg \quad \text{...(iii)}$$

or $$\sin\beta = \cos\beta \Rightarrow \beta = 45°$$

$$T_1 \cos\alpha = mg + T_2\cos\beta$$
$$= mg + \sqrt{2}\,mg\left(\frac{1}{\sqrt{2}}\right)$$

or $$T_1 \cos\alpha = 2\,mg \quad \text{...(iv)}$$

$$T_1 \sin\alpha = T_2 \sin\beta = \sqrt{2}\,mg\left(\frac{1}{\sqrt{2}}\right)$$

$\therefore$ $$T_1 \sin\alpha = mg \quad \text{...(v)}$$

From Eqs. (iv) and (v), we get

$$\tan\alpha = \frac{1}{2} \quad \text{and} \quad T_1 = \sqrt{5}\,mg$$

$$\tan\beta = \tan 45° = 1 \quad \text{and} \quad T_2 = \sqrt{2}\,mg$$

$\therefore$ $$\tan\beta = 2\tan\alpha \quad \text{and} \quad \sqrt{2}\,T_1 = \sqrt{5}\,T_2$$

3. a = slope of v - t graph

$$= -1 \text{ m/s}^2$$

$\therefore$ $$\text{Retardation} = 1 \text{ m/s}^2 = \frac{\mu mg}{m} = \mu g$$

or $$\mu = \frac{1}{g} = \frac{1}{10} = 0.1$$

If μ is half, then retardation a is also half. So using

$$v = u - at$$

or $$0 = u - at$$

or $$t = \frac{u}{a} \quad \text{or} \quad t \propto \frac{1}{a}$$

we can see that t will be two times.

4. Maximum force of friction between A and B

$$(f_1)_{max} = 0.3 \times 60 \times 10 = 180\text{ N}$$

Maximum force of friction between B and ground

$$(f_2)_{max} = 0.3 \times (60 + 40)\,g = 300\text{ N}$$

Both are stationary

$$f_1 = T = 125 \text{ N}$$
$$f_2 = T + f_1 = 250 \text{ N}$$

5. Maximum value of friction between A and B is

$$(f_1)_{max} = 0.25 \times 3 \times 10 = 7.5 \text{ N}$$

Maximum value of friction between B and C

$$(f_2)_{max} = 0.25 \times 7 \times 10 = 17.5 \text{ N}$$

and maximum value of friction between C and ground,

$$(f_3)_{max} = 0.25 \times 15 \times 10 = 37.5 \text{ N}$$
$$F_0 = \text{force on } A \text{ from rod}$$

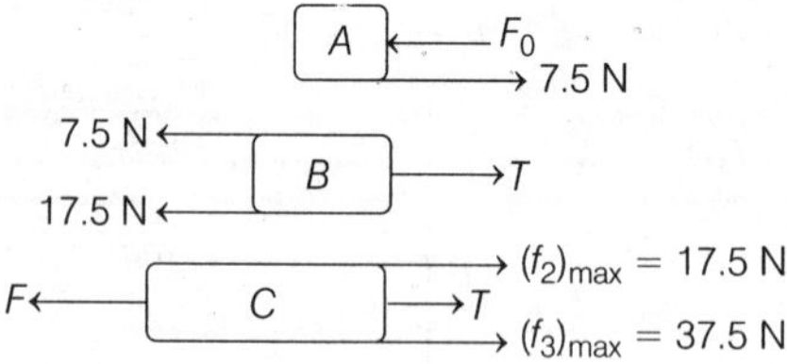

If C is moving with constant velocity, then B will also move with constant velocity

For *B*, $T = 17.5 + 7.5 = 25$ N

For *C*, $F = 17.5 + 25 + 37.5 = 80$ N

For *F* = 200 N

Acceleration of B towards right

$$= \text{acceleration of } C \text{ towards left}$$
$$= a \text{ (say)}$$

Then, $T - 7.5 - 17.5 = 4a$ ...(i)

$200 - 17.5 - 37.5 - T = 8a$ ...(ii)

On solving these two equations, we get

$$a = 10 \text{ m/s}^2$$

6. Since, $\mu_1 > \mu_2$

$\therefore$ $(f_1)_{max} > (f_2)_{max}$

Further if both move,

$$a = \frac{T - \mu mg}{m}$$

μ of block is less. Therefore, its acceleration is more.

7.

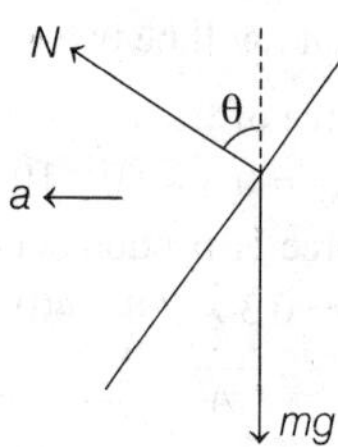

$N \cos\theta = mg = 10$ ...(i)

$N \sin\theta = ma = 5$ ...(ii)

On solving these two equations, we get

$$N = 5\sqrt{5} \text{ N} \quad \text{and} \quad \tan\theta = \frac{1}{2}$$

8. $f_1 \rightarrow$ force of friction between 2 kg and 4 kg

$f_2 \rightarrow$ force of friction between 4 kg and ground

$$(f_{S_1})_{max} = 0.4 \times 2 \times 10 = 8 \text{ N}$$
$$F_{K_1} = 0.2 \times 2 \times 10 = 4 \text{ N}$$
$$(f_{S_2})_{max} = 0.6 \times 6 \times 10 = 36 \text{ N}$$
$$F_{K_2} = 0.4 \times 6 \times 10 = 24 \text{N}$$

At $t = 1$ s, $F = 2\text{N} < 36$ N, therefore system remains stationary and force of friction between 2 kg and 4 kg is zero.

At $t = 4$ s, $F = 8$ N < 36 N. Therefore system is again stationary and force of friction on 4 kg from ground is 8 N.

At $t = 15$ s, $F = 30$ N < 36 N and system is stationary.

9. $f_{max} = 0.3 \times 2 \times 10 = 6$ N

At t = 2 s, $F = 2 \text{ N} < f_{max}$

$\therefore$ $f = F = 2$ N

At t = 8 s, $F = 8 \text{ N} > f_{max}$

$\therefore$ $f = 6$ N

At t = 10 s, $F = 10 \text{ N} > f_{max}$

$\therefore$ $f = 6$ N

$$a = \frac{F - f}{m} = \frac{10 - 6}{2}$$
$$= 2 \text{ m/s}^2$$
$$F = f_{max} = 6 \text{ N at 6 s}$$

For 6 s ≤ t ≤ 10 s

$$a = \frac{F - f}{m} = \frac{t - 6}{2} = 0.5t - 3$$
$$\int_0^v dv = \int a\,dt = \int_6^{10} (0.5t - 3)\,dt$$
$$v = 4 \text{ m/s}$$

After 10 s

$$a = \frac{F - f}{m} = \frac{10 - 6}{2}$$
$$= 2 \text{ m/s}^2$$
$$= \text{constant}$$

$\therefore$ $v' = v + at$

$$= 4 + 2(12 - 10)$$
$$= 8 \text{ m/s}$$

10. Maximum force of friction between 2 kg and 4 kg

$$= 0.4 \times 2 \times 10 = 8 \text{ N}$$

2 kg moves due to friction. Therefore its maximum acceleration may be

$$a_{max} = \frac{8}{2} = 4 \text{ m/s}^2$$

Slip will start when their combined acceleration becomes 4 m/s^2

$$\therefore \quad a = \frac{F}{m} \text{ or } 4 = \frac{2t}{6} \quad \text{or} \quad t = 12 \text{ s}$$

At $t = 3$s

$$a_2 = a_4 = \frac{F}{m} = \frac{2t}{6} = \frac{2 \times 3}{6} = 1 \text{ m/s}^2$$

Both a_2 and a_4 are towards right. Therefore, pseudo forces F_1 (on 2 kg from 4 kg) and F_2 (on 4 kg from 2 kg) are towards left

$$F_1 = (2)(1) = 2\text{N} \Rightarrow F_2 = (4)(1) = 4 \text{ N}$$

From here, we can see that F_1 and F_2 do not make a pair of equal and opposite forces.

11. $N = Mg - F\sin\theta$

$$F\cos\theta = \mu N = \mu[Mg - F\sin\theta]$$

$$\Rightarrow \quad F = \frac{\mu Mg}{\cos\theta + \mu\sin\theta}$$

For F to be minimum, denominator should be maximum.

$$\text{or} \quad \frac{d}{d\theta}(\cos\theta + \mu\sin\theta) = 0$$

$$\Rightarrow \quad -\sin\theta + \mu\cos\theta = 0$$

$$\Rightarrow \quad \tan\theta = \mu$$

Comprehension Based Questions

1. Let $\mu_K = \mu$, then $\mu_S = 2\mu$

According to first condition,

$$F + mg\sin\theta = \mu_S\, mg\cos\theta = 2\mu\, mg\cos\theta \quad \text{...(i)}$$

According to second condition,

$$mg\sin\theta = F + \mu_K\, mg\cos\theta$$
$$= F + \mu\, mg\cos\theta \quad \text{...(ii)}$$

Putting $\theta = 30°$, we get

$$F + mg/2 = 2\mu\, mg\left(\frac{\sqrt{3}}{2}\right)$$

$$\text{or} \quad \sqrt{3}\,\mu\, mg = F + 0.5\, mg \quad \text{...(iii)}$$

$$\frac{mg}{2} = F + \mu\, mg\left(\frac{\sqrt{3}}{2}\right)$$

$$\text{or} \quad 0.5\sqrt{3}\,\mu\, mg = 0.5\, mg - F \quad \text{...(iv)}$$

Dividing Eq. (iii) and (iv), we get

$$F = \frac{mg}{6}$$ **Ans.**

2. Substituting the value of F in Eq. (iii), we have

$$\mu = \frac{2}{3\sqrt{3}} = \mu_K$$

$$\therefore \quad \mu_S = 2\mu = \frac{4}{3\sqrt{3}}$$

3. $$a = \frac{F + mg\sin\theta - \mu_K\, mg\cos\theta}{m}$$

$$= \frac{(mg/6) + (mg/2) - \left(\frac{2}{3\sqrt{3}}\right)mg\left(\frac{\sqrt{3}}{2}\right)}{m}$$

$$= \frac{g}{3}$$ **Ans.**

4. $F' = mg\sin\theta + \mu_S\, mg\cos\theta$

$$= \frac{mg}{2} + \frac{4}{3\sqrt{3}}\, mg\left(\frac{\sqrt{3}}{2}\right) = \frac{7mg}{6}$$ **Ans.**

5. $F'' = mg\sin\theta + \mu_K\, mg\cos\theta$

$$= (mg/2) + \left(\frac{2}{3\sqrt{3}}\right)mg\left(\frac{\sqrt{3}}{2}\right) = \frac{5mg}{6}$$ **Ans.**

6. Acceleration, $a_1 = \dfrac{1350 \times 9.8 - 1200 \times 9.8}{1200}$

$$= 1.225 \text{ m/s}^2$$

Retardation, $a_2 = \dfrac{1200\, g - 1000\, g}{1200}$

$$= 1.63 \text{ m/s}^2$$

$v_f = 0$, h_2, a_2, v, h_1, a_1, $u = 0$

$$h_1 + h_2 = 25 \quad \text{...(i)}$$

$$v = \sqrt{2a_1 h_1} \text{ or } \sqrt{2a_2 h_2}$$

$$\text{or} \quad 2a_1 h_1 = 2a_2 h_2$$

$$\therefore \quad \frac{h_1}{h_2} = \frac{a_2}{a_1} \quad \text{...(ii)}$$

$$= \frac{1.63}{1.225} = 1.33$$

Solving these equations, we get

$$h_1 = 14.3 \text{ m}$$ **Ans.**

7. $v = \sqrt{2a_1 h_1} = \sqrt{2 \times 1.225 \times 14.3}$

$$= 5.92 \text{ m/s}$$ **Ans.**

8. $$\tan\theta = \frac{8}{15}$$

17, 8, θ, 15

$$(f_A)_{max} = 0.2 \times 170 \times 10 \times \cos\theta$$
$$= 300 \text{ N}$$

$$(f_B)_{max} = 0.4 \times 170 \times 10 \times \cos\theta$$
$$= 600 \text{ N}$$

Now,
$(m_A + m_B) g \sin\theta = (340)(10)\sin\theta = 1600$ N
Since, this is greater than $(f_A)_{max} + (f_B)_{max}$, therefore blocks slides downward and maximum force of friction will act on both surfaces

$$\therefore \quad f_{total} = (f_A)_{max} + (f_B)_{max} = 900 \text{ N}$$ **Ans.**

9. $a = \dfrac{(m_A + m_B) g \sin\theta - f_{total}}{m_A + m_B}$

$= \dfrac{1600 - 900}{340} = 2.06 \text{ m/s}^2$

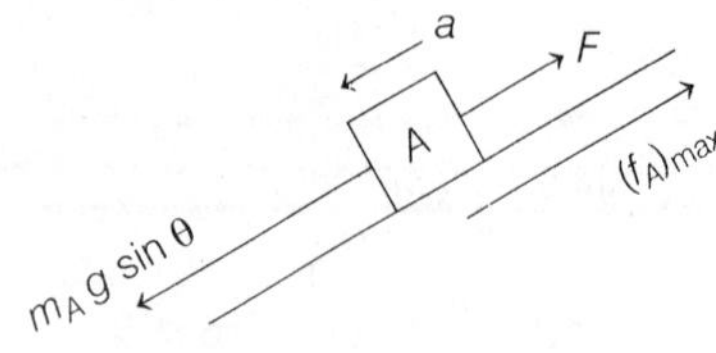

F = force on connecting bar

$$m_A g \sin\theta - F - (f_A)_{max} = m_A a$$

$$\therefore \quad F = m_A g \sin\theta - (f_A)_{max} - m_A a$$

$$= 170 \times 10 \times \sin\theta - 300 - 170 \times 2.06$$

$$\simeq 150 \text{ N}$$ **Ans.**

10. When direction of motion will reverse at the instant, the velocity becomes zero.

$\because \quad v = u + at$

or $\quad 0 = 2 + a \times 3$

$\therefore \quad a = -\dfrac{2}{3}$ m/s²

Thus, acceleration of A is $\dfrac{2}{3}$ m/s² in rightward direction.

11.

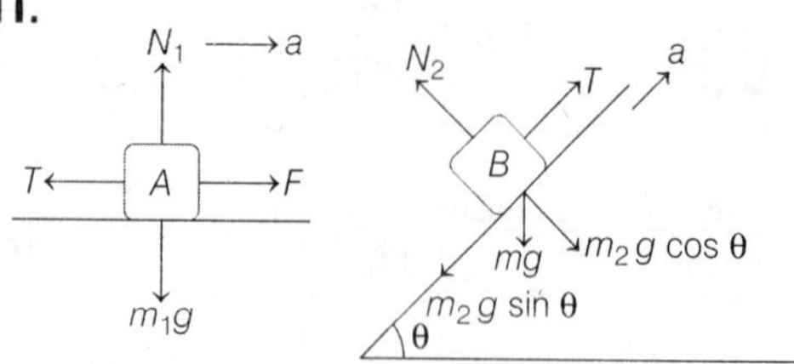

From FBD of A,

$$F - T = m_1 a = 1 \times \frac{2}{3} \quad \text{...(i)}$$

From FBD of B,

$$T - m_2 g \sin\theta = m_2 a \quad \text{...(ii)}$$

$$= 2 \times \frac{2}{3} = \frac{4}{3}$$

or $\quad T - 10 = \dfrac{4}{3}$

$\therefore \quad T = 10 + \dfrac{4}{3} = \dfrac{34}{3}$

$= 11.33$ N

12. From Eq. (i), we get

$$F - T = \frac{2}{3}$$

$\therefore \quad F = \dfrac{2}{3} + 11.33 = 12$ N

Match the Columns

1. $F = 2t$

$$\mu_s mg = 20\mu_s$$
$$\mu_k mg = 20\mu_k$$

(a) Motion starts at 4 s

$\therefore \quad F = \mu_s mg$

$\Rightarrow \quad (2)(4) = 20\mu_s$

$\therefore \quad \mu_s = 0.4$

(b) At 4 s, when motion starts,

$$a = \frac{F - \mu_k mg}{m}$$

$\therefore \quad 1 = \dfrac{8 - 20\mu_k}{2}$

Solving we get, $\mu_k = 0.3$

(c) At $t = 0.1$ s, when motion has not started,

$$f = F = 2 \times 0.1 = 0.2 \text{ N}$$

(d) **At 8 s**

$$a = \frac{F - \mu_k mg}{m} = \frac{2 \times 8 - 0.3 \times 20}{2} = 5 \text{ m/s}^2$$

$\therefore \quad \dfrac{a}{10} = 0.5$ m/s² **Ans.**

2. (a) At $\theta = 0°$, driving force $F = 0$

$\therefore$ friction $= 0$

(b) At $\theta = 90°$, N = 0

$\therefore$ Maximum friction $= \mu N = 0$ or friction $= 0$

(c) Angle of repose,

$$\theta_r = \tan^{-1}(\mu) = 45°$$

Since $\theta < \theta_r$, block is at rest and

$f = mg \sin\theta = 2 \times 10 \sin 30° = 10$ N

(d) $\theta > \theta_r$. Therefore block will be moving

$$f = \mu mg \cos\theta$$
$$= (1)(2)(10)\cos 60° = 10 \text{ N}$$

4. (a) $N - 10 = ma = 5 \times 2$

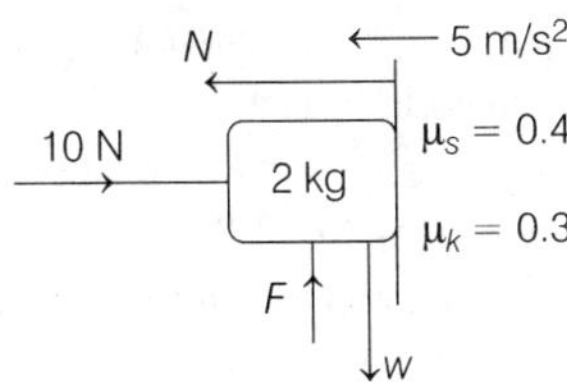

$\therefore$ $N = 20$ N

$\mu_s N = 8$ N

$\mu_k N = 6$ N

$W = mg = 20$ N

(b) When $F = 15$ N

$w - F = 5$ N (downwards)

This is less than $\mu_s N$

$\therefore$ $f = 5$ N (upwards)

(c) $F = w - \mu_s N = 20 - 8 = 12$ N

(d) $F = w + \mu_S N = 20 + 8 = 28$ N

5. (a) Net pulling force F = net resisting frictional force at $C = 10$ N

(b) $f_c = 0$

(c) $N_c = (m_B + m_C)g = 20$ N

(d) $T = F = 10$ N (everywhere)

7. Ground is smooth. So all blocks will move towards right 2 kg and 5 kg blocks due to friction.

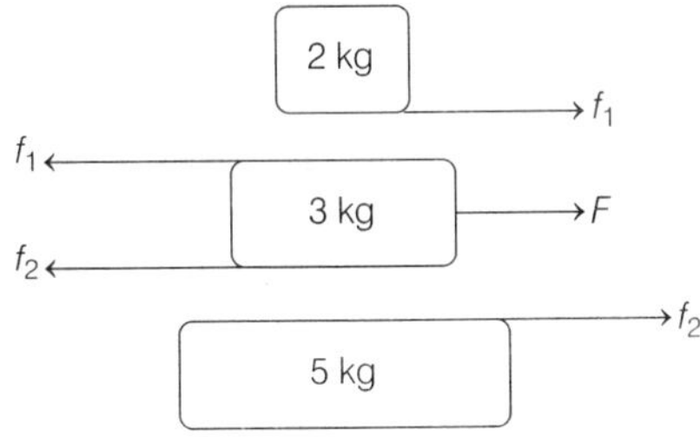

8. $\mu mg \cos\theta = 15$ N

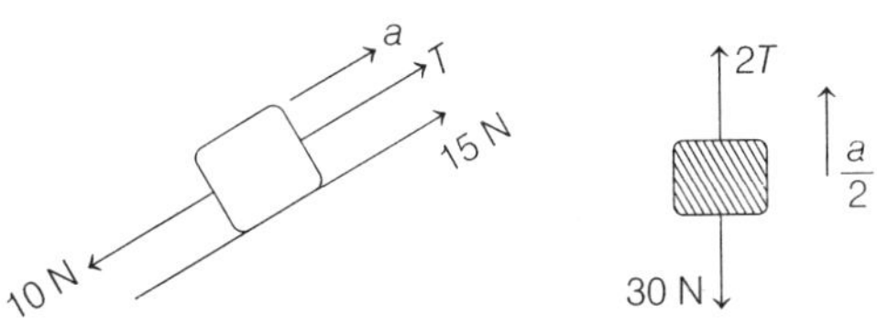

$$T - 10 - 15 = 2a \quad \text{...(i)}$$

$$30 - 2T = 3\left(\frac{a}{2}\right) \quad \text{...(ii)}$$

Solving these two equations we get,

$$a = -3.63 \text{ m/s}^2$$

So, if we take the other figure,

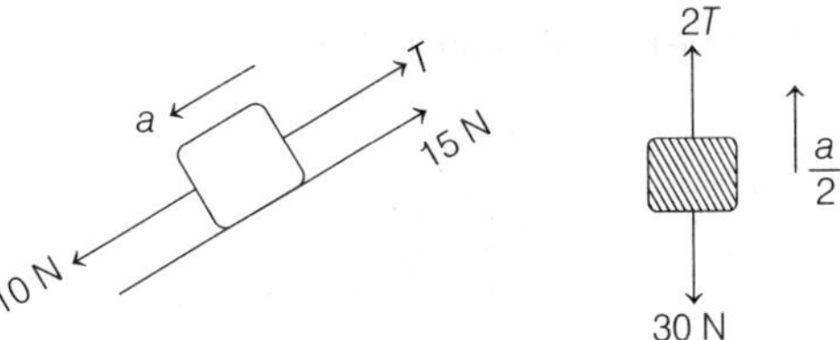

This figure is not feasible. Because for 'a' to be down the plane,

$$10 \text{ N} > T + 15$$

which is not possible

$\therefore$ $a = 0$

and free body diagrams are as shown below.

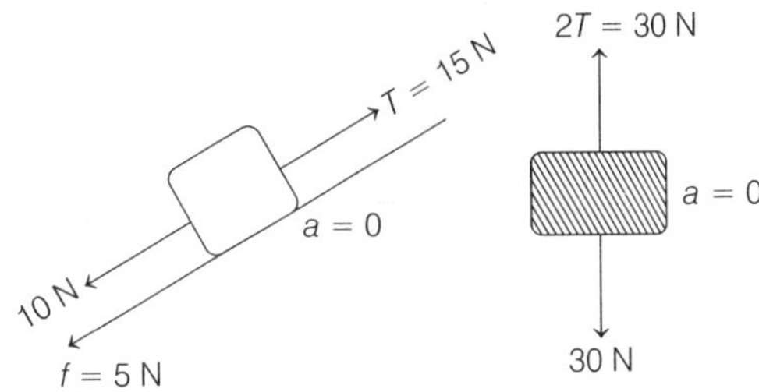

9. The maximum friction on block A is

$$f_{1\,max} = \mu(20 + t) = 10 + \frac{t}{2}$$

(i) When $t = 4$ s, $f_{max} = 12$ N

The horizontal force on block A is $F_A = t = 4$ N, thus static friction acts on the block A.

(ii) When $t = 20$ s

$\because$ $f_{max} = 20 + \frac{20}{2} = 30$ N

$\because$ Horizontal component of F is 20 N and maximum friction is 30 N. Static friction acts on the block A.

(iii) When $t = 40$ s

$$f_{max} = 10 + 20 = 30 \text{ N}$$

In this case, limiting friction acts on the block.

$\because$ $f = 30$ N

$$a = \frac{40 - 30}{5} = 2 \text{ m/s}^2$$

(iv) When $t = 60$ s

$$f_{max} = 10 + 30 = 40 \text{ N}$$

The horizontal component of F is

$$F\cos 45° = t = 60\text{ N}$$

Kinetic friction comes into play.

$$\therefore \quad f = 40\text{ N}$$

and $\quad a = \dfrac{60-40}{5} = 4\text{ m/s}^2$

Free body diagram of block A is,

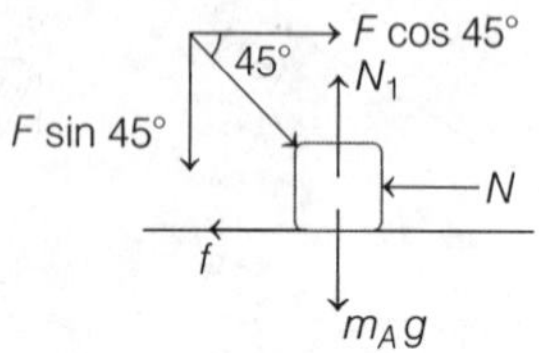

Free body diagram of block B is,

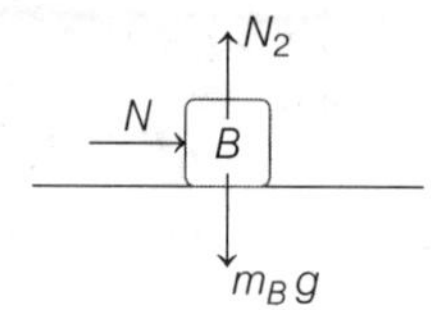

Subjective Questions

1. It is just like a projectile motion with g to be replaced by $g\sin 45°$.

After 2 s,

$$v = \sqrt{v_x^2 + v_y^2}$$

$$= \sqrt{\left(10\sin 45° - \frac{g}{\sqrt{2}} \times 2\right) + (10\cos 45°)^2}$$

$= 10\text{ m/s}$ **Ans.**

2. Suppose T be the tension in the string attached to block B. Then tension in the string connected to block A would be $4T$.

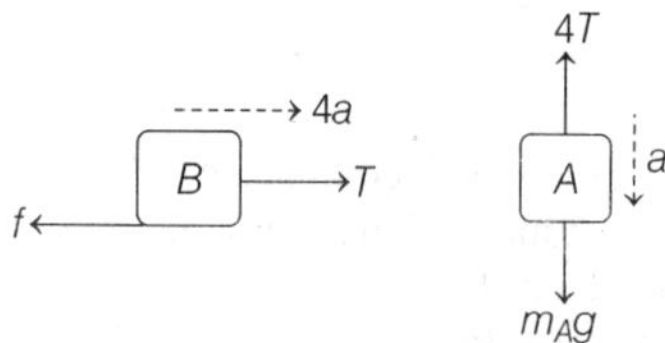

Similarly, if a be the acceleration of block A (downwards), then acceleration of block B towards right will be $4a$.

Equations of motion are

For block A, $\quad m_A g - 4T = m_A a$

or $\quad 50 - 4T = 5a \quad$ ...(i)

For block B, $\quad T - f = 10(4a)$

or $\quad T - (0.1)(10)(10) = 40a$

or $\quad T - 10 = 40a \quad$ ...(ii)

Solving Eqs. (i) and (ii), we get

$$a = \frac{2}{33}\text{ m/s}^2$$ **Ans.**

3. (a) When the truck accelerates eastward force of friction on mass is eastwards.

$$f_{\text{required}} = \text{mass} \times \text{acceleration}$$
$$= 30 \times 1.8 = 54\text{ N}$$

Since it is less than $\mu_s mg$

$$\therefore \quad f = 54\text{ N} \quad \text{(eastwards)}$$

(b) When the truck accelerates westwards, force of friction is westwards.

$f_{\text{required}} = \text{mass} \times \text{acceleration} = 30 \times 3.8 = 114\text{ N}$

Since it is greater than $\mu_s mg$. Hence

$f = f_k = \mu_k mg = 60\text{ N}$ (westwards) **Ans.**

4. Block B will fall vertically downwards and A along the plane.

Writing the equations of motion.

For block B,

$$m_B g - N = m_B a_B$$

or $\quad 60 - N = 6a_B \quad$ ...(i)

$$(N + m_A g)\sin 30° = m_A a_A$$

or $\quad (N + 150) = 30\, a_A \quad$ ...(ii)

Further $\quad a_B = a_A \sin 30°$

or $\quad a_A = 2a_B \quad$ ...(iii)

Solving these three equations, we get

(a) $a_A = 6.36\text{ m/s}^2$ **Ans.**

(b) $a_{BA} = a_A \cos 30° = 5.5\text{ m/s}^2$ **Ans.**

5. (a) N_2 and mg pass through G. N_1 has clockwise moment about G, so the ladder has a tendency to slip by rotating clockwise and the force of friction (f) at B is then up the plane.

(b) $\Sigma M_A = 0$

$$\therefore \quad fl = mg\left(\frac{l}{2}\sin 45°\right) \quad \text{...(i)}$$

$$\Sigma F_V = 0$$

$\therefore \quad mg = N_2 \cos 45° + f \sin 45° \quad ...(ii)$

From Eqs. (i) and (ii),

$$N_2 = \frac{3}{2\sqrt{2}} mg$$

and $$f = \frac{mg}{2\sqrt{2}}$$

or $$\mu_{min} = \frac{f}{N_2} = \frac{1}{3}$$ **Ans.**

6. Here f_1 = force of friction between man and plank and f_2 = force of friction between plank and surface.

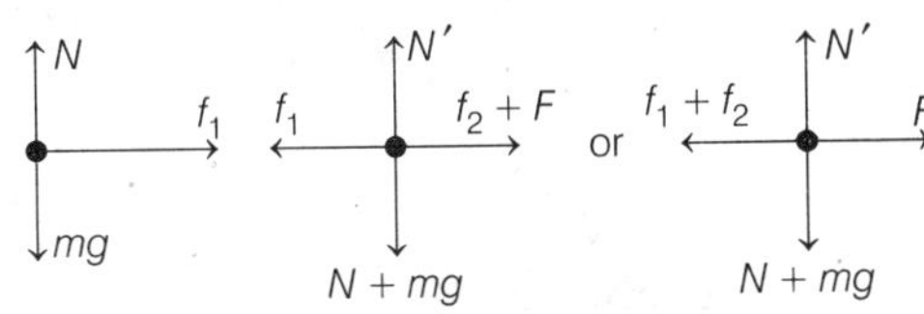

FBD of man FBD of plank

For the plank not to move

$F - (f_2)_{max} \le f_1 \le F + (f_2)_{max}$

or $F - \mu (M + m)g \le ma \le F + \mu (M + m)g$

or a should lie between $\frac{F}{m} - \frac{\mu(M + m)g}{m}$

and $\frac{F}{m} + \frac{\mu(M + m)g}{m}$ **Ans.**

7. $$2a_1 s_1 = 2a_2 s_2$$

or $$\frac{a_1}{a_2} = \frac{s_2}{s_1} = \frac{n}{m}$$

or $$\frac{g \sin \alpha}{\mu g \cos \alpha - g \sin \alpha} = \frac{n}{m}$$

Solving it, we get

$$\mu = \left(\frac{m + n}{n}\right) \tan \alpha$$ **Ans.**

8. Normal reaction between A and B would be $N = mg \cos \theta$. Its horizontal component is $N \sin \theta$. Therefore, tension in cord CD is equal to this horizontal component.

Hence, $T = N \sin \theta = (mg \cos\theta) (\sin \theta)$

$$= \frac{mg}{2} \sin 2\theta$$ **Ans.**

9. Since μ_s between crate and truck is less than 0.9. Therefore, retardation of truck and crate will be different.

Retardation of truck,

$$a_1 = 0.9\, g = 9 \text{ m/s}^2$$

Retardation of crate,

$$a_2 = 0.8\, g = 8 \text{ m/s}^2$$

Displacement of truck, before it finally stops is

$$S_1 = \frac{u^2}{2a_1} = \frac{(15)^2}{2 \times 9} = 12.5 \text{ m}$$

and displacement of crate

$$S_2 = \frac{u^2}{2a_2} = \frac{(15)^2}{2 \times 8} \approx 14.06 \text{ m}$$

$$\therefore \quad S_2 - S_1 = 1.56 \text{ m}$$

10. $\mu_k mg = 0.2 \times 10 \times 10 = 20$ N

For t ≤ 0.2 s

Retardation, $$a_1 = \frac{F + \mu_k mg}{m} = \frac{20 + 20}{10} = 4 \text{ m/s}^2$$

At the end of 0.2 s,

$$v = u - a_1 t$$
$$v = 1.2 - 4 \times 0.2 = 0.4 \text{ m/s}$$

For t > 0.2 s

Retardation $$a_2 = \frac{10 + 20}{10} = 3 \text{ m/s}^2$$

Block will come to rest after time

$$t_0 = \frac{v}{a_2} = \frac{0.4}{3} = 0.13 \text{ s}$$

$\therefore$ Total time = 0.2 + 0.13 = 0.33 s **Ans.**

11. Block will start moving at, $F = \mu\, mg$

or $25t = (0.5)(10)(9.8) = 49$ N

$\therefore \quad t = 1.96$ s

Velocity is maximum at the end of 4 second.

$$\therefore \quad \frac{dv}{dt} = \frac{25t - 49}{10} = 2.5t - 4.9$$

$$\therefore \quad \int_0^{v_{max}} dv = \int_{1.96}^{4} (2.5\, t - 4.9)\, dt$$

$$\therefore \quad v_{max} = 5.2 \text{ m/s}$$ **Ans.**

For 4 s < t < 7 s

Net retardation $$a_1 = \frac{49 - 40}{10} = 0.9 \text{ m/s}^2$$

$$\therefore \quad v = v_{max} - a_1 t_1 = 5.2 - 0.9 \times 3 = 2.5 \text{ m/s}$$

For $t > 7$ s

Retardation $a_2 = \frac{49}{10} = 4.9\ \text{m/s}^2$

$\therefore \quad t = \frac{v}{a_2} = \frac{2.5}{4.9} = 0.51$ s

$\therefore$ Total time $= (4 - 1.96) + (7 - 4) + (0.51)$
$= 5.55$ s **Ans.**

12. Let B and C both move upwards (alongwith their pulleys) with speeds v_B and v_C then we can see that, A will move downward with speed, $2v_B + 2v_C$. So, with sign we can write,

$$\therefore \quad v_B = \frac{v_A}{2} - v_c$$

Substituting the values we have, $v_B = 0$ **Ans.**

13. FBD of A with respect to frame is shown in figure. A is in equilibrium under three concurrent forces shown in figure, so applying Lami's theorem

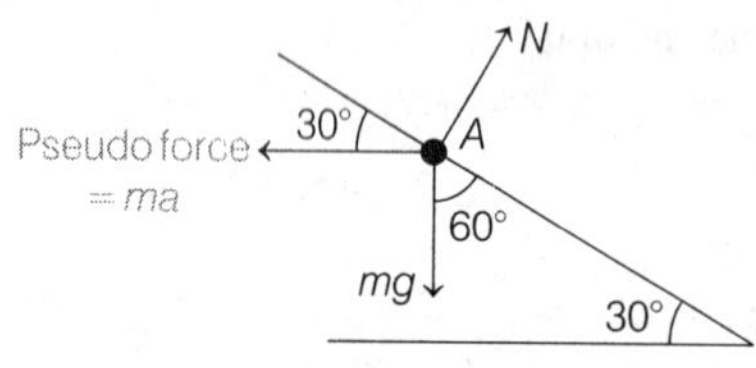

$$\frac{ma}{\sin(90 + 60)} = \frac{mg}{\sin(90 + 30)}$$

$$\therefore \quad a = \frac{g \cos 60°}{\cos 30°} = 5.66\ \text{m/s}^2$$

14. FBD of M_2 and M_3 in accelerated frame of reference is shown in figure.

Note *Only the necessary forces have been shown.*

Mass M_3 will neither rise nor fall if net pulling force is zero.

i.e. $\quad M_2 a = M_3 g$

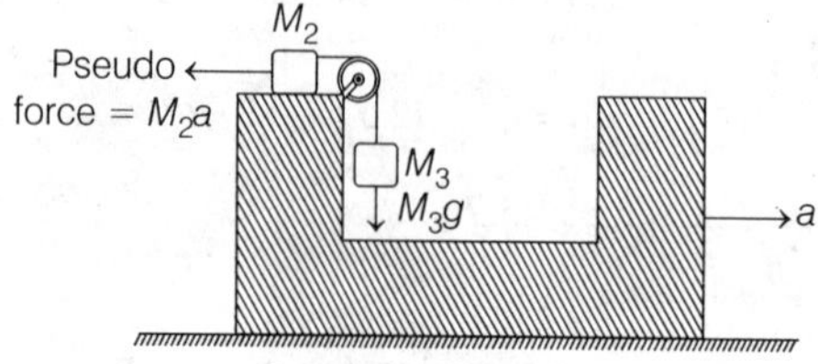

or $\quad a = \frac{M_3}{M_2} g$

$$\therefore \quad F = (M_1 + M_2 + M_3)a$$
$$= (M_1 + M_2 + M_3)\frac{M_3}{M_2} g \quad \textbf{Ans.}$$

15. Retardation $a = \mu_k g = 0.15 \times 9.8 = 1.47\ \text{m/s}^2$

Distance travelled before sliding stops is,

$$s = \frac{v^2}{2a}$$
$$= \frac{(5)^2}{2 \times 1.47} \approx 8.5\ \text{m} \quad \textbf{Ans.}$$

16. $\sqrt{2}\, N = mg \cos\theta$

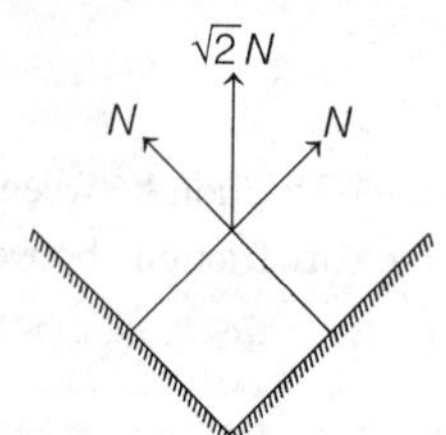

$$\therefore \quad N = \frac{mg \cos\theta}{\sqrt{2}}$$

$$a = \frac{mg \sin\theta - 2\mu_k N}{m}$$
$$= g \sin\theta - \sqrt{2}\, \mu_k g \cos\theta$$
$$= g(\sin\theta - \sqrt{2}\mu_k \cos\theta) \quad \textbf{Ans.}$$

17. $v \cdot \frac{dv}{dx} = \frac{\text{Net force}}{\text{mass}} = \frac{F - \mu_k \rho (L - x) g}{\rho L}$

$$\therefore \quad \int_0^v v\, dv = \int_0^L \frac{F - \mu_k \rho (L - x) g}{\rho L} dx$$

$$\therefore \quad \frac{v^2}{2} = \frac{F}{\rho} - \mu_k gL + \frac{\mu_k gL}{2}$$

$$\therefore \quad v = \sqrt{\frac{2F}{\rho} - \mu_k gL} \quad \textbf{Ans.}$$

18. (a) $v = a_1 t_1 = 2.6$ m/s

$$s_1 = \frac{1}{2} a_1 t_1^2 = \frac{1}{2} \times 2 \times (1.3)^2 = 1.69\ \text{m}$$
$$s_2 = (2.2 - 1.69) = 0.51\ \text{m}$$

Now, $\quad s_2 = \frac{v^2}{2a_2}$

$$\therefore \quad a_2 = \frac{v^2}{2s_1} = \frac{(2.6)^2}{2 \times 0.51}$$
$$= 6.63\ \text{m/s}^2$$

and $\quad t_2 = \frac{v}{a_2} = 0.4$ s

(b) Acceleration of package will be 2m/s^2 while retardation will be $\mu_k g$ or $2.5\ \text{m/s}^2$ not $6.63\ \text{m/s}^2$.

For the package,

$$v = a_1 t_1 = 2.6 \text{ m/s} \Rightarrow s_1 = \frac{1}{2} a_1 t_1^2 = 1.69 \text{ m}$$

$$s_2 = vt_2 - \frac{1}{2} d_2 t_2^2 = 2.6 \times 0.4 - \frac{1}{2} \times 2.5 \times (0.4)^2$$

$$= 0.84 \text{ m}$$

$\therefore$ Displacement of package w.r.t. belt

$$= (0.84 - 0.51) \text{ m} = 0.33 \text{ m}$$ **Ans.**

Alternate Solution For last 0.4 s

$$|a_r| = 6.63 - 2.5 = 4.13 \text{ m/s}^2$$

$$\therefore \quad s_r = \frac{1}{2}|a_r| t^2 = \frac{1}{2} \times 4.13 \times (0.4)^2$$

$$= 0.33 \text{ m}$$

19. Free body diagram of crate A w.r.t ground is shown in figure.

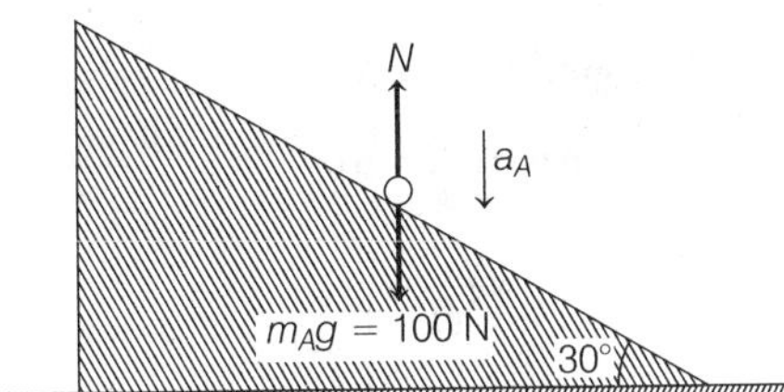

Equation of motion is

$$100 - N = 10 a_A \quad \ldots\text{(i)}$$

$$a_A = a \sin 30° = (2)\left(\frac{1}{2}\right)$$

or $$a_A = 1 \text{m/s}^2$$

Substituting in Eq. (i), we get

$$N = 90 \text{ N.}$$

20. (a) Force of friction at different contacts are shown in figure.

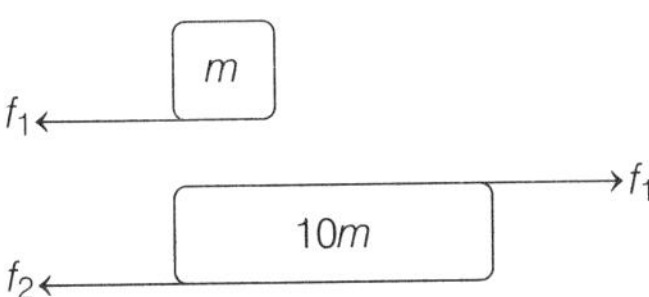

Here, $f_1 = \mu_2 mg$

and $f_2 = \mu_1 (11\, mg)$

Given that $\mu_2 > 11\mu_1$

$\therefore$ $f_1 > f_2$

Retardation of upper block

$$a_1 = \frac{f_1}{m} = \mu_2 g$$

Acceleration of lower block

$$a_2 = \frac{f_1 - f_2}{m}$$

$$= \frac{(\mu_2 - 11\mu_1)g}{10}$$

Relative retardation of upper block

$$a_r = a_1 + a_2$$

or $$a_r = \frac{11}{10}(\mu_2 - \mu_1)g$$

Now, $$0 = v_{\min}^2 - 2a_r l$$

$\therefore$ $$v_{\min} = \sqrt{2a_r l}$$

$$= \sqrt{\frac{22(\mu_2 - \mu_1)gl}{10}}$$ **Ans.**

(b) $0 = v_{\min} - a_r t$

or $$t = \frac{v_{\min}}{a_r} = \sqrt{\frac{20l}{11(\mu_2 - \mu_1)g}}$$ **Ans.**

21. $v_r = \sqrt{v_1^2 + v_2^2}$

Retardation $a = \mu g$

$\therefore$ Time when slipping will stop is $t = \frac{v_r}{a}$

or $$t = \frac{\sqrt{v_1^2 + v_2^2}}{\mu g} \quad \ldots\text{(i)}$$

$$s_r = \frac{v_r^2}{2a} = \frac{v_1^2 + v_2^2}{2\mu g}$$

$$x_r = -s_r \cos\theta = -\left(\frac{v_1^2 + v_2^2}{2\mu g}\right)\left(\frac{v_2}{\sqrt{v_1^2 + v_2^2}}\right)$$

$$= \frac{-v_2\sqrt{v_1^2 + v_2^2}}{2\mu g}$$

$$y_r = s_r \sin\theta = \left(\frac{v_1^2 + v_2^2}{2\mu g}\right)\left(\frac{v_1}{\sqrt{v_1^2 + v_2^2}}\right)$$

$$= \frac{v_1\sqrt{v_1^2 + v_2^2}}{2\mu g}$$

$\mathbf{v}_r$

$\mathbf{v}_1 = v_1$

θ

$-\mathbf{v}_2 = v_2$

In time t, belt will move a distance $s = v_2 t$

or $\frac{v_2\sqrt{v_1^2 + v_2^2}}{\mu g}$ in x-direction.

Hence, coordinate of particle,

$$x = x_r + s = \frac{v_2\sqrt{v_1^2 + v_2^2}}{2\mu g}$$

and $$y = y_r = \frac{v_1\sqrt{v_1^2 + v_2^2}}{2\mu g}$$ **Ans.**

22. FBD of m_1 (showing only the horizontal forces)

Equation of motion for m_1 is

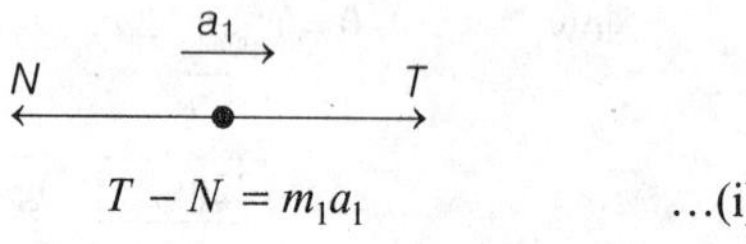

$$T - N = m_1a_1 \quad \text{...(i)}$$

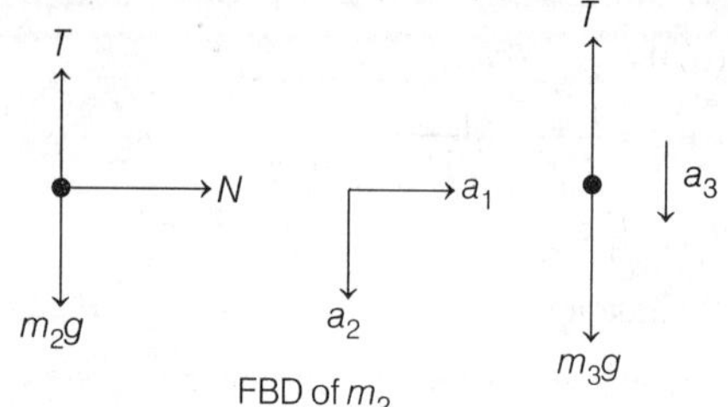

FBD of m_2

Equations of motion for m_2 are

$$N = m_2a_1 \quad \text{...(ii)}$$

and $$m_2g - T = m_2a_2 \quad \text{...(iii)}$$

Equation of motion for m_3 are

$$m_3g - T = m_3a_3 \quad \text{...(iv)}$$

Further from constraint equation we can find the relation,

$$a_1 = a_2 + a_3 \quad \text{...(v)}$$

We have five unknowns a_1, a_2, a_3, T and N solving, we get

$$a_1 = \frac{2m_1m_3\,g}{(m_2 + m_3)(m_1 + m_2) + m_2m_3}$$ **Ans.**

23. Writing equations of motion,

$$T - N = 3ma_1 \quad \text{...(i)}$$

$$N = 2ma_1 \quad \text{...(ii)}$$

$$2mg - T = 2ma_2 \quad \text{...(iii)}$$

$$T - \frac{mg}{2} = ma_3 \quad \text{...(iv)}$$

From constraint equation,

$$a_1 = a_2 - a_3 \quad \text{...(v)}$$

We have five unknowns. Solving the above five equations, we get

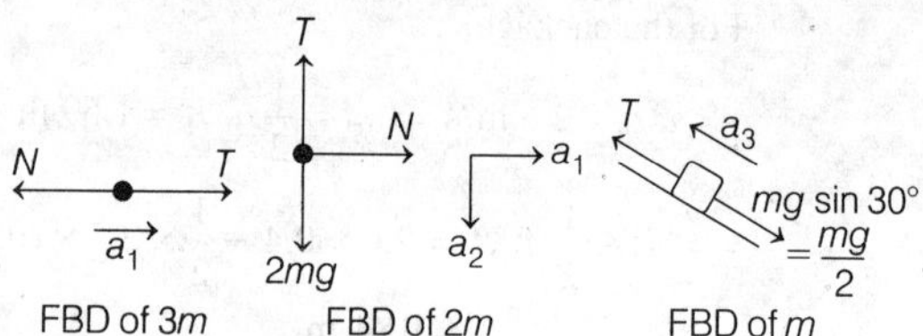

$$a_1 = \frac{3}{17}g, \quad a_2 = \frac{19}{34}g \text{ and } a_3 = \frac{13}{34}g$$

Acceleration of $m = a_3 = \frac{13}{34}g$,

Acceleration of $2m = \sqrt{a_1^2 + a_2^2} = \frac{\sqrt{397}}{34}g$

and acceleration of $3m = a_1 = \frac{3}{17}g$ **Ans.**

24. $a = \dfrac{m_Ag}{m_A + M + m}$

For the equilibrium of B,

$$mg = \mu N = \mu(ma) = \frac{\mu m m_A g}{m_A + M + m}$$

$$\therefore \quad m_A = \frac{(M + m)m}{(\mu - 1)m}$$

$$m_A = \frac{(M + m)}{\mu - 1}$$ **Ans.**

Note $m_A > 0 \; \therefore \; \mu > 1$

25. From free body diagram of cylinder A,

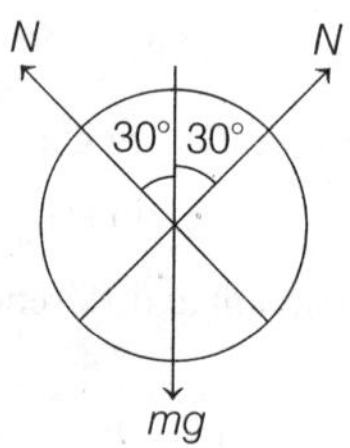

$$2N\cos 30° = mg$$

$$\therefore \quad N = \frac{mg}{\sqrt{3}}$$

From free body diagram of cylinder B,

$$N_0\cos\theta = mg + N\cos 30°,$$

$$N_0\sin\theta = N\sin 30°$$

$$\tan\theta = \frac{N\sin 30°}{mg + N\cos 30°}$$

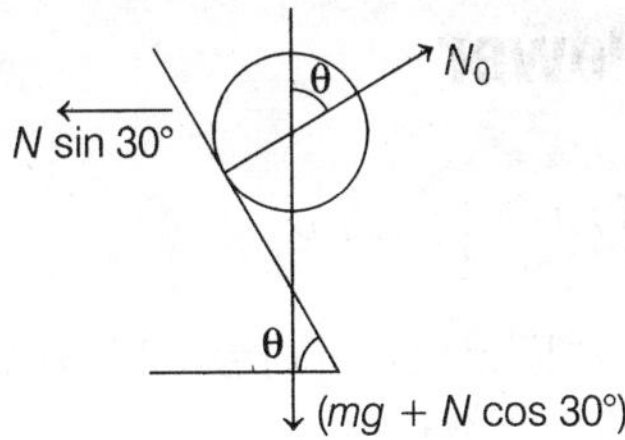

Putting the value of N, $\tan\theta = \frac{1}{3\sqrt{3}}$

$\therefore \quad n = 3$

Note *At minimum value of θ normal reaction between B and C will be zero.*

26. $\mathbf{F}_{net} = \mathbf{F}_{East} + \mathbf{F}_{South} + \mathbf{F}_{down} + \mathbf{F}_0$

$$= 3\hat{\mathbf{i}} + (-1\hat{\mathbf{j}}) + (-1\hat{\mathbf{k}}) + \mathbf{F}_0$$

y (North)

x (Earth)

z (Upward)

Since, the block moves in South-East direction,

$$\mathbf{F}_{net} = x\hat{\mathbf{i}} - x\hat{\mathbf{j}} + 0\hat{\mathbf{k}} \quad [\because \tan\theta = -1]$$

or $\quad x\hat{\mathbf{i}} - x\hat{\mathbf{j}} = 3\hat{\mathbf{i}} - \hat{\mathbf{j}} - \hat{\mathbf{k}} + \mathbf{F}_0$

or $\quad \mathbf{F}_0 = (x-3)\hat{\mathbf{i}} + (1-x)\hat{\mathbf{j}} + \hat{\mathbf{k}}$

$$|F_0| = \sqrt{(x-3)^2 + (1-x)^2 + (1)^2}$$

or $\quad |F_0|^2 = (x-3)^2 + (1-x)^2 + 1$

For minimum F_0, $|F_0|^2$ must be minimum.

Differentiating $|F_0|^2$ w.r.t. x, we get

$$\frac{dy}{dx} = 2(x-3) - 2(1-x) \quad [\text{let } |F_0|^2 = y]$$

For minima, $\frac{dy}{dx} = 0$

or $\quad 2(x-3) - 2(1-x) = 0$

or $\quad 4x + 8 = 0$

or $\quad x = 2$

$$\mathbf{F}_{0(min)} = (2-3)\hat{\mathbf{i}} + (1-2)\hat{\mathbf{j}} + \hat{\mathbf{k}}$$

$$= (-\hat{\mathbf{i}} - \hat{\mathbf{j}} + \hat{\mathbf{k}})\text{ N}$$

$\therefore \quad \mathbf{F}_{0(min)} = \sqrt{(-1)^2 + (-1)^2 + 1^2}$

$$= \sqrt{3} = \sqrt{n}$$

$\therefore \quad n = 3$

27. Here, $\quad a = \frac{F}{m} = \frac{bt - cs}{m} = t - s$

or $\quad \frac{da}{dt} = 1 - v$

or $\quad \frac{d^2a}{dt^2} = \frac{-dv}{dt} = -a$

The solution of equation is $a = a_0 \sin\omega t$.

When, $\omega = 1$ unit.

9. Work, Energy and Power

INTRODUCTORY EXERCISE 9.1

1. $W = \mathbf{F} \cdot \mathbf{S} = \mathbf{F} \cdot (\mathbf{r}_f - \mathbf{r}_i)$

$= (6\hat{i} - 2\hat{j} + \hat{k}) \cdot [(2\hat{i} + 3\hat{j} - 4\hat{k}) - (\hat{i} + 4\hat{j} + 6\hat{k})]$

$= -2 \text{J}$

2. (a) $W_F = FS \cos 45°$

$= (16)(2.2)\left(\frac{1}{\sqrt{2}}\right) = 24.89 \text{ J}$ **Ans.**

(b) $W_N = NS \cos 90° = 0$ **Ans.**

(c) $W_{mg} = (mg)(S) \cos 90° = 0$ **Ans.**

(d) Only three forces are acting. So, total work done is summation of all above work done.

3. $W_T = (T)(x) \cos 0° = Tx$

$W_W = (W)(x) \cos 90° = 0$

$W_N = (N)(x) \cos 90° = 0$

$W_F = (F)(x) \cos 180° = -Fx$

4. $mg - T = ma = \frac{mg}{4}$

$\Rightarrow \quad T = \frac{3mg}{4}$

$\therefore \quad W_T = (T)(l)(\cos 180°)$

$= -\frac{3}{4} mgl$

T a mg

5. $N = mg - F \sin 45° = 18 - \frac{F}{\sqrt{2}}$

Moving with constant speed means net force = 0

$F \cos 45° = \mu N = \frac{1}{4}\left(18 - \frac{F}{\sqrt{2}}\right)$

$\therefore \quad \frac{4F}{\sqrt{2}} = 18 - \frac{F}{\sqrt{2}}$

$\therefore \quad F = \frac{18\sqrt{2}}{5} \text{ N}$

(a) $W_F = FS \cos 45°$

$= \left(\frac{18\sqrt{2}}{5}\right)(2)\left(\frac{1}{\sqrt{2}}\right) = 7.2 \text{ J}$

(b) $W_f = (\mu N)(S) \cos 180°$

$= \left(\frac{1}{4}\right)\left(18 - \frac{F}{\sqrt{2}}\right)(2)(-1)$

$= -7.2 \text{ J}$

(c) $W_{mg} = (mg)(S) \cos 90° = 0$

6. $W = \int_2^{-4} F dx = \int_2^{-4} (-2x)\, dx$

$= [-x^2]_2^{-4} = -[16 - 4] = -12 \text{ J}$ **Ans.**

7. $W = \int_4^2 F dx = \int_4^2 \frac{4}{x^2} dx$

$= -4\left[\frac{1}{x}\right]_4^2 = -4\left[\frac{1}{2} - \frac{1}{4}\right] = -1 \text{ J}$ **Ans.**

8. W = area under F-x graph

From $X = -4$ to $X = -2$

$F = -$ ve (from graph)

$S = +$ ve

$\therefore \quad W_1 = -\frac{1}{2} \times 2 \times 10 = -10 \text{ J}$

From −2 to 4

$F = +$ ve

$S = +$ ve

$\therefore \quad W_2 = +\frac{1}{2}(6 + 2)(10)$

$= +40 \text{ J}$

$\therefore \quad W_T = W_1 + W_2 = 30 \text{ J}$ **Ans.**

9. (a) From $x = 10$m to $x = 5$m

$S = -$ ve

$F = +$ ve (from graph)

$\therefore \quad W_1 = -$ Area

$= -5 \times 3$

$= -15 \text{ J}$ **Ans.**

(b) From $x = 5$m to $x = 10$ m

$S = +$ ve

and $F = +$ ve

$\therefore \quad W_2 = +$ Area $= 5 \times 3$

$= 15 \text{ J}$ **Ans.**

(c) From $x = 10$m to $x = 15$ m

$S = +$ ve

$F = +$ ve

$\therefore \quad W_3 =$ Area

$= 3 \text{ J}$ **Ans.**

(d) From $x = 0$ to $x = 15$ m

$S = +$ ve and $F = +$ ve

$\therefore \quad W_4 = +\text{ Area}$

$= \frac{1}{2} \times 3 \times (12 + 6) = 27 \text{ J}$ **Ans.**

10. (a) From $x = 0$ to $x = 3.0$ m

$S = +\text{ ve}$

$F = +\text{ ve}$

$\therefore \quad W_1 = +\text{ Area} = +4 \text{ J}$

(b) From $x = 3$ m to $x = 4$ m

$F = 0 \Rightarrow W_2 = 0$

(c) From $x = 4$ m to $x = 7$ m

$S = +\text{ ve and } F = -\text{ ve}$

$\therefore \quad W_3 = +\text{ Area} = -1 \text{ J}$

(d) From $x = 0$ to $x = 7$ m

$W = W_1 + W_2 + W_3 = 3 \text{ J}$

INTRODUCTORY EXERCISE 9.2

1. From work energy theorem,

$$W_{net} = W_{mg} + W_{air} = \frac{1}{2} m (v_f^2 - v_i^2)$$

$$\Rightarrow \quad 0 + W_{air} = \frac{1}{2} \times 0.1 [(6)^2 - (10)^2] = -3.2 \text{ J}$$

2. $W_{All} = \Delta \text{ KE} = K_f - K_i$

$$= \frac{1}{2} m (v_f^2 - v_i^2) = \frac{1}{2} \times 2 \times (0 - 20^2)$$

$= -400$ J **Ans.**

4. $v_{x=0} = 0 \quad : \quad v_{x=b} = \alpha\sqrt{b}$

$\therefore \quad W_{All} = \Delta \text{ KE} = K_f - K_i$

$$= \frac{1}{2} m (v_f^2 - v_i^2) = \frac{1}{2} \times m [(\alpha\sqrt{b})^2 - 0]$$

$= \frac{1}{2} m \alpha^2 b$ **Ans.**

5. $W_F = FS \cos 0° = 80 \times 4 \times 1 = 320 \text{ J}$

$W_{mg} = (mg)(S) \cos 180°$

$= (50)(4)(-1)$

$= -200 \text{ J}$

$K_f = W_{All} = 120 \text{ J}$ **Ans.**

6. $K_f - K_i = W_F = \int F dx$

$$0 - \frac{1}{2} m v_0^2 = \int_0^x -Ax dx$$

$$\therefore \quad \frac{1}{2} m v_0^2 = \frac{Ax^2}{2}$$

or $x = v_0 \sqrt{\frac{m}{A}}$ **Ans.**

7. (a) $T = F$, (b) $W_{\text{All forces}} = 40$ J

8. $v = \frac{ds}{dt} = (4t - 2)$

$$W_{all} = \Delta K = K_f - K_i = K_{2s} - K_{0s}$$

$$= \frac{1}{2} m (v_f^2 - v_i^2)$$

$$= \frac{1}{2} \times 2 [(4 \times 2 - 2)^2 - (4 \times 0 - 2)^2]$$

$= 32$ J **Ans.**

9. $W_{all} = \Delta K = K_f - K_i = K_f$ (as $K_i = 0$)

$\therefore \quad W_{mg} + W_{chain} = K_f$

or $W_{chain} = K_f - W_{mg} = \frac{1}{2} m v_f^2 - mgh$

$$= \frac{1}{2} \times 30 \times (0.4)^2 - 30 \times 10 \times 2$$

$= -597.6$ J **Ans.**

INTRODUCTORY EXERCISE 9.3

1. $\Delta U = -W$

So, if work done by conservative force is positive then ΔU is negative or potential energy will decrease. But there is no straight forward rule regarding the kinetic energy.

2. $U_A = -60$ J

$U_B = -20$ J

$\therefore \quad U_B - U_A = 40$ J

INTRODUCTORY EXERCISE 9.4

1. $U = \frac{x^3}{3} - 4x + 6$

$$F = -\frac{dU}{dx} = -x^2 + 4$$

$F = 0$ at $x = \pm 2$ m

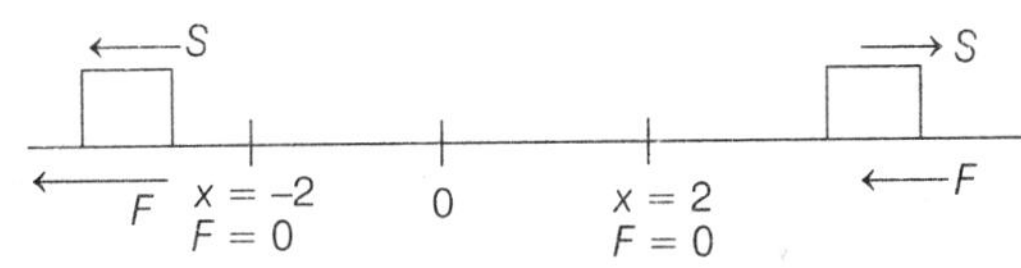

For $x > 2$ m, $F = -$ ve i.e. displacement is in positive direction and force is negative. Therefore $x = 2$ is stable equilibrium position.

For $x < -2$ m, $F = -$ ve

i.e. force and displacement are in negative directions. Therefore, $x = -2$ m is unstable equilibrium position.

2. At A, $x = 0$ and $F = 0$

For $x > 0$, $F = +$ ve. i.e. force is in the direction of displacement. Hence A is unstable equilibrium position.

Same concept can be applied with E also.

At point C, $F = 0$.

For $x > x_C$, $F = -$ ve

Displacement is positive and force is negative (in opposite direction of displacement). Therefore, C point is stable equilibrium point.

3. (a) At $x = 0$, $F = 0$. At P, attraction on $-q$

or $F_1 >$ attraction F_2

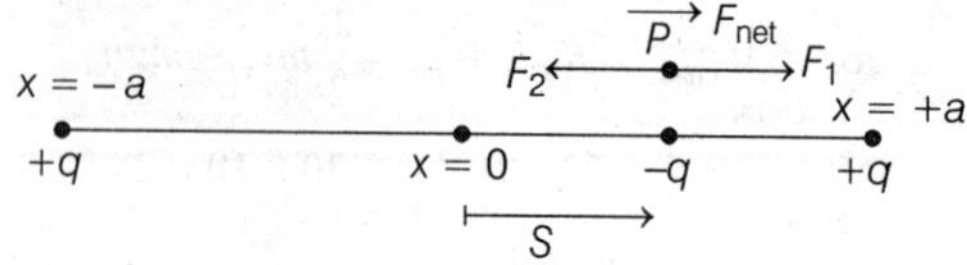

∴ Net force is in the direction of displacement. So, equilibrium is unstable.

(b) F_{net} is in opposite direction of S. Therefore equilibrium is stable.

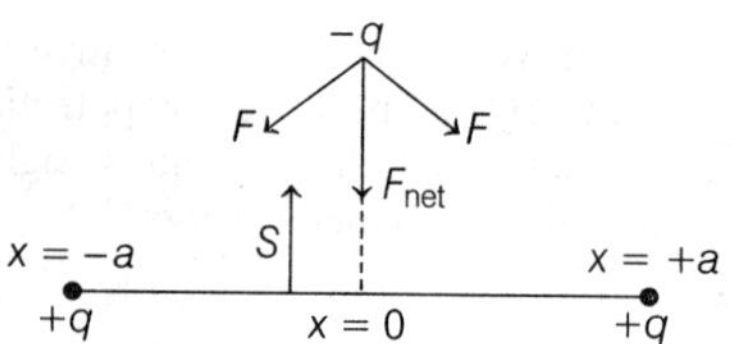

4. U = minimum = − 20 J

at $x = 2$ m

∴ $x = 2$ m is stable equilibrium position **Ans.**

5. $F = (x - 4)$

$$F = 0 \quad \text{at} \quad x = 4\text{ m}$$

When $x > 4$ m, $F = +$ ve

When displaced from $x = 4$ m (towards positive direction) force also acts in the same direction.

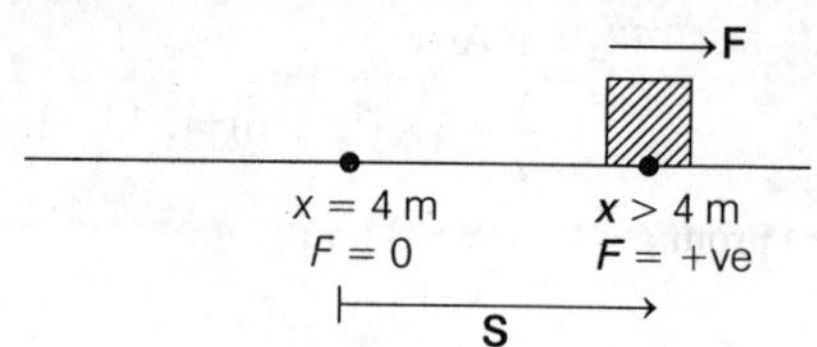

Therefore, equilibrium is unstable.

INTRODUCTORY EXERCISE 9.5

1. (a) $P_{av} = \frac{W}{t} = \frac{\frac{1}{2}mv^2}{t} = \frac{\frac{1}{2}m(at)^2}{t}$

$$= \frac{1}{2}ma^2 t = \frac{1}{2} \times 1 \times (4)^2 (2)$$

$$= 16 \text{ W}$$ **Ans.**

(b) $P_i = Fv = (ma)(at)$

$$= ma^2 t = (1)(4)^2(4)$$

$$= 64 \text{ W}$$ **Ans.**

2. (i) $W = Pt = \frac{1}{2}mv^2$

(ii) $v = \sqrt{\frac{2Pt}{m}}$

(iii) Integrating the velocity, we will get displacement

∴ $$S = \sqrt{\frac{2P}{m}}\left(\frac{t^{3/2}}{3/2}\right) = \sqrt{\frac{8P}{9m}}\, t^{3/2}$$ **Ans.**

3. (a) $\text{KE} = W = \int P\,dt = \int 2t \cdot dt = t^2$

$$\frac{1}{2}mv^2 = t^2$$

∴ $$v = \sqrt{\frac{2}{m}}\, t$$ **Ans.**

(b) $P_{av} = \frac{W}{t} = \frac{t^2}{t} = t$ **Ans.**

Exercises

LEVEL 1

Assertion and Reason

1. F = constant

∴ $$a = \frac{F}{m} = \text{constant}$$

$$v = at = \frac{F}{m}t$$

$$P = F \cdot v = \frac{F^2}{m}t$$

∴ $P \neq$ constant

But $P \propto t$

2. In the figure, work done by conservative force (gravity force) is positive, potential energy is decreasing. But kinetic energy may increase, decrease or remain constant, depending on the value of F.

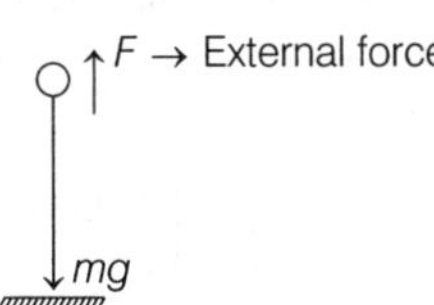

3. **Assertion** $\dfrac{dU}{dt} = \dfrac{d}{dt}(mgh)$

$$= mg\frac{d}{dt}\left(u_y t - \frac{1}{2}gt^2\right)$$

$$= mg(u_y - gt) = mgv_y$$

$\therefore$ $$\left|\frac{dU}{dt}\right| = mg|v_y|$$

$|v_y|$ first decreases then increase with time.

Reason $\dfrac{d\mathbf{p}}{dt} = \mathbf{F} = \mathbf{mg}$ = constant

4. $W_{\text{All}} = \Delta K = K_f - K_i$

$$= \frac{1}{2} m (v_f^2 - v_i^2)$$

$v_f = v_{t_2}$ = Slope of s-t graph at t_2

$v_i = v_{t_1}$ = Slope of s-t graph at t_1

These two slopes are not necessarily equal.

5.

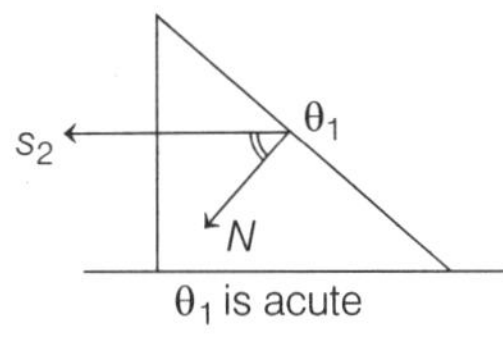

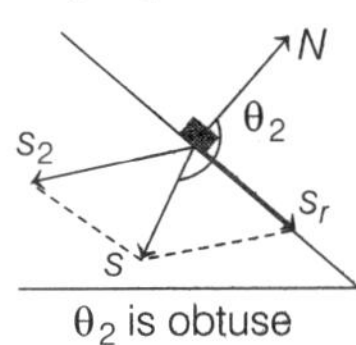

6. $(W_{f_1})_{\text{on } A} = -f_1 s$

$(W_{f_1})_{\text{on } B} = +f_1 s$

$\therefore$ Net work done by $f_1 = 0$

7. Decrease in mechanical energy in first case

$$= E_i - E_f = \frac{1}{2}mv^2 - 0 = \frac{1}{2}mv^2$$

Decrease in mechanical energy in second case

$$= E_i - E_f = \frac{1}{2}mv^2 - mgh$$

Further, μ does not depend on angle of inclination.

8. $W = 0$. That feet remains stationary, which is in contact with the ladder.

9. Change in potential energy is same.

Single Correct Option

1. $T = 2mg$

As soon as string is cut T (on A) suddenly becomes zero. Therefore, a force of $2mg$ acting on upward direction on A suddenly becomes zero.

So, net force on it will become $2mg$ downwards.

$$\therefore \quad a_1 = \frac{2mg}{m} = 2g \quad \text{(downwards)}$$

Spring force does not become instantly zero. So, acceleration of B will not change abruptly.

or $$a_2 = 0$$

2. $T_i = mg$ ...(i)

$$2kx = 2mg$$

$$\therefore \quad kx = mg$$

One kx force (acting in upward direction) is suddenly removed. So, net downward force on system will be kx or mg. Therefore, net downward acceleration of system,

$$a = \frac{mg}{2m} = \frac{g}{2}$$

Free body diagram of lower block gives the equation,

$$mg - T_f = ma = \frac{mg}{2}$$

$$\therefore \quad T_f = \frac{mg}{2} \quad \text{..(ii)}$$

From these two equations, we get

$$\Delta T = \frac{mg}{2}$$ **Ans.**

3. $P = \mathbf{F} \cdot \mathbf{v}$

$$= (-mg\,\hat{\mathbf{j}}) \cdot [u_x\hat{\mathbf{i}} + (u_y - gt)\,\hat{\mathbf{j}}]$$

$$= (-mgu_y) + mg^2t$$

i.e. P *versus* t graph is a straight line with negative intercept and positive slope.

4. $P = \mathbf{F} \cdot \mathbf{v} = Fv\cos\theta = Tv\cos\theta$ **Ans.**

5. $F = 0$ at $x = x_2$. When displaced from x_2 in negative direction, force is positive, i.e. in the opposite direction of displacement. Similarly, when displaced in positive direction, force is negative.

6. Σ (Moments about C) = 0

$$\therefore \quad (k_1x)\,AC = (k_2x)\,BC$$

$$\therefore \quad \frac{AC}{BC} = \frac{k_2}{k_1} \quad ...(i)$$

$$AC + BC = l \quad ...(ii)$$

Solving these two equations, we get

$$AC = \left(\frac{k_2}{k_1 + k_2}\right) l$$ **Ans.**

7. $P = \frac{W}{t} = \frac{mgh + \frac{1}{2} mv^2}{t}$

$$= \frac{(800 \times 10 \times 10) + \frac{1}{2} \times 800 \times (20)^2}{60}$$

$= 4000$ W **Ans.**

8. Work done by friction $= E_f - E_i$

$$= \frac{1}{2} \times 1 \times (2)^2 - 1 \times 10 \times 1$$

$= -8$ J **Ans.**

9. $K_i + U_i = K_f + U_f$

$$\therefore \quad 0 + 6 = \frac{1}{2} \times 1 \times v^2 + 2$$

$$\therefore \quad v = 2\sqrt{2} \text{ m/s}$$

10. $E_i = E_f$

$$0 = m_2 gh - m_1 gh + \frac{1}{2}(m_1 + m_2) v^2$$

$$\therefore \quad v = \sqrt{2gh\left(\frac{m_1 - m_2}{m_1 + m_2}\right)}$$ **Ans.**

11. $W = Mgh + mg\frac{h}{2} = \left(M + \frac{m}{2}\right) gh$

m

M

$\frac{h}{2}$

h

12. (a) Velocity is decreasing. Therefore, acceleration (or net force) is opposite to the direction of motion.

(b) and (c): some other forces (other than friction) may also act which retard the motion.

13. Let retarding force is F.

Then, $\quad Fx = \frac{1}{2} mv^2 \quad ...(i)$

and $\quad F(x') = \frac{1}{2} m (2v)^2 \quad ...(ii)$

Solving these two equations, we get

$$x' = 4x$$ **Ans.**

14. $K_i + U_i = K_f + U_f$

$$\therefore \quad \frac{1}{2} mv_0^2 + 0 = \frac{1}{2} mv^2 + mgh$$

$$\therefore \quad v = \sqrt{v_0^2 - 2gh}$$ **Ans.**

15. $a = \frac{F}{m}$

$$v = at = \left(\frac{F}{m}\right)(2)$$

$$P = F \cdot v = \frac{2F^2}{m}$$ **Ans.**

16. $a = \frac{F}{m}$

$$v = at = \frac{F}{m} t$$

$$P = F \cdot v = \left(\frac{F^2}{m}\right) t$$

or $\quad P \propto t$

i.e. P-t graph is a straight line passing through origin.

17. $K = \frac{1}{2} mv^2 = \frac{1}{2} m (gt^2)$

i.e. $K \propto t^2$

i.e.during downward motion. K-t graph is a parabola passing through origin with K increasing with time. Then, in upward journey K will decrease with time.

18. Upthrust = (Volume immersed) (density of liquid) g

$$= \left(\frac{5}{3000}\right)(1000)(10)$$

$$= \frac{50}{3} \text{ N}$$

Weight = 50 N

$\therefore$ Applied force (upwards) = weight – upthrust

$$= 50 - \frac{50}{3} = \frac{100}{3} \text{ N}$$

$$W = Fs = \frac{100}{3} \times 3$$

$= 100$ J **Ans.**

19. $s = 0$ (in vertical direction)

$$\Rightarrow \quad W = Fs = 0$$

$$\therefore \quad P_{av} = \frac{W}{t} = 0$$

20. $k \propto \frac{1}{l}$

l of shorter part is less, therefore value of k is more

$$W = \frac{1}{2} kx^2$$

$\therefore$ $W_{\text{shorter part}}$ will be more.

21. Let θ_1 is the angle of **F** with positive x-axis.

$$\therefore \quad \tan\theta_1 = \frac{F_y}{F_x} = \frac{15}{20} = \frac{3}{4} = m_1 \quad \text{(say)}$$

Slope of given line, $m_2 = -\frac{\alpha}{3}$

$W = 0$ if $\mathbf{F} \perp \mathbf{s}$ or $m_1 m_2 = -1$

$$\therefore \quad \left(\frac{3}{4}\right)\left(-\frac{\alpha}{3}\right) = -1$$

$$\therefore \quad \alpha = 4 \qquad \textbf{Ans.}$$

22. Decrease in gravitational potential energy of block = increase in spring potential energy

$$\therefore \quad mg\,(x_m \sin\theta) = \frac{1}{2} k x_m^2$$

$$\therefore \quad x_m = \frac{2\,mg\sin\theta}{k} \qquad \textbf{Ans.}$$

23. $\mathbf{v} = \frac{d\mathbf{s}}{dt} = (4\,t)\,\hat{\mathbf{i}}$

$$P = \mathbf{F}\cdot\mathbf{v} = 12\,t^2$$

$$\therefore \quad W = \int_0^2 P dt = \int_0^2 (12)\,t^2 dt$$

$$= 32 \text{ J} \qquad \textbf{Ans.}$$

24. Decrease in potential energy = Work done against friction

$$\therefore \quad mg\,(h+d) = F\cdot d$$

Here, F = average resistance

$$\Rightarrow \quad F = mg\left(1 + \frac{h}{d}\right) \qquad \textbf{Ans.}$$

25. $F = kx \quad \Rightarrow \quad x = \frac{F}{k}$

Now, $$U = \frac{1}{2} kx^2 = \frac{1}{2} k \left(\frac{F}{k}\right)^2$$

or $$U \propto \frac{1}{k}$$

k_B is double. Therefore, U_B will be half.

26. In the frame of car,

$$\therefore \quad m a_0 = kx_0$$

$$\therefore \quad x_0 = \frac{m a_0}{k}$$

$m a_0$ ← [block] → $k x_0$

When car stops, the maximum speed is achieved by the block when spring comes in natural length. Thus, loss in spring potential energy appears as kinetic energy of the block

$$\frac{1}{2} kx_0^2 = \frac{1}{2} mv_{\max}^2$$

$$\Rightarrow \quad v_{\max} = \sqrt{\frac{m}{k}}\, a_0$$

27. According to work-energy theorem,
Loss in kinetic energy = Work done against friction + Potential energy of spring

$$\Rightarrow \quad \frac{1}{2} mv^2 = f x + \frac{1}{2} kx^2$$

where, x is the compression of the spring.

$$\Rightarrow \frac{1}{2} \times 2 \times (4)^2 = 15x + \frac{1}{2} \times 10000x^2$$

$$\Rightarrow \quad 5000x^2 + 15x - 16 = 0$$

$$\therefore \quad x = 0.055 \text{ m}$$

$$= 5.5 \text{ cm}$$

28. $E_i = E_f$

$$0 = \frac{1}{2} \times 10 \times (0.15)^2 - 0.1 \times 10 \times 0.15 + \frac{1}{2} \times 0.1 \times v^2$$

$$\therefore \quad v = 0.866 \text{ m/s} \qquad \textbf{Ans.}$$

29. From $F = kx$

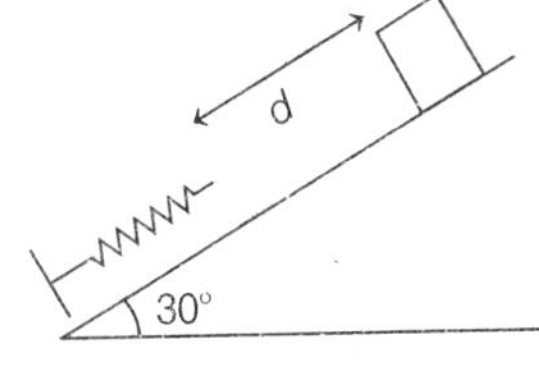

$$k = \frac{F}{x} = \frac{100}{1.0}$$

$$= 100 \text{ N/m}$$

Decrease in gravitational potential energy = increase in spring potential energy

$$\Rightarrow \quad 10 \times 10 \times (d+2) \sin 30° = \frac{1}{2} \times 100 \times (2)^2$$

Solving, we get $\quad d = 2$ m

$\therefore$ Total distance covered before coming momentarily to rest $= d + 2 = 4$ m **Ans.**

30. Speed (and hence the kinetic energy) will increase as long as $mg\sin\theta > kx$.

31. (a) $W_N = NS \cos 90° = 0$

(b) $W_T = TS \cos 0° = (mg \sin\theta)\left(\frac{h}{\sin\theta}\right) = mgh$

(c) $W_{mg} = (mg)(h) \cos 180° = -mgh$

(d) $W_{\text{Total}} = \Delta K = K_f - K_i = 0$

As block is moved slowly or $K_f = K_i$

32. Displacement of floor = 0

33.

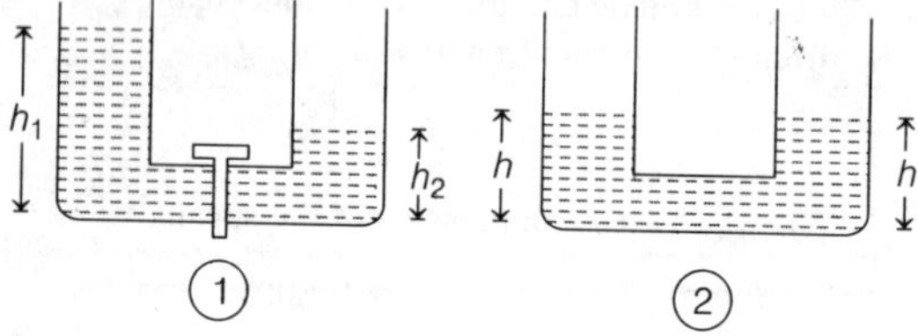

Since, the volume remains same.

$$Ah_1 + Ah_2 = Ah + Ah$$

$$\Rightarrow \quad h = \frac{h_1 + h_2}{2}$$

$$U_1 = \frac{[(\rho Ah_1)gh_1 + (\rho Ah_2)gh_2]}{2}$$

$$U_2 = \frac{(\rho Ah)gh}{2} \times 2$$

$$W_{gr} = -(U_2 - U_1) = U_1 - U_2$$

$$= \frac{\rho Ag}{2}[(h_1^2 + h_2^2) - 2h^2]$$

$$= \frac{\rho Ag}{2}\left[(h_1^2 + h_2^2) - 2\left(\frac{h_1 + h_2}{2}\right)^2\right]$$

$$= \rho Ag\left[\frac{h_1 - h_2}{2}\right]^2$$

34. $P = 2x = Fv = mav = m\left(v\frac{dv}{dx}\right)v$

$$\therefore \quad v^2 dv = \frac{1}{m} 2x\, dx$$

Integrating, we get

$$\frac{v^3}{3} = \frac{x^2}{m}$$

$$\therefore \quad v = \left(\frac{3x^2}{m}\right)^{\frac{1}{3}}$$

35. At highest point,

$$\frac{1}{2} m u_x^2 = K$$

$$\therefore \quad u_x = \sqrt{\frac{2K}{m}}$$

$$R = 4\text{H}$$

$$\frac{2u_x u_y}{g} = \frac{4u_y^2}{2g}$$

$$\therefore \quad u_y = u_x = \sqrt{\frac{2K}{m}}$$

Now,

$$K_i = \frac{1}{2} mu^2$$

$$= \frac{1}{2} m (u_x^2 + u_y^2)$$

$$= \frac{1}{2} m \left(\frac{2K}{m} + \frac{2K}{m}\right)$$

$$= 2K$$ **Ans.**

36. $K_f - K_i = W = \int F dx$

$$\therefore \quad K_f = K_i + \int_{20}^{30} (-0.1x)\, dx$$

$$= \frac{1}{2} \times 10 \times (10)^2 - \left[0.1\frac{x^2}{2}\right]_{20}^{30}$$

$$= 475 \text{ J}$$ **Ans.**

37. KE = decrease in potential energy = mgh

or $\quad \text{KE} \propto m$

or $\quad \frac{(\text{KE})_1}{(\text{KE})_2} = \frac{12}{6} = \frac{2}{1}$

38. $W = U_f - U_i = \frac{1}{2} K (X_f^2 - X_i^2)$

$$= \frac{1}{2} \times 5 \times 10^3 [(0.1)^2 - (0.05)^2]$$

$$= 18.75 \text{ N-m}$$ **Ans.**

39. Mass $\frac{M}{3}$ has its centre of mass $\frac{L}{6}$ below the table surface.

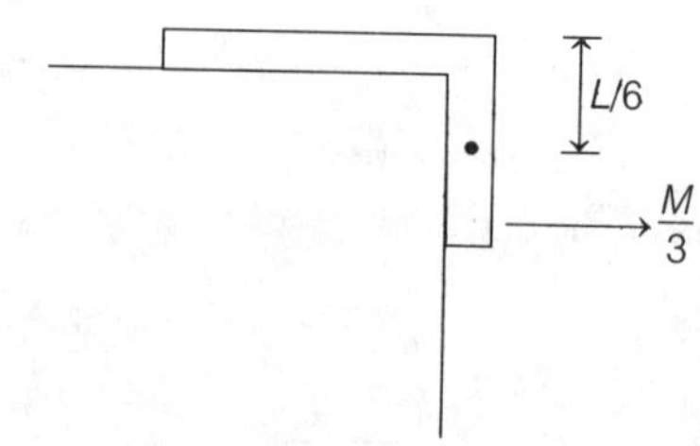

$$\therefore \quad w = mgh = \left(\frac{M}{3}\right)(g)\left(\frac{L}{6}\right) = \frac{MgL}{18}$$

40. $E_i = E_f$

$$\frac{1}{2}mv_0^2 = \frac{1}{2}kx_{max}^2 \Rightarrow x_{max} = \sqrt{\frac{m}{k}}v_0$$

41. $Mg - T = \frac{Mg}{2}$ or $T = \frac{Mg}{2}$

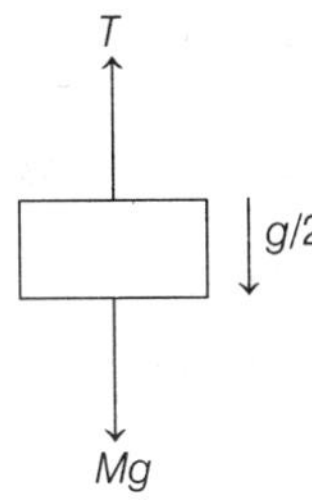

or magnitude of work done $= T \times x = \frac{Mgx}{2}$

42. Ratio of displacement is

$$\frac{1}{2}g(1)^2 : \left(\frac{1}{2}(g)(2)^2 - \frac{1}{2}g(1)^2\right) : \left(\frac{1}{2}g(3)^2 - \frac{1}{2}g(2)^2\right)$$

or $1 : 3 : 5.$

Therefore, ratio of work done will also be 1 : 3 : 5.

As $W = mgs$ or $W \propto s$

43. Change in kinetic energy = work done

= Area under F-x graph

$$\therefore \frac{1}{2} \times 5 \times v^2 = 10 \times 25 + \frac{1}{2} \times 25 \times 10 = 375$$

$$\therefore v = 12.24 \text{ ms}^{-1}$$

44. Let the time of descent of each ball is t_0.

$$\therefore h = \frac{1}{2}g t_0^2 \text{ or } \frac{20 \times 2}{10} = t_0^2$$

$$\therefore t_0 = 2 \text{ s}$$

$\therefore$ Each ball remains in air for four second. Thus, the time interval between balls is 1 s.

2nd
1 s 1 s
1st 3rd
1 s 1 s
4th

The speed of first ball is

$$v = gt = 10 \times 1 = 10 \text{ m/s}$$

$\therefore$ The kinetic energy of the first ball is KE $= \frac{1}{2}mv_0^2$

$$= \frac{1}{2} \times 10 \times 10^{-3} \times 100 = 0.5 \text{ J}$$

45. Work done by conservative force = $-\Delta U$

46. $\tan\theta = \frac{F_y}{F_x} = -\frac{x}{y}$

or $\frac{dy}{dx} = -\frac{x}{y}$ or $\int y\,dy = -\int x\,dx$

or $x^2 + y^2 = c$ is a circular curve.

Thus, the force is along tangent to the path of the block.

The magnitude of the force is

$$F = \sqrt{F_x^2 + F_y^2} = k$$

$$\therefore W = \int_c F\,ds = k\int_c ds$$

$$= k\,2\pi R = 2\pi Rk$$

47. $mgh + \frac{1}{2}mv^2 = \text{constant} = mgH$

(H = initial height)

or $gh + \frac{v^2}{2} = \text{constant}$

48. $\frac{1}{2}mv^2 = (0.9)(mgh)$

$$\therefore v = \sqrt{1.8gh} = \sqrt{1.8 \times 10 \times 2}$$

$$= 6 \text{ m/s}$$

49. $N = mg - F\sin\theta$

Block moves with uniform velocity. Hence, net force = 0

or $F\cos\theta = \mu N = \mu(mg - F\sin\theta)$

$$\therefore F = \frac{\mu mg}{\cos\theta + \mu\sin\theta}$$

$$W = Fd\cos\theta = \frac{\mu\,mgd\cos\theta}{\cos\theta + \mu\sin\theta}$$

50. Maximum acceleration of 2 kg block due to friction can be μg or 5 m/s^2.

Combined acceleration, if both move together with same acceleration would be

$$a = \frac{60}{12} = 5 \text{ m/s}^2$$

Since, both accelerations are equal, upper block will move with acceleration 5 m/s^2 due to friction.

In first two seconds, $s = \frac{1}{2}at^2 = \frac{1}{2} \times 5 \times 4 = 10 \text{m}$

and force of friction, $f = ma = 10 \text{N}$

$$\therefore W_f = fs\cos 0° = 100 \text{J}$$

51. $\frac{3}{4}$ th is lost. Hence, left is $\frac{1}{4}$ th, or

$$v^2 = \frac{v_0^2}{4}$$

$\therefore \quad v = \frac{v_0}{2} = v_0 - at_0 = v_0 - \mu g t_0$

or $\quad \mu = \frac{v_0}{2gt_0}$

52. Work done by tension on M is negative (force and displacement are in opposite directions). But, work done by tension on m is positive. Net work done will be zero.

53. From work-energy theorem,

W = change in kinetic energy

or $\quad W = \frac{1}{2}mv^2$

$\therefore \quad W - v$ graph is a parabola.

54. From work-energy theorem,

Work done = change in kinetic energy

$\therefore Fx = K$ (as F = constant because a = constant)

Therefore, k-x graph is a straight line passing through origin.

55. $F = kx$ or k = slope of F-x graph (F along y-axis)

Here, F is along x-axis.

So, $\quad k = \frac{1.0}{10} = 0.1 \frac{\text{kgf}}{\text{cm}}$

56. Average velocity $= \frac{\text{Total displacement}}{\text{Time}}$

$= \frac{\text{Area under } v\text{-}t \text{ graph}}{\text{Time}}$

Since, $\quad$ area $\neq 0$

$\therefore$ Average velocity $\neq 0$

57. $E = \frac{1}{2}mv^2$

$\therefore \quad \frac{dE}{dv} = mv$

or $\quad p = \frac{dE}{dv} \quad$ [as $mv = p$]

58. $K = \frac{F}{x}$ = slope of F - x graph.

$K \propto \frac{1}{l}$

Length is reduced to half. Therefore, K will become two times. Slope will increase.

59. $k = 4t^2$ or $v^2 \propto t^2$

$\therefore \quad v \propto t$

v varies linearly with time when acceleration or force is constant.

60.

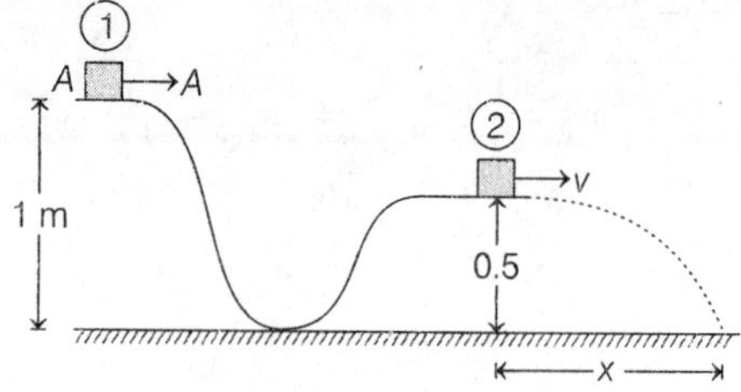

$$mg(1) = \frac{1}{2}mv^2 + mg(0.5)$$

$$v^2 = 2g(1 - 0.5) = g = 10$$

$$\Rightarrow \quad v = \sqrt{10} \text{ m/s}$$

$$t = \sqrt{\frac{2h}{g}} = \sqrt{\frac{2 \times 0.5}{10}} = \sqrt{\frac{1}{10}}$$

Now, $x = vt = 1$ m

61.

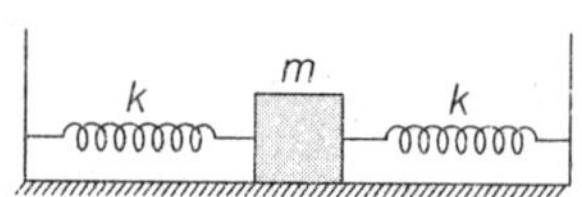

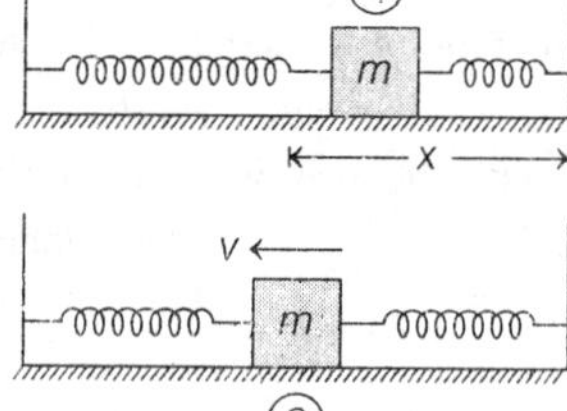

$$\frac{1}{2}kx^2 + \frac{1}{2}kx^2 = \frac{1}{2}mv^2$$

$$kx^2 = \frac{1}{2}mv^2$$

$$v = \sqrt{\frac{2k}{m}}x$$

62. $mgh = \frac{1}{2}kx^2$

$$\frac{40}{1000} \times 10 \times 5 = \frac{1}{2} \times 400x^2$$

$$x = \frac{1}{10} \text{ m} = 10 \text{ cm}$$

63. $\frac{1}{2}m(100)^2 = R(2t)$

Here, R is the retarding force and t, thickness of one plank.

$$\frac{1}{2}m(200)^2 = R(nt)$$

$$n = 8$$

64. $W = \Delta E = \frac{1}{2}k(a+b)^2 - \frac{1}{2}ka^2$

$$= \frac{1}{2}k(b^2 + 2ab)$$

$$= \frac{1}{2}kb(b + 2a)$$

65. $dW = -(\mu mg\cos\theta)\, ds = -\mu mg\, (ds\cos\theta)$

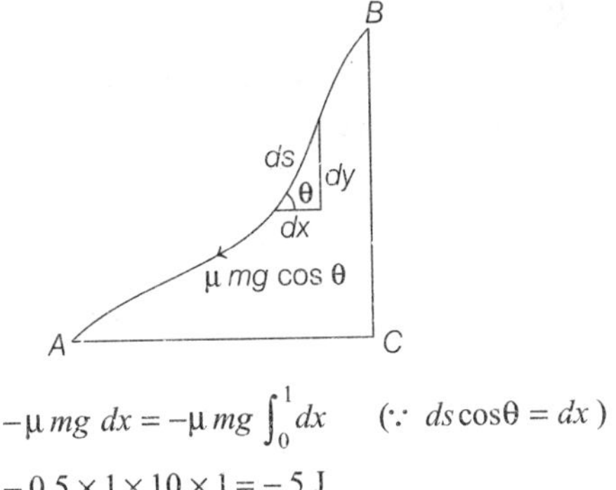

$$= -\mu mg\, dx = -\mu mg \int_0^1 dx \qquad (\because\ ds\cos\theta = dx)$$

$$= -0.5 \times 1 \times 10 \times 1 = -5\ \text{J}$$

66. At maximum elongation, the velocity of the block is zero.

According to work-energy theorem, $W = \Delta T$

or $\quad W_S + W_F = T_f - T_i = 0 - 0 = 0$

or $\quad -\frac{1}{2}kx_{max}^2 + Fx_{max} = 0$

$\therefore \quad x_{max} = \frac{2F}{k} = \frac{2 \times 50}{100} = 1\ \text{m}$

67. At maximum speed, acceleration of the block should be zero.

$\therefore \quad F = kx$

$\Rightarrow \quad x = \frac{F}{k}$

According to work-energy theorem,

$$W = \Delta K = \frac{1}{2}mv_{max}^2 - 0$$

or $\quad W_S + W_F = \frac{1}{2}mv_{max}^2$

or $\quad -\frac{1}{2}kx^2 + Fx = \frac{1}{2}mv_{max}^2$

or $\quad -\frac{1}{2}k\left(\frac{F}{k}\right)^2 + F \times \left(\frac{F}{k}\right)^2 = \frac{1}{2}mv_{max}^2$

or $\quad -\frac{F^2}{2k} + \frac{F^2}{k} = \frac{1}{2}mv_{max}^2$

or $\quad \frac{F^2}{2k} = \frac{1}{2}mv_{max}^2$

$\therefore \quad v_{max} = \sqrt{\frac{F^2}{mk}} = \frac{F}{\sqrt{mk}}$

$$= \frac{50}{\sqrt{1 \times 100}} = \frac{50}{10}$$

$$= 5\ \text{m/s}$$

68. At the maximum compression, velocity of each blocks are zero.

$\therefore$ Gain in PE $= \Delta U =$ Loss in KE

$$= \frac{1}{2}mv_0^2 + \frac{1}{2}mv_0^2 - 0 = mv_0^2$$

$\because$ Spring force is conservative in nature.

$\therefore$ The work done by spring is

$$W_s = -\Delta U = -mv_0^2$$

$\therefore$ The work done on each block by spring is

$$W = \frac{W_s}{2} = -\frac{1}{2}mv_0^2$$

$$= -\frac{1}{2} \times 1 \times 100 = -50\ \text{J}$$

Subjective Questions

1. $K = \frac{p^2}{2m}$

$$K' = \frac{p'^2}{2m} = \frac{(1.5p)^2}{2m}$$

$$= (2.25)\frac{p^2}{2m} = 2.25\,K$$

$\therefore \quad \%$ increase $= \frac{K' - K}{K} \times 100$

$= 125\ \%$ **Ans.**

2. $p = \sqrt{2Km}$

or $\quad P \propto K^{\frac{1}{2}}$

For small % changes,

% change in $p = \frac{1}{2}$ (% change in K)

$= \frac{1}{2}(1\ \%) = 0.5\ \%$ **Ans.**

3. Total work done $= -\frac{1}{2}K(2x_0)^2 = -2Kx_0^2$

$\therefore$ Work done on one mass

$$= \frac{-2Kx_0^2}{2} = -Kx_0^2$$

4. $w_T = (T)(l)\cos\beta$

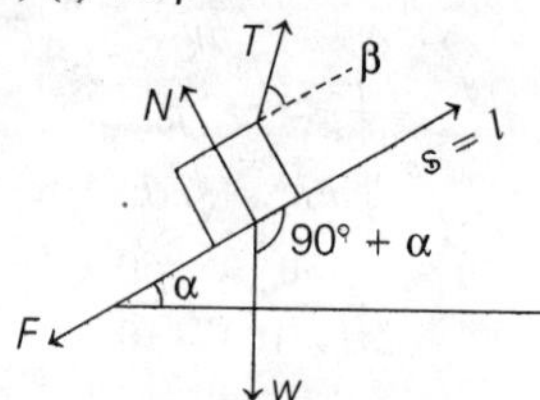

$w_N = (N)(l)\cos 90° = 0$

$w_w = (W)(l)\cos(90+\alpha) = -wl\sin\alpha$

$w_f = (F)(l)\cos 180° = -Fl$

5. $T - mg = ma$

$\therefore \quad T = m(g+a) = 72(9.8+0.98)$

$= 776.16$ N

(a) $W_T = Ts\cos 0°$

$= (776.16)(15)$

$= 11642$ J **Ans.**

(b) $W_{mg} = (mg)(s)\cos 180°$

$= (72\times 9.8\times 15)(-1)$

$= -10584$ J **Ans.**

(c) $K = W_{\text{Total}} = 11642 - 10584$

$= 1058$ J **Ans.**

(d) $K = \frac{1}{2}mv^2$

$\therefore \quad v = \sqrt{\frac{2K}{m}} = \sqrt{\frac{2\times 1058}{72}}$

$= 5.42$ m/s **Ans.**

6. (a) $K = W = \int F dx = \int_0^2 (2.5 - x^2)\,dx$

$= 2.33$ J **Ans.**

(b) Maximum kinetic energy of the block is at a point, where force changes its direction.

or $F = 0$

at $X = \sqrt{2.5}$

$= 1.58$ m

$\therefore \quad K_{\max} = \int_0^{1.58} (2.5 - X^2)\,dx$

$= 2.635$ J **Ans.**

7. $W_f = fs\cos 45°$

Here, $f = mg\sin\theta$, because uniform velocity means net acceleration = 0 or net force = 0

$\therefore \quad W_f = (mg\sin\theta)(s)(\cos 45°)$

$= (1)(10)(\sin 45°)(s)(\cos 45°)$

If $s = vt = 2\times 1 = 2$ m

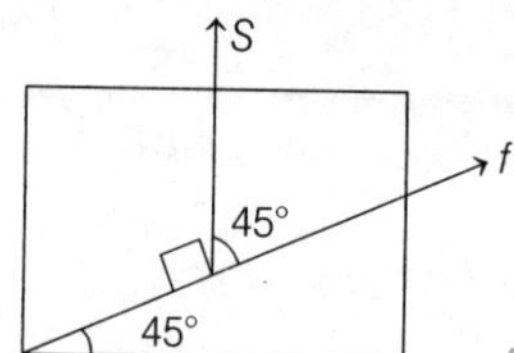

$$W_f = (1)(10)\left(\frac{1}{\sqrt{2}}\right)(2)\left(\frac{1}{\sqrt{2}}\right) = 10 \text{ J}$$ **Ans.**

8. $v_{m_1} = v_{m_2} = v$ (say)

$d_{m_1} = h_{m_2} = 4$ m

Using the equation,

$E_i - E_f =$ Work done against friction

$$0 - \left[\frac{1}{2}\times(10+5)(v^2) - 5\times 10\times 4\right]$$

$= 0.2\times 10\times 10\times 4$

Solving, we get

$v = 4$ m/s

9. **FBD of particle w.r.t. sphere**

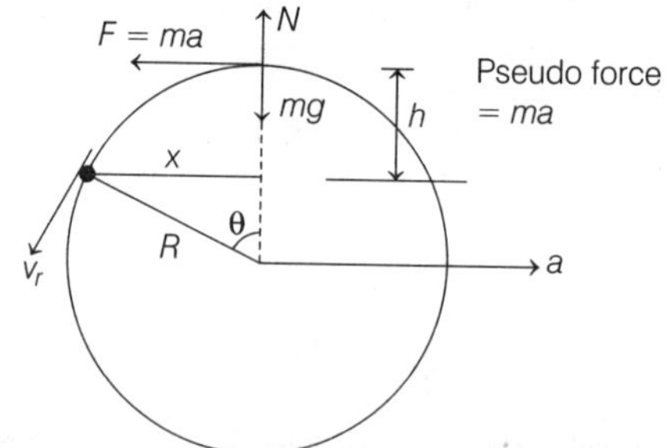

$K_f = \frac{1}{2}mv_r^2 = W_{\text{All}}$

or $\frac{1}{2}mv_r^2 = W_N + W_F + W_{mg}$

$= 0 + Fx + mgh$

$= (ma)(R\sin\theta) + mg[R(1-\cos\theta)]$

$\therefore \quad v_r = \sqrt{2gR(1+\sin\theta-\cos\theta)}$ **Ans.**

10. From constraint relations, we can see that

$v_A = 2v_B$

Therefore, $v_A = 2(0.3) = 0.6$ m/s

as $v_B = 0.3$ m/s (given)

Applying $W_{nc} = \Delta U + \Delta K$, we get

$$-\mu m_A g s_A = -m_B g s_B + \frac{1}{2}m_A v_A^2 + \frac{1}{2}m_B v_B^2$$

Here, $s_A = 2s_B = 2$ m as $s_B = 1$m (given)

$\therefore \; -\mu(4.0)(10)(2) = -(1)(10)(1) + \frac{1}{2}(4)(0.6)^2 + \frac{1}{2}(1)(0.3)^2$

or $-80\mu = -10 + 0.72 + 0.045$

or $80\mu = 9.235$

or $\mu = 0.115$ **Ans.**

11. Let x_{max} = maximum extension of spring

Decrease in potential energy of A

= Increase in elastic potential energy of spring

$\therefore \quad m_A g x_{max} = \frac{1}{2} k x_{max}^2$

$\therefore \quad x_{max} = \frac{2m_A g}{k}$

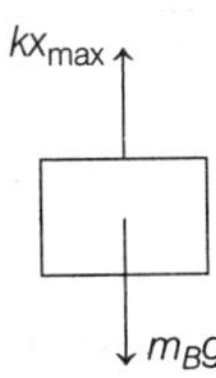

To just lift the block B,

$kx_{max} = m_B g$

$\therefore \quad 2m_A g = m_B g = mg$

$\therefore \quad m_A = \frac{m}{2}$ **Ans.**

12. (a) $K_A + U_A = K_B + U_B$

$\therefore \; 0 + \frac{1}{2} \times 500 \times (0.5 - 0.1)^2 = \frac{1}{2} \times 10 \times v^2 + \frac{1}{2} \times 500 \times (0.3 - 0.1)^2$

On solving, we get

$v = 2.45$ m/s **Ans.**

(b) $CO - \sqrt{(BO)^2 + (BC)^2}$

$= \sqrt{(30)^2 + (20)^2}$

≈ 36 cm $= 0.36$ m

Again applying the equation,

$K_A + U_A = K_C + U_C$

$0 + \frac{1}{2} \times 500 \times (0.5 - 0.1)^2 = \frac{1}{2} \times 10 \times v^2 + \frac{1}{2} \times 500\,(0.36 - 0.1)^2$

On solving, we get

$v = 2.15$ m/s **Ans.**

13. Let X_m is maximum extension of spring. Then, decrease in potential energy of M = increase in elastic potential energy of spring

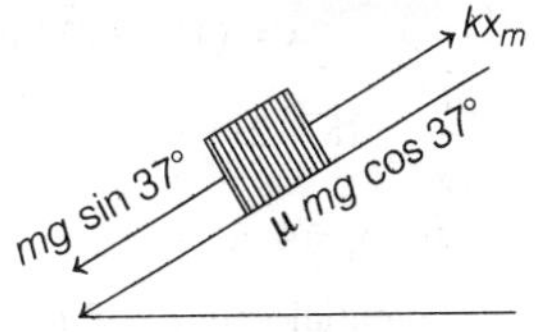

$\therefore \quad \frac{1}{2} kX_m^2 = MgX_m$

or $X_m = \frac{2\,Mg}{k}$

Now, $kX_m = mg \sin 37° + \mu mg \cos 37°$

or $2\,Mg = (mg)\left(\frac{3}{5}\right) + \left(\frac{3}{4}\right) mg \left(\frac{4}{5}\right)$

$\therefore \quad M = \frac{3}{5} m$ **Ans.**

14. (a) $W_{mg} = (mg)(s) \cos 30°$

$= (20)(2)(\sqrt{3}/2)$

$= 34.6$ J **Ans.**

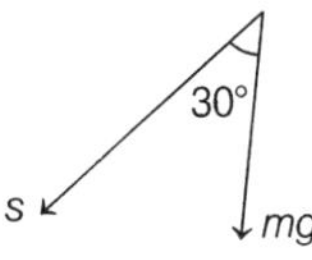

(b) $W_f = fs \cos 180°$

$= (\mu mg \cos\theta)(s)(-1)$

$= -\left(\frac{1}{2}\right)(20)(\cos 60°)(2)$

$= -10$ J **Ans.**

f, 180°, s

15. $F = -\frac{dU}{dr} = \frac{A}{r^2}$ **Ans.**

Integer Type Questions

16. (a) At $x = 6$ m,

$U = (6-4)^2 - 16 = -12$ J

$K = 8$ J

$\therefore \quad E = U + K = -4$ J **Ans.**

(b) $U_{min} = -16$ J at $x = 4$ m

$\therefore \quad K_{max} = E - U_{min}$

$= -4 + 16$

$= 12$ J **Ans.**

(c) $K = 0$

$\therefore \quad U = E$

or $\quad (x-4)^2 - 16 = -4$

or $\quad x = (4 \pm 2\sqrt{3})$ m **Ans.**

(d) $F_x = -\dfrac{dU}{dx} = (8 - 2x)$ **Ans.**

(e) $F_x = 0$ at $x = 4$ m **Ans.**

17. Decrease in potential energy of 1 kg = increase in kinetic energy of both

$$\Rightarrow \quad 1 \times 10 \times 1 = \frac{1}{2} \times (4+1) \times v^2$$

$$\therefore \quad v = 2 \text{ m/s}$$ **Ans.**

18. If A descends X, then B will ascend $2x$. Further, if speed of A at this instant is 2.5 m/s, then speed of B at this instant will be 5 m/s. Now,

Decrease in potential energy of A = increase in potential energy of B + increase in kinetic energy of both

$$\therefore \quad (300)\,x = (50)\,(2x) + \frac{1}{2}\left(\frac{300}{9.8}\right)(2.5)^2 + \frac{1}{2}\left(\frac{50}{9.8}\right)(5.0)^2$$

Solving, we get

$$x = 0.797 \text{ m}$$ **Ans.**

19. If speed of sphere is v downwards, then speed of wedge at this instant will be $v \cot \alpha$ in horizontal direction.

Now,

Decrease in potential energy of sphere

= Increase in kinetic energy of both

$$\therefore \quad mgR = \frac{1}{2}mv^2 + \frac{1}{2}m\,(v \cot \alpha)^2$$

$$= \frac{1}{2}mv^2 \operatorname{cosec}^2 \alpha$$

$$\therefore \quad v = \sqrt{2gR}\,\sin \alpha = \text{speed of sphere}$$

and speed of wedge = $v \cot \alpha$

$= \sqrt{2gR}\,\cos \alpha$ **Ans.**

20. If block drops 12 mm, then spring will further stretch by 24 mm. Now,

$$E_i = E_f$$

$$\therefore \quad \frac{1}{2} \times 1050 \times (0.075)^2 = -45 \times 10 \times 0.012 + \frac{1}{2} \times 45 \times v^2 + \frac{1}{2} \times 1050 \times (0.099)^2$$

Solving, we get $v = 0.37$ m/s **Ans.**

21. Retardation on horizontal surface,

$$a_1 = \mu g = 0.15 \times 10 = 1.5 \text{ m/s}^2$$

Velocity just entering before horizontal surface,

$$v = \sqrt{2a_1 s_1} = \sqrt{2 \times 1.5 \times 0.5} = \sqrt{1.5} \text{ m/s}$$

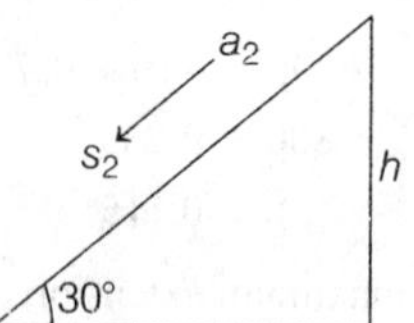

Acceleration on inclined plane,

$$a_2 = g \sin \theta - \mu g \cos \theta$$

$$= 10 \times \frac{1}{2} - 0.15 \times 10 \times \frac{\sqrt{3}}{2}$$

$$= 3.7 \text{ m/s}$$

$$v = \sqrt{2a_2 s_2} = \sqrt{1.5}$$

$$\therefore \quad s_2 = \frac{1.5}{2a_2} = \frac{1.5}{2 \times 3.7} = 0.2 \text{ m}$$

$$h = s_2 \sin 30° = 0.1 \text{ m}$$

Now, work done by friction

= −[initial mechanical energy]

$= -mgh = -(0.05)\,(10)\,(0.1)$

$= -0.05$ J **Ans.**

22. If A moves 1 m down the plane and its speed is v, then B will move 2m upwards and its speed will be $2v$.

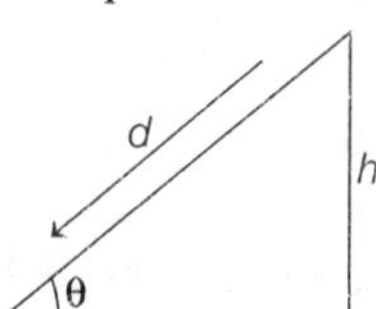

Using the equation,

$E_i - E_f$ = Work done against friction

$$\therefore \quad 0 - \left[\frac{1}{2} \times 30 \times v^2 + \frac{1}{2} \times 5 \times (2v)^2 + 5 \times 10 \times 2 - 30 \times 10 \times \frac{3}{5}\right]$$

$$= 0.2 \times 30 \times 10 \times \frac{4}{5} \times 1$$

Solving this equation, we get

$$v = 1.12 \text{ m/s}$$ **Ans.**

Note $h = d \sin \theta = (1)\left(\dfrac{3}{5}\right) m = \dfrac{3}{5} m$

$m_A = \dfrac{w_A}{g} = 30$ *kg and* $m_B = \dfrac{w_B}{g} = 5$ *kg*

23. (a) Thermal energy = Work done against friction

$= \mu_K mgd$
$= (0.25)(3.5)(9.8)(7.8)$ J
$= 66.88$ J **Ans.**

(b) Maximum kinetic energy
= work done against friction
$= 66.88$ J **Ans.**

(c) $\frac{1}{2}kx_m^2$ = maximum kinetic energy

$$\frac{1}{2} \times 640 \times x_m^2 = 66.88$$

$$x_m = 0.457 \text{ m}$$
$$= 45.7 \text{ cm}$$ Ans.

LEVEL 2

Single Correct Option

1. $W_{All} = \frac{1}{2}mv^2$

$$\therefore \quad W_F + W_{mg} + W_N = \frac{1}{2}mv^2$$

$$\therefore \quad (5 \times 5) + \left(\frac{1}{2} \times 10 \times 5\right) + 0 = \frac{1}{2} \times \frac{1}{2} \times v^2$$

$$\therefore \quad v = 14.14 \text{ m/s}$$ **Ans.**

2. $P = Fv$ = constant

$$\therefore \quad F = \frac{P}{v}$$

$$\therefore \quad mv\left(\frac{dv}{ds}\right) = \frac{P}{v}$$

$$\therefore \quad \int_0^s ds = \frac{m}{P}\int_v^{2v} v^2 dv$$

Solving, we get $s = \frac{7mv^3}{3P}$ **Ans.**

3. $F = kx$

$$\therefore \quad k = \frac{F}{x} = \frac{100}{1}$$
$$= 100 \text{ N/m}$$

$$E_i = E_f$$

$$\therefore \quad \frac{1}{2} \times 10 \times v^2 = \frac{1}{2} \times 100 \times (2)^2 - (10)(10)(2 \sin 30°)$$

Solving, we get

$$v = \sqrt{20} \text{ ms}^{-1}$$ **Ans.**

4. $dm = \left(\frac{m}{\pi/2}\right) d\theta = \left(\frac{2m}{\pi}\right) d\theta$

$$h = R(1 - \cos\theta)$$

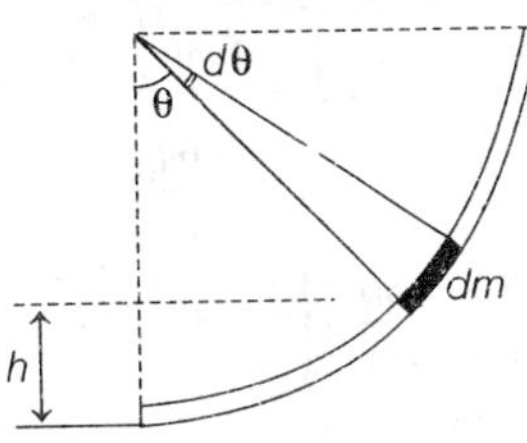

$$dU_i = (dm)gh = \frac{2mgR}{\pi}(1 - \cos\theta)\, d\theta$$

$$\therefore \quad U_i = \int_0^{\pi/2} dU_i = \frac{2mgR}{\pi}\left(\frac{\pi}{2} - 1\right)$$
$$= mgR\left(1 - \frac{2}{\pi}\right)$$

Now, $\quad U_i + K_i = U_f + K_f$

$$\therefore \quad mgR\left(1 - \frac{2}{\pi}\right) = 0 + \frac{1}{2}mv^2$$

or $$v = \sqrt{2gR\left(1 - \frac{2}{\pi}\right)}$$ **Ans**

5. Let X_m is maximum elongation of spring. Then, increase in potential energy of spring = decrease in potential energy of C.

$$\therefore \quad \frac{1}{2}KX_m^2 = M_1 g X_m$$

or $\quad KX_m$ = maximum spring force
$= 2M_1 g = \mu_{min} Mg$

$$\therefore \quad \mu_{min} = \frac{2M_1}{M}$$ **Ans.**

6. $F_{net} = mg \sin\theta - \mu mg \cos\theta$

$= mg \sin\theta - 0.3\, xmg \cos\theta$ ...(i)

At maximum speed $F_{net} = 0$. Because after this net force will become negative and speed will decrease.

From Eq. (i), $F_{net} = 0$ at

$$x = \frac{\tan\theta}{0.3} = \frac{3/4}{0.3}$$
$$= 2.5 \text{ m}$$ **Ans.**

7. At C, potential energy is minimum. So, it is stable equilibrium position.

Further,

$$F = -\frac{dU}{dr} = -(\text{Slope of } U\text{-}r \text{ graph})$$

Negative force means attraction and positive force means repulsion.

8. $E_i - E_f =$ Work done against friction

$$\therefore \quad \frac{1}{2}kx^2 - \frac{1}{2}K\left(\frac{x}{2}\right)^2 = \mu mg\left(x + \frac{x}{2}\right)$$

$$\therefore \quad x = \frac{4\mu mg}{k} \qquad \textbf{Ans.}$$

9. $\mathbf{F} = -\left[\frac{\partial \phi}{\partial x}\hat{\mathbf{i}} + \frac{\partial \phi}{\partial y}\hat{\mathbf{j}}\right] = (-3\hat{\mathbf{i}} - 4\hat{\mathbf{j}})$

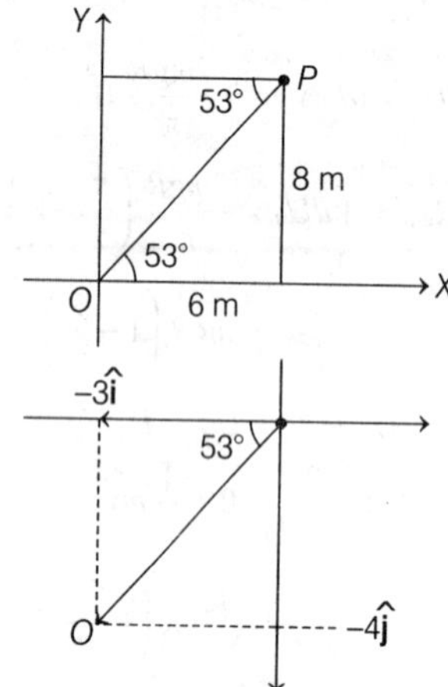

Since, particle was initially at rest. So, it will move in the direction of force.

We can see that initial velocity is in the direction of PO. So, the particle will cross the X-axis at origin.

$$K_i + U_i = K_f + U_f$$

$$\therefore 0 + (3 \times 6 + 4 \times 8) = K_f + (3 \times 0 + 4 \times 0)$$

or $$K_f = 50 \text{ J} \qquad \textbf{Ans.}$$

10.
$$F_{\text{net}} = mg \sin\theta - \mu mg \cos\theta$$

$$= mg \sin\theta - \mu_0 xg \cos\theta$$

$$a = \frac{F_{\text{net}}}{m} = g\sin\theta - \mu_0 xg\cos\theta$$

$$\therefore \quad v \cdot \frac{dv}{dx} = g\sin\theta - \mu_0 xg\cos\theta$$

or $$\int_0^0 v\,dv = \int_0^{x_m} (g\sin\theta - \mu_0 xg\cos\theta)\,dx$$

Solving this equation, we get

$$x_m = \frac{2}{\mu_0}\tan\theta \qquad \textbf{Ans.}$$

11. $F = -\frac{dU}{dx} = \frac{12a}{x^{13}} - \frac{6b}{x^7}$

At equilibrium, $F = 0$ or $x = \left(\frac{2a}{b}\right)^{1/6}$

At this value of x, we can see that $\frac{d^2U}{dx^2}$ is positive.

So, potential energy is minimum or equilibrium is stable.

12. Σ (Moment about O) $= 0$

$$\therefore \quad (kx)\,l = mg\left(\frac{l}{2}\right) \text{ or } x = \frac{mg}{2k}$$

$$U = \frac{1}{2}kx^2 = \frac{(mg)^2}{8k} \qquad \textbf{Ans.}$$

13. $W = Fs$

F and s are same. Therefore,

$$\frac{W_A}{W_B} = \frac{1}{1}$$

From work-energy theorem,

$$\frac{K_A}{K_B} = \frac{W_A}{W_B} = \frac{1}{1}$$

or $$\frac{1}{2}m_A v_A^2 = \frac{1}{2}m_B v_B^2$$

$$\therefore \quad \frac{v_A}{v_B} = \sqrt{\frac{m_B}{m_A}} = \frac{2}{1}$$

14. Work done by conservative force

$$= -\Delta U$$
$$= U_i - U_f$$
$$= [k(1+1)] - [k(2+3)]$$
$$= -3k \qquad \textbf{Ans.}$$

15. After falling on plank downward force on block is mg and upward force is kx. Kinetic energy will increase when $mg > kx$ and it will decrease when $kx > mg$. Therefore, it is maximum when

$$kx = mg$$

or $$x = \frac{mg}{k}$$

and this does not depend on h.

16. $dm = \left(\frac{m}{\pi}\right)d\theta$

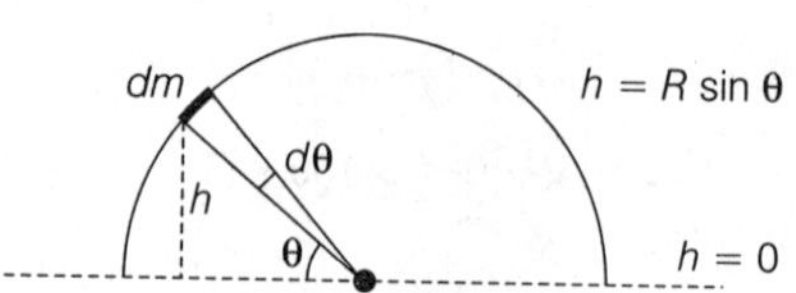

$$\therefore \quad dU = (dm)\,gh = \left(\frac{m}{\pi}d\theta\right)gr\sin\theta$$

$$U_i = \int_0^{\pi} dU = \frac{2mgr}{\pi}$$

Now, $K_i + U_i = K_f + U_f$

$\therefore$ $$0 + \frac{2mgr}{\pi} = \frac{1}{2}mv^2 - mg\left(\frac{\pi r}{2}\right)$$

$\therefore$ $$v = \sqrt{2gr\left(\frac{2}{\pi} + \frac{\pi}{2}\right)}$$ **Ans.**

17. Increase in potential energy per unit time = decrease in kinetic energy of both

$$= -\frac{d}{dt}\left(\frac{1}{2}m_1v_1^2 + \frac{1}{2}m_2v_2^2\right)$$

$$= v_1\left(-m_1\frac{dv_1}{dt}\right) + v_2\left(-m_2\frac{dv_2}{dt}\right)$$

$$= v_1(-m_1a_1) + v_2(-m_2a_2)$$

or $$\frac{dU}{dt} = v_1(-F_1) + v_2(-F_2) \qquad \text{...(i)}$$

Here, $-F_1 = -F_2 = kx = 200 \times 0.1 = 20\text{N}$

Substituting in Eq. (i), we have

$$\frac{dU}{dt} = (4)(20) + (6)(20)$$

$$= 200 \text{ J/s}$$ **Ans.**

18. There is slip, so maximum friction will act on A in the direction of motion (or towards right)

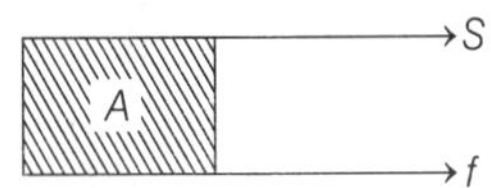

$$f = \mu mg = 0.2 \times 45 \times 10 = 90 \text{ N}$$

$$s = 40 - 10 - 10 = 20 \text{ cm} = 0.2 \text{ m}$$

$\therefore$ $$W = fs = 18\text{J}$$ **Ans.**

19. Constant velocity means net force = 0

Using Lami's theorem in the figure,

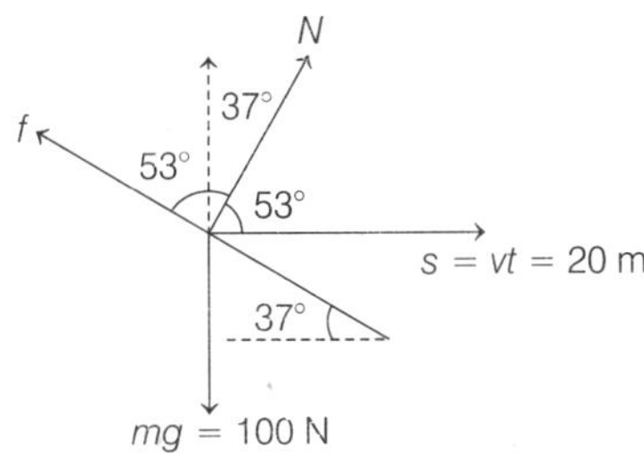

We have, $$\frac{N}{\sin(180° - 53°)} = \frac{100}{\sin 90°}$$

$\therefore$ $$N = 100 \sin 53° = 80 \text{ N}$$

Now, $$W_N = Ns\cos 53°$$
$$= (80)(20)(0.6)$$
$$= 960 \text{ J}$$ **Ans.**

20. In both cases sudden changes in force by cutting the spring would be kx.

$\therefore$ $$a = \frac{\Delta F}{m} = \frac{kx}{m} \qquad \text{(in both case)}$$

In one case, it is downwards and in other case, it is upwards.

21. Since, the particle is released from a small height, θ (angle of radius with vertical) will be very small. Force of friction throughout the journey can be assumed to be μmg. Particle will finally come to rest when whole of its energy ($= mgh$) is lost in the work done against friction. Let particle stops after travelling a distance d. Then,

$$\mu mgd = mgh$$

or $$d = \frac{h}{\mu} = \frac{10^{-2}}{0.01}$$

$$= 1.0 \text{ m}$$

22. Decrease in gravitational potential energy = increase in kinetic energy.

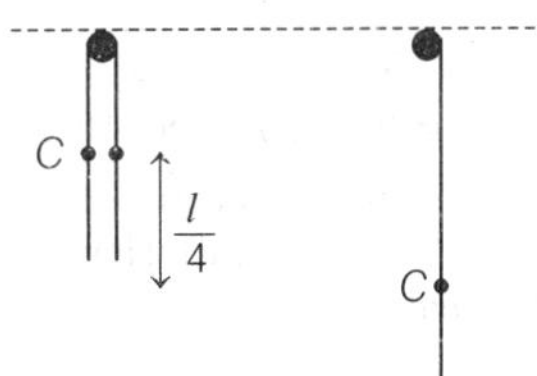

Initially centre of mass of chain was at distance $\frac{l}{4}$ below the pin and in final position, it is at distance $\frac{l}{2}$ below the pin. Hence, centre of mass has descended $\frac{l}{4}$.

$\therefore$ $$mg\frac{l}{4} = \frac{1}{2}mv^2$$

or $$v = \sqrt{\frac{gl}{2}}$$

23. We know that, change in potential energy of a system corresponding to a conservative internal force as

$$U_f - U_i = -W = -\int_i^f \mathbf{F}\cdot d\mathbf{r}$$

Given, $F = ax + bx^2$

We know that, work done in stretching the rubber band by L is $|dW| = |Fdx|$

$$|W| = \int_0^L (ax + bx^2)\, dx$$

$$= \left[\frac{ax^2}{2}\right]_0^L + \left[\frac{bx^3}{3}\right]_0^L$$

$$= \left[\frac{aL^2}{2} - \frac{a \times (0)^2}{2}\right] + \left[\frac{b \times L^3}{3} - \frac{b \times (0)^3}{3}\right]$$

$$= |W| = \frac{aL^2}{2} + \frac{bL^3}{3}$$

24. Power of tension = 0

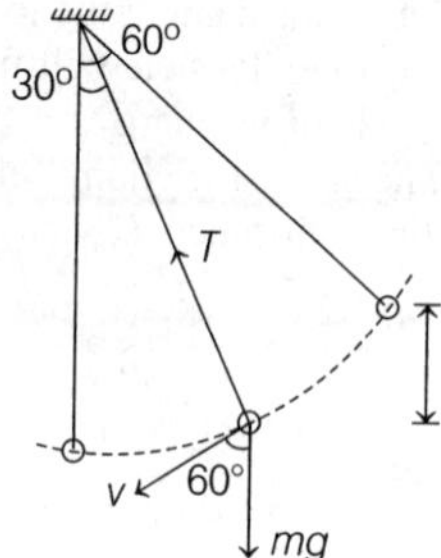

Power of $mg = (mg)(v)\cos 60°$

Here, $v = \sqrt{2gh}$

and $h = l(\cos 30° - \cos 60°)$

25. On M, horizontal components of N and f are balanced (as Mg is vertical). Hence, on $2M$ also they will be balanced.

$\therefore$ Horizontal Kx force on $2M$ should be zero.

26.

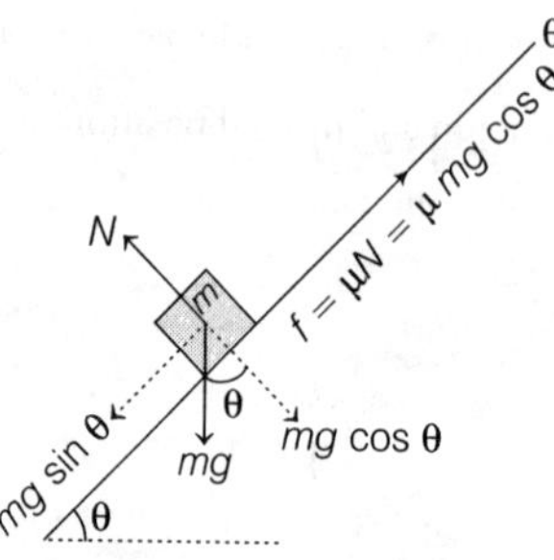

Work done by gravitational force is

$$(mg\sin\theta)d = 10 \times 10 \times \sin 37° \times 10 = 600 \text{ J}$$

Work done by friction is,

$$-fd = (\mu mg\cos\theta)d$$

$$= -0.2 \times 10 \times 10 \times \cos 37° \times 10$$

$$= -20 \times \frac{4}{5} \times 10$$

$$= -160 \text{ J}$$

27. $a \propto -x$

$$a = -\lambda x \qquad (\lambda = \text{constant})$$

$$v\frac{dv}{dx} = -\lambda x$$

$$\int_{v_1}^{v_2} v\,dv = -\lambda \int_0^x x\,dx$$

$$\frac{|v^2|_{v_1}^{v_2}}{2} = -\frac{\lambda x^2}{2}$$

$$\frac{1}{2}mv_2^2 - \frac{1}{2}mv_1^2 = -\frac{\lambda m x^2}{2}$$

(Loss in KE) $\propto x^2$

28. $V(x) = \dfrac{x^4}{4} - \dfrac{x^2}{2}$

$$F = -\frac{dV_{(x)}}{dx} = -[x^3 - x] = 0$$

$\Rightarrow$ $x(x^2 - 1) = 0$

$$x = 0, x = \pm 1$$

$\Rightarrow$ $\dfrac{d^2V_{(x)}}{dx} = 3x^2 - 1$

At $x = \pm 1$, $\dfrac{d^2V_{(x)}}{dx} = +$ ve, i.e.

at $x = \pm 1$, PE is minimum

$$V_{\min} = -\frac{1}{4}$$

$$E = K_{\max} + V_{\min}$$

$\Rightarrow$ $2 = \dfrac{1}{2} \times 1 \times v_{\max}^2 - \dfrac{1}{4}$

$\Rightarrow$ $v_{\max} = \dfrac{3}{\sqrt{2}}$ m/s

29. From energy conservation,

$$\frac{1}{2}kx^2 = \frac{1}{2}(4k)y^2$$

$\therefore$ $\dfrac{y}{x} = \dfrac{1}{2}$

30. Area under F-t graph = momentum

$$= p = \sqrt{2km}$$

$\therefore$ $k = \dfrac{A^2}{2m}$ (A = net area of F - t graph)

$$= \frac{\left\{\left(\frac{4 \times 3}{2}\right) - \left(\frac{1.5 \times 2}{2}\right)\right\}^2}{2 \times 2}$$

$$= 5.06 \text{ J}$$

More than One Correct Options

1. $\mathbf{F} = -\left[\dfrac{\partial U}{\partial X}\hat{\mathbf{i}} + \dfrac{\partial U}{\partial y}\hat{\mathbf{j}}\right] = (-7\hat{\mathbf{i}} - 24\hat{\mathbf{j}})$ N

$$\mathbf{a} = \frac{\mathbf{F}}{m} = \left(-\frac{7}{5}\hat{\mathbf{i}} - \frac{24}{5}\hat{\mathbf{j}}\right) \text{ m/s}$$

$$|\mathbf{a}| = \sqrt{\left(\frac{7}{5}\right)^2 + \left(\frac{24}{5}\right)^2} = 5 \text{ m/s}^2 \qquad \textbf{Ans.}$$

Since, $\mathbf{a}$ = constant, we can apply,

$$\mathbf{v} = \mathbf{u} + \mathbf{a}t$$

$$= (8.6\hat{\mathbf{i}} + 23.2\hat{\mathbf{j}}) + \left(-\frac{7}{5}\hat{\mathbf{i}} - \frac{24}{5}\hat{\mathbf{j}}\right)(4)$$

$$= (3\hat{\mathbf{i}} + 4\hat{\mathbf{j}}) \text{ m/s}$$

$$|\mathbf{v}| = \sqrt{(3)^2 + (4)^2} = 5 \text{ m/s} \qquad \textbf{Ans.}$$

2. $F = -\dfrac{dU}{dx} = 5 - 200x$

At origin, $x = 0$

$\therefore$ $F = 5\text{N}$

$$a = \frac{F}{m} = \frac{5}{0.1} = 50 \text{ m/s}^2$$

Mean position is at $F = 0$

or at, $x = \dfrac{5}{200} = 0.025$ m

$$a = \frac{F}{m} = \frac{5 - 200x}{0.1} = (50 - 2000x) \qquad \text{...(i)}$$

At 0.05 m from the origin,

$x = +0.05$ m or $x = -0.05$ m

Substituting in Eq. (i), we have

$$|a| = 150 \text{ m/s}^2$$

or $= 50 \text{ m/s}^2$

At 0.05 m from the mean position means,

$x = 0.075$

or $x = -0.025$ m

Substituting in Eq. (i), we have

$$|a| = 100 \text{ m/s}^2 \qquad \textbf{Ans.}$$

3. Spring force is always towards mean position. If displacement is also towards mean position, F and s will be of same sign and work done will be positive.

4. Work done by conservative force $= -\Delta U$

Work done by all the forces $= \Delta K$

Work done by forces other than conservative forces $= \Delta E$

5. At equilibrium

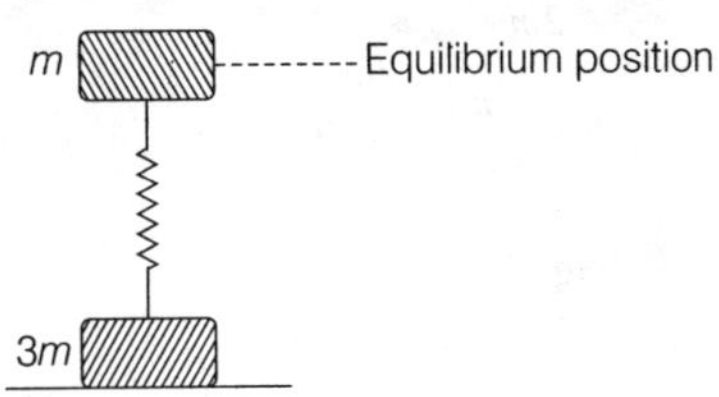

$$k\delta_0 = mg$$

or $\delta_0 = \dfrac{mg}{k}$

where, δ_0 = compression

(b) $\delta_{\text{Total}} = \delta + \delta_0 = \dfrac{3mg}{k}$

$$F_{\max} = k\delta_{\max} = k\left(\frac{3mg}{k}\right) = 3mg \quad \text{(downward)}$$

$N_{\max}$

3 m

3 mg $F_{\max}$

$\therefore$ $N_{\max} = 3mg + F_{\max} = 6mg$ **Ans.**

(d) If $\delta > \dfrac{4mg}{k}$, then upper block will move a distance $x > \dfrac{4mg}{k} - \delta_0$ or $x > \dfrac{3mg}{k}$ from natural length.

Hence in this case, extension

$$x > \frac{3mg}{k}$$

or $F = kx > 3mg$ (upwards on lower block)

So, lower block will bounce up.

6. (a) Decrease in potential energy of B = increase in spring potential energy

$\therefore$ $2mg\, x_m = \dfrac{1}{2} k x_m^2$

$\therefore$ $x_m = \dfrac{4mg}{k}$ **Ans.**

(b) $E_i = E_f$

$$0 = \frac{1}{2}(m + 2m)v^2 + \frac{1}{2} \times k \times \left(\frac{2mg}{k}\right)^2 - (2mg)\left(\frac{2mg}{k}\right)$$

$\therefore$ $v = 2g\sqrt{\dfrac{m}{3k}}$

(c) $a = \dfrac{kx_m - 2mg}{2m}$ (upwards)

$$= \frac{k\left(\dfrac{4mg}{k}\right) - 2mg}{2m} = g$$

(d) $T - 2mg = ma$ ...(i)

$2mg - T = 2ma$ ...(ii)

Solving these two equations, we get

$a = 0$

and $T = 2mg$

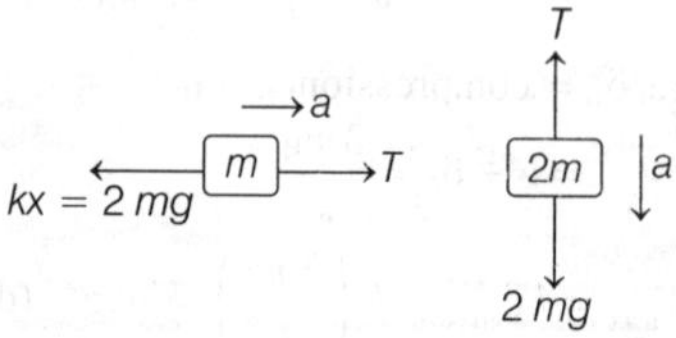

8. (a) Work done by gravity in motion 1 is zero ($\theta = 90°$) and in motion 2 is negative ($\theta = 180°$).

(b) In both cases, angle between N and S is acute.

(c) and (d) : Depending on the value of acceleration in motion 1, friction may act up the plane or down the plane. Therefore, angle between friction and displacement may be obtuse or acute. So, work done by friction may be negative or positive.

9. Work done by conservative forces $= U_i - U_f$

Work done by external forces $= E_f - E_i$

and net work done by all the forces $= K_f - K_i$

10. Total work done is

$$W = W_A + W_B = \frac{1}{2}kx_i^2 - \frac{1}{2}kx_f^2$$

$$= 2 - 0 = 2 \text{ J}$$

$\therefore \quad W_A = W_B = 1 \text{ J}$

11. $\mathbf{a} = \mathbf{b} \times \mathbf{v} \Rightarrow \mathbf{a}$ (acceleration) is always perpendicular to velocity or we can say that force **F** is perpendicular to velocity. Hence, the work done on the particle by the force is zero, its change in kinetic energy is also zero and the speed of the particle remains constant.

Options (b) and (c) are correct.

12. If $F = 0$, $x = \sqrt{2}$ m

When $x > \sqrt{2}$ m, force is directed away from the origin.

When $0 \le x < \sqrt{2}$ m, force is directed towards origin.

If the particle just cross $x = \sqrt{2}$ m, then it starts to accelerate. For minimum value of initial speed, the speed of particle should be zero at $x = \sqrt{2}$ m. This means that KE at $x = \sqrt{2}$ must be zero and it is non-zero at origin.

13. $W = \int F\,dx = \int_2^{\sqrt{2}} (2x^2 - 4)\,dx$

$$= \left[\frac{2x^3}{3} - 4x\right]_2^{\sqrt{2}}$$

$$= \left(\frac{4\sqrt{2}}{3} - 4\sqrt{2}\right) - \left(\frac{16}{3} - 8\right)$$

$$= \frac{-8\sqrt{2}}{3} - \left(\frac{-8}{3}\right) = \frac{-8}{3}(\sqrt{2} - 1)$$

(a) $\because \; W = \Delta K$ or $\dfrac{-8}{3}(\sqrt{2} - 1) = 0 - T_i$

$\therefore \quad T_i = \dfrac{8}{3}(\sqrt{2} - 1)$ J

(b) Also, $W = \left[\dfrac{2x^3}{3} - 4x\right]_{\sqrt{2}}^{0}$

$$= -\left(\frac{4\sqrt{2}}{3} - 4\sqrt{2}\right) = \frac{8\sqrt{2}}{3} \text{ J}$$

But $W = \Delta K$

or $\dfrac{8\sqrt{2}}{3} = K_f - K_i = 0$

$\therefore \quad T_f = \dfrac{8\sqrt{2}}{3}$ J

(c) $T(x = \sqrt{2}) \ge 0$

Comprehension Based Questions

1. $U = E - K = 25 - K$

Since, $K \ge 0$

$\therefore \quad U \le 25$ J

2. $U = E - K = -40 - K$

Since, $K \ge 0$

$\therefore \quad U \le -40$ J

3. Here, $s_A = 2s_B$

$v_A = 2v_B$

and $a_A = 2a_B$

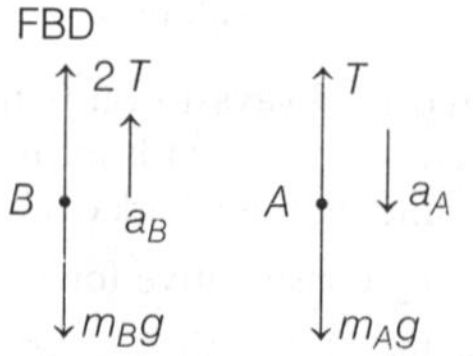

Also, $100 - T = 10a_A = 20a_B$ ...(i)

and $2T - 50 = 5a_B$ ...(ii)

From Eqs. (i) and (ii), we get

$$200 - 2T = 40a_B$$
$$-50 + 2T = 5a_B$$
$$\Rightarrow \quad 150 = 45\, a_B$$
$$\therefore \quad a_B = \frac{150}{45} = \frac{10}{3}\ \text{m/s}^2$$
$$\therefore \quad a_A = \frac{20}{3}\ \text{m/s}^2$$
$$\because \quad 2T - 50 = 5a_B = \frac{50}{3}$$
$$\text{or} \quad 2T = \frac{200}{3}$$
$$\text{or} \quad T = \frac{100}{3}$$
$$W_B = 2T \times s_B = \frac{200}{3} \times 2.5$$
$$= \frac{500}{3}\ \text{J} = 116.67\ \text{J}$$

4. $W_A = -Ts_A = -\frac{100}{3} \times 5$

$$= -\frac{500}{3}\ \text{J}$$
$$= -166.67\ \text{J}$$
$$W_T = W_A + W_B = 0$$

5. $W_g = 100 \times 5 - 50 \times 2.5 = 375$ J

$W = W_T + W_g = 0 + 375 = 375$ J

Match the Columns

1. $\mathbf{s} = \mathbf{r}_f - \mathbf{r}_i = (+2\hat{\mathbf{i}}) - (+4\hat{\mathbf{i}}) = -2\hat{\mathbf{i}}$

Now, apply $W = \mathbf{F} \cdot \mathbf{s}$

2. (a) Net force is towards the mean position $x = 0$ where, $F = 0$ when displaced from this position. Therefore, equilibrium is stable.

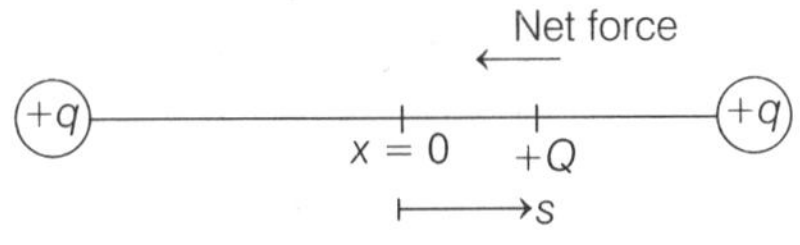

(b) Net force is away from the mean position. Therefore, equilibrium is unstable.

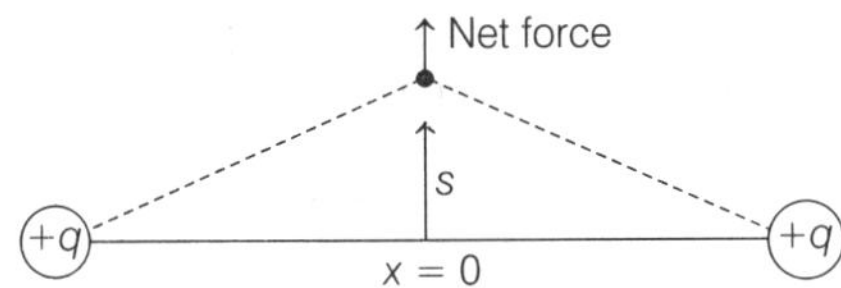

(c) Same logic can be applied as was applied in part (b).

(d) Net force is neither towards $x = 0$ nor away from $x = 0$. Therefore, equilibrium is none of the three.

3. (a) From A to B speed (or kinetic energy) will be increasing. Therefore, net potential energy should decrease.

(b) From A to B, a part of decrease in gravitational potential energy goes in increasing the kinetic energy and rest goes in increasing the potential energy of spring.

(c) and (d) : From B to C kinetic and gravitational potential energy are decreasing and spring potential energy is increasing.

$\therefore$ (decrease in kinetic energy) + (decrease in gravitational potential energy) = increase in spring potential energy.

4. (a)

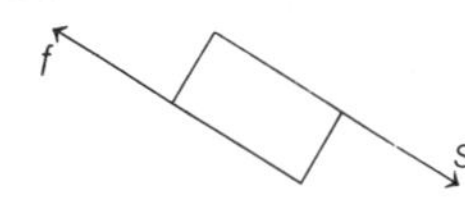

$$W_f = fs \cos 180° = \text{negative}$$

(b)

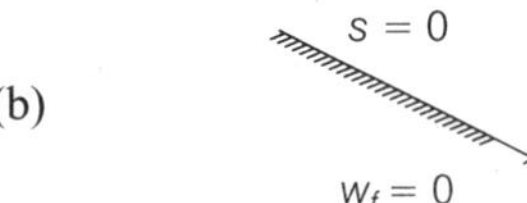

(c) and (d) : No solution is required.

5. (a) $W_1 = \frac{-F^2}{2k_1}$

$$= \frac{-50 \times 50}{2 \times 100} = -12.5\ \text{J}$$

(b) $W_2 = \frac{F^2}{2k_1} = 12.5$ J

(c) $W_3 = \frac{-F^2}{2k_2}$

$$= -\frac{50 \times 50}{2 \times 200} = -6.25\ \text{J}$$

(d) $W_4 = \frac{F^2}{2}\left(\frac{1}{k_1} + \frac{1}{k_2}\right)$

$$= \frac{2500}{2}\left(\frac{1}{100} + \frac{1}{200}\right)$$
$$= \frac{1250}{200} \times 3 = 18.75\ \text{J}$$

Hence, (a) $\rightarrow$ (s), (b) $\rightarrow$ (r), (c) $\rightarrow$ (q), (d) $\rightarrow$ (p)

Subjective Questions

1.

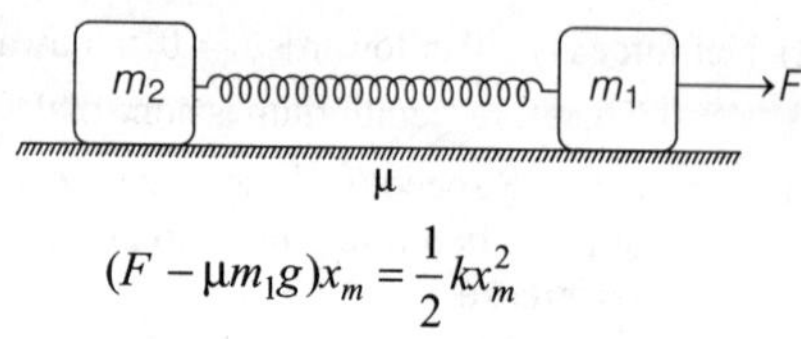

$$(F - \mu m_1 g)x_m = \frac{1}{2}kx_m^2$$

or $$kx_m = 2(F - \mu m_1 g)$$

Second block will shift if $kx_m \geq \mu m_2 g$

$\therefore$ $$2(F - \mu m_1 g) > \mu m_2 g$$

or $$F > \left(m_1 + \frac{m_2}{2}\right)\mu g$$ **Ans.**

2.

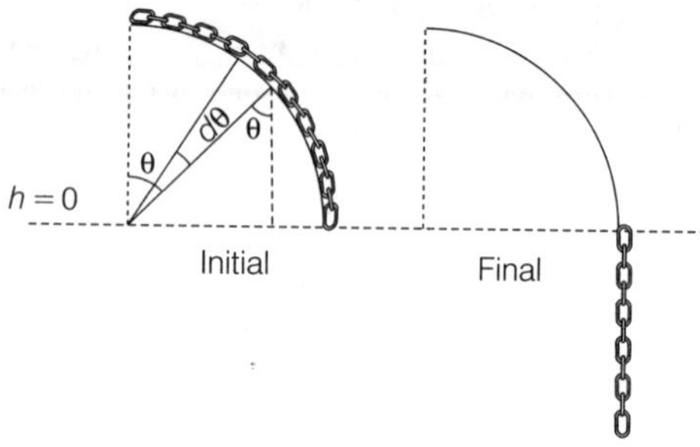

Initial PE,

$$U_i = \int_{\theta = 0°}^{\theta = \pi/2} (r\,d\theta)(\rho)(g)(r\cos\theta)$$

$$= (\rho g r^2)[\sin\theta]_0^{\pi/2} = \rho g r^2$$

Final PE,

$$U_f = \left(\frac{\pi r}{2} \times \rho\right)(g)\left(-\frac{\pi r/2}{2}\right) = -\frac{\pi^2 r^2 \rho g}{8}$$

$$\Delta U = r^2 \rho\, g\left(1 + \frac{\pi^2}{8}\right)$$

$$\Delta U = \text{KE}$$

or $$r^2 \rho g\left(1 + \frac{\pi^2}{8}\right) = \frac{1}{2}\left(\frac{\pi r}{2}\right)(\rho)\, v^2$$

$\Rightarrow$ $$v = \sqrt{4rg\left(\frac{1}{\pi} + \frac{\pi}{8}\right)}$$

or $$v = \sqrt{rg\left(\frac{\pi}{2} + \frac{4}{\pi}\right)}$$ **Ans.**

3. For $t \leq 0.2$ s

$$F = 800 \text{ N} \quad \text{and} \quad v = \left(\frac{20}{0.3}\right)t$$

$\therefore$ $$P = Fv = (53.3\, t) \text{ kW}$$ **Ans.**

For $t > 0.2$ s

$$F = 800 - \left(\frac{800}{0.1}\right)(t - 0.2)$$

and $$v = \frac{20}{0.3}t$$

$\therefore$ $$P = Fv = (160\, t - 533\, t^2) \text{ kW}$$

$$W = \int_0^{0.2}(53.3\, t)\, dt + \int_{0.2}^{0.3}(160\, t - 533\, t^2)\, dt$$

$$= 1.69 \text{ kJ}$$ **Ans.**

4. The work done by friction is $W_f = -\mu\, mgs$

$$= -\mu\, mgvt$$

$$= -0.2 \times 2 \times 9.8 \times 2 \times 5$$

$$= -39.2 \text{ J} = \frac{-39.2}{4.2} \text{ cal}$$

$$= -9.33 \text{ cal}$$

$\therefore$ $$\Delta H = -W_f = 9.33 \text{ cal}$$

5. (a) From energy conservation principle,

Work done against friction = decrease in elastic PE

or $$f(x_0 + a_1) = \frac{1}{2}k(x_0^2 - a_1^2)$$

or $$x_0 - a_1 = \frac{2f}{k} \quad \text{...(i)}$$

From Eq. (i), we see that decrease of amplitude $(x_0 - a_1)$ is $\frac{2f}{k}$, which is constant and same for each cycle of oscillation.

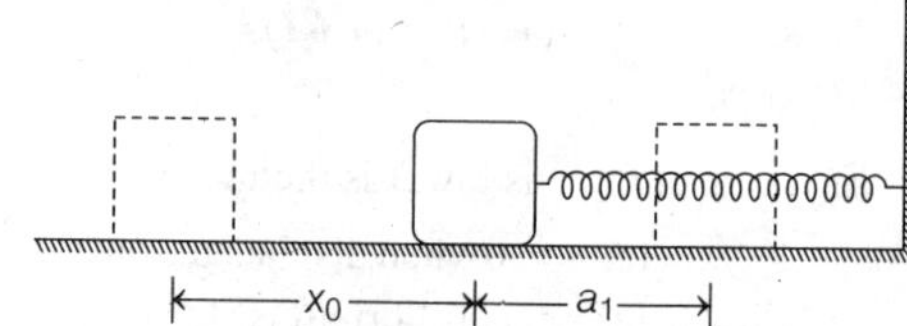

(b) The block will come to rest when $ka = f$

or $$a = \frac{f}{k} \quad \text{...(A)}$$

In the similar manner, we can write

$$a_1 - a_2 = \frac{2f}{k} \quad \text{...(i)}$$

$$a_2 - a_3 = \frac{2f}{k} \quad \text{...(ii)}$$

… …

$$a_{n-1} - a_n = \frac{2f}{k} \quad \text{...(n)}$$

Adding Eqs. (i), (ii),... etc., we get

$$x_0 - a_n = n\left(\frac{2f}{k}\right)$$

or $$a_n = x_0 - n\left(\frac{2f}{k}\right) \quad \text{...(B)}$$

Equating Eqs. (A) and (B), we get

$$\frac{k}{f} = x_0 - n\left(\frac{2f}{k}\right)$$

or $$n = \frac{x_0 - \frac{k}{f}}{\frac{2f}{k}} = \frac{kx_0}{2f} - \frac{1}{2}$$

Number of cycles,

$$m = \frac{n}{2} = \frac{kx_0}{4f} - \frac{1}{4} = \frac{1}{4}\left(\frac{kx_0}{f} - 1\right)$$ **Ans.**

6. Conservation of mechanical energy gives,

$$E_A = E_B$$

or $$\frac{1}{2} m_1 v^2 = \frac{1}{2} kx^2 + m_1 gx$$

or $$2m_1 gH = kx^2 + 2m_1 gx \quad \text{...(i)}$$

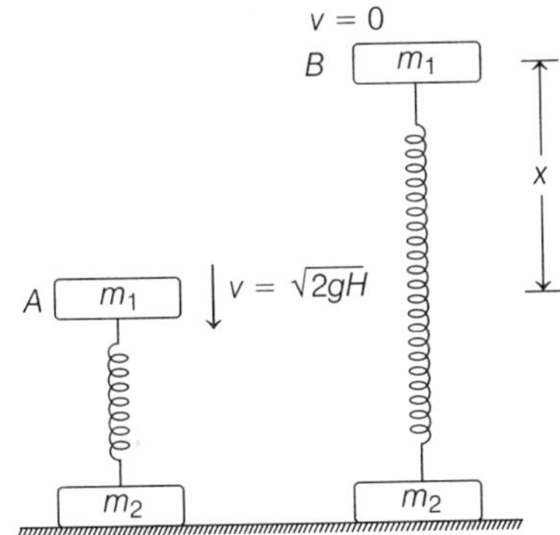

The lower block will rebounce when

$$x > \frac{m_2 g}{k} \quad (kx = m_2 g)$$

Substituting $x = \frac{m_2 g}{k}$ in Eq. (i), we get

$$2m_1 gH = k\left(\frac{m_2 g}{k}\right)^2 + 2m_1 g\left(\frac{m_2 g}{k}\right)$$

or $$H = \frac{m_2 g}{k}\left(\frac{m_2 + 2m_1}{2m_1}\right)$$

Thus, $$H_{min} = \frac{m_2 g}{k}\left(\frac{m_2 + 2m_1}{2m_1}\right)$$ **Ans.**

7. $E_i = E_f$

$$\therefore \quad \frac{1}{2} mv^2 = \frac{1}{2} m\left(\frac{v}{2}\right)^2 + \frac{1}{2} kx^2$$

or $$k = \frac{3v^2 m}{4x^2}$$ **Ans.**

8. $\mu m_A g = 0.8 \times 6 \times 10 = 48$ N

$(m_B + m_C)g = (1 + 2) \times 10 = 30$ N

Since, $(m_B + m_C)g > \mu m_A g, a_A = a_B = 0$

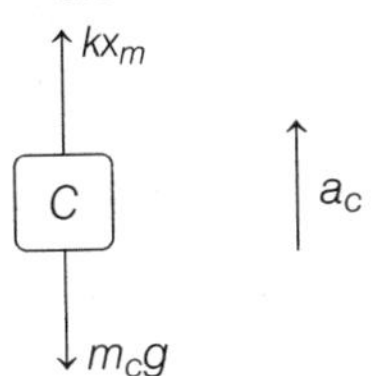

From conservation of energy-principle, we can prove that maximum distance moved by C or maximum extension in the spring would be

$$x_m = \frac{2m_C g}{k} = \frac{2 \times 1 \times 10}{1000}$$

$$= 0.02 \text{ m}$$

At maximum extension,

$$a_C = \frac{kx_m - m_C g}{m_C}$$

Substituting the values, we have

$$a_C = 10 \text{ m/s}^2.$$ **Ans.**

9. Rate at which kinetic plus gravitational potential energy is dissipated at time t is actually the magnitude of power of frictional force at time t.

$$|P_f| = f \cdot v = (\mu mg \cos\alpha)(at)$$

$$= (\mu mg \cos\alpha)[(g \sin\alpha - \mu g \cos\alpha)t]$$

$$= \mu mg^2 \cos\alpha(\sin\alpha - \mu\cos\alpha)t$$ **Ans.**

10. From work-energy principle, $W = \Delta KE$

$$\therefore \quad Pt = \frac{1}{2} m(v^2 - u^2) \quad (P = \text{power})$$

or $$t = \frac{m}{2P}(v^2 - u^2) \quad \text{...(i)}$$

Further

$$F \cdot v = P$$

$$\therefore \quad m \cdot \frac{dv}{ds} \cdot v^2 = P$$

or $$\int_u^v v^2\, dv = \frac{P}{m}\int_0^x ds$$

$\therefore \quad (v^3 - u^3) = \frac{3P}{m} \cdot x$ or $\frac{m}{P} = \frac{3x}{v^3 - u^3}$

Substituting in Eq. (i), we get

$$t = \frac{3x (u + v)}{2 (u^2 + v^2 + uv)}$$ **Hence proved.**

11. (a) Mass per unit length $= \frac{m}{l}$

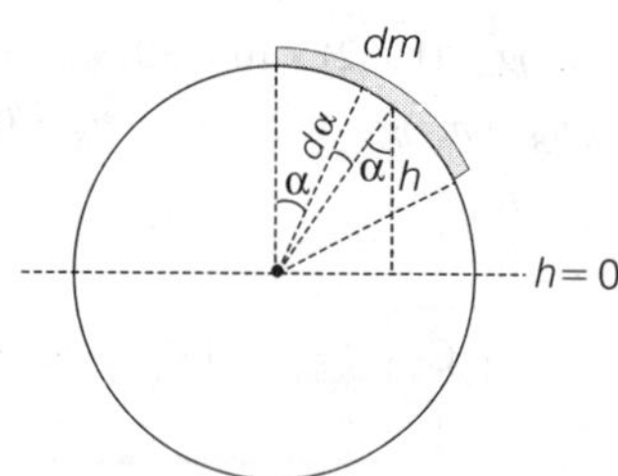

$$dm = \frac{m}{l} R\, d\alpha$$

$$h = R \cos \alpha$$

$$dU = (dm)\, gh = \frac{mgR^2}{l} \cos \alpha \cdot d\alpha$$

$$\therefore \quad U = \int_0^{l/R} dU = \frac{mgR^2}{l} \sin\left(\frac{l}{R}\right)$$

(b) KE $= U_i - U_f$

Here, $\quad U_i = \frac{mgR^2}{l} \sin\left(\frac{l}{R}\right)$

and

$$U_f = \int_\theta^{l/R + \theta} dU = \frac{mgR^2}{l}\left[\sin\left(\frac{l}{R} + \theta\right) - \sin \theta\right]$$

$$\therefore \text{ KE} = \frac{mgR^2}{l}\left[\sin\left(\frac{l}{R}\right) + \sin \theta - \sin\left(\theta + \frac{l}{R}\right)\right]$$

Ans.

(c) $$\frac{1}{2} mv^2 = \frac{mgR^2}{l}\left[\sin\left(\frac{l}{R}\right) + \sin \theta - \sin\left(\theta + \frac{l}{R}\right)\right]$$

or $$v = \sqrt{\frac{2gR^2}{l}\left[\sin\left(\frac{l}{R}\right) + \sin \theta - \sin\left(\theta + \frac{l}{R}\right)\right]}$$

$$v^2 = \frac{2gR^2}{l}\left[\sin\left(\frac{l}{R}\right) + \sin \theta - \sin\left(\theta + \frac{l}{R}\right)\right]$$

$$\therefore 2v \cdot \frac{dv}{dt} = \frac{2gR^2}{l}\left[\cos \theta - \cos\left(\theta + \frac{l}{R}\right)\right] \cdot \frac{d\theta}{dt}$$

$$\frac{dv}{dt} = \frac{\frac{2gR^2}{l}\left[\cos \theta - \cos\left(\theta + \frac{l}{R}\right)\right]}{2v}\left(\frac{d\theta}{dt}\right) \quad \ldots\text{(i)}$$

Here $$\frac{\left(\frac{d\theta}{dt}\right)}{v} = \frac{\omega}{v} = \frac{1}{R}$$

Substituting in Eq. (i), we get

$$\frac{dv}{dt} = \frac{gR}{l}\left[\cos \theta - \cos\left(\theta + \frac{l}{R}\right)\right]$$

At $\quad t = 0, \ \theta = 0°$

Hence, $$\frac{dv}{dt} = \frac{gR}{l}\left[1 - \cos\left(\frac{l}{R}\right)\right]$$ **Ans.**

12. From conservation of energy,

$$m_2 g h_2 = m_1 g h_1 + \frac{1}{2} m_1 v_1^2 + \frac{1}{2} m_2 v_2^2$$

Here, $\quad v_1 = v_2 \cos \theta$

$$\therefore \ 2 \times 10 \times 1 = (0.5)(10)(\sqrt{5} - 1) + \frac{1}{2} \times 0.5 \times v_2^2 \times \left(\frac{2}{\sqrt{5}}\right)^2 + \frac{1}{2} \times 2 \times v_2^2$$

$$\therefore \quad 20 = 6.18 + 0.2\, v_2^2 + v_2^2$$

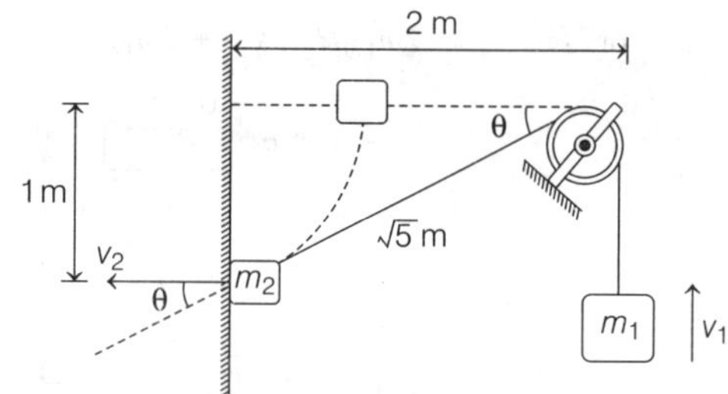

$$v_2 = 3.39 \text{ m/s}$$ **Ans.**

and $$v_1 = v_2 \cos \theta = \frac{2}{\sqrt{5}} \times 3.39$$

or $$v_1 = 3.03 \text{ m/s}$$ **Ans.**

13. Net retarding force $= kx + bMgx$

$\therefore$ Net retardation $= \left(\frac{k + bMg}{M}\right) \cdot x$

So, we can write

$$v \cdot \frac{dv}{dx} = -\left(\frac{k + bMg}{M}\right) \cdot x$$

or $$\int_{v_0}^{0} v \cdot dv = -\left(\frac{k + bMg}{M}\right) \int_0^x x\, dx$$

or $$x = \sqrt{\frac{M}{k + bMg}}\, v_0$$

Loss in mechanical energy,

$$\Delta E = \frac{1}{2}Mv_0^2 - \frac{1}{2}kx^2$$

or $$\Delta E = \frac{1}{2}Mv_0^2 - \frac{k}{2}\left(\frac{M}{k+bMg}\right)v_0^2$$

or $$\Delta E = \frac{v_0^2}{2}\left[M - k\left(\frac{M}{k+bMg}\right)\right]$$

$$= \frac{v_0^2 bM^2 g}{2(k+bMg)}$$ **Ans.**

14. From conservation of mechanical energy,

$$E_i = E_f \quad \text{or} \quad \frac{1}{2}kx_i^2 + mgh_i = \frac{1}{2}mv_f^2$$

$\therefore$ $$v_f = \sqrt{2gh_i + \frac{k}{m}x_i^2}$$

Substituting the values, we have

$$v_f = \sqrt{2 \times 9.8 \times 1.9 + \frac{2300}{0.12}(0.045)^2}$$

$$= 8.72 \text{ m/s}$$ **Ans.**

15. (a) From work-energy theorem,

Work done by all forces = Change in kinetic energy

$\therefore$ $$Fx - \frac{1}{2}kx^2 = \frac{1}{2}mv^2$$

$\therefore$ $$v = \sqrt{\frac{2Fx - kx^2}{m}}$$

Substituting the values, we have

$$v = \sqrt{\frac{2 \times 20 \times 0.25 - 40 \times 0.25 \times 0.25}{0.5}}$$

$$= \sqrt{15} \text{ m/s} = 3.87 \text{ m/s}$$ **Ans.**

(b) From conservation of mechanical energy,

$$E_i = E_f \quad \text{or} \quad \frac{1}{2}mv_i^2 + \frac{1}{2}kx_i^2 = \frac{1}{2}kx_f^2$$

or $$x_f = \sqrt{\frac{mv_i^2}{k} + x_i^2} = \sqrt{\frac{0.5 \times 15}{40} + (0.25)^2}$$

$$= 0.5 \text{ m (compression)}$$

$\therefore$ Distance of block from the wall

$$= (0.6 - 0.5) \text{ m}$$

$$= 0.10 \text{ m}$$ **Ans.**

16. For shifting of B, $kx_0 > mg\sin\theta + \mu\, mg\cos\theta$

or $kx_0 > \sqrt{2} \times 10 \times \frac{1}{\sqrt{2}} + 0.5 \times \sqrt{2} \times 10 \times \frac{1}{\sqrt{2}}$

or $$kx_0 > 15 \quad \therefore \quad x_{0\,\text{min}} = \frac{15}{k}$$

For minimum value of F, the block B will be in the condition of just shift, when the block A is at its extreme position ($v = 0$). Applying work-energy theorem for the block A,

$$W = \Delta K = K_f - K_i = 0 - 0 = 0$$

or $$W_F + W_S + W_f = 0$$

or $$Fx_{0\,\text{min}} - \frac{1}{2}kx_{0\,\text{min}}^2 - \mu\, mgx_{0\,\text{min}} = 0$$

or $$F - \frac{k}{2}x_{0\,\text{min}} - \mu\, mg = 0$$

or $$F - \frac{k}{2} \times \frac{15}{k} - \mu\, mg = 0$$

or $$F - 7.5 - 0.5 \times \sqrt{2} \times 10 = 0$$

$\therefore$ $$F = 7.5 + 5\sqrt{2} = 14.57 \text{ N}$$

17. The equivalent spring constant is

$$k_{eq} = k_1 + k_2 + k_3$$
$$= 40 + 15 + 45 = 100 \text{ N/m}$$

When block will achieve maximum speed, then springs come in relaxed positions.

According to mechanical energy conservation principle,

$$\frac{1}{2}k_{eq}x_0^2 = \frac{1}{2}mv_0^2$$

or $$100 \times (0.1)^2 = 1 \times v_0^2$$

$\therefore$ $$v_0 = 1 \text{ m/s}$$

18. Let for bouncing of the block A, the elongation in the spring is x_1.

$$kx_1 > m_A g \quad \text{or} \quad kx_1 > 100$$

$\therefore$ $$x_1 > \frac{100}{150} \quad \text{or} \quad x_1 > \frac{2}{3}$$

$\therefore$ $$x_{1\,\text{min}} = \frac{2}{3}$$

For $x_{1\,\text{min}}$, the velocity of block B will be zero.

According to conservation principle of mechanical energy,

$$U_i + K_i = U_f + K_f$$

$$\frac{1}{2}kx_0^2 + \frac{1}{2}mv_{0\,\text{min}}^2 = mg(x_0 + x_{1\,\text{min}}) + \frac{1}{2}kx_{1\,\text{min}}^2$$

Here, $x_0 = \frac{mg}{k}$

By putting the value,

$$v_{0\,\text{min}} = \frac{20}{\sqrt{15}} \text{ m/s}$$

$\therefore$ $$n = 5$$

10. Circular Motion

INTRODUCTORY EXERCISE 10.1

1. Direction of acceleration (acting towards centre) continuously keeps on changing. So, it is variable acceleration.

2. In uniform circular motion speed remains constant. In projectile motion (which is a curved path) acceleration remains constant.

3. (a) $a_r = \dfrac{v^2}{R} = \dfrac{(2t)^2}{1.0} = 4t^2$

At $t = 1$ s, $a_r = 4 \text{ cm/s}^2$ **Ans.**

(b) $a_t = \dfrac{dv}{dt} = 2 \text{ cm/s}^2$ **Ans.**

(c) $a = \sqrt{a_r^2 + a_t^2} = \sqrt{(4)^2 + (2)^2}$

$= 2\sqrt{5} \text{ cm/s}^2$ **Ans.**

4. $v_{av} = \dfrac{s}{t} = \dfrac{\sqrt{2}\,R}{(T/4)}$

$= \dfrac{4\sqrt{2}\,R}{(2\pi R)/v}$

$\therefore \quad \dfrac{v_{av}}{v} = \dfrac{2\sqrt{2}}{\pi}$ **Ans.**

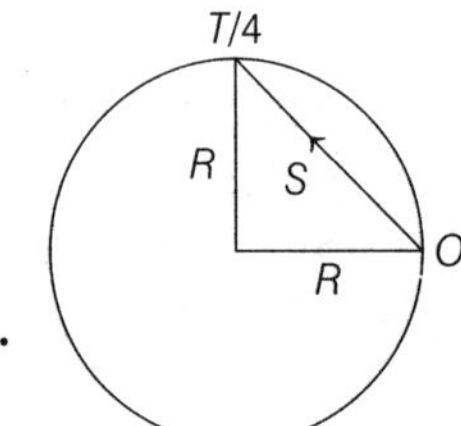

5. $(R\omega^2) = R\alpha$

$\therefore \quad \omega^2 = \alpha$

or $\quad (\alpha t)^2 = \alpha$

$\therefore \quad t = \dfrac{1}{\sqrt{\alpha}} = \dfrac{1}{\sqrt{4}}$

$= 0.5$ s **Ans.**

6. $a_t = \dfrac{dv}{dt} = 8t$

$a_r = \dfrac{v^2}{R} = \dfrac{(4t^2)^2}{54} = \dfrac{8}{27}t^4$

At $t = 3$ s,

$a_t = 24 \text{ m/s}^2$

$a_r = 24 \text{ m/s}^2$

$\tan\theta = \dfrac{a_t}{a_r} = 1$

$\therefore \ \theta = 45°$ **Ans.**

7. (a) $a_r = a\cos 30° = (25)\dfrac{\sqrt{3}}{2}$

$= 21.65 \text{ m/s}^2$ **Ans.**

(b) $a_r = \dfrac{v^2}{R} \Rightarrow v = \sqrt{a_r R}$

or $\quad v = \sqrt{(21.65)(2.5)}$

$= 7.35$ m/s **Ans.**

(c) $a_t = a\sin 30° = (25)\left(\dfrac{1}{2}\right) = 12.5 \text{ m/s}^2$ **Ans.**

INTRODUCTORY EXERCISE 10.2

1. $v = \dfrac{18 \times 5}{18} = 5$ m/s

$\tan\theta = \dfrac{v^2}{Rg} = \dfrac{(5)^2}{10 \times 10} = \dfrac{1}{4}$

$\therefore \quad \theta = \tan^{-1}\left(\dfrac{1}{4}\right)$ **Ans.**

2. $v = \sqrt{\mu R g}$

$\therefore \quad \mu = \dfrac{v^2}{gR} = \dfrac{(5)^2}{10 \times 10}$

$= 0.25$ **Ans.**

3. $v = \sqrt{Rg\tan\theta} = \sqrt{50 \times 10 \times \tan 30°}$

≈ 17 m/s **Ans.**

4. $a \neq 0 \Rightarrow F_{net} = ma \neq 0$

Hence, particle is not in equilibrium.

5. If he applies the breaks, then to stop the car in a distance r

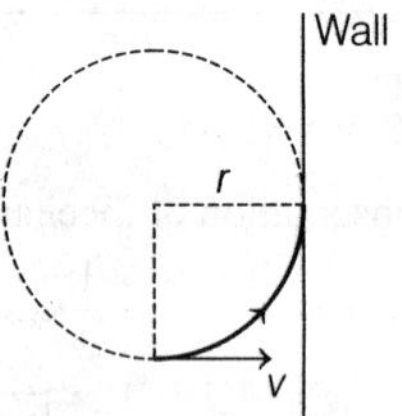

$0 = v^2 - 2a_1 r$

$\therefore \ a_1 = \dfrac{v^2}{2r}$ = minimum retardation required.

(by friction)

If he takes a turn of radius r, the centripetal acceleration required is

$a_2 = \dfrac{v^2}{r}$ (provided again by friction)

Since $a_1 < a_2$, it is better to apply brakes.

6.

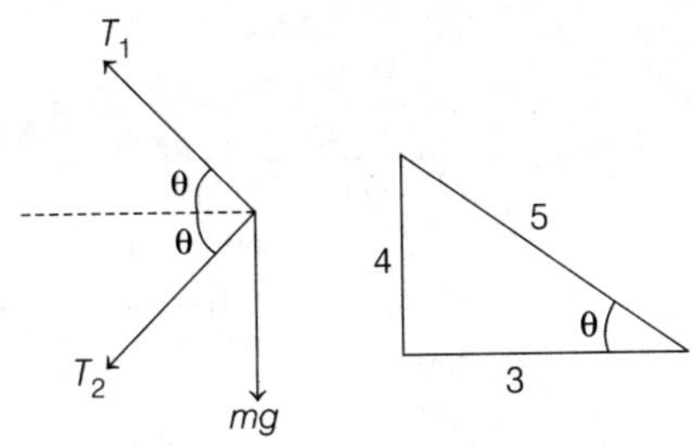

$$T_1 \cos\theta + T_2 \cos\theta = mr\omega^2 \qquad \text{...(i)}$$

$$\omega = (2n\pi)$$

Here, n = number of revolutions per second.

Substituting the proper values in Eq. (i),

$$200 \times \left(\frac{3}{5}\right) + T_2 \times \left(\frac{3}{5}\right) = (4)(3)(2n\pi)^2$$

or $\quad 600 + 3T_2 = 240\, n^2\pi^2 \qquad$ ...(ii)

Further, $\quad T_1 \sin\theta = T_2 \sin\theta + mg$

or $\quad 200 \times \frac{4}{5} = T_2 \times \frac{4}{5} + 4 \times 10$

or $\quad 800 = 4T_2 + 200 \qquad$ ...(iii)

Solving Eqs. (ii) and (iii) we get,

$T_2 = 150$ N and $n = 0.66$ rps

$= 39.6$ rpm

7. (a) $mg - N_1 = \dfrac{mv^2}{R}$

or $mg - \dfrac{mg}{2} = \dfrac{mv^2}{R}$

$\therefore \quad \dfrac{mv^2}{R} = \dfrac{mg}{2} = \dfrac{16\text{kN}}{2} = 8\text{kN}$

Now, $N_2 - mg = \dfrac{mv^2}{R}$ or $N_2 = mg + \dfrac{mv^2}{R}$

$$= mg + \frac{mg}{2} = \frac{3}{2}mg$$

$$= \frac{3}{2}(16\text{ kN}) = 24\text{ kN} \qquad \textbf{Ans.}$$

(b) $mg - N = \dfrac{mv^2}{R}$ or $N = mg - \dfrac{mv^2}{R}$

$$0 = mg - \frac{mv_{\text{max}}^2}{R}$$

$\therefore \quad v_{\text{max}} = \sqrt{gR} = \sqrt{10 \times 250} = 50$ m/s $\qquad$ **Ans.**

(c) $N_2 - mg = \dfrac{mv^2}{R}$

$\therefore \quad N_2 = m\left(g + \dfrac{v^2}{R}\right)$

$$= \frac{16 \times 10^3}{10}\left[10 + \frac{2500}{250}\right]$$

$$= 32 \times 10^3 \text{ N} = 32 \text{ kN} \qquad \textbf{Ans.}$$

INTRODUCTORY EXERCISE 10.3

1. (a) String will slack at height h_1, discussed in article 10.5, where

$$h_1 = \frac{u^2 + gR}{3g} = \frac{5}{3}R \qquad (\text{as } u^2 = 4gR)$$

$$v = \sqrt{u^2 - 2gh_1} = \sqrt{4gR - 2g \times \frac{5}{3}R}$$

$$= \sqrt{\frac{2}{3}gR}$$

2. (a) Velocity becomes zero at height h_2 discussed in article 10.5, where

$$h_2 = \frac{u^2}{2g} = \frac{gR}{2g} = \frac{R}{2}$$

Now, $\quad h_2 = R(1 - \cos\theta)$

$\therefore \quad \dfrac{R}{2} = R(1 - \cos\theta) \Rightarrow \theta = 60°$

(b) $T = mg\cos\theta = \dfrac{mg}{2}$ at $\theta = 60°$

3. (a) $v = \sqrt{u^2 - 2gh} = \sqrt{7gR - 2g(2R)} = \sqrt{3gR}$

(b) $T + mg = \dfrac{mv^2}{R} = \dfrac{m}{R}(mgR)$

$\therefore \quad T = 2mg$

(c) $T - mg = \dfrac{mu^2}{R} = \dfrac{m}{R}(7gR)$

$\therefore \quad T = 8mg$

4. $h = l - l\cos 60° = \dfrac{l}{2} = 2.5$ m

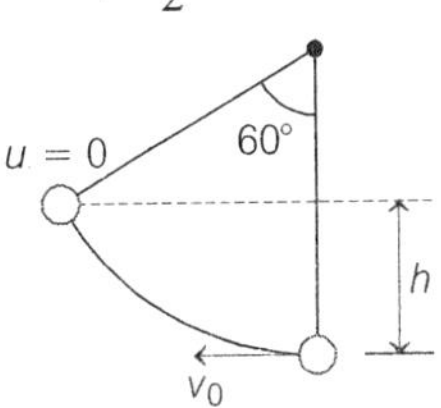

$v_0 = \sqrt{2gh} = \sqrt{2 \times 9.8 \times 2.5} = 7$ m/s $\qquad$ **Ans.**

Exercises

LEVEL 1

Assertion and Reason

2. ***A* to *B*** $s = \sqrt{2}\,R$

and $|\Delta \mathbf{v}| = \sqrt{v^2 + v^2 - 2v \cdot v \cos 90°}$

$= \sqrt{2}\,v$

Average acceleration $= \dfrac{|\Delta \mathbf{v}|}{t} = \dfrac{\sqrt{2}\,v}{t}$

and average velocity $= \dfrac{s}{t} = \dfrac{\sqrt{2}\,R}{t}$

The desired ratio is $\dfrac{v}{R} = \omega$

3. Component of acceleration perpendicular to velocity is centripetal acceleration.

$\therefore \quad a_c = \dfrac{v^2}{R} \quad$ or $\quad R = \dfrac{v^2}{a_c} = \dfrac{(2)^2}{2} = 2\text{ m}$

4. **At *A***

Tangential acceleration is g. Radial acceleration is $\dfrac{v^2}{R}$.

$$\therefore \quad a_{\text{net}} = \sqrt{g^2 + \left(\frac{v^2}{R}\right)^2}$$

5.

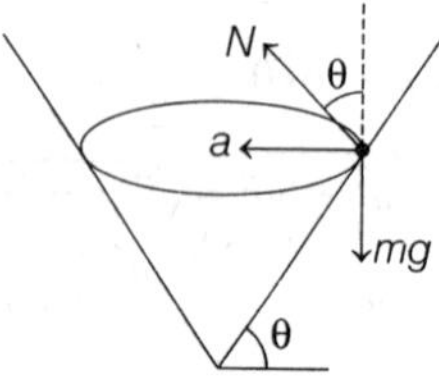

$N \cos\theta = mg$

$\Rightarrow \quad N = mg \sec\theta$

and $\quad N \sin\theta = \dfrac{mv^2}{R}$

6. Weight (plus normal reaction) provides the necessary centripetal force or weight is used in providing the centripetal force.

Single Correct Option

1. $\omega_1 t - \omega_2 t = 2\pi$

$\therefore \quad t = \dfrac{2\pi}{\omega_1 - \omega_2}$

$= \dfrac{2\pi}{(2\pi/T_1) - (2\pi/T_2)}$

$= \dfrac{T_1 T_2}{T_2 - T_1} = \dfrac{(3600)\,(60)}{(3600) - (60)}$

$= \dfrac{3600}{59}\text{ s}$ **Ans.**

2. At $\theta = 180°$, $|\Delta \mathbf{p}| = 2\,mv$ = maximum

At $\theta = 360°$, $|\Delta \mathbf{p}| = 0$ = minimum

3. $h = l - l\cos\theta = l\,(1 - \cos\theta)$

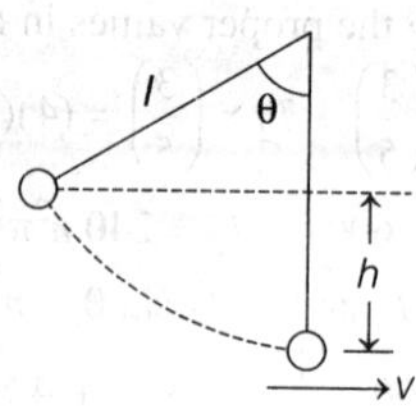

$v^2 = 2gh = 2gl\,(1 - \cos\theta) = v^2_{\text{max}}$

$\therefore \quad K_{\text{max}} = \dfrac{1}{2}mv^2 = mgl\,(1 - \cos\theta)$ **Ans.**

4. $u = \sqrt{5gR}$

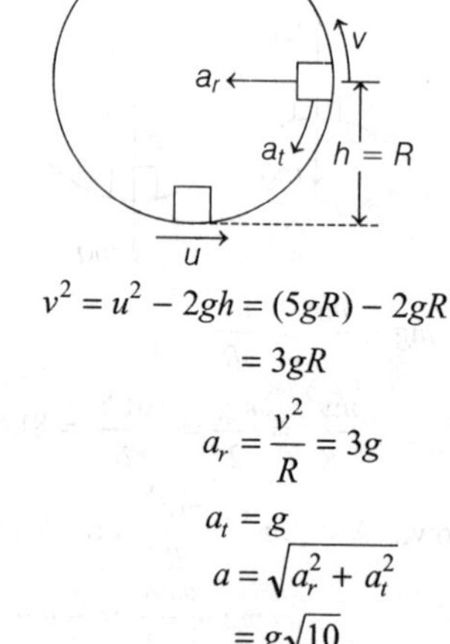

$v^2 = u^2 - 2gh = (5gR) - 2gR$

$= 3gR$

$a_r = \dfrac{v^2}{R} = 3g$

$a_t = g$

$\therefore \quad a = \sqrt{a_r^2 + a_t^2}$

$= g\sqrt{10}$ **Ans.**

5. $N = mR\omega^2$

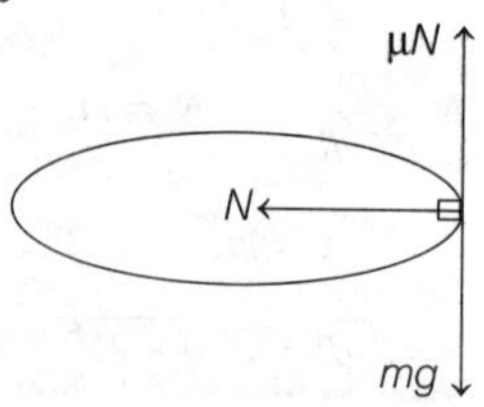

$$\mu N = mg$$

From these two equations. we get

$$\mu = \frac{g}{R\omega^2} = \frac{10}{2 \times (5)^2}$$

$$= 0.2 \qquad \textbf{Ans.}$$

6. $\frac{v^2}{R} = a_t = a$ (Here, $a_t = a$ say)

or $\frac{(at)^2}{R} = a$

$\therefore \quad t = \sqrt{\frac{R}{a}} = \sqrt{\frac{20}{5}} = 2\text{ s}$ **Ans.**

7. $\cos(d\theta)$ components of T are cancelled and $\sin(d\theta)$ components towards centre provide the necessary centripetal force to small portion PQ.

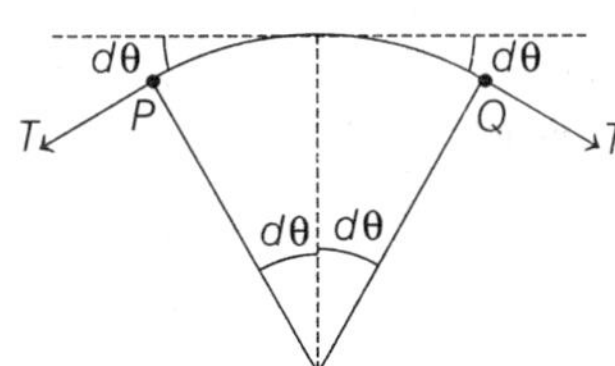

$\therefore \quad 2T \sin(d\theta) = (m_{PQ})(R)\omega^2$

For small angle, $\sin d\theta \approx d\theta$

$\therefore \quad 2T\, d\theta = \left(\frac{m}{2\pi}\right)(2\theta)(R)(2n\pi)^2$

$\therefore \quad T = 2\pi\, mn^2R$

Substituting the values, we get

$$T = (2\pi)(2\pi)(300/60)^2(0.25)$$

$$\approx 250\text{ N} \qquad \textbf{Ans.}$$

8. $\frac{mv^2}{R} = \mu mg$

$\therefore \quad v = \sqrt{\mu Rg} = \sqrt{0.3 \times 300 \times 10}$

$= 30\text{ m/s} = 108\text{ km/h}$ **Ans.**

9. $T\cos\theta = mg$ ...(i)

$T\sin\theta = mr\omega^2 = m(l\sin\theta)\omega^2$ ...(ii)

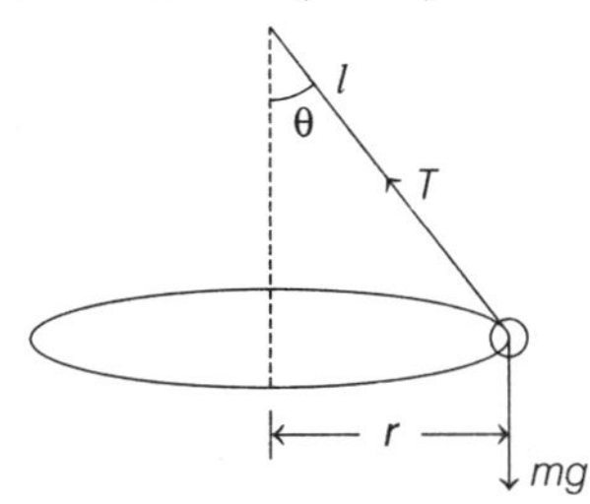

Solving these two equations, we get

$$\cos\theta = \frac{g}{l\omega^2} = \frac{g}{l(2\pi n)^2}$$

$$= \frac{10}{\left[2\pi \times \frac{2}{\pi}\right]^2} \qquad (\because l = 1\text{ m})$$

$\therefore \quad \theta = \cos^{-1}(5/8)$ **Ans.**

10. $T = \frac{mg}{\cos\theta} = \frac{0.1 \times 10}{5/8} = \frac{8}{5}\text{ N}$ **Ans.**

11. $f = ma = m\sqrt{a_t^2 + a_r^2}$

$$= m\sqrt{(R\alpha)^2 + (R\omega^2)^2}$$

$$= m\sqrt{(R\alpha)^2 + [R(\alpha t)^2]^2}$$

$$= 0.36 \times 10^{-3}\sqrt{\left(0.25 \times \frac{1}{3}\right)^2 + \left[0.25\left(\frac{1}{3} \times 2\right)^2\right]^2}$$

$$= 50 \times 10^{-6}\text{ N}$$

$$= 50\,\mu\text{N} \qquad \textbf{Ans.}$$

12. $v^2 = 2gh$

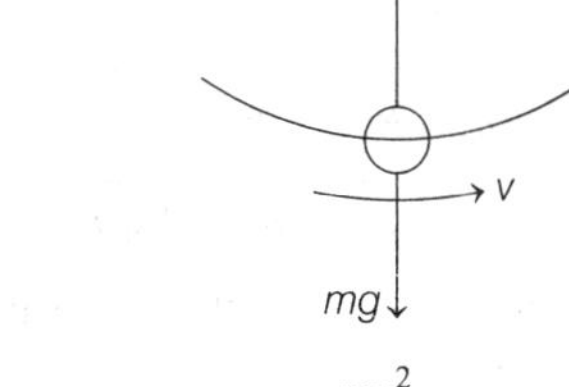

$$T - mg = \frac{mv^2}{l}$$

or $\quad T = mg + \frac{m(2gh)}{l}$

$$= mg\left(1 + \frac{2h}{l}\right) \qquad \textbf{Ans.}$$

13. $(\omega_1 - \omega_2)t = 2\pi$

$$t = \frac{2\pi}{\omega_1 - \omega_2} = \frac{2\pi}{(2\pi/T_1) - (2\pi/T_2)}$$

$$\frac{T_1 T_2}{T_2 - T_1} = \frac{3 \times 1}{3 - 1}$$

$$= 1.5\text{ min} \qquad \textbf{Ans.}$$

14. $\frac{d_B}{d_C} = \frac{v_B t}{v_C t} = \frac{2.5}{2} = \frac{5}{4}$ **Ans.**

15. $\omega_{\text{min}} = \frac{2\pi}{60}$ rad/min and $\omega_{\text{hr}} = \frac{2\pi}{12 \times 60}$ rad/min

$\therefore \quad \frac{\omega_{\text{min}}}{\omega_{\text{hr}}} = \frac{2\pi/60}{2\pi/12 \times 60} = 12$

16.

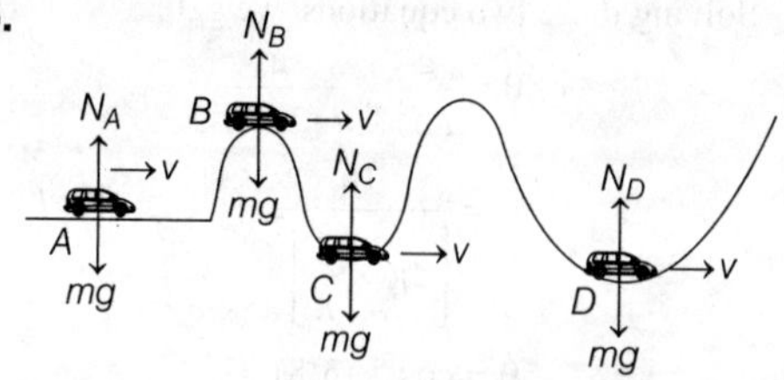

$$A : N_A - mg = 0 \quad \Rightarrow \quad N_A = mg$$

$$B : mg - N_B = \frac{mv^2}{R_B} \quad \Rightarrow \quad N_B = mg - \frac{mv^2}{R_B}$$

$$C : N_C - mg = \frac{mv^2}{R_C} \quad \Rightarrow \quad N_C = mg + \frac{mv^2}{R_C}$$

$$D : N_D - mg = \frac{mv^2}{R_D} \quad \Rightarrow \quad N_D = mg + \frac{mv^2}{R_D}$$

Since, $R_C < R_D, N_C > N_D$

$$N_C > N_D > N_A > N_B$$

17. $\alpha = \frac{d\omega}{dt} = -b$

$$a_t = R\alpha = -Rb \quad \ldots\text{(i)}$$

At $t = \frac{2a}{b}$, $\omega = -a$

$$a_n = R\omega^2 = Ra^2 \quad \ldots\text{(ii)}$$

Now, $a = \sqrt{a_t^2 + a_n^2} = R\sqrt{a^4 + b^2}$

18. Necessary centripetal force to the coin is provided by friction. Thus,

$$mr\omega_{max}^2 = \mu mg$$

or $$r = \frac{\mu g}{\omega_{max}^2}$$

ω_{max} is made three times. Therefore, distance from centre r will remain $\frac{1}{9}$ times.

19. Maximum tension $= m\omega^2 r = m \times 4\pi^2 \times n^2 \times r$

By substituting the values, we get $T_{max} = 87.64$ N

20. $Kx = \frac{mv^2}{r}$

$$\Rightarrow \quad v = \sqrt{\frac{Kxr}{m}}$$

$$T = \frac{2\pi r}{v} = 2\pi\sqrt{\frac{mr}{Kx}}$$

$$\therefore \quad T \propto \sqrt{\frac{r}{x}}$$

$$T' = T\sqrt{\frac{r'x}{rx'}}$$

$$= T\sqrt{\frac{3a \times a}{2a \times 2a}} = \frac{\sqrt{3}}{2}T$$

21. $v^2 = 2gl = 5gR$

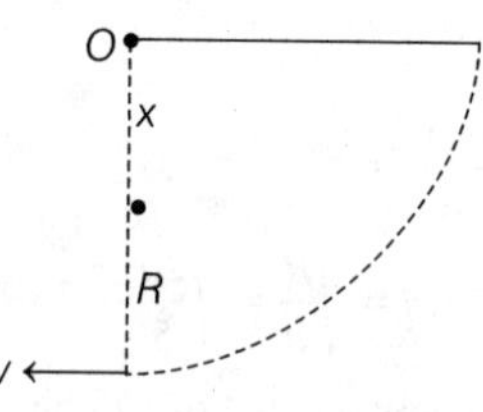

$$\therefore \quad R = 0.4\,l$$

or $$x = l - R = 0.6\,l$$

22. When released from top with zero velocity block leaves contact at

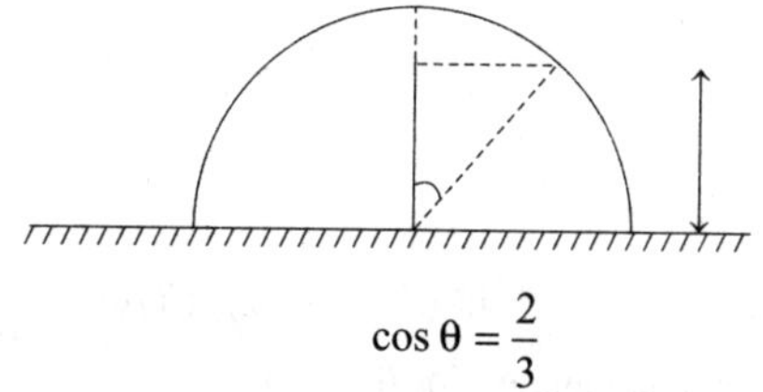

$$\cos\theta = \frac{2}{3}$$

$$\Rightarrow \quad h = r\cos\theta = \frac{2r}{3}$$

23. $\sqrt{2gh} = \sqrt{5gR}$

$$\therefore \quad R = \frac{2h}{5} = \frac{2 \times 5}{5} = 2\text{ cm}$$

24. $|\mathbf{v}_{AB}| = |\mathbf{v}_A - \mathbf{v}_B|$

$$= \sqrt{(R\omega)^2 + (R\omega)^2 - 2(R\omega)(R\omega)\cos\theta}$$

$$= 2R\omega\sin\left(\frac{\theta}{2}\right)$$

25. $T\sin\theta = mr\omega^2$ or $T\sin\theta = m(l\sin\theta)\omega^2$

$$\therefore \quad T = ml\omega^2 = ml(2\pi f)^2$$

$$= ml\left(2\pi \times \frac{2}{\pi}\right)^2 = 16\,ml$$

26. $\frac{v^2}{r} = \frac{4}{r^2}$

$$\Rightarrow \quad v = \frac{2}{\sqrt{r}}$$

$$p = mv = \frac{2m}{\sqrt{r}}$$

27. At the maximum speed, the tangential acceleration of the particle with respect to the block should be zero.

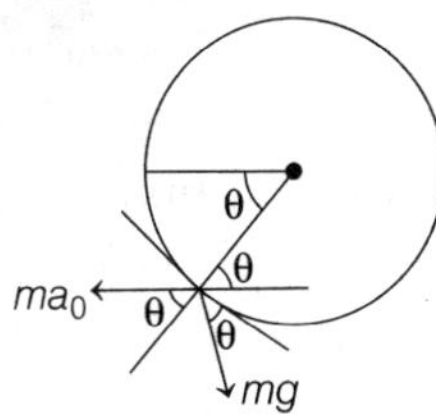

From figure, $ma_0 \sin\theta = mg\cos\theta$

$\therefore \quad \tan\theta = \frac{g}{a_0} = \frac{g}{g} = 1$

$\therefore \quad \theta = 45°$

28. Given, $s = t^3 + 5$

$\therefore$ Speed, $v = \frac{ds}{dt} = 3t^2$

and rate of change of speed, $a_t = \frac{dv}{dt} = 6t$

$\therefore$ Tangential acceleration at $t = 2$ s,

$$a_t = 6 \times 2 = 12 \text{ ms}^{-2}$$

and at $t = 2$ s, $v = 3(2)^2 = 12 \text{ ms}^{-1}$

$\therefore$ Centripetal acceleration

$$a_c = \frac{v^2}{R} = \frac{144}{20} \text{ ms}^{-2}$$

$\therefore$ Net acceleration $= \sqrt{a_t^2 + a_c^2}$

$$= \sqrt{(12)^2 + \left(\frac{144}{20}\right)^2} = 14 \text{ ms}^{-2}$$

29. The bead is moving on a circular path of radius a.

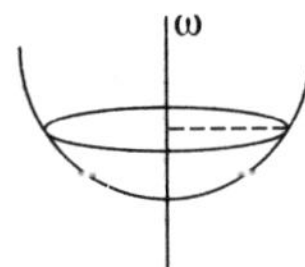

So, the acceleration is $a\omega^2$.

30. For a particle in a uniform circular motion

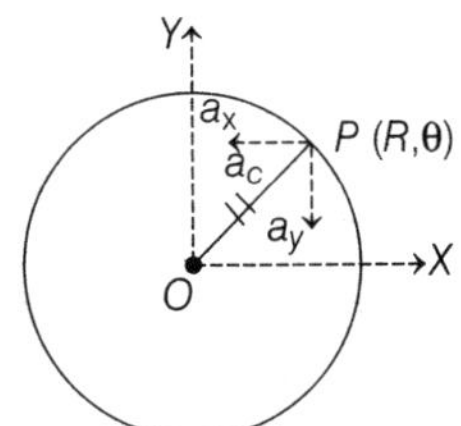

$$\mathbf{a} = \frac{v^2}{R} \text{ towards centre of circle}$$

[centripetal acceleration]

$$\therefore \quad \mathbf{a} = \frac{v^2}{R}(-\cos\theta\,\hat{\mathbf{i}} - \sin\theta\,\hat{\mathbf{j}})$$

or $\quad \mathbf{a} = -\frac{v^2}{R}\cos\theta\,\hat{\mathbf{i}} - \frac{v^2}{R}\sin\theta\,\hat{\mathbf{j}}$

31. $h = l + l\sin\theta = l(1 + \sin\theta)$

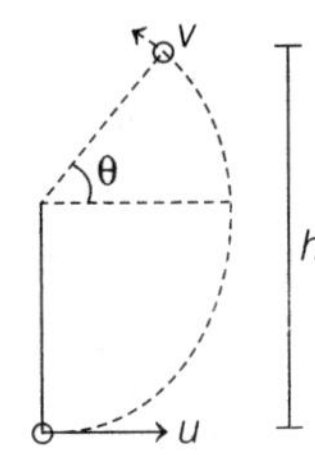

$$v^2 = u^2 - 2gh$$
$$= u^2 - 2gl(1 + \sin\theta)$$

String will slack, where component of weight towards centre is just equal to centripetal force or,

$$mg\sin\theta = \frac{mv^2}{l} = \frac{m}{l}[u^2 - 2gl(1 + \sin\theta)]$$

Substituting $\quad u^2 = \frac{7gl}{2}$, we get

$$\sin\theta = \frac{1}{2} \quad \text{or} \quad \theta = 30°$$

$\therefore$ The desired angle is 90° + 30° or 120°.

32. $T\cos\theta = mg,\ T\sin\theta = mR\omega^2$

or $\quad \tan\theta = \frac{R\omega^2}{g} = \frac{R(2\pi/T)^2}{g}$

$\therefore \quad T = 2\pi\sqrt{\frac{R}{g\tan\theta}}$

But $\quad R = L\sin\theta$

$\therefore \quad T = 2\pi\sqrt{\frac{L\cos\theta}{g}}$

33. $v = \sqrt{2a_t s} = \sqrt{2a_t(\pi R)}$

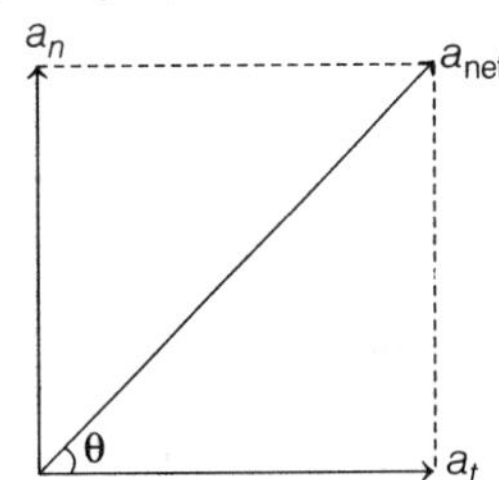

$$\therefore \quad a_n = \frac{v^2}{R} = 2\pi a_t \quad \text{or} \quad \frac{a_n}{a_t} = 2\pi$$

$$\tan\theta = \frac{a_n}{a_t} = 2\pi$$

$$\therefore \quad \theta = \tan^{-1}(2\pi)$$

Subjective Questions

1. $a = \frac{v^2}{R}$

$$\Rightarrow \quad R = \frac{v^2}{a} = \frac{(u\cos\theta)^2}{g} \qquad \textbf{Ans.}$$

2.

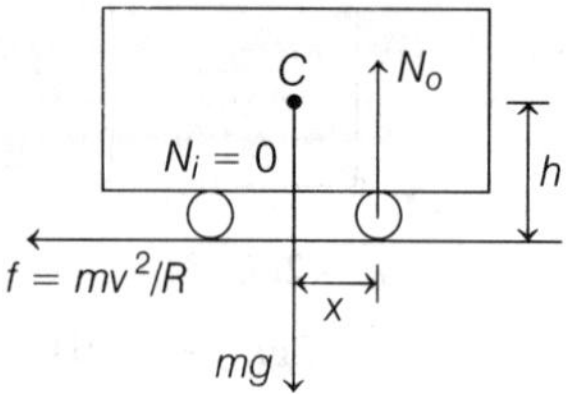

In critical case, normal reaction on inner wheel N_i will become zero. Normal reaction on outer wheel $N_o = mg$. Friction will provide the necessary centripetal force.

$$\therefore \quad f = \frac{mv^2}{R}$$

Taking moment about C,

$$N_o(x) = f(h)$$

$$\text{or} \quad (mg)x = \left(\frac{mv^2}{R}\right)h$$

$$\therefore \quad v = \sqrt{\frac{gRx}{h}}$$

$$= \sqrt{\frac{9.8 \times 250 \times 0.75}{1.5}}$$

$$= 35 \text{ m/s}$$

3. Let ω be the angular speed of rotation of the bowl. Two forces are acting on the ball.

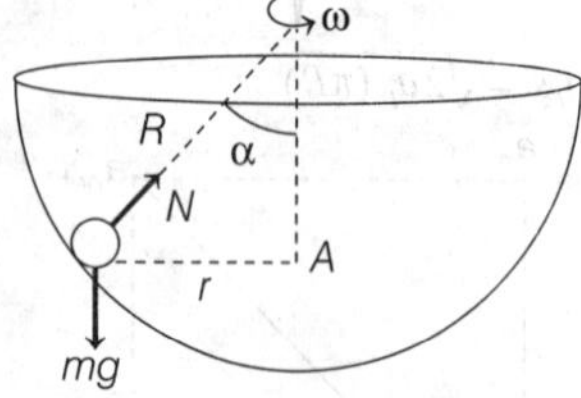

1. normal reaction N
2. weight mg

The ball is rotating in a circle of radius $r (= R\sin\alpha)$ with centre at A at an angular speed ω. Thus,

$$N\sin\alpha = mr\omega^2$$

$$= mR\omega^2 \sin\alpha \qquad \text{...(i)}$$

$$\text{and} \quad N\cos\alpha = mg \qquad \text{...(ii)}$$

Dividing Eq. (i) by Eq. (ii), we get

$$\frac{1}{\cos\alpha} = \frac{\omega^2 R}{g}$$

$$\therefore \quad \omega = \sqrt{\frac{g}{R\cos\alpha}}$$

4. $R = L\sin\theta$

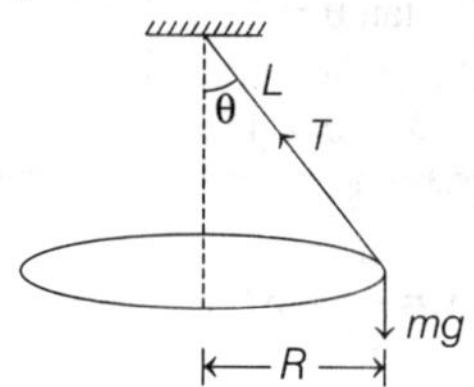

$$T\sin\theta = mR\omega^2 = m(L\sin\theta)\omega^2$$

$$\therefore \quad T = mL\omega^2$$

$$\text{Now,} \quad T\cos\theta = mg$$

$$\therefore \quad \cos\theta = \frac{mg}{T} = \frac{mg}{mL\omega^2} = \frac{g}{L\omega^2}$$

Hence proved.

5. $t = \sqrt{\frac{2h}{g}} = \sqrt{\frac{2 \times 2.9}{9.8}} = 0.77 \text{ s}$

Horizontal distance $x = vt$

$$\therefore \quad v = \frac{x}{t} = \frac{10}{0.77} \approx 13 \text{ m/s}$$

$$a = \frac{v^2}{R} = \frac{(13)^2}{1.5}$$

$$\approx 113 \text{ m/s}^2 \qquad \textbf{Ans.}$$

6. (a) The frictional force provides the necessary centripetal force.

$$\therefore \quad mL\omega^2 = \mu mg$$

$$\text{or} \quad \omega = \sqrt{\frac{\mu g}{L}}$$

(b) Net force of circular motion will be provided by the friction

$$\omega = \alpha t \qquad \text{...(i)}$$

$$F_{net} = m\sqrt{a_t^2 + a_n^2}$$

$$\therefore \quad \mu mg = m\sqrt{(L\alpha)^2 + (L\omega^2)^2} \qquad \text{...(ii)}$$

Here, $a_t = L\alpha$ and $a_n = L\omega^2$

Substituting $\omega = \alpha t$ in Eq. (ii), we have

$$\mu g = \sqrt{L^2\alpha^2 + L^2\alpha^4 t^4}$$

$$\therefore \quad t = \left(\frac{\mu^2 g^2 - L^2\alpha^2}{L^2\alpha^4}\right)^{\frac{1}{4}}$$

Substituting the value of t in Eq. (i), we have

$$\omega = \left[\left(\frac{\mu g}{L}\right)^2 - \alpha^2\right]^{\frac{1}{4}}$$

7. $N \cos\theta = mg$

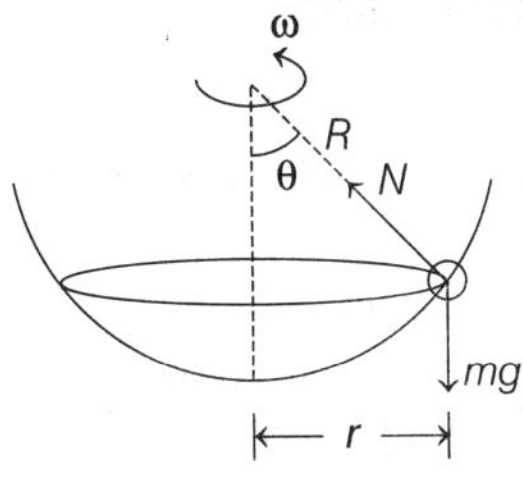

$$N \sin\theta = mr\omega^2 = m\,(R\sin\theta)\,\omega^2$$

Dividing these two equations, we get

$$\cos\theta = \frac{g}{R\,\omega^2} \qquad \text{...(i)}$$

$$\therefore \quad \omega = \sqrt{\frac{g}{R\cos\theta}}$$

At lowermost point, $\theta = 0°$

$$\therefore \quad \omega = \sqrt{\frac{g}{R}}$$

Substituting $\omega = \sqrt{2g/R}$ in Eq. (i), we have

$$\cos\theta = \frac{1}{2}$$

$$\therefore \quad \theta = 60° \qquad \textbf{Ans.}$$

8. (a) 2 kg → T

$$T = m_2 r_2 \omega^2 = (2)\,(2)\,(4)^2 = 64 \text{ N}$$

Centripetal force required to 1 kg block is

$T = 64$ N ← 1 kg → $f = 48$ N

$$F_c = m_1 r_1 \omega^2 = (1)\,(1)\,(4)^2 = 16 \text{ N}$$

But available tension is 64 N. So, the extra force of 48 N is balanced by friction acting radially outward from the centre.

(b) $f_{max} = \mu m_1 g = 0.8 \times 1 \times 10 = 8$ N

2 kg → T T ← 1 kg → 8 N

→ $(m_2 r_2 \omega^2)$ ← $(m_1 r_1 \omega^2)$

$$T = m_2 r_2 \omega^2 = (2)\,(2)\,\omega^2 = 4\,\omega^2 \qquad \text{...(i)}$$

$$T - 8 = m_1 r_1 \omega^2 = (1)\,(1)\,(\omega^2) = \omega^2 \qquad \text{...(ii)}$$

Solving Eqs. (i) and (ii), we get

$$\omega = 1.63 \text{ rad/s} \qquad \textbf{Ans.}$$

(c) $T = m_2 r_2 \omega^2$

2 kg → T

→ $m_2 r_2 \omega^2$

$$\therefore \quad 100 = (2)\,(2)\,\omega^2$$

or $\omega = 5$ rad/s

9. $v^2 = v_0^2 + 2gh$

$$= (0.5\sqrt{gr})^2 + 2gr\,(1 - \cos\theta)$$

$$= (2.25\,gr - 2gr\cos\theta)$$

At the time of leaving contact, $N = 0$

$$\therefore \quad mg\cos\theta = \frac{mv^2}{r} = 2.25\,mg - 2\,mg\cos\theta$$

$$\therefore \quad \cos\theta = \frac{2.25}{3} = \frac{3}{4}$$

$$\therefore \quad \theta = \cos^{-1}(3/4) \qquad \textbf{Ans.}$$

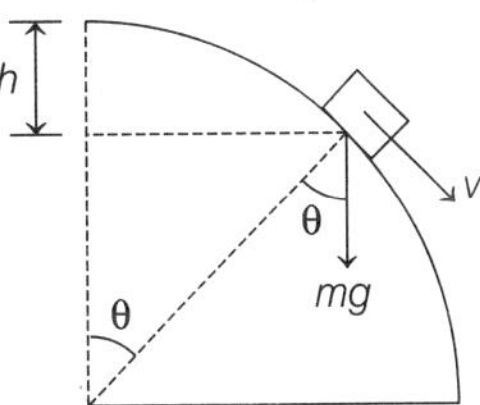

10. $2.5\,mg - mg\cos 30° = \dfrac{mv^2}{r}$

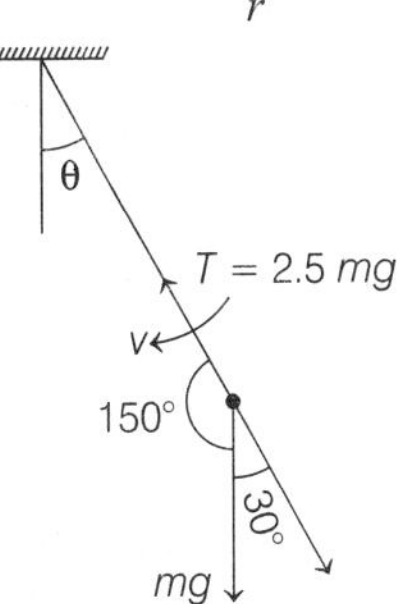

$$\therefore \quad 1.63\,g = \frac{v^2}{r} = \frac{v^2}{2}$$

$$\therefore \quad v = 5.66 \text{ m/s}$$

$$F_{net} = \sqrt{(2.5\,mg)^2 + (mg)^2 + (2)(2.5\,mg)(mg)\cos 150°}$$
$$= 1.7\,mg$$

$$a_{net} = \frac{F_{net}}{m} = 1.7\,g$$
$$\approx 16.75 \text{ m/s}^2$$ **Ans.**

11. $v^2 = v_0^2 + 2\,gh = v_0^2 + 2\,gR\sin\theta$

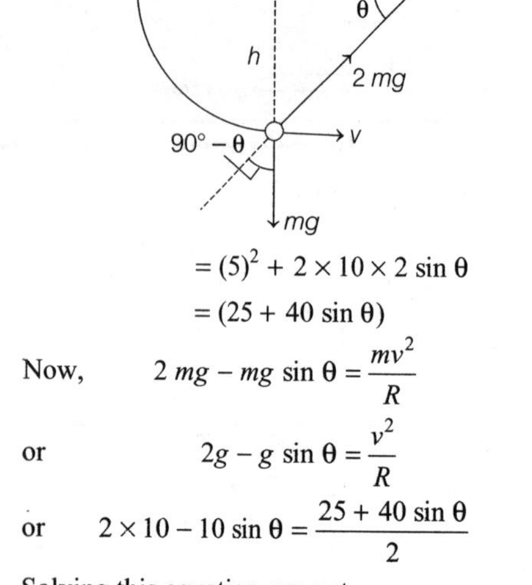

$$= (5)^2 + 2 \times 10 \times 2\sin\theta$$
$$= (25 + 40\sin\theta)$$

Now, $2\,mg - mg\sin\theta = \dfrac{mv^2}{R}$

or $2g - g\sin\theta = \dfrac{v^2}{R}$

or $2 \times 10 - 10\sin\theta = \dfrac{25 + 40\sin\theta}{2}$

Solving this equation, we get

$$\theta = \sin^{-1}\left(\frac{1}{4}\right)$$ **Ans.**

12. From figure,

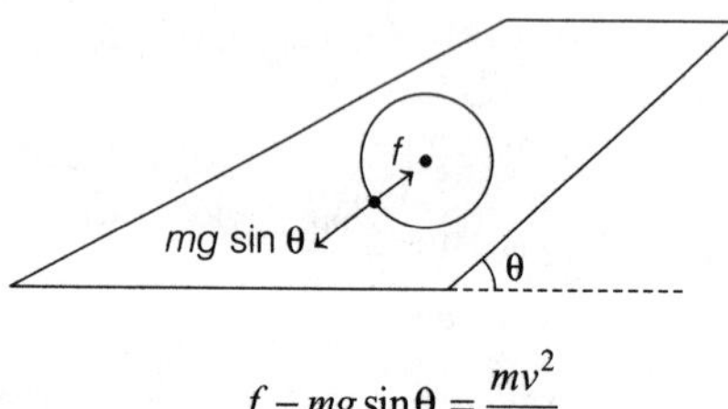

$$f - mg\sin\theta = \frac{mv^2}{r}$$

or $\mu N - mg\sin\theta = \dfrac{mv_{max}^2}{r}$

or $\mu mg\cos\theta - mg\sin\theta = \dfrac{mv_{max}^2}{r}$

or $\mu g\cos\theta - g\sin\theta = \dfrac{v_{max}^2}{r}$ (here, $\theta = 30°$)

$$\therefore \quad v_{max} = \sqrt{gr(\mu\cos\theta - \sin\theta)}$$
$$= \sqrt{gr(\mu\cos 30° - \sin 30°)}$$
$$= \sqrt{10 \times 10\left(\frac{2}{\sqrt{3}} \times \frac{\sqrt{3}}{2} - \frac{1}{2}\right)}$$
$$= \frac{10}{\sqrt{2}} = 5\sqrt{2} \text{ m/s}$$

LEVEL 2

Single Correct Option

1. $E_A = E_B$

$$\therefore \quad \frac{1}{2}mv_A^2 = \frac{1}{2} \times 200 \times (12 - 7)^2 \qquad (\because\ m = 2 \text{ kg})$$

$$\therefore \quad v_A = 60 \text{ m/s}$$

At A, $N = \dfrac{mv_A^2}{R} = \dfrac{(2)(60)^2}{S} = 1440 \text{ N}$ **Ans.**

2. Let us see the FBD with respect to rotating cone (non-inertial)

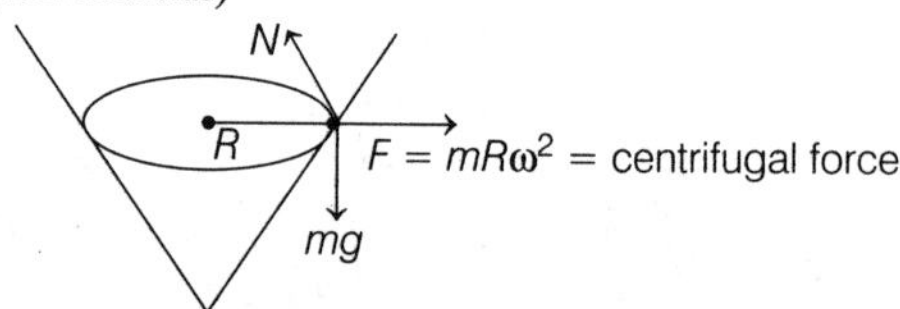

N, F and mg are balanced in the shown diagram. If displaced upwards, F will increase as R is increased. This will have a component up the plane. So, it will move upwards. Hence, the equilibrium is unstable.

3. $\mu mg = mR\omega^2$

$$\therefore \quad \omega^2 = \frac{\mu g}{R} = \frac{(1/3)g}{5a/4} = \frac{4g}{15a}$$ **Ans.**

4. $a_A = g\sin\theta$

$$a_B = \frac{v^2}{R} = \frac{2gh}{R} = \frac{2gR(1 - \cos\theta)}{R}$$

Given, $a_A = a_B$

$\therefore \quad \sin\theta = 2 - 2\cos\theta$

Squaring these two equations, we have

$$\sin^2\theta = 4 + 4\cos^2\theta - 8\cos\theta$$

or $1 - \cos^2\theta = 4 + 4\cos^2\theta - 8\cos\theta$

On solving this equation, we get

$\cos\theta = \dfrac{3}{5}$ or $\theta = \cos^{-1}(3/5)$ **Ans.**

5. At the time of leaving contact

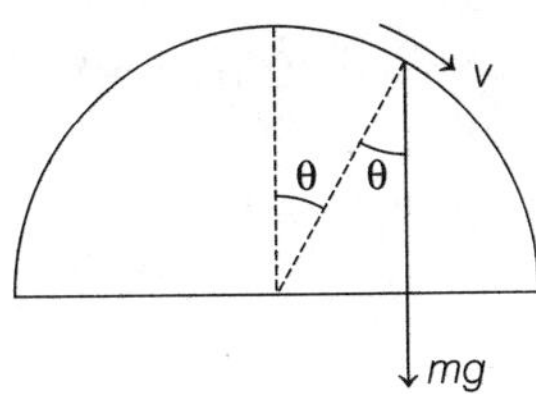

$$N = 0$$

$$\therefore \quad mg\cos\theta = \frac{mv^2}{R} = \frac{m(2gh)}{R}$$

$$\therefore \quad \cos\theta = \frac{2h}{R} = \frac{2\left[\frac{R}{4} + R(1-\cos\theta)\right]}{R}$$

On solving this equation, we get

$$\cos\theta = 5/6$$

or $\theta = \cos^{-1}\left(\frac{5}{6}\right)$ **Ans.**

6. $h_{AB} = R\cos 37° - R\cos 53°$

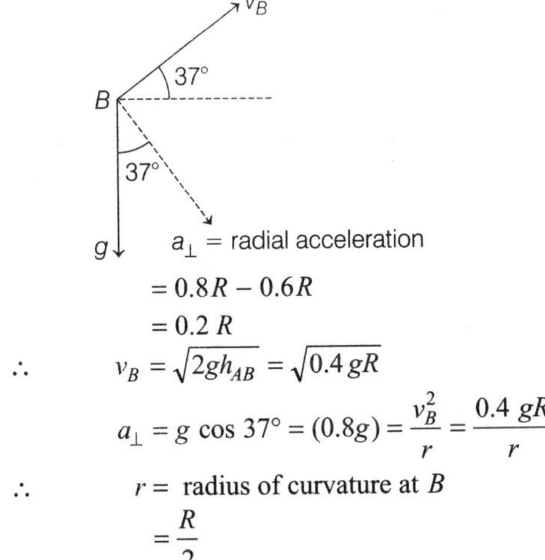

$$= 0.8R - 0.6R$$

$$= 0.2\,R$$

$$\therefore \quad v_B = \sqrt{2gh_{AB}} = \sqrt{0.4\,gR}$$

$$a_\perp = g\cos 37° = (0.8g) = \frac{v_B^2}{r} = \frac{0.4\,gR}{r}$$

$$\therefore \quad r = \text{ radius of curvature at } B$$

$$= \frac{R}{2}$$

7. At the time of leaving contact at P,

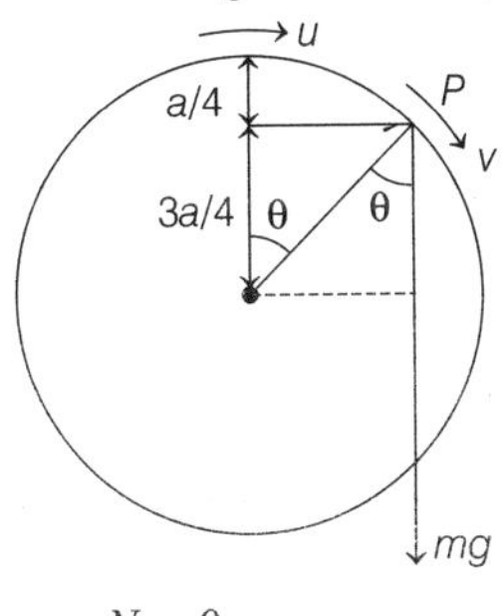

$$N = 0$$

$$\therefore \quad mg\cos\theta = \frac{mv^2}{a} = \frac{m(u^2 + 2gh)}{a}$$

$$\therefore \quad g(3a/4) = \frac{u^2 + 2g(a/4)}{a}$$

$$\therefore \quad u = \frac{\sqrt{ag}}{2}$$ **Ans.**

8. $v = \frac{2\pi r}{T} = \frac{(2\pi)(0.5)}{1.58} \approx 2\text{ m/s}$

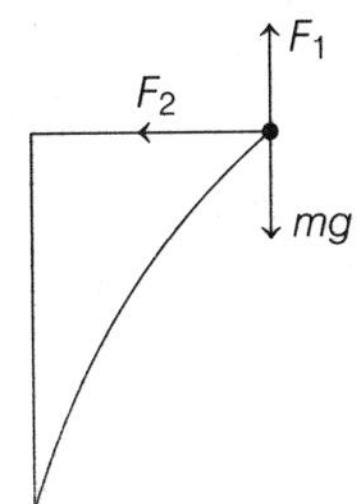

$$F_1 = mg = 100\text{ N}$$

$$F_2 = \frac{mv^2}{r} = \frac{10 \times 4}{0.5}$$

$$= 80\text{ N}$$

$\therefore$ Net force by rod on ball

$$= \sqrt{F_1^2 + F_2^2} = 128\text{ N}$$ **Ans.**

9. $t = T$

$$\therefore \quad \sqrt{\frac{2H}{g}} = \frac{2\pi}{\omega}$$

$$\therefore \quad \omega = 2\pi\sqrt{\frac{g}{2H}} = \pi\sqrt{\frac{2g}{H}}$$ **Ans.**

10. Particle breaks off the sphere at $\cos\theta = \frac{2}{3}$

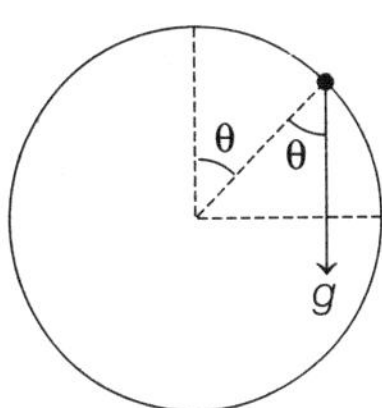

The tangential acceleration at this instant is

$$g\sin\theta = g\sqrt{1-\cos^2\theta}$$

$$= g\sqrt{1-\frac{4}{9}} = \frac{\sqrt{5}}{3}g$$ **Ans.**

11. $h = R\cos\theta$

$$v_0 = \sqrt{2gh} = \sqrt{2gR\cos\theta}$$

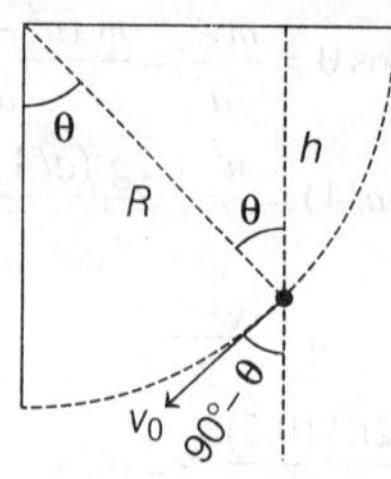

Vertical component of velocity is,

$$v = v_0 \sin\theta$$
$$= \sin\theta\sqrt{2gR\cos\theta}$$

For v to be maximum

$$\frac{dv}{d\theta} = 0$$

$$\therefore \quad [\cos\theta\sqrt{2gR\cos\theta}\,] + \frac{\sin\theta}{2\sqrt{2gR\cos\theta}}(-2gR\sin\theta) = 0$$

$$\therefore \quad 4gR\cos^2\theta - 2gR\sin^2\theta = 0$$

or $\quad 2\cos^2\theta - (1-\cos^2\theta) = 0$

or $\quad \cos\theta = \dfrac{1}{\sqrt{3}}$

$$\therefore \quad \theta = \cos^{-1}\left(\frac{1}{\sqrt{3}}\right) \quad \textbf{Ans.}$$

12. $a_t = a_r$

$$\therefore \quad \frac{dv}{dt} = \frac{v^2}{R} \quad (v = \text{speed})$$

$$\therefore \quad \int_{v_0}^{v} v^{-2}\,dv = \frac{1}{R}\int_0^t dt$$

$$\left[\frac{1}{v_0} - \frac{1}{v}\right] = \frac{t}{R}$$

or $\quad \dfrac{1}{v} = \dfrac{1}{v_0} - \dfrac{t}{R} = \dfrac{R - v_0t}{Rv_0}$

or $\quad v = \dfrac{Rv_0}{R - v_0t}$

$$\therefore \quad \frac{dx}{dt} = \frac{Rv_0}{R - v_0t} \quad (x = \text{distance travelled})$$

or $\quad \displaystyle\int_0^x dx = \int_0^t \frac{Rv_0}{R - v_0t}\,dt$

$$x = Rv_0\left(-\frac{1}{v_0}\right)[\ln(R - v_0t)]_0^t$$

$$= -R\ln\left(1 - \frac{v_0t}{R}\right)$$

$$\therefore \quad 1 - \frac{v_0t}{R} = e^{-x/R}$$

or $\quad t = t = \dfrac{R}{v_0}(1 - e^{-x/R})$

Putting $x = 2\pi R$, we get

$$t = \frac{R}{v_0}(1 - e^{-2\pi}) \quad \textbf{Ans.}$$

13. If $u > \sqrt{5gl}$, then **T** and **a** are in same direction. Hence, **T** · **a** is positive.

If $u = \sqrt{5gl}$, then $T = 0$

$$\therefore \quad \mathbf{T}\cdot\mathbf{a} = 0$$

14. At lowest point **T** and **a** are always in same direction (towards centre).

$\therefore$ **T** · **a** is always positive.

15. $h = l(1 - \cos 60°) = \dfrac{l}{2}$,

$$v^2 = 2gh = gl$$

Now, $T_{max} - mg = \dfrac{mv^2}{l}$ (at bottommost point)

$$\therefore \quad T_{max} = 2mg = \mu_s(4\,mg)$$

$$\therefore \quad \mu_s = 0.5$$

16. $a = \sqrt{a_n^2 + a_t^2}$

$$= \sqrt{\left(\frac{T - mg\cos 30°}{m}\right)^2 + (g\sin 30°)^2}$$

$$= g\sqrt{\left(\sqrt{3} - \frac{\sqrt{3}}{2}\right)^2 + \left(\frac{1}{4}\right)} = g$$

17.

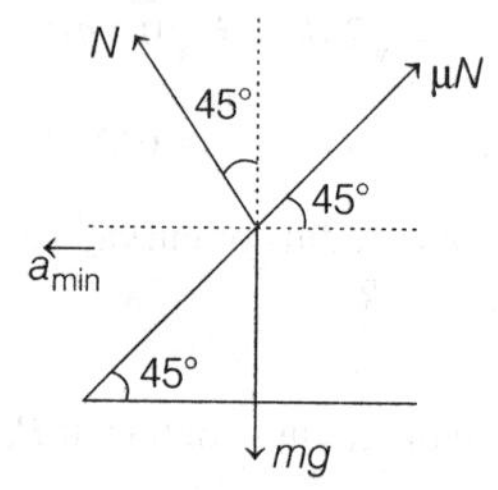

$$\frac{N}{\sqrt{2}} = mg \quad \text{...(i)}$$

$$\frac{N}{\sqrt{2}} - \frac{\mu N}{\sqrt{2}} = \frac{mv_{min}^2}{r} \quad \text{...(ii)}$$

$$\mu = \frac{1}{2} \quad \text{...(iii)}$$

Solving these three equations, we get

$$v_{min} = \sqrt{\frac{gr}{2}}$$

18. Minimum tension is at topmost point (speed = v) and maximum tension at bottommost point (speed = u).

$$\frac{T_{\max}}{T_{\min}} = \frac{mg + \dfrac{mu^2}{L}}{-mg + \dfrac{mv^2}{L}} = 4$$

$$u^2 = v^2 + 2g\,(2L)$$

Solving, we get $v = 10$ m/s

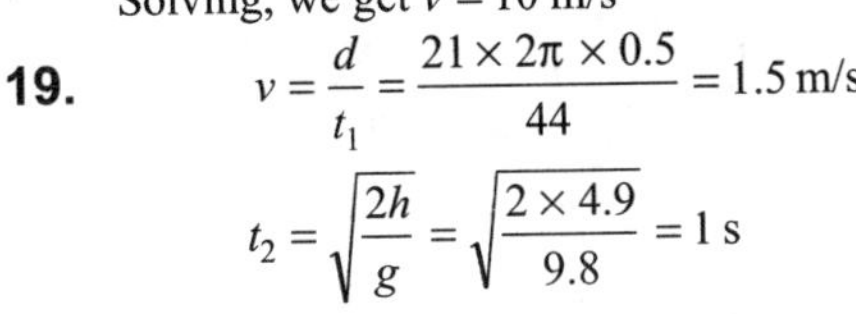

19. $$v = \frac{d}{t_1} = \frac{21 \times 2\pi \times 0.5}{44} = 1.5 \text{ m/s}$$

$$t_2 = \sqrt{\frac{2h}{g}} = \sqrt{\frac{2 \times 4.9}{9.8}} = 1 \text{ s}$$

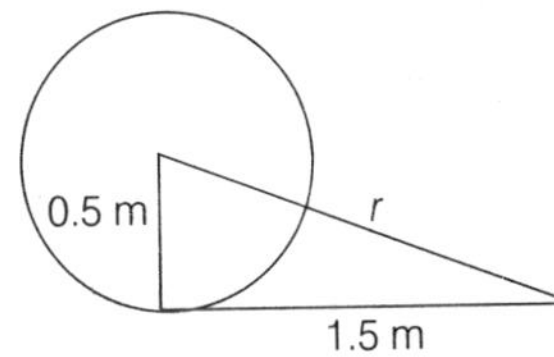

Horizontal distance travelled by drop = $vt_2 = 1.5$ m

$\therefore$ $$r = \sqrt{(1.5)^2 + (0.5)^2}$$

$$= \sqrt{2.5} \text{ m}$$

20. Two forces are acting on girl, tension and weight. Power of tension will be zero and that of weight is,

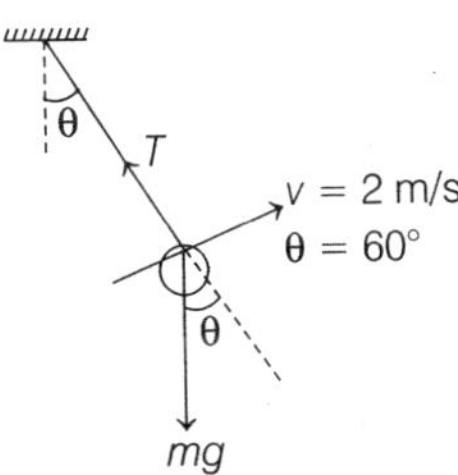

$$P = mgv \cos(90° + \theta) = -mgv \sin 60°$$

$$= -50 \times 9.8 \times 2 \times \frac{\sqrt{3}}{2} = -490\sqrt{3} \text{ W}$$

$\therefore$ Power delivered is $490\sqrt{3}$ W.

21. Since, the particle is released from a small height, θ (angle of radius with vertical) will be very small.

Force of friction throughout the journey can be assumed to be μmg. Particle will finally come to rest when whole of its energy (= mgh) is lost in the work done against friction. Let particle stops after travelling a distance d. Then,

$$\mu mgd = mgh$$

or $$d = \frac{h}{\mu} = \frac{10^{-2}}{0.01} = 1.0 \text{ m}$$

22. $h_{AB} = (r \cos \alpha - r \sin \beta)$

Velocity of particle at B,

$$v = \sqrt{2gh_{AB}}$$

$$= \sqrt{2g\,(r \cos \alpha - r \sin \beta)}$$

Particle will leave contact at B, if component of weight is just equal to centripetal force (towards centre).

or $$mg \sin \beta = \frac{mv^2}{r}$$

or $$\sin \beta = 2 \cos \alpha - 2 \sin \beta$$

$\therefore$ $$3 \sin \beta = 2 \cos \alpha$$

23. $$g \sin \theta = \frac{v^2}{R} = \frac{2gh}{R} = \frac{2gR\,(1 - \cos \theta)}{R}$$

or $$\sin \theta = 2\,(1 - \cos \theta)$$

$$2 \sin \frac{\theta}{2} \cos \frac{\theta}{2} = 2\left(2 \sin^2 \frac{\theta}{2}\right)$$

$\therefore$ $$\tan \frac{\theta}{2} = \frac{1}{2}$$

$$\frac{\theta}{2} = \tan^{-1}\left(\frac{1}{2}\right)$$

or $$\theta = 2 \tan^{-1}\left(\frac{1}{2}\right)$$

Note *In extreme position of pendulum only tangential component of acceleration ($a_t = g \sin \theta$) is present. In lowest position, only normal acceleration ($a_n = v^2/R$) is present.*

24. When body is released from the position P (inclined at angle θ from vertical), then velocity at mean position

$$v = \sqrt{2gl\,(1 - \cos \theta)}$$

$\therefore$ Tension at the lowest point

$$= mg + \frac{mv^2}{l}$$

$$= mg + \frac{m}{l}[2gl\,(1 - \cos 60°)]$$

$$= mg + mg = 2\,mg$$

25. $$\frac{1}{2} mv^2 = as^2$$

or $$F_n = \frac{mv^2}{R} = \frac{2as^2}{R} \qquad \text{...(i)}$$

Further, $v = \sqrt{\frac{2a}{m}} \cdot s$

or $a_t = \frac{dv}{dt} = \sqrt{\frac{2a}{m}} \cdot \frac{ds}{dt} = \sqrt{\frac{2a}{m}} \cdot v$

$= \sqrt{\frac{2a}{m}} \cdot \sqrt{\frac{2a}{m}} \cdot s = \frac{2as}{m}$

$\therefore \quad F_t = ma_t = 2as \quad \text{...(ii)}$

$\therefore \quad F_{net} = \sqrt{F_n^2 + F_t^2}$

$= 2as\sqrt{1 + \frac{s^2}{R^2}}$

26. When a is horizontal

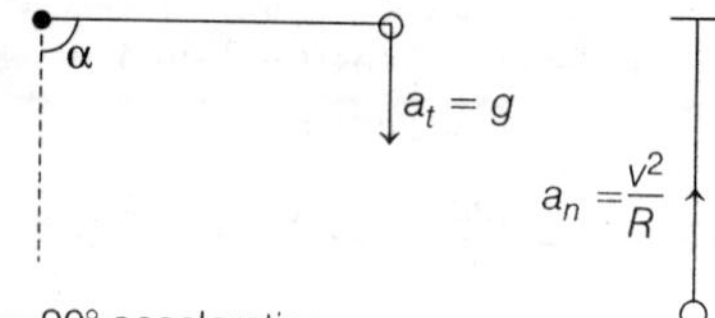

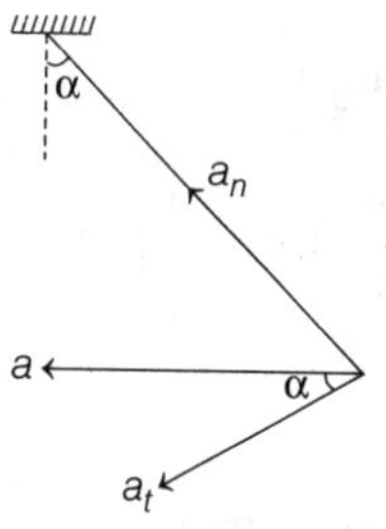

$\tan\alpha = \frac{a_n}{a_t} = \frac{v^2/l}{g\sin\alpha}$

$= \frac{2gh/l}{g\sin\alpha}$

$= \frac{2g\, l\cos\alpha/l}{g\sin\alpha}$

$= 2\cot\alpha$

$\tan\alpha = \sqrt{2}$

or $\cos\alpha = \frac{1}{\sqrt{3}}$

$\therefore \quad \alpha = \cos^{-1}\left(\frac{1}{\sqrt{3}}\right)$

27. $\tan\theta = \frac{h}{b} = \frac{v^2}{Rg}$

$\Rightarrow \quad h = \frac{v^2 b}{Rg}$

28.

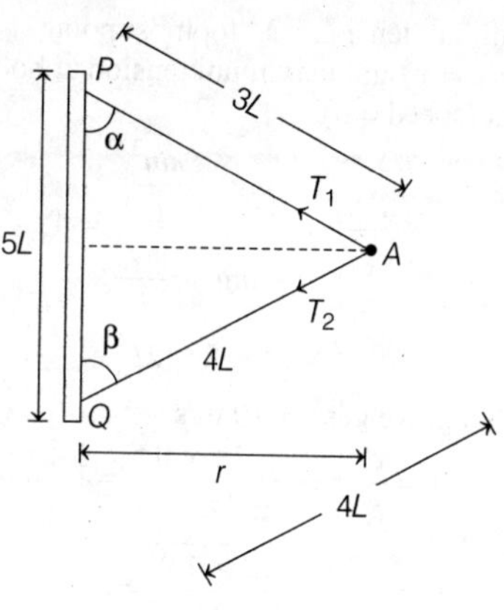

$\angle PAQ = 90°$

$\sin\alpha = \frac{4}{5}, \cos\alpha = \frac{3}{5}$

$\sin\beta = \frac{3}{5}, \cos\beta = \frac{4}{5}$

$r = 3L\sin\alpha = \frac{12L}{5}$

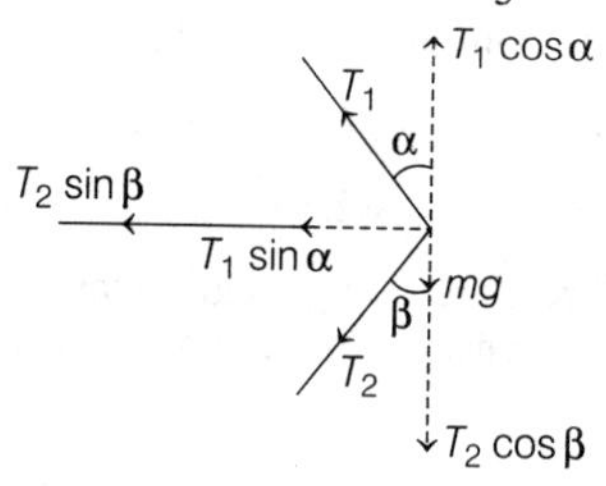

$T_1\cos\alpha = T_2\cos\beta + mg$

$T_1 \times \frac{3}{5} = T_2 \times \frac{4}{5} + mg$

$3T_1 - 4T_2 = 5mg \quad \text{...(i)}$

$T_1\sin\alpha + T_2\sin\beta = m\omega^2 r$

$T_1 \times \frac{4}{5} + T_2 \times \frac{3}{5} = m\omega^2\left(\frac{12L}{5}\right)$

$4T_1 + 3T_2 = 12\, m\omega^2 L \quad \text{...(ii)}$

29.

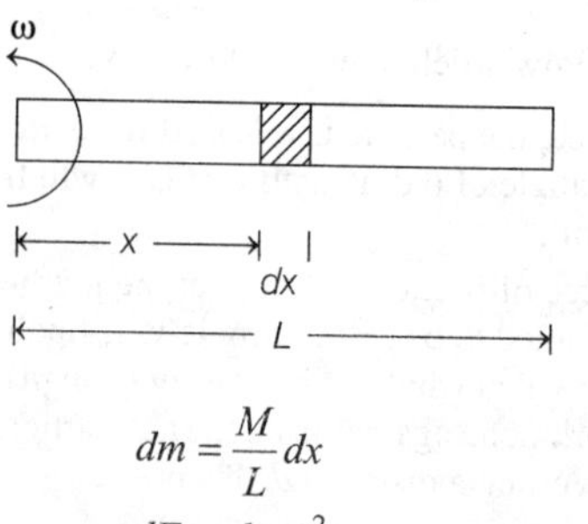

$dm = \frac{M}{L}dx$

$dF = dm\omega^2 x$

$$F = \frac{M}{L}\omega^2 \int_0^L x\,dx$$

$$= \frac{M}{L}\omega^2 \left|\frac{x^2}{2}\right|_0^L$$

$$= \frac{1}{2} M\omega^2 L$$

30.

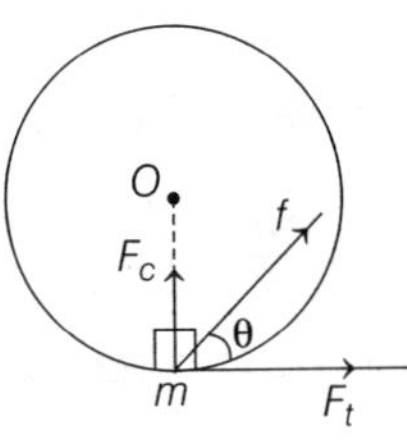

$$\sqrt{F_c^2 + F_t^2} \le \mu mg$$

$$\Rightarrow \quad \left(\frac{mv^2}{r}\right)^2 + (ma_t)^2 \le (\mu^2 m^2 g^2)$$

$$\frac{v^4}{r^2} + a_t^2 \le \mu^2 g^2 \qquad \text{...(i)}$$

$$\tan\theta = \frac{F_c}{F_t} = \frac{mv^2/r}{ma_t} = \frac{v^2}{a_t r}$$

$$\theta = \tan^{-1}\left(\frac{v^2}{a_t r}\right) \qquad \text{...(ii)}$$

31.

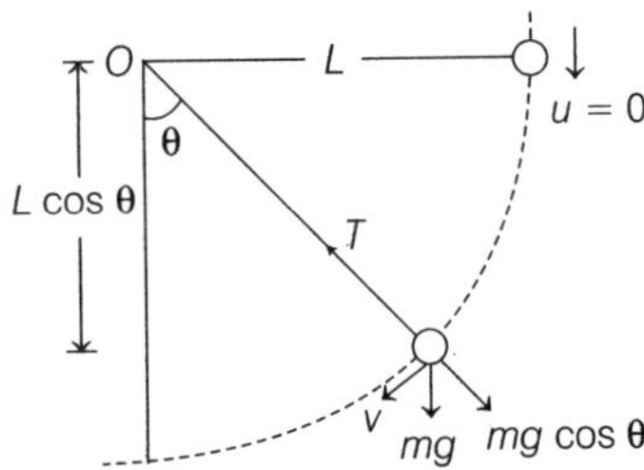

$$v^2 = 0 + 2gL\cos\theta$$

$$T - mg\cos\theta = \frac{mv^2}{L} = 2mg\cos\theta$$

$$T = 3mg\cos\theta$$

$$= 3mg\cos\theta \le 2mg$$

$$\cos\theta \le \frac{2}{3}$$

$$\theta = \cos^{-1}(2/3)$$

32. $$mg(h + L) = \frac{1}{2}mv^2$$

$$\Rightarrow \quad v^2 = 2g(h + L)$$

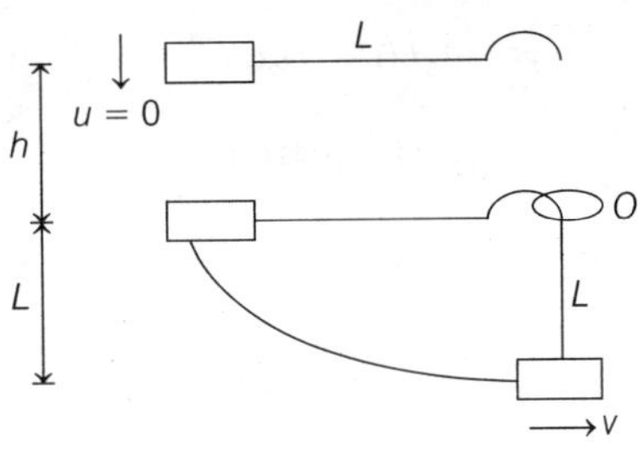

To complete the vertical circle about O,

$$v \ge \sqrt{4gL}$$

$$v^2 \ge 4gL$$

$$2g(h + L) \ge 4gL$$

$$h \ge L$$

$$h_{min} = L$$

33. $$T\sin\theta = mr\omega^2 \qquad \text{...(i)}$$

$$T\cos\theta = mg \qquad \text{...(ii)}$$

$$\therefore \quad \tan\theta = \frac{r\omega^2}{g}$$

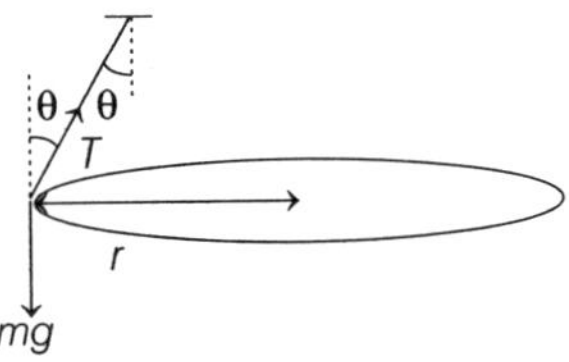

Note *Since, r >> length of pendulum. Hence, radius of bob of pendulum is also r.*

34. $$t_{pc} = \sqrt{\frac{2h}{g}} = \sqrt{\frac{2(2L)}{g}} = 2\sqrt{\frac{L}{g}}$$

$$x = v\,t_{PC} = (\sqrt{gR})\left(2\sqrt{\frac{L}{g}}\right)$$

But $\quad R = L$

$\therefore \quad x = 2L$

Note *At highest point, minimum velocity required is $\sqrt{gR}$.*

35. At P velocity is vertical.

$$\therefore \quad h = \frac{v^2}{2g} = \frac{(5)^2}{2 \times 9.8}$$

$$\approx 1.25 \text{ m}$$

36. When the string rotates by 90°, the speed of ball is

$$v'^2 = v^2 - 2gL = 3gL$$

$$v' = \sqrt{3gL}$$

$$v_1^2 = v^2 - 2gL(1 + \cos\alpha)$$

$$\frac{v^2}{4} = v^2 - 2gL(1 + \cos\alpha)$$

$$2gL(1 + \cos\alpha) = \frac{3v^2}{4}$$

$$= \frac{3}{4} \times 5gL$$

$$1 + \cos\alpha = \frac{15}{8}$$

$$\Rightarrow \quad \cos\alpha = \frac{7}{8}$$

$$\alpha = \cos^{-1}(7/8), \alpha < 45° = \left(\frac{\pi}{4}\right)$$

$$\frac{\pi}{2} < \theta < \frac{3\pi}{4}$$

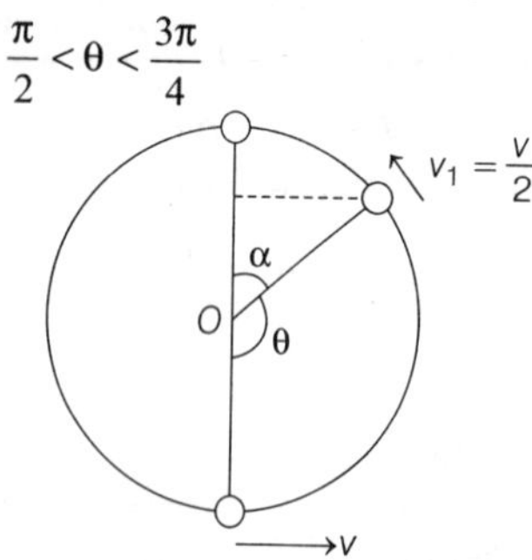

More than One Correct Options

1. Radial acceleration is given by

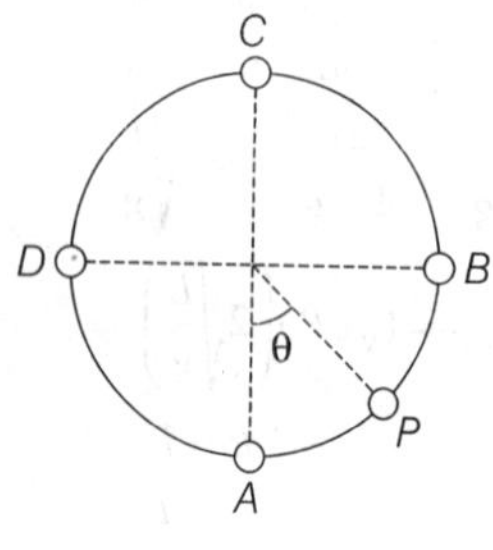

$$a_r = \frac{v^2}{R}$$

At A, speed is maximum.
Therefore, a_r is maximum.
At C, speed is minimum.
Therefore, a_r is minimum.
Tangential acceleration is $g \sin\theta$.
At point $B, \theta = 90°$.
Therefore, tangential acceleration is maximum $(= g)$.

2. $T + mg = \dfrac{mu^2}{l}$

$$\therefore \quad 2\,mg + mg = \frac{mu^2}{l} \quad \text{or} \quad u = \sqrt{3gl}$$

$$v^2 = u^2 + 2\,gh = 3gl + 2g\,(2l)$$

$$= 7\,gl$$

$$\therefore \quad v = \sqrt{7gl}$$

3. $R = h\cot\alpha$

$$N\cos\alpha = mg$$

$$N\sin\alpha = \frac{mv^2}{R}$$

Solving these two equations, we get

$$v = \sqrt{Rg\tan\alpha}$$

$$= \sqrt{(h\cot\alpha)\,(g\tan\alpha)}$$

$$= \sqrt{gh}$$

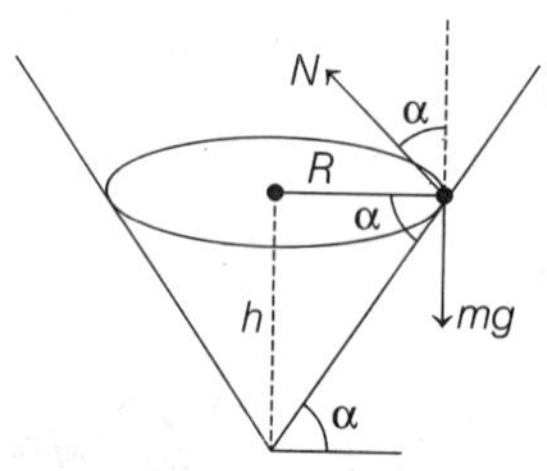

Now, $$T = \frac{2\pi R}{v} = \frac{2\pi\,h\cot\alpha}{\sqrt{gh}}$$

$$= 2\pi\sqrt{\frac{h}{g}}\cot\alpha$$

$$\therefore \quad T \propto \sqrt{h} \quad \text{and} \quad T \propto \cot\alpha$$

5. $N\cos\theta = mg$ ...(i)

$N\sin\theta = mR\omega^2$ ...(ii)

From Eq. (i), we get

$$N = \frac{mg}{\cos\theta} = \text{constant}$$

as $\theta = \text{constant}$

Net force is the resultant of N and mg and both forces are constant.

Hence, net force is constant.

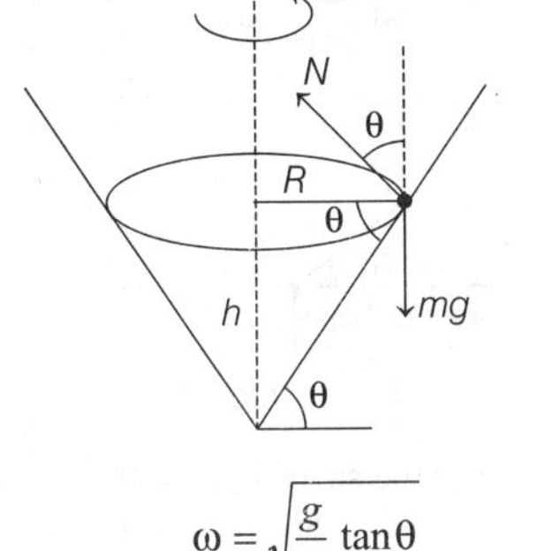

$$\omega = \sqrt{\frac{g}{R}\tan\theta}$$

But $$R = \frac{h}{\tan\theta}$$

$\therefore$ $$\omega = \sqrt{\frac{g}{h}}\tan\theta$$

or $$\omega \propto \frac{1}{\sqrt{h}} \qquad (\theta = \text{constant})$$

6. $R = 1.6\cos 60° = 0.8$ m

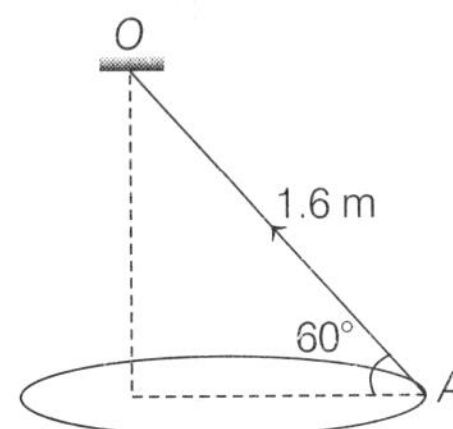

$$T\sin 60° = mg \quad \text{or} \quad T = \frac{2mg}{\sqrt{3}}$$

$$T\cos 60° = \frac{mv^2}{R}$$

$\therefore$ $$\frac{v^2}{R} = \frac{T}{2m} = \frac{g}{\sqrt{3}} = \frac{9.8}{\sqrt{3}}\ \text{m/s}^2$$

$$v = \sqrt{\frac{9.8}{\sqrt{3}} \times 0.8}\ \text{m/s}$$

$$\text{Time period} = 2\pi\frac{R}{v}$$

7. $$\Delta t = \frac{\text{Distance travelled}}{\text{Speed}}$$

$$= \frac{(2\pi R/6)}{v} = \frac{3.14 \times 300}{60 \times 3} = 5.23\ \text{s}$$

(a) $|\Delta \mathbf{v}| = |\mathbf{v}_f - \mathbf{v}_i| = \sqrt{v^2 + v^2 - 2v\cdot v\cos 60°}$

$= 2v\sin 30° = 60$ m/s

(b) $a_i = \frac{v^2}{R} = 12\ \text{m/s}^2$

(c) $|\mathbf{a}_{av}| = \frac{|\Delta \mathbf{v}|}{\Delta t} = \frac{60}{5.23}$

$= 11.5\ \text{m/s}^2$

8. According to work-energy theorem,

$$W_{\text{Total}} = \Delta\text{KE} = \frac{1}{2}mv^2 - \frac{1}{2}mu^2$$

or $$W_F + W_{mg} + W_N = \frac{1}{2}mv^2 \qquad \text{...(i)}$$

$\boldsymbol{W_F}$**:** See miscellaneous example-15 of chapter work, energy and power,

$$W_F = 2000\ \text{J}$$

$\boldsymbol{W_{mg}}$**:** $W_{mg} = -mgh = -mgR\cos 60° = -500$ J

$\boldsymbol{W_N}$**:** $W_N = 0$

Substituting the values in equation (i),

we get $2000 - 500 = \frac{1}{2} \times 10 \times v^2$

$\therefore$ $$v = \sqrt{300} = \text{m/s}$$

9. $U_i + T_i = U_f + T_f$

or $$mgh + \frac{1}{2}mv_0^2 = \frac{1}{2}mv^2$$

$\therefore$ $$v_B^2 = v_0^2 + 2gh$$

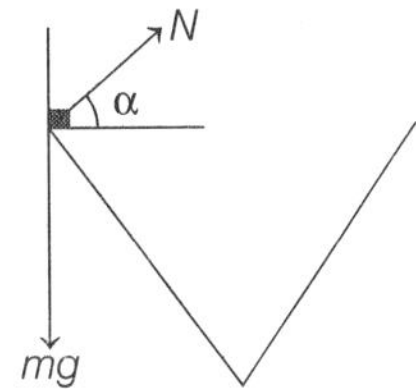

Here, $$N\cos\alpha = \frac{mv_0^2}{r_0}$$

and $$N\sin\alpha = mg$$

$\therefore$ $$\cot\alpha = \frac{v_0^2}{r_0 g}$$

$\therefore$ $$v_0 = \sqrt{r_0 g\cot\alpha}$$

Comprehension Based Questions

1. $\Delta U = \Delta U_{\text{rod}} + \Delta U_{\text{ball}}$

$$= Mg\left(\frac{l}{2}\right) + mgl$$

$$= \left(\frac{M}{2} + m\right)gl \qquad \textbf{Ans.}$$

2. $\omega = \frac{v}{l}$

Now, decrease in rotational kinetic energy = increase in potential energy

$\therefore \quad \frac{1}{2} I\omega^2 = \left(\frac{M}{2} + m\right) gl$

or $\quad \frac{1}{2}\left[\frac{Ml^2}{3} + ml^2\right]\left(\frac{v}{l}\right)^2 = \left(\frac{M}{2} + m\right) gl$

$\therefore \quad v = \sqrt{\frac{\left(\frac{M}{2} + m\right) gl}{\left(\frac{M}{6} + \frac{m}{2}\right)}}$

3. Maximum velocity is at bottommost point and minimum velocity is at topmost point.

$$\frac{\sqrt{u_{min}^2 + 2g(2L)}}{u_{min}} = \frac{2}{1}$$

On solving, we get

$$u_{min} = 2\sqrt{\frac{gL}{3}}$$ **Ans.**

4. $u_{max} = 2\, u_{min} = 4\sqrt{\frac{gL}{3}}$

$\therefore \quad K_{max} = \frac{1}{2} m u_{max}^2 = \frac{8\, mgL}{3}$ **Ans.**

5. $v = \sqrt{u_{max}^2 - 2g(L)}$

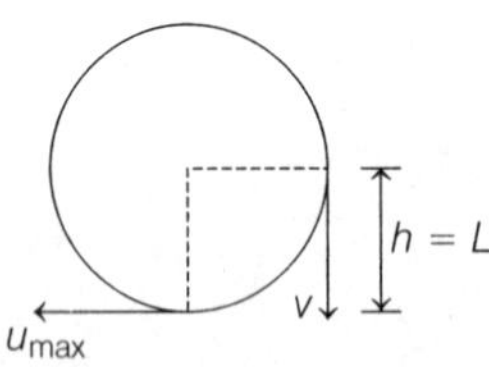

$= \sqrt{\frac{16\, gL}{3} - 2gL} = \sqrt{\frac{10\, gL}{3}}$ **Ans.**

6. In the frame of triangular block,

$T\cos 37° = N\cos 53° + mr\omega^2$

(in horizontal direction)

or $\quad \frac{4}{5}T - \frac{3}{5}N = \omega^2$

or $\quad 4T - 3N = 5\omega^2 \quad$ ...(i)

and $\quad T\sin 37° + N\sin 53° = mg$

or $\quad \frac{3}{5}T + \frac{4}{5}N = 10$

or $\quad 3T + 4N = 50 \quad$ ...(ii)

or $\quad 3\left(\frac{5\omega^2 + 3N}{4}\right) + 4N = 50$

or $\quad \frac{15}{4}\omega^2 + \frac{9}{4}N + 4N = 50$

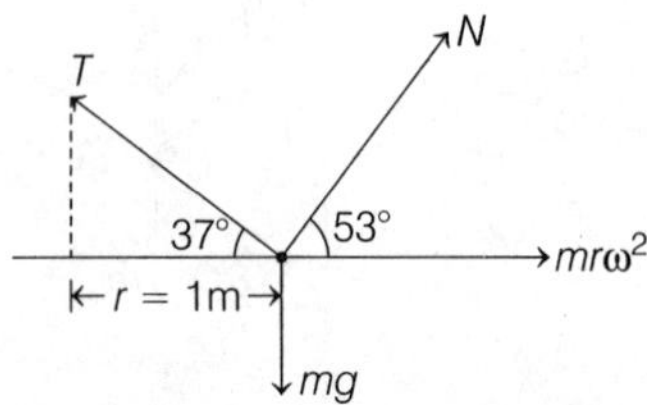

For leaving the surface, $N = 0$

$\Rightarrow \quad \omega^2 = \frac{50 \times 4}{15} = \frac{40}{3}$

$\therefore \quad \omega = \sqrt{\frac{40}{3}}$

$\because \quad \omega = \alpha t$

$\therefore \quad t = \frac{\sqrt{40/3}}{\sqrt{40/3}} = 1\text{s}$

7. $\because\ 3T + 4N = 50$ or $3T = 50 \quad [\because N = 0]$

$\therefore \quad T = \frac{50}{3} = 16.67\text{ N}$

8. Height fallen to Q is $R\sin 30° = \frac{R}{2} = 20\text{m}$

Using conservation of energy,

$E_i - E_f =$ work done against friction

$0 - \left(-mgh + \frac{1}{2}mv^2\right) = 150$

or $\quad v = 10\text{ m/s}$

9. $N - mg\cos 60° = \frac{mv^2}{R}$

$\therefore \quad N = 7.5\text{ N}$

10. In the figure, $x = R\cos\alpha$

and $\quad y = R\sin\alpha$

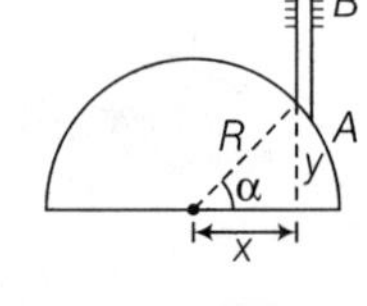

Here, $\frac{dx}{dt} = -R\sin\alpha \frac{d\alpha}{dt}$

or $\quad -v_0 = -R\sin\alpha \frac{d\alpha}{dt}$

or $\quad \frac{d\alpha}{dt} = \frac{v_0}{R\sin\alpha} \quad$ ...(i)

Also, $\quad y = R\sin\alpha$

$\therefore \quad \frac{dy}{dt} = R\cos\alpha \frac{d\alpha}{dt}$

$\frac{dy}{dt} = R\cos\alpha \times \frac{v_0}{R\sin\alpha} \quad$ [from Eq. (i)] or $\qquad \dfrac{dy}{dt} = v_0 \cot\alpha$

$\therefore \qquad v_B = v_0 \cot\alpha$

11. $a_B = \dfrac{dv_B}{dt} = \cot\alpha \dfrac{dv_0}{dt} + v_0 \dfrac{d}{dt}\cot\alpha$

or $\qquad a_B = (\cot\alpha) a_0 - v_0 \operatorname{cosec}^2\alpha \dfrac{d\alpha}{dt}$

$$= a_0 \cot\alpha - v_0 \operatorname{cosec}^2\alpha \left(\frac{v_0}{R\sin\alpha}\right)$$

$$= a_0 \cot\alpha - \frac{v_0^2}{R}\operatorname{cosec}^3\alpha$$

Match the Columns

1. (a) $\qquad v = \sqrt{u^2 - 2gh} = \sqrt{12gl - 2gl}$

$$= \sqrt{10gl} = \sqrt{10 \times 10 \times 1}$$

$$= 10 \text{ m/s}$$ **Ans.**

(b) $a_r = \dfrac{v^2}{R}$ or $\dfrac{v^2}{l}$

$$= \frac{(10)^2}{1} = 100 \text{ m/s}^2$$

$$a_t = g = 10 \text{ m/s}^2$$

$\therefore \quad a = \sqrt{a_r^2 + a_t^2}$

$$= 100.49 \text{ m/s}^2$$

(c) $T = \dfrac{mv^2}{l} = \dfrac{(1)(10)^2}{1} = 100 \text{ N}$

(d) $a_t = g = 10 \text{ m/s}^2$

2. $a_r = \dfrac{v^2}{R} = \dfrac{(2t)^2}{2} = 2t^2$

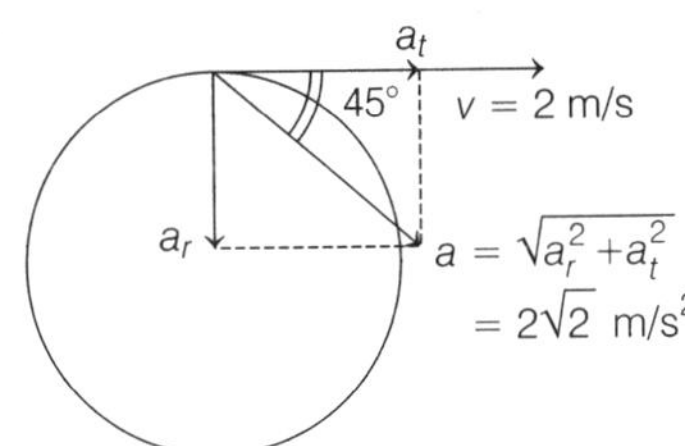

$$a_t = \frac{dv}{dt} = 2 \text{ m/s}^2$$

$$v = 2t$$

$$\omega = \frac{v}{R} = \frac{2t}{2} = t$$

At 1 s,

$$a_r = 2 \text{ m/s}^2,$$

$$a_t = 2 \text{ m/s}^2,$$

$$v = 2 \text{ m/s}$$

and $\qquad \omega = 1 \text{ rad/s}$

(a) $\mathbf{a} \cdot \mathbf{v} = av \cos 45°$

$$= (2\sqrt{2})(2)(1/\sqrt{2}) = 4 \text{ m}^2/\text{s}^3$$

(b) $|\mathbf{a} \times \omega| = a\omega \sin 90°$

$$= (2\sqrt{2})(1)(1)$$

$$= 2\sqrt{2} \text{ m/s}^3$$

(c) $\mathbf{v} \cdot \omega = 0$ as $\theta = 90°$

(d) $|\mathbf{v} \times \mathbf{a}| = va \sin 45° = 4 \text{ m}^2/\text{s}^3$

3. $f = \dfrac{mv^2}{R} = F$

$\therefore \qquad \dfrac{F}{f} = 1$

With increase in speed f will increase but $\dfrac{F}{f}$ will remain same.

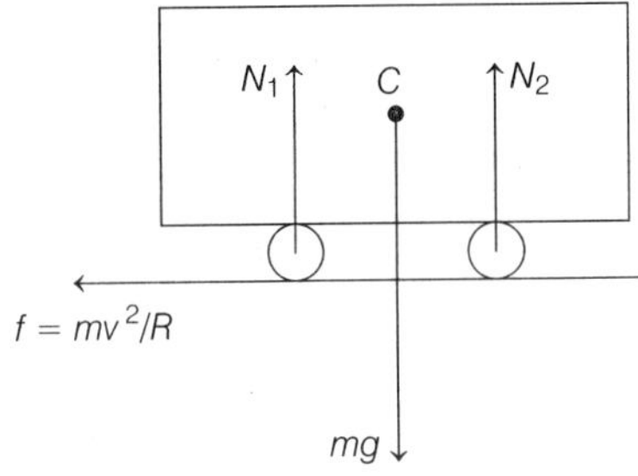

Further, with increase in the value of v, friction f will increase. Therefore, anti-clockwise moment of f about C will also increase. Hence, clockwise moment of N_2 should also increase. Thus, N_2 will increase. But $N_1 + N_2 = mg$. So, N_1 will decrease.

4. $\qquad r = |\mathbf{r}| = \sqrt{(3)^2 + (-4)^2} = 5 \text{ m}$

$$v = |\mathbf{v}| = \sqrt{16 + a^2}$$

$$a_r = |\mathbf{a}| = \sqrt{36 + b^2}$$

In uniform circular motion, $\mathbf{v}$ is always perpendicular to $\mathbf{a}$.

$\therefore \qquad \mathbf{v} \cdot \mathbf{a} = 0$

or $\qquad -24 - ab = 0$

$\therefore \qquad ab = 24 \qquad$ ...(i)

$$a_r = \frac{v^2}{r}$$

$\therefore \qquad \sqrt{36 + b^2} = \dfrac{16 + a^2}{5} \qquad$ ...(ii)

Solving these two equations, we can find the values of a and b.

(d) **r**, **v** and **a** lie in same plane. But $\mathbf{v} \times \mathbf{a}$ is perpendicular to this plane.

$\therefore \quad \mathbf{r} \perp \mathbf{v} \times \mathbf{a}$

or $\quad \mathbf{r} \cdot (\mathbf{v} \times \mathbf{a}) = 0$

5. (a) Since, speed = constant

$\therefore$ Average speed = this constant value = 1 m/s.

(b) Average velocity $= \dfrac{S}{t}$

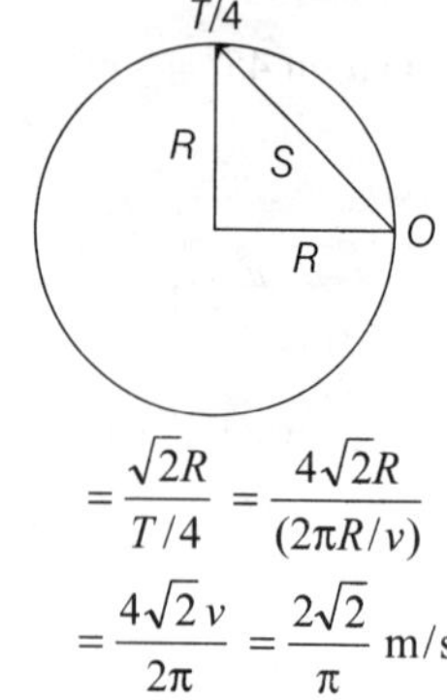

$$= \frac{\sqrt{2}R}{T/4} = \frac{4\sqrt{2}R}{(2\pi R/v)}$$

$$= \frac{4\sqrt{2}\,v}{2\pi} = \frac{2\sqrt{2}}{\pi}\ \text{m/s}$$

(c) $|\mathbf{a}_{av}| = \dfrac{|\Delta \mathbf{v}|}{t}$

$$= \frac{\sqrt{v_f^2 + v_i^2 - 2v_f v_i \cos 90^\circ}}{(T/4)}$$

$$= \frac{4\sqrt{2}v}{T} \qquad (\text{as } v_i = v_f = v)$$

$$= \frac{(4\sqrt{2})\,v}{(2\pi R/v)} = \frac{2\sqrt{2}v^2}{\pi R}$$

$$= \sqrt{2}\ \text{m/s}^2$$

(d) $S = \sqrt{2}R = \sqrt{2}\left(\dfrac{2}{\pi}\right) = \dfrac{2\sqrt{2}}{\pi}$ m

Subjective Questions

1. Minimum velocity of particle at the lowest position to complete the circle should be $\sqrt{4gR}$ inside a tube.

So, $\quad u = \sqrt{4gR}$

$h = R(1 - \cos\theta)$

$\because \quad v^2 = u^2 - 2gh$

or $\quad v^2 = 4gR - 2gR(1 - \cos\theta)$

$= 2gR(1 + \cos\theta)$

or $\quad v^2 = 2gR\left(2\cos^2\dfrac{\theta}{2}\right)$

or $\quad v = 2\sqrt{gR}\cos\dfrac{\theta}{2}$

From $\quad ds = v \cdot dt$, we get

$$R\,d\theta = 2\sqrt{gR}\cos\frac{\theta}{2}\cdot dt$$

or $\quad \displaystyle\int_0^t dt = \frac{1}{2}\sqrt{\frac{R}{g}}\int_0^{\pi/2}\sec\left(\frac{\theta}{2}\right)d\theta$

or $\quad t = \sqrt{\dfrac{R}{g}}\left[\ln\left(\sec\dfrac{\theta}{2} + \tan\dfrac{\theta}{2}\right)\right]_0^{\pi/2}$

or $\quad t = \sqrt{\dfrac{R}{g}}\ln(1 + \sqrt{2}) \qquad$ **Hence proved.**

2. At position θ,

$$v^2 = v_0^2 + 2gh$$

where, $\quad h = a(1 - \cos\theta)$

$\therefore \quad v^2 = (\sqrt{2ag})^2 + 2ag(1 - \cos\theta)$

or $\quad v^2 = 2ag(2 - \cos\theta) \qquad \ldots(\text{i})$

$$N + mg\cos\theta = \frac{mv^2}{a}$$

or $\quad N + mg\cos\theta = 2mg(2 - \cos\theta)$

or $\quad N = mg(4 - 3\cos\theta)$

Net vertical force,

$$F = N\cos\theta + mg$$

$$= mg(4\cos\theta - 3\cos^2\theta + 1)$$

This force (or acceleration) will be maximum when $\dfrac{dF}{d\theta} = 0$

or $\quad -4\sin\theta + 6\sin\theta\cos\theta = 0$

So, either

$$\sin\theta = 0,\ \theta = 0^\circ \ \text{or}\ \cos\theta = \frac{2}{3},$$

$$\theta = \cos^{-1}\left(\frac{2}{3}\right)$$

$\theta = 0°$ is unacceptable

Therefore, the desired position is at

$$\theta = \cos^{-1}\left(\frac{2}{3}\right) \quad \textbf{Ans.}$$

3. $h = l(1 - \cos\theta)$

$$v^2 = v_0^2 - 2gh = 3gl - 2gl(1 - \cos\theta)$$
$$= gl(1 + 2\cos\theta)$$

At 45° means radial and tangential components of acceleration are equal.

$$\therefore \quad \frac{v^2}{l} = g\sin\theta$$

or $\quad 1 + 2\cos\theta = \sin\theta$

Solving the equation, we get $\theta = 90°$ or $\frac{\pi}{2}$ **Ans.**

4. Banking angle, $\theta = \tan^{-1}\left(\frac{v^2}{Rg}\right)$

$$36 \text{ km/h} = 10 \text{ m/s}$$

$$\therefore \quad \theta = \tan^{-1}\left(\frac{100}{20 \times 9.8}\right) = 27°$$

Angle of repose,

$$\theta_r = \tan^{-1}(\mu) = \tan^{-1}(0.4) = 21.8°$$

Since $\theta > \theta_r$, vehicle cannot remain in the given position with $v = 0$. At rest, it will slide down. To find minimum speed, so that vehicle does not slip down, maximum friction will act up the plane.

To find maximum speed, so that the vehicle does not skid up, maximum friction will act down the plane.

Minimum Speed

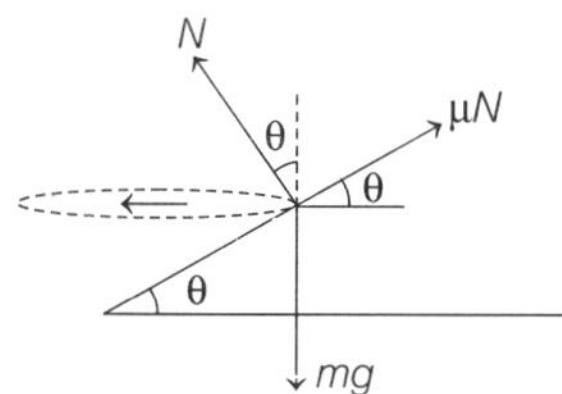

Equation of motion are,

$$N\cos\theta + \mu N\sin\theta = mg \quad \text{...(i)}$$

$$N\sin\theta - \mu N\cos\theta = \frac{m}{R}v_{min}^2 \quad \text{...(ii)}$$

Solving these two equations, we get

$$v_{min} = 4.2 \text{ m/s} \quad \textbf{Ans.}$$

Maximum Speed

Equations of motion are,

$$N\cos\theta - \mu N\sin\theta = mg \quad \text{...(iii)}$$

$$N\sin\theta + \mu N\cos\theta = \frac{m}{R}v_{max}^2 \quad \text{...(iv)}$$

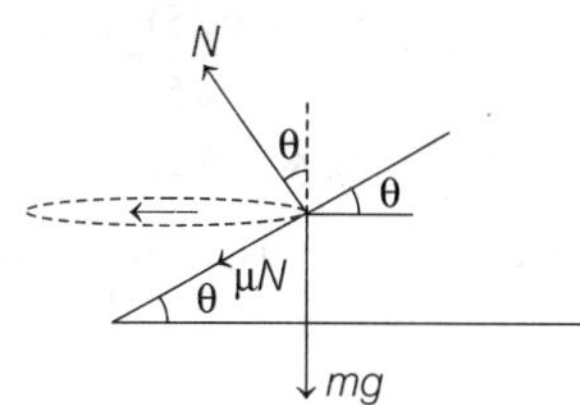

Solving these two equations, we have

$$v_{max} = 15 \text{ m/s} \quad \textbf{Ans.}$$

5. Let v be the velocity at that instant. Then, horizontal component of velocity remains unchanged.

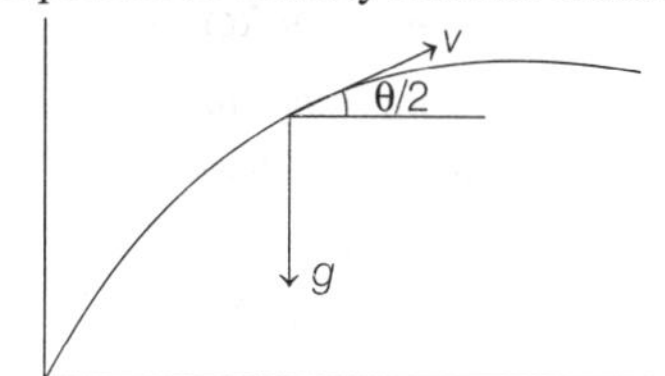

$$\therefore \quad v\cos\frac{\theta}{2} = u\cos\theta \quad \text{or} \quad v = \frac{u\cos\theta}{\cos\frac{\theta}{2}}$$

Tangential component of acceleration of this instant will be

$$a_t = g\cos(\pi/2 + \theta/2) = -g\sin\theta/2$$

$$a_n = \sqrt{a^2 - a_t^2} = \sqrt{g^2 - g^2\sin^2\frac{\theta}{2}}$$

$$= g\cos\frac{\theta}{2}$$

Since, $\quad a_n = \frac{v^2}{R}$

or $$R = \frac{v^2}{a_n} = \frac{\left(\dfrac{u\cos\theta}{\cos\frac{\theta}{2}}\right)^2}{g\cos\frac{\theta}{2}} = \frac{u^2\cos^2\theta}{g\cos^3\left(\frac{\theta}{2}\right)} \quad \textbf{Ans.}$$

6. **After 1 s** $\quad \mathbf{v} = \mathbf{u} + \mathbf{a}t = 20\,\hat{\mathbf{i}} + 10\,\hat{\mathbf{j}},$

$$v = \sqrt{500} \text{ m/s} = 10\sqrt{5} \text{ m/s}$$

$$\mathbf{a} = -10\,\hat{\mathbf{j}}$$

$$a_t = a\cos\theta$$

$$= \frac{\mathbf{a}\cdot\mathbf{v}}{v} = \frac{-100}{10\sqrt{5}}$$

$$= -2\sqrt{5} \text{ m/s}^2 \quad \textbf{Ans.}$$

$$a_n = \sqrt{a^2 - a_t^2} = \sqrt{(10)^2 - (2\sqrt{5})^2}$$

$$= \sqrt{80} \text{ m/s}^2 = 4\sqrt{5} \text{ m/s}^2 \quad \textbf{Ans.}$$

$$R = \frac{v^2}{a_n} = \frac{(10\sqrt{5})^2}{4\sqrt{5}}$$

$$= 25\sqrt{5}\text{ m}$$ **Ans.**

7. (a) Force diagrams of m_1 and m_2 are as shown below

T ← [m_1], $\mu m_1 g$ ← T ← [m_2] → $\mu m_1 g$

(Only horizontal forces have been shown)

Equations of motion are

$$T + \mu m_1 g = m_1 R\omega^2 \quad \text{...(i)}$$

$$T - \mu m_1 g = m_2 R\omega^2 \quad \text{...(ii)}$$

Solving Eqs. (i) and (ii), we have

$$\omega = \sqrt{\frac{2m_1 \mu g}{(m_1 - m_2)R}}$$

Substituting the values, we have

$$\omega_{min} = 6.32\text{ rad/s}$$ **Ans.**

(b) $T = m_2 R\omega^2 + \mu m_1 g$

$$= (1)(0.5)(6.32)^2 + (0.5)(2)(10)$$

$$\approx 30\text{ N}$$ **Ans.**

8. Speed of bob in the given position,

$$v = \sqrt{2gh}$$

Here, $h = (400 + 400\cos 30°)$ mm

$= 746$ mm

$= 0.746$ m

$\therefore$ $v = \sqrt{2 \times 9.8 \times 0.746}$

$= 3.82$ m/s

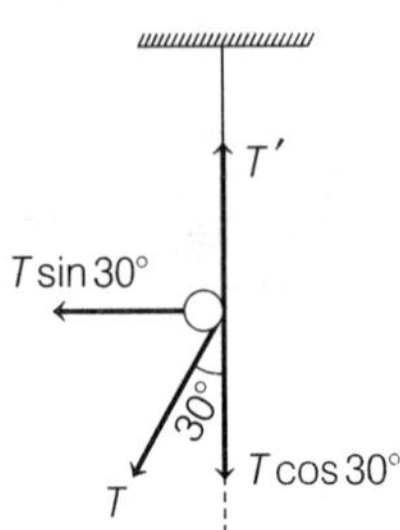

Now $T - mg\cos\theta = \dfrac{mv^2}{r}$

$$T = 2 \times 9.8 \times \cos 30° + \frac{2 \times (3.82)^2}{(0.4)}$$

or $T = 90$ N

$\therefore$ $R = T\sin 30° = 45$ N **Ans.**

$T' = T\cos 30°$

9. Speed of each particle at angle θ is,

$v = \sqrt{2gh}$ (from energy conservation)

where, $h = R(1 - \cos\theta)$

$\therefore$ $v = \sqrt{2gR(1 - \cos\theta)}$

$$N + mg\cos\theta = \frac{mv^2}{R}$$

or $N + mg\cos\theta = 2mg(1 - \cos\theta)$

or $N = 2mg - 3mg\cos\theta$ ...(i)

The tube breaks its contact with ground when $2N\cos\theta > Mg$

Substituting, $2N\cos\theta = Mg$

or $4mg\cos\theta - 6mg\cos^2\theta = Mg$

Substituting, $\theta = 60°$

$$2mg - \frac{3mg}{2} = Mg \quad \text{or} \quad \frac{M}{m} = \frac{1}{2}$$ **Ans.**

Note *Initially normal reaction on each ball will be radially outward and later it will be radially inward, so that normal reactions on tube is radially outward to break it off from the ground.*

10. At distance x from centre,

Centrifugal force $= mx\omega^2$

$\therefore$ Acceleration $a = x\omega^2$

or $v.\dfrac{dv}{dx} = x\omega^2$

or $\int_0^v v\,dv = \omega^2 \int_a^L x\,dx$

or $\dfrac{v^2}{2} = \dfrac{\omega^2}{2}(L^2 - a^2)$

or $v = \omega\sqrt{L^2 - a^2}$ **Ans.**

11. $N = \dfrac{mv^2}{R}$

$$f_{max} = \mu N = \frac{\mu m v^2}{R}$$

$\therefore$ Retardation $a = \dfrac{f_{max}}{m} = \dfrac{\mu v^2}{R}$

$\therefore$ $\left(-\dfrac{dv}{dt}\right) = \dfrac{\mu v^2}{R}$

or $\int_{v_0}^{v} \dfrac{dv}{v^2} = -\dfrac{\mu}{R}\int_0^t dt$

or $v = \dfrac{v_0}{1 + \dfrac{\mu v_0 t}{R}}$ **Ans.**

12. Let R be the radius of the ring

$$h = R(1 - \cos\theta)$$

$$v^2 = 2gh = 2gR(1 - \cos\theta)$$

$$\frac{mv^2}{R} = N + mg\cos\theta$$

or $$N = 2mg(1 - \cos\theta) - mg\cos\theta$$

$$N = 2mg - 3mg\cos\theta$$

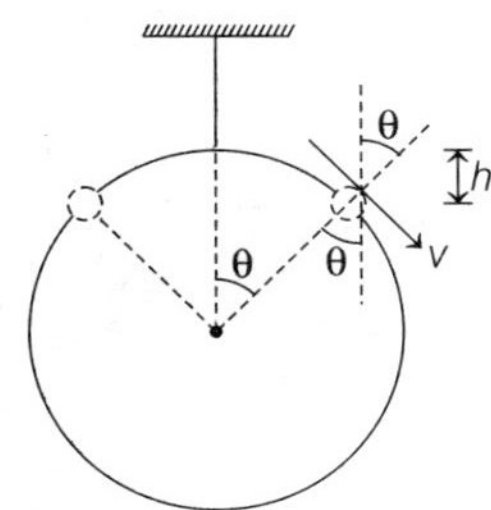

In the critical condition, tension in the string is zero and net upward force on the ring

$$F = 2N\cos\theta = 2mg(2\cos\theta - 3\cos^2\theta) \quad \ldots\text{(i)}$$

F is maximum when $\frac{dF}{d\theta} = 0$

or $-2\sin\theta + 6\sin\theta\cos\theta = 0$

or $$\cos\theta = \frac{1}{3}$$

Substituting in Eq. (i), we get

$$F_{max} = 2mg\left(2 \times \frac{1}{3} - 3 \times \frac{1}{9}\right) = \frac{2}{3}mg$$

$$F_{max} > Mg$$

or $$\frac{2}{3}mg > Mg$$

or $$m > \frac{3}{2}M$$ **Hence proved.**

13. (a) Let v_r be the velocity of mass relative to track at angular position θ.

From work-energy theorem, KE of particle relative to track

= Work done by force of gravity + work done by pseudo force

$$\therefore \quad \frac{1}{2}mv_r^2 = mg(1 - \cos\theta) + m\left(\frac{2g}{9}\right)\sin\theta$$

or $$v_r^2 = 2g(1 - \cos\theta) + \frac{4g}{9}\sin\theta \quad \ldots\text{(i)}$$

Particle leaves contact with the track, where $N = 0$

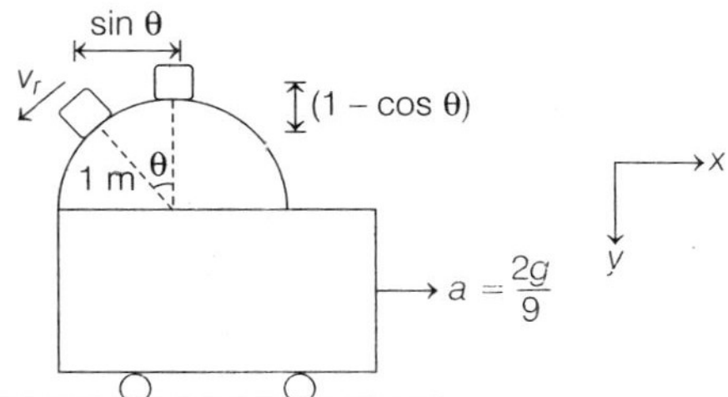

or $$mg\cos\theta - m\left(\frac{2g}{9}\right)\sin\theta = mv_r^2$$

or $$g\cos\theta - \frac{2g}{9}\sin\theta = 2g(1 - \cos\theta) + \frac{4g}{9}\sin\theta$$

or $$3\cos\theta - \frac{6}{9}\sin\theta = 2$$

Solving this, we get

$$\theta \approx 37°$$ **Ans.**

(b) From Eq. (i), we have

$$v_r = \sqrt{2g(1 - \cos\theta) + \frac{4g}{9}\sin\theta}$$

or $$v_r = 2.58 \text{ m/s at } \theta = 37°$$

Vertical component of its velocity is

$$v_y = v_r\sin\theta$$

$$= 2.58 \times \frac{3}{5}$$

$$= 1.55 \text{ m/s}$$

Now, $$1.3 = 1.55t + 5t^2$$

$$\left(\because s = ut + \frac{1}{2}gt^2\right)$$

or $$5t^2 + 1.55t - 1.3 = 0$$

or $$t = 0.38 \text{ s}$$ **Ans.**

$g = 9.81$ $V_0 = -10$

$\Delta x = 100$ $100 = -10t + 4.9t^2$

$4.9t^2 - 10t - 100$

$\frac{m}{s^2}$ m

$10 -$ $t = 3.6, 5.6$

$\frac{g}{y^0}$ $\frac{m}{s^2} - m$

$10 - 4(4.9)(-100)$

$\frac{m}{ms^2}$

$m \div \frac{m}{s^2}$

m